S0-BRE-375

Parallel Processing in Industrial Real-Time Applications

Prentice Hall Series in Innovative Technology

Dennis R. Allison, David J. Farber, and Bruce D. Shriver *Series Advisors*

Bhasker	*A VHDL Primer*
Blachman	*Mathematica: A Practical Approach*
Johnson	*Superscalar Microprocessor Design*
Kane and Heinrich	*MIPS RISC Architecture, Second Edition*
Lawson	*Parallel Processing in Industrial Real-Time Applications*
Nelson, ed.	*Systems Programming with Modula-3*
Nutt	*Open Systems*
Rose	*The Little Black Book: Mail-Bonding with OSI Directory Services*
Rose	*The Open Book: A Practical Perspective on OSI*
Rose	*The Simple Book: An Introduction to Management of TCP/IP-Based Internets*
Shapiro	*A C++ Toolkit*
Slater	*Microprocessor-Based Design*
SPARC International Inc.	*The SPARC Architecture Manual, Version 8*
Strom, et al.	*Hermes: A Language for Distributed Computing*
Treseler	*Designing State Machine Controllers Using Programmable Logic*
Wirfs-Brock, Wilkerson, and Weiner	*Designing Object-Oriented Software*

Parallel Processing in Industrial Real-Time Applications

Harold W. Lawson

Lawson Publishing and Consulting, Inc.
Lidingö, Sweden

with contributions by

Bertil Svensson
Chalmers Technical University, Sweden
Halmstad University, Sweden

Lars Wanhammar
Linköping University, Sweden

Prentice Hall, Englewood Cliffs, New Jersey 07632

Library of Congress Cataloging-in-Publication Data

Lawson, Harold W.
Parallel processing in industrial real-time applications / Harold W. Lawson; with contributions by Bertil Svensson and Lars Wanhammar.
p. cm. — (Prentice Hall series in innovative technology)
Includes bibliographical references and index.
ISBN 0-13-654518-1
1. Parallel processing (Electronic computers) 2. Real-time data processing. I. Svensson, Bertil. II. Wanhammar, Lars. III. Title. IV. Series.
QA76.58.L38 1992 91-48015
004".33—dc20 CIP

Editorial/production supervision: *Harriet Tellem*
Cover design: *Karen Marsilio*
Prepress buyer: *Mary E. McCartney*
Manufacturing buyer: *Susan Brunke*
Acquisitions editor: *Karen Gettman*

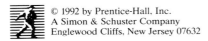

The publisher offers discounts on this book when ordered in bulk quantities. For more information, write:
Special Sales/Professional Marketing
Prentice-Hall, Inc.
Professional & Technical Reference Division
Englewood Cliffs, New Jersey 07632

This book has been developed as the major component of the Swedish National Information Technology Program (IT4) project concerning parallel processors. The Swedish Defense Materiel Administration (FMV) along with the Swedish National Technical Development Board (Nutek) were the governmental sponsors of the project. NobelTech, Ericsson Radar Electronics AB, and Lawson Förlag och Konsult AB were the industrial partners. The project leader was Gunnar Carlstedt of Carlstedt Elektronik AB.

Printed in the United States of America

10 9 8 7 6 5 4 3 2

ISBN 0-13-654518-1

Prentice-Hall International (UK) Limited, *London*
Prentice-Hall of Australia Pty. Limited, *Sydney*
Prentice-Hall Canada Inc., *Toronto*
Prentice-Hall Hispanoamericana, S.A., *Mexico*
Prentice-Hall of India Private Limited, *New Delhi*
Prentice-Hall of Japan, Inc., *Tokyo*
Simon & Schuster Asia Pte. Ltd., *Singapore*
Editora Prentice-Hall do Brasil, Ltda., *Rio de Janeiro*

In memory of

Rear Admiral Grace Murray Hopper

On January 1, 1992, Rear Admiral Hopper died. Her pioneering work in the field of computing will long be remembered. It is with deep respect and appreciation for her guidance in my career that I dedicate this book to her memory.

CONTENTS

FORWARD

Real-time systems permeate the industrialized world. They control life-sustaining instrumentation in the intensive care units of hospitals, monitor the operations of petrochemical plants, and control the on-board navigation and propulsion mechanisms of spacecraft, airplanes, and oil tankers. They are an integral component of global communication networks and financial markets and are embedded in many pieces of equipment that we employ on a day-to-day basis, from the appliances we use to the antilock brakes that have increased the safety of our automobiles.

The next decade will witness significant additional growth of such systems. Just the use of real-time data from the international network of geo-positioning satellites will result in a new generation of real-time mapping and navigation systems that will be deployed in the tens of thousands and will affect our daily lives. Not only will commercial aircraft and ships benefit, but fire and police departments will increase their ability to respond to emergency situations in thousands of cities throughout the world. *Important as real-time systems have become, there is very little formal training in most universities today concerning the specification, design, implementation, testing, evaluation, and evolution of the hardware and software components of real-time systems.*

Parallel processing has a similar history. The availability and use of highly parallel systems is on a steep growth curve. No longer is the use of these systems exclusively restricted to the domain of scientific and technical research and development laboratories. The extremely high-levels of circuit integration in today's VLSI chips, coupled with their inherent availability, reliability, and low cost, have allowed the emergence of a new generation of high-performance, cost-effective highly to massively parallel systems. *Furthermore, there are important classes of real-time systems that either can benefit from or require the performance of parallel systems in order meet their design goals.* However, as is the case of real-time systems, there is very little formal training in most universities today concerning the specification, design, implementation, testing, evaluation, and evolution of the hardware and software components of parallel systems, let alone parallel, real-time systems.

The academic and industrial research and development literature in both real-time systems and in parallel systems is growing at a startling rate, but is fragmented and uneven. New journals in both areas are seemingly being announced every few months. Yet, most of this material does not deal with fundamental principles. It rarely gives the practitioner a basis for understanding and evaluating alternative approaches for dealing with the myriad of technical issues that must be addressed when designing, implementing, and testing parallel, real-time systems.

This engaging and important book by Harold Lawson and his colleagues effectively addresses this need. It provides background in both real-time and parallel systems in a broad, yet unifying way. Harold uses a systematic examination of the various "views" of processes, communications, and synchronization inherent in different processing paradigms as a common thread to discuss real-time and parallel systems. Coupled with his *Behavior Mapping Resource* model, used to characterize the development of all parallel processing systems, he provides the reader with a framework for understanding and evaluating these systems. A framework, which as noted previously, has been missing in the journal literature. He focuses on practical implementations through a rich use of case studies and examples. This book should appeal to those having a background in science, engineering, and computer science and engineering disciplines because of its interdisciplinary orientation. It contains extensive references, glossary, and index entries. It is a must read for those interested in either real-time systems, parallel systems, or both.

Bruce Shriver

PREFACE

The utilization of computer technology in a wide variety of industrial real-time applications has been increasing rapidly during the 1970s and 1980s. The utilization has ranged from relatively simple signal processing and real-time control applications up to sophisticated applications that require significant quantities of computer and human resources.

As the degree of sophistication increases in respect to the goals established for industrial real-time systems, it becomes increasingly important to understand the possibilities of applying parallel processing. In some instances, parallel processing may be the "natural" way of viewing a problem or class of problems to be solved. In other cases, due to heavy processing demands, parallel processing can be the best, perhaps only, means of providing sufficient processing power to meet strict real-time deadlines. There are typically further requirements, such as dependability and responsiveness, implying features such as high reliability, availability, testability, and fault tolerance that dictate the use of a parallel processing approach.

This book is written, first, to both inform and stimulate practicing engineers and scientists who deal with concrete real-time problems that must be solved in industrial environments. The **goal** is to provide a broad, yet unifying, view of the seemingly complex heterogeneous subject area of parallel processing. In this regard, the book treats the fundamental issues, as well as considering parallel processing approaches that have been or can conceivably be applied to solving various problems in the industrial real-time problem domain. The book should provide insight into the subject area, as well as serve as a reference book for continual utilization in evaluating alternative solutions to industrial real-time application problems. In particular, the reader should be able to understand and compare the common denominators as well as the differences between various potential approaches.

Parallel processing is the subject of intensive research and development. As a result, several books have appeared that provide an exhaustive cataloging of the field. A listing of several important books is presented in the Literature Review. This book does not attempt to catalog the general developments in parallel processing by duplicating existing sources. On the other hand, the treatment of those portions of parallel processing research and development as well as products that are or can potentially be of interest for the industrial real-time systems domain are explored in depth.

The book may also be used by faculty and students of engineering and science in an advanced undergraduate or early graduate course. The topic is covered in an interdisciplinary manner by treating subjects normally addressed in signal processing, automatic control, mechatronics, numerical analysis, computer organization, computer architecture, programming languages, software engineering, operating systems, and real-time systems. Thus, a bridge is formed between science, engineering, computer engineering, and computer science disciplines.

A general knowledge of computer systems technology, its utilization and programming, is required. On the other hand, specific knowledge or experience concerning the subject of parallel processing is not required. A working knowledge of fundamental university level mathematics is assumed.

Organization of the book

The book is organized into the following parts:

Part I: Fundamental Issues
Part II: Selected Paradigms, Models, and Artifacts
Part III: Case Studies

In Part I, we consider fundamental issues in a manner that provides a highly structured presentation of the union of industrial real-time systems and parallel processing. Of particular importance is the introduction of a parallel processing development model called the BMR (**B**ehavior **M**apping **R**esource) model, which is utilized to characterize the development of all parallel processing systems. Further, the "fundamental issues" are identified as being the view of **p**rocesses (P), means of **c**ommunication (C), and method of synchronization (S). We also find that these issues, in relationship to the BMR model, are universal for all forms of parallel processing systems. The BMR development model and the PCS issues are used as a thread throughout the book; they provide the reader with an ever present mental model of what is important and how the current material is related to the big picture. Further, the model and issues will assist the reader in understanding relevant current and future developments.

In addition to presenting the BMR model and the PCS issues, the introductory chapter provides a general background to the topic and defines several important concepts and terms. In the remaining chapters of Part I, we consider the general properties of real-time systems, philosophies, paradigms, and models for parallel processing, the applicability of parallel processing to various real-time relevant application domains and the dependability and responsiveness of parallel processing real-time systems. To provide an important perspective, the final chapter provides a brief history of relevant parallel processing developments. In summary, all fundamental information is presented in Part I.

In Part II, we consider several specific hardware and software paradigms, models, and artifacts that are or can be of interest with respect to applying parallel processing in industrial real-time systems. In the prelude to this part, a summary of the various views and mechanisms related to the fundamental PCS (**P**rocess, **C**ommunication, and **S**ynchronization) issues is provided. While the paradigms, models, and artifacts presented in this part are by no means complete, they are representative of the state of the art in behavioral description, mapping, and hardware resources.

In Part III, we present three case studies that illustrate the utilization of parallel processing approaches that have been applied in concrete industrial and/or military real-time applications. Further, we consider a few relevant ongoing research and development efforts that are aimed at providing new paradigms and models for parallel/distributed processing in industrial real-time applications.

In the last chapter, some concluding remarks are made and future trends are considered. A literature review is provided to serve as a starting point for the readers' access to the important sources of relevant literature. Finally, an extensive glossary and an index are included.

The style of presentation

While the subject area of the book is not sufficiently mature to provide the factual form of a typical handbook, our presentation introduces the subject in a highly structured manner. The structuring has permitted us to achieve the central goals of our Swedish National Information Technology project: to categorize ideas, concepts, and practices, providing a basis for understanding as well as for future reference. Wurman (1989) in his book *Information Anxiety* points to the general problem of assimilating knowledge from the enormous quantities of information around us. Certainly, in the subject area of this book, one can observe problems of this nature. Wurman calls for new inventive approaches to the structuring of information that provide convenient maps between what readers understand and the material to be assimilated. In this respect, we present the material of this book in a style aimed at improving information assimilation.

In Part I, each chapter (in Chapter 3, sections of the chapter) begins with a résumé of the major points made in the text with reference to the page(s) where the point is discussed. It is suggested that the reader review these points first. Perhaps they will provide a guide to skip over (or skim over) information with which the reader is well acquainted or be a signal to concentrate on subjects that are not well known. After reading the chapter or sections, the reader should return to the résumé, which also serves as a summary of the material that has been presented. Thus, the structure utilized in addressing the fundamental issues follows the general structure of a good speech; that is, (1) tell the audience what you are going to tell them, (2) tell them, and (3) tell them what you have told them.

In Part II, we shift emphasis from fundamental information gathering to descriptions of specific software and hardware paradigms, models, and artifacts. Part III provides case studies that illustrate how some designers have viewed the use of parallel processing for real-time applications as well as some relevant ongoing research and development. The style of presentation in these latter parts is rather conventional; however, by the chapter division, information on specific artifacts, and projects is rapidly accessible.

In reading the book or in using it as a basis for course literature, it may be desirable to consider particular paradigms, models, artifacts, or case studies as the process of fundamental information gathering in Part I proceeds. Thus, Parts II and III serve as an easily accessible reference work.

The BMR model and reference to the PCS issues permeate the entire book. The BMR model provides a graphic, appearing throughout the book, which, in the spirit of Wurman's observations, aids the reader in extracting the relevance of the current subject with respect to the scope implied by this universal model.

The organization and style of the book have been designed for accessibility and maintainability. The material in Part I can be updated as the state of the art proceeds. Further, the paradigms, models, artifacts, and case studies in Parts II and III can be continually maintained as important advances are identified.

Acknowledgments

Many people have contributed to this book and a warm expression of gratitude is expressed for their advice, discussions, and contributions: In particular, Gunnar Carlstedt, who proposed the project as an ingredient of the Swedish National Information Technology Program and who, as project leader, provided constant guidance in the development of the book. Ingemar Carlsson, Technical Director of the Swedish Defense Materiel Administration (FMV) recognized the importance of the topic for future real-time application development and was a driving force leading to the initiation of the project. The important contributions of Lars Wanhammar in the digital signal processing area and Bertil Svensson in the SIMD PE array architecture area are hereby recognized. Ragnar Arvidsson, Tor Ehlersson, Kurt Lind, and Robert Forchheimer provided information for the application case studies. The author expresses his deep appreciation to Björn Lisper for the use of material from his Parallel Processing course notes used at the Royal Institute of Technology. Lars Bergman has prepared the photographic illustrations for image processing examples and has granted permission to utilize photographs of his daughter, Lina Bergman.

The project was constantly reviewed by a control board consisting of representatives for the governmental and industrial partners. A sincere expression of appreciation is given to Ragnar Arvidsson, Tor Ehlersson, Göran Tengstrand, Mats Zachrison, Christopher Bengtsson, and Dennis Söderberg for their active participation in this project. The author had discussions with many other colleagues who have provided useful information and constructive criticism. The book has been reviewed in detail, at various stages, by Tor Ehlersson, Sven Holte, and Handong Wu. Borko Furht and Ted Lewis have also provided useful comments and suggestions. Further, appreciation is expressed to Robert Babb, Lars Bengtsson, Miquel Bertran, Wolfgang Halang, Jens Riboe, Björn Sikström, Jan Torin, and Pelle Wiberg for their interest in the project.

Employees of the sponsoring organizations, students at the Royal Institute of Technology, Stockholm, and Halmstad University, as well as participants at intensive four day courses, have endured the early versions of this material and have thereby made a significant contribution to its quality.

A deep expression of gratitude is given to those colleagues whose work has formed the basis for a large part of the presentation and is referenced in this book. The author apologizes for all omissions of important and relevant work and solicits communication from interested parties, thus enabling the material to be updated in future editions.

In addition to my word processor, I express my appreciation to my wife Annika for her assistance in preparing the book. Anders Hedin and Lars-Erik Thorelli kindly arranged for my use of facilities at the Department of Telecommunication and Computer Systems, Royal Institute of Technology. Doris Arenander made significant contributions to the style and form of the final version of the book.

Finally to Annika, Adrian, and Jasmine for their understanding and patience during the many (often late night) hours required for preparing this book.

Harold W. Lawson
Lidingö, Sweden

Reference

Wurman, R.S. (1989). *Information Anxiety*, Doubleday, Garden City, New York.

Part I

FUNDAMENTAL ISSUES

Chapter 1

INTRODUCTION

In this chapter, we introduce the general issues related to utilizing parallel/distributed processing in industrial real-time systems.

- the terms philosophy, paradigm, model, and artifact are defined and related to the subject of the book (4)
- analogical reasoning can be used to gain informal insight into parallel/distributed processing situations (5)
- a resource quantity axiom 0, 1 *or* $\approx \infty$ is presented as well as its effect upon allocation, scheduling, and resulting complexities (6)
- common denominator terminology leading to a general view of processes where PE (**P**rocessing **E**lements), M (**M**emory), and C (**C**ommunication) are the hardware process building blocks (14)
- the process abstraction in which data are processed by process procedure(s) and input/output ports connect the process to other processes and/or to the external environment (15)
- a universally applicable BMR (**B**ehavior **M**apping **R**esource) parallel processing development model is introduced; the BMR model is used, as a graphic aid, throughout the book to focus attention on relevant subjects and issues (16)
- application behavior is transformed to one or more models, each having their own structure and behavior (17)

- parallelism is divided into application parallelism (algorithm and data geometry) versus system parallelism (control and data structure) (18)

- goals and reasons for selecting parallel processing alternatives (natural solution, performance, the x-abilities and fault tolerance) (19)

- fundamental resource mapping philosophies are:
  (1) resource adequate, direct mapped versus
  (2) resource limited, dynamically allocated (22)

- the classification of parallel computer systems (SISD, SIMD, MISD, and MIMD) and the importance of granularity, coupling, and general versus special purposeness (24)

- fundamental issues are identified as the view of Processes (P), means of Communication (C), and method of Synchronization (S), which we abbreviate to the PCS issues (26)

The major advances in computer system hardware technologies and the improvements in our knowledge of software technologies achieved during the 1970s and 1980s have provided a basis for seriously considering the utilization of parallel processing in a wide range of industrial real-time applications. While examples of the successful utilization of parallel processing in this application sphere have been achieved, developments can still be considered to be in their infancy. We need to gain a better understanding of philosophies, paradigms, and models for parallel real-time systems. Based upon philosophies, paradigms, and models, we need to develop appropriate artifacts in the form of languages, methodologies, mechanisms, and tools for realizing and dealing with all the conceptual, technical, and practical problems associated with parallel processing-based products.

By *real-time system* we mean a system that assures that controlled activities "progress" and that stability is maintained and further, that the values of outputs **and** the time at which the outputs are produced are important to the proper functioning of the system. Thus, a real-time system responds to defined external circumstances in a time bounded manner. We can differentiate between soft and hard real-time systems. In *soft real-time systems*, the provision of a satisfactory degree of *service* is central and, while important, catastrophes will not result if the service is temporarily degraded. On the other hand, in the more restrictive *hard real-time system*, if a correct output is not available by a specific deadline, a significant, perhaps catastrophic result(s) may occur. In hard real-time systems *predictability* becomes the essential issue. Examples of the soft real-time variety include such systems as airline reservation systems, command and control systems, and telecommunication systems. Aircraft fly-by-wire guidance systems, chemical process control, and antilock braking systems exemplify hard variants of real-time systems.

We shall not make any essential differentiation between *parallel* and *distributed* in respect to the real-time systems we consider. The distinguishing properties are related to physical positioning within the system, the timing requirements, and the methods of transport (that is, communication). The range of applications vary from signal processing up to and including sophisticated control of highly distributed and heterogeneous real-time environments, thus building a real-time complexity hierarchy. In many of the real-time system environments (particularly hard environments), there is an increasing trend to incorporate sophisticated processing directly into products (that is, *embedded systems*). For example, most all forms of real-time control of moving vehicles belong to the embedded system category. In these cases, the physical system structure, including power requirements, become important issues. The general conceptual problem in respect to realizing real-time systems can be visualized as in Figure 1.1.

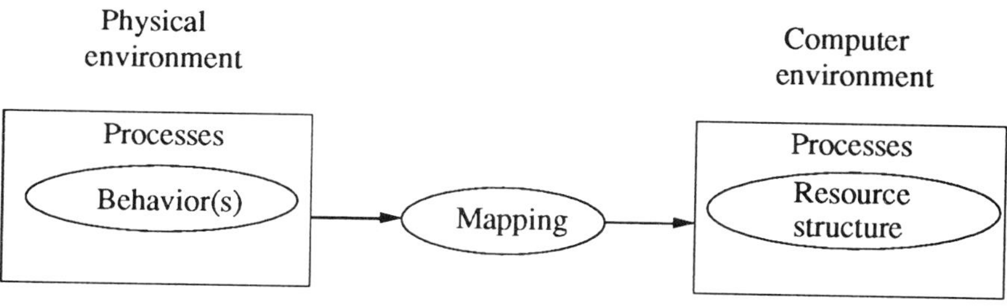

Figure 1.1. General Conceptual Problem

In the real-time application domain, we find a need to have a thorough problem understanding of the environment (physical world realities and relationships), a knowledge of how to describe the process behavior(s) of the physical world, as well as how to map the behavior(s) into a structure of resources for realization via processes in a computer system environment. The resource structure includes relevant hardware components (that is, processing elements, memories, and communications), as well as software related components (languages, methods, mechanisms, tools, and so on).

1.1 PHILOSOPHIES, PARADIGMS, MODELS, AND ARTIFACTS

There are several alternative approaches to addressing the general conceptual problem we have identified. To deal with the related problems at various levels, we are concerned with both abstract and concrete aspects via philosophies, paradigms, models, and artifacts. There is often significant confusion in the technical literature when these terms are used (and misused). In this book, it is essential that the reader have a clear picture of what is intended with these terms. First, let us examine relevant portions in the following dictionary definitions:

philosophy

1. the rational investigation of being, knowledge, and right conduct.
2. a system or school of thought: the philosophy of Descartes.
3. the basic principles of a discipline: the philosophy of law.
4. any system of belief, values, or tenents.
5. a personal outlook or viewpoint.
6. serenity of temper.

paradigm

1. the set of all the inflected terms of a word.
2. a pattern or model.

model

1. a representation, usually on a smaller scale, of a device, structure, and the like.
2. a standard to be imitated.
3. a representative form, style, or pattern.
4. a design or style of a particular product.

artefact or artifact

1. something made or given shape by people, such as a tool or a work of art.

Source: *The Collins Dictionary and Thesaurus*, William Collins Sons & Co Ltd 1987.

These definitions come quite close to our use of the terms in this book. However, to make these terms unambiguous for our purposes, we utilize the following meanings:

philosophy – a general point of view resulting in concepts and strategies that provide a reference point for design decisions (large and small).

paradigm – a specific point of view within the context of a philosophy (a unique pattern or style) from which specific models can be developed.

model – a specific framework (that is, structure) that reflects a paradigm and is the basis for concrete realization.

artifacts – concrete or abstract objects ("things") that are used in realizing models, for example, languages, compilers, assemblers, operating systems, hardware components, and development tools.

From these definitions, the reader should be able to relate to corresponding familiar aspects of computer and/or engineering technology. In this book, we are most interested in surveying relevant philosophies, paradigms, and models. However, we shall consider several artifacts in order to illustrate specific solutions to parallel processing and real-time problems.

1.2 ANALOGICAL REASONING

Via a multidisciplinary approach and the conscious use of *analogical reasoning*, it is expected that the readers will be able to draw informal personal analogies between as well as see the differences among various philosophies, paradigms, models, and artifacts. The *insight* provided by utilizing analogical reasoning is an essential ingredient for understanding as well as for stimulating creative thinking and reasoning. Analogical reasoning is a vital subconscious human activity and is directly in line with contemporary theories of learning mathematics and science as reported by Resnick (1983).

In relationship to creativity, it is interesting to note that Broad (1985) reported that a detailed study of the life long patent production of Thomas A. Edison revealed that Edison had about a dozen central ideas and that via analogical reasoning he managed to generate most of his 1093 patents. Another evidence of the power of analogical reasoning for improving understanding was the development of a successful group-oriented problem-solving approach called *synectics* (Gordon 1961). Gordon introduced four forms of analogies:

personal analogy – one identifies with the elements of the problem and plays the roll of key elements.

direct analogy – one compares parallel facts, knowledge, or technology. Comparisons with biological and physical systems are often rewarding in this regard.

symbolic analogy – one uses objective and impersonal images to describe the problem in a technologically nonaccurate but esthetically satisfying manner.

fantasy analogy – one imagines the best of all possible worlds where everything is possible.

With regard to the subject area of this book, the reader can benefit from the conscious use of these forms of analogical reasoning. By bringing the central concepts and practice related to parallel processing into the human domain as well as in relationship to real-time systems, this book will contribute to a general understanding, as well as to stimulating future product developments and research-related developments in the field.

At the other end of the human reasoning spectrum, we find *formal reasoning* based upon concepts in mathematics and logic. For example, Boute (1989) has described syntactical and semantic formalisms that are useful for formally reasoning about analogue and digital real-time systems. It is quite common for we humans, in most all learning and reasoning situations, to proceed from the informal toward the formal. Analogical reasoning can provide us with the informal (personal) map to the new knowledge. As understanding increases we move toward more formal means of description with a variety of informal, semiformal, and formal steps along the way.

1.3 RESOURCES AND THEIR UTILIZATION

A common denominator related to all forms of processing in industrial applications (human and computerized) is the availability of *resources* and their utilization. In this section, we shall concentrate upon human processes and processing behavior and thus assist in building, via analogies, an informal *map* between the reader's intuitive ability to understand human systems and the subject area of the book.

In human work environments, *processes* to be performed are *assigned* to humans (*processors*) that perform (*execute*) the processes. The processes themselves may be subdivided into one or more interrelated *processes*.

The available processors are resources that may require additional *resources* in order to carry out the execution of the processes that have been assigned. For example, various forms of equipment (machines and tools) may be required.

From a higher-level view of the work situation, we consider both the processors and required equipment as finite resources. Being finite, we need to find effective means of orchestrating their utilization, especially when parallel processing is to be accomplished, that is, mapping desired behavior(s) to the available resource structure.

How many resources of each variety are required? This is an ever present multi-dimensional problem for effective system planning and administration. In principle, there are only three "convenient" quantities of resources:

$$0, 1 \textit{ or } \approx \infty$$

That is, we have **none** (of course, we may not be able to do the work in this case or must do it in some other manner), we have only **one** that must be used for all work, or the number of resources is **virtually infinite**, in which case the question of resource availability is not important. All other finite quantities of resources between one and being virtually infinite introduce problems of *allocation* and *scheduling*, an important axiom to remember.

The quantity of resources problem has a *direct analogy* to parallel processing in real-time systems in that major problems are often encountered in relationship to dimensioning the quantities of processors, registers, memories, memory cells, buffers, input/output ports, communication channels, and the like, to be provided in the system.

There is, in fact, a finite quantity of resources between one and virtually infinite that is of interest. That is, we have available *precisely as many as we need.* In many human work situations, as well as in certain applications of parallel processing for real-time systems, it is possible to calculate precise resource requirements. By having exactly as many as we need, problems of scheduling and resource allocation are either eliminated or become straightforward. There is a direct mapping from problem related processes to the resource structure processes. We can observe this line of thinking in many *signal-processing* applications; however, it should also be interesting in a wider class of real-time applications. A challenge for the use of analogical reasoning!

Unfortunately, we cannot always plan for the availability of exactly as many resources as we need and are thus faced in human work situations, as well as in real-time systems, with the frequently complex processing-related problems of allocating resources, scheduling, time constraints, and so on. It is the strategies related to these problems that occupy a large portion of our creative efforts in producing effective human or computerized systems.

In human as well as in computer-based real-time systems, we are also faced with the important question: *Is it preferable to utilize general-purpose or special-purpose resources?* The capabilities of the resources, processors (that is, humans) and equipment are central issues in human work environments. What degree of general purposeness or special purposeness is best? There is, of course, no one best answer to this important question. Based upon the situation, human or computerized, there exist different answers and degrees of suitability (that is, different alternatives).

1.4 HUMAN PARALLEL PROCESSING ENVIRONMENTS

We now consider three examples of human-related activity that can serve as a concrete basis for building the reader's personal *map* between human situations and analogous parallel processing real-time situations as described in this book.

1.4.1 Human Matrices

We are all impressed by the organization of a section at an athletic stadium when large human matrices produce colorful displays. This human activity has become a tradition and reaches its climax with spectacular displays at Olympic Games. By examining how such a human activity is organized and by fantasizing about how it could be organized or extended to other "processing" endeavors, we can gain significant insight into many of the fundamental problems of parallel processing in real-time environments. Let us illustrate this form of a *massively parallel system* as in Figure 1.2.

Each element of the matrix is a *processor*. Each *processor* is capable, at any given instant, of executing one simple *process*. Thus, we can observe that the processes executed have a fine degree of *granularity* (that is, each process performs very limited processing). As illustrated in Figure 1.2, at a specific point in time, a coordinator (control) provides the timing signal NOW! All the *processors* respond by executing a *process* (in this case the behavior of creating a display). The generalization of this environment to a programmed sequence of varying displays over time is left as an obvious analogical mental exercise for the reader.

From this example, it is not difficult to see the direct analogies to parallel processing problems as well as to fantasize about varieties of "system"-related structures. We could, for example, consider a *local timing* approach. That is, each *processor* is equipped with its own timing device (clock) and follows its "program" execution at specific points in time. For example, to achieve an *n-step* wave across the matrix columns, each *processor* executes a program activity (in some cases, do nothing) at times

$$t, dt, 2dt, 3dt, ..., (n - 1)dt.$$

We can contrast this local timing control with a single *global timing* control for synchronizing the display. Further, we can fantasize about other possibilities, where each *processor* in a column and/or row provides a *signal* to neighboring *processors* upon completion of a change, thus initiating changes by their neighbors. However, this decentralization of control introduces the need for interprocessor communications. We can even conceive of successively passing cards (data) in various patterns through the matrix. Consequently, we begin to move ourselves into the realm of considering network topologies, routing, and asynchronous control.

Figure 1.2. Massively Parallel Human Processing

With this simple human-based example and our fantasized extensions, we can consider several fundamental issues of the organization and timing of regularly structured *massively parallel systems*, for example:

— process granularity
— degree of special versus general purposeness of processors
— centralized versus decentralized control
— global timing versus local timing
— synchronous versus asynchronous timing
— network topology and routing

As a further example of the use of massively parallel human matrices, it is interesting to note that precomputer age evaluation methods for numerical algorithms were often based upon applying multiple processors (humans). An important project in this regard was the human "Computational Unit" of the Manhattan Project at Oak Ridge, Tennessee, during World War II. Many important differential equations were evaluated by humans organized in a matrix of desks, equipped with desk calculators, where in and out baskets on their desks were used as "ports" for communicating partial results to neighbors. Further, redundant calculations were built into the system for improving reliability. In this case, the *granularity* of the processes (the units of work accomplished at each desk) is significantly larger than in our previous human matrix example. We can gain significant insight into parallel processing by considering such human activities. Try organizing some similar human parallel processing systems of your own! Further, what must you consider in order to perform processing in the light of rigid timing constraints?

1.4.2 Models of Production

Further insight can be obtained by drawing analogies between models of highly distributed/parallel industrial production environments and computerized models for real-time systems. Consider the production system of humans and machines in Figure 1.3.

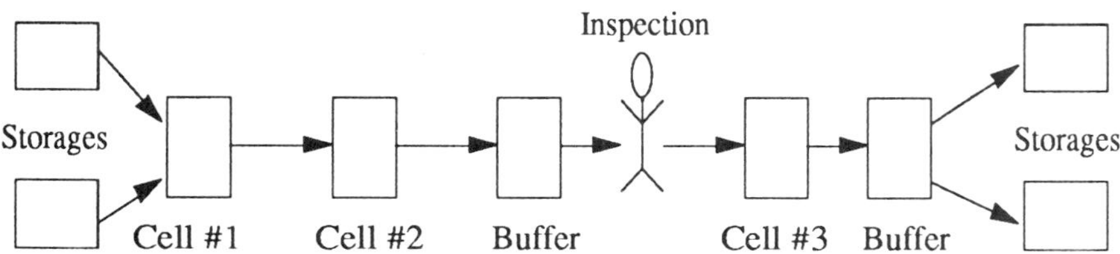

Figure 1.3. Production Line

Here we observe that two sources of raw materials are taken from storages, enter the system, and are first processed in an automated production cell; the partially assembled product is then passed (perhaps by conveyer belt) to the next cell for further assembly. An intermediate buffer storage (normally organized as a queue) is introduced prior to a human inspection process.

When the partially assembled product is controlled, it is passed further to a final automated cell (perhaps for packaging). The final assembled and packaged products are placed into a buffer. From the buffer, the products are further routed to warehouse storage. Observe that a number of highly heterogeneous processes are realized, where each process potentially is of rather coarse *granularity* (that is, each process performs large units of work).

This example of a *distributed/parallel system* containing a variety of processes brings several additional issues into focus, for example:

- — varying degree of granularity
- — special purposeness of the processors
- — pipelines
- — buffering (queues)
- — synchronous and asynchronous timing (again)

Once again, the reader is encouraged to draw several personal analogies from this example.

1.4.3 Pandemonium

As a final human-based example, we consider the pandemonium model of the human brain proposed by Selfridge (1959). Selfridge introduced a view of how the human brain works in recognizing objects. Since we do not know exactly how the brain works, we can consider the contribution by Selfridge as an important *symbolic analogy*. In any event, it is quite useful and suggestive in relationship to important real-time situations. The model is portrayed in Figure 1.4.

A succession of *demons* is applied to the task of recognizing the letter R. Selfridge divides the demons into various specialists that perform various processing tasks. The *image demons* (a cortical signal-processing subsystem) record the initial image of the external signal. The image is analyzed by *feature demons* that look for particular characteristics (for example, presence of angles, curves, lines, and contours). The *cognitive demons* watch responses of the feature demons. Each cognitive demon is responsible for examining the features that are noted in a *feature blackboard* and recognizing one pattern. Cognitive demons, upon recognizing significant features start yelling. Finally, a *decision demon* listens to the pandemonium produced by the cognitive demons and selects the demon that is yelling the loudest as the pattern most likely occurring in the environment.

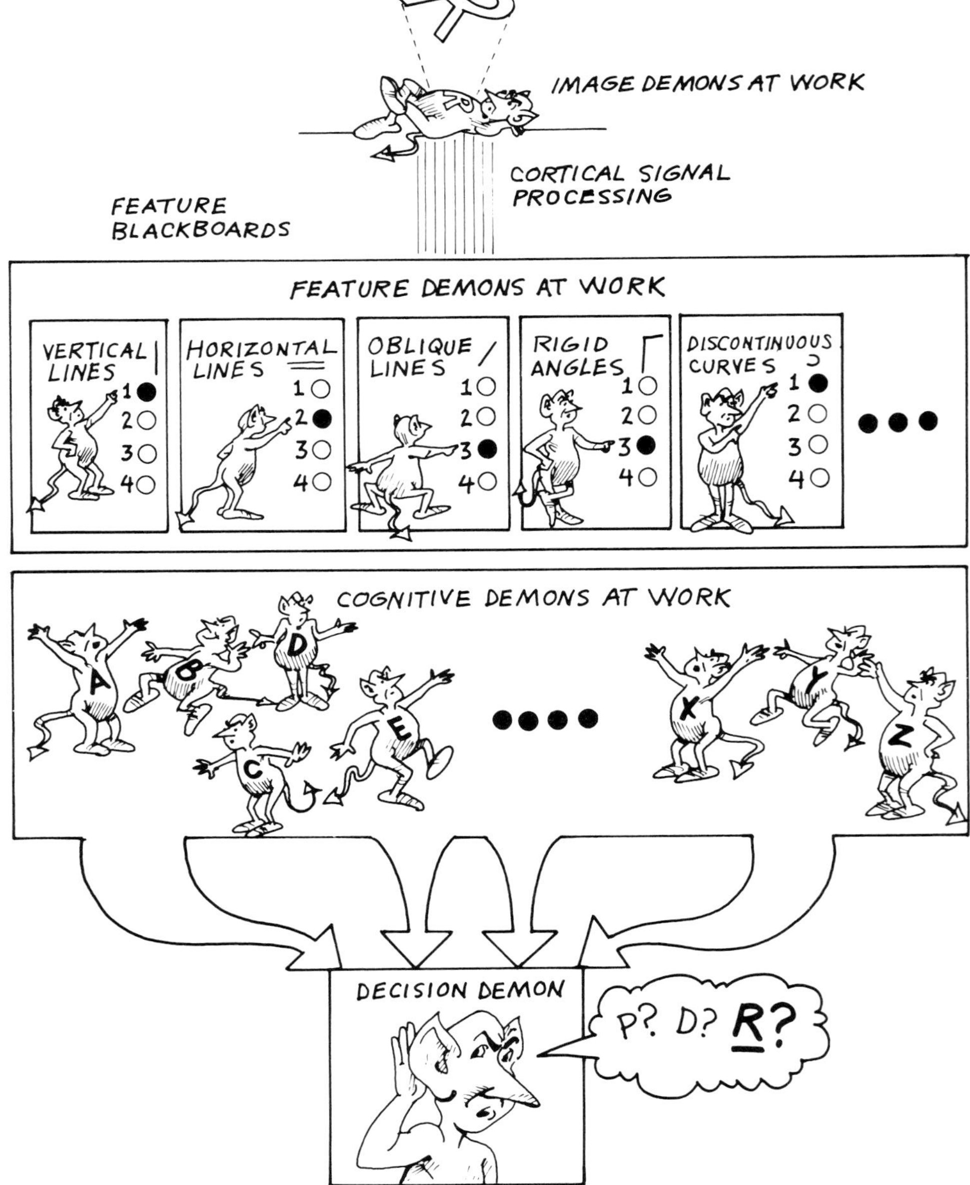

Figure 1.4. Selfridge Pandemonium Model

This third human-oriented example points to further issues that are commonly found in relationship to parallel processing, for example:

— special purposeness of processing
— mixed real-time systems (image processing and decision making)
— hierarchy of processes/processors
— shared memories (blackboards)
— demons (*synonyms,* agents, actors, workers, objects)

For a deeper discussion of the pandemonium model, as well as a stimulating source of human information processing analogies, see Lindsay and Norman (1977).

The fundamental parallel processing issues illustrated via our human-based examples provide a useful starting point concerning the problem of process behavior(s) to resource structure process mapping trade-offs as portrayed in Figure 1.1. The trade-offs must be made in light of the nature of the application and in respect to an appropriate realization philosophy that leads to viable architectural paradigms and models. Further, the trade-offs must lead to the use of philosophy, paradigm, and model appropriate implementation *artifacts*, that is, languages, methods, tools, and mechanisms [see Lawson (1990)]. Providing insight into the selection of appropriate artifacts for various mapping trade-offs is the core subject of this book.

The reader is encouraged to think about other familiar processing situations where parallel processing can be applied, for example, servicing customers in a bank, supermarket, or pharmacy, or the flow of traffic over highways and bridges where vehicles must pass toll gates. Reflect on the effect of the quantity of resources, queuing, the use of general-purpose or special-purpose resources, the control of processing activities, and so on. *Parallelism is all around us! Thus, many aspects of parallelism are quite intuitive.* The consideration of analogies to systems with which we are familiar should provide some guidelines to "thinking parallel" in terms of our design and utilization of parallel computer-based real-time systems.

1.5 COMMON DENOMINATOR CONCEPTS AND TERMINOLOGY

While analogical reasoning can assist in comprehension, the multidisciplinary approach taken in this book naturally leads to terminology problems. When required, we shall pay attention to this problem as the book proceeds. Most importantly, we do not want terminology to stand in the way of appreciation, insight, and deeper understanding of similarities and differences.

Attempts to achieve a common view with respect to computer-related terminology started with the first book that treated computing on a broad basis, *High Speed*

Computing Devices (see Stifler, 1950). Stifler and his colleagues provided the following highly useful definition of **component** in their introductory chapter.

> The term *component* is used throughout this survey to define any physical mechanism or mathematical method which is used as a tool in automatic computation. The term is applied either to an abstract concept or to an item of physical equipment. The scope of the survey includes not only a treatment of the design and operation of physical mechanisms but also the arithmetic and analytical procedures which form the basis of solution of problems reduced to numerical form.

With this spirit of commonality constantly in mind, we present the concepts and terminology utilized in this book. We are in agreement with our wise predecessors and, as implied in the discussion thus far, we make the substitution *process* for *component* in their definition. Whereas the term component implies a static object, our process definition implies both the object as well as the dynamics of its utilization (that is, the behavior).

1.6 RESOURCE STRUCTURE BUILDING BLOCKS

Regardless of the form of computer architecture to be utilized in parallel processing environments, PE (**P**rocessing **E**lements), M (**M**emory) and C (**C**ommunications) *hardware processes* ("components") are the building blocks used in forming the hardware portion of the resource structure. To unify our view of parallel processing systems, we employ a generous interpretation of these building blocks as follows:

processing element (*abbreviation,* PE; *synonym,* processor): A *processing element* is considered to be any device that can perform transformations. Thus it may be a gate, an adder or multiplier, a special-purpose transformation device, or a special- or general-purpose programmed device.

memory (*synonym,* store): A *memory* is any device or media that can be used for storing information over time. Thus, we consider latches, registers, register files, shift registers, memory banks, cache memories, as well as long-term storage devices and media as belonging to the memory category. In some situations, it is useful to define a *memory hierarchy* composed of memories of varying capacities and access rates as well as methods of transport.

communication: *Communication* is defined as any means for transmitting information between processing elements, between memories, or combinations thereof. The physical communication can be accomplished by direct wiring, by buses, or by channels of various types. The act of communicating is accomplished by driver and receiver circuits or such circuits in combination with various means of *synchronization* and *communication protocols*.

1.7 THE PROCESS ABSTRACTION

Since the process notion is used as the most important common denominator of the book, it is essential that we have a clear picture of processes. As we have just considered, processing elements, memories, and communication media are considered to be hardware processes. In these cases, the processes are physical. A straightforward generalization of the process notion is simply to state that all levels above the physical process level are composed of programmed processes that owe their composition to lower-level hardware processes and in some cases even lower-level programmed processes.

Our common definition of the process abstraction is portrayed in Figure 1.5.

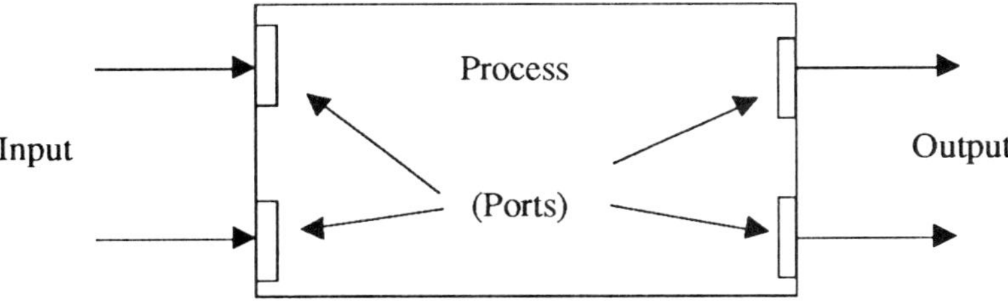

Figure 1.5. Process Abstraction

Here we observe that the process defines input and output *ports* that connect the process to other processes or to the external environment. Further, we assume that the process can contain a data structure (even as primitive as a single bit) and the procedure(s) that, when activated, manipulate the data structure. The *granularity* of the process in terms of the quantity of data and the quantity and complexity of the procedure(s) is sufficient to differentiate both static structure and dynamic process behavior. The generality of this definition permits us to utilize the process as our common denominator (a useful extension of component as introduced by Stifler).

1.8 PARALLEL PROCESSING SYSTEM DEVELOPMENT

Having considered the question of common denominator terminology, hardware resource building blocks and the process abstraction, we now introduce the BMR (**B**ehavior **M**apping **R**esource) model, which highlights the major ingredients of parallel processing systems development. This universal model is portrayed in Figure 1.6.

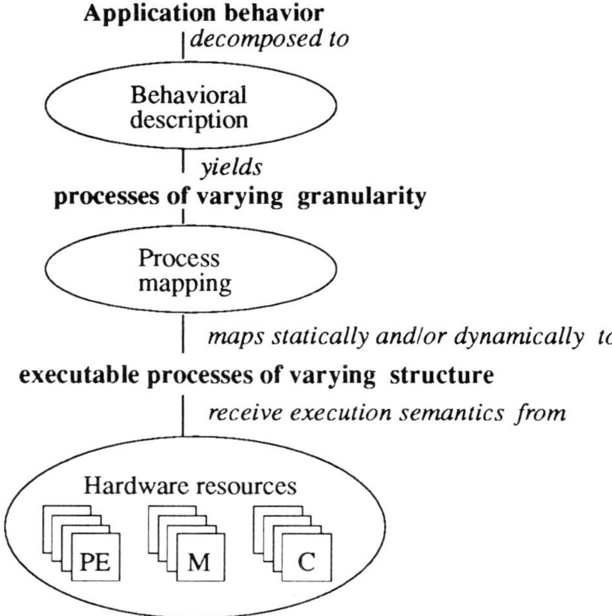

Figure 1.6. Ingredients of Parallel Processing System Development (BMR Model)

We can categorically assert that, regardless of the form of parallel processing utilized, the elements portrayed in this model are *always* present in one form or another. That is, application behaviors are decomposed into behavioral descriptions of some form. From the behavioral descriptions, a process set containing processes of varying granularity is extracted (manually or automatically). The processes of the set are mapped statically or dynamically into executable processes within the framework of some structure. Finally, the processes are given execution semantics (behavior) by the hardware process resources.

Depending on the point of view (philosophy) for realizing a parallel processing system, various *slices* through the elements of the model are made. The slices select various combinations and result in various paradigms and models of parallelism.

> We apply the BMR model throughout the book by highlighting relevant elements as discussion relates to various aspects of parallel processing. Thus, a scaled down version of the model, when appropriate, is incorporated into the text.

1.9 STRUCTURE AND BEHAVIOR OF MODELS

We shall view the development process as the means of transforming the desired application behavior into one or more models, each of which is characterized by its own structure and behavior.

The *structure* of a model (at various levels) is either a static interconnection of the processes (components) or an interconnection developed dynamically (for example, by linking) that exists for some period of time.

The model *behavior*, expressed more explicitly, is the input/output response(s) of a process or collection of processes by means of a procedure(s).

The proper view of these two essential concepts is that the *structure* provides a *framework* in which desired *behaviors* are implemented and operate.

1.9.1 Model Restrictions

In many industrial projects, the application is characterized by requirements as well as the desired structural and behavioral properties of the system via a specification. Further, the *artifacts* to be used for behavioral description ("languages" of various forms) and the hardware environment (specific equipment) are given, thus reducing the degrees of freedom in establishing creative and potentially superior solutions. Even the process allocation activity may be specified (for example, in the case of a specific operating system). If the application to implementation mapping requirements can conveniently be met in light of these artifacts, all is well. Unfortunately, *semantic gaps* often occur based upon the requirement to utilize specific artifacts, making the model implementation difficult and leading to complex and often, in the long run, costly solutions.

While we must work in the realities of the industrial world with respect to standards and practices, due to the diverse nature of the field of parallel processing, it is important to find creative new philosophies and paradigms that provide convenient and efficient structural and behavioral models. Thus, with time, various models should achieve maturity and prove to be generally applicable so they can be applied in a rational industrial manner to wide categories of applications.

1.10 APPLICATION VERSUS SYSTEM PARALLELISM

Parallelism can come in several types. The primary distinguishing characteristic is the case in which general resource structures are applied to problems without any special considerations for the nature of the problem *versus* the case where the parallelism is obtained from the nature of the problem and is captured in the application behavioral description. To view these alternatives, let us consider Table 1.1.

Table 1.1. Application versus System Parallelism

Application parallelism	Algorithm	Data geometry
System parallelism	Control	Data structure and flow

In *application parallelism*, parallelism may be obtained via partitioning of the algorithm(s) and/or via exploiting the geometry of data by partitioning the data into natural units that reflect the nature of the problem and that can be treated conveniently in the resource structure. For example, we can devise application parallelism based upon a pipeline philosophy or upon the philosophy of massive parallel processing in matrix form, as illustrated by our earlier analogies.

In the case of *system parallelism*, the parallelism is obtained purely by the mechanics of the hardware resources, in some cases complemented by sophisticated allocation and scheduling of processes. Parallelism is achieved in relationship to control flow and/or data structure and flow provided by the resource structure and, where relevant, the operating system management of processes. The utilization of system parallelism may be explicit (in which case it is indicated in the behavioral description) or implicit (in which case parallelism is automatically extracted from the behavioral description). One means of automatically extracting parallelism is called *scalar parallelism*, in which case unmodified sequential programs are made parallel with respect to available parallel hardware resources.

In all specific paradigms and models for parallel processing, the key link is process mapping, which will be the determining factor as to how well application and/or system parallelism can be exploited.

1.11 GOALS AND REASONS FOR PARALLEL PROCESSING

The selection of parallel processing for the realization of a real-time application problem or class of problems may be made in order to achieve a variety of goals or for a number of valid reasons. In this section, we point to typical goals and reasons that motivate the utilization of a parallel approach.

1.11.1 Natural Implementation

As described previously, the application may lend itself well to the exploitation of natural parallelism. In the human matrix display analogy that we have previously considered, a parallel processing organization is the natural and only conceivable solution. The distribution of activities via pipelining in the production model also illustrates a natural division into parallel processing activities.

As mentioned earlier, many numerical algorithms and data upon which they operate can be and have been partitioned in order to naturally exploit parallelism (see, for example, Akl, 1989 and Quinn, 1987). Typically, we find that, while certain parts of an algorithm can be treated in parallel, other portions must be treated sequentially; thus, the architecture must be designed in order to permit both forms of processing as required. Further, the performance of the system will be affected by the amount of parallel versus serial processing that is required.

1.11.2 Performance

There are many problems (or subproblems) in the real-time domain that cannot be treated (that is, meet time deadlines) without highly accelerated processing. Improved performance to provide predictability is, of course, often the most important reason for introducing parallel processing.

Due to the fact that hardware technology is constantly becoming less expensive and more compact, it becomes increasingly common to incorporate supercomputing elements in embedded real-time applications. Thus, we must consider supercomputing technology (particularly parallel computing) to be in our real-time resource structure domain. General-purpose (non-time critical) supercomputing, on the other hand, lies outside our domain.

The *ideal* performance goal for the utilization of parallel processing is to achieve a linear **order** of magnitude performance improvement; that is,

$$\text{Speedup} = \Theta(N), \quad \text{where } N \text{ is the number of processors and } \Theta \text{ means "order exactly"}$$

That is, given a set of processes to be performed and the availability of N processing elements, to achieve exactly N-fold improvement in the time required to execute the processes as portrayed in Figure 1.7.

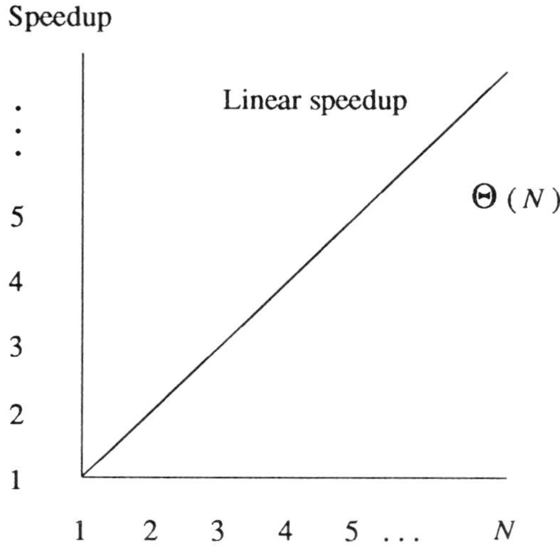

Figure 1.7. Ideal Performance Improvement from Applying Parallel Processors

In practice, the linear speedup goal can rarely be achieved since the computational processes must communicate with each other and their progress is related to each other. Further, system functions that add overhead may be required. Consequently, in the most realistic case, we can hope for the following improvement:

Speedup $= O(N)$, where O means "order at most"

For definitions, of Θ and O and the related "order at least" Ω, see the following. These measures have been introduced by Knuth (1976) as a means of concentrating on "dominating" terms in calculating time and space requirements.

order notation

Assuming f and g are functions over the domain of natural numbers.

1 Omicron (**order at most**), *designated* $O(f(n))$: $O(f(n))$ is the set of all $g(n)$ such that there exist positive constants c and n_0 such that $|g(n)| \leq cf(n)$ for all $n > n_0$

2 Omega (**order at least**), *designated* $\Omega(f(n))$: $\Omega(f(n))$ is the set of all $g(n)$ such that there exist positive constants c and n_0 such that $g(n) \geq cf(n)$ for all $n \geq n_0$

3 Theta (**order exactly**), *designated* $\Theta(f(n))$: $\Theta(f(n))$ is the set of all $g(n)$ such that $g(n)$ is $O(f(n))$ and $g(n)$ is $\Omega(f(n))$.

The notation permits us to concentrate on the *dominating term* in describing time and space complexities and to ignore any multiplicative constants.

1.11.3 The *x*-Abilities

While natural implementation and performance are often the primary goals and reasons for selecting a parallel approach, there are a number of other reasons and goals that are extremely important, which we shall label the *x*-abilities. These include *dependability* and *responsiveness* with related factors [that is, *testability*, *reliability* (robustness), and *verifiability*], *extendability*, and, last but not least among the most important *x*-abilities, *understandability*. We shall consider these *x*-abilities in the book. These goals, unfortunately, are all too often ignored or considered *a posteriori*, leading to important practical and costly economic problems with real-time system products. Thus, there exists a strong motivation to give *a priori* and full consideration to the *x*-ability properties.

1.11.4 Fault Detection and Fault Tolerance

A further frequent dependability and responsiveness goal for hard real-time systems (especially embedded systems) is the question of system *availability*. This leads us to consider various means of planning for the detection and administration of failures during operation (that is, *fault detection* and *fault tolerance*). To achieve fault tolerance, redundant resources are utilized. The system may, for example, be duplicated or triplicated in order to provide redundant processing with majority voting. Alternatively, *flexibility* and *transparency* of program execution may be employed. That is, we attempt to design the architecture of the system so that we are not concerned as to where specific processing takes place, thus enabling the use of fault tolerant techniques, including the reallocation of available resources.

1.11.5 Making Trade-offs

The requirements and goals for a particular real-time project will always involve making trade-offs between the application requirements and goals and the selected architecture. Finally, we must consider the extremely important aspect of achieving *economic* goals. In fact, the effective use of parallel processing can, in many cases, contribute to more economical solutions, for example, by utilizing adequate parallel hardware process resources, thus eliminating the need for complex process mappings with the positive consequence of improving understandability.

1.12 FUNDAMENTAL MAPPING PHILOSOPHIES

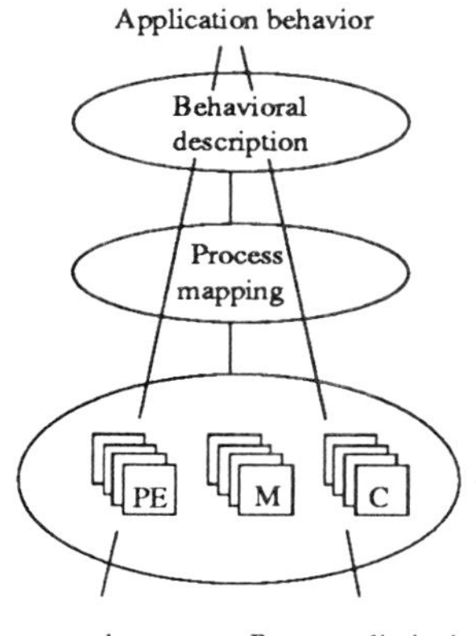

To gain an initial understanding of the fundamental views of exploiting parallel processing in real-time applications, let us consider two slices through our BMR development model as portrayed to the left. That is, we build upon a *resource-adequate* philosophy where application processes are directly (that is statically) mapped to an adequate set of resources *versus* a *resource-limited* philosophy where application processes are dynamically mapped to available resources.

Within both of these general points of view, the *mapping* of application processes to resources involves the activities of *allocation* of processes to specific resources as well as providing process *schedules*, that is, the ordering of the execution of processes. The major differentiating factor is the point in time at which allocation and scheduling transpire, that is, *a priori* (off-line) contra dynamically during system operation.

1.12.1 Direct Mapped versus Dynamically Mapped

The consequences of the two fundamental mapping philosophies are portrayed in Figure 1.8. *Note*: Here we utilize the abbreviation **P** for a programmed process.

Resource-adequate, *direct-mapped* systems reflect the nature of the problem (algorithms and/or geometry of data) where application processes are mapped (allocated and scheduled) directly to specific PE, M, and C hardware processes. As a result of the mapping, the application process logic may be directly embedded into the hardware logic; alternatively, the processes may be programmed and thus interpreted by PEs. In the latter case, no attempt is made to reallocate or alter the schedule of the programmed processes during system operation. Given these properties, it is possible to construct *deterministic* systems. On the other hand, they are typically inflexible. Such systems are controlled by the *time* at which processing takes place according to a fixed schedule.

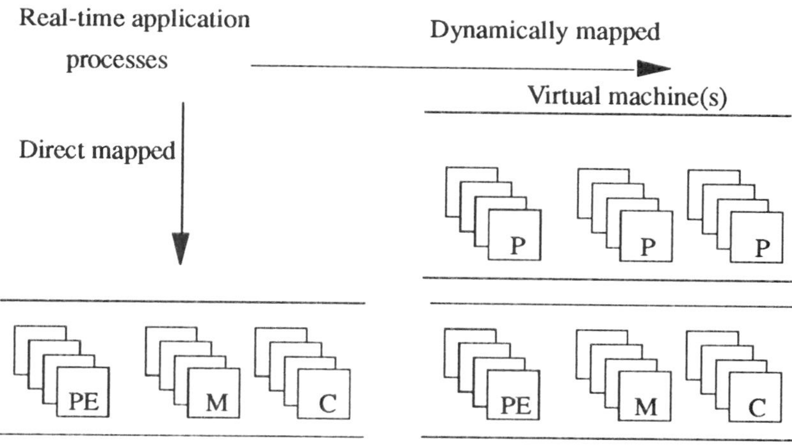

Figure 1.8. Direct Mapped versus Dynamically Mapped

In resource-limited *dynamically-mapped* systems, parallel PE, M, and C hardware processes cooperate to provide a higher level *virtual machine* model upon which the application processes are mapped. In this case, a *process hierarchy* exists. The programmed processes of the virtual machine(s) provide some form of operating system control that is capable of performing dynamic mapping (allocating and scheduling). Such systems are typically driven by the occurrence and processing of *events* in the external environment.

When *events* transpire randomly, both in the nature of the problem as well as in the process execution provided by the resource structure, scheduling becomes quite complex. The complexities arise due to *nondeterministic* properties. Finding schedules that will guarantee the meeting of response time requirements and/or attempts to find *optimal schedules* for time and resource allocation are difficult. In the general case, this problem is *NP-complete* (NP = Non Polynomial), meaning that it is unlikely that an algorithm exists that can find an optimal schedule in $O(N^k)$ (that is, polynomial time), given an arbitrary mix of processes to be executed. For a thorough presentation of NP-complete problems, the reader is referred to Garey and Johnson (1979). It is the resolution of nondeterminism in dynamically mapped solutions that often requires significant design effort and verification in order to achieve reasonable solutions.

There are a variety of trade-offs related to the selection of various alternative paradigms and model solutions within these two fundamental philosophies.

Within the resource-adequate, direct-mapped philosophy, we find various specific points of view, leading, for example, to paradigms and models where pipelining, algorithm, and/or geometric parallellism (perhaps massive) is to be exploited.

Within the resource-limited dynamically mapped philosophy, we find paradigms and models where pipelining, program, and/or data parallelism (again, perhaps massive) is to be exploited.

Various manifestations of these paradigms and model alternatives are examined in the book.

1.13 CLASSIFICATION OF PARALLEL COMPUTER SYSTEMS

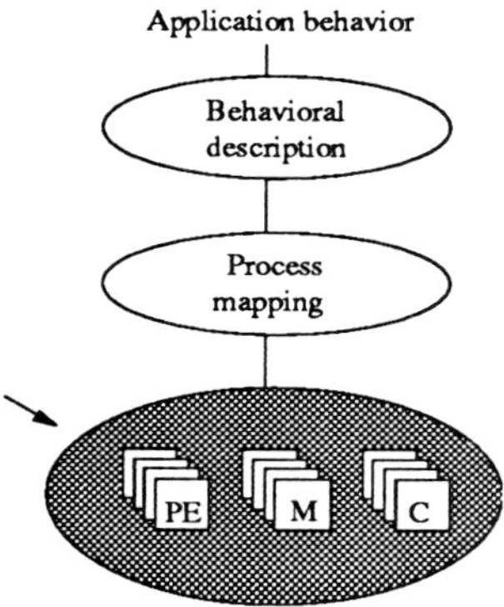

As literature on the field of parallel processing has developed, various means of classification have also evolved. Some of these classifications are highly relevant for our discussions of parallel processing. Thus, we consider some of the more well-known means of classifying and describing parallel hardware resource structures.

1.13.1 Flynn's Classification

The most widely used classification for parallel computer systems was proposed by Flynn (1966). This classification which has endured the test of time is based on the singularity or multiplicity of processed instruction and data streams as follows:

— SISD (**S**ingle **I**nstruction stream, **S**ingle **D**ata stream)
— SIMD (**S**ingle **I**nstruction stream, **M**ultiple **D**ata stream)
— MISD (**M**ultiple **I**nstruction stream, **S**ingle **D**ata stream)
— MIMD (**M**ultiple **I**nstruction stream, **M**ultiple **D**ata stream)

To a large extent, we can consider these alternatives as representing general resource structure points of view (philosophies) where a variety of paradigm and model alternatives can be applied. The first of these, SISD, is considered to be equivalent with the classic and most prevalent computer architecture (the von Neumann model). The latter three can all be considered as parallel processing paradigms. Almost all existing and proposed models of "programmed" parallel computing systems can be classified as either SIMD or MIMD. The MISD architecture may be considered to be a pathological case; however, it can, in fact, be of practical value. It can be used, for example, to categorize redundant fault tolerant systems that contain multiple PEs all of which perform the same operations. We may find uses for this model in various new forms of implementing parallel real-time systems. Utilize your fantasy and invent one!

While the Flynn classification has endured the test of time, it does not reveal all the important architectural properties for parallel real-time systems. The classification implies that some instruction interpretation mechanism is present that provides the control mechanism for sequencing processing activities. In fact, to use this classification for direct-mapped hardware systems, we could motivate the use of SCSD, SCMD, MCSD, and MCMD (where C stands for Control). These designations are much more general and could be used to encompass both forms of control (hardwired and programmed). Let us consider some further properties that must be taken into account.

1.13.2 Granularity (fine, medium, coarse, and very coarse)

It is common to utilize the analogy to food commodities (wheat, oats, sugar, coffee) with regard to the discussions of granularity. Consequently, *fine-grain* parallelism refers to the parallel processing of *microelements* (instructions and/or data) treated in parallel. Thus, in degrees of granularity we proceed up to *very coarse grain* parallelism, as we have noted in our previous human analogies. In processing instructions, for example, we could seek parallelism at the individual instruction level (or microprogram levels), at the level of statements or subroutines, or at the higher process levels. In processing data, we could seek parallelism in processing at the bit level, individual data items, vectors and matrices, records, files, and so on. Granularity is perhaps the single most distinguishing characteristic of parallel/distributed systems. In mixed systems, various units of granularity can be found.

When we introduced the coverage of hardwired control in relationship to Flynn's classification, we were actually emphasizing the importance of fine-grain granularity. One further reflection on the importance of granularity with respect to Flynn's classification has led to the the term SPMD (**S**ame **P**rogram, **M**ultiple **D**ata), which implies a higher degree of granularity (see Mauney and others, 1989).

Since we are considering real-time systems, there is one further essential granularity to consider, *time granularity*. That is, various processing activities must be accomplished within specific time granules. Time granularities, on the other hand, are obviously related to the various other units of granularity that we have introduced.

1.13.3 Coupling (tightly, closely, and loosely)

Another common means of classifying parallel systems is by the degree of coupling between PEs, that is, the network topology and the means of communication. Processing elements can be directly wired together, communicate over buses or cables, or be remotely located and communicate, for example, via radio or microwave signals. Alternatively, communication may occur via shared memories. Thus, the question of coupling is largely related to physical packaging, as well as transport method (that is, communication) and/or memory performance and utilization characteristics. Coupling properties are often used to distinguish between distributed and parallel processing.

1.13.4 General Purpose versus Special Purpose

Parallel processing systems can also be classified as to their degree of general or special purposeness. Certain systems are closely bound to a specific application or application domain and are implemented with a significant special-purpose hardware content. Systems for **D**igital **S**ignal **P**rocessing (DSP) are often the result of a *direct mapping* between the algorithm and hardware components. At the other end of the spectrum, we find general-purpose systems that, via programs, are adapted to deal with a wide variety of application domains. Naturally, there are degrees of general or special purposeness at all points along the spectrum.

1.14 THE FUNDAMENTAL ISSUES

While there may seem to be an extremely large, diverse set of concepts, methods, and mechanisms provided for various parallel processing alternatives, we have introduced a unifying view in terms of the BMR model. We now complement the BMR model with a point of view concerning **the fundamental issues**.

All the parallel processing models (abstract or concrete) and the paradigms upon which they are based can be characterized based upon the approach taken with respect to three *fundamental issues*:

The View of Processes *(P)*

Means of Communication *(C)*

Methods of Synchronization *(S)*

Processes can, in concrete environments, take on a variety of forms and be of varying granularity. As we previously considered in relationship to our BMR model, the decomposition of behavioral descriptions yields processes of varying granularity. Process-related data may be available, respectively delivered, via ports directly (timewise) in synchronous systems or may be accessed from queues in asynchronous systems, in which case the ports can be viewed as an abstraction for a queue.

The port notion becomes an important aspect of interprocess *communication* at all logical and physical model levels. Further, when processes communicate, they must *synchronize* their activities via time or some other appropriate mechanism. When processes operate in resource-limited situations, they have the further need to gain exclusive access to resources of the system. In these situations, *synchronization* is also required as a step toward providing for mutually exclusive use of resources.

As a part of the terminology problem, the terms selected to describe these three fundamental issues vary. This variation leads to confusion. Consequently, the reader should constantly focus on these issues as a means of attaining a proper perspective and as a means of comparing alternative solutions.

We can view the PCS issues in two dimensions within the framework of the BMR model as presented in Figure 1.9. The issues are addressed within the Behavioral Description and Hardware Resource level. That is, each particular behavioral description or hardware resource artifact has (or implies) a view of processes, means of communication, and method of synchronization. Conflicts in the treatment of these fundamental issues among artifacts at various levels often lead to *semantic gaps*, which can result in the use of complex process allocation and scheduling mechanisms. This complexity contributes to uncertainty (nondeterminism).

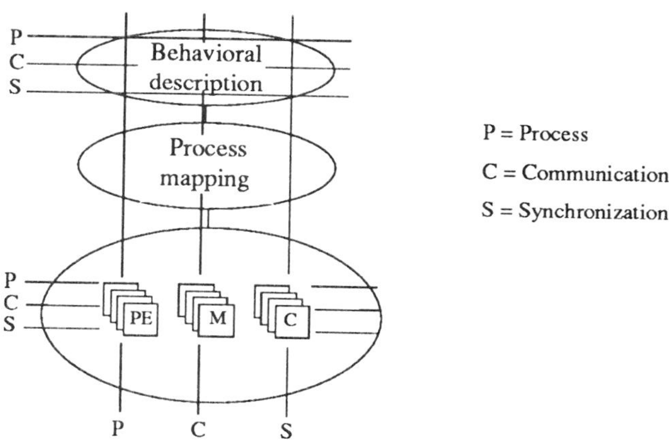

Figure 1.9. The PCS Issues in Two Dimensions

In some cases, the treatment of the PCS issues is transparent (and uniform) through all the levels and results in a system-wide consistency (that is, there are no semantic gaps). This generally results in more predictable results. In some systems, we may find partial couplings horizontally and vertically with respect to subsets of the issues.

Via this figure, we establish a framework for thinking and reasoning about the mechanisms of parallel processing. The figure provides a summary view of the issues that are central to all philosophies, paradigms, and models of parallel processing.

Each paradigm slice through the BMR model (based either upon the resource-adequate or the resource-limited philosophy) must address the PCS issues at all the BMR levels. In dynamically mapped solutions, an operating system takes on the process allocation and scheduling roles. The operating system "virtual machine" level also treats the PCS issues and provides further appropriate mappings to the hardware resources.

The PCS fundamental issues with respect to the parallel processing BMR development model form the major subject of the book. Keeping these pedagogical abstractions constantly in the forefront will assist the reader in obtaining deeper insight (that is, building a personal "map"). Finally, concerning the subject matter of the book,

THERE ARE NO SOLUTIONS; ONLY ALTERNATIVES

We shall examine several alternatives at the general level (philosophy), as well as at the paradigm and model levels. All these solutions provide various views of the PCS issues. The alternatives fit into the direct mapped or dynamically mapped philosophy. Within these two mapping philosophies, we find alternative approaches that apply pipelining, data, and/or program parallelism (sometimes massive), as well as scalar parallelism with respect to varying structures of PE, M and C hardware processes.

To summarize this introductory chapter, the reader is referred, once again, to the summary provided at the beginning of the chapter.

References

Akl, S.G. (1989). *The Design and Analysis of Parallel Algorithms*, Prentice-Hall, Englewood, Cliffs, NJ.

Boute, R.T. (1989). Syntactic and Semantic Aspects of Formal System Description, *Proceedings of EUROMICRO 89: Design Tools for the 90's, Microprocessing and Microprogramming, The EUROMICRO Journal*, Vol. 27, No. 1-5. pp, 155-161.

Broad, W.J. (1985). Edison's Papers Reveal He Invented by Analogy, *International Herald Tribune*, March 14.

Flynn, M.J. (1966). Very High Speed Computing Systems, *Proceedings IEEE*, Vol. 54, No. 12, pp. 1901-1909.

Garey, M.R., and D.S. Johnson (1979). *Computing and Intractability: A Guide to the Theory of NP-Completeness*, Freeman, San Francisco.

Gordon, W.J.J. (1961). *Synectics*, Harper & Row, New York.

Knuth, D.E. (1976). Big omicron and big omega and big theta. *SIGACT News* (April-June), pp. 18-23.

Lawson, H. W. (1990). Philosophies for Engineering Computer-Based Systems, *IEEE Computer,* Vol. 23, No. 12, pp. 52-63.

Lindsay, P.H., and D.A. Norman (1977). *Human Information Processing: An Introduction to Psychology*, Academic Press, New York.

Mauney, J., D.P. Agrawal, Y.K. Choe, E.A. Harcourt, S. Kim and W.J. Staats (1989). Computational Models and Resource Allocation for Supercomputers, *Proceedings of the IEEE*, Vol. 77, No. 12, pp. 1859-1874.

Quinn, M.J. (1987). *Designing Efficient Algorithms for Parallel Computers*, McGraw-Hill, New York.

Resnick, L.B. (1983). Mathematics and Science Learning: A New Conception, *Science*, Vol. 220.

Selfridge, O. (1959). Pandemonium: A Paradigm for Learning, *Symposium on the Mechanization of Thought Processes*, H.M. Stationery Office, London.

Stifler, Jr., W.W. (1950). *High Speed Computing Devices*, McGraw-Hill, New York.

Chapter 2

REAL-TIME SYSTEMS

In this chapter, we consider the general properties of real-time systems in order to provide a context in which we can evaluate the possibilities for applying parallel/distributed processing in industrial real-time applications.

- sensors and actuators represent the view of the external environment (32)
- real-time systems "model" external environments which, in many cases, follow well-known laws of physics (32)
- real-time processes are categorized into (periodic, aperiodic), (static, dynamic) and (critical, essential, nonessential) (34)
- concurrent processes may be executed on one or several PEs; whereas parallel processes imply execution on multiple PEs (35)
- several special requirements are placed upon real-time systems; the foremost requirement is predictability (36)
- various professionals view real-time systems in varying manners (38)
- the programming of real-time systems has historically been based upon low-level languages; however, some higher-level abstractions as well as specific languages for real-time programming have evolved (39)
- resource-adequate, direct-mapped resource structures provide for hardware process realization of the application (DSP applications as well as systolic and wavefront arrays belong to this category) (42)

- continuous operation cyclic systems, while program interpreted, bare some relationship to directmapped systems and can result in predictable solutions (43)

- asynchronous event-driven resource structures are found in resource-limited situations where processes and/or events have been assigned or receive priorities; processing is preemptive and queues of processes and/or events are maintained (45)

- distributed real-time systems are viewed as a form of parallel processing system and are composed of autonomous subsystems that cooperate toward a common goal (47)

- various strategies for deriving schedules for process sets are used for direct-mapped, continuous (cyclic), or asynchronous event-driven paradigm and models (48)

- dynamically mapped solutions result in several approaches to scheduling based upon priorities, processing time requirements, or deadlines (50)

- there are a number of uncertainties concerning the application of parallel processing (particularly for programmed solutions) in real-time system environments (54)

- resource adequacy provided via parallel processing may offer new improved solutions to predictable real-time systems (55)

> Many real-time systems of tomorrow will be large and complex and will function in distributed and dynamic environments. They will include expert system components that will involve complex timing constraints encompassing different granules of time. Moreover, economic, human, and ecological catastrophes will result if these timing constraints are not met. Meeting these challenges imposed by these characteristics very much depends on a focused and coordinated effort in all aspects of system development.
>
> John A. Stankovic (1988)

Having introduced the the subject of parallel processing in the previous chapter, we now continue by examining some generic implementation models and some specific properties of industrial real-time systems. Our goal is to abstract the main stream of developments so that real-time characteristics can be considered as we examine parallel processing alternatives. To establish a degree of commonality for our discussions, let us first introduce a model for the broad class of industrial real-time systems as portrayed in Figure 2.1.

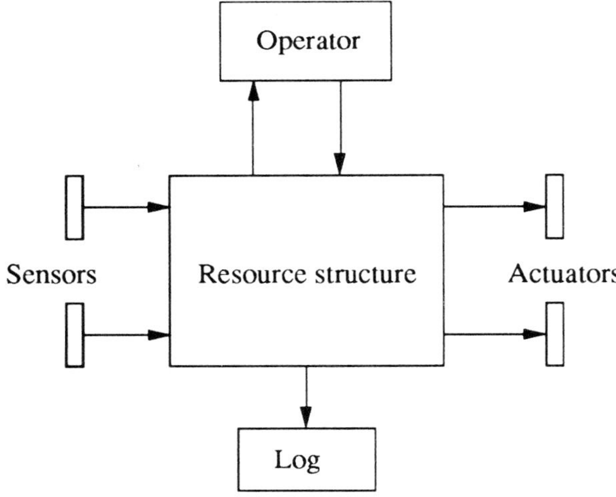

Figure 2.1. Abstract Model of Industrial Real-Time Systems

In general we can state that the *sensors* and *actuators* provide a view of the process behavior(s) in the external real-time environment, respectively the means of controlling process behavior(s) in the external environment. The *resource structure* can be parallel/distributed or centralized.

The real-time system may (optionally) have some means of observing what is going on (externally and internally), as well as for controlling processing from an *operator* interface. Further, we may optionally have some means of keeping a history of what has transpired via some form of *logging* media.

2.1 REAL-TIME APPLICATIONS

The implementation of the behavior of real-time application processes via a resource structure is, in fact, *modeling*, that is, utilizing a model of real-world phenomena that must be evaluated, typically, within specific time limits. In hard real-time systems, many of the phenomena that are modeled obey basic laws of physics and thus the fundamental theoretical models are well known. On the other hand, we are often faced with making approximations to the theoretical results due to limited time, space, and computational precision. Some areas for which real-time application models are typically developed are presented in Figure 2.2.

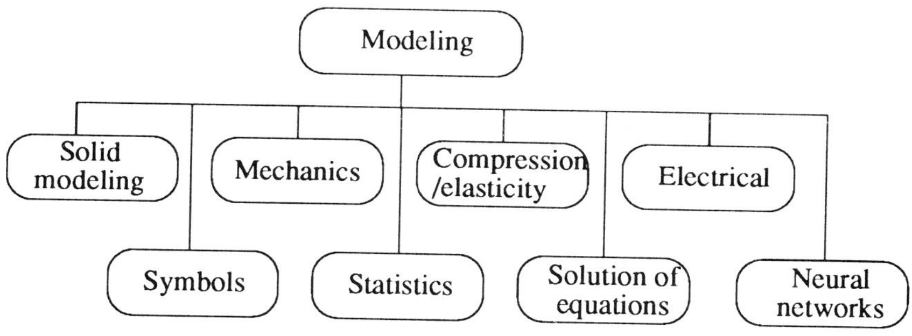

Figure 2.2. Modeling Physical Phenomena

Regardless of the area we model, it is important to be able to identify the relevant objects in each area and then describe the set of transformations that can be performed upon the objects (that is, the processes that can be applied). This leads to various forms of abstract and concrete behavioral description.

In the case of solid modeling, for example, we deal with projections into contours or grids (when dealing with graphics) or from contours and grids to projections (when dealing with vision). When dealing with Newtonian/Langrangian mechanics or the more modern theories of Kane, we are interested in the quantities (mass, speed, acceleration, position, and rotation). The model may deal with compression or elasticity of materials. In modeling electrical elements, the laws of Kirchhoff and Maxwell are utilized. We may treat symbols as the physical objects to be manipulated, in which case the functions applied to the object(s) provide spatial placement into documents, perhaps according to some standard rules for natural languages, engineering symbology, or the like. We frequently develop probabilistic (statistical) models of real phenomena when we cannot base the model on known physical laws or where modeling based upon the laws would result in unnecessarily complex and/or time-consuming computations. We may model by solving linear and differential equations that approximate real-world phenomena. Finally, we may model adaptive control processes via some form of learning mechanism, such as a neural network.

Although there may be several means of abstractly and concretely describing the application, through specification and programming languages, they all result in processes of varying degrees of data and/or program granularity (as portrayed in our BMR development model; see Figure 1.6) that can be exploited in parallel processing real-time situations. Within a specific application domain and based upon the requirements of the system model, we find the need to define various categories of real-time processes.

2.2 REAL-TIME PROCESSES

Given the abstract model of real-time systems and the fact that applications are decomposed (by some means) into processes, let us now consider the various classes of processes that are found in real-time environments. The classes of processes to be supported are determining factors in selecting appropriate behavioral description media, process mapping, and resource structure environments.

2.2.1 Periodic and Aperiodic Processes

First, we can characterize processes as to their periodicity [that is, at what time instance(s) the process occurs]. In this regard, we define the following:

periodic processes, which are to be executed repeatedly at regular intervals
aperiodic processes, which are executed at arbitrary points in time

Periodic processes are time-wise scheduled *deterministic* events, typically where some form of sampling for data acquisition and/or regular control is required. On the other hand, aperiodic processes occur *nondeterministically* due to the existence of some specific condition (event). We can find examples of real-time systems composed solely of periodic or aperiodic processes, as well as systems containing a mixture of both forms.

2.2.2 Static and Dynamic Processes

Processes may be permanent, unchangeable parts of the real-time system or they may be born, live, and die dynamically, leading to the following properties:

static processes, which are a permanent part of the real-time system during its execution

dynamic processes, which are created during the operation of the real-time system as required and removed when no longer needed

A much simpler approach can be applied in the static case, for example, via direct mapping of the problem to an appropriate resource structure. On the other hand, as flexibility requirements increase, particularly in the presence of limited resource structures, dynamic process allocation facilities are required. The combination of dynamic processes and requirements for periodic processes, of course, introduces complexities into the solution.

2.2.3 Relative Importance of Processes

We have previously made the distinction between real-time systems and the more restrictive hard real-time systems. In many complex real-time applications, it is possible to further refine processes into the relative importance categories suggested by Ramamritham, Stankovic, and Zhao (1989):

> **critical processes**, which must meet their deadlines; otherwise, the result(s) could be catastrophic
>
> **essential processes**, which have deadlines and are important to the operation of the system, but will not cause a catastrophe if they are not finished on time
>
> **nonessential processes**, which may miss their deadlines without any effect on the system in the near future, but which could have an effect in the long term (for example, maintenance and bookkeeping-related processes).

Once again, based upon the importance of processes and the mixture of various forms of processes that must be implemented, varying behavioral description, process mapping, and resource structure solutions may be required. The presence of all forms in the same system normally requires a priority mechanism and the use of sophisticated process allocation and scheduling solutions.

2.2.4 Concurrent and Parallel Execution

The terms concurrent and parallel are often used interchangeably; however, we utilize the following delineation:

> **concurrent execution**: The execution of multiple processes that have started but have not completed and thus are active at the same point in time. The processes may be executed by a single or multiple PEs.
>
> **parallel execution:** The execution of multiple processes (or portions of processes) by multiple PEs. The PEs may range from being tightly to being loosely coupled (distributed).

The majority of today's complex real-time system solutions are based upon concurrent process execution utilizing single PEs. It is the possibilities to distribute processes to multiple PEs for true parallel and/or concurrent execution that provides the impetus for this book.

The periodicity requirements for processes, the degree of permanence, and the relative importance, as well as the execution properties of processes, are extremely important properties that must be taken into account in selecting behavioral description media, the appropriate resource structures, and the proper process mapping strategy.

2.3 REQUIREMENTS FOR REAL-TIME SYSTEMS

Implicit in the name real-time systems is the requirement that results be available within a given *time* span after the arrival of input data at the sensors. If the system contains critical processes, then it must abide by tight time constraints to be met under any circumstances, since the failure to meet a deadline will make the results useless. In hard real-time systems, failure to deliver correct results, as described earlier, can lead to a catastrophe. We now identify some important requirements for real-time systems.

2.3.1 Predictability of System Behavior

The time required to perform processing must be predictable, especially for periodic and critical processes. That is, it must lay within maximum time limits in the worst case. We may state that the system must be *deterministic* (its behavior must be exactly predictable in all possible behavioral situations). In certain systems, absolute deterministic behavior, particularly at critical moments, may be essential, for example, in simultaneously controlling the three-dimensional movement of robot arm servomotors.

In some systems the deterministic behavior requirement is far too stringent, and it is often satisfactory to guarantee that processing be performed within specific time limits. Determinism, on the other hand, can be useful in reproducing resource structure behavior. A variety of analytic methods as well as simulation may be utilized in *a priori* verification of predicatability for various problems in varying resource structure environments.

2.3.2 Supervision of Timely Process Execution

It is important to oversee the processes to be executed so that they are executed at the proper points in time. In statically allocated direct-mapped solutions, this must be taken into account in the design. For dynamically mapped solutions in resource-limited environments, supervision can become a difficult problem. It is important to find feasible process allocation and scheduling algorithms, as well as the means of surveillance of processes during their execution. The surveillance may also be necessary to determine if the system has come to a nonprogressing situation, such as one or more processes entering nonterminating loops or a subset of the processes working together, consuming resources but not progressing. A liveness time-out mechanism may be required in order to detect nonprogressing situations.

2.3.3 Synchronization and Communication

There normally exist points in time when processes must synchronize their operation in order to provide correct execution semantics. Synchronization may be required (a) due to an external event (interrupt), (b) due to an internal event (for example, a clock time has been reached), (c) due to the need for processes to have mutually independent utilization rights to a shared resource, (d) due to the need for the processes to communicate with each other in an orderly manner, or (e) due to the need to synchronize output control signals (as introduced above in the control of three synchronized servo-motors). In relationship to the PCS fundamental issues (see Figure 1.9), the solution to these requirements plays a dominant role in real-time system design.

2.3.4 Avoidance of Deadlock

The deadlock situation arises in resource limited situations when two or more processes mutually are holding (that is, have been allocated) resources that are necessary for the progress of each other. Without releasing already held resources, none of the processes can proceed. It is essential to analyze real-time systems in advance for potential deadlock situations.

2.3.5 Detection and Treatment of Transient Overloads

Once again, in resource-limited situations when a surge of demands is placed upon the real-time system, it can be vital to detect the surge and rearrange process allocation and scheduling to meet the demands. In such cases, the relative importance of processes becomes important (normally implemented via some form of priority mechanism).

2.3.6 Safety and Security

Since virtually all real-time systems are utilized in environments that depend upon correct and timely operation, the question of safety and security must be properly addressed. The system must be protected against inadvertent or malicious alteration of data and program code. Further, if operator control is present, some form of security authorization may be necessary.

The requirements we have cited vary from system to system. Certain requirements are present for single PE solutions as well as for distributed/parallel processing solutions. On the other hand, some of the requirements place particular demands upon parallel processing solutions. We shall be examining many of these requirements in the following chapters.

Given the various classes of processes to be implemented in real-time systems and the fundamental requirements, let us consider the primary philosophies for the mapping of real-time processes to a resource structure.

2.4 VARYING VIEWS OF DEVELOPMENT

What the real-time problems are and how the problems are viewed by the "implementors" are key issues. The individuals and groups that design and develop real-time systems are influenced by their education, training and experience (see Lawson, 1990). Thus, depending on their background, they typically tend to view the problem, its behavioral description, and the mapping to a resource structure in different manners (various slices through the BMR development model). These varying views result in different philosophies, paradigms, and models for solving real-time problems.

Engineers and scientists typically address the problem from a detailed knowledge of the physical structure and relationships among the elements of the problem, often relying upon the laws of physics. Computer engineers may view the problem through a knowledge of hardware and software artifacts, which can be configured to provide a resource structure processing environment, whereas computer scientists may view the problem via the artifacts used for description and programming, as well as formal models of application and/or resource structure behavior.

Regardless of the point of view, it is important to emphasize the word **time** in real-time, since it is time that becomes the central issue. How time is treated within the various aspects of our BMR model varies based upon the philosophy and specific paradigms that are applied. However, we can observe that the introduction of the notion of time at the behavioral description level (as a specification) must be matched by a clear picture of the mappings of processes and the timing details of execution semantics provided by the resource structure. *It is the system, as a whole, that must exhibit satisfactory time-dependent behavior.*

Many large, complex real-time system development projects fail or only partially meet their goals due to parochial views taken on the part of diverse project groups. The pieces of the system are addressed separately and a common view of the whole system never evolves.

Given that there exist various views of real-time systems and their implementation, we shall now consider the description of behavior for real-time systems, as well as the three predominant contemporary process mapping and resource structure philosophies.

2.5 REAL-TIME BEHAVIORAL DESCRIPTION

The *behavioral description* of real-time systems differs quite widely based upon the views of the developers, as well as the type of system to be developed. In some instances, a graphical representation of signal flow, process flow, state transitions, and so on, and relevant mathematical equations may be sufficient to structure a direct-mapped solution. On the other hand, for program-based dynamically mapped solutions, both abstract and concrete languages are typically required.

Concerning programmed solutions, Halang and Stoyenko (1990) have reported that, longer than in any other data-processing area, assembly languages have prevailed for the concrete behavioral description of real-time applications. During the 1960s and 1970s, solutions were often confined to assembly languages due to the cost of PEs and memories, causing the need for optimal programming with respect to execution time and space (that is, storage utilization). Despite the arrival of low-cost hardware, the description of real-time behavior has remained largely in the domain of assembly languages and/or low-level languages such as C or PL/M. This use can be attributed to our earlier observation concerning the need for knowledge of the timing properties of the resource structure with respect to the behavioral description.

2.5.1 Abstract Behavioral Descriptions

As more complex real-time systems were conceived, assembly language and low-level language solutions became unwieldy. Thus, the need for higher-level behavioral descriptions grew. This resulted in emphasizing the use of abstract descriptions as well as higher-level languages.

In the area of abstract descriptions for relatively simple control applications based on *programmable logic controllers* (PLCs), the descriptions are normally based on highly problem related graphic representations that are familiar to engineers, for example, *ladder diagrams.*

General software engineering methods and tools have also evolved for abstractly identifying the essence of the real-time system activities. The most predominant system development models are based upon *structured analysis* and *object-oriented analysis.* Both of these methods permit the functional structure and behavior of the real-time system to be described. In some versions of these methods, timing requirements are noted as a form of documentation.

Another popular abstract graphical means of representing real-time system logic is the *Petri net*, which, in some variants, permits timing requirements to be specified and even analyzed. Due to the ability to automatically analyze Petri nets as well as their highly graphical nature, they have become a reasonably widespread notation for real-time system development.

In computer science communities, the question of abstract description of complex systems has led to *process algebras* in which formal descriptions of systems as sets of communicating processes are used to gain a deeper insight into the system and hopefully to verify some of its properties, for example, the absence of deadlock. The application of process algebras to real-time systems, however, can be considered to be in its infancy.

Several developments in this area of abstract descriptions can be relevant for specifying and/or realizing future real-time system solutions for parallel processing environments, which we shall consider in succeeding chapters.

The synthesis of abstract descriptions to concrete descriptions in some cases has been supported by automatic tools that normally provide partial translations to one or more programming languages. In other cases, the abstract description simply serves as a specification and is used as a guide for creating the detailed behavioral description via a programming language.

2.5.2 Real-time Programming Languages

Concerning higher-level programming languages, the most natural initial approach was to augment existing and proven scientific and technical languages with real-time features. Thus, FORTRAN, later Basic, and others where endowed with real-time add-ons. A countertrend was to develop new languages for real-time applications such as Jovial in the United States, as well as Coral 66 and RTL/2 in Great Britain. None of these languages really contained any special real-time features. The access to real-time facilities in these languages is most often provided by the introduction of procedure calls to operating system functions (that is, the process mapping level).

The Pearl (Process and Experiment Automation Realtime Language), developed by West German electrical, chemical, and control system engineers, was presented in 1969 and was the first language to directly address the special problems of real-time systems. This language has evolved into a standard for Basic as well as Full Pearl (see DIN 66253, 1989).

The most intensive effort to supply a high-level real-time language has, of course, been the U.S. Department of Defense sponsored development of Ada. While aimed at real-time problems, the current version of Ada has limited feasibility for real-time systems (particularly hard real-time systems). Compared to Pearl, the language has many elegant features reflecting the computer science orientation of its inventors. On the other hand, the features, for practicing engineers and technicians, often do not reflect their natural way of viewing real-time problems. Due to the specific semantics of Ada's task scheduling, it has been highly criticized as not being a very practical real-time language. Despite the problems with Ada, the language offers some new and important solutions to the structuring and reusability of programs. Further, the language is standardized, well supported, and under continual development, leading to new standardized versions.

Parallel to the development of imperative languages for real-time applications, a number of declarative (nonprocedural fill in the blanks) program generators were developed, often for specific application areas. Some examples are Atlas for automatic test systems, Exact for machine tool controls, and Step5 for programmable logic controllers. The program generators are normally vendor specific and contain preprogrammed function blocks for measurement, control, and automation, which are configured (nonprocedurally) by the user. Some of these products have been supplied for distributed real-time environments and, while limited, they have proved to be successful in many application areas.

Certain higher-level languages such as Modula-2 (see Wirth, 1983) and occam (see INMOS, 1988) have been utilized in the programming of real-time systems. In both cases, a well-defined interface between the language and the underlying process mappings and resource structure is required in order to account for the treatment of time.

A recent procedural-oriented language development is Real-Time Euclid, which, in relationship to all previous languages, is unique in that processes can be analyzed for schedulability. Thus, based upon supplied timing properties, a static determination can be made as to whether the system will meet its timing constraints. Naturally, Real-Time Euclid places restrictions on processes individually and collectively in order to provide accurate timing control (see Stoyenko and Klingerman, 1986).

Another interesting development is the ESTEREL language for synchronous processes (see Berry, Couronné, and Gonthier, 1988, and André and Fancelli, 1990). In contrast to other more general purpose real-time languages, ESTEREL is aimed at dealing with the critical processes of real-time systems. It treats critical processes in a synchronous (deterministic) manner, leaving noncritical (perhaps nondeterministic) processes to a coexisting environment where other processes are treated more conventionally. This recognition of the fundamental time granularity requirement differences between critical (often periodic) processes and noncritical processses can provide useful guidelines for future real-time system development.

The properties of languages for behavioral description are considered again in Chapters 3 and 7. For a further description of real-time languages, the reader is referred to the excellent survey article by Halang and Stoyenko (1990).

As mentioned previously, we see that the development of behavioral description approaches to real-time systems has, in fact, varied, based upon the point of view of the developers. Variations also exist in the selection of process allocation and scheduling strategies for resource structures as exemplified in the following discussion.

2.6 CONTEMPORARY REAL-TIME PARADIGMS AND MODELS

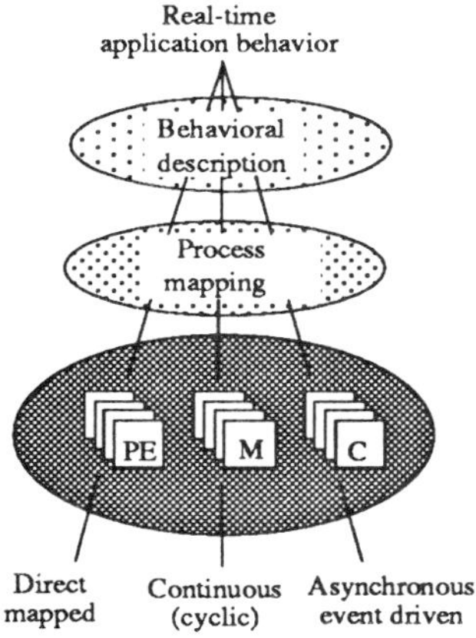

The three main contemporary paradigms and resulting models utilized in real-time systems are the direct mapped, the continuous operation (cyclic), and the asynchronous event driven. Each of these has its place in the real-time system domain, and each has its own set of advantages and disadvantages concerning the types of processes that can be conveniently implemented. Further, each is aimed at dealing with real-time processes at varying degrees of *time granularity*. We shall consider the main attributes of these three paradigms and related generic models shown to the left as slices in relationship to the BMR model.

A common denominator of all the approaches is that they provide mappings of the application *process set* (P) to an appropriate resource structure. The scheduling part of mapping typically involves timing constraints, process precedence constraints, and resource requirements. We shall later in this chapter introduce some of the particular approaches and problems encountered with various scheduling strategies.

2.6.1 Direct-Mapped Systems

The first paradigm follows the direct-mapped philosophy. Typically, very basic PE, M, and C components are used in the resource structure. In simple cases, the application process set (P) may be realized via combinatoric circuits where processing is accomplished by time-controlled signal propagation through corresponding hardware processes. However, we can find even reasonably complex contemporary systems in which the process set is mapped directly to a hardware resource structure; for example, as found in many **D**igital **S**ignal **P**rocessing (DSP) applications. In this case, application processes may be realized by hardware processes or by the PE interpretation of process programs.

Figure 2.3 portrays a generic model for direct-mapped systems. In this model, each process is allocated to a separate PE, which performs the process function directly. The static allocation is based upon a schedule of operations that guarantees appropriate processing order (precedence) and compliance with timing constraints. The Communication (C) is treated by a network of hardwired connections between the incoming signals, processing elements, and generated signals. **S**ynchronization (S) of direct-mapped systems may be synchronous or asynchronous. The systems may or may not retain information in **m**emories (M). The response time from sensor to actuator can typically be accurately calculated and measured.

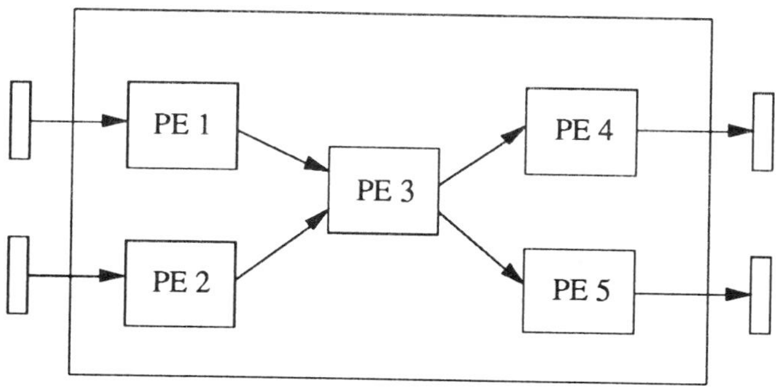

Figure 2.3. Direct-Mapped Model

Real-time systems that must process extremely large volumes of data with tight timing constraints are often only realizable via direct mapping into hardware resources.

Direct-mapped systems support periodic processes in a straightforward manner; however, a general treatment of aperiodic process behavior is difficult to achieve in this framework. In fact, most direct-mapped systems operate continuously without interruption. It is quite possible and often desirable to utilize pipelined processing models in direct-mapped systems, that is, to stage the propagations through the network of PEs so that more time-wise optimal use is made of PE, M, and C components, resulting in a processing speedup.

We shall explore this implementation alternative further when we consider various parallel processing architectures and especially in relationship to certain classes of applications. In this regard, we shall concentrate upon strategies to find optimal solutions in DSP applications, as well as via *systolic* and *wavefront* array solutions.

In the two remaining real-time system implementation paradigms, we shall assume the utilization of conventional computer systems as the basis of the hardware resource structure. The processes to be performed are multiplexed onto (share) the PE, M, and C resources and thus can require *scheduling*, as well as *resource allocation* control over their operation.

2.6.2 Continuous Operation (Cyclic) Systems

A philosophy of allocation and scheduling that is often found in commercial real-time system products and that is based upon programmed solutions is the continuous operation (cyclic scheduled) approach. This simplistic and highly understandable approach is the most predominant form of organizing hard real-time systems where programmed periodic critical processes must be performed and where aperiodic process execution (typically the result of a real-time interrupt), if present, must not contribute to any unpredictable delay of critical process execution.

The process set (P) may contain processes with varying processing times. Thus, the cycles are typically broken up into *time frames*, and a schedule is made based upon the static mapping, where portions of the processing time for each process are allocated slots in the time frames. A major advantage is that process switch overhead is removed or is insignificant. A major disadvantage of current time frame cyclic approaches is that alterations in the temporal behavior of future versions are difficult to accommodate since schedules have historically been developed by hand. This problem is examined again later in this chapter.

The continuous operation cyclic approach is best suited for environments in which input data are to be sampled (or polled) and processed at regular rates. In this regard, continuous operation organizations are somewhat related to direct-mapped approaches, but providing for larger time granularities. Due to their programmability, cyclic-programmed systems provide for greater flexibility than direct-mapped systems. The programmable PEs that are used are often conventional microprocessor CPUs provided with a real-time kernel system software package; however, they may even be specially designed PEs, for example, programmable logic controllers (PLCs) or special-purpose signal-processing PEs.

The use of sampling is closely matched to the treatment of periodic processes as long as sufficient processing power is available to keep up with the periodic requirements. It is even possible to transform aperiodic processes to periodic processes by including processing that periodically samples potential interrupting events. Thus, there is a delay for the processing of aperiodic processes. This may or may not be acceptable, based upon worst-case processing delays that can occur. On the other hand, the continuous operation cyclic system must be partitioned so that if aperiodic processes are entered into execution they do not disturb any critical periodic processes that must be executed. The generic model for continuous operation systems is based upon the provision of cyclic execution of relevant processes as portrayed in Figure 2.4.

Input data from sensors as well as output data to actuators are read/written as required directly from/to the processes that utilize the data. Communication (C) among processes is typically accomplished via shared variables or by conventional argument-parameter mechanisms. Concerning Synchronization (S), the start of each cycle may be synchronized with a specific cyclic frequency, thus establishing a maximum synchronized delay for all processing. When properly constructed, the problem of deadlock can be avoided.

Despite the wide-scale commercial utilization of this approach, very few research results have been published concerning its general applicability (see Lawson, 1992). This can be contrasted to the significant research literature surrounding event-driven behavioral models and systems where a variety of challenging problems exists.

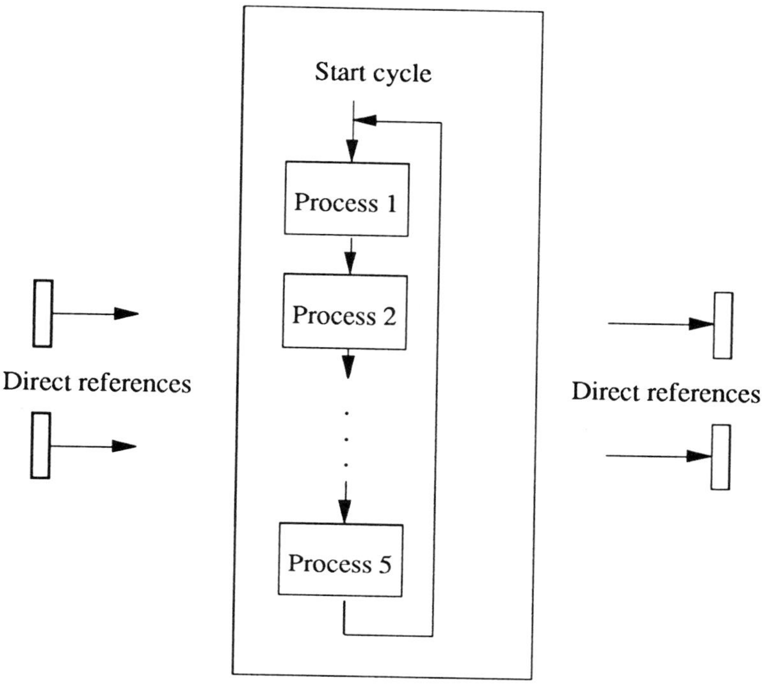

Figure 2.4. Continuous Operation (Cyclic) Model

2.6.3 Asynchronous Event-Driven Systems

Direct-mapped and cyclic paradigms are based upon the use of time-based control. In the paradigm we now consider, processing is based upon the occurrence of events (that is "signals" in a general sense) that indicate that something has happened. These events can be the result of new values being available at the sensors, perhaps indicated via interrupts. On the other hand, the software structure may be organized to generate "pseudo" interrupts (events) that can also be used as the basis for initiating processing. The event occurrence results in one or more processes being scheduled for future execution. Thus the process set (P) is dynamically changing over time.

In these programmed environments, a *process resource allocator and scheduler* (the central part of the operating system) is required to arbitrate the use of the resources and to control the order of process execution. The strategies for dynamic resource allocation and scheduling often provide major challenges to establishing viable resource structure scheduling (the NP completeness problem). The strategies typically attempt to optimize some aspect(s) of the systems behavior. We portray a generic, asynchronous, event-driven model with scheduling in Figure 2.5.

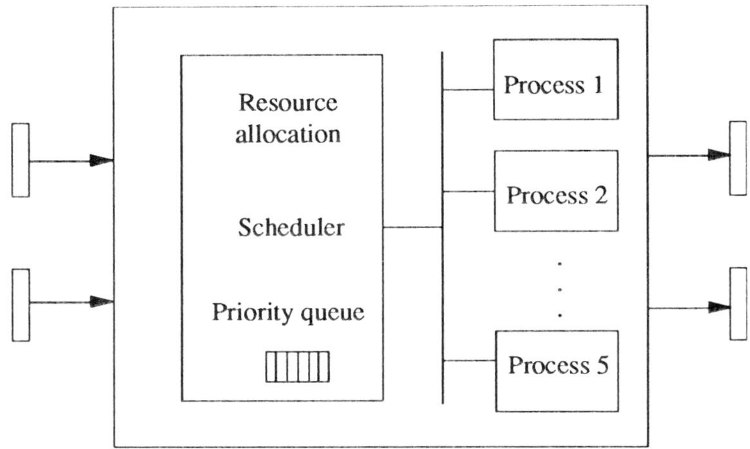

Figure 2.5. Scheduled, Asynchronous, Event-Driven Model

This form of real-time system is frequently referred to as *preemptive*. That is, the PEs that are executing processes may be preempted in order to turn their attention to specific situations (especially in relationship to solutions where events and/or processes are assigned *priorities*). Further, they are referred to as asynchronous since program logic is activated due to event occurrence (external or internally generated) rather than at fixed points in time.

Communication (C) among processes is treated by shared variables and/or via message passing between processes. The controlled cooperation between processes in this form of organization, as well as the controlled access to common resources (mutual exclusion), is typically treated by some form of software (or combined hardware/software) Synchronization (S) mechanism.

While the structure of event-driven systems may be seemingly rather clean, the potential randomness of event occurrence can cause significant problems in terms of dimensioning the resource structure and providing predictability guarantees that all event situations can be processed within specified time limits (or in some cases processed at all). Due to limited resources, the resource allocation and scheduling strategies become the determining factors. Remember the (0, 1, $\approx \infty$) resource utilization axiom that was presented in the introductory chapter.

Despite problems with resource structures and their utilization, this model or variations thereof are often utilized for complex real-time applications (centralized as well as distributed) where mixtures of periodic and aperiodic processes are to be accommodated. Further, the various classes of processes (critical, essential, and nonessential) are typically treated via the utilization of priorities. In these resource-limited situations, the potential deadlock and livelock problems must be taken into account.

The direct-mapped, continuous operation (cyclic) and asynchronous event-driven system paradigms can result in models that vary from the generic forms that have been presented. Further, complex systems (especially distributed systems) may contain a combination of the strategies that have been presented. In any event, the paradigms and generic models provide a useful starting point for comparing the central properties of alternative solutions.

2.7 PARALLEL/DISTRIBUTED REAL-TIME SYSTEMS

Many of the complex real-time systems of today have distributed resource structures and in some cases provide distributed process allocation and scheduling. We have earlier considered the case of distributed logic for controlling the servo-motors in a robot. Distributed systems are found today in moving vehicles such as airplanes, automobiles, in automatic production environments, power network monitoring and control, telecommunications, and military command and control systems, to name a few.

In the introductory chapter, we stated that we do not make any essential difference between parallel and distributed systems. From the real-time system point of view, it is simply a question of the coupling of subsystems and the *time domains* in which they operate. Thus, while there is great confusion and much discussion in the literature concerning this matter, we adopt a simple unified view via the following definition:

> *Parallel/distributed systems are composed of autonomous subsystems that cooperate to achieve common goals. The collection of hardware and software processes may be structured in a variety of manners in order to meet the needs of particular applications.*

This definition also allows for the recursive definition of a subsystem that deals with a subset of the common goals. In the cooperation, the various autonomous subsystems are frequently working in various *time granularities*, resulting in a hierarchy of time domains. Further, in dimensioning parallel/distributed real-time systems, the time and space costs of processing, communication, and memory must be considered.

Given our definition, let us consider a generic model for parallel/distributed real-time systems as portrayed in Figure 2.6. While the requirements and details may change from system to system, we can identify the basic functions of various subsystem processing activities in the real-time environment. Each subsystem in the figure takes on dedicated roles (that is, mixed systems). Subsystems may be based upon uniform general purpose PE, M, and C components that are programmed to perform their dedicated functions. On the other hand, the subsystems may be special purpose, each based upon the most appropriate architecture for behavior to resource structure mappings. We may even find a mixture of the three generic models discussed above (direct mapped, continuous operation cyclic solutions, and asynchronous event driven).

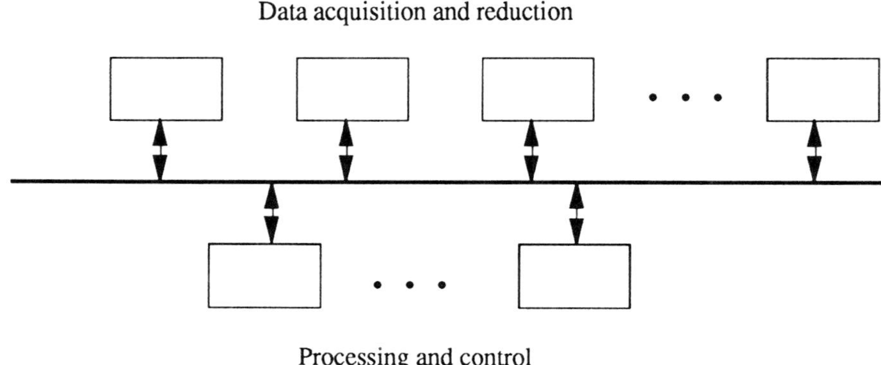

Figure 2.6. Parallel/Distributed Real-Time System Model

Within the *time domain* hierarchy of the system, we find particular subsystems that have very hard time demands such that the goal of *predictability* cannot be accomplished without applying parallel processing. For example, some real-time applications may best exploit subsystems based upon SIMD (**S**ingle **I**nstruction, **M**ultiple **D**ata) architectures, particularly for those portions of an application involving image processing, or neural network approximations. It is this type of mixed environment that forms an important basis for developing the parallel processing insight provided by the current book.

2.8 SCHEDULES FOR PROCESS SETS

The complex distributed/parallel real-time environment we have portrayed requires varying treatment of the fundamental PCS issues with respect to various paradigms and resource structure models. Therefore, it is useful for us to consider some of the contemporary approaches to the scheduling of process sets in real-time applications. Let us consider the general formulation of process sets and scheduling portrayed in Figure 2.7. The figure portrays required *processing time* (that is, time required to complete the process) for which we provide varying interpretations.

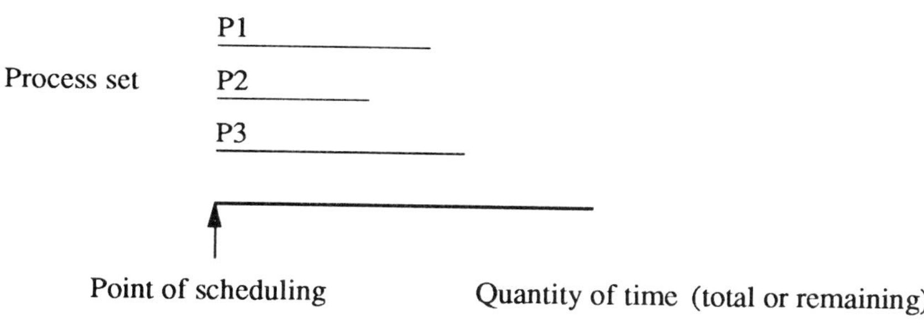

Figure 2.7. Scheduling of a Process Set

In *direct-mapped* systems, based upon processing time requirements, a static allocation and schedule of the process set to one or more PEs is provided, which will guarantee that timing requirements are met. *Thus, the point of scheduling is at system construction time.* It is possible to use various scheduling formulations that manipulate the processing time periods of the processes with respect to the resources, thus seeking an optimum solution.

In *continuous (cyclic)* systems, a static schedule is made where portions of P1, P2, and P3 are executed in various time slots (frames) of the cycle, as portrayed in Figure 2.8. The cyclic schedule "rolls" forward over time (potentially with unused time slot portions). *The schedule is made at the time of system configuration.* With proper dimensioning and treatment of aperiodic processes, it *may* be possible to guarantee that timing requirements are met. However, the designer must pay particular attention to the treatment of interrupts, and potential overloading effects of interrupts must be treated. Further, this type of structure is difficult to maintain when alterations are made to the mix and processes and/or their timing properties.

In *asynchronous event-driven* systems where dynamic mapping is applied, the point of scheduling is at some point during system execution. In this case, processing time represents how much remaining time is required to complete processing (the *latency time*). *The point of scheduling is at some point in the time axis* and is typically made at points in time when processes become delayed waiting for resources or in conjunction with communication to or from other processes. When a schedule is made, the current set of active "executable" processes is considered for scheduling.

Scheduling in these resource-limited environments and the operating systems in which schedulers are embedded have been the subject of significant research since the early 1970s, which has been intensified in the latter part of the 1980s. In the remainder of this section, we shall consider **some** of the main lines of thinking in this respect.

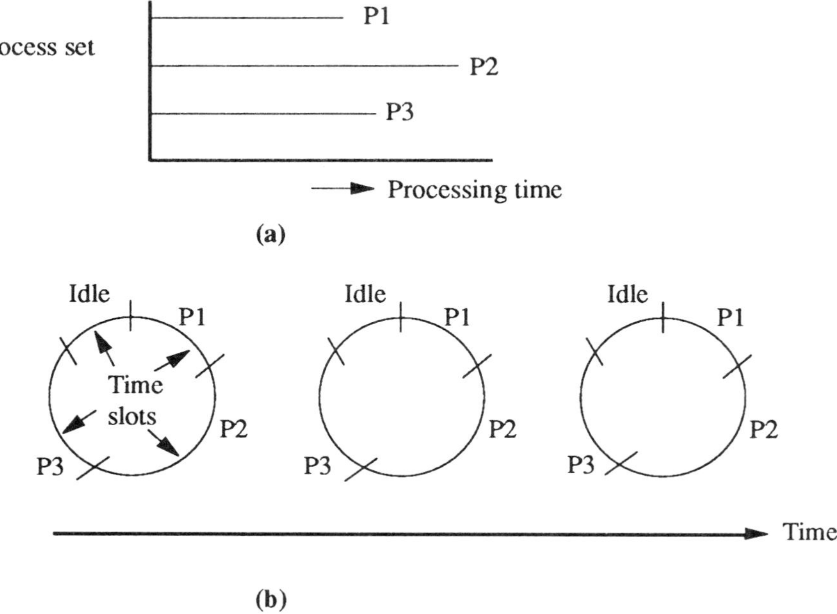

Figure 2.8. (**a**) Process Set; (**b**) Cyclic Time Slot-Based Schedule

2.8.1 Dynamic Scheduling

Our portrayal of latency time in Figure 2.7 is not a sufficient basis for understanding the issues and alternatives of scheduling. First, the calculation of latency time becomes quite complicated due to alternative paths through processes, as well as their dynamic resource and communication needs. Whereas in the simpler direct-mapped and cyclic cases, processes can be more precisely characterized, they are generally more difficult to characterize in the dynamic situation. It often makes sense to characterize processes by the *average execution time* and *worst-case execution time*. Based upon these properties, goals may be set for scheduling.

> *All processes should (**must**) be schedulable based upon average (**worst-case**) processing times.*

Second, to utilize the limited resources in an effective manner, the processes are assigned priorities that indicate their relative importance to the overall functioning of the system. Priorities are often statically assigned to processes or classes of processes. On the other hand, due to the stochastic nature of complex systems, it can be difficult to guarantee that all but the highest-priority process(es) will always meet timing requirements.

2.8.2 Some Process Priority Problems

Let us now examine some process priority problems that can arise. In Figure 2.9, we portray a situation in which a single PE is being scheduled for the processing of the process set. In Figure 2.9a, the highest-priority process P1 with priority 1 must use the services of P3, which has the lowest priority. Thus, due to P1 being suspended to wait for P3, a scheduling decision is made. At this point, P2 is selected for execution since it has a higher priority than P3. Thus, P1 will be *blocked* from execution as long as P2 continues to execute since it is now bound to P3 for its progress. The phenomenon is referred to as *priority inversion.*

One straightforward solution to the problem is portrayed in Figure 2.9b where P3, when "called" upon to provide service for a higher-priority process, temporarily receives the same priority as that process. This is called *priority inheritance* (see Sha, and Lehoczky, 1987) and is clearly illustrated in the figure where P3 temporarily receives the same priority as P1. Thus, P1 cannot be blocked by a lower-priority process. Rajkumar, Sha, and Lehoczky (1988) proposed a slight modification of priority inheritance that provides for a controlled limiting of the amount of blocking permitted, called the *ceiling protocol.*

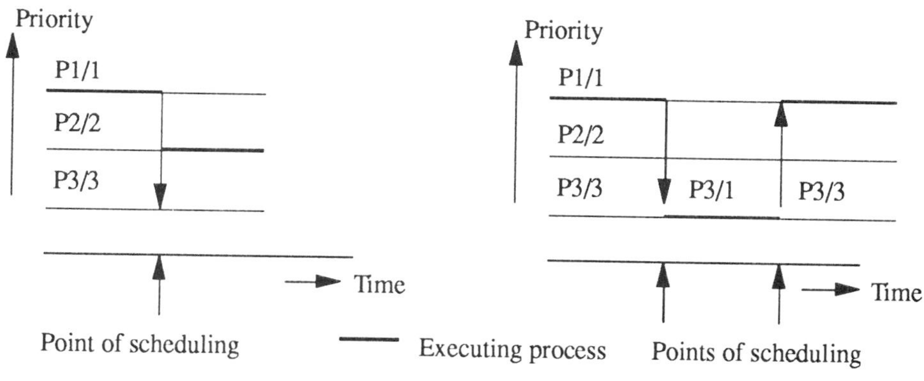

Figure 2.9. (**a**) Priority Inversion (**b**) Priority Inheritance

2.8.3 Scheduling Strategies

As an alternative to utilizing statically assigned priorities for processes, several results have been presented that base dynamic schedules on various time criteria.

Scheduling Periodic Processes

Liu and Layland (1973) provided a single PE *rate monotonic* schedulability equation for *periodic processes* where highest priority is assigned to processes with the shortest processing time requirements. Their result indicates that a set of n independent periodic processes is schedulable if the overall PE utilization is less than

$$n\,(2^{(1/n)} - 1)$$

For large n, this asymptotically approaches 0.693, indicating that all process sets are allocatable if PE utilization is less than 69%. This pessimistic scheduling is based upon the worst possible relationships between the required processing times of the periodic processes. Under more favorable circumstances a higher utilization can be obtained. On the other hand, a subutilization of resources may be necessary in order to meet predictability requirements.

Mixed Periodic and Aperiodic Scheduling

If the response time for aperiodic processes is not critical, they may be run in the background, thus exploiting any available PE overcapacity. Further, if a periodic server process is used to poll the aperiodic processes, the total system may still exploit the rate monotonic scheduling approach. However, it is often the case that aperiodic process requirements are bursty and in some cases require hard deadlines. Lehoczky, Sha, and Stronsnider (1987) have proposed a number of algorithms to deal with this problem. One line of thinking is to use a "deferrable server," in which case a sporadic process is executed immediately and for as long as required, provided that the collection of periodic processes is still schedulable. This strategy assists in improving response time for periodic processes, but does not guarantee that sporadic deadlines will be met during transient overloads.

Deadline Scheduling

Lee and Gehlot (1985) introduced the notion of *temporal scopes* (TS) as a means of describing the relationship of processes to time, as illustrated in Figure 2.10. The quantities identified in the figure are defined as follows:

- — Deadline: the time by which the execution of a TS must be finished
- — Minimum (maximum) delay: the minimum (maximum) time that must or, alternatively, can elapse prior to the start of the execution of a TS
- — Maximum execution time of a TS
- — Maximum elapse time of a TS

By associating these properties with the processes that embody them, the problem of satisfying time constraints becomes one of *deadline scheduling*.

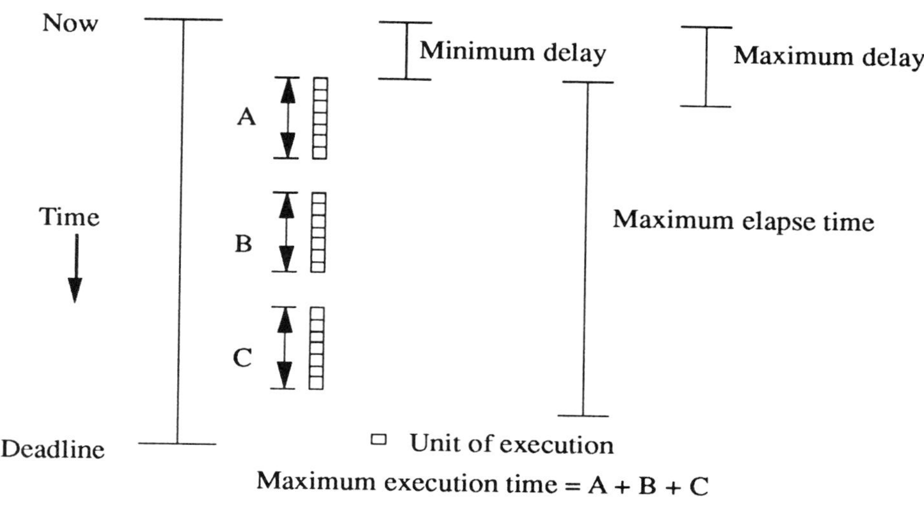

Figure 2.10. Temporal Scopes (TS)

Given the formulation of temporal scopes and deadlines, we can easily develop the *earliest deadline* scheduler in which the processes with the earliest deadline are given the higher priority.

A modification of the earliest deadline scheduler called the *least slack time* scheduler also requires us to know the amount of time remaining for each process in the set before its deadline. Consequently, both deadline and shortest latency are taken into account. This formulation does the best it can with a mix of aperiodic processes. When all deadlines can be met, it yields a result similar to rate monotonic scheduling. However, as one would expect, in overloading situations, earliest deadline and least slack time schedulers degrade in a highly nondeterministic manner.

This concludes our introduction to contemporary approaches to the scheduling of real-time processes. We shall return to this subject later in the book, when we shall concentrate more specifically upon the implications of parallel processing upon real-time scheduling. For a deeper discussion of real-time scheduling, the reader is referred to Burns and Wellings, (1990). Further, Cheng, Stankovic and Ramamritham (1987) have provided a useful survey over scheduling algorithms for hard real-time systems.

2.9 TOWARD PARALLEL PROCESSING ENVIRONMENTS

The direct-mapped system approach is implemented as a parallel network of PE, (possibly M), and C components. However, can the continuous operation (cyclic) and asynchronous event-driven paradigms and models be utilized in parallel processing environments? Are there better paradigms and models for parallel processing environments? It is quite clear that research and development related to extending the contemporary models to highly parallel environments will proceed, as well as searches for new real-time implementation philosophies, paradigms, and models incorporating new means of behavioral description, process allocation, and scheduling and resource structures.

While extensions to existing as well as new approaches will be proposed for parallel real-time systems, it is essential to note that the mapping to parallel processing resource structure environments must be viewed in light of the often strict requirements and constraints placed upon real-time systems that we have considered in this chapter. Once again, the importance of time and the question of predictability must always be taken into account.

2.9.1 Elements of Uncertainty

In relationship to the requirements for predictability, we can point to several phenomena in process allocation and scheduling for resource structures that can contribute to uncertainty and thus result in the inability to provide predictability guarantees. These factors are:

— random interrupts and associated handling
— operating system overhead
— scheduling overhead
— communication delays and overhead
— delays due to memory and/or bus transfers
— dynamic resource allocation
— garbage collection
— reconfiguration of the resource structure
— compiler-generated code

All these phenomena can lead to unpredictable processing situations. In hard real-time systems the existence of such elements of uncertainty is not acceptable. On the other hand, developing real-time systems for parallel processing environments where the uncertainty related to these phenomena can be avoided or minimized is a major research and development challenge.

2.10 FURTHER CHALLENGES

In addition to improving performance by introducing parallel processing, challenging problems remain in terms of the *x*-abilities [understandability, dependability (that is, testability, reliability and verifyability), maintainability, and extendability] as well as in developing fault-tolerant solutions (one of the most important potential gains from introducing parallel processing into real-time environments). These challenges span behavioral description, process allocation, and scheduling and resource structure allocation, with many of them being related to the interaction of these BMR elements. Stankovic (1988) has identified the following future challenges:

— specification and verification techniques that can handle the needs of real-time systems with a large number of interacting components
— design methodologies that can be used to synthesize systems with specified timing properties where these timing properties are considered from the beginning of the design process
— programming languages with explicit constructs to express, with unambiguous semantics, the time-related behavior of modules
— scheduling algorithms that can, in an integrated and dynamic fashion, handle:
(1) complex process structures with resource and precedence constraints
(2) resources (such as communication subnet and I/O devices)
(3) timing constraints of varying granularity
— operating system functions designed to deal with highly integrated and cooperative time-constrained resource management in a fast and predictable manner
— communication architectures and protocols for dealing efficiently with messages that require timely delivery
— architecture support for fault tolerance, efficient operating system functioning and time-constrained communication

One of the main issues that will be debated many times in the future is the question of resource-limited versus resource-adequate environments. With modern hardware process technology, the premise for resource-limited solutions may change in the future, thus permitting solutions to be attained where complex allocation and scheduling can be eliminated or reduced significantly (a major challenge for parallel processing research and development). Thus, as we consider the subject of parallel processing in the following chapter, we should keep in mind the special requirements of real-time systems and the challenges that must be dealt with in order to effectively utilize the potential that parallel processing enables. Further, we should search for areas in which parallel processing offers significant improvements over today's methods for realizing real-time systems, for example, in providing x-ability properties.

References

André, C., and L. Fancelli (1990). A Mixed Implementation of a Real-time System, *Proceedings of Euromicro 90*, North-Holland, New York, pp. 397-402.

Berry, G., P. Couronné, and G. Gonthier (1988). Synchronous Programming of Reactive Systems: An Introduction to ESTEREL, K. Fuchi and M. Nivat (eds.). *Programming of Future Generation Computers*, Elsivier Science Publishers, Amsterdam, pp. 33-55.

Burns, A., and A. Wellings (1990). *Real-time Systems and Their Programming Languages*, Addison-Wesley, Reading, MA.

Cheng, S.-C., J.A. Stankovic, and K. Ramamritham (1987). Scheduling Algorithms for Hard Real-time Systems - A Brief Survey, *Tutorial Hard Real-time Systems* (J.A. Stankovic and K. Ramamritham eds.), IEEE Computer Society Press, Washington, DC.

DIN 66253 (1989). Programmiersprache PEARL - Mehrrechner-PEARL, Beuth-Verlag, Berlin.

Halang, W.A., and A.D. Stoyenko (1990). Comparative Evaluation of High-level Real-time Languages, *International Journal of Real-Time Systems*, Vol. 2, No. 4.

INMOS (1988). *occam 2 Reference Manual*, Prentice Hall, Englewood Cliffs, NJ.

Lawson, H.W. (1990). Philosophies for Engineering Computer Based Systems, *Computer*, Vol. 23, No. 12, pp. 52-63.

Lawson, H.W. (1992). CY-CLONE: An Approach to the Engineering of Resource Adequate Cyclic Real-time Systems, *International Journal of Real-time Systems*,Vol. 4, No. 1, pp. 55-83.

Lee, I., and V. Gehlot (1985). Language Constructs for Distributed Real-time Programming, *Proceedings of the Real-time Systems Symposium*, IEEE Computer Society Press, Los Alamitos, CA.

Lehoczky, J.P., L. Sha, and J.K. Stronsnider (1987). Aperiodic Scheduling in a Hard Real-time Environment, Technical Report, Department of Computer Science, Carnegie Mellon University, Pittsburgh, PA.

Liu, C.L., and J.W. Layland (1973). Scheduling Algorithms for Multiprogramming in a Hard Real-Time Environment, *Journal of the ACM*, Vol. 21, No. 1, pp. 46-61.

Rajkumar, R., L. Sha, and J.P. Lehoczky (1988). Real-time Synchronization Protocols for Multiprocessors, Technical Report, Department of Computer Science, Carnegie Mellon University, Pittsburgh, PA.

Ramamritham, K., J.A. Stankovic, and W. Zhao. (1989). Distributed Scheduling of Tasks with Deadlines and Resource Requirements, *IEEE Transactions on Computers*, Vol. 38, No. 8, pp. 1110-1123.

Sha, L., and J.P. Lehoczky (1987). The Priority Inheritance Protocol: An Approach to Real-time Synchronization, Technical Report, Department of Computer Science, Carnegie-Mellon University, Pittsburgh, PA.

Stankovic, J.A. (1988). Misconceptions about Real-time Computing, *Computer*, Vol. 21, No. 10, pp. 10-19.

Stoyenko, A., and E. Klingerman (1986). Real-time Euclid: A Language for Reliable Real-time Systems, *IEEE Transactions on Software Engineering*, Vol. 12, No. 9, pp. 941-949.

Chapter 3

PARALLEL PROCESSING:
PHILOSOPHIES, PARADIGMS, AND MODELS

INTRODUCTION

In this introductory section we consider the following:

- a common view of behaviors is introduced in order to neutralize the diverse means of behavioral description (59)
- the generic parallel processing model consisting of multiple PEs connected to an interconnection network (ICN) where memory processes are treated as a form of PE (60)
- increasing bandwidth is a common goal in parallel processing systems where solutions can vary among the herd of elephants, army of ants, or eager beaver approaches (61)
- parallelism in real-time processing involves two time domains, the environment and the system views (62)
- scheduling, resource allocation, interprocess communication, synchronization, and the presence of nondeterminancy become important issues in real-time parallel processing solutions (63)

Parallel processing, especially for high-performance general computation, was the subject of intense activity during the 1980s. While many fundamental ideas were developed earlier (as described later in Chapter 6), it is during the 1980s that parallel processing has become of age. In addition to the vast number of parallel architectures, languages, methods, and the like, that have been proposed, many concrete products have been delivered to the marketplace, making the subject area highly relevant for consideration in industrial real-time applications.

The utilization of parallel processing for industrial real-time applications is most often motivated by the need for increased performance in order to meet response time requirements; however, dependability and responsiveness aspects such as faulttolerance and the *x-abilities* that we have identified can also motivate the selection of parallel processing alternatives. As we review the main stream of contemporary parallel processing, it is important to keep eventual use(s) in mind and to be aware of the importance of *predictability* properties and any *uncertainties* that can arise in applying the various parallel processing alternatives. Further, the reader should consider the possibilities of utilizing various parallel processing approaches in their entirety or partially as subsystems in parallel/distributed real-time environments.

In the introductory chapter, we introduced the BMR (**B**ehaviour **M**apping **R**esource Model) and the PCS (**P**rocess, **C**ommunication, and **S**ynchronization) fundamental issues. These two strong abstractions should be kept constantly in focus as we consider the subject of parallel processing.

3.1 A COMMON VIEW OF BEHAVIOR

A significant problem with respect to understandability of all processing systems is the plurality of terminology and concepts utilized in describing the abstract as well as concrete structure and behavior. The existence of multiple views inhibits common understanding, which is a goal of this book. On the other hand, from a functionality point of view, we can ask the question, Are there really fundamental differences?

The processing performed by all computer systems can, in fact, be reduced to a common basis. That is, all systems are designed to provide processing for a set of *situations*. The situations reflect the occurrence of external and/or internal events (including time events) and the state of processing. Thus, **all** computer systems provide some form of *operations* that when properly ordered provides processing behavior for situations. The multiplicity of views of how to conceive of the description of processing structure and behavior for situations is portrayed in Figure 3.1.

The variety of approaches to describing processing variants described in Figure 3.1 is manifested in the quantity of artifacts (languages, methods, methodologies, and the like) that has evolved. A useful way of relating the multiple points of view is that each alternative provides *end-to-end processing protocols* for situations. In line with our earlier goals of using processes as the common denominator, we can view each operation as a process, as well as the collection of operations as a process. Further, our definiton of processes includes both the structure and the behavior.

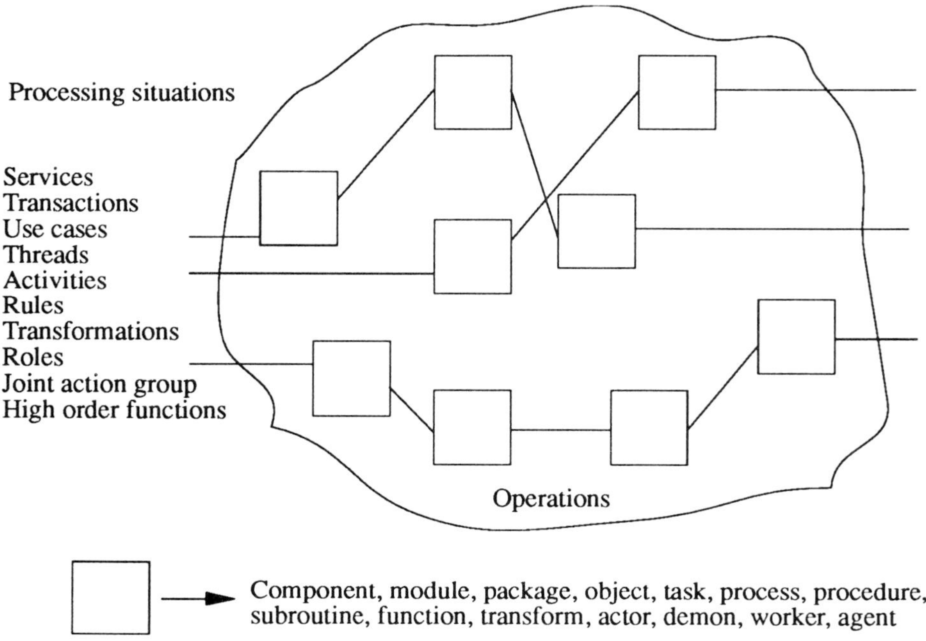

Figure 3.1. A Multiplicity of Views

3.2 GENERIC PARALLEL PROCESSING RESOURCE MODEL

Regardless of whether behaviors are direct mapped or dynamically mapped, the properties and configuration of the hardware processes PE, M, and C provide the concrete realization of a parallel architecture.

To observe the similarity between all approaches, we introduce the generic parallel processing model portrayed in Figure 3.2. In our model the PE and C (interconnection network) processes are clearly visible. On the other hand, we can question where M (memory) processes are placed in this model.

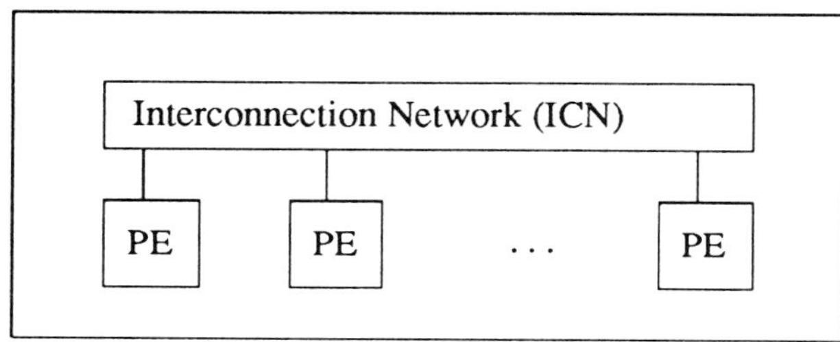

Figure 3.2. Generic Parallel Processing Model

3.2.1 Memories as Processing Elements

The best common denominator means of viewing memory processes is to simply treat them as another form of PE. In this case, the PE, as a hardware process with input and output ports, contains a data structure as well as the logic to perform a finite set of processing operations (protocols) upon the elements of the data structure. By making this simplification, all parallel systems become members of the generic model of parallel systems, that is, a number of PE processes connected by **interconnection network** (ICN) processes.

With this abstraction, we can characterize various memory organizations that are found in diverse parallel architectures as PE processes. For example, the use of *memory interleaving* (described later in this chapter) is simply a means of organizing the local connection network of the PE containing the memory, as well as the process logic of the memory PE, in order to pipeline memory operations.

3.2.2 Increasing Bandwidth

Parallel architectures have been motivated, to a large extent, by the bottleneck caused by traffic between a single PE and Memory processes as found in the classical von Neumann (SISD: **S**ingle **I**nstruction **S**ingle **D**ata Stream) architectural concept. This restrictive processing *bandwidth* can be improved by introducing parallel processing in the following manners:

— parallel processing within PEs (via instruction and/or data pipelining)
— multiple PEs
— interconnection networks permitting for inter-PE transports
— multiple Memory processes

We typically find some combination of these means of increasing the processing bandwidth in all parallel processing architecture resource structures. They each provide some form of system partitioning, which has implications upon processing order and state transitions.

The techniques for instruction and data pipelining have been used for many years and are well established. While these factors contribute to increased bandwidth, they are of less immediate interest than architectures based upon the other three factors. Thus, we factor out the discussion of instruction and data pipelining from this book. On the other hand, pipelining as found in various direct-mapped solutions is described in detail.

3.2.3 Elephants, Ants, and Beavers

Concerning the design of parallel processing systems, one can identify two polar extremes. At one extreme, we have the "herd of elephants" approach, that is, utilizing a small, but multiple number of extremely powerful interconnected PEs (perhaps with significant internal parallel processing). At the other extreme, we have the "army of ants" approach, that is utilizing large numbers of simple interconnected PEs. The "eager beaver" approach represents a compromise somewhere in between the polar extremes and typically employs the ever increasing power of commercially available VLSI-based microprocessor technology.

3.3 PARALLELISM AND REAL-TIME PROCESSING

Given a common view of behavior and the generic model of parallel processing resource structures, let us now relate the question of process parallelism to real-time processing by considering Figure 3.3.

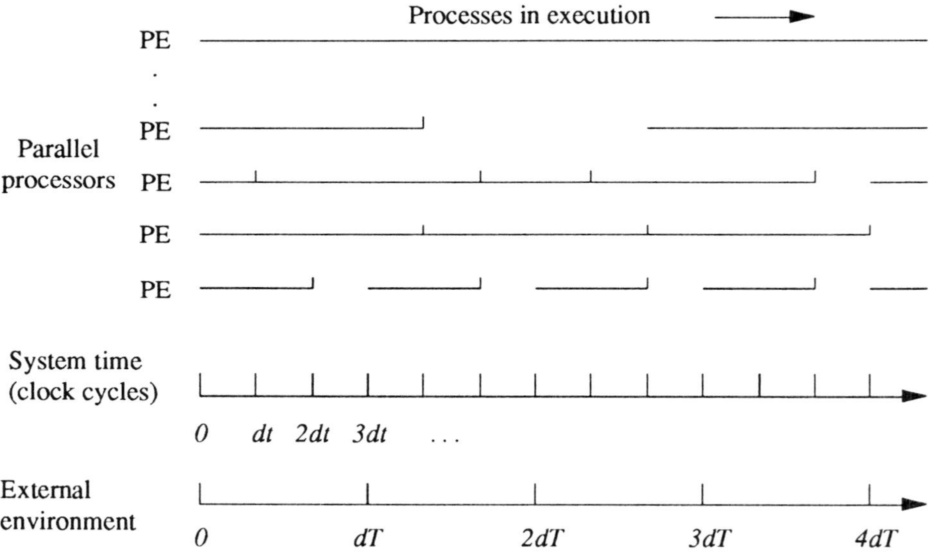

Figure 3.3. Time Dimensions and Parallel Process Execution by PEs

At the bottom, we observe the passing of time in the application environment during which external processes transpire. There are typically particular points along this time continuum (*dT*) that results are required in order to "progress" as well as to maintain application environmental stability. The system view of time (*dt*) is in relationship to a synchronous periodic clock cycle that is used to subdivide processing activities in PEs. (*Note*: In asynchronous systems, there can be multiple views of system time.) Above this level, we have a number of parallel PEs that perform processing functions (that is, processes for computation, decision making, memory, and communication). The processes may be the result of direct mapping of the problem into a parallel hardware structure **and/or** the result of instruction execution. In either case, process execution time becomes a central issue, especially for critical processes.

Regardless of the approach to parallel processing (philosophy and paradigm), the problem is to match the real time of the system environment with the requirements of the application environment and develop appropriate models. Parallel processing in this regard introduces both opportunities and problems.

3.3.1 Schedules, Resources, and Interprocess Communication

The development of process schedules is a key common denominator for all systems. These schedules are mapped out over time. In a real-time environment, we must pay particular attention to response time requirements in this regard. The schedules may be determined statically (perhaps via a computer-aided design tool or a compiler) and/or dynamically (via an operating system scheduler).

Processes need resources in order to accomplish their processing goals. In resource-limited situations, the demands for resources may radically affect the possibilities to achieve response time goals, particularly if critical processes must wait to gain access to shared resources. Remember our 0, 1, $\approx \infty$ axiom from Chapter 1. Direct-mapped solutions aim at being resource adequate, whereas the tradition in dynamically mapped environments is the resource-limited point of view. We can observe that, in the union of real-time and parallel processing systems, it would be useful to delve deeper into concepts and methodologies for resource-adequate situations. Resource adequacy provides an important step toward predictability and reducing or even eliminating uncertainties.

Processes (regardless of level) must communicate with each other. The strategy and means used for this communication play a key role in developing appropriate schedules. Compound process sequences (execution paths) that require communication can become *interleaved* in their execution within and/or across PEs. The interconnection network (ICN), in this case, becomes a vital resource.

Performance in parallel processing environments cannot be measured by PE performance alone. In dimensioning parallel real-time systems, designers must take account of the timing properties and bandwidth of PE, M, and C processes.

3.3.2 Nondeterminism

We have considered this system property earlier. Being somewhat more specific, we can define nondeterminancy to mean that there exist multiple possible process sequences (execution paths) and that we may not be able to prescribe or influence the interleaving of these processes. The compound processes then exhibit nondeterministic behavior. For a real-time system with hard response time requirements to be correct in the face of nondeterminancy, it must be able to produce results (on time) from the compound processes for all permissible interleavings of process executions.

3.4 CHAPTER STRUCTURE

With the relationships between real-time system requirements and parallel processing in mind, let us consider the issues that will be addressed in the remainder of this chapter. The reader can observe the relationship between the various issues and the BMR model presented below.

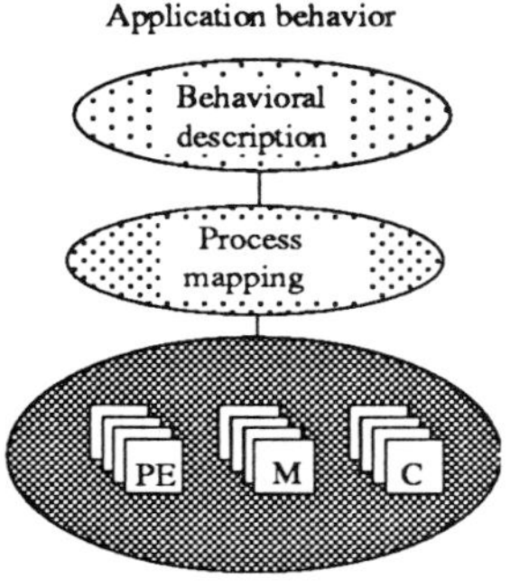

Behavioral description - identifies the main stream of providing behavioral descriptions of application processes for realization in parallel processing environments

Hardware resource structures - considers various combinations of cooperating PE, M, and C processes (that is, alternative hardware architectures)

Interconnection networks - considers interconnection network communication properties

Memory processes and transports - considers the organization of transports between various memory processes that are distributed throughout a system

Process mapping - addresses the general question of allocating processes to various resource structures (static and dynamic) for various parallel processing architectures, including requirements for process scheduling

As these aspects of parallel processing are discussed, the reader should constantly keep in mind the BMR model and the fundamental PCS issues that must be addressed in **all** models (that is, the view of processes, means of communication and method of synchronization).

While it may seem most logical to begin with the behavioral description issues, it is, with some exceptions, the hardware resource architecture alternatives that have, thus far, played the dominant role in establishing various philosophies, paradigms, and models of parallel processing. Thus, in the following section, we address hardware processes in general, and after that consider behavioral description. The subjects of interconnection networks and memory processes, provide a deeper look at these vital parallel processing hardware processes. Finally, process allocation (the key link) ties together behavioral description and the hardware resource structures.

HARDWARE RESOURCE STRUCTURES

By addressing the fundamental PCS issues with respect to the generic parallel processing architecture, we arrive at the following distinguishing characteristics and abstractions.

- how are parallel processing activities controlled? (66)
  - Self-timed control - (wavefront)
  - Time order control - (systolic)
  - Central control - SIMD
  - Individual control - MIMD
- what controls parallel processing execution? (68)
  - Time driven
  - Control driven (instruction sequences)
  - Event driven (event occurrence)
- the unit of parallelism is processes at varying degrees of granularity (68)
- interconnection network and memory processes vary based upon application architecture-dependent alternatives (70)
- systolic and wavefront solutions exploit pipelines where the first is based on synchronous timing and the latter on asynchronism - systolic and wavefront solutions are implemented as arrays of one or more dimensions - DSP algorithms are often implemented in a pipelined manner (72)
- SIMD architectures include PE arrays and VLIW (**V**ery **L**ong **I**nstruction **W**ord) systems where the common characteristic is that a central control fetches instructions and transmits the instructions to multiple PEs (74)
- MIMD architectures include SM (**s**hared **m**emory) multiprocessors as well as DM (**d**istributed **m**emory) multicomputers (78)
- hardware mechanisms for mutual exclusion and synchronization in MIMD environments include disabling interrupts, exchange instruction and spin-locks, fetch&operation, and barriers (80)
- other architectural variants are most often based upon combinations of the features of the hardware processes that have been considered (82)

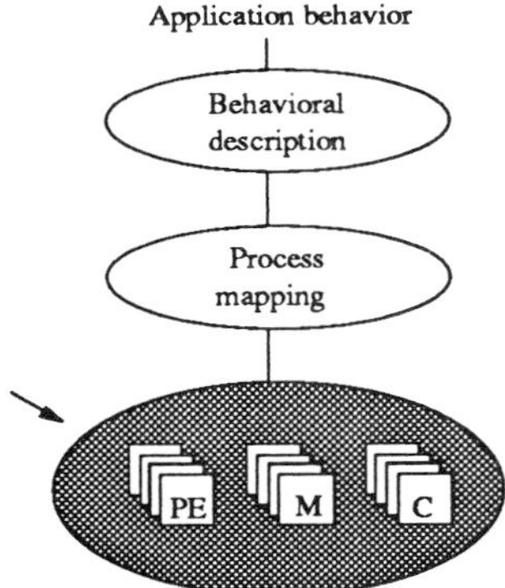

In this section, we characterize the major components (PE, M, and C hardware processes) and their utilization, in particular parallel processing situations. The examination and evaluation of the similarities (and differences) should assist the reader in gaining appropriate insight into the majority of contemporary approaches to the hardware process resource structure portion of the BMR development model portrayed to the left.

Our characterization of parallel processing architectures is based upon answering the following questions and identifying guiding abstractions categorized according to the PCS fundamental issues that have been identified; however, we address them here in another order.

Method of Synchronization

1. How are parallel processing activities controlled?
2. What controls the parallel processing execution?

View of Processes

3. What is the unit of parallelism (that is, process granularity)?

Means of Communication

4. How is the interconnection network (ICN) organized?
5. How are memory processes organized?

Answers to these questions, to a large extent, characterize contemporary approaches to parallel PE, M, and C hardware processes in direct-mapped as well as various dynamically mapped environments.

3.5 HOW ARE PROCESSING ACTIVITIES CONTROLLED?

Given our generic parallel processing model and the generalization of the process notion, we now divide the class of parallel processing architectures according to their means of control as portrayed in Figure 3.4.

The pipeline category is composed of two highly regular forms: wavefront and systolic array systems. These systems are realized by direct mapping from an algorithm to hardware processes, with multiple PEs interconnected via pipelines. In addition to these regular structures, we frequently find pipelined solutions to DSP algorithms based upon providing an application-relevant optimal set of PE, M, and C resources. While we cannot conveniently classify all potential DSP architectures, they often belong to the pipeline category.

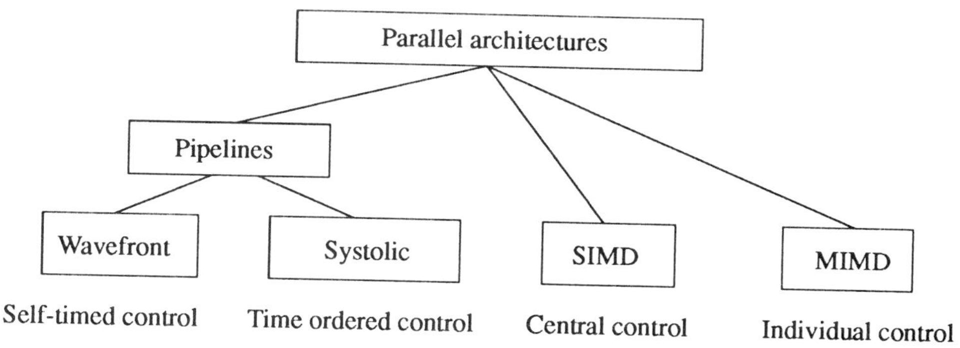

Figure 3.4. Parallel Architectures Classified by **How** Processing Is Controlled

From the four general categories given in the figure, we consider the variants with respect to **how** they are controlled.

wavefront systems are self-timed controlled; that is, there is no form of direct timing mechanism that controls their operation. The processes within the system communicate with each other *asynchronously* .

systolic systems utilize time-ordered control, where the processing activities are subdivided into equal units of time and the processing proceeds among processes *synchronously* in discrete time stages.
(*Note*: The name systolic is taken from the analogy to the regular pumping of blood from the heart, which matches this synchronous thinking.)

SIMD (**S**ingle **I**nstruction **M**ultiple **D**ata) systems in which a centralized control mechanism broadcasts instructions to all system PEs at regular *synchronous* (lockstep) intervals.

MIMD (**M**ultiple **I**nstruction **M**ultiple **D**ata) systems in which individual control is provided in each PE; thus, the PEs proceed at their own rate of speed and communication is *asynchronous.*

While wavefront and systolic systems are often mapped directly into PE, M, and C hardware processes, it is quite possible to use some form of programmed logic in developing the processes to be mapped into PEs, particularly for wavefront systems where self-timing is employed. In the SIMD and MIMD system cases, programmed logic is always utilized as the means of implementing application processes with the available PE, M, and C hardware processes.

3.6 WHAT CONTROLS PROCESSING EXECUTION?

As another synchronization dimension of our hardware resource structure characterization, we describe parallel processing systems by what controls processing activities. These four alternatives are portrayed in Figure 3.5. They are applied to our previous classification of **how** execution is controlled in the following manner:

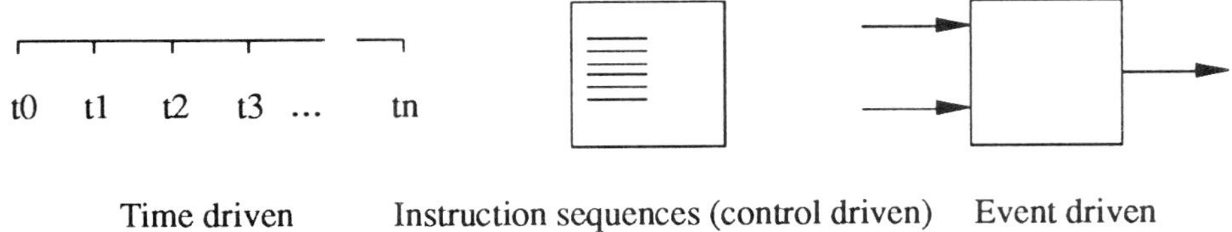

Figure 3.5. Classification by **What** Controls Execution

— in systolic systems, the how and what are basically equivalent (that is, *time driven* implies time-ordered control).
— in *central control* SIMD systems, it is instruction sequences that control execution.
— in wavefront systems, it is the occurrence of events in the form of data availability (*event driven*) that determines the execution sequence in this self-timed control form. If the processes are programmed, sequences of instructions control execution within processes.
— in *individually controlled* MIMD systems, it can be either instruction sequences (*control driven*), the occurrence of one or more *events* (*event driven*), or some combination of the two that controls execution.

3.7 WHAT IS THE UNIT OF PARALLELISM?

Given the methods of synchronizing hardware processes (that is, the how and the what of control), let us now consider one of the most distinguishing characteristics, *process granularity*, that is, the granularity of the processes executed via the PE processes in a parallel processing system. Considering the general range of program and data elements that are granularity candidates, we derive the classification portrayed in Figure 3.6. Most of the terms used in this Figure should be recognizable; however, the terms used in the very coarse grain entries require some further explanation. By *cluster* we mean a set of cooperating processes, and by *data set* we mean a collection of related data contained in multiple files.

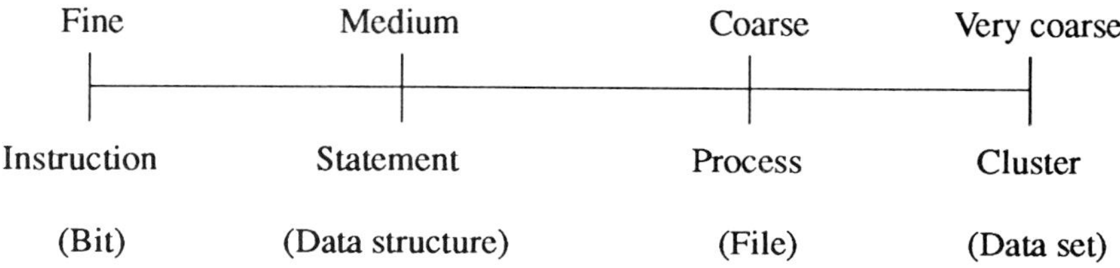

Figure 3.6. Classification by Degrees of Program and Data Granularity

Particular resource structures are aimed toward exploiting parallelism at one or more of the granularity levels with respect to programs and/or data. In general, we can state that fine-grain parallelism is predominant in those cases where large numbers of PEs cooperate (army of ants approach), whereas the coarser the degree of granularity, typically the fewer the number of cooperating PEs (herd of elephants approach). Another general conclusion is that fine-grain parallelism is found in tightly coupled systems, and as processing becomes increasingly loosely coupled, the granularity of data and program processes increases.

3.7.1 Processes as a Granularity Common Denominator

We find varying terminology in the technical literature for the granularity units identified in Figure 3.6. For example, one may utilize the term *object* as the unit of parallelism, with thoughts directed to the generalization of object-oriented methodologies and programming languages. Objects could also be utilized as a unifying concept to describe all units of parallelism. However, once again, we revert to *process* as the single central unifying concept. Thus, for example, to the control unit of a CPU, an instruction is a process. (The control unit itself is a process.) Statements can be viewed as processes as well as larger units, such as entire programs or even several cooperating programs acting jointly as a single process.

Even the various units of data as identified in our figure are viewed as processes. The data implicitly, if not explicitly, are embedded in a process with ports that encapsulates the operations (protocols) for accessing and altering the data.

Thus, once again, we utilize the process (as portrayed in Figure 1.5) as the unifying concept of any activity to be executed by PEs in our parallel systems. As indicated in the BMR model (Figure 1.6), the application behavior is decomposed into processes at varying degrees of granularity. Further, in accordance with the BMR model, the resource structure provides sets of hardware processes that via cooperation provide execution semantics for the decomposed application processes.

3.7.2 Varying Process Granularities

We now relate these discussions to specific categories that have evolved.

- — in systolic and wavefront systems as well as in DSP applications, the granularity matches that decided upon by the designers in considering the nature of processes and data of the application; however, fine-grain and medium-grain data granularities are most dominant.
- — in SIMD architectures, the unit of granularity is generally fine grain or at most a restricted form of medium data granularity (uniform data elements).
- — in MIMD systems, the unit of parallelism varies at program and data levels. Further, the mechanisms to treat various units of granularity exist in hardware, software, or some combination thereof.

In all parallel processing variants, the interaction of the three fundamental PCS issues (processes, communication, and synchronization) has a major influence upon the efficiency that can be obtained for various degrees of granularity.

We have thus far treated the view of processes (P) of varying granularity and the method of synchronization in hardware processes. Next we introduce C (communication) and M (memory) related issues in a general manner, since both topics are addressed in detail in separate sections in this chapter.

3.8 HOW IS THE INTERCONNECTION NETWORK ORGANIZED?

The ICN (interconnection network) is the media used for accomplishing physical transports between cooperating hardware processes. It goes without saying that the availability of fast, reliable transports via the interconnection network in a parallel system is the key to achieving improved performance and in many cases reliability and fault tolerance. In Figure 3.7, we provide a common abstract view of interconnection networks.

The ports (terminals) to the network process are the points of interface for connected PE and M processes. The connection at a terminal may be another C process (that is, connection to other ICNs). Each terminal has a unique address. When information is to be transmitted in the network, it is transmitted from a sending terminal to one or more receiving terminals. The *address* is used as the controlling information in routing the information to the proper destination(s). Regardless of the ICN architecture, routing is based on a mapping of *address* to *path* through the network.

Based upon this general abstraction, we shall consider later in this chapter, various realizations of single-stage and multistage networks (MINs), point-to-point topologies, and various methods of transmission (that is, circuit switched and packet switched) that are distinguishing properties of ICN architectures.

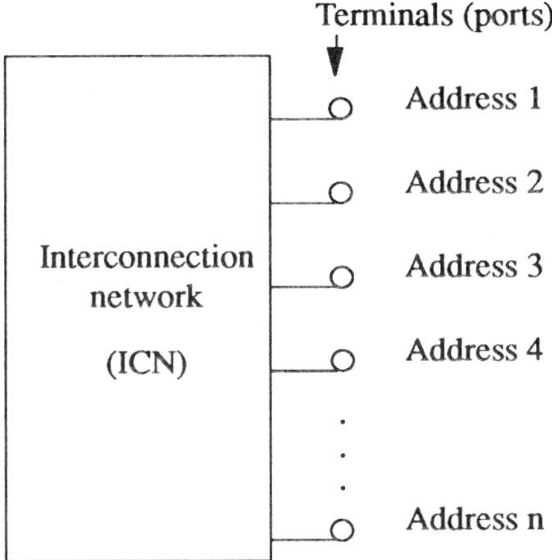

Figure 3.7. Abstract View of an Interconnection Network

3.9 HOW ARE MEMORY PROCESSES ORGANIZED?

Remembering our general notion of memory processes as PEs, let us view a hierarchy of memory processes as portrayed in Figure 3.8. The levels of the memory (hierarchy) utilized in particular parallel processing architectures vary.

— in systolic systems and many DSP applications, explicit M processes may not be required, assuming that data are constantly moved through the system, in which case it is equivalent to a combinational circuit. However, typically, some form of local memory is distributed throughout the system. We can find latching buffers used to even out timing control. (*Note*: An alternative to latches is to introduce appropriate timing delays into the "circuit".)

— in wavefront systems, we typically find registers and/or local memory of some form.

— in SIMD systems, we typically find that registers and/or local memories are always utilized. There are many systems that even exploit a global memory (that is, main memory), which is managed by a conventional host machine.

— in MIMD systems, which are normally based upon commercially available hardware processes, we can find all the levels that have been identified. In this case, the local memory is typically a *cache* memory.

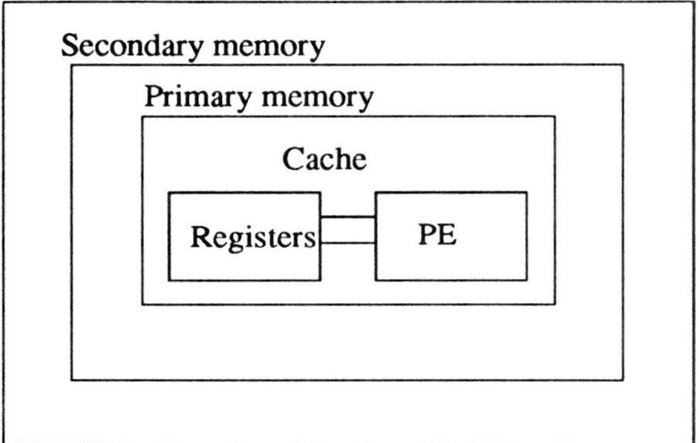

Figure 3.8. Hierarchy of Memory Processes

Transports among various memory processes may be explicit or implicit. In the implicit case, transports transpire due to the use of a *virtual address* mechanism that partitions (maps) *address spaces* of the memory hierarchy.

Having presented the central classification questions with respect to the PCS fundamental issues and having established some useful abstractions, we now proceed by exemplifying and examining some properties and models of the architectural classes that have been introduced.

3.10 PIPELINED SYSTEMS

Wavefront and systolic pipeline solutions are highly related. In both cases, the goal is to improve processing bandwidth by the use of an ICN that directly connects communicating (cooperating) PE processes together, as illustrated in Figure 3.9.

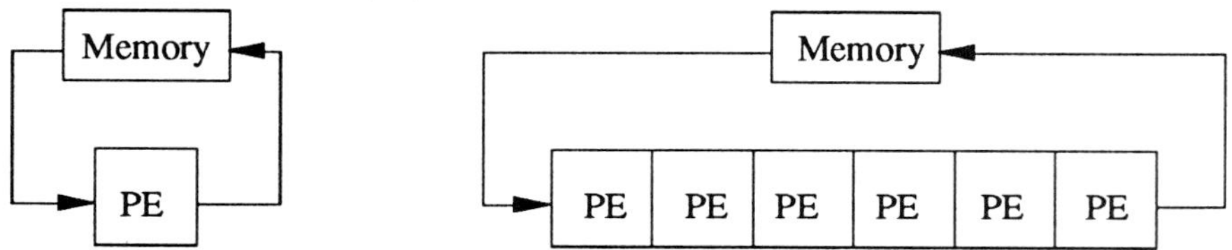

Figure 3.9. Basic Principle of Pipelined Processing

Via interconnected PE processes, according to either wavefront or systolic principles, multiple processing stages can be accomplished in parallel without referring back to the memory processes where data are stored. Thus, assuming that the throughput from using the single PE variant is $O(N)$, the introduction of a direct-mapped solution, in this case, can increase performance $O(6N)$. Naturally, there is an overhead to set up the wavefront or systolic structure; however, when full capacity is reached, assuming that the timing relationship between processing and memory access is well balanced, the system can be "pumped" at high rates of speed.

3.10.1 Wavefront and Systolic Mechanisms

To explicitly illustrate and compare the mechanisms involved in wavefront systems and systolic systems, we introduce the evaluation of a function containing two embedded functions

$$r \leftarrow f(g(a, b), h(c, d))$$

It is clear from this definition (assuming no side effects from variable interaction) that the functions $g(a, b)$ and $h(c, d)$ are candidates for parallel processing; whereas the function f must be evaluated sequentially after collecting the results of g and h in order to produce the result r.

The parallel evaluation of the functions according to the (a) wavefront and (b) systolic mechanisms is illustrated in Figure 3.10. In both cases, the PE behaviors are identical to the processes they perform (g, h, and f) and the ICN is realized as the actual wired connections.

In the systolic case, it is fairly clear that the time to evaluate the functions is placed under the time press of the clock signals. Further, buffers may be required to latch up results at various stages of processing. On the other hand, the advantage of the asynchronous self-timed control as used in the wavefront case is that the functions can take as long a time as required. Handshaking (wait and receive, respectively, send) logic provides for the necessary control.

It is clear that systolic structures are best suited for a uniform (typically fine grain) granularity where processing occurs in regular, short time intervals. A wavefront system can also be based on simple processes being performed by the PEs; however, sophisticated processes (perhaps statically programmed for a programmable PE) can be coupled together in pipelined fashion (one or more dimensions). To achieve higher performance in the wavefront case, a good balance between processing times is required.

3.10.2 Pipelines for DSP Applications

In DSP applications, specific pipelined architectures aimed at optimal exploitation of hardware process resources are typically developed. When the equations to be solved exhibit a regular structure, the DSP solution may yield a systolic or wavefront array solution. On the other hand, the equations may be transformed into an architecture of less regular but more optimal form according to selected optimization criteria and optimization algorithms.

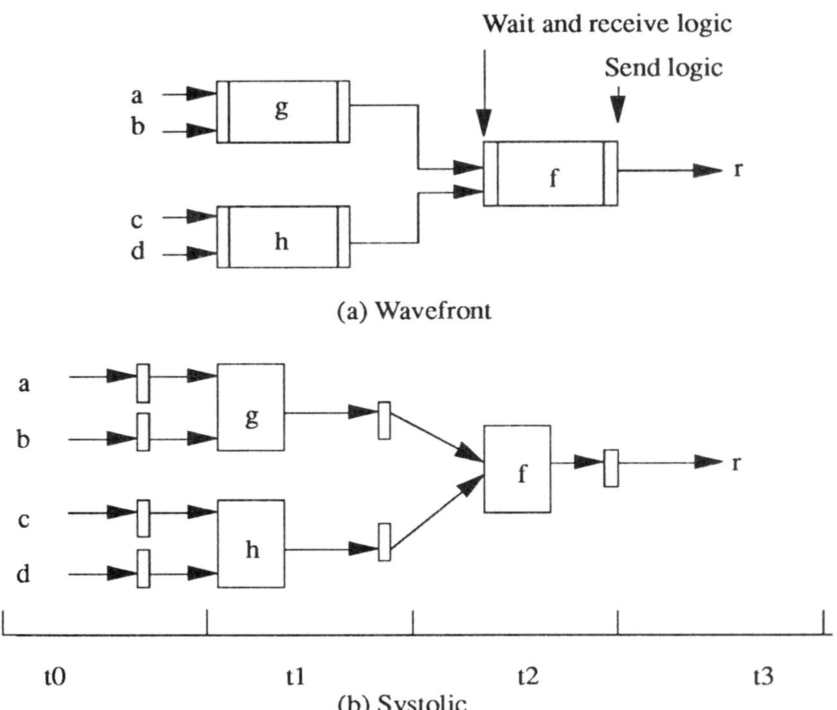

Figure 3.10. Wavefront and Systolic Principles

3.11 SIMD ARCHITECTURES

The most distinguishing characteristic of Single-Instruction, Multiple-Data architectures is the utilization of central control for the operation of multiple PEs as they execute process instructions in a synchronized (lockstep) manner. In this regard, the categorization shown in Figure 3.11 yields two variants.

The PE array category is represented by a large number of designs that have evolved for accelerating processing operating on words at a time (*word parallel*) or bits (*bit serial*), as well as various processing mechanisms and memory process organizations (that is, *associative processing*). Another variant of SIMD is the VLIW approach in which a single, long instruction word is used to simultaneously control several PEs in executing conventional programs.

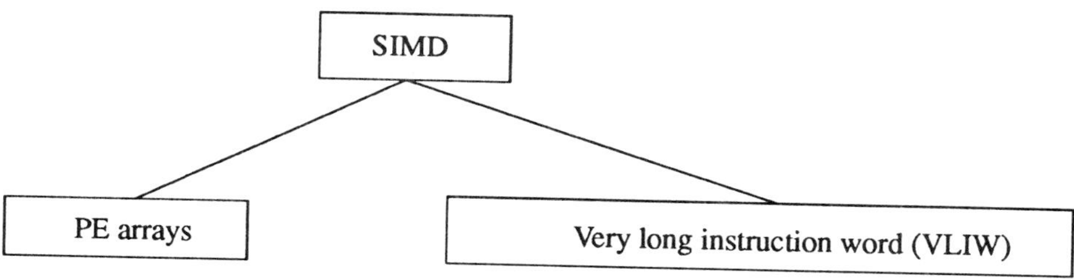

Figure 3.11. SIMD (**S**ingle **I**nstruction **M**ultiple **D**ata) Architectures

In both forms of SIMD architectures, instructions are accessed sequentially from a program memory via a single location counter and transmitted to all the PEs. At this point the similarities between PE arrays and VLIW architectures terminate. In PE arrays, the parallelism is visible to and directly controlled by the user, whereas in VLIW systems, the parallelism is automatically extracted from conventional sequential programs (*scalar parallelism*). Further, in PE arrays, the same instruction is *broadcast* to all PEs, whereas in VLIW architectures, separate instructions are delivered directly to corresponding PEs, where each PE is controlled by a part of the long instruction word.

3.11.1 PE Arrays

In PE arrays, one instruction works on several data items simultaneously by using several **P**rocessing **E**lements (PEs), where each PE carries out the same operation as illustrated in Figure 3.12.

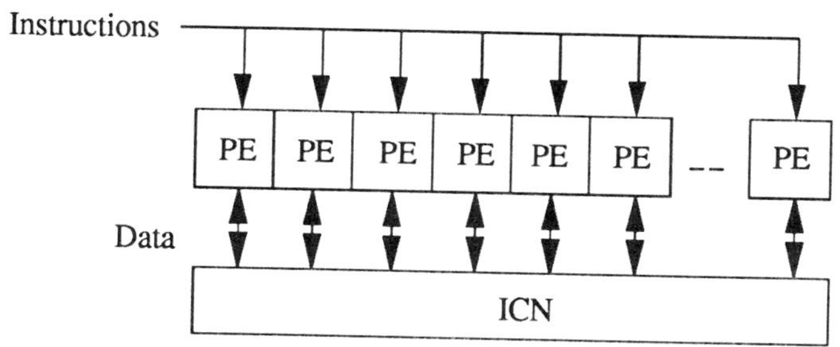

Figure 3.12. Principle for PE Array Parallel Processing

A PE-array processor has a single control unit that reads instructions pointed to by a single program counter, decodes them, and sends control signals to the PEs. The PEs typically operate on data in their local memories and/or data received from the interconnection network. The ICN provides flexibility in choosing source and destination for data to and from the PEs, as required in many algorithms. A critical aspect of PE arrays is the I/O system, which provides for converting, typically at very high rates, input/output data between the format of the outside world and the internal format of the array. The design of an appropriate I/O system is highly application dependent.

The PEs typically perform a limited set of processing functions. The most common ICN topology is the *two-dimensional mesh,* which is illustrated in Figure 3.13. The main reason for this popularity is the obvious support for close local connections between PEs, which are exploited in several application areas. As the reader will observe, however, based on the dimension of the mesh, there can exist a relatively large maximum-distance path (defined as the *diameter*) between an arbitrary pair of PEs wishing to communicate. However, the diameter can be reduced as illustrated in the figure via wrap-a-round, thus forming a *torus*. For example, a rectangular torus PE array of size N ($N = 1024$) has a diameter of 32 (that is, $\sqrt{N}$). In some applications, even this distance is not acceptable and other ICN alternatives are utilized, as described later in the book.

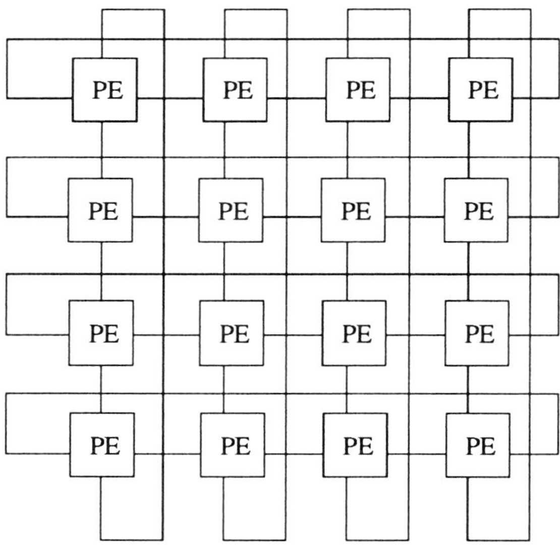

Figure 3.13. Torus Two-Dimensional Mesh (Wrap-a-Round at the Edges)

Most PE arrays have been designed to improve performance in one specific class of application, for example, high-speed numerical computation or image processing. In this regard, we may think of the PE-array system as being *direct mapped.* However, more recently, there have been attempts to extend the range of applications for this parallel processing architectural form, thus providing more general-purpose properties. To provide overall control of the PE arrays, as well as to execute sequential operations, it is common to utilize a conventional host computer, which then views the PE array system as an attached processor, as illustrated in Figure 3.14. Here we observe that programs (typically written in augmented imperative languages) are executed on the host computer with linkage to the PE array for those operations that are to be executed in the PE array environment.

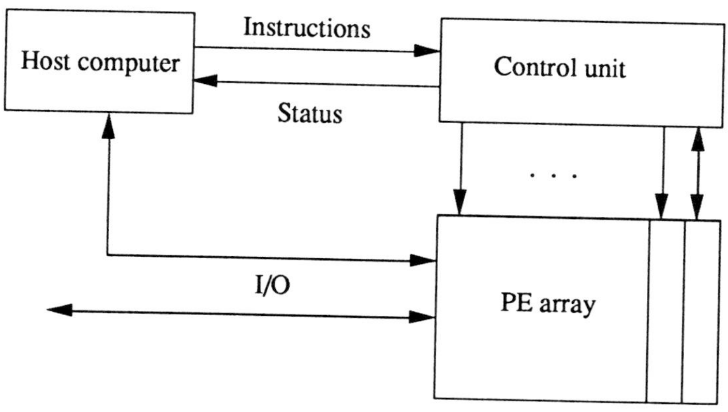

Figure 3.14. Host Computer - PE Array Relationship

3.11.2 Very Long Instruction Words

The VLIW (Very Long Instruction Word) architectures differ from others in that multiple PEs are controlled by separate portions of a long instruction word (256 to 1024 bits) as portrayed in Figure 3.15. Each field of the instruction word is delivered directly to control a specific PE. Thus, in contrast to PE arrays, each PE can be performing different instructions. The instruction field is subdivided into fields that control local processing in the PE. The PEs are connected to shared memory processes (not shown here) and each PE contains local registers. The instructions are rather conventional (that is, those found in typical microprocessor-based CPUs). Unlike other parallel architectures, no special importance is attached to an interconnection network for communicating between the PEs. The connections are quite local and quite special purpose. Thus, the VLIW model implements *scalar parallelism* and has more in common with the internal PE pipelining than with more general parallel processing paradigms. We examine this special architecture in Part II.

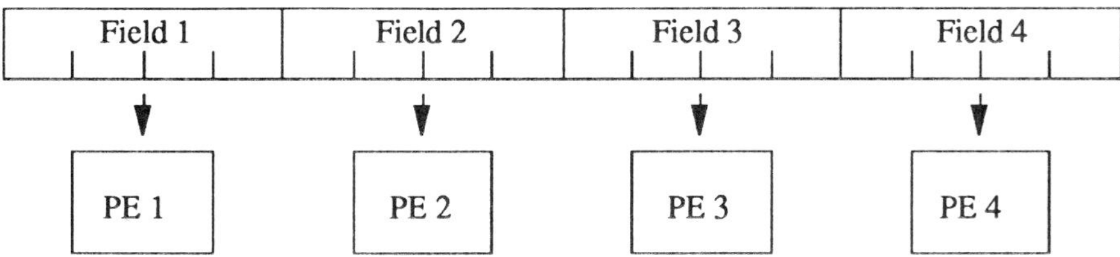

Figure 3.15. Very Long Instruction Word Model

3.12 MIMD ARCHITECTURES

The MIMD (**M**ultiple **I**nstruction, **M**ultiple **D**ata) category contains a multitude of both commercial products, mostly delivered during the 1980s, as well as research projects. All the architectures in this category are based upon individual control, where the PEs operate as asynchronous *agents* and where execution is synchronized, when required, via hardware and/or software mechanisms. Despite this general functional similarity of MIMD architectures, they are distinguishable as indicated in Figure 3.16.

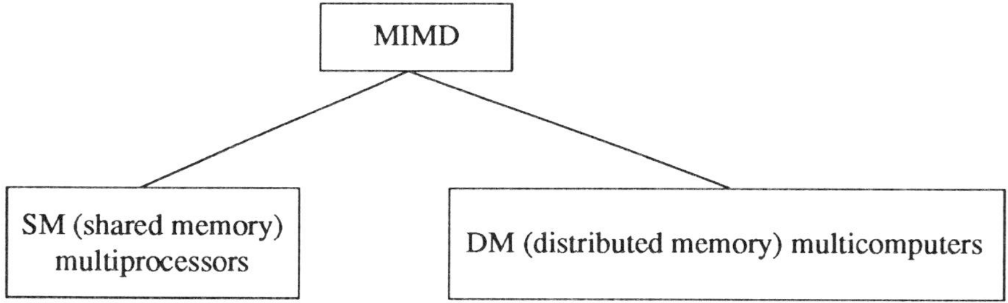

Figure 3.16. MIMD Parallel/Distributed Architectures

3.12.1 Multiprocessors versus Multicomputers

The main physical difference between SM (Shared Memory) *mutiprocessors* and DM (Distributed Memory) *multicomputers* lies in the manner in which interactions between the PEs transpire. In multiprocessor systems, all PEs share a common main memory process and address space, whereas, in the multicomputer case, each PE has its own local memory processes and communication must take place by message passing. Consequently, in multicomputer systems, a PE cannot directly address the memory processes belonging to another PE. It is these properties that are often used to differentiate between these two MIMD architectures, portrayed in Figure 3.17.

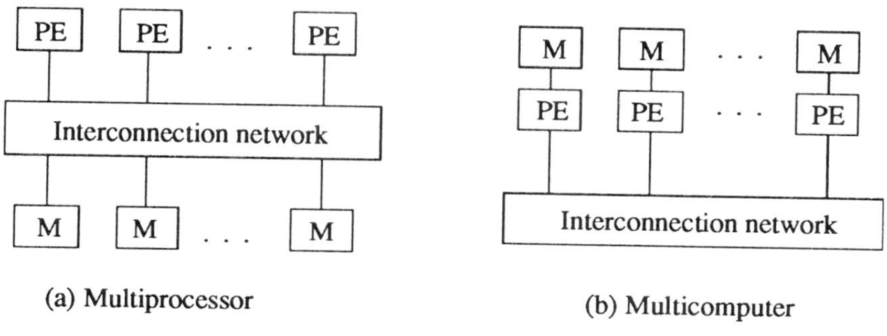

Figure 3.17. Multiprocessor and Multicomputer Architectures

The SM versus DM properties of multiprocessors versus multicomputers are evident from the figure. However, the multiprocessor category also includes a multicomputer architectural structure with unique memory referencing properties. In this case, a SM is physically distributed, with a portion of the SM contained in each PE forming a *single address space*. Memory references are direct in the portion of the address space held locally in the PE, but must transpire via message passing when referencing addresses in the M processes associated with other PEs.

In the multiprocessor case, each PE may contain a local *cache memory* that improves bandwidth, but introduces new problems as described in the section concerning memory processes and transports.

3.12.2 LANs and WANs

Multicomputers can be coupled to and/or include various forms of LANs (**L**ocal **A**rea **N**etworks) and WANs (**W**ide **A**rea **N**etworks). While LANs and WANs are interconnection networks that provide parallel/distributed processing, they are typically **not** utilized to accelerate the execution of a single subsystem application. On the other hand, the multicomputers in the LAN and/or WAN may be cooperating at a higher system level, as we have illustrated for distributed real-time systems in Chapter 2 (see Figure 2.6). The granularity of program and units of data that are treated in highly distributed systems tends to be quite coarse.

3.12.3 Some Important MIMD Issues

The subject of MIMD parallel processing architectures has received the largest attention of the research community, and a vast amount of literature is available concerning research efforts and commercial products. A number of issues that are typically dealt with in this context and to which we shall address ourselves in this chapter are:

— mutual exclusion (sharing of common resources)
— process synchronization and communication
— scheduling and allocation strategies (load balancing and the like)

The treatment of these issues often involves mechanisms in the hardware, operating systems, programming languages, compilers, run-time systems, and even program linkers and loaders.

3.12.4 Mutual Exclusion and Synchronization Mechanisms

In this section, we consider the basic hardware mechanism alternatives; software mechanisms are considered under the topic of concurrent programming in the next section. Within the hardware processes we find that microprograms, memory controllers, communication switches, and so on, may participate in implementing mutual exclusion and synchronization.

Disabling Interrupts

Historically, the mutual exclusion problem was handled by the hardware interrupt mechanism. That is, a process wishing to gain exclusive access to a shared variable(s) or resource simply requested an interrupt. When the interrupt was honored, further interrupts could not occur, thus guaranteeing mutually exclusive access.

This simple technique works in single-PE environments; however, if more than one PE exists, the treatment of interrupts can become much more complicated. The simplest solution to the parallel PE situation is to centralize interrupts (and resource management) to one PE so that no interleaving of critical sections can occur. This centralizing of control has severe disadvantages from the fault tolerance and performance points of view. On the other hand, if interrupt handling is distributed throughout the parallel system, the solution must be programmed very carefully. Further, the resulting system is often difficult to test and maintain.

Spin-locks

Another hardware-based mechanism for providing mutual exclusion is the utilization of a single (atomic) time-indivisible instruction that provides for mutual exclusion. Both test and set instructions and exchange instructions belong to this category. The net effect is to permit the locking of a variable that guarantees only one process will be granted access until it releases the lock. During the time that the lock is set, other processes issuing the instruction will be forced to wait.

The spin-lock provides a parallel synchronization mechanism based upon the locking instruction (test and set or exchange). Assuming that the granularity of use of the lock is small, this method can be quite satisfactory and is commonly exploited. However, if the lock is retained for long periods of time, the waiting times that waste memory bandwidth and processor cycles may not be acceptable. As an alternative solution, one of the software synchronization mechanisms (described later) is superior, since processing time can be utilized while blocked processes are waiting, thus eliminating the *busy waiting* that occurs with the use of spin-locks.

Fetch and Operation

One hardware solution to multiple processes accessing a common data structure is the implementation of a special form of Fetch instruction. Thus, an indivisible instruction F&Operation (where Operation is any one of the typical memory cell access or manipulation functions) has been introduced. Multiple processes residing on multiple PEs can issue such instructions, for example, to index through a common array data structure. Each reference F&A (I,1) will yield consecutive values to index the array. Assuming that the array is, in fact, a sequential queue, this will provide a parallel means of adding elements to the queue, and F&S (I,1) Fetch and Subtract will provide a parallel means of removing elements from the queue. The assurance of proper updating and referencing is provided by incorporating some form of combining of operations in the interconnection network, as described later in this chapter.

Barriers

Another important synchronization mechanism for the execution of parallel processes is the use of a barrier. In this case, the mechanism forces a number of processes to wait until all have reached some common point. To illustrate this mechanism, consider the problem of solving a linear system of equations of the form

$$X_{i+1} = AX_i + B$$

where X_{i+1}, X_i, and B are vectors of size N and A is a matrix of size N x N. Let us assume that each iteration the calculations of vector X_{i+1} is performed by N processes, where each process calculates one vector element. A typical imperative code for this problem is as follows:

```
repeat
  par_for J := 1 to N do
  begin
        XTEMP [J] := B[J];
        for K := 1 to N do
          XTEMP [J] := XTEMP [J] + A [J,K] * X [K];
  end;
```

```
    barrier_synchronize
    par_for J := 1 to N do
        X [J] := XTEMP [J];
    barrier_synchronize
until false;
```

At the beginning of this repetitive loop, N processes are initiated by the **par_for** statement. Each process calculates a new value, which is stored in XTEMP. The last parallel loop copies back the elements of XTEMP to the vector X. This requires barrier synchronization of all the processes in the first and second **par_for** loops. Note that the vector B and matrix A are shared and only read, whereas, all elements of X are read in order to calculate the new vector element; further, all elements of are updated in each iteration.

The hardware mutual exclusion and synchronization mechanisms we have presented are complemented by the software mechanisms presented in the next section.

3.13 OTHER ARCHITECTURAL VARIANTS

While we have considered the main stream of contemporary hardware architectures for parallel processing, other architectural concepts are worth noting. However, in most cases, we can observe that the architectures are built upon the concepts and models that we have already described. For example, *dataflow* architectures (presented in Chapter 12) are based upon asynchronous event-driven processes and, while they build upon a completely different processing model, their structural realization is largely analogous to wavefront or to MIMD systems that are controlled by events.

As we move into the future development of complex parallel/distributed real-time systems, we are likely to see new architectures that build upon combinations of the architectures that have been identified. Undoubtedly, we shall even see architectures built on new philosophies, paradigms, and models that will advance the state of the art.

Once again, the reader should return to the summary at the beginning of this section to review the section highlights.

BEHAVIORAL DESCRIPTION

We consider various aspects of the description of the structure and behavior of application and hardware processes.

- human intellectual processes of thinking-reasoning-describing are introduced (84)

- a variety of structural and behavioral models for parallel computation have been developed and can assist in viewing certain aspects of parallel processing problems — several of the abstractions are congruent and can be mapped to each other (85)

- hardware description languages are utilized for describing the structure and behavior of PE, M, and C processes at various levels of physical and logical abstraction (85)

- the description of applications to be realized by direct mapping as in digital signal processing applications involves characterizing the application via appropriate equations — further, for DSP applications, signal-flow diagrams are typically employed (88)

- programmed processes are normally quite influenced by the underlying programming paradigm to be employed — we consider the general properties of imperative, concurrent, object-oriented, functional, logic, and dataflow programming paradigms — with few exceptions the time dimension is absent in contemporary programming languages (90)

- programming languages are categorized as synchronous or asynchronous, reflecting their utilization in particular parallel processing environments (95)

- programming of PE arrays is quite dependent upon the SIMD architecture and supported programming languages — we identify some typical instructions and means of programming language support (95)

- concurrent programming contains mechanisms for treating competition for resources, as well as means for providing cooperation via interprocess communication — software mechanisms for mutual exclusion, synchronization, and communication at various levels include semaphores, critical regions, conditional critical regions, messages, monitors, rendezvous, remote procedure call, and ports (97)

- functional programs, based upon lambda calculus, are transformational and built upon the notion of referential transparency — via higher-order functions and lazy evaluation, functional program execution can be accelerated (110)

- logic and functional programs show interesting potential for parallel processing since they can be decomposed into fine-grain processes by compilers (110)

- logic programs, based upon relations, include the notions of clauses, goals, Horn clauses, unification, and inferences — the unification process introduces nondeterminancy (112)

- language variants aimed at parallel/distributed real-time applications have been developed (114)

The fundamental intellectual activities involved in capturing the behavior of an application are

Thinking - Reasoning - Describing

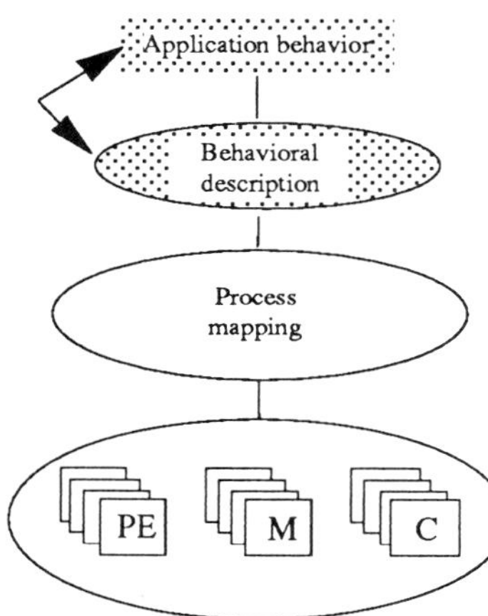

These human processes are universal. Due to the complexities and our immaturity in dealing with parallel processing for real-time applications, they become essential ingredients in producing successful philosophies, paradigms, and model solutions. Based upon the background and experience of the humans involved in these processes, the nature of the application, model restrictions on structure and behavior, and the like, the result of the human processes yields various slices (or portions thereof) in respect to a behavioral description level or through the entire BMR development model.

The thinking-reasoning-describing processes are typically supported by formal or semiformal abstractions of the problem, as well as, when appropriate, hardware description and/or programming languages. However, it is important to remember that the common goal of all processing systems is the treatment of situations as portrayed in Figure 3.1. Behavioral description is the first step in forming an appropriate processing structure.

In the current section, we consider the general ingredients of several behavioral description approaches that are or can be applied in parallel processing situations. The specific properties of a variety of behavioral description artifacts are presented in Chapter 7.

3.14 ABSTRACT MODELS

In the parallel processing abstract model domain, we find, for example:

— signal-flow graphs
— communicating finite-state machines
— Petri nets
— computation graphs
— dataflow models
— P-V semaphore synchronization systems
— process algebras
— cellular automata
— parallel RAM (PRAM) models

Each of these abstraction approaches is enthusiastically supported by professionals in the field. Some of them are based on highly formal methods. By formal method, we mean that there is a corresponding symbology that can be logically manipulated in order to prove certain properties, for example, completeness, consistency, freedom from cycles (that is, liveness in program terms), freedom from deadlock, and others. Some of the abstract models also form the kernel of the philosophy upon which various semiformal methods are based, as well as for particular paradigms and models applied in hardware description and programming languages.

While each of the abstractions explicitly or implicitly provides a view of processes, means of communication, and method of synchronization, it typically tends to emphasize the importance of one of the issues.

In many cases, the abstract concepts are quite similar and even congruent (that is, one can often find mappings between the various models illustrating that the differences are often linguistic and not conceptual).

Certain of these abstractions will surface again later in this chapter. Krishnamurthy (1989) provides a comprehensive description and comparison of the majority of these formalisms and others. Most of the formalisms can be utilized to model hardware or software processes.

3.15 DESCRIPTION OF HARDWARE PROCESSES

We now consider the description of hardware processes, that is, the description of PE, M, and C processes for direct-mapped applications. With respect to the BMR model, the application is captured in terms of the *HDL (Hardware Description Language).* The goal in this case is often to produce a specific solution, such as an ASIC (Application-

Specific Integrated Circuit). (*Note*: Hardware descriptions can be employed when creating general-purpose PE, M, and C processes. However, in this book, we are only concerned with their use for direct mapped solutions.)

3.15.1 Hardware Description Languages

As we have moved into the era of VLSI, structured design has become an absolute requirement and considerable effort has been expended in developing design aids. Hardware Description Languages (HDLs) are one specific example. Several HDLs have been in use for over 10 years, such as CDL, ISP, and AHPL; however, their primary application has been in the verification of architecture and not in synthesizing concrete components. They do not have the ability to model designs with a high degree of accuracy since their timing model is not precise and/or their language constructs imply certain specific hardware structures.

To provide for the description and synthesis of integrated circuits, the U.S. Department of Defence in the VHSIC (Very High Speed Integrated Circuit) program supported the development of the VHDL languages in which three styles are provided. The behavioral description style of VHDL programming is aimed at description and simulation of architectural structures and provides most of the features of a higher-level programming language plus facilities for the treatment of time. In contrast to the behavioral description style, the combined use of the structural and dataflow styles provides behavioral information that forms the basis for concrete hardware synthesis. VHDL has become a standard and a multitude of implementations have appeared. We examine some specific properties of the three VHDL styles in Chapter 7. For a general overview of VHDL, a number of books are now available (see, for example, Armstrong, 1989).

3.15.2 Hardware Abstraction Levels

We now consider the general notions associated with describing various levels of hardware structures and behaviors. With respect to VHDL, the structure and behavior of six levels are identified as indicated in Table 3.1. The levels represent various views of *modeling* digital systems to be realized in VLSI technology. However, we often find corresponding structures (or subsets thereof) in considering non-VLSI hardware technologies.

The PMS level takes its name from work of Siewiorek, Bell, and Newell (1982) where P-processor, M-memory, and S-switch are utilized as abstractions for higher-level architectures. We can consider these notions to be equivalent to our PE, M, and C process notions. PMS is the high-level architectural model of the hardware.

The chip level (referred to by others as module level) is used to model the input/output response of a device (that is, the algorithm that implements the chip). The chip level can then be further described in terms of the lower levels of structure and behavior.

Table 3.1. Structure and Behavior at Various Levels

Hardware Descrition Level	Described Structural Primitives	Representation of Behaviors
PMS Processor Memory Switch	CPUs Memories Buses	Performance properties of primitives
Chip	Mircroprocessors RAMs, ROMs UARTs Parallel ports	I/O response Algorithms Micro-operations
Register	Registers ALUs Counters Multiplexors	Truth Tables State Tables Micro-operations
Gate	Gates Flip-flops	Boolean equations
Circuit	Transistors, R, L, and C	Differential equations
Silicon	Geometrical objects	None

At the bottom of the hierarchy, the geometrical shapes represent areas of diffusion, polysilicon, and metal on the silicon surface. The structure (interconnection) of these processes is related to materials and fabrication where behavioral description is not explicitly required. As we move upward in the hierarchy, we develop further structural primitives, each of which has its corresponding means of behavioral representation used in modeling the corresponding phenomenon. *At each level, the notion of process and relevant ports can be defined as well as means of communication and method of synchronization*. (This property provides proof that the process is a highly useful common denominator.)

The reader will observe that, although the basis of structure and behavior changes from level to level, there exist similarities as well as differences. The similarities in terms of structure and behavior should also be observed as we move upward and consider higher-level programmed processes. This hierarchical view from top to bottom or bottom to top, if you prefer, provides insight.

3.16 DIRECT-MAPPED SYSTEMS

It is the application processes representing the underlying algorithms and data that become the objects of realization. The required problem behavior is often expressed as a set of equations that is mapped into regular structures (systolic or wavefront) or synthesized into more optimal forms, as in the case of digital signal-processing applications. For example, a DSP *algorithm* is a computational rule, f, that, when applied to an ordered input sequence, $x(nT)$, maps it onto an ordered output sequence, $y(nT)$, according to

$$x(nT) \rightarrow y(nT), \quad y(nT) := f(x(nT))$$

The computational rule is an unambiguously specified sequence of operations on an ordered data set as summarized in Figure 3.18. It uses a basic set of operations (fundamental processes), for example, additions and multiplications. The algorithm also requires a detailed description of the numerical accuracy and number ranges, as well as of the rounding and overflow nonlinearities involved.

DSP algorithm		
Sequence of operations	Basic set of arithmetic and logic operations	Ordered data set

Figure 3.18. The Three Parts of a DSP Algorithm

A DSP algorithm is a process acting on binary numbers. Often, several algorithms on different hierarchical levels can be identified within a DSP system. Generally, a DSP algorithm can be described by transforming equations into a set of expressions, as follows:

$$x_1(n) := f_1[\ -\ , x_1(n-1), x_1(n-2), \ldots, x_p(n-1), x_p(n-2), \ldots, a_1, b_1, c_1, \ldots]$$
$$x_2(n) := f_2[\ -\ , x_1(n-1), x_1(n-2), \ldots, x_p(n-1), x_p(n-2), \ldots, a_2, b_2, c_2, \ldots]$$
$$x_3(n) := f_3[x_1(n), x_1(n-1), x_1(n-2), \ldots, x_p(n-1), x_p(n-2), \ldots, a_3, b_3, c_3, \ldots]$$

•

•

•

$$x_N(n) := f_N[x_1(n), x_1(n-1), x_1(n-2), \ldots, x_p(n-1), x_p(n-2), \ldots, a_N, b_N, c_N, \ldots]$$

The assignment sign ": =" is used to indicate that the expressions are given in computational order. These expressions will be evaluated repeatedly. Note that the arguments on the right side of the first two expressions only contain previously computed values and that some arguments are absent. Therefore, these two expressions can be computed immediately. Once these expressions have been evaluated, the remaining expressions can be computed.

Characteristic for most DSP algorithms is that the sequence of operations is data independent, has high input and output data rates, and must be executed within a fixed, given sampling period. *These criteria dominate the selection of appropriate process granularities, means of communication, and methods of synchronization.*

To illustrate the required flow in DSP applications, it is common to use an abstract representation (the signal-flow graph) as a guide for establishing appropriate structure and behavior of the resulting system.

Signal-flow graphs can be used to represent the algorithm either in the time domain or in the frequency domain. The **Z**-transform is used to describe discrete-time systems in the frequency domain. It is similar to the Laplace transform, which is utilized to describe analog systems. Figure 3.19 shows a signal-flow graph for a second-order section in the frequency domain.

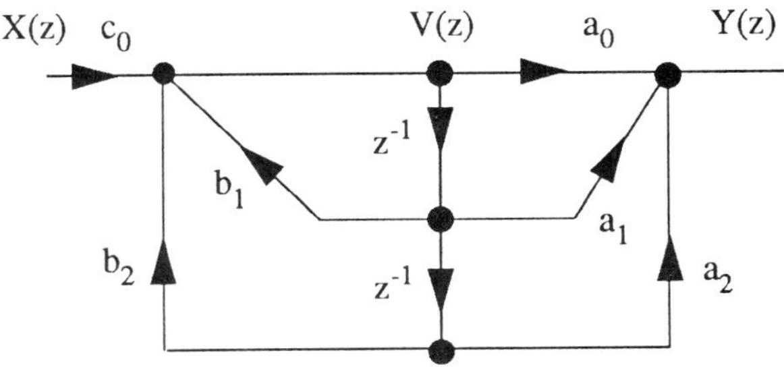

Figure 3.19. Second-order Section in Direct Form II

This graph depicts the following frequency domain equations:

$$V(z) = c_0X(z) + b_1z^{-1}V(z) + b_2z^{-2}V(z)$$
$$Y(z) = a_0V(z) + a_1z^{-1}V(z) + a_2z^{-2}V(z)$$

The corresponding equations in the time domain are

$$v(n) = c_0x(n) + b_1v(n-1) + b_2v(n-2)$$
$$y(n) = a_0v(n) + a_1v(n-1) + a_2v(n-2)$$
$$v(n-2) = v(n-1)$$
$$v(n-1) = v(n)$$

In Chapter 4, we shall consider a procedure for deriving the time-domain description from the signal-flow graph. This description can easily be coded in a suitable programming language, but it can also be used as a basis for a direct-mapped implementation approach, perhaps described in a hardware description language resulting in an ASIC.

3.17 PROGRAMMED PROCESSES

As we turn our attention to programmed processes, it is important to, once again, keep in mind that the result of a behavioral description is in fact a means of defining processes that become allocatable and schedulable units. That is, the processes will be allocated statically and/or dynamically to PEs. The processes may exhibit coarse granularity down to extremely fine granularity in terms of the allocatable and executable units. Further, in addition to the view of processes, there is always a means of communication and method of synchronization that are explicit or implicit with respect to each behavioral description artifact.

3.17.1 Parallelism Visibility versus Transparency

A distinguishing property in relationship to programmed processes is the degree to which the underlying parallelism provided by the hardware resource structure is made visible to the programmer.

— for SIMD PE arrays, the architecture is highly visible and to be exploited, the programmer must explicitly identify (by special operators or procedure calls) the invocation of specific parallel hardware facilities.

— for VLIW architectures, the potential parallelism is extracted automatically by the compiler.
— the parallelism in MIMD systems is exploited in a visible or transparent manner via explicit, or compiler-generated implicit use of communication and synchronization primitives.

Later in this section, we consider the general trends in providing behavioral descriptions for PE arrays. The special properties of *scalar parallelism* extraction for VLIW architectures are addressed in Chapter 9. We next consider the main paradigms that are or can be applied to parallel processing solutions in MIMD environments.

3.17.2 Programming Paradigms

The selection of a particular programming paradigm for the implementation of a parallel processing system is "tone setting" with respect to the PCS issues. The semantics of the various paradigms and the languages in which the paradigm is embedded provide specific points of view.

During the 1980s a variety of programming paradigms became popular, including concurrent programming, object-oriented programming, functional programming, logic (relational) programming, and to some extent dataflow programming. These paradigms, as enumerated in Figure 3.20, complement the previous and still dominant imperative programming paradigm. It is important for us to understand the fundamental concepts upon which these paradigms are developed and, further, to keep in mind the potential advantages and disadvantages from a parallel processing point of view. Therefore, we first summarize the major conceptual aspects of the paradigms. A number of books provide good descriptions of modern programming paradigms, (for example, see Watt, 1990).

The major differentiating characteristic is whether the programming language is based upon step-by-step *procedural* descriptions of processing (*imperative*) or whether the language is based upon the provision of properties of the problem (*declarative*). As indicated in the figure, within both of these categories, we can find variants that have been specifically developed for the purpose of providing concurrent execution.

Imperative Programming

This is the oldest paradigm and has its origins in the 1950s when language designers recognized that variables and assignment commands constitute a simple but useful abstraction for the memory fetch and update operations of machine instruction repertoires. Due to the close relationship to machine architectures they can be implemented very efficiently, at least in principle. This paradigm remains the dominant one with a wide variety of higher- and lower-level language variants having been

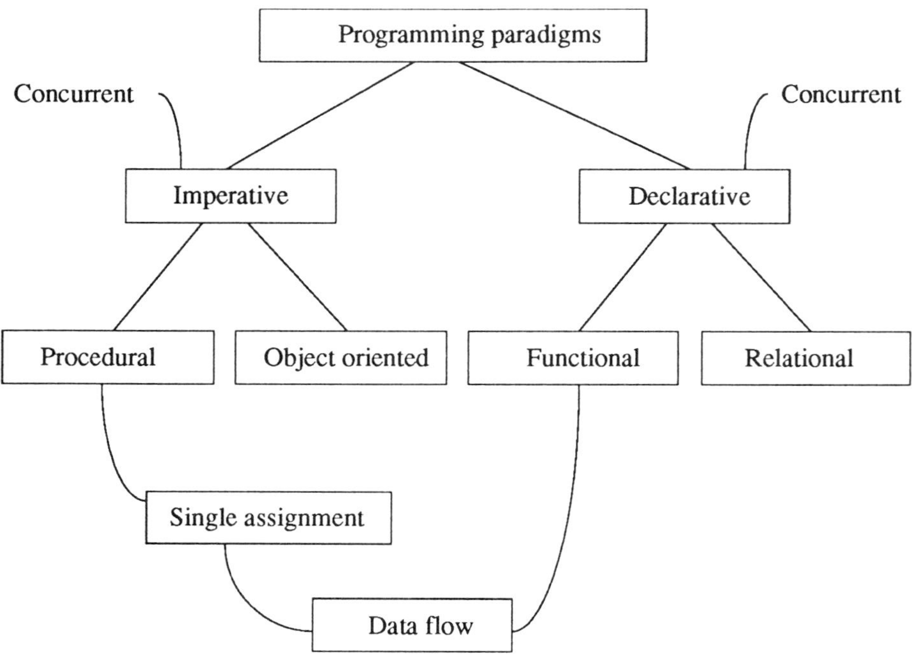

Figure 3.20. Contemporary Programming Language Paradigms

developed. The great majority of professional programmers are skilled in this paradigm and/or the related concurrent programming and object-oriented paradigms. Thus, there is significant inertia required to change to new paradigms. On the other hand, the imperative paradigm is related to the very purpose and nature of computer programming. Programs are written to model real-world processes affecting real-world objects, and such objects often posses a state that varies with time. Variables naturally model such objects, and imperative programs naturally model such processes.

Concurrent Programming

Even though concurrent programming is often referred to in the literature, one could really question whether it is a paradigm in its own right. On the other hand, it lays at the center of the PCS issues of parallel processing. While the techniques are still emerging, concurrent programs are often structured to conform with one particular parallel/concurrent hardware or virtual machine architecture. Concurrency is indicated via some explicit syntactical structure in the language that identifies separate execution sequences. The execution sequences are often referred to as *threads*; however, these sequences simply represent means of treating situations as portrayed in Figure 3.1.

The essence of concurrency has to do with *competition* between processes for resources in resource-limited environments and *interprocess communication* among cooperating processes. The concepts of this paradigm are found to some extent in the programming language domain and to some extent in the operating system domain. The concepts are most often associated with imperative languages, where concurrency is typically programmed explicitly via language features or system procedure calls. However, the notion of concurrency is also central for parallel processing related to declarative paradigms, even when concurrency is achieved implicitly and typically at fine levels of granularity.

Object-oriented Programming

This paradigm is based upon the concepts of *objects* and *object class*. An object encompasses a data structure(s) and operations (referred to as *methods*) that have the exclusive rights to access the data structure(s). Object-oriented programming originated as a discipline for improving upon classical procedural programming; however, it is possible to construct programs entirely from objects and classes leading to a distinctive style of programming. The object-oriented style imposes a modular structure on programs. The object notion is highly analogous to our process definition. As mentioned earlier, we could be tempted to use the term object instead of process throughout this book. Thus, depending on the point of view taken, all entities in a computer environment are objects. Further, as Doyle (1976) describes in an interesting manner in his book concerning the behavior of objects in a variety of physical environments, "Every Object is a System" providing once again, the proper generalized point of view.

Functional Programming

The general view of programs is that they provide a means of implementing a mapping. The program takes input values and maps them into output values. In imperative programming, mappings are achieved indirectly. In functional programming, the mapping of input to output is achieved much more directly. A program is a function (or a group of related functions), typically composed of simpler functions. The relationships between functions are quite straightforward; one function can call upon another, or the result of one function can be used as an argument to another function. Variables, commands, and side effects as found in the imperative approach do not exist; instead, the programs are written entirely with a language of expressions, functions, and declarations. In contrast to imperative programming, there is no memory model. On the other hand, there are two concepts that provide for accelerating execution of functional programs: *higher-order functions* and *lazy evaluation.*

Relational (Logic) Programming

In contrast to the view that programs provide a mapping, logic programming is *relational* where programs implement relations. Since relations are much more general than mappings, logic programming is potentially higher level than imperative or functional languages. A central notion of logic programming is *unification*, which provides the fundamental means of establishing (that is, binding) relationships and evaluation of clauses of the language.

Dataflow Programming

In principle, dataflow programming is highly related to functional programming in that it is side effect free and performs mappings. The best analogy is the pipeline, where data flows through processes that perform transformations. The flow is controlled by the availability of data (asynchronous) rather than by a control mechanism based upon time or sequences of instructions. As indicated in Figure 3.20, dataflow has also evolved from the procedural language side. In this case, dataflow properties are achieved by making restrictions on when variables are defined (explicitly, there is only one single assignment point). When conventional procedural languages are employed, they are converted into a form that builds pipelines during execution.

The dataflow paradigm has not been as widely spread nor developed as the other paradigms and is most often quite dependent upon a particular architectural model of parallel program execution. We examine this technology from architecture and language viewpoints in Chapter 12.

In summary, it is useful for us to once again take the common view of processing situations as portrayed in Figure 3.1, which can, in fact, be applied to all the paradigms that have been introduced.

Absence of the Time Dimension

In the world of real-time systems, the imperative programming paradigm has been dominant, and very few practitioners have attempted to move outside this domain. Real-time system development has, to a large extent, remained in the domain of assembly language programming, where the developers have attempted to obtain the maximize utilization of available PE, M, and C resources in meeting real-time response demands, while at the same time being able to extract reasonably accurate timing information.

Most of the work on programming languages and their paradigms has not directly addressed the question of time, which is of the essence in real-time applications. As noted by Halang and Stoyenko (1990), three exceptions in which time is explictly treated are Pearl, Real-Time Euclid, and ESTEREL. The nonimperative paradigms we have characterized all have significant potential benefits to offer in future parallel real-time system development. Thus, we are in need of developments that lead to the advantages that can be obtained from newer programming paradigms, but that also provide the basis for real-time system realization. This will undoubtedly be a major research area in the future.

3.17.3 Asynchronous versus Synchronous Parallel Programs

The programming language paradigms we have described lend themselves, in some cases, to convenient realization in an asynchronous, contra synchronous execution environment (see Perrot, 1987).

Synchronous Parallel Program Environment

The regularity of the data enables the same operations to be applied in parallel by constraining hardware processes to act in unison. This class of language is applied to optimizing the use of instruction and data pipelined machines (particularly vector processing), as well as in SIMD PE arrays where hardware parallelism is highly visible. While some special-purpose languages have evolved for synchronous parallel programming, imperative languages have most often formed the basis for developments in this area.

Asynchronous Parallel Program Environment

The independent parts of a program can compete for common resources. Further, they cooperate and communicate with each other in order to improve the efficiency of program execution as well as the utilization of the resource structure. This class of languages is applicable for the programming of MIMD architectures. In addition to research efforts to produce special-purpose parallel processing hardware for functional and logic languages, many implementations have been provided for commercially available MIMD machines. Further, for wavefront systems, asynchronous behavioral descriptions (expressed in higher-level programming languages) are of interest for this direct-mapped form of architecture. In this regard, one can observe similarities between the dataflow and wavefront paradigms.

In further discussions, we assume that the reader is familiar with one or more imperative programming languages.

3.18 PROGRAMMING OF PE ARRAYS

Since programs are executed in PE arrays in a lock-step manner, synchronization is implicit. Communication, on the other hand, is highly dependent upon the topology of the ICN, which connects the PEs together, and upon the coupling of instruction sequences. Further, we can observe a multilevel view of processes. The general process structure is typically implemented in a host processor, whereas each instruction executed in the PE array is a parallel process in its own right.

The description of application behavior is typically bound to the properties of the specific PE-array architecture, as well as to the support provided for particular programming languages. Despite this "customized" environment, we now identify some typical properties at both the instruction level and programming language levels.

3.18.1 Instruction Level

The instruction level of a PE array provides powerful instructions, performing tasks that typically require procedures with loops on sequential computers. Examples of instructions are:

- *Maximum value of a field* (vector, matrix, and so on). On a bit-serial array this is found by traversing the bitslices from most to least significant bit and successively discarding values with a zero if there are others still active with a one.
- *Exact match,* or *closest match,* between a constant and the values of a field.
- *Pairwise multiply* between the elements of two vectors, matrices, and so on.

The effect of executing instructions can be limited to a certain PE subset. The subset is specified by an array of zeros and ones, called a *selector.* Selectors are often determined through an associative process, that is, PEs are selected on the basis of the contents of their respective memories.

Based on the type of operands and type of result, six basic instruction categories used to manipulate data in the memory array can be identified:

Instruction type	*Example*
field ⇒ field	Increment field, permute field
field ⇒ selector	Maximum/minimum value of a field
field,field ⇒ field	Multiply fields, pairwise max of vector elements
field,field ⇒ selector	Pairwise equality between vector elements
constant,field ⇒ field	Multiply by constant, AND with constant
constant,field ⇒ selector	Exact match, closest match, greater than

3.18.2 Programming Languages

Higher-level languages for SIMD processor arrays are often referred to as *data parallel languages.* Typically, they are similar to conventional imperative languages but allow the programmer to organize data so that operations may be applied to many elements of data simultaneously. This is accomplished by adding new data types and extending the meaning of existing program syntax when applied to parallel data. Extension of the control structure is frequently provided.

When programming in data parallel style, emphasis is placed on the use of large, uniform data structures, such as arrays, whose elements can be processed all at once. For example, the statement **A** = **B** + **C** indicates many simultaneous addition operations if **A**, **B**, and **C** are declared to be arrays. Each corresponding array element is contained in the memory of separate PEs, or at least in the memory of a different "virtual" PEs.

The result is that much of the parallel code looks just like sequential code. The compiler examines the declarations to determine whether **B** + **C** will require a single addition operation (in a host processor) or thousands (in the PE array).

Scalar and parallel values may be mixed in a program, for example, when multiplying every element of an array by a constant. In this case, the scalar value is broadcast simultaneously to all processors. Further, an operation on parallel data may yield a scalar result, for example, when finding the sum or maximum of all the elements of an array. In this case, a reduction operation is performed that can be supported, in various manners, by the hardware processes (for example, by the ability to form and evaluate a binary tree).

Conditionals are implemented in PE arrays by limiting the impact of operations to a certain subset of the PEs. This is often achieved through the use of a *selector*.

A more detailed description of PE-array programming as well as the specific properties of various PE-array architectures is provided in Chapter 10.

3.19 CONCURRENT PARALLEL PROGRAMMING

We now consider some of distinguishing characteristics of concurrent programming paradigms with respect to the behavioral description of parallel processing.

Many of the concepts used in modern programming languages for partitioning programs into concurrently and/or parallel executable processes have their origins in operating system practice and theory that evolved during the 1960s and 1970s and are based upon extensions to the imperative programming paradigm. Concurrency is applied in situations in which processes must:

— (a) compete for shared resources
— (b) cooperate and communicate, in which case the processes must be properly synchronized

The underlying concepts and mechanisms for treating asynchronous process properties have been studied theoretically and have been the basis for process algebras such as CSP (Communicating Sequential Processes) (see Hoare, 1985), CCS (Calculus of Communicating Systems) (see Milner, 1989) and UNITY (Unbounded Nondeterministic Iterative Transformations) (see Chandy and Misra, 1988).

Further, the underlying concepts appear in such well-known languages as Modula-2 (see Wirth, 1983), Ada (see Barnes, 1984) and occam (see Inmos, 1988). The specific notions of CSP and CCS as well as several languages are reviewed in Chapter 7. In this chapter, we shall consider the essence of the problems of mutual exclusion, synchronization and communication from the software point of view, which is portrayed in Figure 3.21. Hardware mechanisms for synchronization and communication have been described in the previous section.

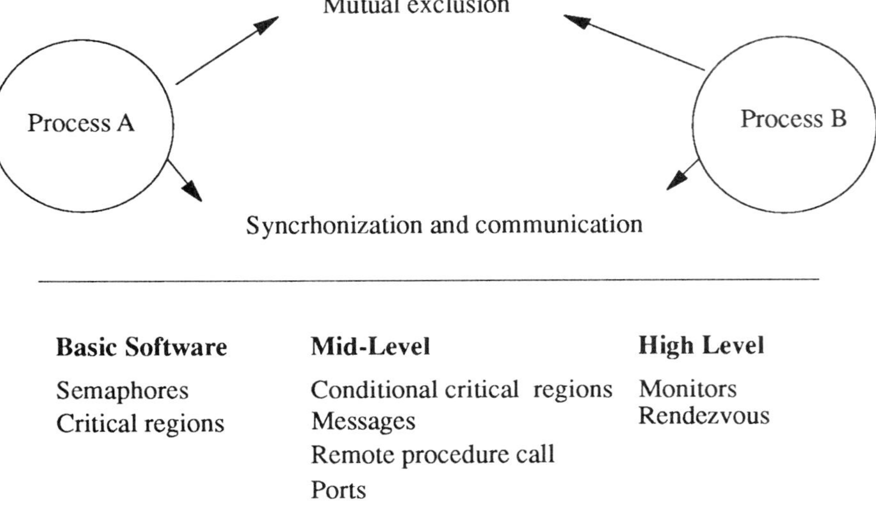

Figure 3.21. Software Mechanisms for Competing and Cooperating Processes

The subjects of mutual exclusion and synchronization and communication are highly related, since in both cases we do not want the processes to interfere with each other during critical operations. Without controlling hardware and/or software solutions, the potential unorderliness can lead to catastrophic results.

3.19.1 Mutual Exclusion

When two or more processes need to share a common variable(s) or resource of some form (buffers, peripheral devices, and the like), sole access is required in order to avoid problems of disrupting interaction during access. This problem arises in concurrent systems operating within a single PE, as well as in multiple-PE parallel systems. In both cases, the exact order of process execution cannot be determined in advance (the order is *nondeterministic*). Thus, processes are structured to contain *critical sections* at which time sole access to shared variables or resources is guaranteed. Several solutions have been suggested for implementing mutual exclusion, each of which provides specific advantages and disadvantages; however, we can state that all solutions must provide the following guarantees:

— for single-PE environments, at any moment there can be at most one process inside a critical section.
— for multiple-PE environments, there may be more than one critical section in operation; however, they must not be related to the same resources or communications.
— the stopping of one process outside its critical section does not affect the other processes.
— no assumption can be made about the relative speeds of the processes.
— processes about to enter a critical section should not block each other indefinitely (that is, become deadlocked).

We now consider several system software- and language-related methods that have been proposed or utilized for solving the mutual exclusion problem.

Semaphores

To avoid the problem of the busy form of waiting implicit in the test and set or exchange instruction solution, Dijkstra (1968) proposed a mechanism (normally, but not always, implemented in software) that can be utilized to provide orderly access to shared resources based upon operations on a *semaphore variable*. The use of "semaphore" comes from the analogy to the use of railway semaphore signals, which provide a means of gaining exclusive access to a track when several trains (processes) must follow the same track (shared resource).

Dijkstra introduced two operations on semaphore variables: P(MUTEX) and V(MUTEX), where MUTEX is the name of a mutual exclusion semaphore variable and the operations P and V have, in essence, the meaning Request and Release, respectively. (*Note*: P and V are based upon Dutch words.) These two operations, which have received synonyms such as (WAIT, SIGNAL), (REQUEST, RELEASE) and (UP, DOWN), are defined as follows:

P(MUTEX) - causes the semaphore's value to be decremented by 1
(provided that it is not already zero).
V(MUTEX) - causes the semaphore's value to be incremented by 1
(provided it is not already 1).

By intializing the semaphore variable to 1, the first process that requests a resource managed via the semaphore will execute a P(MUTEX), which decrements the semaphore to zero and permits the process to enter its critical section. Otherwise, if the value is already zero, another critical section is using the resource and the requesting process is put to sleep. It can be awoken later when the resource is released via a V(MUTEX) operation. The general structure of the semaphore variable and a process containing a critical section is portrayed as follows:

```
var   MUTEX : SEMAPHORE ;
      MUTEX := 1;  (* initialization *)

      (* process *)
      P(MUTEX) ;
      critical section
      V(MUTEX) ;
```

It is common to utilize operating system control over semaphore variables to establish orderly accessing to shared resources, for example, to build a queue of waiting (sleeping) processes that avoids busy waiting. Thus, if requesting processes are awakened in the order that they request the resource, a fairness is achieved in the allocation of the resource. To achieve this orderliness, the following behavioral semantics of the P(MUTEX) and V(MUTEX) operation are utilized:

```
P(MUTEX) =   if MUTEX = 1 then
                 MUTEX := 0
             else
                 wait on the queue associated with MUTEX;

V(MUTEX) =   if QUEUE ≠ EMPTY then
                 remove a process from the queue
             else
                 MUTEX := 1
```

We have considered examples of semaphores in which a single resource is requested. In this form, we only require the use of a single control, resulting in the *binary semaphore* structure that has been illustrated. A generalization of this mechanism is the *counting semaphore*, which can be used to satisfy requests for a pool of similar resources, for example, a buffer pool. A graphical means of portraying the semantics of semaphore operations is presented in Figure 3.22.

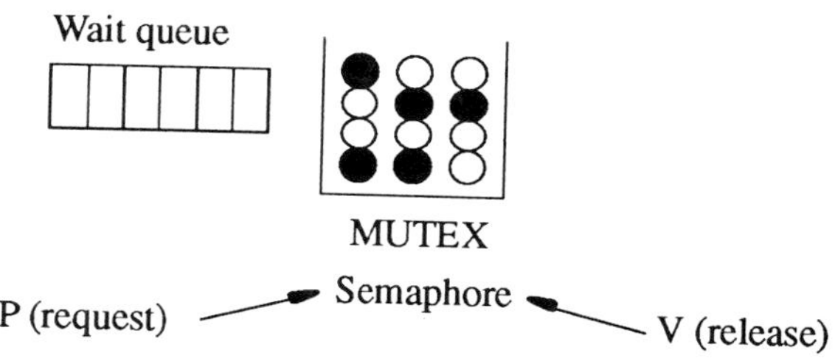

Figure 3.22. Semaphore-based Mutual Exclusion

Here we can observe that a P operation is a form of request and a V operation a release. We can view the MUTEX semaphore variable as an *urn* in which a number of *marbles* are contained. In the binary semaphore case, there is only one marble. In the counting semaphore case, there are as many marbles as there are resources in the pool. Thus, resources can be granted (black marbles) up to the limit. If further requests are made and there are no resources (marbles) available, requesting processes are placed on a wait queue. When resources are released, if there are processes waiting for the resource, they will be removed from the queue. *Note*: Various disciplines and strategies can be used in queue removal.

Semaphore variables are logically complete but often lead to complex constructions, which reduces understandability and the program becomes sensitive to minor changes. Programming errors (for example, if a P operation is written where a V should appear) can lead to the processes being blocked indefinitely. Care must be exercised since testing and debugging become significantly more difficult!

Critical Regions

To avoid the detailed, error-prone programming of P and V operations, Hoare (1972) suggested a language construct from which the compiler could generate semaphore variables and appropriate P and V operations automatically. He proposed the following:

with RESOURCE **do** S ;

This code appears at each instance where a statement or block of statements S is used as a critical region. Thus, all occurrences of program code that identify RESOURCE will be provided with P and V operations on a commonly generated semaphore variable.

Conditional Critical Regions

A further refinement of the critical region ideas led to *conditional critical regions,* which are expressed as follows:

```
with RESOURCE when B do S ;
```

where B is a Boolean expression and S is a critical region requiring RESOURCE. If B is false, the process is delayed. Thus, a condition must be fulfilled in addition to a resource being available. This solution provides a discipline with respect to granting the resource and in the removal of processes from the wait queue, as indicated in Figure 3.22.

Monitors

In the previous software solutions to the mutual exclusion problem (semaphores and critical regions), the statements performing operations on shared resources are spread throughout the program, thus making it difficult to study the structure of the programs and see the ways in which shared resources are utilized. To improve upon this situation, Dijkstra (1972), Brinch-Hansen (1973), and Hoare (1974) proposed the higher-level concept of monitors (sometimes called secretaries). The monitor collects all the critical sections into a single structure in the form of procedures (or functions) of the monitor. Processes then invoke these procedures (with appropriate arguments) when they wish to gain access and operate upon a shared resource. As with *P* and *V* operations, only one process is granted access to the shared resource at a time. The general structure of a monitor and invocation of a monitor procedure are portrayed in the following code:

```
monitor MONITORNAME ;
(* declaration of local data *)

        procedure PROCNAME (parameter list) ;
                begin (* procedure body *) end ;

        (* declaration of other local procedures *)

begin
        (* initialization of local data *)
end ;

MONITORNAME.PROCNAME (actual parameters)
```

The monitor contains a declaration of local data (the data to be shared in the case of shared variables) or control information concerning access to a shared resource (for example, a peripheral device). The procedures that can manipulate the shared resource are then declared with appropriate parameter lists. The body of the monitor is executed at the beginning and provides any necessary initialization of the shared resource. Once initialized, processes can invoke the procedures (entry points) of the monitor, passing actual parameters, as illustrated. In terms of the graphic presentation of Figure 3.22, the MUTEX semaphore variable and queues are contained within the monitor.

The utilization of monitors makes the programming of mutual exclusion much less error prone, and errors are easier to detect. An extension of the monitors with *condition variables* permits the construct to be utilized for building orderly queues of processes.

In mutual exclusion, processes are normally competing for the use of resources; however, the solutions to the mutual exclusion problem serve as a starting point for process synchronization and communication.

3.19.2 Process Synchronization and Communication

We shall now consider cases in which the processes wish to cooperate with each other and are generally aware of the purpose of each other. They may be synchronized around the occurrence of a particular event (for example, a specific time has arrived) or they may wish to synchronize in order to communicate with each other (pass messages) in a producer-consumer relationship. These two areas of synchronization and communication, which often build on the same primitives as mutual exclusion, are so closely related that they are most often presented as parts of the same problem. To gain a first view of these problems as well as to concretely demonstrate the use of conditional critical regions, let us consider the producer-consumer problem of a bounded buffer.

A Bounded Buffer

A bounded buffer is a buffer containing a limited quantity of message space (resources) that can be used for producing or consuming messages. In conditional critical region form, the program code follows the following structure.

bounded buffer for controlled production and consumption

```
var RESOURCE :    record
                      BUFFER : array [0..N-1] of MESSAGE ;
                      POINTER : 0..N-1 ;
                      (*position of next item to be consumed*)
                      COUNT : 0..N
                      (*number of items in the buffer*)
                  end ;
```

```
with RESOURCE do (*intialization*)
begin
        COUNT := 0 ;  POINTER := 0
end ;

(*in the producer*)

(*produce item*)
with RESOURCE
        when COUNT < N do
        begin
                BUFFER [(POINTER + COUNT) mod N)] := ITEM ;
                COUNT := COUNT + 1
        end ;

(*in the consumer*)

with RESOURCE
        when COUNT > 0 do
        begin
                ITEM := BUFFER [POINTER] ;
                COUNT := COUNT - 1 ;
                POINTER := (POINTER + 1) mod N
        end ;
(*consume item*)
```

Notice that the producer will produce new items up to the limit of the buffer size, but will then be blocked. The consumer will take items from the queue if there are any; otherwise, it will be blocked. Thus, a convenient, buffered message-passing scheme has been provided.

Let us now consider another example of process synchronization where processes are activated at particular points in time. In this example, we demonstrate monitors and utilize a *condition variable* as a means of dealing with orderly queues in monitors. In our example, we declare a condition variable and two related operations as follows:

TIMEQUEUE : CONDITION and the operations

TIMEQUEUE.SIGNAL and TIMEQUEUE.WAIT

The WAIT operation deactivates a process and indicates the time at which it is to be awoken. The deactivated process is appended to a condition variable queue (organized by the time for awakening). The SIGNAL operation causes the resumption of the first process on the queue associated with the condition variable. If no processes are waiting, the signal has no effect. The program code is as follows:

time-wise scheduling of process reactivation

```
monitor CLOCK ;
type   RANGE = 0..MAXINT ;
var    ALARM : RANGE ;
         TIMEQUEUE : CONDITION ;

       procedure HOLD(T:RANGE) ;
       var ALARM : RANGE ;
       begin
              if T > 0 then
              begin
                     ALARM := TIME + T ;  (*wake up time*)
                     TIMEQUEUE.WAIT(ALARM) ;
                     (*appended by priority, i.e. wake up time*)
                     TIME := ALARM
                     (*advances to restart time of newly awoken process*)
              end
       end ;      (*HOLD*)

       procedure NEXT ;
       begin
              repeat
                     TIMEQUEUE.SIGNAL
              until TIME <> TIMEQUEUE.PRIORITY or
                        TIMEQUEUE.LENGTH = 0
              (*remove all processes which should be woken up at this
                time, checking to make sure there are sleeping processes*)
       end ;      (*NEXT*)

       begin
              TIME := 0
       end       (*CLOCK*)
```

A process wishing to wait until a specified time can call the procedure HOLD with the amount of time it wishes to wait. If that time has not already elapsed, it will be placed in the queue TIMEQUEUE in time order. Time is advanced to the restart time of a newly awoken process (activated as a result of a SIGNAL). The procedure NEXT is utilized to remove processes from the time queue one at a time until all processes that should be resumed at that instant have been resumed. Further, PRIORITY (time in this case) and LENGTH operations on the condition variable assist in the removal. While this simulated clock example does not deal with all problems, it does represent an interesting solution upon which real solutions to time-wise synchronization can be constructed.

Message Passing

We have considered the case where processes cooperate via a bounded buffer, which is fine for single-PE environments and may be feasible in shared memory MIMD environments; however, the general problem of producing and consuming messages in MIMD parallel processing environments is normally treated by message-passing mechanisms and primitives. To communicate in an orderly fashion, the processes must be synchronized in some manner.

From the programming language viewpoint, message passing is a logical transport function. The management of the transport is typically dealt with by the kernel part of the operating system and, if the transport is across PEs, in cooperation between the kernel and the interconnection network. The kernel may utilize cyclic buffers to administer transmission in those cases where the producer is freed to continue operation after sending a message. In various programming languages, the transport facilities are provided directly in the language or via some form of SEND and RECEIVE statement or procedure call semantics. The mechanisms used in message transport can be simple *mailboxes* or can provide for a sequence of message transmissions via a *pipe*.

As an outgrowth of the study of mutual exclusion and synchronization problems in general, a number of theoretic solutions eventually found their way into concrete programming language features for supporting message passing. In particular, we can follow the development of guarded commands proposed by Dijkstra (1975) and utilized in CSP (**C**ommunicating **S**equential **P**rocesses) by Hoare (1985) and by Brinch-Hansen (1978) in his language DP (**D**istributed **P**rocesses). These developments have had a strong influence on the message passing mechanisms developed in Ada (see Barnes, 1984) and in occam (Inmos, 1988).

Guarded Commands

The original idea for guards was to provide a structured means of describing nondeterministic behavior. An alternative list of guarded commands have the following general structure:

```
[ GUARD1 -> COMMAND1
[] GUARD2 -> COMMAND2
[] GUARD3 -> COMMAND3
[] ----
]
```

The delimiter [] is used to separate guarded commands. Each command (set of executable statements) is guarded by a predicate expression and will only be executed if the predicate is true. If more than one are true at the same time, the decision as to which command is selected is arbitrary (hence *nondeterministic*). It is also possible to indicate a repetitive set of guarded commands as follows:

```
* [ GUARD1 -> COMMAND1
  [] GUARD2 -> COMMAND2
  [] GUARD3 -> COMMAND3
  [] ----
  ]
```

In this case the set of commands will be iterated as long as at least one of the guards is true.

Communicating Sequential Processes

The important ideas by Dijkstra influenced Hoare and, in CSP, Hoare introduced the notion of guards as a means of synchronizing input and output operations between processes (that is, process communication). This extension is evident in the following CSP example of a producer and consumer of a character string:

```
X :: (*process name)
        *[ C: CHARACTER ;
           PRODUCER ? C -> CONSUMER ! C
         ]
```

In this case, a process is acting as an intermediary between the producer and the consumer. The process continuously iterates, where in each iteration it waits for a character from the producer (PRODUCER ? C) and then outputs the character to a consumer (CONSUMER ! C). Thus, the symbol ? means to wait for the delivery of a character from PRODUCER, and the ! means to transmit the character to CONSUMER.

This simple example shows how guards were used as predicates to control this input/output operation and how process communication is achieved in CSP. In general, we can state that CSP process communication abides by the following:

1. An input command in process A specifies, as its source, the name of another process B.
2. An output command in process B specifies, as its destination, the process A.
3. The target variable of the input command matches the value denoted by the expression of the output command.

Rendezvous

In CSP, each process must name the process with which it wishes to communicate, thus providing a symmetry in the synchronization relationship. Synchronization according to this form is known as a *rendezvous*. No buffer is utilized to hold information as it is passed directly between the processes. Whichever process encounters its input or output command first must wait for the other process to reach its corresponding output or input command in which the waiting process is named. Only at this point will both processes execute their communication statement (a *rendezvous* takes place). An extended rendezvous, permitting two-way communication at the rendezvous point, is the central communication and synchronization mechanism of the Ada programming language. These aspects of Ada are illuminated in Chapter 7.

Ports

The rendezvous method of message passing requires explicit identification of the communicating processes. As an alternative, we can utilize the *port* (sometimes referred to as a *socket*) concept, where processes can be connected to input and output ports of other processes over which messages are transported. In this case, the sending process does not need to identify the receiving process (or vice versa). The port becomes the neutral entity over which they communicate. In these asynchronous systems, the input ports typically provide an abstraction for a queue. Some languages have utilized this form of synchronization and communication in preference to the more cumbersome and overhead-ridden rendezvous.

Remote Procedure Call

Making message passing explicit in program text may have some disadvantages. One mechanism that can be used to avoid this problem in the use of remote procedure calls. In this case, the semantics of the procedure call is retained regardless of whether the procedure being invoked is executing in the same PE or in another PE. In the latter case, the run time and/or operating system determines the locality of the called procedure and provides semantics for the procedure call via synchronizing with the remote procedure for argument passing. In fact, the Ada and Concurrent C language communication and synchronization rendezvous mechanisms are remote procedure calls. (When required, remote procedure is implemented by message passing.)

In summarizing the concurrent parallel programming discussion, we can state that: *The means of communication and method of synchronization are critical issues since they control the degree of process granularity for efficient parallel execution, the ease of writing correct programs and verifying them to be correct.*

The subject of concurrent programming has received significant attention in professional literature and therefore we have been dwelled upon this subject in this chapter. For further detailed studies of these problems, the reader is referred to Perrot (1987) and Ben-Ari (1990). Survey articles have been provided by Andrew and Schneider (1983) and by Dinning (1989).

We now examine the principle properties of programming language paradigms that became popular during the 1980s.

3.20 OBJECT-ORIENTED PROGRAMMING

The need to structure imperative programs has always been important with respect to dealing with the mounting complexity of large programs. Structuring imperative programs for the purpose of parallel processing is absolutely essential. The concepts of object-oriented programming have their origin in the Simula programming language (see Dahl, Myhrhaug, and Nygaard, 1970). These gentlemen developed the notion of class, subclasses, objects with attributes, and inheritance, which are central to modern object-oriented programming. During the 1970s, as the need for structuring became more acute, the importance of *information hiding* by *encapsulation* was described by Parnas (1972) as a means of isolating a global variable and the procedures or functions that access the variable. Thus, other parts of the program could not gain arbitrary access to the variable but must call upon the functions or procedures. These notions became one of the early premises for software engineering.

The object-oriented approach is potentially very appealing from a parallel processing point of view since a discipline is enforced by which objects communicate with each other by regularized procedure calls or by message passing. In this regard, objects can simply be viewed as communicating processes and thus can be treated by many of the general notions we have presented for the concurrent programming paradigm. In addition to embedding object-oriented concepts into higher-level languages such as Simula and later Smalltalk, Eiffel, and to some extent Ada, the concepts have been incorporated into the C language resulting in Objective C, which resembles Smalltalk, and C++, which resembles Simula. Due to the often strict time and resource utilization demands placed upon real-time applications, many real-time development projects have turned to these low-level object-oriented languages like C++. Another interesting development in this area is Concurrent Smalltalk (see Yokote, 1989) in which monitor concepts (called secretaries) are provided for concurrency control.

The earliest, boldest effort to exploit the properties of object orientation and parallel processing was the Intel 432 project, which has been neatly described by Organick (1983). Ada programs were decomposed into objects of varying granularity. The hardware architecture maintained rather complex data structures in order to administrate program execution. Despite the problems encountered in this pioneering effort, they could demonstrate increases of performance due to successively adding more PEs in a specially developed MIMD architecture.

While the Intel 432 experienced problems, we will undoubtedly see further developments of parallel architectures that are designed to take advantage of the attractive object-oriented paradigm notions.

3.21 FUNCTIONAL PROGRAMMING

Since software is the major contributor to costs in nontrivial real-time projects, it is important to understand the concepts of new nontraditional paradigms and to consider their potential applicability in parallel processing and real-time systems.

In both functional and logic programming, the key to exploiting parallelism is based on decomposing programs into fine-grain processes that are coupled together based upon language mechanisms. The potential for parallelism with fine-grain processes is quite significant. We could compare logic and functional programming as being *reactional* or *tranformational*. That is, logic programs react to situations by unifying and applying appropriate implications and assertions. On the other hand, functional languages are based upon transformations of inputs to outputs. Given this general characterization, let us introduce some of the principles of these two paradigms.

In exploiting functional programming, the problem is expressed by functions and recursion, which are the major tools of the functional programmer. Modern functional programming style is based upon pattern matching, which provides a powerful form of selecting functions to be evaluated. Consider the following:

```
datatype  shape = point
                | circle of  real              (* radius *)
                | box of  (real * real)        (* width , height *)

fun       area (point) = 0.0
        | area (circle, r) = pi * sqr (r)
        | area (box (w,h)) = w * h
```

Here we have defined a function area that is of type shape and maps into a value of type real. If we invoke the function area with the pattern 'point', the first definition is selected and the function result is 0.0. If, for example, we invoke area with 'circle' 5.0, the second alternative is selected by pattern matching, and the value 5.0 is bound to r for the purpose of evaluating the function expression. Likewise invoking 'box' (2.0, 3.0) selects and evaluates the third alternative after bindings to w and h. Note that this concept, while similar to a CASE construct in an imperative language, is much more powerful.

3.21.1 Lambda Calculus

All functional languages are based upon the use of lambda calculus, which was developed by the logician Alonzo Church in the 1930s. The primary aim was to develop a model for communication between different parts in a sequential functional derivation. This was accomplished by utilizing names for objects so that they could be referred to or *substituted* in certain contexts without changing meaning (that is, *referential transparency*). Thus, Church provided a notation and a calculus (rules for evaluation and substitution).

Programs constructed in functional languages are composed of expressions that are rewritable functions and constructor functions that can be utilized recursively. Since functional languages are side effect free, a subexpression in a total expression can be replaced by any other equivalent expression with the same value without affecting the value of the total expression (that is, referential transparency of lambda calculus). Further, functions are first class values in the language and can appear anywhere that a value is defined.

The execution of a functional program proceeds by reduction and evaluation of expressions. In *lazy evaluation* (*call by need* or *output driven*), a functional expression may be partially reduced before all its arguments are completely evaluated. Function arguments are only evaluated and supplied upon demand (only when they are needed). This can be placed in contrast to the situation in imperative languages where, most typically, all arguments are completely evaluated prior to the invocation of a function (procedure).

All modern functional languages also provide for *higher-order functions* in which functions can appear as arguments. Further features of functional languages include the ability to repeatedly apply a function to one argument at a time. This provides a convenient shorthand notation for implementing extremely powerful functions over sets of values.

The reader will observe that functional languages are characterized by rather clean, well-structured concepts, making them a good candidate for parallel processing paradigms. Thus, there are many efforts to develop parallel processing models based upon functional languages. For example, Kahn and McQueen (1977) generalized the notion of lazy evaluation to include parallelism. In their approach, each function call in an expression is viewed as a process in a network. Such a process can be modeled as a producer-consumer process to evaluate arguments. This model is directly utilizable in parallel processing environments since several producer-consumer processes can be made to run in parallel.

For thorough descriptions of functional programming languages, see Wikström (1987) and Watt (1990).

3.22 LOGIC PROGRAMMING

Logic programming refers to the use of formulas from first-order predicate logic as statements of a programming language. That is, logic investigates relationships between premises and conclusions of arguments. To prove that a conclusion follows from a set of premises, a number of *inference* steps are given, showing how the premises lead to the conclusion by following certain rules.

Logic programs are organized into *clauses,* which describe facts (assertions), relationships (implications), and conclusions (goals). It is important that each clause contain no more than one conclusion, and when this restriction is present, the clauses are called *Horn clauses.* A logic program is, in fact, a set of Horn clauses or procedures. Because the fundamental operation during the execution of a logic program is the application of a Horn clause, or procedure, the performance of logic programming systems is typically measured in terms of *LIPS (Logical Inferences per Second).*

The Prolog language was introduced in 1972 (see Colmerauer and others, 1973, and Rousell, 1975) as an extension to the fundamental ideas of logic programming in order to provide a viable language for solving practical problems. There are a variety of books and articles that provide very good descriptions of logic programming and Prolog (see, for example, Sterling and Shapiro, 1986 as well as Clocksin and Mellish, 1981).

The Japanese Fifth Generation Computer project selected to utilize logic programming languages as the primary implementation media. This selection was based on a number of factors (see Shapiro, 1983).

— symbolic logic is a natural vehicle for specifying a system
— it is easier to specify and verify a system if the specification and the programming language follow the same formalism
— logic programs can be seen as a generalization of relational data bases
— provides a single-assignment language, which may be more easily implemented in parallel processing environments
— close relationship between the deduction mechanism of expert systems and Prolog's deduction mechanism

Given this background, let us examine some of the rudiments of logic programming and demonstrate how the simple language structure provides a good means for exploiting parallel processing. For a more complete discussion, the reader is referred to one of the many books available on this topic, for example, see Conery (1987).

The Basic Concepts

The fundamental clauses used in logic programs are one of the following four types:

Clause Type	Example
Implication	$p \leftarrow q \wedge r.$
Assertion	p.
Goal	$\leftarrow q \wedge r.$
Null clause	null

The text of a program consists of implications and assertions. Goal statements and null clauses are derived by an interpreter as it executes the program.

Execution Semantics and Parallelism

Execution begins when an initial goal statement is provided. The interpreter computes all values for variables of the goal through a series of resolutions. If a null clause can be derived, the substitutions used in the derivation provide values for the variables of the initial goal. The execution can be represented as a goal tree, where multiple descendants of a node indicate a choice of clauses for resolving the goal at that node.

Unification

A key step in the interpretation of a logic program is the *unification* of a goal atom with the head of a clause. The unification of two terms means that the most general ("simplest") unifier is sought. If no common unifier exists, the unification fails. We can, in fact, view unification as providing both the communication and synchronization mechanism of logic programming systems.

Implicit Parallelism

There are two major forms of *implicit parallelism* in logic programs, which are quite simply related to a speedup of the search of the goal tree. This can be accomplished via exploiting the AND and/or OR relationships.

Nondeterministic Results

In pure logic programs, the result of a unification and goal search may yield several alternative solutions (that is, multiple program clauses that satisfy the goal). This multiplicity, while important in such operations as data base searches, is not appropriate in real-time applications if a decision is to made as to what to do. There are several other limitations to using pure logic programming or even Prolog in real-time environments; however, the nondeterminism property is one important aspect that must be dealt with in any practical utilization of logic programming for time-critical applications.

3.22.1 Concurrent Logic Programs

The early versions of Prolog did not provide any further program structure than implication and assertions. Thus, building systems based upon Prolog programs was not possible. In later developments, Shapiro (1987) created Concurrent Prolog to which various means of mutual exclusion as well as process synchronization and communication have been added via *Guarded Horn Clauses*. This solution is based upon applying the Dijkstra guarded commands described earlier in the chapter. Another concurrent logic program approach called Parlog has been described by Gregory (1987).

3.22.2 Additional Logic and Functional Approaches

A variant of Prolog that is worth noting in respect to using logic programming for real-time applications is STRAND (Foster and Taylor, 1989). Another interesting development for real-time applications is Erlang (Armstrong and Virding, 1990) which is a functional language having a syntactical family resemblence to Prolog. In these cases, many of the dynamic execution properties leading to nondeterminism have been removed.

Finally, for an excellent overview of contemporary research in programming language paradigms, the reader is referred to a special issue of the ACM Computing Surveys (Wegner, 1989).

References

Armstrong, J.R. (1989). *Chip-Level Modelling with VHDL*, Prentice Hall, Englewood Cliffs, NJ.

Armstrong, J.L., and S.R. Virding (1990). Erlang-An Experimental Telephony Programming Language, *Proceedings of the XIII International Switching Symposium*, Stockholm, Vol. III, pp. 43-48.

Andrew, G.R., and F.B. Schneider (1983). Concepts and Notions for Concurrent Programming, *Computing Surveys*, Vol. 15, No. 1, pp. 3-43.

Barnes, J.G.P. (1984). *Programming in Ada*, 2nd ed., Addison-Wesley, Reading, MA.

Ben-Ari, M. (1990). *Principles of Concurrent and Distributed Programming*, Prentice Hall, Englewood Cliffs, NJ.

Brinch-Hansen, P. (1973). *Operating System Principles*, Prentice Hall, Englewood Cliffs, NJ.

Brinch-Hansen, P. (1978). Distributed Processes: A Concurrent Programming Concept, *Communications of the ACM*, Vol. 21, pp. 934-940.

Chandy, K.M., and J. Misra (1988). *Parallel Program Design: A Foundation*, Addison-Wesley, Reading, MA.

Clocksin, W.F., and C.S. Mellish (1981). *Programming in Prolog*, Springer-Verlag, New York.

Colmerauer, A., K. Kanoui, R. Pasero, and P. Roussel (1973). Un systéme de comunication homme-machine en Francais. Rapport, Groupe Intelligence Artificielle, Universite d'Aix Marseille, Luminy.

Conery, J.S. (1987). *Parallel Execution of Logic Programs*, Kluwer Academic Publishers, Norwell, MA.

Dahl, O.-J., B. Myhrhaug, and K. Nygaard (1970). Simula 67 Common Base Language, N.S-22, Norwegian Computing Center, Oslo, Norway.

Dijkstra, E.J. (1968). Co-operating Sequential Processes, In F. Genuys (ed.), *Programming Languages*, Academic Press, New York.

Dijkstra, E.J. (1972). Hierarchical Ordering of Sequential Processes, *Operating Systems Techniques* (eds. C.A.R. Hoare and R.H. Perrot), pp. 72-79, Academic Press, New York.

Dijkstra, E.J. (1975). Guarded Commands, Non-Determinism and a Calculus for the Derivation of Programs, *Communications of the ACM*, Vol. 18, No. 8, pp. 453-457.

Dinning, A. (1989). A Survey of Synchronization Methods for Parallel Computers, *Computer*, Vol. 22, No. 7, pp. 66-77.

Doyle, P. (1976). *Every Object Is a System*, Greshem Press, Old Woking, Surrey, England.

Foster, I., and S. Taylor (1989). *STRAND: New Concepts in Parallel Processing*, Prentice Hall, Englewood Cliffs, NJ.

Gregory, S. (1987). *Parallel Logic Programming in PARLOG*, Addison-Wesley, Reading, MA.

Halang, W.A., and A.D. Stoyenko (1990). Comparative Evaluation of High-level Real-time Languages, *International Journal of Real-time Systems*, Vol. 2, No. 4.

Hoare, C.A.R. (1972). Towards a Theory of Parallel Programming, *Operating System Techniques*, (eds. C.A.R. Hoare and R.H. Perrot), pp. 61-67, Academic Press, New York.

Hoare, C.A.R. (1974). Monitors: An Operating System Structuring Concept, *Communications of the ACM*, Vol. 17, No. 10, pp. 549-557.

Hoare, C.A.R. (1985). *Communicating Sequential Processes*, Prentice Hall, Englewood Cliffs, NJ.

INMOS (1988). *occam2 Reference Manual*, Prentice Hall, Englewood Cliffs, NJ.

Kahn, G., and D. McQueen (1977). Coroutines and Networks of Parallel Processors, in *Information Processig '77*, North-Holland, Amsterdam.

Krishnamurthy, E.V. (1989). *Parallel Processing: Principles and Practices*, Addison-Wesley, Reading, MA.

Milner, R. (1989). *Communication and Concurrency*, Prentice Hall, Englewood Cliffs, NJ.

Organick, E.I. (1983). *A Programmer's View of the Intel 432 System*, McGraw-Hill, NY.

Parnas, D.L. (1972). On the Criteria to Be Used in Decomposing Systems into Modules, *Communications of the ACM*, Vol. 15, pp. 1053-1058.

Perrot, R.H. (1987). *Parallel Programming*, Addison-Wesley, Reading, MA.

Roussel, P. (1975). PROLOG: Manuel de reference et d'utilisation. Groupe Intelligence Artificielle, Universite d'Aix Marseille, Luminy, September.

Shapiro, E. (1987). *Concurrent Prolog: Collected Papers*, Vols. 1-2, MIT Press, Cambridge, MA.

Siewiorek, D., C.G. Bell, and A. Newell (1982). *Computer Structures: Principles and Examples*, McGraw-Hill, New York.

Sterling, L., and E. Shapiro (1986). *The Art of Prolog*, MIT Press, Cambridge, MA.

Watt, R.W. (1990). *Programming Language Concepts and Paradigms*, Prentice Hall, Englewood Cliffs, NJ.

Wegner, P. (1989). Introduction to the Special Issue on Programming Language Paradigms, *ACM Computing Surveys*, Vol. 21, No. 3, pp. 253-258.

Wikström, A. (1987). *Functional Programming Using Standard ML*, Prentice Hall, Englewood Cliffs, NJ.

Wirth, N. (1983). *Programming in Modula-2*, Springer-Verlag, New York.

Yokote, Y. (1989). *The Design and Implementation of Concurrent Smalltalk*, World Scientific Series in Computer Science, Vol. 21, Singapore.

INTERCONNECTION NETWORKS

We introduce the seemingly complex, but crucial subject of interconnection networks via a structured presentation of the major concepts and issues. The following central points are made:

- the selection of interconnection network is highly application and architecture dependent (119)
- transport is accomplished by circuit switching or packet switching (121)
- networks can be directly and fully connected (as in the case of the crossbar), or, alternatively, directly or indirectly partially connected (122)
- network operations include communication on a **one-to-one**, **one-to-all** (that is, broadcast), or **all-to-one** basis (123)
- permutations and switches are building blocks of partially connected networks (124)
- partially connected networks can be single stage (including buses) or multistage (126)
- interconnection networks can be controlled globally or locally with respect to the management of switches (129)
- store and forward and wormhole routing in packet-switched networks are presented and compared (130)
- packet-switched networks can enter deadlock (130)
- performance properties of networks include small diameter, uniformity, extendability, short wires, and redundant paths (for fault tolerance), as well as bandwidth and narrowness (132)
- cost properties include minimum number of wires, efficient layout, simple routing algorithm, fixed degree, and fit to available technology (133)
- Clos networks, rings and trees, grids (meshes) and toruses, shuffle-type topologies (including Omega and Benes networks), plus Boolean **n**-cube and hypercube variants, Banyan and delta networks, and hashnets are presented (133)

- the hot-spot problem, where traffic becomes concentrated to one or a few receivers, is described, along with hardware and software combining solutions (137)

- we analyze the performance properties of multiprocessor ICNs with respect to crossbars, bus architectures, and multistage variants (141)

- an analytical method is presented for analyzing the performance properties of multicomputer ICNs and exemplified by analyzing the three-dimensional torus topology (143)

- as a general summary of interconnection network properties and value judgments, the following comparison has been made by Tabak (1990).

Property	Bus	Hypercube	Crossbar	Multistage
Speed	low	moderate	high	high
Cost	low	moderate	high	moderate
Reliability	low	high	high	high
Configurability	high	low	low	moderate
Complexity	low	moderate	high	moderate

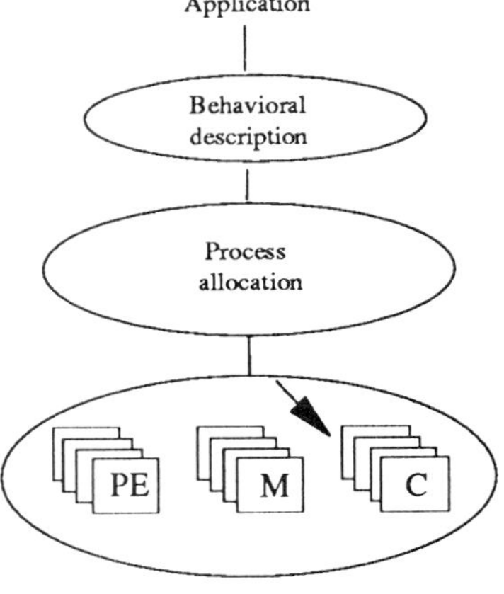

We have earlier considered an abstract model of interconnection networks in Figure 3.7 where a number of PE processes are attached to the ICN via ports (terminals) and where each PE has a unique terminal address. From an application program point of view, we **may** be interested in keeping the details of the ICN hidden from the application. That is, the transportation service provided over the network is treated as a black box. On the other hand, certain types of applications, including most all time-critical real-time systems, may be better mapped onto systems having a specific ICN structure. We observed, for example, how the mesh network (see Figure 3.13) is the natural basis for many SIMD PE-array architectures. In direct-mapped situations there is little attempt to generalize the interconnections since they are determined solely to serve that particular application. However, the best network selection may be based upon one of the topologies described in this chapter. It is essential to understand the principles and the advantages and disadvantages, as well as the performance, predictability, cost, and reliability properties, of various ICN approaches, especially in relation to their utilization in real-time systems.

3.23 NETWORK PROPERTIES

Much of the early theory in networks and switching systems evolved from telephone and power system applications where networks are the primary system ingredient. Some important early work in the telecommunications area that has influenced computer-related developments were by Clos (1953) and Benes (1965).

As ICNs have become an important ingredient in parallel computer systems, the subject area has become highly relevant and a multitude of research and development results have been reported. The reader is referred to the book by Siegel (1990), the overview article by Feng (1981), and the special issue of *IEEE Computer* (see Bhuyan, 1987) for a general coverage of ICNs. In the parallel processing context, we can state that:

> The art of designing parallel processing systems deals, to a large extent, with finding communication network models and methods that, at a reasonable cost, provide rapid communication for the types of appli-cations for which the system is to be applied.
>
> Björn Lisper (with permission, translated from Swedish)

As with other resources, in the hard real-time environment, ICN predictability as well as fault-tolerance properties become essential issues.

3.23.1 What Is Connected to What?

Based upon the application and architecture, we find that ICNs are utilized to couple:

1. PEs to M processes (*Note*: We have earlier equated M and PE.)
2. PEs to PEs

In the first case, we find that the ICN is used as the means of connecting PEs to shared **m**emories (SM) as in the case of multiprocessors. In the second case, we find a variety of ICN structures for **d**istributed **m**emory (DM) multicomputer systems, as well as in SIMD PE-array architectures (including the mesh). Further, special-purpose interconnections are developed for DSP, systolic, and wavefront systems. While the question of what is connected to what varies in detail, the abstract model of the ICNs presented in Figure 3.7 can be used as the common denominator where PEs are coupled to PEs. What varies, is the structure and behavior of connections inside the network, which we now consider.

We begin our presentation by considering the major properties of interconnection networks as portrayed in Figure 3.23.

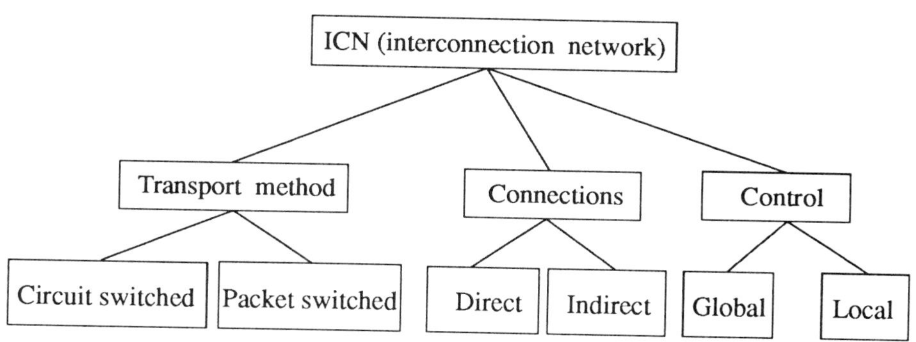

Figure 3.23. Categorization of Interconnection Network Properties

3.24 TRANSPORT METHOD

The method used for message transmission between PEs can either be packet-switched or circuit-switched. The telephone and post office systems can be used as analogies for these two forms. The packet-switched system is similar to the postal system, where users of the network communicate by transmitting addressed packets. The routing and flow of the packets at any given point in time are dependent upon the pattern of communication. The circuit-switched system, like the telephone system, establishes connections and, when established, the users are free to communicate as long as the connection remains established.

3.24.1 Circuit Switched

The path for a message is completely reserved before the message is sent. When the path is established, the PEs (via the terminals to which they are connected) are coupled together and can begin to communicate. Circuit-switched transmission can be administered quite effectively by, for example, simple handshaking. On the other hand, the risk for collision is large due to the fact that the path for transmission is locked up during the entire transmission. During this time, no other transmission that must use the path or parts thereof can begin their transmission until the previous transmission is completed. This can lead to poor utilization of the network. As we consider later, circuit switching is appropriate for networks with global control. However, locally controlled circuit switching, where a request for path selection is made first and the message is sent after the path has been coupled, provides a feasible approach.

3.24.2 Packet Switched

The path a message takes is not reserved in advance. The message is sent through the network one stage at a time with switching transpiring locally in the network. This means that the network processing elements (switches) must be able to locally buffer messages or portions thereof. Further, it is possible that the messages on their way through the network must wait on another message that is utilizing a planned connection path. In general, this means that a packet-switched network must have more intelligent coupling processes (that is, switches). Acknowledgment of messages, becomes more expensive due to the fact that the acknowledgement must transpire via a separate message, thus increasing network traffic. To reduce traffic, an unacknowledged transmission or *datagram* can be implemented in packet switched networks, which, on the other hand, can have consequences for reliability. Packet-switching requires more administration than circuit-switched transmission. On the other hand, the network can be exploited better since a message only locks up a smaller part of its path as it proceeds through the network. Therefore, packet switching is most appropriate for local control.

3.24.3 Comparison

An important advantage of circuit switching is that the routing algorithms are only executed rarely, so overhead may be less. On the other hand, an important advantage of packet switching is that a connection only consumes network resources (wires and routers) when a message is actually being transmitted. Thus, circuit switching generally works best where large quantities of data are to be transmitted, whereas packet switching has a definite advantage when the quantities of data being transmitted are small or can be divided into small packages. Another important consideration from the predictability point of view is that circuit-switched systems can be made deterministic, whereas packet switched systems are inherently nondeterministic.

3.25 NETWORK CONNECTIONS

In the ideal model, every PE can communicate with any other PE without time delay and independent of the other PE's communication. Unfortunately, conflict-free transport requires a physical communication link between every element in the system. This direct *full connectivity* can be realized through the use of a full crossbar network, which is illustrated in Figure 3.24.

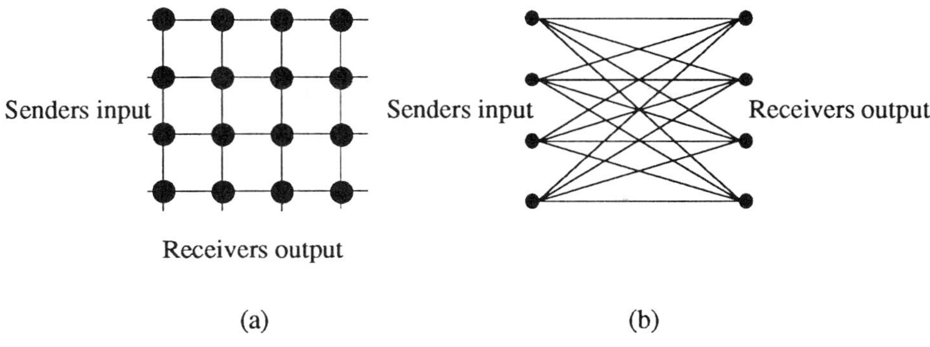

Figure 3.24. Conflict-free Full Crossbar Connection Network

In the first variation (a), the edges represent the input and output sets and the nodes represent the crosspoints or switches. In the second variation (b), a *bipartite graph*, the nodes represent the input and output sets and the edges represent the crosspoints. In the example provided, the ICN can accommodate four intercommunicating PEs or, for example, two PEs used for processing operations and two memory PEs. While the crossbar is the most general connection network, the number of crosspoints required is N^2 since there is one crosspoint between every input and output (sender-receiver pair). Thus, such networks become quite expensive for large N. However, they should be seriously considered as a candidate for achieving predictability goals in parallel processing real-time systems.

Due to the limitations of full connectivity, the next best alternative is to approximate full connectivity with a direct- or indirect-coupled *partial connectivity network*. The general result of the approximation is that longer communication times are required. Thus, a trade-off is made between hardware and time.

Before examining the properties of partially connected networks, let us examine the types of operations that are typically performed within the network framework.

3.25.1 Network Operations

The two principal forms of communication that should be achievable within the connection network are:

one-to-one - that is, a PE communicates with another PE
one-to-all - that is, a PE can *broadcast* to all PEs

One-to-one communication is the most fundamental form. However, broadcasting, in certain situations, is extremely valuable. Consider, for example, the PE array implementation of matrix multiplication where the same element in a multiplicand participates in the summation of many elements in the result. By broadcasting the element to many parallel PEs, summation can start in parallel. Lacking full direct connectivity, a broadcast to *n* PEs can be emulated in *n* stages with the assistance of one-to-one communication. On the other hand, some ICNs permit the implementation of broadcasting in a direct manner, thus providing one-to-all efficiently.

To implement one-to-one as well as one-to-all (broadcast), it is important that the connection network provide *reachability*, that is, a given PE can reach all other PEs in the system (the network is connected). In the case of one-to-one communication, it is desirable to allow as many PEs as possible to communicate with each other at the same time. A special case of this parallel communication is where every PE in the system communicates to another *unique* PE. If the number of receiving PEs, N, is equal to the number of sending PEs, the communication pattern is a *permutation* that is accomplished via a binary mapping of the senders address to that of the receivers. That is, a mapping $\{1, \ldots N\} \Rightarrow \{1, \ldots N\}$. Permutations are an important building block for networks based upon partial connections. We shall examine the general principles for permutations, but first, for completeness sake, we consider another general operation requirement.

Another case of one-to-one communication arises when many PEs want to send to the same address at the same time, that, is **all-to-one** communication. An example of this, which we considered earlier, is when many PEs executing processes wish to synchronize on a semaphore variable for the purpose of gaining access to a resource or communicating. The solution, as described earlier, leads to a serialization of access (mutual exclusion and waiting). This concentration of messages to common destinations can lead to "traffic jams" called *hot spots* (described more thoroughly later), which may result in an undesirable serialization of communication.

3.25.2 Permutations and Switches (Network Building Blocks)

A *permutation* is achieved by applying a function to the binary address of the input element (sender), thus generating the address of the output element (receiver). For example, given the bit structure

$$x = \{b_n, b_{n-1}, \ldots, b_1\}$$

a variety of permutations can be applied to x. These permutations include *exchange permutations*, *perfect shuffles*, *butterfly permutations*, *bit reversal permutations*, and *shift permutations*. All permutation functions provide partial connections. To grasp the general principle, consider the perfect shuffle permutation in Figure 3.25, where the permutation is portrayed as direct connections and indirectly via 2 x 2 switched connections.

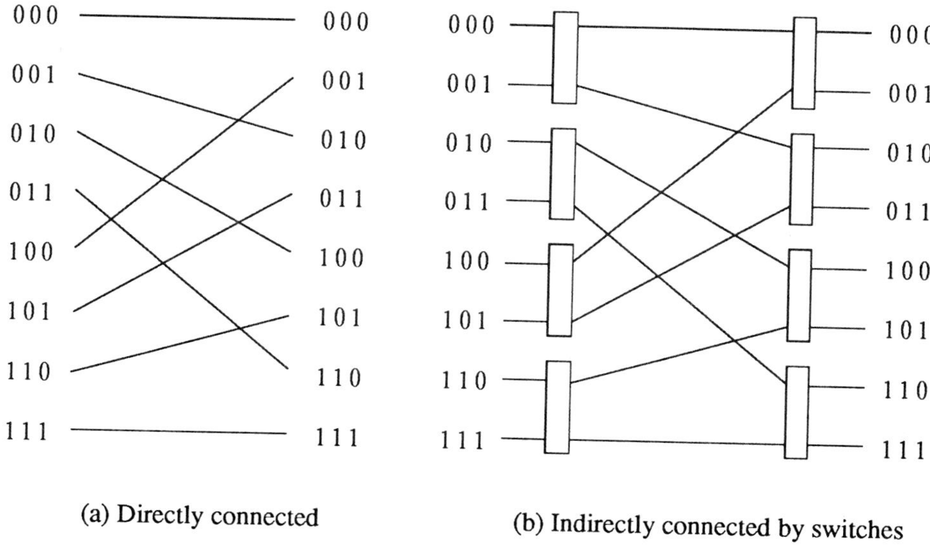

(a) Directly connected

(b) Indirectly connected by switches

Figure 3.25. Perfect Shuffle Permutation

The perfect shuffle takes its name from the analogy to cutting a playing card deck in two parts and then interleaving the remaining cards in each part. Formally, we can express this version of the shuffle as

$$x = \{b_n, b_{n-1}, \ldots, b_1\}$$

$$shuffle(x) = \{b_{n-1}, \ldots, b_{n-2}, \ldots, b_1, b_n\}$$

Thus, our shuffle corresponds to a simple circular left shift of the address [that is, binary representation of (x)], yielding the following mappings:

$$\{000, 001, 010, 011, 100, 101, 110, 111\} \Rightarrow$$

$$\{000, 010, 100, 110, 001, 011, 101, 111\}$$

The perfect shuffle is illustrated in Figure 3.25b via 2 x 2 connections, which in the permuted addresses are utilized in controlling the switch point (a point at which an exchange is made).

The simple processing operation of circular left shift is typical of the various practical permutation mappings, where the realization is most often based upon complementing, shifting, and/or partitioning the binary address representation.

A *switch* in its elementary form can be considered to be a 2 x 2 crossbar that implements simple permutative couplings and, if required, broadcasting, as portrayed in Figure 3.26.

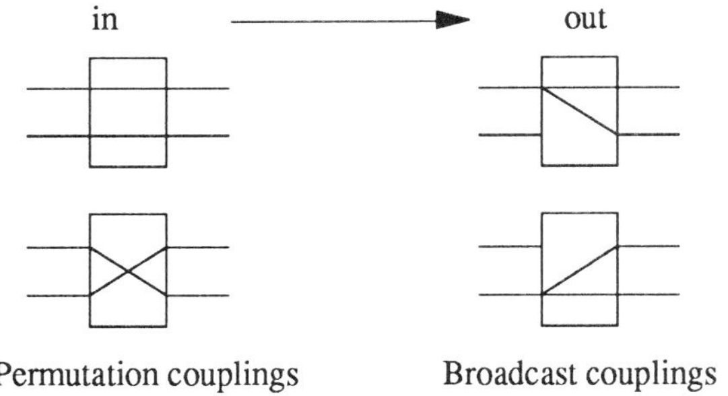

Figure 3.26. A 2 x 2 Switch Providing Permutative and Broadcast Switching

The control of a switch setting can be represented by one single bit if only the permutative connection is provided. If both permutative and broadcast switching is required, the switch must be controlled by two bits representing all four combinations that are illustrated. *Note*: Some systems provide larger switches, for example 4 x 4, in which case more bits are required to control the source to destination coupling in the switch.

In some switches, additional logic may be implemented to administer and/or to take care of special network-related problems. Thus, for economic reasons, the size of the switch may be increased to deal with larger quantities of input and output connections.

Having considered these important network building blocks, let us now consider the general characterization of various connection network alternatives.

3.25.3 Single-stage Network

The single-stage network is composed solely of direct connections between PEs. The couplings can either couple PEs pairwise (point to point) or be common for several PEs. In the latter case, we find a *bus system*. In bus systems there is a serialization of communications among those PEs sharing the bus, and if several PEs wish to communicate at the same time, some of them must wait. One can even consider a bus hierarchy in which local groups of PEs communicate on a local bus that is successively coupled to a higher-level bus. Between every higher- and lower-level bus, a bi-directional control unit is required that recognizes if a message is being transmitted from the higher level to a lower-level bus, or vice versa. These three variations of single-stage networks are portrayed in Figure 3.27.

A crossbar is a single-stage, direct, fully connected network where the PEs share couplings on a pairwise basis. Single-stage networks that are not fully connected lack direct connections between certain PEs and are normally connected according to a permutation (for example, the perfect shuffle as illustrated in Figure 3.25). Communication, in these cases, must be accomplished *iteratively*, that is, by passing the message through the net-work several times. Naturally, the iteration takes a longer time. There may even arise conflicts during the iteration if messages converge toward the same link (hot spot) and will utilize the link in the same iteration stage. In this situation, a message must wait.

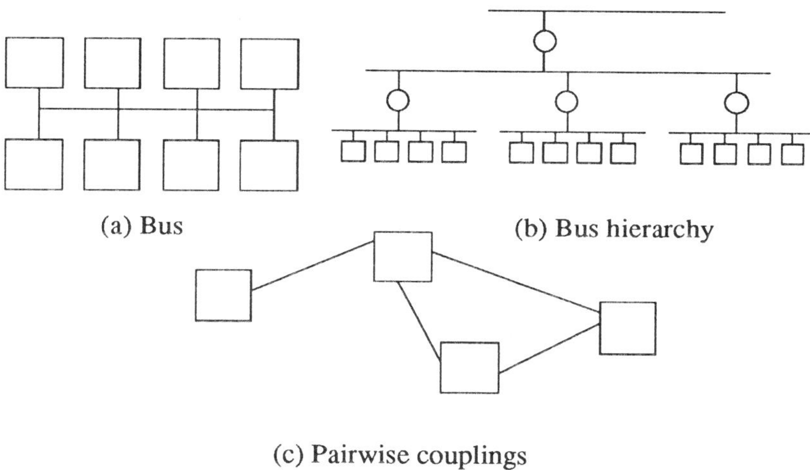

Figure 3.27. Single-stage Networks

3.25.4 Multistage Network

A multistage network is composed of a number of switches that are coupled together as well as to the PEs in the network. Via switch settings, various paths through the network are opened. Multistage networks are often composed of single-stage networks coupled together with switches (thus, the name multistage). The basic idea is to manage the couplings (even if several stages are required) between PEs, once again without requiring the use of full connectivity (the crossbar). This means that some of the paths share common parts. Messages that are transmitted over these common routes can select to utilize the common part at the same time. Thus, a conflict occurs and some message(s) must wait.

3.25.5 Examples of Pairwise Couplings

To demonstrate the structure of single-stage and multistage networks (with direct and indirect connections), let us first consider the *shuffle-exchange network*, portrayed in Figure 3.28 which consists of a shuffle permutation function (the arrows) and a single exchange function (the boxes). In an N element network, any destination can be reached in $\log N$ iterations (the *diameter* = $\log N$). For N = 1024, the diameter is 10, whereas for the two-dimensional mesh (considered earlier in Figure 3.13) it was 32. Thus, the maximum-distance value of the shuffle-exchange network is low compared to the two-dimensional mesh. The reader should once again view the permuting switches as (2 x 2) crossbars.

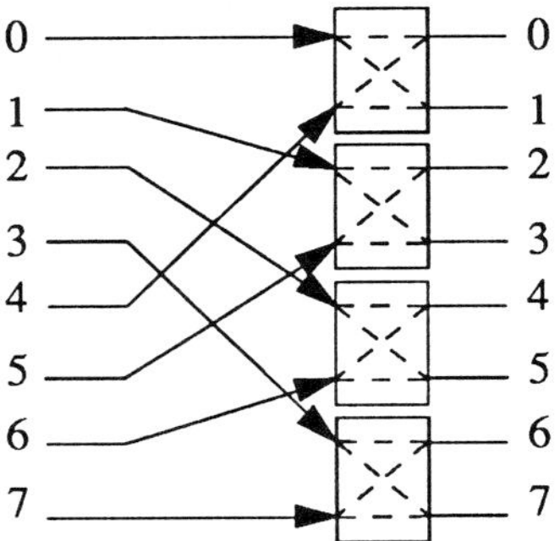

Figure 3.28. Shuffle-Exchange Network

To illustrate direct connections between PEs, we consider a *direct binary n-cube network* as portrayed in Figure 3.29a where the point-to-point connected PEs are at the corners of an n-dimensional cube, and each PE contains an n-way switch (n = 3 in this case). The maximum distance (diameter) to any other PE is again $\log N$.

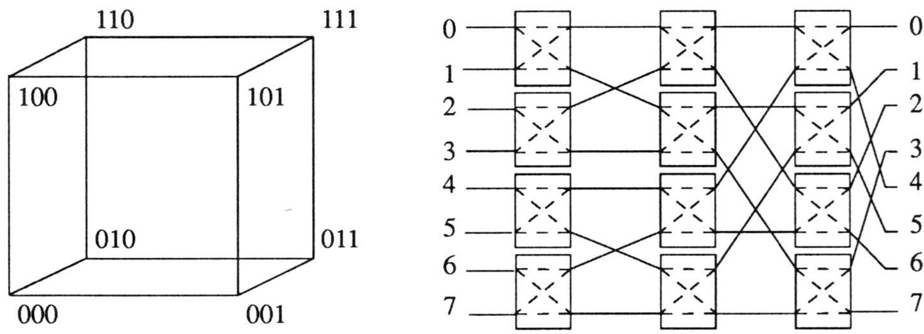

Figure 3.29. (a) Direct and (b) Indirect Binary Three-cube

The direct cube can be simulated by the *indirect binary n-cube network*, which is a multistage network with multiple stages of two-way switches. Figure 3.29b shows the network for $N = 8$, which requires three steps (that is, $\log N$).

From these examples, the reader can observe the principal differences between ICNs for connecting multiple PEs directly point to point and indirectly in single and multistage variations.

3.25.6 Comparison

A bus-based system provides best performance when transports being sent from the individual PEs are separated time-wise from the beginning. Broadcasting can be realized quite effectively in such a system. A single-stage network with pairwise couplings is well utilized if the communication patterns are such that as few iterations as possible are required. Fewer iterations even lead to a reduction of the risk for conflicts. The ideal case is that all communication is accomplished in one single step, which obviously results in no conflicts.

A multistage network is best exploited if access patterns are such that paths that simultaneous messages follow never have any common parts. Thus, no conflicts occur. In contrast to single-stage networks, there is never more than one iteration in a multistage network (with the exception of special provisions for fault tolerance). All eventual performance degradation comes from message collisions. In direct point-to-point variants, messages traverse (max $\log N$) "links" on their way to a destination, whereas, in the multistage network case, messages always traverse $\log N$ "switched" stages.

3.26 CONTROL OF NETWORKS

The control of a network (in particular the setting of switches) can be accomplished globally or locally. *Note*: In further discussions, we utilize the terms *router* (and *routing*) as a collective name for the structure and behavior of links and switches.

3.26.1 Global Control

A single outer mechanism controls the network. This form of control is excellent for SIMD PE arrays where one common central instruction stream is used for controlling the operations performed in all PEs (including their communications). The centralized control periodically sets the switches in order to enable communications that follow.

3.26.2 Local Control

Every message has self-contained information identifying where it is to be transmitted (normally an address in a message header). Thus, local control is well suited to asynchronous MIMD systems. With local control, every unit (switch in a multistage network) decides upon the path for the messages. This decision-making process constitutes *routing*. The strategy used for routing can be quite straightforward; however, sophisticated routing algorithm strategies can exploit information on message frequency in order to transmit messages over paths that are less loaded with traffic. These more sophisticated strategies are called *adaptive routing*.

3.26.3 Routing in Packet-switched Networks

Simple switched connections have limitations in terms of viability in large networks. To deal with large networks, autonomous switching elements are normally provided to achieve *routed communication*. The routers are located in some sparse pattern in the network topology. The routers perform services much like those of the postal service, which forwards mail from branch office to branch office. However, when routed communication is utilized, an *uncertainty* for communication delay is introduced. The time requirements are based upon the topology of the routers connections, the *routing algorithm,* and the volume of traffic. On the other hand, for each particular topology and routing strategy, it is often quite straightforward to analytically determine the **average** and **worst-case** performance properties. We now examine some packet-switching routing strategies and problems.

Store and Forward

Messages are stored locally in the router before they are forwarded. Thus, the router process must contain buffers for storing messages. Since the size of buffers is limited, messages must have a limited size in this form of network. A queueing mechanism is provided where waiting messages can be retained and *flow control* can be used to inhibit the transmission of further messages to the router when the buffer is full. It follows that the routers must be rather complicated to support this form of packet-switched transmission.

3.26.4 Network Deadlock

An important problem that must be addressed in the case of packet-switched networks containing internal buffers is the potential occurrence of deadlock as portrayed in figure 3.30. The routers enter a situation where they are mutually demanding buffer space of each other and there is no space available. Consequently, they cannot proceed.

(*Note*: Network deadlock is just one of a number of deadlock situations that can develop in resource-limited environments. The simplest solution to the general resource problem is to acquire and retain all resources required when they are needed. In the section of process allocation, we consider a more refined method of resource acquisition and release.)

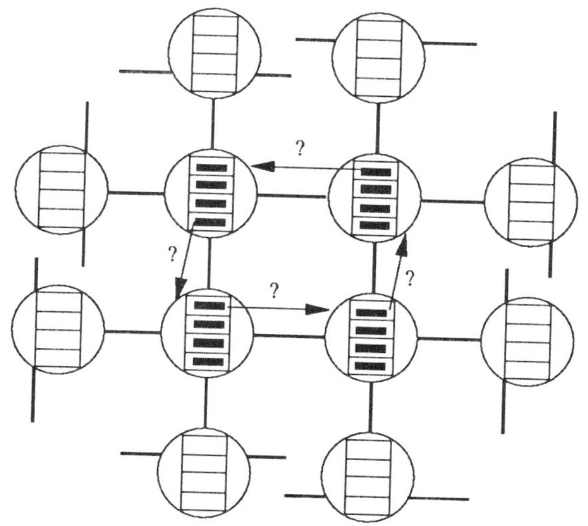

Figure 3.30. Network Deadlock

Wormhole Routing

In packet-switched networks, one good solution to the network deadlock problem is the use of wormhole routing. In this strategy, messages are subdivided and transmitted in smaller portions called *flits,* where each flit is a few bits in length. First, the message head (with address selection information) is transmitted. When a head arrives at a router, the router decides which connection is to be used for further transmission, and it is sent along without waiting for the remaining portions of the message. When the remaining flits arrive, they are immediately sent out on the selected connection in the order they arrive. At the end of the message, a flit is used to identify that the message is complete. This final flit signals the router to prepare to receive the next message head.

A message in this strategy will be spread over many switches during transmission (that is, the worm is spread out and seeking the hole). In extreme cases, flits are received at the final destination before the final flits leave the sender. Wormhole routing is unbuffered, thus eliminating collisions and resulting in a circuit-switched-like behavior. The message will be spread over the network rather than collected into a buffer. *In effect, a pipeline is formed over the network connections.*

A variant of wormhole routing called *virtual cut-through,* on the other hand, does utilize buffers. Otherwise, it operates, quite similarly. In this case, once a message head has been routed to its destination, a path with required buffers is reserved for the remainder of the transmission. Thus, buffers cannot grow arbitrarily, as is the case in a straightforward store and foreward routing scheme. A further interesting solution has been provided by Yantchev and Jesshope (1989) for two-dimensional packet-switched networks where *virtual networks* are implemented in which deadlock avoidance can be attained.

Comparison

Wormhole routing is flexible, can be implemented with simple switches (as with circuit switched networks), and permits variable-length messages. On the other hand, a larger portion of the connection network becomes tied up at the same time, which is avoided with the store and forward strategy. However, some of the other variants, such as virtual cut-through and virtual networks, may provide useful solutions yielding both low latency and freedom from deadlock.

3.26.5 Alternative Routing

Since the performance of the connection network is vital, it can be beneficial to take account of the presence of other messages in the network (loading) and to attempt to improve upon the network utilization by an *adaptive routing algorithm,* as introduced previously. Some form of intelligent flow control attempts to predict traffic requirements based upon the immediate history of transmissions. In this case, the switch must be rather sophisticated and contain a reasonable amount of local memory. Alternative routing is also an important property for attaining fault tolerance, as described in Chapter 5; however, in this case, it is a corrective action instead of a planning action based upon loading.

3.27 PERFORMANCE AND COST PROPERTIES OF NETWORKS

Several commonly utilized alternative network topologies will be reviewed in this section; however, it is useful to define some general performance and cost properties; see, for example, Hillis (1985).

The following factors determine network performance:

small diameter — the diameter is the maximum number of times that a message can be forwarded between routers when traveling from one PE to another. If the distance is small, then processes are likely to be able to communicate more quickly.

uniformity — it is desirable that all pairs of PEs communicate with equal ease or at least that the traffic patterns between all pairs of routers be reasonably balanced.

extendability — it should be possible to build a network of any given size or, as a minimum, it should be possible to build an arbitrarily large version of the network.

short wires — if the network can be efficiently embedded in two- or three-dimensional space such that all the wires are relatively short, then the physical distance between routers can be small.

redundant paths — if there are many possible paths between each pair of PEs, a partially defective network may continue to function in a fault-tolerant manner. Also, if a path is blocked because of traffic, a message can be directed along another route.

The diameter, as we have considered several times, is one of the normal *metrics* used to characterize the performance properties of networks. The following metrics are also utilized in characterizing network performance.

bandwidth — the total number of messages that can be sent or received by PEs in the system in a basic unit of time.

narrowness — a measure of congestion in the network, which is obtained by calculating the maximum number of interconnections required for all possible two-way partitionings of the network.

In implementing a connection network, the following cost factors must be taken into consideration.

minimum number of wires — each physical connection costs money. Thus, if the number of wires is small, the cost is likely to be small, also.

efficient layout — if the topology can be tightly and neatly packed into a small space, the packaging job becomes easier.

simple routing algorithm — if the routers are locally controlled, they are not as costly.

fixed degree — if each router connects to a fixed number of others, then one router design can serve for all sizes of networks.

fit to available technology — if the topology can be built easily with available components, it will be less expensive.

3.28 REVIEW OF SELECTED NETWORK TOPOLOGIES

A large number of network topologies have been proposed and explored in the technical literature, thus leading to an often confusing situation in evaluating and selecting an appropriate topology. We find, for example, *grids* (synonymous with mesh considered earlier), *trees*, *rings*, *hypercubes*, *omega networks*, *delta networks*, *indirect binary n-cubes* (described earlier), *Banyan networks*, *hypertoruses*, *twisted toruses*, *k-folded toruses*, *x-trees*, *shuffle exchanges* (described earlier), *k-way shuffles*, *De Brujn network*, *reverse exchanges*, and *butterfly networks*, to name some of the most well known. All the network topologies are based upon some form of partial connection. There are proponents for each of the various network structures. Which network is optimal or provides satisfactory performance depends upon the problem assumptions, the requirements, and available implementation technology.

3.28.1 Clos Networks

The simplest and most obvious network topology is to connect every node to every other node, as we have illustrated in Figure 3.24 (that is, use crossbars). When N is small, say less than 100, this can be a practical solution. The most straightforward implementation of a crossbar requires N^2 switches. However, when the connections are one to one, it has been shown that multistage networks with the capabilities of crossbars can be constructed from fewer switches. The Clos networks belong to this category. A five-stage Clos network with 1000 communicating components requires only 146,300 switches, as opposed to 1,000,000 required for a full crossbar.

3.28.2 Rings and Trees

Partially connected ring and tree topologies are portrayed in Figure 3.31. Perhaps the simplest and least expensive partially connected network topology is the ring. The disadvantage with the ring network is that the diameter increases linearly with the number of processors; consequently, the topology is only practical for small N. It is easy to lay out rings, and the routing algorithm is extremely simple and its worst-case performance is predictable.

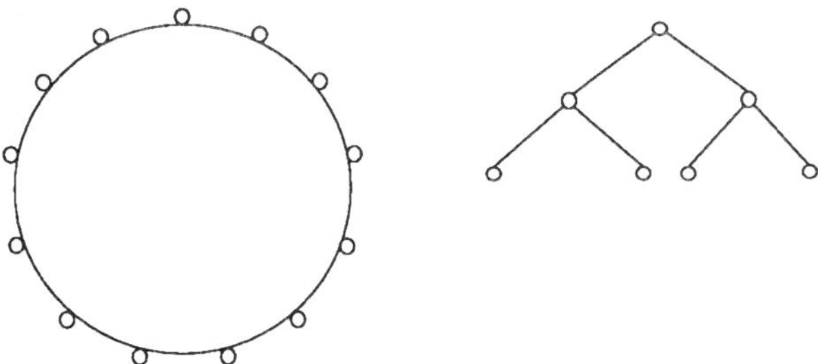

Figure 3.31. Rings and Trees

The m-ary tree network provides another inexpensive topology, where m is most commonly 2. The advantages of trees include a low diameter (order log N), fixed degree, and efficient layout in two dimensions. A disadvantage can be the communications bottleneck at the root of the tree; however, there are a variety of algorithms providing local communication that avoid this problem. Alternatively, the base of the tree can be augmented with additional connections to prevent root congestion. The x-tree topology adds connections that jump from one branch to another. *Fat trees* add parallel connections to increase the capacity near the roots.

3.28.3 Grids (Meshes) and Toruses

Two-dimensional layout in most implementation technologies naturally suggests a two-dimensional grid (mesh) as found in many SIMD PE array solutions. As considered earlier, the grid network topology has a relatively large diameter ($2\sqrt{N}$), which, by connecting edges to form a torus, is reduced to ($\sqrt{N}$). The grid (torus) topology is well matched to many problems, specifically problems that closely match the geometry of physical space. Hydrodynamics, aerodynamics, electrodynamics, quantum chromodynamics, image processing, wire routing, and graphics are some important areas of application. Typical for these problems is that calculations are performed on an n -dimensional lattice where the communication patterns are local to the lattice. Technological limitations force a two-dimensional or at most three-dimensional network. However, higher-dimensional lattices can be projected onto these grids.

3.28.4 Shuffle-type Network Topologies

Shuffle-type networks, introduced previously, are characterized by diameters that scale logarithmically with N. The butterfly communication pattern often used in Fast Fourier Transform computations belongs to this category. When the nodes of the butterfly network are rearranged so that each layer is drawn in the same pattern, an *omega network* is formed. A single layer of an omega network is a *perfect shuffle* or *shuffle exchange* (as illustrated earlier), although these terms are often used for the entire omega network. Further, by connecting log N omega networks in series, a network is formed that is capable of relaying any permutation and is also referred to as an omega network. A general form of the omega network has been independently proposed in the telephone literature called the *Benes network* in which large switches are employed as a complement to permuted connections. The basic structures of shuffle-type topologies are illustrated in Figure 3.32.

A somewhat repackaged form of the omega network is referred to as the *Boolean n-cube* or *hypercube* since the graph is formed by the corners and edges of an n-dimensional hypercube. Here $n = \log N$. The n-cube pattern can be formed by reordering the butterfly pattern so that one corner of the cube corresponds to one row of the butterfly. A generalization of the omega or, more precisely, of the shuffle exchange is the k-way shuffle, which for $k > 2$ has a smaller diameter. The *reverse exchange* and

De Brujn network are variations or are isomorphic to the omega network. The recursive generation of hypercubes is portrayed in Figure 3.33.

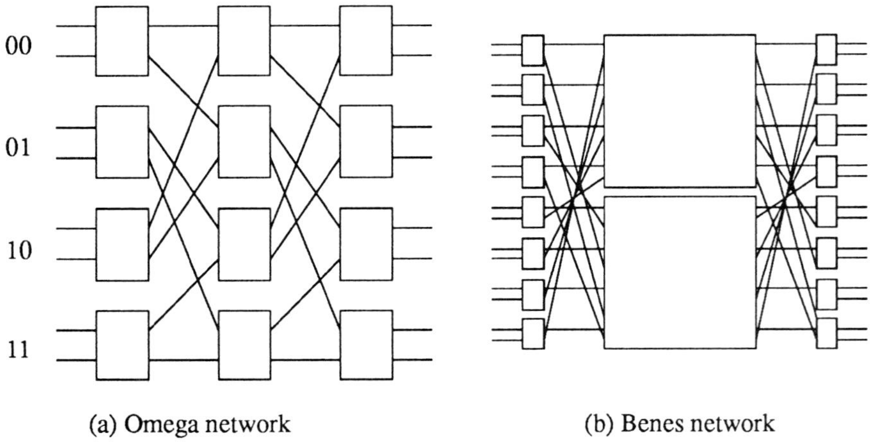

(a) Omega network (b) Benes network

Figure 3.32. Omega and Benes Networks

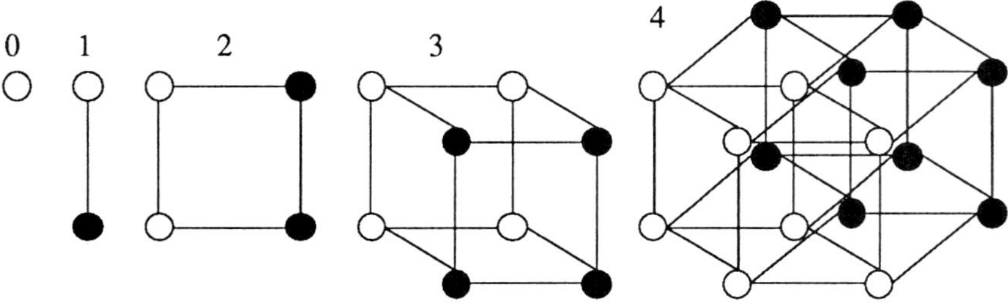

Figure 3.33. Recursive Construction of a Hypercube (order 0 to order 4)

The omega networks and its relatives are popular since simple local algorithms can be used for routing messages through them. Omega networks are uniform, have reasonably small diameter, and contain redundant paths. Most importantly, they have been studied in depth and are relatively easy to visualize. A disadvantage of the n-cube variety is that the degree per node grows with N.

3.28.5 Banyan and Delta Networks

As mentioned previously, n-cube networks provide redundant paths; however, the redundancy also adds to the cost. *SW-Banyan networks* are a class of logarithmic networks that contains exactly one path between any input/output pair. A version of the Banyan called the *delta network* provides for simpler routing than the Banyan.

3.28.6 Hashnets

As an alternative to regular network topologies, one can consider connecting everything randomly. Random networks perform rather well when compared with other proposed routed networks. The primary advantage of *hashnets* (the name given to randomly interconnected networks) is that they can be analyzed probabilistically. However, routing may become chaotic when several passes have been applied, and it is hard to guarantee that connections can be made in a calculatable time. Thus, the applicability of hashnets in real-time environments is questionable. On the other hand, hashnets can be made fault tolerant.

This concludes our overview of some of the popular network structures. We return later in the book to considering more specific utilization of ICNs. However, we now consider the hot-spot problem mentioned earlier, after which we wind up the section by considering the performance analysis of some network structures.

3.29 THE HOT-SPOT PROBLEM

One important problem that can be found in all networks is the biasing of traffic from a number of sources to one particular sink. This sink becomes a *hot spot,* with the implications for the network being that message buffers and message queues become full. Thus, hot spots lead to radically reduced network performance and even, in the worst case, cause a complete jam. To illustrate the hot-spot problem, let us consider the Omega network portrayed in Figure 3.34 with N ports on each side of the network.

In describing and analyzing the hot-spot problem, let us first consider that the traffic pattern is initially uniform at a rate r ($0 \leq r \leq 1$) per network cycle. Once steady state has been reached, assume that a traffic pattern develops in which a fraction p ($0 \leq p \leq 1$) of all messages is directed toward a specific sink (the hot sink). Thus, each source transmits $r(1 - p)$ messages that are uniformly distributed and rp messages to the hot sink. The hot sink receives messages of both the uniformly distributed $r(1 - p)$ and the concentrated message variety rpN.

Due to the rpN component, the rate of messages to the hot sink can approach or even exceed 1. At this point, the queues in the interchange box closest to the hot sink become full, which causes a chain reaction backward in the network, with preceding boxes becoming full. Even the buffers in the PEs become full because they cannot place any messages into the network. This phenomenon is called *tree saturation* and is well illustrated in the figure.

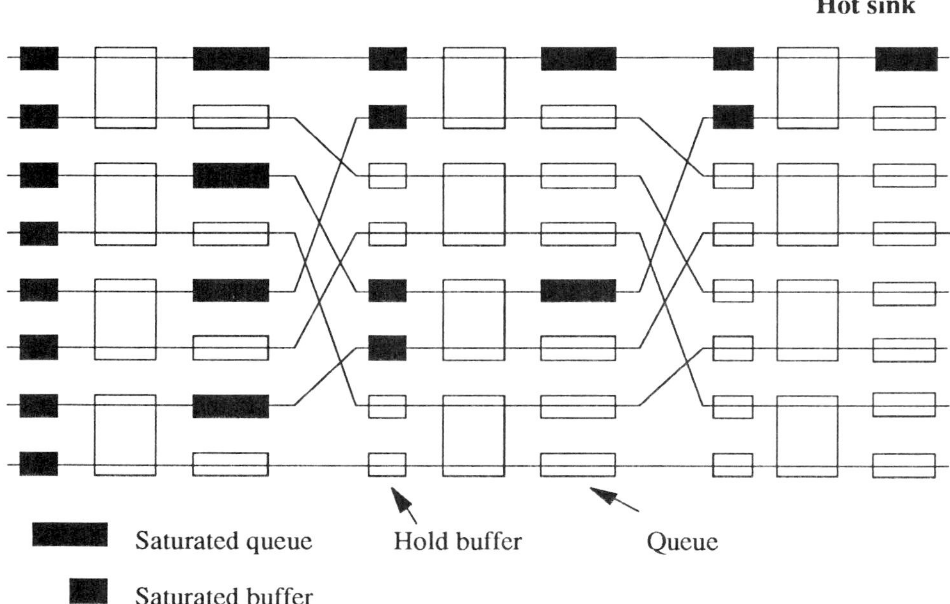

Figure 3.34. Omega Network Saturated by a Hot Sink

Once tree saturation exists, every message from every source to any sink must cross the saturated tree and thus suffers delay. This occurs in steady state when the rate of traffic to the hot sink, $r(1 - p) + rpN$, reaches 1. Further, this situation occurs independently of the topology and dimensioning of queue sizes and other parameters.

3.29.1 Radically Reduced Bandwidth

To understand the effect of hot spots on bandwidth BW, consider the following:

$$BW = \frac{N}{1 + p(N - 1)}$$

The effect on BW as a function of N for various p is given in Figure 3.35. We can observe that in a system with 1000 PEs, hot-spot traffic of 1% can limit the total BW to less than 10%. (*Note*: This assumes that hot-spot requests can continue to be issued from a PE even if that PE still has an unsatisfied hot-spot request pending.)

It has been shown by simulation that the onset of hot-spot contention can occur rapidly. On the other hand, recovering from a transient hot-spot situation can take a long time. Large networks are particularly vulnerable and if measures are not taken to maintain uniform traffic; the onset and hot-spot contention result in a continuous tree saturation situation. Consequently, in large multistage networks where no provision is made for hot spots, the traffic patterns may not perform well, thus negating the advantages of parallel processing.

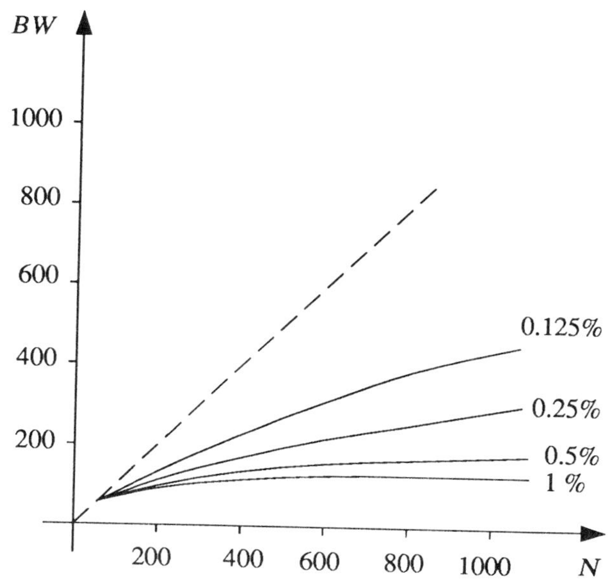

Figure 3.35. *BW* as a Function of the Number of PEs for Various Hot-spot fractions

3.29.2 Solutions to the Hot-spot Problem

Hardware Combining

One means of dealing with the hot-spot problem is to add hardware into the interchange boxes that attempts to combine equal requests. This approach was developed as a result of work on parallel processing in the Ultracomputer and IBM RP3 projects (see Gottlieb, Lubachevsky, and Rudolph, 1983). These computers provide hardware features for synchronization via the Fetch and Operation form of instruction discussed earlier in relationship to hardware synchronization mechanisms. Hot-spot problems arise as a result of con-centrated references to synchronization variables.

The approach taken is to attempt to eliminate the problem caused by identical references to identical entities and destinations (identical memory locations when PEs are connected to memory processes). However, when the hot spot develops due to sources accessing many different entities that are in the same destination, combining does not help.

The combining solution adds logic to switches that detect identical references and perform processing operations in the switches, as exemplified in Figure 3.36. In this case, we observe that when a Fetch and Operation (Add) in this case is processed by the switch, it retains the value to be added. If a successive operation arrives affecting the same location (variable), the operation is performed locally prior to the forwarding from the switch. Further, when a resultant value (Y) is being returned, it is returned unaltered to the first issuer and in incremented form to the second issuer.

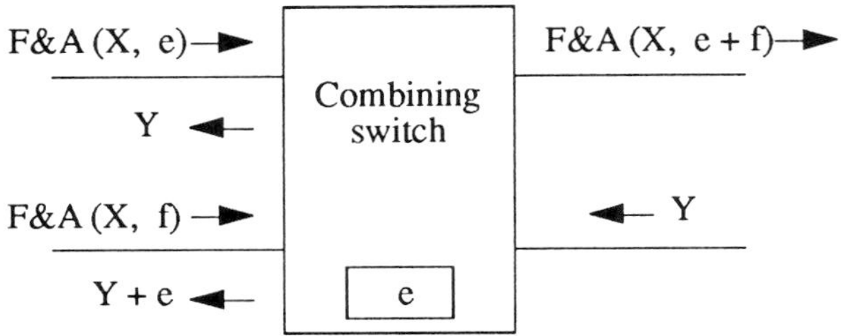

Figure 3.36. Hardware Combining Switch

Combining has been explored on a pairwise and on a three-way basis. If combining can be accomplished, simulation has shown that three-way combining can reduce the effect of hot spots. On the other hand, the hardware in the interchange boxes for identifying and combining requests adds a significant cost to the solution.

Software Combining

As an alternative to hardware combining, we can consider software combining, which is based upon a more intelligent distribution of data into memories of the network according to variables that are shared. For example, in the case that many PEs are all accessing a single copy of the sum of vector (where each PE is processing a part of the vector), **or** when a shared variable representing the number of processors N is being decremented by all PEs as a means to determine the completion of processing. In such cases, we may solve the problem by making a tree of such variables and assigning each to different memory modules.

Processing proceeds by each processor updating its leaf copy of the variable and checking to see if all other leaf PEs at the same level of the tree have been updated (accomplished by decrement counting in the superior node). In this case, the PE updates the variable at a higher-level node (once again checking to see if all PEs at that level have updated), and so forth. Thus, the shared variable becomes distributed. If the problem structure permits this solution, it can be used to make radical improvements over a system that provides neither hardware nor software combining.

For a further investigation of the hot-spot problem and solutions, the reader is referred to DeCegama (1989).

3.30 NETWORK PERFORMANCE

The analysis of various forms of interconnection networks (ICNs) is quite essential in obtaining timing information for planning real-time systems in which parallel processing is to be exploited. Thus, we now consider some measurements that are of interest in this regard. We shall relate our analysis of performance to the two primary MIMD forms of parallel processors (multiprocessors, both loosely and tightly coupled, and multicomputers). Our analysis of SM (**s**hared **m**emory) multiprocessors draws upon the presentation of Bhuyan, Yang, and Agrawal (1989), and the analysis of DM (**d**istributed **m**emory) multicomputer networks draws upon the presentation by Reed and Grunwald (1987).

3.30.1 Multiprocessor ICNs

The analysis of the three forms of ICN typically found in multiprocessors containing N PEs and M Memory modules is considered. This includes N x M crossbars, **M**ultistage **I**nterconnection **N**etworks (often referred to as MIN's), as well as multiple-bus intercon-nection networks.

Performance Parameters

To compare the properties of the various ICNs the following parameters are defined:

bandwidth (BW) — this is the most common performance parameter for measuring synchronous ICNs. It is defined as the mean number of *active* memory modules in one transfer cycle of the ICN. In this case, active means that a processor is successfully performing a memory operation (either read or write) in the memory cycle. BW also takes into account the memory access conflicts caused by the random nature of PE requests.

probability of acceptance (P_A) — defined as the ratio of the expected bandwidth to the expected number of requests generated per clock cycle as follows:

$$P_A = \frac{BW}{pN}$$

throughput (*Thr*) — defined as the average number of packets delivered by the network in a unit time. For multiprocessor ICNs the throughput is the mean number of memory access completions per unit time.

processor utilization (P_u) — defined as the expected value of the percentage of time a PE is active. A PE is active if it is doing internal processing without referencing global memory. Processing power can be derived from P_u, which is simply the sum of PE utilizations divided by the number of PEs.

These parameters are related to each other by the following:

$$P_u = \frac{BW}{N\lambda T}$$

$$P_u = \frac{Thr}{\lambda}$$

where N is the number of PEs, T is the time taken for a memory read or write operation, and λ is the memory request rate.

To make an analytical model tractable, some approximation assumptions are required (often leading to disputes of validity, but necessary).

uniform reference model — the URM implies that, when a PE makes a memory request to the global memory, the request will be directed to any one of the M memory modules with the same probability $1/M$ (requests are uniformly distributed amongst the M modules). If the memory provides M-way interleaving, the assumption is more accurate than if interleaving is not provided. (*Note*: Interleaving is discussed later in this chapter.)

request rate — defines how often a PE accesses global memory. In synchronous systems, the request rate can be specified as the probability that a PE generates a memory request at the beginning of a cycle. In asynchronous systems, the memory request may be generated at any point in time. In this case, an exponential *thinking time* is normally assumed.

request independence assumption — states that, for synchronous systems, a memory request generated in a cycle is independent of previous cycles. This assumption is not true since a request that was rejected in a previous cycle will be resubmitted in the current cycle. However, it is claimed that this assumption, which simplifies analysis, still keeps the results reasonably accurate.

Analysis Techniques

From these parameters and assumptions, a variety of analytical methods have been applied in order to extract and compare the properties of the three networks with respect to synchronous versus asynchronous timing, as well as circuit-switched versus packet-switched transport. For a detailed description of the techniques that have been applied and all results, the reader is referred to the paper by Bhuyan, Yang, and Agrawal (1989).

Hardware Features of the ICNs

The features of the hardware required for each of the three variations that are analyzed are provided in Table 3.2.

Table 3.2. Comparison of Three Multiprocessor Network Alternatives

	Crossbar	MINs	Multiple-Bus
No. switches or connections	$N * M$	$N \log N$	$B * (N + M)$
Load of buses	N	1	B
No. of wires	M	N	B
Arbiter	M 1-of-N arbiters	$N \log N$ 1-of-2 arbiters	1 B-of-M and M 1-of-N arbiters
Fault tolerance and expansion	Fair	Poor, but fair with additional hardware	Good

We observe that the number of switches required for the crossbar is $N \times M$ in contrast to $N \log N$ for MINs. The number of connections necessary for an $N \times M \times B$ multiple-bus system is proportional to $B(N + M)$. Since each bus must drive $N + M$ modules, the bus load is proportional to $N + M$, while the bus load of a MIN is one due to the one-to-one connection.

All the networks require some form of arbitration to resolve request conflicts. In the crossbar, M N-user 1-server arbiters are required, each of which selects one of N outstanding requests for memory during a memory cycle. The MINs, on the other hand, require two 2-user, 1-server arbiters for each switching element for $(N/2) \log_2 N$ switches.

Arbitration for multiple-bus systems requires M-users, B-servers in order to assign B buses to outstanding requests. Once a bus is granted a request to memory, only one of the PEs that requests the memory can proceed while the others, if any, are delayed. Thus, $M + 1$ arbiters, one arbiter of M-users, B-servers type and M arbiters of N-users, 1-server type are required.

With respect to expandability and reliability, multiple-bus systems show advantages over the other two because of their reconfigurability and multiple-data paths between every PE and memory. They can still operate in degraded mode after a failure of a subset of the buses.

To make MINs fault tolerant, additional hardware such as additional stages or duplicated data paths must be added. It is easier to reconfigure a crossbar than a MIN. For example, in the case of a fault, a particular row or a column can be removed and the network can operate in degraded mode.

3.30.2 Multicomputer ICNs

Multicomputer systems do not share memory; thus, the network must efficiently support message passing. Due to the high latency for message passing, compared to memory access, optimization of message traffic is crucial. Reed and Grunwald (1987) have provided methods for evaluating the performance of network alternatives.

As we considered earlier, the direct point-to-point connection network topology provides a maximum internode distance (diameter), but the number of link visits (*LV*) becomes an important property for analyzing network performance. Thus, the following appropriate measure is defined:

$$LV = \sum_{l=1}^{l_{max}} l \cdot F(l)$$

where $F(l)$ is the probability of an arbitrary message crossing l communication links (that is, the routing distribution) and l_{max} is the network diameter. Thus, different choices of $F(l)$ lead to different message routing distributions and, in turn, different mean internode distances.

Message Routing Distributions

In analyzing symmetrically connected networks (that is, networks having an isomorphism that maps any node onto any other node), three message routing distributions are considered:

uniform message routing — probability of sending a message from node i to node j is the same for all i and j ($i \neq j$). Makes no assumption about the nature of computation and can be seen as an upper bound.

sphere of locality — assumes processes that exchange messages with high frequency are in close physical proximity. A node sends messages to other nodes inside its sphere of locality with some high probability Φ and nodes outside of its sphere with probability ($1 - \Phi$). Reflects the locality of communication of many programs (for example, nearest neighbor).

decreasing probability routing — the probability of sending a message to a node decreases as the distance of the destination node from the source node increases. The distribution function $\Phi(l) = Decay(d, l_{max}) \cdot d^l$, where ($0 < d < 1$), l_{max} is the network diameter, and d is a locality parameter. We may view $Decay(d, l_{max})$ as a normalizing constant for the probability Φ, chosen such that the probabilities sum to 1. As d approaches 1, the cumulative distribution function of Φ approximates a linearly increasing function of the distance from the source node. Conversely, as d approaches 0, the cumulative distribution function Φ approaches a nearest-neighbor pattern. Small d values mean that messages travel small distances (that is, locality exists), whereas as large d values mean that messages travel longer distances.

Visiting Ratios

While the distributions can be used to calculate mean internode distances, they do not reflect link utilization for which visiting ratios are defined. Visiting ratios can be used to locate those devices (links or nodes) in a network that most limit performance — the bottlenecks. A visit is either a link crossing or computation at a destination node.

With a uniform message routing distribution, the visit ratios must be the same. That is, the probability of visiting each destination node is the same, and V_{PE}, the visit ratio for K nodes, is

$$V_{PE} = \frac{1}{K}$$

It may seem surprising to learn that this ratio also applies for the nonuniform distributions we have described. This conclusion can be drawn from two features of the networks and routing distributions: network symmetry and similar message-routing behavior at all nodes. That is, if all network nodes behave similarly and the network is symmetric, each node is equally likely to be visited.

Based upon the internode distance LV, which represents the average number of visits to all communications links by a message and the number of communication links, we can further define the communication link ratios:

$$V_{CL} = \frac{LV}{Numlinks\ (K, Net\_type)}$$

This quantity can be viewed as a measure of the message intensity supported by one link. If V_{CL} is near 1, then nearly all messages must cross each link at some point along the paths to their respective destinations. Unfortunately, this measure is only accurate when the ICN contains only one type of link (for example, in a ring). In a binary tree, for example, one would expect that traffic would be different, leading to different link ratios for each level.

An Analysis Example

Due to the wide variety of point-to-point networks, it is useful to observe how we can apply the measures discussed above to evaluate alternatives. To illustrate the evaluation process, we take a look at a generalization of the binary hypercube: the torus as portrayed in a three-dimensional variation in Figure 3.37.

In general, a D-dimensional torus is a lattice of width w — connecting each of its w^D nodes to a ring of size w in each of the D orthogonal dimensions, as illustrated in the figure. Since each of the w^D nodes is connected to D rings, there are $2Dw^D$ total link connections to the Dw^D communication links.

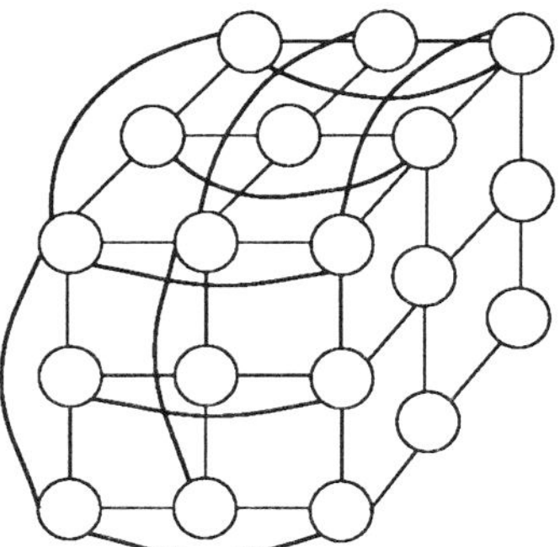

Figure 3.37. Three-dimensional torus

Message routing in a torus is straightforward if source and destination addresses are viewed as D-digit, base w numbers. Each digit represents a ring of w nodes, and a message is routed to its destination by successively sending the message to the correct location on each of the D rings. Thus, the network diameter is $D \lfloor w/2 \rfloor$, that is, D times the maximum internode distance in any dimension using that dimension's ring.

Note: When $w = 2$, the torus reduces to the binary hypercube. If w is fixed and D increases, the network diameter increases only logarithmically with the number of nodes. This represents the primary advantage of the binary hypercube topology. The offsetting disadvantage is that the number of connections per node must also increase with the network size.

Initially, it appears that the mean internode distance for uniform message routing is simply D times that for a simple ring. However, this is not the case. In the torus, some dimensions need no address resolution; that is, the source and destination nodes share the same address on that ring. Thus, the simplest view overestimates the mean path length. To compensate, we must include the case of zero moves in each dimension and scale the sum of the moves in each dimension to obtain the true mean path length. The average distance moved in each dimension is

$$LV^{uniform}_{one\ dimension} = \frac{\sum_{k=0}^{w-1} min\left\{ k, w-k \right\}}{w}$$

$$= \frac{w^2-1}{4w} \quad w\ odd$$

The minimum function in the sum reflects the routing of messages along the shorter of the two potential paths in the ring. Because the dimensions are independent, the true mean path length is D times this distance scaled to exclude nodes that route messages to themselves:

$$LV^{uniform}_{torus} = D\left(\frac{w^D}{w^D - 1}\right)LV^{uniform}_{one\ dimension}$$

Due to network symmetry and the existence of only one communication type, we can immediately obtain the link visit ratios:

$$V^{uniform}_{CL} = \frac{LV^{uniform}_{torus}}{Dw^D}$$

$$= \frac{w^2 - 1}{4w(w^D - 1)} \quad w\ odd$$

The derivation of mean path lengths and visit ratios for nonuniform message routing distributions, while conceptually straightforward, is computationally difficult. Reed and Grunwald develop a solution based upon the assumption that the sending node is at the center of the D-dimensional hyperspace and that, once again, w is odd. The details of this solution can be found in their paper.

It is hoped that the analytical method demonstrated here for the torus case will inspire the reader to utilize corresponding approaches to other networks when the need arises. Based upon their analytical method, Reed and Grunwald also report on network performance bounds for various forms of ICNs. Further, they apply their method to benchmarking the networks of two commercially available multicomputer systems.

This concludes our presentation of interconnection networks. As a final summary for the section, we can quote Reed and Grunwald (1987):

> You cannot find an interconnection network that is optimal for all applications but, by employing the methods described here, you can choose one that fits the requirements of certain classes of application.

In respect to this situation, the current section should have shed some light on the issues of this vital parallel processing subject area.

References

Benes, V. (1965). *Mathematical Theory of Connecting Networks and Telephone Traffic*, Academic Press, New York.

Bhuyan, L.N. (ed.) (1987). Interconnection Networks for Parallel and Distributed Processing, *Computer (special issue)*, Vol. 20, No. 6, pp. 9-12.

Bhuyan, L.N., Q. Yang, and D.P. Agrawal (1989). Performance of Multiprocessor Interconnection Networks, *Computer*, Vol. 22, No. 2, pp. 25-37.

Clos, C. (1953). The Study of Non-Blocking Switching Networks, *Bell System Techical Journal*, No. 32. pp. 406-24.

DeCegama, A.L. (1989). *The Technology of Parallel Processing: Parallel Processing Architectures and VLSI Hardware*, Vol. 1, Prentice Hall, Englewood Cliffs, NJ.

Feng, T.Y. (1981). A Survey of Interconnection Networks, *Computer*, Vol. 14, No. 12, pp. 12-27.

Gottlieb, A., B.D. Lubachevsky, and L. Rudolph (1983). Basic Techniques for the Efficient Coordination of Very Large Numbers of Cooperating Sequential Processors, *ACM Transactions on Programming Languages and Systems*, Vol. 5, No. 2, pp. 164-189.

Hillis, W.D. (1985). *The Connection Machine*, MIT Press, Cambridge, MA.

Hockney, R.W. and C.R. Jesshope (1988). *Parallel Computers 2: Architecture, Programming and Algorithms*, Adam Hilger, Bristol and Philadelphia.

Reed, D.A., and D.C. Grunwald (1987). The Performance of Multicomputer Interconnection Networks, *Computer*, Vol. 20, No. 6, pp. 63-73.

Siegel, H.J. (1990). *Interconnection Networks for Large-scale Parallel Processing*, McGraw-Hill, New York.

Tabak, D. (1990). *Multiprocessors*, Prentice Hall, Englewood Cliffs, NJ.

Yantchev, J., and C.R. Jesshope (1989). Adaptive, Low Latency, Deadlock-Free Packet Routing for Networks of Processors, *IEE Proceedings*, Vol. 136, No. 3, pp. 178-186.

MEMORY PROCESSES and TRANSPORTS

We consider some of the main line issues in the transport of information between various levels of memories. The following points are addressed:

- transports at the register level are by load and store operations — above this level transports are either explicit or implicit (that is, via virtual addressing mechanisms) (150)

- parallelism is achieved at the physical memory access level via partitioning of the cells (interleaving), which if properly exploited increases memory bandwidth — randomness of accessing that can occur in parallel processing environments reduces the advantages of interleaving (151)

- caching provides implicit transports between primary memory and a cache memory — information transported is organized into blocks of cells for which copies exist in both memories (153)

- performance of cache memories is tied to the hit rate, that is, how often addressing selects cache memory cells, thus avoiding cache faults and the need to reference primary memory — studies have indicated that hit rates can be as high as 95% and that the optimal block sizes for cache memories are 64 or 128 bytes (153)

- keeping data correct in primary memory in the presence of alterations in cache memory (via store instructions creating dirty pages) leads to two strategies — the write-back policy that writes the block back only on demand when the block is to be replaced and the write-through policy that writes back immediately (155)

- when caches are used in a multiprocessor environment, there is an increase in memory contention, communication, and latency — further, the dirty page problem becomes more serious and leads to the need for mechanisms to maintain cache coherence (156)

- the simplest solution to the cache coherence problem is to use a single cache for all PEs which, of course, leads to a severe bottleneck — alternatively, to avoid using the cache for shared data that may or may not be reasonable based upon the application and the effect upon performance (156)

- for bus-oriented systems, some form of snooping protocol that monitors transactions on the bus can be applied where the protocol varies based upon whether a write-back or write-through policy is to be followed (157)

- another alternative is to use a directory that provides the state of blocks in the system — a variety of forms have been proposed — this is the only reasonable approach for multiprocessors based upon multistage ICNs (157)

- the potential for deadlock and the Ping-Ponging effect associated with cached mutual exclusion lock variables are two caching-related problems that must be considered (158)

- to extend the number of PEs that can be usefully exploited in bus-based systems, bus hierarchies have been defined in which clusters of PEs with their own cluster cache memories are organized in a tree manner — higher-level nodes in the bus hierarchy can be a source of bottlenecks; thus, locality of program execution is a highly desirable property (158)

- associative memories divide memory into uniform-sized units where each unit is associated with a dedicated (often simple bit serial) PE — operations can be performed in parallel on the contents of memories associated with each PE — associative memories provide predictable behavior (159)

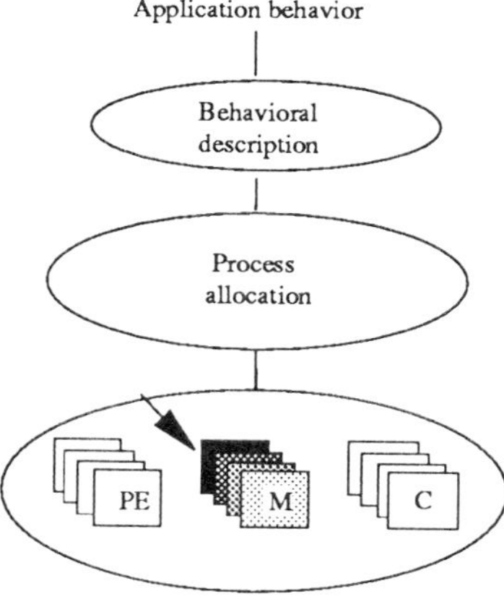

The reader will recall that the M components (**M**emories) in a system have been identified as a form of PE process. That is, they contain a data structure and a set of operations that can be performed on the data structure. In its full generality, we apply this notion to registers, cache memories, primary memories, or secondary memories (that is, external storage devices). Thus, there exists a hierarchy of memory processes having varying capacities and providing various levels of access times, as previously portrayed in Figure 3.8.

3.31 REAL AND VIRTUAL MEMORIES

At the low end of the memory hierarchy, we find registers whose values are transported to and from a higher-level memory via load and store operations. To extend the range of addressable memory beyond the scope of local memory, one or more levels of *virtual memory* may be introduced. In this case, a *cache* memory is used for retaining the most frequently addressed memory cells. Implicit transports are then provided in order to transfer referenced cells, *blocks* of cells, *pages* of cells, or *segments* of cells to and from the even higher-level primary and perhaps secondary memory.

The virtual memory concept permits us to view the computing system as having a large address space. This facility is provided at the cost of address translations and the cost associated with the logic for treating addressing exceptions (an addressed cell not found in the local memory). At the block and page level of virtual memory, the translation and exception handling are typically treated by hardware processes, whereas at higher levels of addressing, the operating system comes into play in order to manage the outermost virtual memory and provide transports over appropriate input/output channels to secondary memories. The hierarchy we have identified represents an increasing degree of granularity that matches, to some extent, the presentation of granularity in Figure 3.6. However, when data and/or program instructions are divided into uniform-size blocks, pages, or segments, the units may or may not conveniently represent the true granularity of the application relevant data and/or programs.

We shall not address the outermost levels of virtual memory processes in this book; instead, we confine our discussion to issues that are most centrally related to parallel processing issues. In this case, it is the use of cache memories and transports to and from shared primary memories that has become the central issue related to performance and capacity in parallel processing systems. For a more detailed discussion of the entire range of virtual memory systems, the reader is referred, for example, to Baer (1980). Before addressing cache memories, however, let us consider an important, often overlooked form of memory parallelism.

3.32 PARALLELISM IN MEMORY PROCESSES

Historically, the drive to achieve speedup and increased capacity in conventional computer systems resulted in the use of pipelining for instructions and/or data. This drive to improve bandwidth also resulted in the development of parallelism in the memory organization itself.

3.32.1 Interleaving

We can draw an analogy between the interconnection networks that have been described earlier and the *interleaving* strategy used in designing memory processes. Interleaving of memory into a network of memory cells has been utilized for many years in uniprocessor environments as a means of reducing effective memory access time. The interleaving works best when accesses are made in rapid succession to consecutive memory locations. For example, in the sequential fetching of instructions or in accessing con-secutive array elements, an increase of effective bandwidth of the memory can be attained.

Memory interleaving and the allocation of cells to memory banks is based upon which portion of the address is used for designating the memory bank, as portrayed in Figure 3.38.

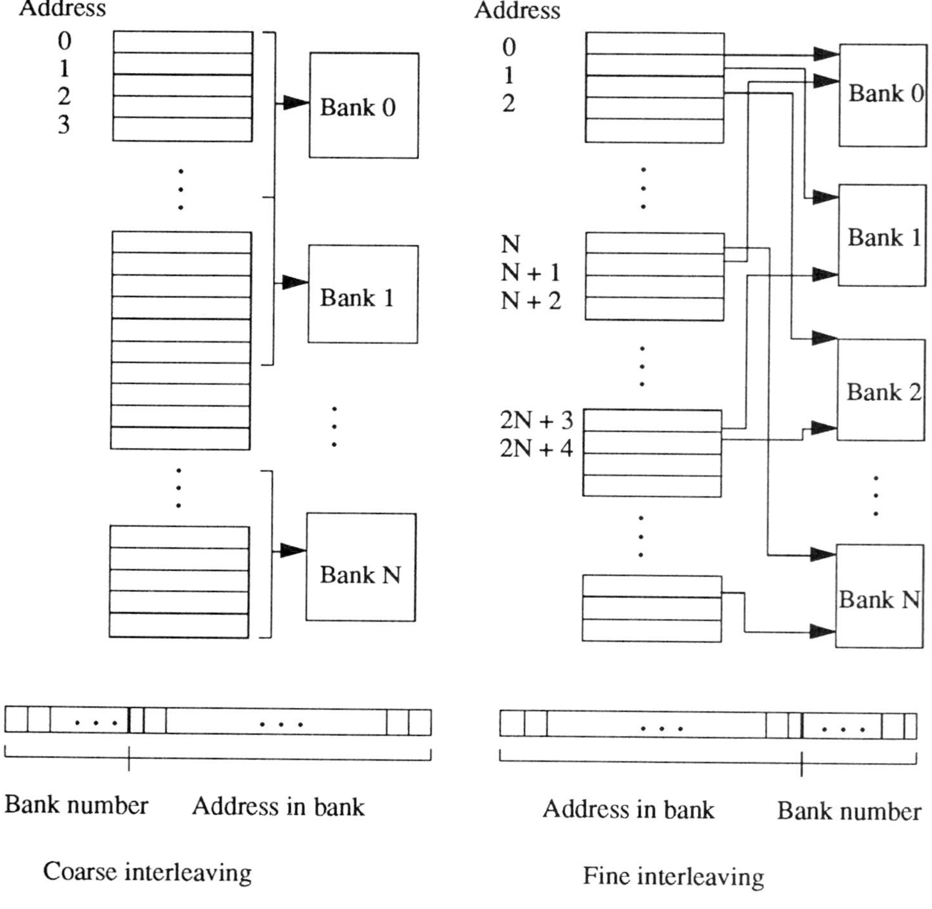

Figure 3.38. Memory Interleaving (Coarse and Fine Grain)

When the higher-order bits are used for the bank address, coarse-grain interleaving is attained where each *n*-word memory module contains a block of *n* consecutive locations. When the low-order bits are used for bank addresses, the effect is to assign consecutive cells to different modules. In either case, the interleaving is accomplished as a mapping via address decoding. The fine-grain (consecutive address) form has been most prevalent for uniprocessor systems. While these regular memory reference patterns develop for single PE situations, the randomness of parallel PEs making requests to a shared primary memory reduces the effectiveness of interleaving. On the other hand, interleaving is still applied in parallel processing environments. Exploitation of memory interleaving becomes a challenge for the designers of the parallel hardware and especially for the designer of the software processes.

3.33 CACHING AND SHARED MEMORY ENVIRONMENTS

We begin by examining the general properties of cache memories and then move on to the special properties that must be taken into account in shared memory (SM) caching environments.

3.33.1 Cache Memory Principles

A cache memory is organized into *blocks* of cells typically varying from as little as 16 cells up to 256 cells. The local cache memory has a limited capacity for retaining blocks of cells; consequently, the entire addressable memory is located elsewhere and only copies of actively referenced cells are retained locally. Blocks will be loaded on demand; as long as only read references are made, the block is said to be "clean." The block becomes "dirty" when a write is made into one or more cells of the block in cache memory. In this latter case, at some point in time, in order to maintain consistency with the primary memory, the entire block or portions thereof are written back to the primary memory. In single-PE environments, we can wait until there is a demand to replace a dirty block in cache and then write the entire block back to main memory (*write-back policy*) or we can write immediately when a store is made into a particular cell (*write-through policy*). However, as we shall consider in multiple-PE environments, more elaborate schemes are required.

Various cache organizations differ primarily in the way blocks of the main memory are mapped into blocks in the cache. Some secondary effects of the organization have to do with cache size, block size, the write-back policy, and the replacement algorithm.

3.33.2 Evaluation of a Cache System

How well a cache system performs is influenced by the cache size, block size, and addressing structure. Evaluations have shown that the effect of the replacement algorithm and the write-back policy has been minimal. The common metric used to measure the efficiency of a cache system is the *hit rate* (h), which is defined as the ratio

$$h = \frac{\text{number of memory references to the cache}}{\text{total number of memory references}}$$

Thus $(1 - h)$ is the *miss ratio*. From this we can calculate a total access time t_a, assuming t_c is the cache access time and t_m is the access time to the primary memory.

$$t_a = ht_c + (1 - h)t_m$$

This measure is rather idealistic since it does not include any calculation for memory interference (that is, competition at the memory level for the same cells) during write backs and block faults. Further, more general parameters such as the number of memory references per instruction and the locality of code and data have been excluded. However, t_a is sufficiently accurate for evaluation purposes. (*Note*: t_a may not be sufficiently accurate for predictability purposes in real-time systems.)

For a given cache size, there exists an optimal block size, as presented in Figure 3.39 showing the miss ratio versus block size for a fixed buffer capacity. Measurements have indicated that block sizes of 64 or 128 bytes are best; however, the block size does not seem to be the dominant factor since the curves are quite flat. On the other hand, total cache size seems to play the most dominant role since the miss ratio decreases significantly with increased buffer size. From these data and other experiments, one can conclude that caches of size 8 to 16K with block size of 64 to 128 bytes will yield hit ratios of over 95%.

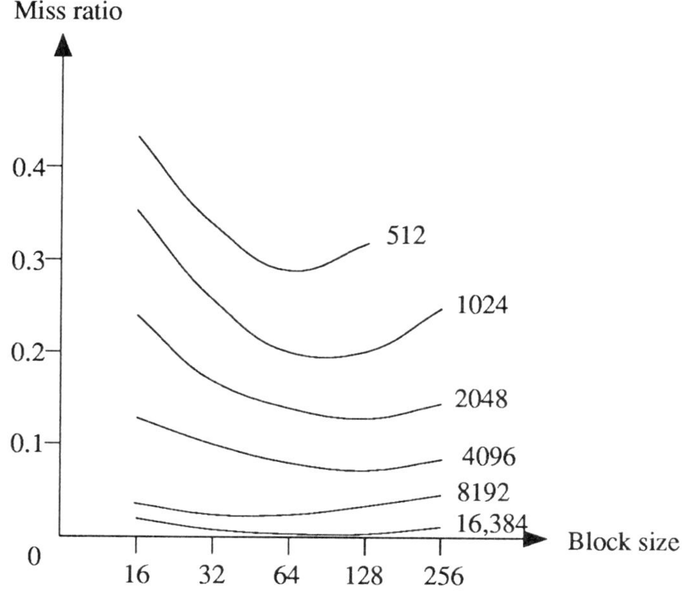

Figure 3.39. Miss Ratio versus Block Size for a Given Cache Capacity

For a review the general philosophy and implementation of cache memories, the reader is referred to Baer (1980) and the survey by Smith (1982).

3.33.3 Cache Memories in Parallel Processing Environments

Early parallel processing MIMD machines, particularly those utilizing multistage ICNs, did not exploit cache memory processes. However, this method of accelerating performance and increasing capacity in uniprocessor environments has been carried forward into contemporary MIMD shared memory bus-based architectures (see Bell, 1985). The use of a cache memory in this environment is quite appealing since, if the majority of program and data references can be made locally, the traffic over the interconnection network can be reduced, thus increasing memory bandwidth and contributing to a general overall performance lift. If, for example, PE memory references have a 95% *hit rate*, only 5% of PE requests will reach the bus. In this situation, the requirements for bus bandwidth are reduced by a factor of 20, thus permitting the inclusion of 20 times as many PEs, as compared to shared memory systems without cache memory.

On the other hand, **there is no free lunch**. The increased traffic can lead to increased *memory contention*, *communication contention*, and *latency time* (the time for memory requests to move through the network). A further price to be paid is the problem of *cache coherence*; that is, if cooperating processes are executing in different PEs and an update of a commonly known shared memory data object is made, it can be essential that all programs that may be affected by the change be provided with the updated value. Thus, there may potentially be several copies of the data object residing in local caches that need updating. Several strategies have been suggested for dealing with assuring the coherence of data in caches in the context of bus-based architectures as well as in multistage ICN environments. Dubois, Scheurich, and Briggs (1988) and Stenström (1990) have surveyed the problems and strategies.

3.33.4 Consistency in Write-Through and Write-Back Caches

The coherence problem is best illustrated by showing the effect of Load and Store operations under varying situations as presented in Figure 3.40. In (a), we see that if a shared data item X is loaded by programs operating in PE1 and PE2 they will load the same value of X. The problem comes when the program in one of the PEs executes a Store operation.

In caches implementing a write-through strategy (b), the data item X' is updated in both the cache and the shared memory (that is, written through to the shared memory). When this writing has taken place, a reference by PE2 to X in its cache will not yield the latest value of X' (that is, it is inconsistent).

In caches implementing a write-back strategy (c), there is no updating of X in the shared memory until the modified data in cache are replaced or invalidated.

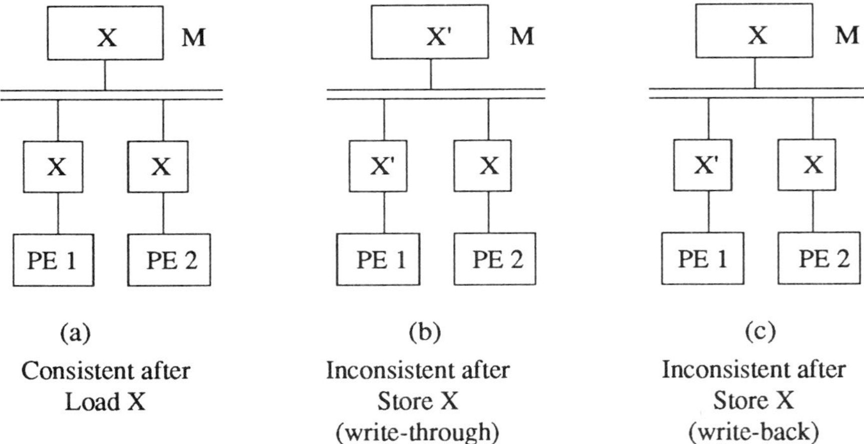

Figure 3.40. Consistency in Write-Through and Write-Back Caches

3.33.5 Solutions to the Cache Coherence Problem

A variety of *cache coherence* solutions that have been applied or suggested. They are presented here in their approximate order of complexity.

A Single Cache

The simplest solution is to resort to having one single cache memory that is shared by all PEs. The cost associated with this solution is that the cache memory reference time (latency) is increased via the need to introduce common means of PE cache memory communication.

Avoid Caching Shared Data

Another straightforward solution is to avoid placing shared data in the multiple caches. Thus, only a single shared copy of critical *noncachable* items such as locks, shared data structures, process queues, and data protected by critical regions exists. This solution has a number of side effects:

— shared data items must be tagged so that PEs recognize them
— requires compiler and perhaps loader logic to produce (cachable, noncachable) tags
— can lead to fragmentation in page-based systems
— introduces problems with I/O
— cache must be flushed when referencing processes are "migrated"

A variation of avoiding the caching of shared data is to keep the locks associated with shared variables in shared memory (that is, noncachable), utilize the cache only within critical sections, and then flush the cache at exit. The side effects of this variant are:

— to avoid complex tagging, the entire cache must be flushed
— flushing must be done at I/O operations
— only applicable for small caches

Snooping on the Bus

For bus-based systems, the table that records the status of each block can be efficiently distributed among the PEs. It is possible to take advantage of the unique properties of the bus, that is, to exploit its single time unit resolution, which provides an instantaneous overview of current traffic. Further, broadcasting properties of the bus can be exploited in order to implement a *snoopy cache controller*, that is, a controller that implements a *cache coherence protocol* on the bus. There are various schemes for snooping:

write-through caches — where all snoopy controllers watch for stores on the bus. If a store is made to a location cached in remote caches, then the copies of the block in remote caches are either invalidated or updated via broadcasting. This scheme maintains coherence even in I/O situations.

write-back-caches — which is based upon an *ownership protocol.* In this case, when a store is executed, the ownership is moved to the PE in which the store was made. After this, the main memory can be updated, and either the other caches are invalidated (write-back/invalidate) or the new data are broadcast to all caches (called write-back/broadcast).

Directory Schemes

Snoopy protocols are not suitable in multistage ICN environments since significant amounts of broadcasting would radically reduce network performance. Further, due to variable and potentially long latency, a single time unit view of all traffic (available in bus-based solutions) is not feasible. In these cases, directories are utilized to store information about where copies of blocks reside. Various directory schemes have been proposed. One method involves the maintenance of a central *cache directory.* A directory controller can find out which caches have a copy of a particular block. A second scheme uses a *present flag vector* associated with each memory block, indicating which caches have a copy of the block. The central directory scheme is independent of whether the write-through or write-back policy is applied; however, in the flag vector approach, additional information is required. A third scheme associates the block state information and flag vector with the primary memory copy. Stenström (1990) analyzes the storage requirements and performances of these three approaches.

3.33.6 Caching Problems

As knowledge and experience have grown with respect to the application of caching techniques in parallel processing environments, a number of problems have been detected that must be taken into account with respect to safe and predictable architectures.

Deadlock

Cache memory operations in attempting to keep data coherency can run into the locking problem in a manner similar to the network deadlock problem that was discussed earlier in this chapter. In this case, entire pages of memory may become locked.

Lock Ping-Ponging

Some particular problems have been observed with respect to the behavior of caches when a lock variable used for mutual exclusion is manipulated by multiple PEs. This problem can be appreciated if we consider the case where X in Figure 3.40c is a lock variable. Let us say that X has been altered by a test and set type instruction in PE1, which assumes that it now has exclusive use of the resource guarded by X. In the meantime, PE2 may test and set the same lock variable via its cache copy of X before X is updated in primary memory from the PE1 alteration of X. When this situation occurs, it has been observed that an alternating (Ping-Ponging) effect of seizing and releasing the lock variable arises. Further, if the lock is being used to guard a central queue of processes to be executed, the results may be a catastrophic reduction of performance if many PEs are all going after the same lock. A number of investigations have been made as to means of addressing these particular cache problems. See Anderson (1989) for a good presentation of the problems and potential solutions.

3.33.7 Cache Hierarchies

A major tendency in multiprocessor systems that exploit a cache memory organization is to introduce cache hierarchies, especially for bus-based systems. Since the capacity and contention on a single bus limit the number of PEs that can effectively be exploited to approximately 20 to 30 PEs, given the current technology balance, the only means to increase the number of PEs effectively is to introduce a tree hierarchy of clusters of PEs with caches. Whether this hierarchy can be effectively exploited is, once again, dependent upon the application. A bus hierarchy was portrayed in Figure 3.27.

When cache hierarchies are introduced, the updating via write-back or write-through and related snoopy cache protocols must treat the tree hierarchy nature of the system. In this case, updates must move as high up in the tree as necessary when a store operation affects shared data. Higher-level nodes may become a bottleneck if the problem cannot successfully exploit locality to clusters of PEs. Of course, they may tend to communicate across clusters at the same point in time, also causing temporary bottlenecks. Solutions to the problem of intense traffic at critical higher-level nodes have been investigated, which typically involve adding additional (parallel) buses at higher levels. An example of such a development is the DDM (Data-Diffusion Machine); see Hagersten, Haridi, and Warren (1990). Naturally, such a solution adds to the complexity of cache protocols, as well as, introducing additional hardware expenses.

3.34 ASSOCIATIVE MEMORY

Another form of memory that can be and has been successfully utilized in real-time parallel processing situations is the associative memory. In this case, the memory is partitioned in such a way that each PE is given a dedicated portion of the memory to process, as portrayed in Figure 3.41.

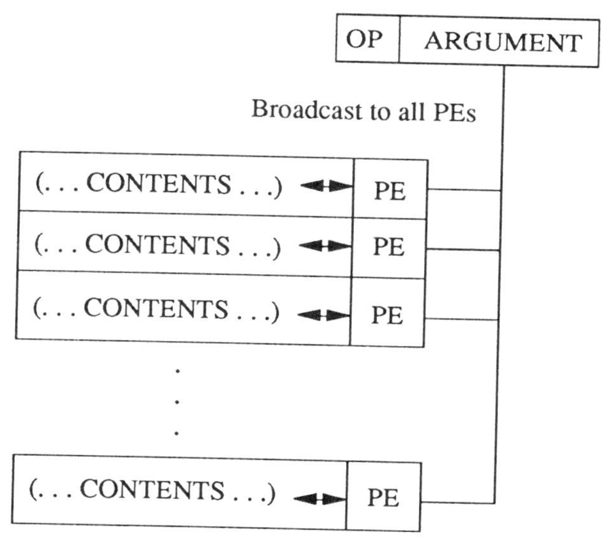

Figure 3.41. Associative Memory Organization

Instructions are provided simultaneously to all the PEs. Quite often the PEs are trivial and operate in a bit-serial manner. On the other hand, they may be programmed to do comparison, searches, and so on. It is even possible (and often highly desirable) to apply variable-length arithmetic operations in parallel. This form of memory has been exploited, for example, in radar applications in tracking multiple objects in parallel. Due to their regular structure and regular means of control, associative memories provide absolute predictability. We can compare this with the highly complex nondeterministic properties of most of the traditional multilevel memory solutions that have been described. Associative memories, which have been applied mostly in SIMD PE array systems, are further described in Chapter 10.

In summarizing this section, we can observe that the forms of memory processes utilized must be analyzed carefully when they are to be employed in parallel processing real-time situations. The predictability of maximum latency may be as important as the improvements of bandwidth.

References

Anderson, T.E. (1989). The Performance of Spin-waiting Alternatives for Shared-memory Multiprocessors, *Proceedings of the 1989 International Conference on Parallel Processing*, Pennsylvania State University Press, University Park, PA.

Baer, J-L. (1980). *Computer Systems Architecture*, Computer Science Press, Patomic, MD.

Bell, C.G. (1985). Multis: A New Class of Multiprocessor Computers, *Science*, Vol. 228, pp. 462-467.

Dubois, M, C. Scheurich, and F.A. Briggs (1988). Synchronization, Coherence, and Event Ordering in Multiprocessors, *Computer*, Vol. 21, No. 2, pp. 9-21.

Hagersten, E., S. Haridi, and D.H.D. Warren (1990). The Cache-Coherence Protocol of the Data Diffusion Machine (eds. M.Dubois and S. Thakkar) *Cache and Interconnect Architectures in Multiprocessors*, Kluwer Academic Publishers.

Smith, A.J. (1982). Cache Memories, *Computing Surveys*, Vol. 14, No. 3, pp. 473-530.

Stenström, P. (1990) A Survey of Cache Coherence Schemes for Multiprocessors, *Computer*, Vol. 23, No. 6, pp. 12-24.

PROCESS MAPPING

In this section, we examine the most important issues of process mapping, that is, allocation and scheduling. The following major points are addressed.

- allocation and scheduling are related to **where**, respectively **when** processes are executed in resource-adequate, direct-mapped, or in resource-limited, dynamically mapped environments — both mapping aspects determine **how** to control the utilization of PE, M, and C hardware processes (162)

- a unified model of process allocation is presented where the process set is viewed as an abstract network — each process is represented as a tuple composed of its instructions (or control logic), an activation record in which variables and state information are retained and ports connecting to other processes (163)

- from the abstract network of processes, allocation can be static or dynamic — process grouping strategies include centralized, distributed, and hybrid forms (165)

- transparency in allocation solutions means that communicating processes are not aware of their physical placement — thus, we differentiate between logical and physical communication — physical communication occurs locally or is converted to a message communication over an ICN (166)

- the properties of the application processes as well as their mapping to a resource structure determine performance — the effect of sequential code requirements, process granularity, process overhead, and synchronization overhead are examined (167)

- the static allocation of DSP algorithms takes place in two steps; first, scheduling of the operations in the algorithm and, second, optimization within a class of architectures — optimization criteria include sample period, processor, delay, or resource utilization (171)

- allocation of image data within PE arrays is typically organized in a rectangular (subimage) or line-by-line (linear) form (176)

- in programmed process solutions for dynamically mapped environments, a set of mechanics is associated with the administration of processes in which each process contains an activation record — the structural coupling (dynamic behavior) of processes is maintained via a thread of control that links processes (177)

- process mechanics can involve significant overhead when the details of resource utilization must be maintained in activation records — to minimize these requirements, lightweight processes are utilized that factor out resource-related state information and place it at higher levels (normally called task level) (179)

- operating systems for MIMD environments are based upon the following philosophies
    1. master-slave, client-server, or farmer-worker
    2. separate operating system organization (distributed)
    3. floating operating system (180)

- the special considerations for real-time process allocation in parallel processing environments are introduced, including requirements for the allocation of the interconnection network as a resource (183)

- the problems of process deadlock and a solution providing ordered resource allocation are addressed (186)

- the problem of process liveness where two or more processes enter continuous nonterminating loops is discussed (187)

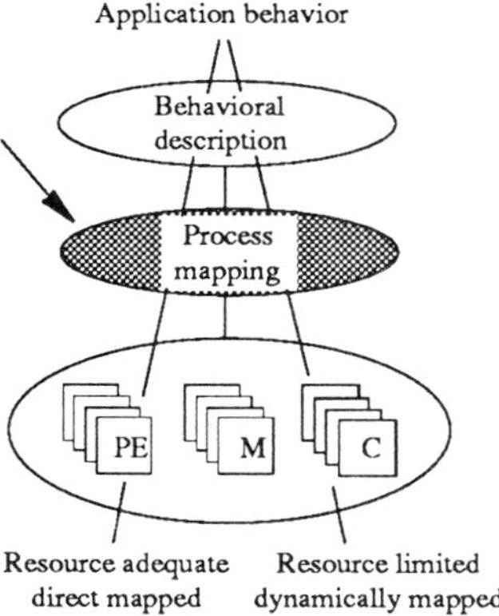

We have observed that parallel processing hardware processes provide alternative hardware resource structure paradigms and models. Further, behavioral descriptions provide various means of expressing the process behavior to be implemented. Thus, we are ready to examine the issues related to *mapping* application process behaviors to process behaviors implemented via parallel hardware structures, that is, to find appropriate allocation and scheduling strategies. As indicated in Chapter 1, there are two main mapping philosophies, as indicated in the BMR model to the left.

With respect to both mapping philosophies, *allocation* has to do with the *space domain*, that is, **where** processes from the process set reside (statically or dynamically), and scheduling has to do with the *time domain*, that is, **when** processes are executed. These two aspects of mapping become interrelated, especially when specific time requirements must be met, thus dictating the usage of particular approaches to allocation. In this chapter, we consider various formulations of the allocation and scheduling of processes with respect to particular space and time requirements, as well as with respect to particular hardware resource structures.

We have, thus far, introduced various hardware resource models, including systolic and wavefront arrays, SIMD PE arrays, and VLIW processors, as well as MIMD multiprocessors and multicomputers. The mapping to be applied varies among these alternatives; however, as a common denominator, we can view the problem of allocation and scheduling of application processes according to the mechanisms for controlling the use of PE, M, and C hardware processes, as illustrated in Figure 3.42. The main differences between various solutions is **how** control is constituted, **where** it takes place, and **when** control is applied in the mapping of processes.

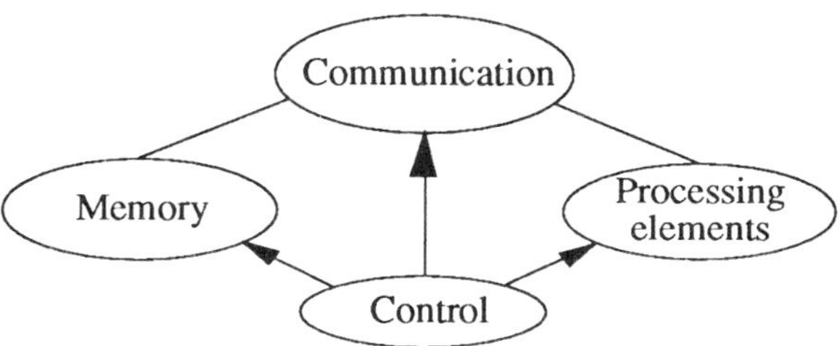

Figure 3.42. Allocation and Scheduling as the Control of Hardware Processes

While the underlying architectural models vary along with the how, where, and why of control, it is useful to observe that there are, in fact, a set of unifying concepts and mechanisms that can be applied in order to build a basis for various allocation and scheduling formulations.

3.35 A UNIFIED MODEL OF PROCESS ALLOCATION

In our unified model of allocation, we represent the *structure* of a set of processes as an abstract network, which is exemplified in Figure 3.43. This model abstraction is sufficient to cover all forms of processes of varying, granularities as well as their mappings to various physical architectures (direct mapped or dynamically mapped). From the figure, we can extract the following information:

1. That a process (P) is composed of the tuple

P::= {*instructions*, *activation record*, *ports*}

where a process is represented as set of *instructions* that when executed provides process behavior (via process procedures), an *activation record* in which all information about the *state* of the process (including any variables owned by the process) is retained, as well as the *port* connections to the *activation records* of other processes.

2. Alternatively, we can represent a process with the following tuple:

P::= {*control logic*, *activation record*, *ports*}

in the case that process behavior is provided by *control logic* directly mapped (embedded) into the PE; thus, the link to an instruction stream is vacuous (empty).

3. Remembering that all (M) memories are treated as PEs, observe that we have mapped the process representation P (as defined in 1), the *instruction* stream, and various *activation records* into separate PEs. Further, we imply an inter-PE communication mechanism for connecting activation records together via process *ports*.

4. The state of the entire system at any particular instance of time is defined as

$$\text{State} = \sum_{i=1}^{N} P_i$$

The state is the sum of all the process tuples. Finally, we can conclude that when all essential process tuple information is mapped into separate PEs:

> *A system can be viewed as being realized via a set of cooperating hardware processes PE_1 to PE_n that contains the set of application processes.*

From this common bottom line point of view, we can build up various formulations.

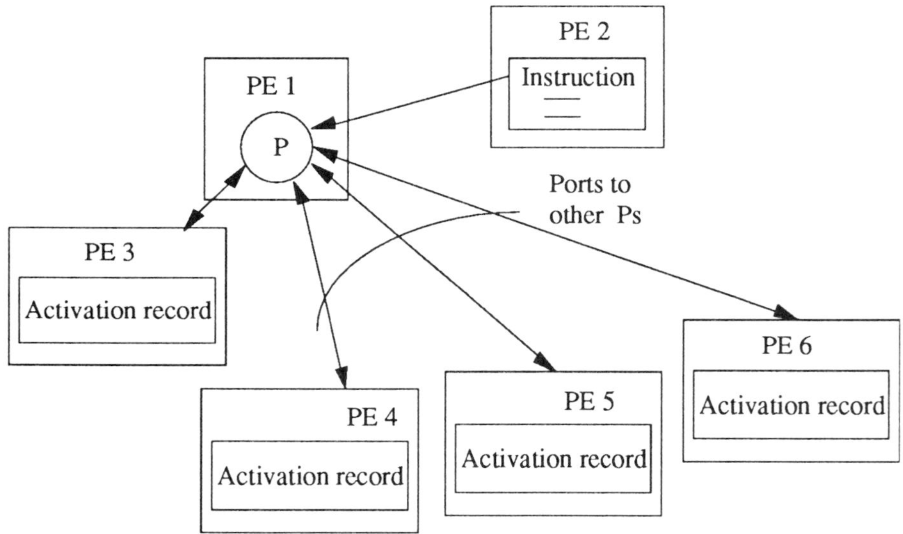

Figure 3.43. Abstract Network of Processes, Instructions, Activation Records and Ports Allocated to Processing Elements

3.35.1 Allocation of Processes to PEs

While the problem of allocating processes varies based upon the real or virtual architecture selected for providing execution semantics, we can always identify the *process grouping strategies* portrayed in Figure 3.44.

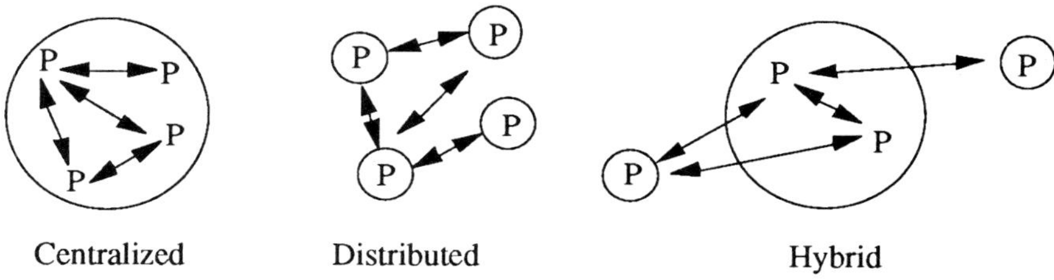

Figure 3.44. Alternative Allocations of Process State

1. **Place all the processes into one central PE.** That is, we *multiplex* all tuple elements of all Ps into a single PE. The problem of allocation for our abstract network becomes one of *addressing* the P-tuple elements in a memory space. We have a multiplicity of Ps in one PE.
2. **Distribute processes to multiple PEs.** That is, allocate the Ps *instruction* (or *control logic*) and *activation records* into individual PEs separated by *communication links* for the ports.
3. **To combine process allocation into centralized and decentralized parts.** Thus, we use the allocation principles of 1 and 2 to create a hybrid of both centralized and distributed form.

From these few fundamental notions, we can generate all the forms of architectural paradigms and models we have considered earlier (direct mapped, SIMD, and MIMD variants). Further, when virtual architectures are utilized, we can apply the same principles at multiple levels.

3.35.2 Static Allocation

The static allocation of processes to multiple PEs must be done in relationship to the properties of the problem to be solved. The *resource adequacy* philosophy is applied. Direct-mapped solutions belong to this category; however, we can even interpret cases where processes are statically allocated in SIMD PE array and MIMD architectures for particular periods of time without any attempt to reallocate during execution. Thus, in effect, they are utilized in a static, resource-adequate manner.

Statically allocated solutions can be completely distributed with one process per PE and very little or no contention for resources (such as shared memories or communication paths). In such cases, the allocation can be made based purely upon the problem requirements. However, when multiple processes are allocated into PEs and M and C resources become shared, many complications arise that must be accounted for at the time of constructing the static allocation solution. Such solutions must match the problem needs with the hardware resource structures that have been provided.

When programmed solutions are used in creating static resource adequate solutions, a *process map* is normally provided by the compiler and/or program loader so that the PEs can be directed to processes in order to provide execution service.

3.35.3 Dynamic Allocation

In *resource-limited* situations, the question of allocation of processes to PEs becomes much more complicated, leading to the need for more general means of sharing resources, priorities for determining processes execution order, and the need to transport instructions and/or activation records around in the system, as well as more sophisticated means for communication and synchronizing process execution.

3.35.4 Transparent Allocation Solutions

It is often desirable to allocate processes such that they are not aware of their physical position. To achieve this form of independent program structure, we must either:

— utilize a common address space for the entire hardware system **or**
— provide a transparent transport mechanism

There are, of course, varying performance and costs for providing each form of transparency.

Logical Transport among PEs

From the process point of view, a communication is accomplished via a *message* of some form. In fact, a message is composed from contents or partial contents of an activation record and is transmitted to an activation record. The system software and the PE treat the communication by converting the logical transport to a physical transport across a transport link, as portrayed in Figure 3.45.

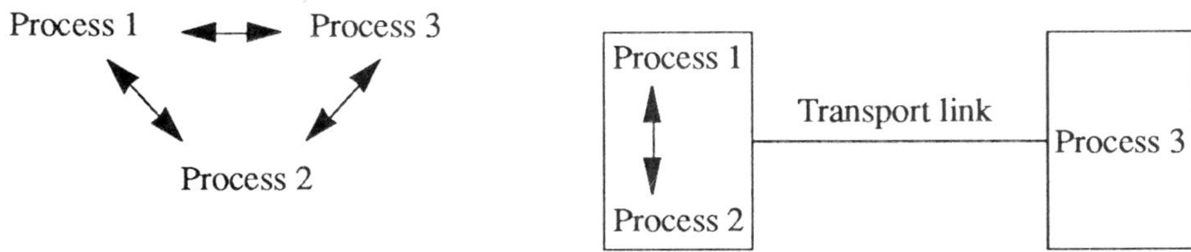

Figure 3.45. Interprocess Communication (Logical and Physical)

Physical Transport among PEs

When the communication is between processes in the same PE, the communication is accomplished via the use of commonly known memory addresses. When the communication must be transported over an ICN, the transmission can be *synchronous* or *asynchronous*.

In synchronous systems, the sending process transmits a message to a receiving process and waits until the receiving process responds with an acknowledgment that the message has been received. Correspondingly, the receiver waits for a message and then sends an acknowledgment. The sender resumes execution only when receipt of the message is confirmed.

In asynchronous systems the sending process does not wait for the receiving process to receive the message. If the receiver is not ready to receive the message at the time of its arrival, the message may be buffered or simply lost (a questionable situation, especially for hard real-time systems). Buffering can be provided in hardware or, more appropriately, in shared memory mailboxes.

In the behavioral description section, we considered several concurrent programming language properties that result in the transparent communication execution, including remote procedure calls, rendezvous, and ports. In essence, all these mechanisms result in message passing.

With our unified model of process allocation in mind as a common denominator, let us proceed to consider further formulations and issues related to process mapping.

3.36 ALLOCATION AND SPEEDUP

How and **where** processes are allocated can have a radical effect upon performance. Remembering the three basic alternatives presented in Figure 3.44 (centralized, distributed, and hybrid), we take a closer look at the effect of process allocation upon performance. While the presentation relates largely to MIMD environments, the formalisms that are presented can be useful for reasoning about most all paradigms and models.

3.36.1 Amdahl's Law

One of the early conjectures concerning whether centralized elephants or decentralized armies of ants (or even nowadays eager beavers) are best for achieving accelerated performance was presented by Amdahl (1967). Amdahl presented the case against parallel processing by showing that a small number of sequential operations can effectively limit the speedup of a parallel algorithm.

For example, if 10% of the operations must be performed sequentially, then the maximum speedup is 10 no matter how many PEs are provided in the parallel processing environment. This argument is quite strong since if parallel computers can never run 10, 15, or 20 times faster than single PE computers; then the expression "wait for a faster technology" makes a lot of sense. Of course, the amount of horsepower we can get out of the elephants is reaching its limit in current hardware technology. Further, there do exist algorithms that contain almost no sequential processing. In any event, Amdahl's law is important since it serves as a means of determining whether an algorithm is a good candidate for allocation to parallel hardware resources.

3.36.2 Speedup Bounds for Parallel Processes

In Chapter 1, we indicated that the maximum attainable speedup is $\theta(N)$, that is, linear. Whether linear or close to linear performance improvement can be reached or even approximated is determined by a number of factors, including:

— the need to synchronize PEs (PEs may have to wait for each other)
— the nature of the problem with respect to data structures and algorithms
— contention between PEs when requiring the use of a common resource

Given these factors, we now examine some important relationships that define the $O(N)$ performance that can be achieved as presented by Worlton (1987) and reviewed by Johnson (1989).

$$\text{Speedup} = \frac{1}{R + (1-R)\left[\dfrac{Y}{KG} + f\left(\dfrac{K}{N}\right)\left(\dfrac{1}{K} + \dfrac{O}{KG}\right)\right]}$$

where:

G	=	the process granularity
K	=	number of processes between synchronization
N	=	number of PEs
O	=	process overhead
R	=	residual sequential code
Y	=	synchronization overhead

$$f\left(\frac{K}{N}\right) = \begin{cases} \dfrac{K}{N} & K \text{ divisible by } N \\ \dfrac{K}{N} + 1 & \text{otherwise} \end{cases}$$

Process overhead (O) is the additional time required to complete a process due to the fact that it is being executed on a parallel processor. Synchronization overhead (Y) is the additional time required to properly pace the parallel/concurrent execution of the processes. Assuming that both of these effects are negligable and that the number of processes is divisible by the number of PEs, we may simplify to

$$\text{Speedup} = \frac{1}{R + \dfrac{1-R}{N}}$$

This expression, which conveys Amdahl's law, directly reflects the effect of residual sequential code (R) upon speedup. Graphically, we can observe this effect in Figure 3.46.

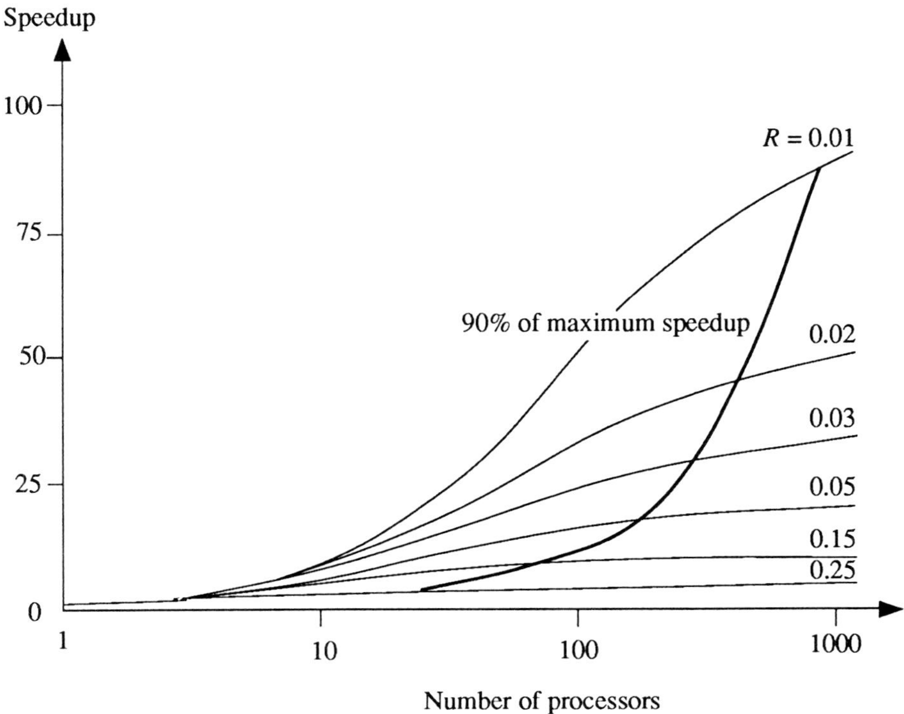

Figure 3.46. Effect of Residual Sequential Code on Speedup

The heavy line in the figure indicates the point at which each curve reaches 90% of its asymptotic value. It is easy to see that this asymptote is the reciprocal of (R). The diagram points to the fact that residual sequential code places a rather significant constraint on the effectiveness with which any particular algorithm can make use of large numbers of PEs. For example, with 5% residual code, 90% of the ideal speedup

(18 out of a possible 20) for an infinite number of PEs is reached when only 171 PEs are utilized. Assuming (R) is as little as 2%, a speedup of 45 out of a possible 50 is reached with only 441 PEs.

In continuing our analysis, we assume that the amount of residual sequential code is negligable. If we fix the number of processes (K) and allow the number of PEs to become arbitrarily large, the speedup approaches

$$\text{Speedup} = \frac{K}{1 + \dfrac{Y + O}{G}}$$

We can observe that the speedup is independent of the number of processors; consequently, the parallel processing efficiency (speedup) divided by (N) goes to zero in this limit. However, this case is more of theoretical than practical interest since it points to the difficulty of mapping a fixed-size application onto an ever larger number of PEs.

If we assume one process per PE, the speedup reduces to

$$\text{Speedup} = \frac{N}{1 + \dfrac{Y + O}{G}}$$

If we then define a relative overhead, Q, such that

$$Q = \frac{Y + O}{G}$$

we observe that, in this case, the parallel processing efficiency is $1/(1 + Q)$. Thus, if the relative overhead can be made small and held constant as (N) increases, a strategy of assigning one process per PE and then increasing the problem size as the number of PEs is increased should result in a good speedup and high efficiency. This scaled problem approach to parallel processing has been described by Gustafson, Montry, and Benner (1988).

On the other hand, if the number of PEs is fixed while the number of processes grows without bound, the limiting speedup is

$$\text{Speedup} = \frac{N}{1 + \dfrac{O}{G}}$$

This case resembles the previous one, with the added simplification that the effect of synchronization overhead has disappeared. This may be a deceptively simple example in that an arbitrarily large number of processes on a fixed-size machine may incur significant process overhead.

The formulations that have been provided suggest that *a successful parallel algorithm will minimize both residual sequential code and relative overhead.* However, this may be a difficult challenge. Contriving a parallel implementation of an inherently sequential algorithm can result in a significant process overhead. Further, increasing process granularity in order to reduce relative overhead will place an upper bound on the number of PEs onto which a fixed-size problem may be mapped.

It is important to keep these performance-related factors in mind as we examine the various processes allocation and scheduling formulations. As a useful summary of the analysis of performance and overhead factors, consider the visualization of trade-offs in Figure 3.47 as introduced by Leu (1987), where the middle line represents an optimally balanced solution.

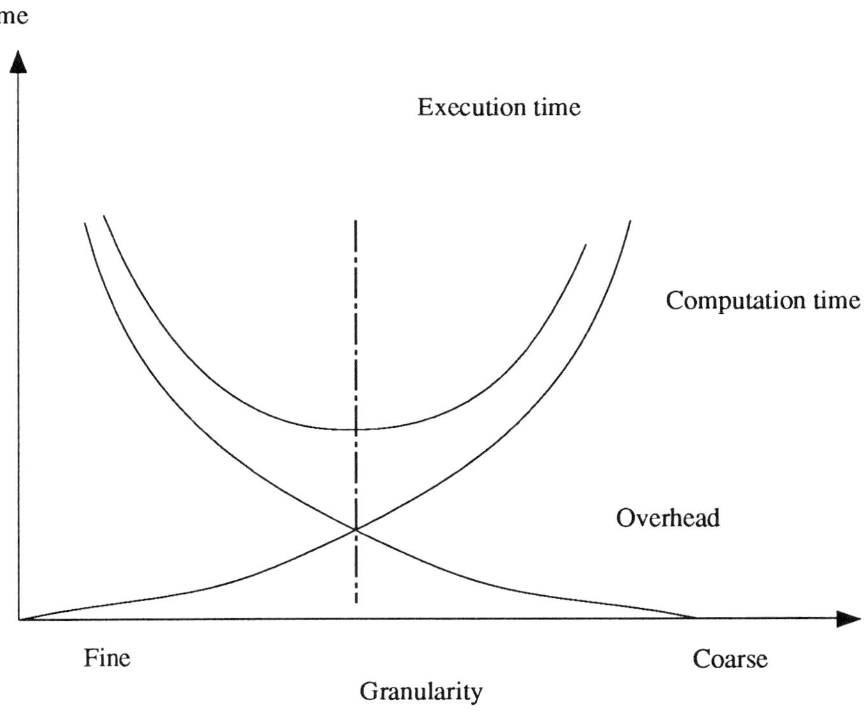

Figure 3.47. Trade-off between Parallelism and Overhead

3.37 DIRECT-MAPPED ALLOCATION

We now consider the mainstream ideas used for static allocation and mapping in DSP applications. The formulations presented here will be further elaborated in Chapter 4 and 8.

Most DSP algorithms are amenable to static scheduling, and it is even possible to synthesize optimal sets of hardware resources. The synthesis of an optimal architecture starts from a given DSP algorithm represented by its equations and signal-flow graph. By applying a systematic procedure (described in Chapter 4), the basic operations (processes) and the order in which they will be computed are extracted.

The *first* allocation step is to derive a schedule of the operations (processes) that involves distributing the operations in the *time domain* so that an *adequate* but *minimum* quantity of hardware resources is required. Often, only the number of PEs is minimized, but it is also possible to minimize the (M) **m**emory and (C) **c**ommunication resources. In fact, it is possible to minimize the total hardware resource requirements by proper scheduling. The *schedule* determines the number and type of PE, M, and C processes required for a class of optimal architectures.

The *second* allocation step involves an optimization within this class of architectures.

Let us relate these two steps to the BMR model. The synthesis process is essentially downward (from application algorithm to hardware resources). However, for direct-mapped solutions, these steps are highly interdependent. For example, the scheduling assumes certain costs for PE, M, and C components. Further, the selection of a particular algorithm restricts the class of usable architectures. Therefore, the synthesis process must, in practice, be followed by an evaluation phase and a subsequent design iteration. The design process may have to be reiterated several times to achieve a satisfactory solution. The design process may also require an extention to a lower-level of resource abstraction, for example, to the logic and electrical circuit level (as presented in Table 3.4).

3.37.1 Various Forms of Optimality

Due to the complexity of the problem, scheduling and resource allocation and assignment are often treated separately. The following criteria of optimality are commonly used for static scheduling.

- Sample period optimality
- Processor optimality
- Delay optimality
- Resource optimality

A schedule is *sample period optimal* if it has a sample period equal to the minimal possible sample period. It is *processor optimal* if it uses a minimal number of PEs of the different types as the processors. The minimal number of PEs of type i is defined as

$$\left\lceil \frac{D_i}{T_{min}} \right\rceil$$

where D_i is the total execution time of all operations of type i and T_{min} is the minimal sampling period. A schedule is *delay optimal* if it has a delay from input to output equal to the delay bound. The delay bound is the shortest possible delay from input to output of the algorithm. Finally, a *resource optimal* schedule yields a minimal quantity of resources for a given performance constraint, for example, sample rate and latency.

PE assignment involves the selection of a particular PE in a pool of PEs that should execute a certain process. Ideally assignment should be done at the same time as scheduling, but, as mentioned previously, this is not possible in the majority of scheduling techniques. The separation makes it difficult to evaluate the cost function associated with the schedule. For instance, the maximal number of concurrent processes is not necessarily the same as the required number of PEs.

Let us consider an example and various alternatives to assignment. Consider the periodic algorithm whose *schedule* is shown in Figure 3.48 for one period. Each row in the figure represents a PE. The sampling period is assumed to be 3 and there are at the most two concurrent operations.

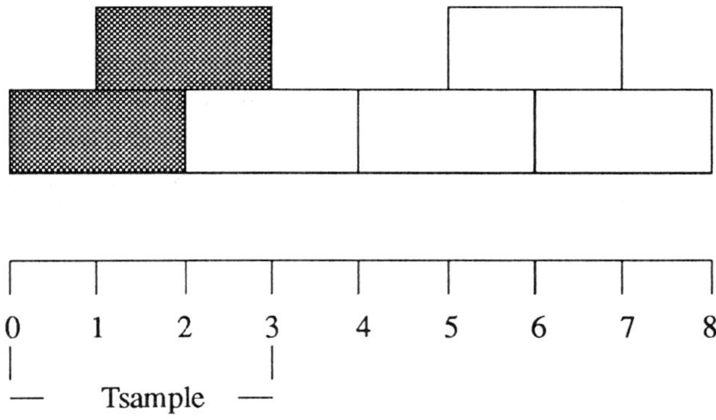

Figure 3.48. Time Schedule

Figure 3.49 portrays the same time schedule folded modulo 3. However, there are still at the most two concurrent operations. Each row represents a PE. Obviously, two PEs do not suffice. A process that is folded modulo 3 must be continued on the same row in the diagram, that is, continued in the same PE.

In this case, we cannot find a sample schedule that utilizes less than three PEs assuming that the schedule is nonpreemptive (typically the case in direct-mapped solutions).

At the architectural level, the main interest is the overall organization of the system, which usually is described in terms of PE, M, and C processes. These hardware processes are characterized by parameters such as memory capacity, access time, word length, transmission rates, and processor performance. At this level, the designer is also interested in the global dataflow between the high-level primitives in the system, with the objective of estimating the system performance and identifying potential bottlenecks in data transmission within the system.

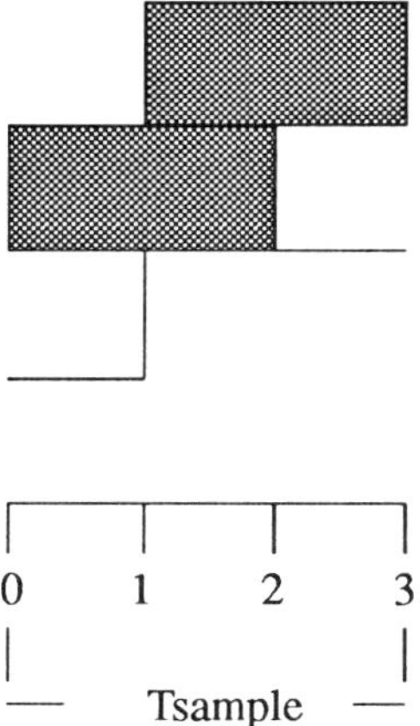

Figure 3.49. Schedule Folded Modulo Tsample

At the end of the architectural design phase, timing relationships between the hardware processes become more interesting. Also, test pattern generation and fault simulation are addressed at this point.

In summary, we can state once again that the starting point for the synthesis of an optimal architecture is the schedule of operations. *The synthesis problem is essentially to efficiently map the processes onto the PEs, which can execute the basic set of operations (processes), provide (M) memories and suitable (C) communication channels, and provide proper synchronization, control, and test circuitry.*

3.37.2 Points in the Resource-time Domain

In general, the relationship between the operations (processes) in the algorithm and the PEs is established by a direct mapping of the operations executed in each *time slot* onto the PEs. The schedule implicitly determines the required number and type of PEs, memories, and communication channels. Therefore, we assume that the scheduling of the operations is optimal in some sense. However, the scheduling assumes an underlying computational architecture. Thus, *scheduling* and *architecting* are highly interdependent design processes.

A class of related algorithms can be obtained by changing the set of basic (atomic) operations. For example, a sum of products can be interpreted as an inner product. The algorithms may have different numerical properties due to differences in quantization, and the like, and be more or less suited for implementation using a particular architecture. The sets of arithmetic operations commonly used in DSP algorithms are add/sub, add/sub-and-shift, multiply, multiply-and-accumulate, vector product, two-port adaptor, and butterfly. For sake of simplicity, we assume for now that the schedule is fixed. In practice, the schedule may have to be reiterated for different sets of basic operations, processors, and architectures.

There are several approaches to map the basic operations onto the PEs. The simplest choice is to select a generalized PE type that can execute all types of operations. That is, all PEs are homogeneous. The mapping of operations is simplified since each operation can be mapped onto any of the, at that moment, available PEs.

Another choice is to select dedicated PEs that can execute only one or a few types of operations. The performance of these PEs can be optimized with respect to the given requirements; however, they may not be efficiently utilized if they are too specialized. Hence, by proper scheduling and by utilizing different PE alternatives, a number of feasible implementations or points in the resource-time domain can be found.

The maximal utilizable quantity of resources is limited by the parallelism in the algorithm, while the minimum is the single PE case. It is desirable that PEs be kept simple. Normally, it is necessary that all PEs perform constant-time operations. In between these two extreme cases, there may be a number of possible solutions, as portrayed in Figure 3.50. T_{sample} in this case is the required sampling period, whereas T_{min} represents the minimum that is achievable (based on application parallelism).

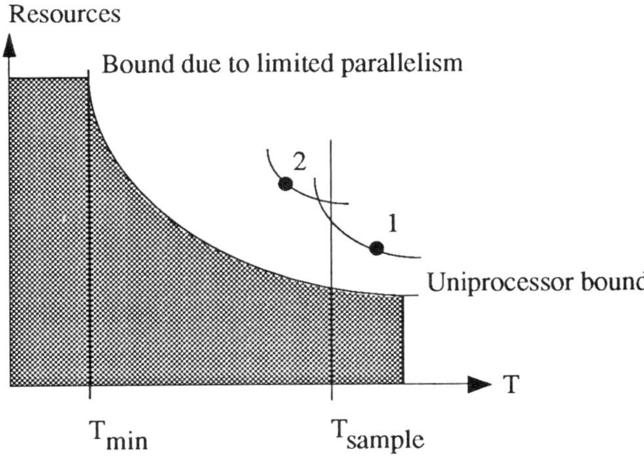

Figure 3.50. Resources versus Sample Rate for Different Schedules

Solution 1 does not meet the time requirements, whereas solution 2 meets the timing requirements but is not necessarily optimal. Thus, a closer analysis of these two solutions may, via resource-time trade-offs, yield a satisfactory solution that meets time requirements and is optimal. One final observation in relationship to this figure is that we can consider the mapping extremes of only one PE given at the uniprocessor bound and one operation per PE given at the bound due to limited parallelism. The reader may find it useful to relate these extremes to our resource axiom (0, 1, $\approx \infty$).

Note: For direct mapping to systolic and wavefront arrays, the requirement that the algorithm match the systolic or wavefront structure is very stringent. Generally, while details may vary somewhat, there are not as many variations in architectural choice. Either the application algorithm and geometry of its data fit the systolic or wavefront structure or they do not. It is not fruitful to create semantic gaps by forceful process allocation in order to utilize an inappropriate set of hardware resources (another important axiom to remember).

3.38 PE ARRAY ALLOCATION

For PE arrays, we have a **preallocated** set of processes permanently assigned to PEs (that is, the individual instructions representing processes). In terms of our unified allocation model, what is altered is their activation records (data). Thus, allocation primarily involves the mapping of data rather than processes. Further, scheduling is not an issue within the PE array since the processes all execute in unit time. Higher-level processes are, on the other hand, typically scheduled within the framework of a host machine.

To achieve highest efficiency, a SIMD PE array processor requires that the problem expose at least the same degree of parallelism as the array. In nearly all applications that call for large amounts of computing power, this is the case. However, it is not always necessary that the machine be as parallel as the problem (that is, be resource limited). Further, difficulties may be encountered concerning communications and input/output, especially in attempting to utilize the entire parallelism offered by the system. Thus, for PE arrays, we find the need to **map** the problem (in terms of its data requirements) onto PE array structures.

To demonstrate mapping, let us assume a 128 x 128 grid of PEs to be used for image processing. One typical means of allocation is to assign a PE to each pixel. Thus, images are divided and processed in square parts, sized 128 x 128 (see Figure 3.51a). This method implies a quite complicated I/O system which must reorder data. A *staging memory* is typically required to assist in the necessary transformations. This allocation approach also creates neighborhood access problems at the edges of the subimages that must be taken care of at the lowest level of programming.

Another alternative is to organize the PE array ensemble as *linear arrays*, where one PE takes care of one column of the image (see Figure 3.51b). Processing proceeds by sweeping over the lines. This approach simplifies I/O significantly, at least in the case where the image is inputted and outputted in line-scan format. Normally, the PEs have enough memory to allow the whole image to be stored in the array permitting each PE to access an entire pixel column. Thus, vertical neighbor pixels are in the same PE and horizontal ones are in neighboring PEs. The result is that long-distance communication in the vertical direction is achieved at no cost (within the same PE).

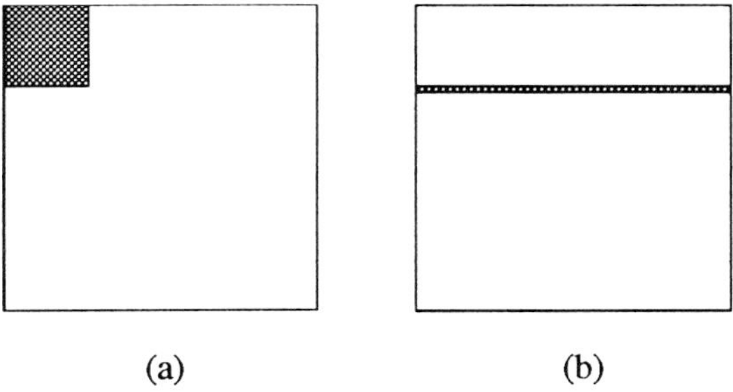

Figure 3.51. Processing Part of an Image: (a) Subimage by Subimage; (b) Line by Line

The linear array approach to image processing has a limit (by definition): the number of PEs cannot exceed the number of pixels of a line. However, duplication of arrays can be made to enhance performance if needed. This can be accomplished via parallel arrays or arrays working in a pipeline fashion.

To make this collection of mapping methods more complete, we should also mention that each PE in a two-dimensional grid or torus can process a small, coherent part of the image. Reordering of data during input/output is also required in this case; however, it can be done one line at a time, thus requiring less staging memory. The neighborhood access patterns are different for different pixels within the subimage, but the instantaneous pattern is the same for the entire set of physical PEs.

Within PE array solutions, *virtual processors* can be mapped to physical processors in several ways, yielding various consequences for input/output and computations. Choosing organization and mapping carefully are as important as using as many PEs as possible in the solution of a problem. For example, it can be beneficial to use fewer, but more powerful PEs and a simple and efficient mapping and input/output scheme. Further issues and solutions to PE array allocation are considered in Chapter 10.

3.39 MIMD ALLOCATION

For resource-limited environments where dynamic mapping is utilized, the allocation of processes to PEs, as well as process scheduling strategies, is performance critical. When a potentially large set of active processes can exist simultaneously, the allocation and scheduling activities must be based on the proper management of queues of processes leading to nondeterministic properties.

In real-time environments these aspects must be strictly controlled in order to properly dimension systems where predictability is an essential issue.

3.39.1 Process Representation and Mechanics

The creation of sets of processes that are to be executed concurrently is programmed explicitly in concurrent imperative program code or extracted implicitly as in the case of declarative style languages. Again, we should remember that concurrent means that two or more processes are *active* (however, not necessarily executing) in the same time domain. Whether the concurrent processes are executed in parallel via multiple PEs is dependent upon the availability of a parallel PE resource structure, the related operating systems allocation strategy, scheduling strategy, run-time environment, and the necessary ICN hardware resources.

Multiprocessing is realized in concurrent single-PE systems by maintaining a thread of control for each active process. Further, information that is processed by the process (data), as well as control (state) information about the process, is partitioned into activation records. This partitioning is illustrated in Figure 3.52.

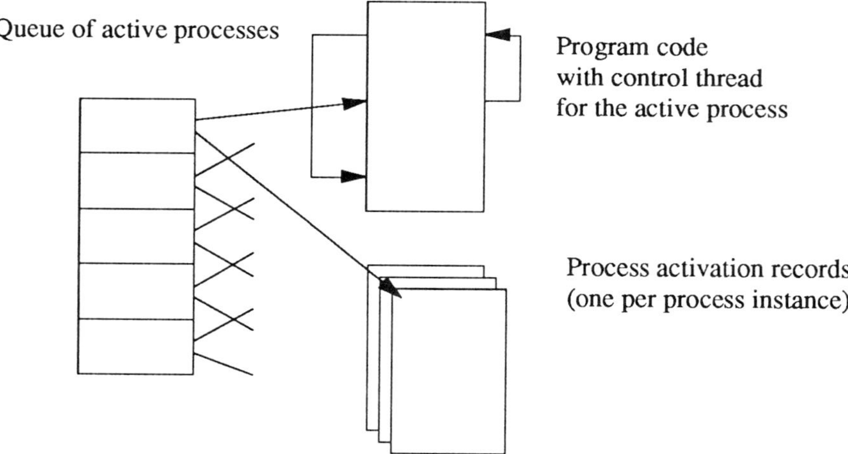

Figure 3.52. Processes as Threads of Control and Activation Records

Whether the processes reside in a single memory connected to a single PE or reside in multiple PEs with shared or nonshared memories, all processes are represented in memory via a separate thread of control and separate activation record. These are the fundamental elements used to characterize processes in dynamically mapped environments.

The activation record can contain a significant amount of state information. The state information is used for scheduling the process as well as for initiating, suspending, reinitiating, and terminating process execution. This collection of state information is typically referred to as the PCB (**p**rocess **c**ontrol **b**lock), PSD (**p**rocess **s**tate **d**escriptor), or simply the process context. The typical set of information is as follows:

— **process state** (new, ready, running, blocked, halted)
— **program counter** (address of the next instruction of the process to be executed)
— **PE registers** (local registers used by the process)
— **memory management information** (base and bound registers or page tables)
— **I/O status information** (outstanding I/O requests, I/O devices allocated to the process, list of open files)
— **scheduling information** (process priority, deadlines, elapsed time pointers to scheduling queues)
— **protection information** (process status in the protection hierarchy, if any)

Due to the fact that each process instance has its own activation record, it is possible to reutilize process program code for new process instances. All relevant process information is partitioned into the new process activation record, and the new instance establishes a new thread of control through the existing process code. This is a normal phenomenon for recursive or reentrant processes.

In addition to the active process queue illustrated in the figure, an inactive queue is also maintained for processes that are waiting for resources or for events. Each such process also has an associated inactivated control thread and activation record, which become activated when the process is activated by the scheduler.

3.39.2 Lightweight Processes

From the list of process activation record-related information given above, it is easy to see that there can be significant overhead in managing processes. The overhead leads to the need to find more expedient forms of processes that avoid maintaining significant amounts of process context (particularly with respect to context switch).

To produce more effective operating system environments for MIMD resource-limited environments (including parallel/distributed environments), a new type of process structure has been introduced called *lightweight processes*. Much of the resource allocation state information is factored out of process representations when they are not required. The lightweight process shares its parent's activation record. Thus, the management of lightweight processes is much simpler and much more efficient. Lightweight processes represent a trade-off between full process generality and efficiency requirements. The overhead is not much more than for a normal procedure call.

Having considered the question of the allocation of processes, including necessary mechanics in MIMD systems, we now turn our attention in the following sections to considering static and dynamic allocation strategies.

3.39.3 Allocation and Scheduling Strategies

In the single-PE environment, all processes must be allocated for execution within the single PE. While many scheduling strategies are possible within the single-PE environment (such as priority based, round robin, rate-monotonic, that is, shortest execution time, and others), the nature of the resource as well as the class of problems to be solved dictates, to a large extent, the approach utilized. However, when multiple-PE resources are introduced, the questions of allocation and scheduling strategy become more complicated.

The simplest approach to parallel/distributed processing environment allocation is, of course, the static approach that is, where the application processes are assigned to particular PEs based upon an optimal or satisfactory partitioning of the problem in terms of the available resources and required communications and synchronizations. By static allocation, a good *load balance* may be obtained. The linkers and loaders initialize the system with the process code. In some cases, there may be an identity between each process and PE. In other cases, PEs are directed to active process queues by some centralized and/or decentralized scheduler. Activation and deactivation of processes dynamically creates, alters, and deletes activation records, which are the process representations. This approach has been utilized in the MIMD-based avionics real-time system described as a case study in Chapter 15.

When a dynamic strategy is required, several approaches can be applied in attempting to find a suitable *load balancing* of processes. Some approaches provide load balancing for general sets of processes, while others attempt to achieve load balancing based upon the properties of the application. Thus, there are various philosophies for multiprocessing operating systems.

3.39.4 Operating System Organization Philosophy

Hwang and Briggs (1984) identify three major philosophies for organizing the operating system functions in parallel processing environments.

Master-Slave Organization

One of the PEs is selected to be a *master*; it always executes the OS. Other PEs are denoted as *slaves*. If a slave PE requires an OS service, it must request it and wait until the current program running in the master is interrupted. Obviously, this can introduce idle time in the slave. Further, the system is sensitive to failure of the master. The main advantage of this organization is its simplicity with regards to the required hardware resources as well as software solutions. It can be an effective variant where the workload is well defined or for asymmetrical systems, where the slave PEs have less capability than the master PE.

Separate Operating System Organization

The operating system kernal is run separately on each PE. Many of the OS routines are distributed in a number of copies among the local memories of the PEs. Although this variant is less prone to catastrophic failures, it wastes storage by keeping multiple copies of routines and data. On the other hand, it contributes to deadline predictability and responsiveness (fault tolerance) and thus must be seriously considered for real-time environments.

Floating Operating System Organization

The assignment of the master floats from one PE to another. A better *load balancing* between PEs may be obtained by utilizing this strategy. However, this organization is more complicated to implement. It is obviously more flexible than the master-slave organization. In the case of failures, graceful degradation of the system may be possible; a failure of any single PE is generally not catastrophic. At the same time, this organization contributes to significant nondeterminism and must be evaluated carefully for its use in time-critical real-time environments.

While any one of these operating system philosophies may be appropriate for particular applications, a natural means of viewing the utilization of resources in a resource-limited situation is via a model like the master-slave model or models such as *client-server* or *farmer-worker*. A good human analogy for the client-server model is the service provided by tellers in a bank (servers) and the queues of customers (clients) that wait to gain access to a server. It is not hard to fantasize about various capabilities of the tellers and requests for particular types of service. For example, all tellers may be able to deal with any type of transaction or can only provided limited specific services. Customers place varying demands on the tellers in terms of volume of transaction, and the like. These issues and the use of analogical reasoning as presented in Chapter 1 provide a useful mechanism for thinking and reasoning about this form of scheduling solution. In the farmer-worker model, the farmer, in order to serve requests, farms out processes to workers. So take your pick as to which analogy pleases your own thinking and reasoning processes.

To illustrate the principles, in this regard, let us consider these models as portrayed in Figure 3.53 as client-server, or farmer-worker, variants.

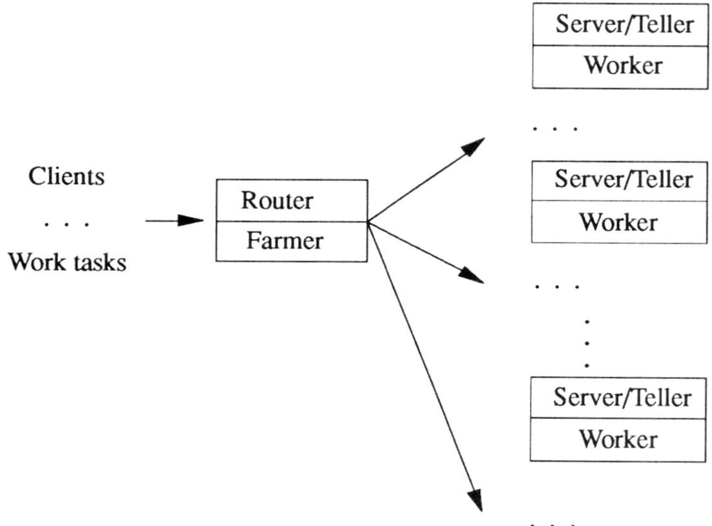

Figure 3.53. Scheduled Client-Server/Farmer-Worker Model

We consider the case where all arriving clients (work tasks) are first handled by a router (farmer) that will provide for a sequencing of the clients requests for services with respect to the available server (teller), or worker, resources. In the bank situation, the routing may be achieved by a ticket machine providing a service number.

The properties of routers for client-server models in the human and computer domain have been studied quite intensively and many results are available (see Conway, Maxwell, and Miller, 1967). Simulations of such models normally assume a stochastic Poisson distributed arrival rate of clients.

Client-server (farmer-worker, master-slave) models are directly translatable into parallel processing resources. In fact, we can find them in use today in MIMD environments. We take a closer look at the farmer-worker model in Chapter 11.

Group Scheduling

As larger quantities of parallel processing resources have been made available, it has been natural to consider scheduling the utilization of resources in groups (slaves, tellers, or workers), rather than as individual resources. In this case, multiple resources (clusters) are allocated together for a well-defined collection of processes. Where this is possible, it can lead to significantly reduced resource scheduling overhead. On the other hand, the effective utilization of group scheduling must come as a result of a close match with the nature of the application.

3.40 REAL-TIME PARALLEL PROCESSING SCHEDULING

As considered earlier, real-time systems are typified by the requirement for functional correctness, as well as their ability to meet timing constraints. In Chapter 2, we considered the main points of view for scheduling real-time processes with respect to single-PE environments. However, the approaches to scheduling in single-PE environments are not always directly applicable in parallel processing environments. Mok and Dertouzos (1978) showed that algorithms that are optimal for single-PE systems, such as *rate monotonic* for periodic processes, are not optimal for increased numbers of PEs. Further, earliest deadline or least slack time solutions are similarly nonoptimal. Due to the NP-completeness of the scheduling problem, adequate, suboptimal solutions are all that can be expected.

3.40.1 Allocating Periodic Processes

The general consensus among those who have investigated periodic process allocation is that it is better to allocate periodic processes statically, rather than to let them migrate and potentially downgrade system performance. Even on tightly coupled system with a single dispatcher, it is better to keep the processes on the same PEs rather than to be tempted to utilize an idle PE and risk unbalancing the system.

If static allocation is employed, the rate-monotonic algorithm or another optimal single-PE algorithm can be utilized to test for schedulability on each PE. Naturally, processes that are highly related should be mapped into the same PE.

3.40.2 Allocating Aperiodic Processes

One is tempted to keep things simple even in the presence of aperiodic processes by statically allocating processes to PEs, where each PE contains its own scheduler/dispatcher, and to apply the same strategy as in the single-PE case. In the presence of blocking problems, *inheritance* or *ceiling protocols* could be applied. However, in the parallel environment, *remote blocking* can occur; that is, a process is blocked by a process running on another PE. Further, static assignment does not allow for utilizing the extra power of multiple PEs in dealing with transient overloads.

To deal with the exploitation of extra PE power, Stankovic, Ramamritham, and Cheng (1985) have suggested a *bidding protocol* approach in which periodic processes are statically allocated, but where aperiodic processes can migrate as follows:

— each aperiodic process arrives at some PE node in the network that is running its own scheduler.

— the node at which the aperiodic process arrives then checks to see if this new process can be scheduled, together with its existing load. If it can, the process is said to be *guaranteed* by this node.

— if the node cannot guarantee new processes, it looks for alternative nodes that may be able to guarantee it. It does this by having a knowledge of the state of the entire network and by *bidding* for spare capacity in other nodes.
— the process is thus moved to a new node where there is a high probability that it will be scheduled. Due to race conditions, the new node may not be able to schedule it once it has arrived. Thus, the guarantee test must be applied again and, if it fails, the process must move again.
— the result is that an aperiodic task is scheduled (guaranteed) or it fails to meet its deadline.

The approach applied employs a heuristic algorithm for determining where a nonguaranteed process should be moved and, while not optimal, does provide a high probability of success. Naturally, this approach assumes that the aperiodic processes can be moved. However, in some systems, aperiodic processes may be bound to particular PEs, as in the case of I/O connections.

3.40.3 Remote Blocking

To eliminate or reduce the effect of remote blocking, processes should not use remote resources, implying that processes should be grouped according to their resource requirements. Of course, processes should also be grouped according to their periods, where harmonic periods are grouped together. This leads to conflicts, and compromises must be sought.

In single-PE systems, it is proper for higher-priority processes to preempt lower-priority processes; however, in parallel environments this is not necessarily desirable. Interactions in relationship to priority can occur, for example, when processes running on separate PEs share a common critical section. In such cases, we can again enter the problem of priority inheritance, resulting in the blocking of higher-priority processes. To minimize this remote preemption, the critical section can be made nonpreemptable (or at least only preemptable via other critical sections), as proposed by Mok (1983). Alternatively, we can define the priority of the critical section to be higher than all processes in the system. Rajkumar, Sha, and Lechoczky (1988) have applied a ceiling protocol to this problem.

3.40.4 Transient Overloading

Although migration of aperiodic tasks can be used for the effective utilization of PEs, we may still be left with the following situations:

— aperiodic deadlines are missed, rather than periodic ones.
— aperiodic deadlines are not missed in an order that reflects importance.

The first point may be acceptable depending upon the application; however, the second is important if the application has any hard deadlines for sporadic activity. A compromise can be reached between static and flexible allocation if static allocation is employed in normal circumstances, with controlled migration being employed during transient overloads. In this case, each PE attempts to schedule all assigned periodic and aperiodic processes. If a transient overload occurs (or is predicted), the set of aperiodic and/or periodic processes that will miss their deadlines is isolated. Further, an attempt will be made to move these processes to another PE and then return them during the next cycle.

This approach may or may not be acceptable. Naturally, it is better to dimension the system to eliminate the need for such migration (that is, toward resource adequacy). On the other hand, as a means of error recovery after a transient burst, this approach provides an increased chance that the deadlines missed will be less important.

3.40.5 Distributed Processing Environments

As we move from the shared-memory (SM) multiprocessor-type system to DM multicomputers, it is normal to encounter allocation difficulties; however, in the case of scheduling, the differences are not too significant. One major difference that can occur, of course, is in the case of migration, where the time required to migrate a process is increased. A good solution to the time-delay problem is, instead of applying migration, to simply retain duplicate copies of the processes program code in the separate PEs. This duplication can be done by static allocation or dynamically in anticipation of the requirements. When the actual process is to be scheduled for execution, only relevant state information (the activation record) need be transmitted across the network.

3.40.6 Scheduling Intercommunication Network Access

Messages being transferred over an ICN compete for the use of the ICN. In hard real-time systems, it will be important to schedule the use of the ICN in a manner that is consistent with the scheduling of the processes in the PEs; otherwise, parallel processing can be counterproductive. If this care is not taken, priority inversion may come into play in utilizing the ICN resource. In this regard, it is important to note that standard FIFO message-passing protocols cause problems.

Although the ICN is just another resource, some important issues distinguish the scheduling of the use of network channels from processor scheduling (see Stankovic, 1988).

- — unlike a processor, which has a single point of access, a communication channel has many points of access, that is, one terminal for each attached physical node.
- — while preemptive algorithms may be appropriate for scheduling processes on a single processor, preemption during message transmission will mean that the entire message will need retransmitting.

— in addition to deadlines imposed by the application processes, deadlines may also be imposed by buffer availability — the contents of a buffer must be transmitted before new data can be placed in it.

— in processor scheduling, it is common to use the concept of priority to distinguish hard real-time processes from softer ones. Furthermore, it is usually assumed that the scheduler can support a sufficient range of priority levels, say to support rate-monotonic scheduling. For some ICNs (for example, buses) only a limited number of distinct priority levels is allowed to resolve bus contention.

Some investigations have been made concerning the use of rate monotonic scheduling in the context of bus scheduling. However, in general, research concerning the relationship of ICNs and real-time systems has not been widely pursued (especially for hard real-time systems).

3.41 PROCESS DEADLOCK AND LIVENESS

We now turn our attention to two scheduling and allocation problem areas. The first of these (process deadlock) occurs in resource-limited environments; however, the liveness problem can occur in resource-limited or resource-adequate environments.

Deadlock occurs when two or more processes have been allocated resources and all require further resources in order to progress. It may happen that, specifically, the resources required for progressing are held by another process(es) who in turn is waiting on the availability of resources held by the other process(es). DEADLOCK occurs and none of the processes can proceed. (We considered this problem earlier in relationship to the buffer resources of a store and forward ICN.)

The simplest solution to the deadlock problem is to assure that a process has all the resources it requires prior to being activated. This solves the problem but introduces the further problem of poor resource utilization. Thus, other solutions that guarantee deadlock freeness should be and have been explored.

3.41.1 Circular Waiting

To avoid circular waiting, a linear ordering on all resource types can be enforced. Each resource type that can be allocated is assigned a number in this ordering. Given that R is the set of resource types,

$$R = \{r_1, r_2, \cdots, r_n\}$$

and that a function F given a resource type returns its position in the linearly ordered set, we can apply the following discipline.

If a process has a resource r_j and requests a resource r_k, the request will only be honored if

$$F(r_j) < F(r_k)$$

Alternatively, a process requesting a resource r_j must release all resources r_i, where

$$F(r_i) < F(r_j)$$

This technique will guarantee that circular waits will never develop; however, based upon the process requirements, it may place severe restrictions on the progress of processes.

3.41.2 Liveness

Another undesirable phenomenon that can potentially arise in parallel processing environments is that two or more processes enter nonterminating loops or seize a large quantity of resources without progressing. In these situations, the system appears to do nothing or becomes highly degraded. Such situations naturally should be verified prior to installation of the software. On the other hand, as a security measure, the scheduler(s) should implement some form of time limitation for process execution, after which the process is preempted and fault procedures are followed.

3.42 RESOURCE ADEQUACY

Given the complications of allocation and scheduling of real-time processes in parallel processing environments, one might ask the simple question, As hardware resources become less and less expensive, is it wise to continue to seek solutions to optimize the utilization of resource-limited systems? Granted, these problems are intellectually challenging, but since they cannot be completely solved in the general case (are NP-complete), there will always be a degree of uncertainty and unpredictability concerning the implementation of time-critical real-time processes in such environments. Dijkstra (1989) has also pointed to this situation:

> It is only too easy to design resource sharing systems with such intertwined allocation strategies that no amount of applied queuing theory will prevent most unpleasant performance surprises from emerging. The designer who counts performance predictability among his responsibilities tends to come up with designs that need no queuing theory at all.

One can speculate that alternatives providing a compromise between the resource-adequate philosophy of direct-mapped solutions, and the flexibility afforded by program interpretation, can lead to new philosophies, paradigms, and models. With these final comments, we conclude our discussion of the critical area of process allocation and scheduling as well as our presentation of parallel processing.

References

Amdahl, G. (1967). Validity of the Single Processor Approach to Achieving Large Scale Computing, *AFIPS Conference Proceedings*, Vol. 30, pp. 483-485, Thompson Books, Washington, DC.

Burns, A., and A. Wellings (1990). *Real-time Systems and Their Programming Languages*, Addison-Wesley, Reading, MA.

Conway, R.W., W.L. Maxwell, and L.W. Miller (1967). *Theory of Scheduling*, Addison-Wesley, Reading, MA.

Dijkstra, E.W. (1989). "The Next Forty Years." Personal Note EWD 1051.

Gustafson, J.L, G.R. Montry, and R.E. Benner (1988). Development of Parallel Methods for a 1024-Processor Hypercube, *SIAM Journal of Scientific and Statistical Computing*, Vol. 9, No. 4.

Hwang, K., and F.A. Briggs (1984). *Computer Architecture and Parallel Processing*, McGraw-Hill, New York.

Johnson, G.M. (1989). Exploiting Parallelism in Computational Science, *FGCS (Fifth Generation Computing Systems)*, Vol. 5, Nos. 2-3, pp. 319-337.

Lehoczky, J.P., L. Sha, and J.K. Stronsnider (1987). Aperiodic Scheduling in a Hard Real-Time Environment, Technical Report, Department of Computer Science, Carnegie Mellon University, Pittsburgh, PA.

Leu, J.S. (1987). Strategies for Retargeting Existing Sequential Programs for Parallel Processing, Ph.D. Dissertation, North Carolina State University.

Liu, C.L., and J.W. Layland (1973). Scheduling Algorithms for Multiprogramming in a Hard Real-time Environment, *Journal of the ACM*, Vol. 21, No. 1, pp. 46-61.

Mauney, J., D.P. Agrawal, Y.K. Choe, E.A. Harcourt, S. Kim, and W.J. Staats (1989). Computational Models and Resource Allocation for Supercomputers, *Proceedings of the IEEE*, Vol. 77, No. 12, pp. 1859-1874.

Mok, A.K., (1983). Fundamental Design Problems of Distributed Systems for Hard Real-time Environments, Ph.D. Thesis, Laboratory for Computer Science, Massachussets Institute of Technology, MIT/LCS/TR-297, Cambridge, MA.

Mok, A.K., and M.L. Dertouzos (1978). Multiprocessor Scheduling in a Hard Real-time Environment, *Proceedings of the 7th Texas Conference on Computer Systems.*

Rajkumar, R., L. Sha, and J.P. Lehoczky (1988). Real-time Synchronization Protocols for Multiprocessors, Technical Report, Department of Computer Science, Carnegie Mellon University, Pittsburgh, PA.

Sha, L., and J.P. Lehoczky (1987). The Priority Inheritance Protocol: An Approach to Real-time Synchronization, Technical Report, Department of Computer Science, Carnegie-Mellon University, Pittsburgh, PA.

Sha, L., J.P. Lehoczky, and R. Rajkumar (1986). Solutions to some Practical Problems in Prioritizing Preemptive Scheduling. In *Proceedings IEEE Real-Time Symposium*, IEEE Computer Society Press, Washington, DC.

Stankovic, J.A. (1988). Real-time Computing Systems: The Next Generation, COINS Technical Report 88-06, Department of Computer and Information Science, University of Massachusetts, Amherst, MA.

Stankovic, J.A., K. Ramamritham, and S. Cheng (1985). Evaluation of a Flexible Task Scheduling for Distributed Hard Real-time Systems, *IEEE Transactions on Computers*, Vol. 32, No. 12, pp. 1130-1143.

Worlton, J. (1987). Toward a Science of Parallel Computation, *Computational Mechanics-Advances and Trends*, AMD Vol. 75, ASME, New York, pp. 23-35.

Chapter **4**

APPLICATION DOMAINS

We examine a few areas of application in which parallel processing can effectively be exploited in real-time environments. The following aspects are treated in the chapter.

- that the need for high-speed computation in real-time applications will increase as research into important scientific and engineering applications is intensified (190)
- that a good algorithm is measured in terms of its running time, number of PEs utilized, cost, and efficiency (193)
- direct-mapped problems are considered with an emphasis upon the decomposition of digital signal-processing applications — systolic and wavefront examples are provided (195)
- SIMD PE array applications in the area of image and graphic processing are explored, including an example of solving two-dimensional FFTs (**F**ast **F**ourier **T**ransforms) (209)
- an MIMD application involving the solutions of recurrence and tridiagonal systems of equations is considered (220)
- other application domains are briefly described, including fractal geometry, parallel simulation, data bases, and information retrieval (224)

The physics Nobel laureate Kenneth G. Wilson has identified several of the "Grand Challenges to Computational Science" (see Wilson, 1989). In research areas such as accurate weather forecasting, astronomy, astrophysics, materials science, electronic structure of molecules, molecular biology, and fluid dynamics, even the fastest of today's supercomputers is orders of magnitude too slow to provide the processing power required for accurate experimentation. Wilson also points out that it is not just the lack of processing power, but the need of good algorithm development, programming languages, and parallel thinking that is the key to future development.

While the goals we set for today's industrial real-time systems are modest compared to the advanced computations called for by Wilson, it is important to reflect on the rapid developments that permit us to introduce real-time control systems into physical environments in the world around us. Thus, if breakthroughs are made in being able to compute important phenomena (for example, the electronic structure of molecules), it could affect some important classes of real-time system development in the future. Thus, we can conclude that advanced real-time systems will always be faced with the need for utilizing high-performance parallel processing systems.

4.1 NUMERICAL PROBLEMS

In Chapter 2 (figure 2.2), we observed that real-time applications involve the modeling of various real-world phenomena. While we should by **no** means limit our view of real-time applications to numerical problems, they are inherent in many scientific and engineering applications of computers, including, of course, providing the heart of many industrial real-time systems. In these applications, algorithms are applied to, for example, finding zeros of functions, solving systems of equations, and calculating eigenvalues, and to perform a variety of numerical tasks, including differentiation, integration, interpolation, approximation, and Monte Carlo simulations.

In many cases, it is the speedup of the numerical computations incorporated in time-critical processes that dictates the need for parallel processing. Thus, it is quite common to seek solutions based upon *application parallelism* as well as *system parallelism.*

Research and development results concerning parallel numerical algorithms have been reported by, among many, Ortega and Voigt (1987), Quinn (1987), and Akl (1989). Quinn, for example has subdivided algorithmic parallelism into:

— pipelined algorithms (including systolic and wavefront)
— partitioned algorithms
— relaxed algorithms

The *pipelined algorithms* are applicable to a wider class of numerical problems than digital signal processing and wavefront and systolic array solutions. At larger granularities we can find pipelining in the application of dataflow concepts, as presented in Chapter 12.

By *partitioned algorithms*, we mean situations where one computational process is divided among multiple PEs and where the final combination of partial solutions requires synchronization among the subprocesses. The partitioning can be prescheduled at compile time or self-scheduled at run time. By *relaxed algorithms*, Quinn means those algorithms that can proceed without the need for explicit synchronization.

In the current chapter, we shall only consider a few numerical problems and approaches to solving them in the framework of particular parallel processing hardware resource paradigms. Thus, the reader is referred to the excellent general literature in this area for a deeper presentation of the parallel processing of numerical problems.

To portray the notion of an application domain and its effect upon the selection of paradigms, consider the BMR model in Figure 4.1, where we have indicated a slice through the various elements. Looking from the top down or bottom up, it portrays the fact that within an application domain a particular resource structure model, behavioral description approach, and process allocation strategy is normally best suited to meet application requirements. Thus, we examine application and system parallelism with respect to the general categories of paradigms and models that have been presented in Chapter 3.

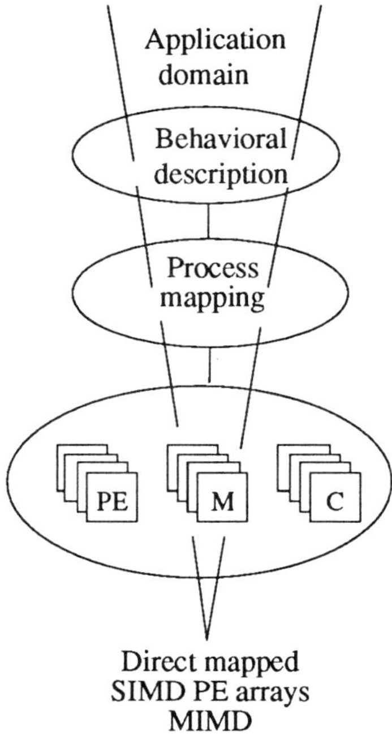

Figure 4.1. Application Domains for Various Paradigms

4.2 GOOD ALGORITHMS

Wilson called for good algorithm development as a key factor. But what are good algorithms? Further, how can we measure their "goodness"?

These are questions for which we must seek quantitative answers in terms of speedup, cost, and efficiency with respect to available resources. In analyzing algorithms, as defined by Akl (1989), the measurements of goodness are normally related to *running time*, *number of PEs utilized*, *cost*, and *efficiency*. In addition to these standard metrics, a number of technology-related measures may also be used when it is known that the algorithm is destined to run a computer based on a particular paradigm and hardware resource technology. Therefore, let us establish a general frame of reference for evaluating parallel algorithms.

4.2.1 Running Time

We define *running time* as the time taken by the algorithm to solve a problem on a parallel computer, that is, the elapsed time from the moment it starts to the moment it terminates. If various PEs do not begin and end their computation simultaneously, then the running time is equal to the elapsed time until the last PE terminates.

(*Note*: In real-time environments, systems do not terminate; they continue. Consequently, we shall equate termination, in this regard, as some specific point in the real-time cycle during which the algorithm is applied. The measured algorithm may, for example, be contained in a periodic process or in an aperiodic process with a deadline.)

4.2.2 Counting Steps

The definition of what constitutes a step varies among theoretical models of computation. The RAM (**r**andom **a**ccess **m**achine) and its extension to PRAM (**p**arallel version) are often utilized. These models are based upon a read-only input tape, a write-only output tape, and a program(s). Memories consist of an unbounded sequence of registers. Simple instructions of the form load, store, read, write, add, subtract, test, jump, and halt are provided. From this model, worst-case (as well as expected) time and space complexities are calculated. We shall not explore this model further; however, it is used widely by those who work in the field of algorithm analysis and complexity. Further information is provided by, among others, Quinn (1987).

It is clear that the running of a parallel algorithm normally contains *computational* as well as *routing* steps. For a problem of size n, the parallel worst-case running time of an algorithm is a function of n, which will be our basis for comparison.

4.2.3 Lower Bound and Upper Bound

In answering the question, Is this algorithm the fastest for a problem?, we normally seek to establish a *lower bound* on the number of steps required to solve the problem in the worst case. If the number of steps an algorithm executes is the fastest possible and is of the same *order* as the lower bound, it is said to be *optimal.* If a new algorithm is faster than all known algorithms for the problem, then we say that it has established a new *upper bound* on the number of steps to solve the problem in the worst case.

Let us now contrast two algorithm examples with respect to lower and upper bounds as well as optimality:

— To date, no algorithm is known for multiplying two n x n matrices in n^2 steps. Standard textbook algorithms require $O(n^3)$. However, the upper bound on this problem is established by an algorithm requiring $O(n^x)$ operations at most, where $x < 2.5$.

— By contrast, several sorting algorithms exist that require $O(n \log n)$ operations and are hence optimal.

Another point of view in defining speedup in evaluating a parallel algorithm is to compare it with the best known sequential algorithm for solving the same problem. Thus speedup can be defined as

$$\text{Speedup} = \frac{\text{worst-case running time of fastest known sequential algorithm}}{\text{worst-case running time of the parallel algorithm}}$$

4.2.4 Number of Processors

The number of PEs used in a parallel solution is important due to the practical matters of cost and maintenance, as well as the all-important aspect of reliability. Therefore, the larger the number of PEs required to solve a problem, the more expensive the solution becomes.

4.2.5 Algorithm Cost

The cost of a parallel algorithm is given as the product

$$\text{Cost} = \text{parallel running time x number of PEs used}$$

The cost equals the number of steps executed by all PEs in solving the problem in the worst case (assuming that all PEs execute the same number of steps). If this assumption is not true, then the cost is an upper bound on the total number of steps executed.

Assume that a lower bound on the number of sequential operations required in the worst case to solve a problem is known. If the cost of a parallel algorithm for that problem matches this lower bound within a constant multiplicative factor, then the algorithm is *cost optimal*. On the other hand, a parallel algorithm is *not cost optimal* if a sequential algorithm exists whose running time is smaller than the parallel algorithm's cost.

4.2.6 Model Independent Lower Bounds

If we let $\Omega\ (T(n))$ be a lower bound on the number of sequential steps required to solve a problem of size n; then $\Omega\ (T(n)/N)$ is a lower bound on the running time of any algorithm that uses N PEs to solve that problem. Relating this to our earlier discussion of the lower bound for sorting algorithms:

> Since $\Omega\ (n \log n)$ is the sequential lower bound, the equivalent lower bound on any parallel algorithm using n PEs is $\Omega\ (\log n)$.
> *Note*: Omega Ω (order at least) is defined in Chapter 1.

4.2.7 Algorithm Efficiency

When no optimal algorithm is known for solving a problem, the *efficiency* of a parallel algorithm for that problem is used to evaluate its cost as follows:

$$\text{Efficiency} = \frac{\text{worst-case running time of fastest known sequential algorithm}}{\text{cost of parallel algorithm}}$$

Usually, efficiency ≤ 1; otherwise, a faster sequential algorithm can be obtained from the parallel version.

The analysis of algorithms that has been presented can be generally applied in considering parallel algorithms versus sequential algorithms and has been presented in order to provide the reader with a reference for evaluating the goodness of algorithms. We now consider the characteristics of a few real-time, system-relevant application areas.

4.3 DIRECT-MAPPED APPLICATIONS

As considered in Chapter 3, it is the application processes representing the underlying algorithms and data that become the object for realization. The required problem behavior is often expressed as a set of equations that is mapped into regular pipelined structures (systolic or wavefront) or synthesized into some form of optimal solution, as in the case of DSP applications. Since digital signal processing is considered to be a basic means of realizing an important class of real-time system functions, it will be examined somewhat closer than the other direct-mapped forms.

4.3.1 Characteristics of Signal Processing

Signal-processing techniques includes various methods and techniques for extracting information obtained either from nature itself, via sensors, or from other machines. Generally, the aim of signal processing is to reduce the information content in a signal to facilitate a decision about what information the signal carries. In other instances the aim may be to retain the information content and to transform the signal into a form that is more suitable for transmission, storing, and the like, often as a partial function in a distributed real-time environment.

Modern signal processing is mainly concerned with digital techniques, but it also includes analog and sampled-data techniques, which often are used in the interfaces between digital systems and the outside analog world. Switched-Capacitor (SC) techniques are well suited for many signal-processing tasks. Major applications are found in the interfaces between analog and digital systems, where filters, A/D, and D/A converters are needed. An important advantage is that such SC circuits can be integrated together with digital CMOS circuits on the same chip. Hence, a fully integrated, direct-mapped DSP *system-on-a-chip* is feasible.

The major reason behind the (increasing) use of discrete time and digital signal-processing techniques is that problems caused by errors, for example, drift and ageing of the components, are circumvented. For analog systems, especially for frequency selective filters, realizations with minimal circuit element sensitivity have been developed. Thus, by utilizing high-quality components, high-performance filters can be implemented. At the other end of the spectrum, inexpensive and simple filters can be realized with inexpensive, low-tolerance components. On the other hand, there is a practical limit for the performance of analog components, for example, the tolerance of a resistor. Even with the best components available, many important functions cannot be implemented in an economical way. Fortunately, no such lower bounds exist for DSP techniques.

The flexibility of digital signal processing, which is indirectly due to the *independence of coefficient sensitivity,* makes it easy to change and even dynamically adapt the on-line processing to changing situations, for example, with adaptive filters. Thus, expensive tuning procedures can also eliminated. Further, the coefficient sensitivity in an algorithm determines a lower bound on the round-off errors or *signal quality*.

In practice, an arbitrary good signal quality can be maintained by using sufficiently high numerical accuracy. Note that the accuracy in floating-point numbers is determined by the mantissa. Generally, a high dynamic range (large exponent) is not required in good signal-processing algorithms. Hence, DSP algorithms are often implemented utilizing fixed-point arithmetic.

Latch-up and different types of oscillations resulting from normal disturbances may appear in analog systems, but most often analog systems return to normal function when the disturbance disappears. Corresponding phenomena are also present in DSP algorithms, but also some unique phenomena, due to finite word-length effects, are present. In fact, a major design problem is to maintain the stability of the system and recover to normal operation in the presence of external disturbances. Therefore, algorithms that guarantee that the system will return to normal operation when the disturbance has vanished are of special importance. Disturbances that cause the abnormal behavior can originate from transients via power supply lines, ionic radiation, initial values in the memories at start-up, or abnormal input signals. The most important filter algorithms with this guaranteed stability are wave digital filters and nonrecursive FIR-filters (**F**inite **I**mpulse **R**esponse).

The development of VLSI technology is an important prerequisite for making advanced and complex DSP techniques viable, but also economically competitive. The use of VLSI technology also contributes to increased system reliability. Thus, we find increasing interest in the development of ASIC (**A**pplication **S**pecific **I**ntegrated **C**ircuits), as well as in the methods to design, implement, and test the circuits. In this respect, the development of VHDL provides a significant step forward.

While DSP algorithms are often implemented via programmed solutions in single-PE environments, in this section and in this book, we shall emphasize the direct-mapped solutions, with particular emphasis on the VLSI hardware resource solution space.

Computational Properties of DSP Algorithms

On the surface, most DSP algorithms look very simple since they consist of a set of simple arithmetic expressions that are being evaluated repeatedly. Complicated data structures are seldom used. These facts are often misunderstood by novice hardware designers, who may be tempted to modify the algorithm to suit the artifact idiosyncrasies of the hardware, design techniques, and tools. Such uninitiated and often undocumented changes of the algorithm must be avoided, because underlying the DSP algorithm is a complex set of requirements that may be difficult to appraise directly from a simple change in the algorithm. For example, intricate bit manipulations and nonlinear operations are used in most speech-coding systems. A simple change of a quantization scheme may drastically affect the speech quality. In fact, the quality of most DSP algorithms is directly related to various finite word-length effects. Another, even more important aspect concerns the stability of the algorithm with respect to various types of nonlinearities.

Most recursive algorithms with nonlinearities are unstable and will produce different types of unwanted oscillations, *parasitic oscillations*. Temporary malfunction of the hardware may also cause parasitic oscillations. Sophisticated theories and methods are therefore included in the algorithm design to assure that such oscillations cannot persist. As mentioned previously with respect to disturbances, examples of filter algorithms that suppresses all parasitic oscillations include wave digital filters and nonrecursive FIR filters. To avoid these dangerous pitfalls, it is necessary to use a design method that guarantees integrity at each design step involved in transforming the DSP algorithm into a working system.

We shall now consider, via an example, the mainstream approach to decomposing a signal-flow graph to a direct-mapped solution.

4.3.2 Decomposition to Node Values

Equations and signal-flow diagrams provide the starting point for deriving the expressions for node values in a computable order. In our discussion of behavioral description, we considered in Figure 3.22 a second-order section in direct form II. Figure 4.2 shows the corresponding, fully specified signal-flow graph where the ordering of the additions is indicated and the required quantization in the recursive loop is shown.

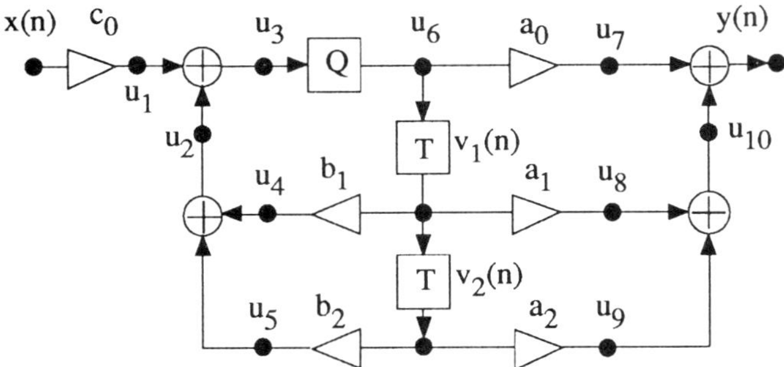

Figure 4.2. Fully Specified Signal-flow Graph with Node Numbers

The decomposition of the signal-flow graph into a precedence form that more clearly indicates the computational order of the differential equations is accomplished by applying the steps of the following algorithm.

1. Collapse unnecessary nodes in the fully specified signal-flow graph by removing all branches with transmittance = 1. Note that transmittances = -1, in many cases, can be propagated into adjacent branches. This will yield an equivalent, and eventually simpler, signal-flow graph with fewer nodes and branches.
2. Assign node variables to all nodes in the fully specified signal-flow graph as follows:
   - Input nodes with the sequence variables, $x_i(n)$.
   - Output nodes with the sequence variables, $y_i(n)$.
   - The contents in the delay elements with the sequence variables, $v_i(n)$.
   - The outputs from the basic operations, which are all the remaining nodes, with the variables, u_i.

The computational order for the branches, corresponding to arithmetic operations, is determined in steps 3 to 7.

3. Remove all branches with delay elements in the signal-flow graph.
4. Select all initial nodes in the (remaining) signal-flow graph and denote this set of nodes by N_i, as shown in the following. The algorithm is not sequentially computable if there are no initial nodes left in the remaining part of the signal-flow graph.

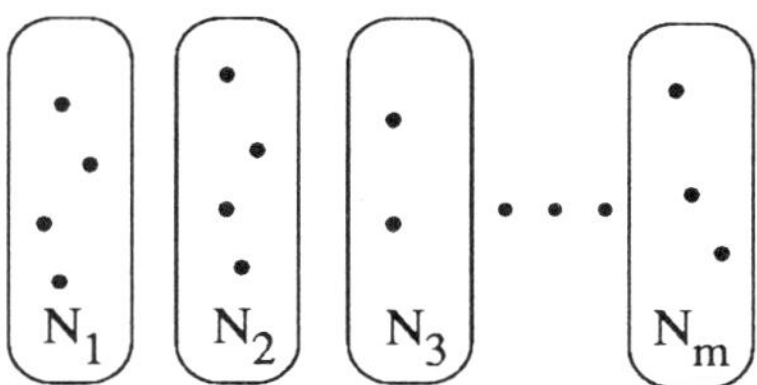

5. Delete all basic operations that are executable, that is, operations for which all inputs are initial nodes.
6. If there are any nodes left, repeat the procedure from step 4.
7. Connect the nodes with branches (basic operations) according to the signal-flow graph. Note that the node variables $v_i(n)$ always belong to the first set of nodes, while the node variables, u_i, belongs to the other sets.

A method for updating the variables corresponding to the delay elements is given in steps 8 to 12.

8. Extract all branches with delay elements in the original signal-flow graph.
9. Group the terminal nodes in the (remaining) signal-flow graph. A pathological case exists if there are no terminal nodes; that is, the signal-flow graph has a closed loop of delay elements.
10. Delete all branches connected to terminal nodes.
11. If there are any nodes left, repeat the procedure from step 9.
12. Connect the nodes with delay branches according to the signal-flow graph obtained is step 7.

We shall not illustrate the step-by-step development of the algorithm; however, we provide the final result from applying the algorithm to the example, in Figure 4.2, as portrayed in Figure 4.3.

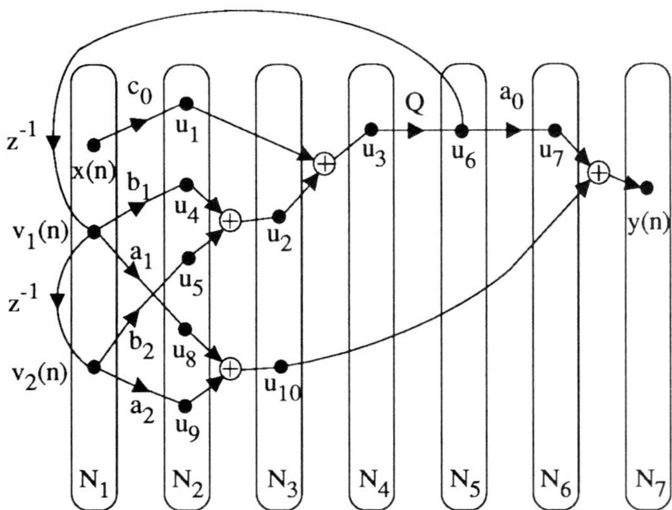

Figure 4.3. Direct Form II Expressed in Precedence Form

4.3.3 Nonsequentially Computable Algorithms

If the process of applying the decomposition algorithm is terminated prematurely due to the lack of initial nodes, the remaining precedence graph contains a delay-free loop. An example is shown in Figure 4.4.

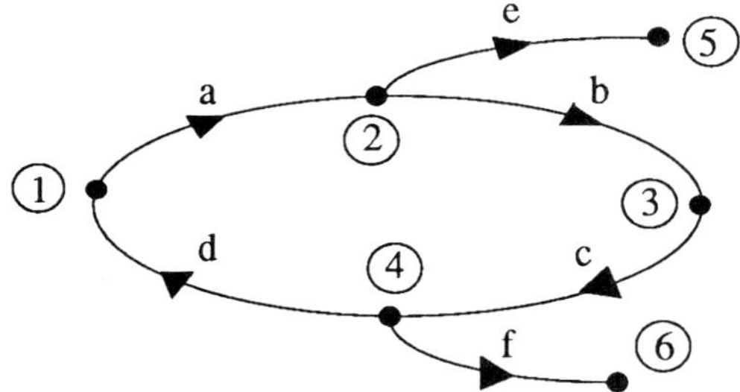

Figure 4.4. Nonsequentially Computable Algorithm

The presence of a delay-free loop indicates that part of the algorithm is *nonsequentially computable* (see Fettweis, 1976). Such algorithms cannot be implemented as a computer program or in digital hardware. Hence, these algorithms have no practical use which leads us to the following theorem:

A necessary and sufficient condition for an algorithm to be sequentially computable is that every directed loop in the signal-flow graph contain at least one delay element.

4.3.4 Difference Equations in Computable Order

For our example, the difference equations in a computational order can directly be obtained from the precedence graph in Figure 4.3. Note that the node values in N1 are known at the beginning of the sample interval. Hence, the operations with output nodes belonging to set N2 have all the necessary inputs and can therefore be executed. Next, the operations, with output nodes belonging to set N3, have all inputs available and can be executed. This process is repeated until the last set of nodes has been reached. The operations belonging to the different sets are executed sequentially, while the operations within a set can be executed in parallel. Finally, we update all delay elements. Thus, the resulting set of differential equations is as provided in Figure 4.5.

Nodes	Equations
N2	$u_1 := c_0x(n)$ $u_4 := b_1v_1(n)$ $u_5 := b_2v_2(n)$ $u_8 := a_1v_1(n)$ $u_9 := a_2v_2(n)$
N3	$u_2 := u_4 + u_5$ $u_{10} := u_8 + u_9$
N4	$u_3 := u_1 + u_2$
N5	$u_6 := [u_3]Q$
N6	$u_7 := a_0u_6$
N7	$y(n) := u_7 + u_{10}$
N1	$v_2(n+1) := v_1(n)$ $v_1(n+1) := u_6$

Figure 4.5. Difference Equations for Direct Form II

The order of the basic operations can always be interchanged within a set, and in some cases some operations can be performed at a later instance of time, for example, u_{10} can be computed after u_3. The system of difference equations in Figure 4.5 can therefore be simplified to:

$$u_6 := [c_0x(n) + b_1v_1(n) + b_2v_2(n)]Q$$
$$y(n) := a_0u_6 + a_1v_1(n) + a_2v_2(n)$$
$$v_2(n+1) := v_1(n)$$
$$v_1(n+1) := u_6$$

The number of memory cells needed depends on the order of the computations, as well as the number of the PEs required to perform the basic operations; however, the quantity required is bounded from above by the number of nodes.

By associating appropriate execution times to the operations, represented by the branches in the precedence graph, a longest (time) directed path is defined. The time taken by this path is the shortest time in which the algorithm can be computed. This path is the *critical path*. Generally, one or several equally long critical paths may exist.

The longest directed paths in Figure 4.3 are easily identified by inspection and assuming that all operations take one time unit,

MULT(b_1)-ADD-ADD-QUANT-MULT(a_0)-ADD = 6 time units, and
MULT(b_2)-ADD-ADD-QUANT-MULT(a_0)-ADD = 6 time units.

Apparently, in the first time step, five multiplications can be done in parallel. In the second time step, only two additions can be done, and so on. However, it is not necessary to perform an operation earlier than the result is required. Consequently, the operations should be scheduled such that the total quantity of resources, in terms of power consumption, chip area, and other factors, is minimized.

4.3.5 Maximal Sampling Rate

The maximal sample rate of a signal-flow graph is determined by the recursive parts in a signal-flow graph. In principle, nonrecursive parts of the signal-flow graph, for example, input and output branches, do not limit the sample rate; however, to achieve this limit, excessive delays may have to be introduced. This problem will be discussed later in more detail.

The *minimal sample period* (see Renfors and Neuvo, 1981, and Fettweis, 1976) is

$$T_{min} = \max_{i}\{\frac{1}{N_i}\sum_{i} D_{opi}\}$$

where D_{opi} is the total delay due to the arithmetic operations and N_i the number of delay elements in the directed loop i, respectively.

The minimal sample period is also referred to as the *iteration bound*. This bound can be directly found from the signal-flow graph by inspection. Loops that yield T_{min} are called *critical loops*.

The signal-flow graph in Figure 4.6 has two loops. Loop 1 is the critical loop if

$$\frac{T_b + T_e + 2T_{add}}{2} > T_c + T_e + T_{add}$$

Otherwise, loop 2 is the critical loop.

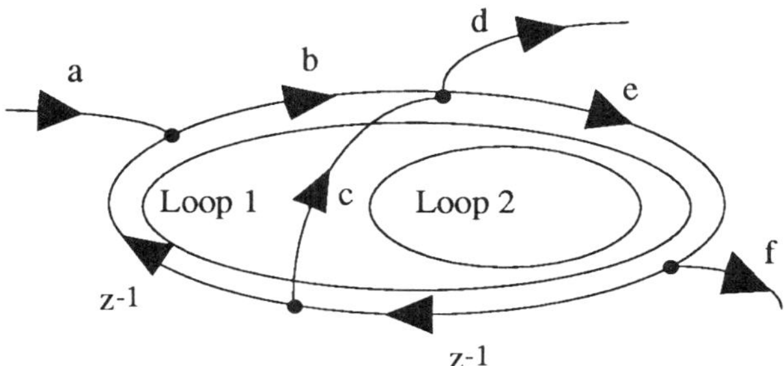

Figure 4.6. Signal-flow Graph with Two Directed Loops

The maximal sampling frequency is always bounded by the critical loop(s). However, input, output, and other nonrecursive branches in the signal-flow graph may have a critical path with a computational time that is longer than T_{min}. For example, one or several of the paths $T_a + T_b + T_d$, $T_a + T_b + T_e + T_f$, $T_c + T_d$, and $T_c + T_e + T_f$ in Figure 4.6 may be longer than T_{min}. In that case, the critical path(s) will limit the sample rate. Despite this limit, the theoretical sampling rate may still be achieved in one of two ways.

The first method involves interleaving of the computations and requires a duplication of the resources used in the critical path so that the effective computation rate is T_{min}. In this approach, computational resources must be added, since several critical paths are computed simultaneously.

The second method can be used if the application is such that the latency of the system is allowed to be increased; that is, additional delay may be introduced between the input and the output of the system. This means that the original critical path can be removed by inserting the additional delay elements so that a new and shorter critical path(s) is obtained.

Note that the maximal sample rate is, in principle, infinite for a nonrecursive structure, for example, an FIR filter. However, this requires that the critical path be broken up into infinitesimal small pieces. Thus, the delay of the filter will be infinite.

4.3.6 Creating Pipelines

Pipelining is accomplished by inserting delay(s) into the critical path so that it is divided into several paths of equal length. The data throughput is determined by the length of the new decreased path length. By pipelining, the parallelism is increased, which can result in a more efficient utilization of the computational resources. Pipelining can be applied at different hierarchical levels of the system. In digital circuits, pipelining corresponds to inserting latches between different levels of the logic circuits so that each pipelining level has the same computational delay.

Note that the parallelism in a structure is a fundamental property and cannot be changed. By inserting delay elements, possibly by pipelining, into the critical path, **a new structure** with a higher degree of parallelism is obtained.

Pipelining is introduced in the following two steps:

1. Introduce delay elements in series with the nonrecursive branch(es).
2. The delay elements are propagated into the branches so that they are divided into equal lengths of time.

Note: The order of an operation and delay element can be interchanged as long as the operator is time invariant. Further, pipelining can be applied for both linear and nonlinear operations.

Loop Folding

The operations inside a (possibly infinite) FOR loop correspond to the operations within one sample interval in a DSP algorithm. Loop-folding techniques have traditionally been utilized by compilers to increase the performance of compiled code. We now illustrate that loop folding is a form of pipelining that can be used in real-time systems to decrease latency or even reduce the cost of the implementation.

Figure 4.7 provides an example in which the kernel of a simple loop containing three multiplications and two additions is provided. (We assume that start and end are delay elements.) The loop has a critical path of length 3 and the operations are scheduled in three different control steps; thus, the sample period is three time units. We need two multipliers and one adder. It is not possible to rearrange or reschedule operations within the loop to further minimize the resources.

Now, consider that the operations are divided into two sections so that the critical paths are broken down into two pieces of length 2 and 1, respectively. The loop is folded as shown in Figures 4.8 and 4.9. There are two options; either we can minimize loop time (sample period) or minimize the resources. Figure 4.8 shows the first case; the loop time is decreased to 2. In the second case, illustrated in Figure 4.9, the resources are minimized. Only one multiplier and one adder are required. The drawback is that latency from input to output has been increased from the original 3 to 6. Unfortunately, excessive delay is a major problem in most signal-processing applications.

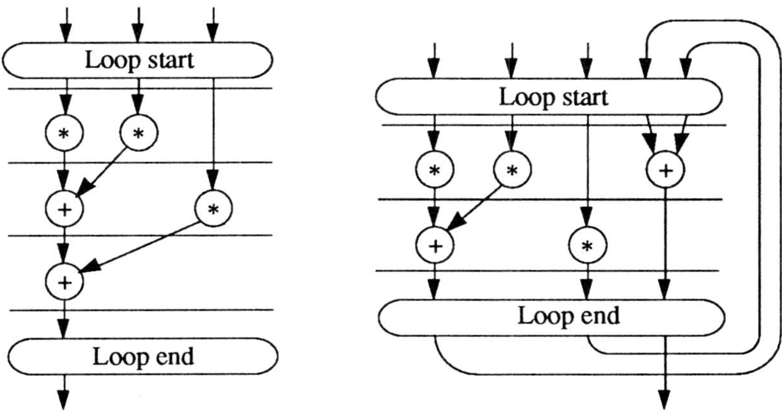

Figure 4.7. Original Loop **Figure 4.8.** Loop-folding to Minimize Loop Time

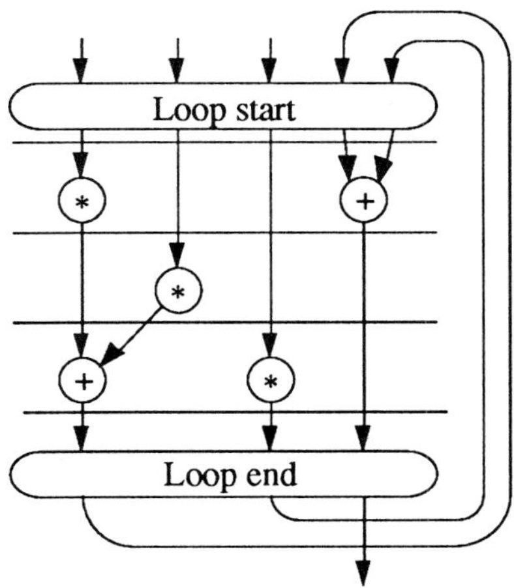

Figure 4.9. Loop-folding to Minimize Resources

Loop-folding is equivalent to recognizing the fact that some operations that belong to an interval or iteration can be started earlier than others and be executed at the same time as operations from previous intervals. We do not need to execute all operations in an interval before we start to execute operations from the next. This resembles scheduling a cyclic graph instead of a DAG (**d**irected **a**cyclic **g**raph) as described in Chapter 8.

PE Assignment

Both the algorithm and the hardware can be pipelined (that is, application and system parallelism can be exploited). In classical pipelines, only one operation is executed by each pipeline stage (PE), where the stages are separated by latches. Hence, a special PE is allocated to each stage of the (algorithm) pipeline. This leads to fixed and simple communication pattern between the PEs. This case can be referred to as a *structural pipeline*. A more general case is when the whole task is partitioned into several smaller subtasks that are pipelined. These subtasks can be executed by a structural pipeline. However, a more efficient manner of organizing the hardware, in terms of resources utilization, is to allow the pipeline stages to share resources. This system-level parallelism can be referred to as *functional pipelining*.

This concludes our introduction to the principal concepts of DSP applications and their mappings into pipelined structures. We shall delve deeper into the questions of schedules and optimality in Chapter 8.

4.3.7 Systolic Array Example

To illustrate a specific direct mapping of an algorithm to the systolic array form, let us consider the multiplication of a matrix $A = (a_{ij})$ with a vector x represented by the transpose $(x_1, ..., x_n)^T$. Mead and Conway (1980) have shown that the product $y = (y_1, ..., y_n)^T$ can be computed according to the following recurrences:

$$y_i^{(1)} = 0$$
$$y_i^{(k+1)} = y_i^{(k)} + a_{ik}x_k$$
$$y_i = y_i^{(n+1)}$$

Thus, assuming A is an n x n band matrix with a bandwidth $w = p + q - 1$ (as illustrated for a case $p = 2$ and $q = 3$ in Figure 4.10), the recurrences can be evaluated by pipelining the x_i and y_i through the systolic array consisting of w linearly connected inner product step PEs, as illustrated in Figure 4.11.

The general computation proceeds by pumping the y_i (which are initially zero) to the left, while the x_i are pumped to the right and the a_{ij} are pumped down in a staggered manner. When a_{ij} elements are entered into a PE, they are multiplied by x_k and summed to y_i.

Observe how critical the topology and use of uniform time periods is in achieving this type of computation. Some general properties of systolic systems have been identified by Kung (1982) as follows:

— the design makes multiple use of each input data item.
— the design utilizes extensive concurrency.

— there are only a few types of simple cells (PEs).
— data and control flows are simple and regular.

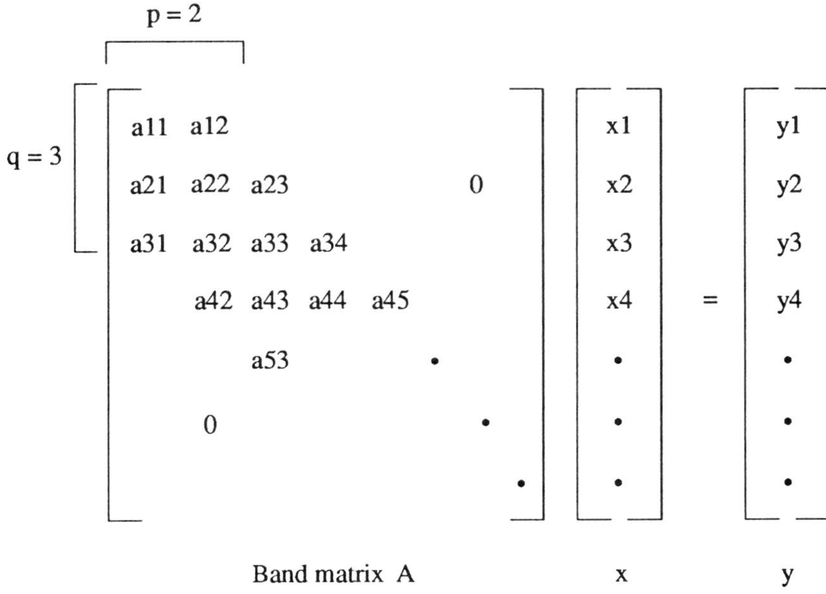

Figure 4.10. Multiplication of a Band Matrix by a Vector

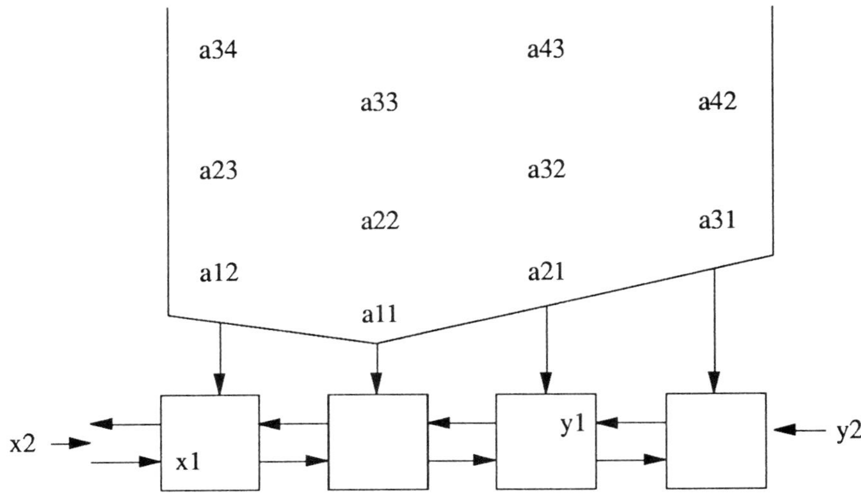

Figure 4.11. Systolic Array for the Band Matrix Multiplication Example

However, in very large systolic arrays, cell synchronization can be difficult to achieve due to clock skew problems. A good way to avoid this problem is to introduce the use of asynchronously controlled wavefront solutions.

4.3.8 Wavefront Array Example

To compare the systolic and wavefront array concepts in a practical example, we now consider a full matrix multiplication algorithm that can be executed on a square, orthogonal N x N wavefront array, as portrayed in Figure 4.12.

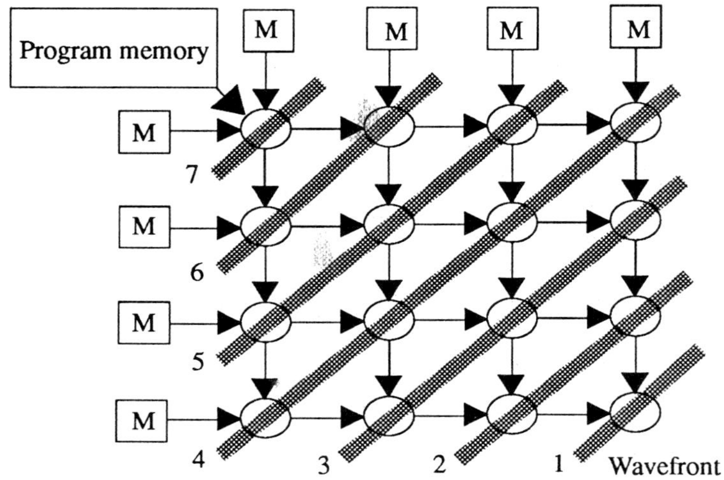

Figure 4.12. Wavefront Processing for Matrix Multiplication

Let $A = (a_{ij}), B = (b_{ij})$, and $C = A \times B = (c_{ij})$, where all are N x N matrices. Kung and others (1987) have shown that the matrix A can be decomposed into columns A_i and the matrix B into rows B_j; therefore,

$$C = A_1 * B_1 + A_2 * B_2 + \cdots + A_N * B_N$$

where the product $A_1 * B_1$ is the outer product. The matrix multiplication can then be achieved in N sets of wavefronts (recursions), each executing one outer product:

$$C^{(k)} = C^{(k-1)} + A_k * B_k$$

Initially, the elements of A are stored in M modules to the left (in columns), and those of B (in rows) in M modules on the top. Processing starts with PE (1, 1); thereafter appropriate, data are propagated to the neighbouring PEs, that is, PE (1, 2) and PE (2, 1), which execute their respective operations. The front of activity will be at PE (3, 1), PE (2, 2) and PE (1, 3). Thus, a computation wavefront moves down over the PE array. Once the wavefront is traversed, the first recursion is completed. Similar recursions can be executed concurrently with the first one by pipelining more wavefronts in succession immediately after the first wavefront. The wavefronts of successive recursions never interact, since once a PE performs its operations for one recursion it is available for the recursion.

Many useful computations can be performed by applying systolic and wavefront structures. On the other hand, the exploitation of a specific structure is most often tied to the application. Applications in the fields of DSP (**d**igital **s**ignal **p**rocessing), matrix arithmetic, and various nonnumeric processing have been successfully implemented. An interesting systolic array synthesis tool that exploits two-level pipelining (that is, external to as well as internal to the PEs) has been reported by Lisper (1990).

From a system point of view, it can be interesting to consider the use of multiple interconnected wavefront and systolic structures (*chaining*). In this case, we may wish to combine simpler operations performed by individual structures into a larger system, thus avoiding memory referencing, again improving upon bandwidth and performance.

This concludes our brief presentation of some representative uses of direct-mapped paradigms.

4.4 SIMD PE-ARRAY APPLICATIONS

The exploitation of the SIMD PE-array paradigm requires that application parallelism and system parallelism be well matched. On the other hand, the details of particular realizations of PE arrays vary. Consequently, some parallel algorithms function better on particular systems than upon others. This complicates the job of finding representative applications for PE-array resource structures. While PE arrays can be applied to a wide range of numerical (and even nonnumerical) computations, they have been widely applied (and well suited to) the problems of image and graphic processing. Thus, we shall illustrate some properties of these areas and how SIMD PE arrays can be utilized to advantage. Further application examples are provided in Chapter 10.

4.4.1 Characteristics of Image Processing

Images are represented as an array of picture elements, pixels (each pixel carrying a grayscale or color value). In most cases, rectangular pixels are used, but also hexagonal ones are sometimes provided. It is self-evident that the processing of images permits an enormous amount of geometric data parallelism; typical image sizes are 512 x 512 or 1024 x 1024 pixels.

The term *image processing* normally refers to the processing of natural images, that is, images derived from the external environment by devices such as cameras and scanners. Also, images constructed from measured data, for example, those achieved by back-projection in computer-aided tomography, magnetic resonance techniques, or ultrasound, are regarded as natural. *Graphic processing* or *computer graphics*, on the other hand, deals with the creation and manipulation of artificial images.

The image-processing area is usually divided into:

— image coding
— image enhancement and restoration
— image analysis and pattern recognition

The purpose of image coding is to compress the information in an image as much as possible. A key notion is the transformation of pictures to a form in which they are represented by less correlated data. In this representation, less significant data may be removed without too much distortion being introduced. The major tools in this area are reversible linear transforms like the Fourier transform.

The purpose of image enhancement and restoration is to derive a resultant image that is better in some sense than the original. In image enhancement, the judgment of what is considered "better" is often based upon the ability of a human observer to derive information from the image. Contrast enhancement, smoothing, and sharpening are examples of techniques used (see Figure 4.13). Pseudocoloring can be used to accentuate features in a gray-scale image. Restoration of an image normally refers to the process of reconstructing a degraded image by using some *a priori* knowledge of the phenomenon that caused the degradation. Examples of degradation phenomena are blurring by motion, defocus or noise, and geometrical degradation by aberrations of the optical system. Once again, the computations involved in the various filtering techniques also typically rely upon Fourier transforms.

Pattern recognition is the area that shows the largest range of variation. It also represents the greatest challenge for automatization in an industrial environment, for example, in contexts like automatic assembly or the control of automotive vehicles. A pattern recognition task calls for analysis of a picture leading to a description of it in terms of features. The computation of features normally involves a variety of picture-to-picture transformations. Many of these are useful as image enhancement operations.

When attempts to automate image interpretation were first made in the 1960s and early 1970s, the difficulty of the task and the enormous amount of computations required came as a surprise. A reason for this is that we humans are so good at seeing. This in turn implied that studies of biological visual systems might be fruitful when developing methods as well as architectures for computerized vision. No doubt, partial understanding of early stages in our visual system has influenced researchers to approach the image analysis and recognition task as consisting of different levels of processing. In Chapter 1, we considered one example, the Selfridge pandemonium model.

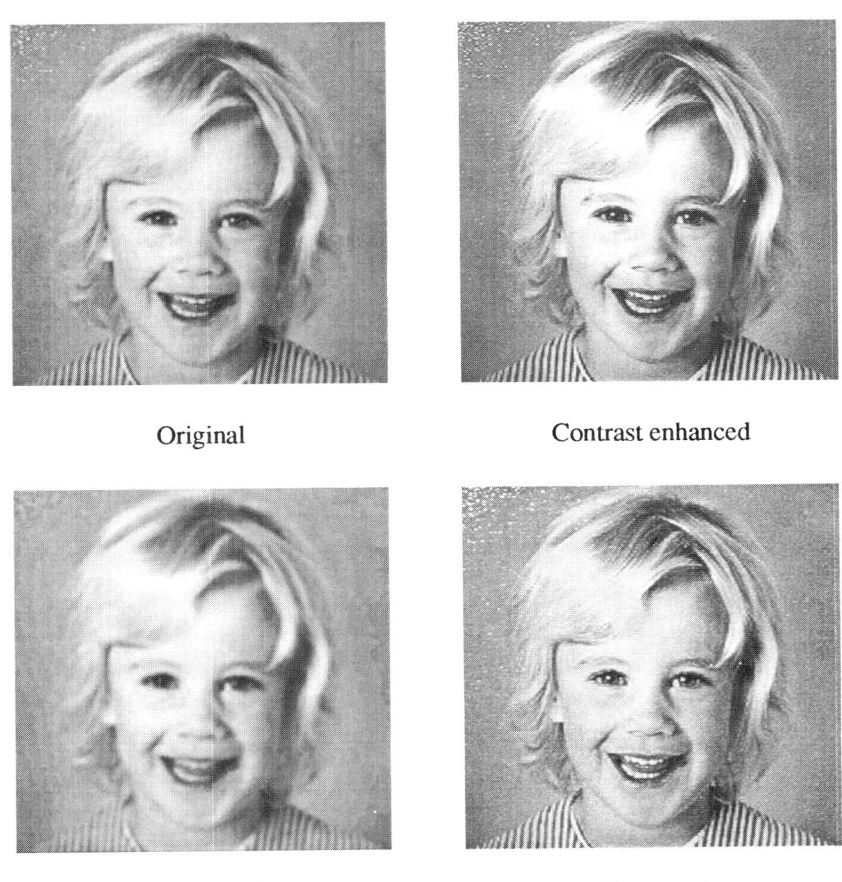

Figure 4.13. Contrast Enhancement, Smoothing, and Sharpening

4.4.2 Levels of Image Processing for Pattern Recognition

Image-processing functions for pattern recognition are normally considered to belong to one of four categories:

- — preprocessing
- — segmentation
- — description
- — recognition

The categories also represent a scale from low to high level, the first two considered as low level, the third as intermediate level, and the last as high-level image-processing functions, as portrayed in Figure 4.14.

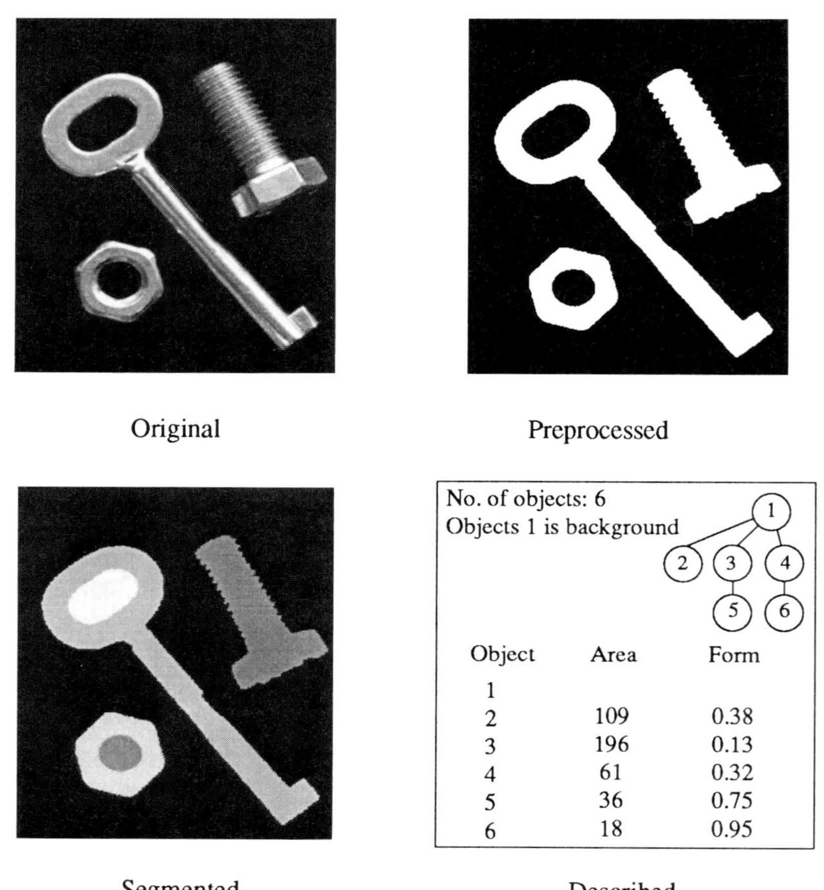

Object	Area	Form
1		
2	109	0.38
3	196	0.13
4	61	0.32
5	36	0.75
6	18	0.95

Figure 4.14. Preprocessing, Segmentation, and Description Steps

Low-level operations have images as input and images as output. It is well known from experience that parallelism is readily exploited — and absolutely necessary in these real-time tasks. Preprocessing includes enhancement and extractions of features. In the human visual system, this is done already in the first layers of neurons; that is, in the retina. The extraction of discontinuities is of paramount importance for subsequent steps of the perceptive system. Segmentation is the process of dividing the picture into different regions based upon the extracted discontinuities and similarities. It is often an iterative process exposing a high degree of parallelism.

Intermediate-level operations take preprocessed and segmented images and produce various kinds of descriptions and measurements on which decisions on higher levels can be based.

Image processing on the highest level includes methods like statistical pattern recognition and symbolic graph matching. In statistical pattern recognition, identification of an object or a scene is based on its location in the n-dimensional space spanned by the measured features. In symbolic graph matching, the scene at hand is described in the form of a graph (for example, showing spatial relationships) that is matched to a set of object model graphs.

4.4.3 Low- and Medium-level Operations

We now consider some examples of operations that are frequently used in image-processing systems. Most of them can be classified as low level, a few as medium level. We also make some comments on available forms of parallelism and on desirable architectural features.

Neighborhood Operations

In neighborhood operations, each pixel is replaced by a function of neighboring pixels within a window (the neighborhood), normally rectangular, in most cases even quadratic.

Operations of this type include convolution (the image matrix is convolved with the smaller window matrix), median filtering, and arbitrary logic operations on binary images. In the convolution group, also known as linear filters, we find mean value filtering (convolution with a kernel of all identical weights), template matching, and cross-correlation computations, for example.

Three forms of parallelism are available for neighborhood operations, as identified by Danielsson and Levialdi (1981). The first is *pixel bit parallelism*, meaning that all bits of a data item are treated in parallel. (Many specialists are so accustomed to this case, which is applied in the parallel arithmetic and logic of almost all conventional computers, that they often forget to regard it as a form of parallelism.)

The second is *neighborhood parallelism*. If all elements of the neighborhood, say 3 x 3 or 5 x 5, are available in parallel without explicit addressing, processing can be speeded up significantly. One of the first dedicated picture processors to be built, Picap I designed by Kruse (1973), used this principle. A 3 x 3 neighborhood was made available through the use of line-length shift registers.

The third form is *image parallelism*, meaning that several — maybe all — pixels of the image are treated in parallel using multiple PEs. The amount of parallelism available in this dimension is orders of magnitude greater than in the other two. Therefore, it is not surprising that, concurrent with the ability to build larger and larger systems, interest in parallelism in image processing has concentrated on this form.

Early examples of architectures using image parallelism are the STARAN processor (Potter, 1978), the British commercial system DAP from ICL (Reddaway, 1979), and the Swedish research machine LUCAS (Svensson, 1983). It is interesting to note that they are all bit serial and thus without pixel bit parallelism, the form of parallelism that is normally taken for granted.

Region Operations

The higher-level recognition tasks demand region information from the lower-level processing as a basis for their decisions. That is, the lower levels should be able to find, label, and extract parameters of regions that may be defined, for example, by intensity, texture, local gradients, or intraregion similarity.

In *labeling operations,* each region in an image is given a unique number. In the output image, each pixel is labeled with the number of the region to which it belongs (see Figure 4.15). Sequential machines typically scan the image pixel by pixel, from left to right, line by line, looking at the labeling of the previous row. After this processing, regions initially assumed to be separate but later found to be identical, must be merged by a relabeling process, again pixel by pixel. Image parallel architectures should be able to perform labeling with a high degree of parallelism by some kind of spreading process from a seed pixel in each region.

Parameter extraction involves computing a quantitative measure of some property (area, perimeter, form factor, moment) over a region. The ability to sum all elements of a matrix fast — or often to count the number of 1's in a binary matrix — is an important architectural feature for these tasks. It is self-evident that parallel approaches are necessary for this purpose. In our terminology, parameter extraction is an intermediate-level operation.

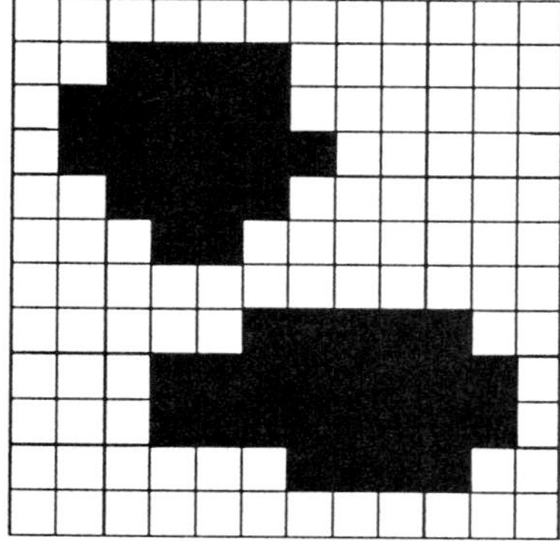

1	1	1	1	1	1	1	1	1	1	1	1
1	1	2	2	2	2	1	1	1	1	1	1
1	2	2	2	2	2	1	1	1	1	1	1
1	2	2	2	2	2	2	1	1	1	1	1
1	1	2	2	2	2	1	1	1	1	1	1
1	1	1	2	2	1	1	1	1	1	1	1
1	1	1	1	1	1	1	1	1	1	1	1
1	1	1	1	1	3	3	3	3	3	1	1
1	1	1	3	3	3	3	3	3	3	3	1
1	1	1	3	3	3	3	3	3	3	3	1
1	1	1	1	1	1	3	3	3	3	1	1
1	1	1	1	1	1	1	1	1	1	1	1

Figure 4.15. Labeling in a Binary Picture

Image Transforms

Two-dimensional transforms are frequently used for the purpose of image enhancement, restoration, and coding. They can also be used to prepare for description and pattern recognition.

The result of a two-dimensional Fourier transform applied to an image is a matrix describing the spatial frequencies of the original (a *frequency image*). Discarding the high frequencies and transforming back from the frequency to the image domain results in a low-pass filtering of the image. Low-pass filtering can also be achieved by a convolution operator. For large convolution kernels, a trip to the frequency domain (using, of course, the fast Fourier transform algorithm) may be advantageous, but this is strongly dependent of the architecture of the computer. Certain interconnection networks (perfect shuffle, *n*-cube, and similar structures) between the PEs of a parallel machine speed up the processing of the fast Fourier transform and similar transforms.

4.4.4 Two-dimensional FFT Example

Due to the importance of the two-dimensional Fourier transform for image processing, we now examine a possible solution within the PE array framework.

The **F**ast **F**ourier **T**ransform (FFT) algorithm is, in fact, the basis for most signal- and image-processing applications. FFT is a method for efficiently computing the **D**iscrete **F**ourier **T**ransform (DFT) of a time series (discrete data samples). A straightforward calculation of the DFT on a sequential computer takes $O(N^2)$ time, where N is the number of samples, whereas only $O(N \log_2 N)$ time is needed when the FFT method is used. The algorithm is well suited for parallel computation. Using N PEs, the processing time can be reduced to $O(\log_2 N)$.

The FFT is a clever computational technique to compute the DFT. The DFT of a time series is obtained as a weighted combination of the DFTs of two shorter time series. These, in turn, are computed in the same manner until the DFT of a single point is needed. This is the sample point value itself.

Figure 4.16 shows the decomposition of a time series and Figure 4.17 illustrates the calculation. Further decomposition yields the computational flow graph of Figure 4.18. This graph may be arranged as in Figure 4.19, showing that the perfect shuffle-exchange pattern is ideally suited for the computation. A binary cube pattern also solves all communication problems.

FFT on a perfect shuffle-connected, PE-array computer (LUCAS) is described in (Fernström, Kruzela, and Svensson, 1986). Assuming a 10-MHz clock, the execution time for a 256-point FFT with 16-bit data on a 128-PE array is 0.33 ms. In this case, bit-serial multipliers are utilized. By performing first row and then column FFTs independently on a matrix of input data, we obtain a two-dimensional FFT. A transform of a 256 x 256 image requires 512 one-dimensional transforms (256 in each direction), thus taking 170 ms. Half of the transforms are computed entirely within the PEs, all at the same time.

Fast Fourier transforms may also be computed with other PE-array topologies. On the linear array-organized PICAP3, a transposition of the array must be made between the transformations in the x- and y-directions, allowing all one-dimensional transformations to be computed within the PEs. Lindskog (1989) reports a calculated execution time of 93.5 ms using a 32-PE array on a 512 x 512 complex data image. On the coarse-grained PICAP3, the transposition phase takes about 20% of the total time. (*Note*: PICAP3 was designed to provide powerful floating-point operation units as PEs.)

FFTs have been the object of attention in other architectures as well, including both direct-mapped solutions and MIMD-based solutions. In these cases the ICN structure and means of communication determine the level of performance that is achievable.

Having characterized the field of image processing and examined one of the central algorithms, we now briefly look at the graphics area where SIMD PE arrays can also be effectively applied.

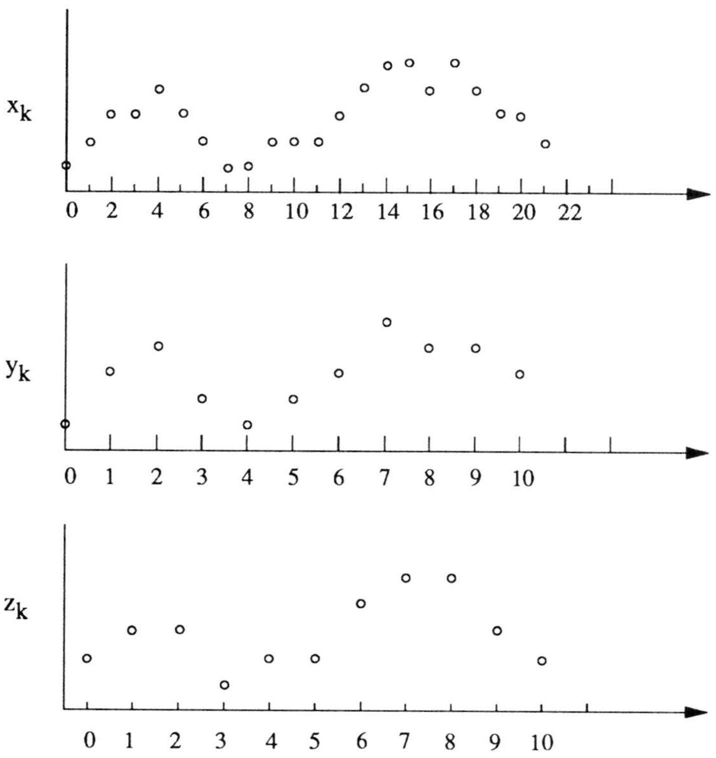

Figure 4.16. Decomposition of a Time Series into Two Half as Long Series

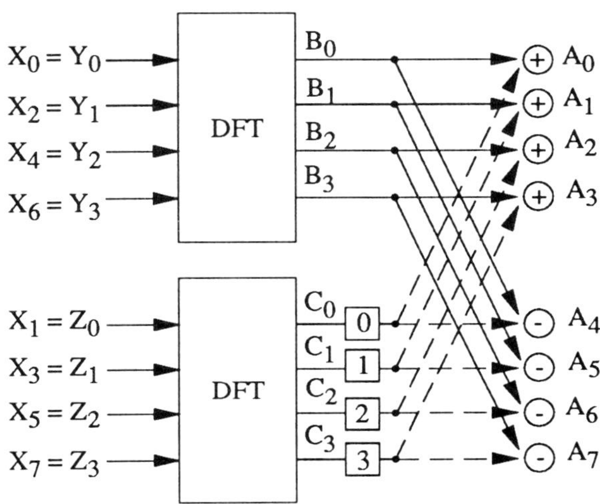

Figure 4.17. Signal-flow Graph Illustrating How Calculation of an 8-Point DFT Can Be Reduced to the Calculation of Two 4-Point DFTs. A number within a square represents multiplication by $e^{-2\pi j/N}$ raised to the number. In the lower half, the value arriving by the dotted line is subtracted from the value arriving by the solid line. In the upper half the two values are added.

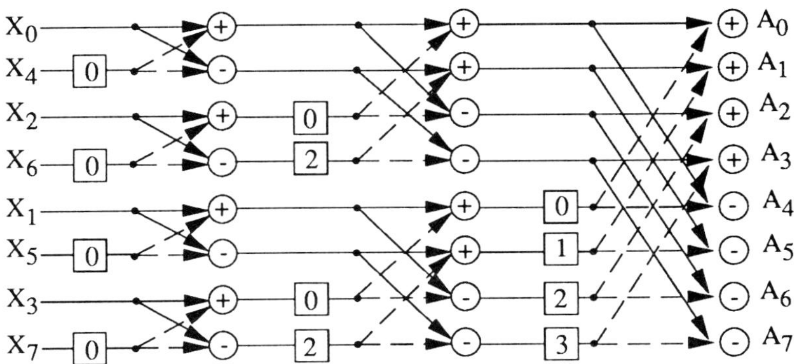

Figure 4.18. Calculation of an 8-Point DFT using the FFT Algorithm

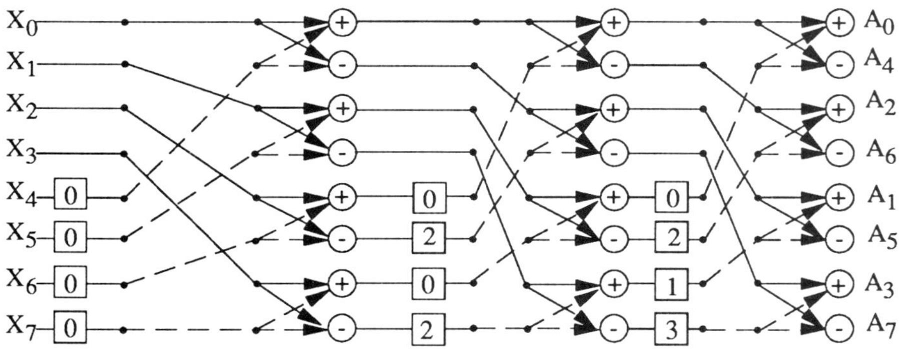

Figure 4.19. Adaptation of the FFT Algorithm to the Perfect Shuffle-exchange Interconnection Structure

4.4.5 Characteristics of Graphic Processing

In *graphic processing* or *computer graphics*, artificial images are created and manipulated. Typically, the images are two-dimensional views of three-dimensional artificial worlds. Manipulation includes tasks like scaling, rotation, and translation, which are required, for example, when the viewpoint or viewing direction in the three-dimensional world is changed. Manipulation may include recomputing the pixel values of surfaces when the imagined light source changes or moves. Since a raster image typically has a thousand by a thousand raster points (pixels) and manipulation of the image implies recomputing the value of each point, it is self-evident that an enormous amount of computing power is required. Approximately 100 floating-point operations per pixel are needed to calculate, transform, clip, project, and shade an image. If a 1000 by 1000 pixel screen is to be updated every twentieth of a second, 2 billion floating-point operations per second (2 Gflops) are needed. Graphic processing is indeed one of the major application areas for parallel processing technology.

As an example, let us consider the *ray-tracing* technique, a rather simple algorithm for picture generation, but extremely computational intensive. It is used to simulate complex lighting effects such as reflected illumination (where light bounces from one object to another), mirrorlike (specular) reflection, transparency effects (refraction), and shadowing. Examples of applications where the demand for realism is great are computer-aided design work and flight simulators. In the latter case, the image sequence must be generated in real time, since the image shown at a particular instant to the pilot undergoing instruction will depend on feedback from the aircraft's controls.

The ray-tracing method works by sending a simulated light ray from each point on the screen through a pinhole out into the environment, which contains the objects and light sources (see Figure 4.20). The ray passes through the environment and is the subject of a number of surface reflections and refractions. The intensity at each pixel is given by the sum of intensities of all the reflected and refracted contributions generated as the viewing ray is traced backward from the viewpoint toward the light source(s). The object surfaces may be smooth or textured, the light sources may be of point type or extended, and so on. Actually, by using the basic laws of optics in this rather straightforward way, realistic shading models can be constructed for graphics displays.

Ray tracing lends itself very well to parallel implementation since all points on a screen can be traced independently. In a multiprocessor system, each processor may take care of one portion of the screen. However, since not all PEs need the same time to compute their part of the screen, some of them can be idle while others are still working. Consequently, the static work distribution scheme may be replaced by a dynamic load-balancing scheme, according to which new data (coordinates) are sent to the PE that has just finished its computation. In this way, all processors can be kept busy.

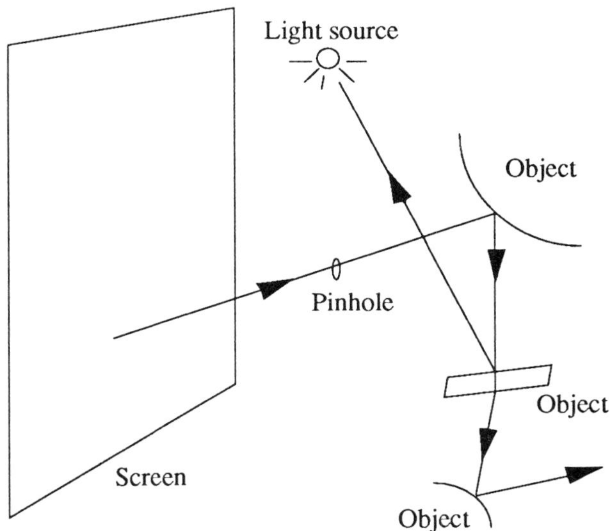

Figure 4.20. Ray Tracing

Many graphic processing tasks may be divided into several stages that can be pipelined. For example, a solid-modeling computation consists of the following sequential steps: first, the clipping stage, which only retains objects that are potentially visible from the point of observation. Next, hidden surface elimination, which determines the frontmost object for every pixel on the screen. This is typically the most computationally intensive stage. The final step is coordinate transformation. Each step in the pipeline may be parallelized.

We have considered how several important numerical, image, and graphic problems can be addressed with varying SIMD PE array hardware resource structures. In the next section, we consider the solution of large systems of equations with MIMD architectures.

4.5 MIMD - MULTIPROCESSOR AND MULTICOMPUTER

The solution of ordinary or partial differential equations quite frequently involves the application of discrete numerical methods to tridiagonal equations. In fact, sets of such equations or a single, large tridiagonal system of equations constitutes a large part of engineering and physics problems. Therefore, they are of direct interest for industrial real-time applications.

Conventional Gaussian elimination **must** be evaluated term by term due to sequential recurrences. We shall now examine a modification of Gaussian elimination that is straightforward and suitable for MIMD computers, where the number of PEs is much smaller than the number of equations. The method presented was introduced by Kowalik and Kumar (1985).

4.5.1 Parallel Algorithms for Recurrence Equations

Recurrence Equations

Consider the following set of recurrence equations:

$$x_1 = d_1$$

$$b_j x_{j-1} + x_j = d_j, \quad \text{for } 2 \leq j \leq n$$

which can be represented by a matrix equations $Ax = d$; where A is bidiagonal as illustrated in Figure 4.21.

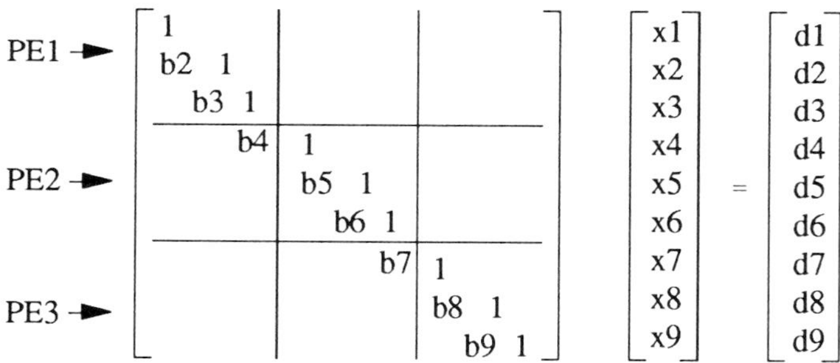

Figure 4.21. Recurrence Equation in Matrix Form

In this example, we observe that $n = 9$, $p = 3$ and $k = n/p = 3$ (p = number of PEs). The following algorithm is applied during phase 1 of the method for obtaining the vector x, where we eliminate $b2$, $b3$, $b5$, $b6$, $b8$, and $b9$ by applying three PEs simultaneously.

```
PE i,    (1 ≤ i ≤ p)
f(i-1)k+1 := b(i-1)k+1,               -not computed for i = 1
For j := (i-1)k + 2 to i k  do
        begin
        fj := - bj fj-1,              -not computed for i = 1
        dj := dj - bj dj-1
        end
```

The result of phase 1 is an almost diagonalized system, but now nonzero elements $f5$, $f6$, $f8$, and $f9$ have been created as portrayed in Figure 4.22.

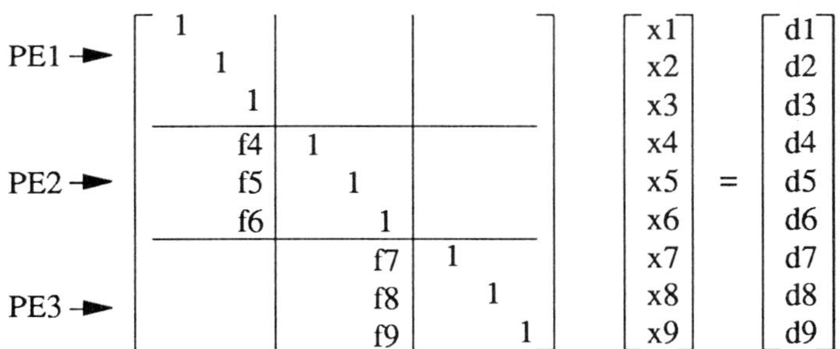

Figure 4.22. Almost Diagonalized System of Equations

To decouple the system, we must find the values of $x3$ and $x6$ by solving equations 3 and 6. Due to the fact that there are only p - 1 of them, we can solve these equations using one of the PEs. In general, in phase 2 we solve the following set:

$$x_k = d_k$$
$$f_j x_{j-k} + x_j = d_j, \quad j = 2k, 3k, \ldots, (p - 1)k$$

The remaining system of equations is then decoupled and can be solved in parallel by p - 1 PEs in phase 3.

PE i, $(2 \leq i \leq p)$
For j := (i-1)k + 1 to i k-1 do
$x_j := d_j - f_j \, x_{(i-1)k}$

Finally, PE1 can compute the value of

$$x_{pk} := d_{pk} - f_{pk} \, x_{(p-1)k}$$

4.5.2 Parallel Algorithms for Tridiagonal Equations

The recurrence method can be extended to solve a single set of tridiagonal equations:

$$b_j x_j - 1 + a_j x_j + c_j x_{j+1} = d_j, \qquad 1 \leq j \leq n$$
$$b_1 = c_n = 0$$

Once again, let us assume $n = 9$ and $p = 3$. Since we are dealing with MIMD systems, it is not necessary that $k = n/p$ be an integer; however, this simplifies the notation. The initial matrix is provided in Figure 4.23.

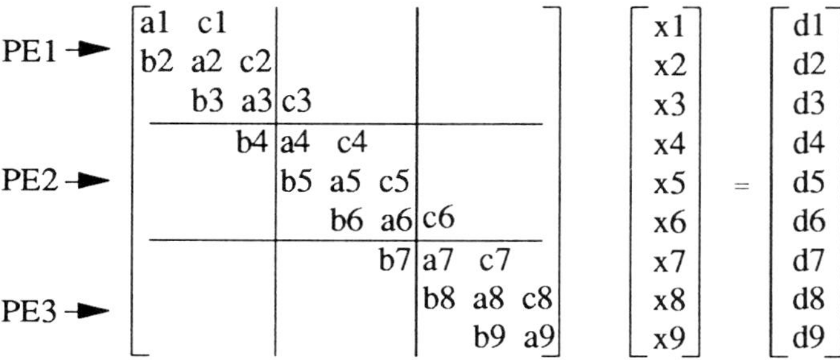

Figure 4.23. Matrix for Tridiagonal Equations

This initial matrix is processed in phase 1 and produces the new equations given in Figure 4.24. Each PE is in operation, and we can see, for example, that PE2 eliminates *b*5, *b*6, *c*4, and *c*3, in that order. (*Note*: We exclude the program details for the various phases of this algorithm.)

In phase 2, *p* tridiagonal equations are solved using Gaussian elimination on a single PE. That is, phase 2 decouples the system of equations shown in Figure 4.24 into *p* subsystems. Finally, in phase 3 the remaining $n - p$ variables are calculated.

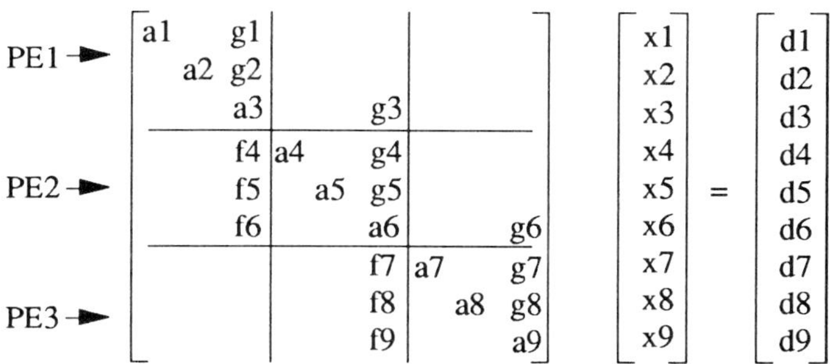

Figure 4.24. Matrix after the First Phase

Kowalik and Kumar report that, with the assumption that the execution time is twice that for the multiplication, addition, or subtraction, the total solution time for solving n equations with p PEs is proportional to $T_p = 20k + 10p$ + constant. For the single PE case, $T_1 = 10n$ + constant. Thus, the theoretical speedup is approximately

$$\text{Speedup} = \frac{T_1}{T_p} \approx \frac{n}{2k + p}$$

or assuming that p is much smaller than n and k, we obtain

$$\text{Speedup} = 0.5p$$

The algorithm is reported to be numerically safe for diagonally dominant matrices. Further, the speedup would increase somewhat if the values of f's and g's become progressively smaller, and their computation can be avoided when they drop below a threshold numerical value. The programs for the algorithm were programmed in Fortran for the HEP (the first commercially available MIMD computer), and execution confirmed both the speedup factors and the property of speedup improvements when f's and g's became sufficiently small.

The approach for solving equations given here for MIMD environments should be contrasted to the computational paradigms provided for by systolic and wavefront arrays and SIMD PE arrays. Once again, we repeat our earlier observation:

THERE ARE NO SOLUTIONS; ONLY ALTERNATIVES

By changing the computational circumstances and requirements, varying alternative solutions will always prove to provide a range of not possible, possible, reasonable, adequate, good, and superior solutions. Some of them may be quite straightforward and lead to convenient implementations, whereas others may require significant effort when the application problem — resource structure semantic gaps are large.

4.6 OTHER APPLICATION DOMAINS

We exemplified the parallel processing properties of a few application domains with particular emphasis upon signal, numerical, image, and graphic problems. There are a variety of application domains that are both relevant for the union of parallel processing and industrial real-time applications that deserve the reader's attention. Thus, we enumerate a few domains and point the reader to literature that can provide a starting point for a deeper study of these domains. For an excellent source of problem solving with parallel processing, the reader is referred to the book by Fox, and others (1988).

4.6.1 Fractal Geometry

The utilization of traditional mathematics for the description of nature and natural phenomena has the limitation of reducing objects to regular structures. To develop a mathematics that provides a closer relationship to the irregular structures found in nature and natural phenomena, Mandelbrot (1977) developed *fractal geometry*. Thus, Mandelbrot attempts to describe many of the pathelogical shapes that scientists have observed and termed, for example, grainy, hyrdalike, in between, pimply, pocky, ramified, tangled, and wiggly.

The computation of fractal sets is one of the favorite algorithms used to illustrate the computational properties of diverse parallel processing architectures. For practical use, fractal sets have been applied in many interesting new applications, for example, as a method in analyzing terrains, which is extremely important in military real-time applications.

4.6.2 Parallel Simulation

In certain real-time systems, especially those for which periodic advice and/or insight is required, it may be necessary to simulate certain phenomena during real-time operations. For example, in a ground-based flight simulator, virtually all sensor inputs and actuator outputs are simulated; however, the simulator attempts to model real time. In the control of production processes where live sensor and actuator data are being processed, we may wish to simulate the effect of making alterations in the production system (based upon historical and live data). Thus, we may wish to ask questions like "What would be the benefit of coupling in or decoupling various production resources?" or "Will a specific alteration be safe?" In a military Command Control and Communications System C^3I, it is of particular interest to simulate sensors and actuators for war gaming, as well as in live situations, for gaining insight and simulating the effect of alternative maneuvers. These latter situations can be time critical.

In the situations we have portrayed, simulation performance becomes an important issue and thus one of the important applications for parallel processing in advanced real-time applications.

Let us now review some of the current thinking in the relatively new field of *parallel simulation*, which has become popular due to the availability of commercial parallel processing systems.

For complex simulations, traditional DES (**d**iscrete **e**vent **s**imulation) can require significant processing time even on extremely fast uniprocessing hardware. Multiprocessors seem to be an attractive means of reducing simulation time; however, existing discrete simulation algorithms are not adequate for parallel execution. A new approach is required to design adequate algorithms for parallel execution. Thus, new distributed and parallel simulation paradigms are aimed at exploiting inherent parallelism and thereby reducing simulation time.

Two main paradigms have been proposed for parallel discrete event simulation (PDES), one *conservative* and the other *optimistic*. The conservative paradigm was proposed by Peacock, Wong, and Manning (1979) and by Chandy and Misra (1979) and has been called the Chandy-Misra approach to PDES. It is conservative since it makes sure that events treated in parallel have no side effects. The optimistic paradigm was proposed by Jefferson (1985) and is known as the time-warp approach. In this approach, potential side effects are ignored and simulation proceeds until it is shown that an event side effect has caused an improper result, in which case the simulation is rolled back.

Additional approaches to the simulation problem have led to centralized event-list schemes; however, by making this critical part sequential, the real advantages of utilizing parallel processing are negated. The event-list is a dominating factor.

Due to the critical role of simulation in tomorrow's sophisticated real-time systems, this area of parallel simulation will undoubtedly receive increasing attention. A survey of the area has been provided by Fujimoto (1990).

4.6.3 Real-time Data Bases

The majority of contemporary industrial real-time systems are oriented toward providing satisfactory computational, and stability properties. However, there are real-time applications where a data base is maintained and where rapid information retrieval becomes a requirement. One good example is the real-time tracking of multiple targets by a radar system. In Chapter 3, we indicated the parallel search and comparison properties of associative processing solutions that can be applied in radar object tracking.

State of the art traditional database systems are typically not utilized in industrial real-time applications due to two inadequacies: poor performance and lack of predictability (see Son, 1990).

We can, in fact, deal with RTDB (**r**eal-**t**ime **d**ata **b**ases) at two levels: first as a totally "fluent" collection of data. That is, data are only relevant for limited periods of time, after which they are of no value other than for logging purpose. These unique aspects of RTDB have not been widely exploited thus far in real-time applications. Most work has centered around "transaction"-oriented approaches, where some form of more long-term consistency is desirable. Thus, many of the problems inherent in solutions with traditional data bases and real-time allocation and scheduling remain.

Within the category of transaction-based data bases, we find that they do not schedule their transactions to meet response requirements and normally lock data tables in order to assure consistency in the data base. Scheduling transactions in a real-time data base must consider both data consistency (including temporal ordering) and timing constraints. Even here, research in this area is at an early stage.

The obvious solution is to introduce some form of priority scheme in dealing with data-base transactions. Thus, the data base is simply treated as a resource. In lock-based concurrency data-base control algorithms, a direct application of a real-time scheduling protocol may result in *priority inversions,* as we described earlier. To avoid such inversions, the mechanisms of priority inheritance and priority ceilings, which have also been described, may be applied in the data-base context. In fact, Son (1990) reports that the combination of the two provides for freedom from deadlock and a worst-case blocking of at most a single lower-priority transaction.

In highly distributed environments, one could consider utilizing a global ceiling protocol manager at a specific site, which would have all information and make all decisions about ceiling blocking. The temporal consistency would be assured, since every data object maintains most up-to-date values. On the other hand, holding locks across a network has many disadvantages, including delaying local processing, which is undoubtedly counterproductive for real-time data-base systems.

Before completing our small menu of additional real-time application areas, we should note that other areas such as *sorting and searching,* which are quite naturally implemented via parallel processing, may well be part of a real-time application. Further, the area of *neural networks* (requiring large-scale parallel computation) may be incorporated into tomorrow's real-time systems. Some neural network properties are considered in Chapter 10.

While of necessity brief, this chapter should provide a stimulus for further investigation of solutions to the diverse problems that can arise in parallel processing real-time environments.

References

Akl, S.G. (1989). *The Design and Analysis of Parallel Algorithms*, Prentice Hall, Englewood Cliffs, NJ.

Ballard, D.H., G.E. Hinton, and T.J. Sejnowski (1983). Parallel Visual Computation, *Nature*, Vol. 306, November 3, 1983, pp. 21-26.

Chandy, K.M., and J. Misra (1979). Distributed Simulation: A Case Study in Design and Verification of Distributed Programs, *IEEE Transactions on Software*, Vol. SE-5, No. 5, pp. 440-452.

Crochiere, R.E. (1974). *Digital Network Theory and Its Application to the Analysis and Design of Digital Filters*, Ph.D. Dissertation, Department of Electrical Engineering, M.I.T., Cambridge, MA.

Crochiere, R.E., and A.V. Oppenheim (1975). Analysis of Linear Digital Networks, *Proceedings of the IEEE*, Vol. 63, pp. 581-595.

Danielsson, P.E., and S. Levialdi (1981). Computer Architectures for Pictorial Information Systems, *Computer*, November, pp. 53-67.

Fernström, C., I. Kruzela, and B. Svensson (1986). *LUCAS Associative Array Processor – Design, Programming and Application Studies*, Lecture Notes in Computer Science, Vol. 216, Springer-Verlag, New York.

Fettweis, A. (1976). Realizability of Digital Filter Networks, Archiv. Elektr. Übertragungstechnik, Vol. 30, No. 2, pp. 90-96.

Fox, G., M. Johnson, G. Lyzenga, S. Otto, J. Salmon, and D. Walker (1988). *Solving Problems on Concurrent Processors*, Vol 1: *General Techniques and Regular Problems*, Prentice Hall, Englewood Cliffs, NJ.

Fujimoto, R.M. (1990). Parallel Discrete Event Simulation, *Communications of the ACM*, Vol. 33, No. 10, pp. 30-53.

Golub, G.H., and C.F. Van Loan (1989). *Matrix Computations*, 2nd ed., Johns Hopkins University Press, Baltimore, MD.

Jefferson, D.R. (1985). Virtual Time, *ACM Transactions on Programming Languages and Systems*, Vol. 7, No. 3, pp. 404-425.

Johnson, G.M. (1989). Exploiting Parallelism in Computational Science, *FGCS (Fifth Generation Computing Systems)*, Vol. 5, Nos. 2-3, pp. 319-337.

Kowalik, J.S., and S.P. Kumar (1985). Parallel Algorithms for Recurrence and Tridiagonal Equations, appearing in S.J. Kowalik (ed.), *Parallel MIMD Computation: The HEP Supercomputer and Its Applications*, pp. 295-307, MIT Press, Cambridge, MA.

Kruse, B. (1973). A Parallel Picture Processing Machine, *IEEE Transactions on Computers*, Vol. C-22, pp. 1075-1087.

Kung, H.T. (1982). Why Systolic Architectures?, *IEEE Computer*, Vol. 15, No. 1.

Kung, S.Y., S.C. Lo, N. Jean, and J.N. Hwang (1987). Wavefront Array Processors — Concept to Implementation, *IEEE Computer*, Vol. 13, No. 7, pp. 18-33.

Lindskog, B. (1989). PICAP3. A Linear SIMD Array with Floating-point Arithmetic, Report LiTH-ISY-I-0971, Linköping University, Sweden.

Lisper, B. (1990). Synthesis of Time-optimal Systolic Arrays within Cells with Inner Structure, *International Journal of Parallel and Distributed Computing*, Vol. 10, No. 2, pp. 182-187.

Mandelbrot, B.B. (1977). *The Fractal Geometry of Nature*, W.H. Freeman and Company, San Francisco.

Mead, C., and L. Conway (1980). *Introduction to VLSI Systems*, Addison-Wesley, Reading, MA.

Ortega, J.M., and R.G. Voigt (1987). A Bibliography on Parallel and Vector Numerical Algorithms, *National Aeronautics and Space Administration*, CR 178319, June.

Peacock, J.K., J.W. Wong, and E.G. Manning (1979). Distributed Simulation Using a Network of Processors, *Computer Networks*, Vol. 3, No. 1, pp. 44-56.

Potter, J.L. (1978). The STARAN Architecture and Its Application to Image Processing and Pattern Recognition Algorithms, *Proceedings AFIPS NCC*, 1978, pp. 1041-1047.

Quinn, M.J. (1987). *Designing Efficient Algorithms for Parallel Computers*. McGraw-Hill, New York.

Reddaway, S. (1979). The DAP Approach. *Infotech State of the Art Report on Supercomputers*, Infotech International, Ltd., Maidenhead, Berks, UK.

Renfors, M., and Neuvo, Y. (1981). The Maximal Sampling Rate of Digital Filters under Hardware Speed Constraints, *IEEE Transactions on Circuits and Systems*, CAS-28, No. 3, pp. 196-202.

Son, S.H. (1990). Scheduling Real-time Transactions, *Proceedings of the EUROMICRO Workshop on Real Time*, IEEE Computer Society Press, Los Alamitos, CA.

Svensson, B. (1983). Image Operations Performed on LUCAS — An Array of Bit-serial Processors, *Proceedings of the 3rd Scandinavian Conference on Image Analysis*, Copenhagen, Denmark, July 1983, pp. 308-313.

Wilson, K. G. (1989). Grand Challenges to Computational Science, *FGCS (Fifth Generation Computer Systems)*, Vol. 5, Nos. 2-3, pp. 171-189.

Chapter 5

DEPENDABILITY and RESPONSIVENESS

- A number of relevant terms are defined, including fault, error, failure, reliability, availability, performability, maintainability, testability, correctability, safety, and security (231)

- dependability in hardware processes is considered from three points of view:
  reconfigurable wafer-scale integration (232)
  scan testing including BIST (built-in self-test) (234)
  probability diagnosis for isolating faults (236)

- sources and categories of faults are identified (238)

- a space-time view of fault-tolerant systems is presented and a variety of fault-tolerance methods is placed into these domains (239)

- static and dynamic hardware and software redundancy is described (240)

- ICN fault tolerance is examined via an extrastage cube network example — a variety of other techniques is identified (244)

- fault-tolerance possibilities for systolic and wavefront arrays are considered (247)

- the verification of hardware and software processes is introduced (247)

The provision of dependable and responsive industrial real-time systems is becoming an absolute requirement, in particular, as systems are placed in critical roles in which damages due to an undependable and/or unresponsive system can be devastating. In this chapter, we shall concentrate upon *dependability* from the point of view of providing functioning parallel hardware processes. Further, we consider strategies to achieve hardware and software *responsiveness* in the presence of faults during the operation of parallel/distributed real-time systems. However, let us first clarify some general terminology, which is often confusing but for which an understanding is needed. Several of the terms involve measures and are examples of the x-abilities we have introduced.

fault — the phenomenon that causes an error.

error — result of a fault; the system is placed in an undesirable state.

failure — the system function does not agree with the specified function.

reliability — denoted $R(t)$, is the conditional probability that a system can perform its specified function at a time t, given that it was operational at time $t = 0$. $R(t)$ is a function of the fault processes affecting the system and any mechanisms that prevent system failure when a fault occurs.

availability — denoted $A(t)$, is a measure used for systems that are subject to failure and repair. It is the probability that a system is operational at time t.

performability — is the possibility to operate a system containing faults at a degraded level of performance.

maintainability — is the ability to perform maintenance off line and/or on line, in which case the system may be operating at a degraded performance level.

testability — is the ability to perform tests to isolate faults at the time of production, as well as in off-line and/or on-line operation.

correctability — is the ability to correct faults during normal system operation (in the real-time case, also without delaying critical process deadlines).

safety and *security* — are the *abilities* to protect the system from inadvertent misuse or from malicious attempts to destroy system functionality.

Note that the defined measures are independent of whether faults isolated by testing (off line or on line) are related to hardware or to software problems. However, the major efforts in testing and fault tolerance, to date, have been placed on hardware faults, where many techniques have evolved. Due to the abstract and diverse nature of software, techniques for treating software faults have not been as widely refined; however, in some cases, as we shall consider, there are analogous approaches with respect to the treatment of hardware and software faults.

As emphasis has been placed on dependability and responsiveness issues, research and development in these areas has led to many conferences, publications, and the like, which we can classify as "Design for x," where x is any one of the above measures that we have enumerated. The common denominator for x that is often not explicitly considered is *understandability*, which naturally is a prerequisite for the effective treatment of each of the above-named measures.

5.1 DEPENDABLE PARALLEL HARDWARE PROCESSES

The provision of dependable parallel hardware resources is an essential starting point for providing dependable real-time systems. In this regard, the quality of the hardware processes is related to their fundamental design, as well as the manufacturing processes used for their creation.

For newly created hardware processes (and parallel ensembles thereof), testing and fault isolation are essential. Further, as we shall consider, in VLSI-based solutions, static restructurability becomes essential.

Once reliable hardware processes are available and become part of a parallel processing system, they must be continually tested, off line for maintenance purposes and on line as a part of the fault-tolerance strategy.

Our purpose here is not to present the details of hardware design, production, and testing at various stages. We restrict ourselves to highlighting some of the aspects that should be considered in relation to the theme of the book.

5.1.1 Reconfigurable WSI Structures

During the 1980s, we observed the beginning of efforts to increase the degree of circuit integration into WSI (**W**afer-**S**cale **I**ntegration). However, as the feature size of integrated-circuit elements has been miniaturized, the probability of defects has increased. This phenomenon has been observed in the ongoing attempts to produce larger M (memory processes). As we move toward utilizing regular integrated-circuit structures in providing combined PE, M, and C processes, it is important to appreciate the possibilities to provide dependable WSI systems in the presence of increased defect probabilities.

Koren and Singh (1990) have reviewed the contemporary approaches to providing dependable WSI systems from wafers containing large numbers of hardware processes, some percentage of which are defective. We review a few general strategies for restructuring processes in the presence of defects (that is, defect-tolerant designs). On the other hand, we shall not consider the physical means by which restructuring is accomplished.

The first reconfiguration scheme is based upon changing PE (**p**rocessing **e**lements) into CE (**c**onnection **e**lements) in the presence of a faulty PE, as illustrated in Figure 5.1. In this case, when a faulty PE is detected, all other PEs in the corresponding row and column are altered to become connection elements and only act as a transport mechanism. While this scheme is simple, it is only reasonable to consider in the presence of a small number of defective PEs. Since an entire row and column must be disabled for each faulty PE, multiple faults degrade the array quickly. Further, depending upon the granularity of the PEs, significant amounts of integrated-circuit real estate can be sacrificed.

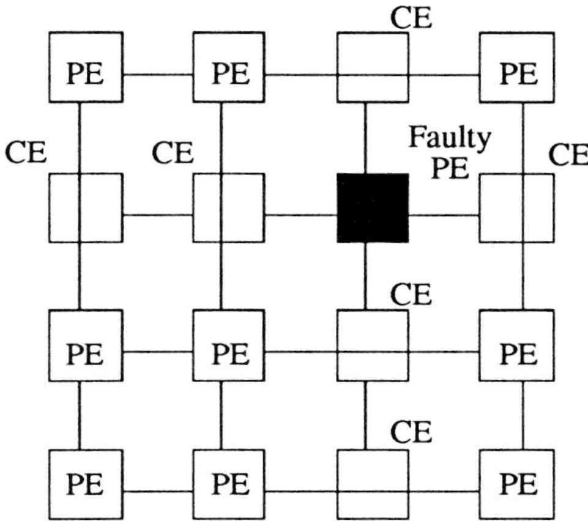

Figure 5.1. Row and Column Exclusion Scheme
(PE, **P**rocessing **E**lement, and CE, **C**onnection **E**lement)

In Figure 5.2, we consider another simple scheme that adds spare columns to the array. The PEs are reindexed in their rows so as to skip over the faulty PEs. Once the reindexing is accomplished, the appropriate vertical connections can be made. For s spare columns, this scheme can tolerate up to s faults in each row. However, complicated switch and interconnection structures are required in order to support this form of reconfiguration. Further, reconfiguration can lead to long links. This factor may be important, especially for synchronous systems, since it changes the timing relationships for communicating between PEs.

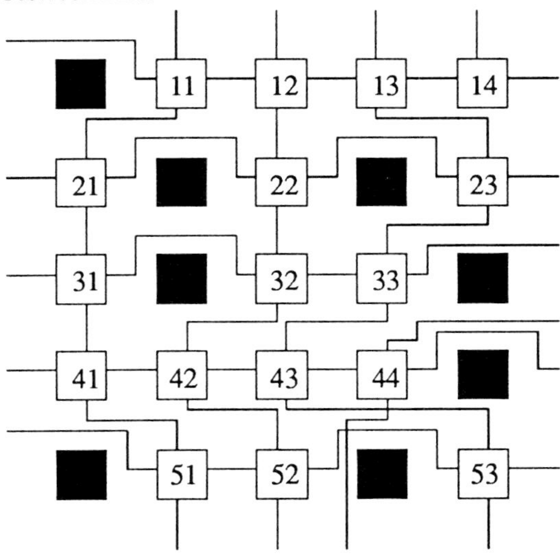

Figure 5.2. Improved Reconfiguration Strategy

The final scheme we shall consider is called the interstitial redundancy, scheme which is presented in Figure 5.3. In this approach, redundant PEs are placed systematically as spares in the array. Each spare can replace any neighboring primary PE. Since reconfiguration is local, restructured interconnections stay short.

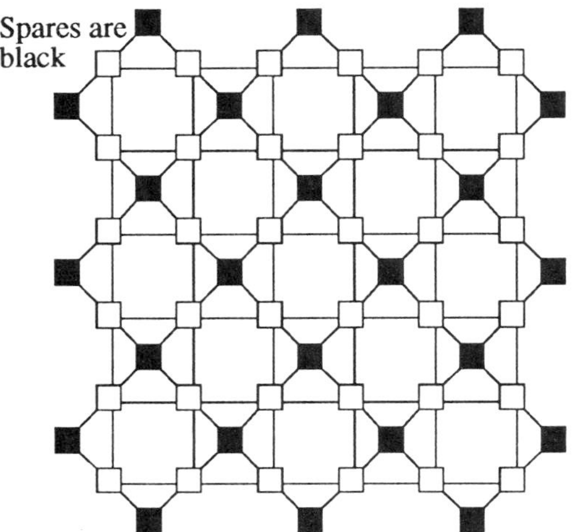

Figure 5.3. Interstitial Redundancy Scheme

Testing may be at the point of manufacture (as we have described) or may be made periodically as a part of the off-line diagnosis, on-line fault isolation and/or maintenance procedures. In all cases, the goal is to provide functioning hardware. Where testing has shown that portions of the system are not functioning, the testing procedures should, where possible, lead to reconfiguration of the hardware processes. With reconfiguation, in some cases, performability goals in the form of the degraded system performance are achieved. These static reconfiguration approaches to WSI may suggest analogous approaches to treating dynamic reconfiguration.

5.1.2 Scan Testing

The testing of hardware processes has historically been an area that can be characterized by a high degree of pragmatic, special-purpose solutions. The combinatoric test vector problems of large circuits leads to long test sequences that seldom can guarantee complete test coverage (that all cases are tested). Further, as circuits become highly integrated, observability (getting at pins, pads, and so on) becomes more difficult, requiring high-precision testing devices such as a bed-of-nails prober. Thus, one can make a strong case for integrating testing close to the individual hardware processes so that testing can be carried out in parallel and without physical probe requirements.

The fundamental idea of adding logic to a circuit in order to scan in test cases was introduced by Williams and Parker (1982). (Their publication also provides an excellent survey of testability.) The scan testing idea spread widely in the industry for testing at the printed circuit board level. However, each manufacturer went its own way concerning the detailed implementation. This resulted in nonstandard components, nonstandard test equipment, and the like. During the 1980s a number of manufacturers met to address this situation. The result has been the introduction of the JTAG (**J**oint **T**est **A**ction **G**roup) IEEE standard, which provides important guidelines for some but not all aspects of scan testing techniques.

The JTAG Standard

The JTAG standard is concerned with (B-S) **b**oundary **s**can testing. The general architecture of the standard is portrayed in Figure 5.4. At the top of the circuit, we observe that input and output signals are connected to NDI and NDO, which propagate the normal data inputs and outputs. NDI and NDO are passed through BSRs (**B**oundary **S**can **R**egisters). If scan testing is not enabled (that is, bypassed), the circuit simply exercises the application logic. The remainder of the logic mechanisms of the circuit implement B-S testing.

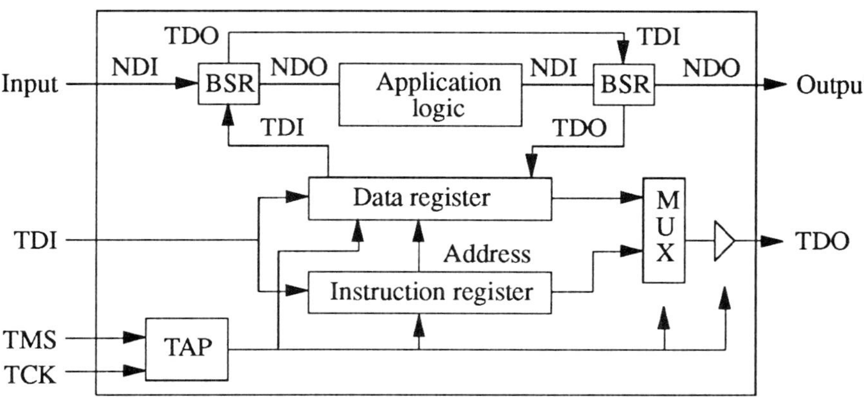

Figure 5.4. Standard Boundary Scan Architecture

The TAP (**T**est **A**ccess **P**ort) is implemented as a four-wire interface; thus, each device using boundary scan requires four pins for this interface. The TDI and TDO (**T**est **D**ata **I**n and **O**ut) pins serve as the beginning and end of the boundary scan chain. The input signals to the TAP are clocked at the rising edge of the TCK (**t**est **c**lo**ck**). The TAP shifts in instructions and data registers. TMS (**T**est **M**ode **S**elect) is a serial input that is used to control the boundary scan. A variety of instructions is provided that permits various enabling and disablings of the couplings indicated (including the bypassing of testing).

This standardized structure facilitates the development of software support tools in the test equipment. However, it is important to note that it has not defined a standard for the testing procedures. Whetsel (1988) provides a more thorough presentation of the JTAG standard.

Toward BIST (Built-in Self-test)

It is interesting to consider the ideas of the JTAG standard as a means of providing self-testing circuits. Assuming that the granularity of the application logic of a circuit is sufficiently coarse, the overhead for adding self-testing may well be motivated. Davidson (1988) reports a figure of 10% to 15% overhead as a typical goal. The added circuitry naturally increases the cost for the ICs and slows down the circuit. On the other hand, it provides significant returns in manufacturing as well as in field testing and maintenance. The incorporation of JTAG ideas in the circuit requires, of course, that the testing mechanisms (including test patterns) be completely built into the circuit.

For parallel processing real-time systems, the incorporation of BIST may become a requirement. Further, one can easily think of a control structure (perhaps microprogrammed) that will exercise all circuits of a system all the time. A subset of the system is doing active processing while the remainder is simultaneously being tested. With intelligent strategies, the active versus tested circuits can be varied to provide good dynamic test coverage for fault detection. This is the first important step toward building fault-tolerant parallel processing systems.

5.1.3 Probablistic Diagnosis

We now turn our attention to methods for detecting faults in operational hardware systems. In particular, we shall examine a probabilistic method that can be used in isolating single or multiple intermittent faults. The method is quite straightforward and general and can be applied in minor variants to:

— bus faults
— instruction execution faults
— switching network faults
— architecture (topology) related faults

Further, these probabilistic methods developed by Narraway (1990) can be used during system development and acceptance testing, and for both off-line and on-line diagnosis.

The diagnostic process is a set-theoretic intersection procedure, where it is assumed that there exists a sequence of system-descriptive objects, A_i, such that when a fault exists, A_i embodies information concerning the fault location F, such that

$$F = \bigcap_{i=1}^{N} A_i$$

Identification of F is complete at the Nth object being presented. The mean $\tilde{N}$ and the associated variance s^2 are of particular interest in gauging the performance of any diagnostic process based on the equation. The process of calculating the intersection can be mechanized by calculating a sequence of derived sets D_k starting at A_1 of a sequence. Let us illustrate this process by the following example:

Assume that a bus has a sticking bit F, which is stuck at logical 1 intermittently. Objects for the calculation A_i are obtained from bus words b_i, for which it is known that some bit has failed to achieve a desired logic level. The elements of A_i are the bits of bus word i that are at logic 1. A sequence of objects A_i obtained by the process eventually has an intersection in bit F. Consider, as an example, an 8-bit bus single faulty bit diagnosis, where $N = 4$ and bit 2 sticks at logic 1 as follows:

bit	7	6	5	4	3	2	1	0		7	6	5	4	3	2	1	0
A1			1	1		1		1	D1			1	1		1		1
A2			1			1	1	1	D2			1			1		1
A3	1			1	1	1	1	1	D3						1		1
A4	1	1	1	1		1			D4						1		

In this case, we have succeeded in isolating the single bit fault, where bit 2 is stuck at logic 1 by successively anding the elements D_k in the sequence with the new incoming A_i. This method can be applied to isolating multiple faults.

Narraway reports that this probabilistic diagnosis has yielded favorable results in almost all cases examined. Of central importance is the probability of isolating a fault over a sequence. Thus, we define a cumulative probability for diagnosis exactly on the Nth faulty data set $P_d(N)$ as follows:

$$P_d(N) = P_c(N) - P_c(N-1)$$

The mean $\tilde{N}$ and variance s^2 can thus be calculated as follows:

$$\tilde{N} = \sum_{N=1}^{\infty} N \, P_d(N)$$

and

$$s^2 = \sum_{N=1}^{\infty} N^2 \, P_d(N) - (\tilde{N})^2$$

Given these probability functions, Narraway generalizes their use for all forms of topological structures where stuck-at faults are to be isolated. This includes bus structures, paths in a network, spanning trees, and sequences of instructions.

5.2 RESPONSIVENESS AND FAULT TOLERANCE

> Parallel and distributed computing systems provide a unique opportunity for trading real-time performance and fault tolerance, as well as space and time, because of their inborn redundancy that can be used for higher system efficiency or dependability. The multiplicity of resources does not come without headaches. The multiplicity of resources makes deterministic computation difficult, and we need to deal with the issue of nondeterminism that occurs due to unpredictable communication delays, data-dependent program execution and computation times.
>
> Miroslaw Malek (1990)

In this section, we explore the questions of real-time system responsiveness in the presence of faults as well as those aspects (positive and negative) that accrue due to the introduction of parallel processing. The paper by Malek (1990), the text by Burns and Wellings (1989), and a special issue of *IEEE Computer* (see Singh and Murugesan, 1990) are important sources for further details.

5.2.1 Sources and Categories of Faults

Faults can be attributed to the following sources:

— inadequate specification
— introduced from design errors in software components
— introduced by failure of one or more hardware components
— introduced by transient or permanent interference in supporting communication subsystems

The first two sources of faults are, in general, unanticipated faults and their avoidance is directly related to the quality of the design and implementation, as well as the possibilities to verify critical properties of the software. The latter two fault sources are more predictable and should be taken into account in the design of a reliable real-time system. The following fault categories can be distinguished.

transient faults — the fault starts at a particular time, remains in the system for some period, and then disappears. Typically, these faults arise due to some disturbance, for example, from electrical fields or radio interference.

permanent faults — the fault starts at a particular time and remains until it is repaired, for example, a broken connection or a software error.

intermittent faults — faults that occur from time to time, for example, a hardware component that is heat sensitive and works for a time, stops working properly, cools down, and then starts to operate again.

5.2.2 Space and Time View of Fault Tolerance

The issues related to space and time seem to be predominant in designing responsive fault-tolerant systems. That is, fault tolerance requires some form of extra space or extra time, or both, as portrayed in Figure 5.5.

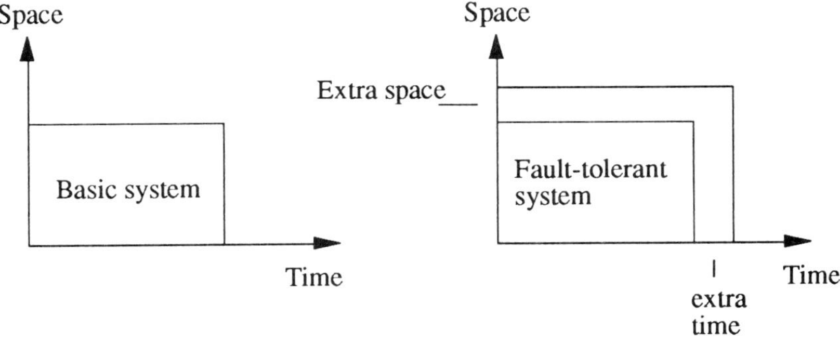

Figure 5.5. Space-Time Trade-off in Basic and Fault-tolerant Systems

In our earlier discussions of JTAG and built-in testing, we observed these space-time trade-offs in respect to fault detection in hardware processes. In fact, the same trade-offs can be made for software processes.

Although both the space and time dimensions are always involved, designers often treat time as an inexpensive resource and concentrate upon space optimization. This trade-off is **not** appropriate for real-time systems, where *time* often plays the most critical role.

Various approaches to fault-tolerance can be placed into the space-time domain approximately as portrayed in Figure 5.6.

5.2.3 Redundancy of Hardware and Software

Let us consider some of the approaches portrayed in the figure. Concerning hardware redundancy, Anderson and Lee (1981) describe the following methods:

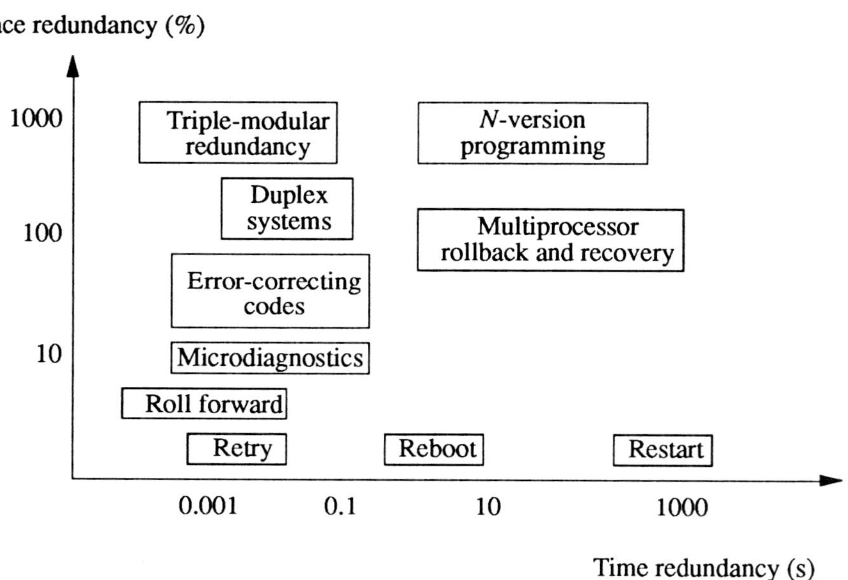

Figure 5.6. Space-Time Overhead for Fault-tolerance Approaches

Static Hardware Redundancy

In this case, an attempt is made to determine if a component is not working properly by examining its results in comparison to other identical components (that is, modular redundancy is introduced). Typically, three identical components are utilized (TMR, triple modular redundancy). The results are compared via majority-voting circuits. If one of the results differs from the other two, it is masked out. Of course, this approach assumes that the fault is not due to internal errors in the component but is transient or is due to component deterioration. This technique can be extended to *N-modular redundancy*.

Dynamic Component Redundancy

Dynamic component redundancy provides an explicit or implicit means of indicating that the component is not functioning properly. In this regard, it provides *error detection* as opposed to *error masking*, as in the TMR case. Historically, dynamic component redundancy has been accomplished by the use of *checksums* at points of transmission and, in the case of memories, by the utilization of *parity bits*. These classical methods can be complemented with BIST approaches, which were described earlier. The BIST approach has significant advantages with respect to isolating the source of faults.

In terms of the parallel processing systems we have considered in this book, hardware redundancy of the static and/or dynamic variety should be considered for hardware process-based, direct-mapped systems, as well as for the PE, M, and C components of programmed solutions. In the direct-mapped case, static redundancy is quite appropriate, since a hardware solution is most often based upon the use of small sets of identical components. In programmed solutions, at the hardware level it is quite common to provide parity and checksum solutions. However, a modular redundancy analogous solution can be found in the software domain.

5.2.4 Dynamic Software Redundancy

N-version Programming

Since software is not subject to deterioration (other than by humans making alterations), it is most common to concentrate on detecting design faults. One method of attacking this problem proposed by Chen and Avizienis (1978) is the creation of N versions of the program ($N \geq 2$). Thus, N individuals or groups produce the software without interaction. The method assumes that the problem can be unambiguously specified and that programs that have been developed independently will fail independently. It is important that the solution be made in different programming languages so that common language implementation errors do not creep in. Once implemented, the programs execute concurrently with the same inputs, and their results are compared by a *driver process* that is responsible for:

— invoking each of the versions
— waiting for the versions to complete
— comparing and acting on results

It may be impossible to wait for all programs to complete; therefore, it is important to develop intermediate points in the computation at which point comparisons can be made. Thus, a part of the specification must include points at which the programs communicate and synchronize with the driver process. Chen and Avizienis recommend the following components for this purpose:

— comparison vectors
— comparison status indicators
— comparison points

Comparison vectors are the data structures representing the outputs of the respective programs (*votes*) to be used for the purpose of comparison. Comparison status indicators are sent from the driver process to the versions, for possible reaction from the versions. The structure of this communication is illustrated in Figure 5.7. The reactions may result in:

— continuation
— termination of one or more versions, or
— continuation after changing one or more votes to the majority value

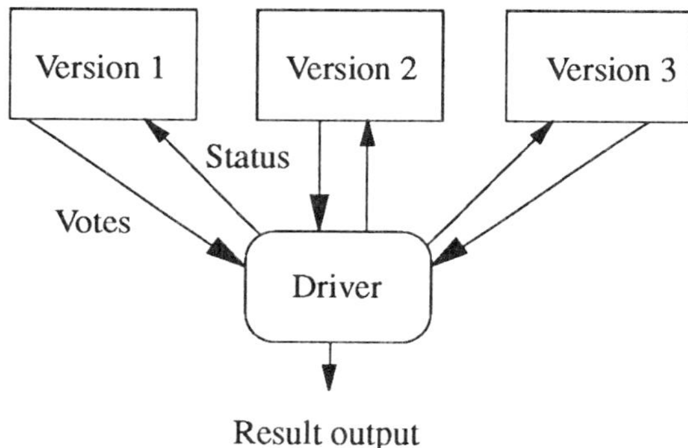

Figure 5.7. *N*-Version Programming

The voting comparison method must often resort to inexact voting due to the varying computational precisions and other factors, which will result in minor differences between "correct" results. Thus, methods such as taking the median value of *N* results or allowing a tolerance range can be applied. In addition to computational precision, we can find, in some cases, varying results based upon different numerical methods; for example, a quadratic equation may have more than one solution.

The advantages of utilizing parallel processing for *N*-version programming should be quite clear. The various versions are assigned to their own PEs. In this case, the questions of (C) communication and (S) synchronization in the real-time system become essential issues. In MIMD environments, barrier synchronization may be usefully exploited.

Error Detection, Confining Damages, and Error Recovery

The *N*-version program is a correlary to the *N*-modular redundancy approach described in hardware solutions. We shall now consider some of the internal means of detecting software errors, assessing and confining damages, and error recovery. These aspects are more fully described in Anderson and Lee (1981).

Software Error Detection

There are several manners in which software errors are detected. Errors may arise as the result of hardware detecting attempts to execute an illegal instruction, arithmetic overflow, or protection violation. The run-time system may also be the source of error detection, catching such errors as array bound errors or null pointer references.

A *watchdog timer* is often used in real-time systems, in which case the software component must continually reset the timer to indicate that it is functioning properly; otherwise, it is assumed to be in error.

In *hard deadline* systems, the missing of a deadline may also be treated as an error situation.

Controls in the form of a watchdog timer or missed deadline, of course, are not guarantees that the software component functions properly and should be used in combination with other controls. For example, *reversal checks* can be made in simple cases where the transformation input to output and back again is *isomorphic*. It may also be desirable to use *coding checks*, that is, software equivalents of the checksum methods used in communication. More general knowledge of the application and system can also lead to *reasonableness checks*, that is, by checking value ranges or the use of *assertions* that describe relationships that should always be true. Finally, structural checks over data objects such as arrays, lists, or queues may be made based upon element counts, the use of redundant pointers, or extra status information.

Damage Confinement and Damage Assessment

There may be a delay between the occurrence of a fault and the error being detected; thus, it is important to be able to confine and assess the damages. Damage confinement is often referred to as *firewalling*. The modular decomposition of problems, where modules hide the details of implementation and have clean interfaces to other modules, is one means of providing firewalls.

The use of protection mechanisms and access permissions related to the capabilities of reading, writing, and executing can also be useful in containing damages to data and program structures.

Software Error Recovery

This is the point at which fault tolerance begins. The goal is to turn an erroneous system state into one that can continue its normal operation, perhaps with degraded service. In this regard, a foreward or backward recovery strategy my be applied.

For *foreward recovery*, an attempt is made to correct the system state. This, of course, is dependent on precise error isolation and the means to make the correction (damage assessment). Self-correcting Haming codes are a good example of the possibility to do foreward recovery. Another example is the use of redundant pointers.

In *backward recovery*, an attempt is made to restore the system to a safe previous state (*recovery point*); at this point an alternative section of the program is executed. The technique used is called *checkpointing*, which implies that all critical system state information be saved regularly, thus leading to questions of efficiency in checkpointing as well as restarting. Various approaches to *incremental checkpointing* as well the use of a *recovery cache* have been applied or proposed.

When concurrent processes interact with each other, state restoration can become extremely complicated, leading to a *domino effect*. If the concurrent processes are executed in a parallel processing environment, the use of rollback may become more tedious, especially in attempting to unwind the effect of communications.

Recovery Block Approach

In this approach, the software is composed of *recovery blocks*, which at entrance build an automatic *recovery point* and at exit an *acceptance test*. The failure of an acceptance test results in the program being restored to the recovery point at the beginning of the block and an alternative module being executed. Facilities for specifying and compiling the code for recovery blocks are not typically found in programming languages. However, Shrivastava (1979) developed a concurrent Pascal expression of recovery blocks, allowing the nesting of blocks (that is, recovery can be specified at various levels).

There should be excellent opportunities to explore the utilization of the recovery block thinking in parallel processing environments where various alternative blocks can be executed in parallel.

5.2.5 Fault Tolerance in Interconnection Networks

A fault-tolerant network is one that continues to provide service, in at least some of the cases, even when the network contains one or more faulty processes. The fault(s) may be either permanent or transient. A network is *single-fault tolerant* if it can function in the presence of a single fault. More generally, an *i-fault tolerant* network can operate in the presence of multiple faults. Such networks are called *robust*. For a survey of fault tolerance in networks, the reader is referred to the special issue of *IEEE Computer* (see Bhuyan, 1987).

The obvious means of providing fault tolerance is to duplicate (or perhaps even triplicate) the entire ICN. The networks can operate in parallel with DRS (double redundancy) or TRS (triple redundancy). This may be the best and most straightforward solution for reasonably small but critical networks (especially for hard real-time systems with high reliability demands). On the other hand, a variety of techniques has been applied to achieve some degree of fault tolerance within various ICNs. We shall consider one of several examples presented by Adams, Agrawal, and Siegel (1987), where the strategy is to provide additional control for bypassing switches when the switches or the output communication paths to which they are connected have been determined to be faulty. Consider the augmented extrastage cube network portrayed in Figure 5.8.

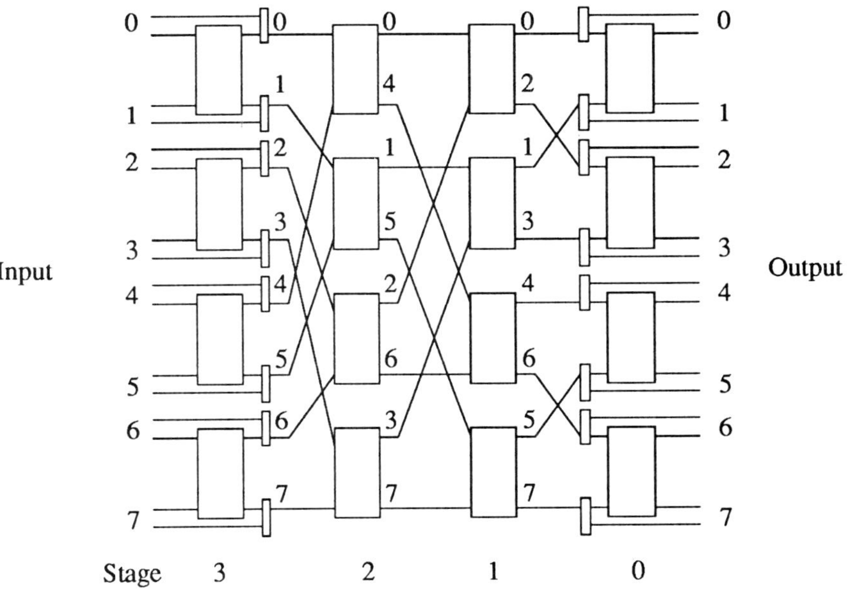

Figure 5.8. Extrastage Cube Network for $N = 8$

In this case, the general cube is extended with an extra stage to the input side of the network along with multiplexers and demultiplexers at the input and output stages, respectively. Dual connections to and from the PEs of the network are required. Stage n is connected like stage 0; that is, links that differ in the low-order bits are paired. Stage n and stage 0 can be bypassed (disabled). A stage is *enabled* when its switches are being used to provide interconnection and is *disabled* when its switches are being bypassed. The enabling and disabling in stages n and 0 are accomplished as shown in Figure 5.9.

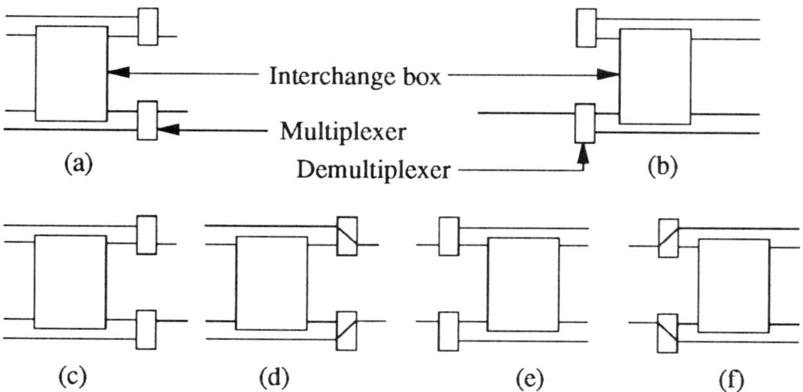

Figure 5.9. Input and Output Stage Switch Setting: (a) multiplexer for enabling and disabling; (b) output stage switch with demultiplexer for enabling and disabling; (c) input stage switch enabled; (d) input stage switch disabled; (e) output stage switch enabled; (f) output switch disabled

Normally, the network will be set so that stage n is disabled, stage 0 is enabled, and the resulting structure is the generalized cube. If a fault is detected, the network is reconfigured. A fault in a switch in a stage n switch requires no change in network configuration; stage n remaining disabled. If the fault occurs in stage 0, then stage n is enabled and stage 0 is disabled (that is, stage n replaces the function of stage 0). For a fault in a link or in a switch in stages n - 1 to 1, both stages n and 0 will be enabled. This dual enabling provides two distinct paths between any source and any destination, at least one of which must be fault free in order to provide a single-fault-tolerant network. However, multiple fault tolerance can be achieved by individually enabling and disabling the stage n and stage 0 switches.

Various Techniques for Multistage Networks

Given this concrete example, we now enumerate some of the techniques that have been utilized or explored in terms of providing fault-tolerant multistage networks:

- — adding of an extra stage with or without bypassing
- — adding extra links
- — slightly increasing the number of network ports
- — varying switch size and number of stages in an interrelated manner
- — increasing switch size and adding corresponding links
- — replication of the network (as considered previously)

The use of these techniques, and others, is reviewed by Adams, Agrawal, and Siegel (1987).

5.2.6 Fault Tolerance in Wavefront and Systolic Systems

The fabrication of regular arrays introduces the problems we have considered earlier with respect to reconfigurability in VLSI circuits. Hedlund and Snyder (1984) have specifically addressed these problems.

Concerning responsiveness during operation, in a wavefront array, once a fault has been detected, the faulty PE is stopped and all subsequent PEs will automatically cease. In the case of systolic arrays, a global error-halt signal is required, which must be broadcast to all PEs. Rolling back the computation to a new starting point is more straightforward in the wavefront case. On the other hand, during the systolic array operation, depending upon the topology, it may be possible to utilize multiple processing elements in providing the redundant processing required for fault detection, as illustrated by Malek (1990). Finally, the ease of fault tolerance for wavefronts by programming the PEs to dynamically reroute around PEs containing fault conditions makes them a good candidate for responsive wafer-scale integration. In this case, analogies to the reconfiguration of WSI systems can be useful.

5.3 HARDWARE AND SOFTWARE VERIFICATION

Verification involves proving the truth of something by presenting evidence. In respect to the hardware and software processes we are concerned with, we can define:

verifiabillity — the ability to determine if a process (or set of cooperating processes) behaves in a manner consistent with the specified behavior (that is, it is correct).

Formal verification methods for both hardware and software processes have received significant attention during the 1980s. Several of the formal methods described in Chapter 7 have been applied in this respect.

For hardware process, several aspects need to be verified, including low-level design rules, timing, high-level design rules, firmware, and functional correctness. Camurati and Prinetto (1987) provide a good introduction to formal verification in the hardware domain.

Work on software verification has concentrated on timing (temporal) properties and, in many cases, the properties related to the treatment of queues in nondeterministic environments. Some early pioneering work in this area was introduced by Hoare (1969, 1972). For additional relevant work, the reader is referred to the work of Manna and Pnueli (1981) on temporal logic, the work of Jahanian and Mok (1986) in developing RTL (real-time logic), Guttag, Horning, and Wing (1985) for their work on Larch, and Barbacci and Wing (1987) for their work on Durra.

References

Adams, G.B., D.P. Agrawal, and H.J. Siegel (1987). Fault-tolerant Multistage Interconnection Networks, *Computer*, Vol. 20, No. 6, pp. 14-27.

Anderson, T., and P.A. Lee (1981). *Fault Tolerance Principles and Practice*, Prentice Hall, Englewood Cliffs, NJ.

Barbacci, M.R., and J.M. Wing (1987). Specifying Functional and Timing Behaviour for Real-time Applications. *PARLE Parallel Architectures and Languages Europe*, Vol. II, Springer-Verlag, New York.

Bhuyan, L.N. (ed.) (1987). Interconnection Networks for Parallel and Distributed Processing, *Computer (special issue)*, Vol. 20, No. 6.

Burns, A., and A. Wellings (1989). *Real-time Systems and Their Programming Languages*, Addison-Wesley, Reading, MA.

Camurati, P., and P. Prinetto (1987). Formal Verification of Hardware Correctness: An Introduction, *Computer Hardware Description Languages and their Applications*, M.R. Barbacci and C.J. Koomen (eds.), Elsevier Science Publishers, B.V. (North-Holland), New York.

Chen, L., and A. Avizienis (1978). N-Version Programming: A Fault Tolerance Approach to Reliability of Software Operation, *Digest of Papers, The Eighth Annual Conference on Fault-tolerant Computing*, Toulouse, France.

Davidson, S. (1988). Merging BIST and Boundary Scan at the IC Level, *Proceedings of Wescon/88*, Anaheim, CA.

Guttag, J.V., J.J. Horning, and J.M Wing (1985). The Larch Family of Specification Languages, *IEEE Software*, Vol. 2, No. 5, pp. 24-36.

Hedlund, K.S., and L. Snyder (1984). Systolic Architectures — A Wafer-scale Approach, *Proceedings of the 1984 IEEE Conference on Computer Design*, pp. 604-610.

Hoare, C.A.R. (1969). An Axiomatic Basis for Computer Programming, *Communications of the ACM*, Vol. 12, No. 10, pp. 576-583.

Hoare, C.A.R. (1972). Proof of Correctness for Computer Programming, *Acta Informatica*, Vol. 1, No. 1, pp. 271-281.

Jahanian, F., and A.K. Mok (1986). Safety Analysis of Timing Properties in Real-time Systems. *IEEE Transactions on Software Engineering*, Vol. 12, No. 9, pp. 890-904.

Koren, I., and A.D. Singh (1990). Fault Tolerance in VLSI Circuits, *Computer*, Vol. 23, No. 7, pp. 73-83.

Malek, M. (1990). Responsive Systems: A Challenge for the Nineties, *Proceedings Euromicro 90*, North-Holland, Amsterdam, pp. 10-16.

Manna, Z., and A. Pnueli (1981). Verification of Concurrent Programs: The Temporal Framework, in R.S. Boyer and J.S. Moore (eds.), *The Correctness Problem in Computer Science*, Academic Press, New York.

Narraway, J.J. (1990). Probabilistic Diagnosis, *Proceedings of the EUROMICRO Workshop on Real Time*, IEEE Computer Society Press, Los Alamitos, CA, pp. 152-161.

Shrivastava, S.K. (1979). Concurrent Pascal with Backward Error Recovery, *Software Practice and Experience*, Vol. 9, No. 12, pp. 1021-1034.

Singh, A.D., and S. Murugesan (1990). Fault-tolerant Systems: Special Issue, *Computer*, Vol. 23, No. 7.

Whetsel, L. (1988). A Proposed Standard Test Bus and Boundary Scan Architecture. *Proceedings of Wescon/88*, Anaheim, CA.

Williams, T., and K.P. Parker (1982). Design for Testability — A Survey, *IEEE Transactions on Computers*, Vol. C-31, No. 1, pp. 2-15.

Chapter ***6***

HISTORICAL PERSPECTIVE

In this chapter, we review **some** of the historical factors that lay behind the current state of the art in parallel processing. We primarily point to the developments in the 1960s and 1970s.

- factors that have contributed to the rapid development in the 1980s have been identified: availability of high performance, large capacity hardware structures, better knowledge of parallelism, and availability of custom and semicustom integrated-circuit technology (251)

- parallelism in hardware processes (CPUs and I/O communication) have existed for a long time (252)

- military and space requirements have driven the development of parallel processing, including its exploitation for real-time systems (252)

- the ILLIAC-IV was the first SIMD machine to be realized (254)

- the development of the FFT algorithms was the most important development for digital signal processing during the 1960s (256)

- original work on concurrency in software resulted in the development of coroutines, **fork** and **join** statements, as well as the introduction of P and V synchronization primitives (256)

- during the 1970s several experimental and commercial parallel processing machines became available — in the MIMD category, C.mmp, Cm*, and HEP — in the SIMD category, STARAN, as well as the introduction of dataflow architectural concepts (258)

- further work based on P and V synchronization primitives resulted in monitors, and the introduction of guarded commands led to the development of CSP (261)

- the availability of regular integrated-circuit components as well as the new awareness of custom and semicustom development potential in the late 1970s provided an important starting point for the 1980s (261)

- the microprocessor became the important new instrument for moving into the era of programmed digital signal processors (261)

Denning (1986) notes several interesting developments concerning early views of parallel processing. He reports that in the 1920s Vanevar Bush at the Massachusetts Institute of Technology demonstrated a general analog computer capable of solving arbitrary differential equations; it consisted of components operating in parallel. von Neumann's papers indicate that in the 1940s he considered methods for solving differential equations on a discrete grid; all grid points were updated in parallel using the differential equation to determine how neighbors affect each other. Many early researchers in the field of intelligent machines proposed computing substrates based on regular networks of automata. During the 1960s, several works were reported on a class of models called parallel program schemata. Thus, a starting point was established prior to the current intense developments in the area.

In the previous chapters of this part of the book, we have concentrated upon parallel processing developments that primarily arose during the 1980s and that led to making parallel solutions interesting for real-time environments. We can attribute the possibilities to exploit parallel processing in contemporary and future systems to the following three enabling factors:

(1) *New high-performance and large-capacity component and packaging technologies permitting volume replication*
(2) *A better understanding of application and system parallelism in general and concurrent programming operating systems in particular*
(3) *The general accessibility to custom and semicustom integrated circuits*

While we have experienced an intensification of interest and concrete results during the 1980s, it is important to note that the goals of utilizing parallel processing, even for certain real-time applications, have a history dating back to the 1950s and 1960s. In the absence of the three factors we have sighted for contemporary advances, developments where often speculative and did not lead to concrete, widely utilized parallel processing products in general and real-time system products in particular.

The other chapters of the book provide a sufficient view of the history of the 1980s. Many of the advances have been covered in dealing with the fundamental issues in the previous chapters of Part I. In Part II, we consider the selected paradigms and artifacts for parallel processing with respect to the BMR model, where specific developments of the 1980s are documented.

In this chapter, we provide a perspective on some of the major developments that occurred prior to the 1980s. Several of the books that provide a deep cataloging of parallel processing offer in-depth historical accounts. For example, for hardware resource structures, the presentation by Hockney and Jesshope (1988) is recommended, whereas for a presentation of software and programming developments, the presentation by Perrott (1987) and the articles collected by Gehani and McGettrick (1988) are extremely valuable.

6.1 DEVELOPMENTS PRIOR TO 1970

The need for and early support of research and development for parallel processing in real-time applications were related to military-sponsored projects. However, hardware parallel processing was, and still is, utilized in improving the overall performance of conventional, commercially available computer systems.

6.1.1 CPU - I/O Parallelism

The major utilization of parallelism in commercial products was to divide CPU processing and input/output activities into concurrent activities. During the 1950s, supercomputer projects of the day, including such machines as the Univac Larc and the IBM Stretch, included separate parallel processing for input/output files. Even some less ambitious systems incorporated special-purpose *file processors* that operated in parallel. During the the late 1950s and in the 1960s, almost all commercial computers utilized *channel programs* executed in special-purpose channel processors that operate independent of the CPU and synchronize for start-up, completion, and error recovery. Probably the most advanced commercial product of the 1960s with regard to parallel CPU and I/O was the CDC 6600, which incorporated up to 10 *programmable peripheral processors* for performing qualified input/output functions.

In Chapter 3, we presented *memory interleaving*, which must also be considered as an early example of parallel processing arising from some of the earliest computer system designs of the 1950s and 1960s.

6.1.2 Military and Space Requirements

While parallel processing was being accomplished in the commercial realm, it was recognized that many problems, particularly military and space related, could not efficiently or effectively be handled by the conventional computer architectures. Thus, in the United States, the Department of Defense sponsored several research and some development projects during the 1960s aimed at providing new architectures for exploiting parallel processing. A good checkpoint on these activities is provided by the proceedings of the symposium on "Parallel Processor Systems, Technologies, and Applications" held in June 1969 (see Hobbs, and others, 1970). The introductory chapter of the symposium proceedings provides a good overview of the state of the art as of 1970.

The reasons given for exploring parallel processing were basically the same as the reasons and goals for parallel processing that were cited in Chapter 1. Even in this pre-VLSI era, there was optimism as to breakthroughs in LSI technology that would enable further development of parallel processing. The definition of parallel processing offered in the introductory chapter of the symposium proceedings is still valid today and directly in line with the common viewpoint that is promoted in this book.

> In this paper, the term "parallel processing" is interpreted broadly to include any type of system organization in which multiple operations are accomplished simultaneously, or multiple hardware control or processing units are working simultaneously. This broad definition permits consideration of widely different types of organizations and systems including multicomputer systems, multiprocessors, associative processors, array or network processors, and functionally partitioned systems.

While the ambition was evident, the *enabling factors* cited at the beginning of this chapter were not as yet present. One could not conveniently embed the "electronic monsters" of the pre-1970 era into many real-time applications.

Several categorization schemes were presented in the 1960s, including the Flynn (SISD, SIMD, MISD and MIMD) classification we have utilized. As a practical classification, Hobbs, and others examined the existing developed or proposed parallel systems and divided them into the following categories:

Type I	Multicomputers and Multiprocessors
Type II	Associative Processors
Type III	Parallel Network of Array Processors
Type IV	Functional Machines

The type I parallel systems include all multicomputers and multiprocessors except highly parallel machines (that is, ones with more than 10 processors and where the processors are integrated to allow them to work on the same algorithm). This category included several complete computer systems interconnected to facilitate data transfer and the assignment of processing tasks. (Today, we would call them *loosely coupled.*) However, the category also includes multiprocessors that share common memory and common input/output equipment. Both symmetric and asymmetric variations are included in this type. It even includes the parallel I/O activity variety found in commercial computers. In fact, most of the systems cited as belonging to this category where available as commercial products.

The type II associative processors are based upon the use of associative memories (that is, memories that permit parallel search and retrieval based upon the contents of the individual memory cells as described in Chapter 3). By complementing the memory cells with processing operations, functions can be directly applied to the data in parallel. Since the same operation is performed on every memory cell, we can categorize associative processors as SIMD. Proposals were made for associative processors during the 1960s; however, very few resulted in concrete, usable hardware products. Some products did arrive in the 1970s as described later.

The type III network of array processors involves a large number of processing units interconnected in some kind of network, frequently a matrix. Usually, each element communicates with immediate neighbors (above, below, to the right, and to the left). There were several machines of this SIMD type proposed in the late 1950s and the 1960s; however, only a few resulted in functioning hardware. In this functioning category is the ILLIAC IV system.

The type IV functional organization is one in which a number of functional units are provided to perform different types of operations concurrently on a different data item within a single program or on different programs. The examples cited are mostly high-performance pipelined machines of the era where the functions are hardwired. (*Note*: The VLIW architecture that arrived in the 1980s fits conveniently into this category.)

We now take a closer look at some of the properties of the ILLIAC IV, since this project provided concrete results and has been tone-setting for many further developments in the field of massively parallel processing. Further, it was envisioned that the machine could be utilized in time-critical real-time applications.

6.1.3 The ILLIAC IV

This famous machine was the fourth in a series of projects at the University of Illinois aimed at improving the state of the art in parallel processing. As a government-sponsored research project, the university contracted the development of the hardware and certain support software to the Burroughs Corporation. A general overview of the architecture is portrayed in Figure 6.1.

The system contains an array of 256 coupled processing elements (in four autonomous quadrants of 64 each) driven by instructions from a common control unit (CU). Each of the PEs has 2,048 words of 64-bit memory with a 240-nanosecond cycle time. Each PE is capable of 64-bit floating-point multiplication in 400 nanoseconds and addition in 240 nanoseconds.

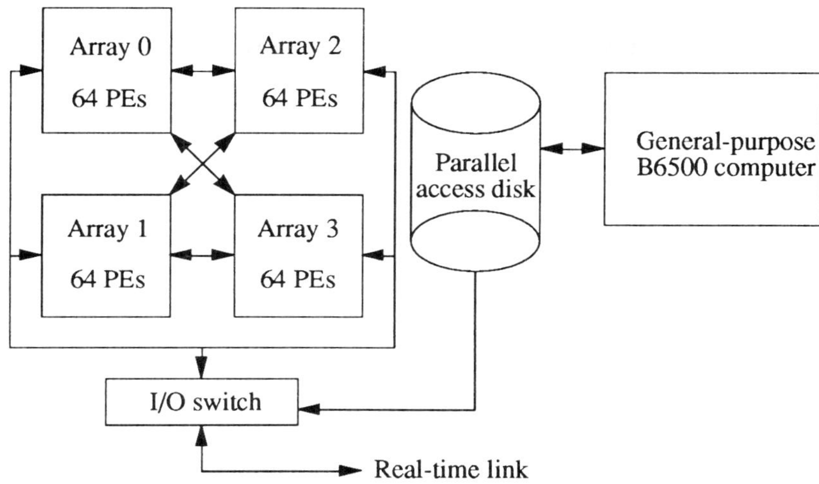

Figure 6.1. The ILLIAC IV System

The machine is partitionable to a 32-bit structure, where each quadrant can be considered as 128 parallel operating units. Further, an 8-bit fixed-point capability is provided in each PE.

The PE instruction set is similar to a conventional computer with extensions for (1) enabling the communication of data to neighboring PEs by means of routing instructions and (2) permitting PEs to set their own mode registers to effectively enable or disable themselves. Instructions are decoded by a common control unit (CU), with control signals being sent to the PE array. In addition to instruction control, the CU can broadcast data to each PE.

The problem of generating high-speed input/output was and still is today a limiting factor for parallel processing. In the ILLIAC IV project, a head per track disk with a 40-millisecond rotation speed was developed (a technological achievement in its own right). Further, the system contained a Burroughs B6500 for performing input/output operations, compilation, and operating system services.

It was envisioned that the ILLIAC IV would provide radically improved performance for a variety of application areas, including the solution of complex differential equations for modeling weather problems (an enormous real-time problem!), linear programming, statistical communication algorithms, and convolution and correlation equations. Knapp, Ackind, and Thomas (1970) provide a detailed analysis of the ILLIAC IV for use in urban defense radar systems. The major radar system functions to be assigned to the ILLIAC IV included (1) radar beam forming and control, (2) scan for objects,

(3) confirmation, (4) cloud track, (5) designation, and (6) object track. This application is certainly one of the most significant early attempts at exploiting massively parallel processing in a nontrivial real-time application.

Although the ILLIAC IV never reached its final goals, a machine was built with one 64-PE quadrant and was the subject of intensive utilization and research until the early 1980s. The project has influenced many subsequent developments. A good retrospective overview of the ILLIAC IV by its original designers has been provided (see Barnes, and others, 1968).

6.1.4 Digital Signal Processing and Direct Mapping

During the 1940s and 1950s, the need for improved automatic control and signal-processing techniques in real-time applications, for example, fire control and radar systems, provided, a strong impetus for the development of sample-data and digital techniques (see Kaiser, 1966). A major reason for the impetus is that by utilizing numerical (digital) algorithms instead of analog components it became possible to circumvent the problems associated with component tolerances and ageing, as we noted in Chapter 4. Hence, with the introduction of digital technology, more sophisticated signal-processing methods became viable. However, significant developments in the field of signal processing for exploiting digital parallel processing have been highly dependent upon the first and third enabling factors given at the beginning of the chapter, that is, component and packaging technology as well as access to semicustom and custom integrated-circuit technology. Up to the beginning of the 1970s, the field was dominated by analog and hybrid analog-digital techniques.

The major event of the 1960s, which has been an important stimulus for research in the digital signal-processing area, was the introduction of reversible linear transformation algorithms for the FFT (**F**ast **F**ourier **T**ransform) by Cooley and Tukey (1965). The importance of ICN interconnection networks and permuted partial communication for algorithm implementation had its birth.

The applicability of more general concepts for direct mapping via the automated synthesis of parallel processes was recognized by Bredt and McCluskey (1970). They explored the use of *flow tables* (borrowed from switching theory) to analyze and synthesize control mechanisms for parallel processes.

6.1.5 Software and Programming Considerations

The software and programming considerations for associative processors (type II) and array processors (type III) were normally developed as special-purpose solutions that dealt with exploiting the special properties of these new forms of computational devices. On the other hand, there was some general research concerning the properties of algorithms and parallelism that was to become important during the 1970s.

Conway (1963a) introduced the first notions of synchronization and communication techniques in the form of *coroutines*, where each **coroutine** is, in fact, a process. Synchronization was provided by the use of **resume** and **return** statement semantics. These ideas where later integrated into the Simula programming language by Dahl and Nygaard (1966). While coroutines provided an interesting fresh view of program synchronization and communication, they could not be used for parallel processing since their semantics allow for the execution of only one routine at a time. It is worth noting that Wirth (1966) also contributed to the further development of the coroutine concepts.

Another early proposal for concurrency was the introduction of the **fork** and **join** statements by Conway (1963b) and Dennis and Van Horn (1966). Unlike the coroutine approach, the invoking routine and the designated routine proceed concurrently at the fork and synchronize again at the join.

As noted in Chapter 3, one of the most significant results of the 1960s was the introduction of the *synchronization primitives* called P and V operating on *semaphore variables* by Dijkstra (1968). This work spanned significant future investigations of the question of the software process synchronization.

Early research on finding *implicit* parallelism in procedural language structures as well as in dataflow was also done during the 1960s. In this regard, we can note, among many, the works of Adams (1970), Gonzalez and Ramamoorthy (1970), Baer and Russell (1970), and Reigel (1970). Another important contribution was the original ideas that led to the development of logic and functional programming languages by Robinson (1965 and 1969).

6.1.6 A Retrospective Observation

As an interesting reflection on the state of the art in 1970 and potential future development, we note some general observations by Hobbs, and others (1970). They point to several key considerations that can significantly favor a parallel processor configuration that would not otherwise be technically favored:

1) A hardware fabrication breakthrough may allow one parallel processor design approach to take precedence over all others.
2) One approach may be successful in a particular company because of its compatibility with that company's present generation of computers.
3) Software algorithms may be developed that provide high equipment utilization for one particular approach.
4) Government support of a particular approach may result in one parallel processor approach dominating regardless of whether it is technically superior or not.

Certainly, the development trends speculated in the first three points have not as yet yielded any single best approach. With regard to the fourth point, the U.S. government support (via the Advanced Research Projects Agency) during the later part of the 1980s has been given to a plurality of projects, each offering various forms of advantages in their particular domains of applicability. Other governmental and private organizations in North America, Europe, and the Far East have also supported diverse development of parallel processing architectures. There is not likely to be any one best approach in the forseeable future. Once again:

THERE ARE NO SOLUTIONS; ONLY ALTERNATIVES

6.2 PARALLEL PROCESSING IN THE 1970s

With regard to the three enabling factors identified at the beginning of the chapter, major advances in components and packaging technology transpired during the 1970s. Further, accessibility to semicustom and custom integrated-circuit technology had its beginnings, along with the recognition of the importance of new solutions to the concurrency problems of synchronization and communication. Many of the developments in the 1970s can be classified as further developments from the 1960s, being based upon the new integrated-circuit technologies and packaging techniques. However, there was an increase of interest in MIMD multiprocessor architectures, with shared resources belonging to the type I category of Hobbs, and others. Further, several speculative projects were initiated to explore a new philosophy based upon *dataflow* as a means of organizing and exploiting parallel processing.

The general intensification of interest in parallel processing during the 1970s can be noted by the introduction of an annual conference sponsored by the IEEE Computer Society and the Association of Computing Machinery. The ninth annual conference transpired in August 1980. The proceedings of this conference containing 65 summaries of results provide another checkpoint in the state of the art (see Kuck, Lawrie, and Sameh, 1980).

While many of the results of parallel processing projects and products during the 1970s were not specifically aimed at solving industrial real-time problems, many of them did contribute to the state of the art of parallel processing in general. Many lessons can be learned from the earlier attempts to move into the era of parallel processing; thus, in the remainder of this chapter we will briefly review some of the 1970s projects that have influenced contemporary developments. Once again, a more detailed account is provided by Hockney and Jesshope (1988).

6.2.1 Carnegie-Mellon C.mmp and Cm*

Some of the most significant MIMD parallel processing research projects during the 1970s transpired at Carnegie-Mellon under the direction of Gordon Bell and in cooperation with Digital Equipment Corporation.

The first of these projects (C.mmp) provided a symmetrical multiprocessor parallel processing environment consisting of 16 PDP-11 computers and 16 memory modules with **total** crossbar interconnection between all processors and memories (see Wulf and Bell, 1972).

Next, the Cm* project provided a new multiprocessor architecture based upon LSI-11 computers that could be organized into a hierarchical structure. Each computing element contained a processor and a memory. While communication between computing elements was via hierarchical connections, the collective memories of up to 50 processing elements formed a single global memory for the system (see Swan, Fuller, and Siewiorek, 1977).

These pioneering efforts have been further described by Satyanarayanan (1980), and a retrospective view of their development has been provided by Jones and Schwarz (1980).

6.2.2 Heterogeneous Element Processor - HEP

Among the first commercially available MIMD systems was the Heterogeneous Element Processor, designed by Smith (1978) and produced by the Denelcor Corporation. The system consisted of up to 16 PEs connected, via a package-switching network, to a maximum of 128 memory modules. One of the major ideas of the HEP was related to the synchronization of requests to the large shared memory provided by the system. Every word of data contains a full/empty switch that prohibits the reading of data until it is filled and only permits writing of data when the cell is empty. The processing elements themselves operated in parallel via separate internal pipelines for various functions. Thus, parallelism is achieved both locally and globally.

HEP was programmed mostly in FORTRAN, where special language features and machine instructions were provided to establish parallel streams of processes that build upon the **fork** and **join** statement semantics. To assure some form of fairness in the parallel processes being executed, processes are switched on every clock cycle.

The pioneering HEP product has provided an inspiration for further development of parallel MIMD products; however, the product was discontinued in 1985 due to financial difficulties at Delencor.

6.2.3 Dataflow Architectures

During the 1970s several researchers proposed a completely new way of viewing the organization and execution of programs. We devote Chapter 12 to developments in the dataflow area. The fundamental idea is to decompose a program into a set of *packets,* each containing an operator and its operands. These packets are transmitted to PEs, evaluated, and returned to storage. The order of the evaluation in the processing elements does not have to correspond to the order in which the operations are syntactically given in the program, thus providing a form of scalar parallelism. As mentioned in the earlier discussion of programming paradigms in Chapter 3, there is a relationship between the functional way of viewing processing and the dataflow concepts.

6.2.4 STARAN and Bit-slice Associative Processing

The architectural concepts implemented in the Goodyear STARAN computer (Batcher, 1974, 1976, 1977, 1979) can be traced back to a paper by Shooman (1960). This early paper introduced the idea of treating several data items simultaneously in a bit-slice fashion. This "parallel processing with vertical data" is contrasted with the usual *word serial/bit parallel* processing mode found in conventional computers and is also referred to as *word parallel/bit serial processing*.

The ability to treat all data items in a memory area simultaneously — albeit only one bit at a time — allows large quantity tests and selections to be performed very quickly, forming the basis for **associative processing**. Data items are selected for processing not only by their addresses in memory, but by the fact that part of their contents match a given pattern.

The first STARAN model (completed in 1972) contained processing arrays with 256 1-bit processing elements (PEs) connected to memory modules of 256 words, each 256 bits long. The normal data access is a bit slice, each PE accessing one bit from the corresponding memory word. Through a FLIP network, the bit slice can be shuffled in various ways, for example, to suit the butterfly data access pattern of the fast Fourier transform. Furthermore, a word instead of a bit-slice can be accessed by the same 256 processors, making STARAN an **orthogonal computer**. This trick is made possible by scrambling the logical words and logical bit slices into the physical chips in such a way that the bits of one word are all in different chips, and the bits of one bit slice are all in different chips. Several other access patterns can also be derived by individual chip addressing and passes through the FLIP network.

Early applications programmed for STARAN were air traffic control (a hard real-time application), described in Rudolph and Batcher (1982), and image processing, described in Goodyear (1976) and Potter (1978). The former application demonstrates the ability of this kind of architecture to keep track of and compare hundreds of constantly changing records simultaneously. The latter application shows that uniform processing of low-precision data suits an array of bit-serial processing elements.

Although not a commercial success, STARAN demonstrated the power of large arrays of bit-serial PEs. Application work performed on several similar designs conceived in the late 1970s and operational in the early 1980s has continued to show a large range of application areas. See, for example, Reddaway (1979) on the DAP product and Svensson (1983) on the LUCAS project.

6.2.5 Software and Programming Considerations

The use of the **fork** and **join** statement approach found its way into developments during the 1970s. In particular, Ritchie and Thompson (1974) made extensive use of these concepts for controlling process concurrency in UNIX.

The original work of Dijkstra concerning P and V synchronization became the subject of intense development during the 1970s. A major contribution in the form of *monitors* was made by Hoare (1974), and these concepts were incorporated into a programming language by Brinch Hansen (1975). The monitor concept proved to be quite useful in structuring complex real-time systems (see Lawson, Bertran, and Xampeny, 1977).

Further, Dijkstra (1975) introduced the notion of guarded commands, which has affected thinking in the area of program organization for concurrent execution. Among other work, these notions influenced Hoare (1978) in his development of CSP.

In the area of functional programming, the major event and the beginning point for much of today's research was the paper by Backus (1978) entitled "Can Programming be Liberated from the von Neumann Style?" In the area of logic programming, the major developments were the introduction of Prolog by Kowalski (1974) and the continuing theoretical contributions of Robinson (1979).

6.2.6 VLSI-inspired Developments

The 1970s can be marked as the era of major advances in integrated-circuit technology. In addition to major advances in memory technologies, the microprocessor was born and rapidly became a widely utilized component.

The first and third factors cited at the beginning of this chapter started to become reality during the late 1970s. More regularly structured VLSI components became available, as well as the beginning of the availability of custom and semicustom VLSI. The most significant contribution in providing an awareness of the possibilities of VLSI was made by Mead and Conway (1980).

6.2.7 Digital Signal Processing

While the FFT algorithm (Cooley and Tukey, 1965) was the most important development of the 1960s, the microprocessor was destined to become the most important development for digital signal processing during the 1970s. The microprocessor formed the basis for the first programmable signal-processing elements and has been extremely successful. At this point, digital electronic components started to find their way in as a replacement for analog-based signal-processing technology in a wide variety of real-time environments.

6.3 ENTERING INTO THE 1980s

Finally, we began the chapter by indicating three enabling technologies that have provided the impetus for the rapid and diverse developments of parallel processing in the 1980s. This development was speculated on by Mead and Conway (1980), who wrote in their pioneering book *Introduction to VLSI Systems*:

> VLSI electronics presents a challenge, not only to those involved in the development of fabrication technology, but also to computer scientists and computer architects. The ways in which digital systems are structured, the procedures used to design them, the trade-offs between hardware and software, and the design of computational algorithms will all be greatly affected by the coming changes in integrated electronics. We believe this will be a major area of activity in computer science through the 1980s.

Their prediction was certainly correct, as attested by the writing of this book, which brings into focus many of the developments of the 1980s that can be of interest for industrial real-time applications. Perhaps the 1990s will be marked as an era where the developments in parallel processing of the 1980s will find broader use in terms of real-time system products.

References

Adams, D.A. (1970). A Model of Parallel Computations, *Parallel Processor Systems, Technologies, and Applications,* Spartan/Macmillan, New York, pp. 311-334.

Backus, J. (1978). Can Programming Be Liberated from the von Neumann Style, *Communications of the ACM*, Vol. 21, No. 8, pp. 613-641.

Baer, J.L., and E.C. Russell (1970). Preparation and Evaluation of Computer Programs for Parallel Processing Systems, *Parallel Processor Systems, Technologies, and Applications,* Spartan/Macmillan, New York, pp. 375-416.

Barnes, G.H., R.M. Brown, M. Kato, D.J. Kuck, D.L. Slotnick, and R.A. Stokes (1968). The ILLIAC IV Computer, *IEEE Transactions on Computers*, Vol. C-17, No. 8, pp. 746-757.

Batcher, K.E. (1974). STARAN Parallel Processor System Hardware, *Proceedings of AFIPS National Computer Conference*, 1974, pp. 405-410.

Batcher, K.E. (1976). The FLIP Network in STARAN, *Proceedings of the 1976 International Conference on Parallel Processing,* Waldenwoods, MI.

Batcher, K.E. (1977). The Multidimensional Access Memory in STARAN, *IEEE Transactions on Computers*, Vol. C-26, No. 2, pp. 174-177.

Batcher, K.E. (1979). The STARAN Computer, *Infotech State of the Art Report on Supercomputers*, Infotech International Ltd., Maidenhead, Berkshire, UK.

Bredt, T.H., and E. J. McCluskey (1970). Analysis and Synthesis of Control Mechanism for Parallel Processes, *Parallel Processor Systems, Technologies, and Applications* Spartan/Macmillan, New York, pp. 287-296.

Brinch Hansen, P. (1975). The Programming Language Concurrent Pascal, *IEEE Transactions on Software Engineering*, Vol. SE-1, No. 2, pp. 199-206.

Conway, M.E. (1963a). Design of a Separable Transition-diagram Compiler, *Communications of the ACM*, Vol. 6, No. 7, pp. 396-408.

Conway, M.E. (1963b). A Multiprocessor System Design, *Proceedings of AFIPS 1963 Fall Joint Computer Conference*, Vol. 24, pp. 139-146.

Cooley, J.W., and J.W. Tukey (1965). An Algorithm for the Machine Computation of Complex Fourier Series, *Mathematics of Computation*, Vol. 19, pp. 297-301.

Dahl, O., and K. Nygaard (1966). SIMULA - An Algol Based Simulation Language, *Communications of the ACM*, Vol. 9, pp. 671-678.

Denning, P.J. (1986). Parallel Computing and Its Evolution, *Communications of the ACM*, Vol. 29, No. 12, pp. 1163-1167.

Dennis, J.B., and E.C. Van Horn (1966). Programming Semantics for Multiprogrammed Computations, *Communications of the ACM*, Vol. 9, No. 3, pp. 143-155.

Dijkstra, E.W. (1968). Cooperating Sequential Processes, *Programming Languages*, F. Genuys (ed.), Academic Press, New York, pp. 43-112.

Dijkstra, E.W. (1975). Guarded Commands, Nondeterminancy, and Formal Derivation of Programs, *Communications of the ACM*, Vol. 18, No. 8, pp. 453-457.

Gehani, N., and A.D. McGettrick (1988). *Concurrent Programming*, Addison-Wesley, Reading, MA.

Gonzalez, M.J., and C.V. Ramamoorthy (1970). Recognition and Representation of Parallel Processable Streams in Computer Programs, *Parallel Processor Systems, Technologies, and Applications,* Spartan/Macmillan, New York, pp. 335-376.

Goodyear (1976). Digital Image Processing and STARAN, Report GER-16336, Goodyear Aerospace Corporation, Akron, Ohio.

Hoare, C.A.R. (1974). Monitors: An Operating System Structuring Concept, *Communications of the ACM*, Vol. 17, No. 10, pp. 549-557.

Hoare, C.A.R. (1978). Communicating Sequential Processes, *Communications of the ACM*, Vol. 21, No. 8, pp. 666-677.

Hobbs, L.C., D.J. Theis, J. Trimble, H. Titus, and I. Highberg, eds. (1970). *Parallel Processor Systems, Technologies, and Applications,* Spartan/Macmillan, New York.

Hockney, R.W., and C.R. Jesshope (1988). *Parallel Computers 2: Architecture, Programming and Algorithms*, Adam Higler, Bristol, England, and Philadelphia.

Jones, A.K., and P. Schwarz (1980). Experience Using Multiprocessor Systems - A Status Report, *Computing Surveys*, Vol. 12, pp. 121-165.

Kaiser J. F. (1966). *Digital Filters*, Chapter 7 in F.F. Kuo, and J.F. Kaiser (eds.), *System Analysis by Digital Computer*, John Wiley & Sons, Inc., New York.

Knapp, M.A., G.M. Ackins, and J. Thomas (1970). Application of the ILLIAC IV to Urban Defense Radar Problem, *Parallel Processor Systems, Technologies, and Applications,* Spartan/Macmillan, New York, pp. 23-70.

Kowalski, R.A. (1974). Predicate Logic as a Programming Language, *Information Processing 74, IFIP Congress*, pp. 569-574, August.

Kuck, D.J., D.H. Lawrie, and A.H. Sameh, eds. (1980). *Proceedings of the 1980 International Conference on Parallel Processing*, IEEE Catalog NO. 80CH1569-3.

Lawson, H.W., M. Bertran, and J. Xampeny (1977). Structured Design and Implementation of the Central Control of a High Voltage Power Dispatching System, *Proceedings of the IFAC Symposium on Automatic Control and Protection of Electrical Power Systems*, Melbourne, February.

Mead, C., and L. Conway (1980). *Introduction to VLSI Systems*, Addison-Wesley, Reading, MA.

Perrott, R.H. (1987). *Parallel Programming*, Addison-Wesley, Reading, MA.

Potter, J.L. (1978). The STARAN Architecture and Its Application to Image Processing and Pattern Recognition Algorithms, *Proceedings of AFIPS National Computer Conference*, 1978, pp. 1041-1047.

Reddaway, S. (1979). The DAP Approach. *Infotech State of the Art Report on Supercomputers*, Infotech International. Ltd., Maidenhead, Berkshires, UK.

Reigel, E.W. (1970). Parallelism Exposure and Exploitation, *Parallel Processor Systems, Technologies, and Applications*, Spartan/Macmillan, New York, pp. 417-438.

Ritchie, D.M., and K. Thompson (1974). The UNIX Timesharing System, *Communications of the ACM*, Vol. 17, No. 7, pp. 365-375.

Robinson, J.A. (1965). A Machine-oriented Logic Based on the Resolution Principle, *Journal of the ACM*, Vol. 12, pp. 23-41.

Robinson, J.A. (1969). Mechanizing Higher Order Logic, *Machine Intelligence 4* (eds., B. Meltzer, and D. Michie), American Elsevier, New York, pp. 151-170.

Robinson, J.A. (1979). *Logic: Form and Function*, North-Holland, Amsterdam.

Rudolph, J.A., and K.E. Batcher (1982). A Productive Implementation of an Associative Array Processor: STARAN, in D.P. Siewiorek, C.G. Bell, and A. Newell, *Computer Structures: Principles and Examples*, McGraw-Hill, New York, pp. 317-331.

Satyanarayanan, M. (1980). *Multi-processors: A Comparative Study*, Prentice Hall, Englewood Cliffs, NJ.

Shooman, W. (1960). Parallel Computing with Vertical Data, *Proceedings AFIPS Conference* pp. 110-115.

Smith, B.J. (1978). A Pipelined Shared Resource MIMD Computer, *IEEE Proceedings of the International Conference on Parallel Processing*, pp. 6-8.

Svensson, B. (1983). LUCAS Processor Array: Design and Applications, Ph.D. thesis, Department of Computer Engineering, University of Lund, Sweden, April 1983.

Swan, R.J., S.H. Fuller, and D.P. Siewiorek (1977). Cm*: A Modular Multi-microprocessor, *Proceedings of the National Computer Conference*, Vol. 46, pp. 637-644.

Wirth, N. (1966). Program Structures for Parallel Processing, *Communications of the ACM*, Vol. 9, No. 5.

Wulf, W.A., and C.G. Bell (1972). C.mmp: a Multi-Mini-Processor, *Proceedings of AFIPS Fall Joint Computer Conference*, Vol. 41, No. 2, pp. 765-777.

Part II

SELECTED PARADIGMS, MODELS and ARTIFACTS

PRELUDE

Part I dealt with fundamental issues where we have considered mainstream developments in parallel processing and real-time systems. In this part, we examine several specific paradigms, models, and artifacts. The paradigms represent various couplings between processing models and resource structures. These couplings are represented as vertical slices through the BMR model, as illustrated in the following:

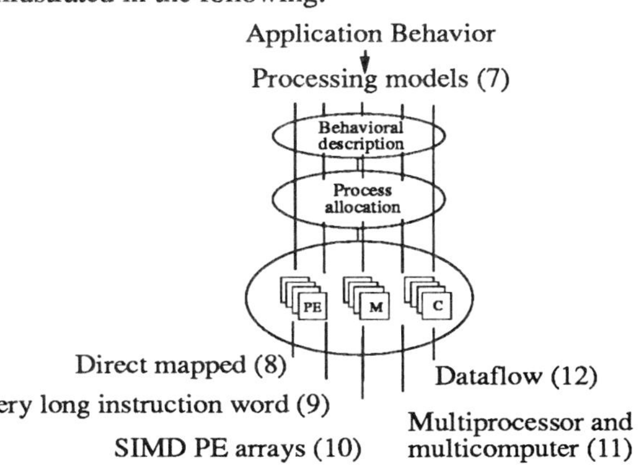

The processing model portion of a paradigm represents the specific approach taken in describing the behavior of the application in order to make application behavior processable by a resource structure.

As we have considered in Part I, certain processing models are closely related to specific resource structure paradigms. This is the case for SIMD PE array architectures (Chapter 10) and dataflow architectures (Chapter 12). In the case of direct mapping (Chapter 8), the actual resource structure is determined in conjunction with the properties of the algorithm and its potential mappings to a family of optimal architectures.

When general-purpose resource structures are provided, a variety of processing models can be mapped into the resource structure, leading to a multiplicity of processing paradigms. The VLIW (Chapter 9) as well as multiprocessor and multicomputer architectures (Chapter 11) permit processing paradigm flexibility. In Chapter 7, we concentrate mostly upon processing models that can be applied to these multiple-purpose resource structures. However, we also consider the VHDL hardware description language that provides an important form of processing model.

In describing the resource structure portion of paradigms and related artifacts, we consider, in addition to the relevant PE, M, and C processes, artifacts used in process mapping and, when appropriate, development environments and tools used in assisting in application development. For example, operating systems for parallel processing environments are described in Chapter 11 where MIMD (multiprocessor and multicomputer) architectures are addressed.

A Word of Warning Concerning Artifacts

While specific artifacts of the trade are essential, they should not be viewed in isolation. Viewing an application problem solely in terms of one or a few of the artifacts often hinders proper development. Unfortunately, the tendency toward *artifact fixation* is prevalent among many professionals (see Lawson, 1990). The problems are too often viewed through a specific set of hardware resources, via a specific formal method, software methodology, programming language, and/or a specific operating system. The reader must keep in mind that what can and cannot be accomplished by applying specific artifacts (and especially combinations of artifacts) limits the degrees of freedom in exploring appropriate solutions in the problem-relevant solution space.

Summarizing the PCS Issues

As we considered in Chapter 1 and observed in the remainder of Part I, the major differences between philosophies, paradigms, and models for exploiting parallel processing lie in the treatment of the PCS issues. After considering the fundamental issues in Part I and in preparation for considering some specific paradigms, models, and artifacts in Part II, we summarize the various views of these fundamental issues.

Not all the views are mutually exclusive, and we find variations on the approaches that have been enumerated. However, our categorization can be useful in providing a general basis for comparison. In particular, the reader will notice that the same views often appear with respect to communication and synchronization. This is due to the fact that the act of communication also implies the act of synchronization. Thus, many of the mechanisms treat both C and S aspects.

Given this preamble to Part II, the reader should be well prepared to examine specific paradigms, models, and artifacts presented in this book, as well as to categorize and contrast other approaches that are encountered.

View of Processes

Fine grain	*Medium grain*	*Coarse Grain*
Instructions	Closures	Procedures*
Operations	Lightweight processes*	Processes*
(arithmetic, logic, etc.)		Tasks*

* Can have varying semantic content that determines actual granularity.

Means of Communication

Physical	*Logical*
Port connections	Abstract ports (queues)
Shared memory	Procedure call (Remote)
Interconnection network	Message passing (Buffered)
Unbuffered message passing	Channels
	Unification

Method of Synchronization

Low Level	*Medium Level*	*High Level*
Time	Semaphores	Monitors
Events (including Interrupts)	Critical regions	Rendezvous
Instructions	Messages	Abstract ports (queues)
Spin-locks	Remote procedure call	Process creation
Barriers	Unification	Process termination
		Coroutines
		FORK-JOIN
		COBEGIN-COEND

Reference

Lawson, H.W. (1990). Philosophies for Engineering Computer-based Systems, *IEEE Computer*, Vol. 23, No. 12, pp. 52-63.

Chapter 7

PROCESSING MODELS

In this chapter, we consider the properties of specific artifacts that can be utilized for abstract and concrete descriptions of application model behavior. Most of the artifacts described in this chapter can best be related to SISD or MIMD resource structure paradigms, where various views of behavioral description result in processing models that can be isolated from specific hardware resource structures.

Since behavioral description leading to specific models of processing plays a central role in our thinking-reasoning-describing processes, it is useful to reflect upon the following observation by McKeeman (1976).

> The universe and its reflection in the ideas of man have wonderfully complex structures. Our ability to comprehend this complexity and perceive an underlying simplicity is intimately bound with our ability to symbolize and communicate our experience. The scientist has been free to extend and invent new languages whenever old forms became unwieldy or inadequate to express his ideas. His readers, however, have faced the double task of learning his new language and the structures he described. There has, therefore, arisen a natural control: a work of elaborate linguistic inventiveness and meagre results will not be widely read.

In our presentation of various artifacts for behavioral description, we will **not** concentrate upon the linguistic inventiveness of the languages (this is better left to more detailed tutorial descriptions or manuals). We shall instead concentrate upon the structures and behavior that can be described by various artifacts.

7.1 FORMAL METHODS

While the use of formal methods for describing the behavior of complex systems has not been widespread in industrial environments, some methods have been utilized for analyzing parallel processing or at least concurrent behavior. There are several important and useful properties of these formal artifacts. The hope is that, by providing a highly regular linguistic expression of the behavior, we can prove certain properties of the system under consideration. In some cases, the goal of the linguistic artifact is extended into being a guide for or the basis of deriving (synthesizing) the processes to be allocated to hardware resources. There are two important starting points with regard to the formal methods that we consider: first the work of Dijkstra in introducing guarded commands in his language DILAG (see Dijkstra, 1975) and, second, another line of thinking based upon the use of graphical networks for representing control flow, as introduced by Petri (1962).

7.1.1 CSP (Communicating Sequential Processes)

The CSP language was developed by Hoare (1978, 1985) and is based upon a few process-related concepts: that processes have disjoint address spaces and that communication is accomplished by synchronous message passing, where process synchronization is accomplished between processes in their communication "act."

Disjoint Process State Space

The central notion is that a program is viewed as communicating processes P_1 to P_n ($n > 1$), where their individual state spaces are disjoint and there are **no** shared variables or common addresses.

Communication by Synchronous Message Passing

Communication and process synchronization are achieved by message passing via input/output constructs. A process P1 (source process) sends a message to P2 (target process) by executing an output command of the form P2!x (with the semantics send x to P2). The identifier x identifies the type of message supplied from P1's variable x (source variable), and it is received in the target variable y of P2 via an input command P1?y. The net effect is an assignment statement between the two processes. These mechanisms are symmetric (the sender and receiver must mutually identify each other).

Selective Communication

Based upon Dijkstra's guarded commands, the selective communication construct specifies the selection of one of the alternative processes for communication subject to some condition in the form

<guard> → <command list>

The guard consists of a list of declarations and Boolean expressions optionally followed by a semicolon and a message-passing statement. The guard fails if any of its

Boolean expressions are FALSE or if the process named in its input command has terminated. In the case of termination, the guard neither fails nor succeeds if the Boolean expression is TRUE, but the message-passing statement cannot be executed without a delay. A skeleton form is as follows:

P_i :: [**if** B_i1 ; $a_j1 \rightarrow S_i1$
[] B_i2 ; $a_j2 \rightarrow S_i2$

[] B_in ; $a_jn \rightarrow S_in$
fi]

P_i, $i \neq j$ is a unique process
$B_i1, \ldots, B_in$ are guards (Boolean expressions) over the local state of P_i
$a_j1, \ldots, a_jn$ are communication commands naming some target process (P_j)
and
$S_i1, \ldots, S_in$ are loop-free and communication-free statements.

The semantics are such that if at least one guard B_in is true an arbitrary one is nondeterministically selected and the corresponding open command (or open alternative) is executed. If all guards fail, the command aborts. If all guards neither fail nor succeed, execution is delayed until some guard succeeds.

Repeated Selective Communication

Many problems can be neatly structured by the use of repeated selective communication which is indicated with an * as follows:

P_i :: *[**if** B_i1 ; $a_j1 \rightarrow S_i1$
[] B_i2 ; $a_j2 \rightarrow S_i2$
.
.
.
[] B_in ; $a_jn \rightarrow S_in$
fi] .

In this case, the inner part, which is an alternative command, is executed repeatedly until all the guards fail. When all the guards fail, the repetitive command terminates and control is transferred to the succeeding statement.

An Example

As an example of utilizing CSP, let us consider a semaphore process that loops continuously acting as an intermediary for other processes. (*Note*: CSP has no embedded notion of semaphores or monitors; consequently, these functions, if desired, must be constructed from basic CSP processes.)

```
SEMAPHORE ::
        VALUE : INTEGER; VALUE = 1;

        *[  A?V( ) → VALUE = VALUE + 1
          [] B?V( ) → VALUE = VALUE + 1
          [] VALUE > 0 ; A?P( ) → VALUE = VALUE - 1
          []  VALUE > 0 ; B?P( ) → VALUE = VALUE - 1
          ] .
```

At each iteration either a V( ) signal or a P( ) signal from one of the processes A or B may be accepted. In this case, no values (messages) are required, since no data value is to be passed between the processes. Note that a P signal cannot be accepted if the first part of the guard in which it is contained is false; that is, VALUE is less than or equal to 0. The processes A or B communicate with the semaphore process as follows:

SEMAPHORE ! V( ) and SEMAPHORE ! P( )

When a process A or B executes the V( ), it must wait until the semaphore process selects the corresponding guarded command. Only at this point can a rendezvous occur and the VALUE be increased by 1.

In Summary

CSP provides a formal basis for studying processes, interprocess communication, and synchronization. It provides a crisp and clean concept of processes, in which the states of processes are isolated from each other. The programming language occam, presented later in the chapter, is a direct descendant of CSP and provides a concrete means of expressing behavior in a CSP-consistent manner. Further, CSP has also influenced the synchronization concepts found in Ada and other programming languages.

Being a pioneering effort, the work naturally has its limitations and much subsequent work has been done in refining CSP notions. For example, Keiburtz and Silberschatz (1979) provided some concrete critique. They note that the property of unbuffered synchronous message passing, while clean, is not very practical and can lead to significant performance degradation in parallel systems. They also note that the clean termination of processes is not always easy to assure in CSP. Further, to deal with communication protocols, additional "signal" handling must be provided, which is not straightforward.

7.1.2 CCS (Calculus of Communicating Systems)

One interesting formal model of concurrency has been developed by Milner (1980) and subsequently described in his book Milner (1989). CCS algebraically describes behavior as a concurrent system, provides specifications, serves as a programming language, and is well suited for verification. CCS is related to developments in lambda - calculus, flow graphs, and flow algebras. CCS is based upon the following ideas:

— systems are sets of asynchronous executing processes
— establishing behavioral equivalence-congruence under observation
— synchronized communication

The first idea relates processes to being self-controlled agents. The second idea is related to the selection of different algebraic rules based upon various forms of behavioral equivalence of programs, whereas the third idea is related to parallel composition, synchronization, and nondeterminism. Central to CCS are the use of binding of variables, name localization, substitution, evaluation, passing values, establishing equivalences, recursion, and fixed points. CCS provides both a functional and an operational model.

The Principles of CCS

There are two sets of objects in CCS:

1) a set of basic computing agents performing actions
2) a set of operators, both dynamic and static, for structuring and building a combination of agents

The basic computing agents can perform certain named actions. The names are chosen from a denumerable set of labels $\Delta = \{\alpha, \beta, \gamma, ...\}$. Also corresponding to each action in Δ, is a coaction, whose names are chosen from another denumerable set of labels Δ' called *conames*, where Δ' is disjoint from and in bijection with Δ.

Further, it is so defined that any action a can **only** synchronize with its coaction (called a *partner*). When they synchronize, there is an interaction that produces a silent coupling action, denoted by τ.

When coupling takes place, the two synchronized actions α and α' are neither visible nor available as external input or output. The coupling provides both communication and synchronization. This situation is described by a *restriction* on the use of α and α' and is denoted by $\backslash\alpha$.

Given these straightforward basic ideas from CCS, a number of operators that operate upon computing agents and combinations of computing agents are defined, including:

— the null operator (NIL)
— sequential composition and recursion
— summation
— parallel composition
— restriction
— relabeling

The true value of CCS is that almost all interesting concurrent behaviors can be described with a few rules, thus making it attractive for verfying properties of concurrent systems.

In Summary

Many concurrent algorithms can be expressed in CCS with clarity. Further, attempts have been made to utilize CCS as a programming language. A language called COSY has been developed based on CCS for concurrent programming (see Best, 1986). Further, proof methods based on CCS have been applied to the development of systolic systems by Hennessy (1986). CCS does not provide any notion of time; however, in an extension called TPCCS (TP = **T**ime and **P**robability), Hansson and Johnsson (1990) have illustrated the usefulness of CCS within the domain of real-time systems.

7.1.3 Petri Nets

Petri nets where introduced by Petri (1962) as a means of graphically representing a flow of control. They were developed specifically in order to formally analyze concurrent systems. Murata (1989) provides a good introduction to Petri nets. The power of Petri nets comes from their dual representation: both a graphical form that enables the use of intuition and improves understanding and human communication, as well as a mathematical expression from which formal analysis and simulation can be derived.

Petri nets have been used widely for analyzing communication protocols and for proof of deadlock-free systems, as well as verification of mutual exclusion. Thus, they are of direct interest for understanding some of the important problems we have considered in behavioral description and resource allocation.

To capture the intuitive nature of Petri nets, let us consider the Petri net portrayed in Figure 7.1.

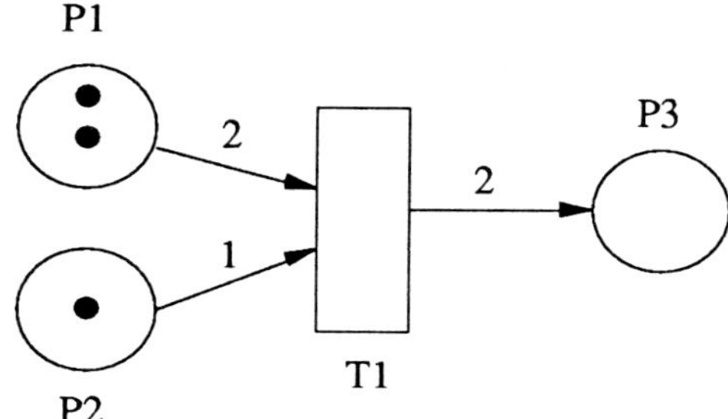

Figure 7.1. A Petri net

The circles are called *places* and the rectangles are called *transitions*. The edges (arcs) that connect places and transitions have a degree. The system is activated solely by the presence of *tokens*. A transition is enabled to *fire* (be activated) if each input place has at least as many tokens as the weight of the edge from the place to the transition. The transition can be fired if the number of tokens in each of its output places will not exceed its capacity after firing. Thus, in our example, the transition is fired if an only if P1 contains two tokens and P2 contains at least one token and the output place can accept two tokens. When the transition fires, the number of tokens in each input place is reduced by the weight of the arc and the number of tokens in each output place is increased by its arc's weight.

From the example, it can easily be seen why Petri nets are frequently referred to as PT nets (**P**lace/**T**ransition) nets. More formally, a Petri net is represented as a six-tuple:

PT (P, T, E, M_0, K, W)

where P — is a set of places (normally represented by circles or ovals)
T — is a set of transitions (normally represented by rectangles or bars)
E — is a set of directed edges (arcs) from a place to a transition or a transition to a place
M_0 — denotes an initial token marking
K(P) — denotes the maximum number of tokens a place P can hold (the default is infinity)
W(E) — denotes the weight assigned to an edge E (default is 1)

A basic Petri net is nondeterministic and there is no explicit concept of time. The order of firing of enabled transitions is random, as well as the selection between conflicting transitions. Further, multiple transitions can occur concurrently. However, to utilize Petri nets in a practical manner, it is possible to make worst-case assumptions about transitions.

Analysis of Petri-nets

Given an expression of the Petri net, it is possible to employ both analytical and search methods to the representations in order to determine important properties.

First, via *search techniques*, reachability and/or coverability can be determined. We can determine if the net is *bounded* (that is, the maximum number of tokens is <= infinity). A determination can be made if the net is *safe* (that is, the maximum number of tokens is <= 1 in all places). Further, we can prove if a transition is *dead* (never fired after considering all possible paths). In general, all possible paths and their composition can be determined.

Petri nets can be treated *analytically* via matrix and state equations, where it is also possible to prove that a net is bounded and/or safe, if a transition is dead, as well as the mutual exclusion of places and the freedom from deadlocks.

An Example

To gain an appreciation of Petri nets, let us consider a simple but highly illustrative application in regulating a railroad crossing gate (see Leveson and Stolzy, 1987). In Figure 7.2, we observe the three actors in the system, the train, the computer, and the crossing gate.

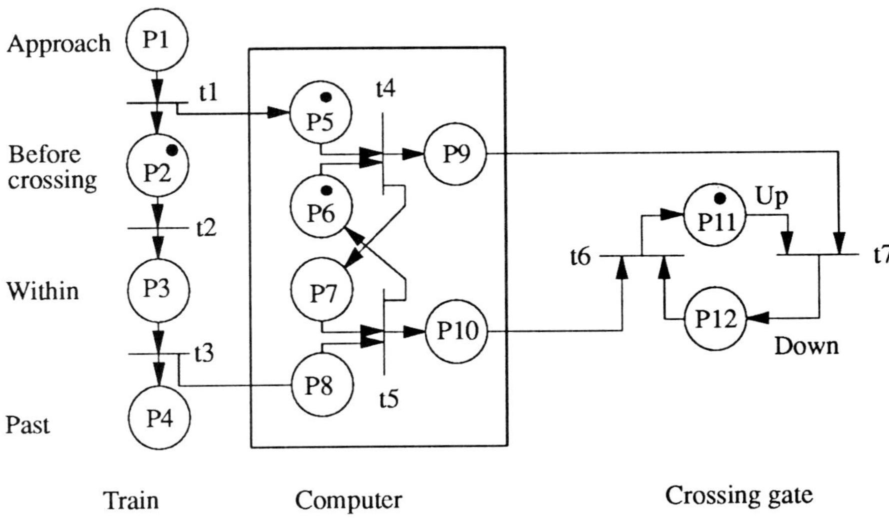

Figure 7.2. Petri Net Example of a Railroad Crossing

In this Petri net representation, we utilize a simple bar for transition instead of a rectangle. We observe the state of the system at a point when a train has approached the crossing, resulting in tokens being placed in P2 and P5. Note that, in the state prior to this transition, tokens appeared in P1, P6, and P11. Thus, when a token was placed in P1 as the train approached, it caused the firing of the transition (t1), thus resulting in the current state portrayed in the figure. In the next state, transition (t4) will be fired, resulting in a token being placed in P9, after which a firing will cause the firing of transition (t7), causing the gate to go down. After this, the train will move into the state where a token is placed in P3 and then into P4, at which point transitions will be fired in an appropriate order to lift the gate and restore the system state to initial conditions.

The value of Petri nets as a graphic media is quite clear from this example. Further, as Leveson and Stolzy (1987) note, it provides a highly useful means of performing a safety analysis. Thus, their value in analyzing real-time systems is quite apparent.

Colored Petri Nets

While Place/Transition nets are useful for proving assertions for small systems, simple net semantics can lead to an excessive volume. Colored Petri nets (CP nets) have been introduced in order to address this problem. In CP nets, tokens become colored sets and places are labeled to indicate specifically the type of tokens they can contain. Further, arcs are labeled with expressions to identify the tokens added or removed at a place when a transition takes place. Finally, transitions can be labeled with a *guard* (Dijkstra's idea again), which must be satisfied in order for the transition to fire. For further explanation of colored Petri nets, see Jensen (1987).

Timed Petri Nets

As mentioned earlier, Petri nets, in general, have no concept of *time,* which naturally limits their usability for time-based analysis. However, during the 1980s much attention was given to developing Petri nets where time becomes an explicit factor. This has led to the development of both *deterministic timed nets* as well as *stochastic Petri nets (SPN).*

In Summary

This is only a brief introduction to the subject of Petri nets, which has become a hot area of interest among those working in analyzing various properties of real-time systems. Several projects have resulted in the development of automatic and/or semiautomatic synthesis of both program- and/or hardware-level control structures (see, for example, Peng, Kuchinski, and Lyles, 1989). Further, Rosenberg (1987) provides references to over 2000 papers in the Petri net area.

7.2 SOFTWARE METHODOLOGIES

A wide variety of software methodologies is available in the commercial marketplace. The methodologies also provide support for thinking-reasoning-describing; however, there is no explicit attempt to, in the "Descartian spirit," prove specific properties of a system other than by simulation and testing. Within a methodology, one always finds some form of language (often graphical as well as textual) that is used for describing processing models. Several of the methodologies are supported by tools used as an aid in software specification, development, and even throughout the life cycle of products.

All the methodologies provide means of suppressing details (they provide *abstraction*). Consequently, all processing models must necessarily represent a compromise between added detail and understandability. In some cases, the methodology provides for extracting partial implementation details in an automatic or semiautomatic manner. The methodologies can be categorized as follows:

7.2.1 Top-down Functional Decomposition

This class of methodologies, typically represented by the work of De Marco (1979) and characterized by an initial mapping of required functions onto software entities within an architecture, generally goes under the name SA (Structured Analysis). The decomposition of component functions is made in a top-down manner. Such an approach is well suited for applications where *operation* is the significant feature of the desired solution to a given requirement. It emphasizes the sequential, procedural aspects of the solution. The basic decomposition criteria of the functional decomposition methodologies is that the units of design (functions, modules, or components) represent steps in the software processing. These components will therefore be biased toward satisfying the needs of operations at the expense of satisfying the needs of the real-world objects that are operated upon. Concurrency of software functions and real-time properties, with some exceptions, are often not explicitly dealt with by these methodologies. However, it is worthwhile to note the exceptions.

A variant of structured analysis called SA/RT has been developed; however, it primarily provides a means of annotating real-time properties in a structured analysis diagram, rather than automatically incorporating them into the final solution (see Ward and Mellor, 1985). Thus, they serve as a goal for real-time processing requirements.

In the United Kingdom, a widely used methodology for real-time system development and, in later years, including parallel processing environments is Mascot 3. In this case, abstract entities for decomposition, that is, activities (equivalent to processes), IDA (integrated data areas), channels, pools, and servers, are explicitly provided. The problem is decomposed into these elements. Since these entities provide a set of semantics for the PCS issues we have identified, it is realistic to consider Mascot as a method for decomposing parallel programs. Further, various translations to occam and Ada have been developed for Mascot designs (see, Jackson 1986).

7.2.2 Data structure-Driven Design

This class is typically represented by JSD (Jackson Structured Design) (see Jackson, 1975) in general and JSP (Jackson Structured Programming) in particular. In JSP, design proceeds by first defining data structures and then structuring the software components based upon these data structures. This approach clearly identifies the real-world objects on which system operations must act, but does not provide much help in designing the operations. This implies that it does not provide any explicit guidance for identifying common operations or in coping with complex operations. On large systems the designer must work with several sets of data for which the chances of a "structure clash" (structural incompatibilities) are quite considerable.

In JSD, a graphical means of representing higher-level objects "processes" has been added where a network of processes is developed to process the data structures. Specifically, input processes can be used to detect actions in the external environment and pass them on to the system; likewise, output processes pass responses from the system to the external environment. Processes are linked together via asynchronous data streams. While JSD does not provide any specific time model, it has been successfully utilized for some large real-time projects (at least in respect to system functionality). Further, automatic translations to code skeletons for occam2 and Ada have been developed (see Lawton and France, 1988).

7.2.3 Object-oriented Design

The OOD (Object-Oriented Design) methodology provides a balanced treatment of both data structures and operations (functions), yielding a straightforward mapping between the statement of the problem (the requirements) and the solutions (the design). A fundamental difference with respect to functional decomposition and data structure-driven methods is that in OOD the basic unit of design (component or module) is an abstraction of a real-world object, not simply a step in the processing or data structure.

Object-oriented design is based upon the identification of objects from the requirements (or problem space), together with the operations that either they perform or that are performed on them. Real-world objects are entities that are in some way tangible whether real (for example, vehicle) or abstract (for example, speed). The design approach is to create software "objects" and operations that directly parallel or (abstract) the real-world objects and operations. The mapping between the statement of the problem and solution is, by design, highly visible. This mapping provides understandability for design validation and verification and also, to some extent, for coping with the complexity of large systems. However, we can observe that systems with large quantities of interacting objects may well remain complex simply due to the volume of objects. Remember, we humans have difficulty focusing on more than a few objects at a time.

Many of the purist supporters of the object-oriented approach consider that, to qualify as being object oriented (as opposed to object based), mechanisms must be provided for the concepts of *class*, *instances*, and *inheritance*, which are central notions that contribute to the object style of programming.

The HOOD (**H**ierarchical **O**bject **O**riented **D**esign) methodology developed under contract from the **E**uropean **S**pace **A**gency (ESA) is one of the concrete developments in this area. A number of object types are defined to which problems can be decomposed. The objects are described in terms of an ODS (**O**bject **D**esign **S**keleton), which has been developed for a direct and convenient translation into Ada. Thus, HOOD is rather specifically oriented toward the Ada context, and systems developed with HOOD must live within the limits of what can be accomplished within the Ada framework. For further information, see HOOD (1989).

Another example of the use of object-oriented software engineering is ObjectOry (see Jacobson, 1992). In ObjectOry there is a clear delineation between problem analysis, implementation, and testing. These are viewed as "industrial processes" and much effort has been extended to provide appropriate support for these activities, especially for large-scale projects. An important difference between ObjectOry and other methodologies is the fact that ObjectOry provides for analysis of the problem at a rather high abstraction level without the influence of implementation details. For example, there are no specific notions of synchronization or communication at the analysis level. These details are added during implementation when the solution is specialized toward particular implementation artifacts. This separation of concerns is provided via the use of a number of abstract design entities to which problems are mapped by Use-Cases (end-to-end processing protocols). To demonstrate the use case concept, consider Figure 7.3.

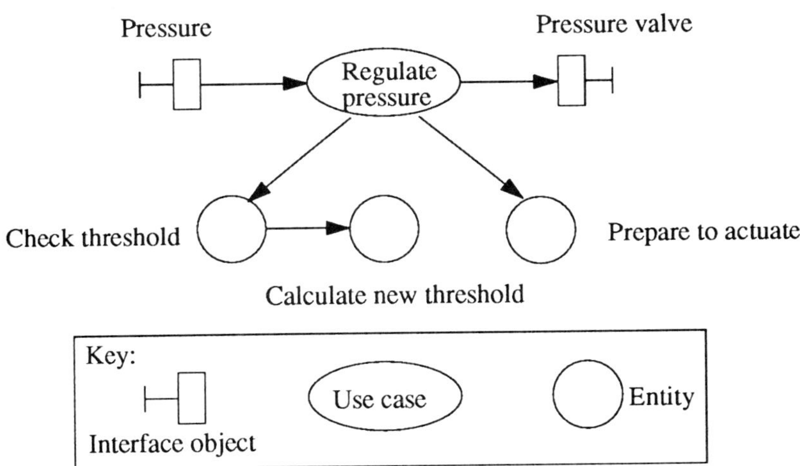

Figure 7.3. Use Case Description a la ObjectOry

A Use Case is composed of a number of interconnected objects. Interface objects provide contact points with the external environment, which for real-time systems are directly translatable to sensors and actuators. Entities are objects that contain processing and may maintain data and state information, whereas active objects provide processing but do not maintain data and state information.

A Use Case provides "a" particular *path* of system utilization for a situation. The set of all Use Cases provides a specification for the system. This information, which is captured at an early analysis state, is utilized in the later stages of design, implementation, and testing, as well as in providing traceability.

We have provided two examples of contemporary OOD approaches. Several books are available that deal with object-oriented methodologies, for example, Booch (1990) and Coad and Yourdan (1990).

(*Note*: The reader will observe a strong family resemblance between the concept of object and our generalized notion of process as utilized in this book.)

7.2.4 Dimensional Design

An interesting (not so well known) design representation that can be applied for abstract as well as concrete behavioral description is DD (**D**imensional **D**esign). This graphical system and program logic representation has been developed by Witty (1981) and has been further developed by Bertran (1988).

The concepts of DD are quite straightforward which contributes to their understandability and usability. The basic idea is to represent treelike structures in a systematic manner as a two-dimensional projection of three-dimensional space (portrayed in Figure 7.4). The object can be an abstract object, a comment, or a concrete object such as a predicate, a procedure, an operator, or a data structure. The pseudo three-dimensional representation results in three directed lines from the object. In various object class contexts, we assign particular meanings (attributes) to the connected objects. One useful interpretation is given at the right in the figure. In this case, parallel objects are connected horizontally, sequences of objects are connected vertically, and subsidiary objects ("composed of") are defined at an angle. These attribute interpretations are strong enough to represent the majority of conventional data and program structures, as well to define abstract system structures, including parallel structural and behavioral relationships.

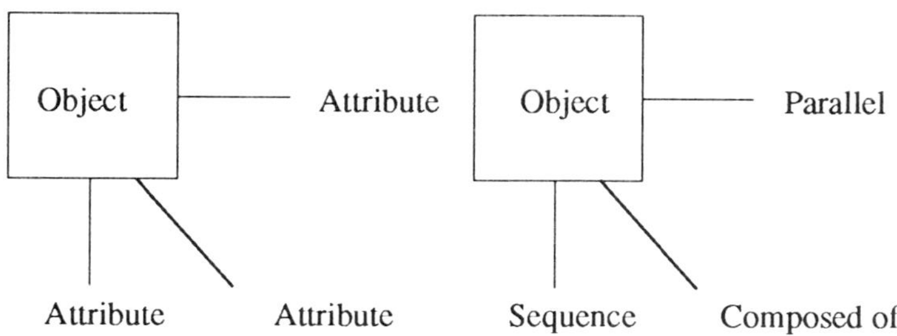

Figure 7.4. Dimensional Design Object and an Interpretation

Other useful interpretations of the attributes for objects can include an object inheritance attribute, or the "is A" relationship typically found in Entity-Relationship descriptions. It may be desirable to introduce graphical conventions for lines (dotted, dashed, thick), which represent specific assigned attributes. The attribute assignment and graphical interpretations are conventions established by DD users. They can and should be selected so as to provide for appropriate human-to-human communication about the objects they describe.

Experience with these DD techniques for the design and implementation of a real-time power dispatching system (see Bertran, 1988) have proved their usefulness as a means of describing system and program logic as well as for communicating the logic in a small group. When used for stepwise refinement, the first pass through the design results in a set of structured comments. Later passes add refinements via the "composed of" relationship, which successively provide more details (including program code at the leaves of the DD tree). In Figure 7.5, we consider a DD representation of the use case that was illustrated for ObjectOry (Figure 7.3).

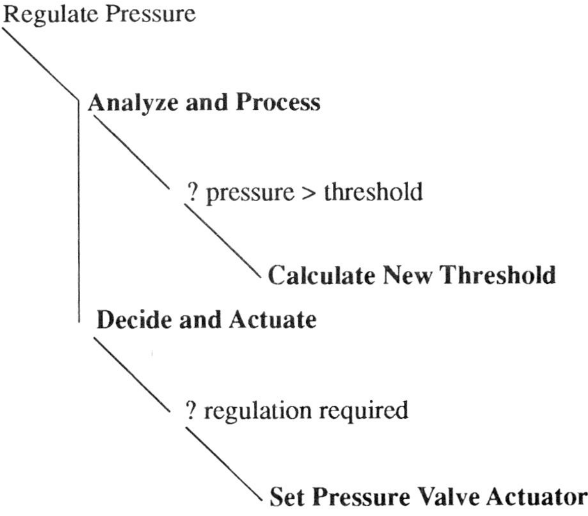

Figure 7.5. Dimensional Design of a Use Case

Note that comment objects have been provided in boldface. An important advantage of DD is that it can be further refined within the same notation to contain successive logic details of the processes. A support tool for the use of DD notation in the design and simulation of both synchronous and asynchronous concurrent systems has been developed by Bertran and others (1990). Further, Lawson (1992) describes how DD, as well as Objectory's use cases, can be usefully applied in describing the behavior of real-time processes. This work is also introduced in Chapter 16. It is interesting to note that the DD design representation has been adopted as one of the methodologies within the European Esprit software maintenance project.

7.3 HARDWARE DESCRIPTION LANGUAGES

The design and development of hardware processes has historically been accomplished by specialists dealing with the physical component technology on one hand and with the realization (including optimization) of digital logic on the other. Various levels of abstraction (for example, microprograms) have been added as the complexity of the functions to be accomplished has increased (see Lawson, 1976).

The description of hardware *structure* and behavior via languages that can be used to simulate and synthesize hardware processes has been pursued since the mid 1960s. While the languages and tools for supporting hardware design and development activities may leave a lot be desired in practical (highly optimized) hardware realization, some important advances have been made during the 1980s.

We are not concerned here with the use of hardware description languages for the design and development of general-purpose computer products composed of PE, M, and C processes. We are, however, quite interested in hardware description languages as a means of realizing direct-mapped architectures, for example, DSP applications as described in Chapter 8. Further, as hardware description languages become more powerful, we may in the future see their use in designing and developing reasonably high level real-time systems. This is due to the fact that they now provide facilities equivalent to contemporary imperative programming languages, as well as provide means of explicitly dealing with *time*.

7.3.1 Hardware Description Language Developments

Larsson (1989) presents a general introduction to the development of both informal and formal hardware description language developments. In the hardware description language category, we find *register transfer languages,* such as CDL (**C**omputer **D**esign **L**anguage) developed by Chu (1965) and DDL (**D**igital **D**esign **L**anguage) developed by Duley and Dietmeyer (1968). This class of language is aimed at describing data-path behavior. The languages have been created with traditional computer system structures in mind. Thus, they assume synchronous control, a central clock, and global memory. Consequently, SISD and SIMD architectures are favored. While the behavioral description is at the register transfer level, the specification can be seen as a guideline for gate-level design. Behaviour and structure are intertwined in an implementation-bound thinking related to how registers are controlled.

A step above register transfer languages, we find the development of ISP (**I**nstruction **S**et **P**rocessor) (Barbacci, 1981). This language is used to describe the behavior of instruction decoders and instruction interpretation. ISP assumes a global clock, global memory, and a sequential model of computation.

The next category are *structure description languages* in which structure information describes how modules are interconnected internally and externally via ports. van Cleemput (1977) developed SDL (Structure **D**escription **L**anguage), which permits hierarchical net-oriented descriptions of module interconnectivity. Lim (1982) proposed HISDL as an extension to SDL in which interconnections are specified either as component oriented or net oriented. Further, iterative and recursive constructs can be used to describe highly regular structures.

A **b**lock **d**escription **l**anguage (BDL) has been developed by Slutz, Okita, and Wiseman (1984) in which properties (that is, name-value pairs) can be assigned to nets (called signals in BDL), as well as to ports, block instances, and block definitions. While there is no ability to specify iterative or recursive structures, the ability to organize hierarchies is quite apparent.

7.3.2 VHDL

As mentioned in the discussion of behavioral description in Chapter 3, the VHDL language was developed as a part of the Very High Speed Integrated circuit program of the U.S. Department of Defense. The IEEE has sponsored further development of the VHDL and has moved it into the status of a standard in 1987. We introduce some of the central concepts of VHDL.

VHDL encompasses **three** styles of usage: structural description, dataflow description, and behavioral description. The language structure (but not the semantics) is inspired by Ada. In all three styles, the basic unit is a design entity.

Design Entities

A logic circuit is viewed as a *design entity,* which can be as simple as an AND gate or as complicated as a microprocessor. The description of design entities in all three styles is divided into the *interface description* and *architectural bodies.* The use of design libraries is encouraged. The interface description localizes all points of contact with the external environment by declaring **entities,** whereas the architectural body describes the **architecture** of components. As with Ada packages, declarations can be used to conveniently declare types, functions, and subtypes, which are placed in a library and subsequently accessed via **use** statements. Further, to provide convenient replication of components (instances), a **generic** facility is provided. Type checking is performed on all declarations and their use.

Structural Description

The structure is described by **component** declarations and signal connections in terms of **port** maps. Components can be conveniently described as being composed of lower-level components. Structural descriptions are processed by an analyzer for their consistency and may then be placed into the design library. Together with a dataflow description, they can be used for the synthesis of actual hardware components.

Dataflow Description

The dataflow description is used to describe realistic hardware behavior as the flow of data between memories and gating elements (M and PEs in our generalized view of hardware processes). Timing properties are taken into account by describing signal waveforms. Random logic or separately controlled digital logic can be created. Functions to be performed are isolated in **block** declarations. The activation of logic is controlled by **guarded** statements. All signal assignments transpire concurrently. Dataflow description complements the structural description, thus providing a concrete basis for simulating a design, as well as synthesizing physical hardware processes.

Behavior Description

When a pure behavior is provided in the **architecture** description, it provides a basis for simulating functionality; however, it does not provide any direct correspondence between the behavior and the real hardware. This style provides an excellent modeling tool. The facilities available are comparable to most higher-level programming languages, with the addition of facilities for the treatment of time. Thus, as noted previously, we can conclude that this form of description is interesting for describing and realizing real-time systems, especially of the direct-mapped variety.

Treatment of Time

To provide a general idea of the treatment of time, let us consider a VHDL fragment for modeling the waveforms for the three-phase clock portrayed in Figure 7.6.

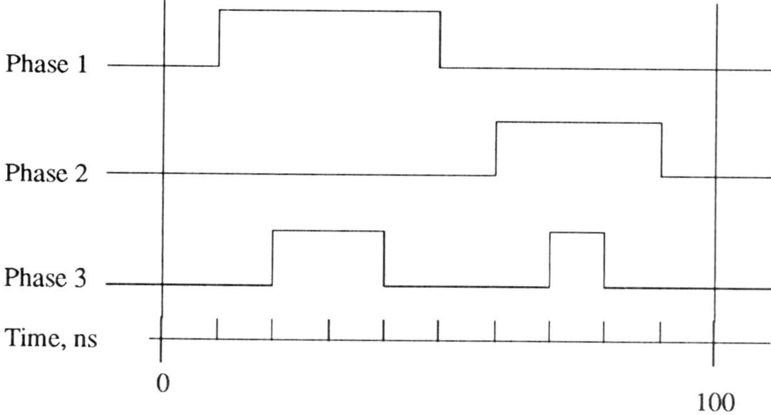

Figure 7.6. Three-phase Clock Example

The process model is encoded as follows:

```
-- process for multi-phase clock
three_phase: process
begin
        phase1 <=       '1' after 10ns,
                        '0' after 50ns;

        phase2 <=       '1' after 60ns,
                        '0' after 90ns;

        phase3 <=       '1' after 20ns,
                        '0' after 40ns,
                        '1' after 70ns,
                        '0' after 80ns;
        wait for 100ns;
end process;
```

Notice that the wait statement provides a cyclic start point to run the process in every 100 ns period. Another important facility is to be able to declare units of time, as illustrated in the following type declaration. All units of time are automatically scaled to femtoseconds (fs).

```
type TIME is range 0 to 2** 31-1
        units
                fs;
                ps      = 1000 fs;
                ns      = 1000 ps;
                us      = 1000 ns;
                ms      = 1000 us;
                s       = 1000 ms;
                min     = 60 s;
                hr      = 60 min;
        end units;
```

In Summary

We have outlined the major facilities available in VHDL. For further information, the reader can consult the language standard IEEE (1987) or the popular descriptions by Armstrong (1989) and Lipsett, Schaefer, and Ussery (1989). For those interested in constructing models with VHDL, the work of Armstrong (1989) and Coelho (1989) is recommended. Leung and Shanblatt (1989) provide a practical example of VHDL utilization for the control of robots.

7.4 PROGRAMMING LANGUAGES

In this section, we consider a few languages that have been or can be utilized in parallel processing environments, as well as languages that have been utilized or proposed for real-time systems. Two languages, occam and Ada, are considered in reasonable depth; however, our presentation is restricted to illustrating the concepts and styles of these programming languages.

7.4.1 Occam

The occam language (see INMOS, 1988) highly reflects the thinking of the concepts of CSP (Communicating Sequential Processes) and a specific hardware resource, the transputer. Perhaps more than any other programming language, occam is based upon the exploitation of the process concept. There are two central features: *processes* and *channels* over which processes communicate. (*Note*: The occam language has been further developed in recent years; however, we utilize the original syntax for this introductory description.)

Primitive Processes

The simplicity of the language is reflected in the fact that there are only three main primitive processes (input, output, and assignment) from which other processes can be composed. The three main process forms are denoted as follows:

Output:	channel ! expression
Input:	channel ? variable
Assignment	variable := expression

These processes are complemented with the **SKIP** and **STOP** processes. A **SKIP** process starts, performs no action, and terminates, whereas a **STOP** process starts, performs no action, but never terminates.

Combining Processes

The primitive processes can be combined via the *constructors*:

SEQ	sequential
PAR	parallel
ALT	alternative
IF	
WHILE	
FOR	

Structural indentation in the source text is significant. In the following fragment, the assignment and output processes are part of the **SEQ** constructor:

```
SEQ
  message := TRUE
  to.bus ! message
```

The constructor, in this case, combines processes to form a new process that executes its primitive processes in the order they are listed and terminates after the last primitive process has terminated.

```
PAR
  to.bus ! ANY
  from.bus ? message
```

This indicates that the processes are to be executed in parallel; thus there is no order relationship between them. The reserved word **ANY** is used to transmit a *don't care* content onto a channel.

```
ALT
  from.bus1 ? message
    to.bus1 ! message
  from bus2 ? message
    to bus2 ! message
```

The **ALT** indicates that one of the inputs will be chosen and perform the associated process (indented by two spaces). If multiple channels have available input, one is chosen nondeterministically. By convention, if a value is sent on both "from.bus1" and "from.bus2" at the same time, the first one will be chosen. More generally, *guarded commands* are utilized that reflect Boolean expressions, input processes, and/or time conditions.

```
IF
  found
    to.bus ! ok
  TRUE
    to.bus ! error
```

The guard in this case is provided by testing "found"; if true, "ok" is output to the bus; otherwise, "error" is given as the output. Note the syntax with the predicate row below the **IF**. If the **TRUE** clause were not included and "found" is false, the process would not terminate.

```
WHILE TRUE
  j := j + 1
```

This construction will execute the assignment state forever since the condition of the **WHILE** is **TRUE**.

```
SEQ  i = [ 0 FOR counter ]
  from.bus ? packet [i]
```

This sequence accepts input from "from.bus" and places it into the vector "packet." The formal description is variable = [base **FOR** count], so variable will start at base and be incremented "count" times.

Channels are used to communicate values between two processes and to synchronize their activities. When a process outputs onto a channel, it waits for the input process to be ready. An input process must wait for an output process to be ready when accepting data from a channel, that is, the communication is synchronized. When the actual data sent are not of interest (that is, only synchronization is desired), the **ANY** constant is utilized.

Further Features

The occam language contains several additional features, including the primitive data types **BOOL**, **BYTE**, **INT**, **INT16**, **INT32**, **INT64**, **REAL32**, and **REAL64** and arrays of the primitive types. There are also scope rules associated with declarations. Further, it is possible to define a **FUNCTION,** which is a valued process.

An occam program acts upon variables, channels, and timers. A variable has a value and may be assigned a value in an assignment or input. Channels communicate values; further, the communication of time can be treated in a highly consistent manner since the timer function is treated as a channel. This permits the convenient construction of occam programs that synchronize upon time in the same manner as they synchronize for the communication of values. Thus, there are facilities for declaring and utilizing **CHAN** (channels) and **TIMER**.

Occam processes are to placed into specific transputer PEs via a **PLACED** command. It is also possible to control the specific placement of a variable, channel, timer, or array in memory via the **PLACED** command. When priority is to be assigned to processes executing within the same transputer, **PRI** priority can be assigned. Further, there is a dynamic **ALT** for run-time alteration of priorities.

Some Illustrative Process Structures

To illustrate the naturalness and power of occam with respect to the transputer, let us examine a few interesting process structures:

```
PLACED PAR
    PROCESSOR 1
      terminal (term.in, term.out)
    PROCESSOR 2
      editor (term.in, term.out, files.in, files.out)
    PROCESSOR 3
      network (files.in, files.out)
```

In this case, we have assigned three processes, terminal, editor, and network, to three specific transputers, where each process uses the local memory of the processor and will communicate over channels.

```
PRI PAR
  terminal (term.in, term.out)
  editor (term.in, term.out)
```

Here we have specified that the two processes terminal and editor will be executed concurrently on the same transputer, but that process terminal (by its lexical order) will be given priority over process editor.

```
PAR
    farmer ()
    PAR i = 0 FOR 4
      worker (i)
```

In this case we have created a farm where there are concurrent farmer and worker processes. When this structure is expanded, we find the following structure:

```
PAR
    farmer ()
    PAR
      worker (0)
      worker (1)
      worker (2)
      worker (3)
```

which corresponds to the farm structure of parallel processes portrayed in Figure 7.7. We shall examine this form of parallel process organization more thoroughly in Chapter 11.

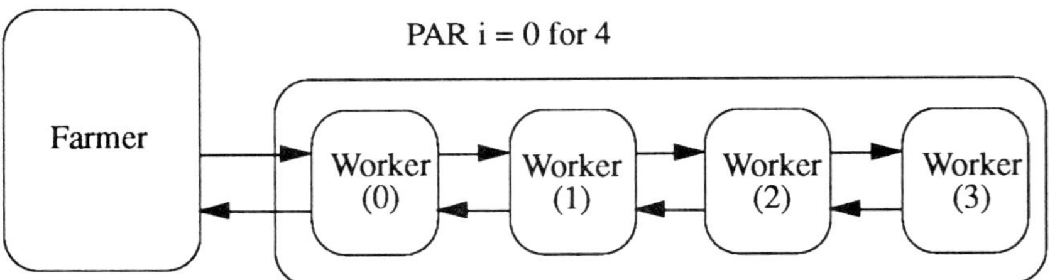

Figure 7.7. A Farm of Parallel Processes

The processes described in occam can be destined to run on *naked* transputer hardware, in which case occam programs directly reflect the behavior of the system (direct-mapped philosophy). On the other hand, it is possible to express occam programs that will reside in a more general environment, in which case they will be scheduled based upon the resources made available in the transputer environment (dynamically mapped philosophy). In this latter case, an operating system such as Helios or TRANS-RTXc, also described in Chapter 11, is utilized.

This concludes our brief overview of occam. The reader has observed the direct relationship between processes and the transputer. For further details on occam, the reader is referred to INMOS (1988) and to Jones and Goldsmith (1988).

7.4.2 Ada

The Ada language has been developed as a standard by the U.S. Department of Defense as a means of programming critical software. The language provides strong typing for reliability purposes, *packages* for the decomposition of large systems into modules, and built-in primitives for concurrent programming. The model of concurrent programming (*tasking*) is provided as a part of the programming language syntax and semantics. We extract some of the major concepts of Ada that are relevant for concurrent programs.

Rendezvous Mechanism

Ada provides synchronous (unbuffered) communication via the rendezvous mechanism. As the name implies, rendezvous provides an image of two people who choose a place to meet. The first one to arrive at the scene must wait for the second. In this human analogy, the notion is symmetric and the place of rendezvous is neutral. The Ada rendezvous, however, belongs to one of the two tasks called the *accepting task*. The other task (the *calling task*) must know the identity of the accepting task and provide the name of the location of the rendezvous (the *entry*). On the other hand, the accepting task has no obligation to know the identity of the calling task. Both tasks are executing concurrently and they only synchronize at the time of a rendezvous.

The Ada asymmetric rendezvous model has the advantage that *servers* can be programmed in a natural manner. For example, a printing task can accept requests for printing from any other task in the system. One can observe from this example that, if a symmetric model was to be applied (as in CSP), the server task would have to be altered everytime a new task was added for which printing services were to be provided.

A task in Ada is divided into two sections (the *specification* and the *body*). The specification is solely composed of entry declarations. The syntax of an entry is like a procedure declaration. This format was provided in order to provide for the convenient substitution of a concurrent entry for a sequential procedure without otherwise changing the program. For example:

```
task Buffer is
        entry Append (I: in Integer);
        entry Take (I: out Integer);
end Buffer;
```

When a task specification has been declared and made available to other tasks, they may call the entry using the following notation:

```
Buffer.Append (I);
```

This entry requires the use of the accept statement (a central rendezvous mechanism) in the task body of the task owning the entry, as follows:

```
task body Buffer is
begin
  ...
   accept Append (I: in Integer) do
     ... statements in the accept body
   end Append;
  ...
end Buffer;
```

We can contrast the rendezvous mechanism with the normal procedure call semantics in which case the procedure is invoked immediately. When the calling task has executed its entry call and the accepting task has executed an accept statement, the rendezvous can commence, and it proceeds as follows:

— the calling task passes the **in** parameters to the accepting task and becomes blocked pending completion of the rendezvous.
— the accepting task executes the statements in the accept body.

— the **out** parameters are passed back to the calling task.
— the rendezvous completes and the two tasks are no longer suspended.

It is important to note that the completion of the rendezvous does not necessarily cause a task to commence execution. This decision is left to the underlying scheduling mechanism. The server task must execute a new accept statement (usually done inside of a loop) in order to denote its readiness for a new rendezvous.

When multiple calling (producing) tasks attempt to rendezvous with the entry of a single server task (consumer), the tasks are queued in the order of their arrival at the entry. The accept statement always engages the first task in the queue. After completing the accept statement (rendezvous), the server task must execute a new accept statement in order to provide service to tasks waiting on the entry queue.

The rendezvous mechanism provides a clean interface between tasks. In summary, we can state that it provides an asymmetric synchronous unbuffered means of communication with two-way dataflow.

It is, however, also permissible for tasks to share global variables, thus bypassing the controlled rendezvous task synchronization. Such use of global variables must be done with caution.

Select Statement

To provide conditions under which entries will be accepted in a server task, the select statement is provided. The effect of the select statement is to function as a *guard*. This mechanism has been inherited from Dijkstra via CSP. To illustrate its use in the classical bounded buffer example, consider the following Ada fragment:

```
task body Buffer is

...

begin
  loop
     select
       when Count < N =>
          accept Append (I: in Integer) do
              (code to append)
          end Append;
          (code to increment buffer counter)
     or
```

```
            when Count > 0 =>
                accept Take (I: out Integer) do
                    (code to remove)
                end Take;
                (code to reduce buffer counter)
        end select;
    end loop;
end Buffer;
```

The select statement permits the Buffer task to choose between two guarded alternatives. As we can see, the guards are Boolean expressions prefixed to accept statements. If the expression is TRUE, the alternative is called an *open alternative* and a rendezvous with the accept statement is permitted. If the expression is FALSE, the alternative is said to be a *closed alternative* and rendezvous is not permitted. If more than one alternative is true, a nondeterministic selection will be made.

We can now consider several conditions under which the Buffer task behaves. If the buffer is empty (Count = 0), the select statement is reduced to an ordinary accept statement on the remaining open alternative Append. If the buffer is full (Count = N), there will only be one open alternative, Take. We can observe that at least one alternative will always be open since it is impossible that Count = 0 and Count = 1 simultaneously. In the situation 0 < Count < N, both alternatives are open. If there are no tasks waiting in the entry queues, the accepting task will wait for the first task that calls an entry. If there are calling tasks waiting in only one queue, a rendezvous occurs with the first task in that queue. However, if there are calling tasks waiting in both queues, the accepting task nondeterministically choses to rendezvous with the first task in one of the two queues.

The language leaves the nondeterministic selection to a reasonable solution; for example, the implementation may always select the first open alternative. In any event, the programmer is not to rely upon a particular order of selection.

Syntactically, a select statement consists of an arbitrary number of guarded accept statements separated by the reserved word **or**. If a guard is omitted, it is assumed to mean **when True** =>. Following the last select alternative, one of the following may appear:

— **else**, followed by a sequence of statements
— **delay T**, followed by a sequence of statements (T is a real-valued expression)
— **terminate**

Only one of these alternatives may appear. The semantics of the **select** statement under varying alternatives is as follows:

- the guards are evaluated. The set of alternatives whose guards evaluate to TRUE is the set of open alternatives. It is a fatal error if the set of open alternatives is empty (unless there is an **else** alternative).
- if there are calling tasks waiting on entry queues for open alternatives, a rendezvous is commenced with the first task on one of those queues.
- if all queues for open alternatives are empty, the accepting task is suspended. As soon as some task calls an entry in the set of open alternatives, the rendezvous is commenced with this calling task. Note that the set of open alternatives does not change, because the guards are not reevaluated during the execution of the select statement.
- the rendezvous transpires as described earlier.
- upon completion of the rendezvous, the accepting task executes the statements following the **accept** body.
- **select** with **else** alternative. If there are no open alternatives, or if there are open alternatives but no calling task exists in one of their entry queues, the sequence of statements in the else alternative is executed.
- **select** with **delay** alternative. If there are no calling tasks in the entry queues of the open alternatives, the accepting task will wait as described previously, but only for the amount of time given in the **delay** clause. When this time has expired, the sequence of statements in the **delay** alternative is executed. It is important to note that the accepting task need not be awakened exactly when the delay has expired. Only if the entry queues are still empty after the delay has expired can the tasks be rescheduled and execute the statements in the **delay** alternative.
- **select** with **terminate** alternative. The semantics of this alternative is quite complex. Roughly, it means that, if this **select** statement is suspended and all tasks that could possibly call its entries have completed execution and are waiting on **select** statements with **terminate** alternatives, then this entire set of tasks is terminated.

In summary, the **select** statement provides a programming primitive for concurrency. It performs a relatively low level operation, checking for calls and choosing among them, but various options make it possible to express a variety of algorithms.

Programming with the Rendezvous

The rendezvous mechanism provides for the realization of several paradigms and as such provides the Ada programmer with a rather general mechanism. In its simplest form, the rendezvous implements a *remote procedure call*. That is, the calling task calls upon a procedure that is not present within itself, but belongs to another independent task. The **select** is the generalization of this paradigm.

The delay alternative implements a *timeout*, that is, a limit on the amount of time one is willing to wait. It can be used in control systems that require the program to sense the absence of a response and not just to interpret a response, as illustrated in the following Ada fragment, that can raise an alarm.

```
task body T is
begin
  loop
     select
       accept Sensor_1 do ... ;
     or
       accept Sensor_2 do ... ;
     or
       ...
     or
       delay 0.1;     - - 100 milliseconds
       Raise_Alarm;
     end select;
  end loop
end T;
```

The **else** alternative is equivalent to a delay of zero and provides a mechanism for a form of *polling*, that is, to check if there is a message that needs to be processed, or otherwise to continue with normal processing.

The accept bodies may be empty, in which case the bodies may be utilized for synchronization purposes, as illustrated in the following fragment, which emulates a binary semaphore:

```
task body Semaphore is
begin
   loop
      accept Wait;
      accept Signal;
   end loop;
end Semaphore;
```

Another aspect of the rendezvous mechanism is the ability to nest **accept** statements, as portrayed in the following fragment:

```
task body T1 is
begin
   ...
   accept Synch_2 do      - - T2 calls this entry
      accept Synch_3;      - - T3 calls this entry
   end Synch_2;
   ...
end T1;
```

By utilizing nested accept statements in this example, we are able to synchronize three tasks (T1, T2, and T3). T2 will remain suspended until the rendezvous with T3 has occurred. If T3 calls T1 first, it will wait in the entry queue until T2 arrives. Compare this with a nonnested version in which T2 could be rescheduled before T3 calls its entry.

Many other constructs are possible by the use of the rendezvous facility. It is important to keep in mind that the queues are associated with *entries* and not with the accept statement.

Utilization of Select in Calling Tasks

We have examined the case where the accepting task can use else and delay alternatives to avoid being suspended forever while waiting for a rendezvous. A similar facility is available for calling tasks; however, the calling task can only suspend waiting for one entry (that is, there are no multiple-entry calls). An example of a timeout for a calling task is provided in the following fragment:

```
task body T is
begin
   loop
      select
        Sensor.Sample ( ... );
     or
        delay 1.0;  - - seconds
        Notify_Operator;
      end select;
   end loop;
end T;
```

If the call is not accepted within the specified time interval, the attempt is abandoned and the statements following the **delay** are executed. This does not mean that the calling task will be suspended for the time interval since the rendezvous itself could take an arbitrarily long time, and even upon completion of the rendezvous the calling task might not be immediately scheduled.

An interesting structure is the use of the the **else** alternative in the caller to poll as to whether one server among multiple servers is available, as illustrated in the following fragment:

```
task body T is
begin
   loop
      select
        Server_1.E  (...);
      else
        null;
      end select;
      select
        Server_2.E(...);
      else
        null;
      end select;
      ...
   end loop;
end T;
```

In this example, the calling task engages a server only if it is immediately available. Otherwise, the attempt is abandoned and the task continues to the next select statement. It is possible to construct a variant that will rendezvous with exactly one server.

Dynamic Task Creation

We have been examining static task examples thus far, where all relevant task information is created when the program is loaded. It is useful to be able to declare a *task type*, in which case a task template is created from which instances can be created as new task objects. This facility is illustrated in the following code fragment, which creates an array of buffer tasks.

```
task type Buffer-Type is
   entry Append (I: in Integer);
   entry Take (I: out Integer);
end Buffer_Type;

Buffers: array (1..20) of Buffer-Type;
```

```
procedure P(Buff: in Buffer_Type) is
   I: Integer := ... ;
begin
   Buff.Append(I);              - - call entry in parameter
end P;

Buffers(I+1).Append(E1);        - - direct call

P(Buffers(J));                  - - task parameter
```

An array of buffers is created, each of which has its own pointers and counter. The two executable statements show a call to an entry point of an element of the task array and a call to a procedure. Note how the identity of the task can be computed at run time. Additional flexibility in managing tasks can be obtained by the utilization of a pointer to task types. In Ada, once a pointer (called *access type*) has been declared, additional objects of the type can be allocated during execution. Using conventional data structure techniques, it is then possible to maintain lists of tasks, as illustrated in the following fragment:

```
type Node;
type Buffer_Ptr is access Node;
type Node is
   record
      Buff: Buffer_Type;
      Next: Buffer_Ptr;
   end record;

procedure Allocate (Ptr: in out Buffer_Ptr) is
   Temp: Buffer_Ptr := Ptr.Next;
begin
   Ptr.Next := new Node;
   Ptr.Next.Next := Temp;
end Allocate;
```

In this example, a node is declared that contains a field of task type Buffer_Type and a pointer to the same node type. The procedure allocates a new node (including a new task) and links it after the node pointed to by the parameter.

Real-time Scheduling

In spite of the fact that Ada was designed for use in real-time systems, it has been widely criticized. Frequently, the concerns are practical with regards to the speed of rendezvous or the treatment of interrupts. More serious are the concerns with Ada's tasking model, which is nondeterministic, making it difficult to determine if tasks will meet their deadlines. Further, Ada seemingly provides no direct support for priorities, and tasks are queued in FIFO order without regard to importance (that is, priority). Consequently, high-priority tasks can be blocked indefinitely by lower priority tasks due to priority inversion, which was described in Chapters 2 and 3.

To get around these problems, a number of vendors have provided through the pragma facilities of Ada coupled with a proprietary run-time system some form of priority-based scheduling implementation. However, these issues are also being addressed at the language standardization level.

Significant effort has been made in developing scheduling strategies that can accommodate Ada tasking and still provide for predictable systems. One important effort has been related to the rate-monotonic scheduling approach, described in Chapters 2 and 3. The reader is referred to the paper by Sha and Goodenough (1990) for a detailed description of rate-monotonic scheduling and its application to Ada.

Finally, from this brief presentation of Ada features used in achieving tasking, the complexity of the language becomes evident. Ada, due to its general purposeness, provides many alternative ways of doing similar processing operations.

7.4.3 Other Concurrent Programming Languages

We have only selected two contemporary programming languages for closer examination; however, a vast number of languages have been developed for expressing the behavioral description for parallel/distributed processing. For an excellent survey of the state of the art, the reader is referred to a special issue of the **ACM Computing Surveys** (see Wegner, 1989). We now briefly enumerate and characterize some of these developments related to the C family of languages.

The C language has become an important language in both real-time and parallel processing environments. There are two important developments with C that are worth noting. First C++ and Objective C have extended C in the direction of object orientation, as noted earlier in the chapter. The other major development is the introduction of Concurrent C and Concurrent C++. Concurrent C provides programming facilities in a style similar to the Ada rendezvous (with improvements). Concurrent C++ extends the concepts of an object-oriented language. For a description of concurrent programming and the Concurrent C and C++ variants, the reader is referred to Gehani (1989).

In Summary

In concluding this chapter, we can note that, while much work has been done on various paradigms for behavioral description, we cannot and most likely will not be able to single out any best approach. *There are several alternatives.* Certainly, the approach based upon CSP, occam, and the transputer represents the most, to date, unified approach by covering all aspects of our BMR model. It will be interesting to follow the development of VHDL, which provides facilities for dealing with time, particularly if its behavioral description style will lead to a widely accepted real-time programming language. Despite the problems we have noted for Ada, there has been and will be significant efforts to use Ada as the programming language for real-time parallel/distributed systems of the future.

We considered the main lines of behavioral description for contemporary real-time systems in Chapter 2. Some research and development in the area of real-time languages will be addressed in Chapter 16.

Finally, it will be interesting to follow the development of new paradigms based upon nonprocedural languages, for example, functional and logic based with respect to real-time parallel processing systems.

References

Armstrong, J.R. (1989). *Chip-Level Modelling with VHDL*, Prentice Hall, Englewood Cliffs, NJ.

Barbacci, M. (1981). Instruction Set Processor Specification (ISPS): The Notation and Its Applications, *IEEE Transactions on Computers*, Vol. C-30, No. 1, pp. 24-40.

Berry G. (1985). The Synchronous Programming Language ESTEREL and Its Mathematical Semantics, *Proceedings of the Seminar on Concurrency*, Springer-Verlag, New York, LNCS 197.

Bertran, M. (1988). On a Formal Definition and Application of Dimensional Design, *Software Practice and Experience*, Vol. 18, No. 11, pp. 1029-1045.

Bertran, M., J. Forga, F. Oller, and J.A. Frau (1990) PADDS: An Environment for the Design of Concurrent Systems by Simulation (personal note).

Best, E. (1986). COSY - It's relationship to Nets and CSP, *Lecture Notes in Computer Science*, No. 225, Springer-Verlag, New York.

Booch, G. (1990). *Object-Oriented Development*, Benjamin Cummings, Menlo Park, CA.

BSIVDM90 (1990). *VDM Specification Language - Proto-Standard*, Technical Report, British Standards Institution, BSI IST/5/50.

Chu, Y. (1965). An ALGOL-like Computer Design Language, *Communications of the ACM*, Vol. 8, No. 10.

Coad, P., and E. Yourdan (1990). *Object-Oriented Analysis*, Prentice Hall, Englewood Cliffs, NJ.

Coelho, D.R. (1989). *The VHDL Handbook*, Kluwer Academic Publishers, Hingham, MA.

DeMarco, T. (1979). *Structured Analysis and System Specification*, Prentice Hall, Englewood Cliffs, NJ.

Dijkstra, E.W. (1975). Guarded Commands, Non-Determinancy and Formal Derivation of Programs, *Communications of the ACM*, Vol. 18, pp. 453-457.

Duley, J. R., and D.L. Dietmeyer (1968). A Digital System Design Language (DDL), *IEEE Transactions on Computers*, Vol. C-17, No. 9, pp. 850-860.

Gehani, N. (1989). *The Concurrent C Programming Language*, Prentice Hall, Englewood Cliffs, NJ.

Hansson, H., and B. Johnsson (1990). A Calculus for Communicating Systems with Time and Probabilities, *Proceedings of the 11th IEEE Real-time Systems Symposium*, IEEE Computer Society Press, Los Alamitos, Calif.

Hennessy, M. (1986). *Algebraic Theory of Processes*, MIT Press, Cambridge, MA.

Hoare, C.A. R. (1978). Communication Sequential Processes, *Communications of the ACM*, Vol. 21, pp. 666-667.

Hoare, C.A.R. (1985). *Communicating Sequential Processes*, Prentice Hall, Englewood Cliffs, NJ.

HOOD Reference Manual Issue 3.0, Sept. (1989). Document No. WME/89-179/JB. HOOD Working Group, European Space Agency.

IEEE (1987). *IEEE Standard VHDL Reference Manual*, IEEE Std. 1076-1987.

INMOS (1988). *occam 2 Reference Manual*, Prentice Hall, Englewood Cliffs, NJ.

ISO8807 (1988). *LOTOS - A Formal Description Technique Based on the Temporal Ordering of Observational Behaviour*, International Organization for Standardization.

Jackson, K. (1986). Mascot3 and Ada, *Software Engineering Journal*, Vol. 1, No. 3, pp. 121-135.

Jackson, M.A. (1975). *Principles of Program Design*, Academic Press, New York.

Jacobson, I. (1992). *Object-Oriented Software Engineering*, Addison-Wesley, Reading, MA.

Jensen, K. (1987). Coloured Petri Nets, *Lecture Notes on Computer Science*, Vol. 254, Springer-Verlag, New York, pp. 248-299.

Jones, G., and M. Goldsmith (1988). *Programming in occam 2*, Prentice Hall, Englewood Cliffs, NJ.

Keiburtz, R.B., and A. Silberschatz (1979). Comments on "Communication Sequential Processes," *ACM Transactions on Programming Languages and Systems*, Vol. 1, No. 2, pp. 218-225.

Larsen, P.G. (1990). A Formal Event Structuring Approach to Real-time Design, *Proceedings of the Euromicro Workshop on Real Time*, IEEE Computer Society Press, Los Alamitos, CA.

Larsson, T. (1989). *A Formal Hardware Description and Verification Method*, Ph.D. thesis, Department of Computer and Information Science, Linköping University, Sweden.

Lawson, H.W. (1976). Function Distribution in Computer System Architectures, *Proceedings of the Third International Symposium on Computer Architecture*, Clearwater, FL.

Lawson, H.W. (1992). CYCLONE - An Approach to the Engineering of Resource Adequate Cyclic Real-time Systems, *International Journal of the Real-time Systems*, Vol. 4, No. 1, pp. 55-83.

Lawton, J.R., and N. France (1988). The Transformation of JSD Specifications into Ada, *Ada User*, Vol. 8, No. 1, pp. 29-44.

Leung, S.S., and M.A. Shanblatt (1989). *ASIC System Design with VHDL: A Paradigm*, Kluwer Academic Publishers, Hingham, MA.

Leveson, N.G., and J.L. Stolzy (1987). Safety Analysis Using Petri-Nets, *IEEE Transactions on Software Engineering*, Vol. 13, No. 3, pp. 386-397.

Lim, W. (1982). HISDL - A Structure Description Language, *Communications of the ACM*, Vol. 25, No. 11.

Lipsett, R., C. Schaefer, and C. Ussery (1989). *VHDL: Hardware Description and Design*, Kluwer Academic Publishers, Hingham, MA.

McKeeman, W.M. (1976). Programming Language Design, *Lecture Notes in Computer Science, Compiler Construction, An Advanced Course*, 2nd ed., G. Goos and J. Hartmanis (eds.), Springer-Verlag, New York.

Milner, R. (1980). A Calculus of Communicating Systems, *Lecture Notes in Computer Science*, No. 92, Springer-Verlag, New York.

Milner, R. (1989). *Communication and Concurrency*, Prentice Hall, Englewood Cliffs, NJ.

MoD005 (1989). *Standard for Military Safety-Critical Software - 00-55*, The UK Ministry of Defence, Draft.

Murata, T. (1989). Petri-Nets: Properties, Analysis and Applications, *Proceedings of the IEEE*, Vol. 77, No. 4, pp. 544-580.

Peng, Z., K. Kuchinski, and B. Lyles (1989) CAMAD: A Unified Data Path/Control Synthesis Environment, *Design Methodologies for VLSI and Computer Architecture* (ed. D.A. Edwards), North-Holland, Amsterdam.

Petri, C. (1962). Kommunikation mit Automaten, Bonn: Institut für Instrumentelle Mathematik, Schriften des 11M Nr. 3.

Rosenberg, G. (1987). Advances in Petri-Nets, *Lecture Notes on Computer Science*, Vol. 266, Springer-Verlag, New York.

Sha, L., and J.B. Goodenough (1990). Real-time Scheduling Theory and Ada, *IEEE Computer*, Vol. 23, No. 4, pp. 53-62.

Slutz, E, G. Okita, and J. Wiseman (1984). Block Description Language (BDL), *Design Automation Conference Proceedings*.

van Cleemput, W. (1977). A Hierarchical Language for the Structural Description of Digital Systems, *Design Automation Conference Proceedings*.

Ward, P.T., and S.J. Mellor (1985). *Structured Development of Real-time Systems*, (Vols. 1, 2 and 3), Yourdon Press, New York.

Wegner, P., ed. (1989). Special Issue on Programming Language Paradigms, *ACM Computing Surveys*, Vol. 21, No. 3.

Witty, R. (1981). *Small Scale Software Engineering*, Ph.D. dissertation, Department of Computer Science, Brunel University, Uxbridge, UK.

Chapter 8

DIRECT-MAPPED ARCHITECTURES

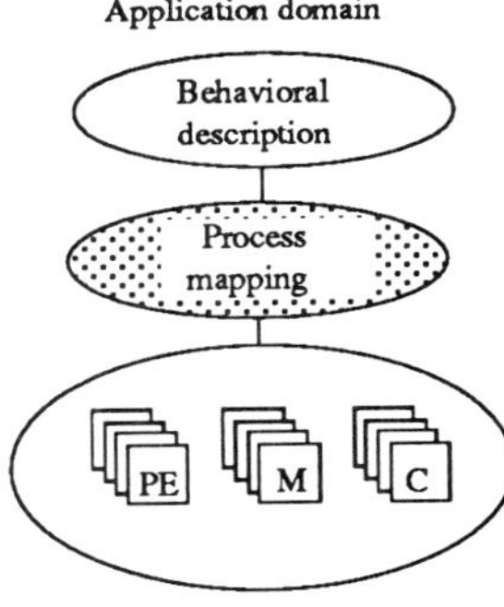

Generally, a DSP algorithm can be mapped to an architecture either by a direct mapping or by first mapping the algorithm to an intermediate, representation which is followed by mapping to a programmed architecture. The first approach aims at high-performance systems, while the second method attempts to reduce the design effort and cost by using standard programmable components (digital signal processors). In this chapter, we consider direct-mapping techniques.

As we considered in Chapter 3, the synthesis of an optimal architecture starts from a given DSP algorithm. The first design step is a scheduling of the operations (processes) in the algorithm. The purpose of the scheduling is to distribute the operations in time so that an adequate but yet minimum quantity of hardware resources is required. Often, only the number of PEs is minimized, but it is also possible to minimize the memory and communication requirements. In fact, it is possible to minimize the total hardware requirements by proper scheduling. The schedule determines the number and type of PE, M, and C processes for a class of optimal architectures. The second design step involves optimization within this class of architectures.

The synthesis process is essentially downward as illustrated in Figure 8.1. However, these steps are highly interdependent. For example, scheduling assumes certain costs for PE, M, and C hardware processes. Further, the selection of a particular algorithm restricts the class of usable architectures. Therefore, the synthesis process must, in practice, be followed by an evaluation phase and a subsequent design iteration. The design process may need to be reiterated several times to achieve a satisfactory solution. The design process may also require extension to lower levels, for example, to the logic and/or electrical circuit level.

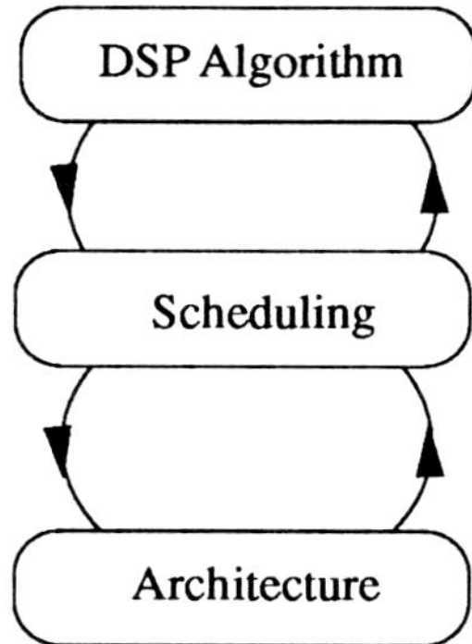

Figure 8.1. Mapping of an Algorithm onto an Architecture

In this chapter, we first reconsider scheduling and resource allocation in general and then present various formulations of the scheduling problem as well as some common optimization techniques. Finally, we shall present methods to synthesize optimal circuit architectures based upon these schedules. Once again, appropriate scheduling techniques are important for designing an architecture that matches a given algorithm.

8.1 SCHEDULING AND RESOURCE ALLOCATION

Scheduling of operations (processes) is a common problem that appears in a variety of settings as described in Part I. The processes to be scheduled are characterized by their start or release time, duration, and deadline and whether they arrive at random time instances or periodically. Recall that hard real-time processes are processes for which the deadline must be met. Further, if all processes are known in advance, it is possible to perform scheduling before run time, yielding a *static* schedule that will not change. Static schedules need only be done once. Conversely, a *dynamic* schedule must be used whenever the process characteristics are not completely known. The scheduling must be done dynamically at run time by a scheduler that runs concurrently with the program. This may cause a significant overhead since most scheduling problems are computationally intensive. Execution of processes in the dynamic environment becomes NP-complete. *Most DSP algorithms are amenable to static scheduling.* In fact, for such algorithms it is possible to synthesize optimal architectures. We therefore focus our interest on static scheduling problems.

As considered in Chapter 3, resource allocation should ideally be done in conjunction with the process scheduling, but due to the complexity of the problem, they are most often treated as separate problems.

8.2 SCHEDULING FORMULATIONS

In this section we will discuss various formulations of the scheduling problem:

— Single interval
— Direct blocking
— Loop folding (discussed in Chapter 4)
— Periodic scheduling

8.2.1 Single Interval

The starting point for scheduling is the fully specified SFG (signal-flow graph). The first step is to extract all algorithmic delay elements, as shown in Figure 8.2. The remaining part, which contains only the arithmetic operations, is denoted by *N*.

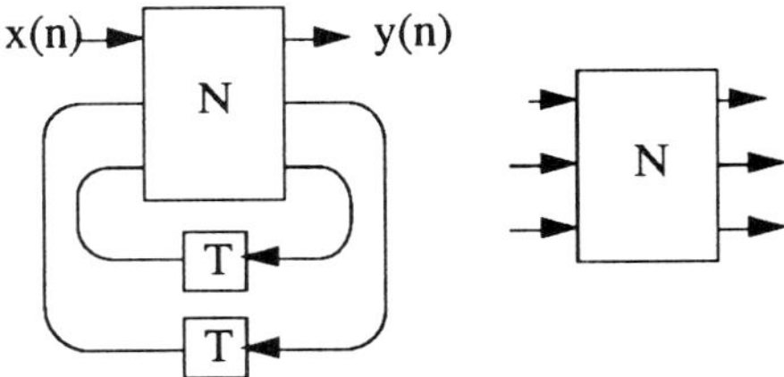

Figure 8.2. Signal-flow Graph with Extracted Delay Elements

Once the delay elements have been removed, this network can be interpreted as a precedence graph for the arithmetic operations during one sample interval. It appears that an analysis of the precedence graph reveals the computational parallelism, time-critical path (CP), the maximal sample rate, and so on. However, it is not sufficient to consider one sample interval since this view does not reveal the true computational properties of the algorithm. We will demonstrate its shortcomings by some examples (see Crochiere and Oppenheim, 1975).

In the most simple formulation, all inputs to the DAG (directed acyclic graph) are assumed to be applied at time zero, and all outputs are assumed to be ready at the end of the sample interval; that is, the boundaries of the interval are uniform, as shown in Figure 8.3.

The algorithm in Figure 8.3 is assumed to be recursive. The input and output pairs, (1, 1') and (2, 2'), are in the original SFG connected via delay elements. For the sake of simplicity, we assume that all operations have a unit delay. The time-critical path is indicated with thick lines. The computational paths in the DAG will form constraints on the sample period. With this formulation we cannot employ a sample period shorter than the time-critical path, in this case 3. Note that this is not the minimal sampling period.

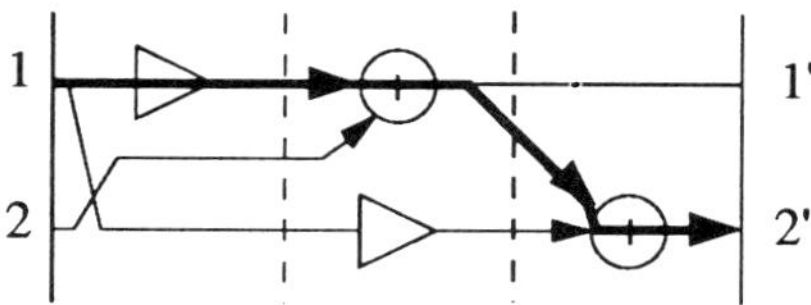

Figure 8.3. Schedule with Uniform Boundaries

Another alternative is to introduce nonuniform boundaries. Here, the only restriction is that the paths from an input to the corresponding output, 1-1' or 2-2', must be of equal length. This is due to the fact that the shape of the borders at the start and the end must be compatible in order to allow the schedule to be periodically repeated. In Figure 8.3, the longest path of this type is 2 long. This fact can be used to achieve the schedule in Figure 8.4. In this case, the computational paths have been skewed in time (retiming) in such a way that the sample period becomes 2, which is equal to the minimal sampling period.

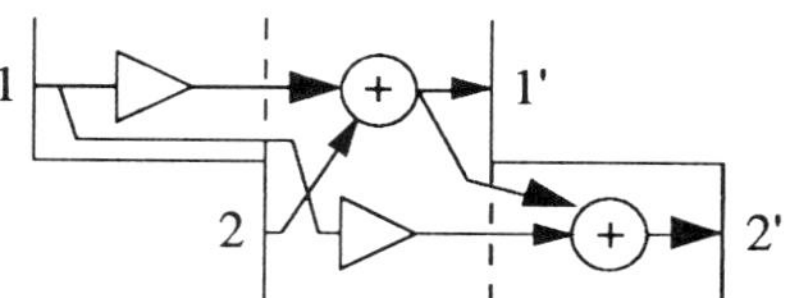

Figure 8.4. Schedule with Nonuniform Boundaries

Another problem with this view is that the paths from the inputs to the outputs correspond to loops in the original SFG with only one delay element. This means that if the critical loop of the SFG contains more than one delay element the critical path restricting the sample period cannot be found.

Example 1

Figure 8.5 shows a second-order section in *direct form II*. The basic operations are multiplication and addition. The multiplication is assumed to take 4 time units and addition takes 1 time unit. The required sample period is T_{sample} = 10 time units. The critical loop, CL, and the critical path, CP, of this algorithm are 6 and 11 time units, respectively. Hence, to achieve the desired sample rate, we must either duplicate some computational resources or introduce pipelining.

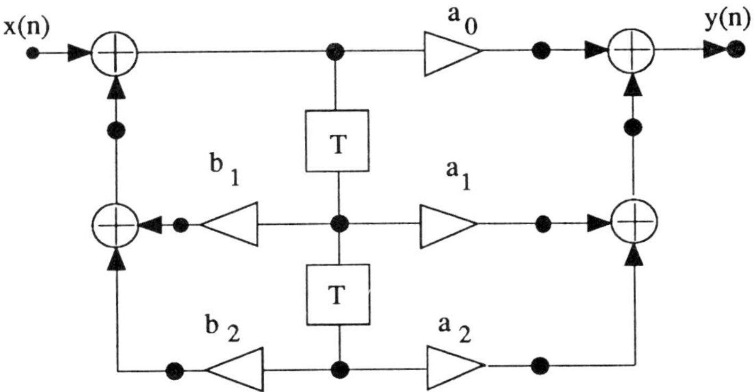

Figure 8.5. Second-order Section in Direct Form II

In this case, we choose to introduce pipelining. The pipelined structure is shown in Figure 8.6 and the precedence graph of the pipelined algorithm is shown in Figure 8.7. It is convenient to add a time axis to the precedence graph. The dots indicate the starting and finishing times of the operations.

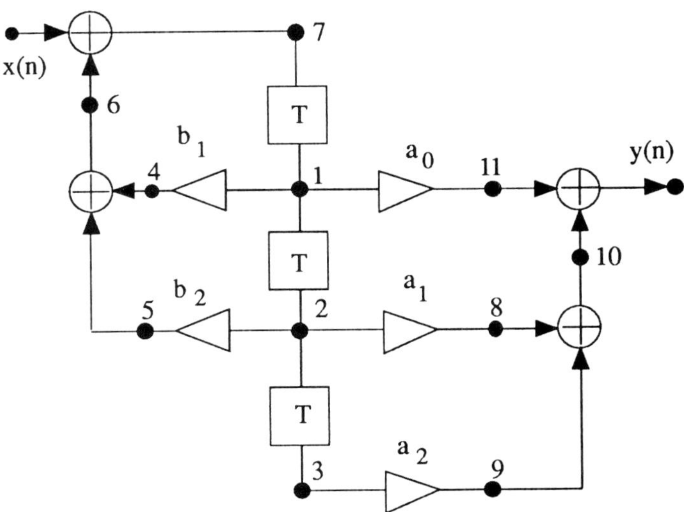

Figure 8.6. Second-order Section with Pipelining

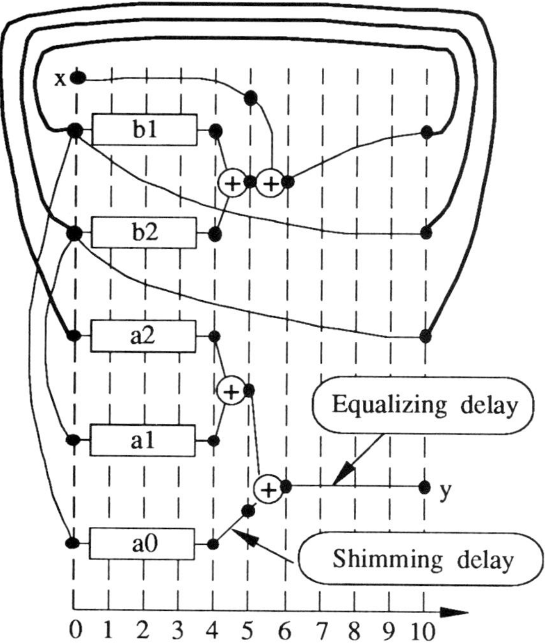

Figure 8.7. Direct Form II in Precedence Form
(*Note*: Addition requires 1 time unit; multiplication requires 4 time units)

Equalizing and *shimming* delays have been inserted in order to meet the specified sampling period by extending all computational paths to 10 time units. An equalizing delay of four time units has been placed after the last adder in the recursive loop. Further, a shimming delay with unit time has been placed after the multiplication with a_0. The output, y, has been delayed by an equalizing delay of 4 time units, so that the difference between the input and output is 10 time units. The dark lines in the figure indicate algorithmic delay elements, which carry signal values from one sample interval to the next. Note that algorithmic delay elements do not necessarily represent the storing of signals in physical memories.

The precedence graph in Figure 8.7 can be directly interpreted as a schedule for the arithmetic operations. Five multipliers and two adders are needed. The number of storage units is 34. Clearly, a better schedule can be found.

The operations can be scheduled to minimize the number of operations of the same type that occur at the same time. The scheduling is done by interchanging the order of operations and delays within the same branch.

An improved schedule is shown in Figure 8.8. The number of storage units has increased to 38 time units, while the number of multipliers and adders required is reduced to 3 and 1, respectively. Thus, less computational resources, but more storage is needed for this schedule.

Generally, a trade-off between computational resources and memory must be made, but communication costs need to be taken into account. Further, note that the average number of multipliers needed is only (5 * 4)/10 = 2. This indicates that it might be possible to use only two multipliers with a more efficient schedule.

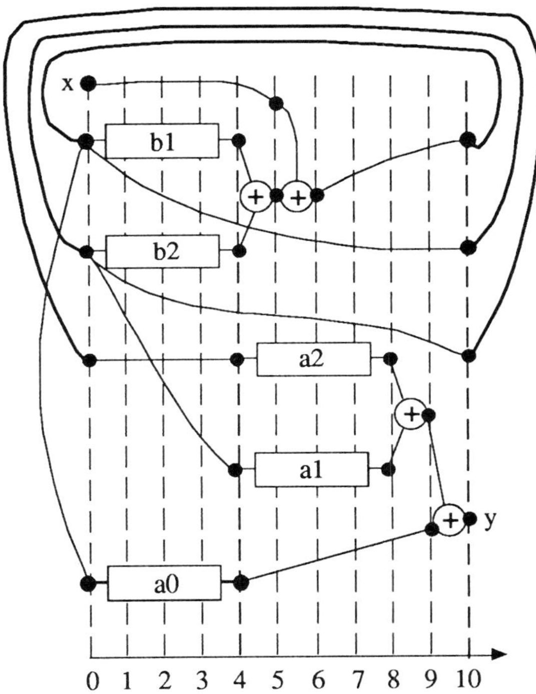

Figure 8.8. Improved Schedule Requiring Fewer PEs

8.2.2 Direct Blocking

The precedence graph represents the operations that must be executed during a single sample interval. However, the DSP algorithm will, in principle, be executed indefinitely. From a computational point of view, the repeated execution of the algorithm can be represented by an infinite sequence of networks, each representing the operations within a single sample interval, as shown in Figure 8.9 (see Wanhammar, 1986, Wanhammar, Afghani, and Sikström, 1988, and Heemstra and Herrmann, 1989). The networks are connected via the inputs and outputs of the (algorithmic) delay elements since the values that are stored in the delay elements are used as inputs in the next sample interval. Note that the algorithmic delay elements do not represent an operation or physical memory; they only represent a renaming of signal values between two sample intervals. The precedence graph contains a number of delay-free paths of infinite length. The longest average path is the critical path (CP). The average computational time of the CP is equal to the iteration bound. This value can also be determined by computing the average time for N_{CP} networks, where N_{CP} = the number of delay elements in the critical path. Note that the input branches $x(n)$ and the output branches $y(n)$ do not belong the critical path.

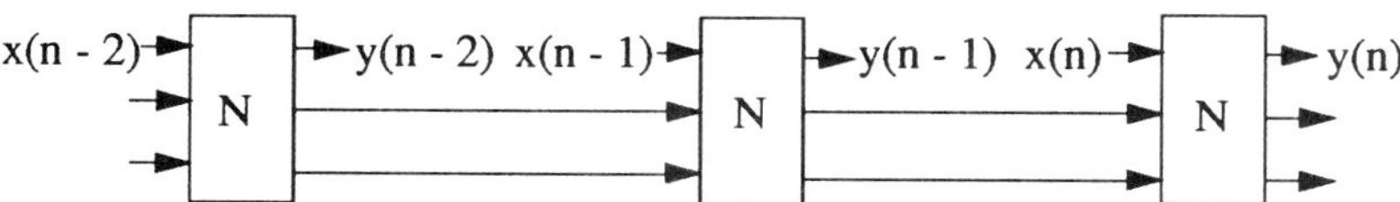

Figure 8.9. Direct Blocking of Three DAGs

This formulation of the scheduling problem allows the operations to be freely scheduled across the sample interval boundaries. Hence, inefficiencies in resource utilization due to the artificial requirement of uniform boundaries are avoided.

8.2.3 Periodic Scheduling

In the single interval and direct blocking formulations we did not take into account that the schedule is inherently periodic. It is therefore convenient to connect k networks in a closed loop, as shown in Figure 8.10 (Wanhammar, Afghani, and Sikström, 1988). The networks are fully specified signal-flow graphs with proper shimming delays. Equalizing delays are inserted into each of the computational paths so that the loop times becomes equal to kT_{sample}.

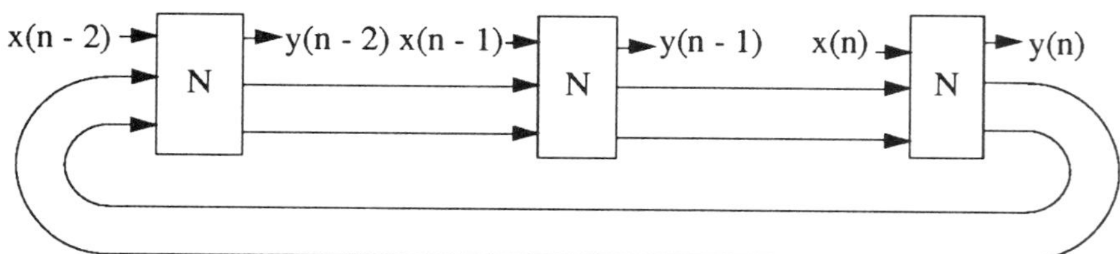

Figure 8.10. Circularly Concatenated Intervals (k = 3)

This problem formulation forces the schedule to be periodic. Unfortunately, it is not yet known how to determine the best choice of k. Only some partial results are available.

The minimal sample period, T_{min}, is achieved by utilizing $k = N_{CP}$ and an unlimited amount of resources. However, a more interesting case is to obtain T_{min} with the use of a minimal number of resources. This is achieved if only one CP exists and a proper scheduling is done, with

$$k = mN_{CP}$$

where m = integer. To find the actual resource minimum, the best of all optimal schedules using minimal resources must be found for all reasonable values of m. Typical values for m are in the range from 1 to 3.

If several CPs exist, the scheduling will instead be done for

$$k = m\{N_{1CP}, N_{2CP}, \ldots\}$$

where { } denotes the least common multiple. Generally, a search over all reasonable values of k must be done in order to find a minimum resource schedule. Experience shows that only small values of k need be considered.

Periodic scheduling is the most general possible problem formulation and it can be used to achieve resource optimal schedules using arbitrary constraints on, for example, sample rate and latency.

Example 2

Figure 8.11 shows an initial schedule for two sample intervals of the second-order section used in example 1. The initial schedule is obtained by connecting two precedence graphs.

The storage requirements and the number of multipliers and adders are the same as in example 1. A better schedule, shown in Figure 8.12, is obtained by propagating the delays throughout the network such that the number of concurrent multiplications is reduced. In this case, we obtain a schedule that utilizes only two multipliers and one adder. A count of the delays in Figure 8.12 yields 92/2 = 46 units per sample. However, some delays can be shared between branches so that only 71/2 = 35.5 units of delay are required per sample.

Example 2, shows that hardware resources can be minimized by proper scheduling of the operations. However, there are still several interesting problems to be answered. For example, what are suitable cost measurements in terms of PE, M, and C processes and over how many sample intervals should the planning be done? Further, it is important to note that cyclic planning problems are much more difficult than acyclic.

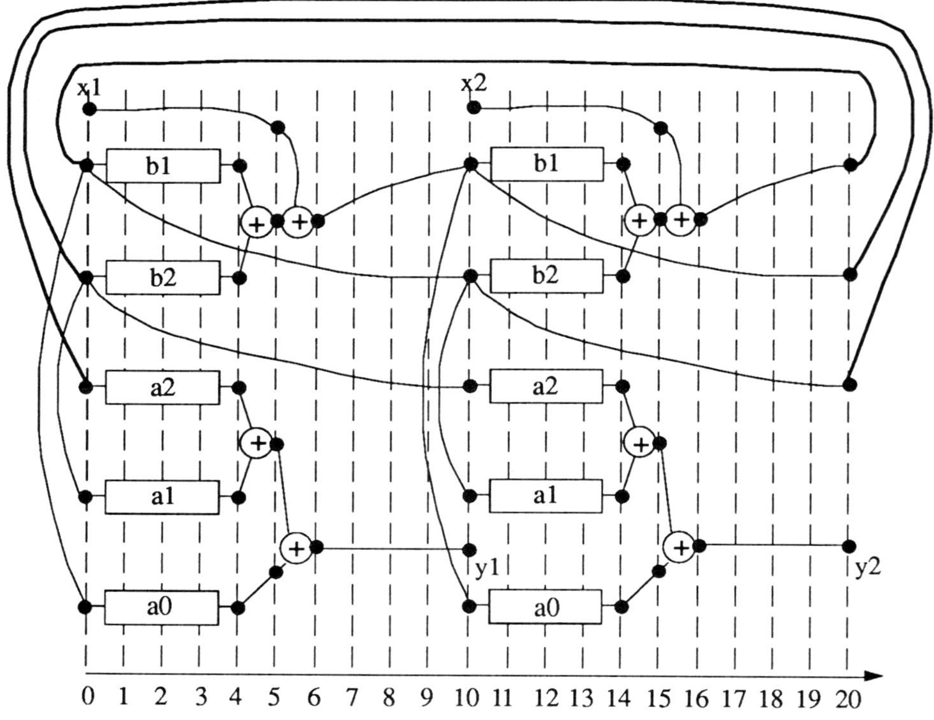

Figure 8.11. Initial Schedule for Two Sample Intervals

8.3 SCHEDULING METHODS

Scheduling methods are basically combinatorial optimization techniques that search the solution space for a solution with favorable properties. Optimization methods can be characterized as:

— Heuristic - nonheuristic
— Constructive - iterative

Heuristic methods use some form of rules to limit the search in the solution space in order to shorten the required search time. This is often necessary due to the fact that most scheduling problems have been shown to be NP-complete. A drawback of heuristic methods is that they can get stuck in local optima. Conversely, *nonheuristic* methods will eventually find the optimal solution since they traverse the whole solution space, but they will, in general, require excessive run time.

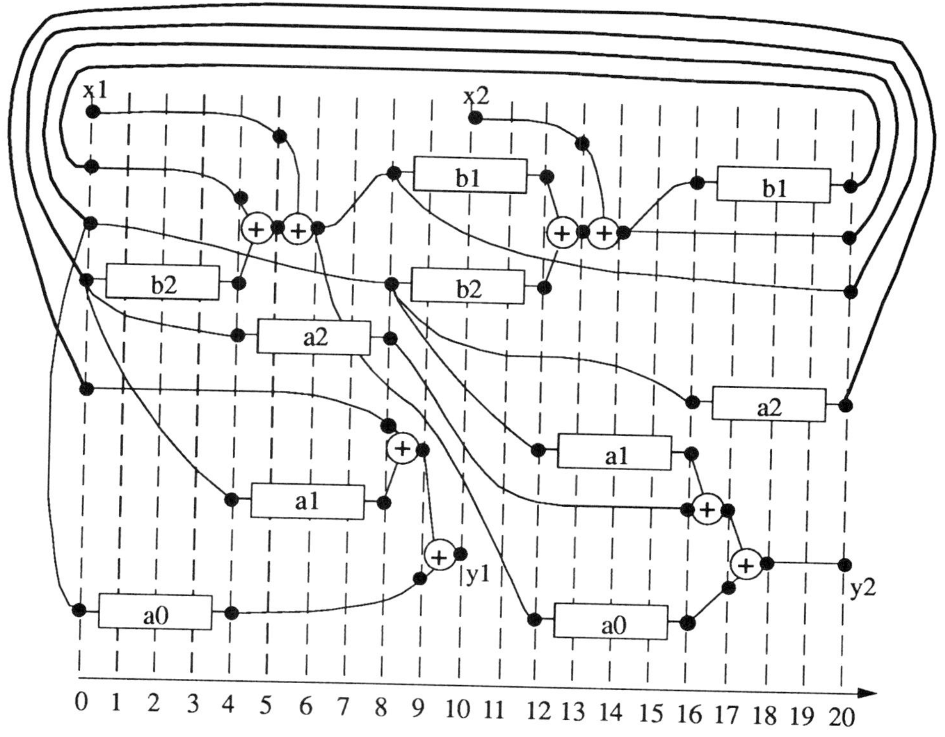

Figure 8.12. Schedule for Two Sample Intervals

Constructive methods construct a solution, whereas *iterative* methods iteratively produce better solutions from older ones. Constructive methods can be used to find an initial solution for an iterative method.

The following optimization techniques are utilized and/or are relevant for DSP scheduling:

— ASAP and ALAP scheduling
— Linear programming methods
— Critical path list scheduling
— Force-directed scheduling
— Cyclostatic scheduling
— Simulated annealing

Some of these techniques can and should be considered for the allocation and scheduling of processes in other computational paradigms.

8.3.1 ASAP and ALAP Scheduling

ASAP (As Soon As Possible) scheduling (Heemstra and Herrmann, 1989) simply schedules operations as soon as possible, that is, a computation can start when its predecessors are ready. The aim is to obtain the shortest possible execution time without considering resource requirements. However, it is possible to postpone certain operations if there are more operations in a time step than can be handled by the available resources. The operations on the time-critical path must be given higher priority to be executed first in order to reach the shortest possible execution time.

In ALAP (As Late As Possible) scheduling the operations are scheduled as late as possible. ASAP and ALAP scheduling are often used to calculate the time range in which the operations can be scheduled. For example, the two schedules in Figure 8.13 shows that only the multiplications m_1 and m_2 and the addition a_1 can be rescheduled.

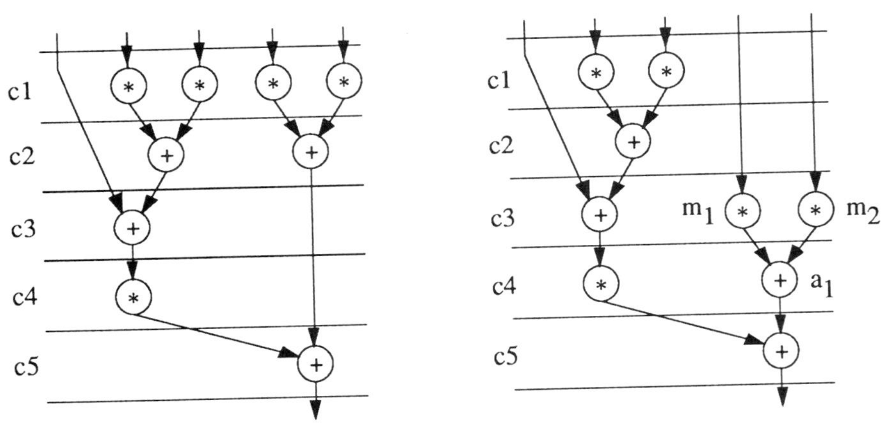

Figure 8.13. ASAP and ALAP Schedules

8.3.2 Linear Programming

The precedence relations represents a set of constraints (inequalities). Integer linear programming methods (Lee, Hsu, and Lin, 1989) can be utilized to efficiently solve such large sets of inequalities. Using linear programming methods, the optimal solution is obtained. However, large problems with many operations might be intractable to solve due to the NP-completeness of the scheduling problem.

8.3.3 Critical Path List Scheduling

Critical path list scheduling (Davidson and others, 1981, Heemstra and Herrmann, 1989) is a special case of list scheduling. In a first step, an ordered list of operations is formed.

Second, the operations are picked one by one from this list and assigned to a free resource (PE). The operations are ordered in the list according to the length of the path from the start nodes to the operations.

The method takes into account that the operations on the time critical path must be given a higher priority in order to achieve the minimal sample period. The aim is to obtain as short execution time as possible.

8.3.4 Force-directed Scheduling

Force-directed scheduling has been developed by Paulin and Knight (1989). In force-directed scheduling, the operations are distributed in time so that the required amount of resources is minimized under a fixed execution time constraint. Paulin and Knight have also proposed a similar method called **force-directed list** scheduling, FDLS, which minimizes execution time with a fixed amount of resources.

The force-directed scheduling techniques are based on an analogy with the equilibrium of a system of masses that is connected via springs. More precisely, forces = costs associated with the cost of assigning an operation to time step *j*. However, assigning an operation will have an influence on the possible time frames in which the adjacent operations can be assigned. Therefore, indirect forces are added that take into account the cost that the assignment will cause for the other operations by restricting their time frames. Scheduling is done by sequentially assigning the operation with the least combined force and then the whole set of forces is recalculated for the remaining operations. Force-directed scheduling is a heuristic method that will not, in general, be able to achieve rate optimal schedules.

8.3.5 Cyclostatic Scheduling

Cyclostatic scheduling techniques have been developed by Schwartz and Barnwell (1986). Process scheduling and PE assignment are considered in one single step. The PE schedule for the operations in one sample interval is considered as a pattern in the processor-time space. The PEs are indexed in a cyclic ring; that is, if we have N PEs, the PEs are indexed modulo N. Hence, the PEs are assumed to be connected via a regular array type of network.

A cyclostatic schedule is characterized by a pattern in the processor-time space. When executing the algorithm, the pattern is repeated and displaced in both the time and processor domains. This imposes a constraint on the cyclostatic schedule, which can be found by a depth-first search for such schedules. Only solutions that are PE optimal are considered. Note that an optimal cyclostatic schedule may not exist. In that case the technique fails. The search has a worst-case exponential complexity due to the NP-completeness of the scheduling problem. However, the constraints on real problems, for instance the precedence relations, make the solution space smaller.

8.3.6 Simulated Annealing

Metropolis and others (1953) proposed an algorithm for simulation of how a solid reaches thermal equilibrium. Almost 30 years later, Kirkpatrick, Gelath, and Vecchi (1982) and Černy (1985) realized that there is a simple analogy between certain combinatorial optimization problems and the slow cooling of a solid until it reaches its thermal equilibrium. For example, an almost perfect monolithic Si crystal is grown from a seed crystal that is dipped into the silicon melt, and a large crystal rod is formed if the seed is pulled out of the melt sufficiently slowly. At high temperatures, the molecules in the crystal will move about randomly. When the temperature is slowly reduced, the molecules will tend to move to positions corresponding to a lower-energy state (perfect crystal), and it becomes less likely that they move away from these positions as the temperature decreases. However, there is a small possibility that a molecule may temporarily move to a position with higher energy. Such moves to unfavorable positions are important for the annealing process in order to allow the perfect crystal be formed. This means that the optimization algorithm does not get stuck in local minima. This property distinguishes simulated annealing from gradient methods, which seek a solution in the direction of the largest derivative, that is, the latter methods tries to decrease the cost function as fast as possible. Finally, at zero temperature the molecules will occupy states corresponding to the global energy minimum. The process of cooling a physical system until it reaches its low-energy ground state is called *annealing*. By simulating such a cooling process, near global-optimum solutions to very large optimization problems can be found. Simulated annealing is useful for solving large combinatorial problems with many degrees of freedom (van Laarhoven and Aarts, 1987 and Otten and van Ginneken 1989).

The basic algorithm for simulated annealing is displayed at the top of the following page.

The algorithm randomly generates new states, *state(i)*, for the problem and calculates the associated cost function, *Cost(i)*. The simulation of the annealing process starts at a high fictive temperature, T_M. A new state, j, is randomly chosen, and the difference in cost is calculated, $\Delta Cost(i, j)$. If $\Delta Cost(i, j) \le 0$, that is, the cost is lower, then this new state is accepted. This forces the system toward a state corresponding to a local or possibly a global minimum. However, most large optimization problems have many local minima, and the optimization algorithm is therefore often trapped in a local minima. To get out of a local minima, an increase of the cost function is accepted with a certain probability, that is, if

$$\exp(-\Delta Cost(i, j)/T_M) > \text{Random}(0, 1)$$

the new state is accepted. The simulation starts with a high temperature, T_M. This makes the left side of the equation to be close to 1. Hence, a new state with larger cost

```
Procedure Simulated_Annealing;

  begin
    Initialize;
    M := 0;
    repeat
          repeat
             Perturb(state(i) → state(j), ΔCost(i, j));
             if ΔCost(i, j) ≤ 0 then accept
             else
             if exp(-ΔCost(i, j)/T_M) > Random(0, 1) then accept;
             if accept then  Update(state(j));
          until Equilibrium;  { Sufficiently close }
          T_M+1 := f(T_M);
          M:= M+1;
    until Stop_Criterion = True; { System is frozen }
  end;
```

is likely to be accepted. The probability of accepting a worse state is decreased as the temperature is decreased. For each temperature, the system must reach an equilibrium; that is, a number of new states must be tried before the temperature is reduced by, typically, 10%. It can be shown that under certain conditions, the algorithm will find the global minima and not get stuck in local minima.

Simulated annealing can be directly applied to optimize a periodic schedule. We can find an initial solution (initial schedule) with almost any of the earlier presented methods. The optimal solution is found by moving the operations randomly within their feasible time frames so that the cost function is minimized. Generally, the problem in optimization is to construct a good cost function that has both local and global properties such that the global minima are reached.

8.4 IDEAL DSP ARCHITECTURES

Many DSP architectures have been proposed for various applications. Some of the most common types have previously been discussed. Of particular interest are architectures with multiple PEs. The fact that DSP algorithms generally lack data-dependent branching operations facilitates perfect scheduling of the operations and planning of the interprocessor and memory communication. *Hence, to any given DSP algorithm of this type, there is a corresponding class of ideal multiprocessor architectures.*

An *ideal DSP architecture* belongs to a class of architectures that implements the given schedule. Thus, an ideal architecture has PEs that are able to execute the operations according to the schedule and are supported with appropriate communication channels and memories. Note that there may be several architectures that implement a given schedule and that a new class of architectures is obtained if the schedule is altered.

The *processing elements* usually perform simple, memoryless transformations of the input data to a single output value. If several PEs always operate on the same inputs, it may be favorable to merge these into one PE with multiple inputs and outputs. At this point it is interesting to note that the execution time for PEs and the cycle time (read and write) for memories, manufactured in the same technology, are of the same order. Hence, to fully utilize a multiple-input PE, as shown in Figure 8.14, one memory, or memory port, must be provided for each input value.

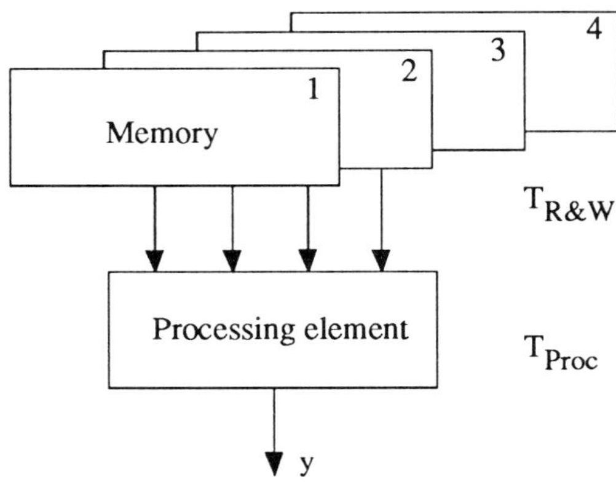

Figure 8.14. Processing Element with Multiple Inputs

The *memory elements* store data so that the PE, with respect to the algorithm, can access appropriate data without loss of any computational time slots. Since the PEs normally require several simultaneous inputs, we assume the memories are partitioned into several independent memories or have several ports that can be accessed in parallel. Furthermore, the storage must be efficient. The important issues are the access mechanism for the memories, the bandwidth, and the number of ports.

The *interconnection network*, ICN, must provide the necessary communication channels that are needed to supply the processing elements with proper data and parameters and store the results in the proper memories. It is favorable if the data movement can be kept simple, regular, and uniform. Major design issues involve the topology of the communication network and its bandwidth.

Control is an important issue in all architectures. There are two types of control signals: a signal for setting up control and communication paths and another signal for loading information into the memories. The first type of signal needs only to be valid in time intervals during which the second type of signal has significant transitions. The latter type of signal is used to capture (latch) values and store them into the memories. Since they define the basic units of time, they are referred to as *clocks*.

Control strategy mainly is concerned with the manner in which control signals direct the dataflow in the system. In a centralized control scheme, all the control signals come from a single source. Obviously, the central controller is a critical part in a system and may become a bottleneck that affects the performance and reliability of the entire system. The central controller must therefore be carefully designed to achieve good system performance. These drawbacks can be somewhat alleviated by the use of a distributed control strategy in which a small controller is associated with each operational unit in the system. In multiprocessor systems, control of crossbar interconnection networks is usually decentralized, while control of multiple-bus interconnection networks can be either centralized or decentralized.

At present, there is no generalized architecture suitable for the design of control units. Anceau (1986) describes various realization techniques utilized in microprocessors. However, the simple and static computational structure that characterizes most DSP algorithms allows the use of far less complex control schemes than is required in modern general-purpose computers. Many DSP algorithms have an inherent hierarchy that can be directly mirrored by the control structure.

As described earlier, the timing philosophy is one of the most important attributes characterizing a computing system. We have described two types of possible timing schemes: synchronous and asynchronous.

Synchronous techniques, which are widely used, are characterized by the existence of a central, global clock that broadcasts clock signals to all units in the system so that the entire system operates in a lock-step fashion. On the other hand, asynchronous techniques operate without a global clock. The communications among operational units are performed by means of interlock hand shaking. As a result, they have good expansibility and modularity, but are difficult to design.

Self-timed circuitry is often used in CMOS circuits because of its performance and area efficiency. Synchronization in self-timed systems is obtained by a causal hand-shaking operation instead of by using a global clock.

8.5 SYNTHESIS OF OPTIMAL ARCHITECTURES

It is useful to depict the scheduling of the operations as shown in Figure 8.15. According to this fictive schedule, five PEs are required. Two of the PEs perform operations with a duration of 2 time units, while the other three PEs take 3 time units.

The period of the schedule (sample period) is 6 time units. In general, it is assumed that a transaction between PEs and memories, or directly between PEs, can take place at every start and finish of an operation. The schedule in Figure 8.15 corresponds to a shared-memory architecture of the type shown in Figure 8.16. Generally, the memory has several input and output ports and the two interconnection networks are of crossbar type, but, in practice, substantial simplifications are possible.

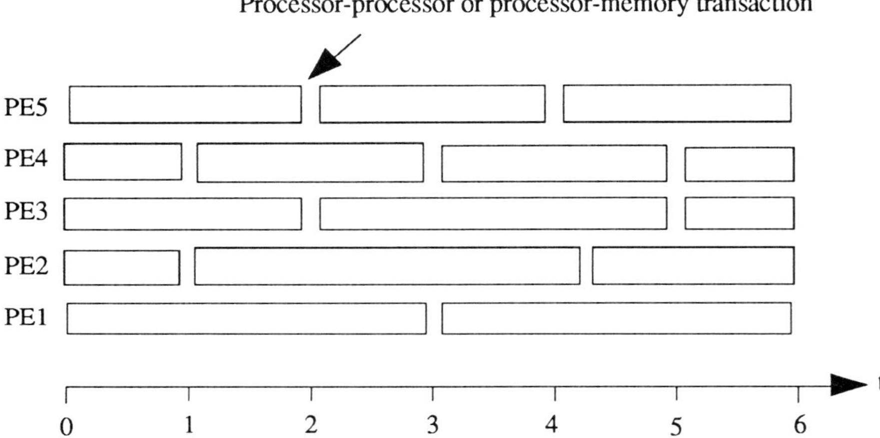

Figure 8.15. Schedule for the Operations: Planning cycle is 6 time units

By definition, an optimal architecture can execute the algorithm according to the given schedule. The ICN and memories must therefore be organized so that no computational degradation takes place. Hence, the schedule not only determines the necessary PE resources, but it also determines the quantity and organization of the memories and required communication channels. Due to the static computational structure of most DSP algorithms, all communication between PEs and memories can be planned ahead of execution. Therefore, only those communication channels that are actually used need to be realized. Generally, there is a significant flexibility in designing the interconnection network.

The architecture in Figure 8.16 is a shared-memory architecture that suffers from the well-known memory bandwidth bottleneck. Since the cycle time for the memories and the execution time for the PEs, are of the same order, a shared-memory architecture can only accommodate a few PEs. However, most DSP systems can be partitioned into subsystems that can be realized by using only a few bit-serial PEs. Furthermore, the number of necessary memories depends on the number of input values that simultaneously must be provided to the processors. Thus, the number of memories may be excessively large.

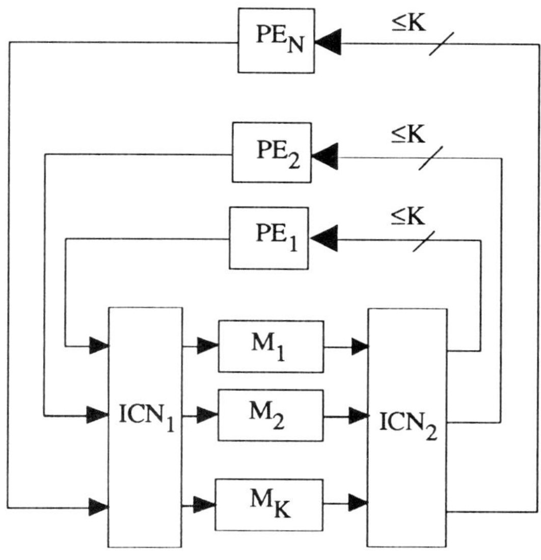

Figure 8.16. General Shared-memory Architecture

However, it has been shown in Wanhammar, Afghahi, and Sikström (1988) and Wanhammar (1992) that this imbalance between processing capacity and communication bandwidth can be avoided by using bit-serial PEs and serial-parallel converters inside the ICNs, as shown in Figure 8.17. This scheme also allows the bit-serial PEs to be supplied with inputs using only a single or a few memories. In fact, the number of memories is equal or less than the largest number of inputs to any of the processors. Often, a single memory is sufficient to support several PEs.

Each memory is connected to its own set of shift registers (cache memory) via a bit-parallel bus, which can be made very short by placing the shift registers adjacent to the memories (RAM). Hence, the interface between the memories and the serial-parallel converters is simple and regular and consumes little chip area. Thus, the complex and irregular part of the two interconnection networks, in Figure 8.16, is bit-serial. Normally, both of the ICNs can be substantially simplified. In fact, ICN_1 consists of only a bit-serial wire from each processor. A control signal is used to load the value in the shift register onto the memory bus. However, in some cases, shimming delays must be inserted into the two networks in order to synchronize the bit flows with the RAMs. The network, ICN_2, is also bit serial, but it may contain both switches and shimming delays. It is efficient to use bit-serial communication for the main part of the system rather than bit parallel, since the former consumes less chip area for wiring and drivers.

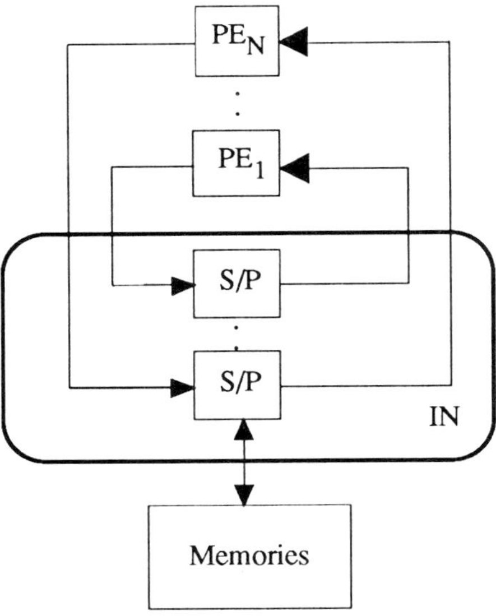

Figure 8.17. Balanced Shared-memory Architecture with bit-serial PEs

Example 3

The schedule, which was derived in example 1 for a pipelined second-order section in direct form II, has been redrawn in Figure 8.18. The scheduling period is 20 time units and the sample period is T_{sample} = 10 time units. Multiplication takes 4 time units and addition takes 1 time unit. The scheduling is done with the objective of minimizing the number of PEs. The sharing of delays has been explicitly shown in Figure 8.18. From the schedule it is evident that 76 time units of storage are required. In a general shared-memory architecture, the number of required memories is five, since five memory transactions take place at time slot 0. However, the hardware requirements may be reduced if the time instances of the inputs and outputs may be changed. For example, if the inputs are rescheduled to time slot 5 and 13, only four independent memories are required, since four memory transactions takes place at both time slots 8 and 16. The storage is reduced to 68 units. In this case, even more efficient schedules are possible.

Now, using the balanced shared-memory architecture of the type shown in Figure 8.17, several memory-PE transactions can take place in a single time slot (Dinha and others, 1984a,b). Only two memories are required, since the maximal number of inputs to any PE, the adders, is two. The balanced architecture, with three PEs, two memories with three shift registers each, is shown in Figure 8.19.

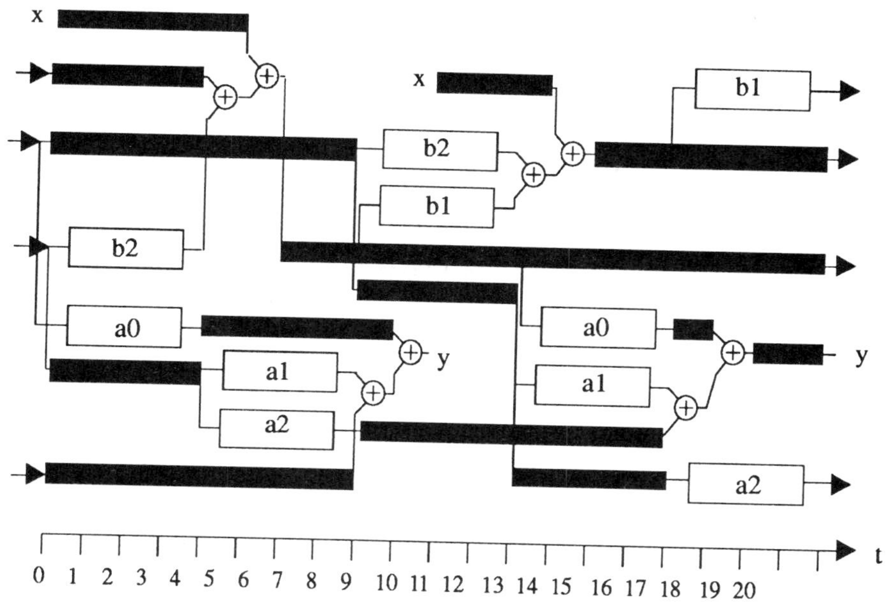

Figure 8.18. Schedule for Pipelined Second-order Section in Direct Form II

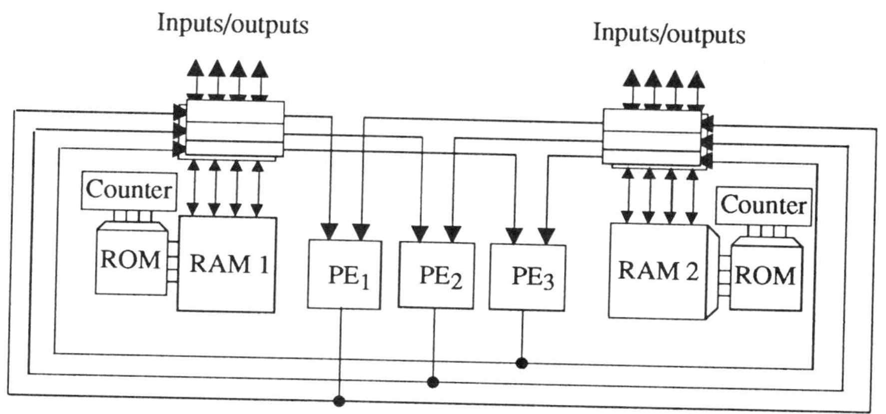

Figure 8.19. Balanced Multiprocessor Architecture with Three bit-serial PEs and Two Memories

Notice that for some cases, a larger number of PEs is required than is indicated by the number of concurrent operations.

This concludes our presentation of DSP direct-mapped architectures. A number of interesting as highly useful approaches to static mapping have been introduced. The approaches given here may well be applied at high levels of real-time systems, particularly in systems requiring absolute predictability.

References

Anceau F. (1986). *The Architecture of Microprocessors*, Addison-Wesley, Reading, MA.

Černy, V. (1985). Thermodynamical Approach to the Travelling Salesman Problem: An Efficient Simulation Algorithm, *Journal of Optimization Theory and Applications*, Vol. 45, pp. 41-45.

Crochiere, R.E., and A.V. Oppenheim (1975). Analysis of Linear Digital Networks, *Proceedings of the IEEE*, Vol. 63, No. 4, pp. 581-595.

Davidson, S., D. Landskov, B.D. Shriver, and P.W. Mallett (1981). Some Experiments in Local Microcode Compaction for Horizontal Machines, *IEEE Transactions on Computers*, Vol. C-30, No. 7, pp. 460-477.

Dinha, F., B. Sikström, U. Sjöström, and L. Wanhammar (1984a). A Multi–processor Approach to Implement Digital Filters, *Nordic Symposium on VLSI in Computers and Communications*, Tampere, Finland, June 13–16.

Dinha, F., B. Sikström, U. Sjöström, and L. Wanhammar (1984b). LSI Implementation of Digital Filters — A Multi-processor Approach, *International Conference on Computers, Systems and Signal Processing*, Bangalore, India, Dec. 10-12.

Heemstra de Groot, S.M. and O.E. Herrmann (1989). Evaluation of Some Multiprocessor Scheduling Techniques of Atomic Operations for Recursive DSP Filters, *Proceedings of the European Conference on Circuit Theory and Design*, Brighton, UK, Sept. 5-8, pp. 400-404.

Kirkpatrik, S., C.D. Gelath, Jr., and M.P. Vecchi (1982). Optimization by Simulated Annealing, IBM Research Report RC 9355.

van Laarhoven, P.J.M., and E.H.L. Aarts (1987). *Simulated Annealing: Theory and Applications*, D. Reidel Publishing Co, Dodrecht, Holland.

Lee, J.-H., Y.-C. Hsu, and Y.-L. Lin (1989). A New Integer Linear Programming Formulation for the Scheduling Problem in Data Path Synthesis, *Proceedings of the IEEE International Conference on Computer-aided Design*, Santa Clara, Calif., Nov. 5-9, pp. 20-23.

Metropolis, M., A.W. Rosenbluth, M.N. Rosenbluth, A.H. Teller, and E. Teller (1953). Equation of State Calculations by Fast Computing Machines, *Journal of Chemical Physics*, Vol. 21, pp. 1087-1092.

Otten, R.H.J., and L.P.P.P. van Ginneken (1989). *The Annealing Algorithm*, Kluwer Academic Publishers, Hingham, MA., 1989.

Paulin, P.G. and J.P. Knight (1989). Algorithms for High-level Synthesis, *IEEE Design and Test of Computers*, Dec. 1989, pp. 18-31.

Schwartz, D.A. and T.P. Barnwell III (1986). Cyclo-Static Solutions: Optimal Multiprocessor Realizations of Recursive Algorithms, *VLSI Signal Processing, II*, IEEE Press, New York, 1986.

Wanhammar, L. (1986). On Algorithms and Architecture Suitable for Digital Signal Processing, *Proceedings of the European Signal Processing Conference, EUSIPCO–86*, The Hague, The Netherlands, Sept. 1986.

Wanhammar, L. (1992). *DSP Integrated Circuits*, Prentice Hall, Englewood Cliffs, NJ. (in preparation).

Wanhammar, L., M. Afghahi and B. Sikström (1988). On Mapping of DSP Algorithms onto Hardware. *Proceedings of the IEEE Conference on Circuits and Systems*, Espoo, Finland, June 7-9, Vol. 2, pp. 1967-1970.

Chapter 9

VERY LONG INSTRUCTION WORD ARCHITECTURES

VLIW (Very Long Instruction Word) machines can be viewed as a straightforward extension of the von Neumann architecture that provides a degree of *fine-grain scalar parallelism*. The original concepts were developed as a means of compacting sequential microcode into parallel (horizontal) microcode. However, it was discovered that an analogous approach could be taken in providing wide instruction words at the classical machine instruction set level. Some view VLIW machines as a further develop-ment of RISC architectures (see Wayner, 1989).

9.1 FUNDAMENTAL CONCEPTS

The VLIW solution is to construct one big processor with n arithmetic units that connect to a common register file. The fact that each unit can be activated during the same instruction cycle leads to long instruction words.

The major premise leading to the exploitation of the parallel arithmetic units is the ability to partition the problem (program) into several parallel operations that can be performed at the same time. Where computations are interdependent and/or where conditional branching occur, the possibilities of exploiting the multiple arithmetic units become limited. There is no general solution to the interdependence issue; however, the treatment of conditional branching is a part of the VLIW philosophy. Program segments containing arithmetic operations and conditional branches are executed together. The branching can result in the nullification of some of the computations that have been performed.

Compiler recognition of parallel structures in the program code is the key to success of this approach. A technique called *trace scheduling* (see Fisher, 1981, and Ellis, 1986) has been developed for this purpose.

9.2 MULTIFLOW TRACE COMPUTER

As a concrete example of this form of parallel architecture, we consider the Multiflow TRACE computer (see Fischer, 1987). Unfortunately, this product is no longer available in the marketplace; however, it remains as a highly useful example of this type of architecture. The Multiflow TRACE provided an upgradable and compatible family with up to 28 fast functional units operating simultaneously upon a synchronous execution stream. The central PE contains multiple integer/logical units, floating-point add/logic units, and a floating-point square root unit.

Memory is demand paged and virtually addressed with 4 gigabytes per user process. In contrast to coarse-grain parallelism systems, high-level regularity in the user code is not required in order to exploit the hardware parallelism. All functional units are completely synchronized in each clock cycle. The true cost of every operation is visible at the instruction repertoire level, permitting the compiler to optimize operation scheduling. Instruction pipelining permits new operations to begin on every functional unit during each instruction. Functional units are never required to wait upon each other.

Fine-grain parallelism at the level of adds, loads, stores, and other primitive operations can be achieved. Since such parallelism typically occurs throughout the programs, regardless of the application, increased performance can be achieved across a broad range of programs. On a TRACE 7 member of the product family, each instruction word (256-bits) controls seven different functional units as illustrated in figure 9.1. On a TRACE 28, where each instruction is 1024 bits wide, 28 different functional units are controlled.

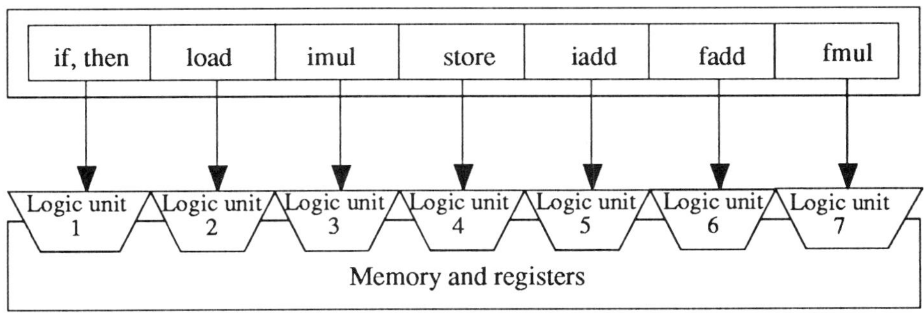

Figure 9.1. Functional Unit Control for the TRACE 7

Due to the fact that the cost of computer memory has dropped radically in relationship to the cost of logic, the construction of VLIW architectures becomes practical and attractive. Complex program scheduling logic is not required, resulting in the sequential form of computation to which users are accustomed. Execution patterns are static and are completely deterministic, thus simplifying both testability and fault isolation.

9.2.1 Code Compaction

The trace scheduling compilers combine operations into long instruction words by determining which operations can be overlapped. The compilers support the FORTRAN and C languages and can guarantee compatability with existing programs. They do not have to be rewritten to take advantage of the parallel functional units, as in the case of most other approaches to supercomputing. An example of how source code could be combined into instruction words is provided in Figure 9.2.

Source code:	Sequential operations:	
(1) C=A+B	OP1	(LOAD A)
	OP2	(LOAD B)
	OP3	(C=A+B)
	OP4	(STORE C)
(2) K=I*J	OP5	(LOAD I)
	OP6	(LOAD J)
	OP7	(K=I*J)
	OP8	(STORE K)
(3) L=M-K	OP9	(LOAD M)
	OP10	(L=M-K)
	OP11	(STORE L)
(4) Q=C/K	OP12	(Q=C/K)
	OP13	(STORE Q)

Wide instructions words

	OP1		OP2			
	OP5		OP6		OP3	
	OP9	OP7	OP4			
			OP8	OP10		OP12
	OP11		OP13			

Figure 9.2. Instruction Combining

In the example, 13 sequential instructions are reduced to 5 wide instructions. The unshaded parts of the instructions are available for other parts of the code. As mentioned, branching becomes an important issue in relationship to exploiting the potential of the VLIW architecture. Trace scheduling addresses this problem. A *trace* is defined to be a loop-free execution sequence of instructions for which the compiler predicts conditional branches. Identification of program structure and combining instructions proceeds as follows:

— The compiler first finds the most frequent parts of the program (the first trace) by predicting the outcome of the program's conditional operations.
— This first trace block is processed as one long code block containing data-ready operations.
— Compensation code is added to ensure that the program executes properly by dealing with trace separation and reconnection boundaries.
— The compiler considers the most frequently used portion of the remaining code (second trace), and so on, until the entire program has been compiled, as illustrated in Figure 9.3.

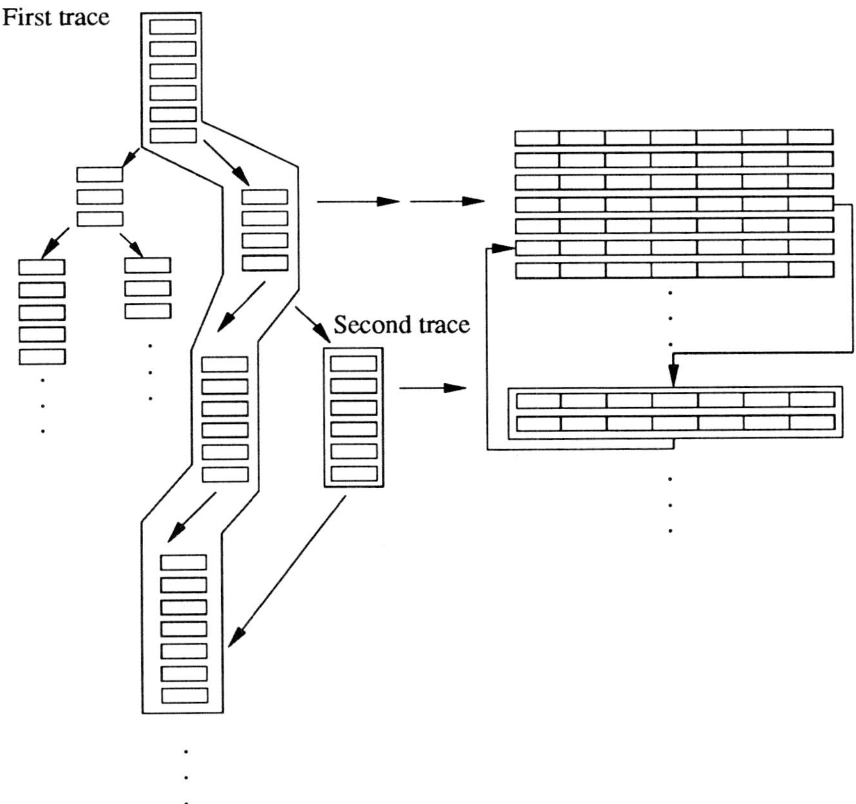

Figure 9.3. Multiple Traces and Combining

9.2.2 Operating System

The TRACE/UNIX operating system, a version of the Berkeley 4.3 BSD has been extended and enhanced for scientific applications. TRACE/UNIX provides a kernel that manages the machine. **All programs** running on the TRACE, including utilities and the kernel, are accelerated via VLIW overlapped instructions.

In summary, we observe that the combined VLIW architecture and trace scheduling compiler technology make this approach an interesting parallel processing alternative. The key distinction lies in the fact that Multiflow optimizes nonparallel code, where conventional vectorizing or multiprocessing systems cannot perform well. The major marketing premise of Multiflow has been that the majority of the application programs contain "junk" code that cannot be easily parallelized or vectorized. It is for these cases that the scalar parallelism of Multiflow can be exploited. While the Multiflow corporation has terminated operations, it will be interesting to follow developments in this area, especially if other actors enter the computer marketplace with similar solutions.

In the area of real-time systems, the VLIW approach naturally provides a straightforward means of obtaining accelerated performance for existing real-time system and application programs.

References

Ellis, J.R. (1986). *Bulldog: A Compiler for VLIW Architectures*, MIT Press, Cambridge, MA.

Fischer, J.A. (1981). Trace Scheduling: A Technique for Global Microcode Compaction, *IEEE Transactions on Computers*, Vol. C-30, No. 7, pp. 478-490.

Fischer, J.A. (1987). VLIW Architectures: Supercomputing via Overlapped Execution, *Proceedings of the Second International Conference on Supercomputing*, pp. 3-8, May.

Wayner, P. (1989). VLIW: Heir to RISC?, *Byte*, pp. 259-262, August.

Chapter **10**

PE ARRAY ARCHITECTURES

The main concepts and principles of SIMD (**S**ingle **I**nstruction stream, **M**ultiple **D**ata) PE arrays have been described in Chapter 3. In this chapter, we consider more thoroughly the distinguishing characteristics of this SIMD class: array topology, processing element design, input/output structure and programming style and languages. Throughout the text, the architectural principles are illustrated with various examples of existing designs, commercial machines, or research machines. A number of specific application examples are also provided. To assist the reader in obtaining a collected view of each of the PE-array artifacts used in the examples, product and research project summaries are provided in the final section of the chapter.

10.1 PE-ARRAY TOPOLOGIES

The topology of the PE array is defined, to a large extent, by the structure of the interconnection network. Further, the choice of topology is heavily influenced by the demands of the applications. Looking back over the brief history of PE arrays, one may observe that many of the architectures have been designed for **specific** application domains. Typically, the designers have tried to combine the communication demands of the specific application with more general processing demands.

We shall introduce the most common topologies and consider the interconnection structures of several existing (or previously existing) research and commercial machines. The list is by no means exhaustive, but has been chosen to demonstrate the variety of topologies.

10.1.1 Mesh-connected Arrays

The *two-dimensional mesh,* which was introduced in Chapter 3 and illustrated in Figure 3.13, is the most common topology of PE arrays. The main reason for this popularity is its obvious support for close local connections, which are exploited in several application areas. The main drawback of the two-dimensional mesh is the relatively large maximum-distance value, *Dmax*. With wraparound connections at the edges as in Figure 3.13, *Dmax* for an *N* PE array is equal to the square root of *N* (for example, for a 1024 PE array, *Dmax* is 32).

The first PE array to be implemented was *ILLIAC IV*, "the first Supercomputer," as described in the Chapter 6. It was intended to have 256 powerful PEs, divided into four quadrants, with 64 PEs in each. However, only one quadrant was constructed. The topology is shown in Figure 10.1. As the reader can observe, it is a two-dimensional mesh with modified horizontal wraparound connections. Rather than being connected to PE number 8, PE number 15 is connected to the next PE in order, number 16. Thus, the interconnection structure of ILLIAC IV can be described as a one-dimensional nearest-neighbor structure (a long row of PEs) with additional connections eight steps forward and backward (the vertical connections in the figure).

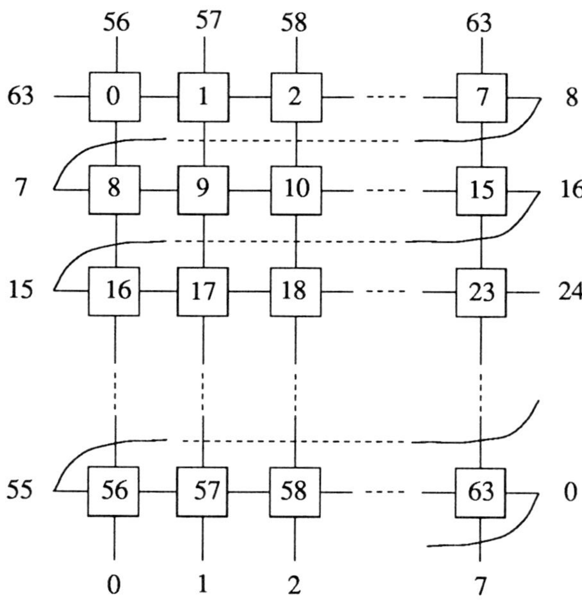

Figure 10.1. Topology of ILLIAC IV

The *Distributed Array Processor DAP* produced by ICL (International Computers Limited) and AMT (Active Memory Technology Ltd.), as well as the *Massively Parallel Processor MPP* from Goodyear Aerospace are the prime examples of large-scale two-dimensional PE arrays. Both use bit-serial PEs. DAP is manufactured in 1024 (32 by 32) and 4096 (64 by 64) PE arrays, while the only MPP machine that was constructed has a 16384 (128 by 128) PE array.

The DAP architecture provides an additional interconnection facility in that two sets of data paths ("highways") pass along the rows of PEs and along the columns of PEs, respectively, as portrayed in Figure 10.2. Via these data paths a row (or column) of bits can be broadcast in one cycle so that each row (column) of PEs receives the same data pattern. Another use is in extracting data from the array, where the basic operation is to AND together all the rows or columns, respectively. The reader can observe that provisions have been made to overcome the shortcoming of the ordinary two-dimensional array, its poor long-distance communication performance.

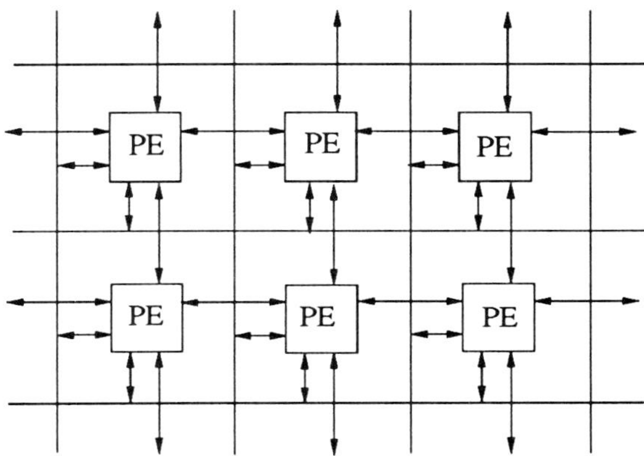

Figure 10.2. Connectivity for a Small Section of the DAP:
Horizontal and vertical lines are row highways and column highways, respectively

A variation of the two-dimensional mesh, the *X-grid*, has been chosen in two recent designs: BLITZEN, a research machine from North Carolina State University (see Blevins and others, 1990) and *MasPar MP-1*, a commercial product from MasPar Computer Corporation, California (Blank, 1990). In the network, portrayed in Figure 10.3, only four single-bit paths per PE are used for the communication with eight neighbors. This is accomplished by the use of a tristate node at each X intersection. For example, routing to the north direction (upward in the figure) can be achieved by sending a value out to the northeast and accepting a value from the southeast. All PEs route in the same direction at the same time. Thus, each PE sends data on one wire, receives data on one of the other three wires, and places the remaining two wires in the high-impedance state. This makes eight paths possible with only four wires. Via this topology, diagonal data movement is improved by a factor of 2.

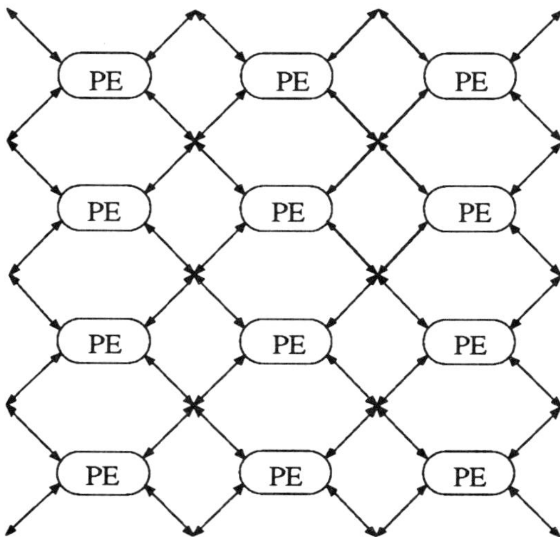

Figure 10.3. X-grid network

10.1.2 Shuffle-exchange Networks, Direct and Indirect Binary *N*-cubes

Shuffle-exchange and cube structures are common topologies in multicomputers and have also been proposed in shared-memory multiprocessors as an alternative to buses where the number of PEs is large (see Chapters 3 and 11). As will be shown here, they may also be usefully applied in PE arrays, although they are not as common as the two-dimensional arrays.

The *shuffle-exchange network* and cube structures were described in Chapter 3 and illustrated in Figures 3.28 and 3.29. Typical for the use of shuffle-exchange and cube networks in PE arrays is that they are combined with one- or two-dimensional regular arrays. An example of a research machine utilizing a combination of shuffle-exchange and other structures is the *LUCAS* system. An early commercial PE array, *STARAN*, combines a variation of the indirect cube network with a linear array. A contemporary commercial system, the *Connection Machine*, combines a direct cube structure with various regular structures of differing dimensions.

LUCAS (**L**und **U**niversity **C**ontent **A**ddressable **S**ystem) was designed and built as a research vehicle to study organization principles, PE design, programming, and application development of PE array machines. Therefore, the interconnection network was made reconfigurable so that varying topologies could be utilized. Eight different sources can be wired to the input of each PE, as shown in Figure 10.4. This allows several simple network structures to be implemented simultaneously. Application development and programming in areas like image, signal, and database processing could be accomplished within the framework of a machine with both shuffle-exchange network and nearest-neighbor connections (in one dimension).

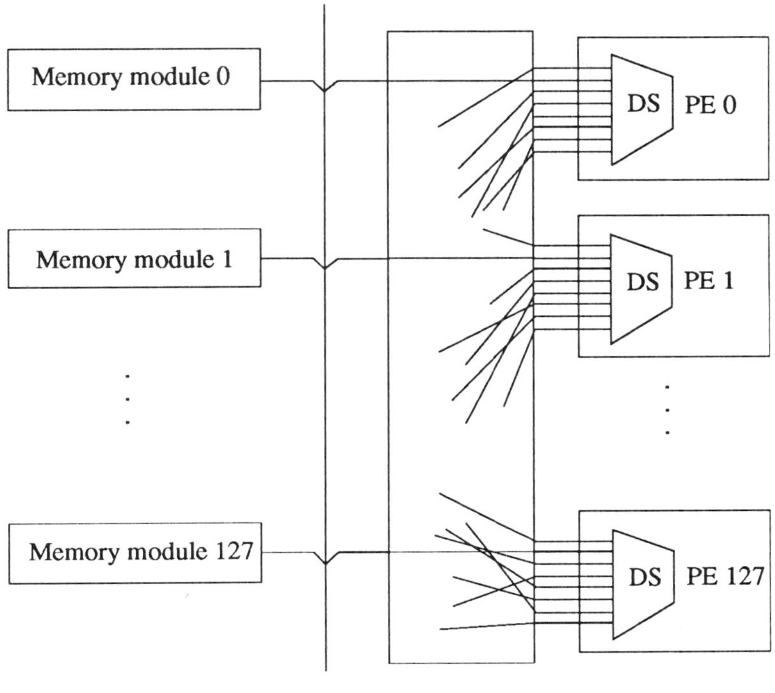

Figure 10.4. Reconfigurable Interconnection Structure of LUCAS (All data selectors, DS, are controlled by the same code)

STARAN, manufactured by Goodyear Aerospace Corporation in the 1970s, used a "flip network" between memory modules and PEs. This network is functionally identical to the indirect binary n-cube. More important than the ability to reach any memory module from any PE were the many different access patterns that were made available through the network in combination with a clever permutation addressing scheme.

The *Connection Machine Model CM-2* from Thinking Machines Corporation (1989a) uses a 12-dimensional direct binary cube to support general patterns of communication among 4096 nodes (in a fully configured system), where each node incorporates 16 bit-serial PEs. The *routers* – one at each node – are capable of dealing with contention for hypercube wires by routing the message to alternative routes.

While the router network supports completely general patterns of communication by message passing, additional special hardware supports certain commonly used regular patterns of communication. This is called the *NEWS network*, because one of its uses is to implement a two-dimensional grid (North, East, West, and South connections).

However, grids of any dimension up to 31 are supported. For example, possible grid configurations for 64K PEs include 256 x 256, 1024 x 64, 65536 x 1, 64 x 32 x 32, and 16 x 16 x 16 x 16. The structured NEWS communication is significantly faster than general routing.

Figure 10.5 shows a node of 16 PEs including router, NEWS, and hypercube interface.

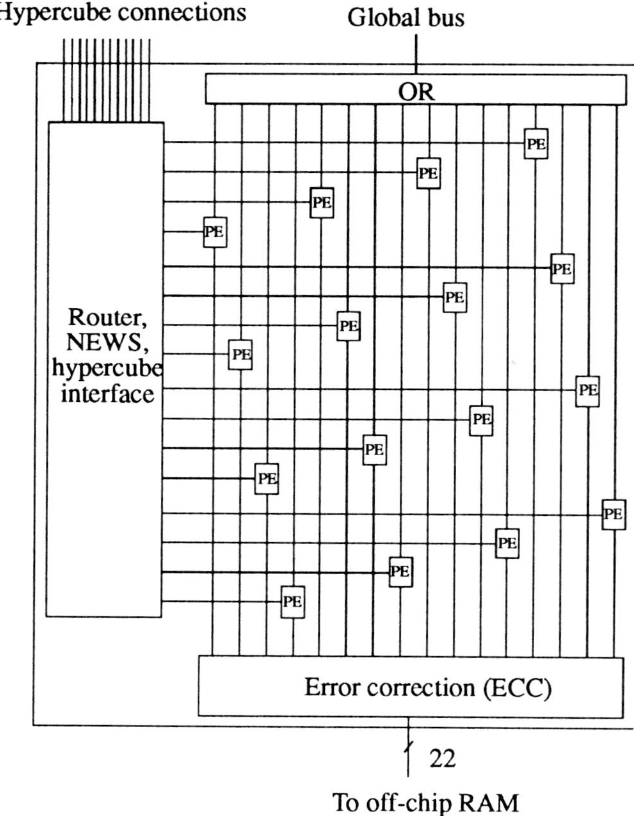

Figure 10.5. CM-2 Processor Chip

When the number of elements in the parallel data structure is greater than the number of physical PEs, the system operates in *virtual PE* (resource-limited) mode. This means that each hardware PE simulates (by sequential execution) a number of virtual PEs, each with a correspondingly smaller memory. The virtual PE mode is supported by microcode.

As an example of the way in which a data structure and a communication demand may be mapped onto the architecture, imagine a set of 2^{22} virtual PEs (about 4 million) that we wish to organize as a 2048 x 2048 square grid. We assume a 64K Connection Machine system.

First, a two-dimensional grid of shape, say, 64 x 64 is embedded in the Boolean 12-cube. This can always be done using Gray-coding of the grid coordinates, implying selection of a subset of the wires that form the 12-cube. Each of the 64 x 64 nodes has 16 physical PEs arranged as a 4 x 4 grid. Within each physical PE we now need 64 virtual PEs, which we imagine are arranged as an 8 x 8 grid.

For each virtual PE to send a value to its east neighbor, three different types of communication need to take place. Within each group of 64 virtual PEs (implemented in a single physical PE), 56 of them have their East neighbor within the same physical PE, in which case communication is accomplished by having each physical PE rearrange data within its own memory. The remaining eight values are to be sent to the physical PE to the east. In some cases this is within the same 16 PE node; in some cases it is not.

Within each group of 16 physical PEs, 12 of them must send data to another physical PE that is within the same chip. This transfer is thus independent of the entire router/hypercube-wire mechanism. Remaining to be transmitted is only 1/32 of the total communications. Each node has to send 32 messages to its East neighbor along one NEWS hypercube wire.

All three types of communication are supported by specialized hardware on the CM-2, allowing the communication to take place without use of the slower general routing mechanism. This is true for grid communication patterns of any dimension that are handled by microcode.

In summary, a very general network, the Boolean cube, has been selected as the basic communication structure for the CM-2, but special hardware support has been added for the most common regular structures – the multidimensional grids.

10.1.3 Linear Arrays

Several linear arrays of PEs have been utilized, mainly in low-level image processing. The earlier mentioned general-purpose systems LUCAS and STARAN provide a linear array structure in addition to shuffle and flip networks, respectively. Examples of pure linear arrays, that is, with only nearest-neighbor interconnections in one dimension, are LAPP (Forchheimer and Ödmark, 1983), SLAP (Fisher and Highnam, 1985), and AIS-5000, the latter of which is characterized at the end of the chapter. LAPP integrates a row of photodiodes and PEs into a single chip and is designed for high-speed, low-cost industrial quality-measurement and inspection. The LAPP structure and an industrial application are presented as a case study in Part III.

The *AIS-5000* is a commercially available system from Applied Intelligent Systems, Inc. It provides up to 1024 processing elements arranged in a one-dimensional chain that, for computer vision applications, can be as wide as the image itself. Processing of images is done line by line.

10.2 PROCESSING ELEMENT (PE) DESIGN

In the design selection of a PE array, there exists a traditional trade-off problem, the balance between the power of the PEs and the size of the array. One extreme is based on massive parallelism and very simple, bit-serial PEs. This philosophy is represented by DAP, MPP, Connection Machine, and AIS-5000, for example. At the other end of the scale we find designs like PICAP3 (described later) with a moderate number of specialized floating-point PEs. Surprisingly, the two extremes may be combined in the same design: the Connection Machine CM-2 represents both schools in that it, in addition to its tens of thousands of bit-serial PEs, also contains thousands of 32-bit floating-point PEs. The two sets of PEs share the same communication structure and memory.

There is also a relationship between the power of the PEs and the interconnection structure. Multibit PEs may require multibit data paths to match their processing bandwidth. This, in turn, restricts the degree of connectivity of the array.

10.2.1 Simple Bit-serial PEs

The machines that provide the highest degree of parallelism are also characterized by the simplest PE designs. The DAP and the Connection Machine both have bit-serial PEs that can perform a full adder operation and various other logical operations on 1, 2, or 3 bits. They also have a small set of 1-bit registers to store intermediate results, as well as an activation flip-flop. The PEs of LUCAS and AIS-5000 also belong to this category. As an illustration of the degree of complexity found in these PEs, Figures 10.6a and 10.6b illustrate the bit-serial PEs of LUCAS and the Connection Machine CM-2, respectively.

10.2.2 Enhanced Bit-serial PEs

Multiplication is a common operation in many of the applications in which PE arrays are utilized, for example, in signal and image processing. A serious drawback of simple bit-serial PEs is that multiplication time grows quadratically with the data length. However, there is a method of performing bit-serial multiplication that requires no more

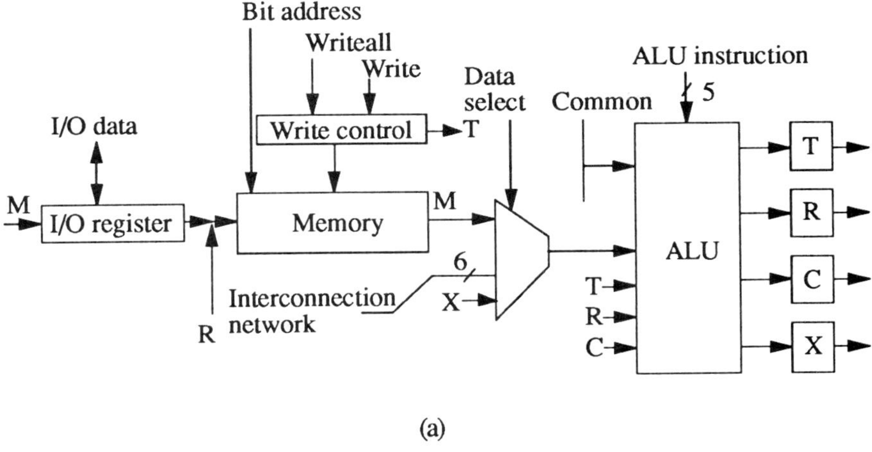

(a)

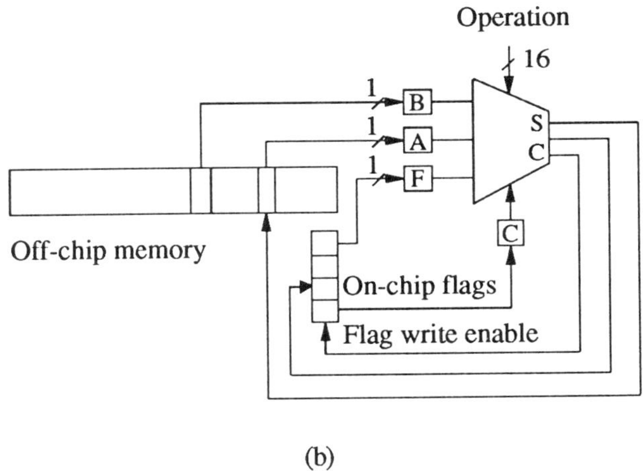

(b)

Figure 10.6. Examples of Bit-serial PEs: (a) LUCAS, (b) Connection Machine

time than is needed to read the operands (bit by bit, of course) and store the result (also bit by bit). The method, based on a carry-save adder technique, requires as many full adders as the data length. Figure 10.7 shows the design for multiplication of two 2's complement integers. It is operated by first shifting in the multiplicand, most significant bit first, into the array of M flip-flops. The bits of the multiplier are then successively applied to the input, least significant bit first, and the product bits appear at the output, also least significant bit first.

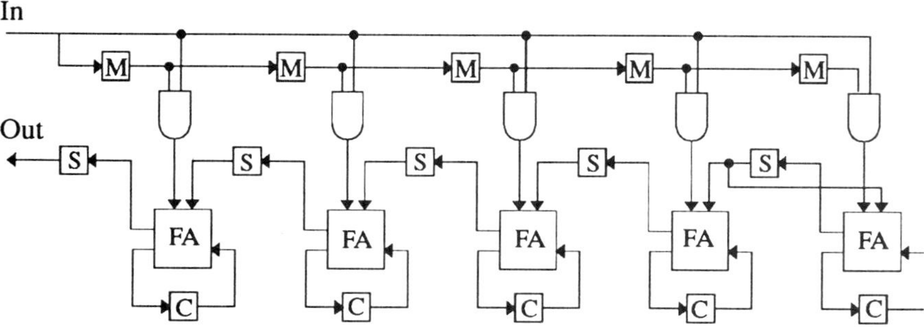

Figure 10.7. Principle of Bit-serial Multiplier Used in the PEs of REMAP

The design, which was proposed but not implemented in the LUCAS project, will be utilized in the *REMAP* system, an implementation of a configurable modular PE array building upon the experiences of LUCAS (Bengtsson and others, 1991). A similar multiplier design has been proposed for the *Centipede*, a further development of the AIS-5000 concept.

10.2.3 Bit-parallel and Floating-point PEs

While still conforming to the PE-array principle, the proposed and partially implemented *PICAP3* design (now terminated) contained PEs that are considerably more complex than those that we have considered thus far (see Figure 10.8). Each PE provides 32-bit integer and floating-point arithmetic, a four-port register file, and a set of complicated gate arrays to implement functions such as local addressing, microword decoding, memory control, and parity check. A PICAP3 system is anticipated to have up to 64 PEs.

The PE design of the commercial *MasPar MP-1* provides an interesting compromise between the simple bit-serial PEs and full-fledged floating-point PEs. The PE (see Figure 10.9) is designed around a 4-bit data bus and a 4-bit ALU. During a floating-point or integer instruction on longer data words, successive 4-bit nibbles pass through the ALU to generate the full-precision result. The registers that contain the mantissas of floating-point numbers are provided with shifting capability to allow alignment of data before addition and subtraction. To prevent operations from being memory bound, a large set of registers is provided on-chip in each PE. Forty 32-bit registers are available to the programmer and an additional eight 32-bit registers are used internally to implement the instructions.

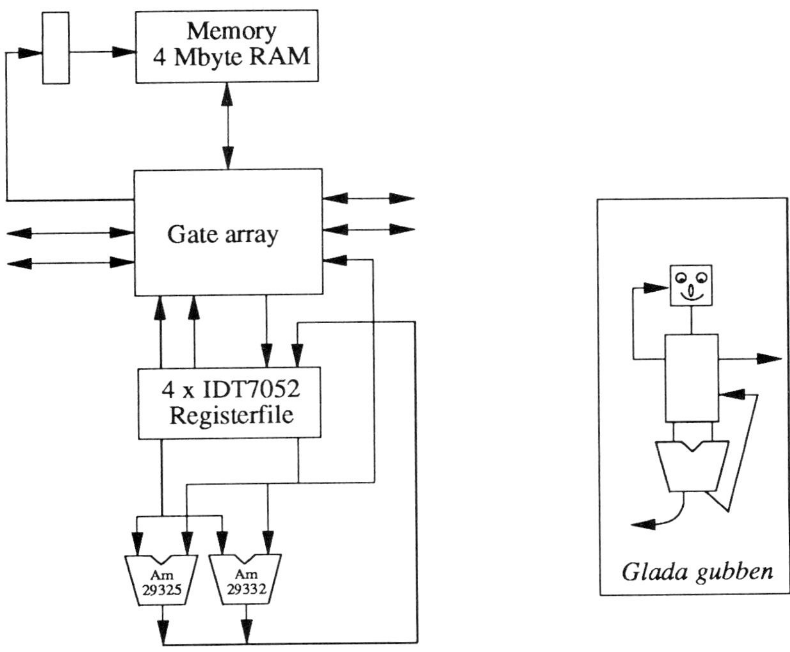

Figure 10.8. A PE "Glada gubben" (Merry man) in PICAP3.32

10.3 RESOURCE ALLOCATION

To achieve highest efficiency, a PE array requires that the problem expose at least the same degree of parallelism as the array. In nearly all applications that call for large amounts of computing power, this is the case. However, it is not necessarily a requirement that the machine be as parallel as the problem (that is, a resource-limited situation). In addition, there may be difficulties concerning communications and input/output when attempting to utilize the entire parallelism potential provided by the machine. The purpose of this section is to illustrate trade-off situations and demonstrate the various consequences of the decisions made. The general issues for *resource allocation* in PE arrays were introduced in Chapter 3.

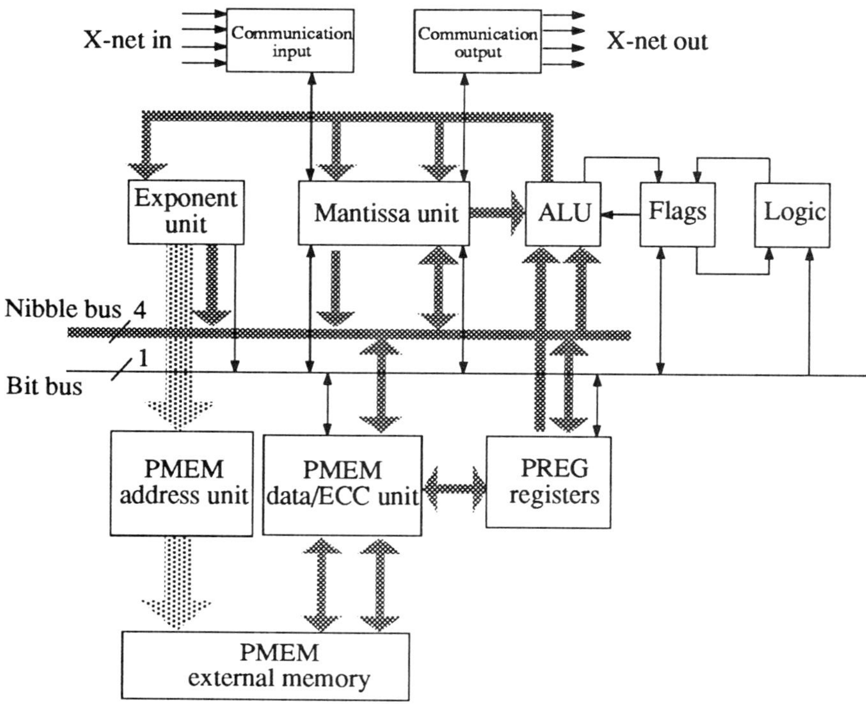

Figure 10.9. Schematic View of the MasPar MP-1 PE: Illustrated is the 4-bit ALU, the 1-bit LOGIC unit, the 16-bit EXPONENT unit, and the 64-bit MANTISSA unit. Also shown are the set of forty 32-bit PREG registers, the memory interface, and the X-grid-based communication.

10.3.1 Image-processing Approaches

Our first illustration of resource allocation is concerned with image processing. In MPP, with its 16,384 PEs arranged as a 128 x 128 grid, one PE is typically assigned to each pixel. Thus, images are divided into square parts, sized 128 x 128, when processed (see Figure 10.10a). This method implies a quite complicated I/O system in order to reorder data. The *staging memory* that accomplishes I/O in the MPP represents a large part of the machine (a part that was actually added late in the design phase). The method also introduces neighborhood access problems at the edges of the subimages, which must be taken care of at the lowest level of programming.

In LUCAS and AIS-5000, which are organized as linear arrays, the row of PEs at any instant of time takes care of one line of the image (see Figure 10.10b). This simplifies I/O significantly, at least in the case when the image is input and output in line-scan format. Normally, the PEs provide sufficient memory to allow the entire image to be stored in the array (that is, the memory of each PE contains a whole pixel column). Vertical neighbor pixels are in the same PE; horizontal ones are in neighboring PEs. Long-distance communication in the vertical direction is achieved at no cost (within the same PE).

The linear-array approach to image processing has a limit (by definition); that is, the number of PEs cannot exceed the number of pixels of a line. However, duplication of arrays can be made to enhance performance if required. For example, the arrays can be structured as parallel arrays or arrays organized in a pipeline fashion.

To make the review of mapping methods complete, it should be noted that each PE in a two-dimensional array can process a small, coherent part of the image, as illustrated in Figure 10.10c. Reordering of data during input/output is also needed in this case, although it can be done a line at a time, thus requiring less staging memory. The neighborhood access patterns are different for different pixels within the subimage, but the instantaneous pattern is the same for the entire set of physical PEs.

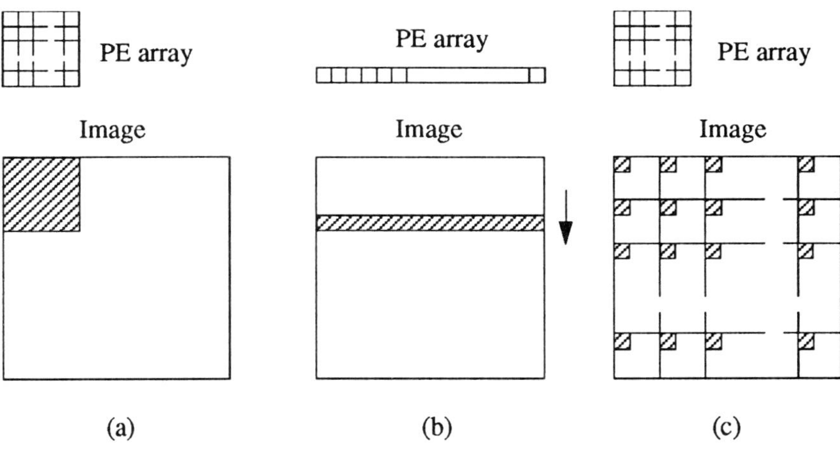

Figure 10.10. Processing Part of an Image: (a) subimage on whole array, (b) line by line, and (c) subimage on PE

The three examples (subimage on whole array, line by line, and subimage on PE) demonstrate that virtual PEs can be mapped to physical PEs in several ways, yielding varying consequences for input/output and computations. Choosing the organization and mapping carefully is as important as using as many PEs as possible in the solution of a problem. For example, it might be beneficial to use fewer, but more powerful PEs coupled with a simple and efficient mapping and input/output scheme.

10.3.2 Neural Net Approaches

PE arrays are candidates for performing the computations of neural network models efficiently. The computations involved in such models are uniform and arithmetically simple. This suggests that simple PEs are sufficient and that the PE-array type of architecture is appropriate.

The number of interconnections in an artificial neural network is often orders of magnitude greater than the number of available PEs. In addition, extensive *training sets* are normally used, however, in some models they can be run independently of each other. Thus, the problem parallelism exceeds the machine parallelism by orders of magnitude, leaving the system designer with a multidimensional design space in the resource-limited allocation task.

A popular neural net model is the multilayer feedforward network with error back-propagation, as illustrated in Figure 10.11. In the first phase of computation, the input to the network is provided and values propagate through the network to compute the output vector. In these computations, each neuron first computes a weighted sum of all its inputs. Next, each neuron applies an activation function to the sum, resulting in an activation value (or output) of the neuron. Usually, a sigmoid function with a smooth thresholdlike curve is used as the activation function.

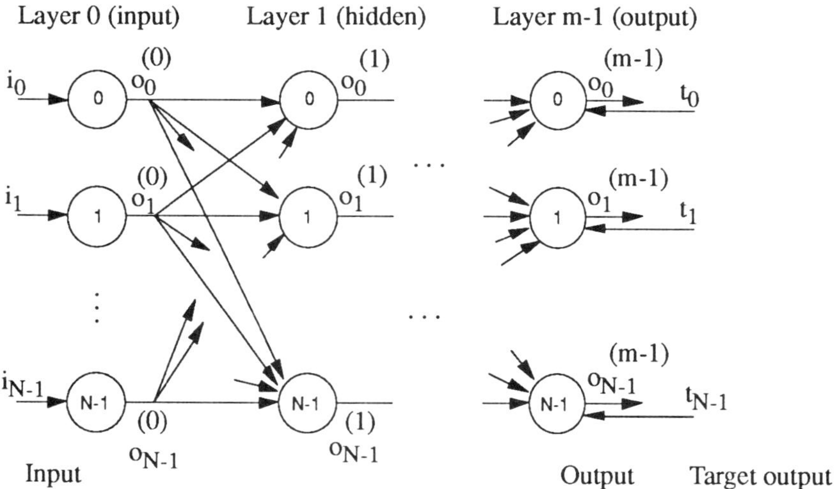

Figure 10.11. Neural Network of the Multilayer Feedforward Type

The output vector of the network is compared with a target vector, which is provided by a teacher, resulting in an error vector. In the second phase, the values of the error vector are first propagated back through the network. The error signals for hidden units are thereby determined recursively: Error values for layer l are determined from a weighted sum of the values of the next layer, $l + 1$, again using the connection weights — now "backward." The weighted sum is multiplied by the derivative of the activation function to give the error value.

Finally, appropriate changes of weights and thresholds can be made. The weight change in the connection to unit i in layer l from unit j in layer l-1 is proportional to the product of the output value and the error value.

The mapping of neural network computations on PE arrays has been studied by, among others, Brown, Garber, and Vanable (1988), Svensson and Nordström (1990), Singer (1990), and Nordström and Svensson (1992). Nordström and Svensson identify six different ways of achieving parallelism:

(i) each node in a layer can be mapped to one PE,
(ii) each interconnection can be mapped to a PE,
(iii) the training examples can be mapped to different PEs,
(iv) different training sessions (for example, different starting weights) can be started on different PEs,
(v) the different layers can be pipelined, and
(vi) the forward and backward passes can be run simultaneously on different patterns.

Svensson and Nordström (1990) use method (i). Brown and co-workers use method (ii) since they run a rather small network on a fairly large array. Singer runs several training sessions simultaneously, that is, method (iii), which turns out to be the most efficient method on the Connection Machine (minimizes the need for communication).

10.4 INPUT/OUTPUT FOR PE ARRAYS

In many applications, especially in real-time situations, high data rates into or out of the PE array are required. To obtain a well-balanced architecture, the design of the I/O system is as important as the design of PEs and array topology.

Input/output can be discussed in terms of different classes of data formats:

(1) *Conventional format*: Word-sequential, bit-parallel format, the traditional data format used by conventional computers.

(2) *Processing format*:
 (2a) Bit-slice or bit-plane format, which is the processing format of arrays with bit-serial PEs, or
 (2b) Word-slice or word-plane format, which is the processing format of arrays with bit-parallel PEs.
(3) *Application format*, for example, the format of an image or a data base (often this is a multidimensional array).

The input/output system serves as an interface between the different formats. In real-time applications, with PE arrays directly connected to input and output devices, the interface between the application data format (3) and the processing format (2) is extremely important; however, transfer between the word-at-a-time format of the front-end PE and the array PEs must also be efficient.

We illustrate the transfer between the different formats in the LUCAS I/O system. See Figure 10.12 and Figure 10.6a. A set of 8-bit I/O registers (shift registers) is connected to the memory array, one register per memory word. The I/O registers can be read or written from the front-end processor or dedicated I/O processor in the conventional word-at-a-time format. A data input process can be divided into two phases: one to fill the I/O registers from the front-end or I/O processor, and one to shift the contents out of the I/O registers and into any field of the memory array. The first phase requires one write cycle of the front-end or I/O processor to transfer 8 bits; the second phase requires eight memory array write cycles, where, during each cycle, an entire bit slice is transferred.

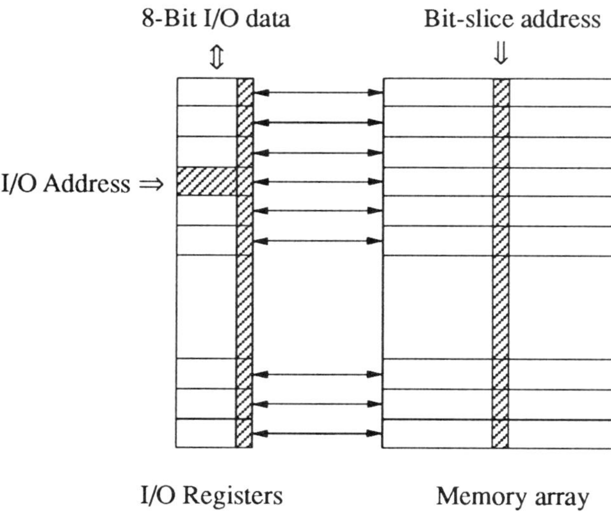

Figure 10.12. Input/Output structure of LUCAS

A variation of this input/output scheme that is used in some designs does not permit the addressing of the I/O registers. Instead, data are shifted in and out of the register set. Such I/O register systems may also be used for basic communication between the PEs.

PASIC, (see Figure 10.13), is an example of a design with a bit-parallel shift register along the row of PEs. This can be utilized for image output as well as for inter-PE communication. However, for image input there is a direct, word-parallel, bit-serial interface between the photosensor array (128 x 128 pixels in the present version) and the linear array of PEs. Thus, PASIC is an example of a design that provides special facilities to interface between the data format of the application and the processing data format, resulting in a significantly higher input speed. PASIC is primarily intended for low-level vision processing where high-speed image I/O is required. PASIC integrates its image sensor and PE array on one chip and is a further development of the LAPP concept, which is treated as a case study in Part III.

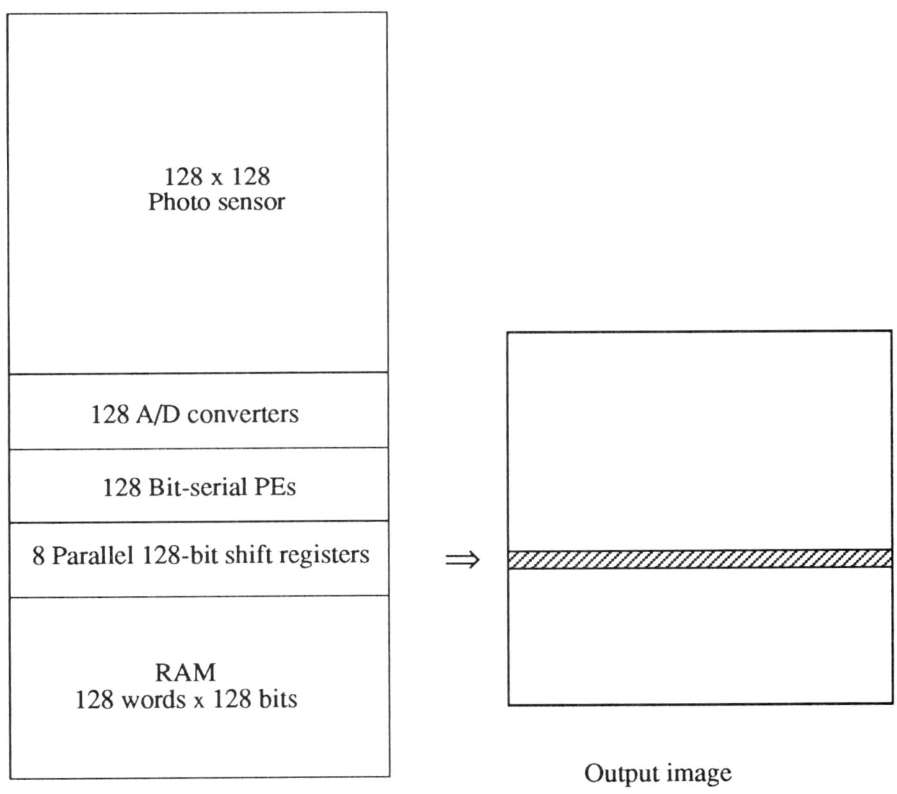

Figure 10.13. PASIC Overview: a one-chip PE-array including image sensor

The high-speed I/O facility of the two-dimensional AMT DAP PE array is depicted in Figure 10.14. One of the 1-bit registers in the PEs, the D register, may be loaded from the memory or written back to the memory, but does not otherwise take part in PE operations. The D plane may be shifted toward the north edge of the array so that successive rows of the plane are output at that edge; at the same time, successive data words may be presented as input at the southern edge. The shifting is done independently of the normal array instruction stream and may be done at a faster clock rate. Shifting is controlled by one of a number of input/output couplers, rather than by the array control unit, and may be thought of as a DMA facility.

After the shifting of a plane is finished, it is stored to – or the next plane is loaded from – the array. This is done by a request to the array control unit, thus delaying the normal instruction stream for one clock cycle. Reordering of the data may be required, which is accommodated via double-buffer arrangements.

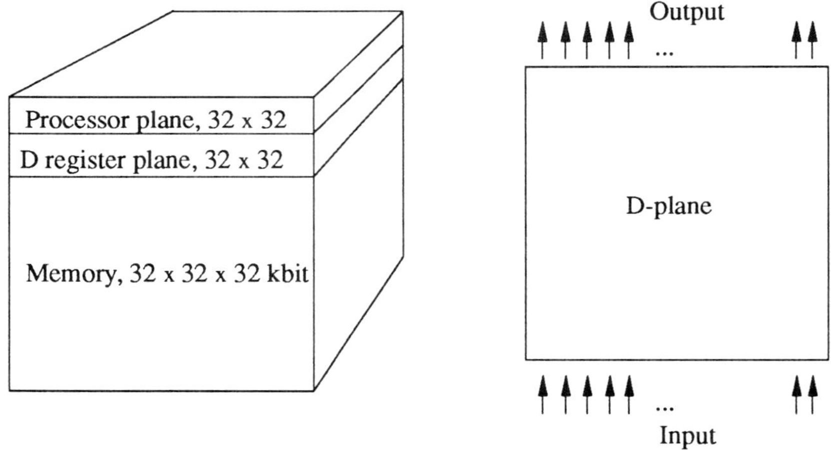

Figure 10.14. AMT DAP 500

10.5 PROGRAMMING OF PE ARRAYS

The data-parallel style for programming of PE arrays was introduced in Chapter 3 (Behavioral Description). The instruction level provides powerful instructions working on entire sets of data simultaneously. These instructions form the basis for data-parallel high-level languages. These languages permit the programmer to organize data in relation to the array of PEs so that operations may be applied to many data elements simultaneously. In this section, we present specific properties of various data-parallel languages and conclude with comments on the experiences with this programming style.

10.5.1 High-level Languages

High-level languages for PE arrays are often referred to as *data-parallel languages.* Typically, they are quite similar to conventional languages but permit the programmer to organize data so that operations may be applied to many elements of data simultaneously. This is accomplished by adding new data types and extending the semantic meaning of existing program syntax when applied to parallel data. Extension of the control structure is often also provided.

When programming in data-parallel style, emphasis is put on the use of large, uniform data structures, such as arrays, whose elements can be processed all at once. For example, the statement **A=B+C** indicates many simultaneous addition operations if **A**, **B**, and **C** are declared to be arrays. Each array element is in the memory of a different PE, or at least in the memory of a different virtual PE.

Thus, much of the parallel code looks like sequential code. The compiler examines the declarations to determine whether **B+C** will require a single addition operation (in the front-end PE) or thousands (in the PE array).

Scalar and parallel values may be mixed in a program, for example, when multiplying every element of an array by a constant. In this case the scalar value is broadcast to all PEs at once. Also, an operation on parallel data may yield a scalar result, for example, when finding the sum or maximum of all the elements of an array. In this case a reduction operation is performed, which can be supported in various manners by the hardware (for example, by the ability to form a binary tree).

Conditional operations are implemented in PE arrays by limiting the impact of operations to a certain subset of the PEs. This is often achieved through the use of a parallel data type called the *selector.*

Pascal/L and Parallel Pascal

Pascal/L (see Fernström, 1983) is an extension of Pascal for parallel processing developed for the LUCAS project. In Pascal/L the parallelism of the architecture has a direct correspondence in the syntax of the language. Consequently, constructs in the language are directly implementable as elementary operations of the PE array.

There are two kinds of parallel variables: **selectors** and **parallel arrays**. A selector defines a Boolean vector distributed over the memory modules and is intended to control the parallelism of operations. (At execution time, the activity registers are set in those PEs where the corresponding selector element has the value TRUE.) A parallel array consists of a fixed number of components that are all of the same type and that are located in the **M**emory **M**odules (MM).

For example:

```
var    SEL          : selector [0..999] := (0..399 -> TRUE);
       WEIGHTS      : parallel array [0..999,0..999] of integer (12);
```

declares a selector with elements in the first 400 MMs selected and a 1000 x 1000 matrix of 12-bit integers located in the first 1000 MMs, 1000 components in each MM.

An indexing scheme allows simultaneous access to a column or a subset of the column components of a two-dimensional array. For example, WEIGHTS[*,5] selects column 5 of WEIGHTS, and WEIGHTS[SEL,5] selects a subset of column 5 of WEIGHTS. A parallel array may be used without any index at all (and no brackets), in which case all components of the array are referenced. Parallel variables are allowed in expressions and assignments; for example, 4+WEIGHTS[*,5] adds 4 to all components of column 5.

New control structure concepts are included in Pascal/L to permit control of selection and repetition along the parallel dimension. The **where do elsewhere** construct defines different actions to take place in different memory modules, depending on the contents of a selector:

```
where SEL   do WEIGHTS[*,10] := 2*WEIGHTS[*,10]
            elsewhere WEIGHTS[*,10] := 0;
```

The **case where** statement and the **while and where do** statement provide the two further control structure extensions.

In expressions and assignments where the corresponding components of the parallel variables are located in different memory words, the variables must be aligned. The type of alignment needed is defined by the programmer in terms of standard alignment functions, which correspond to the data movements over the interconnection network.

For example, if the perfect shuffle connection is included,

```
M[*,0] := shuffle(M[*,1])
```

To support associative processing, a number of standard functions and procedures are defined. The **first** function is used to find the first component of a selector with the value TRUE. It returns a new selector with only this element true. The **next** procedure assigns the value FALSE to the first TRUE element of the selector. This is useful when processing selected elements sequentially. The **some** function, finally, returns the value TRUE if there is at least one TRUE element of the selector; otherwise, it returns the value FALSE.

Parallel Pascal (Reeves, 1984) was designed with the MPP as the initial target architecture and was the first high-level programming language to be implemented on the MPP. The extensions are similar to those of Pascal/L. They include also a set of standard functions that implement reduction operations: **sum, product, all, any, max,** and **min**, all operating on arrays.

For example, given the definition

```
var  a:  array [1..100,1..5] of integer;
     b:  array[1..100] of integer;
     c:  integer;

b := sum(a,2)
```

computes the sums of the rows of a, and

```
c := sum(a,1,2)
```

computes the sum of all elements of the array a.

FORTRAN-8x, DAP FORTRAN, CM FORTRAN

Extensions to FORTRAN-77 for parallel processing have been proposed in a draft ANSI standard, FORTRAN-8x. Many of the features in the proposal emerged from DAP FORTRAN. FORTRAN for the Connection Machine (CM FORTRAN), which we shall exemplify, implements the array features of FORTRAN-8x.

The most important difference between FORTRAN-77 and FORTRAN-8x is that expressions in FORTRAN-8x can treat entire arrays as atomic objects. For example, in the statement A = B + C, A, B, and C may be scalars, vectors, matrices, or multidimensional arrays.

Arrays are stored in the Connection Machine with one element per virtual PE. Thus, arrays map directly onto the multidimensional communications grid.

CM FORTRAN also includes functions that inquire about array attributes, perform data reduction, or perform other complicated array operations. Examples of reduction operations are SUM, PRODUCT, MAXVAL, MINVAL, ANY, ALL, and COUNT. Examples of high-level operations are DOTPRODUCT (vector dot product) and MATMUL (matrix multiplication).

A reduction operation may utilize a MASK argument so that only selected PEs participate in the operation. For example, the expression SUM(A, MASK=A.GT.0) sums only the positive elements of the array A.

Like the Pascal-based languages discussed previously, CM FORTRAN has an extended control structure. For example, in the code

```
WHERE (B .NE. 0)
   C = A / B
ELSEWHERE
   C = 1.0E30
END WHERE
```

where A, B, and C are all conforming arrays, the result of A/B is assigned to C in each PE containing a nonzero element of B, and 1.0E30 is assigned to C in all other PEs. As a further example, the following code clears the part of the matrix H that is below the diagonal:

```
FORALL (I = 1:N, J = 1:N, I .GT.J) H(I,J) = 0.0
```

Note the use of a mask expression in addition to the index variables I and J.

Our description of CM FORTRAN (as well as C* and *Lisp next) is based mainly on the Connection Machine Technical Summary (Thinking Machines Corporation, 1989a). Further details can be found in (Thinking Machines Corporation, 1989b) and the CM programming manuals. Hockney and Jesshope (1988) provide a rather detailed treatment of data-parallel versions of FORTRAN and Lisp.

C*

*C** is a parallel dialect of C that was developed at Thinking Machines Corporation but that has also been implemented for other machines. Two new storage classes are added that describe where the data reside. The keywords used are **mono** and **poly**. Scalar (**mono**) data reside in the memory of the front end, and parallel (**poly**) data reside in the memory of the PE array. Existing operators are extended to operate on parallel data. Two rules are added to the usual rules of C evaluation: The *replication rule* states that a scalar value is automatically replicated where necessary to form a parallel variable. The *As-If-Serial rule* states that a parallel operator is executed for all active PEs as if in some serial order. The latter is a simple way of stating the guarantee that, from the programmer's point of view, the PEs do not interfere with each other (while still permitting a parallel implementation).

The C* compiler for the Connection Machine computer system is implemented as a translator to ordinary C code, which is then compiled by an ordinary C compiler for the front-end computer. The C* compiler parses the C* source code, performs type and data flow analyses, and then translates parallel code into a series of function calls that invoke operations on the machine instruction level.

*Lisp

The **Lisp* language is an extension of Common Lisp for programming the Connection Machine in a data-parallel style. It supports primitives that correspond directly to the operation of the hardware. Therefore, it is possible to write code that executes very efficiently.

As in the extensions to other languages treated, a new, parallel data type has been added. A **pvar** (parallel variable) is a Common Lisp data object that has a value in each PE, virtual or physical, of the Connection Machine.

There are two ways of viewing a pvar. In one model, each PE is simultaneously running the same Common Lisp program, and the pvar represents a variable that exists in all PEs which is operated upon simultaneously in all PEs. In the other model, the pvar represents an array whose size is the same as the number of PEs. The elements of the array are located in consecutive PEs.

As described earlier in this chapter, the Connection Machine provides very flexible communication between PEs by packet switching. *Lisp provides functions for exploiting this communications system. The **pref** !! function allows each active PE to simultaneously read the value of a pvar in any PE. Even if two or more PEs attempt to read the data of a single PE, they all receive the same correct data. ***pset** allows each active PE to simultaneously write the value of a pvar to any other PE. If two or more values are destined for the same place, the user can specify how they are to be combined (for instance, by adding the values together).

*Lisp also includes reduction functions, for example, ***min**, ***sum**, and ***logior** (bitwise logical OR). For example, **(*all (*sum** (!! **1)))** will sum together the quantity 1 in all PEs in the Connection Machine. The result will be the number of virtual PEs in use at that moment.

10.5.2 Conclusion

Data-parallel programming is astonishingly straightforward and may be applied successfully to many more problems than was originally conceived. It has been a long-lasting conception that efficiency could be achieved **only** in certain very regular calculations. Several years of use of data-parallel machines have changed this view. Hillis and Steele (1986), after having presented several examples of data-parallel algorithms, state:

> Our current view of the applicability of data parallelism is somewhat broader. That is, we are beginning to suspect that this is an appropriate style wherever the amount of data to be operated upon is very large.

> One potentially productive line of research in this area is searching for counterexamples to this rule: that is, computations involving arbitrarily large data sets that can be more efficiently implemented in terms of control parallelism involving multiple streams of control. Several of the examples presented in this article first caught our attention as proposed counterexamples.
>
> Having one processor per data element changes the way one thinks. We found that our serial intuitions did not always serve us well in parallel contexts. For example, when sorting is fast enough, the order in which things are stored is often unimportant. Then again, if searching is fast, then sorting may be unimportant. In a more general sense, it seems that the selection of one data representation over another is less critical on a highly parallel machine than on a conventional machine since converting all the memory from one representation to another does not take a large amount of time.

Not only are data-parallel algorithms easier to find than was expected; they are also easier than expected to program in high-level languages. Very small changes to the conventional languages are needed. The data-parallel style of thinking and description of processing leaves us with programs that are easy to read and effective to execute. In general, there are no efficiency problems with various data set sizes since the concept of virtual PEs takes care of the potential problems in an elegant manner.

10.6 APPLICATION EXAMPLES

Computations that involve large uniform data sets and that are especially well suited for PE arrays are present in many of the problem areas where single-PE computers are found to be insufficient. Parallel solutions are sought to improve performance. Image and signal processing were among the application areas mentioned in Chapter 4; further, FFT computations were illustrated. The reader might want to reexamine these examples. We now provide some further examples to illustrate the applicability and processing power of some of the designs described in this chapter. Two further image-processing examples are introduced, one example of a learning network simulation and one example to illustrate the computation of a graph problem on a PE array.

10.6.1 Image-processing Examples

With a suitable architecture that utilizes a high degree of parallelism, image-processing tasks with real-time requirements may be solved even with rather small-sized systems. We will demonstrate this via two examples.

A PASIC Example

An edge-detection task typically used as a preprocessing step in pattern recognition is described as a demonstration of the capabilities of PASIC by Chen and others (1990).

The prototype PASIC system, as described previously, works with an image size of 128 x 128 pixels, each providing 8-bit resolution. Recall that the PEs are arranged as a linear array; thus processing is accomplished one image line at a time.

The edge-detection algorithm is as follows:

1. *Median filtering and smoothing:* Median filtering is done in two steps; first, 1 x 3 vertical neighborhood, then 3 x 1 horizontal neighborhood on the result of the previous. Smoothing is performed by adding two horizontal neighbors, followed by adding two vertical neighbors of the result.
2. *Gradient calculation:* The gradients in the x- and y-directions are computed using the Sobel operator (see Figure 10.15a). The gradient magnitude is approximated by the sum of the absolute values of the two gradients.
3. *Thresholding and thinning:* A binary picture is created by thresholding. This picture now shows the edges. By an iterative thinning process of four steps, the widths of the edges are reduced to one pixel (if originally not wider than five pixels).

The execution times of the different steps, assuming a clock rate of 20 MHz, are shown in Figure 10.15b. The resulting total execution time of less than 5 ms allows for a frame rate of more than 200 frames per second on this one-chip system. If the chip (and image size) is scaled up, the processing time grows linearly so that, for a 512-PE system working on 512 x 512 images, the maximum frame rate would be 50 frames per second.

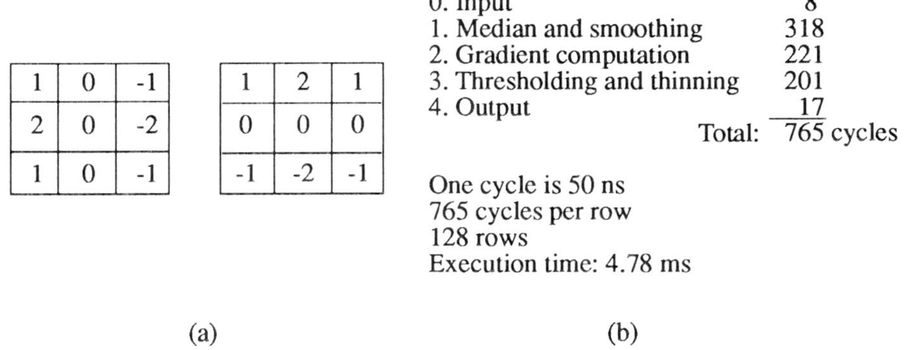

1	0	-1
2	0	-2
1	0	-1

1	2	1
0	0	0
-1	-2	-1

(a)

Step	Cycles
0. Input	8
1. Median and smoothing	318
2. Gradient computation	221
3. Thresholding and thinning	201
4. Output	17
Total:	765 cycles

One cycle is 50 ns
765 cycles per row
128 rows
Execution time: 4.78 ms

(b)

Figure 10.15. (a) Sobel Operator;
(b) Execution Times for the Different Steps of Edge Detection

It should be noted that, since the PEs are bit serial, the execution time for the major part of this algorithm grows linearly also with the number of bits per pixel. In many applications, fewer than 8 bits may be utilized with good results.

A LUCAS Example

An edge-detection task run on LUCAS, using tracking to obtain true edges, is described by Svensson (1983). As with the preceding algorithm, it may be performed in real time. In this particular algorithm, no smoothing of the image is done before edge detection. The gradient image, derived in a manner similar to the one described previously, is thresholded at two different levels. The low threshold yields *all potential* edge points, while the high threshold yields only the strongest points (the *safe* edge points). Now the safe points are propagated iteratively to connected pixels marked in the image of potential points. The procedure is illustrated in Figure 10.16 and an example of a run is given in Figure 10.17.

The computation time on a 128 by 128 pixel image with 8-bit gray scale is 1.4 ms using a 20-MHz clock. The final tracking phase is extremely efficient with this type of architecture and represents only 14% of the total time. As in the PASIC case, scaling up the system and the images will result in linearly increasing computation times.

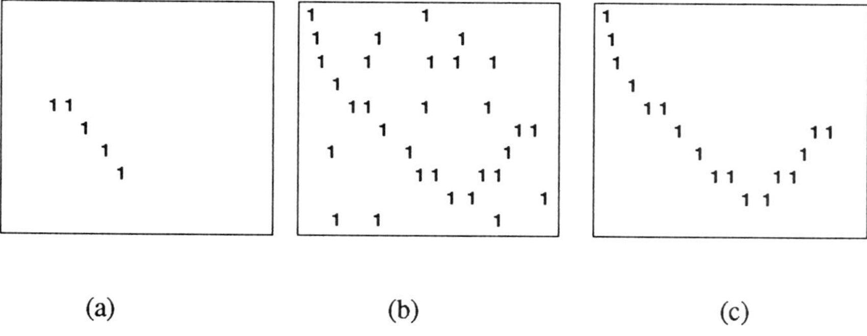

(a) (b) (c)

Figure 10.16. Tracking Process: Result of thresholding at high level (a) and at low level (b); result of tracking the 1's of (a) in (b) is shown in (c)

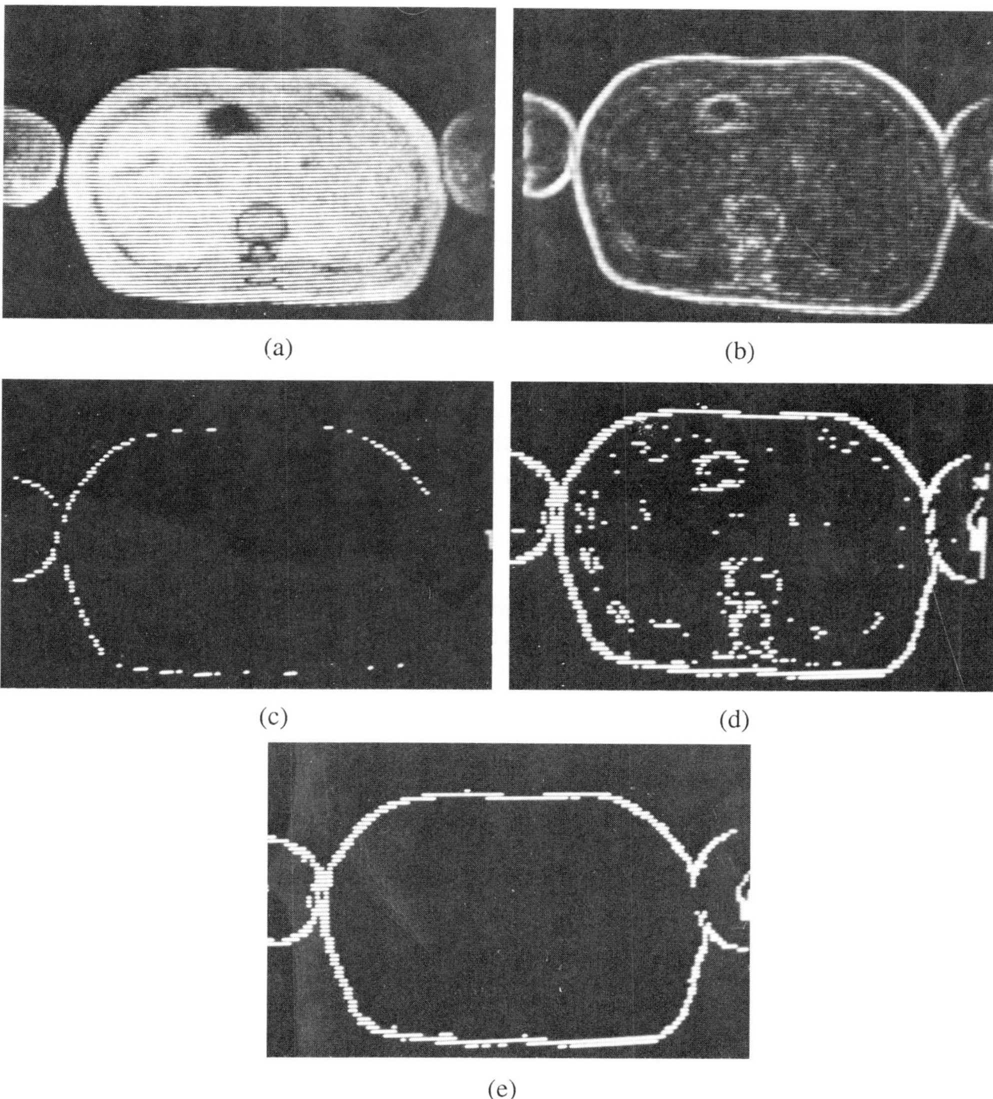

Figure 10.17. Edge Detection of a Magnetic Resonance Image by Tracking: (a) original image; (b) gradient image derived by Robert's cross-difference operator; (c) result of thresholding image (b) at level 160; (d) result of thresholding image (b) at level 64; (e) result of tracking the points in the image (c) along the points in image (d)

10.6.2 Learning Network Example

The error back-propagation scheme for training a multilayer neural network was briefly described earlier in the chapter. The computations mainly involve matrix-by-vector multiplications where the matrices contain the connection weights and the vectors contain activation values or error values. Such a multiplication contains N^2 scalar multiplications and N computations of sums of N numbers.

The fastest possible processing is to perform all N^2 multiplications in parallel requiring N^2 PEs and unit time, and then form the sums by using trees of adders. The addition requires $N(N - 1)$ adders and $O(\log N)$ time. This is, however, an unrealistic method depending on both the number of PEs required and the communication problems that are introduced. Instead, it is more practical to take the approach of having as many PEs as neurons in a layer N and storing the connection weights in matrices, sized N by N, one for each layer. The PE with index j has access to row j of the matrix by accessing its own memory word.

The computations performed on an array of bit-serial PEs are described in (Svensson and Nordström, 1990), where the calculation times for different network sizes are derived. Bit-serial multipliers of the type presented in Figure 10.7 are utilized. Some results from the study are presented in Table 10.1. In the table, b is the data length and N is the number of neurons per layer.

Table 10.1. (a) Training Time per Layer (ms); (b) Recall Time per Layer (ms) (10-MHz clock frequency is assumed)

		N		
		256	1024	4096
	8	2.4	9.9	40.6
b	12	3.6	14.4	58.6
	16	4.7	18.9	76.6

(a)

		N		
		256	1024	4096
	8	1.0	4.2	17.6
b	12	1.4	5.8	24.2
	16	1.8	7.5	30.7

(b)

A common measure of the performance of neural net hardware is the number of CPSs (Connections Per Second). In a net with N neurons per layer, N^2 connections are used and/or updated in each layer. The MegaCPS figures for bit-serial array PEs of different sizes are given in Table 10.2.

Table 10.2. Number of MegaCPS (Million Connections per Second) for Different Network Sizes and Data Precisions

Training

		N		
		256	1024	4096
b	8	27	106	413
	12	18	73	286
	16	14	55	219

Recall

		N		
		256	1024	4096
b	8	66	250	953
	12	47	180	694
	16	36	140	546

If external RAM is utilized, 64 PEs of the complexity we introduce can easily be integrated on one VLSI chip. A 1024 PE array will have 16 such chips, each with approximately 100 pins. Memory can be implemented using chips with 64k x 4 bits, yielding a memory chip count of 256. With appropriate mounting technology, this type of network may be implemented on one board. It would, for example, run a four-layered feed-forward network with 1024 neurons per layer at the speed of 29 training examples or 81 recall examples per second.

10.6.3 Graph Problem

Problems that can be identified as graph theoretic arise in diverse areas, for example, traffic planning and network analysis. A common task is to find the shortest path between any two vertices of a graph. The connection between two vertices may be unidirectional or bidirectional. In the first case, the graph is called a *directed graph.* Also, a cost (or path length) may be associated with each path. Such graphs are called *weighted.*

Solutions of problems of this kind often take the form of searching large trees or updating matrices. Opportunities to exploit data parallelism are numerous. As an example, we will consider the problem of finding *the shortest path between all pairs of vertices in a weighted directed graph.*

In a weighted directed graph the paths between the vertices are unidirectional and a length is associated with each path. Figure 10.18 provides an example of such a graph. The graph may also be described in the form of a matrix. The absence of a direct path between a pair of vertices is marked in the matrix with "infinite" (if).

To solve the problem on a PE array, we will parallelize an algorithm developed by Floyd (1962), which is considered as one of the two most efficient algorithms for sequential computers. It is well suited for parallel implementation. On sequential computers a computation time $O(n^3)$ is required, where n is the number of vertices. On a parallel computer with n PEs, it should be possible to perform the algorithm in a time $O(n^2)$.

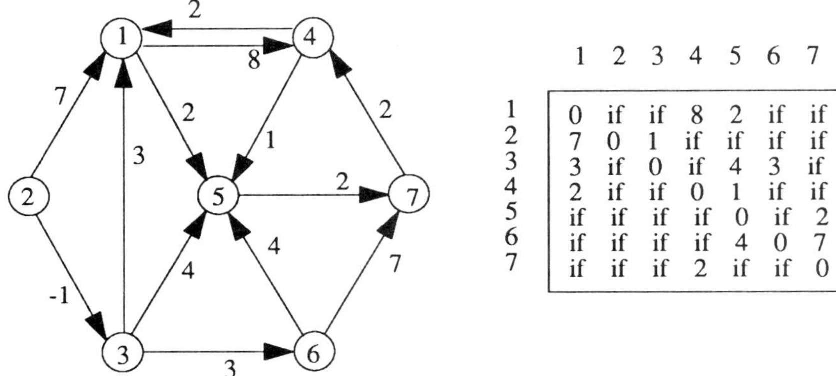

	1	2	3	4	5	6	7
1	0	if	if	8	2	if	if
2	7	0	1	if	if	if	if
3	3	if	0	if	4	3	if
4	2	if	if	0	1	if	if
5	if	if	if	if	0	if	2
6	if	if	if	if	4	0	7
7	if	if	if	2	if	if	0

Figure 10.18. Weighted Directed Graph and Its Distance Matrix

The algorithm works as follows. Starting with the original n by n matrix D of direct distances, n different matrices $D_1, D_2, ..., D_n$ are constructed sequentially. Matrix D_k is obtained from matrix D_{k-1} by inserting vertex k in a path wherever this results in a shorter path.

On a parallel computer with n PEs, an entire column of the matrix may be updated simultaneously. In the kth iteration, column p of D_k is obtained in the following way (using Pascal/L notation for matrix elements):

$$D_k(, p) := \min [D_{k-1}(, p), D_{k-1}(, k) + D_{k-1}(k, p)]$$

A Pascal/L program for the entire algorithm is provided on the following page.

It is easily seen that the execution time of the program is $O(n^2)$. The task that is performed n^2 times is an "add fields" instruction followed by a "mark field greater than field" instruction and a selector masked "move field." These are all performed in constant time.

The algorithm requires a representation for an infinite value. A number that is a little smaller than half the greatest number that is possible to represent in the given field length may be chosen. In the worst case, two such numbers are added, which can be done without yielding overflow.

We have shown how a good sequential algorithm may be ported in a straightforward way to a parallel environment. For other graph-theoretical problems, however, new algorithms have to be developed. For examples, see Svensson (1983).

```
Program FLOYD;
const noofvertices = 128;
var    Dmatrix: parallel array [1..noofvertices,1..noofvertices] of
                                                    integer(8);
       k, p : integer;
begin
    for k:=1 to noofvertices do
    begin
        for p:=1 to noofvertices do
        begin
            where (Dmatrix[*,k]+Dmatrix[k,p]) < Dmatrix[*,p] do
            Dmatrix[*,p]:= Dmatrix[*,k]+Dmatrix[k,p];
        end;
    end;
end.
```

10.7 IMPLEMENTATION CONSIDERATIONS

As forecast by Mead and Conway (see Chapter 6), the development of **V**ery **L**arge **S**cale **I**ntegration technology (VLSI) has had an important influence on the design and implementation of PE arrays and has on the whole been a necessary prerequisite for producing arrays of general usefulness.

As an increasing number of PEs are implemented on the same chip, the number of connections to other chips (at least in nearest-neighbor connected systems) also increases, even if at a slower rate. This may cause practical connection problems between chips. Even worse problems, however, arise in the connections between PEs and memory if the memory is placed in separate chips. Local addressing, which we encountered, for example, in PICAP3, is totally impossible if several PEs are implemented on the same chip. Thus, we shall probably see a development toward integrated memory and processor chips. The combination of the two problems points to the solution of implementing a whole array on a wafer, that is, **W**afer **S**cale **I**ntegration (WSI).

WSI, however, introduces another problem. It is acceptable for wafers that are intended for VLSI fabrication to contain defects. To cope with this situation, techniques are being developed to switch out faulty PEs and make a continuous array of the correct ones, or to include redundancy in the array so that the probability of producing a functioning array increases (see the discussion of reconfigurable WSI structures in Chapter 5).

10.8 OVERVIEW OF REPRESENTATIVE DESIGNS

To assist the reader in obtaining a collected view of each of the designs used to illustrate various PE array properties in this chapter, we now provide brief descriptions of the machines and references to original and important descriptions. The machines appear in approximately chronological order (design and first publishing). The reader will also find related information in Chapter 6.

10.8.1 ILLIAC IV

ILLIAC IV, "the first supercomputer," was the first PE array to be implemented. Designed at University of Illinois under the leadership of Daniel Slotnick and implemented by Burroughs Corporation, it was intended to have 256 powerful PEs, divided into four quadrants of 64 PEs each. However, only one quadrant was constructed. The implementation was completed in 1972. The machine had the status of a research machine, and only one system was built.

The topology is portrayed in Figure 10.1. It is a two-dimensional mesh with modified horizontal wraparound connections. The interconnection structure can also be described as a one-dimensional nearest-neighbor structure (a long row of PEs) with additional connections eight steps forward and backward. Very powerful processing elements capable of 64-bit floating-point operations were utilized.

ILLIAC IV was operational at NASA Ames Research Center from 1972 to 1981 and remained the world's most powerful computer for its entire lifetime. The original paper on the ILLIAC IV hardware is by Barnes and others (1968).

10.8.2 STARAN

Designed in approximately 1970, first implemented in 1974, and manufactured by Goodyear Aerospace Corporation, Akron, Ohio, USA, STARAN was a commercial product during the late 1970s. Some tens of installations in various configurations were delivered.

The number of PEs is 256 per array. Several arrays may be combined. The topology is a "flip" network in combination with a linear array. The flip network is a variation of an indirect binary n-cube. The PEs belong to the category of bit-serial, simple PEs. The central publications are by STARAN's chief architect, Ken Batcher (1974, 1976, and 1977).

10.8.3 DAP (Distributed Array Processor)

DAP was designed in the mid 1970s by Stewart Reddaway of International Computers Limited (ICL), UK. The first implementation dates to 1978. It has been a commercial product during the entire 1980s, first from ICL, and later from Active Memory Technology Ltd. (AMT), UK. The architecture and implementations are still under development.

The number of PEs is typically 1024 or 4096. The topology was shown in Figure 10.2. It is a two-dimensional mesh, 32 x 32 or 64 x 64 PEs. Row and column "highways" are added. A system and I/O overview is shown in Figure 10.14. The PEs belong to the category of bit-serial, simple PEs.

The DAP project and the scientific use of several DAP installations have been important for the development of data-parallel programming languages and the understanding of the wide applicability of highly parallel, regular processing arrays in real-time applications.

The main ideas behind DAP have been documented by its chief designer, Stewart Reddaway (1979), and a description of the current line of DAP products from AMT is provided by Hunt (1989).

10.8.4 MPP (Massively Parallel Processor)

The Massively Parallel Processor, MPP, was designed by Goodyear Aerospace Corporation, USA, in the late 1970s, mainly for the processing of satellite images. The only implementation made was delivered to NASA in 1982.

The number of PEs is 16,384. The topology is a two-dimensional mesh, 128 x 128 PEs. The PEs are bit serial, enhanced with variable-length shift registers to speed up multiplication. Descriptions of MPP and its use can be found in Batcher (1980) and Potter (1985).

10.8.5 LUCAS

The design of LUCAS (**L**und **U**niversity **C**ontent **A**ddressable **S**ystem) at the University of Lund, Lund, Sweden, was made in 1980. LUCAS was a research project aimed at exploring architecture, programming, and applications of bit-serial associative arrays, thus, only one implementation of the architecture has been made.

The implemented number of PEs is 128. The topology of the array is modifiable and was shown in Figure 10.4. Eight different sources can be chosen to each PE. In application studies, LUCAS has been utilized with perfect shuffle-exchange network and nearest-neighbor connections in one dimension.

The PEs belong to the category of bit-serial, simple PEs. Being a research machine, LUCAS provides a modifiable ALU function set (PROM). The PE structure is shown in Figure 10.6a. The I/O structure is shown in Figure 10.12.

A high-level microprogramming language was designed and implemented. A data-parallel language based on Pascal was designed (Pascal/L).

Applications have been run in the areas of image processing, data-base manipulation, signal processing, matrix computations, and graph-theoretical problems. Specific examples from image, signal, and graph processing have been presented in this chapter.

The LUCAS project resulted in the production of three Ph.D. theses by its inventors, Svensson (1983), Kruzela (1983), and Fernström (1983). Some further important publications include Fernström and others (1983), and Fernström, Kruzela, and Svensson (1986), and Ohlsson and Svensson (1983).

10.8.6 Connection Machine CM-2

The Connection Machine architecture was first described as a doctoral thesis at the Massachusetts Institute of Technology, Cambridge, Massachusetts, USA. The production, design and manufacturing have been made by Thinking Machines Corporation in Cambridge. Model CM-2 is the second variant of the architecture.

The design and the introduction of the CM-1 were in the mid 1980s. CM-2 was introduced in 1988.

The number of PEs in a fully equipped system is 65,536. The topology is a 12-dimensional direct binary cube that supports general patterns of communication among 4096 nodes (in a fully configured system), where each node incorporates 16 bit-serial PEs. The *routers* – one at each node – are capable of dealing with contention for hypercube wires by routing the message alternative ways.

Additional special hardware supports certain commonly used regular patterns of communication. This is called the *NEWS network,* because one of its uses is to implement a two-dimensional grid (North, East, West, and South connections). However, grids of any dimension up to 31 are supported. For example, possible grid configurations for 64K PEs include 256 x 256, 1024 x 64, 65536 x 1, 64 x 32 x 32, and 16 x 16 x 16 x 16. The structured NEWS communication is significantly faster than general routing.

The basic PEs of CM-2 belong to the category that we have called bit serial, simple. The PE design is shown in Figure 10.6b. Floating-point PEs with 32-bit precision (up to 2048 of them) are distributed over the machine (one floating-point PE located at each group of 32 bit-serial PEs), and boost floating-point performance. The two sets of PEs share the same communication structure and memory.

The major reference is the Ph.D. thesis by Hillis (1985). Further relevant publications include Tucker and Robertson (1988) and Thinking Machines Corporation (1989a, b).

10.8.7 AIS-5000 and Centipede

AIS-5000 is the largest of a series of linearly organized processing arrays from Applied Intelligent Systems, Inc., Ann Arbor, Michigan, USA. Centipede is a further development of the AIS-5000 architecture, which has not yet reached production. The design of the AIS-5000 dates back to the mid 1980s and was first described to the international scientific community in 1988.

The system is a linear array of 1024 simple, bit-serial PEs. Each PE contains its own bit-wide RAM of (currently) 32k bits. The system integrates 128 PEs on each board, thus the entire PE array is a small desktop system. Its main use is in industrial vision systems where the speed requirements are far greater than what can be met by ordinary sequential PEs.

The reader is referred to Schmitt and Wilson (1988) and Wilson (1988) for further descriptions.

10.8.8 PICAP3

The PICAP3 architecture is a result of the combined image processing and computer architecture research at Linköping University, Sweden, under the leadership of Per-Erik Danielsson. The chief designer of the PICAP3 architecture is Björn Lindskog. The design was, in its first version, completed in 1987. It was partly implemented (two PEs) in 1988. Unfortunately, the project has terminated.

The machine was designed to provide 64 PEs organized as a linear array. Each PE comprises 32-bit integer and floating-point arithmetic (Am29332 and Am29325), a four-port register file, and a set of complicated gate arrays to implement functions like local addressing, microword decoding, memory control, and parity check. No more than four PEs with associated memories (4 Mbyte each) can be implemented on one circuit board. The PE design is shown in Figure 10.13. The design was optimized for multi-dimensional signal processing.

A two-dimensional FFT calculation is demonstrated in Chapter 4 of this book. The Ph.D. thesis by Lindskog (1988) and Licentiate thesis by Segerström (1990) provide further details.

10.8.9 MasPar MP-1

The MasPar MP-1 family is a recent commercial product from MasPar Computer Corporation, Sunnyvale, California, USA. It was introduced on the market in 1989. An MP-1 array may have from 1024 to 16,384 PEs. The topology is named X-net, similar to the X-grid of Blitzen (see description of Blitzen that follows).

The PEs belong to the category of bit-parallel PEs. A MasPar PE (shown in Figure 10.9) is designed around a 4-bit data bus and a 4-bit ALU. During a floating-point or integer instruction on longer data words, successive 4-bit nibbles pass through the ALU to generate the full-precision result. The registers that hold the mantissas of floating-point numbers are provided with shifting capability to allow alignment of data before addition and subtraction. A large set of registers is provided on-chip at each PE.

Forty 32-bit registers are available to the programmer, and an additional eight 32-bit registers are used internally to implement the instructions.

Like the Connection Machine, MasPar supports the concept of virtual PEs; however, the solution is different. In the Connection Machine, the repeated execution of an instruction on one PE required to emulate virtual PEs is managed by a microprogrammed sequencer and is transparent to the macroinstructions issued by the front-end computer. MasPar has taken the alternative view, well known from RISC philosophy, of letting an optimizing compiler generate the detailed control unit instruction sequence.

Further information has been published by Blank (1990), Nickols (1990), and Christy (1990).

10.8.10 BLITZEN

BLITZEN is the name of an architecture and implementation project at the Research Triangle of North Carolina. The participating organizations are North Carolina State University at Raleigh, Duke University at Durham, and Microelectronics Center of North Carolina, Research Triangle Park, North Carolina, USA.

The BLITZEN architecture was designed in 1987-1988 and is based upon the experiences of the MPP architecture (see the preceding). Implementations of prototype systems typically providing 1024 PEs have been achieved in 1990. A full custom VLSI chip incorporates 128 bit-serial PEs.

The topology used is the X-grid, a two-dimensional array with an X-shaped grid of interconnections as portrayed in Figure 10.3. With every PE sending data out on one wire and receiving data on a different wire, paths can be formed in eight compass directions. This eight-neighbor grid is an improvement over the four-neighbor grid used in MPP.

The PEs represent a further development of the PEs of MPP, which are enhanced bit-serial PEs. Among other improvements, local addressing has been included.

Blevins and others (1990), and Davis and Jennings (1990) provide sources of further information.

10.8.11 PASIC

PASIC is an integration of a two-dimensional image sensor and a linear PE array. It has been developed as a research project at Linköping University, Sweden. The design was first presented in 1989.

The PEs form a linear array into which image data may be loaded in parallel from a square photodiode array on chip. The PEs belong to the category of bit-serial, simple PEs. The system architecture is shown in Figure 10.13. The first prototype is intended to have 128 PEs and a 128 x 128 pixel photodiode array. The system is aimed at low-level image processing.

Descriptions of PASIC can be found in Chen and others (1990) and in the Licentiate thesis by Åström (1990).

References

Barnes, G.H., R.M. Brown, M. Kato, D.J. Kuck, D.L. Slotnick, and R.A. Stokes (1968). The ILLIAC IV Computer, *IEEE Transactions on Computers*, Vol. C-17, No. 8, pp. 746-757.

Batcher, K.E. (1974). STARAN Parallel Processor System Hardware, *Proceedings of the AFIPS National Computer Conference*, 1974, pp. 405-410.

Batcher, K.E. (1976). The FLIP Network in STARAN, *Proceedings of the 1976 International Conference on Parallel Processing,* Waldenwoods, MI.

Batcher, K.E. (1977). The Multidimensional Access Memory in STARAN, *IEEE Transactions on Computers*, Vol. C-26, No. 2, pp. 174-177.

Batcher, K.E. (1980). Design of a Massively Parallel Processor, *IEEE Transactions on Computers*, Vol C-29, pp. 836-840.

Bengtsson, L., A. Linde, T. Nordström, B. Svensson, M. Taveniku, and A. Åhlander (1991). Design and Implementation of the REMAP^3 Software Reconfigurable SIMD Parallel Computer, *Fourth Swedish Workshop on Computer Systems Architecture*, Linköping, Sweden, January, 1992. Available as Research Report CDv-9105 from Centre for Computer Science, Halmstad University, Halmstad, Sweden.

Blank, T. (1990). The MasPar MP-1 Architecture, *Proceedings of the IEEE CompCon Spring 1990*, pp. 20-24.

Blevins, D.W., E.W. Davis, R.A. Heaton, and J.H. Reif (1990). BLITZEN: A Highly Integrated Massively Parallel Machine, *Journal of Parallel and Distributed Computing*, Vol. 8, No. 2, pp. 150-160.

Brown, J.R., M.M. Garber, and S.F. Vanable (1988). Artificial Neural Network on a SIMD Architecture, *Proceedings of the 2nd Symposium on the Frontiers of Massively Parallel Computation*, pp. 43-47, Fairfax, VA.

Chen, K., A. Åström, T. Ahl, and P.E. Danielsson (1990). PASIC: A Smart Sensor for Computer Vision, *Proceedings of* 10*th International Conference on Pattern Recognition*, Atlantic City, NJ, June.

Christy, P. (1990). Software to Support Massively Parallel Computing on the MasPar MP-1, *Proceedings of the IEEE CompCon Spring 1990*, pp. 29-33.

Davis, E.W., and J.M. Jennings (1990). Evaluation of New Architectural Features in a Massively Parallel SIMD Machine, *Proceedings of the 1990 International Conference on Parallel Processing*, St. Charles, IL.

Fernström, C. (1983). *The LUCAS Associative Array Processor and Its Programming Environment*, Ph.D. thesis, Department of Computer Engineering, University of Lund, Sweden, May.

Fernström, C., I. Kruzela, L. Ohlson, and B. Svensson (1983). An Associative Parallel Processor Used in Real-time Signal Processing, *Proceedings of the Second European Signal Processing Conference*, pp. 793-796, September.

Fernström, C., I. Kruzela, and B. Svensson (1986). *LUCAS Associative Array Processor – Design, Programming and Application Studies*, Lecture Notes in Computer Science, Vol. 216, Springer-Verlag, New York.

Fisher, A.L., and P.T. Highnam (1985). Real-time Image Processing on Scan Line Array Processors, *IEEE Computer Society Workshop on Computer Architecture for Pattern Analysis and Image Database Management*, Miami Beach, FL, pp. 484-489.

Floyd, R.W. (1962). Algorithm 97: Shortest path, *Communications of the ACM*, Vol. 5, pp. 345.

Forchheimer, R., and A. Ödmark (1983). A Single Chip Linear Array Picture Processor, *Proceedings of 3rd Scandinavian Conference on Image Analysis*, Copenhagen, July, pp. 320-325.

Hillis, W. D. (1985). *The Connection Machine*, MIT Press, Cambridge, MA.

Hillis, W.D., and G.L. Steele (1986). Data Parallel Algorithms, *Communications of the ACM*, Vol. 29, No. 12, pp. 1170-1183.

Hockney, R.W., and C.R. Jesshope (1988). *Parallel Computers 2: Architecture, Programming and Algorithms*, Adam Hilger, Bristol, UK and Philadelphia.

Hunt, D.J. (1989). AMT DAP – a Processor Array in a Workstation Environment, *Computer Systems Science and Engineering*, Vol. 4, No. 2, pp. 107-114.

Kruzela, I. (1983). *An Associative Array Processor Supporting a Relational Algebra*, Ph.D. thesis, Department of Computer Engineering, University of Lund, Sweden, May.

Lindskog, B. (1988). PICAP3 – *An SIMD Architecture for Multi-Dimensional Signal Processing*, Ph.D. Thesis, Linköping Studies in Science and Technology, No. 207, Linköping University, Sweden.

Lindskog, B. (1989). PICAP3. A Linear SIMD Array with Floating-Point Arithmetic, Report LiTH-ISY-I-0971, Linköping University, Sweden.

Nickols, J.R. (1990). The Design of the MasPar MP-1: A Cost Effective Massively Parallel Computer, *Proceedings of the IEEE CompCon Spring 1990*, pp. 25-28.

Nordström, T., and B. Svensson (1992). Using and Designing Massively Parallel Computers for Artificial Neural Networks, *Journal of Parallel and Distributed Computing*, Vol. 14, No. 3.

Ohlsson, L. and B. Svensson (1983). Matrix Multiplication on LUCAS, *6th Symposium on Computer Arithmetic*, IEEE Computer Society Press, pp. 116-122.

Potter, J.L. (ed.) (1985). *The Massively Parallel Processor*, MIT Press, Cambridge, MA.

Reddaway, S. (1979). The DAP Approach. *Infotech State of the Art Report on Supercomputers*, Infotech International Ltd., Maidenhead, Berkshire, UK.

Reeves, A.P. (1984). Parallel Pascal: An Extended Pascal for Parallel Computers, *Journal of Parallel and Distributed Computing*, Vol. 1, pp. 64-80.

Schmitt, L.A., and S.S. Wilson (1988). The AIS-5000 Parallel Processor, *IEEE Transactions on Pattern Analysis and Machine Intelligence*, Vol. 10, No. 3, pp. 320-330.

Segerström, J. (1990). *Konstruktion av Processormodul för PICAP3 – Problem och Möjligheter*, Licentiate Thesis, Linköping Studies in Science and Technology, Thesis No. 207, Linköping University, Sweden (in Swedish).

Singer, A. (1990). Implementations of Artificial Neural Networks on the Connection Machine, Technical Report RL90-2, Thinking Machines Corporation, Cambridge, MA, January.

Svensson, B. (1983). *LUCAS Processor Array: Design and Applications*, Ph.D. thesis, Department of Computer Engineering, University of Lund, Sweden, April.

Svensson, B., and T. Nordström (1990). Execution of Neural Network Algorithms on an Array of Bit-serial Processors, *Proceedings of* 10*th International Conference on Pattern Recognition*, Atlantic City, NJ, June 16-21.

Thinking Machines Corporation (1989a). Connection Machine Model CM-2 Technical Summary. TMC, Cambridge, MA.

Thinking Machines Corporation (1989b). *Getting Started in CM Fortran*. TMC, Cambridge, MA.

Tucker, L.W., and G.G. Robertson (1988). Architecture and Applications of the Connection Machine, *Computer*, Vol. 21, No. 8, pp 26-38.

Wilson, S.S. (1988) One dimensional SIMD architectures – the AIS-5000, in *Multicomputer Vision*, S. Levialdi, ed., Academic Press, New York, pp. 131-149.

Åström, A. (1990). *A Smart Image Sensor. Description and Evaluation of PASIC*, Licentiate thesis (No. 257), Department of Electrical Engineering, Linköping University, Sweden.

Chapter **11**

MULTIPROCESSOR and MULTICOMPUTER ARCHITECTURES

As presented in Part I, the MIMD architecture category includes both SM (shared memory) multiprocessors as well as DM (distributed memory) multicomputers, which exploit point-to-point ICNs (interconnection networks) or which are coupled via a LAN or WAN. While certain aspects of these MIMD variants deserve special attention, there does exist the MIMD family relationship. The family relationship is exploited in that processing models, programming languages, operating systems, development environments, and tools can and have been constructed that can be utilized ("ported onto") several different members of the MIMD family.

In Chapter 7, we considered several processing models as well concrete programming languages that can be applied in providing software for MIMD environments. In this chapter, we briefly examine allocation and scheduling aspects that are interesting for the entire MIMD family. Next, we consider, based on the division SM (shared memory) and DM (distributed memory), the general properties of these two classes as well as the specific properties of some representative commercially available artifacts. Afterward, we consider the process allocation and scheduling aspects of MIMD systems by examining several operating system alternatives (including real-time variants). Finally, we consider some of the development environments and tools that have been provided for this family of systems.

11.1 MIMD ALLOCATION AND SCHEDULING

The allocation and scheduling of processes based upon available hardware resources as well as the orderly management of process communication and synchronization are typically provided by an operating system. A reasonably common view of these functions can be taken within the variants of the MIMD family. This is due to the fact that the operating system, by its role as a virtual machine, imposes its own view of PCS issues, which are mapped onto specific hardware resources. Behavioural descriptions must be translated with respect to the operating system virtual machine views. Thus, a generally applicable virtual machine semantics is provided for varying hardware resources. More concretely, the operating system (and compiled program code) provides for the utilization of shared memory or some form of message passing in accomplishing C (communication) and S (synchronization) behavior. At the higher level of behavioral description abstraction, the actual C and S mechanisms may be explicit or implicit.

The provision of appropriate operating systems for resource-limited real-time parallel processing environments provides a major challenge. The question of predictability is always difficult, especially in systems where mixed categories of processes (periodic, aperiodic, critical, essential, and so on) are to be accommodated. Later in this chapter, we consider some of the mainstream operating system approaches for parallel processing, including those aimed at supporting real-time system functions.

Despite problems with predictability, MIMD architectures when applied in a distributed real-time system can provide important services. They may, for example, be utilized as a test harness to drive hard real-time equipment that is under test or to provide accelerated simulation performance in human-machine systems (or both simultaneously such as vehicle simulators). MIMD-based systems may be used for sophisticated decision making, perhaps in relationship to large quantities of historical data-base information where time requirements are not as stringent. Further, there exist MIMD systems which can be coupled together in a "naked mode," in which case a high degree of predictability can be achieved.

11.2 SHARED-MEMORY ARCHITECTURES

The SM (Shared Memory) MIMD variant includes both bus-based and multistage interconnection network implementations. They may be configured in multiprocessor fashion, where the switch connecting PE and M processes is between the memory and the PEs or in multicomputer fashion, where the switch is between PEs but where the total shared-memory space is divided among the M processes connected locally to each PE. In the multiprocessor category, we find bus-based artifacts such as the Encore Multimax, Sequent, and Elexsi, and in the multistage case, the BBN Butterfly, which exploits a partially connected permutation-based ICN (arranged in a butterfly structure). The common denominator of the two multiprocessor architectural approaches is their utilization of a shared memory that is addressable by all the PEs in the system. Memory latency is uniform for the bus based architectures and nonuniform in the multistage ICN-based variants.

11.2.1 Bus-based Multiprocessor Systems

Several parallel computers based upon the use of a single high-speed bus and shared main memory were introduced during the 1980s. Bell (1985) refers to this class of parallel computer as *multis*. He explains *multis* as a natural evolution from *minis* and *micros*. A *multis* is based upon contemporary MOS microprocessors. However, there are members of this family that have been marketed and that are based upon specially designed PE, M, and C components, for example, the Elexsi multiprocessor, which utilizes custom-made ECL technology.

During the 1980s, a number of standard (or de facto standard) buses became available for connecting multiple PEs together, for example:

— Intel Mulitbus II (IEEE 1296)
— Motorola VME Bus (IEEE 1014)
— Texas Instrument Nu Bus (IEEE 1011)
— IEEE P896 Futurebus
— Scalable Coherent Interface (SCI bus) (IEEE 1596)

Most of the standard buses of this form have a capacity of approximately 10 million transactions per second (with the exception of the SCI bus). Several shared-memory products have come to the marketplace in which one of these standard buses has been utilized. On the other hand, due to the critical nature of bus performance, there is strong motivation to opt for the design of special bus logic that does not contain the overhead and complexities associated with the utilization of standard bus structures. In this regard, we can consider the Encore Nanobus, which transmits at 100 megabytes per second, and the ECL technology-based Elexsi high-speed bus, which can transfer data at 320 megabytes per second.

Whether a standard or special-purpose bus is utilized, it is the bus capacity that is the dominating factor in determining the limits of potential speedup, which is linear until the bus becomes saturated (naturally, exclusive of various overheads, including the effect of residual code and process administration, as discussed in Chapter 3).

11.2.2 Processing Elements

The majority of the shared memory (*multis*) products are based upon the use of MOS microprocessor-chip sets such as the National 32032 series, the Motorola 68020 series, and the Intel 80386 series. Each of these chip sets contains all key characteristics of past-generation mainframes, including 32-bit addressing, virtual memory control, and complete instruction sets, including floating-point arithmetic. The performance of the chip sets is approximately equal to that of a minicomputer.

11.2.3 Encore Multimax

To gain a perspective concerning bus-based multicomputers, we have selected, from several, the Encore Multimax (see Encore, 1989). Multimax is a modular, expandable microprocessor using the Nanobus (100 MB/second). The Nanobus provides the primary communication paths between hardware process modules. Twenty slots are provided in which one of four types of cards can be placed, as illustrated in Figure 11.1.

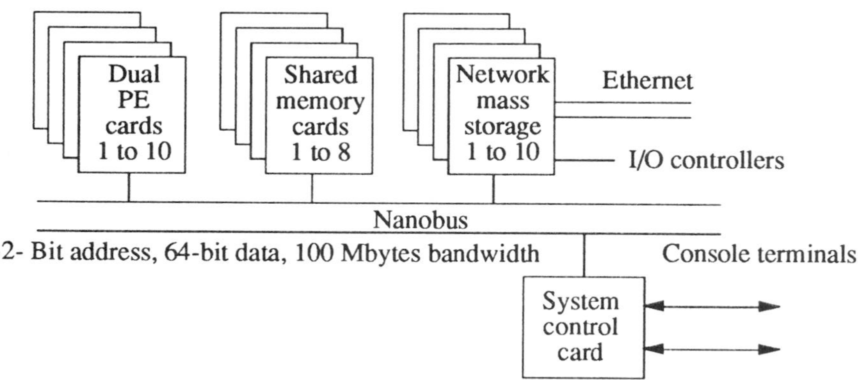

Figure 11.1. Encore Multimax

Hardware Processes

The **D**ual **P**rocessor **C**ards (DPC) contain two PEs per card. The Encore Multimax series 310 and 320 (APC version) is based upon the use of the National 32232, which provide two MIPS each. The Multimax 510 series (XPC version) utilizes the NS32532 rated at 8.5 MIPS. Both versions have floating-point accelerator hardware available. Each processor has its own cache memory. In the APC version, the cache is 64K-bytes and in the XPC version 256K-bytes.

The processor provides a MMU (**m**emory **m**anagement **u**nit) supporting demand-paged virtual memory management (4K-byte page size). The MMU provides for 32 bits (4 Gbyte) of virtual addressing per process.

The **S**hared-**M**emory **C**ards (SMC) provide 16 Mbytes of random-access memory in two independent banks of 1M-bit MOS RAM chips. Each card provides two-way interleaving between banks and four-way interleaving between boards. Systems having at least four SMCs permit eight-way interleaving. (Setup of interleaving is controlled at system start-up by the **S**ystem **C**ontrol **C**ard, SCC.) The capacity of memory in various configurations varies from 16 to 160 Mbytes.

The **E**thernet/**M**ass **S**torage **C**ards (E/MSC) allocate one channel to Ethernet as well as up to nine additional connections to disk and tape drives. The System Control Card serves as the source of bus timing signals and provides bus arbitration, interval, and time-of-year clock. Further, it supervises hardware fault diagnosis and interfaces to panels as well as local and remote terminals. A vital function performed by the SCC is to construct a configuration map of existing system resources. As mentioned previously, it can assign memory interleaving characteristics recognized by the memory modules.

The quantity of DPC, SMC, and E/MSC cards can be varied to meet varying demands.

Support for Process Synchronization

Hardware synchronization is provided by means of interlocked test-and-set instructions. Spinlocks, barriers, and monitors are constructed over the hardware facilities.

Operating Systems

UMAX 4.2 and UMAX V variants of UNIX operate symmetrically so that programs running on different PEs gain simultaneous access to operating system functions. The MACH operating system is also available.

The Multimax was the first MIMD machine to support true symmetric parallel programming support. Thus, instead of a master-slave asymmetric structure, operating system kernel functions are distributed to multiple PEs and can be executed simultaneously. This is done at the cost of increasing the use of locks; however, it provides a better basis for load balancing and exploiting available resources. This support is available for various programming languages, including Ada.

11.2.4 BBN Butterfly

The BBN Butterfly is based upon the use of a butterfly-permuted, partially connected ICN structure. While the memories are local to each PE in the system, they form the continuum of a single address space. Unlike the uniform memory latency of PEs in bus-based multiprocessors, machines like the Butterfly have uniform latency locally, but must use message passing for accessing memory in other PEs. The ICN switch for a 64-processor GP-1000 is portrayed in Figure 11.2.

The GP-1000 can be composed of from 1 to 128 PE nodes, where each PE contains a Motorola MC68020 microprocessor, MC68882 floating-point unit, MC68851 memory management controller, 4 Mbytes of local memory, and Butterfly switch interfaces.

Properties of Memories

Via the Butterfly switch, each PE can directly access the memory on any PE board. Thus, at the maximum of 128 PEs the maximum total memory is 512 Mbytes. Local memory references require approximately 0.5 μs whereas remote memory accesses (in another node) require approximately 5 μs.

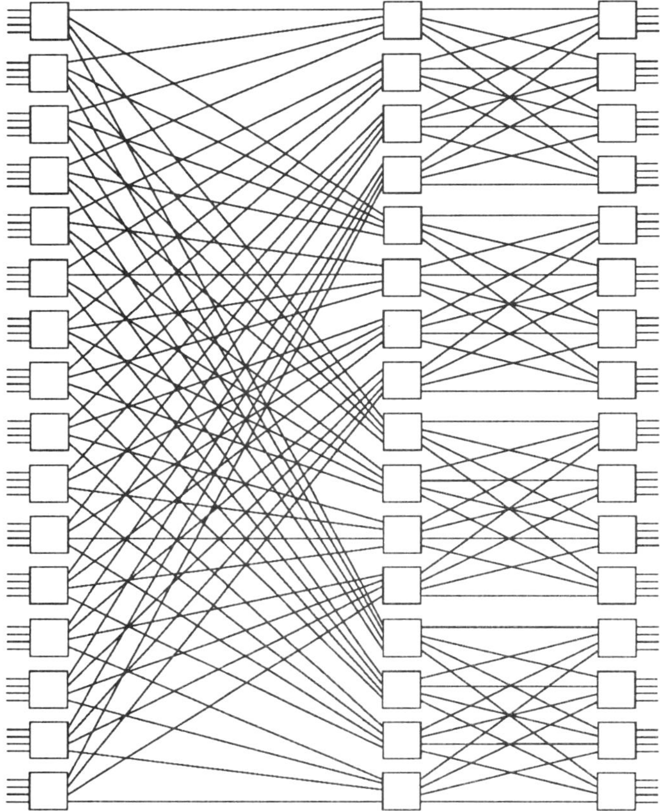

Figure 11.2. BBN Butterfly GP-1000 Switch for 64-processors

The memory addressing properties of the Butterfly introduces a trade-off. that is, knowing where data are located (so they can be processed locally) versus allowing the system to process data regardless of location (causing programs to run more slowly). Forcing the programmer to allocate all data in specific PEs makes the system inflexible and limits growth. Further, it forces the programmer to concentrate upon artifact issues rather than upon the problem. On the other hand, judicious planning in allocating data can alter the performance of the system by a factor of 10 or more.

BBN provides a tool called Uniform System that assists the programmer in making decisions concerning memory allocation. One very important property of this tool is that it can distribute global variables throughout the PE cluster in order to minimize the problems with *hot spots* (described in Chapter 3). Further, frequently referenced read-only data (for example, pointers to buffers and environment tables) may be copied into each PE, thus avoiding remote references.

Support for Process Synchronization

The Butterfly architecture supports an atomic "clear-then-**operation**" (operation = add, and, or) memory primitive. These operations are the building blocks for higher-level multiprocessing synchronization mechanisms such as barriers, monitors, and semaphores.

Operating Systems

The GP1000 supports Mach1000 as its operating system. To accommodate real-time processing, Mach1000 provides facilities for dedicating certain PEs to tasks (see Mach definition of task). These dedicated PEs permit the separation of the cooperating parallel processes to be freed from the normal scheduling. Dedicated PEs may be allocated and freed as needed.

11.3 DISTRIBUTED MEMORY ARCHITECTURES

DM (**D**istributed **M**emory) multicomputer systems incorporate complete computers providing PE, M, and local C processes that are coupled together over some form of interconnection network (ICN). The computers do not share any common memory processes and thus must communicate via message passing. We exemplify this category by first examining a DM architecture with a specific topology, the hypercube-connected computers. Second, we consider transputer architectures in which the transputer component building blocks can be interconnected into a variety of possible topologies.

11.3.1 Intel iPSC Hypercube

The Intel iPSC Hypercube is based upon a further development of the Caltech Cosmic Cube (see Seitz, 1985). We shall consider the second generation of this product called the iPSC/2. DeCegama (1989) provides a more complete description of this and other hypercube products.

Hardware Processes

An iPSC can contain up to 128 nodes, each of which is a complete computer system with processor, memory, and communications facilities. The architecture of a node is presented in Figure 11.3.

The CPU is an Intel 80386 microcomputer that provides pipelining for instruction fetching, decoding, execution, and memory management functions. Numeric coprocessors, the Intel 80387 and/or the Witek 1167 numeric chip, can be attached for accelerated performance. The memory subsystem can contain 1-, 2-, 4- or 8-Mbyte modules. At the price of reducing node connections, an additional 8-Mbyte module can

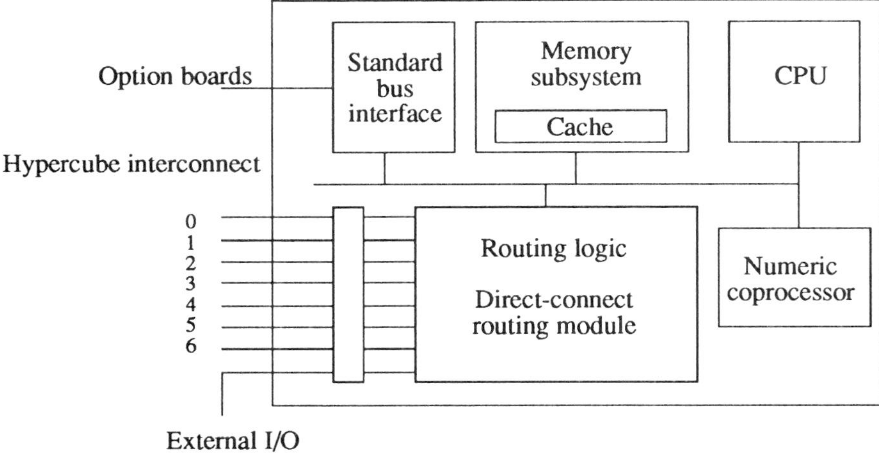

Figure 11.3. Architecture of an iPSC/2 Node

be incorporated, providing a total of 16-Mbytes. Further, a cache memory of 64 Kbytes is incorporated into the PE.

To provide a means of incorporating special-purpose boards into the system, a tightly coupled Standard Bus Interface module is provided, which can be adapted to native bus conventions of the option board. One example is the incorporation of a vector accelerator board (the iPSC - VX), which is used in configuring a 16-node iPSC-D4/VX machine in which each node is an iPSC/2 node plus VX board.

Internode Communications

The routing logic is realized via the **D**irect-**C**onnect routing **M**odule (DCM) from which messages are transferred to and from other nodes. To optimize use of the network, the DCM utilizes a special algorithm for messages of greater than 100 bytes. In this case, the DCM first sends out a header to the destination node. The receipt of the header triggers a path that is set up in all intermediate nodes, thus clearing a path for the message. Once the header reception is acknowledged, the message is streamed at hardware rates (without packaging) to the destination node in wormwhole fashion (see Chapter 3). The routing logic interface is a single, 32-bit-wide DMA interface that supports transfers between the routing module and the node memory. It steals cycles from the 80386 for the transfers.

The nodes in the hypercube network are assigned such that the address of any two nearest-neighbor nodes differs by one binary digit, as illustrated for the three-dimensional case in Figure 11.4. The reader will observe that the channels connecting nearest

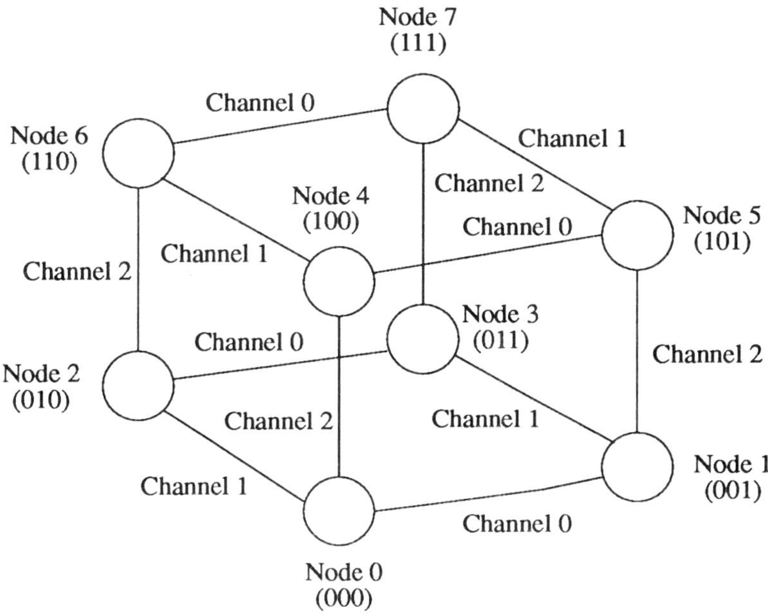

Figure 11.4. Channel and Node Naming Conventions

neighbors are named for their corresponding dimension. The dimension of a channel between two nodes is determined by taking the binary exclusive OR of the two node addresses where the bit position that remains 1 is the dimension of that channel. For example, the connection of node 5 and 7 (101 and 111) yields the exclusive OR result 010, the channel name (a bit in position 1).

The channels 0 to 6 are utilized for connections to other nodes in the system; however, channel 7 is utilized for external I/O connections to devices such as a disk farm, graphics devices, and real-time input and output functions. The transmission in the network operates completely synchronously. In addition to data being transmitted over the network, separate status information is constantly being transmitted (even when data transfer is not taking place). The status provides information concerning the readiness of adjacent nodes (RDY) for established paths, as well as indicating the end of messages (EOM). Due to the fact that status information is interspersed with message data, the end of message can easily be detected by routers on the fly. This dynamic mechanism eliminates the need for message size counters and removes limits for maximum-size messages.

Routing Algorithm

The transmission of each message involves a sending node and a receiving node. The route that the message takes through the network is unique between any two nodes. The combination of channels that composes a path is defined by a Caltech-developed routing algorithm (*e*-cube). The algorithm guarantees that no circularities occur in message routing, thus preventing any form of hardware deadlock. To achieve deadlock freedom, messages in hypercubes can be routed in increasingly higher dimensions until the destination is reached. Paths may consist of increasingly higher numbered channels, which do not have to be contiguous. Routing to lower-numbered channels is not permitted.

The routing operation is broken into four phases: establishing a path, acknowledgment, message transmission, and, finally, releasing connections. In initiating a transfer, a serializer in the source node calculates a channel (exclusive OR discussed earlier) and requests the corresponding outgoing channel. The DCM arbitrates between all local requesters for the same channel and grants one at a time on a round-robin basis.

Operating Systems

The NX/2 operating system runs on each node in the iPSC2 configuration. Each application process has a 1-Gigabyte address space. There may be up to 20 processes in each node, where each process has its own address space. UNIX COFF (**C**ompatible **O**bject **F**ile **F**ormat) files can be read by the NX/2 loader. The NX/2 manages the numeric coprocessor (if attached), where each process is assigned a coprocessor state. NX/2 operates the Direct-Connect message-passing hardware; further, it provides flow control, message buffering, and deadlock avoidance.

11.3.2 INMOS Transputer

The first major effort to provide a **unified** family of building blocks for parallel processing, including the industrial real-time application area, transpired during the 1980s, resulting in the INMOS *transputer* technology (see INMOS, 1986). Transputers can and have been utilized to construct network- and communication-oriented parallel computer systems with a variety of topologies. A significant number of designs have been made for real-time systems. In 1991, INMOS introduced a new member of the transputer family (the T9000), which provides a major step forward in the state of the art of MIMD multicomputer architectures (see INMOS, 1991). Thus, it is important to examine the underlying ideas of transputer development.

Transputer Philosophy

We observe that the INMOS transputer technology is based upon the utilization of conventional von Neumann architectural concepts, with the important extension of specific support for a concurrent (and parallel) process-oriented view of computation. The transputer product is based upon a holistic philosophy, and the technology provides means for developing resource structures from integrated hardware and software components. A network of transputers corresponds directly to a network of processes, with each transputer supporting one or more processes in a time-shared fashion.

Early Transputer Products

The fundamental hardware building block is the transputer chip, which is produced in a family of 16- and 32-bit devices. A general view of the early transputer chip structure (prior to the T9000) is provided in Figure 11.5.

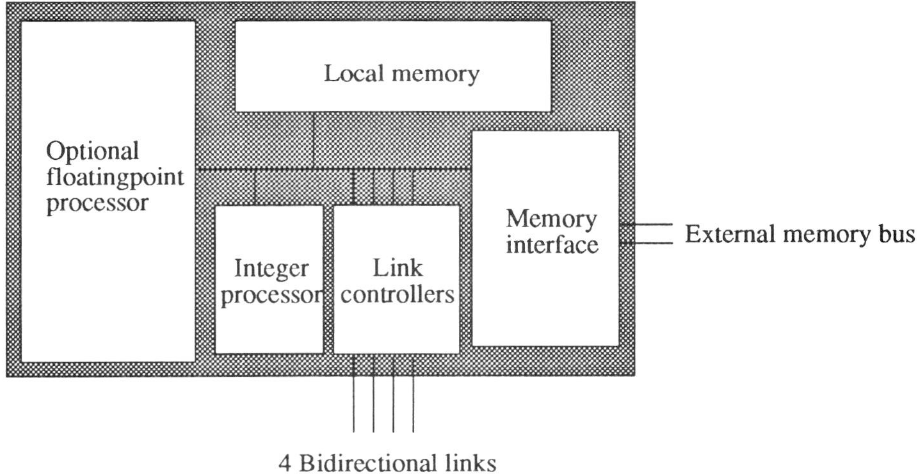

Figure 11.5. Transputer Chip Structure

Each chip is an autonomous unit that is capable of local execution and simultaneous communication to neighboring chips or to the outside world. Four serial links with two-way communication are provided, as well as a bit-serial communication protocol. A local memory is provided for both programs and data. It is also possible to interface the chip to an external memory via a bus connection from which programs and data can be accessed. Computation is provided by an integer processor and, in some versions of the chip, by an optional floating-point processor.

The instruction repertoire is quite simple in structure and has a direct relationship to the occam programming language, which in turn is related the CSP (Communicating Sequential Processes), as described in Chapter 7. Instructions are 8 bits, comprising a 4-bit function code and a 4-bit data value. Operands that are longer than 4 bits are built up 4 bits at a time in an operand register.

Processes defined in occam can be assigned to execute either in multiplexed fashion thus sharing a transputer chip, or assigned to dedicated transputer chips or mixtures thereof. When processes are multiplexed onto a single transputer, a microprogrammed scheduler provides a simple (nonpriority-based) strategy for managing separate queues for active processes and inactive processes (processes waiting for reactivation at a specific time).

Processes can execute locally and communicate with other processes either locally or simultaneously in neighboring chips. While local memory is limited, it is possible to define processing upon partitioned sets of data, for example, to achieve *geometric parallelism.*

To illustrate a possible configuration of transputer chips with software processes, consider the 4 x 4 completely connected system portrayed in Figure 11.6.

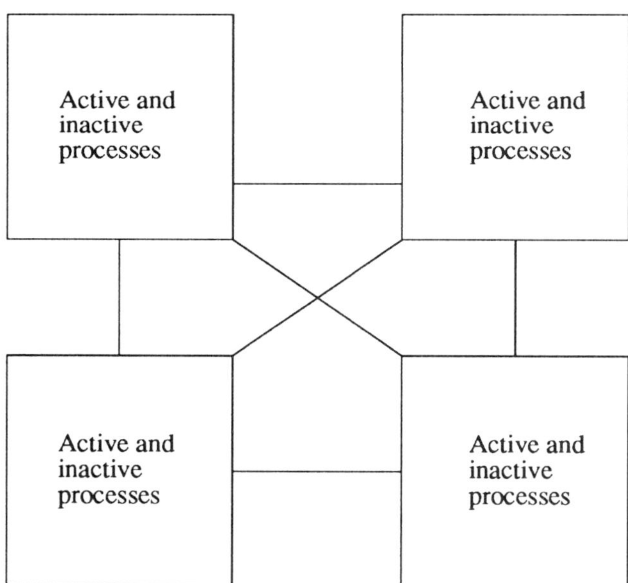

Figure 11.6. Completely Connected Transputer System

Within the limitations of four serial links per chip, it is possible to create arbitrary topologies for parallel systems. However, the bit-serial nature of transmission limits the maximum attainable transmission speed. While the transputer has become an important object for parallel processing experimentation, there are a growing number of commercially available transputer-configured products with appropriate software engineering and application development tools available in the marketplace.

Although occam was intended to be the primary programming language for the transputer, other procedural languages and some object-oriented languages are supported. Further, special operating system support for parallel processing has been developed, as described later.

Transputer Networks

Transputers can and have been configured into butterflies, hypercubes, grids, balanced trees, rings, and pipelines, to name a few common topologies. To assist in building networks, a 32 x 32 crossbar switch component is available as a part of the family. Due to the generality of the transputer philosophy, it has become a major instrument for experimentation in which several projects have been aimed at reconfigurable transputer networks.

In the late 1980s, INMOS components moved into an era of mass production and the price/performance ratio for their chips continues to improve. It is the express goal of INMOS to produce transputer chips that are not significantly more expensive then memory chips and where each chip contains a significant amount of local memory. If this is accomplished, new realistic paradigms for real-time parallel processing will undoubtedly be enabled.

T9000 Transputer

The introduction of the T9000 components has brought INMOS into a new era. We can observe that major advances have been made both in the internal architecture of the transputer chip and especially in improvments and new possiblities for building ICNs of the multicomputer as well as multiprocessor variety.

The features of the T9000 transputer chip illustrated in Figure 11.5 are still present; however, several new features have been added, as follows:

— instruction pipelining based upon parallel processing of groups of instructions
— an on-chip memory of 16K bytes, which can be used as normal RAM or as an instruction and data cache
— a small workspace cache for process local variables
— a programmable memory interface for adapting the system to communicate with various external memory configurations
— a virtual channel processor that manages the multiplexing of messages sent over the links between transputers
— control links that are used in error procedures

Compatibility is maintained with previous-generation transputers. On the other hand, there are new facilities and instructions, for example, the introduction of signal and wait instructions operating upon sempahore variables. Further, facilities for handling local error conditions and for controlling the use of operating system calls have been developed. In this latter case, a P-mode (protected mode) has been provided.

While the new features of the transputer chip are important, it is in the area of support for parallel and distributed processing that INMOS has made a big step forward.

Constructing Multiprocessors

While the multicomputer nature of the early transputer family has been a dominating factor, within the T9000 framework it is also possible to configure a crossbar-based shared memory solution. This feature is in recognition of the fact that in some applications the rapid access to large volumes of data may be essential. This behavior is difficult to achieve in the classical transputer channel communication model. In this respect, there are several features of the T9000 that are dedicated to managing caches and for constructing a memory hierarchy where the programmable memory interface is a key component.

Message-passing Mulitcomputers

The backbone of the new channel communiction approach is the C104 communications support device portrayed in Figure 11.7. We observe that the 32 x 32 crossbar switch, provided in the earlier line of components, is incorporated into the C104. In addition to the switch, we observe two CLink registers (two are also incorporated in each T9000). These control links are provided for separate control connections and are employed in error procedures.

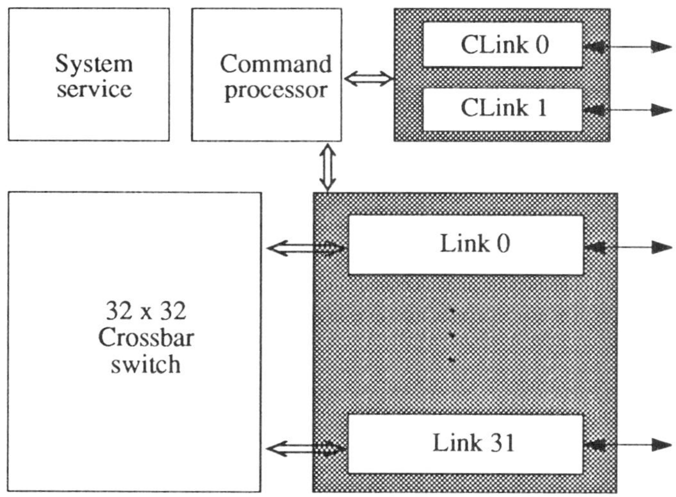

Figure 11.7. C104 Communications Support Device

The C104 becomes an active agent in the wormhole-routing, packet-switched approach used in communicating among transputers. This packet structure and routing are illustrated in Figure 11.8. Here we observe the contents of a packet following the packet header at various transmission stages. As described in Chapter 3, during wormhole routing, a path is established for the packet from the sender to the receiver, as clearly indicated in the figure. Implicit in this figure also is that the T9000 and C104 components can belong to arbitrarily large networks, where 32 x 32 crossbars are parts thereof.

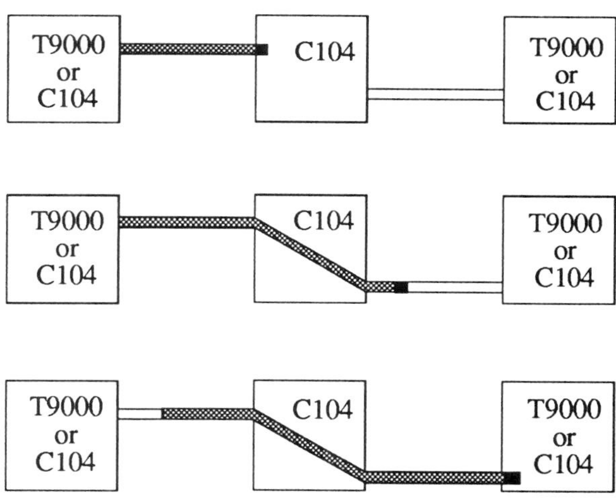

Figure 11.8. Wormhole-routed Packet

To obtain more efficiency in the use of the network links, a major new aspect of the T9000 is the VCP (**V**irtual **C**hannel **P**rocessor). Its role in relationship to communications is portrayed in Figure 11.9. We obseve that the header is divided into parts where the first part selects an output link of the C104 and the second part indicates the receiving virtual channel within the T9000. Headers are deleted as the message is moved along its route. This removal process occurs at each link along the way. There are 256 virtual channel register sets provided in each T9000. Since the virtual channel header is 2 bytes long, 65,536 channels can be emulated via the virtual facilities. The allocation of virtual channel addresses over a system of T9000s provides some flexibility as to how the addresses are assigned to each individual T9000. Via multiplexing the use of a link, multiple virtual messages can be sent across the same link.

Given this sampling of some of the important new features of the T9000, we now move on to consider operating system artifacts for MIMD architectures.

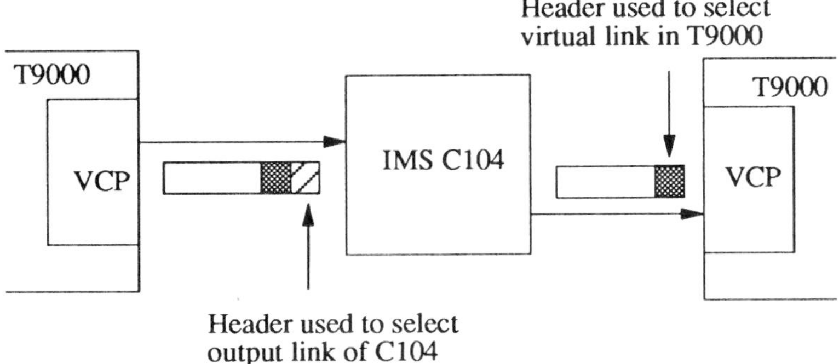

Figure 11.9. Virtual Channel Processors and Headers

11.4 OPERATING SYSTEM ARTIFACTS

In this section, we address some of the strategies and specific operating systems that are available for parallel processing MIMD systems. We begin by considering the farmer-worker model of allocation and scheduling and then proceed to some well-known operating systems. In the case of UNIX, it has been a question of upgrading an existing uniprocessor operating system. MACH and Helios have been designed, from the start, as parallel/distributed operating systems. In the case of Helios, it was originally developed specifically for the transputer. Next, we consider real-time operating system kernels aimed directly at parallel processing, the TRANS-RTXc and VRTX. Finally, we review the features of a distributed version of UNIX called CHORUS, which is targeted for real-time system utilization.

11.4.1 Farmer-Worker Model

To concretely illustrate the farmer-worker approach to allocation and scheduling, we consider an artifact, the Par.C System, which is supplied by Parsec Developments of Leiden, Holland. The Par.C System exploits the transputer technology via the utilization of the farmer-worker approach, which can be used as a model for realizing concrete parallel processing architectures. The farmer-worker concepts may well be exploited in certain real-time environments, particularly where the capacity of the resource structure is known and the loading of the system can be controlled.

The Farmer Approach

The general concepts have been introduced in Chapter 3. The Farmer approach involves the utilization of a Producer that continually produces command messages that are to be handled by a Calculator (which can be one of many parallel calculators) and a Consumer, which collects the results of calculations. This model was introduced and related to the client-server model view in Figure 3.53.

The straightforward logical structure of the Farmer is mapped onto the physical structure of the available network. The Farmer makes the physical structure transparent to the user. The Producer, Consumer, and Calculator functions are provided by the user. The Producer runs on the Root processor and produces messages that are sent to the Farmer running on every processor. The Farmer takes care of the distribution of messages over all available Calculators, one per processor. The resulting messages coming from the Calculators are collected by the Farmer and propagated back to the Consumer, also running only on the Root processor.

Booting and Program Loading

The Par.C package, running on a host computer, investigates the structure of the physically connected network while booting the system. This results in a boot tree, which is then utilized to load the Farmer program into the individual transputers. To illustrate this, consider the simple network and possible boot trees portrayed in Figure 11.10.

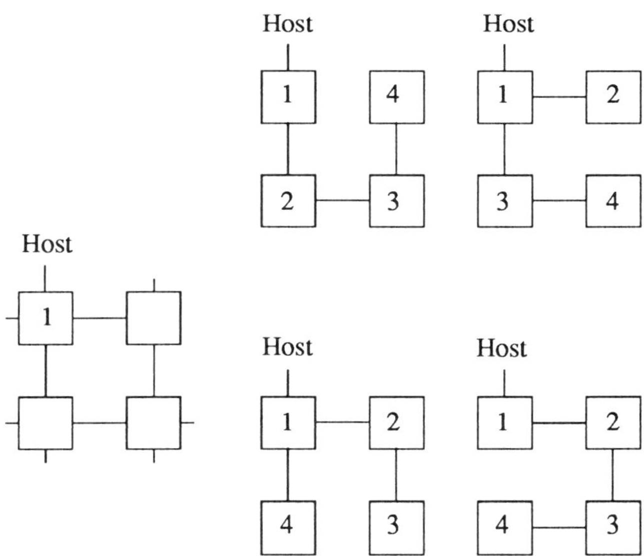

Figure 11.10. Simple Network and Possible Boot Trees

The Farmer will make use of the boot-tree information by only communicating over links that are provided from the boot tree. These connections are sufficient, since messages can only come from and travel back to the Root of the tree (that is, the PE connected to the host). The configuration for the second boot tree is portrayed in Figure 11.11.

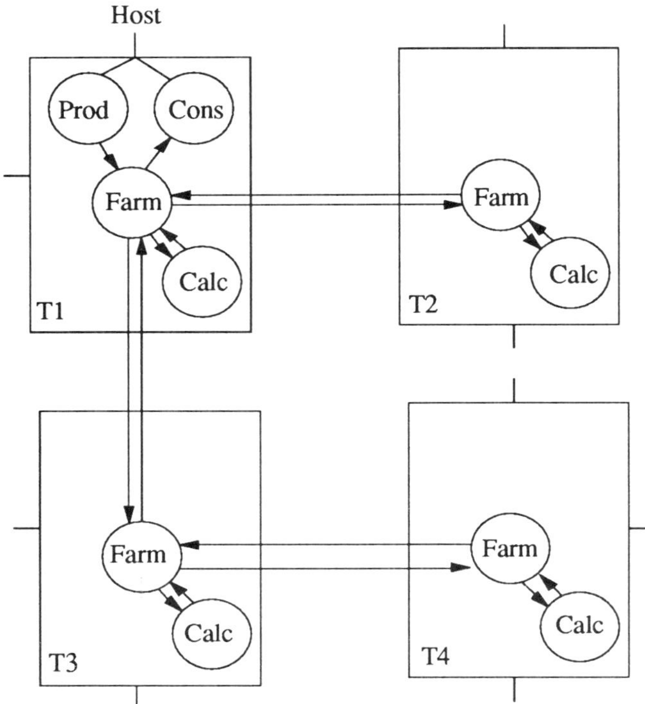

Figure 11.11. Farmer Configuration for the Simple Network

Structure of the Farmer Process

Each Farmer process is connected to a Calculator and to Farmer processes on the other transputers (if present). Only the Farmer process running on the Root is connected to the Producer and Consumer processes. A further examination of the Farmer process is provided in Figure 11.12.

The main tasks of the Farmer are the distribution of command messages and the collection of result messages. Since these tasks are independent of each other, separate parallel processes for Distribute and Collect are provided. For efficiency of resource utilization, buffers are provided. The data coming down the tree to be distributed are sent to a free Request buffer. This is a special buffer that signals a request for new data back to the Distribute process after it has sent on the previous data block. Data are only sent

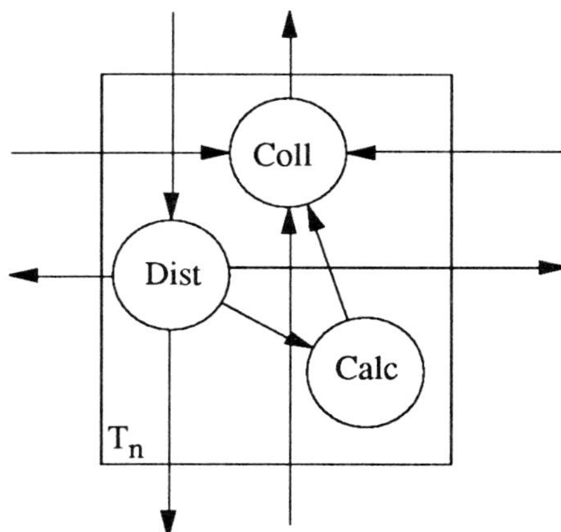

Figure 11.12. Overview of the Farmer Process

to this request buffer when the Distribute process knows that it is ready to receive the message. Together with the automatic synchronization of the channel communication, this mechanism assures that the PEs do not get overloaded with messages that cannot be handled. The Distribute process only accepts a message coming down the tree when it knows that it can propagate it to one of the Request buffers. (This seems to be a good solution to using buffering, but still provide a high degree of predictability.)

The Collect process multiplexes the resulting messages coming from the Calculator and from the Farmers in the subtrees. The buffers for this process only require simple buffers since actions do not have to be triggered for this process.

Farmer Process Pseudocode

Let us now examine some pseudocode for the Distribute and Collect functions of the Farmer, which provides an expression of the essential structure and behavior. In the code, displayed at the top of the following page, the keyword "select" is utilized to denote that actions need only be taken when one of the channels (distinguished by alt) is ready to communicate.

Improving Efficiency via Internal Pointers

The Farmer, as it has been described, operates by sending messages between the different parallel communicating processes. The Farmer can be made more efficient by utilizing pointers to the messages in communications that transpire within the same PE, thus reducing the number of bytes that must be transmitted. This difference between passing data and pointers is illustrated in Figure 11.13.

DISTRIBUTE:

```
forever {
        select {
                alt Receive request from Calculator on this PE :
                        Adjust the number of free buffers ;
                alt Receive request from one of the active buffers :
                        Adjust the number of free buffers ;
                alt (If at least one buffer is free)
                     Receive message from the BootLink:
                        {If Calculator on the PE is free
                                Send message to Calculator process;
                         else
                                Send message to one of the free active links ;
                        }
                }
        }
```

COLLECT:

```
forever {
        select {
                alt Receive message from own Calculator :
                        Set source-ID in message header ;
                alt Receive message from an active Link (i) ;
                }
        Send message to Bootlink ;

        }
```

In the first case, each process utilizes its own private memory to store the data. Message exchange transpires by copying the memory of the sender to the memory of the receiver. When messages contain significant amounts of data, it may be more efficient to utilize the second alternative, in which case data are not moved but pointers are passed around between the processes. Naturally, copying still must occur for communications that take place over the links.

When the data solution is utilized, we have assured that the data area must be transmitted before new data can arrive, thus avoiding any form of overwrite. In the pointer case, the common data must be managed to avoid memory contention. Thus, new memory space must be allocated for arriving messages and deallocated by a process transferring the message to the next PE.

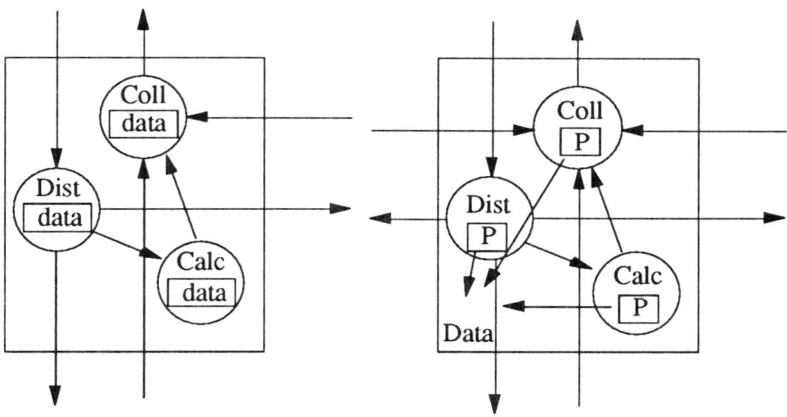

Figure 11.13. Communicating: (a) data versus (b) pointers

Extending the Farmer Model

The Farmer can be extended by utilizing a more complex headers for messages. When a destination_ID is utilized, the message can be routed from one PE to another, thus providing for a simple message passer, including the possibility of sending messages of varying size. Other data can be included in order to obtain statistics; for example, the path length can be used to determine how many Farmers the message has passed by having each Farmer increment this number before passing the message. A message_type can be used to determine that different actions should be taken on different messages. For example, this facility could be used to broadcast specific messages to all Calculators in the network.

One of the interesting statistics that can be obtained from an expanded header are timings of the system. By setting the start time when a message is sent out by the Producer, the Consumer can calculate the time required to handle the message. The time spent in the Calculator can also be determined for analysis purposes. These timings can be used by another program, for instance to determine the number of Calculators actually working or the communication overhead in this particular system and program. Some insight into the possibilities for dynamic load balancing can be obtained by altering the amount of work required to process each single command message.

The expanded header includes the following elements:

```
struct header {
        int             message_ID ;
        char            source_ID ;
        char            destination_ID
        int             message_size ;
        char            path_length ;
        char            message_type ;
        clock_t  DT_Calculator ;
        clock_t  DT_Message ;
}
```

Message Passer Based on the Farmer

The Farmer described earlier carries messages from a master PE to and from several other slave PEs in a tree network. It can be extended to send messages from one specific PE to another. For this purpose, messages have to be routed from the source PE to the destination PE. This can be realized using the numbering scheme for the transputer network, which makes it possible to determine the direction a message should travel to get from the source to the destination.

A message produced by a user program is handled by the Collect process from the Farmer. This process determines whether the message should go up-tree or not. If so, the message is sent to the Collect process on the PE connected to the bootlink. If the message has to move down-tree or to this particular PE, the message is sent to the Distribute process on the same PE. For this communication, an extra channel has to be defined to carry messages from the Collect process to the Distribute process, as portrayed in Figure 11.14.

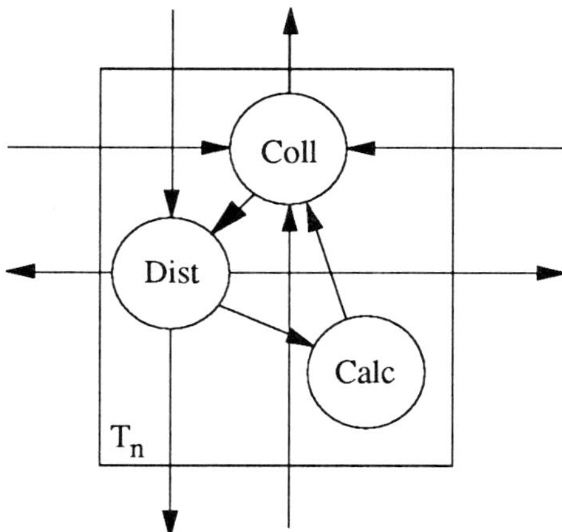

Figure 11.14. Extra Channel for Message Passer

The Distribute process in the Message Passer receives messages from the bootlink and from the Collect process. These messages must go down-tree or to their own user Calculator process. The task of the Distribute process is to send the message to the correct channel, using the destination_ID contained in the message.

Pseudocode for the Message Passer

We now consider the pseudocode of the Distribute and Collect functions of the Message Passer, which is provided on the following page.

In summary, we can see that the farmer-worker model, with varying degrees of refinement and extension, provides a rational means of constructing parallel/distributed software solutions. In transputer environments, the addition of the virtual channel facilities of the T9000 enhances the value of this model since it provides for the management of message passing.

11.4.2 UNIX on Parallel Processors

The popularity of UNIX for multiprocessing and time-sharing applications has made it a practical alternative upon which to base real-time operating systems. This popularity is due to the flexibility, portability, and availability of numerous support tools for boosting programmer productivity. The UNIX paradigm is based upon the use of *processes*, *files*, and *pipes* (communication facility), where the user views processing as a system of cooperating processes. Synchronization of processes (added to the original UNIX versions) is provided for via *semaphores*, *message queues*, and *named pipes*. The two mainstreams of UNIX development in the 1980s have resulted in AT&T's System V and 4.3 BSD from the University of California (usually referred to as Berkley UNIX). In Berkley UNIX, the additional communication facility of *Internet domain sockets* is provided.

Much of the elegance and power of UNIX comes from its multiprocessing design philosophy. UNIX encourages the programmer to construct applications by piecing together collections of small programs that will be executed as processes. Pipes connect the output of one process to the input of another. Further, the UNIX "shell" command language syntax permits the user to invoke more than one process and, by using an appropriate terminator, have them run concurrently ("process & process....") or in a pipelined manner ("process | process ...."). The basic structure of UNIX is portrayed in Figure 11.15.

```
DISTRIBUTE:

     forever {
          select {
               alt Receive request from Calculator on this PE :
                    Adjust the number of free buffers ;
               alt Receive request from one of the active buffers :
                    Adjust the number of free buffers ;
               alt (If at least one buffer is free)
                   Receive message from the Bootlink:
                    Set Message_Received flag ;
               alt (If at least one buffer is free)
                   Receive message from COLLECT :
                    Set Message_Received flag ;
               }

               IF (Message_Received flag set)
                  { Reset Message_Received flag ;
                    IF  (destinationCalculator on this PE)
                              Send message to Calculator process;
                         else
                              Send message to one of the determined links ;
          }


COLLECT:

     forever {
          select {
               alt Receive message from own Calculator :
                    Set source-ID in message header ;
               alt Receive message from an active Link (i) ;
               }
          IF (destination is reachable by Bootlink)
               Send message to Bootlink ;
          else
               Send message to DISTRIBUTE ;

           }
```

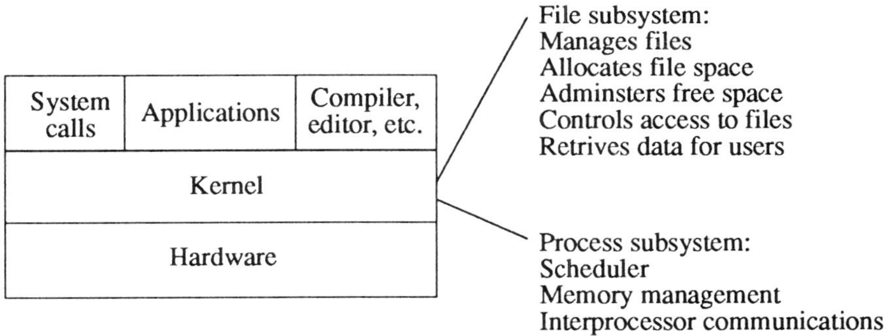

Figure 11.15. Structure of UNIX

All files in UNIX are treated as an unformatted stream of bytes that are transmitted over pipes. Device drivers are written to interface with particular external suppliers and consumers of byte streams, thus making them look like files. Files can also be contained within memory, thus providing rapid access. Programs, as collections of processes coupled by pipes, can interact with files without dealing with hardware specifics.

The scheduling and resource allocation algorithms for standard UNIX implementations attempt to achieve a fairness of processing by time slicing the use of available resources. This approach is suitable for time-sharing systems but, of course, is not appropriate for real-time systems. Extended versions of UNIX are being applied in various parallel processing environments. Further, there are also several extended versions of UNIX that are aimed at real-time parallel processing. Typically, these real-time extensions involve binding a statically allocated subset of the parallel processing resources in order to deal with periodic processes and events initiated by interrupts.

UNIX for parallel processing environments has been developed for message passing and shared-memory programming styles. In extending UNIX to parallel processing environments, the following requirements have been identified by Russell and Waterman (1987):

— mutual exclusion primitives

— synchronization capabilities

— a multiprocessor process scheduling capability

— interprocess communication

— flexible memory management and cache coherence

— easy reconfiguration and expandability

When properly exploited, command pipelines in a multiprocessor UNIX version may achieve better than linear speedup if all the stages run simultaneously on separate PEs, thereby avoiding context switching overhead that occurs in a uniprocessor environment. When fine-grain interaction is important, however, care must be taken to ensure that the sender is producing data at approximately the same rate as the receiver is consuming the data. Otherwise, the faster process will be forced to wait for the slower and run the risk of being locally context-switched in favor of other runable processes.

11.4.3 MACH Operating System

The UNIX paradigm was not initially designed for today's parallel processing environments; consequently various "fixes" have been made in order to provide support for parallel/distributed processing environments. To continue the UNIX philosophy but provide a better basis for parallel/distributed processing, the Mach operating system, developed at Carnegie-Mellon University, was funded by DARPA (**D**efense **A**dvanced **R**esearch **P**roject **A**gency). A description of the original ideas is provided by Rashid (1986), and a detailed description of MACH's support for concurrency and parallelism has been provided by Black (1990).

Mach supports the goal of running a single operating system on many different classes of machines in a variety of configurations, all with a consistent user interface. Mach uses four fundamental abstractions:

— *port*: a queue or communication channel for messages protected by the kernel. All communication traffic within Mach makes references to ports as read or write destinations using the primitives *Send* and *Receive*.

— *task*: contains the resources associated with a process (address space, file descriptors, port-access capabilities). Does not perform computations itself, but serves as a framework in which *threads* can operate.

— *thread*: control unit most basic to PE utilization, containing the minimal processing state associated with a computation (a program counter, a stack pointer, and other hardware register state information). A UNIX process corresponds to a Mach task containing a single thread. A Mach task may contain multiple threads, but each thread is associated with exactly one task. Multiple threads within a task may execute in parallel. A thread, in this context, is called a *lightweight process*.

— *message*: consists of a fixed-length header and a typed collection of data objects used in communication between threads. A message can be of any size and may contain port-access capabilities in addition to data.

Mach provides for shared-memory techniques as well as message passing. Further, RPC (**r**emote **p**rocedure **c**all) is provided for interfacing programs written in various programming languages. The *virtual memory system* features include read/write and copy-on-write sharing of memory between tasks. The following information is utilized in administrating virtual memory:

— *address map*: describes the region of memory that comprises the task's address space. Every region refers to either a *virtual memory object* or a *share map*.

— *virtual memory object*: represents the backing storage for a memory region. It maintains information as to what pages of the object are currently resident and where to find nonresident pages.

— *share map*: provides a level of indirection above the virtual memory objects, thereby allowing the same memory object to be shared by multiple tasks.

— *resident page*: used to keep track of the state of the machine's physical pages, that is, free, reclaimable, in use, and in which virtual memory object.

Mach's interprocess communication facility provides for simple types (strings, reals, integers of various sizes, and so on), which differentiates it from its predecessor UNIX, where all communication is via unformatted byte streams.

Interprocessor communication messages may contain collections of ports, port access rights, and other data. A *copy-on-write* method is utilized to pass messages. Thus, the only time data are actually copied (not just pointed to) is when either the sender or the receiver attempts to modify the data. In such an event, only a copy of the modified page of data is made. The remainder of the data buffer continues to be shared. This method reduces updating overhead.

Both UNIX and Mach have been used as the operating system basis for parallel processing systems. In commercially available product versions, facilities have often been added to bind portions of the hardware resource structure in order to accommodate real-time processes. Finally, the use of UNIX in real-time environments has been described by Furht and others (1991).

11.4.4 HELIOS

Helios (see Perihelion, 1989) was originally designed as an operating system for the transputer; thus, it was designed for multiple PE use at its origin. However, Helios has been ported to other parallel processing configurations that utilize different communication and memory management mechanisms. While providing UNIX-like thinking at the user level, the underlying implementation of Helios is entirely different. Helios is based upon a client/server approach.

Helios support two types of parallel processing objects:

— *processes* that resemble threads of lightweight processes: a process shares memory with other processes and process context switches are rapid. (*Note*: On transputer chips a process maps directly into an occam process, where process management is supported by firmware on the chip.) Semaphores are used to lock shared data structures and Helios makes no attempt to keep track of any processes that have been created.

— *tasks*, which have names created by Helios system calls: different tasks may not share memory; tasks communicate by message passing and are often allocated to different PEs.

Each task can be seen as either a job for a particular user or a system task. A task often contains several processes; in particular, server tasks normally have a process for each client.

Another early design decision was to utilize Xwindows for graphic support in Helios. Since Xwindows is also based on a client-server model, it is suited for use in Helios; further, it has become an industry standard.

Helios itself is not a real-time operating system in that it does not provide any mechanisms for guaranteed response times. However, it is often applied in real-time environments since it can work in conjunction with a dedicated remote PE. The remote PE contains code for treating interrupts and buffering events for further transmission to another PE running Helios. However, for complex systems processing, predictability cannot be assured.

Helios is adaptable to configurations for massive parallelism and, in particular, Helios can operate in mixed environments.

Client-Server Model

The client-server model serves as the basis for Helios operation. Interprocess communication is handled by message passing, where the underlying mechanism is hidden by system software layers. For example, a client wishing to access a system resource sends a message to a server process requesting the access to be made on its behalf. The server replies with another message indicating success or failure; on success, the client accesses the resource by sending further messages to the server. Processes that have the roles of clients or servers may reside in different PEs. Transparency in message delivery is provided where the actual location of a server is not known to a client (that is, it is topology independent).

Servers, each having a name, are organized into PE clusters. Further, each PE cluster is also named such that a server can be identified by its full name or identified generically by a shortened subset of the name. For example, a specific name NetX/Cluster2/01/task may be given, whereas /task relates to the nearest server. Locating a server is the result of a distributed search.

The naming scheme permits a degree of fault tolerance since all messages sent by Helios have an associated timeout. When a message fails to get through within a specific time limit, the system does an automatic retry a specific number of times, after which a new distributed search is performed in attempting to identify a new server route.

Implementation and Utilization Characteristics

Helios is a true distributed operating system where each PE node contains a Helios kernel that treats memory management and message passing. Each PE node contains two servers, the *process manager* and the *loader*. The process manager takes care of process creation within the PE as well as general housekeeping, and the loader takes care of loading and unloading of program modules and resident libraries (loaded on demand).

Further, servers run on one or several PE nodes. Certain servers must run on nodes with particular hardware attached, for example, a file manager requiring a disk device or a window manager requiring that a video memory be attached. Servers not requiring special hardware connections can be distributed in order to accommodate load balancing.

A dumb link facility permits Helios to communicate with PEs that have been loaded into naked hardware via a private protocol called the occam server program. In this manner, the occam program controls the use of transputer links where PEs dedicated to special functions or PEs that are too small to accommodate a Helios kernel can be connected to the system.

Alternatively, an occam program can be converted to run under Helios, in which case Helios controls (multiplexes the use of links) for message passing. Thus, direct use of the links interferes with Helios scheduling of these resources. On the other hand, the placement of tasks can be allocated to specific PEs via the shell or be distributed to PEs by the Task Force Manager.

In the transputer case, the majority of networks are connected to a host system. Helios treats the host system in the same manner as a transputer processing node via running a program in the host (IO Server). This C program causes the host processor to appear to the rest of the network as another node running Helios. Thus, messages sent to and from the host are dealt with in the same manner as those transmitted to other transputer nodes. The IO server normally provides services for consoles, files systems, serial ports, and the like. Thus, Helios can be adapted to the conventions of other file systems and networks (for example, file servers on an Ethernet using the standardized TCP/IP protocols).

A Helios network may contain an arbitrary number of transputer nodes and host nodes; thus, the transputer links may be regarded as a local area network connecting different hosts.

The Helios operating system has been implemented via the C language. Access to parallel processing functionality is via system calls. A number of languages other than C and occam have been ported to Helios systems, including FORTRAN and Pascal.

Network Servers

Helios provides support for network servers where clusters of subnetworks, possibly with some collective network resources, can be managed. Each subnet contains a network server that is responsible for booting or rebooting the PEs of the subnetwork. The network servers are addressed via their position in the network hierarchy. Via this division, it is possible, for example, to have some of the subnets out of operation.

Task Force Manager

When scheduling and placement of tasks are left to Helios, the Task Force Manager is utilized. Like the network server, there is a TFM for each subnet that has **no** knowledge of the network outside the subnet. The management provided is for task forces, which are simply collections of tasks. TFM is responsible for maintaining a reasonably balanced loading in the face of resource, including communication, requirements.

Helios cannot support dynamic reloading of tasks once they have started execution. Thus, once allocated to a PE, tasks are fixed making initial placement critical. The following criteria are used in the mapping algorithm:

— optimal allocation of resources
— polarization of different user Task Forces
— maximize efficiency of interprocess communication
— minimize multiprogramming

Mapping is accomplished in two phases. In phase (a), allocation is based upon the first two criteria, where task requirements for specific resources dictate their binding to particular PEs (for example, the use of a UART). In phase (b), the last two criteria are applied. In this case, the assumption has been made that more can be gained by allocating tasks to separate PEs than by maximizing interprocess communication with local message passing.

Based upon the problem, one of two mapping programs is applied. The multiprogramming *mmapper* algorithm applies heuristics in the situation where the number of tasks exceeds the capacity of the subnetworks (resource limited). The *cmapper* program is applied when there are adequate resources; via random permutations *cmapper* attempts to place tasks in PEs in order to minimize communication distance (diameter). When the number of PEs in a network becomes large (for example, more than 40), both of these algorithms experience difficulties. The resolution of the problem is quite natural, since allocations are made on a subnet basis (divide and conquer).

In conclusion, we can observe that Helios is an interesting operating system for the transputer environment and has found its way into other parallel processing environments. It certainly has been an important pioneering effort.

11.4.5 RTX Kernels

One of the most straightforward means of creating operating system functionality for real-time systems has been to employ a real-time kernel, typically referred to as RTX (**R**eal-**T**ime e**X**ecutive). Several RTX variants have been supplied that provide specific real-time operating system services. Typically, they provide interrupt handling, some straightforward priority-based scheduling, process communication, synchronization, timing, and memory management facilities. They are frequently supported with testing and debugging environments.

RTX kernels have been usefully employed in many uniprocessor environments. One of the most successful commercial products has been VRTX (V = Versatile), provided originally in 1981 by Ready Systems of Sunnyvale, California. One of the first multiprocessor real-time kernels was developed for early-generation transputer systems, namely TRANS RTXc (1991) by Intelligent Systems International of Leuven, Belgium.

TRANS RTXc, which is written in the C language for transputers, takes advantage of the special properties of the transputer for process communication. Thus, one can begin by assuming that all processes are contained in one transputer (PE). Further, via a configuration tool (RTXcgen), processes can be distributed out to other transputers where communication is altered from memory-based communication to communication over the links provided in a transputer architecture. *Note*: Source code is not altered!

A fixed priority scheme is employed. Further, the priorities are assigned during RTXcgen configuration. Message passing and synchronization are provided via the utilization of semaphores with associated queues. Facilities are provided for locking and unlocking resources and to arbitrate process possession when the resource is freed. Memory is managed by partitioning memory space into identifiable partitions, where each partition contains a number of blocks of the same size. There is no means of dynamically extending memory requirements; thus, adequate memory must be reserved for worst-case conditions.

TRANS RTXc provides a convenient manner of implementing real-time systems for transputer parallel processing environments. Further implementations for other parallel processing hardware resources will also be available.

For the new generation of transputer products, that is, the T9000, Ready Systems has developed a multiprocessor version of their popular VRTX. VRTX32/T is supported by a range of tools for design, simulation, and visualization. A graphical icon langauge is provided for expressing concurrent software entities, mechanisms for intertask synchronization and communication, and scheduler mechanisms.

11.4.6 CHORUS/MiX

The CHORUS/MiX operating system is provided by Chorus Systémes of Saint-Quentin-En-Yvelines, France. CHORUS provides a real-time distributed UNIX environment, which will now be made available in the T9000 generation of transputers.

CHORUS is based upon a small real-time distributed nucleus used to integrate distributed processing and communication at the lowest level. The facilities provided include thread scheduling, real-time event handling, network transparent interprocess communications, and memory management. The facilities are exploited by independent servers (subsystems) that coexist with the nucleus. In fact, we can view a CHORUS system as a set of cooperating servers.

Due to the highly distributed approach taken by CHORUS and the availability of the new virutal communication facilities of the transputer, the marriage of these two should lead to new solutions in the area of distributed/parallel systems (includng some real-time variants).

11.5 DEVELOPMENT ENVIRONMENTS AND TOOLS

The effective utilization of computer systems for industrial real-time systems is highly dependent upon the availability of software development environments and tools. Due to the inherent problems in developing parallel solutions, the role of the development environments and tools becomes an essential ingredient of any project. The environments and tools, in some cases, provide for automatically or semiautomatically generating, testing, and documenting software components for parallel/distributed environments. Further, the "visualization" of algorithms and processes has become an important part of many tools. In this section, we examine a few typical contemporary approaches.

11.5.1 ADAS

ADAS is a set of computer-aided design tools that supports a methodology for the architecture-level synthesis and analysis of software algorithms and their hardware implementations. Use of ADAS is intended to be an iterative process, where successive designs are refined.

Software and hardware are modeled as directed graphs in a manner quite similar to Petri nets (see Chapter 7), where the following attributes are given for the graph:

— firing delay, token consumption rate, token production rate
— firing threshold, firing condition
— arc queue lengths, speed and capacity of "components"
— associated C or Ada functional model
— stochastic behavior

ADAS provides detailed simulation results for performance evaluation of a design. Further, tools are provided for consistency checking the hardware and software graphs.

Each of the components of the architecture model is described by speed and capacity characteristics and **not** by modeling any special hardware technologies.

A Simulation Management Facility (SMF) provides for managing simulations over a range of speeds, system dimensions, and algorithms. SMF then provides facilities for tabulating user-specified metrics.

System simulation is essentially an approximation of system behavior. The granularity of a simulation is the amount of simulated time that can be realized in a unit of real time. According to Yalamanchili and Carpenter (1989), loosely coupled systems can be modeled in ADAS with high-simulation granularity, whereas tightly coupled systems usually require a lower-simulation granularity.

11.5.2 Express System

The Express system has been produced by Parasoft of Mission Viejo, California, and is built on the philosophy that the developers of parallel solutions will be familiar with using development environments that are based upon existing operating systems, such as MS-DOS, UNIX, VMS, and Macintosh. Consequently, Express permits users to develop their parallel programs in these environments and then "port" them into an attached parallel system. In this case, the original system serves as a host environment, and all the normal commands provided by that environment are available to the Express user. Express was originally aimed at Multicomputer systems where a point-to-point ICN is used, such as a hypercube, butterfly, or torus. We can view Express as an intermediary, as portrayed in Figure 11.16.

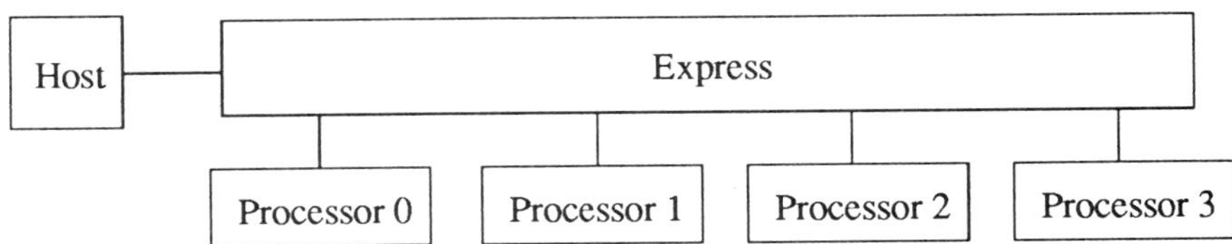

Figure 11.16. Host and Parallel System

Express provides a normalized model that is largely independent of the actual host and parallel processing hardware. Express hides the details of the ICN from the user, thus avoiding the necessity to know exactly what processes are going to be executed on specific PEs. The Express parallel processing features may also by integrated with operating systems for parallel operating system environments such as Mach and Helios, which were described earlier. In this case, the user sees the basic utilities of the underlying parallel OS, while still being able to take advantage of Express parallel processing features.

Parallel Processing Toolkit

Express should be viewed as a set of utilities and tools designed for parallel processing that provides the following facilities:

- — high- and low-level communication primitives for sending messages between processors, peripherals, and other system components
- — at the lowest level, providing simple node-addressed message passing, while many other levels are possible, including a semiautomatic problem decomposer for "domain-decomposed" algorithms
- — transparent I/O system allowing any node in the machine to access the OS facilities, which would normally be available to the host processor; several modes of operation tailored to the particular problem
- — parallel graphics system providing device-independent, run-time configurable graphics primitives and higher-level packages (contouring, three dimensional), which are available for multiple-output devices
- — a source-level debugger for parallel programs; allows direct interactive access to program execution on the parallel machine via breakpoints, stack tracing, printing of selected variables, and so on.
- — a graphical system for visualizing, evaluating, and enhancing the performance of parallel programs; analysis performed on subroutine use, communication overhead, load balancing, interprocessor timing differences, and so on.

A library of code examples is provided for guidance and suggestions as to the "domain decomposition" of problems.

Subroutine Farming

Many parallel programs are organized such that an initial sequential part of the program is executed, followed by portions that can be executed in parallel and finally executing a sequential part. In the Express environment, the logical means of treating this type of situation is to execute the sequential portions on the host and then farm out the parallel parts to available parallel PEs, as described earlier in this chapter. This farming is done via the Subroutine Farm Interface. The user indicates what data are to be sent and what is expected in return, along with the subroutine call. Express generates all necessary communication calls and handles the "packaging" of the subroutine on the parallel computer. By altering the subroutine call, the program can be changed from a completely sequential version running on the host to one that exploits the available parallel processing facilities.

Complete Parallel Systems

In contrast to the subroutine farming example, where the host performs all input/output services, and the like; Express will generate the software for parallel systems that will deal directly with input/output devices. In this case, utilities are provided to assist in such activities as dynamically adapting the problem to the dimension of the parallel processing network (the number of nodes), mapping of larger data sets to small constituent parts, interface with I/O system, and combining functions for the accumulation of resultant data.

The Parasoft Express system provides some interesting capabilities. Naturally, all facilities have a price. Thus, the utilization of Express or other tools for developing parallel real-time systems must be viewed with respect to our ever present consideration of predictability; a requirement in many real-time environments.

11.5.3 PARET Modeling Tool

The complexity of parallel processing systems provides a major intellectual challenge, and it is extremely important to gain insight and intuition with respect to the structure and behavior of parallel systems. Analogical reasoning helps us; however, it is very important be able to visualize parallel algorithms in execution and the systems upon which they are executed. A number of tools have been developed in this area.

PARET (**P**arallel **A**rchitecture **R**esearch and **E**valuation **T**ool) was developed by Nichols and Edmark (1988) for multicomputer systems. The tool provides for studying the interaction of algorithms and architectures, the effects of varying physical resources on system performance, and alternative mapping, scheduling, and routing strategies (both static and dynamic). This interactive animation system allows the user to exercise various multicomputer models.

This concludes our small sampling of the development environment tools. A vast number of methods and tools have been and will be made available in this area.

References

ADAS (1988) *ADAS Version 2.5 User Manual*, Center for Digital Systems Research, Research Triangle Institute, North Carolina.

Bell, C.G. (1985). Multis: A New Class of Multiprocessor Computers, *Science*, Vol. 228, pp. 462-467, April.

Black, D.L. (1990). Scheduling Support for Concurrency and Parallelism in the Mach Operating System, *Computer*, Vol. 23, No. 5, pp. 35-43.

DeCegama, A.L. (1989). *The Technology of Parallel Processing: Parallel Processing and VLSI Hardware*, Vol. 1, Prentice Hall, Englewood Cliffs, NJ.

Encore (1989). *Multimax Technical Summary*, Encore Computer Corp., 726-01759 Revision E, January.

Furht, B., D. Grostik, D. Gluck, G. Rabbat, J: Parker, and M. McRoberts (1991). *Real-Time Unix Systems-Design and Application Guide*, Kluwer Academic Publishers, Boston-Dordrecht-London.

INMOS (1986). Transputer Reference Manual.

INMOS (1991). The T9000 Transputer - Products Overview - Manual, SGS-Thomoson Microelectronics.

Nichols, K.M., and J.T. Edmark (1988). Modeling Multicomputer Systems with PARET, *Computer*, Vol. 21, No. 5, pp. 39-48.

Perihelion (1986). *The Helios Operating System*, Prentice Hall, Englewood Cliffs, NJ.

Rashid, R.F. (1986). Threads of a New System, *Unix Review*, Vol. 4, pp. 37-49, August.

Russell, C.H., and P.J. Waterman (1987). Variations on UNIX for Parallel-processing Computers, *Communications of the ACM*, Vol. 30, No. 12, pp. 1048-1055.

Seitz, C.L. (1985). The Cosmic Cube, *Communications of the ACM*, Vol. 28, No. 1, pp. 22.

TRANS RTXc (1991). TRANS RTXc User Manual, Intelligent Systems International, Leuven, Belgium.

Yalamanchili, S., and T. Carpenter (1989). Modelling and Analysis of Multicomputer Architectures, *American Institute of Aeronautics and Astronautics*, 89-3014-CP, pp. 344-350.

Chapter 12

DATAFLOW ARCHITECTURES

The fundamental ideas for dataflow architectures come from extending the *dataflow graphs* utilized by compilers into an internal representation of program structure. The dataflow graph is a directed graph in which the nodes are functions to be executed and the arcs represent data dependencies between functions. The fundamental notion that evolved was to develop an architecture that could execute these graphs directly, instead of generating code for classical architectures. On the other hand, we can observe that dataflow architectures are highly influenced by a particular programming language style.

12.1 FUNDAMENTAL CONCEPTS

In the original dataflow model proposed by Dennis (1974), data values involved in a computation are carried by *tokens* placed on the arcs of the graph. The nodes of the graph are *actors,* which respond to the presence of a token on their input arcs by "firing," that is, applying the actor function to the values carried by the input tokens. The results are carried by tokens placed on each output arc of the actor. These principal elements of dataflow architectures are illustrated in Figure 12.1. The calculation of the result is left as an exercise to the reader.

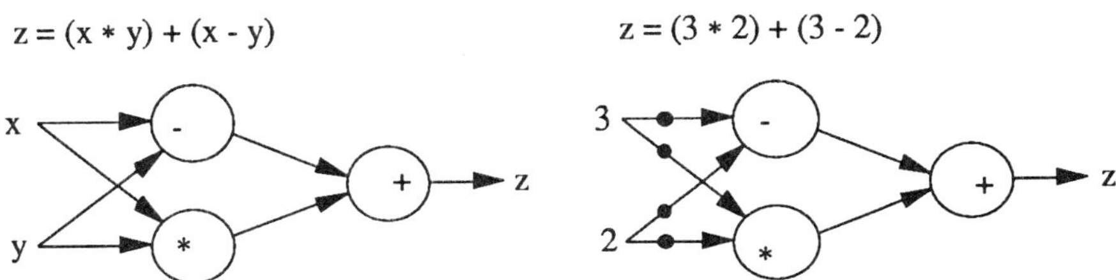

Figure 12.1. Dataflow Graph and Evaluation Initiated by Token Availability

An actor, the places for its input tokens (operands), and the result token destination are contained in an *activity template*. The activity templates corresponding to our previous example are portrayed in Figure 12.2.

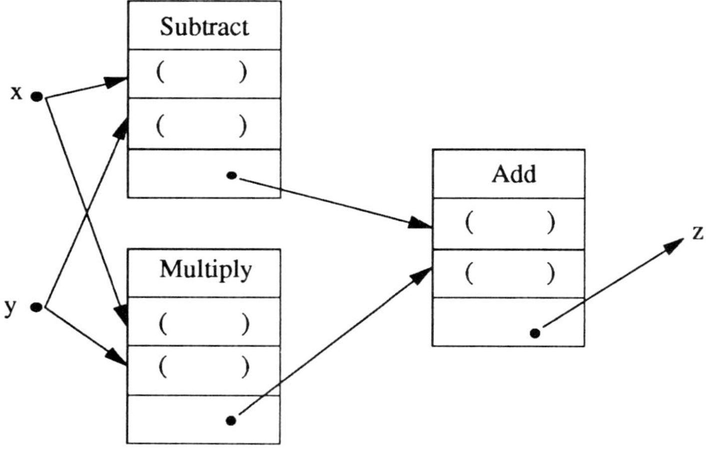

Figure 12.2. Activity Templates and Their Token (Operand) Dependence

Naturally, tokens require storage space. In general, the dataflow model makes no limitations upon the token storage queues built at the arcs for data ready to be processed or on the behavior within the nodes. However, an arbitrarily long FIFO queuing mechanism is, in practice, impossible to implement.

While a variety of specific dataflow architectures has been proposed, we can identify the essential ingredients by examining Figure 12.3.

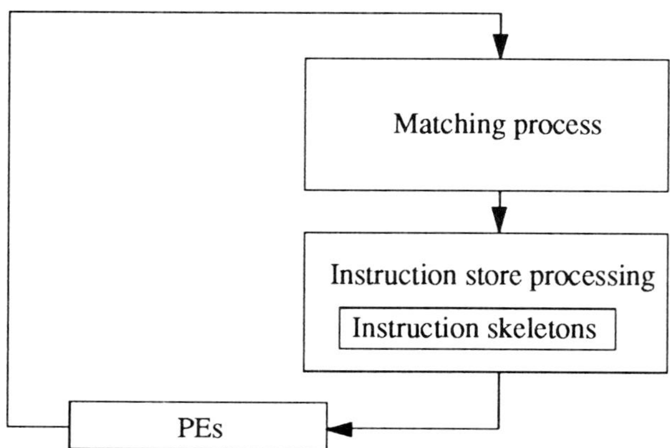

Figure 12.3. Dataflow Architecture Example

A number of PEs act as instruction execution agents for templates organized in the circular pipeline manner implied by the figure. Completed templates (packages) that are executable circulate in this ring, with computed values being returned to the matching unit, where tokens are delivered causing other template skeletons to be fired.

It is possible to radically increase the level of concurrency by coupling several of the basic dataflow processors (each being a PE) together via an ICN. The generic architecture for this more advanced dataflow architecture has the same structure as all other parallel processors (see Figure 3.2), that is, a number of PEs (where some are M processes) connected together via an ICN. However, memory processes in this case contain data and the activity template skeletons to be processed with corresponding data arguments.

An important property of the ICN variants is that delays (even large) do not affect the performance as long as enough enabled activity templates are available in each PE. Thus, program parallelism is used to compensate for communication delays.

12.2 STATIC VERSUS DYNAMIC DATAFLOW MODELS

Two basic approaches to placing practical limitations on the general dataflow model have been explored. First, the *static dataflow* model provides a fixed amount of token storage per arc. Second are dataflow models providing for more general behavior, such as the *dynamic tagged token* model introduced by Arvind, Gostelow, and Plouffe (1978), which provides dynamic storage allocation for tokens from a common pool. In this case, tokens must carry tags to indicate their logical position within arcs. A further implementation of dynamic dataflow machine has been made by Yuba and others (1984).

In the dataflow models (static and dynamic) there is no notion of sequential control flow. Many actors (templates) of the dataflow graph may be ready to fire at the same time. Based upon the algorithm, this opens the door to the possibility of large-scale parallelism, with hundreds or even thousands of PEs concurrently processing various parts of a graph.

As mentioned, a variety of mechanisms have been proposed for the detailed semantics of this form of processing, including the use of associative memory elements for token matching in order to provide parallel searching for all tokens affected by a newly computed result. The reader is referred to the one of the survey articles on this subject by Treleavan, Brownbridge, and Hopkins (1982), Arvind and Culler (1986), or Veen (1986) for further details.

12.3 PROGRAMMING OF DATAFLOW MACHINES

In principle, languages developed for dataflow are highly related to functional programming. Some special requirements have been identified by Ackerman (1982).

— **side-effect free**: the language is functional and, once the values of all the inputs are available to an expression or function, the execution cannot influence the results of any other operations that are ready to execute.

— **locality of effects**: the scope of a variable is to be restricted to ensure that operations do not have far-reaching data dependencies.

— **single assignment rule**: a variable may appear on the left-hand side of an assignment only once within its scope, and the same variable cannot appear on both sides of the assignment statement (for example, we cannot write X := X + 1). Via this restriction, assignments are transformed to mathematical equalities.

— **construct for parallel repetition**: a loop-free repetition statement for calculations that do not depend upon each other and thus can be calculated in parallel.

A number of dataflow languages have been proposed, including Lucid (see Wadge and Aschcroft, 1977). Lucid can be translated conveniently into dataflow architectures; however, it has been implemented on other more conventional computers. It leads to a pipeline style of thinking in organizing processing behaviors. Another language that has been used for research projects at the Massachusetts Institute of Technology is VAL (see Ackerman and Dennis, 1979). In the following sections, we will examine a small example that is written in VAL (**Va**lue-Oriented **L**anguage).

12.4 STATIC DATAFLOW MODEL

We now consider the properties of one interesting, alternative dataflow model, a static dataflow model that leads to a pipelines of tokens being executed. This static dataflow model has been described by Dennis (1987).

Each dataflow instruction is signaled by the completion of specific predecessor instructions and is activated when the right number of signals has been received. The signals provide an indication that data on which the instruction will operate are available at specific (statically assigned) memory locations. At any point in time there can be at most one instance of execution of a particular instruction.

Each PE has storage for the dataflow instructions, data memory for values, functional units for basic scalar operations, and a mechanism for controlling the activation of instructions. The principle structure of the PE is illustrated in Figure 12.4a.

The PE holds a collection of dataflow instructions, some of which are marked as ready for execution. Instructions selected for execution are inserted into an *execution pipeline* by "fire" signals. The execution pipeline is similar to the pipelining used in some conventional CPUs and contains stages for address calculation, operand fetch, operator applications, and storage of results. Upon completion of execution, an instruction generates a "done" signal that gives notice to successor instructions, possibly marking some of them as ready for execution.

In Figure 12.4b, we observe the three parts of the basic structure of instructions: the *execution part* providing the operation to be performed, the data to be utilized, and the disposition of the result. The *signaling part* enumerates successor instructions and specifies which of these are to be signaled upon completion of instruction execution; the *enable part* identifies how many signals must be received before the instruction is ready to fire. The C field specifies the number of signals yet to be received before the instruction can be fired (it is decreased by one for each signal), and the R field is used in resetting the C field when the instruction is executed.

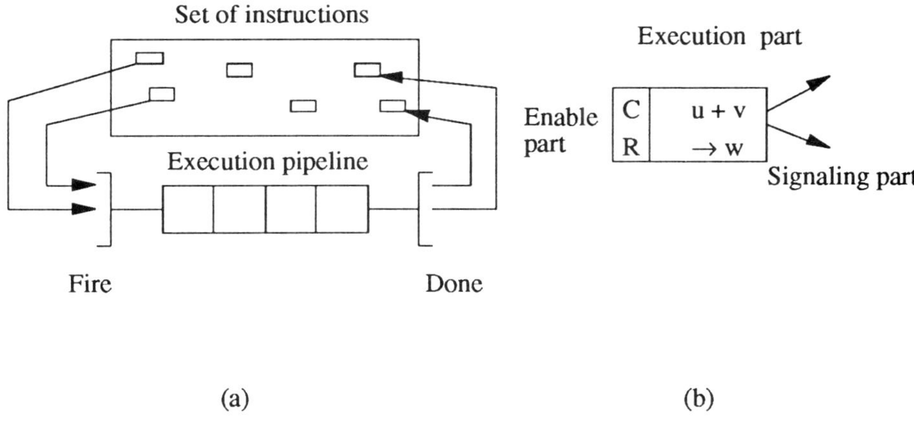

Figure 12.4. Dataflow Instruction Execution

From this description, it is easy to see that the dataflow PE is able to achieve sustained operation at nearly full performance. Scalar parallelism within the application task is sufficient to keep the execution pipeline full with productive work. *No general-purpose architecture has been able to achieve this goal. Note*: This is due to the implicit graph structure of processing including all acyclic properties. Thus, the pipeline of instructions to be executed is quite long. In conventional CPU pipelines, pipelines must be emptied and restarted at unconditional branch and at true conditional branch instructions. The lack of branching keeps the pipeline busy, which is an interesting property of this model. Further, since data are allocated statically, there is very little overhead in data referencing.

This model has been applied to aerodynamic simulations, a global weather model, and other scientific applications. The programming of this architectural model is via a functional or specific dataflow programming language. To illustrate a simple program, consider the following fragment written in VAL (see Ackerman and Dennis, 1979).

```
forall i in [1, n]
X :=    if i = 1 then A[i]
        elseif i = n then A[n]
        else 0.5 * (A[i-1] + A[i+1])
        endif ;
construct X
endall
```

The **forall** - **endall** statement is the primary parallel building block of VAL. In this example, for each value of *i* the body of the forall expression defines a value of X that is the ith element of the resulting array value. On the dataflow pipeline model, the computation could be performed by reading elements of A from the array memory, performing the evaluations of conditional expressions in the pipeline, and storing the elements of the constructed array in the array memory.

12.5 REAL-TIME DATAFLOW ARCHITECTURES

It is interesting to note that dataflow concepts have been considered as an appropriate means of organizing real-time processing (see Barkhodarian (1987), Lent and Kurmann (1989), Takesue (1990) and Ojstersek and Zumer (1990)). In the static dataflow variant, this seems to be a reasonable and interesting approach.

Ojstersek and Zumer propose a general model for real-time processing that can effectively treat periodic processes by decomposing them into concurrent "grains" that enjoy the parallelism attainable by dataflow architectures. They have added special nodes for interfacing to the external environment, as well as a synchronization node. The synchronization node acts much like a barrier and provides a clean point at which outputs can be simultaneously delivered to the external controlled object, as well as to define clean starting points for the input of signals. The model they have proposed is portrayed in Figure 12.5.

A Data Flow Control Language (DFCL) has been developed for the programming of periodic tasks. To make the resultant execution completely deterministic, only one periodic process is described and implemented. A parallelism profile can be easily determined based upon the longest path length and the total number of atomic operations performed. From this information, the number of PEs required to achieve a particular performance level can be determined. A Gant chart can be used to observe how grains are scheduled to the PEs.

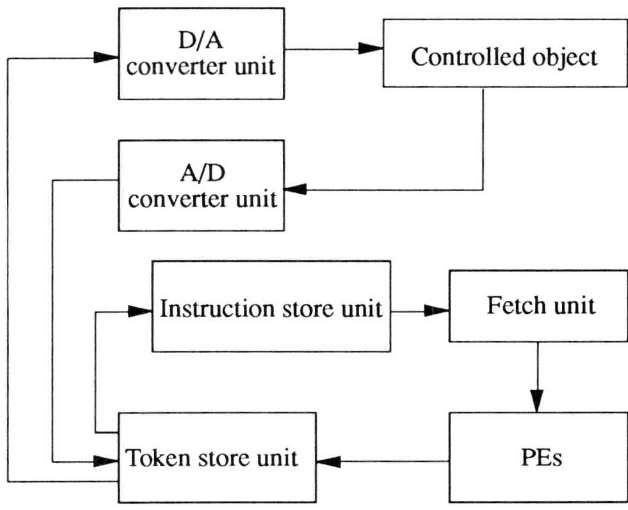

Figure 12.5. Model of the Dataflow Real-time Architecture

Lent and Kurmann (1989) have experimented with dataflow concepts in the implementation of a grinding machine controller. Unique in their approach is the separation of data tokens and control tokens. Control tokens carry time stamps that control the time at which firing will occur. Further, unlike the conventional dataflow model firings, where all inputs must be available (AND condition), their model provides for firing when subsets of inputs are available (OR condition). This approach has, in fact, also been proposed for general-purpose dataflow machines (see Wu, 1990).

Takesue (1990) introduces a priority and maximum execution depth-based solution in another dataflow variant aimed at real-time systems. The approach, unlike those of the others, deals with the question of random (aperiodic) processing requirements.

12.6 IN SUMMARY

In summary, we can observe that dataflow architectures are based upon some interesting observations concerning program structure and processing requirements. They provide a useful means of obtaining high utilization of PE resources. On the other hand, they require a particular view of behavioral description. The ideas, thus far, have not resulted in any major change in thinking in the commercial computer field; however, they may find a range of important applications in the future.

References

Ackerman, W.B. (1982). Data Flow Languages, *Computer*, Vol. 12, No. 2, pp. 15-25.

Ackerman, W.B., and J.B. Dennis (1979). *VAL - A Value-oriented Algorithmic Language: Preliminary Reference Manual*, Report MIT/LCS/TR-218, Laboratory for Computer Science, 545 Technology Square, Cambridge, MA.

Arvind, and D.E. Culler (1986). Dataflow Architectures, *Annual Reviews in Computer Science*, Palo Alto, CA., Vol. 1, pp. 225-253.

Arvind; K. Gostelow, and W. Plouffe (1978). *The Preliminary Id Report: An Asynchronous Programming Language and Computing Machine*, Technical Report 114, Department of Computer and Information Science, University of California, Irvine.

Barkhodarian, S. (1987). RAMPS: A Real-time Structured Small Scale Data Flow System for Parallel Processing, *Proceedings of the 1987 International Conference on Parallel Processing*, Pennsylvania State University Press, PA.

Dennis, J.B. (1974). First Version of a Data Flow Procedure Language, in B. Robinet (ed.), *Lecture Notes in Computer Science, Vol. 19: Programming Symposium*, pp. 362-376, Springer-Verlag, New York.

Dennis, J.B. (1987). Dataflow Computation: A Case Study, in V. Milutinovic (ed.), *Computer Architecture: Concepts and Systems*, Elsevier, New York.

Lent, B., and H. Kurmann (1989). The OR Dataflow Architecture for a Machine Embedded Control System, *International Journal of Real-time Systems*, Vol. 1, pp. 107-132.

Ojstersek, M., and V. Zumer (1990). Automatic Grain Size Determination for a Macro Dataflow Real-time System, *Proceedings of the EUROMICRO Workshop on Real Time*, IEEE Computer Society Press, Los Alamitos, CA.

Takesue, M. (1990). Dataflow Computer Extension toward Real-time Processing, *International Journal of Real-time Systems*, Vol. 1, pp. 333-350.

Treleavan, P.C., D.R. Brownbridge, and R.P. Hopkins (1982). Data-Driven and Demand-Driven Computer Architectures, *ACM Computing Surveys*, Vol. 14, No. 1, pp. 93-143.

Veen, A.H. (1986). Dataflow Machine Architecture, *ACM Computing Surveys*, Vol. 18, No. 4, pp. 365-396.

Wadge, W.W., and E.A. Ashcroft (1985). *Lucid, the Dataflow Programming Language*, Academic Press, New York.

Wu, H. (1990). *Extension of Data Flow Principles for Multiprocessing*, Ph.D. thesis, Royal Institute of Technology, Stockholm, TRITA-TCS-9004.

Yuba, T., T. Shimada, K. Hiraki, and K. Kashiwagi (1984). *A Dataflow Computer for Scientific Computation*, Electrotechnical Laboratory, 1-1-4 Umesono, Sakuramura, Niiharigun, Ibaraki, 305, Japan.

Part III

CASE STUDIES

Chapter 13

DIRECT-MAPPED SOLUTION IN A RADAR SYSTEM

To demonstrate the thinking and reasoning leading to the implementation of portions of a complex system in a direct-mapped manner, we present the signal processor (SP) for the Giraffe Radar System developed by Ericsson AB in Mölndal, Sweden. We begin by examining the general properties of the Giraffe Radar System and then focus upon requirements, structure, mapping, and an example of one functional implementation.

13.1 RADAR SIGNAL PROCESSING

To detect targets, a ground-based search radar transmits radio-frequency pulses to illuminate any target, at any distance, in the direction the antenna points. Distance to a target is measured by the time it takes for the pulse to travel to the target and return (by speed of light). See Figure 13.1.

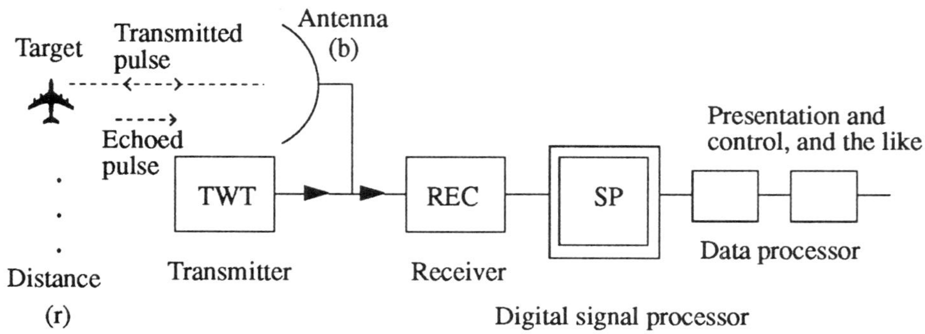

Figure 13.1. Radar System

As the antenna scans the search volume, a possible target on a bearing **b** at a distance **r** is hit by a number of pulses. The pulses are reflected (echoed) back, amplified, and frequency converted in the receiver. After A/D conversion, they are processed in the signal processor (SP).

Based upon the reflected signal, the SP attempts to extract that target echo among all other signals that is also echoed back or intentionally transmitted to the radar. In a Doppler radar, the Doppler velocity of the echoed signal is the key to sorting unwanted echoes (called clutter) from the targets. The signal is enhanced by matched integration of all received signals reflected from the target. For a general background description of radar systems, the reader is referred to Barton (1988) and Skolnik (1970).

The Ericsson Giraffe is a pulse Doppler radar system with pulse compression. It is of *full coherent type* with a receiver comprising frequency conversion down to zero intermediate frequency. In the last mixer stage, two versions of the same frequency signal, with orthogonal phase, are generated. These signals, called the **i**nphase (I) and the **q**uadrature (Q) video, are the inputs to the SP (see Figure 13.2). The SP produces distance and bearing measurements to the detected targets as its output.

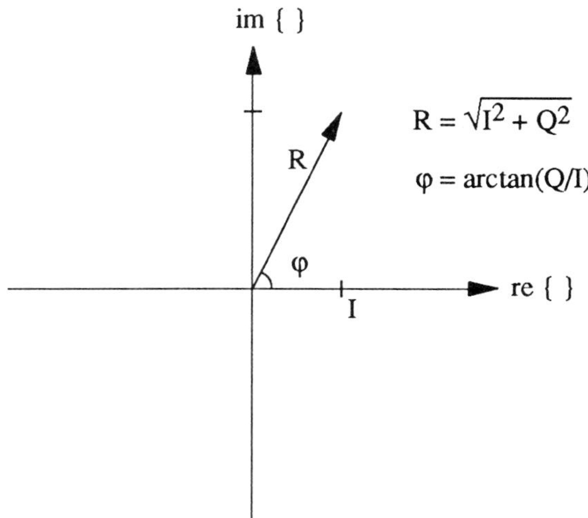

Figure 13.2. Distance and Bearing Measurements

13.1.1 The IQ-Plane

The I and Q video signals can be viewed as composants to a signal vector in the IQ-plane. A signal coming from a stable stationary target yields signal vectors with constant amplitude and phase for a number of pulses received during the antenna illumination (scanning) of a target. When the signal vector comes from a moving target, the signal vector rotates from pulse to pulse (that is, the signal vector changes from pulse to pulse).

The Signal Processor's Task

At every range, there may be a target to reveal. This is achieved by sampling the I and Q vectors for every single range resolution cell by processing this sample (called *range bins*) together with a number of previously sampled vectors from the same range.

To cover the full instrumented range of the radar, several millions of range bins per second must be processed, from which only hundreds of target detections can be expected. Thus, we may view the SP as a super sorting machine that must find needles in a hay stack.

The important task for a signal processor in a pulse Doppler radar is to suppress all constant signal vectors (that is, fix target echoes) and subsequently to reveal any moving targets.

13.2 SYSTEM REQUIREMENTS

The main functional requirement on the Giraffe SP is to provide an instantaneous optimized detection function with respect to aircraft targets. Detections are to be made in the surveilled (scanned) areas under varying conditions (rain, fair weather, ground clutter, man-made clutter, and so on). Further, the SP must be able to simultaneously detect hovering helicopters at shorter ranges. Since the Giraffe employs coding on the transmitted pulses, the SP must decode the received signal (called pulse compression).

These and other functional requirements lead to a functional block diagram, which is portrayed in Figure 13.3. First, every input target signal vector is converted to digital representation in the ADC (**A**nalogue to **D**igital **C**onversion) block and then parallel processed for:

- — clutter suppression to reveal moving targets (MTI CHANNEL)
- — hovering helicopter signal matching or signal matching without clutter removal (HLC/NMTI CHANNEL)

These two parallel operations are then merged for detection and sorting of targets in the THRESHOLD DETECTION block. Where HLC processing is required, only the MTI CHANNEL is utilized for air target detection. For longer ranges, where the NMTI CHANNEL is available, it is utilized for air target detection in clutter-free areas since it has a slightly higher sensitivity than the MTI CHANNEL. These functions and others permit the THRESHOLD DETECTION to produce the air and Hlc target-detection outputs.

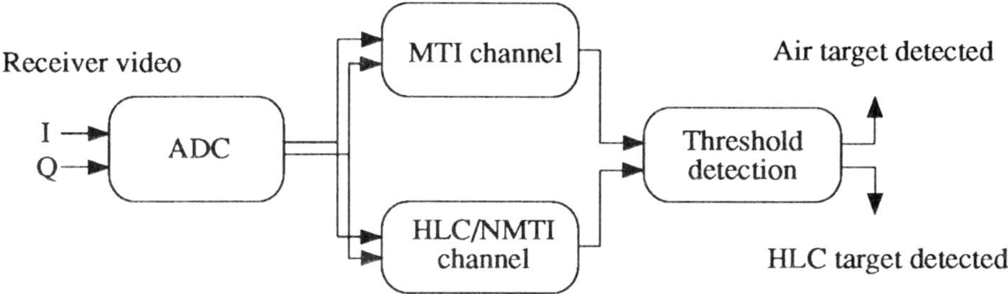

Figure 13.3. Dataflow Block Diagram for the SP

13.2.1 Performance Requirements

Due to the fact that signal processing must be performed for every range bin, the Giraffe radar SP operations must be accomplished in extremely hard (that is, tight) real time. All the operations on a single signal vector (rotating, filtering, equalizing, integration, thresholding, and so on) must be done during the dwell time in the corresponding single range bin. This means that the operations must be performed in less than 0.3 μs, which is the sampling frequency for the Giraffe radar.

The performance demands are primarily for data throughput and are not as stringent with respect to delay. Thus, a pipeline delay of several tens of microseconds is quite acceptable. The data input rate to the SP is approximately 50 Mbit/s. On this input, about 450 operations for each range bin must be executed; consequently, the total volume of executed operations is about 1.5 Gop/s. This figure presumes that all nonlinear and iterative calculated functions have been accomplished via operation saving table look-up operations. At the end of the SP, the expected output of up to some hundred targets per second makes an output data rate of less than 10 kbit/s.

There are a number of other tasks for the SP to perform that, while requiring real-time processing, operate in a the millisecond time frame or longer. Some examples are as follows:

— calculations of the speed of rain clutter
— monitoring and control of receiver gain
— changing mode of operation
— built-in self-test and supervision of execution

Further, a number of functions can be demanded from an operator. For example, the initiation of a thorough test procedure to pinpoint a faulty circuit board.

13.2.2 Dependability Requirements

The SP has been designed to meet both testability and maintainability requirements. Testability means that SP must be able to detect and localize hardware errors. Maintainability means that it will meet MTBF (**M**ean **T**ime **B**efore **F**ailure) and MTTR (**M**ean **T**ime **T**o **R**epair) specifications.

13.2.3 Algorithm Requirements

The DSP algorithms that must be applied by the SP have inherent limitations in terms of the order of processes and processing resource consumption. The algorithms to be performed on the signal flow are of four basic types: vectorial or scalar, linear or nonlinear are as follows.

Vector Rotation

Vector rotation is a vectorial *linear* operation. A new signal vector (I', Q') is calculated from the old signal vector (I, Q), rotated by an angle α:

$$I' = I \cos \alpha - Q \sin \alpha$$
$$Q' = Q \cos \alpha + I \sin \alpha$$

In general, α and then $\sin \alpha$ and $\cos \alpha$ are known in advance for a large number of single vectors; consequently, only four multiplications and two additions must be performed.

Coherent Limitation

Coherent limitation is a *nonlinear* operation. The signal vectors are compared with a circle in the IQ-plane. Signal vectors (I, Q) with amplitude larger than L must be shortened to amplitude L. No phase shift will be done.

if $I^2 + Q^2 > L^2$
then $I' = L \cos(\arctan(Q/I))$
$Q' = L \sin(\arctan(Q/I))$
else $I' = I$
$Q' = Q$

This type of algorithm is most conveniently solved via table look-up.

Recursive Integration

Recursive integration (same as IIR-filtering) is a scalar linear operation (see Oppenheim and Schaffer, 1975, Rabiner and Gold, 1975 or Peled and Liu, 1976). The algorithm calculates a new output value $Y[n, r]$ as a sum of a fraction of the previous output value $Y[n - 1, r]$ and another fraction of the input value $X[n, r]$.

$$Y[n, r] = 1/k \bullet Y[n - 1, r] \quad + \quad (k - 1)/k \bullet X[n, r]$$

The fraction $1/k$ is subject to change between different operation modes. n is the current pulse and $n - 1$, the previous pulse.

Thresholding

Thresholding is a scalar and nonlinear operation. The signal echos are compared with a threshold value.

if	(Video [r, b,...] > Threshold)
then	AirTarget [r, b] := 1
else	AirTarget [r, b] := 0

13.3 MAPPING THE SYSTEM REQUIREMENTS TO RESOURCES

In relationship to the BMR model, we can observe that the mapping of functional performance and other requirements requires several iterations. The first mapping goal is to balance the functional and performance requirements in relationship to the choice of algorithms in the time and space domain. A logical order of functions (processes) is established via this first mapping, which can be directly mapped (allocated) to subfunctions that are implemented in the resource structure. The mapping to an appropriate resource structure is accomplished via the static allocation of processes (operations). In iterating through the BMR model in search of a solution, the mappings result in two forms of parallelism:

— several levels of parallelism with respect to channels
— several levels of pipelining with respect to functions

13.3.1 Algorithm Mapping

The mapping of algorithms is highly dependent upon how the algorithm is to be implemented. Linear operations may be performed in any order. For example AB + AC may be computed by factoring A to A(B + C) without any effect on the result (assuming that precision is properly treated). However, to improve performance, nonlinear algorithms have been applied in several cases. This early choice of algorithm implementation reduces the degrees of freedom in SP mapping. Where nonlinear algorithms have been selected to reduce operations, there are only a few possible algorithm sequences remaining. Figure 13.4 shows the resulting structure for the MTI channel.

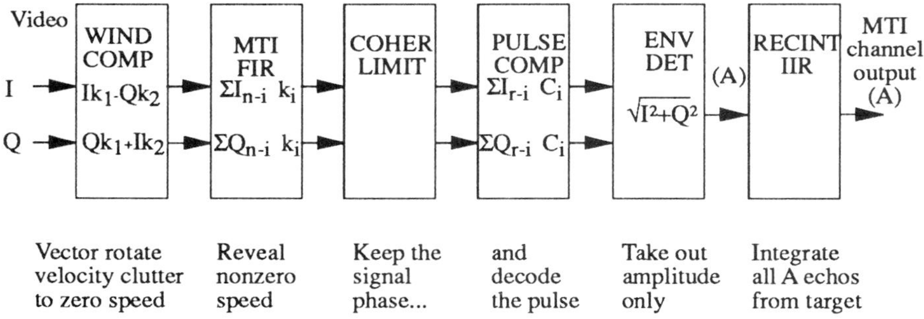

Figure 13.4. MTI Channel Algorithm Sequence

The COHERent LIMITation is a nonlinear operation that decreases the data word length and equalizes the signal amplitudes. Since this operation is exploited, the order of the PULSE COMPression operation (that is, the decoding of a transmitted pulse) and the MTI filtering cannot be exchanged. One consequence of this immobility of operations is that the PULSE COMPression must be done in both MTI- and HLC/NMTI-Channels (they cannot be factored out). On the other hand, by applying COHERent LIMITation in both instances, performance is improved.

13.3.2 Real-time Hierarchy

The control of and the operations of the SP are divided into the time hierarchies portrayed in Figure 13.5. The upper two timing levels are coupled to the antenna rotation speed, while the lower two levels are coupled to the sampling frequency. To synchronize between these two levels, higher-level processes are required to wait for the completion of lower-level operations. However, under certain circumstances, the lower-level operations are aborted and restarted at the initiation of a higher-level operation.

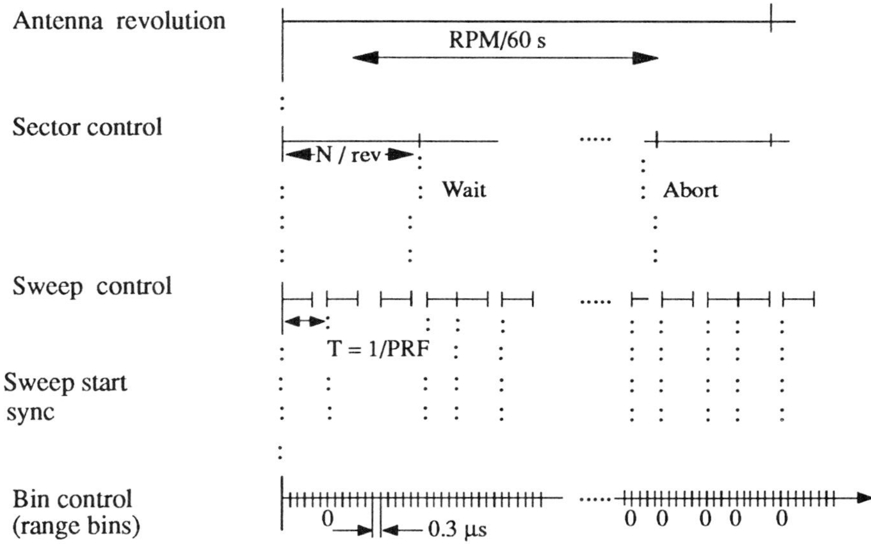

Figure 13.5. Real-time Hierarchy of the SP

13.3.3 Pipelining and Parallelism

Pipelining is exploited in the function structure (operation execution) as well as within the hardware resource structure. Where operations at the lowest level of the real-time hierarchy could not be conveniently divided for pipelining, parallelism is introduced in order to meet performance requirements. A specific example of parallelism (and pipelining) will be introduced later in this case study.

13.3.4 Granularity

The granularities that can be conveniently dealt with are highly related to the available resource structure building blocks. The SP is mapped onto PCPs (printed circuit boards) with standard TTL integrated circuits. This leads to available PE and C granularities of 4, 8, 16, ... bit word lengths.

Memories are local to each function and designed for the worst-case size requirements on a per function basis. Dependent upon the IC utilized, data-referencing granularity of 2K x 8 bits or 4K x 4 bits, or others, is exploited.

Most functions require one or more PCBs for their implementation. Inter-PCB communication is limited by the maximum PCB I/O connectors, permitting approximately 150 signals. Since this communication facility is completely customized, the signals are utilized for fine-grain granularity on a bit-wise basis.

13.3.5 Program Implementation

Programmed control is utilized for some sweep control, sector control, and antenna control processing, as portrayed in Figure 13.5. The majority of the functions are distributed to individual programmed PEs which are embedded into the hardware resource structure.

Control at the range bin level is always performed by direct-mapped hardware resources utilizing both centralized and decentralized state machine programs (microprograms). The centralized control must be synchronized with the data path pipelining delays.

13.3.6 PCS Views

The implementation of the SP within the framework of a hardware resource structure is guided by the point of view of the Process, Communication, and Synchronization fundamental issues. Processes are equated to static DSP-oriented operations. Communication among processes is, as described previously, fully customized in relationship to the data structure. However, the data transmit protocol is accomplished in a systolic manner with data exchange in every range bin. The data range bin number is implicit by data order. Synchronization is accomplished by a start sweep sync that indicates the zero range bin (see Figure 13.5).

The PCS views we have indicated apply to the radar video data. For the control of processes and built-in test, a separate view exists. Communication in these cases takes place via buses. However, most of the synchronization is accomplished via the sweep start sync signal.

13.4 A FIR FILTER EXAMPLE

To examine a concrete use of pipelining and parallelism, we shall examine one-half of the Moving Target Indicator FIR filter processor, which is portrayed in Figure 13.6.

To meet the demanding real-time processing requirements of the MTI filter function (as portrayed in the MTI CHANNEL, see Figure 13.4), four PE and M hardware processes are interleaved, as shown in Figure 13.6. Two such FIR filter processors are used in the MTI channel, one for the I-video and the other for the Q-video.

The MULT&ACC component can only perform two operations per input data item. Since eight-tap FIR filtering is required, it can operate only on every fourth data input. However, via this hardware structure of four PE and M pairs, the filter can process all inputs and produce outputs at the systolic range bin rate.

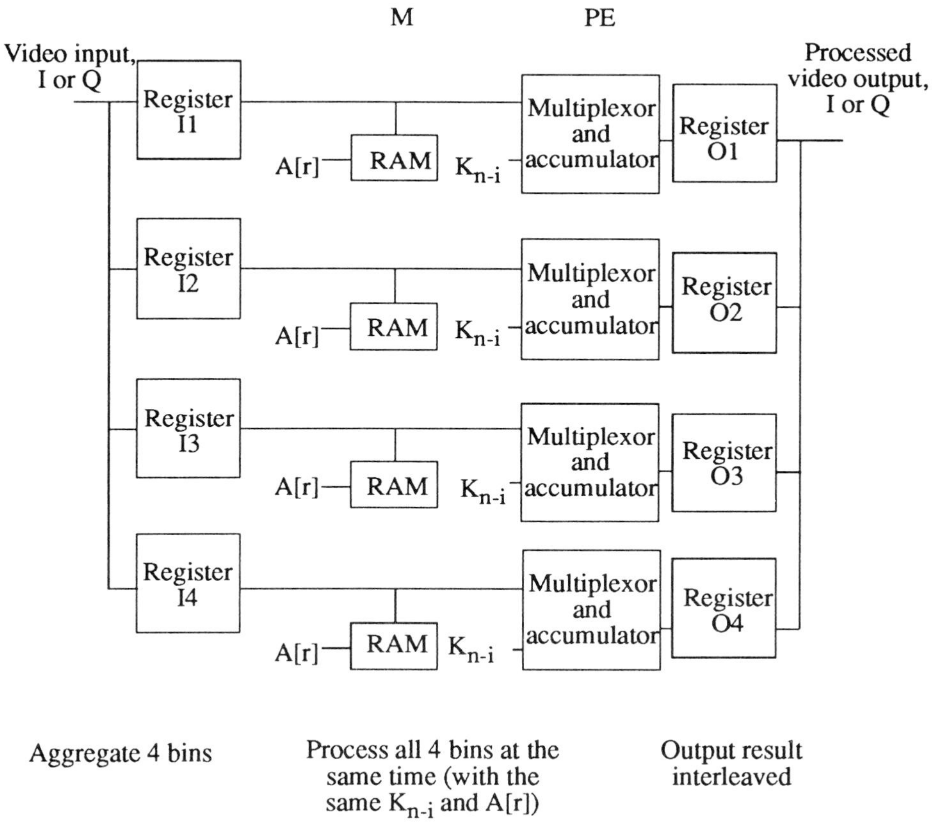

Figure 13.6. Block Diagram for FIR Filter Processor

Input REGisters serve as time synchronizers in order to permit the four PE and the RAM-based M components to use common control data: A[r] and K_{n-1}. The output REGisters resynchronize output to the input data rate of 0.3 μs.

13.5 IN SUMMARY

The SP hardware resource structure is designed for the worst case with respect to each PE, M, and C hardware process. Despite this dimensioning, the PE and C facilities are nearly always fully utilized, whereas the M facilities are not always fully exploited. These results are based upon the direct-mapped philosophy in which we can observe that there is very little difference between maximum and minimum performance in system requirements.

As a final commercial note, more than 300 Giraffe Radar Systems have been delivered to 13 different countries in various versions for mobile, coastal, and naval defense applications.

References

Barton, D.K. (1988). *Modern Radar System Analysis*, Arctech House, Inc., Norwood, MA.

Oppenheim, A.V., and R.W. Schaffer (1975). *Digital Signal Processing*, Prentice Hall, Englewood Cliffs, NJ.

Peled, A., and B. Liu (1976). *Digital Signal Processing: Theory, Design and Implementation*, Wiley, New York.

Rabiner, L.R., and B. Gold (1975). *Theory and Application of Digital Signal Processing*, Prentice Hall, Englewood Cliffs, NJ.

Skolnik, M.I. (1970). *Radar Handbook*, McGraw-Hill, New York.

Chapter **14**

SINGLE-CHIP LINEAR ARRAY PICTURE PROCESSOR

LAPP 1100, developed by Integrated Vision Products AB of Linköping, Sweden, is an example of a small-scale, special-purpose processor array of the SIMD type. The same chip contains both a linear photodiode camera and a parallel image processor. The system concept is thereby called the Linear Array Picture Processor (LAPP).

In this chapter we describe the LAPP 1100 system in some detail and provide an example of its use in an industrial application, the inspection of a motor block subassembly in automobile production, where the LAPP camera is mounted on a moving robot arm. The linear array nature of the photodiode sensor demands either that the object or the camera be moved in a direction orthogonal to the array.

14.1 LAPP 1100 SYSTEM DESCRIPTION

The architecture of LAPP 1100 is depicted in Figure 14.1. The degree of parallelism of the array is 128. Via threshold circuitry, the Photodiode Array supplies the image information to an internal 128-bit-wide bus. Fourteen registers (R0 to R13) may be used for the storage of image lines or intermediate results. Three computational units, GLU, NLU, and PLU, perform image operations where results are placed in the 128-bit-wide Accumulator register. The contents of the Accumulator may be stored in one of the registers or used as a second operand in two-operand instructions.

Communication into and out from the chip is performed via a 16-bit I/O bus. The contents of the Accumulator may be altered by input or written as output over the bus in eight consecutive 16-bit parts. Alternatively, quantitative status information may be output, for example, the number of 1's in the Accumulator, which is useful when measuring the perimeter or area of an object. The I/O bus is also the path over which array instructions are transmitted.

Using LAPP 1100 typically implies working with binary images, although gray-scale information from the Photodiode Array may be obtained as well. However, the instruction set has been primarily designed for processing binary images.

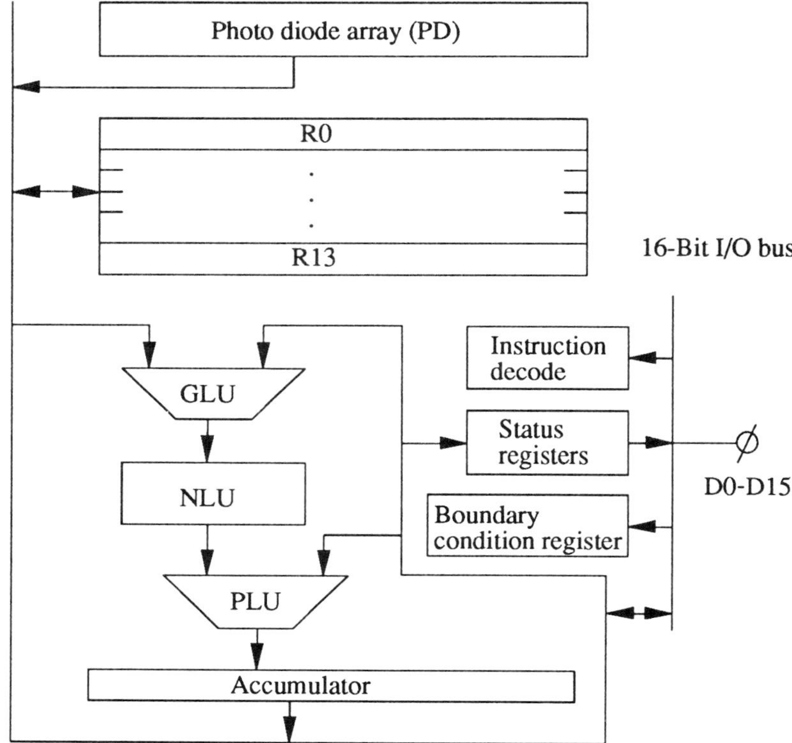

Figure 14.1. LAPP 1100 Architecture

14.2 LAPP 1100 INSTRUCTIONS

As mentioned previously, the processing capabilities of LAPP 1100 are spread over three computational units: the **G**lobal **L**ogical **U**nit, GLU, the **N**eighborhood **L**ogical **U**nit, NLU, and the **P**oint **L**ogical **U**nit, PLU. The motivations for and characteristics of these units are best described by an example.

Imagine an image-processing task where interest is to be focused on the leftmost object of the image. In such a task there is a need to *extract the leftmost object* in a line of the image, where images are input and processed line by line. The task may be performed in three steps, as shown in Figure 14.2.

Figure 14.2. Extraction of Leftmost Object (1's are black, 0's are white)

First, the right edges of all the objects are found and marked by identifying the two-point neighborhood (1 0). This is an example of a neighborhood operation, performed by the NLU. The NLU is also capable of matching a three-point neighborhood, using 1, 0, and X (don't care). Next, a mask that will be utilized to mask out all objects except the leftmost one is created. The mask is created by filling with 1's to the right from the leftmost 1, and then inverting the result. This is a global (GLU) operation, LFILL (fill right from leftmost object), followed by a point (PLU) operation, LDI (invert before load). Finally, a logical AND (which is a PLU operation) between the mask and the original line will provide the desired result, that is, mark the leftmost object.

From this simple example we can observe that an important characteristic of the instruction set is the ability to perform global operations (operations that require signals to propagate a long distance) efficiently. We may regard LAPP 1100 as an example of how a SIMD array may be "tuned" to a specific application area after careful study of the computational needs of that area.

The most important instructions of LAPP 1100 are summarized in Table 14.1. As can be seen from the schematic diagram in Figure 14.1, the three units GLU, NLU, and PLU are cascaded. Thus, in each instruction cycle one operation from each class can be performed in this particular order. (We have already considered one example of this processing order.)

14.2.1 PLU (Point Logical Unit)

The PLU instructions make up the simplest class of instructions. They operate positionwise on two image registers, the output of the NLU and the Accumulator (see Figure 14.1). An example of a PLU instruction is XOR, which may be used to test whether two image registers have identical contents.

Table 14.1. Instruction Set of LAPP 1100

PLU Instructions

LD	load acc with NLU input
AND	bitwise logical AND
OR	bitwise logical OR
XOR	bitwise logical XOR
LDI	invert NLU before LD
ANDI	invert NLU before AND
ORI	invert NLU before OR
XORI	invert NLU befor XOR

NLU Instructions

DOT	detect isolated 1's
HOLE	detect isolated 0's
INV	invert
LEDGE	detect left edges
REDGE	detect right edges
LSHIFT	shift left
RSHIFT	shift right

GLU Instructions

MARK	mark connected objects
LMARK	mark left border object
RMARK	mark right border object
FILL	mark holes
LFILL	fill right from leftmost object
RFILL	fill left with rightmost object

Combined Instructions

LSCAN	detect leftmost object pixel
RSCAN	detect rightmost object pixel
SHRINK	shrink objects
EXPAND	expand objects
INCA	increment acc arithmetically
DECA	decrement acc arithmetrically

Transfer Instructions

ST	transfer acc to register
STPD	transfer PD to register

Miscellaneous Instructions

INITPD	initiate photodiode array
TSTZ	set interrupt flag if acc = 0
TSTNZ	set interrupt flag if acc <> 0
SETB	define border values

14.2.2 NLU (Neighborhood Logical Unit)

Neighborhood operations are frequently used in image-processing applications. Filtering operations that suppress noise or extract lines and edges are typical examples of the use of neighborhoods. The NLU operation has only one source operand. For each position in the operand, a comparison with a three-point correlation mask is made. 0, 1, and X (don't care) are used in the mask. This yields 27 different masks. Some of these have straightforward image interpretations and are given their own mnemonics, as shown in Table 14.1. For example, the mnemonic LEDGE corresponds to the mask (01X) and is used as a left-edge detector.

14.2.3 GLU (Global Logical Unit)

The Global Logical Unit supports extraction of features of a more global nature than can be extracted directly with the neighborhood operations. For example, while the extraction of the leftmost leftedge in the image can be done using only NLU and PLU operations, the cost of a large number of consecutive operations varies from case to case. The GLU unit supports seven global instructions, all derivatives of the connectivity operation MARK. This operation takes two operands (see Figure 14.3). The upper operand (the Accumulator) is regarded as a reference image. Only those objects in the lower operand that are "connected" vertically to objects in the reference image are allowed to be part of the resulting image.

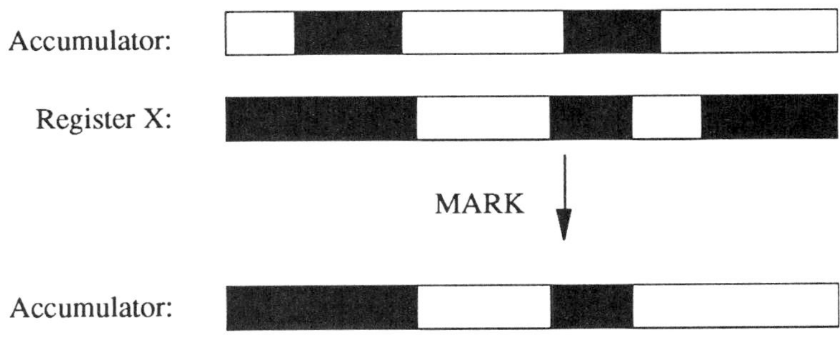

Figure 14.3. The MARK Instruction (keeps those objects in the lower operand that are connected to objects in the upper operand)

The MARK operation is useful in, for example, the process of extracting and keeping apart several objects that simultaneously show up in the image. Other GLU operations may be used to test for homogeneity of binary objects, fill holes in objects, find the first occurrence of an edge, and so on.

14.2.4 Combined, Transfer, and Miscellaneous Instructions

The three types of instructions may be combined in any possible way. Table 14.1 lists a few combinations that are often used and therefore have been given their own mnemonics. The transfer instructions and miscellaneous other instructions, all self-explanatory, complete the instruction set.

14.3 A SMALL EXAMPLE

As a demonstration of the instruction set, we provide a program that will detect small "holes," that is, small clusters of 0's surrounded by 1's. One useful application is the checking of PCBs (printed circuit boards).

Algorithm description: Each pixel along the border of a circle is tested (see Figure 14.4). If all tested pixels are object pixels and the center pixel is background (0), then a small hole has been detected and the center pixel is set to 1; otherwise, it is set to 0. The algorithm is implemented using the code displayed on the following page.

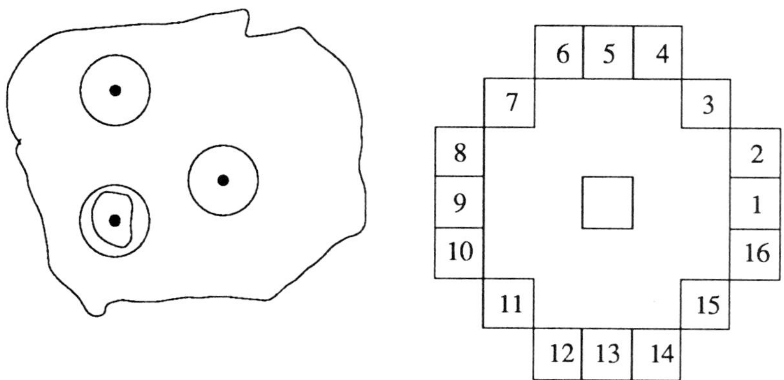

Figure 14.4. Small Hole Detector

14.4 AN INDUSTRIAL APPLICATION

A typical application of the LAPP camera has been developed at Volvo Corporation in Skövde, Sweden, by Carl Johan Bergsten. In the fabrication of motor blocks, a LAPP system is used for inspection of silicon strings used for tightening. The camera is mounted on a moving robot arm, that is, this is an example of a mobile, special-purpose parallel processor working in an industrial real-time system.

```
          **                        ; get lines 0-6 to registers R0-R6
hole:     INITPD                    ; initiate diode array
          LD (111) R0               ; test 4, 5, 6
          AND (111) R6              ; test 12, 13, 14
          ST R0                     ; store intermediate result
          LD RSHIFT R1              ; test 7, 11
          AND RSHIFT R5             ;
          LD RSHIFT A               ; shift into place
          AND R0                    ; combine results
          ST R0                     ; store intermediate results
          LD LSHIFT R1              ; test 3, 15
          AND LSHIFT R5             ;
          LD LSHIFT A               ; shift into place
          AND R0                    ; combine results
          ST R0                     ; store intermediate result
          LD RSHIFT R2              ; test 8, 9, 10
          AND RSHIFT R3             ;
          AND RSHIFT R4             ;
          LD RSHIFT A               ; shift into place
          LD RSHIFT A               ;
          AND R0                    ; combine results
          ST R0                     ; store intermediate result
          LD LSHIFT R2              ; test 2, 1, 16
          AND LSHIFT R3             ;
          AND LSHIFT R4             ;
          LD LSHIFT A               ; shift into place
          LD LSHIFT A               ;
          AND R0                    ; combine results
          ANDI R3                   ; combine with center pixel
          **                        ; other operations
          **                        ; move contents of R1-R6 to R0-R5
          STPD R6                   ; get next line
          jmp hole
```

Silicone strings are used for tightening between different parts of the cylinder. The strings are applied by a moving robot arm. The task for the visual inspection system is to check, shortly after the application of the silicone, that the string is of constant width, has the right position, and has no interrupts. The solution (see Figure 14.5) uses a LAPP camera mounted on the same robot arm, scanning the whole string by cross-sectional lines.

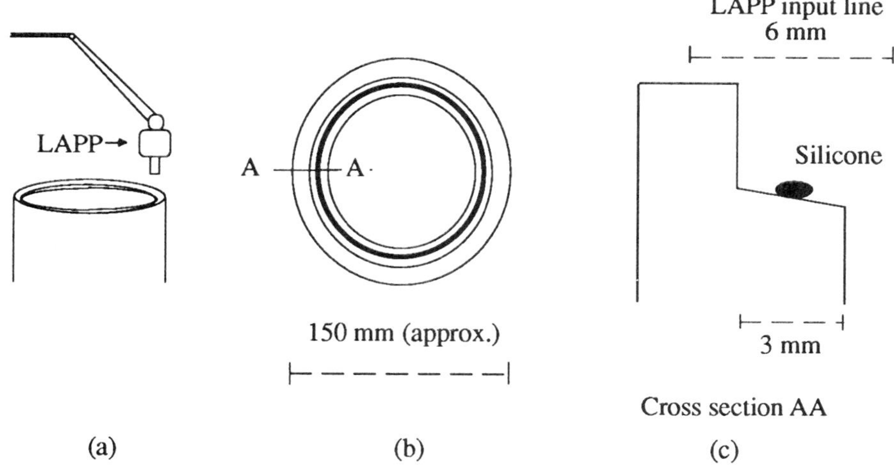

Figure 14.5. Inspection of Silicone Strings on Motor Blocks: (a) principal view of the application; (b) top view of the cylinder, with the silicone string applied; (c) cross section, also showing the position of the input line to the camera

The resulting light intensity over one input line (after filtering to remove noise) is shown in Figure 14.6. The system allows the threshold to be chosen adaptively in real time. Thus, different illumination situations are managed, making the setup insensitive to variations in the lighting of the environment.

Approximately 1000 exposures are taken on one revolution. The totality of exposures make up an image, as shown in Figure 14.7. However, such an image is never actually created in the computer; instead, the width and positioning of the string are determined on the fly, one line at a time, by also taking into consideration the appearance of neighboring lines.

The camera moves around the perimeter with a speed of 124 mm/s. Thus, the entire perimeter is scanned in about 3 seconds. This time is actually determined by the maximum speed of the robot arm. In later implementations, a rotating disc will replace the moving robot arm of the prototype arrangement, resulting in a tenfold speed enhancement. The parallel processing facility, tightly coupled with the image sensor, will still provide sufficient speed.

Thus, the sensor-processor combination of LAPP 1100 is capable of performing simple measuring or inspection tasks at very high speed and, perhaps the most important feature in industrial environments, it adapts itself to different lighting conditions in real time.

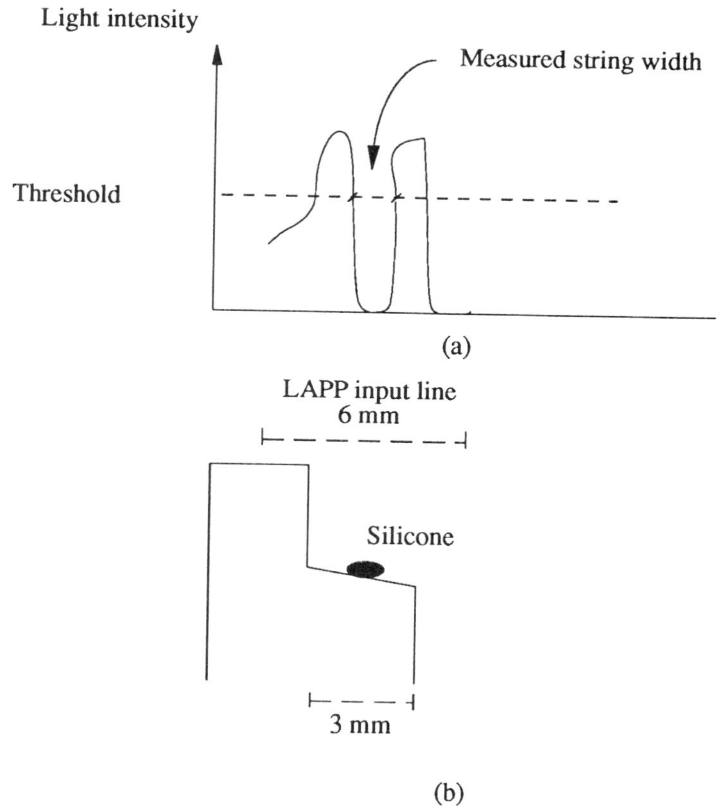

Figure 14.6. Light Intensity in LAPP Input Line (after filtering to remove noise)

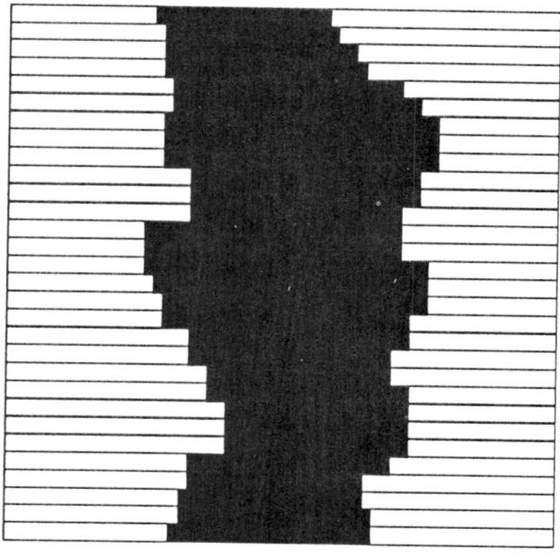

Figure 14.7. Sequence of Input Lines (after filtering)

In summary, the LAPP camera provides a useful tool for many low-level image-recognition tasks. It has been described by Forchhiemer and Ödmark (1983).

References

Forchhiemer, R., and A. Ödmark (1983). A Single Chip Linear Array Picture Processor, *Proceedings of the 3rd Scandinavian Conference on Image Analysis*, Copenhagen, July, pp. 320-325.

Chapter 15

AN MIMD AVIONICS SYSTEM

In this chapter we consider the design and implementation of an MIMD system designed for military aircraft use in the late 1970s and early 1980s. The SDS80 computer and support system represent one of the earliest efforts to apply parallel processing in a sophisticated real-time application. SDS80 was developed by Ericsson based upon specifications and purchase orders from the Swedish Defence Materiel Administration. The system is operational and is installed in the high-technology Swedish aircraft JAS, where it is used, among other functions, for the radar and display subsystems. We shall consider the major properties of SDS80 as well as the rationale behind important design decisions. The reader should pay particular attention to the approaches used in providing a system for real-time operation, for example, how the goals of reliability and predictability have influenced various aspects of behavioral description, mapping, and the resource structure.

15.1 LEARNING FROM EXPERIENCE

Experience with the computer and electronics system of a previous military aircraft (JA37 Viggen) indicated that a large portion of the costs were due to the maintenance requirements for software. Viggen contained several different computer systems, each with its own assembly language and set of development tools. These experiences led to the following requirements for the standardized system SDS80:

- — use of a higher-level language, Pascal/D80, with real-time additions
- — a program development environment, PUS80
- — a modularly constructed computer, D80, providing microprogrammed support for Pascal/D80 as well as multiprocessor capabilities

15.2 THE PASCAL D80 LANGUAGE

The language is based on standard Pascal with additions for real-time processing. To achieve the high level of performance required, the language facilities that have been implemented are static in nature.

Parallel processes can be declared and there is support for communication between processes, including the ability to start and stop processes.

A programmed system can be divided into a number of modules, where the following structure is utilized:

Subsystem - Processor - Process - Module - Procedure and Function

The language permits separate compilation of individual program modules, which provides for flexible program development.

Special emphasis has been given to error handling. Via the language, the system can deal with both hardware and software faults. The programmer is given the opportunity to define error routines where he or she can describe how the program will behave for each type of error.

The language provides the possibility to address variables with physical addresses, which is necessary in a system where input/output units are coupled to specific memory addresses. Further, efficient bit field manipulation is supported in the language.

Pascal/D80 also provides for *in-line code,* where portions of the program can be written in assembly language in order to provide accelerated performance when absolutely required.

In general, we observe that a decision was made to provide a highly predictable environment supported by language and compiler facilities that lifted the level of programming abstraction.

15.3 PROGRAM DEVELOPMENT ENVIRONMENT PUS80

Realizing that effective programming is not solely achieved via a higher-level programming language, an appropriate programming development environment was provided.

PUS80 is composed of hardware and a number of help programs. The hardware consists of a host computer and a communication computer connected to the target computer. A VAX computer serves as the host. Loading and debugging of programs from the host are accomplished via the communication computer. However, loading and absolute debugging **can** be performed solely within the framework of the communication computer (without the VAX host).

The development environment provides strict control over the systems that are developed. The methods for program development have been standardized and emphasis has been placed upon the importance of uniform and good documentation of all programs.

Program development in SDS80 takes place in steps. Programs are developed and tested first as a sequential program within the framework of an emulator on the host computer. When no formal errors can be found, the program is tested in the target computer. When testing reveals no errors, the program is integrated into its partial system structure and the entire system is tested. The partitioning of testing simplifies the isolation of errors, which are found much earlier in the development cycle than if testing only occurred at the system level.

15.4 THE D80 COMPUTER SYSTEM

The computer has been developed for the use of higher-level languages. It is a 32-bit stack machine with instructions that support the language structure. Since the application area is real-time systems, emphasis has been placed upon high performance. To meet requirements for efficient higher-level language operation, high-level instructions are executed directly by microprograms.

The computer is modularly constructed and can be coupled together to cover a range of less sophisticated up to advanced system requirements. Computing power is adjusted to the application requirements by coupling sufficient numbers of processors into the system (that is, toward resource adequacy). Synchronization between the processes is based on semaphores, which are handled by the use of high-level instructions such as "claim-semaphore" and "release-semaphore."

To accommodate parallel processes, the CPU contains three memories: an operand stack memory, local data memory, and process administration memory. This structure makes it possible to switch between different contexts rapidly. For example, a procedure call takes 3.75 μs and a return takes 1 μs. A process switch including semaphore handling takes 3 to 8 μs.

A number of standard functions are incorporated in D80 as building blocks. Through connecting these standard functions to an internal bus (intermodule bus), D80 can contain up to 15 parallel PEs. The structure of D80 is portrayed in Figure 15.1.

CM is a global data memory attached to the IM bus. CU controls communication on the intermodule bus via the polling of all units and the processing of message exchanges between the various units. Communication to and from the communication computer and target computer is managed by the CU. A real-time clock with a resolution of 64 μs is also provided as a CU function.

Due to the fact that SDS80's application area is military aircraft, D80's input/output channels are connected to the military standard bus (MIL-STD-1553B). The channel is programmable and can execute in parallel with processors and other channels. A processor can directly communicate with a channel via a normal read or write instruction in the intermodule bus address space where the channels are mapped.

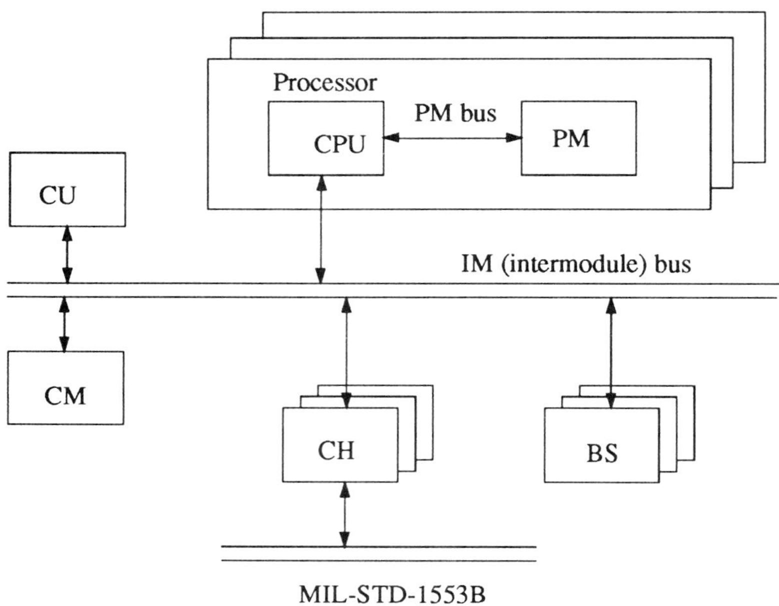

Figure 15.1. Architecture of D80

The **B**ulk **S**torage (BS) memory is nonvolatile and can contain programs for several D80 subsystems. BS can also be utilized for the purpose of registering. The memory is implemented as 4 Mbytes but is extendable. BS is addressed in the same manner as channels via the intermodule address space.

A D80 processor consists of a CPU and a local **p**rogram **m**emory (PM), which contains the executable program code. Each CPU can address 4 Mbytes of PM. Further, each CPU has hardware support to administer up to 15 concurrent processes, where each process has a unique priority. Each process, in turn, can handle up to 15 procedure call levels. A local data memory in the CPU contains local variables of the processes.

The D80 processor via the Pascal-oriented instruction repertoire provides support for floating-point arithmetic. Via effective addressing mechanisms for local variables plus hardware support for parallel processes and multiprocessor properties, a computer with high performance has been attained.

A D80 with one CPU and a 8-MHZ system clock frequency can normally execute 1 million instructions per second. To meet high performance requirements, modern techniques have been utilized to minimize the physical properties of volume, weight, and power dissipation. This has been accomplished via customized development of VLSI components and compact CMOS memories.

A two-processor configuration with 256-Kbyte memory for each CPU, communication unit, and 1553 I/O channel is contained in two double-sided PC boards in double European format and dissipates less than 100 watts. Computers of this type are utilized in the JAS military aircraft.

A simpler version of D80, called D80M, based upon a commercial microprocessor has also been developed for SDS80. This system has **no** direct support for automatic management of parallel processes and therefore process management is handled by the operating system. D80M can only execute as a single processor. A D80M can be an attractive alternative for an inexpensive system that does not demand an entire D80.

15.5 PROPERTIES OF THE INTERMODULE BUS INTERFACE

The synchronous intermodule bus (IM) is controlled from the CU. The other units attached to the IM bus are polled on a round-robin basis. The IM bus is accessed when a CPU has a directive to send or has obtained a directive to initiate receipt. The CPU then accesses the bus as soon as it is polled.

When a machine instruction is executed in the CPU that is directed toward the IM bus, the CPU enters a wait state until it is polled and hence can access the bus. During wait state, the CPU is idle. Directives sent out on the IM bus consist of:

— directives to another CPU, to interrupt the CPU, resume processes, and so on
— read or write operations in the IM bus address space

When the CU receives a directive, it is queued in a directive queue and the corresponding receiver unit is initiated to access the IM bus and receive the directive. The initiation is noted and treated immediately after the current machine instruction is completed. At this point, the execution of the ongoing process is suspended, the directive is fetched, and appropriate actions are taken. Normal execution will be resumed in the active process with the highest priority. Thus, reception of a directive can suspend or resume a process.

15.6 ERROR HANDLING AND MONITORING FUNCTIONS

When a restart of the D80 computer is done, a safety control is initiated. The control contains:

— check and verification of correct function of all basic computer functions
— check of functions for supervision of the CPU and error handling

The control is performed by test microprograms in the CPUs, the CU, and the 1553B-channels, as well as via assembler programs. Further, monitoring at run time is achieved by built-in monitoring of program execution and special instructions to test the hardware during normal operations.

Run-time monitoring functions operate in parallel with normal program execution and consume no extra time. If an error is detected, a branch is taken to a user-defined error routine. If no such routine has been defined, the error is propagated to the previous routine. Finally, if no error routine is found, the process is stopped. Reactivation of that process can normally only be done by reseting the CPU.

15.7 DEVELOPMENT OF AN ADA VERSION

The reader can observe that a rational set of trade-offs, given the technology of the late 1970s and early 1980s, was made in developing the SDS80. Due to the development and standardization of the Ada language for military applications, the Swedish Defence Materiel Administration specified and ordered the development of an Ada-based version, the SDS80A.

A new processor D80A was developed as the backbone of this new system in which direct microprogram support is provided for Ada constructs. Due to this direct support, a rendezvous between two tasks (without parameter transfer), that is, an entry call, start, and completion of an accept statement, including required task scheduling, takes 40 μs within the same processor and 45 μs between two processors.

The support environment for the Ada version (AIDE, **A**da **I**ntegrated **D**evelopment **E**nvironment) is much more sophisticated than the PUS80 predecessor. AIDE has been designed to support life-cycle operations and contains tools for configuration management, as well as a window-oriented human-machine interface. In addition to code generation tools for D80A, a D80A emulator is provided in the host environment. The disposition of memory and task working space can be specified at program generation time, thus enabling the development of predictable code. Consequently, application run-time characteristics can be measured in advance via the debugger and D80A emulator. A successor, the AIDE-F environment, is based on UNIX workstation environments.

Acknowledgments

The material in this chaper is largely based upon material developed at Ericsson AB in Mölndal, Sweden. The author hereby acknowledges the work of and expresses appreciation to Lars Bengtsson, Kurt Lind, Toomas Käer, and Olle Wikström.

Chapter ***16***

RESEARCH and DEVELOPMENT PROJECTS

The increase in interest in the field of real-time systems and its intersection with parallel/distributed processing has spawned a significant number of research and development efforts around the world. As the final case study chapter, we review some of these projects in order to provide a general understanding of the thinking and reasoning involved in developing philosophies, paradigms, and models that will provide some of the advances in the field.

As noted several times in the book, various philosophies for developing real-time systems represent slices through the BMR model in which points of view are taken in respect to behavioral description, process mapping, and resource structures. Further, in our interest domain, the philosophy **must** provide a point of view concerning the treatment of TIME.

We have differentiated between the major implementation philosophies:

1. Resource limited; nondeterministic execution of processes **and**
2. Resource adequate; deterministic execution of processes.

The first philosophy is generally taken when real-time systems are *event* driven. Two examples of current distributed/parallel system-relevant research in this area are the Alpha project (see Jensen and Northcutt, 1990) and the ARTS project (see Tokuda and Mercer, 1989). Both of these projects started at Carnegie-Mellon University and several aspects of their design have common roots. They are both oriented toward *best-effort* scheduling with the limited resources available (see Locke, 1986). Alpha is now commercially available and ARTS is an ongoing research project.

The second philosophy is based upon the provision of *adequate resources* that can deal with real-time requirements within specific time frames, resulting in systems that are driven by *time* rather than by *events*. The systems are dimensioned so that the deterministic execution of processes (either directly in hardware or via precisely timed programs) can be provided. As we have considered, this line of thinking is prevalent in digital signal processing; however, it is also interesting to apply this approach for programmed solutions.

An interesting solution that provides direct mapping (with very limited system software support) in a distributed environment is the MARS system (see Kopetz and others, 1989). Another example in which a new view of behavioral description and TIME is taken is Cy-Clone (**Clone** of the **Cy**lic Paradigm) (see Lawson, 1992). In both cases, the mapping of process sets is static and based upon deterministic *precisely timed programs*.

A third philosophy represents a compromise between the previous two, where certain resources are bound for periodic processes and where additional resources are multiplexed in order to treat aperiodic processes resulting from events, transactions, and the like. A good example of current distributed/parallel system research in this area is the Spring Architecture (see Stankovic, 1990). We also find this line of thinking in the development and implementation of the ESTEREL programming language (see Berry, Couronné, and Gonthier, 1988).

Each philosophy is relevant and useful based upon system goals. In particular, various philosophies and resulting paradigms and models will be appropriate for varying *time granularity* and other requirements of the application system. In this chapter, we first examine the Real-Time Euclid language, which has been developed as a basis for extracting precise timing profiles from real-time behavioral descriptions. In succession, we then examine Alpha, ARTS, MARS, Spring, and Cy-Clone.

16.1 REAL-TIME EUCLID

Real-Time Euclid provides timing information at the source program level (see Klingerman and Stoyenko, 1986). In Real-Time Euclid, processes must be static and nonnested. Each process definition must contain activation information that pertains to its behavior. The temporal scope concept in this case is called a *frame*. Periodic and aperiodic processes are specified as follows:

```
periodic <frameInfo> first activation <time Or event>
atEvent <conditionID> <frameInfo>
```

The clause <frameInfo> defines the periodicity of the process (including the maximum rate for sporadic processes) and is expressed in real time units at the head of the program. A periodic task can be activated either via the occurrence of a start time or by an interrupt. The <time Or event> clause is one of the following:

```
atTime <real-time expression>
atEvent <real-time expression>
atTime <real-time expression> or atEvent <conditionID>
```

where <conditionID> is a condition variable associated with an interrupt initiating sporadic processes. To gain an understanding of the use of these facilities, we consider a cyclic temperature controller. It has a periodicity of 60 units (its periodicity is once per minute, assuming the time unit is 1 second). The controller is to be activated after 600 units (10 minutes) or when a startMonitoring interrupt arrives.

```
realTimeUnit := 1.0 % time unit = 1 seconds

var Reactor: module
var startMonitoring : activation condition atLocation 16 # A10D
  % defines a condition variable mapped onto a specific interrupt

        process TempController : periodic frame 60
                                 first activation time 600
                                 or atEvent startMonitoring

        % import list
        %
        % execution part
        %
        end TempController
end Reactor
```

No loop semantics are provided in the program since the looping is supplied by the cyclic scheduler, which underlies the execution of Real-Time Euclid programs.

Given information about processes to be included in the real-time system, further timing information is calculated for each process. Information obtained is as follows:

— total CPU requirements for executing noninterruptible parts
— total CPU requirements for executing interruptible parts
— total time spent performing device operations
— maximum time spent waiting for interprocess communication
— worst-case time for being blocked* by another process
— worst-case time for being blocked* waiting for a device to become available
— relative size of each process's interruptible parts

(*) being blocked means, for example, waiting to gain access to a monitor process.

This introduction provides some idea of the Real-Time Euclid approach, which has been applied in uniprocessor environments. While the extension to parallel processing environments is obviously much more challenging, the notions presented by Real-Time Euclid can provide a useful as one starting point.

Comment: While it is quite useful to be able to describe timing properties, they must always be interpreted in the context of the underlying system software and hardware processes that provide execution semantics. Thus, whether the timing is realizable or not depends upon the entire system. Halang and Stoyenko (1991) have addressed this broder perspective and introduced *schedulability analysis* as a means of determining if predictability demands can be met. We now consider a few all-encompasing real-time system philosophies, paradigms, and models.

16.2 THE ALPHA PROJECT

The Alpha project stems from original research led by E. Doug Jensen on the Archons project at Carnegie-Mellon University beginning in 1979. Further Alpha development has been sponsored by the Department of Defense and supported by the Concurrent Computer Corporation and Digital Equipment Corporation. A number of industrial, military, and academic partners are participating in the further development and application of Alpha. Alpha has been designed for use in large, complex real-time system environments. It is oriented toward doing the best that it can with the "limited" resources that are available. Further, Alpha can be used as a "superstructure" to piece together large real-time systems from smaller parts. The parts managed by Alpha may be developed based upon other operating systems, such as VRTX, VxWorks, or UNIX.

16.2.1 Alpha Paradigm and Model

The Alpha paradigm presents a programming model that is viewed as a single logical system structured in a network-transparent fashion. The network contains an indeterminate number of physical nodes. The principal abstractions that are provided are *objects*, *operation invocation*, and *threads*.

Objects are abstract data types (code plus data) that can be coupled into threads of execution via operation invocation. The object operation invocation mechanism is a fundamental facility upon which the Alpha kernel is based. All objects are known and accessible in a transparent manner so that objects and threads may be easily transported in order to meet performance and/or fault-tolerance requirements. Threads are the unit of schedulability. A thread in Alpha can extend over distributed processing facilities, in which case it inherits resources and timing requirement properties along its way. The relationship of objects, operation invocation, and threads is portrayed in Figure 16.1.

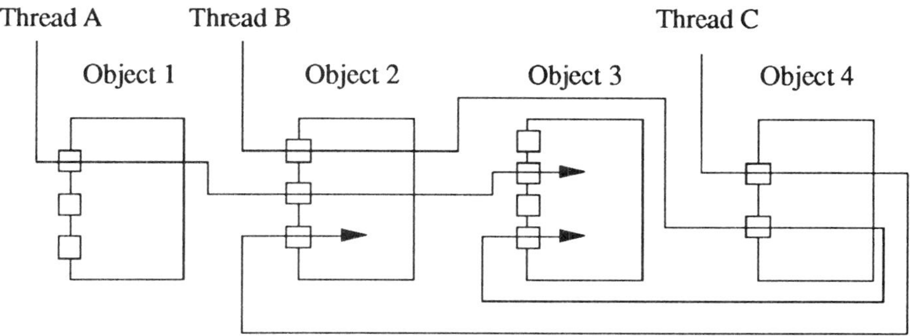

Figure 16.1. Alpha Objects, Operation Invocation, and Threads

As we can observe, three schedulable threads are defined that have, via operation invocation, attached objects to themselves. Threads represent the Alpha view of Processes, and each thread maintains its own execution stack. The kernel keeps track of relevant state information for each thread. Communication within threads is via operation invocation, which is treated as a synchronous RPC (remote procedure call). The threads collectively are treated as asynchronous processes and may communicate with each other. Unlike threads in Mach (see Chapter 11), Alpha threads are not bound to a specific address space and thus can be connected over distributed PEs.

Alpha employs *thread attributes* that follow the thread dynamically as new objects are coupled into the thread. The attributes provide information concerning urgency, fault-tolerance requirements, exception scopes, time/value information, constraints, and the like. These attributes are used by the scheduler, which selects the most important threads for execution. Thus, scheduling is not simply based upon classical priority mechanisms or upon the timing properties of processes (as used in rate monotonic scheduling). As a part of the fault-tolerance strategy, facilities are provided to repair threads that may be broken due to a node failure. Further, in secure system versions, threads may be local and protected as required by constraining operation invocation.

A major goal of the Alpha philosophy has been to separate policy from mechanism. Thus, while objects, operation invocation, and threads provide mechanisms, the policies that utilize them may be altered based upon system requirements of functionality, performance, and cost.

Due to the wide-scale support that has developed for Alpha, its further development should be continuously evaluated in order to determine its applicability for real-time system projects.

16.3 THE ARTS PROJECT

The ARTS (**A**dvanced **R**eal-Time **T**echnology) project has been established in order to provide a test bed for developing and verifying distributed real-time systems. It is an experimental environment that has been implemented in its first version via a set of SUN3 workstations connected to a real-time network based on the IEEE 802.5 token ring and Ethernet.

16.3.1 ARTS Paradigm and Model

The ARTS view of behavioral description is also an object-oriented approach in which objects contain a *time fence* (time limit) and an exception handler (to be invoked in case the object execution exceeds its time fence). The ARTS/C++ language provides these object declaration facilities. This timing information is used at every synchronous or asynchronous invocation of an object in order to detect the origin of timing errors.

As with the Alpha project, a separation of scheduling mechanisms and policy has been followed. In the ARTS case, the separation has been provided so that test bed experimentation can be performed in applying various scheduling approaches.

To implement the mechanism-policy separation, an **I**ntegrated **T**ime **D**riven **S**cheduler (ITDS) has been designed to treat both hard and soft real-time activities found in a wide variety of real-time applications. For hard activities, the ITDS model permits the designer to predict whether the given tasks can meet their deadlines or not. For soft activities, a determination can be made as to whether worst-case response times satisfy application requirements. ITDS works with "capacity preservation," where requirements for hard periodic and sporadic tasks are first taken into account via static rate-monotonic scheduling and where remaining capacity is available for assignment to soft real-time tasks according to some policy. A policy must provide the following structures and rules:

— a defined structure for ready queues
— execution of a thread
— selection of processes to be executed
— blocking of a thread
— killing of a thread
— an aperiodic server algorithm

Provisions for monitoring, debugging, measurement, and evaluation have been essential ingredients of ARTS. Logical and timing errors are difficult to track in distributed systems due to the lack of instantaneous and accurate global state or event ordering. In ARTS, the real-time kernel in each node time stamps event messages, thus making system dynamic properties more observable. Time-stamped event information is tapped from the event-message buffer and given to a reporter, which transmits relevant information to a remote visualizer. These properties of the ARTS real-time monitor are portrayed in Figure 16.2.

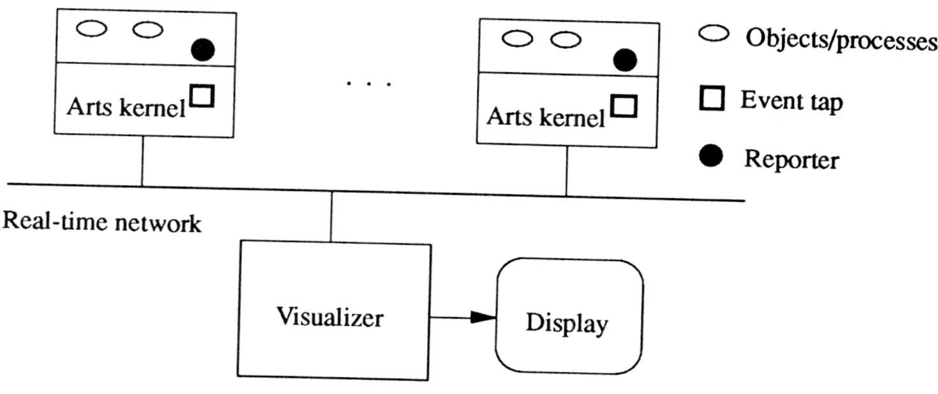

Figure 16.2. ARTS Real-time Monitor

In general *priority inheritence* is used as the means of avoiding the blocking of higher-priority tasks by lower-priority tasks. This policy carries over to network communication, where a separate protocol machine (Communication Manager) is implemented, providing eight levels of task priorities ("remember the resource quantity axiom"!). In any event, preemption of network use has been provided in order to direct utilization of the limited communication resource to the highest-priority tasks.

As with Alpha, a number of interesting ideas have been incorporated in ARTS and it will be interesting to follow its further development and utilization.

16.4 THE MARS PROJECT

The MARS (**Ma**intainable **R**eal-Time **S**ystem) project had its origin at the Technische Universitat Berlin and later at the Technische Univeristat Wien. The project has been led by Herman Kopez and is neatly summarized by Kopetz, and others (1989). A number of key points have driven the design of MARS:

— the limited time validity of real-time data
— predictable performance under peak loads
— fault tolerance and
— maintainability and extensibility

These properties of MARS are achieved via a direct-mapped, resource-adequate approach where static schedules are made off line for which complete timing properties are known. Predictability can be guaranteed due to the provision of resource adequacy for peak-load conditions.

MARS is designed for a distributed environment. Thus, to provide a common point of reference, MARS defines a global time base (called *system time*) that is maintained throughout the distributed network.

16.4.1 MARS Paradigm and Model

The behavior of the system to be modeled is viewed as being transaction oriented, where a *transaction* represents the single execution of a specified set of tasks between a stimulus and a response. Conceptually, a transaction is an acylic graph where the *tasks* are nodes and messages appear as arcs. The tasks may appear in different hardware components as portrayed in Figure 16.3.

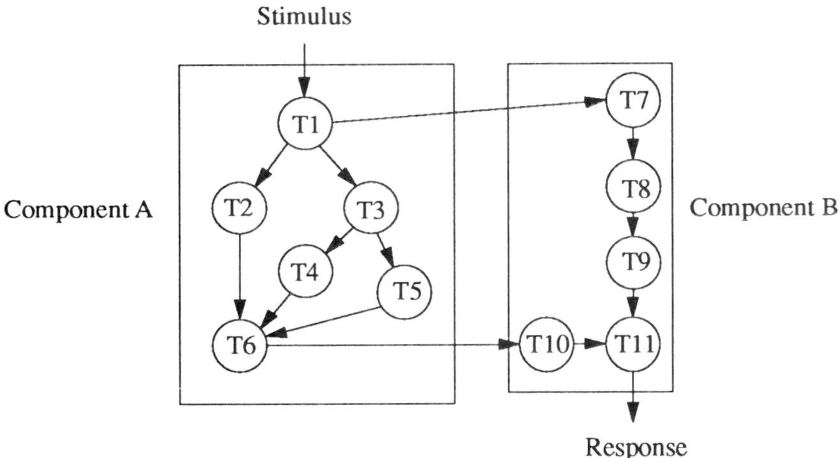

Figure 16.3. Transaction from Stimulus to Response

In MARS, the view of processes is that of a task which can have any degree of granularity. In the communication structure, messages are passed between tasks either locally within a component (a node) or between components (nodes). The components are self-contained computers, which are connected together via a bus into a *cluster*, as illustrated in the simplified architectural model of Figure 16.4. Extensibility is provided by replacing a node in a cluster with a new cluster, as illustrated in the figure.

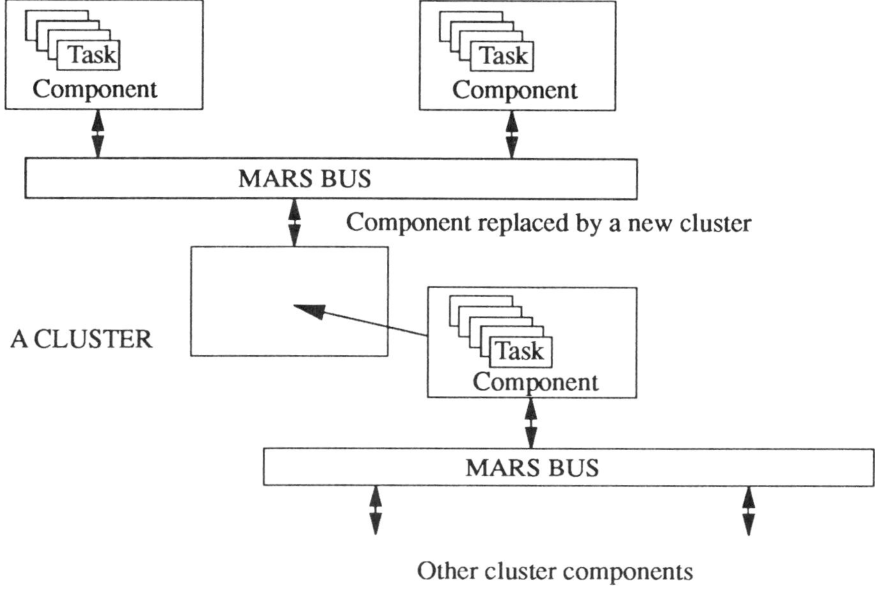

Figure 16.4. MARS Cluster and Extension with a New Cluster

The communication on the MARS bus is by a TDMA (**T**ime **D**ivision **M**ulti-**A**ccess), where time is divided into slots and where calculation of worst-case timing not only includes task processing times for transactions, but the time delays for bus utilization.

An interesting strategy is taken concerning the lifetime of real-time data, that is, the **r**eal-**t**ime **d**ata**b**ase (RTDB). Since real-time data are related to the instantaneous situation, they do not have to be and should not be treated in the same manner as an archivial data base. In the RTDB, the passage of time invalidates data. Further, losing the RTDB causes a suspension of control. Within the framework of MARS, communication takes place via unacknowledged *datagrams,* where a *time validity stamp* is placed on each datagram. Via this strategy, unpredictability due to communication delays arising from typical end-to-end protocols is avoided. The timing properties of the transaction processing replace the need for an acknowledgment-type protocol. Further, to improve reliability, datagrams are sent twice. The local operating system kernel in each PE is responsible for extracting relevant datagram contents. Further, a control is made as to determine whether the information contained in the datagram is still valid and useful.

The MARS operating system is written in the C programming language, where an identical copy runs locally and autonomously in each MARS component. Its primary functions are to administer CPU, memory, and bus resources, as well as to hide hardware details from application tasks. The kernel also maintains the global system time and oversees the efficiency of message passing.

Significant attention has been given to providing design support and evaluation tools for MARS. Once again, the further development and utilization of MARS are well worth examining. Many MARS concepts have already influenced the design of commercially available systems.

16.5 THE SPRING PROJECT

The Spring project at the University of Massachusetts employs both the resource-adequate and resource-limited philosophies in a distributed real-time operating system structure (see Stankovic, 1990).

16.5.1 Spring Paradigm and Model

The paradigm is characterized by the following properties:

- — resource segmentation/partitioning
- — functional and spatial partitioning
- — selective preallocation
- — *a priori* guarantee for critical tasks
- — an on-line guarantee for essential tasks
- — integrated CPU scheduling and resource allocation
- — use of the scheduler in a planning mode
- — separation of importance and timing constraints
- — end-to-end scheduling
- — utilization of significant information about tasks at *run time,* including timing, task importance, and fault-tolerance requirements, and the ability to dynamically alter this information

The Spring architecture model is viewed as being part of a SpringNet, which is portrayed in Figure 16.5. Each node is a multiprocessor containing one or more application processors (AP), one or more system processors, and an I/O subsystem. The *functional* properties of the Spring architecture, as manifested by the properties of the paradigm, have been simulated, whereas the component (hardware process) level requirements have not been implemented.

Relating to Figure 16.5, it is important to note that application processors execute previously guaranteed and relatively high level application tasks. System processors offload the scheduling algorithm and other OS overhead from the application tasks.

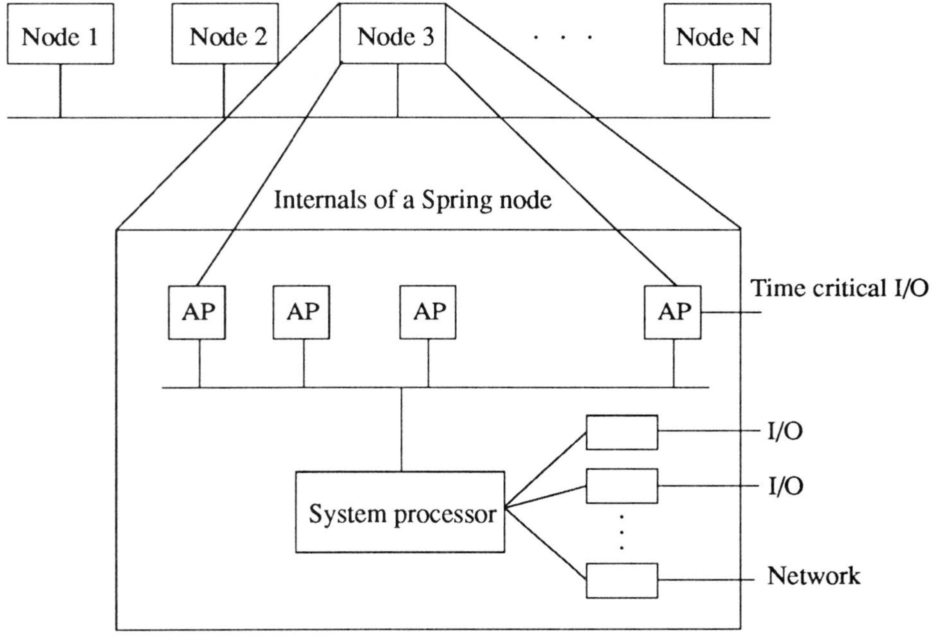

Figure 16.5. SpringNet Architecture

Further, this separation implies *that external interrupts and OS overhead do not cause uncertainty in executing guaranteed tasks.* The I/O subsystem is partitioned away from the Spring kernel and handles noncritical I/O, slow I/O devices, and fast sensors.

With regard to resource segmentation, all tasks and groups of tasks are resource and time bounded, meaning that they are composed of well-defined segments. Further, both the worst-case execution times and the worst-case resource requirements are known. Kernel primitives are also bounded. This information is available to the scheduler and provides *microscopic predictability.*

As a part of the functional and spatial partitioning, we can observe that each node in the SpringNet is a multiprocessor and that, for fault-tolerance purposes, the role of system processor can be taken over by an AP. Further, via functional partitioning, a problem can be divided into smaller parts, allowing varying degrees of granularity. Application tasks are protected from unpredictable interrupts that can lead to nondeterminism.

Concerning selective preallocation, the paradigm suggests that some of tasks that have real-time constraints be dealt with statically by binding I/O devices directly to the task, whereas a dynamic scheduling algorithm is applied in the front end for other tasks.

Critical tasks (and task groups) with very fast I/O requirements are preallocated and thus guaranteed. The notion of guaranteeing timing constraints is central to the paradigm. Essential tasks are analyzed dynamically and guaranteed, if required, on line. The scheduler integrates CPU and resource allocation in such a fashion that blocking can never occur, as can be experienced in, for example, earliest deadline schedulers.

The scheduler is used in a planning mode when a new task is invoked. Since the total load on the system is known, intelligent decisions can be made when a deadline cannot be guaranteed. Due to the fact that plan scheduling takes place in parallel, some interesting race conditions must be attended to.

By the separation of timing and importance, critical tasks are guaranteed; further, essential tasks are assigned a level of importance that may vary as system conditions change. Thus, essential tasks that miss their deadlines will be the less important tasks of that category.

The use of the scheduling of task groups as opposed to individual tasks permits the meeting of collective deadlines on an end-to-end basis, for example, a set of tasks overseeing a moving robot. Finally, significant amounts of semantic information about a task or task group are maintained for utilization at run time. Kernel primitives are utilized to inquire about and to alter this information.

The computation of worst-case execution times is essential to provide guarantees. Thus, precise timing properties for CPUs, cache memories, MMUs (**m**emory **m**apping **u**nits), floating-point coprocessors, DSP chips, and other front-end I/O processors must be attainable. *It is preferable to have a slower but predictable machine than a faster but unpredictable one*. These aspects are often difficult to analyze for complex architectures that have been designed to emphasize performance. On the other hand, simpler hardware processes are viewed as appropriate candidates. While these aspects have been studied in the project, there is still much to do in order to provide an adequate basis for determining execution properties.

In reviewing the properties of the Spring, we can observe that the paradigm proposed is based upon careful hardware and software design in order to provide both *microscopic* and *macroscopic* predictability. The designers have stated that they are well aware that the weakest link in an entire system can undermine careful design and analysis. Thus, they are attempting to address all the issues in an integrated fashion.

16.6 THE CY-CLONE PROJECT

The Cy-Clone (Clone of the Cyclic paradigm) project has been initiated by Lawson (1992) and is based upon the resource-adequacy, direct-mapped philosophy. The original concepts were derived from experiences in designing an Automatic Train Control system for the Swedish National Railways (SJ). The current work, which has resulted in Cy-Clone, has been supported by the Swedish Defence Materiel Administration (FMV).

A novel approach to real-time behavioral description and the treatment of TIME are hallmarks of Cy-Clone. Further, Cy-Clone is proposed as a basis for concrete industrial implementation as well as for academic research. The philosophy, paradigm, and model lead to an artifact independent set of concepts, which can be realized via a variety of specific artifacts.

As described in Chapter 2, the traditional cyclic paradigm, due to its inherent simplicity, has been the predominant approach used in developing the vast majority of hard real-time systems. Cyclic solutions have been widely **and** justly criticized due to the fact that they are inflexible, particularly in relationship to maintenance and upgrading of the systems (see Sha and Goodenough, 1990). These problems are not present in Cy-Clone solutions.

16.6.1 Cy-Clone Paradigm

As described in Lawson (1990), it is essential to work from the problem definition and characteristics in the development of computer-based systems. For real-time systems, the general problem is to provide an appropriate processing model of the external environment. *The processing model must fulfill the periodic and aperiodic needs of the environment by both progressing via processing and by maintaining stability in the environment.*

Cy-Clone reduces the processing and stability requirements of real-time systems in respect to TIME to the view provided in Figure 16.6. The cyclic (continuous) nature of processing is reflected in every time interval. Most essential is that a *dT* is defined that is the maximum time interval permitted for processing, but which is acceptable for maintaining stability in the environment. The *dT* time interval provides a *moving window* over the environment. In various applications, as well as within parts of a specific application, *dT* may be measured in seconds, milliseconds, microseconds, or even smaller time granules. The time interval *dT* may be altered dynamically as the application moves from stage to stage or mode to mode of operation. For example, we may define a large *dT* at STARTUP, a finer *dT* during NORMAL OPERATION, and a very fine *dT* during EMERGENCY situations.

Cy-Clone views all real-time processing as *time constrained parsing* of the environment within the limits of the *current dT*. In all cases, the current situation is determined and the system reacts. Each stage or mode is composed of parallel *parse rules* (one for each potential situation within the stage or mode). *Within the Cy-Clone paradigm, we will see to it that sufficient resources are provided so that **all** parses for all sets of parse rules can be accommodated within their respective dT limits.* This point of view permits us to deal with both periodic and aperiodic processes without any need for their differentiation. There is no need for a complex interrupt handling mechanism

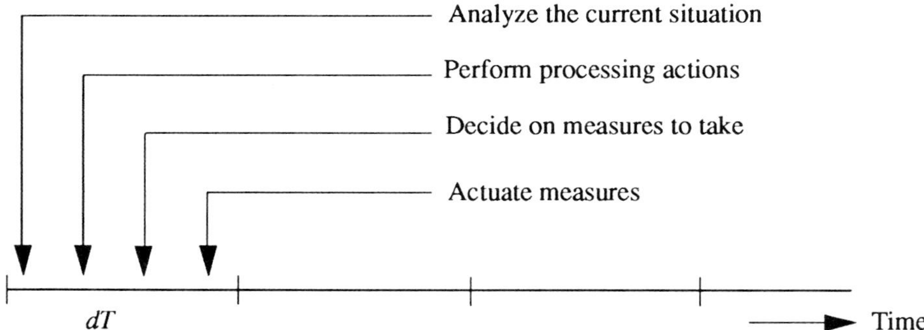

Figure 16.6. Cyclic Nature of Real-time Systems

and preemptive processing, thus providing significant simplifications. The only interrupt that is implemented is the RT-clock synchronizing signal at the *current dT*.

The Cy-Clone point of view leads to a concentration upon the problem rather than the artifacts. Attention is focused upon the processing required in *dT* intervals. The stage or mode relevant "state" (that is, situation) is reconsidered during each cycle. The net result is simple programmed solutions (short program segments) where *tricks of coding* are not introduced for obtaining efficiency with respect to a particular programming language, system software, or hardware artifact.

Cy-Clone provides for the mapping of rules into processes that are allocated to **one** or **more** PEs as required in order to meet *dT* timing demands. The transformation from single-processor to multiprocessor solutions is handled by CAE and CAD tools.

As mentioned, the Cy-Clone problem-oriented view has been successfully exploited in the development of a successful Automatic Train Control system (see Lawson, 1990). Further, the approach is highly analogous to the design of hardware systems, where the same activities portrayed in Figure 16.6 are applied in meeting clock cycle requirements. A further symbolic analogy can be found in the pandemonium model of the human brain as described in Chapter 1. The pandemonium model involves several categories of demons performing various tasks in recognizing objects where a *blackboard* is used for all communication. The fact that many demons operate in parallel and independent of each other creates temporary pandemonium situations. This is clearly analogous to both hardware design and Cy-Clone-based systems. That is, we move from defined states to pandemonium (parallel rule evaluation) for an interval and then establish a stabile state in each cycle.

Although we begin from a Clone of the Cyclic paradigm, we wind up with a rather different result in which the inflexible time-frame mapping of processes is eliminated. Further, in comparison with other philosophies and paradigms for real-time systems, there is no need for explicit priority or for preemptive processing.

The major trade-off made in Cy-Clone is that we are willing, when necessary, to introduce additional hardware (as required) in order to provide adequate resources.

In return, we simplify, thus making the system software structure more understandable, with all the positive side-effect benefits that thereby accrue.

Note: It is not clear that Cy-Clone solutions actually require more hardware resources. They operate without operating system functions, thus eliminating significant memory (as well as overhead) requirements. One measure that provides optimism in this regard is that the ATC (**A**utomatic **T**rain **C**ontrol) system requires only 8K of ROM programs to provide full control functionality.

16.6.2 Cy-Clone Model

The model can be utilized as a basis for a variety of concrete implementations via specific hardware artifacts. According to Flynn's classification, we can categorize the architectural model as SISD (**S**ingle **I**nstruction **S**tream, Single **D**ata **S**tream) with convenient extension to MIMD (**M**ultiple **I**nstruction Stream, **M**ultiple **D**ata **S**tream). The major elements of the generic architectural model are portrayed in Figure 16.7.

The important properties of the model are as follows:

— We factor out real-time processing involving extremely large quantities of simultaneous data, for example, image processing, signal conditioning and complex digital filtering. These are seen as Data Reduction Subsystems, which deliver "reduced data" to the real-time system (similar to the image demons in the pandemonium analogy).

— The human-computer interface is treated as a means of "viewing" the internal operation of the real-time system as well as the means of "operator control." Further, long-term (nondeterministic) planning algorithms that are not time critical may be executed in this computer.

— An optional network connection is provided when the system in question is a subsystem in a distributed network (LAN or WAN or both).

— The Blackboard contains "Reduced" Environment Variables and includes all values that are used to represent the current "environmental situation." They can be thought of as the nonqueued *ports* to and from the system. However, the variables can represent other common system-relevant state information. We are not concerned whether these variables are stored in a (possibly multi-port) shared memory as registers (latches), as a shift register, or as separate register files that are commonly accessible via a bus. Various realizations of the Blackboard can result in different concrete structures; however, sufficiently rapid and predictable access is the important implementation issue. The Blackboard is the *real-time data base* (RTDB) of the application.

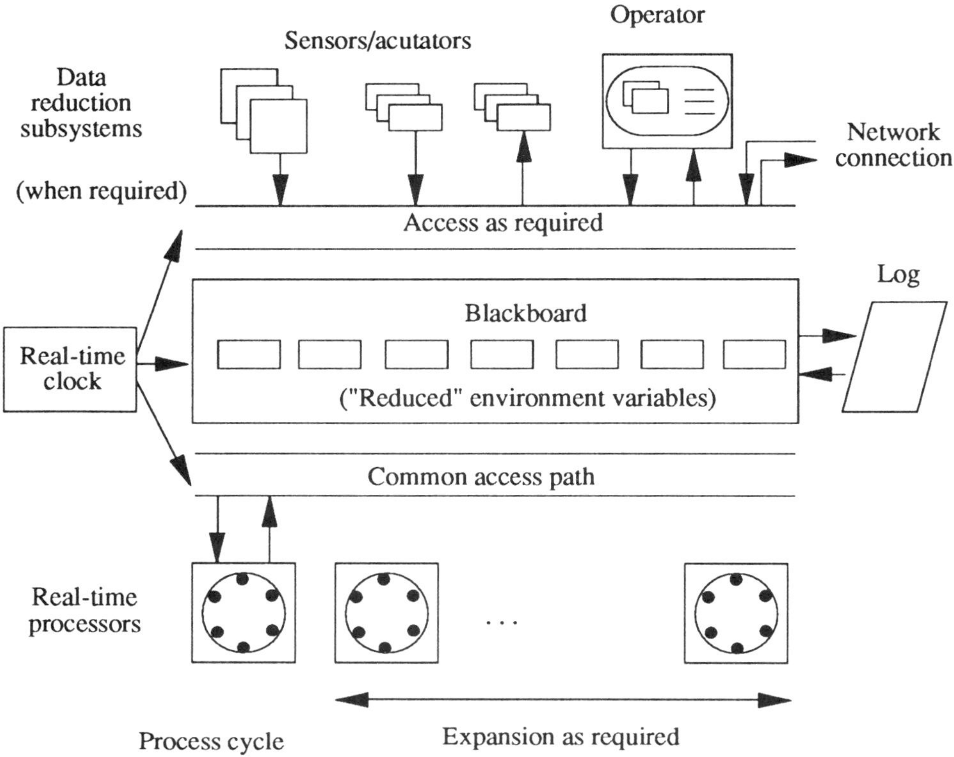

Figure 16.7. Cy-Clone Generic Architectural Model

— The real-time processors are stored program computers (PEs) that continually execute programmed process loops at *dT* rates of speed. The initial model is a single processor version (SISD), in which case the Blackboard may be incorporated into the local memory. All processes are executed by this single processor.

— As processing demands increase, more powerful PEs can be incorporated. However, it is also possible to add new processors and execute in parallel MIMD form. The common access path to Blackboard environmental variables must be characterizable so that precise timing and utilization profiles can be developed. Various concrete multiprocessor solutions can be provided.

— A form of *problem-oriented cache* can be realized by transmitting cycle-relevant data to the local memories of respective PEs at the beginning of each *dT* cycle.

— A separate real-time clock is distributed for synchronization purposes, as well as for keeping time in various time units when necessary and for providing the *current dT* synchronization point signal.

— The log, when required, can be implemented as a timed read-out and possibly read-in of the environmental variables. The log can be used for off-line analysis as well as for establishing (re-creating) environmental situations. "Freezing" the set of environment variables at the start of each *dT* may be useful for this function. An important by-product of the ability to perform log read-in is the potential use for testing, debugging, and evaluating the system, particularly in the event of failure.

— The Cy-Clone paradigm and architectural model, due to the lack of complexity, lend themselves to various straightforward means of testing, verification, fault tolerance, and security. With regard to fault tolerance, double or triple modular redundancy methods can easily be applied since a major result synchronization point (*dT*) provides a clean point for majority logic comparisons. Further, it is possible to consider partitioning the logic in a manner such that critical processes are assigned to redundant components, whereas noncritical processes are assigned to single components. In a similar manner, some logic (parse rule sets) in the system can be completely isolated from outside interrogation (locked up) if a high degree of security is required.

16.6.3 Behavioral Description

An object approach can be taken in providing Cy-Clone behavioral descriptions. One appropriate object-oriented concept is the ObjectOry notion of use cases as described in Chapter 7. Use cases define a particular path of use of the system and can be conveniently utilized as an abstract representation of a rule. Further, the *set* of all use cases (parse rules) represents the specified functionality of the system, where subsets represent relevant rules for stages or modes. In a relatively straightforward manner, use cases can be decomposed into the parsing *process set* to be executed in the Cy-Clone cyclic manner.

Another interesting design representation that can be applied for abstract as well as concrete Cy-Clone solutions is *dimensional design* (DD), which is also described in Chapter 7. Using the *parallel* and *composed of* attributes of DD objects but redefining the vertical connection to a *"mode shift"* attribute for mode objects, we arrive at a quite natural means of viewing the structure of a Cy-Clone real-time system. The system is viewed as a composition of parallel rules, as portrayed in Figure 16.8. The actual implementations of the rules are viewed as further refinements. They can be constructed using an appropriate imperative programming language, particularly one that does not have heavy semantics with respect to the PCS issues. As a research project, it would be quite interesting to consider the use of a functional language in this context.

Appropriate CAE and CAD tools can be developed around DD-like representations. Further, understandability can be provided at the human-computer interface, where the instrumentation of Cy-Clone solutions should be much simpler than for systems permitting a wide variety of program structures. In fact, an analog to the Logic Analyzer used for testing hardware is quite appropriate for Cy-Clone rule-based systems.

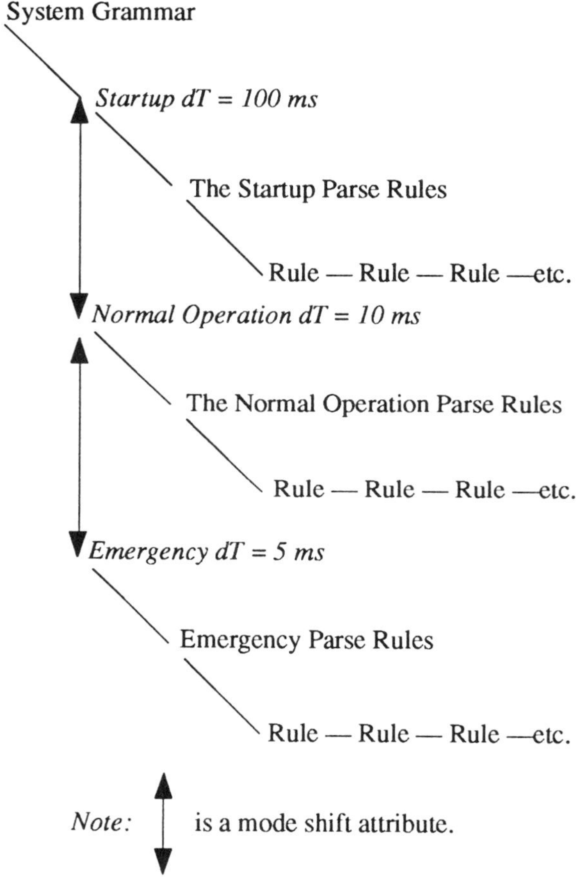

Figure 16.8. System Grammar as a Collection of Mode-related Parallel Parsing Rules

16.6.4 Hardware Resource Example

As described previously, Cy-Clone provides a philosophy, paradigm, and model. The model can be realized in a variety of manners. In terminating this brief description of Cy-Clone, we consider an interesting realization based upon the use of a cyclic memory (shift register, fiber-optic cable, and so on) as the media for containing the RTDB (**r**eal-**t**ime **d**ata **b**ase) portrayed in Figure 16.9. This realization provides some extremely interesting properties, especially with respect to understandability, fault tolerance, and modular extendability.

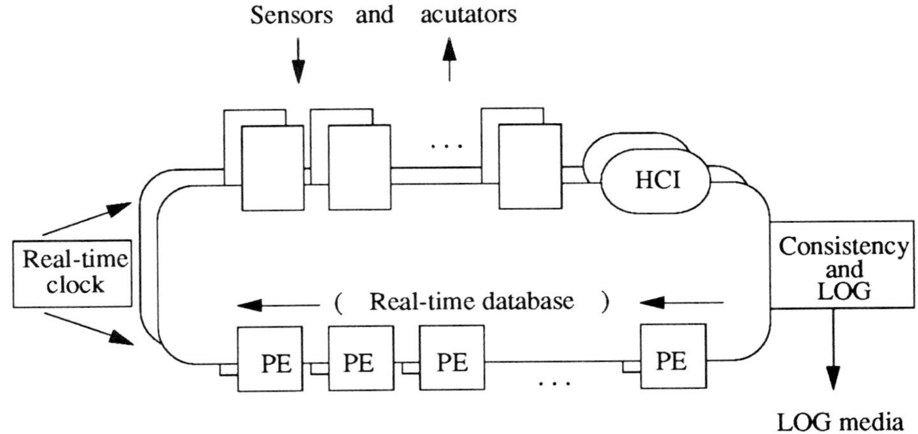

Figure 16.9. Feasible Cy-Clone Hardware Resource Architecture

In the figure, we have purposely duplicated the cyclic memory, which contains the **r**eal-**t**ime **d**ata **b**ase (RTDB), as well as duplicated the PEs, sensors and actuators, and HCI (**H**uman-**C**omputer **I**nterface) for fault-tolerance considerations. In such a system, the RTDB continually circulates. Based upon the import requirements of the rules contained in each PE, at the beginning of dT, each PE pulls out (parses) relevant data from the database. As output results are produced, they are exported into the RTDB up to the end of dT. Sensors and acuators as well as the HCI can access the RTDB at the frequencies they require.

With respect to fault tolerance, double (or even triple) modular redundancy on each PE, sensor, actuator, and HCI can be applied. Thus, checks are made to determine if data being placed into the RTDB are consistent. In the case of inconsistency, a majority logic result can be placed into the RTDB; alternatively, a special VOID inconsistency marker can be entered. To continually check the RTDB, a bit-wise consistency comparitor is placed into the loop. Further, in this logic, we extract data from the RTDB that are to be logged on the log media. If necessary, we can duplicate or triplicate the RT-clock logic and clock signal connections. The important point is that the simplicity of this structure leads to a convenient, understandable, fault-tolerant solution. Further, with a proper hardware construction philosophy, systems can be made modularly extendable.

In summary, Cy-Clone provides a philosophy, paradigm, and architectural model for developing a generic class of cyclic, continuous-operation, real-time systems. The Cy-Clone approach emphasizes understandability. Understandability is improved by removing complex factors such as priority interrupt structures, dynamic resource allocation, and scheduling processes. Understandability is further enhanced by providing graphical human-machine communication that permits internal as well as external visibility.

References

Berry, G., P. Couronné, and G. Gonthier (1988). Synchronous Programming of Reactive Systems: An Introduction to ESTEREL, K. Fuchi and M. Nivat (eds.), *Programming of Future Generation Computers*, pp. 33-55, Elsivier Science Publishers, New York.

Halang, W.A., and A.D. Stoyenko (1991). *Constructing Predictable Real Time Systems*, Kluwer Academic Publishers, Boston-Dordrecht-London.

Jensen, D., and J.D. Northcutt (1990). Alpha: A Non-proprietary Operating System for Mission-critical Real-time Distributed Systems, *Proceedings of the 1990 IEEE Workshop on Experimental Distributed Systems*, IEEE Computer Society Press, Los Alamitos, CA, October.

Klingerman, E., and A.D. Stoyenko (1986). Real-time Euclid: A Language for Reliable Real-time Systems, *IEEE Transactions on Software Engineering*, Vol. SE-12, No. 9, pp. 941-949.

Kopetz, H., A. Damm, C. Koza, M. Mulazzani, W. Schwabi, C. Senft, and R. Zainlinger (1989). Distributed Fault-tolerant Real-time Systems: The MARS Approach, *IEEE Micro*, pp. 25-158, February.

Lawson, H. W. (1990). Philosophies for Engineering Computer-based Systems, *Computer*, Vol 23, No.12, pp. 52-63.

Lawson, H.W. (1992). Cy-Clone - An Approach to the Engineering of Resource Adequate Cyclic Real-time Systems, *International Journal of Real-time Systems*, Vol. 4, No. 1, pp. 55-83.

Locke, C.D. (1986). *Best-effort Decision Making for Real-time Scheduling*, Ph.D. thesis, CMU-CS-86-134, Department of Computer Science, Carnegie-Mellon University, Pittsbugh, PA.

Selfridge, O. (1959). Pandemonium: A Paradigm for Learning, *Symposium on the Mechanization of Thought Processes*, H.M. Stationery Office, London.

Sha, L., and J.B. Goodenough (1990). Real-time Scheduling Theory and Ada, *Computer*, Vol. 23, No. 4, pp. 53-62.

Stankovic, J.A. (1990). The Spring Architecture, *Proceedings Euromicro'90 Workshop on Real Time*, IEEE Computer Society Press, Los Alamitos, CA, pp. 104-113.

Tokuda, H., and C.W. Mercer (1989). ARTS: A Distributed Real-time Kernel, *Operating System Review*, Vol. 23, No. 3, pp. 29-53.

Chapter **17**

CONCLUDING REMARKS and FUTURE DIRECTIONS

In this book we have considered the mainstream philosophies, paradigms, models, and some of the artifacts related to parallel/distributed processing. Further, we have considered the actual or potential utilization of parallel/disributed processing in industrial real-time applications. We conclude by summarizing and looking toward the future.

17.1 A QUICK SUMMARY

The reader is encouraged to once more scan through the summaries provided in each chapter of Part I (each section in Chapter 3). They provide a useful reference of important points. A quick summary of the contents of the book is portrayed in Figure 17.1.

This figure can be related to the BMR model, where application behavior, by some means, is described and decomposed into processes of varying granularity. From this figure, we can **roughly** identify the following philosophies, paradigms, and models.

philosophy (general point of view) — The general point of view leads us to questions of description style and mapping philosophy, leading to the division of direct-mapped and dynamically mapped approaches. Here we also make the **important** distinction between resource adequate and resource limited.

paradigm (specific point of view) — In this case, we select some specific form of parallelism that will serve as a basis for how performance will be expedited. We have identified pipelines, parallel, and scalar as the three major paradigms. The paradigms often determine, or restrict the selection of appropriate description and programming styles to be applied (explicitly or implicitly).

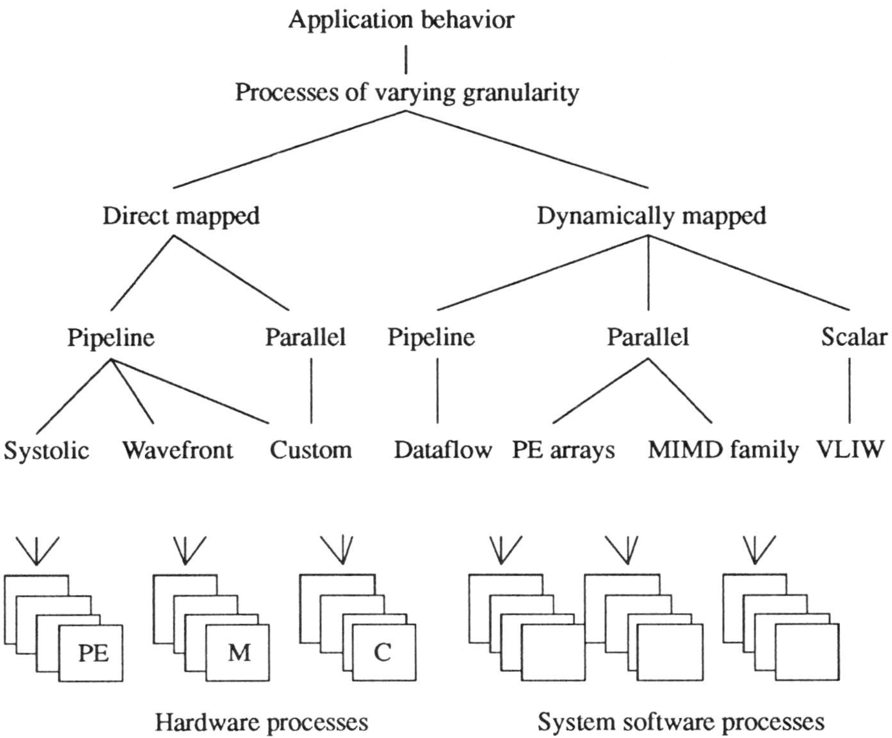

Figure 17.1. Collective Summary of Parallel Processing

model (specific framework, structure) — At the model level we identify specific architectural structures and related styles. Note that in the direct-mapped variant we have identified a custom style, which collectively describes special-purpose solutions (for example, as described in Chapter 8).

Within the alternatives that have been considered in this book, we have continually referred to BMR model applicability as well as to the PCS fundamental issues. These two notions extend over all the specific developments described in this book and should become a permanent part of the readers mental capital as a means of understanding and contributing to future developments.

As we consider the use of parallel processing for real-time systems or portions thereof, we must pay particular attention to the properties we have identified in the book, in particular the *x-abilities*.

17.2 FUTURE DEVELOPMENT OF DIRECT-MAPPED PROCESSING

It is quite clear that the future of direct-mapped processing is highly related to further developments in VLSI technology, including the methods and tools related to specification, design, and synthesis of hardware resource structures. One interesting development in this area is the DSP Station, in which a holistic view of DSP development is taken. DSP algorithms can be simulated and analyzed; further, they can be optimized by a method that combines integer linear programming and general simulated annealing (see Chapter 8). Designs can be synthesized to commercially available DSP PEs, to bit-serial hardwired ASICs or to bit-parallel programmable ASICs. The philosophy, paradigm, and models for the DSP Station has been heavily influenced by experiences with CATHEDRAL II (see Rabaey and others, 1988).

It is also important to follow VHDL developments. A variety of tools for simulation and synthesis have arrived on the marketplace. Another interesting development to follow is the possibility for applying the VHDL behavioral description style to a wider class of programmed solutions.

The iWARP joint project between Intel Corporation and Carnegie-Mellon University is also worth following (see Borkar and others, 1990). Both systolic and memory-based communication are incorporated in a distributed memory machine. iWARP provides high-speed communication and supports tightly coupled computing as found in systolic arrays, as well as the message-passing style of computation found in wavefront arrays. It is envisioned that iWARP is suitable for a wide range of direct-mapped solutions.

17.3 FUTURE DEVELOPMENT OF THE MIMD FAMILY

It is always difficult to speculate about the future. In Chapter 6, we learned how several potential trends failed to be realized (at least to this point in time). Denning (1986) speculates that developments, especially with respect to MIMD solutions, will proceed in four stages, of which stage 1 and to a some extent stage 2 have occurred. Let us briefly summarize his view:

Stage 1 — parallelism introduced into the hardware of a single computer via multiple functional units, multibank memories, and data and instruction pipelines. Operating systems using the ready queue mechanism are altered to handle multiple servers in shared-memory systems.

Stage 2 — parallel execution of cooperating programs on different computers become explicit where programs exchange data over high-speed links rather than by passing addresses of shared data segments. Operating systems altered to deal with the management of distributed networks. Progress limited more by algorithm technology than programming technology (that is, can applications be decomposed to run on parallel processors?).

Stage 3 — new languages will make parallelism implicit and their compilers will take over the burden of partitioning programs. To date, experience has remained at the research level, and there is reason to believe that languages and compilers are currently incomplete with respect to solving real problems. The inability to deal with heterogeneous pieces or to define boundaries between them will motivate stage 4.

Stage 4 — there will be a very high level interface capable of interacting with scientists and engineers at the same level of abstraction as scientists do with each other. The interfaces will help formulate precise descriptions of problems in a given problem domain using natural languages, pictures, speech, and formal notation. The interface will decompose the problem descriptions into natural pieces for parallel processing.

If we examine current research and development interests in the field of parallel processing, we observe many activities already starting to take place in stages 3 and 4. Making these last two stages relevant for real-time applications places further demands on their development with respect to the special real-time requirements, including the ever present predictability requirement.

17.3.1 Portability and Reusability of Program Code

One serious concern of the computer industry is related to the portability and reusability of program code. Due to the unbalance in project costs between software and hardware, it is difficult to entice software developers to create programs on a one-off basis. To achieve rationality in operations, **currently** there is a need to reutilize the code for multiple projects and port it into varying environments. Many new commercial parallel processing ventures failed during the 1980s due to the problem of not being able to entice software developers to produce software products for their parallel processing hardware. This situation leads us to one of two views, either the separation or the integration of hardware and software concerns.

17.3.2 Case for Separating Hardware and Software Concerns

The von Neumann SISD architecture has been commercially successful due to the fact that a separation of concerns has been possible. That is, many software systems have been developed and ported between the architectural variants. Further, during the 1980s, we started to observe a greater awareness and utilization of software components (to a large extent inspired by the development of Ada and the general interest in object-oriented analysis, design, and programming languages).

The possibilities to contribute new solutions in the area of parallel processing are wide open. We find many creative professionals involved in such endeavors. As we considered in the first chapter, many solutions build upon analogies to other solutions. One such proposal by Valiant (1990) introduces a bulk-synchronous parallel BSP model. Valiant proposes this model as a standard upon which several parties can agree upon in moving from the von Neumann uniprocessor model to parallel processing in general-purpose computation. The major features of the model are as follows (Valiant, 1990):

1. A number of *components*, each performing processing and/or memory functions.
2. A *router* that delivers messages point to point between pairs of components; and
3. Facilities for synchronizing all or a subset of the components at regular intervals of L time units where L is the *periodicity* parameter. A computation consists of a sequence of *supersteps*. In each superstep, each component is allocated a task of some combination of local computation steps, message transmissions and (implicitly) message arrivals from other components. After each period of L time units, a global check is made to determine whether the superstep has been completed. If it has, the machine proceeds to the next superstep. Otherwise, the next period of L units is allocated to the unfinished superstep.

Valiant is suggesting the replacement of the multitude of synchronization and communication mechanisms found in current MIMD solutions with a single simple mechanism. There is, in fact, an interesting simliarity between the BSP model and Cy-Clone, presented in the previous chapter. In Cy-Clone, dT serves as the periodicity parameter. However, since the BSP model is aimed at general-purpose computation, it would not provide the predictability properties that are achieved by applying the well controlled Cy-Clone approach.

We can conclude that, while the separation of concerns makes a lot of sense for general-purpose computing, in the real-time sphere, unless the predictability properties can be extracted when moving software among hardware environments, the separation of these concerns will not provide appropriate solutions for hard real-time systems. In real-time environments, one can make a case for attempts at radically reducing software complexity by creating highly integrated hardware and software environments.

17.3.3 Case for Integrating Hardware and Software Concerns

The separation of concerns is based on the point of view that software is complex and thus costly to develop and support in project and product life cycles. Unfortunately, separation leads to generality, which can in turn lead to nondeterminism when implemented in a variety of resource-limited environments. One can make a strong case for the implementation of hard real-time systems in resource-adequate environments. Hardware is traded off against software in order to reduce software complexity and to achieve determinism. This can be achieved, to some extent, today with transputers coupled together in sufficient quantities to deal with the computational problems.

Further research and development in this area will yield further viable philosophies, paradigms, models, and artifacts for developing hard real-time systems. For example, Lawson and Svensson (1992) have proposed a further development of Cy-Clone where various time-controlled architectures can be integrated into a distributed/parallel environment.

For a further discussion of the future aspects of parallel processing systems, the excellent paper by Hey (1990) is highly recommended.

17.4 FUTURE DIRECTIONS FOR PE ARRAYS

Conventional computers have evolved from big machines residing in a few computer centers, via minicomputers and desktop computers, to embedded, yet powerful systems. We shall undoubtedly see massively parallel computers utilized in a distributed manner and coupled to workstations or integrated into larger industrial systems solving real-time applications.

An example of an effort to implement a minaturized massively parallel computer is the *BLITZEN* project at the Research Triangle of North Carolina (see Chapter 10). A highly integrated chip has been designed comprising as many as 128 bit-serial processing elements, each with 1K bit of on-chip memory. A board containing a few dozen, maybe a hundred, of these chips can be easily plugged into the backplane of a workstation or used in industrial environments where small size and large computing power are needed.

A likely development is that such massively parallel systems will be integrated with sensors and actuators in order to cope with the high input/output data rates. We have already demonstrated two examples, the LAPP and the PASIC systems (see Chapters 10 and 14). There will certainly be more.

It is quite possible that systems composed of many cooperating PE arrays, each integrated with some sensory or motor function or serving some other specialized task in the system, will evolve (see Figure 17.2). The different arrays are controlled by their own streams of instructions; thus, the total system may be characterized as MIMSIMD (Multiple Instruction Streams, Multiple SIMD). The cooperation between the modules will typically require very high bandwidth interarray communication.

These ideas conform with Arbib's (1989) "sixth generation computers" concept:

> The study of animal and human brain suggests overall architectural principles for "sixth generation computers." Each such machine will comprise a network of more specialized devices, with many of these devices structured as highly parallel arrays of interactive, neuron-like, possibly adaptive, components.

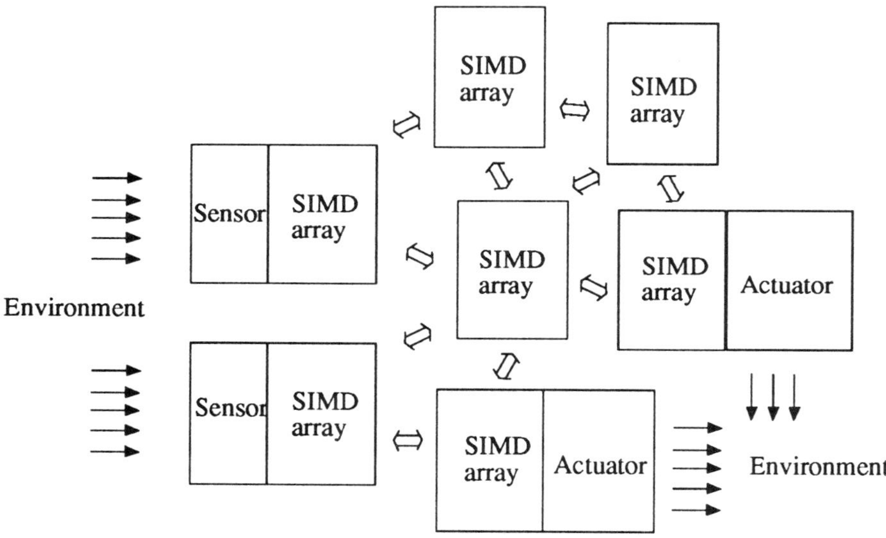

Figure 17.2. A MIMSIMD system integrated with sensors and actuators

According to Arbib, and quite in line with the Pandemonium model presented in Chapter 1, systems will be characterized by:

(a) *Cooperative computation:* the computer will be a heterogeneous network of special-purpose and general-purpose subsystems. Some of the subsystems (such as the front ends for perceptual PEs (see (b)), and devices for matrix manipulation) will be highly parallel;

(b) *Perceptual robotics:* increasingly, computers will have intelligent perceptual and motor interfaces with the surrounding world; and

(c) *Learning:* Many of the subsystems will be implemented as adaptive "neural style" networks.

It is also worth noting that much interest is being directed toward *optical* realizations of PE-array functions, especially as a solution to the communication problem. Beams of light may cross each other without interfering, making it possible to communicate between millions of PEs at once. The early practical systems utilizing optical technology will no doubt be hybrid electronic/optical systems.

17.5 A FINAL NOTE

In this book, we have introduced relevant developments in parallel processing up to the beginning of the 1990s. Further, we have continuously addressed the suitability of various philosophies, paradigms, models, and artifacts for real-time applications. It is the hope of the author that the book has provided a stimulating, fresh view of these topics and filled its role of both informing and stimulating creativity.

It is clear that in developing tomorrow's complex real-time systems parallel processing will play an important role. Distributed/parallel environments containing a variety of subsystems, each built according to appropriate philosophies, paradigms, and models, will undoubtedly be common practice the future. To paint this picture more explicitly, let us postulate the structure of a sophisticated yet realistic distributed mechantronical system, as portrayed in Figure 17.3. Parallel processing-based solutions can appear in many contexts in this environment, including the signal processing aspects of smart power subsystems.

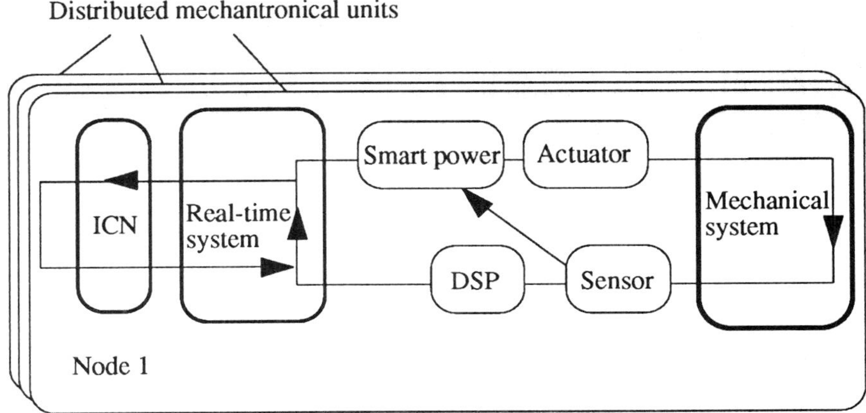

Figure 17.3. A Heterogeneous Distributed Mechantronics System

The multiplicity of solution spaces in environments of the type we have portrayed will place enormous demands upon our intellectual ability to realize reliable and responsive real-time solutions. The importance of *understandability* as a common denominator goal in this regard cannot be overly emphasized.

Finally, one last time:

THERE ARE NO SOLUTIONS; ONLY ALTERNATIVES

The development of appropriate alternatives will depend upon building upon existing approaches as well as finding new approaches. The challenge is there; we hope that **you** will be among those that help in discovering, developing, and/or applying tomorrow's alternatives.

References

Arbib, M.A. (1989). Schemas and Neural Networks for Sixth Generation Computing, *Journal of Parallel and Distributed Computing*, Vol. 6, pp. 185-216.

Borkar, S., R. Cohn, G. Cox, T. Gross, H.T. Kung, M. Lam, M. Levine, B. Moore, W. Moore, C. Peterson, J. Susman, J. Suton, J. Urbanski, and J. Webb (1990). Supporting Systolic and Memory Communication in iWARP, *Proceedings of the 17th Annual Symposium on Computer Architecture*, pp. 70-81, IEEE Computer Society Press, Los Alamitos, CA.

Denning, P.J. (1986). Parallel Computing and Its Evolution, *Communications of the ACM*, Vol. 29, No. 12, pp. 1163-67.

Hey, A.J.G. (1990). Supercomputing with Transputers - Past, Present and Future, *Proceedings of the ACM International Conference on Supercomputing*, ACM SIGARCH - Computer Architecture News, Vol. 18, No. 3.

Lawson, H.W. and B. Svensson (1992). An Architecture for Time-Critical Distributed/Parallel Processing, *Proceedings DSA92, Fourth Swedish Workshop on Computer System Architecture*, Linköping, Sweden, January.

Rabaey, J., H. DeMan, J. Vanhoof, G. Goossens, and F. Catthoor (1988). CATHEDRAL II: A Synthesis System for Multiprocessor DSP Systems, in *Silicon Compilation*, D. Gasjki (ed.), Addison-Wesley, Reading, MA.

Valiant, L. (1990). A Bridging Model for Parallel Computation, *Communications of the ACM*, Vol 33, No. 8, pp. 103-111.

LITERATURE REVIEW

The specific literature used as a basis for the book has been referenced at the end of each chapter. However, it is extremely important to have a good list of sources of material in order to follow developments in the field of parallel processing, especially as it is related to industrial real-time applications. Consequently, this literature review presents an overview of major relevant sources of professional publications, books, and survey articles. Naturally, the books and survey articles provide good starting points for your own further search of relevant specific technical contributions.

PROFESSIONAL PUBLICATIONS

A wide variety of professional publications cover various aspects of the theme presented in the book. The publications range from highly theoretical down to highly practical contributions. On the other hand, the potential reader should not let the title of the publication (Journal or Transaction) stand in the way of inquisitive search of the literature. Further, in a new area such as parallel processing, which affects many other subjects, articles tend to appear in diverse publication sources.

Given this background, **some** of the important general sources of relevant publications are as follows:

Proceedings of the IEEE
IEEE Journal of Selected Areas of Communications

IEE Proceedings
IEE Software Engineering Journal

IEEE Transactions on Computers
IEEE Transactions on Communications
IEEE Transactions on Circuits and Systems
IEEE Transactions on Software Engineering
IEEE Transactions on Systems, Man and Cybernetics
IEEE Transactions on Computer Aided Design
IEEE Transactions on Robotics and Automation
IEEE Transactions on Information Theory
IEEE Transactions on Parallel and Distributed Systems
IEEE Transactions on Pattern Analysis and Machine Intelligence
IEEE Computer
IEEE Control Systems
IEEE Communications
IEEE Circuits and Devices
IEEE Design and Test
IEEE Expert
IEEE Network
IEEE Micro
IEEE Software
IEEE Spectrum

Journal of the ACM
ACM Communications
ACM Transactions on Computer Systems
ACM Computing Surveys
ACM Transactions on Programming Languages and Systems

Advanced Robotics, The International Journal of the Robotics Society of Japan

ACM Special Interest Group Publications, especially
SIGARCH (Architecture)
SIGMETRICS
SIGPLAN Notices (Programming Languages)

Euromicro Journal
SIAM Journal on Computing

International Journal of Real-time Systems, Kluwer Academic Publishers

Journal of VLSI Signal Processing, Kluwer Academic Publishers

Distributed Computing, Springer International, Berlin

Journal of Parallel and Distributed Computing, Academic Press, Inc.

Parallel Computing, North-Holland

Concurrency: Practice and Experience, John Wiley & Sons, Ltd.

Neural Networks, Pergamon Press

PERIODIC CONFERENCES, WORKSHOPS, AND SYMPOSIUMS

There are a large number of professional meetings that relate to the theme of the book. Several of them are held regularly and the proceedings form a valuable source of relevant information.

ACM International Conference on Supercomputing
ACM/IEEE/IFIP International Conference on Pattern Recognition
ACM/IEEE Design Automation Conference
ACM/IEEE Symposium on Computer Architecture
ACM SIGMETRICS International Conference on Measurement and Modeling of Computer Systems

American Control Conference

IEEE Real-time System Symposium
IEEE Frontiers of Massively Parallel Computation
IEEE International Conference on Computer Design
IEEE CompEuro
IEEE Conference on Robotics and Automation

Euromicro Symposium on Microprocessing and Microprogramming
Euromicro Workshop on Real Time

ESPRIT PARLE: Parallel Architectures and Languages

CONPAR: Conference on Algorithms and Hardware for Parallel Processing

International Conference on Parallel Processing, Pennsylvania State University Press

THEORETICAL CONTRIBUTIONS

Here we consider a few publications that have provided a basis for important theories that are relevant to the topic of the book but that are not conveniently placed into other literature categories.

Garey, M.R., and D. S. Johnson (1979). *Computing and Intractability: A Guide to the Theory of NP-Completeness*, Freeman, San Francisco. A complete description of the NP-complete theory and methods for approximative solutions. Approximately, 200 NP-complete problems are enumerated, including many scheduling problems that are relevant in resource-limited environments.

Lamport, L. (1978). Time, Clocks and the Ordering of Events in a Distributed System, *Communications of the ACM*, Vol. 21, No. 7, pp. 558-565. A classic theoretical presentation of synchronization in distributed systems.

BOOKS, SURVEY ARTICLES, CASE STUDIES, SPECIAL ISSUES

The comments provided for the majority of the following publications are meant as a general classification of contents and are purely based upon subjective judgments by the author. The lack of comments should **not** be interpreted to mean that the material is in any way less important or less relevant.

Real-time Applications and Systems

Books

Allworth, S.T., and R.N. Zobel (1987). *Introduction to Real-time System Design,* Macmillan, New York. An introduction to real-time systems. A real-time virtual machine is defined using the MASCOT methodology. The virtual machine provides support for real-time parallel processing environments. Issues of scheduling, reliability, interfaces, performance, and design methodology are considered.

Bowen, B.A., and W.R. Brown (1985). *System Design: Volume II of VLSI Systems Design for Digital Signal Processing*, Prentice Hall, Englewood Cliffs, NJ.

Burns, A., and A. Wellings (1990). *Real-time Systems and Their Programming Languages*, Addison-Wesley, Reading, MA. A rather general treatment of the subject emphasizing software aspects. Ada, occam2, and Modula-2 are used as languages for explaining concrete concepts. Concentrates more on the artifacts used for developing real-time systems than upon real-time application problems.

Furht, B., D. Grostik, D. Gluch, G. Rabbat, J. Parker, and M. McRoberts (1991). *Real-Time Unix Systems-Design and Application Guide*, Kluwer Academic Publishers, Boston-Dordrecht-London. Describes the general problems in building preemptive (event driven) operating systems as well as the implementation of REAL/IX which is a product of the MODCOMP corporation of Ft. Lauderdale, Florida. Properties of REAL/IX are analyzed and several application examples are presented. Highly recommended.

Halang, W.A., and A.D. Stoyenko (1991). *Constructing Predictable Real Time Systems*, Kluwer Academic Publishers, Boston-Dordrecht-London. A valuable contribution. Describes how predicatable real-time systems can be created via constraints placed upon behavioral description, operating system, and hardware. *A priori* assessment of behavior is accomplished via schedulability analysis. Highly recommended.

Levi, S.-T., and A.K. Agrawala (1990). *Real time System Design*, McGraw-Hill, New York. Contemporary book covering several central software system concepts of real-time systems. Covers areas such as real-time reasoning, time-based resource allocation and scheduling, time knowledge and clocks, fault tolerance under time constraints.

Ripps, D.L. (1989). *An Implementation Guide to Real-Time Systems*, Yourdan Press Computing Series, New York. Describes how to design and use a traditional real-time operating system. It provides a cookbook on the design and implementation of a kernel. No specific attention is given to parallel/distributed environments.

Soucek, B. (1989). *Neural Networks and Concurrent Real-time Systems: The Sixth Generation*, Wiley-Interscience, New York. Provides an introduction to real-time systems and neural networks. Several examples of the use of neural networks in real-time applications are provided. An extensive reference list is included in each chapter.

Stankovic, J.A., and K. Ramamritham (1988). *Tutorial: Hard Real-Time Systems*, IEEE Computer Society Press, Los Alamitos, CA. In lieu of an encompassing textbook covering the subject of hard real-time systems, this combined tutorial and collection of important articles is highly useful. The subject is covered from a variety of viewpoints. Highly recommended.

Special Issues

Krishna, C.M., and Y.H. Lee (1991). Real-Time Systems, *IEEE Computer*, Vol. 24, No. 5.

Schoppers, M. (1991). Real-Time Knowledge-Based Control Systems, *Communications of the ACM*, Vol. 34, No. 8.

General Parallel Processing Literature

The following literature provides general and in some cases comprehensive overviews of the subject of parallel/distributed processing. Many of these books have provided useful sources for the preparation of this book.

Books

Almasi, G.S., and A. Gottlieb (1989). *Highly Parallel Computing*, Benjamin/-Cummings, Redwood City, CA. An important contribution to the technical literature on parallel processing. Provides some sample applications. Presents both hardware and software issues related to a variety of parallel processing architectures. Highly recommended for serious study.

Anderson, A.J. (1989). *Multiple Processing*, Prentice Hall, Englewood Cliffs, NJ. A well-written, thorough textbook covering computer architectures for parallel processing.

Babb, R.G. (1988). *Programming Parallel Processors*, Addison-Wesley, Reading, MA. Provides a programmer's view of eight commercially available multiprocessors. Each machine is described according to architecture, operating system, and programming paradigm. A common benchmark program is used to compare the eight architectures.

Baer, J.L. (1980). *Computer System Architecture*, Computer Science Press, Rockville, MD. One of the earliest computer architecture books on fundamental concepts of supercomputers and parallel processing. Broad treatment of the field, somewhat outdated.

Coulouris, G.F., and F. Dollimore (1988). *Distributed Systems: Concepts and Design*, Addison-Wesley, Reading, MA.

DeCegama, A.L. (1989). *The Technology of Parallel Processing: Parallel Processing Arhcitectures and Hardware*, Vol. 1, Prentice Hall, Englewood Cliffs, NJ. A highly useful **encyclopedia** of the field of parallel processing. Represents an enormous effort on the part of the author to review both the professional literature and practice in the field. Two further volumes are in preparation.

Hayes, J. P. (1988). *Computer Architecture and Organization*, 2nd ed., McGraw-Hill, New York.

Hockney, R.W., and C.R. Jesshope (1988). *Parallel Computers 2: Architecture, Programming and Algorithms*, Adam Higler, Philadelphia, PA. This second edition extends the previous edition, which concentrated largely on supercomputers. A very thorough book covering many aspects of parallel processing from hardware, software, and application points of view. Introduces a classification formalism as well as a normalized performance measurement. Recommended for serious study.

Hwang, K., and F.A. Briggs (1984). *Computer Architecture and Parallel Processing*, McGraw-Hill, New York.

Hwang, K., and D. DeGroot, (eds.) (1989). *Parallel Processing for Supercomputers & Artificial Intelligence*, McGraw-Hill, New York. Despite the name "artificial intelligence" in the title, this book provides a collection of articles covering a wide range of parallel processing-related topics.

Kain, R.Y. (1989). *Computer Architecture, Hardware and Software: Volume II*, Prentice Hall, Englewood Cliffs, NJ.

Krishnamurthy, E.V. (1989). *Parallel Processing: Principles and Practices*, Addison-Wesley, Reading, MA. A book containing an enormous information volume per page. Covers, in a summary form, almost all major theoretical and practical aspects of parallel processing. Only recommended for serious study. The information density makes reading somewhat difficult.

Lewis, T.G. and El-Rewini, H. (1992). *Introduction to Parallel Computing*. Prentice Hall, Englewood Cliffs, NJ. A textbook covering the fundamentals of parallel computing. Provides a good introduction to various paradigms of parallel programming. Highly recommended.

Lipovski, G.J., and M. Malek (1987). *Parallel Computing: Theory and Practice*, Wiley-Interscience, New York. Presents a well-structured point of view concerning parallel processing. Some very useful thoughts on testing and fault tolerance are presented. The Texas Reconfigurable Computer is examined in detail; however, several other architectures are presented.

Mullender, S. (1989). *Distributed Systems*, ACM Press, New York, and Addison-Wesley, Reading, MA. A collection of work on distributed systems by experts in the field. Areas such as communication, naming, security, data storage, transactions, replication, methodology, and architecture are considered. Introductions and examples are provided. Assumes a familiarity with computer organization, computer networks, and operating systems.

Siewiorek, D., C.G. Bell, and A. Newell (1982). *Computer Structures: Principles and Examples*, McGraw-Hill, New York. An extremely valuable contribution. The PMS (Processor-Memory-Switch) notation is defined and used as a common means of categorizing computer architectures. Numerous architectures is presented. The book needs updating to take account of the parallel processing developments of the 1980s.

Stone, H. S. (1990). *High-performance Computer Architecture*, Addison-Wesley, Reading, MA. A well-structured book that describes important design concepts and principles for high-speed (including parallel) computers. Particularly useful are the methods of evaluating important concepts and mechanisms. Highly recommended.

Tabak, D. (1990). *Multiprocessors*, Prentice Hall, Englewood Cliffs, NJ. Concentrates solely on multiprocessor systems, from the hardware and system software points of view. An excellent introduction to the subject.

Treleavan, P.C., (ed.) (1989). *Parallel Computers - Object-oriented, Functional and Logic*, Wiley, New York. Presents parallel processing projects incorporated into the European Esprit programme. Recommended for a view of European research projects.

Survey Articles and Special Issues

Enslow, P.H. (1977). Multiprocessor Organization, *ACM Computing Surveys*, Vol. 9, No. 1, pp. 103-129. A very early contribution to the professional literature.

Haynes, L.S., R.L. Lan, D.P. Siewiorek, and D.W. Mizell (1982). A Survey of Highly Parallel Computing, *IEEE Computer*, Vol. 15, No. 1, pp. 9-24. A bit out of date but highly recommended.

Patt, Y. N. (1991). Experimental Research in Computer Architecture, *IEEE Computer*, Vol. 24, No. 1.

Singhal, M., and T. L. Casavant (1991). Distributed Computing Systems, *IEEE Computer*, Vol. 24, No. 8.

Specific Parallel Processing Architectures and Systems

Books

Fountain, T. (1987). *Processor Arrays: Architectures and Applications*, Academic Press, New York. A good introduction to the principles and practices of SIMD PE-array architectures. Several specific systems are described.

Hillis, W.D. (1985). *The Connection Machine*, MIT Press, Cambridge, MA. Selected for publication as an ACM Distinguished Dissertation, this book provides an excellent overview of parallel processing issues and provides the foundation for the development of the Connection Machine. Very worthwhile reading.

Iannucci, R.A. (1990). *Parallel Machines: Parallel Machine Languages*, Kluwer Academic Publishers, Boston, MA. Presents a framework for understanding the tradeoffs between the conventional view and the dataflow view of processing. Introduces a viable approach to scalable general purpose parallel computation.

Kowalik, S.J., (ed.) (1985). *Parallel MIMD Computation: The HEP Supercomputer and its Applications*, MIT Press, Cambridge, MA. A collection of articles that describes the archictecture and use of one of the first commercially available MIMD machines.

McCanny, J., J. McWhirter, and E. Swartzlander, Jr. (eds.) (1989). *Systolic Array Processors*, Prentice Hall, Englewood Cliffs, NJ.

Nossek, J.A. (ed.) (1991). *Parallel Processing on VLSI Arrays*, Kluwer Academic Publishers, Boston, MA. A collection of eight invited contributions.

Potter, J.L., (ed.) (1985). *The Massively Parallel Processor*, MIT Press, Cambridge, Mass. A collection of articles explaining the architecture and applications of the Goodyear MPP computer system.

Wulf, W.A., R. Levin, and S.P. Harbison (1981). *HYDRA/C.mmp: An Experimental Computer System*, Mc-Graw-Hill, New York. Explains the concepts of one of the first experimental MIMD systems of Carnegie- Mellon University.

Survey and Case Study Articles

Siewiorek, D.P., V. Kini, H. Mashburn, S. McConnel, M. Tsao, R. Joobbani, and H. Bellis (1978). A Case Study of C.mmp, Cm* and C.vmp, Parts I and II, *Proceedings of the IEEE*, Vol. 66, No. 10, pp. 1178-1220. Explains and compares various experimental MIMD architectures developed at Carnegie-Mellon University.

Treleaven, P.C., D.R. Brownbridge, and R.P. Hopkins (1982). Data-Driven and Demand-Driven Computer Architecture, *ACM Computing Surreys*, Vol. 14, No. 1, pp. 93-143. The first overview of these topics. Still useful as an introduction.

Veen, A.H. (1986). Dataflow Machine Architecture, *ACM Computing Surveys*, Vol. 18, No. 4, pp. 365-396. Provides an overview of various approaches to dataflow architectures and surveys research projects.

Interconnection Networks

Books

Dubois, M., and S. Thakkar (eds.) (1990). *Cache and Interconnect Architectures in Multiprocessors*, Kluwer Academic Publishers, Boston, MA. A collection of invited papers concerning cache coherency protocols for general interconnects.

Reed, D.A., and R.J. Fujimoto (1987). *Multicomputer Networks - Message-based Parallel Processing*, MIT Press, Cambridge, MA. Provides a useful approach to understanding the structure and evaluation of the properties of MINs. Analytic and simulated results are reported. Concrete applications and commercial systems are studied.

Siegel, H.J. (1990). *Interconnection Networks for Large-scale Parallel Processing*, Mc-Graw-Hill, New York. First published in 1985. The first comprehensive book on the subject. A classic contribution now in its updated and improved second edition.

Solman, M., and J. Kramer (1987). *Distributed Systems and Computer Networks*, Prentice Hall, Englewood Cliffs, NJ. Provides a detailed description of hardware and software architectures for distributed systems and communication networks in LAN and WAN environments.

Survey Articles and Special Issues

Bhuyan, L.N. (ed.) (1987). Interconnection Networks for Parallel and Distributed Processing, *IEEE Computer*, Vol. 20, No. 6.

Feng, T.Y. (1981). A Survey of Interconnection Networks, *IEEE Computer*, Vol. 14, No. 2, pp. 12-27. Presents and discusses the design issues of ICNs for parallel processing. A detailed description of network topologies and switching methods is provided. A bit outdated, but still quite useful.

Liu, M. T. (ed.) (1991). Special Issue on Protocol Engineering, *IEEE Transactions on Computers*, Vol. 40, No. 4.

Behavioral Description

Books

Ben-Ari, M. (1990). *Principles of Concurrent and Distributed Computing*, Prentice Hall, Englewood Cliffs, NJ. Presents the major issues in concurrent programming in a highly readable manner. Recommended for deeper concurrent programming insight than has been provided in this book.

Brinch Hansen, P. (1977). *The Architecture of Concurrent Programs*, Prentice Hall, Englewood Cliffs, NJ.

Burns, A. (1985). *Concurrent Programming in Ada*, Cambridge University Press, New York. Contains a detailed discussion of the Ada tasking model and a brief overview of the Ada langauge. A large number of examples are provided.

Bustard, D., J. Elder, and J. Welsh (1988). *Concurrent Program Structures*, Prentice Hall, Englewood Cliffs, NJ. An in-depth presentation of concurrent programming with many examples. The Pascal Plus language is used as the concrete media for presentation. Recommended for serious reading concerning concurrent programming.

Chandy, K.M., and J. Misra (1988). *Parallel Program Design: A Foundation*, Addison-Wesley, Reading, MA. Presents an important new theory of concurrent/parallel programming called UNITY. A solid base for the theory is provided. Recommended for serious study.

Conery, J.S. (1987). *Parallel Execution of Logic Programs*, Kluwer Academic Publishers, Boston, MA.

Gehani, N. (1984). *Ada: Concurrent Programming*, Prentice Hall, Englewood Cliffs, NJ.

Gehani, N. (1989). *The Concurrent C Programming Language*, Prentice Hall, Englewood Cliffs, NJ. Introduces a superset of the C and C++ programming languages for concurrent and distributed programming using the extended rendezvous model from Ada. One chapter provides an excellent survey over the evolution of synchronization primitives.

Gehani, N., and A.D. McGettrick (eds.) (1988). *Concurrent Programming*, Addison-Wesley, Reading, MA. An important collection of articles that provides both insight and details related to varying views of concurrent programming. Highly recommended.

Hoare, C.A.R. (1985). *Communicating Sequential Processes*, Prentice Hall, Englewood Cliffs, NJ. Defines a theory of concurrency that is suitable for mathematically competent programmers. CSP has affected many other developments. Recommended for deeper thinking in this subject area.

Holt, R. C. (1983). *Concurrent Euclid, The Unix System, and Tunis*, Addison-Wesley, Reading, MA. Introduces concurrency problems and solutions via the Concurrent Euclid language. Provides a good overview of the Unix operating system, as well as a modified version called Tunis, which provides an environment for the implementation of Concurrent Euclid.

Inmos Ltd. (1984). *Occam Programming Manual*, Prentice Hall, Englewood Cliffs, NJ.

Jones, G., and Goldsmith, M. (1988). *Programming in Occam-2*, Prentice Hall, Englewood Cliffs, NJ. After introducing occam2 syntax and semantics, a variety of programming methods is examined in detail. Several practical examples are provided. Recommended for the serious occam and transputer enthusiast.

Milner, R. (1989). *Communication and Concurrency*, Prentice Hall, Englewood Cliffs, NJ. A thorough description of the CCS calculus developed by Milner for describing communicating concurrent processes. Highly recommended for a sound theoretical presentation.

Perrott, R.H. (1987). *Parallel Programming*, Addison-Wesley, Reading, MA. A well-structured presentation of the major issues in synchronous and asynchronous parallel programming. Easy to read.

Wadge, W.W., and E.A. Ashcroft (1985). *LUCID, The Dataflow Programming Language*, Academic Press, New York. Presents a dataflow programming style that can be applied within dataflow architectures or simulated within the framework of conventional architectures.

Watt, D.A. (1990). *Programming Language Concepts and Paradigms*, Prentice Hall, Englewood Cliffs, NJ. This excellent presentation of programming language concepts and paradigms is highly recommended. Many relevant issues of parallel processing are addressed in the book.

Williams, S.A. (1990). *Programming Models for Parallel Systems*, Wiley, New York. Provides a brief description of the central concepts for programming of parallel systems. Recommended for a general introduction.

Yokote, Y. (1989). *The Design and Implementation of Concurrent Smalltalk*, World Scientific Series in Computer Science, Vol. 21, Singapore. A very good introduction to concurrent object-oriented programming. Explains the philosophy behind the implementation of Concurrent Smalltalk as well as the implementation approach. Highly recommended.

Survey Articles, Tutorial Articles and Special Issues

Andrews, G.R., and F.B. Schneider (1983). Concepts and Notions for Concurrent Programming, *ACM Computing Surveys*, Vol. 15, No. 1, pp. 3-43. An excellent overview of the mechanisms for concurrent programming covering fundamental ideas of processes, communication, and synchronization. Highly recommended.

Bal, H.E., J.G. Steiner, and A.S. Tanenbaum (1989). Programming Languages for Distributed Computing Systems, *ACM Computing Surveys*, Vol. 21, No. 3, pp. 261-322. A thorough investigation of the state of the art of languages for distributed computing systems (defined by the authors as multicomputers that communicate by message passing). Fifteen representative distributed languages are described and a comprehensive bibliography is supplied. Well worth studying.

Cohen, J. (ed.) (1992). Special Section on Logic Programming, *Communications of the ACM*, Vol. 35, No. 3. An useful collection of papers on logic programming including an excellent historical and tutorial account by J.A. Robinson.

Davis, A. (1988). A Comparison of Techniques for the Specification of External System Behaviour, *Communications of the ACM*, Vol. 31, No. 9. Provides coverage of various techniques for describing the behavior of real systems. Illustrates the importance of the careful application of scientific approaches to practical problems. Various examples are provided to explain different methods.

Korson, T., and J.D. McGregor (1990). Understanding Object-oriented: A Unifying Paradigm, *Communications of the ACM* Vol. 33, No. 9, pp. 40-60. Provides useful definitions of the terms object based and object oriented. Describes the history and current trends in the use of the paradigm. This is an introductory article for a special issue on object-oriented design and many other excellent articles appear in the issue.

Murata, T. (1989). Petri Nets: Properties, Analysis and Applications, *Proceedings of the IEEE*, Vol. 77, No. 4, pp. 541-580. An overview article with 315 references covering Petri nets. Petri nets are defined and exmplified for communication protocols and multiprocessor systems. Important properties of Petri nets and methods for determining reachability, boundedness, and liveliness are described. Timed and stochastic Petri nets are covered.

Wing, J.M. (1990). A Specifier's Introduction to Formal Methods, *IEEE Computer*, Vol. 23, No. 9, pp. 8-24. A very useful introduction to the state of the art and practice in the area of formal methods. Highly recommended.

Allocation and Scheduling (Compilers and Operating Systems)

Books

Joseph, N., V.R. Prasad, and N. Natarajan (1984). *A Multiprocessor Operating System*, Prentice Hall, Englewood Cliffs, NJ.

Zima, H., and B. Chapman (1991). *Supercompilers for Parallel and Vector Computers*, Addison-Wesley, Reading, MA. An in-depth treatment of modern restructuring tools (supercompilers) that detects implicit concurrency and transform programs into concurrent code. Covers both shared memory and distributed memory systems.

Special Issue and Survey Article

Boykin, J., and S.J. LoVerso (eds.) (1990). Recent Developments in Operating Systems, *IEEE Computer*, Vol. 23, No. 5. Contains a number of articles that deal with parallel/distributed operating systems, including papers on Mach and Amoeba.

Mauney, J., D.P. Agrawal, Y.K. Choe, E.A. Harcourt, S. Kim, and W.J. Staats (1989). Computational Models and Resource Allocation for Supercomputers, *Proceedings of the IEEE*, Vol. 77, No. 12, pp. 1859-1874. An overview of many of the central issues related to resource allocation of processes is provided. Several concrete examples and an excellent reference list are provided.

Image and Signal Processing

Books

Bayoumi, M.A. (ed.) (1991). *Parallel Algorithms and Architectures for DSP Applications*, Kluwer Academic Publishers, Boston, MA. A collection of contributions which address related issues and problems of DSP algorithms and architectures.

Choudhary, A.N., and J.H. Patel (1990). *Parallel Architectures for Integrated Vision Systems*, Kluwer Academic Publishers, Boston, MA. Examines issues in designing hierarchical and partitionable architectures for vision systems. A model of computation for problems in integrated vision systems (IVS) is developed.

Uhr, L. (ed.) (1987). *Parallel Computer Vision*, Academic Press, New York.

Special Issue

Choudhary, A.N., and S. Ranka (1992). Parallel Processing for Computer Vision and Image Understanding, *IEEE Computer*, Vol. 25, No. 2. Contains a variety of highly useful state of the art contributions.

Parallel Algorithms and Problem Solving

Books

Akl, S.G. (1989). *The Design and Analysis of Parallel Algorithms*, Prentice Hall, Englewood Cliffs, NJ. A well-written book on the subject. Good practical examples are provided. The emphasis is more on algorithms and underlying architectures than on mathematical properties. Recommended for those seeking a straightforward introduction to this subject.

Fox, G., M. Johnson, G. Lyzenga, S. Otto, J. Salmon, and D. Walker (1988). *Solving Problems on Concurrent Processors*, Vol 1: *General Techiques and Regular Problems*, Prentice Hall, Engelwood Cliffs, NJ. An excellent book with a wealth of information concerning problem solving in many aspects of natural science. The emphasis is upon solutions in hypercube architectures, which reflects the experience of the authors. Highly recommended for a serious study of parallel processing applications.

Quinn, M.J. (1987). *Designing Efficient Algorithms for Parallel Computers*, McGraw-Hill, NewYork. Provides a well-structured introduction to the topic. Emphasis is placed upon algorithms for architectural variants. Recommended for an overview of the subject area.

Fault Tolerance, Testing, and Verification

Books

Anderson, T., and P.A. Lee (1981). *Fault-tolerance Principles and Practice*, Prentice Hall, Englewood Cliffs, NJ.

Siewiorek, D.P., and R.S. Swarz (1982). *The Theory and Practice of Reliable System Design*, Digital Press, Bedford, MA.

Survey Articles and Special Issue

Randell, B., P.A. Lee, and P.C. Treleavan (1978). Reliability Issues in Computing System Design, *ACM Computing Surveys*, Vol. 10, No. 2, pp. 123-65.

Schneider, F.B. (1990). Implementing Fault-tolerant Services Using the State Machine Approach: A Tutorial, *ACM Computing Surveys*, Vol. 22, No. 4, pp. 299-319.

Singh, A.D., and S. Murugesan (eds.) (1990). Fault-tolerant Systems, *IEEE Computer*, Vol. 23, No. 7. A number of informative articles are presented on various aspects of testing, error control, and fault tolerance in software and hardware structures. Recommended for a good overview of the state of the art.

Evaluation of Parallel Processing

Books

King, P.J.B. (1990). *Computer and Communication Systems Performance Modeling*, Prentice Hall, Englewood Cliffs, NJ. A good introduction to the subject. Treats both the theory and application in a straightforward manner. Highly recommended.

Lazowska, E.D., J. Zahorjan, G.S. Graham, and K.C. Sevic (1984). *Quantative System Performance*, Prentice Hall, Engelwood Cliffs, NJ. An excellent book for gaining an understanding of queuing network models and their application.

Marsan, M.A., G. Balbo, and G. Conte (1986), *Performance Models of Multiprocessor Systems*, MIT Press, Cambridge, MA. This book addresses the modeling and performance of MIMD multiprocessor systems via analytical methods. Emphasis is placed upon stochastic processes and queuing models. Recommended for a general insight into the subject.

Simmons, M., R. Koskela, and I. Bucher (1989). *Instrumentation for Parallel Computing Systems*, ACM Press, New York, and Addison-Wesley, Reading, MA. A collection of workshop articles.

GLOSSARY

It is difficult to obtain complete agreement on the definition of terms, especially in areas like parallel processing and real-time systems. The nomenclature that has been used throughout this book and provided here has been taken, to a large extent, from a cross section of existing definitions in the professional literature.

actuators — the means of controlling behavior in the external environment. Can involve digital to analog conversion when required.

address space — The set of all possible addresses available to a *process*. In some systems, the address space can be further categorized into a *virtual address space* and a *physical address space*.

Amdahl's law — Presents a case against parallel processing by observing that the maximum speedup achievable is limited by the proportion of the program code that must be executed sequentially.

aperiodic process — A process that can be initiated at any arbitrary point in time (compare with *periodic process*).

application parallelism — The natural parallelism that can be extracted from the application. The parallelism may be due to the geometry of data to be processed and/or the natural decomposition of processing algorithms.

ASAP and ALAP scheduling — As Soon as Possible and As Late as Possible scheduling refer to the scheduling of a process when its predecessor processes are ready, or postponing scheduling a process for a time step if there are more processes to be executed than available PEs.

associative memory — A memory whose contents are accessed by a key rather than via an address.

asynchronous — A means of synchronizing processes (software and/or hardware) in which explicit signals are transmitted between processes that mark the point at which processing can commence and when it has terminated. In the context of communication, often referred to as hand shaking.

balance — A state in which the PE bandwidth is in close match with the memory, interconnection network, and I/O system such that no specific hardware process(es) limits performance.

bandwidth — The number of bits per second that can be processed by a memory, an arithmetic unit, input/output system, or interconnection network.

barrier — A parallel programming synchronization mechanism that forces a number of processes to wait until all have reached some common point (see *event, read/write lock, semaphore*, and *spinlock*).

behavior — How a process or set of processes (external or internal to the computer system) reacts under particular situations (conditions).

bit serial — A means of processing data one bit at time. For example, a bit-serial adder, which adds one bit at a time (compare with *word parallel*).

block — A collection of contiguous data and/or program code that is treated as a single entity of cache memory.

BMR (behavior-mapping-resource) model — The model introduced in this book in order to unify views of various parallel processing alternatives.

broadcast — The transmission on a one-to-many (perhaps all) basis. Accomplished by various means dependent upon the ICN that is utilized.

bus — An interconnection in which all transmitters and receivers are directly connected to a common set of lines.

cache coherence — Describes a state, essential on shared-memory multiprocessors that employ separate *cache memory* for each processor, in which cached data are kept consistent across caches. To keep the data consistent, a coherence protocol is utilized.

cache directory — The collection of tags in a cache that is utilized for associative access to cached data.

cache memory — A small, high-speed memory placed between slower main memory and the processor. A cache increases effective memory transfer rates and processor speed. It contains copies of data recently referenced by the processor and fetches several bytes of data from memory in anticipation that the processor will access the next sequential series of bytes. Caches additionally reduce the number of transfers on system buses, allowing more processors to be effectively utilized in a *multiprocessor* system.

central control — The placement of control of a system (for example, an ICN interconnection network or PE array) in a central position (compare *individual control*).

circuit switched — A transport method for ICN (interconnection networks) where complete connections are established between sender and receiver and held for the duration of the communication. The telephone switching system is a good example (compare with *packet switched*).

closely coupled — Describes a *multicomputer* architecture in which component processors share the same bus, but run separate operating systems and are assigned private blocks of memory (see *loosely coupled* and *tightly coupled*).

coarse-grain parallelism — Parallel execution in which the amount of computation per process is several times larger than overhead and communication expended per process (compare with *fine-grain parallelism*).

communication — Any process involved in transmitting information between PEs, between M processes, or combinations thereof. Physical communication can be accomplished by direct wiring, by buses, or by channels of various types.

concurrent execution — The execution of multiple processes that have started but not completed and thus are active at the same point in time. The processes may be executed by a single or multiple PEs (compare with *parallel execution*).

concurrent programming — Programming required to deal with competition between processes for resources in resource-limited environments and interprocess communication among cooperating processes (compare with *parallel programming*).

conditional critical regions — A method of implementing controlled P and V synchronization primitives in which a condition is evaluated and, if true, a request for the resource (P) is made.

constructive method — A scheduling method that constructs a solution, as opposed to methods that attempt to successfully develop better solutions.

context switch — Saving of the state of a currently executing process and restoring the state of another process enabling a PE(s) to switch among processes.

CPS (connections per second) — A measure of performance for neural net hardware.

critical path list scheduling — An ordered list of processes (operations) is formed, followed by the selection of operations for scheduling according to the length of path from the start of operations; time-critical paths are given higher priority.

critical processes — Process that must meet their deadlines; otherwise, the results can be catastrophic (see also *essential* and *nonessential processes*).

critical regions — A portion of program code under which mutually exclusive use of a resource is guaranteed.

crossbar network — An interconnection network in which each input is connected to each output through a path that contains a single switching node.

cycle time — The length of a single cycle of a computer function, such as a memory or PE cycle.

cyclic systems — A paradigm for organizing the execution of processes in repetitive loops.

cyclostatic scheduling — PE schedules for processes (operations) in one sample interval are developed for multiple PEs.

DAG directed acyclic graph — A direct graph without cycles

dataflow architecture — An architecture that is based upon the notion that data events drive processing asynchronously. The order of execution does not have to abide by program ordering.

deadlock — The state in which two or more processes are deferred indefinitely because they are mutually holding resources required for each others progress.

dependability — The stabile provision of properly functioning hardware and system software resources (compare with *responsiveness*).

Dhrystone — A programming benchmark that measures processor (and compiler) efficiency in executing a typical benchmark. Dhrystone does not use floating-point, I/O, or operating system calls, and contains little code that could be optimized by vector processors.

diameter — The maximum number of times that a message must be forwarded between routers when traveling from one PE to another.

direct binary *n*-cube — A network organized in the form of a cube in n dimensions where the connections are made directly from PE to PE, for example, in a hypercube multcomputer (compare with *indirect binary n-cube*).

direct blocking — A scheduling formulation that permits the scheduling of processes (operations) over multiple sample interval boundaries without regard to artificial boundaries.

direct-mapped systems — A direct mapping between application behavior and the resource structure.

direct-mapping cache — A *cache memory* in which only one address comparison is needed to locate any data in the cache because any block of main memory data can be placed in only one possible position in the cache (compare with *fully associative cache*).

distributed systems — Systems where hardware resources are physically distributed over a long distance. Long in this case means a loose coupling. When cooperating in the solution of the same problem, they are not differentiated from *parallel processing systems*.

DSP (digital signal processing) — The use of discrete-time digital techniques for the reduction of information content in signals in order to facilitate decisions and/or to condition the signals for further processing, including storage and transmission.

dynamic processes — Processes that are created during the system operation as required and removed when no longer needed.

dynamic schedule — A scheduling strategy that is dictated by the fact that process execution characteristics are not completely known in advance, for example, asynchronous event-driven systems.

earliest deadline scheduling — A scheduling method where at every time step the process whose deadline is closest is scheduled.

ECC (error correction code) — Designates a technique of encoding and checking extra bits associated with each data word so that any single-bit error in the data word can be identified and automatically corrected.

embedded systems — Systems that are incorporated into other noncomputer systems, for example, machines, tools, or automobiles.

essential processes — Processes that have a deadline and, while important to the operation of the system, will not cause a catastrophe if they do not meet their deadlines.

Ethernet — A network consisting of a wideband coaxial cable to which participating nodes are connected by means of electrically isolated transceivers. These transceivers assist in synchronizing transmissions by sensing the presence of contending signals on the Ethernet and requiring their own nodes to retry conflicting transmissions. Ethernet communications are accomplished by means of data packets, each of which carries the identity of both sender and intended receiver.

event — A parallel programming synchronization mechanism that allows a group of cooperating processes to wait for a common flag to be set (typically by another process) and then to proceed simultaneously (see also *barrier, read/lock, semaphore,* and *spinlock*). The term event is also used to indicate an occurrence of a situation in the external environment.

event driven — Refers to systems where the occurrence of events is used to control processing.

exchange instruction — A single-time indivisible instruction that tests the value of an exclusion variable (for example Test and Set). Used to provide mutual exclusion. Can lead to busy waiting.

extra-stage cube network — An indirect cube network in which an extra stage has been added to provide for network reconfiguration in the presence of single faults.

fine-grain parallelism — A form of parallel execution where the amount of work per process is small compared with the amount of work per process required for communication and overhead (compare with *coarse-grain parallelism*).

force-directed scheduling — The processes (operations) are distributed over time such that the required quantity of resources is minimized under a fixed execution time constraint.

fully associative cache — A cache memory in which any block of data from main memory can be placed anywhere in the cache. Address comparison must take place against each block in the cache to find any particular block (compare with *direct-mapping cache*).

functional languages — A language that implements a mapping from input to output values. A program is a function or group of related functions. There are no memory model and no side effects of program execution. Higher-order functions and lazy evaluation can be used to achieve accelerated performance.

Gflops (gigaflops) — Processing at 1 billion floating-point operations per second.

global memory — A memory that is directly accessible by every PE in a *multiprocessor* system.

granularity — A measure of the quantity of processing performed by an individual process each time it is executed by a PE(s).

guard — The introduction of a predicate that guards the execution of a program unit (a statement, block, process, and so on); provides a highly useful programming style.

hard real-time systems — A real-time system in which stringent timing requirements are placed. The missing of a deadline can have catastropic results (compare with *soft real-time systems*).

HDL (hardware description languages) — Languages used to describe the structural and behavioral properties of hardware processes; can deal with one or several levels of abstract and/or concrete hardware logic.

heuristic method — Optimization method involving a search method, where rules are applied in order to shorten required search time.

Horn clauses — A restricted form of predicate logic clause in which only one conclusion is permitted, an essential property for logic programming.

hot spot — Phenomenon observed in multiprocessors due to memory access statistics being slightly skewed from a uniform distribution to favor a particular memory location or module.

hypercube — A parallel processor whose interconnection structure treats individual PEs as the nodes in a multidimensional cube and interconnects two PEs if the corresponding nodes of the cube are neighbors.

ideal DSP architectures — A class of architectures that implements a given schedule. Contains PEs that can execute processes (operations) according to a schedule that is supported by appropriate C and M processes.

image processing — A computation performed on a digitized representation of an image for the purpose of enhancing the image or extracting information from the image.

imperative languages — Programming languages where programs are based upon imperative commands that are obeyed by a processor on a statement by statement basis; refers often to the languages used in programming the von Neumann class of architectures.

ICN (interconnection network) — The system of logic and conductors that connect together the hardware processes via terminal addresses in a parallel processing system.

indirect binary *n*-cube — A network organized in the form of a cube in *n* dimensions, where the connections are made indirectly in *n* switched stages (compare with *direct binary n-cube*).

individual control — The localization of control to individual PEs as in MIMD architectures (compare with *central control*).

interleaving — Assigning consecutive addresses alternately between two or more memory controllers. Interleaving speeds up memory transfers due to the fact that each interleaved bank can begin processing the next sequential word before the antecedent word in the previous bank has been completed.

interrupts — Events that arise in the external or internal environment and that can cause interruption of ongoing processing in order to direct attention to a condition that has arisen.

iterative methods — Refers to a method that iteratively seeks to produce better scheduling solutions from older ones.

lambda calculus — A calculus introduced by A. Church in the 1930s in order to develop a communication model for separate parts of a sequential functional derivation; provided rules for substitution and evaluation.

latency — The delay between a request and the time the request is satisfied.

lightweight processes — A set of processes that shares a memory area and that can be threaded together into varying dynamic execution structures. The processes are scheduled by their own local scheduler.

linear arrays — A means of organizing PE arrays in a linear manner where nearest-neighbor connections are in one dimension; for image-processing applications, this PE array organization normally maps conveniently to line-by-line scanning devices.

linear programming — The solution of large sets of inequalities (constraints) that leads to an optimal solution; when applied to scheduling for large problems, they tend to become intractable to solve due to NP-completeness of the scheduling problem.

liveness — The fact that a process(es) is (are) making progress. That is, it is behaving correctly, has not erroneously entered an infinite loop, or by its incorrect operation singularly or collectively has bound resources.

logic languages — A programming language based upon the use of relations expressed in the first-order predicate calculus.

loosely coupled — Describes a *multicomputer* architecture in which component processors share neither bus, memory, nor operating system. Assemblages of computer systems interconnected on a network are *loosely coupled* (see *closely coupled* and *tightly coupled*).

memory — Any device or media that can be used for storing information over time, for example, latches, registers, memory banks, and cache memories, as well as long-term storages.

memory management — The protocols (hardware and even software) that allow virtual addresses to be mapped into physical addresses as well as administrating movement between levels of memory.

mesh — An ICN (interconnection network) that is organized in a rectangular manner, where each node can communicate with its north, south, east and west neighbors; wraparound may be provided at the edges, thus forming a torus.

message passing — An explicit form of communication between processes where information is transmitted in the form of a message; can be contrasted with communication via a shared memory.

Mflops (megaflops) — Processing at millions of floating-point operations per second.

MIMD (multiple instruction stream, multiple data stream) — A parallel computer system composed of multiple independent PEs.

MIPS (millions of instructions per second) — A measure of the computation rate of a PE or a collection of parallel PEs. There is, unfortunately, no agreed-upon standard for the measurement of MIPS. The maximum number of instruction fetches per second is not a viable metric: obviously, a simple instruction (such as a no operation) takes negligible time as compared to typical productive instructions.

miss ratio — The ratio of cache misses to total cache accesses.

MMU (**m**emory **m**anagement **u**nit) — The logic that controls page mapping and protection. Implements virtual address to physical address mapping.

monitor — A programmed process that provides for the orderly control of access to shared resources in the system.

MSYPS (millions of sychronizations per second) — A measure of the rate at which a multiprocessor performs synchronization among its PEs.

multicomputer — Describes computing systems that make use of more than one processor in a *loosely coupled* or *closely coupled* manner (compare with *multiprocessor*).

multiprocessing — An extension of *multiprogramming* characterized by the parallel execution of multiple processes.

multiprocessor — Describes a *tightly coupled* computing system that makes use of more than one PE and where a common memory is shared among the PEs (compare with *multicomputer*).

multiprogramming — Identifies the act of running multiple programs with simulated simultaneity. Multiprogramming implies multiplexing, that is, sharing the processor(s) by rapid, transparent switches among several *programs* (see also *multiprocessing*, *multitasking*, and *parallel programming*).

multistage network — An ICN (**i**nter**c**onnection **n**etwork) in which multiple stages are connected together with switches that direct network messages based upon appropriate portions of an address according to a permutation.

multitasking — Identifies tactics that permit multiplexing several simultaneous processes whose activity must be synchronized at certain points (see also *multiprogramming* and *parallel programming*).

mutual exclusion — The guarantee that a process will be given sole access to a resource without any outside interference.

narrowness — A measure of congestion in a network obtained by calculating the maximum number of interconnections required for all two-way partitionings.

nondeterministic — The exact properties of process execution within a system cannot be determined in advance of their execution.

nonessential processes — Processes that may miss their deadlines without any near-term effect; however, long-term consequences may occur (see *critical processes* and *essential processes*).

nonheuristic — Refers to a method for scheduling that considers the entire solutions space and will eventually find an optimal solution but will, in general, require excessive execution time.

NP-complete — A class of problems for which there exists no current algorithm that can solve any problem in the class in a time guaranteed to be less than exponential to the size of the problem.

object-oriented — A paradigm in which real-world objects are modeled via program structures that contain both the data (information) that represent the object as well as the operations (procedures) that operate upon the data.

omega network — A network based upon the use of a perfect shuffle or shuffle-exchange permutation in each layer of the network.

operation — The fine-grain processes found in DSP (**d**igital **s**ignal **p**rocessing) applications.

order notation — A notation utilized to characterize orders of magnitude in measuring time and space properties of algorithms.

P and V synchronization — Primitive operations that are used for requesting and releasing a shared resource.

packet switched — A transport method where messages are sent through an ICN (interconnection network) one portion at a time. Thus, communication paths do not have to be reserved in advance. The postal system provides a useful analogy (compare with *circuit switched*).

page — A set of contiguous bytes used as the unit of physical *memory management* and protection.

page fault — An exception generated when an executing process refers to a page that is not currently in physical memory or when a page is referenced with inappropriate permissions (for example, trying to write a read-only page) (see *paging*).

paging — The action of bringing pages of an executing *process* into *physical memory* when referenced. When a process executes, all its pages are said to reside in *virtual memory*. However, only the actively used pages need to reside in *physical memory.*

parallel execution — The physical execution of processes in parallel; can be compared with concurrent execution, which may or may not actually transpire in parallel.

parallel processing systems — Systems where multiple hardware resources are applied in solving the same problem. Typically, they are phyically close (tightly coupled) (compare with *distributed systems*).

parallel programming — Identifies the tactics used by programmers to restructure a program to take advantage of multiple processors simultaneously and thus increase speed of execution (see also *multiprogramming* and *multitasking*).

PE arrays — Regular arrays of logic used in SIMD architectures that typically provide for highly parallel execution of fine or at most medium-grain processes; a synchronized central program instruction control is utilized.

perfect-shuffle interconnection — An interconnection structure that connects PEs according to a permutation that corresponds to a perfect shuffle of a deck of cards.

periodic process — Process that is to be executed at regular intervals and that typically has a specific deadline.

periodic scheduling — Refers to a scheduling formulation that takes account of periodicity via the connection of k networks into a closed loop. It is the most general formulation and can be used to achieve resource optimal schedules.

permutation — One-to-one mapping from a set of objects onto the same set of objects.

pipeline — A series of operations, performed one after another, in sequence, to achieve improved results. Pipelined computation has great potential for parallel execution because each stage of the pipeline can run on its own dedicated PE. This eliminates context switching and allows multiple, independent computations to overlap in time.

port — In a physical hardware process, it represents that actual wired connections to the physical device. As an abstract software object, it is used as a means indicating communication, perhaps permitting the development of queues of data to be communicated.

predictability — The ability to predict how a system will behave under all circumstances that can arise.

primary storage — Synonymous with *physical memory* (compare with *secondary storage*).

priority — The degree of importance associated with a process. Is used to effect its scheduling in relationship to other processes.

priority inheritance — A means to prevent the blocking of process execution by processes having a lower priority; for example, P2 inherits the priority of P1 when P1 has requested a result of P2 and is waiting for the result.

priority inversion — Refers to the situation where a process of lower priority can block the execution of a higher priority process; for example, P1 is waiting for P3 to return a result; meanwhile P2, which has a higher priority than P3 but lower than P1, is executed; thus, P1 is blocked by a lower-priority process.

process — In its general form applied in this book, a process is related to all components, hard and soft, where transformations are made on information taken from input ports and placed in output ports. In the programming context, a process is a major schedulable control *thread* in an address space, able to share memory and run in parallel with other control threads.

process priority — The priority assigned to a *process* for scheduling purposes.

processing element — Any device that can perform transformations; it may be a gate, adder, multiplier, special-purpose device, or general-purpose programmed device.

protocol — A set of rules or conventions that govern how PEs communicate, synchronize, or maintain coherent information in caches or in local memories.

R/C ratio — The ratio of a processes running time to its overhead and communications; a measure of process granularity.

read/write lock — A specialized form of *semaphore* that provides access to data structures for a single writer or multiple readers. Read/write locks prohibit write access until all pending reads are complete and prohibit read access while any write is in progress.

remote procedure call — The mechanism by which a process calls upon a process located in another PE; input and output arguments are delivered by message passing to and from the remotely invoked process.

rendezvous — A synchronization method in which two processes agree to synchronize at a particular point (the rendezvous); the rendezvous may be symmetric, in which case the two processes have mutual knowledge of each other (by name), or asymmetric, in which a server process does not know the identity of those processes to which it provides service.

resource structure — The collection of PE, M and C processes that provides execution semantics for a collection of processes that have been mapped in terms of the resource structure.

responsiveness — The ability of a system to continue to function, perhaps at reduced capacity, in the presence of faults (compare with *dependability*).

routing — Refers to the structure and behavior of links and switches in a network in transmitting messages through a network; can be controlled globally or locally; further routing may be adaptive and try to dynamically optimize network resource utilization.

schedules — Refers to an execution order of processes that can be developed statically or dynamically.

scheduling formulation — Refers to various approaches to addressing the scheduling problem (for example, single interval, direct blocking, loop folding, rate monotonic, earliest deadline, and periodic scheduling).

secondary storage — Synonymous with disk or other high-speed mass storage (compare with *primary storage*).

self-timed control — The provision of local timing control where the occurrence of events (for example, data result calculations) drives the execution in an asynchronous manner.

semaphore — A mechanism for synchronizing program execution by putting requesting processes to sleep until the requested resource(s) is available.

sensor — Provides a view of the process behaviors in the external system.

shuffle exchange — An interconnection network that consists of perfect shuffles and pairwise exchanges.

signal-flow graphs — Graphical representations of the processing required for signals in terms of operations and delays.

SIMD (single instruction stream, multiple data stream) — A processor structure in which a single instruction manipulates an entire data structure via multiple PEs.

simulated annealing — The use of a combinatorial optimization method that is analogous with the slow cooling of a solid until it reaches thermal equilibrium; has a major advantage in that it will avoid becoming stuck in local optima.

single interval — The reduction of a signal-flow graph to a precedence graph by removing delays and its subsequent analysis in terms of one single sample interval; restriction to a single interval may seem to reveal computational parallelism, but it has shortcomings with respect to the computational properties of the algorithm to be implemented.

single-stage network — A network composed of direct connections between PEs; the couplings can be pairwise (point-to-point) or common for several PEs (that is, a bus).

SISD (single instruction stream, single data stream) — A uniprocessor of the von Neumann type.

slack time — A scheduling approach that selects processes (operations) based upon those having least slack time (that is, the time interval from the present time to the deadline minus the remaining processing time).

soft real-time systems — Systems where service is to be supplied in real time; however, the missing of a deadline will not result in a catastrophe (compare with *hard real-time systems*).

speedup — The ratio of the time to execute an efficient serial program for a calculation to the time to execute a parallel program for the same calculation on *N* PEs.

spinlock — A parallel program synchronization mechanism that allows a memory location serving as a lock to be set by an acquiring process and forces other processes wishing to acquire the lock to loop continuously until the lock is released by the current holder (see also *barrier, event, read/write lock,* and *semaphore*).

static process — Process that is a permanent part of a real-time system during its execution.

static scheduling — A scheduling strategy that can be applied when the execution properties of all processes (operations) are known in advance.

store and forward — A network where messages can be stored locally in a router buffer before they are forwarded.

structure — The static interconnection of processes or an interconnection established dynamically, for example, by a linking that exists for some period of time.

switches — Network processes that switch connections between input and output ports of the processes; for example, 2 x 2 or 4 x 4 connections; a complete connection crossbar provides a switch of *N* x *N* connections.

synchronization — An operation in which two or more processes exchange information to coordinate their activity. Alternatively, a point in time at which the activity of one or more processes are synchronized.

synchronous — A means of controlling the execution of processes based upon regular intervals (clock periods).

system parallelism — The parallelism that is explicitly available in the hardware resource structure and, if present, system programs that control access to the hardware resources, for example, an operating system.

systolic array — A parallel processing system with a highly structured, iterative interconnection pattern where time controls the steps of execution.

TCP/IP (Transport Control Protocol/Internet Protocol) — TCP and IP have been the standard Department of Defense Internet communications protocols. They have also become the standard UNIX networking protocols.

terminals — The connection points for PEs in an ICN (interconnection network); each terminal has an associated address for its identification.

Test and Set — A primitive instruction that performs READ/MODIFY/WRITE operations for synchronization of processes.

thrashing — A situation in which pages are requested faster than they can be supplied, with the consequence that the requesting processor remains idle, waiting for service from *secondary storage* (see *working set*).

thread — Generically, a control sequence of connected processes developed during program execution. Often referred to in association with connected *lightweight processes.*

tightly coupled — Describes *multiprocessor* computing systems in which component processors share the same bus, operating system, and memory (see also *closely coupled* and *loosely coupled*).

time-ordered control — Organizing control according to time such that processes are executed based solely upon synchronous timing properties.

timing philosophy — The application of synchronous versus asynchronous approaches to dealing with the control of process execution.

torus — A network topology in which an N-dimensional lattice determines communication patterns. The torus is formed by connecting a grid in multiple dimensions around its opposite edges.

trace scheduling — Refers to a method of compacting microprograms or programs by isolating loop-free sequences that can be run in parallel; used in VLIW architectures.

transient overload — The arrival of more events to be processed than a real-time system is dimensioned to treat.

unification — The process of binding processes together based upon the properties of their arguments; the central mechanism for communication and synchronization in realizing logic programs.

virtual address space — The set of all possible *virtual addresses* that a process can use to identify the location of an instruction or data element.

virtual channels — Association of multiple logical channcel with physical channels. Provides for the sharing of transmission bandwidth. In flow control algorithms, it is utilized to decouple buffers and for physical channel utilization.

virtual memory — The set of storage locations that is referred to by virtual addresses. Makes disk storage locations appear to the programmer to exist in physical memory.

virtual PE — In the PE-array context, used as a means of exploiting memories associated with PEs for mapping virtual copies of PEs, thus extending the range of problem size that can be accommodated.

VLIW (very long instruction word) — The use of large instruction words that control parallel hardware resources; various traces through a program are executed in parallel; provides for a straightforward implementation of scalar parallelism.

wavefront array — A regular structure, where parallel processes are activated by events (normally data availability) and, as a result of computation, produce new events that control further processing.

Whetstone — A common FORTRAN benchmark program, originally developed by the British Ministry of Defence, which measures floating-point performance of a computer system. Also, shorthand notation for results of a program, more accurately reported in "Whetstone instructions per second" or "Kilo Whetstone instructions per second." Two separate performance figures are quoted for most machines, one for single-precision floating point, another (typically smaller) for double precision.

word parallel — Processing of multiple bits in a word in parallel. For example a parallel adder (compare with *bit serial*).

working set — The minimum amount of physical memory required by a process or collection of cooperating processes to prevent *thrashing*.

wormwhole routing — Messages are broken up into small units called flits and transmitted successively after a path has been established through the network based upon a header flit; the need for buffering as in store and forward is eliminated.

write back — Cache memory management technique where cache contents are actually updated only when the block in which data are to be written must be swapped out.

write through — A cache management technique whereby data from a write operation are copied simultaneously in both cache and main memory. This procedure keeps cache and main memory always in step with one another.

INDEX

Lecture Notes in Artificial Intelligence 3533

Edited by J. G. Carbonell and J. Siekmann

Subseries of Lecture Notes in Computer Science

Moonis Ali   Floriana Esposito (Eds.)

Innovations in Applied Artificial Intelligence

18th International Conference on
Industrial and Engineering Applications of
Artificial Intelligence and Expert Systems, IEA/AIE 2005
Bari, Italy, June 22-24, 2005
Proceedings

Series Editors

Jaime G. Carbonell, Carnegie Mellon University, Pittsburgh, PA, USA
Jörg Siekmann, University of Saarland, Saarbrücken, Germany

Volume Editors

Moonis Ali
Southwest Texas State University
Department of Computer Science
601 University Drive, San Marcos, TX 78666-4616, USA
E-mail: ma04@txstate.edu

Floriana Esposito
Università di Bari
Dipartimento di Informatica
Via Orabona 4, 70126 Bari, Italy
E-mail: esposito@di.uniba.it

Library of Congress Control Number: 2005927487

CR Subject Classification (1998): I.2, F.1, F.2, I.5, F.4.1, D.2, H.4, H.2.8, H.5.2

ISSN 0302-9743
ISBN-10 3-540-26551-1 Springer Berlin Heidelberg New York
ISBN-13 978-3-540-26551-1 Springer Berlin Heidelberg New York

Springer is a part of Springer Science+Business Media

springeronline.com

Printed in Germany

Typesetting: Camera-ready by author, data conversion by Scientific Publishing Services, Chennai, India
Printed on acid-free paper SPIN: 11504894 06/3142 5 4 3 2 1 0

Preface

"Intelligent systems are those which produce intelligent offsprings."

AI researchers have been focusing on developing and employing strong methods that are capable of solving complex real-life problems. The 18th International Conference on Industrial & Engineering Applications of Artificial Intelligence & Expert Systems (IEA/AIE 2005) held in Bari, Italy presented such work performed by many scientists worldwide.

The Program Committee selected long papers from contributions presenting more complete work and posters from those reporting ongoing research. The Committee enforced the rule that only original and unpublished work could be considered for inclusion in these proceedings.

The Program Committee selected 116 contributions from the 271 submitted papers which cover the following topics: artificial systems, search engines, intelligent interfaces, knowledge discovery, knowledge-based technologies, natural language processing, machine learning applications, reasoning technologies, uncertainty management, applied data mining, and technologies for knowledge management. The contributions oriented to the technological aspects of AI and the quality of the papers are witness to a research activity clearly aimed at consolidating the theoretical results that have already been achieved. The conference program also included two invited lectures, by Katharina Morik and Roberto Pieraccini.

Many people contributed in different ways to the success of the conference and to this volume. The authors who continue to show their enthusiastic interest in applied intelligence research are a very important part of our success. We highly appreciate the contribution of the members of the Program Committee, as well as others who reviewed all the submitted papers with efficiency and dedication. Two reviewers evaluated each paper to assure the high quality of the accepted papers.

The Co-chairs, Donato Malerba and Giovanni Semeraro, deserve our gratitude. A special thanks goes to the members of the Organizing Committee, Nicola Fanizzi and Stefano Ferilli, as well as to Nicola Di Mauro and Teresa Basile who worked hard at solving problems before and during the congress. We extend our sincerest thanks to CIC Services staff for their contribution.

We wish to thank the Dipartimento di Informatica of the University of Bari for encouraging and supporting us in organizing the event. The financial support of the University of Bari, Italy, which partially covered the publication costs of this book, is gratefully acknowledged. We also extend our appreciation to

President Denise Trauth and Provost Perry Moore of Texas State University-San Marcos for their support of this conference.

Bari, June 2005

Moonis Ali
Floriana Esposito

Organization

IEA/AIE 2005 was organized by the Department of Computer Science, University of Bari.

Conference Organization

General Chair	Moonis Ali (Texas State University-San Marcos, USA)
Program Chair	Floriana Esposito (Università degli Studi di Bari, Italy)
Program Co-chairs	Donato Malerba (Università degli Studi di Bari, Italy) Giovanni Semeraro (Università degli Studi di Bari, Italy)
Organizing Committee	Nicola Fanizzi (Università degli Studi di Bari, Italy) Stefano Ferilli (Università degli Studi di Bari, Italy)
Publicity Responsible	Berardina Nadja De Carolis (Università degli Studi di Bari, Italy)
Conference Secretariat	Olimpia Cassano (Centro Italiano Congressi, CIC Sud, Italy)

Program Committee

Agosti M.
Baumeister J.
Belli F.
Borzemski L.
Bratko I.
Cadoli M.
Chang K.H.
Chen Z.
Chung P.
Dapoigny R.
Dasigi V.G.
del Pobil A.P.
Drummond C.
Famili F.
Frasconi P.
Gaglio S.
Gams M.
Giordana A.
Goker M.
Hendtlass T.
Hinde C.
Honkela T.
Ishizuka M.
Ito T.
Kietz J.-U.
Koronacki J.
Kumara S.
Laurini R.
Lesser V.
Loganantharaj R.
López de Mántaras R.
Matthews M.
Mello P.
Missikoff M.
Mitra D.
Moniz Pereira L.
Monostori L.
Nguyen N.T.
Okuno H.G.
Potter W.D.
Ras Z.
Saitta L.

Shadbolt N.
Shih T.K.
Silva de Azevedo H.J.
Sim K.M.
Soda G.
Stock O.
Tanaka T.
Tatar M.M.
Torasso P.
Turini F.
Wotawa F.
Yang C.

Additional Reviewers

An B.
Angulo C.
Anselma L.
Apolloni B.
Appice A.
Arcos J.-L.
Atzmueller M.
Atzori M.
Bacchin M.
Baglioni M.
Basile T.M.A.
Bassis S.
Berardi M.
Biennier F.
Bordeaux L.
Caruso C.
Castellanos M.
Ceci M.
Cerquides J.
Chan P.C.
Curk T.
d'Amato C.
Degemmis M.
Demsar J.
Di Mauro N.
Di Nanna B.
Di Nunzio G.M.
Dorigo M.
Faruque A.
Gaito S.
Geffner H.
Goy A.
Hung C.-C.
Iannizzi D.
Iannone L.
Jakulin A.
Ju An Wang A.
Juvan P.
Karnavas Y.L.
Kurkovsky S.A.
Lamata M.T.
Lamma E.
Leban G.
Létourneau S.
Licchelli O.
Lisi F.A.
Lombardo V.
Lops P.
Martelli A.
Melucci M.
Milano M.
Orio N.
Palmisano I.
Petrone G.
Picardi C.
Pretto L.
Raffaetà A.
Redavid D.
Riguzzi F.
Rinzivillo S.
Roli A.
Sadikov A.
Sanchez Miralles A.
Sanz Bobi M.
Schaerf A.
Seow K.-T.
Shoniregun C.
Silaghi M.
Sorlin S.
Storari S.
Thirunarayan K.
Torra V.
Torroni P.
Torta G.
Tzacheva A.
Varlaro A.
Vento M.
Vladusic D.
Yang Y.
YuanShi W.
Zaluski M.

Table of Contents

Invited Contributions

Computer Vision

Image Analysis

Speech Recognition

Robotics

Agents

Planning

Human-Computer Interaction and Natural Language Processing

Reasoning

Machine Learning

Data Mining

Genetic Algorithms

Neural Networks

Decision Support and Heuristic Search

Fuzzy Logic

Knowledge Management

Applications

Applications of Knowledge Discovery

Katharina Morik

Univ. Dortmund, Computer Science Department, LS VIII

1 Introduction

Knowledge Discovery from Databases (KDD) – also named Data Mining – is a growing field since 10 years which combines techniques from databases, statistics, and machine learning. Applications of KDD most often have one of the following **goals**:

- Customer relationship management: who are the best customers, which products are to be offered to which customers (direct marketing or customer acquisition), which customers are likely to end the relationship (customer churn), which customers are likely to not pay (also coined as fraud detection)?
- Decision support applies to almost all areas, ranging from medicine over marketing to logistics. KDD applications aim at a data-driven justification of decisions by relating actions and outcomes.
- Recommender systems rank objects according to user profiles. The objects can be, for instance, products as in the amazon internet shop, or documents as in learning search engines. KDD applications do not assume user profiles to be given but learns tehm from observations of user behavior.
- Plant asset management moves beyond job scheduling and quality control. The goal is to optimize the overall benefits of production.

Of course, most of these goals existed already before KDD. They have been achieved by human expertise, reporting on the basis of database OLAP, and to a small degree by numerical modeling. The new situation stems from applying learning algorithms to the huge amount of stored data which enables a data-driven inspection – the contribution of KDD. The goals are achieved by data analysis **tasks**:

- Outlier detection is a necessary part of data cleaning but can also deliver interesting results. It always depends on domain knowledge whether an outlier is due to a failure in data entry or is a finding of a surprising effect. Outliers presuppose a general model from which they deviate.
- Subgroup detection looks for small groups that deviate significantly from the majority.
- Frequent set mining finds frequent correlations of objects. It became famous in basket analysis applications (which items are sold together frequently?) but has been successfully applied to determining situation-action or action-outcome correlations, as well, particularly in bioinformatics.

M. Ali and F. Esposito (Eds.): IEA/AIE 2005, LNAI 3533, pp. 1–5, 2005.

- Classification is and an overwhelming number of problems can be formulated as classification tasks. Given oberservations together with class labels, a decision function is learned which can then be applied to new, unlabeled data.
- Regression differs from classification in that it is not a label but a real value which is attached to the observations and will be predicted to unlabeled, new data.
- Clustering partitions the data without the need for any labels but based on similarity between the observations.

When the tasks are determined which fulfil the goal of an application, the KDD process starts. According to the CRISP model [2], the data inspection and preparation handles failures, missing values, feature selection, and feature generation. According to a poll of KDnuggets in October 2003[1], 64% of data miners use more than 61% of their time for this preprocessing. Machine learning algorithms perform not only the central data mining step, i.e., the one corresponding to a task, but also contribute to data cleaning and data preparation. For instance, the MiningMart system offers to apply decision tree learning in order to replace NULL values by predicted values [10]. Also feature selection is automatically performed by some learning algorithms (e.g., decision tree learning). However, most real-world applications benefit from selecting relevant features beforehand. Most often, this is done in a wrapper approach where the cross-validation of a learning algorithm's result evaluates the feature set, and the feature set is systematically decreased (or increased). The Yale system offers such a wrapper loop using genetic programming as the search procedure in the space of possible feature sets [13].

As soon as the data are well prepared and transformed adequately, the task can be performed using one of the algorithms which are readily available. According to a poll of KDnuggets in February 2005, top-down induction of decision trees are still the favorite method (14% of the votes), frequent set mining (or association rules) with 7% and the support vector machine (SVM) with 4% have only started to be commercially applied.

KDD can be characterised in contrast to statistical analysis by the following:

- KDD exploits given data which are collected for purposes different from analysis. In contrast, statistics acquire data carefully by well designed questionnaires which cover the relevant features and do not ask for irrelevant information. If data of a process are to be analysed, experiment design takes care that relevant observations are measured from a process. Hence, feature selection and generation is much more important in KDD than in statistics.
- KDD deals with huge numbers of observations, each characterised by a large number of features. In contrast, many statistical studies investigate only some hundred or thousand observations, each described by very few attributes. Hence, the design of efficient algorithms for data management and analysis is much more important in KDD than in statistics.

[1] www.kdnuggets.com

In terms of the mathematical models used, however, KDD and statistics have a lot in common.

2 Applications

Application fields range from banking, bioinformatics and telecommunication to scientific analysis, e.g., in medicine or astronomy. Here, two standard applications are described stressing the importance of system support for preprocessing and the re-use of KDD cases. Both applications are from the field of telecommunication with the goal of enhancing customer relationship management, an important market in Europe [2]. The first application is on marketing services of the Polish telecommunication company (NIT) to customers (goal: customer acquisition). The task was classification of customers into those who want to subscribe a particular service and those who don't. The class label is derived: the customer already subscribes the service or accepts it when it is offered by NIT's call center. The data stem from the customer databases and that of a call center. The distributed data have to be integrated and a record for each customer has to be established. The stored phone calls and the contract data of the customers are transformed into customer profiles. For instance, frequencies of calls at certain hours of the day, the average length of a phone call, frequencies of calls to special numbers (long distance calls, numbers with prefixes, internet access via phone modem) are calculated. The now labeled user profiles are used by a decision tree learner predicting customers who most likely want to subscribe the service. The integration of the distributed data bases and the aggregation of user profiles was at first a tedious process, designed by a data mining expert. Hence, re-using the steps of this process is necessary in order to speed up data mining. For instance, the same procedure must be run about 4 times a year in order to adapt to changes in customer behavior. These runs of the overall case no longer require a data mining expert but should just be pressing a button. Moreover, almost the same procedure can be done for all the services of NIT. After the first set-up of the KDD case for one service, it should be easy for non-expert users to create these similar cases. For the re-use of cases, their documentation in a form which is easy to understand by non-experts is most important. This aspect is not yet taken serious enough by commercial tools [3].

The second application is also on customer relationship management, but on customer churn. If as many customers leave their contracts as new services are sold, the benefit does not increase. Hence, detecting which customers are about to

---

[2] According to Marco Richeldi from TILab, Italy, the European customer relationship management market increased from 0.5 billion US dollars in 1999 to 3.5 billion US dollars in 2004 – cf. the presentation at http://www-ai.cs.uni-dortmund.de/MMWEB/content/oneDaySeminar.html.

[3] Comparing SAS and MiningMart, a study showed that case design and case adaptation was much easier using MiningMart [3,4]. The MiningMart system is GNU-licensed available at http://www-ai.cs.uni-dortmund.de/MMWEB/downloads/downloads.html.

leave and take some initiative in keeping them, is an important goal. The task was again classification of customers into those who are likely to stop their contract within the next 6 months, and those who continue. Running a learner on past data, where the customer's behavior 6 months later is known, delivered a decision tree which predicts customer churn for the current data set. Again, generating the customer profiles from the raw data is a long chain of steps, creating many new views of the database. Easing the implementation of such preprocessing chains is an important issue. In a case study, the time of developing the case when using the MiningMart system was compared to the time needed when using standard commercial tools. The conceptual level at which preprocessing is designed using MiningMart [4] effectively reduced development time (from 12 days to 2.5 days, two data miners working the full day) [12, 11]. Preprocessing determines the quality of the learning results. Its documentation and design at a conceptual level offers a great potential to speeding up the development and re-use of a KDD process.

3 New Directions

KDD is a dynamic field. New application types are approaching:

- Integration of databases and documents in the WorldWideWeb has been put forward by the database community. Now methods are demanded which are capable of exploiting the huge collection of documents and their link structure for enhanced mining of data such as, e.g. bank transactions or genome data bases.
- Distributed data mining is characterized by distributed computing and distributed data, where the communication links have bandwidth constraints and data sources are object to privacy concerns [6, 1]. A famous scenario is the on-board computing of cars and its interaction with central services. Travellers using their mobile phones for computing is another new scenario which challenges data mining. Peer-to-peer networks also put new tasks on the agenda of KDD.
- Beyond time series, there are many time phenomena which ask for a careful analysis, e.g., classifying or clustering very large sets of time series [7], monitoring streams of data [5], detecting a change of the data producing process (concept drift), and learning episodes from time-stamped data [8].

Here, an application is sketched which again stresses the importance of preprocessing[5]. The scenario is a meeting of some persons, each with a computer storing music (audio data) organised in taxonomies, e.g., according to genre, preference, casual use. Of course, the users' taxonomies do not fit together. When the users

[4] The user interactively designs the case using a graphical interface. The MiningMart system then compiles the case down to SQL procedures.

[5] This application is currently developed by Michael Wurst and me together with 9 students. The system is called Nemoz and will be published at SourceForge.

start an ad hoc network they exchange songs according to the own preferences. The learned classification rules for the own taxonomy nodes are applied to parts of the taxonomies of other peers in order to find recommendable songs there. In addition, (parts of) taxonomies of other peers can be incorporated into the own music organisation. The enabling technique is to learn from audio data. As raw data, nothing can be learned from such time series – the second note being a C is not a suitable feature for personal preferences or genres. The series need to be transformed before classification or clustering can become successful. An automatic procedure of creating feature transformations according to a classification task has been developed [9]. Again, the preprocessing was the key issue in handling a new and complex application.

References

1. G. Agrawal. High-level interfaces for data mining: From offline algorithms on clusters to streams on grids. In *Workshop on Data Mining and Exploration Middleware for Distributed and Grid Computing*, Minneapolis, MN, September 2003.
2. Pete Chapman, Julian Clinton, Randy Kerber, Thomas Khabaza, Thomas Reinartz, Colin Shearer, and Rüdiger Wirth. Crisp–Dm 1.0. Technical report, The CRISP–DM Consortium, August 2000.
3. Cezary Chudzian, Janusz Granat, and Wieslaw Traczyk. Call Center Case. Deliverable D17.2b, IST Project MiningMart, IST-11993, 2003.
4. Janusz Granat, Wieslaw Traczyk, and Cezary Chudzian. Evaluation report by NIT. Deliverable D17.3b, IST Project MiningMart, IST-11993, 2003.
5. Sudipto Guha, Adam Meyerson, Nina Mishra, Rajeev Motwani, and Liadan O'Callaghan. Clustering data streams: Theory and practice. *IEEE Transaction Knowledge Data Engineering*, 15(3), 2003.
6. H. Kargupta and P. Chan. Distributed data mining. *AI Magazine*, 20(1):126, 1999.
7. Eamonn Keogh, Stefano Lonardi, and Bill Chiu. Finding suprising patterns in a time series database in linear time and space. In *Procs. Int. Conf. on Knowledge Discovery in Databases*, 2002.
8. Heikki Mannila, Hannu Toivonen, and A.Inkeri Verkamo. Discovery of frequent episodes in event sequences. *Data Mining and Knowledge Discovery*, 1(3):259–290, November 1997.
9. Ingo Mierswa and Katharina Morik. Automatic feature extraction for classifying audio data. *Machine Learning Journal*, 58:127–149, 2005.
10. Katharina Morik and Martin Scholz. The MiningMart Approach to Knowledge Discovery in Databases. In Ning Zhong and Jiming Liu, editors, *Intelligent Technologies for Information Analysis*. Springer, 2004.
11. Marco Richeldi and Alessandro Perrucci. Churn analysis case study. Deliverable D17.2, IST Project MiningMart, IST-11993, 2002.
12. Marco Richeldi and Alessandro Perrucci. Mining Mart Evaluation Report. Deliverable D17.3, IST Project MiningMart, IST-11993, 2002.
13. Oliver Ritthoff, Ralf Klinkenberg, Simon Fischer, and Ingo Mierswa. A hybrid approach to feature selection and generation using an evolutionary algorithm. In John A. Bullinaria, editor, *Proceedings of the 2002 U.K. Workshop on Computational Intelligence (UKCI-02)*, pages 147–154, Birmingham, UK, september 2002. University of Birmingham.

Spoken Language Communication with Machines: The Long and Winding Road from Research to Business

Roberto Pieraccini and David Lubensky

IBM T.J. Watson Research Center, 1101 Kitchawan Road,
Route 134, Yorktown Heights, NY 10598, USA
{rpieracc, davidlu}@us.ibm.com

Abstract. This paper traces the history of spoken language communication with computers, from the first attempts in the 1950s, through the establishment of the theoretical foundations in the 1980s, to the incremental improvement phase of the 1990s and 2000s. Then a perspective is given on the current conversational technology market and industry, with an analysis of its business value and commercial models.

1 Introduction

One of the first speech recognition systems was built in 1952 by three AT&T Bell Laboratories scientists [1].The system could recognize sequences of digits spoken with pauses between them. The pioneers of automatic speech recognition (ASR) reported that [...] *an accuracy varying between 97 and 99 percent is obtained when a single male speaker repeats any random series of digits.* However, the system required to be adjusted for each talker [...] *if no adjustment is made, accuracy may fall to as low as 50 or 60 percent in a random digit series.* The Automatic Digit Recognition machine, dubbed Audrey, was completely built with analog electronic circuits and, although voice dialing was a much attractive solution for AT&T towards cost reduction in the long distance call business, it was never deployed commercially.

It took more than three decades for the algorithms and the technology of speech recognition to find a stable setting within the framework of statistical modeling. And it took two more decades of incremental improvement to reach an acceptable level of performance.

Only towards the beginning of this century, nearly fifty years after Audrey, did we witness the emergence of a fairly mature market and of a structured industry around conversational applications of the *computer-speech* technology. The principles on which modern speech recognition components operate are not dissimilar to those introduced in the late 1970s and early 1980s. Faster and cheaper computers and the availability of large amounts of transcribed speech data allowed a relentless incremental improvement in speech recognition accuracy. Even though automatic speech recognition performance is not perfect, it offers tremendous business benefits in many different applications.

There are many applications of speech recognition technology, ranging from dictation of reports on a desktop computer, to transcription of conversations between

M. Ali and F. Esposito (Eds.): IEA/AIE 2005, LNAI 3533, pp. 6 – 15, 2005.

agents and callers, to speech-to-speech translation. Although many applications are commercially exploited in different niches of the market, the industry is mostly evolving around *conversational systems*, aimed at customer self-service in call centers, or providing effective control of devices in automotive or mobile environments.

2 A Brief History of Automatic Speech Recognition Research

The early history of speech recognition technology is characterized by the so-called linguistic approach. Linguists describe the speech communication chain with several levels of competence: acoustic, phonetic, lexical, syntactic, semantic, and pragmatic. Although the precise mechanism that grants humans, among all animals, the mastering of a sophisticated language was, and still is, mostly inscrutable, there was a fairly general agreement in the scientific community that, for building speech understanding machines, *that mechanism* should be replicated. Thus, most of the approaches to the recognition of speech in the 1960s were based on the assumption that the speech signal needs to be first segmented into the constituent phonetic units. Sequences of phonetic units can then be grouped into words, words into phrases and syntactic constituents, and eventually one can reach a semantic interpretation of the message.

Although an obvious solution, the linguistic approach never produced satisfactory results since the acoustic variability of speech prevented the accurate segmentation of utterances into phonetic units. The phonetic variability of words, mainly due to coarticulation phenomena at the word junctures and speaker variability, concurrently with errorful strings of decoded phonetic hypotheses, caused errors in the lexical transcriptions, which propagated to erroneous syntactic and semantic interpretations.

At the end of the 1960s, practical usability of speech recognition was extremely doubtful, and the seriousness of the field was severely mined by the lack of practical results. That prompted John Pierce, executive vice-president of Bell Laboratories, renowned scientist and visionary in the field of satellite communications, to launch into a contentious attack to the whole field in an infamous letter to the Journal of the Acoustical Society of America [2].

Although Pierce's letter banned speech recognition research at Bell Laboratories for almost a decade, it did not arrest the enthusiasm of a few visionaries who saw the potential of the technology. ARPA[1], the Advance Research Project Agency of the US Department of Defense, against the opinion of an advisory committee headed by Pierce, started in 1971 a $15 million 5 year research program that went under the name of SUR: Speech Understanding Research. At the end of the program, in 1976, four systems [3] were evaluated, but unfortunately none of them matched the initial requirements of the program—less that 10% understanding error with a 1000 words vocabulary in near real time. Three of the systems were based on variations of classical AI rule-based inference applied to the linguistic approach. One of them was built by SDC, and the other two—HWIM and Hearsay II—were developed by BBN and

[1] The name of the research agency changed through the years. It was ARPA at its inception in 1958; it became DARPA—D as in Defense—in 1972. President Bill Clinton changed its name back to ARPA in 1993. The initial D was added again in 1996. Today, in year 2005, it is still called DARPA.

CMU respectively. The fourth system, Harpy [4], built by CMU, went very close to match the program requirements. In fact, Harpy was capable of understanding 95% of the evaluation sentences, but its real time performance was quite poor: 80 times real time—a 3 second sentence required 4 minutes of processing on a 0.4 MIPS PDP-KA 10. Rather than using classical AI inference, Harpy was based on a network of 15,000 interconnected nodes that represented all the possible utterances within the domain, with all the phonetic, lexical, and syntactic variations. The decoding was implemented as a *beam-search* variation of the dynamic programming algorithm [5] first published by Bellman in 1957.

Harpy was not the first application of dynamic programming to the problem of speech recognition. A dynamic programming algorithm for matching utterances to stored templates was experimented first by a Russian scientist, Vintsyuk [6], in 1968, and then by Sakoe and Chiba [7] in Japan in 1971. However, in the hype of the AI years of the 1970s, the dynamic programming—or Dynamic Time Warping (DTW)—approach was considered a *mere engineering trick* which was limited to the recognition of few words at the expense of a large amount of computation. It was a brute-force approach which did not have the elegance, and the *intelligence* of systems based on rule inference. However, DTW was easier to implement—it did not require linguistic expertise—and its performance on well defined speech recognition tasks was generally superior to the more complex rule based systems.

In the mid 1970s Fred Jelinek and his colleagues at IBM Research started working on a rigorous mathematical formulation of the speech recognition problem [8] based on fundamental work on stochastic processes carried out a few years earlier by Baum at IDA [9]. The IBM approach was based on statistical models of speech—Hidden Markov Models, or HMM—and word n-grams. The enormous advantage of the HMM approach as compared with all the other methods is in the possibility of learning automatically from virtually unlimited amounts data. However, it was not until the early 1980s, thanks to the experimental work and tutorial paper [10] by Larry Rabiner and his colleagues at Bell Laboratories, that the HMM approach became mainstream in virtually all speech research institutions around the world.

3 The Power of Evaluation

In the 1980s and 1990s speech recognition technology went through an incremental improvement phase. Although alternative techniques, such as artificial neural networks, were investigated, HMM and word n-grams remained the undisputed performers. However, towards the end of the 1980s, a general disbelief about the actual applicability of speech recognition to large vocabulary human-machine spoken language dialog was still present in the speech recognition research community.

Automatic dictation systems of the late 1980's and a few other industrial hands-eyes busy applications were the only demonstrable products of speech recognition technology. In 1988, a company called Dragon, founded by Jim and Janet Baker, former IBM researchers, demonstrated the first PC-based, 8,000 words speech recognition dictation system. The system was commercialized in 1990, but did not find much appeal in the market; the computational limitations still required users to speak with pauses between words. Although next generation of dictation products did not require a user to pause between words, the market for this application never really took off, and still remains a niche market[2].

In the second half of the 1980s most of the research centers started following the HMM/n-gram paradigm. However the efforts remained fragmented and it was difficult to measure progress. Around this time DARPA funded a new effort [11] focused at improving speech recognition performance. The major difference from the previous program, the 1971 SUR, was in the new focus that DARPA put in the on-going evaluation of speech recognition systems from the program participants. A common task with a fixed vocabulary, associated with shared training and test corpora, guaranteed the scientific rigorousness of the speech recognition performance assessment, which was administered through regular yearly evaluations by NIST, the National Institute of Standards and Technology (NIST). The new program, called Resource Management, was characterized by a corpus of read sentences belonging to a finite state grammar with a 1000 word vocabulary. Word accuracy, a well defined standard metric, was used for assessing the systems and measuring progress. A controlled, objective, and common evaluation paradigm had the effect of pushing the incremental improvement of speech recognition technology. In a few years, program participants pushed the word error rate from 10% to a few percent.

The Resource Management task was the first in a series of programs sponsored by DARPA with increasingly more complex and ambitious goals. Airline Travel Information Systems (ATIS) [12] followed in the early 1990s, and was focused on spoken language understanding. The common evaluation corpus in the ATIS project included *spontaneous queries* to a commercial flight database, whereas Resource Management sentences were *read* and defined by a fixed finite state grammar. ATIS forced the research community to realize, for the first time, the difficulties of spontaneous speech. Spontaneous speech is not grammatical, with a lot of disfluencies, such as repetitions, false starts, self corrections, and filled pauses. Here is an example of a spontaneous sentence from the ATIS corpus:

From um sss from the Philadelphia airport um at ooh the airline is United Airlines and it is flight number one ninety four once that one lands I need ground transportation to uh Broad street in Phileld Philadelphia what can you arrange for that.[3]

With ATIS, the speech recognition and understanding community realized that classical natural language parsing based on formal context free or higher order grammars failed on spontaneous speech. Statistical models, again, demonstrated their superiority in handling the idiosyncrasies of spoken language. A new paradigm invented at AT&T Bell Laboratories [13] and aimed at the detection of semantically meaningful phrases was soon adopted, in different forms, by several other institutions and demonstrated superior performance when compared with traditional parsing methods.

The ATIS program, which ended in 1994, while fostering the incremental improvement in the speech recognition and understanding performance, did not provide

---

[2] Besides providing accessibility to disabled individuals, speech recognition based dictation found most of the adopters within the professional community of radiologists.

[3] This sentence was judged to be the most ungrammatical spontaneous sentence among those recorded by the MADCOW committee in the early 1990s , during the DARPA ATIS project. A t-shirt with this sentence imprinted on the back was made available to program participants.

a satisfactory answer to the general problem of human-machine spoken communication. ATIS dialogs were mostly *user initiated*: the machine was only intended to provide answers to questions posed by the user. This is not a typical situation of regular conversations, where both parties can ask questions, provide answers, and change the course of the dialog. This situation, known as *mixed-initiative* dialog, contrasts with the other extreme case, where the machine asks questions and the user can only provide answers, known as *system-initiative*, or directed-dialog.

Aware of the important role of mixed initiative dialog systems in human-machine communication, DARPA followed the ATIS program with the launch of another project known as the DARPA Communicator [14]. Other programs with complex speech recognition tasks based on corpora, such as *Switchboard* (human-human conversational speech) and *Broadcast News* (broadcast speech) followed, until the most recent EARS[4] (Effective Affordable Reusable Speech-to-text). On-going DARPA evaluations push researchers to invent new algorithms and focus not only on speech recognition accuracy but also computational efficiency.

4 The Change of Perspective and the Conversational Market

While in the mid 1990s the research community was improving the speech recognition performance on more and more complex tasks, two small startup companies appeared on the quite empty market landscape. The first was Corona, renamed successively Nuance, a spin-off from the Stanford Research Institute (SRI). The second, an MIT spin-off, was initially called Altech, and then renamed SpeechWorks[5]. While the research community was focusing on complex human-like conversational dialog systems, SpeechWorks and Nuance took a different perspective. If the task is simple enough for the available speech recognition technology to attain reasonable accuracy, the interface can be engineered in such a way as to provide an excellent user experience, certainly superior to that offered by conventional touch-tone Interactive Voice Response (IVR). Simple applications, such as package tracking, where the user is only required to speak an alphanumeric sequence (with a checksum digit), and slightly more complex applications such as stock quote and flight information were their commercial targets.

The notion of user-centered design, as opposed to technology driven, became the guiding principle. Users want to accomplish their task with the minimal effort. Whether they can talk to machines with the same freedom of expression offered in human-human conversations, or they are gracefully directed to provide the required information in the simplest way, proved to be of little concern to users. Getting to the end of the transaction in the shortest time is the most important goal. Notwithstanding the efforts of the research community, free-form natural-language speech was, in the mid 1990s, still highly error prone. On the other hand, limiting the response of users to well crafted grammars provided enough accuracy to attain high levels of automation. In a way, SpeechWorks and Nuance pushed back on the dream of natural-language mixed-initiative conversational machines, and engaged in the most realistic

4 http://www.darpa.mil/ipto/programs/ears/

5 SpeechWorks was acquired by Scansoft in 2003.

proposition of directed-dialog with a meticulously engineered user interface. SpeechWorks and Nuance's goal was to build *usable* and not necessarily *anthropomorphic* systems.

The first telephony conversational applications showed business value, and attracted the attention of other players in the industry. Travel, Telecom, and Financial industries were the early adapters of directed dialog systems and deployed widely by SpeechWorks and Nuance, while the *holy-grail* of natural language communication remained in the research community. UPS, FedEx, American and United Airlines, E-trade, and Schwab were amongst the early adapters to speech enable their non-revenue generating lines of business. In the late 1990s, analysts predicted that speech market (including hardware, software, and services) will soon become a multi billion dollar business.

The concept of properly engineered directed-dialog speech applications became an effective replacement for touch-tone IVRs, and an enabler for customer self-service. A new professional figure emerged, the Voice User Interface (VUI) designer. The VUI designer is responsible for the complete specification of the system behavior, the exact wording of the prompts, and what is called the *call flow,* a finite state description of the dialog. The application development methodology was then structured according to classical software engineering principles. Requirement gathering, specification, design and coding, followed by usability tests, post-deployment tuning, and analysis, enabled speech solution providers to develop scalable, high quality, commercial grade solutions with strong Return on Investment (ROI).

In the early 2000s, the pull of the market towards commercial deployment of more sophisticated systems, and the push of new technology developed at large research centers, like IBM and AT&T Labs, prompted the industry to move cautiously from the directed-dialog paradigm towards more sophisticated interactions. IBM successfully deployed the first commercial mixed-initiative solution with T. Rowe Price, a major mutual funds company, using natural language understanding and dialog management technologies developed under the DARPA Communicator program [15]. This type of solutions is capable of handling natural language queries, such as *I would like to transfer all of my money from ABC fund to XYZ fund* as well resolving elliptical references, such as *Make it fifty percent* and allow users to change the focus of dialog at any point in the interaction.

The technology developed at AT&T known as HMIHY (How May I Help You) [16], or *call-routing*, aims at the classification of free-form natural language utterances into a number of predefined classes. Still far from providing sophisticated language understanding capabilities, HMIHY systems proved to be extremely useful and effective for routing of incoming calls to differently skilled agents, and are becoming the standard front-end for sophisticated conversational systems.

While the technology of speech recognition was assuming a more mature structure, so was the market for its commercial exploitation. Companies like SpeechWorks and Nuance initially assumed most of the industry roles, such as technology vendors, platform integrators, and application builders. At the same time, larger companies with a long history of research in speech recognition technologies, such as AT&T and IBM, entered the market. Other smaller companies appeared with more specific roles, such as tool providers, application hosting and professional services, and the whole speech recognition market started to exhibit a clear layered structure.

As the number of companies involved in the conversational market increased, the number of deployed systems rose to hundreds per year, and the need for industrial standards quickly emerged. By ensuring interoperability of components and vendors, standards are extremely important for the industry and for growing the market. VoiceXML, a markup language for the implementation of dialog systems in browser-client architectures, based on the same http transport protocol of the visual Web, was invented in the late 1990s and became a W3C recommendation (VoiceXML 1.0[6]) in 2000, followed by VoiceXML 2.0[7] in 2004. Other standards followed, such as MRCP[8] (Media Resource Control Protocol), a protocol for the low level control of conversational resources like speech recognition and speech synthesis engines, SRGS[9] (Speech Recognition Grammar Specification), a language for the specification of context-free grammars with semantic attachments, CCXML[10] (Call Control Markup Language), a language for the control of the computer-telephony layer, and EMMA[11] (Extensible Multi Modal Annotation), a language for the representation of semantic input in speech and multi-modal systems.

5 Business Cases and Business Models of Conversational Systems

Despite of its mature appearance, the conversational solutions market is still in its infancy. Transactional conversational solutions have not yet reached mainstream: only about 5% of the IVR ports in the US are speech enabled today. Thus, the conversational speech technology market is potentially very large, but penetration is still slow. When the technology will reach a reasonable level of market penetration, possibly during the next few years, conversational access will change the dynamics of e-commerce. Telecom, banking, insurance, travel, transportation, utilities, retail, and government industries are the major potential adopters of conversational technologies. Products and services offered to consumers have become more and more complex during the past few decades, requiring the above industries and businesses to develop sophisticated support infrastructure. While interaction with a consumer could lead to increased revenue opportunity, the cost of providing support for simple inquiries and transactions would require higher investments for infrastructure and agent wages. In fact, in a typical call center, labor contributes to over 70% of the total operational cost. Enabling customer *self-service* through conversational interfaces has considerably awakened the interest of the enterprises as a means to reduce operational expenses. However, as excessive automation may actually reduce customer satisfaction, finding a good trade-off between reducing cost and maintaining the quality of customer care is extremely important. That requires extensive knowledge of the business, understanding of customer needs, as well as the implementation of best practices in the call center transformation and voice user interface design.

---

[6] http://www.w3.org/TR/voicexml/
[7] http://www.w3.org/TR/voicexml20/
[8] http://www.ietf.org/internet-drafts/draft-shanmugham-mrcp-06.txt
[9] http://www.w3.org/TR/speech-grammar/
[10] http://www.w3.org/TR/ccxml/
[11] http://www.w3.org/TR/emma/

The overall market is maturing slowly, primarily due to a number of false starts when the technology was not ready, or with poorly engineered highly ambitious systems. That created the perception in the marketplace that speech recognition technology is not ready, it is costly to deploy and maintain, and it's difficult to integrate with the rest of the IT infrastructure. As the industry progresses with standards and more robust technology, these negative perceptions are becoming less valid. Successful industry-specific engagements and customer education can help increase the speed of the technology acceptance curve in the marketplace. Conversational self-service, unlike the Web, is still an emerging interface and as such every customer application is special and should be analyzed and developed carefully and methodically following specific best practices.

The value proposition offered by conversational applications is mainly the return on investment (ROI) created by the reduced costs of services obtained through full or partial automation. Historically, one of the first examples of a large ROI obtained by speech technology is the deployment, by AT&T, of a simple routing system which allows choosing among different types of calls by saying *collect*, *third party billing*, *person to person*, *calling card*, or *operator* [17]. The system, which was deployed in 1992, automated more than a billion calls per year that were previously handled by operators, and is said to have saved AT&T in excess of $600 million a year.

Attainment of ROI is straightforward and easily predictable in those situations when speech recognition is introduced in call centers without automation or very limited self-service. The ROI is not always obvious when the conversational system replaces an existing touch tone IVR. However, even in those situations, a higher automation rate can be obtained by using speech technology and by a complete redesign of the user interface. Furthermore, a well designed voice interface leads to higher customer satisfaction and retention, which alone can justify the choice.

As far as the business model for speech technology is concerned, licensing of core technology is certainly the one with the highest profit margin. After the initial R&D investment, vendors would benefit from a steep revenue/cost function, since the number of sold licenses is loosely dependent on the revenue production costs, such as marketing, sales, and product improvement. As the market matures, software core technology may be commoditized in the presence of market competition. If performance of products from different vendors is comparable, differentiation will come in the form of specific content (e.g. grammars, language models, dialog modules, etc.), tools to support design, development, and tuning of applications, and integration of the software with third party IT infrastructure.

Application builders have traditionally adopted the *time-and-material* model, customers pay hourly rates for initial development of the solution and subsequent maintenance and upgrades Unfortunately, the cost and the amount of specialized resources needed for the development of conversational systems is fairly high, and this model does not scale well with the increased market demand for conversational solutions. This situation has prompted the industry to develop the concept of *pre-packaged applications*, which are offered today by a large number of speech technology vendors. Pre-packaged applications address specific vertical sectors of the industry, such as finance, banking, and health. They are configurable and customizable, and since they are typically built and tuned on prior customer engagements, deployment risks are generally lower.

We're now seeing an emerging trend towards a hosting model for conversational solutions. The trend is for small and medium size businesses as well as large enterprises. Hosting is also referred to as an on-demand/utility model where clients lease solutions, and there are many different business models for every customer budget.

Finally, the overall optimization of contact centers is another interesting model for conversational solutions. This is not a hosting, but rather an outsourcing model, where companies such as IBM, Accenture, and EDS, who specialize in running large IT organizations, manage call centers for large clients. These outsourcing deals typically achieve cost reduction through call center consolidation, and multi-channel self-service, including Web, IVR, e-mail, and chat. Conversational solutions are viewed as complementary to the Web in terms of self-service, and can often outweigh the benefits realized through the Web itself.

6 Conclusions

Automatic speech recognition research, which started more than 50 years ago, found commercial deployment within a structured and maturing market only during the past few years. The vision of building machines we can talk to as we talk to humans was not abandoned, but pushed back in favor of a more pragmatic use of the technology. What enabled the change from technology to user centered design was the realization that users do not necessarily need a full replication of human–like speech and language skills; good user experience is instrumental to market adoption. Highly engineered solutions, focused on the delivery of effective transactions, and compatible with the performance of the current speech recognition technology proved to be key to the industry of conversational technology.

References

[1] Davis, K., Biddulph, R., Balashek, S. (1952), "Automatic recognition of spoken digits", J. Acoust. Soc. Amer, V. 24, pp. 637-642.

[2] Pierce, J. R. (1969) Whither Speech Recognition, J. Acoust. Soc. Amer, V. 46, pp. 1049-1050.

[3] Klatt, D. H (1977), "Review of the ARPA Speech Understanding Project," J. Acoust. Soc. Amer., V. 62, No. 4, pp. 1345-1366.

[4] Lowerre, B., Reddy, R., (1979) 'The Harpy Speech Understanding System', in Trends in Speech Recognition, ed. W. Lea, Prentice Hall.

[5] Bellman, R. (1957), "Dynamic Programming," Princeton University Press.

[6] Vintsyuk, T.K., (1968), "Speech discrimination by dynamic programming," Kibernetika 4, 81-88.

[7] Sakoe H., Chiba S., (1971) "A dynamic-programming approach to continuous speech recognition," paper 20 c 13.Proceedings of the International Congress on Acoustics, Budapest.

[8] Jelinek F., (1976) "Continuous Speech Recognition by Statisical Methods," IEEE Proceedings V. 64, N.4, pp. 532-556.

[9] Baum L. E., (1972) "An inequality and associated maximization technique in statistical estimation for probabilistic functions of Markov processes," Inequalities, V. 3, pp. 1-8.

[10] Levinson, S. E., Rabiner, L. R. and Sondhi, M. M., (1983) "An introduction to the application of the theory of probabilistic functions of a Markov process to automatic speech recognition," Bell Syst. Tech. Jour., V. 62, N. 4, Apr 1983, pp. 1035-1074.

[11] Price P., Fisher W. M., Bernstein J., Pallett D. S., (1988) "The DARPA 1,000-Word Resource Management Database for Continuous Speech Recognition," Proceedings ICASSP 1988, p. 651-654.

[12] Hirschmann, L. (1992), "Multi-site data collection for a spoken language corpus," In Proc. of the 5th DARPA Speech and Natural Language Workshop, Defense Advanced Research Projects Agency, Morgan Kaufmann.

[13] Pieraccini, R., Levin, E., (1993) "A learning approach to natural language understanding," in NATO-ASI, New Advances & Trends in Speech Recognition and Coding, Springer-Verlag, Bubion (Granada), Spain.

[14] Walker M. et al., (2002) "DARPA Communicator: Cross System Results for the 2001 evaluation," in Proc. if ICSLP 2002, V. 1, pp 269-272

[15] Papineni K., Roukos S., Ward T., (1999) "Free-Flow Dialog Management Using Forms," Proc. Eurospeech, pp. 1411-1414.

[16] Gorin A. L., Riccardi G., Wright J. H., (1997) "How May I Help You?" Speech Communication, V. 23, pp. 113-127.

[17] Cox R. V., Kamm C. A., Rabiner L. R., Shroeter J., Wilpon J. G., (2000) "Speech and Language Processing for Next-Millennium Communications Services," Proc. of the IEEE, V. 88, N. 8, Aug. 2000.

Motion-Based Stereovision Method with Potential Utility in Robot Navigation

José M. López-Valles[1], Miguel A. Fernández[2], Antonio Fernández-Caballero[2], María T. López[2], José Mira[3], and Ana E. Delgado[3]

[1] Departamento de Ingeniería de Telecomunicación, E.U. Politécnica de Cuenca
Universidad de Castilla-La Mancha, 16071 – Cuenca, Spain
josemaria.lopez@uclm.es
[2] Departamento de Informática, Escuela Politécnica Superior de Albacete
Universidad de Castilla-La Mancha, 02071 – Albacete, Spain
{miki, caballer, mlopez}info-ab.uclm.es
[3] Departamento de Inteligencia Artificial, E.T.S.I. Informática,
UNED, 28040 - Madrid, Spain
{jmira, adelgado}@dia.uned.es

Abstract. Autonomous robot guidance in dynamic environments requires, on the one hand, the study of relative motion of the objects of the environment with respect to the robot, and on the other hand, the analysis of the depth towards those objects. In this paper, a stereo vision method, which combines both topics with potential utility in robot navigation, is proposed. The goal of the stereo vision model is to calculate depth of surrounding objects by measuring the disparity between the two-dimensional imaged positions of the object points in a stereo pair of images. The simulated robot guidance algorithm proposed starts from the motion analysis that occurs in the scene and then establishes correspondences and analyzes the depth of the objects. Once these steps have been performed, the next step is to induce the robot to take the direction where objects are more distant in order to avoid obstacles.

1 Introduction

Perception is a crucial part of the design of mobile robots. We want mobile robots to operate in unknown, unstructured environments. To achieve this goal, the robot must be able to perceive its environment sufficiently to allow it operate with that environment in a safe way. Most robots that successfully navigate in unconstrained environments use sonar transducers or laser range sensors as their primary spatial sensor [1] [2] [3]. On the hand, autonomous navigation [4] can be divided up into two elements: self-localization, and obstacle avoidance [5] [6]. Self-localization is always necessary if the target cannot be guaranteed to be in the field of view of the robot's sensing device. Self-localization using vision is not the hardest part of navigation because only a few visual cues are required. Obstacle avoidance is a lot more difficult, because it is in general not possible to guarantee that an obstacle will be detected.

There has been some work on the control strategies to be used where the required path is known and obstacle positions are known with some level of uncertainty [7].

M. Ali and F. Esposito (Eds.): IEA/AIE 2005, LNAI 3533, pp. 16 – 25, 2005.

Most research has concentrated on using the concept of free-space [8]. A free-space area is a triangular region with the cameras and a fixated scene feature as its vertices. If the robot moves while holding the feature in fixation, a free-space volume will be swept out.

The goal of the stereo vision method with application in mobile robotic is to calculate depth to surrounding objects by measuring the disparity between the two-dimensional imaged positions of the objects points in a stereo pair of images. Since a single 3D point will project differently onto a camera's sensor when imaged from different locations, the 3D world position of the point can be reconstructed from the disparate image locations of these projections. Many algorithms have been developed so far to analyze the depth in a scene. Brown et al. [9] describe a good approximation to all of them in their survey article.

Depth analysis is faced by different methods; but all of them have as a common denominator that they work with static images and not with motion information. In this paper, we have chosen as an alternative not to use direct information from the image, but rather the one derived from motion analysis. This alternative should provide some important advantages when working with mobile robots in dynamic environments. Autonomous robot guidance in dynamic environments requires, on the one hand, the study of relative motion of the objects of the environment with respect to the robot, and on the other hand, the analysis of the depth towards those objects.

In this paper, firstly a stereo vision method is proposed. Then, we present a simulation of a robot that uses motion-based and correlation-based stereo vision to navigate and explore unknown and dynamic indoor environments. The system uses as input the motion information of the objects present in the scene, and uses this information to perform a depth analysis of the scene. After estimating the scene depth distribution, an algorithm, which imposes the search for maximum depth criteria to guide an autonomous robot, is proposed. Keeping this purpose in mind, the algorithm tracks those areas where depth is maximal.

2 Motion-Based Stereovision Method

Our argumentation is that motion-based segmentation facilitates the correspondence analysis. Indeed, motion trails obtained through the permanency memories [10] [11] charge units are used to analyze the disparity between the objects in a more easy and precise way.

2.1 Accumulative Computation for Motion Detection

The permanency memories mechanism considers the jumps of pixels between grey levels, and accumulating this information as a charge. This representation is also called accumulative computation, and has already been proved in applications such as moving object shape recognition in noisy environments [12] [13], moving objects classification by motion features such as velocity or acceleration [14], and in applications related to selective visual attention [15]. The more general modality of accumulative computation is the charge/discharge mode, which may be described by means of the following generic formula:

$$Ch[x,y,t]=\begin{cases}\min(Ch[x,y,t-\Delta t]+C, Ch_{max}), & if\ "property\ P[x,y,t]"\\ \max(Ch[x,y,t-\Delta t]-D, Ch_{min}), & otherwise\end{cases} \tag{1}$$

The temporal accumulation of the persistency of the binary property $P[x,y,t]$ measured at each time instant t at each pixel $[x,y]$ of the data field is calculated. Generally, if the property is fulfilled at pixel $[x,y]$, the charge value at that pixel $Ch[x,y,t]$ goes incrementing by increment charge value C up to reaching Ch_{max}, whilst, if property P is not fulfilled, the charge value $Ch[x,y,t]$ goes decrementing by decrement charge value D down to Ch_{min}. All pixels of the data field have charge values between the minimum charge, Ch_{min}, and the maximum charge, Ch_{max}. Obviously, values C, D, Ch_{min} and Ch_{max} are configurable depending on the different kinds of applications, giving raise to all different operating modes of the accumulative computation.

Values of parameters C, D, Ch_{max} and Ch_{min} have to be fixed according to the applications characteristics. Concretely, values Ch_{max} and Ch_{min} have to be chosen by taking into account that charge values will always be between them. The value of C defines the charge increment interval between time instants t-1 and t. Greater values of C allow arriving in a quicker way to saturation. On the other hand, D defines the charge decrement interval between time instants t-1 and t. Thus, notice that the charge stores motion information as a quantified value, which may be used for several classification purposes. In this paper, the property measured in this case is equivalent to "motion detected" at pixel of co-ordinates [x,y] at instant t.

$$Ch\ [x,y,t]=\begin{cases}Ch_{max}, & \text{if } Mov[x,y,t]=1\\ \max(Ch\ [x,y,t-1]-D, Ch_{min}), & \text{if } Mov[x,y,t]=0\end{cases} \tag{2}$$

Initially the charge for a pixel is the minimum permitted value. The charge in the permanency memory depends on the difference between the current and the previous images grey level value. An accumulator detects differences between the grey levels of a pixel in the current and the previous frame. When a jump between grey levels occurs at a pixel, the charge unit (accumulator) of the permanency memory at the pixel's position is completely charged (charged to the maximum charge value). After the complete charge, each unit of the permanency memory goes decrementing with time (in a frame-by-frame basis) down to reaching the minimum charge value, while no motion is detected, or it is completely recharged, if motion is detected again. Thus, "motion detected" may be obtained by means of the following formula:

$$Mov\,[x,y,t]=\begin{cases}0, & if\ \ GLB\,[x,y,t]=GLB\,[x,y,t-1]\\ 1, & if\ \ GLB\,[x,y,t]\neq GLB\,[x,y,t-1]\end{cases}, \tag{3}$$

which is easily obtained as a variation in grey level band between two consecutive time instants t and t-1. In order to diminish the effects of noise due to the changes in illumination in motion detection, variation in grey level bands at each image pixel is treated as follows:

$$GLB[x,y,t]=\left\lfloor\frac{GL[x,y,t]*n}{(GL_{max}-GL_{min}+1)}\right\rfloor+1, \tag{4}$$

where $GL[x,y,t]$ is the grey level of pixel (x,y) at t,
n is the number of grey level bands,
GL_{max} is the maximum grey level value, and
GL_{min} is the minimum grey level value.

2.2 Disparity Analysis for Depth Estimation

The retrieval of disparity information is usually a very early step in image analysis. It requires stereotyped processing where each single pixel enters the computation. In stereovision, methods based on local primitives as pixels and contours may be very efficient, but are too much sensitive to locally ambiguous regions, such as occlusions or uniform texture regions. Methods based on areas are less sensitive to these problems, as they offer an additional support to do correspondences of difficult regions in a more easy and robust way, or they discard false disparities. Although methods based on areas use to be computationally very expensive, we introduce a simple pixel-based method with a low computational cost.

In our case, the inputs to the system are the permanency memories of the right and left images of the stereo video sequences. When an object moves in the scene, the effect in both cameras is similar to the charge accumulated in the memory units. If little time has elapsed since an object moved, the charge will be close to the maximum value in both permanency memories, and if a lot of time has elapsed since it moved, the charge would be much lower or even equal to the minimum value in both memories. Thus, we may assume that units with equal instantaneous charge values in their permanency memories correspond to the same objects.

For each frame of the sequence, the right permanency memory is fixed in a static way, and the left permanency memory will be displaced pixel by pixel on the epipolar restriction basis over it, in order to analyze the disparities of the motion trails. By means of this functionality, for all possible displacements of one permanency memory over the other, the correspondences between motion trails are checked and the disparities are assigned. In order to know up to what extent we have to displace one image over the other looking for correspondences, we have to take into account the disparity restriction. This restriction tells us that motion trails cannot raise a disparity value greater than a maximum permitted disparity.

Once the last displacement according to the disparity restriction has been calculated, each unit analyzes which is the displacement value where the value of its charge variable has been maximal. This displacement value is assumed the most confident disparity value for the pixels that form the region containing the pixel. This way the unicity restriction is imposed, as for each processing unit the final value has only one unique disparity value. This is a constraint based in the geometry of the visual system and in the very nature of the objects of the scene. It tells us that to any pixel of the right image there is only one corresponding pixel on the left image. This means that, if there are several pixels candidates to correspondents, we have to choose the most confident one. Once motion trails of the moving objects that appear in the stereo sequence provide the correspondences, from their disparity and the system's geometry it is possible to estimate the depth of the elements in the scene.

3 Simulation for Autonomous Robot Navigation

For sure, the precision of the depth estimation is not too accurate due to the horizontal and vertical discreetization of the cameras, but the information is good enough for the autonomous navigation task. From this perception, a system capable of analyzing the depth of the situation of an object enables controlling the traction system to direct it towards the region more far away from the cameras.

The robot guidance algorithm proposed starts from the motion analysis that occurs in the scene and then establishes correspondences and analyzes the depth of the objects, as described in the previous sections. Once these steps have been performed, the next step is to induce the robot to take the direction where objects are more distant, in order to avoid obstacles.

The algorithms have been tested in a simulated scenario, a square corridor (see figure 1). On the external walls of the corridor, there are some square figures simulating windows and doors, whilst on the interior walls there are only doors. The reason for the inclusion of doors and windows is to have some objects moving when the cameras advance on the robot. In this scenario, the robot walks through the interior of the corridor.

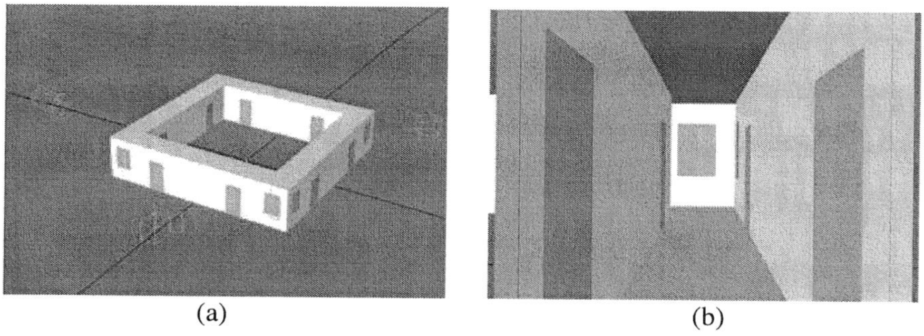

(a) (b)

Fig. 1. Corridor scenario. (a) Aerial view. (b) In the interior of the corridor

The corridor scenario is composed of 500 image stereo frames. 125 pairs of frames are enough for studying a straight stretch and a turn on one corner. We have separately analyzed the straight stretches and the turns. The values of the main parameters used in this simulation were number of grey level bands $n = 8$, maximum charge value $Ch_{max} = 255$, minimum charge value $Ch_{min} = 0$, and charge decrement interval $D = 16$.

3.1 Analysis of the Turns in the Three-Dimensional Environment

Figure 2 shows the result of applying our algorithms in the moment when the robot has to turn one of the corners. In column (a) some input images of the right camera are shown, in column (b) we have the images segmented in grey level bands, in column (c) motion information as represented in the right permanency memory is

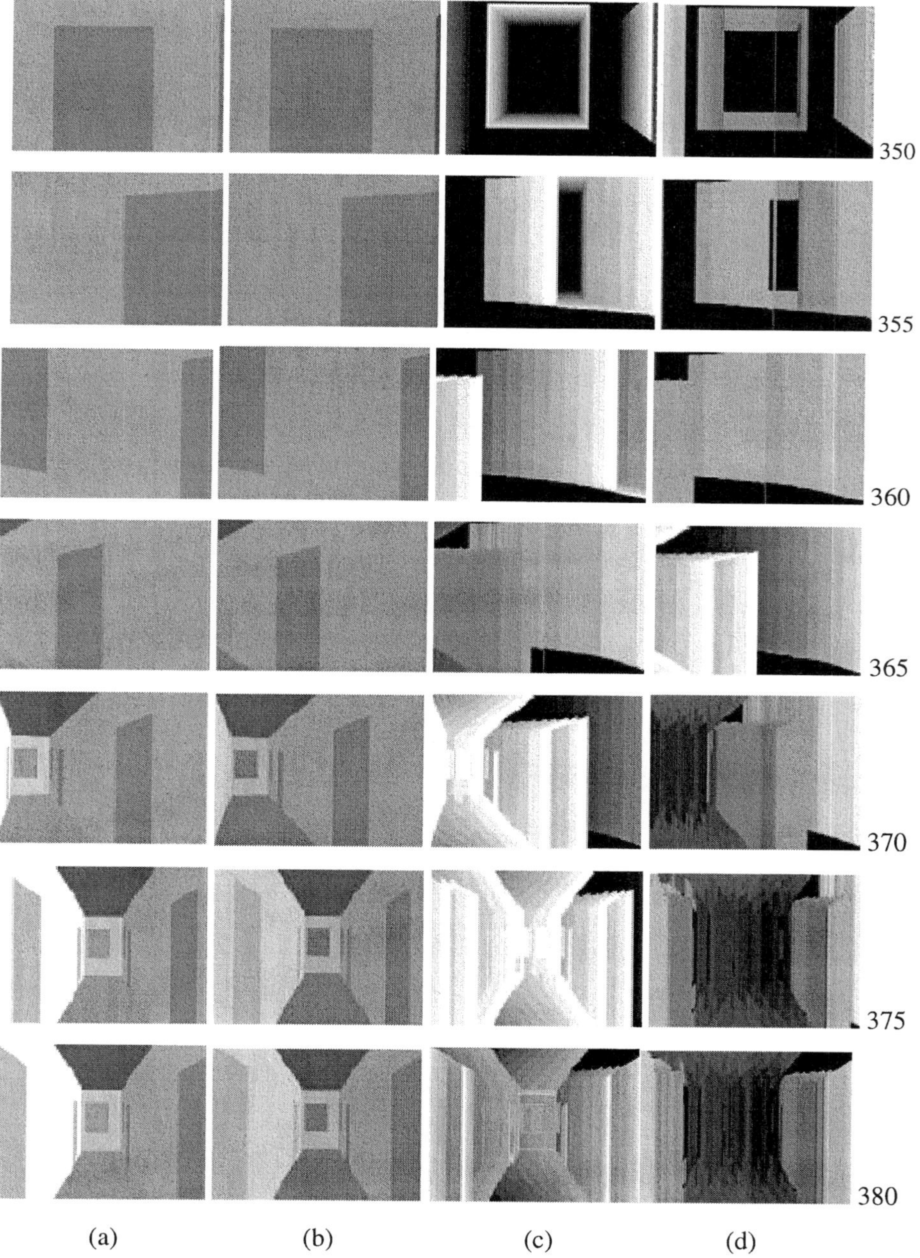

Fig. 2. Results for the turns in the corridor scenario (frames 350 to 380). (a) Input images of the right camera. (b) Images segmented in grey level bands. (c) Motion information in right permanency memory. (d) Scene depth

Fig. 3. Results for the straight stretch in the corridor scenario (frames 265 to 350). (a) Input images of the right camera. (b) Images segmented in grey level bands. (c) Motion information in right permanency memory. (d) Scene depth

offered, and in column (d) the final output, that is to say, the scene depth as detected by the robot, is presented.

When looking at the results offered on figure 2, we may make some remarks. Firstly, between frames 350 and 365, as the robot is turning, all objects of the environment appear displaced in the image, offering long trails in the permanency memory. These motion trails are analyzed to calculate the object's depths in the output image. In frames around the 370, the end of the corridor appears again. This issue causes a great impact in the permanency memory. This effect is interpreted by the algorithm to provide the depth of the scene, which gives very high values as it may be appreciated at the output image. From frame 375 on, the corridor does not move in horizontal direction any more. Nevertheless, the effect of the previous turn is still present in the permanency memory. Thus, the depth may still be calculated easily. Between frames 375 and 380, the horizontal movements of the end of the corridor are losing strength in the permanency memory. Nevertheless, the algorithm contains sufficient information to estimate its depth. From frame 380 on, we are in the situation of straight stretches.

3.2 Analysis of the Straight Stretches in the Three-Dimensional Environment

In this case, the walking of a robot through a straight-line corridor is simulated. The proper movement of the robot enables considering the static objects in the scenario as elements moving towards the cameras. Figure 3 shows the results of applying the algorithms to the straight stretch in the simulated three-dimensional environment.

In frame 265, although in the input image the first door present in the straight stretches of the corridors does not appear any more, its presence is still under consideration in the permanency memory. This is why its depth is calculated in the output image. Also in the output image corresponding to frame 265, the end of the corridor appears with a much lower illumination due to its remoteness. Associated to frame 280, the central smooth walls do not offer any motion information. That is the reason why there is no information in the permanency memory and in the output image. Again, in this frame the doors and the windows of the end appear in dark grey color. Gradually, from frame 300 to frame 350, the color of the objects at the end gets clearer due to the approach motion to the cameras.

3.3 General Remarks

From the results obtained in figures 2 and 3, there are several general conclusions and remarks we may consider. Firstly, motion analysis in the z-axis, obtained by accumulative computation from motion detection and disparity analysis from depth estimation, enables knowing which objects are approaching the cameras or moving away. This is really important in autonomous robot navigation, and especially for the obstacle avoidance task. In second place, our system enables the generation of a sort of three-dimensional map of the robot's environment. This way, objects that are static by nature are detected due to the relative motion of the cameras with respect to the environment.

4 Conclusions

In this paper, we have introduced a method for robot navigation that uses motion-based and correlation-based stereo vision to explore unknown and dynamic indoor environments. The method uses as input the motion information of the objects present in the scene, and uses this information to perform a depth analysis of the scene. For the purpose of autonomous robot navigation, we have chosen the alternative not to use direct information from the image, but rather to exploit all information derived from motion analysis. This alternative provides some important advantages when working with mobile robots in dynamic environments. The idea of stereo and motion computation on grouped grey level regions may be compared to the work of Matas on maximally extremal regions [16], which has proved to be very effective.

Firstly, through motion information it is easier to use correspondences than by grey level information of the frames. The results are also more accurate and robust. This is due to the instantaneous motion features, such as position, velocity, acceleration and direction of the diverse moving objects that move around the robot. Thus, motion information of an object will be different from any other moving object's one. Nonetheless, when observing motion features of a concrete object in both stereo sequences at the same time instant, we appreciate that these features are extremely similar. This is the reason why it is easy and robust to establish correspondences between the motion information of an object at the right image respect to the object at the left image. There exist very few ambiguity possibilities. A second advantage of using motion information relates to the nature of static objects. A translation or turn movement of the proper robot makes that walls or furniture move in relation to the robot, and of course respect to the observing cameras. This relative motion is different if the objects are close to or far away from the robot. Therefore, it will be very easy to discriminate among objects in the scene far away or close to the robot. The method proposed takes the advantage of algorithms based on pixels, as its output is a dense map of disparities. Besides, it also takes the advantage of algorithms based on higher level primitives by putting into correspondence complete regions of the image – see, permanency memories - and not only pixels.

Acknowledgements

This work is supported in part by the Spanish CICYT TIN2004-07661-C02-01 and TIN2004-07661-C02-02 grants.

References

1. Brooks, R.A., "A robust layered control system for a mobile robot", IEEE Journal of Robotics and Automation, vol. 2, no. 1, (1986): 14-23.
2. Dudek, G., Milios, E., Jenkin, M. & Wilkes, D., "Map validation and self-location for a robot with a graph-like map", Robotics and Autonomous Systems, vol. 26, (1997): 159-187.

3. Nickerson, S., Long, D., Jenkin, M., Milios, E., Down, B., Jasiobedzki, P., Jepson, A., Terzopoulos, D., Tsotsos, J., Wilkes, D., Bains, N. & Tran, K, "ARK: Autonomous navigation of a mobile robot in a known environment", International Conference on Intelligent Autonomous Systems, (1993): 288-293.
4. Jaillet, L., Siméon, T., "A PRM-based motion planner for dynamically changing environments", Proceedings of the IEEE International Conference on Intelligent Robots and Systems, IROS 2004, (2004).
5. Györy, G., "Obstacle detection methods for stereo vision as driving aid", Proceedings of the 11th IEEE International Conferece on Advanced Robotics, ICAR 2003, (2003): 477-481.
6. Park, S.-K., Kim, M., Lee, C.-W., "Mobile robot navigation based on direct depth and color-based environment modeling", Proceedings of the IEEE International Conference on Robotics and Automation, ICRA 2004, (2004).
7. Hu, H. & Brady, M., "Dynamic planning and environment learning of an industrial mobile robot" , IEEE Transactions on Robotics and Automation, (1996).
8. Rueb, K.D. & Wong A.K.C., "Structuring free space as a hypergraph for roving robot path planning and navigation", IEEE Transactions on Pattern Analysis and Machine Intelligence, vol. 9, no. 2, (1987): 263-273.
9. Brown, M. Z., Burschka, D. & Hager, G. D., "Advances in Computational Stereo", IEEE trans. on Pattern Analysis and Machine Intelligence, vol. 25, no. 8, (2003).
10. Fernández, M.A., Fernández-Caballero, A., López, M.T., Mira, J., "Length-speed ratio (LSR) as a characteristic for moving elements real-time classification", Real-Time Imaging, vol. 9, (2003): 49-59.
11. Mira, J., Fernández, M.A., López, M.T., Delgado, A.E., Fernández-Caballero, A., "A model of neural inspiration for local accumulative computation", 9th International Conference on Computer Aided Systems Theory, Springer-Verlag, (2003): 427-435.
12. Fernández-Caballero, A., Fernández, M.A., Mira, J., Delgado, A.E., "Spatio-temporal shape building from image sequences using lateral interaction in accumulative computation", Pattern Recognition, vol. 36, no. 5, (2003): 1131-1142.
13. Fernández-Caballero, A., Mira, J., Férnandez, M.A., Delgado, A.E., "On motion detection through a multi-layer neural network architecture", Neural Networks, vol. 16, no. 2, (2003): 205-222.
14. Fernández-Caballero, A., López, M.T., Fernández, M.A., Mira, J., Delgado, A.E., López-Valles J.M., "Accumulative computation method for motion features extraction in dynamic selective visual attention", 2nd International Workshop on Attention and Performance in Computational Vision, Springer-Verlag, (2004): to appear.
15. Fernández-Caballero, A., Mira, J., Delgado, A.E., Fernández, M.A., "Lateral interaction in accumulative computation: A model for motion detection", Neurocomputing, vol. 50, (2003): 341-364.
16. Matas, J., Chum, O., Martin, U., Pajdla, T., "Robust wide baseline stereo from maximally stable extremal regions", Proceedings of the British Machine Vision Conference, vol. 1, (2002): 384-393.

Object Tracking Using Mean Shift and Active Contours

Jae Sik Chang[1], Eun Yi Kim[2], KeeChul Jung[3], and Hang Joon Kim[1]

[1] Dept. of Computer Engineering, Kyungpook National Univ., South Korea
{jschang, hjkim}@ailab.knu.ac.kr
[2] Scool of Internet and Multimedia, NITRI (Next-Generation Innovative Technology Research Institute), Konkuk Univ., South Korea
eykim@konkuk.ac.kr
[3] School of Media, College of Information Science, Soongsil University
kcjung@ssu.ac.kr

Abstract. Active contours based tracking methods have widely used for object tracking due to their following advantages. 1) effectiveness to descript complex object boundary, and 2) ability to track the dynamic object boundary. However their tracking results are very sensitive to location of the initial curve. Initial curve far form the object induces more heavy computational cost, low accuracy of results, as well as missing the highly active object. Therefore, this paper presents an object tracking method using a mean shift algorithm and active contours. The proposed method consists of two steps: object localization and object extraction. In the first step, the object location is estimated using mean shift. And the second step, at the location, evolves the initial curve using an active contour model. To assess the effectiveness of the proposed method, it is applied to synthetic sequences and real image sequences which include moving objects.

1 Introduction

An active contour model is a description of an object boundary which is iteratively adjusted until it matches the object of interest [1]. Recently, the models are successfully used for object detection and tracking because of their ability to effectively descript curve and elastic property. So, they have been applied to many applications such as non-rigid object (hand, pedestrian and etc.) detection and tracking, shape warping system and so on [2, 3, 4].

In the tracking approaches based on active contour models, the object tracking problem is considered as a curve evolution problem, i.e., the initial curve, initialized by the object boundary of the previous frame, is evolved until it matches the object boundary of interest [2, 3]. Generally, the curve evolutions are computed in narrow band around the current curve. This small computation area induces low computation cost. And the initial curve near the object boundary guarantees practically that the curve converges to object boundary. However their tracking results are very sensitive to conditions of the initial curve such as location, scale and shape. Among these conditions, location of the initial curve has a high effect on the results. The initial curve far from the object needs more heavy computational cost to converge and induces errors such as noises and holes which have similar feature to object boundary. Moreover, it lost the highly active objects that have large movements.

M. Ali and F. Esposito (Eds.): IEA/AIE 2005, LNAI 3533, pp. 26 – 35, 2005.

Accordingly, this paper proposes a method for object tracking using mean shift algorithm and active contours. The method consists of two steps: object localization and object extraction. In the first step, the object location is estimated using mean shift. And the second step, at the location, evolves the initial curve using an active contour model. The proposed method not only develops the advantage of the curve evolution based approaches but also adds the robustness to large amount of motion of the object.

The remainder of the paper is organized as follows. Chapter 2 illustrates how to localize the object using mean shift algorithm and active contours based object detection method is shown in chapter 3. Experimental results are presented in chapter 4. Finally, chapter 5 concludes the paper.

2 Object Localization

2.1 Mean Shift Algorithm

The mean shift algorithm is a nonparametric technique that climbs the gradient of a probability distribution to find the nearest dominant mode (peak) [5, 6]. The algorithm has recently been adopted as an efficient technique for object tracking [6, 7].

The algorithm simply replacing the search window location (the centroid) with a object probability distribution $\{P(I_{ij}|\alpha_o)\}_{i,j=1,\ldots,IW,IH}$($IW$: image width, IH: image height) which represent the probability of a pixel (i,j) in the image being part of object, where α_o is its parameters and I is a photometric variable. The search window location is simply computed as follows [5, 6, 7]:

$$x = M_{10}/M_{00} \qquad \text{and} \qquad y = M_{01}/M_{00}, \tag{1}$$

where M_{ab} is the $(a + b)th$ moment as defined by

$$M_{ab}(W) = \sum_{i,j \in W} i^a j^b P(I_{ij} \mid \alpha_o).$$

The object location is obtained by successive computations of the search window location (x,y).

2.2 Object Localization Using Mean Shift

The mean shift algorithm for object localization is as follows:

1. Set up initial location and size of search window W and repeat Steps 2 to 4 until terminal condition is satisfied.
2. Generate a distribution over a photometric variable, object probability distribution, within W.
3. Estimate the search window location using Eq. (1).
4. (If the second iteration, modify the size of W as bounding box size of initial curve.)
5. Output the window location as the object location.

If the variation of the window location is smaller than a threshold value, then the terminal condition is satisfied.

In the mean shift algorithm, instead of calculating the object probability distribution over the whole image, the distribution calculation can be restricted to a smaller image region within the search window. This results in significant computational savings when the object does not dominate the image [5].

2.3 Adaptation of Search Window Size

The search window size of general mean shift algorithm is determined according to object size. It is efficient to track the object whose motion is smaller than the object size. However, in many case, objects have large motion due to their activity and low frame rate. The smaller search window than the object motion fails to track the object. Accordingly, in this paper, the size of the search window in the first iteration of the mean shift algorithm is adaptively determined in direct proportional to the amount of object's motion, which is determined as follows:

$$\begin{aligned} W_{width} &= \max\left(\alpha\left(\left|m_x^t - m_x^{t-1}\right| - B_{width}\right), 0\right) + \beta B_{width} \quad \text{and} \\ W_{height} &= \max\left(\alpha\left(\left|m_y^t - m_y^{t-1}\right| - B_{height}\right), 0\right) + \beta B_{height}, \end{aligned} \tag{2}$$

where α and β is a constant and superscript of m means frame index.

3 Object Extraction

3.1 Active Contours Based on Region Competition

Zhu and Yuille proposed a hybrid approach to image segmentation, called region competition [8]. Their basic functional is as follows:

$$E[\Gamma, \{\alpha_i\}] = \sum_{i=1}^{M} \left\{ \frac{\mu}{2} \int_{\partial R_i} ds - \log P(\{I_s : s \in R_i\} \mid \alpha_i) + \lambda \right\}, \tag{3}$$

where Γ is the boundary in the image, $P(\cdot)$ is a specific distribution for region R_i, α_i is its parameters, M is the number of the regions, s is a site of image coordinate system, and μ and λ are two constants.

To minimize the energy E, steepest descent can be done with respect to boundary Γ. For any point $\vec{v}$. On the boundary Γ we obtain:

$$\frac{d\vec{v}}{dt} = -\frac{\delta E[\Gamma, \{\alpha_i\}]}{\delta \vec{v}}, \tag{4}$$

where the right-hand side is (minus) the functional derivative of the energy E.

Taking the functional derivative yields the motion equation for point $\vec{v}$:

$$\frac{d\vec{v}}{dt} = \sum_{k \in Q_{(\vec{v})}} \left\{ -\frac{\mu}{2} k_{k(\vec{v})} \vec{n}_{k(\vec{v})} + \log P(I_{(\vec{v})} \mid \alpha_k) \vec{n}_{k(\vec{v})} \right\}, \tag{5}$$

where $Q_{(\vec{v})} = \{k \mid \vec{v} \text{ lies on } \Gamma_k\}$, i.e., the summation is done over those regions R_k for which $\vec{v}$ is on Γ_k. $k_{k(\vec{v})}$ is the curvature of Γ_k at point $\vec{v}$ and $\vec{n}_{k(\vec{v})}$ is the unit normal to Γ_k at point $\vec{v}$.

Region competition contains many of the desirable properties of region growing and active contours. Indeed we can derive many aspects of these models as special cases of region competition [8, 9]. Active contours can be a special case in which there are two regions (object region R_o and background region R_b) and a common boundary Γ as shown in follows:

$$\frac{d\vec{v}}{dt} = -\mu k_{o(\vec{v})}\vec{n}_{o(\vec{v})} + \left(\log P(I_{(\vec{v})} \mid \alpha_o) - \log P(I_{(\vec{v})} \mid \alpha_b)\right)\vec{n}_{o(\vec{v})} \tag{6}$$

3.2 Level Set Implementation

The active contour evolution was implemented using the level set technique. We represent curve Γ implicitly by the zero level set of function $u : \Re^2 \rightarrow \Re$, with the region inside Γ corresponding to $u > 0$. Accordingly, Eq. (6) can be rewritten by the following equation, which is a level set evolution equation [2, 3]:

$$\frac{du(s)}{dt} = -\mu k_s \|\nabla u\| + \left(\log P(I_s \mid \alpha_o) - \log P(I_s \mid \alpha_b)\right)\|\nabla u\|, \tag{7}$$

where

$$k = \frac{u_{xx}y_y^2 - 2u_y u_x u_{xy} + u_{yy}u_x^2}{(u_x^2 + u_y^2)^{3/2}}.$$

The curve evolution is achieved by iterative calculation of level values $u(s)$ using Eq. (7). In curve evolution, the stopping criterion is satisfied when the difference of the number of the pixel inside curve $\vec{v}$ in the successive iteration is less than a threshold value. The threshold value is used a constant chosen experimentally.

3.3 Object Extraction Using Active Contours

The aim of the object extraction is to find closed curve that separates the image into object and background regions. The object to be tracked is assumed to be characterized by a probability distribution, an object probability distribution $P(I_s \mid \alpha_o)$, over some variable such as intensity, color, or texture. Unlike in the object region, the background is difficult to be characterized a simple probability distribution. The distribution is not clustered in a small area of a feature space due to their variety. However, it is spread out across the whole space uniformly for a variety of background regions. From that, we can assume that the photometric variable of background is uniformly distributed in the space. Thus, the distribution $P(I_s \mid \alpha_b)$ can be proportional to a constant value.

Active contour model based object boundary extraction algorithm is as follows:

1. Set up initial level values u, and repeat Steps 2 to 3 until terminal condition is satisfied.
2. Update level values using Eq. (7) within narrow band around curve, zero level set.
3. Reconstruct the evolved curve, zero level set.
4. Output the final evolved curve as the object boundary.

To set up the initial level values, we use a Euclidian distance mapping technique. Euclidian distance between each pixel of the image and initial curve is assigned to the pixel as a level value. In general active contours, the search area for optimal boundary curve is restricted to the narrow band around curve. This not only save computational cost but also avoid the local optima when the initial curve is near the object boundary. However it makes the evolving curve miss the boundary when the curve is far from the object.

After updating the level values, the approximated final propagated curve, the zero level set, is reconstructed. Curve reconstruction is accomplished by determining the zero crossing grid location in the level set function. The terminal condition is satisfied when the difference of the number of pixel inside contour Γ is less than a threshold value chosen manually.

4 Experimental Results

This paper presents a method for tracking object which have distributions over some photometric variable such as intensity, color, or texture. This section focuses on evaluating the proposed method. In order to assess the effectiveness of the proposed method, it was tested with a synthetic image sequence and hand image sequences, and then the results were compared with those obtained using the active contours for distribution tracking proposed by Freedman et al. [2].

Freedman's method finds the region such that the sample distribution of the interior of the region most closely matches the model distribution using active contours. For matching distribution, the method examined Kullback-Leibler distance and Bhattacharyya measure. In this experiment, we only have tested former.

4.1 Evaluation Function

To quantitatively evaluate the performance of the two methods, The Chamfer distance was used. This distance has been many used as matching measure between shapes [10]. To calculate the distance, ground truths are manually extracted from images to construct accurate boundaries of each object. Then, the distances between the ground truth and the object boundaries extracted by the respective method are calculated.

The Chamfer distance is the average over one shape of distance to the closet point on the other and defined as

$$C(F,G) = \frac{1}{3}\sqrt{\frac{1}{n}\sum_{i=1}^{n} v_i^2}\,, \tag{8}$$

where F and G are sets of pixels on object boundary detected by the proposed method and manually, respectively. In Eq. (8), v_i are the distance values from each point on F to the closet point on G and n is the number of points in the curve. The distance values v_i were described in [10].

4.2 Tracking in Synthetic Sequences

To demonstrate the ability of the method to track textured regions, a synthetic image sequence is used. In the sequence, the background is composed of horizontal strips, while the object is composed of diagonal strips. For photometric variable which describe the object, a simple texture vector may be chosen based on the directions of (nonzero) intensity gradients in the neighborhood of a pixel.

Fig. 1 and 2 show tracking results in the synthetic sequence extracted using the proposed method and Freedman's method, respectively. In the first frame, an initial curve was manually selected around the object, and then the curve was evolved using only active contours. The Chamfer distances of the two methods are shown in Fig. 3. In the case of the proposed method, object localization using mean shift is considered as the first iteration. The distance in the proposed method decreases more dramatically and the method satisfies the stopping criteria after less iteration than Freedman's method. Due to it, Freedman's method takes lager time to track the object than the

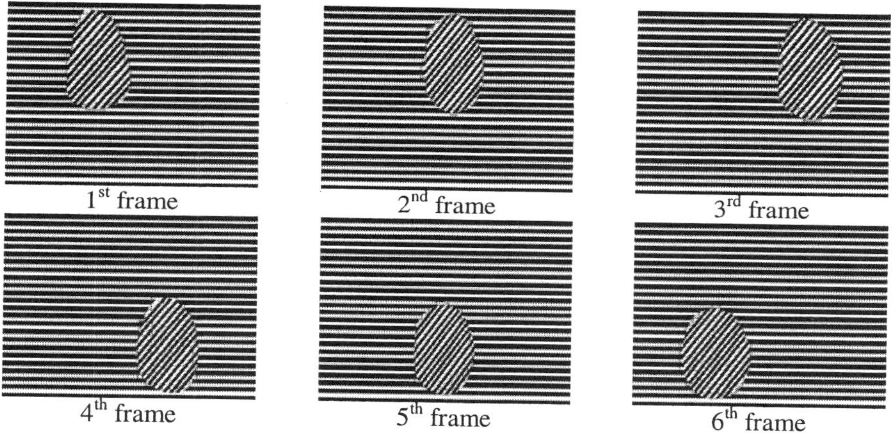

Fig. 1. Tracking with the proposed method in synthetic images

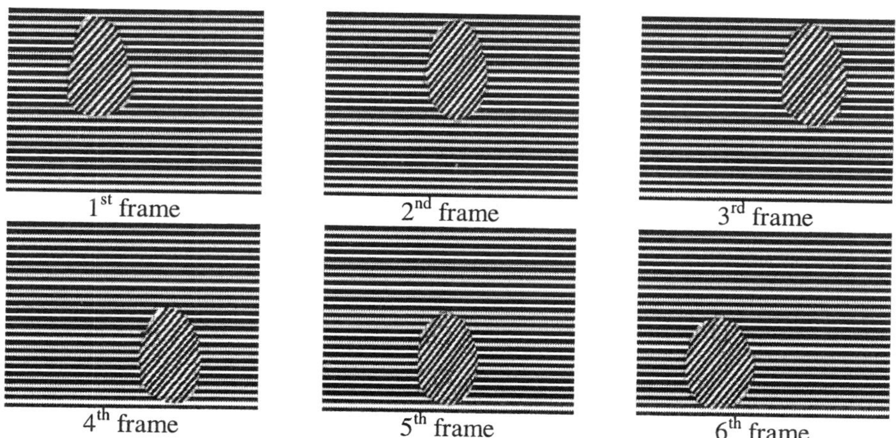

Fig. 2. Tracking with the Freedman's method in synthetic images

proposed method as shown in Table 1. When visually inspected, the proposed method produces superior detection results to the Freedman's method. As shown in Fig. 1 and 2, the proposed method detects object boundary accurately. On the contrary, the Freedman's method produces some holes and tough boundaries. This is because active contours detect whole local optima passed by curve during curve evolution but the proposed method moves the initial curve near the global optimum using mean shift algorithm before curve evolution.

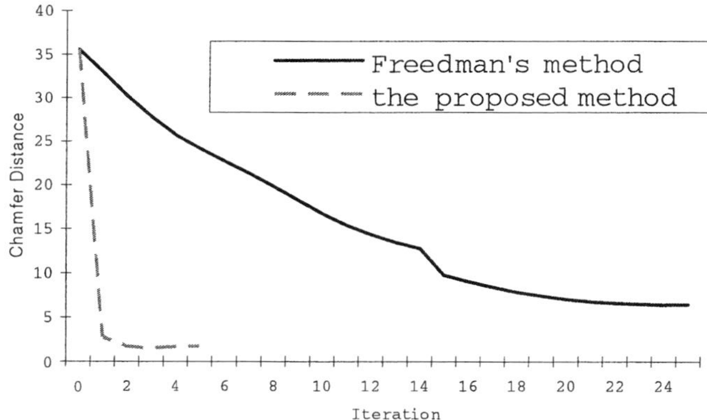

Fig. 3. Comparison of two methods in term of the Chamfer distance

Table 1. Time taken for tracking in synthetic images (sec.)

	1st frame	2nd frame	3rd frame	4th frame	5th frame	6th frame
Freedman's method	0.031000	0.157000	0.172000	0.281000	0.313000	0.282000
proposed method	0.031000	0.047000	0.063000	0.063000	0.093000	0.125000

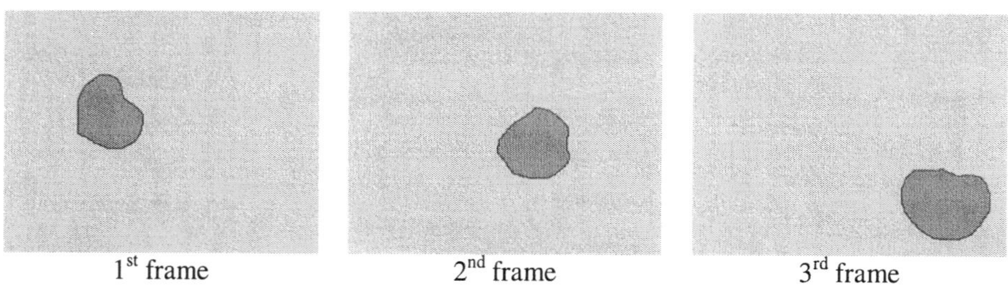

Fig. 4. Tracking in synthetic images include a large amount of motion

One of the problems of almost active contours is that the search areas for optima are limited to the narrow band around curve. Because of it, the active contours have difficulties to track objects that have large amount of motion. The other side, in the proposed method, the initial curve is moved near the global optimum before curve evolution. Accordingly, the method is more effective to track the objects that have large amount of motion. Fig.4 shows the tracking results in a synthetic sequence designed to demonstrate the ability of the proposed method to track objects that have large amount of motion. For photometric variable which describe the object, a simple texture vector may be chosen RGB color value of a pixel. As shown Fig. 4, the proposed method tracks the object while Freeman's method fails to track it.

Table 2. Time taken for tracking in hand sequence (sec.)

	1st frame	2nd frame	3rd frame	4th frame	5th frame	6th frame
Feedman's method	0.192000	0.360000	0.359000	0.453000	0.188000	0.438000
proposed method	0.192000	0.188000	0.187000	0.218000	0.156000	0.188000

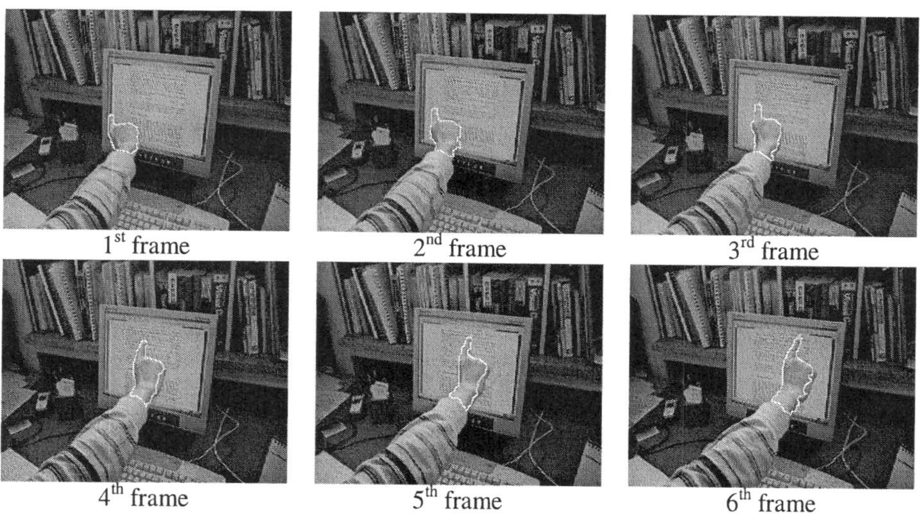

Fig. 5. Tracking with the proposed method in hand sequence

4.3 Tracking in Hands Images

To assess the effectiveness of the proposed method to real image sequence, it is applied to hand tracking. For photometric variable which describe the hands, we use skin-color information which is represented by a 2D-Gaussian model. In the RGB space, color representation includes both color and brightness. Therefore, RGB is not necessarily the best color representation for detecting pixels with skin color. Brightness can be removed by dividing the three components of a color pixel (R, G, B) according to intensity. This space is known as chromatic color, where intensity is a normalized color vector with two components (r, g). The skin-color model is obtained from 200 sample images. Means and covariance matrix of the skin color model are as follows:

$$m=(\bar{r},\bar{g})=(117.588,79.064),$$

$$\Sigma=\begin{bmatrix} \sigma_r^2 & \rho_{X,Y}\sigma_g\sigma_r \\ \rho_{X,Y}\sigma_r\sigma_g & \sigma_g^2 \end{bmatrix}=\begin{bmatrix} 24.132 & -10.085 \\ -10.085 & 8.748 \end{bmatrix}.$$

The hand tracking result in real image sequence is shown in Fig. 5. The proposed method is successful in tracking through the entire 80-frame sequence. Freedman's method also succeeds in the hand tracking in the sequence, because the sequence has high capture rate and hand has not a large movement. However Freedman's method takes lager time to track the hand than the proposed method as shown in Table 2.

5 Conclusions

In this paper, we have proposed an active contour model based object tracking with mean shift algorithm. In the approaches based on active contour models, the object tracking problem is considered as a curve flow problem and their results are very sensitive to condition of initial contour. Bad initial condition induces a heavy computational cost, low accuracy of results, and missing the object that has a large movement. Accordingly, the proposed method consisted of two steps: object localization and object extraction. The first step finds the object location using a mean shift algorithm. And at the location, the initial curve is evolved using an active contour model to find object boundary. The experimental results shown demonstrate that the proposed method yields accurate tracking results despite low computational cost.

Acknowledgement

This work was supported by the Korea Research Foundation Grant (KRF-2004- 041-D00643).

References

1. Fenster, S. D., Kender, J. R.: Sectored Snakes: Evaluating Learned Energy Segmentations. IEEE Transactions on Pattern Analysis and Machine Intelligence. Vol. 23, No. 9 (2002) 1028-1034
2. Freedman, D., Zhang, T.: Active Contours for Tracking Distributions. IEEE Transactions on Image Processing. Vol. 13, No. 4 (2004) 518-526
3. Chan, T. F., Vese, L. A.: Active Contours Without Edges. IEEE Transactions on Image Processing. Vol. 10, No. 2 (2001) 266-277

4. Gastaud, M., Barlaud, M., Aubert, G.: Combining Shape Prior and Statistical Features for Active Contour Segmentation. IEEE Transactions on Circuits and Systems for Video Technology. Vol. 14. No. 5 (2004) 726-734
5. Kim, K. I., Jung, K., Kim, J. H.:Texture-Based Approach for Text Detection in Image Using Support Vector Machines and Continuously Adaptive Mean Shift Algorithm. IEEE Transactions on Pattern Analysis and Machine Intelligence. Vol. 25, No. 12 (2003) 1631-1639
6. Bradski, G. R.: Computer Vision Face Tracking For Use in a Perceptual User Interface. Intel Technology Journal 2nd quarter (1998) 1-15
7. Jaffre, G., Crouzil, A.: Non-rigid Object Localization From Color Model Using Mean Shift. In Proceedings of the International Conference on Image Processing, Vol. 3 (2003) 317-319
8. Zhu, S. C., Yuille, A.: Region Competition: Unifying Snakes, Region Growing, and Bayes/MDL for Multiband Image Segmentation. IEEE Transactions on Pattern Analysis and Machine Intelligence. Vol. 18, No 9 (1996) 884-900
9. Mansouri, A.: Region Tracking via Level Set PDEs without Motion Computation. IEEE Transactions on Pattern Analysis and Machine Intelligence. Vol. 24, No. 7 (2002) 947-961
10. Borgefors, G.: Hierarchical Chamfer Matching: A Parametric Edge Matching Algorithm. IEEE Transactions on Pattern Analysis and Machine Intelligence. Vol. 10. No. 11 (1998) 849-865

Place Recognition System from Long-Term Observations

Do Joon Jung and Hang Joon Kim

Department of Computer Engineering, Kyungpook National University,
702-701, 1370, Sangyuk-dong, Buk-gu, Daegu, Korea
{djjung, hjkim}@ailab.knu.ac.kr
http://ailab.knu.ac.kr

Abstract. In this paper, we propose a place recognition system which recognize places from a large set of images obtained over time. A set or a sequence of images provides more information about the places and that can be used for more robust recognition. For this, the proposed system recognize places using density matching between the estimated density of the input set and density of the stored images for each place. In the proposed system, we use global texture feature vector for image representation and their density for place recognition. We use a method based on a Gaussian model of texture vector distribution and a matching criterion using the Kullback-Leibler divergence measure. In the experiment, the system successfully recognized the places in several image sequence, the success rate of place recognition was 87% on average.

Keywords: Place Recognition, Steerable Pyramid, Density Matching.

1 Introduction

Place recognition (or localization) is a fundamental problem in mobile robotics and wearable computing. Most mobile robots must be able to locate themselves in their environment in order to accomplish their task [1]. An essential function of a wearable computing is to find the user's location and orientation relative to the real-world environment [2]. A number of researchers around the world have begun to work in the mobile computing and wearable computing for solving this kind of problem.

Place has been recognized using some methods based on computer vision like a panorama-based method and an image sequence matching method in the indoor environment [2], [3]. In the panorama-based method, place is recognized using matching between input video frames and panoramic images captured beforehand. In the image sequence matching method, place is recognized using matching of the color information between reference frames and current frames. These methods have shortcoming because just using the color information of images. Therefore, the place recognition performance is decreased according to the intensity variation and camera motion.

M. Ali and F. Esposito (Eds.): IEA/AIE 2005, LNAI 3533, pp. 36–43, 2005.

In this paper, we propose a place recognition system which recognizes places using textural information of images and their spatial layout [4]. A set or a sequence of images provides more information about the places and that can be used for more robust recognition. Therefore, the proposed system recognize places using density matching between the estimated density of the input set and density of the stored images for each place. In the proposed system, an image is represented as an 80 dimensional vector. To represent the image, we use a steerable pyramid [5] with 4 orientations and 4 scales applied to the intensity image. Thereafter, we would like to capture global image properties, while keeping some spatial information. Therefore, we take the mean value of the magnitude of the local features averaged over large spatial regions. We further reduce the dimensionality using PCA. We use a method based on a Gaussian model of texture vector distribution and a matching criterion using the Kullback-Leibler divergence measure for place recognition. We consider the 15 places, and the images are acquired while a person navigates the environment. In the experiment, the system successfully recognized the places in several image sequence, the success rate of place recognition was 87% on average.

2 Proposed System

2.1 Overview of the System

In the proposed system, we used wearable system which consists of a webcam, a mobile PC and a Head Mounted Display (HMD). While user navigate a building, a mobile PC recognizes a place through the images captured from the webcam and the user receive a feedback which is the recognized place on the HMD. Figure 1 shows the overview of the proposed system.

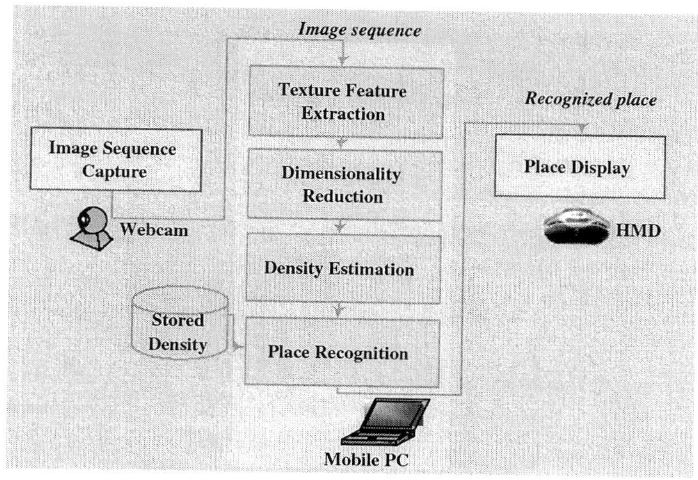

Fig. 1. System overview

In the proposed system, while user navigates the places like figure 2, the system recognizes the place through images obtained from the webcam. The images have motion-blur and saturation because images are captured during user moving the places and the webcam performance is not good. But the proposed system is more robust system because the system use textural information of large set of observations.

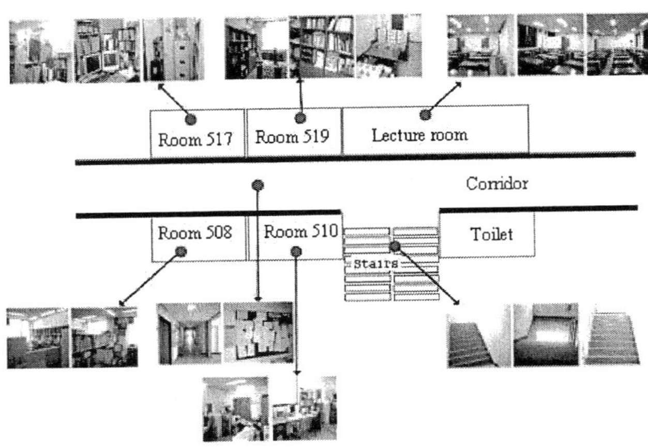

Fig. 2. Example of places

In the proposed system, we extract textural information using wavelet image decomposition. We use a steerable pyramid [5] with 4 orientations and 4 scales applied to the intensity image. Thereafter, we would like to capture global image properties, while keeping some spatial information. Therefore, we take the mean value of the magnitude of the local features averaged over large spatial regions. We further reduce the dimensionality using PCA for reducing the computation time. We use a method based on a Gaussian model of texture vector distribution and a matching criterion using the Kullback-Leibler divergence measure for place recognition. We assume a parametric density form (Gaussian) with parameters estimated from the training data.

2.2 Image Representation

In the proposed system, we use textural properties of the image and their spatial layout for image representation [4]. Texture properties and their spatial layout are represented by a vector but the vector has high dimensionality. Therefore, we generate feature vector which represents an image through dimensionality reduction using PCA for reducing computation time.

Texture Feature Extraction. While navigating an environment, image is obtained the camera mounted on helmet. Therefore, the image has multi-scale and multi orientation. For considering this property, we use a wavelet image decomposition to compute texture features. Each image location is represented by output of filters turned to different orientations and scales. We use a steerable pyramid [5] with 4 orientations and 4 scales applied to the intensity image. The steerable pyramid is a linear multi-scale, multi orientation image decomposition that provides a useful front-end for many computer vision and image processing applications. Figure 3 shows the steerable pyramid of image. This particular steerable pyramid contains 4 orientation subbands, at 2 scales. The local representation of an image at an instant t is then given by the $v_t^L(x) = \{v_{t,k}(x)\}_{k=1,..N}$, where $N = 16$ is the number of subbands. We would like to capture global image properties, while keeping some spatial information. Therefore, we take the mean value of the magnitude of the local features averaged over large spatial regions as follows:

$$m_t(x) = \sum_{x'} |v_t^L(x')| w(x' - x), \tag{1}$$

where $w(x)$ is the averaging window. The resulting representation is downsampled to have a spatial resolution of $M \times M$ pixels (here we use $M = 4$), Therefore, m_t has size $M \times M \times N = 256$.

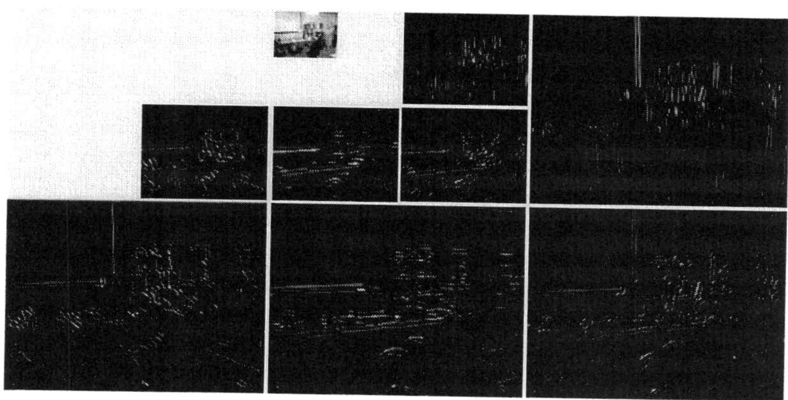

Fig. 3. Steerable pyramid of image

Dimensionality Reduction. PCA has been used for dimensionality reduction and analysis the data structure of high dimensional data. This is problem which finding the eigenvectors of data. There are two methods for solving this problem. One is matrix calculation method and the other method is using Neural Network (NN) recursively [6], [7].

PCA is data transform to axis which represents data better more good. Data vector is called to Principal Components (PCs) in the transformed dimensional space [6]. In the proposed system, we use the PCA for mapping the high dimensional texture pattern to low dimensional data lossless the information. In the proposed system, obtained image size is 76800 (320×240) dimension and we extract texture feature vector 256 dimension. We select 80 PCs because the eigenvalue is significantly decreased at 80 PCs. Therefore, we represent the vector of texture space to 80 dimensional vector using PCA for reducing the computation time.

2.3 Place Recognition Based on Density Matching

The recognition accuracy of current discriminant architectures for visual recognition is hampered by the dependence on holistic image representation. The formulation of visual recognition as a problem of statistical classification has led to various solutions of unprecedented success in areas such as face detection, face, texture, object, and shape recognition, or image retrieval [8]. In the proposed system, place is recognized by comparing sets of observations. We use a method reported in [9] for comparing sets of observations. We estimate Kullback-Leibler divergence between densities inferred from training data (the model densities) and densities inferred from samples under test. Because, a natural measure of the difference between the actual and the desired probability distributions is the relative entropy, Kullback-Leibler divergence. We use a method based on a Gaussian model of texture vector distribution and a matching criterion using the KL-divergence measure for place recognition. In the general case of two multivariate distributions, evaluating $D_{KL}(p_k \parallel p_0)$ is a difficult and computational expensive task, especially for high dimensions. Therefore, we use a closed form expression for two normal distributions p_k and p_0 which is reported in [10] as follows:

$$D_{KL}(p_0||p_k) = \frac{1}{2}\log\left(\frac{|\sum_k|}{|\sum_0|}\right) + \frac{1}{2}\mathrm{Tr}(\sum\nolimits_0 \sum\nolimits_k^{-1} + \sum\nolimits_k^{-1}(\bar{x}_k - \bar{x}_0)(\bar{x}_k - \bar{x}_0)^T) - \frac{d}{2}, \tag{2}$$

Where d is the dimensionality of the data (number of pixels in the image),$\bar{x}_k$ and $\bar{x}_0$ are the means of the training set for the kth subject and of the input set, respectively, and $\sum_k$ and $\sum_0$ are the covariance matrices of the estimated Gaussians for the kth subject and for the input set, respectively. For using this method, we assume a parametric density form (Gaussian) with parameters estimated from the training data. Moreover, we estimate the parameters of the distribution of our test sample. Thereafter, compute $D_{KL}(p_0 \parallel p_k)$, we exchange the indices 0 and k in equation (2).

3 Experimental Results

The experimental environment was inside building where possible noises were existed and the lighting condition was changing. We consider the 15 places for testing the place recognition system. The places are a corridor, 6 rooms, a seminar room, a lecture room, an office, stairs, a toilet, 2 classrooms, a PC room. Examples of representative views associated with individual places are depicted in Figure 4.

Fig. 4. Examples of representative views of 15 out of 15 places

Table 1. Processing time of each module

Module	Texture extraction	Dimensionality reduction	Place recognition
Processing time	0.07 sec	0.01 sec	0.05 sec

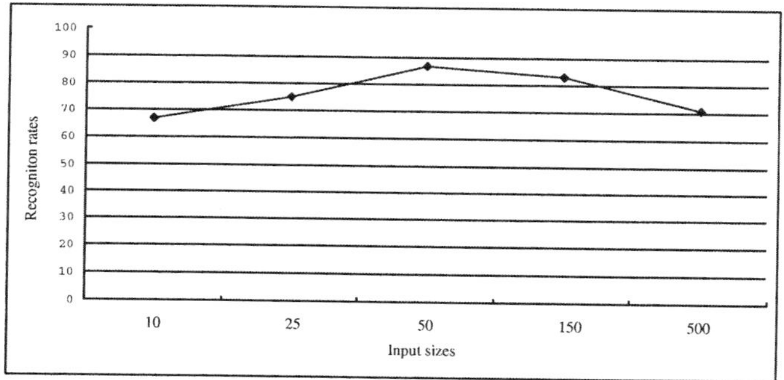

Fig. 5. Recognition rates for different input sizes

Many different users captured the images used for the experiments described in the paper while visiting 15 different places at different times of day. The locations were visited in a fairly random order. The proposed place recognition system consists of three equipments: a webcam, a mobile PC, and a Head Mounted Display (HMD). The webcam used in the system was a Smilecam Su-320 color video camera, the HMD was cy-visor DH-4400VP, and the mobile PC performed on Pentium 1.7GHz PC running Windows Xp. In the test, image sequence was acquired with the size of each frame is 320×240 pixels. The system could be processing about 7 frames per second on average. Table 1 shows the processing time of each module.

To estimate the behavior of the system for different input sizes, we recently captured test images into sets of 10, 25, 50, 150, 500 frames (0.4, 1, 2, 6, and

Table 2. Place recognition result

Places	P_1	P_2	P_3	P_4	P_5	P_6	P_7	P_8	P_9	P_{10}	P_{11}	P_{12}	P_{13}	P_{14}	P_{15}
P_1	174	8		5			6		8	6				4	
P_2		189		12			7			5					
P_3		2	152					15				12			5
P_4				194			4		17						
P_5					178	7					15				
P_6						182				8	13				
P_7							174		5						
P_8			3					187					25		
P_9	14			16					172	11					5
P_{10}	22	15					8			194					3
P_{11}					14	19					177				
P_{12}			17		14							181			
P_{13}							22						178		
P_{14}			7											187	7
P_{15}			3					2						11	171

P_1 : *Room* 517, P_2 : *Room* 519, P_3 : *Lecture room*, P_4 : *Room* 523, P_5 : *Corridor*, P_6 : *Toilet*, P_7 : *Room* 518, P_8 : *Seminar room*, P_9 : *Room* 508, P_{10} : *Room* 510, P_{11} : *Stairs*, P_{12} : *PC room*, P_{13} : *Office* 411, P_{14} : *Class room* 415, P_{15} : *Class room* 418.

20 seconds), respectively. According to the input size, performance is different. The input size 50 frames show the best result and a large number of input sets generate poor performance. Figure 5 shows the recognition rates for different input sizes.

For the test, while navigating the places with wearable system, we obtained 20 image sequences and counted the recognized place. The success rate of place recognition was 87% on average. In the table 2, the success count of the each place recognition was as shown.

4 Conclusions

Place recognition is one of critical issues to be solved in the research field of wearable computing and robot navigation and manipulation. Accordingly, in this paper, a place recognition system is proposed to identify familiar places. While navigating in an environment, a user (or a robot) can receive augmented information about where it is from a wearable computer. Without any auxiliary devices, the proposed system utilizes only computer vision technique, and the use of textural information over long period of time which make the proposed system more reliable. Our system for recognition from a set of observations is based on classifying a model built from the set, rather than classifying the individual observations. We used global texture feature for image representation and their density for place recognition. We used a method based on a Gaussian model of texture vector distribution and a matching criterion using the Kullback-Leibler divergence measure. The proposed place recognition system recognizes the place in the image sequence obtained from the webcam and display the recognized place on the HMD. In the proposed system, we considered the 15 places inside the building. In the experiment, the system successfully recognized the place, the success rate of place recognition was 87% on average. Although the system working on the mobile PC, it could be processing the 7 frames per second in real time. Further, we will test the proposed system on a PDA phone and we will test with much more places.

Acknowledgements

This work was supported by Korea Research Foundation Grant (KRF-2004-041-D00639)

References

1. Ulrich, I., Nourbakhsh, I.: Appearance-based place recognition for topological localization. *In Proceeding of ICRA '00 : IEEE International Conference on Robotics and Automation*, vol. 2 (2000) 1023–1029
2. Kourogi, M., Kurata, T., Sakaue, K.: A panorama-based method of personal positioning and orientation and its real-time applications for wearable computers. *In Proceeding of ISWC '01 : Fifth International Symposium on Wearable Computers*, (2001) 107–114
3. Aoki, H., Schiele, B., Pentland A.: Realtime Personal Positioning System for a Wearable Comptuers. *In Proceeding of ISWC '99 : International Symposium on Wearable Computer*, (1999) 37–43
4. Torralba, A., Murphy, K.P., Freeman, W.T., Rubin, M.A.: Context-based vision system for place and object recognition. *In Proceeding of ICCV '03 : IEEE International Conference on Computer Vision*, (2003) 273–280
5. Somoncelli, E. P., Freeman, W. T.: The steerable pyramid: a flexible architecture for multi-scale derivative computation. *International Conference on Image Processing*, vol. 3 (1995) 444–447
6. Turk, M., Pentland, A. : Eigenfaces for recognition. *Journal of Cognitive Neuroscience*, vol. 3 (1991) 71–86
7. Duda, R.O., Hart, P.E., Stork, D.G.: Pattern Classification. Wiley Interscience, 2000
8. Vasconcelos, N., Ho, P., Moreno, P. : The Kullback-Leibler Kernel as a Framework for Discriminant and Localized Representations for Visual Recognition. *In Proceeding of ECCV '04: 8th European Conference on Computer Vision*, vol. 3 (2004) 430–441
9. Shakhnarovich, G., Fisher, J.W., Darrell, T. : Face recognition from long-term observations. *In Proceeding of ECCV '02: 7th European Conference on Computer Vision*, vol. 3 (2002) 851–865
10. Yoshizawa, S., Tanabe, K.: Dual differential geometry associated with the Kullback-Leiber information on the Gaussian distributions and its 2-parameter deformations. *SUT Journal of Mathematics*, (1999) 113–137

Real-Time People Localization and Tracking Through Fixed Stereo Vision

S. Bahadori[1], L. Iocchi[1,2], G.R. Leone[1], D. Nardi[1], and L. Scozzafava[1]

[1] Dipartimento di Informatica e Sistemistica,
University of Rome "La Sapienza", Rome, Italy
lastname@dis.uniroma1.it
[2] Artificial Intelligence Center,
SRI International, Menlo Park, CA, USA

Abstract. Detecting, locating, and tracking people in a dynamic environment is important in many applications, ranging from security and environmental surveillance to assistance to people in domestic environments, to the analysis of human activities. To this end, several methods for tracking people have been developed using monocular cameras, stereo sensors, and radio frequency tags.

In this paper we describe a real-time People Localization and Tracking (PLT) System, based on a calibrated fixed stereo vision sensor. The system analyzes three interconnected representations of the stereo data (the left intensity image, the disparity image, and the 3-D world locations of measured points) to dynamically update a model of the background; extract foreground objects, such as people and rearranged furniture; track their positions in the world.

The system can detect and track people moving in an area approximately 3 x 8 meters in front of the sensor with high reliability and good precision.

1 Introduction

Localization and tracking of people in a dynamic environment is a key building block for many applications, including surveillance, monitoring, and elderly assistance. The fundamental capability for a people tracking system is to determine the trajectory of each person within the environment.

In recent years this problem has been primarily studied by using two different kinds of sensors: i) markers placed on the person to transmit their real world position to a receiver in the environment; ii) video cameras. The first approach provides high reliability, but is limited by the fact that it requires markers to be placed on the people being tracked, which is not feasible in many applications.

There are several difficulties to be faced in developing a vision-based people tracking system: first of all, people tracking is difficult even in moderately crowded environments, because of occlusions and people walking close each other or to the sensor; second, people recognition is difficult and cannot easily be integrated in the tracking system; third, people may leave the field of view of

M. Ali and F. Esposito (Eds.): IEA/AIE 2005, LNAI 3533, pp. 44–54, 2005.

the sensor and re-enter it after some time (or they may enter the field of view of another sensor) and applications may require the ability of recognizing (or re-acquiring) a person previously tracked (or tracked by another sensor in the network of sensors).

Several approaches have been developed for tracking people in different applications. At the top level, these approaches can be grouped into classes on the basis of the sensors used: a *single* camera (e.g. [17, 18]); *stereo* cameras (e.g. [4, 6, 2, 3]); or *multiple* calibrated cameras (e.g. [5, 13]).

Although it is possible to determine the 3-D world positions of tracked objects with a single camera (e.g. [18]), a stereo sensor provides two critical advantages: 1) it makes it easier to segment an image into objects (e.g., distinguishing people from their shadows); 2) it produces more accurate location information for the tracked people.

On the other hand, approaches using several cameras viewing a scene from significantly different viewpoints are able to deal better with occlusions than a single stereo sensor can, because they view the scene from many directions. However, such systems are difficult to set up (for example, establishing their geometric relationships or solving synchronization problems), and the scalability to large environments is limited, since they may require a large number of cameras.

This paper describes the implementation of a People Localization and Tracking (PLT) System, using a calibrated fixed stereo vision sensor.

The novel features of our system can be summarized as follows: 1) the background model is a composition of intensity, disparity and edge information; and is adaptively updated with a *learning factor* that varies over time and is different for each pixel; 2) plan-view projection computes *height maps*, which are used to detect people in the environment and refine foreground segmentation in case of partial occlusions; 3) *plan-view positions* and *temporal color-based appearance models* are integrated in the tracker and an optimization problem is solved in order to determine the best matching between the observations and the current status of the tracker.

2 System Architecture

The architecture of the PLT System, shown in Figure 1, is based on the following components:

- *Stereo Computation*, which computes disparities from the stereo images acquired by the camera.
- *Background Modelling*, which maintains an updated model of the background, composed of intensities, disparities, and edges (see Section 3).
- *Foreground Segmentation*, which extracts foreground pixels and *image blobs* from the current image, by a type of background subtraction that combines intensity and disparity information (see Section 3).
- *Plan View Projection*, which projects foreground points into a real world (3-D) coordinate system and computes *world blobs* identifying moving objects in the environment (see Section 4).

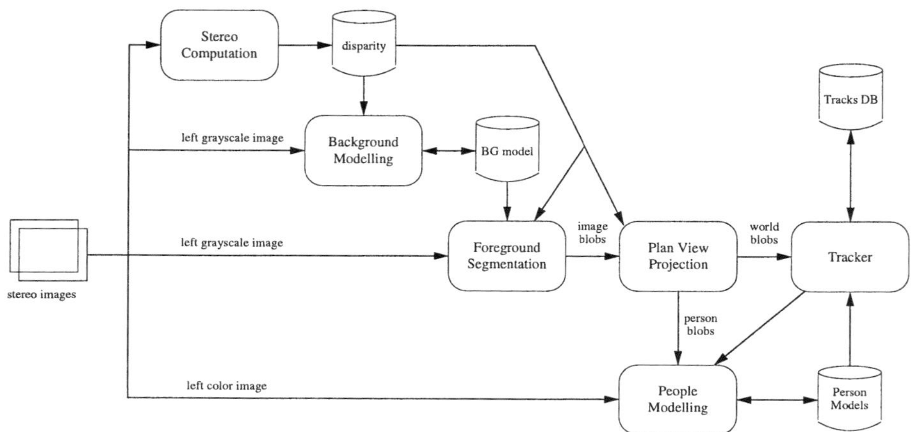

Fig. 1. PLT System Architecture

- *People Modelling*, which creates and maintain appearance models of the people being tracked (see Section 5).
- *Tracker*, which maintains a set of *tracked objects*, associating them with *world blobs* by using an integrated representation of people location and appearance and a Kalman Filter for updating the status of the tracker (see Section 6).

The stereo vision system is composed of a pair of synchronized fire-wire cameras and the Small Vision System (SVS) software [10], which provides a real-time implementation of a correlation-based stereo algorithm. We assume that the stereo camera has been "calibrated" in three ways: correcting lens distortion (done by the SVS software), computing the left-right stereo geometry (also done by the SVS software) and estimating the sensor's position and orientation in the 3-D world (done by standard external calibration methods). Given this calibration information, the system can compute several important things, such as the location of the ground plane and the 3-D locations of all stereo measurements.

For best results in the localization and tracking process, we have chosen to place the camera high on the ceiling pointing down with an angle of approximately 30 degrees with respect to the horizon. This choice provides for a nice combination of tracking and person modelling.

In the following sections we describe in further details the components of our system, except for the *Stereo Computation* module, whose description can be found in [10].

3 Background Modelling and Foreground Segmentation

When using a static camera for object detection and tracking, maintaining a model of the background and consequent background subtraction is a common technique for image segmentation and for identifying foreground objects. In order to account for variations in illuminations, shadows, reflections, and background changes, it is useful to integrate information about intensity and range and to dynamically update the background model. Moreover, such an update must be different in the parts of the image where there are moving objects [17, 16, 8].

In our work, we maintain a background model including information of intensity, disparity, and edges, as a Gaussian probability distribution. Although more sophisticated representations can be used (e.g. mixture of Gaussians [16, 8]), we decided to use a simple model for efficiency reasons. We also decided not to use color information in the model, since intensity and range usually provide a good segmentation, while reducing computational time.

The model of the background is represented at every time t and for every pixel i by a vector $X_{t,i}$, including information about intensity, disparity, and edges computed with a Sobel operator. In order to take into account the uncertainty in these measures, we use a Gaussian distribution over $X_{t,i}$, denoted by mean $\mu_{X_{t,i}}$ and variance $\sigma^2_{X_{t,i}}$. Moreover, we assume the values for intensity, disparity, and edges to be independent each other.

This model is dynamically updated at every cycle (i.e., for each new stereo image every 100 ms) and is controlled by a *learning factor* $\alpha_{t,i}$ that changes over time t and is different for every pixel i.

$$\mu_{X_{t,i}} = (1 - \alpha_{t,i})\, \mu_{X_{t-1,i}} + \alpha_{t,i}\, X_{t,i}$$

$$\sigma^2_{X_{t,i}} = (1 - \alpha_{t,i})\, \sigma^2_{X_{t-1,i}} + \alpha_{t,i}\, (X_{t,i} - \mu_{X_{t-1,i}})^2$$

The learning factor $\alpha_{t,i}$ is set to a higher value (e.g. 0.25) for all pixels in the first few frames (e.g. 5 seconds) after the application is started, in order to quickly acquire a model of the background. In this phase we assume the scene contains only background objects. Notice that the training phase can be completely removed and the system is able to build a background model even in presence of foreground moving objects since the beginning of the application run. Of course it will require a longer time to stabilize the model.

After this training phase $\alpha_{t,i}$ is set to a lower nominal value (e.g. 0.10) and modified depending on the status of pixel i. In regions of the image where there are no moving objects, the learning factor $\alpha_{t,i}$ is increased (e.g. 0.15) speeding up model updating. While in the regions of the image where there are moving objects this factor is decreased (or set to zero) In this way we are able to quickly update the background model in those parts of the image that contain stationary objects and avoid including people (and, in general, moving objects) in the background. The numerical values used for $\alpha_{t,i}$ depend on the characteristics of the application and can be used to tune the reactivity of the system in background model update.

In order to determine regions of the images in which background should not be updated, the work in [8] proposes to compute *activities* of pixels based on intensity difference with respect to the previous frame. In our work, instead, we have computed *activities* of pixels as their difference between the edges in the current image and the background edge model. The motivation behind this choice is that people produce variations in their edges over time even if they are standing still (due to breathing, small variations of pose, etc.), while static objects, such as chairs and tables, do not. However, note that edge variations correctly determine only the contour of a person or moving foreground object, and not all the pixels inside this contour; therefore, if we consider as *active* only those pixels that have high edge variation, we may not be able to correctly identify the internal pixels of a person. For example, if a person with uniform color clothes is standing still in a scene, there is high probability that the internal pixels of his/her body have constant intensity over time, and a method for background update based only on intensity differences (e.g., [8]) will eventually integrate these internal pixels into the background.

To overcome this problem we have implemented a procedure that computes *activities* of pixels included in a contour with high edge variation. This computation is based on first determining *horizontal and vertical activities* $H_t(v)$ and $V_t(u)$, as the sum over the pixels (u, v) in the image, of the variation between current edge E and edge component of the background model μ_E, for each row/column of the image.

$$H_t(v) = \sum_u |E_{t,(u,v)} - \mu_{E,t,(u,v)}| \qquad V_t(u) = \sum_v |E_{t,(u,v)} - \mu_{E,t,(u,v)}|$$

Then, these values are combined in order to assign higher activity values to those pixels that belong to both a column and a row with high horizontal and vertical activity:

$$A_t(u, v) = (1 - \lambda)\, A_{t-1}(u, v) + \lambda\, H_t(v)V_t(u)$$

In this way, the pixels inside a contour determined by edge variations will be assigned a high activity level. Note also that, since the term $H_t(v)V_t(u)$ takes into account internal pixels for people with uniformly colored clothes, the learning factor λ can be set to a high value to quickly respond to changes. In our implementation the learning factor λ used for updating activities is set to 0.20.

The value $A_t(u, v)$ is then used for determining the learning factor of the background model: the higher the activity $A_t(u, v)$ at each pixel $i = (u, v)$ the lower the learning factor $\alpha_{t,i}$. More specifically, we set $\alpha_{t,(u,v)} = \alpha_{\texttt{NOM}}\,(1 - \eta A_t(u, v))$, where η is a normalizing factor.

Foreground segmentation is then performed by background subtraction from the current intensity and disparity images. By taking into account both intensity and disparity information, we are able to correctly deal with shadows, detected as intensity changes, but not disparity changes, and foreground objects that have the same color as the background, but different disparities. Therefore, by combining intensity and disparity information in this way, we are able to avoid false positives due to shadows, and false negatives due to similar colors, which typically affect systems based only on intensity background modeling.

The final steps of the foreground segmentation module are to compute connected components (i.e. *image blobs*) and characterize the foreground objects in the image space. These objects are then passed to the Plan View Segmentation module.

4 Plan View Segmentation

In many applications it is important to know the 3-D world locations of the tracked objects. We do this by employing a *plan view* [3]. This representation also makes it easier to detect partial occlusions between people.

Our approach projects all foreground points into the plan view reference system, by using the stereo calibration information to map disparities into the sensor's 3-D coordinate system and then the external calibration information to map these points from the sensor's 3-D coordinate system to the world's 3-D coordinate system.

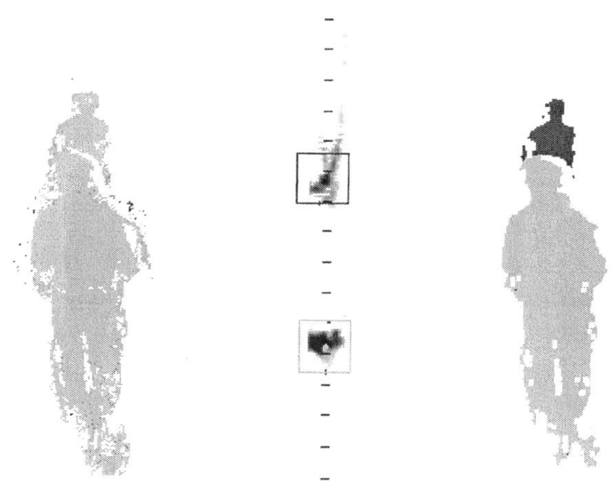

Fig. 2. a) Foreground segmentation (1 *image blob*); b) Plan View Projection (2 *world blobs*); c) Plan View Segmentation *2 person blobs*

For plan view segmentation, we compute a *height map*, that is a discrete map relative to the ground plane in the scene, where each cell of the height map is filled with the maximum height of all the 3-D points whose projection lies in that cell, in such a way that higher objects (e.g., people) will have a high score.

The *height map* is smoothed with a Gaussian filter to remove noise, and then it is searched to detect connected components that we call *world blobs* (see Fig. 2b where darker points correspond to higher values). Since we are interested in person detection, *world blobs* are filtered on the basis of their size in the plan view and their height, thus removing blobs with sizes and heights inconsistent with people. The Plan View Segmentation returns a set of *world blobs* that could be people moving in the scene.

It is important to notice that Plan View Segmentation is able to correctly deal with partial occlusions that are not detected by foreground analysis. For example, in Figure 2 a situation is shown in which a single *image blob* (Fig. 2a) covers two people, one of which is partially occluded, while the Plan View Segmentation process detects two *world blobs* (Fig. 2b). By considering the association between pixels in the image blobs and world blobs, we are able to determine image masks corresponding to each person, which we call *person blobs*. This process allows for refining foreground segmentation in situations of partial occlusions and for correctly building person appearance models.

5 People Modelling

In order to track people over time in the presence of occlusions, or when they leave and re-enter the scene, it is necessary to have a model of the tracked people. Several models for people tracking have been developed (see for example [7, 15, 12, 9]), but color histograms and color templates (as presented in [15]) are not sufficient for capturing complete appearance models, because they do not take into account the actual position of the colors on the person.

Following [7, 12], we have defined *temporal color-based appearance models* of a fixed resolution, represented as a set of unimodal probability distributions in the RGB space (i.e. 3-D Gaussians), for each pixel of the model. Computation of such models is performed by first scaling the portion of the image characterized by a *person blob* to a fixed resolution and then updating the probability distribution for each pixel in the model. Appearance models computed at this stage are used during tracking for improving reliability of data association process.

6 Tracking

Tracking is performed by maintaining a set of *tracked people*, updated with the measurements of *person and world blobs* (extracted by the previous phases). We use a probabilistic framework in which tracked people $P_t = \{N(\mu_{i,t}, \sigma_{i,t}) \,|\, i = 1..n\}$ and measurements $Z_t = \{N(\mu'_{j,t}, \sigma'_{j,t}) \,|\, j = 1..m\}$ are represented as multi-dimensional Gaussians including information about both the person position in the environment and the color-based person model. The update step is performed by using a Kalman Filter for each person. The system model used for predicting the people position is the constant velocity model, while their appearance is updated with a constant model. This model is adequate for many normal situations in which people walk in an environment. It provides a clean way to smooth the trajectories and to hold onto a person that is partially occluded for a few frames.

With this representation data association is an important issue to deal with. In general, at every step, the tracker must make an association between m observations and n tracked people. Association is solved by computing the Mahalanobis distance $d_{i,j}$ between the predicted estimate (through the Kalman Filter) of the ith person $N(\mu_{i,t|t-1}, \sigma_{i,t|t-1})$ and the jth observation $N(\mu'_{j,t}, \sigma'_{j,t})$.

An association between the predicted state of the system $P_{t|t-1}$ and the current observations Z_t is denoted with a function f, that associates each tracked person i to an observation j, with $i = 1..n$, $j = 1..m$, and $f(i) \neq f(j)$, $\forall i \neq j$. The special value $\perp$ is used for denoting that the person is not associated to any observation (i.e. $f(i) = \perp$). Let $\mathcal{F}$ be the set of all possible associations of the current tracked people with current observations. The best data association is computed by minimizing $\sum_i d_{i,f(i)}$. A fixed maximum value is used for $d_{i,f(i)}$ when $f(i) = \perp$.

Although this is a combinatorial problem, the size of the sets P_t and Z_t on which this is applied are very limited (not greater than 4), so $|\mathcal{F}|$ is small and this problem can be effectively solved.

The association f^*, that is the solution of this problem, is chosen and used for computing the new status of the system P_t. During the update step a weight $w_{i,t}$ is computed for each Gaussian in P_t (depending on $w_{i,t-1}$ and $d_{i,f(i)}$), and if such a weight goes below a given threshold, the person is considered *lost*. Moreover, for observations in Z_t that are not associated to any person by f^* a *new* Gaussian in entered in P_t.

The main difference with previous approaches [2, 11, 13] is that we integrate both plan-view and appearance information in the status of the system, and by solving the above optimization problem we find the best matching between observations and tracker status by considering in an integrated way the information about the position of the people in the environment and their appearance.

7 Applications and Experiments

The system presented in this paper is in use within the RoboCare project [1, 14], whose goal is to build a multi-agent system that generates services for human assistance and develops support technology which can play a role in allowing elderly people to lead an independent lifestyle in their own homes. The RoboCare Domestic Environment (RDE), located at the Institute for Cognitive Science and Technology (CNR, Rome, Italy), is intended to be a testbed environment in which to test the ability of the developed technology.

In this application scenario the ability of tracking people in a domestic environment or within a health-care institution is a fundamental building block for a number of services requiring information about pose and trajectories of people (elders, human assistants) or robots acting in the environment.

In order to evaluate the system in this context we have performed a first set of experiments aiming at evaluating efficiency and precision of the system. The computational time of the entire process described in this paper is below 100 ms on a 2.4GHz CPU for high resolution images (640x480)[1], thus making it possible to process a video stream at a frame rate of 10 Hz. The frame rate of 10 Hz is sufficient to effectively track walking people in a domestic environment, where velocities are typically limited.

For measuring the *precision* of the system we have marked 9 positions in the environment at different distances and angles from the camera and measured the distance returned by the system of a person standing on these positions. Although this error analysis is affected by imprecise positioning of the person on

[1] Although some processing is performed at low resolution 320x240.

the markers, the results of our experiments, averaging 40 measurements for each position, show a precision in localization (i.e. average error) of about 10 cm, with a standard deviation of about 2 cm, which is sufficient for many applications.

Furthermore, we have performed specific experiments to evaluate the integration of plan-view and appearance matching during tracking. We have compared two cases: the first in which only the position of the people is considered during tracking, the second in which appearance models of people are combined with their location (as described in Section 6). We have counted the number of *association errors* (i.e. all the situations in which either a track was associated to more than a person or a person is associated to more than a track) in these two cases. The results of our experiments have shown that the integrated approach reduces the *association errors* by about 50% (namely, from 39 in the tracker with plan-view position only to 17 in the one with integrated information, over a set of video clips with a total of 200,000 frames, of which about 3,500 contain two people close each other).

8 Conclusions and Future Work

In this paper we have presented a People Localization and Tracking System that integrates several capabilities into an effective and efficient implementation: dynamic background modelling, intensity and range based foreground segmentation, plan-view projection and segmentation for tracking and determining object masks, integration of plan-view and appearance information in data association and Kalman Filter tracking. The novel aspects introduced in this paper are: 1) a background modelling technique that is adaptively updated with a learning factor that varies over time and is different for each pixel; 2) a plan-view segmentation that is used to refine foreground segmentation in case of partial occlusions; 3) an integrated tracking method that considers both plan-view positions and color-based appearance models and solves an optimization problem to find the best matching between observations and the current state of the tracker.

Experimental results on efficiency and precision show good performance of the system. However, we intend to address other aspects of the system: first, using a multi-modal representation for tracking in order to better deal with uncertainty and association errors; second, evaluating the reliability of the system in medium-term re-acquisition of people leaving and re-entering a scene.

Finally, in order to expand the size of the monitored area, we are planning to use multiple tracking systems. This is a challenging problem because it emphasizes the need to re-acquire people moving from one sensor's field of view to another. One way of simplifying this task is to arrange an overlapping field of view for close cameras; however, this arrangement increases the number of sensors needed to cover an environment and limits the scalability of the system. In the near future we intend to extend the system to track people with multiple sensors that do not overlap.

Acknowledgments

This research is partially supported by MIUR (Italian Ministry of Education, University and Research) under project RoboCare (A Multi-Agent System with Intelligent Fixed and Mobile Robotic Components). Luca Iocchi also acknowledges SRI International where part of this work was carried out and, in particular, Dr. Robert C. Bolles for his interesting discussions and useful suggestions.

References

1. S. Bahadori, A. Cesta, L. Iocchi, G. R. Leone, D. Nardi, F. Pecora, R. Rasconi, and L. Scozzafava. Towards ambient intelligence for the domestic care of the elderly. In P. Remagnino, G. L. Foresti, and T. Ellis, editors, *Ambient Intelligance: A Novel Paradigm*. Springer, 2004.
2. D. Beymer and K. Konolige. Real-time tracking of multiple people using stereo. In *Proc. of IEEE Frame Rate Workshop*, 1999.
3. T. Darrell, D. Demirdjian, N. Checka, and P. F. Felzenszwalb. Plan-view trajectory estimation with dense stereo background models. In *Proc. of 8th Int. Conf. On Computer Vision (ICCV'01)*, pages 628–635, 2001.
4. T. Darrell, G. Gordon, M. Harville, and J. Woodfill. Integrated person tracking using stereo, color, and pattern detection. *International Journal of Computer Vision*, 37(2):175–185, 2000.
5. D. Focken and R. Stiefelhagen. Towards vision-based 3-d people tracking in a smart room. In *Proc. 4th IEEE Int. Conf. on Multimodal Interfaces (ICMI'02)*, 2002.
6. I. Haritaoglu, D. Harwood, and L. S. Davis. W4S: A real-time system detecting and tracking people in 2 1/2D. In *Proceedings of the 5th European Conference on Computer Vision*, pages 877–892. Springer-Verlag, 1998.
7. I. Haritaoglu, D. Harwood, and L. S. Davis. An appearance-based body model for multiple people tracking. In *Proc. of 15th Int. Conf. on Pattern Recognition (ICPR'00)*, 2000.
8. M. Harville, G. Gordon, and J. Woodfill. Foreground segmentation using adaptive mixture models in color and depth. In *Proc. of IEEE Workshop on Detection and Recognition of Events in Video*, pages 3–11, 2001.
9. J. Kang, I. Cohen, and G. Medioni. Object reacquisition using invariant appearance model. In *Proc. of 17th Int. Conf. on Pattern Recognition (ICPR'04)*, 2004.
10. K. Konolige. Small vision systems: Hardware and implementation. In *Proc. of 8th International Symposium on Robotics Research*, 1997.
11. J. Krumm, S. Harris, B. Meyers, B. Brumitt, M. Hale, and S. Shafer. Multi-camera multi-person tracking for easyliving. In *Proc. of Int. Workshop on Visual Surveillance*, 2000.
12. J. Li, C. S. Chua, and Y. K. Ho. Color based multiple people tracking. In *Proc. of 7th Int. Conf. on Control, Automation, Robotics and Vision*, 2002.
13. A. Mittal and L. S. Davis. M2Tracker: A multi-view approach to segmenting and tracking people in a cluttered scene using region-based stereo. In *Proc. of the 7th European Conf. on Computer Vision (ECCV'02)*, pages 18–36. Springer-Verlag, 2002.

14. Robocare project. `http://robocare.istc.cnr.it`.
15. K. Roh, S. Kang, and S. W. Lee. Multiple people tracking using an appearance model based on temporal color. In *Proc. of 15th Int. Conf. on Pattern Recognition (ICPR'00)*, 2000.
16. C. Stauffer and W. E. L. Grimson. Adaptive background mixture models for real-time tracking. In *IEEE Conf. on Computer Vision and Pattern Recognition (CVPR'99)*, pages 246–252, 1999.
17. Christopher Richard Wren, Ali Azarbayejani, Trevor Darrell, and Alex Pentland. Pfinder: Real-time tracking of the human body. *IEEE Trans. on Pattern Analysis and Machine Intelligence*, 19(7):780–785, 1997.
18. T. Zhao and R. Nevatia. Tracking multiple humans in crowded environment. In *IEEE Conf. on Computer Vision and Pattern Recognition (CVPR'04)*, 2004.

Face Recognition by Kernel Independent Component Analysis

T. Martiriggiano, M. Leo, T. D'Orazio, and A. Distante

CNR- ISSIA via Amendoda 122/D-I,
70126 BARI, Italy
{leo, dorazio, martiggiano, distante}@issia.ba.cnr.it

Abtract. In this paper, we introduce a new feature representation method for face recognition. The proposed method, referred as Kernel ICA, combines the strengths of the Kernel and Independent Component Analysis approaches. For performing Kernel ICA, we employ an algorithm developed by F. R. Bach and M. I. Jordan. This algorithm has proven successful for separating randomly mixed auditory signals, but it has never been applied on bidimensional signals such as images. We compare the performance of Kernel ICA with classical algorithms such as PCA and ICA within the context of appearance-based face recognition problem using the FERET database. Experimental results show that both Kernel ICA and ICA representations are superior to representations based on PCA for recognizing faces across days and changes in expressions.

1 Introduction

Face recognition has become one of most important biometrics technologies during the past 20 years. It has a wide range of applications such as identity authentication, access control, and surveillance.

Human face image appearance has potentially very large intra-subject variations due to 3D head pose, illumination, facial expression, occlusion due to other objects or accessories (e.g., sunglasses, scarf, ect.), facial hair, and aging. On the other hand, the inter-subject variations are small due to the similarity of individual appearances. This makes face recognition a great challenge. Two issues are central: 1) what features to use to represent a face and 2) how to classify a new face image based on the chosen representation. This work focuses on the issue of feature selection. The main objective is to find techniques that can introduce low-dimensional feature representation of face objects with enhanced discriminatory power. Among various solutions to the problem (see [1] for a survey), the most successful are the appearance-based approaches, which generally operate directly on images or appearances of face objects.

Principal Component Analysis (PCA), Linear Discriminant Analysis (LDA) and Independent Component Analysis (ICA) are three powerful tools largely used for data reduction and feature extraction in the appearance-based approaches [2] [3] [4].

Although successful in many cases, linear methods fail to deliver good performance when face patterns are subject to large variations due to 3D head pose, illumination, facial expression, and aging. The limited success of these methods should be

M. Ali and F. Esposito (Eds.): IEA/AIE 2005, LNAI 3533, pp. 55 – 58, 2005.

attributed to their linear nature. As a result, it is reasonable to assume that a better solution to this inherent nonlinear problem could be achieved using non linear methods, such as the so-called kernel machine techniques [5].

Yang [6], Kim *et al.* [7] investigated the use of Kernel PCA and Kernel LDA for learning low dimensional representations for face recognition. Experimental results showed that kernel methods provided better representations and achieved lower error rates for face recognition.

2 Overview of Present Work

In this paper, motivated by the success that ICA, Kernel PCA and Kernel DLA have in face recognition, we investigate the use of Kernel Independent Component Analysis (Kernel ICA) for face recognition. Kernel ICA combines the strengths of the Kernel and ICA approaches. Here, we employ an algorithm developed by F. R. Bach and M. I. Jordan [8]. This algorithm has proven successful for separating randomly mixed auditory signals. We use Kernel ICA to find a representation in which the coefficients used to code images are statistically independent, i.e., a factorial face code. Barlow and Atick discussed advantages of factorial codes for encoding complex objects that are characterized by high-order combinations of features [9], [10].

3 Experimental Results

The face images employed for this research are a subset of the FERET face database. The FERET dataset contain images of 38 individuals. There are four frontal views of each individual: a neutral expression and a change of expression from one session, and a neutral expression and change of expression from a second session that occurred three weeks after the first. Examples of the four views are shown in fig. 1.

Fig. 1. Example from the FERET database of the four frontal image viewing conditions: neutral expression and change of expression from session 1; neutral expression and change of expression from session 2. Reprinted with permission from Jonathan Phillips

The algorithms are trained on a single frontal view of each individual. The training set is comprised of 50% neutral expression images and 50% change of expression images. The algorithms are tested for recognition under three different conditions: same session, different expression (Test Set 1); different day, same expression (Test Set 2); and different day, different expression (Test Set 3).

Face recognition performance is evaluated by the nearest neighbor algorithm. Coefficient vectors b in each test set were assigned the class label of the coefficient vector in the training set that was most similar as evaluated by the Euclidean distance measure δ_{euc} and the cosine similarity measure $\delta_{\cos}$, which are defined as follows:

$$\delta_{euc}(b_{test}, b_{train}) = \sqrt{\sum_i (b_{test_i} - b_{train_i})^2}, \quad \delta_{\cos}(b_{test}, b_{train}) = \frac{-b_{test}^T \cdot b_{train}}{\|b_{test}\| \|b_{train}\|}$$

where $\|.\|$ denotes the norm operator.

Figures 2 and 3 report the face recognition performances with the Kernel ICA, ICA factorial code representations (for performing ICA, we employ the FastICA algorithm developed by A. Hyvärinen [12]) and PCA representations (the eigenface representation used by Pentland *et al.* [2]). In figure 2 and 3 the performances have been evaluated with the δ_{Euc} and the $\delta_{\cos}$ similarity measures, respectively.

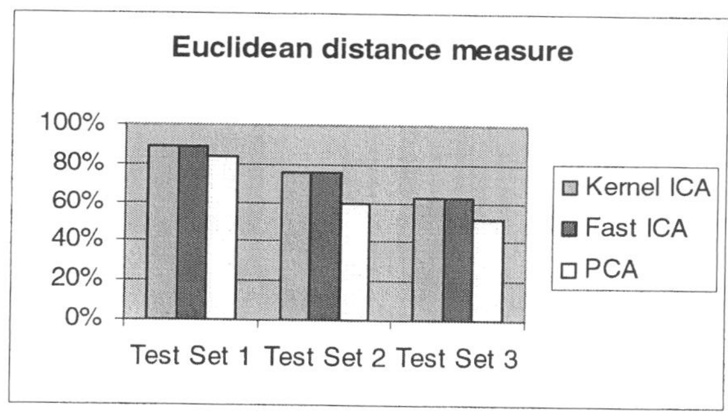

Fig. 2. Recognition performance of the Kernel ICA, ICA factorial code representations and PCA representations corresponding to the δ_{Euc} similarity measure

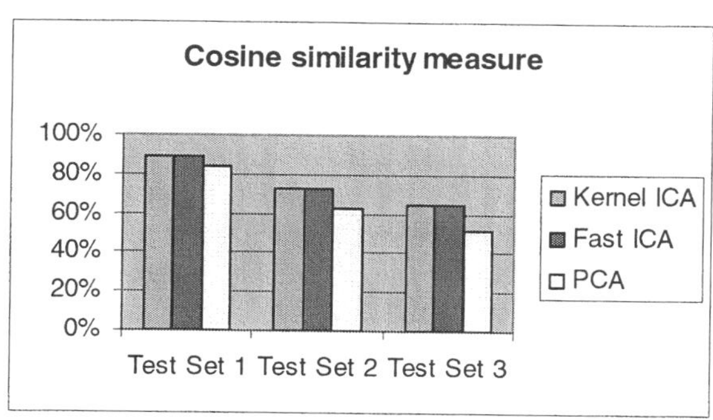

Fig. 3. Recognition performance of the Kernel ICA, ICA factorial code representations and PCA representations corresponding to the $\delta_{\cos}$ similarity measure

There is a trend for the Kernel ICA and ICA representation to give superior face recognition performance to the PCA representation. The difference in performance is statistically significant for Test Set 2 and Test Set 3, when the test and training images differ not only in expression but also in lighting, scale and the date on which they were taken. Therefore, the high-order relationships among pixels, estimated by Kernel ICA and ICA, improve notably the performance when the face recognition is more difficult.

The lack of a substantial difference between the performances of the Kernel ICA and ICA algorithms, as found in their mono-dimensional applications, is probably due to the PCA preprocessing which is necessary in order to reduce the dimensionality of the data. In our opinion, the new orthogonal representation of the data provided by PCA precludes the kernel methods to improve their ability of represent the knowledge. In other words the evaluation of ICA produces the same results if it is applied directly after PCA or after a further transformation of PCA in a non-linear space (kermel method).

References

1. Zhao, W., Chellappa, R., Rosenfeld, A., Phillips, P.J.: Face Recognition: A literature survey. Technical Report CART-TR-948. University of Maryland, Aug. 2002.
2. Turk, M.A., Pentland A.P.: Eigenfaces for recognition. Journal of Cognitive Neuroscience, vol. 3, no. 1, pp. 71–86, 1991
3. Belhumeur, P.N., Hespanha, J.P., Kriegman, D.J.: Eigenfaces vs. Fisherfaces: recognition using class specific linear projection. IEEE Transactions on Pattern Analysis and Machine Intelligence, vol. 19, no. 7, pp. 711–720, 1997
4. Bartlett, M.S., Movellan, J.R., T.J., Sejnowski.: Face Recognition by Independent Component Analysis. IEEE Transactions on Neural Networks, vol. 13, NO. 6, November 2002.
5. Ruiz, A., López de Teruel P.E., : Nonlinear kernel-based statistical pattern analysis. IEEE Transactions on Neural Networks, vol. 12, no. 1, pp. 16–32, January 2001
6. Kim, K.I., Jung K., Kim H.J.: Face Recognition Using Kernel Principal Component Analysis. IEEE Signal Processing Letters, vol. 9, no. 2, February 2002
7. Yang, M.H.: Kernel eigenfaces vs. Kernel fisherfaces: Face Recognition using kernel methods. In Proc. 5th Int. Conf. Automat. Face Gesture Recognition, Washington, DC, May 2002, pp. 215-220
8. Bach, F.R., Jordan M. I., Kernel Independent Component Analysis, J. Machine Learning Res., vol. 3, pp. 1-48, 2002
9. Barlow, H.B.: Unsupervised learning Neural Comput., vol. 1, pp. 295-311, 1989
10. Atick, J.J.: Could information theory provide an ecological theory of sensory processing? Network, vol. 3, pp. 213-251, 1992
11. Phillips, P.J., Moon H., Rizvi S.A., Rauss P.J.: The FERET evaluation methodology for face-recognition algorithms. IEEE Transactions on Pattern Analysis and Machine Intelligence, vol. 22, no. 10, pp. 1090–1104, 2000
12. Hyvärinen, A.: Fast and Robust Fixed-Point Algorithms for Independent Component Analysis. IEEE Transactions on Neural Networks 10(3):626-634, 1999

Head Detection of the Car Occupant Based on Contour Models and Support Vector Machines

Yong-Guk Kim[1], Jeong-Eom Lee[2], Sang-Jun Kim[2], Soo-Mi Choi[1], and Gwi-Tae Park[2]

[1] School of Computer Engineering, Sejong University, Seoul, Korea
[2] Dept. of Electrical Engineering, Korea University, Seoul, Korea
gtpark@korea.ac.kr

1 Introduction

Head detection is a relatively well studied problem in computer vision. Several methods for head detection are proposed such as motion based method [6], disparity map [7], skin color method [8] and a head-shoulder contour [9]. Those methods are mainly based on stereo vision and color information for detecting the head. Our application domain is the telematics, especially within the car. In such environment, the illumination level is very variable. Moreover, we may need to use infrared illumination to capture the occupant in the night. Therefore, it is difficult to utilize the color information.

In this paper, we propose a new algorithm that can detect occupant's head in a car by using head-shoulder contour model and support vector machines (SVM) classifier. The position of the head provides diverse information about the occupant, such as pose, size, position, and so on. So, that information could be critical for the smart airbag system in deciding whether to deploy it or not, and controlling intensity of deployment. Our system has a simple single camera and consists of two parts: the first is to extract a head-shoulder contour model [4] of occupant from an accumulative difference image, and the second part detects the head by using SVM classifier.

2 Head Detection Algorithm

In our application, since the occupant sometimes could move very little, it is often difficult to extract the motion of the occupant by using the common difference image. To sidestep such problem, a new scheme is adopted, namely the accumulative difference image. Difference images are accumulated until the difference value is greater than the predefined threshold. In this way, the motion information of the occupant can be acquired regardless of an amount of the occupant's motion. An example of it is shown in Fig. 1(b).

As shown in Fig. 1(b), the difference image often contains small holes or gaps. To fill in those small holes and gaps, the binary morphological operations such as dilation and erosion [5] are necessary. A silhouette image is obtained after those operations as illustrated in Fig. 1(c). At this time we have down-sampled the image to reduce the processing time. And for extracting feature points from a silhouette, we first search a center of gravity point of blob in the silhouette image. And then, draw several lines from the center of the blob by intervals of 2.5 degrees, and extract cross

M. Ali and F. Esposito (Eds.): IEA/AIE 2005, LNAI 3533, pp. 59 – 61, 2005.

points of a line and the contour of blob as feature points. Here, the feature points indicate the sampled points at the fixed interval along the contour. This feature points are illustrated in Fig. 1(d).

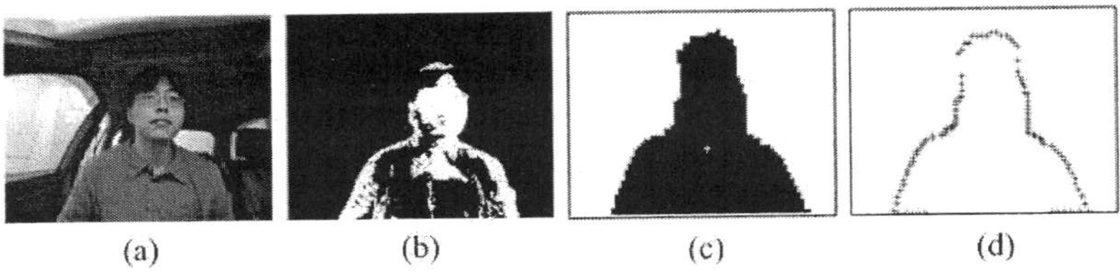

Fig. 1. A procedure from input sequential images to contour(a) a sample image in sequence ; (b) a accumulative difference image;(c) a silhouette image; (d) feature points of contour

The head-shoulder contour models can be derived from the feature points. Since the size of the head is varied according to the distance from the camera, we decide to adopt three different models to cover diverse cases. Notice that each model is made up of different number of feature points, 97, 81 and 65, respectively, from large to small model.

To detect the head using SVM, it has to be trained using the correct head model and the incorrect head mode. Once the machine is trained, the feature points of the contour are feed to it, and the input contour is matched to the head model as shown in Fig. 2. When the input comes in, the system checks whether it matches to the large model. If not match well, then it goes to the regular one. Finally, it matches to the small model. The central point of the contour is regarded as the center of the detected head.

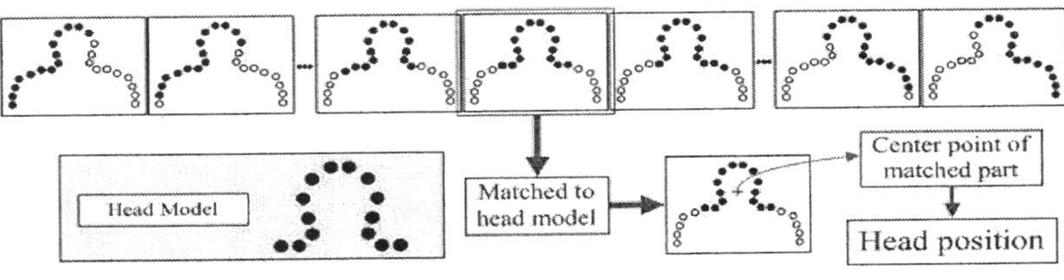

Fig. 2. The head detection procedure using SVM

3 Results and Conclusions

The performance of the head detection algorithm is evaluated with our image database, which consists of sequential image sets captured within a car at 15fps. And the public domain implementation of SVM, called Lib SVM, and two standard kernels (i.e., polynomial kernel and radial basis function (RBF) kernel) [3] were used for this study.

Correct detection rate (CDR) and false detection rate (FDR) are used to evaluate head detection performance. The CDR is the percentage of the heads detected correctly as head when head detection occurs after making contour, and the FDR is the percentage of the frames where non-heads are detected as head when contour is made.

Result suggests that CDR for the simple pattern was 100% and FDR was zero. However, CDR for the complex pattern was remained at 100%, and yet FDR was increased to 5.71% because that pattern contained diverse arm movements. We found no distinctive difference between polynomial and radial basis function kernel. The result images of the experiment are shown in Fig. 3.

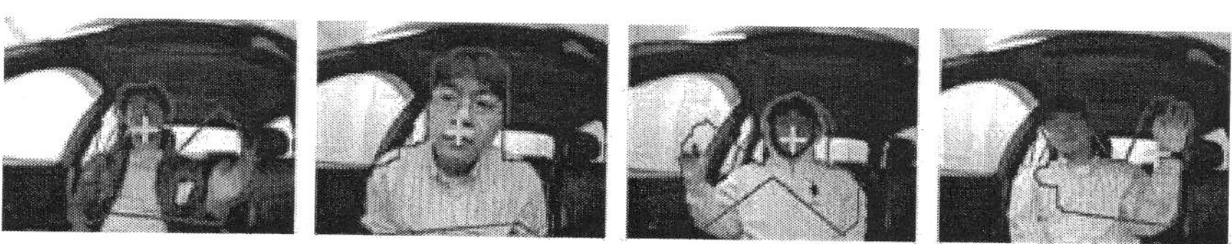

Fig. 3. Three different cases of head detection

We describe a new method to detect the head of the car occupant. Given the variable illumination conditions within the car, the color information for detecting the head (or face) is not sufficient. Our method is based upon using only the grey image, since the infrared illumination could be utilized in the night. Although it is known that SVM could be useful for detection the face, such method can be slower when the size of the training set images is increased to cover diverse pose and size variation of the face. Since the contours in our study are lighter than the conventional face images in terms of SVM processing, it fits to the embedded system installed in the car. On the assumption that the occupant is alone in a car, this method is promising.

Acknowledgments. This work was supported by Hyundai Autonet Co..

References

1. http://www.nhtsa.dot.gov
2. V. Vapnik, "*The Nature of Statistical Learning Theory*", Springer-Verlag, NY, USA, pp.45-98, 1995
3. http://www.csie.ntu.edu.tw/~cjlin/libsvm/index.html
4. A. Blake and M. Isard, "*Active Contours*", Springer-Verlag, London, 1998
5. G. Baxes, "*Digital Image Processing: principles and applications*", John Wiley & Sons, New York, USA, 1994.
6. Y. Owechkp, N. Srinivasa, S. Medasani, and R. Boscolo, "Vision-Based Fusion System for Smart Airbag Applicaions", IEEE, Intelligent Vehicle Symposium, vol. 1, pp. 245-250, 2002
7. B. Alefs, M. Clabian, H. Bischof, W. Kropatsh, and F. Khairallah, "Robust Occupancy Detection from Stereo Images", IEEE Intelligent Transportation Systems Conference, 2004
8. R. Patil, P. E. Rybski, T. Kanade, and M. M. Veloso, "People Detection and Tracking in High Resolution Panoramic Video Mosaic", Proceedings of IEEE/RSJ International Conference on Intelligent Robots and Systems(IROS 2004), vol. 1, pp. 1323-1328, 2004
9. W. Huang, R. Luo, H. Zhang, B. H. Lee, and M. Rajapakse, "Real Time Head Tracking and Face and Eyes Detection", IEEE Region 10 Conference on Computers, Communications, Contorl and Power Engineering, vol. 1, pp. 507-510, 2002

A Morphological Proposal for Vision-Based Path Planning*

F.A. Pujol[1], J.M. García[1], M. Pujol[2], R. Rizo[2], and M.J. Pujol[3]

[1] Depto. Tecnología Informática y Computación,
{fpujol, juanma}@dtic.ua.es,
[2] Depto. Ciencia de la Computación e Inteligencia Artificial,
{mar, rizo}@dccia.ua.es,
[3] Depto. Matemática Aplicada,
Universidad de Alicante, Ap. Correos 99, 03080 Alicante, España
mjose@ua.es

Abstract. Many different path planning methods have been proposed over recent years, although there are only a few that deal with computer vision techniques. In this work we implement a path planning algorithm which takes into account a vision processing system. Thus, we develop a method that uses Mathematical Morphology to provide near-optimal paths throughout an environment. The experiments show that our path planning algorithm is able to locate good solution paths after a training process, which is necessary to fix some parameters. This will make possible its adaptation to a practical robot system.

1 Introduction

In recent years, an increasing amount of robotic research has focused on the problem of planning and executing motion tasks autonomously, i.e., without human guidance [1], [2]. Enabling a robot to navigate autonomously opens the door to develop powerful robotic products. As a consequence, vision-based path planning provides a more practical approach to robot control.

In relation to this, Mathematical Morphology (MM) has proven to be useful for a variety of image processing problems (e.g., shape and size extraction, noise removal) [3], [4]. This paper shows a method to implement path planning tasks for a robot by using MM techniques. To do this, a method to develop collision-free paths using MM operations is described in Section 2. Then, in Section 3 the experimentation verifies the accomplishment of our research objectives. Finally, we conclude with some important remarks in Section 4.

2 A Vision-Based Path Planning Algorithm

In this section we propose a MM-based path planning algorithm. First, a map that separates obstacles from free-space is obtained, as shown below:

* This work has been supported by the Spanish MCYT, project DPI200204434C0401 and by the Generalitat Valenciana, projects GV04B685,GV04B634.

M. Ali and F. Esposito (Eds.): IEA/AIE 2005, LNAI 3533, pp. 62–64, 2005.

1. Apply a Gaussian smoothing to the original image.
2. Create a set of symbols for each pixel (from the gradient and the variance).
3. Merge the results by means of the creation of a new image, where lower intensity pixels represent a higher probability of being classified as an obstacle.
4. Binarize the image.
5. Repeat the following steps:
   - Implement a morphological dilation (3×3 square structuring element).
   - Change black tones to a grey tone, with increasing intensity.
6. Obtain a map where higher intensity pixels constitute obstacle-free zones.

As soon as this map is obtained, the algorithm chooses the pixel with the lowest probability of collision in a 3×3 neighborhood. Hence, the selection of the next pixel in the path will be completed by using a normalized weight w_i which ensures that the new pixel has the lowest probability of collision:

$$w_i = \exp\{a * (dist_{old} - dist_{new})\} . \tag{1}$$

where $dist_{old}$ is the Euclidean distance from the current pixel to the destination one, $dist_{new}$ is the Euclidean distance from the selected new pixel to the destination one and a is a real constant, so that $0 \leq a \leq 1$.

As a consequence, the robot will move to the pixel with the highest weight w_i; this operation will be repeated until it arrives to the destination or there is some failure due to a collision with non-detected obstacles. Therefore, factor a provides the best weights w_i to complete the path planning task.

3 Experimentation

Let us consider now the results of some experiments for our model. First, Fig. 1 (a) shows a world created for the robot to wander throughout it and Fig. 1 (b) shows the resulting map after the initial processing method.

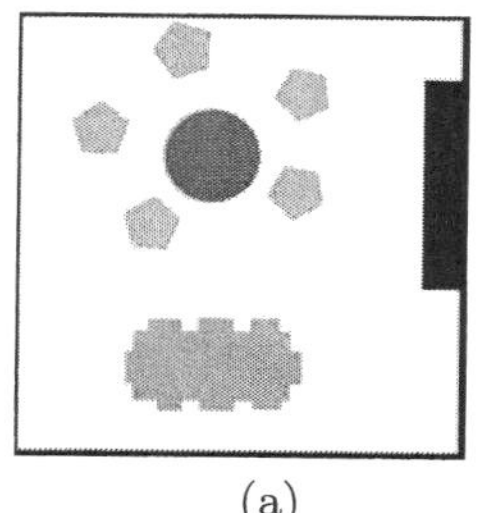

(a)

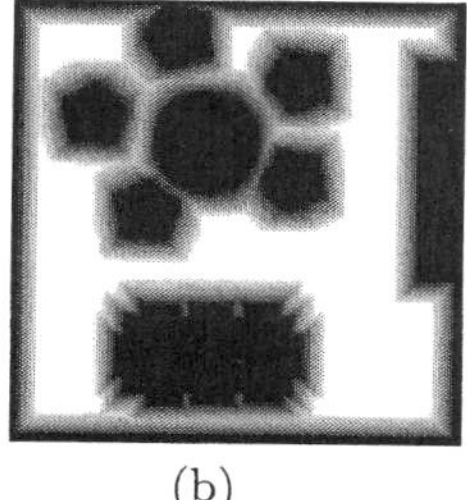

(b)

Fig. 1. The environment for path planning: (a) World 1 (b) A morphological map

From this map, a path is followed after estimating the weights w_i; in addition, factor a should be defined. In Fig. 2 some example paths (where factor a varies

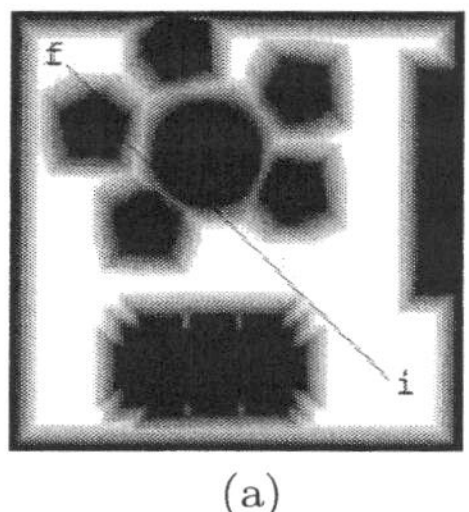

(a)

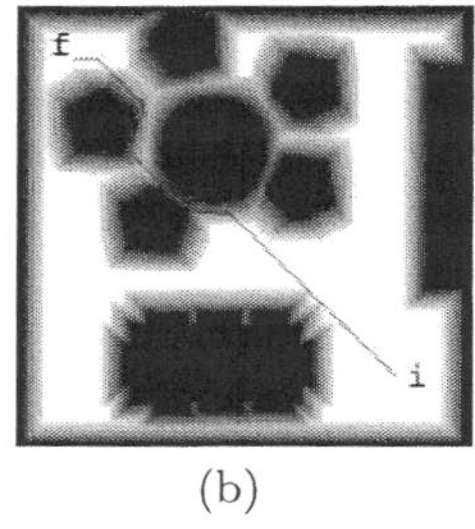

(b)

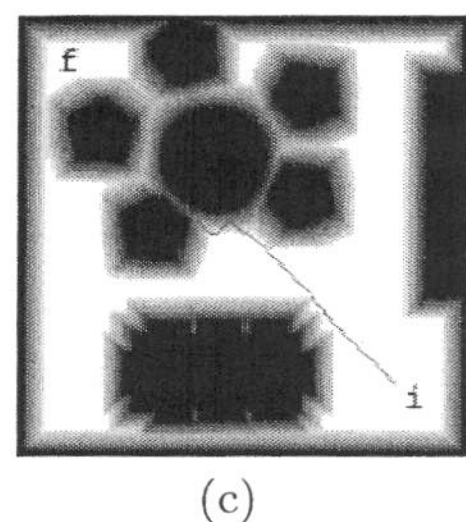

(c)

Fig. 2. Some paths followed in the environment: (a) $a = 1.0$ (b) $a = 0.1$ (c) $a = 0.05$

from 0.05 to 1.0) are shown. Note that 'i' refers to the initial point of the path, and 'f' indicates the final point of the path.

From these examples, if a has a high value (Fig. 2 (a)), the algorithm will select a path that easily reaches the destination point, although it is not collision-free. On the contrary, when a has a low value (Fig. 2 (c)), the robot may stop before completing its task, since it is preferred not to move close to the obstacles. As a consequence, a has a better behavior when the robot follows a semi-optimal path that keeps it away from collision (in this example, $a = 0.1$, see Fig. 2 (b)). Nevertheless, the choice of an appropriate factor will depend mainly on the map of the environment resulting from the initial method.

4 Conclusions

The research work in this paper aims to address the path planning problem and contribute to the development of practical planning systems. Throughout the document, we have developed a vision-based algorithm for the generation of a map in unknown environments using MM operations. The experimentation shows that the main goals of our research task have been accomplished. As a future work, we found it necessary to consider a real robot system that make possible a more accurate designing method so that the robot internal hardware and software could be efficiently implemented.

References

1. Zufferey, J.C.; Floreano, D.; van Leeuwen, M.; Merenda, T.: Evolving Vision-Based Flying Robots. In Proceedings of the Second International Workshop on Biologically Motivated Computer Vision, LNCS 2525, Berlin, Springer-Verlag (2002), 592–600
2. Lin, Z.C., Chow, J.J.: Near Optimal Measuring Sequence Planning and Collision-Free Path Planning with a Dynamic Programming Method. International Journal of Advanced Manufacturing Technology, **18** (2001) 29–43
3. Serra, J.: Use of Mathematical Morphology in Industrial Control. Microscopy Microanalysis Microstructures, **7** (1996) 297–302
4. Goutsias, J., Heijmans, H. J. A. M.: Fundamenta Morphologicae Mathematicae. Fundamenta Informaticae, **41** (2000) 1–31

A New Video Surveillance System Employing Occluded Face Detection

Jaywoo Kim[1], Younghun Sung[1], Sang Min Yoon[2], and Bo Gun Park[3]

[1] Interaction Lab. Samsung Advanced Institute of Technology,
440-600, P. O. Box 111, Suwon, Rep. of Korea
{jaywoo, younghun.sung} @samsung.com
http://www.sait.samsung.co.kr/sait/src/saitEnIndex.html
[2] Computing Lab. Samsung Advanced Institute of Technology,
440-600, P. O. Box 111, Suwon, Rep. of Korea
sangmin.yoon@samsung.com
[3] Automation & Systems Research Institute Seoul National University,
151-742, Seoul, Rep. of Korea
gun@diehard.snu.ac.kr

Abstract. We present an example-based learning approach for detecting a partially occluded human face in a scene provided by a camera of Automated Teller Machine (ATM) in a bank. Gradient mapping in scale space is applied on an original image, providing human face representation robust to illumination variance. Detection of the partially occluded face, which can be used in characterization of suspicious ATM users, is then performed based on Support Vector Machine (SVM) method. Experimental results show that a high detection rate over 95% is achieved in image samples acquired from in-use ATM.

1 Introduction

The need for the video surveillance system which can distinguish the suspicious users from normal users only by users' face images has been raised up for ATM application. If ordinary face detection algorithms are used in the application, it will have high possibility that both the normal face and the face with sunglasses, the mask, and/or the muffler, i.e. the partially occluded face are detected as the normal face. There are several issues to solve this problem and make the surveillance function feasible for the ATM. One is illumination variation. The illumination environment which encompasses ATM varies time to time, and place to place, because normally ATM is located toward a window or a road. The surveillance system may misconceive the normal face taken in a back light condition as the partially occluded face and generate a false alarm. Another problem is computational load. The surveillance system in ATM usually uses a personal computer inside of the ATM. This computer can share its computing power only when it is not working on transactional activity. This fact regulates the time limitation for the surveillance system to detect the occluded face within few hundred milliseconds, from ATM-card-in signal to first transactional key input. The key factor to solve the problem is reduction of classification processing time.

M. Ali and F. Esposito (Eds.): IEA/AIE 2005, LNAI 3533, pp. 65 – 68, 2005.

In the paper, we introduce the noble SVM based classification algorithm which specifically distinguishes the partially occluded face from the normal face or non facial images. It overcomes the illumination variation problem by adopting illumination robust representation method such as gradient map represented in scale space. In addition, we use Principle Component Analysis (PCA) method to reduce computational burden for the classification. Consequently, the system is able to detect the partially occluded face in real time and in various illumination conditions.

2 System Framework

The flow diagram of the surveillance system for ATM using occluded face detection technology is shown in Fig. 1.

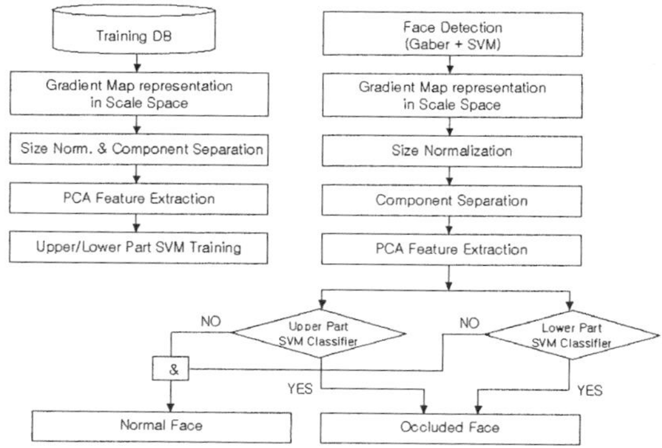

Fig. 1. Flow diagram for the proposed system. The left upper diagram describes training flow and the right diagram describes detection flow

Since the surveillance system for ATM should endure large illumination variance and the edge representation is known to be robust to the illumination variation, we developed a gradient map method for face representation. The gradient map is obtained by gradient operators, which are defined as follows [1][2][3]. However, the drawback still exists. The illumination variation against the occluded face with sunglasses in the gradient map is larger than that in the intensity image, because the characteristic of the gradient map is discrete, not continuous. This is why we introduced another representation method in addition to the gradient map. The representation in scale space is known to be making smoother and abstractive expression of the image. Especially the smoothing effect of the gradient map image represented in scale space is greater than that of intensity image. In addition, the gradient mapped face image in scale space is even more robust to illumination change. Once the full face is presented in the gradient map in scale space, we separated the face image into two parts; i.e. an upper part and a lower part. To extract the feature from the separated images, PCA has been used because of its simplicity and efficiency [4]. The central idea of PCA is to find a low dimensional subspace which captures most of image variation and therefore allows the best least square approximation. After obtaining the PCA features, we constructed the SVM training set. SVM implicitly maps the data into a dot product space via a nonlinear mapping function. Thus SVM learns a hyper-plane which separates the data by a large margin. We included position, scale and rotation varying images of the occluded face in the training image set.

3 Experiment Results

The proposed system was tested in two databases. One is Purdue University's AR DB [5] and the other is SAIT DB which is obtained from the real ATM environment allowing natural illumination change. Two criteria are selected for performance measure; i.e. a detection rate and a false alarm rate. The detection rate is the ratio of the positively-detected occluded faces over total occluded faces. The false alarm rate is the ratio of falsely-detected occluded faces over positively-detected occluded faces.

3.1 Results in AR DB

AR DB is the image database obtained from the restricted indoor environment where the light condition is controlled and the pose is fixed. 1560 frontal face images were used in the training for both the face region detection SVM and the classification SVM. Table I shows the performance of the system in AR DB. Table 1 is the experiment result when the trained images are used for the test and Table 2 is the experiment result when the untrained 636 images are used for the test.

Table 1. Experiment results in AR DB when the trained images are used for occluded face detection

	Detection rate	False alarm rate
Upper part	99.21 %	0.41 %
Lower part	99.41 %	0.12 %

Table 2. Experiment results in AR DB when the untrained images are used for occluded face detection

	Detection rate	False alarm rate
Upper part	97.28 %	1.2 %
Lower part	97.96 %	0.41 %

3.2 Results in SAIT DB

In order to confirm whether the proposed system can be commercialized, the system was tested in SAIT DB. Totally 4819 images were collected for both the face region detection SVM training and the classification SVM training. Table 3 and Table 4 show the performance of the system in SAIT DB. Table 3 is the experiment result when the trained images are used for the test and Table 4 is the experimental result when the untrained 1500 images are used for the test.

Table 3. Experiment results in SAIT DB when the trained images are used for occluded face detection

	Detection rate	False alarm rate
Upper part	98.99 %	0.10 %
Lower part	98.56 %	0.44 %

Table 4. Experiment results in SAIT DB when the untrained images are used for occluded face detection

	Detection rate	False alarm rate
Upper part	95.50 %	1.08 %
Lower part	96.20 %	2.76 %

4 Conclusion

We proposed an occluded face detection method based on a noble face representation that can reasonably work for the application requiring high illumination variance robustness and short computation time. This system could be improved further in several aspects based on field observations. One is high false alarm rate of the mask, compared with the muffler or the sunglasses. This happens because the training patterns of the mask are simple and often cause imprecise localization. The other problem is the high reflective sunglasses case. Sometimes the eye-like pattern appears on the high reflective sunglasses which the system misconceives as real eyes. In commercialization process, decreasing the threshold value for SVM classifiers can deal successfully with this problem. However, the training patterns that cover more field cases and more reliable representation method for complex patterns will lead better detecting performance.

References

1. Jain, A. K.: Fundamentals of Digital Image Processing. Prentice Hall, New Jersey (1989) 348-351
2. Davis, L. S.: A Survey of Edge Detection Techniques. Computer Graphics and Image Processing, Vol. 4 (1975) 248-270
3. Frei, W., Chen, C. C.: Fast Boundary Detection : a Generalization and a New Algorithm. IEEE Trans. Computer, Vol. 26, No. 2 (1977)
4. Yoon, S. M., Kee, S. C.: Detection of Partially Occluded Face using Support Vector Machines. MVA (2002) 546-549
5. Martinez, A. M.: Recognition of Partially Occluded and/or Imprecisely Localized Faces using a Probabilistic Approach. CVPR, Vol. 1 (2000) 712-717

Intelligent Vocal Cord Image Analysis for Categorizing Laryngeal Diseases*

Antanas Verikas[1,2], Adas Gelzinis[1], Marija Bacauskiene[1], and Virgilijus Uloza[3]

[1] Department of Applied Electronics, Kaunas University of Technology, Studentu 50, LT-3031, Kaunas, Lithuania
[2] Intelligent Systems Laboratory, Halmstad University, Box 823, S-301 18 Halmstad, Sweden
[3] Kaunas University of Medicine, Kaunas, Lithuania
antanas.verikas@ide.hh.se, adas.gelzinis@ktu.lt
marija.bacauskiene@ktu.lt, uloza@kmu.lt

Abstract. Colour, shape, geometry, contrast, irregularity and roughness of the visual appearance of vocal cords are the main visual features used by a physician to diagnose laryngeal diseases. This type of examination is rather subjective and to a great extent depends on physician's experience. A decision support system for automated analysis of vocal cord images, created exploiting numerous vocal cord images can be a valuable tool enabling increased reliability of the analysis, and decreased intra- and inter-observer variability. This paper is concerned with such a system for analysis of vocal cord images. Colour, texture, and geometrical features are used to extract relevant information. A committee of artificial neural networks is then employed for performing the categorization of vocal cord images into *healthy*, *diffuse*, and *nodular* classes. A correct classification rate of over 93% was obtained when testing the system on 785 vocal cord images.

1 Introduction

The diagnostic procedure of laryngeal diseases is based on visualization of the larynx, by performing indirect or direct laryngoscopy. A physician then identifies and evaluates colour, shape, geometry, contrast, irregularity and roughness of the visual appearance of vocal cords. This type of examination is rather subjective and to a great extent depends on physician's experience. Objective measures of these features would be very helpful for assuring objective analysis of images of laryngeal diseases and creating systematic databases for education, research, and everyday life decision support purposes. In addition to the data obtained from one particular patient, information from many previous patients—experience—plays also a very important role in the decision making process. Moreover, the

* We gratefully acknowledge the support we have received from the Lithuanian State Science and Studies Foundation.

M. Ali and F. Esposito (Eds.): IEA/AIE 2005, LNAI 3533, pp. 69–78, 2005.

physician interpreting the available data from a particular patient may have a limited knowledge and experience in analysis of the data. In such a situation, a decision support system for automated analysis and interpretation of medical data is of great value. Recent developments in this area have shown that physicians benefit from the advise of decision support systems in terms of increased reliability of the analysis, decreased intra- and inter-observer variability [12].

This paper, is concerned with an approach to automated analysis of vocal cord images aiming to categorize diseases of vocal cords. We treat the problem as a pattern recognition task. To obtain an informative representation of a vocal cord image that is further processed by a pattern classifier, a set of texture, colour, and geometrical features are used. The choice of the feature types was based on the type of information used by the physician when analyzing images of vocal cords.

A very few attempts have been made to develop computer-aided systems for analyzing vocal cord images. In [9], a system for automated categorization of manually marked suspect lesions into *healthy* and *diseased* classes is presented. The categorization is based on textural features extracted from co-occurrence matrices computed from manually marked areas of vocal cord images. A correct classification rate of 81.4% was observed when testing the system on a very small set of 35 images.

2 Data

Vocal cord images were acquired during routine direct microlaryngoscopy employing a Moller-Wedel Universa 300 surgical microscope. A 3-CCD Elmo colour video camera of 768 × 576 pixels was used to record the laryngeal images. This study uses a set of 785 laryngeal images recorded at the Department of Otolaryngology, Kaunas University of Medicine during the period from October 2002 to December 2003. The internet based archive—database—of laryngeal images is continuously updated.

2.1 Ground Truth

We used a "ground truth" taken from the clinical routine evaluation of patients. A rather common, clinically discriminative group of laryngeal diseases was chosen for the analysis i.e. mass lesions of vocal cords. Visual signs of vocal cord mass lesions (colour, shape, surface, margins, size, localization) are rather typical, clinically evident and descriptive.

Mass lesions of vocal cords could be categorized into six classes namely, *polypus*, *papillomata*, *carcinoma*, *cysts*, *keratosis*, and *nodules*. This categorization is based on clinical signs and a histological structure of the mass lesions of vocal cords. In this initial study, the first task was to differentiate between the *healthy* (*normal*) class and pathological classes and then, differentiate among the classes of vocal cord mass lesions. We distinguish two groups of mass lesions of vocal cords i.e. nodular—*nodules*, *polyps*, and *cysts*—and diffuse—*papillomata*, *keratosis*, and *carcinoma*—lesions. Thus, including the *healthy* class, we have to

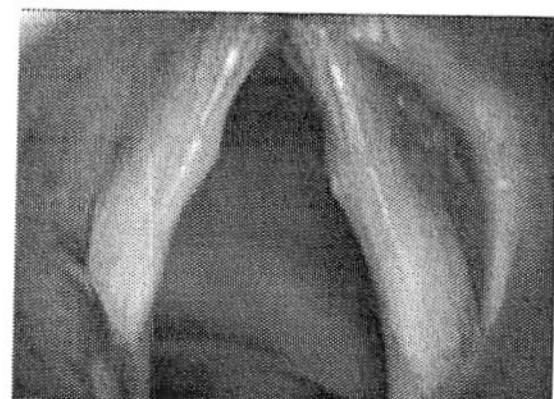 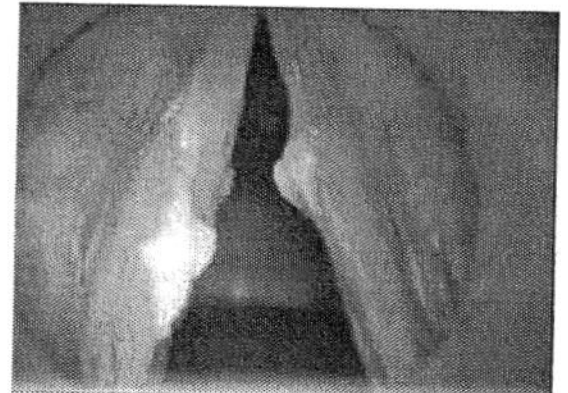 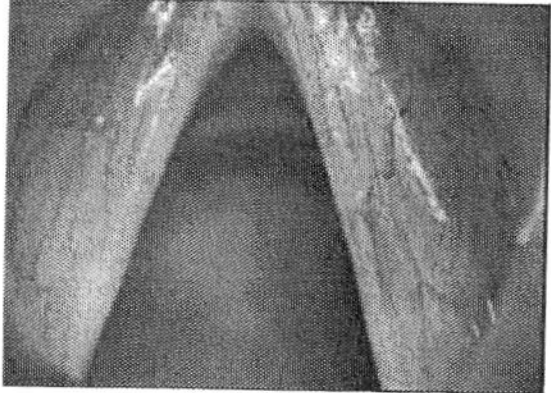

Fig. 1. Images from the *nodular* (left), *diffuse* (middle), and *healthy* (right) classes

distinguish between three classes of images. Categorization into the aforemention six classes will be the subject-matter of further research. Amongst the 785 images available, there are 49 images from the *healthy* class, 406 from the *nodular* class, and 330 from the *diffuse* class. It is worth noting that due to the large variety of appearance of vocal cords, the classification task is difficult even for a trained physician. Fig. 1 presents characteristic examples from the three decision classes considered, namely, *nodular*, *diffuse*, and *healthy*.

3 The Approach

To obtain a concise and informative representation of a vocal cord image that is further categorized by a pattern classifier, a set of texture, colour, and geometrical features is used. A committee of artificial neural network serves as a pattern classifier categorizing the obtained representation of a vocal cord image.

3.1 Colour Features

Since we measure distances in a colour space, we use an approximately uniform $L^*a^*b^*$ colour space for representing colours. The Euclidean distance measure can be used to measure the distance (ΔE) between the two points representing the colours in the colour space:

$$\Delta E = [(\Delta L^*)^2 + (\Delta a^*)^2 + (\Delta b^*)^2]^{1/2} \tag{1}$$

We characterize the colour content of an image by the probability distribution of the colour represented by the 3-D colour histogram of $N = 4096$ ($16 \times 16 \times 16$) bins and consider the histogram as a random N-vector. Most of bins of the histograms were empty or almost empty. Therefore, to reduce the number of components of the N-vector, the histograms built for a set of training images were summed up and the N-vector components corresponding to the bins containing less than N_α hits in the summed histogram were left aside. Hereby, when using $N_\alpha = 10$ we were left with 491 bins. To obtain an even more compact description of the histogram, the N-vector is projected onto a set of basis vectors and only first $K \ll N$ projection coefficients are used in the description. A metric taking into account the underlying properties of the colour space is used to calculate the basis vectors. To define the underlying properties of the colour space, we use a symmetric, positive definite matrix $\mathbf{A} = [a_{ij}]$, characterizing the colour-based similarity of histogram bins. The entry a_{ij} expressing the similarity between colours of bins i and j—the mean points of the bins—is given by

$$a_{ij} = 1 - (d_{ij}/d_{max})^{\beta} \tag{2}$$

where d_{ij} is the Euclidean distance between the colour i and j, given by Eq. (1) and β is a constant. To be able to exploit the matrix $\mathbf{A}$ for the calculation of the basis vectors, the matrix is factored into $\mathbf{A} = \mathbf{U}^T\mathbf{U}$ and the set of basis vectors used to extract colour features is then obtained in the following way [13].

First, having a set of vocal cord images, the eigenvectors $\boldsymbol{\psi}_k$ of the matrix $\boldsymbol{\Sigma}_\mathbf{A} = E(\mathbf{U}\mathbf{h}_C\mathbf{h}_C^T\mathbf{U}^T)$, where $\mathbf{h}_C$ is the histogram N-vector and $E(.)$ stands for the expectation, are computed. The basis vectors $\boldsymbol{\varphi}_k$ are then given by $\boldsymbol{\varphi}_k = \mathbf{U}^{-1}\boldsymbol{\psi}_k$ and the kth colour feature ξ_{Ck} is computed as

$$\xi_{Ck} = \mathbf{h}_C^T\mathbf{A}\boldsymbol{\varphi}_k \tag{3}$$

Using only the first K_C basis vectors a histogram vector $\mathbf{h}_C$ is approximated by $\widehat{\mathbf{h}_C} = \sum_{k=1}^{K_C} \xi_{Ck}\boldsymbol{\varphi}_k$.

3.2 Extracting Texture Features

There are many ways to describe image texture. Gabor [1] as well as wavelet [14] based filtering, Markov random fields, co-occurrence matrices [8], run length matrices [7], and autoregressive modelling [10] are the most prominent approaches used to extract textural features. The multi-channel two-dimensional Gabor filtering, co-occurrence matrices, run length matrices, and the singular value decomposition (SVD) are the approaches employed to extract texture features in this work.

An image $z(x,y)$—$L^*(x,y)$, $a^*(x,y)$, or $b^*(x,y)$—filtered by a Gabor filter of frequency f and orientation θ is given by

$$zg_{f,\theta}(x,y) = \mathrm{FFT}^{-1}[Z(u,v), G_{f,\theta}(u,v)] \tag{4}$$

where FFT^{-1} is the fast inverse Fourier transform, $Z(u,v)$ is the Fourier transform of the image $z(x,y)$, and $G_{f,\theta}(u,v)$ stands for the Fourier transform of the Gabor filter $g_{f,\theta}(x,y)$. Using the three filtered components $z_Lg_{f,\theta}(x,y)$, $z_ag_{f,\theta}(x,y)$, and $z_bg_{f,\theta}(x,y)$, an average filtered image

$$\overline{zg}_{f,\theta}(x,y) = [z_Lg_{f,\theta}(x,y) + z_ag_{f,\theta}(x,y) + z_bg_{f,\theta}(x,y)]/3 \tag{5}$$

is then obtained and a 40-bin histogram of the image $\overline{zg}_{f,\theta}$ is calculated. Thus, having N_f frequencies and N_θ orientations, $N_f \times N_\theta$ of such histograms are obtained from one vocal cord image. The first two bins and the bins corresponding to those containing less than N_β hits in the histogram accumulating all the training images are left aside. The remaining bins are concatenated into one long vector $\mathbf{h}_G$. The kth Gabor feature ξ_{Gk} is then computed as

$$\xi_{Gk} = \mathbf{h}_G^T\boldsymbol{\vartheta}_k \tag{6}$$

where $\boldsymbol{\vartheta}_k$ is the eigenvector corresponding to the kth largest eigenvalue of the correlation matrix $E(\mathbf{h}_G\mathbf{h}_G^T)$ estimated from the training set of vocal cord images. Only the first K_G Gabor features are utilized. We used $N_\beta = 1000$ in this study.

To extract the SVD based features, the three image bands L^*, a^*, and b^* are concatenated into a matrix of $3V \times H$ size, where V and H is the image size in the vertical and horizontal direction, respectively. The kth SVD based feature ξ_{Sk} is then given by the kth singular value of the matrix. Only the first K_S singular values have been utilized in this study.

In the co-occurrence matrix based approach, we utilized the 14 well known Haralick's coefficients [8] as a feature set. The coefficients were calculated from the average co-occurrence matrix obtained by averaging the matrices calculated for 0°, 45°, 90°, and 135° directions. The matrices were computed for one, experimentally selected, distance parameter. Seven features, short-run emphasis, long-run emphasis, grey-level non-uniformity, run-length non-uniformity, run percentage, low grey level run emphasis, and high grey level run emphasis [7] have been extracted based on the run-length matrices. Since red colour dominates in the vocal cord images, the $a^*(x, y)$ (red-green) image component has been employed for extracting the co-occurrence and run-length matrices based features.

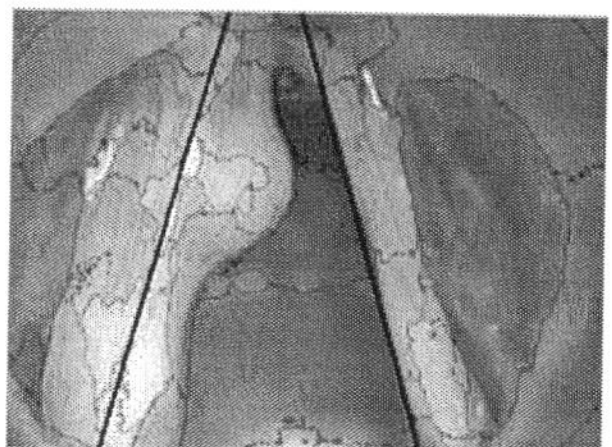
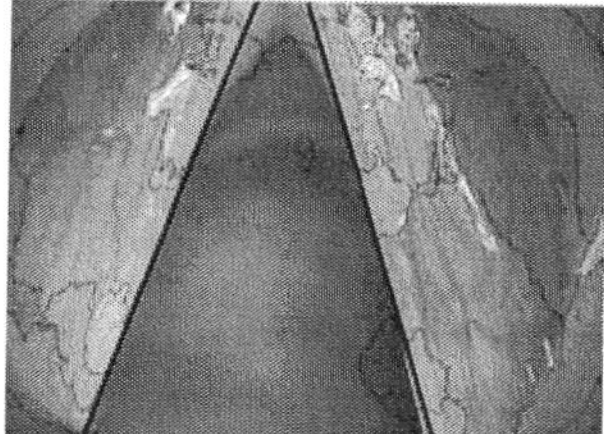

Fig. 2. Vocal cord images coming from the *nodular* (left) and the *healthy* (right) classes along with two lines used to calculate the geometrical feature ξ_{G1}

3.3 Geometrical Features

Currently we use only two geometrical features, which are mainly targeted for discriminating the *healthy* class from the other two. To extract one of the features, a vocal cord image is first segmented into a set of homogenous regions. Two lines, ascending in the left-hand part and descending in the right-hand part of the image are then drawn in such a way as to maximize the number of segmentation boundary points intersecting the lines. Fig. 2 presents two examples of the segmentation boundaries found and the two lines drawn according to the determined directions. The first geometrical feature ξ_{G1} is then given by the sum of the squared number of the boundary points intersecting the two lines. The second geometrical feature ξ_{G2} is obtained in the same way, except that colour edge points are utilized instead of the segmentation boundary points.

We segment vocal cord images by applying the mean shift procedure [4] in the concatenated 5-dimensional *spatial-range* space. There are two dimensions—x, y—in the spatial and three—$L^*a^*b^*$—in the range space.

3.4 Pattern Classifier

Three alternatives have been investigated in this work for classifying vocal cord images, namely the k nearest neighbour ($k - NN$) rule, a committee of neural networks and a committee of committees of networks. We used the $k - NN$ classifier as a basic classifier, since it is known that provided $k \to \infty$ and $k/n \to 0$, where n is the number of samples, the expected error probability of the $k - NN$ rule approaches the Bayes error probability [5]. In this work, the Euclidean distance measure has been utilized and the number of the nearest neighbours k providing the best performance was determined experimentally. The rationale behind using the committee of committees structure is as follows.

Numerous previous works on classification committees have demonstrated that an efficient committee should consist of networks that are not only very accurate, but also diverse in the sense that the network errors occur in different regions of the input space [15]. Manipulating training data set [16, 17], employing different subsets of variables and different architectures are the most popular approaches used to achieve the diversity of networks. In this work, three techniques, namely, manipulating training data set, training from different initial weights, and employing different subsets of input variables are jointly used for achieving the diversity. To build a neural classifier, usually a neural network is trained several times using different initial weights and only the network providing the best performance is utilized. Instead of leaving aside all the other outcomes, we aggregate them into a committee. To build different committees, we manipulate training data set and input variables. Thus the committee of networks exploits the diversity of the different training outcomes, while a committee of committees benefits from the diversity due to the use of different training sets and input variables.

L-fold training data set partitioning, Bootstrapping [2], AdaBoosting [6], Pasting Votes [3] are the most prominent techniques used for manipulating training data set. In this work, we resorted to the simple L-fold random data set partitioning into training and test sets. We used a single hidden layer perceptron as a committee member with the number of hidden nodes found by cross-validation.

A variety of schemes have been proposed for combining multiple neural networks into a committee [18]. In this study, we employed two simple aggregation approaches, namely, the weighted averaging and the majority voting rule. The aggregation weights for weighted averaging approach were obtained based on the classification accuracy estimated on the training set. Let us assume that p_i is the correct classification rate of the ith network. The aggregation weight w_i is then given by $w_i = p_i^\gamma$, with γ being a parameter. The same combination rules have been applied for both committees and committees of committees.

4 Experimental Investigations

After some experiments, we have chosen to use $N_f = 7$ frequencies and $N_\theta = 6$ orientations for extracting Gabor features. The distance parameter d used to calculate co-occurrence matrices was found to be $d = 5$. Values of the parameter γ used to calculate the aggregation weights ranged from 10 to 15, being larger for larger committees. Since we used $I = 13$ different initializations, such was the committee size. The size of the committee of committees was specific for each input pattern $\mathbf{x}$ analyzed. To classify $\mathbf{x}$, all the committees that have not used the $\mathbf{x}$ in their training sets were aggregated. In all the tests, we have used 100 different random ways to partition the data set into Training–D_l and Test–D_t sets. Thus, 100 different committees were build for a particular feature set. The cross-validation experiments performed have shown that 11 hidden nodes was the appropriate network size for all the feature sets tested.

The mean values and standard deviations of the test set correct classification rate presented in this paper for the $k - NN$ classifier and the committee of networks were calculated based on those 100 trials. Ten trials have been used to estimate those statistics for the committee of committees case. Out of the 785 images available, 650 images were assigned to the set D_l and 135 to the test set D_t. We used the Bayesian inference technique to train neural networks [11]. Although training of the system is rather time consuming, the computational complexity in the operation mode is not high, since usually only one image needs to be processed at a time.

4.1 Classification Results

Table 1 summarizes the test data set correct classification rate obtained using different classifiers and single types of features. In the parentheses, the standard deviation of the correct classification rate is provided. In the table, "*Classifier*" stands for the type of classifier, "*Features*" for the feature set used, and "*Committees*" means committee of committees. Numbers in the parentheses next to the denotations of the feature sets stand for the size of the feature sets. In all the tests, the results of which are presented in Table 1, the majority voting aggregation rule has been applied.

The upper part of Table 1 is for the case when first nine colour, Gabor and SVD features were used. This approximate number was determined using a single neural network. No significant reduction in classification error rate was observed when using larger number of those features. Observe, that the first nine features of the aforementioned types have been employed. All the co-occurrence and run length matrices based features have been utilized in this test.

The middle part of Table 1 presents the results obtained using features selected by the $k - NN$ classifier. The sequential forward selection procedure has been utilized to select the features. The procedure starts with one feature and adds one feature at a time—the one providing the highest increase in correct classification rate. All the co-occurrence and run length matrices based features and the first 25 features of the remaining types were involved in the selection procedure. The feature subset chosen was that providing the highest correct clas-

Table 1. The average test data set correct classification rate for different classifiers and feature sets

N#	Features\Classifier	$k-NN$	Committee	Committees
1.	Colour (9)	70.32 (3.25)	84.07 (2.71)	87.77 (1.10)
2.	Co-occurrence (14)	67.39 (3.38)	79.85 (2.84)	82.93 (0.84)
3.	Gabor (9)	64.33 (3.35)	71.64 (3.22)	75.29 (0.96)
4.	Run Length (7)	54.39 (3.98)	60.41 (3.03)	62.68 (0.76)
5.	SVD (9)	60.64 (4.29)	65.11 (3.27)	68.54 (0.87)
6.	Colour (14)	80.25 (3.39)	87.50 (2.25)	90.06(0.79)
7.	Co-occurrence (9)	71.72 (2.86)	78.32 (2.64)	80.76 (0.88)
8.	Gabor (14)	69.17 (3.28)	74.43 (2.79)	78.73 (0.69)
9.	Run Length (2)	58.09 (4.23)	56.59 (3.42)	58.22 (0.87)
10.	SVD (11)	65.48 (4.04)	64.55 (3.08)	68.28 (1.16)
11.	Colour (8) + Gabor (6) + Geom (2)	75.92 (3.28)	88.36 (2.70)	90.96 (1.10)
12.	Colour (14) + Gabor (8) + Geom (2)	84.33 (3.49)	88.56 (2.55)	90.57 (0.95)
13.	Colour (14) + Gabor (6)	82.68 (3.46)	87.83 (2.54)	90.83 (0.68)
14.	Colour (15) + Co-oc (5) + Geom (2)	83.31 (3.49)	89.29 (2.13)	90.83 (0.94)
15.	All (14+3+4+2+3+2=28)	85.61 (3.02)	89.34 (2.01)	91.97 (0.70)

sification rate. If several subsets exhibited approximately the same performance, the smallest one was chosen.

The lower part of Table 1 presents classification results obtained when simultaneously utilizing features of the different types for training neural networks or calculating the distance in the $k-NN$ classifier. The first 8 colour, 6 Gabor, and 2 geometrical features were utilized in alternative N# 11. For the other alternatives, 12-15, the features were selected using the $k-NN$ classifier. The first 25 colour, the first 25 Gabor and the geometrical features have been utilized to select features for alternative N# 12. The only difference between alternatives N# 12 and N# 13 is that the geometrical features were excluded from the set of available features in the latter case. In alternative N# 14, all the co-occurrence matrix based features were used instead of the Gabor ones. In the last case, the selection was made amongst the first 25 colour, 25 Gabor, 25 SVD and all features of the other types. There were selected 14 colour, 3 co-occurrence 4 Gabor, 2 run length, 3 SVD, and 2 geometrical features in this test.

As it can be seen from Table 1, when used alone, the colour features provided the highest correct classification rate amongst all the types of features tested. The co-occurrence matrix based features clearly outperformed the other types of texture features. The $k-NN$ classifier was much more sensitive to feature selection results than a committee or a committee of committees. The classifier specific feature selection improved the performance of the $k-NN$ classifier considerably. Though the colour features possess the largest discrimination power, the texture features also contribute to reducing the classification error. The geo-

Table 2. The average test data set correct classification rate obtained when combining committees trained on different feature types

Rule\N#	1-2	1-3	1-5	1-5, 11, 12	11, 12, 14
Voting	88.28 (0.97)	88.54 (1.03)	88.66 (1.00)	92.23 (0.65)	92.36 (0.57)
Average	88.54 (0.52)	88.66 (0.65)	88.92 (0.64)	93.12 (0.72)	92.23 (0.45)

metrical features increase the correct classification rate even further, mainly due to an improved differentiation between the *healthy* and the other classes. Fig. 2 illustrates the position of two lines found when calculating ξ_{G1} for the images coming from the *nodular* and *healthy* classes. As it can be seen from Fig. 2, the lines are quite well aligned with the cord edges, in the *healthy* class case.

Table 2 presents the average test data set correct classification rate obtained when combining committees trained on different feature types. As it can be seen from Table 2, combining committees trained on various sets of input variables enables further boosting of the classification accuracy. Two aggregation alternatives are considered in this test, namely, the majority voting and weighted averaging. The weighted averaging aggregation approach provided a slightly higher correct classification rate. Bearing in mind the high similarity of the decision classes, the obtained over 93% correct classification rate is rather encouraging.

5 Conclusions

This paper is concerned with an automated analysis of vocal cord images aiming to categorize the images into the *healthy*, *nodular*, and *diffuse* classes. To obtain a comprehensive representation of the images, features of various types concerning image colour, texture, and pattern geometry are extracted. The representation is then further analyzed by a pattern classifier performing the categorization. Amongst the four alternatives tested for extracting texture features, namely the co-occurrence matrices, Gabor filtering, singular value decomposition, and the run length matrices, the texture features obtained from the co-occurrence matrices proved to be the most discriminative ones. As expected, when used alone, the colour features provided the highest correct classification rate amongst all the types of features tested.

The k nearest neighbour ($k - NN$) rule, a committee of neural networks and a committee of committees of networks have been employed for solving the classification task. The $k - NN$ classifier was much more sensitive to feature selection results than a committee or a committee of committees. A committee of committees trained on various sets of input variables proved to be the most accurate classification scheme. Three techniques, namely, manipulating training data set, training from different initial weights, and employing different subsets of input variables were jointly used for obtaining diverse networks aggregated into a committee of committees. A correct classification rate of over 93% was obtained when classifying a set of unseen images into the aforementioned three classes. Bearing in mind the high similarity of the decision classes, the correct classification rate obtained is rather encouraging.

References

1. Bovik, A.C., Clark, M., Geisler, W.S.: Multichannel texture analysis using localized spatial filters. IEEE trans Pattern Analysis Machine Intelligence **12** (1990) 55–73
2. Breiman, L.: Bagging predictors. Machine Learning **24** (1996) 123–140
3. Breiman, L.: Pasting small votes for classification in large databases and on-line. Machine Learning **36** (1999) 85–103
4. Comaniciu, D., Meer, P.: Mean shift: A robust approach toward feature space analysis. IEEE Trans Pattern Analysis Machine Intelligence **24** (2002) 603–619
5. Devroye, L., Gyorfi, L., Lugosi, G.: A Probabilistic Theory of Pattern Recognition. Springer-Verlag, New York (1996)
6. Freund, Y., Schapire, R.E.: A decision-theoretic generalization of on-line learning and an application to boosting. Journal of Computer and System Sciences **55** (1997) 119–139
7. Galloway, M.M.: Texture analysis using gray level run lengths. Computer Graphics and Image Processing **4** (1975) 172–179
8. Haralick, R.M., Shanmugam, K., Dinstein, I.: Textural features for image classification. IEEE Trans System, Man and Cybernetics **3** (1973) 610–621
9. Ilgner, J.F.R., Palm, C., Schutz, A.G., Spitzer, K., Westhofen, M., Lehmann, T.M.: Colour texture analysis for quantitative laryngoscopy. Acta Oto-Laryngologica **123** (2003) 730–734
10. Lu, S.W., Xu, H.: Textured image segmentation using autoregressive model and artificial neural network. Pattern Recognition **28** (1995) 1807–1817
11. MacKay, D.J.: Bayesian interpolation. Neural Computation **4** (1992) 415–447
12. Ohlsson, M.: WeAidUa decision support system for myocardial perfusion images using artificial neural networks. Artificial Intelligence in Medicine **30** (2004) 49–60
13. Tran, L.V.: Efficient Image Retrieval with Statistical Color Descriptors. PhD thesis, Linkoping University, Linkoping, Sweden (2003)
14. Unser, M.: Texture classification and segmentation using wavelet frames. IEEE trans Image Processing **4** (1995) 1549–1560
15. Verikas, A., Lipnickas, A., Bacauskiene, M., Malmqvist, K.: Fusing neural networks through fuzzy integration. In Bunke, H., Kandel, A., eds.: Hybrid Methods in Pattern Recognition. World Scientific, Singapore (2002) 227–252
16. Verikas, A., Lipnickas, A.: Fusing neural networks through space partitioning and fuzzy integration. Neural Processing Letters **16** (2002) 53–65
17. Verikas, A., Gelzinis, A., Malmqvist, K.: Using unlabelled data to train a multilayer perceptron. Neural Processing Letters **14** (2001) 179–201
18. Verikas, A., Lipnickas, A., Malmqvist, K., Bacauskiene, M., Gelzinis, A.: Soft combination of neural classifiers: A comparative study. Pattern Recognition Letters **20** (1999) 429–444

Keyword Spotting on Hangul Document Images Using Two-Level Image-to-Image Matching

Sang Cheol Park, Hwa Jeong Son, Chang Bu Jeong, and Soo Hyung Kim

Department of Computer Science, Chonnam National University,
300 Yongbong-dong, Buk-gu, Kwangju 500-700, Korea
{sanchun, sonhj, cbjeong, shkim}@iip.chonnam.ac.kr

1 Introduction

A lot of printed documents and books has been published and saved as a form of images in digital libraries. Searching for a specified query word on document images is a challenging problem. The OCR software helps the images to be converted to the machine readable documents to search a full context [1]. Another approach [1, 2] is image-based one, in which both the document images and word information are saved in a database. The searching procedure is accomplished through comparing the features of query word image with the word images extracted from document images in the database. In this paper, we propose an accurate and fast keyword spotting system for searching user-specified keyword in Hangul document images by a two-level image-to-image matching method.

2 Proposed System

The character segmentation is based on projection analysis, constrained by the prior knowledge. The bounding box of Hangul character usually has a shape of square, and the width of the box is nearly invariant. From this prior knowledge, we estimate the number of characters in a word image by the value of the width of the image divided by the height.

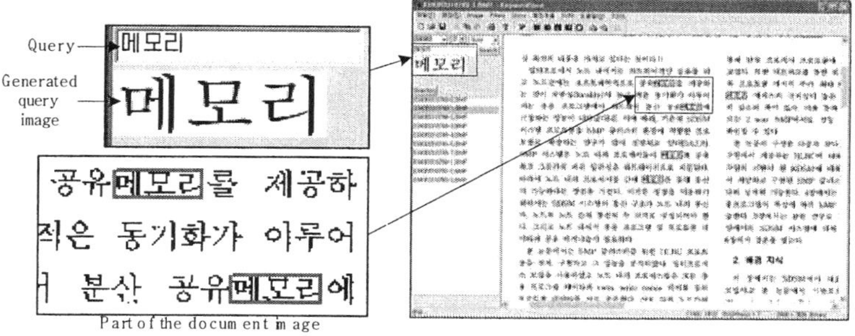

Fig. 1. User interface for the the proposed system

M. Ali and F. Esposito (Eds.): IEA/AIE 2005, LNAI 3533, pp. 79 – 81, 2005.

The query word image is generated by the system in a font appearing most frequently in the document images. Whenever the user types a character, the system creates a character image.

We normalize a character image into 32×32 size before extracting the features. Three types of features are applied in the paper. First, to use a mesh feature we define a N×M mesh grid. The element of feature is the number of black pixels in each mesh grid. Second, the four profiles are obtained by counting the white pixels in the four directions-rightward, downward, leftward and upward respectively, until the black pixels are encountered. Each profile is represented as an one-dimensional array with 32 values. By averaging the 32 values, a 4-dimensional feature set is obtained. Third, we calculate the wavelet coefficients by using a standard two-dimensional Harr wavelet in a 5-level decomposition. Since the coefficient which has large absolute value are more significant in representing the image, we calculate the index and the value of coefficients in descending order of the absolute value, and use these as the feature of the character image.

In a matching procedure we compare a character of a query image with one of a word image in a database. Two characters are considered as similar when the distance (Manhattan distance) between the two is lower than a character threshold value and then the next pair of characters is compared in the same manner. Finally, we determine two images as a similar pair when the mean of the character feature vectors' distance is lower than a word threshold.

To speed up, we use two-level matching strategy. In the 1st matching level, the feature vector should be selected to raise the recall rate and speed. To increase the speed, a low dimensional feature is used. In the 2nd matching level, the system should get the high recall and precision rate even though the speed is lower than that of the first stage. We use the high dimensional feature vector to raise the recall and precision rate, while preserving the searching speed.

3 Experimental Result

For the experiment 8 document images are downloaded from the website of Korea Information Science Society [3] and the font size of a character is 8 or 10 in the document images which were scanned at 300 DPI. We distill only the Hangul word images out of the document images to get the 1600 experiment word images. 30 query images are used. We implemented the proposed system using a Visual C++ programming language on a Pentium-4 2.80GHz PC.

To analysis the performance of the system using the 4, 8, 16, and 30-dimensional feature vectors extracted from mesh, profile, and wavelet in each dimension, we observed the recall and precision rate with the growing of a threshold value.

The system has higher precision rate and speed where the profile feature is used in each low dimension. With using 30-dimensional mesh feature, the proposed system gets higher recall and precision rate, and searches more 27,000 words than using 32-dimensional profile feature. Hence we select the low dimensional profile features and 30-dimensional mesh feature for the 1st and 2nd matching stage respectively.

Table 1 shows the performance of using combinations of low dimensional profile feature and 30-dimensional mesh feature. We used the 4-dimensional profile and 30-dimensional mesh features for the proposed system.

Table 1. Performance of various combinations of features

Combination		Recall	Precision	Speed
The 1st stage	The 2nd stage	(%)	(%)	(words / second)
4D profile	30D mesh	89.69	89.84	519,951
8D profile		89.86	89.71	467,673
16D profile		90.02	90.16	447,640

22 character segmentation errors occur among 1600 word images (accurate rate of 98.56%). There are two types of errors in the searching stage: False Acceptance Ratio(FAR) and False Rejection Ratio(FRR) which are 0.13(63/47379)% and 10.31(64/621)% respectively. FRR is depending on font styles and pixels whose information is changed, and FAR is caused in the case that the feature can't represent the difference of two images.

4 Conclusion

We have proposed a system that provides better performance than those of conventional keyword spotting systems on Hangul document images. The proposed system has a recall rate of 89.69%, a precision rate of 89.84% and a searching speed of 519,951 words a second. The experimental results show that the proposed system provides better performance than that of conventional keyword spotting systems on Hangul document images.

Acknowledgement

This research was supported by the Program for the Training of Graduate Students in Regional Innovation which was conducted by the Ministry of Commerce, Industry and Energy of the Korean Government.

References

[1] Doermann, D.: The indexing and retrieval of document images: a survey, Computer Vision and Image Understanding, vol. 70, no. 3, pp. 287-298, 1998.

[2] Oh, I.S., Choi, Y.S., Yang, J.H., and Kim, S.H.: A keyword spotting system of korean document images, Proc. 5th International Conference on Asian Digital Libraries, Singapore, p. 530, Dec. 2002.

[3] http://www.kiss.or.kr/

Robust Character Segmentation System for Korean Printed Postal Images

Sung-Kun Jang[1], Jung-Hwan Shin[1], Hyun-Hwa Oh[2], Seung-Ick Jang[3], and Sung-Il Chien[1]

[1] School of Electronic and Electrical Engineering, Kyungpook National University, Daegu, 702-701 South Korea
{skjang, jhshin, sichien}@ee.knu.ac.kr
[2] Samsung Advanced Institute of Technology, Yongin, 449-901 South Korea
hyunhwa.oh@samsung.com
[3] Electronics and Telecommunications Research Institute, Daejon, 305-350 South Korea
sijang@etri.re.kr

Abstract. This paper proposes a character segmentation system for Korean printed postal images. The proposed method is composed of two main processes, which are robust skew correction and character segmentation. Experimental results on real postal images show that the proposed system effectively segments characters to be suitable for the input of OCR system.

Keywords: Postal automation system, character segmentation, skew correction, character components.

1 Introduction

The development of electronic business, which uses more efficient and cost-effective forms of communications, has contributed to creating a more paperless society. In fact, everyday physical post letter is largely being replaced by electronic mail. Contrary to our expectations, the number of postal matters is rising steadily due to advertising matters, bills, etc., and most of them are printed by machine for reasons for the convenience of users. In order to cope effectively with the increase of postal matters, many researches are focused on address image recognition system for postal automation system [1]. The postal automation system includes five main modules: destination address block location, text line separation, character segmentation, character recognition, and finally address interpretation. Specifically, the performance of character segmentation significantly affects the accuracy of character recognition.

Character segmentation for Korean printed image [2-4] is complex due to the inherent feature of the Korean character, which represents a syllable and has a 2-dimensional composition of one or more consonants and a vowel, which is horizontal, vertical, or their composite. Unlike the document image, postal image is difficult to segment characters from character strings due to a variety of fonts and their sizes. Furthermore, in the up-to-date fashion of Korean fonts, the composites of a vowel and consonants are densely formed to meet the aesthetical demand. This trend causes the appearance of touching patterns and makes it difficult to segment characters. And, it is quite probable that the envelope may be misaligned during the scanning process.

M. Ali and F. Esposito (Eds.): IEA/AIE 2005, LNAI 3533, pp. 82 – 84, 2005.

Such skew may cause problems in subsequent procedures of character segmentation and character recognition. Therefore, robust skew correction algorithm is proposed for better character segmentation.

2 Character Segmentation System

In this paper, a robust character segmentation system to extract Korean characters from a skewed postal image is proposed. The proposed system is composed of two main modules for skew correction and character segmentation (see Figure 1). In primary skew correction, in order to see the direction of character strings in a skewed input image, two or more adjacent characters in the identical character string are merged and resulted in a region by the horizontal dithering. To determine a major skew angle, we form an accumulator array. For the skew angle of each region, the relevant elements of the accumulator array are incremented by the weighted value with respect to the size of the region. The peak-valued element in the accumulator array is averaged and that value corresponds to the major rotation angle of the input image. After applying the primary skew correction, the secondary skew correction is needed. To estimate a correct skew angle in case the adjacent character strings are osculated, the skew angle estimation method based on the base line of a character string is found to be more robust. In addition, the skew angle is calculated by the same procedure used for the primary skew correction. Then, the character strings, which are enclosed by rectangles, are segmented using connected component analysis and horizontal projection profile.

To ensure the robust performance of a character segmentation system, two steps of operation are employed. First, character components are extracted from the character strings in the skew-corrected image by using connected component analysis and vertical adjacency analysis. The character components of Korean fonts are classified into two types, which are over-segmented character, such as a consonant, a vowel, a part of a consonant or vowel, and character itself, such as a digit or Korean character. Then, the character components are merged into reasonable characters by the proposed character-component merging algorithm. In the proposed algorithm, many merging-path candidates, which are possible combinations of the character components using shape information of characters and a digit recognizer based on multilayer perceptron (MLP) [5], are evaluated and then character candidates are determined by selecting eight best merging-paths according to the evaluated merging score.

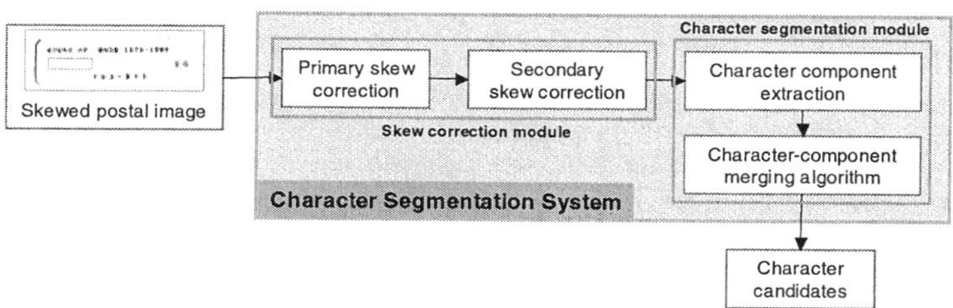

Fig. 1. The structure of character segmentation system

3 Experimental Results and Conclusions

To evaluate the performance of the proposed character segmentation system, five hundred postal images (9688 words) were randomly selected as the test samples from 5000 postal images, which are standard postal images called ETRI DB, which are gathered by ETRI in Korea and used as a reference DB for postal image processing among Korean researches.

The performance of our proposed system was evaluated by checking whether correctly segmented characters exist within the determined eight best merging-path candidates, the first place to the eighth place. Especially, we counted the number of the words, which are composed of successfully segmented characters only. In other words, the words are excluded even if they contained an incorrect segmented character. As shown in Table 1, within the third place, the proposed method successfully segments 9425 words (97.28%) from the test images. Moreover, within the eighth place, it segments 98.50% of words successfully. Compared to the result of the system without a digit recognizer, the correction rate has improved 3.57% within the third place, 3.63% with in the fifth place, and 2.67% within the eighth place.

Considering the characteristics of postal images containing many digits, we increased the success rate of character segmentation by adding a digit recognizer on to the proposed system. In addition, we expect that the proposed system will be quite useful for enhancing the performance of the character recognizer.

Table 1. Number of correctly segmented words from test postal images with and without digit recognizer

	Proposed system with digit recognizer	Proposed system without digit recognizer
Within 3rd place	9425 (97.28%)	9079 (93.71%)
Within 5th place	9514 (98.20%)	9162 (94.57%)
Within 8th place	9543 (98.50%)	9284 (95.83%)
Out of 8th place	145 (1.50%)	404 (4.17%)
Total number of words	9688	

References

1. Kim, H.Y., Lim, K.T., Kim, D.S.: Postal Envelope Image Recognition System for Postal Automation. The KIPS Transactions Part B. Vol.10-B, No. 4 (2003) 429-441
2. Lee, J.S., Kwon, O.J., Bang, S.Y.: Highly Accurate Recognition of printed Korean Characters through an Improved Two-stage Classification Method. Pattern Recognition. Vol. 32. (1999) 1935-1945
3. Liang, S., Ahmadi, M., and Shridhard, M.: Segmentation of Touching Characters in Printed Document Recognition. Second Int'l Conf. Document Analysis and Recognition. (1993) 569-572
4. Jang, S.I., Jeong, S.H., Nam, Y. S.: Classification of Machine-Printed and Handwritten Addresses on Korean Mail Piece Images Using Geometric Features. 17th International Conference on Pattern Recognition (ICPR'04), 2004, pp. 383-386
5. Haykin, S.: Neural Networks. Macmillan College Publishing Company, New Jersey (1994)

Case Based Reasoning Using Speech Data for Clinical Assessment

Rocio Guillén and Rachel Usrey

Computer Science Dept., California State University San Marcos, CA, USA

Abstract. The question of detecting pertinent information about an individual from properties of their speech is not a new one. Much research has been done to explore the manifestation of emotions in voice. The work presented in this paper proposes to apply these efforts in the domain of depression assessment using Case Based Reasoning. Cases are constructed using the recordings of responses to a questionnaire from English speaking Males and Females, and Spanish speaking Males and Females. We apply the exemplar and instance approach to classify new test cases. Experimental results show that the construction of cases using sound waveform statistics can be utilized by a case based reasoner to classify new instances correctly.

Keywords: Case-Base Reasoning, Speech recognition, Decision Support.

1 Introduction

Case Based Reasoning (CBR) is an approach that has been successfully applied to the medical domain as a tool to assist in the diagnosis and search for solutions or treatment [7]. The flexibility this approach provides makes it specially useful for depression assessment. Given that no two people or patients are exactly alike, no two cases will be exactly alike. CBR makes it possible to apply inexact comparisons and still have a useful result. In our work cases are constructed from subjects' responses to a depression survey recorded as wave (.wav) files that are given a score indicating whether or not the subject exhibits symptoms of severe depression. To identify the effectiveness of the cases we used two basic case based reasoning approaches: exemplar and instance. Exemplar returns the most similar case from the historical database and offers that as the solution to the new case. Instance retrieves multiple cases from the historical database that meet predefined parameters and the most common solution is offered as the solution to the new case [8], [9].

Building the cases from the recordings (.wav files) from real subjects motivated the investigation of approaches utilized in analyzing voices, and in particular emotion. Most of these approaches involve the statistical analysis of features in three categories: acoustic, prosodic, and language. Acoustic features deal with the nature of sounds, such as wavelength and frequency of the sound,

M. Ali and F. Esposito (Eds.): IEA/AIE 2005, LNAI 3533, pp. 85–94, 2005.

and speech rate. prosodic features include attributes pertaining to the energy of speech, voice quality, speech rate, articulation, flow of syllables, stress, and pronunciation. Language features relate to the word choices themselves.

Among the different methods used to analyze acoustic and prosodic features are maximum likelihood Bayes classifier (MLB), kernel regression (KR), linear discriminant classifier and k nearest neighbor (KNN). Lee *et. al.* [1] used a 10-feature set based on pitch and energy of the speech variables, distinguishing male and female test data. This set consisted of the mean, median, standard deviation, maximum of both the pitch and energy, and the minimum of pitch and the range of energy. The features chosen for our research are based on the latter because we are interested in distinguishing between female and male voices and its effects in the classification results.

The addition of language information shows significant improvement of emotion detection over the acoustic information only. Lee uses two training sets for evaluation of linguistic data. A salience measure was applied to the utterances to identify words related to the emotional content of speech. While the results achieved with the combination and linguistic information are significant, they did not apply directly to our work. The speech data we analyzed does not contain emotionally salient language because the recordings are of numerical responses to the questionnaire. The acoustic results in isolation verify the usefulness of the sound statistics of pitch (max, median, mean, standard deviation) and energy (max, min, median, mean, standard deviation).

In the following sections we present our case-based reasoning system for classification of new cases, i.e., new wave (.wav) files represented as statistical vectors,describe the construction of these vectors, describe the application of the exemplar and instance approach, describe experiments and results, and conclude with a discussion of the results produced.

2 Case-Based Reasoning System

Extensive research has been done into the study and identification of emotion in voice through evaluation of sound. Such studies have shown that elements such as pitch, timbre, rate and even stress placed upon syllabus can be used to determine the emotion of the speaker. Lee et. al. [1] showed that there exists a significant difference between even male and female speakers with respect to the accuracy of detection of emotion. Feature selection has indicated the importance of the statistics of pitch and energy , or fundamental frequency and sound level respectively, as containing valid information pertinent to emotional content [2], [3]. The fact that assessing measurements collected from voice data suggests the possibility that using the same or related statistical data can reveal information about a person's mental state. Though a possible indicator of depression, the measured emotional content in voice data, as previously described, cannot be used to measure depression directly. Depression is not an emotional state in itself, but may manifest in any subset of possible emotions. While work has been done using computers in the assessment of depression, the research has been

Table 1. Training and test sets

Language Category	Database Cases	Test Cases
English Female	60	11
English Male	48	11
Spanish Female	41	11
Spanish Male	26	11

directed to the domain of speech content. A Voice Interactive Depression Assessment Study (VIDAS) [4] has explored the validity of applying the approach of waveform analysis in the limited domain of depression assessment, while ignoring the subjective speech content of the waveform file itself. The emphasis of our work has been not on *what* is said, rather in *how* it is said. Data obtained from the analysis of waveforms was used to generate cases, and case based reasoning was applied to evaluate the potential for depression in the given subject.

The question we attempted to answer is whether it is possible to categorize wave (.wav) files, recorded from people being assessed for depression, in such a way that we are able to build cases to be used by a case based reasoner, and classify new instances correctly. The construction of cases was done to assess whether the pitch and energy statistics contain usable information for the depression assessment task; the case based reasoning component focused on the two primary classical case based reasoning functions namely, retrieval of cases and reuse of solutions [5], [9].

2.1 Case Structure

For our analysis, we obtained data originally collected in the VIDAS study, which consisted of 20 recorded responses and a total score for each subject. Voice recordings were stored as wave (.wav) files, a type of digital sound storage. The wave (.wav) files were analyzed using SFSWin [10]. The sound data was normalized, next the fundamental frequency waveform (FF) and amplitude envelope tracks (AE) were generated using 1 ms time frames. The normalization of the wave (.wav) files adjusts the volume to a standard volume level, we used such normalization as a baseline to compare recordings made at different times, under different circumstances. The maximum, minimum, median, mean, and standard deviation of the pitch (FF) and energy (AE) of the sound waveforms were read directly from the graphs. This generated 4380 sets of statistics, or 219 cases consisting of 20 questions.

The 219 cases were then divided according to the designated language categories. We randomly selected 30% of each category as test cases (test set). The remainder constituted the historical database (training set). The final distribution of the records is shown in Table 1.

Then a vector was created for further analysis containing thirteen values including: Question#, Pitch (max,min,median,mean std_dev) in Hz, Energy (max,min, median,mean std_dev) in Db, Survey Score, Category (scale), Patient Id.

The max, min, median, mean, and standard deviation of both pitch (fundamental frequency) and energy of the sound wave were chosen because they offered the best chance to identify emotional content in voice [2]. A complete case then consists of twenty vectors, one for each question in the survey. A case example follows (pitch statistics are measured in Hz and energy statistics are measured in Db).

	Pitch Statistics					Energy Statistics							
Q#	Max	Min	Med	Mean	StdD	Max	Min	Med	Mean	StdD	Score	Cat	Id
1	146	55	130	114.9	30.9	77.0	32.4	59.8	60.6	10.1	16	2	g13

⋮

	Pitch Statistics					Energy Statistics							
Q#	Max	Min	Med	Mean	StdD	Max	Min	Med	Mean	StdD	Score	Cat	Id
20	302	65	160	161.4	55.8	79.0	45.3	66.8	66.3	7.9	16	2	g13

Because of the differences in the identification performance between male and female voices shown in the Introduction section, we postulated that there was also likely to be a vocal distinction between native Spanish and English speakers. The rhythms and syllable stress patterns are two such language distinctions. Therefore, each case was placed into one of four similar groups, as determined by the gender of the speaker and the language spoken (English or Spanish).

For this reason, all of the historical cases were stored in knowledge databases grouped by language and gender; English speaking female, English speaking male, Spanish speaking female, and Spanish speaking male.

Although the basic concept behind case-based reasoning is using the specific to extrapolate a solution for another specific, some generalization techniques have been successfully applied in a case-based reasoning context [6]. Therefore, in addition to examining the twenty vectors that come from a patient's response to the CES-D questionnaire, we also made a more general voice analysis. Instead of twenty separate vectors, the statistical waveform data was combined into a single twelve-feature vector for each patient including.

Pitch(max,min,median,mean std_dev of means of individual questions, and avg std dev of individual std dev) in Hz
Energy (max,min,median,mean std_dev of means of individual questions, and avg std dev of individual std devs) in Db
Survey Score, Category (scale), Patient Id

An example of a single-vector case for Patient d28 with Score = 42, Category = 3 is shown below.

Pitch Statistics						Energy Statistics					
Max	Min	Med	Mean	StdD	Avg StdD	Max	Min	Med	Mean	StdD	Avg StdD
442	50	204	179.41	31.87	48.40	99.98	31.57	79.56	78.19	3.43	9.1

2.2 Scale

The classification of the historical cases and the correctness of the test cases classification was determined by the score given in the original VIDAS study. The score is a numerical value, which, if above certain threshold, indicates "symptoms of severe depression". The original threshold as defined by the CES-D questionnaire was 15; any score above 15 indicates severe depression. However the researchers involved in the depression study considered this as an oversimplification of the diagnosis process. That is, there was a "gray area" within the scale depending on social, cultural, and economic circumstances. Based upon the new scale, the scores were divided into three categories: 1) 0-15 no symptoms of depression, 2) 16-24 further evaluation necessary, 3) > 24 severe symptoms of depression.

Every case was assigned a category value based upon the patient's score. The category was used as the means by which the classification results were evaluated.

3 Reasoning and Retrieval

In this section we discuss the implementation of the case-based reasoning system. Since our problem is a classification problem we applied both exemplar and instance approaches [8], which have been identified by Aamodt and Plaza [5] as being appropriate for this type of examination.

In a case-based reasoning system, a test case is input to the reasoner, the reasoner retrieves cases from the database for further analysis to suggest a solution. The exemplar approach retrieves from the historical database the case that most closely resembles the test case. This case is then offered as a solution. Application of the exemplar approach in our work consisted of comparing cases feature by feature and calculating a difference as a percentage. Such percentage was then used to select the case that most closely resembled the given test case. The case with the least percentage difference was returned as the solution.

The instance approach examines the historical database and returns a selection of cases meeting specific requirements based upon predefined metrics. In our work, the metric range is based upon the standard deviation of each feature category per question within each language category and depression group. The selection of historical cases returned is then used by the case-based reasoner to suggest a solution based upon the most popular solution therein. The popular solution is the one that occurs most often within the returned historical cases. If cases have been retrieved, but no majority vote is obtained, i.e., a tie occurs, a secondary evaluation is performed on the cases retrieved. If no cases are retrieved, an error condition is returned. For our implementation, the exemplar approach was applied as the secondary evaluation.

Given that our research is focused on the initial possibility of building useful cases for depression assessment with waveform analysis statistics, error conditions do not prevent the successful classification of new cases. The exemplar and instance approaches perform better with larger databases [5], but due to the limited number of cases available with which to construct the historical databases we expected our system would return a certain number of results as the error condition.

3.1 Implementation

Our system for the twenty-vector implementation included four database files, four test case files, and four twenty-vector metric files, one for each language group. There was also a separate metric file that contained all four language group single-vector metrics. The system generated four output files: a temporary storage file and three results files. The former was created for the cases retrieved in the instance approach. The latter included one file for the exemplar approach results, and two for the instance approach results. Of the two instance approach results files, one was for the twenty-vector cases with the twenty-vector metric and the other was for the twenty-vector cases with the single-vector metric. The solution for the most similar case in the exemplar approach was stored within the program variables.

The single-vector implementation included a historical database file and test case file for each language group; a single metric file contained all four language group single-vector metrics. Three output files were created, one temporary storage file for the instance approach, and two result files,one for the exemplar approach results and one for the instance approach results.

The results files for both the exemplar and the instance implementations contained the score assigned by VIDAS and the depression category recommended by the case-based reasoning system for each patient in the test groups. We analyzed these results and calculated the percentages of correct classification presented in the Experimental Results section.

3.2 Evaluation

The basis for evaluation of emotion on voice research is human recognition rates (see Introduction section). human subjects were able to correctly identify emotion present in both real and laboratory recordings about 70% of the time. The goal of most automated systems is to emulate their human equivalent. However, assessment of depression is a complex task involving many tools, and expert knowledge. The goal of the work presented was to explore the possibility of developing a new tool to aid in depression assessment by analyzing the patient's voice. We have not found a baseline for comparing and evaluating our results. Thus, patterns and consistencies in the classification rates, and performance above random classification are used to evaluate the success of our hypothesis. By assigning depression categories at random in the original scale, 1 or 2, the probability of correct classification is 50%. In using the new scale a random assignment of one of these scores to a patient would give a probability of 33% correct classification rate.

4 Experimental Results

In this section we describe in detail experiments using the exemplar and instance approaches.

Table 2. Multiple result solution

Percentage Difference	Patient Id	Solution Category
145.97	A24	3
145.97	P06	3
145.97	D17	2
	Majority Solution:	**3**

4.1 Exemplar Approach

The exemplar approach [5] compares the input, i.e., the unclassified test case, with the historical cases in the database. The historical case that most closely matches the test case is returned as the solution, i.e., output. The unclassified patient's statistical vector is compared element by element to each case, represented as a vector, in the database. The percentage difference between the two vectors is then evaluated to identify the most similar case(s). This is the similarity measure utilized in our experiments for both the twenty-vector cases and the single-vector cases. The category of the historical case with the lowest percentage difference with the test case is returned. This approach always returns at least one result. If multiple historical cases are returned, a majority vote is taken. For instance, Table 2 shows the results of comparing the vector representing the test case for patient A70 with the cases, represented as vectors, in the training set.

The historical cases, i.e., vectors for patient A24, patient P06, and patient D17 were returned as the nearest matches. All of them with the same percentage difference 145.9 with respect to the test case vector representing patient A70. The most popular solution category among those returned, in this case “3”, is offered as the classification solution to the test case. If the majority vote is inconclusive, then the case is determined to be inconclusive.

Results Exemplar Approach. Tests were run on 11 test cases represented as single-vectors and represented as twenty-vectors. Single-vector twelve-feature cases are the result of combining the twenty sets of feature statistics into a single set (see Case Structure subsection above), while attempting to preserve the integrity of the original cases. Max and min remained true by selecting the absolute max and min of each feature. Median and mean were altered slightly by taking the median and mean of each category, the results show that the difference would ultimately be statistically insignificant. Combining the standard deviation information proved to be more complex. We took the standard deviation of the mean category as well as the average of the origianl generated standard deviations. The salience of each of these methods was evaluated by comparing these results to one another.

The results obtained for both the twenty-vector cases and the single-vector representation show that using the original scale resulted in the best performance, while explorations of the standard deviation features proved inconclusive. The latter present no definite trend in either the positive or negative direction.

Table 3. Correct classification results

Twenty-Vector Cases			Combination Single-Vector Cases					
			All Stats		Avg StdD		StdD Mean	
Scale:	Original	New	Original	New	Original	New	Original	New
English Female	72.73%	45.45%	72.73%	36.36%	63.64%	45.45%	54.55%	18.18%
English Male	54.55%	36.36%	45.45%	36.36%	45.45%	27.27%	45.45%	27.27%
Spanish Female	45.45%	45.45%	72.73%	63.64%	45.45%	27.27%	54.55%	36.36%
Spanish Male	54.55%	45.45%	54.55%	27.27%	72.73%	36.36%	63.64%	27.27%

The original scale achieved or surpassed the random classification rate of 50% in 69% of the tests. Using the new scale, classification scales above the random 33% rate were achieved 63% of the time. The correct classification of the test cases, i.e., new instances of patient sound data for the twenty-vector and single-vector representations are presented in Table 3.

4.2 Instance Approach

We used the same test cases and historical database as the exemplar approach, so that direct comparison of the results can be made. The test cases were inputted into the system one at a time, then compared element by element to each case of the historical database. All cases that matched the test case within a specified range for each element, called a metric (cf. similarity measure), were set aside for further processing. Once all cases in the historical database were compared, the reasoner looked for the majority category from those cases it previously set aside. If a majority was found then it was the recommended solution. If no majority was found, the exemplar approach was applied to the cases that were set aside. If no cases were set aside an error was returned.

Results Instance Approach. Two metrics were developed for use with this approach, a twenty-vector ten-feature metric and a single-vector twelve-feature metric. For the twenty-vector metric, the historical database questions were grouped according to language category, depression category, and question number. Then the standard deviation was calculated for each feature in these groups, resulting in three metric values for each question in each depression and language category. As no clear pattern emerged from these data, the median was chosen as the initial metric range. This resulted in a twenty-vector metric with a range for every element in the twenty-vector case. Partial twenty-vector metric statistics for the English Speaking Female group are presented in Table 4 that shows Q# the question number, cat the depression category, and the pitch and energy statistics, bold indicates the ranges selected. The same method was applied to the single-vector representation.

Overall, using the original scale resulted in the best performance, while explorations of the standard deviation features proved inconclusive, presenting no definite trend in either the positive or negative direction. The original scale achieved or surpassed the random classification rate of 50% in 70% of the tests.

Table 4. Partial statistics English Speaking Female group

		Pitch Statistics					Energy Statistics				
Q#	Grp	Max	Min	Med	Mean	StdD	Max	Min	Med	Mean	StdD
1	1	98.73	**41.90**	39.97	40.09	23.93	**5.12**	8.65	5.87	**5.46**	1.68
1	2	**103.32**	33.63	53.70	25.99	35.97	9.07	10.23	12.32	11.06	**1.76**
1	3	105.08	42.50	**44.68**	**36.31**	**30.85**	4.87	**9.81**	**6.71**	5.45	2.5
2	1	99.19	56.22	29.40	**35.19**	**27.11**	5.14	6.70	**5.58**	4.96	2.04
2	2	111.25	16.70	62.95	52.27	25.05	9.16	**6.91**	7.58	8.26	2.47
2	3	**105.09**	**40.50**	**38.94**	27.67	33.39	**5.85**	8.04	5.53	**5.47**	**2.16**
3	1	**103.07**	**48.43**	41.47	36.44	28.04	4.51	7.04	5.56	5.08	1.54
3	2	117.09	33.91	49.54	33.34	34.25	8.73	12.68	10.38	10.27	**1.88**
3	3	101.87	55.88	**42.28**	**34.35**	**32.23**	**5.21**	**8.92**	**6.18**	**5.94**	2.06

Table 5. Correct classification results original and new scale

	Twenty-Vector Cases									
Original	Scale					New	Scale			
	median stdD	std Dev/2	std Dev/4	sqrt (stdD)	ln (stdD)	stdD stdD	Dev/2 Dev/2	Dev/4 Dev/4	(stdD) (stdD)	(stdD) (stdD)
Eng. Female	72.7%	63.6%	45.4%	27.2%	36.3%	45.4%	45.4%	18.1%	27.2%	9.0%
Eng. Male	81.8%	72.7%	54.5%	63.6%	63.6%	54.5%	45.4%	36.3%	54.5%	45.4%
Span. Female	45.4%	54.5%	45.4%	63.6%	54.5%	27.2%	45.4%	45.4%	54.5%	54.5%
Span. Male	72.7%	72.7%	72.7%	45.4%	54.5%	45.4%	45.4%	45.4%	45.4%	36.3%

Using the new scale, classification rates above the random 33% rate were achieved 80% of the time. The correct classification of test cases for the twenty-vector test case using the original and the new scale is shown in Table 5.

The reasoner failed to return a result in 20% for sqrt(stdD) and in 34% for ln(stdD) of the total test cases. These errors will likely be reduced or eliminated by expanding the historical database.

5 Discussion

In all the tests performed the original scale was shown to consistently have performed better, which was not surprising given the richness in the categories. Exploration of the metric range proved very helpful. The original application of the median standard deviation with each field proved to be too broad. In the case of the single-vector combination cases, the solution returned was often simply the majority solution with the database. The narrowing of the scope of the metric provided mixed results. Using the twenty-vector cases, narrowing the scope caused a decrease in the classification rate of the English Female group, and an increase in the Spanish Female group. The rates of the English Male and Spanish male groups remained relatively steady. Using the combination, or single-vector cases, a slight increase was observed in the English Female and Spanish Female groups. The others, remained steady. The scores using the twenty-vector metrics were generally higher in both the exemplar and instance approach. However, some difficulty arises from the lack of general trend or pattern in them. A first approach to exploring the problem further would be to evaluate these cases with a larger knowledge base as a possible source for these difficulties may be due to the sample size.

While the results were lower with the combination statistics, than with the twenty-vector statistics, a potentially constructive pattern did emerge. With the Instance approach, the English speaking female data was consistently classified at better rate than the other language groups. This could be attributed, in part, to having more of these cases in the database, which is consistent with the original description of the Instance approach; as it is intended for use with a large knowledge base. It remains to be tested whether increasing the size of the knowledge base will in fact increase the positive classification rate.

We can conclude from the experiments carried out that the construction of cases using sound waveform statistics can be utilized by a case based reasoner to classify new instances correctly in clinical assessment, increasing the knowledge base should increase the successful classification rate. Further experiments using speech data in other domains would allow us to determine whether the approach described is general enough.

References

1. Lee, C.M., Narayanan, S.S., Pieraccini,R.: Combining Acoustic and Language Information for Emotion Recognition In *Proceedings of the International Conference on Spoken Language Processing*, 2002.
2. Polzin, T., Waibel, A.: Emotion-sensitive human-computer interfaces *SpeechEmotion*, 201-206, 2000.
3. Yacoub, S., Simske, S., Lin, X., Burns, J.: Recognition of Emotions in Interactive Voice Response Systems *Proceedings of 8th European Conference on Speech Communication and Technology*, Geneva, Switzerland, 2003.
4. Gonzalez, G. Voice Interactive Depression Assessment Study (VIDAS), 2003, URL *http://www.csusm.edu/obrt.*
5. Aamodt, A., Plaza, E. Case-Based Reasoning Foundational Issues, Methodological Variations, and Systems Approaches, *AI Communications*, **7**(1):39-59, 1994.
6. Schmidt, R., Gierl, L. Prototypes for Medical Case-Based Reasoning Systems *Proceedings of the 20th Annual Conference of the International Society for Clinical Biostatistics*, Munich, Germany, 1999.
7. Schwartz, A.B., Martins, A., Barcia, R.M., Lee, R.W. PSIQ-A CBR Approach to the Mental Health Area *Fifth German Workshop on Case-Based Reasoning: Foundations, Systems and Applications*, Kaiserslautern, 217-224, 1997.
8. Aha, D., Kibler, D., Alert, M. Instance-based learning algorithms *Machine Learning*, **6**(1):37-66, 1991.
9. Leake, D.B., Leake. *Case-Based Reasoning: Experiences, Lessons, & Future Directions* AAAI Press, Menlo Park, CA, 1996.
10. SFSWin, URL *http://www.phon.ucl.ac.uk/resource/sfs,*

Feature-Table-Based Automatic Question Generation for Tree-Based State Tying: A Practical Implementation

Supphanat Kanokphara and Julie Carson-Berndsen

Department of Computer Science,
University College Dublin,
Ireland
{supphanat.kanokphara, julie.berndsen}@ucd.ie

Abstract. This paper presents a system for automatically generating linguistic questions based on a feature table. Such questions are an essential input for tree-based state tying, a technique which is widely used in speech recognition. In general, in order to utilize this technique, linguistic (or more accurately phonetic) questions have to be carefully defined. This may be extremely time consuming and require a considerable amount of resources. The system proposed in this paper provides a more elegant and efficient way to generate a set of questions from a simple feature table of the type employed in phonetic studies.

1 Introduction

Tree-based state tying technique is widely used to cluster HMM states into classes and tie all states in the same class in order to reduce the data sparseness problem [1]. The requirement for this technique is only a set of phonetic questions. While this strategy is good, poorly-defined phonetic questions may lead to lower accuracy in the resulting system. In order to use this approach to its full advantage, the phonetic questions must be defined by an expert who is familiar with the units and has a strong linguistic background. This may slow down the implementation of speech recognition systems since manual definition of phonetic questions is a time consuming task and, unless the data is thoroughly cross-checked, may be inconsistent and contain errors which may lead to degradation in the system.

Many researchers aware of this problem and have investigated alternative ways to generate questions automatically without any human intervention [2], [3]. The basic idea is to determine phone classes according to the database in a data-driven manner. However, the disadvantage of a data-driven approach is they might generate poor quality questions if the corpus is not of an appropriate quality.

To deal with the shortcomings of the manual and data-driven approaches simultaneously, we suggest a separation of the question generation procedure into 2 different steps, namely *feature tagging* and *feature co-occurrence tagging*. Feature tagging is the process of examining the relationship between a unit (in this case, phone) and its corresponding features. This process has two possible outputs: classes of units defined

M. Ali and F. Esposito (Eds.): IEA/AIE 2005, LNAI 3533, pp. 95 – 97, 2005.

according to their features or units tagged with their respective features. Feature co-occurrence tagging is the process of examining how features overlap (or co-occur) and defining classes of units which model the co-occurring features. For example, in English, a lip rounding feature can co-occur with a vocalic manner feature but not with a stop manner feature. The feature co-occurrence tagging step is carried out automatically given the tagged feature set. By doing this, the requirement for linguistic experts for phonetic questions is certainly reduced; in some cases the linguistic expert may not even be necessary because feature tagging is quite common in linguistics and thus tagged feature sets are already available for many languages in the form of feature tables [4], [5]. This novel approach addresses the shortcomings mentioned above since feature tagging is based entirely on linguistic knowledge and hence robust to bad quality corpora.

2 Feature-Table-Based Automatic Question Generation

Due to space limitations, the algorithm will not be fully explained here but interested reader can find it from [6]. In [6], we generate all possible feature co-occurrence classes and prune linguistically ill-formed classes later. This is considered to be computational inefficiency because many linguistically ill-formed classes have to be constructed. In this paper, we introduce another tree-based clustering to generate feature co-occurrence classes. This allows us to prune out some classes while they are constructed. Moreover, when a node is pruned, its entire child nodes are also pruned thus reducing system complexity.

The tree is constructed in a left-to-right, top-down fashion. All of the nodes on a particular level are expanded before moving down to the next level. For the purposes of this paper, we assume that each node of a decision tree is a feature co-occurrence class and every leaf node is a linguistically well-formed class. The depth of a tree is equal to the number of tiers (i.e. a particular level in the tree represents a specific tier) and the number of branches for each node is equal to the number of features on the next tier. The tree expansion continues until tier N is reached and nodes which remain at tier N are assumed to be linguistically well-formed classes.

It is important to note that this tree is not the same as tree-based state clustering. Tree-based state clustering forms a phone set according to the probability score and a question at each node is chosen in maximum likelihood sense. Our tree clusters a phone set orderly according to a feature table. In tree-based state tying, a question (phone class) for a child node is a subset of its parent node question, i.e. liquid → l, etc. In our system, a phone class of a node does not have to be a subset of its parent node. This allows our tree to construct feature co-occurrence phone class automatically.

Actually, the phone recognition results from the algorithm in this paper and [6] are the same. The difference is just time for building phonetic questions. Phonetic questions can be constructed much faster than the ones in [6]. Therefore, we expanded our feature table to include gender tier. With this gender tier, we can expand our acoustic model to be gender-dependent. This increases phone recognition accuracy from 71.14% to 72.49%.

3 Conclusion

This paper has proposed a novel way to generate a set of questions for tree-based state tying. This strategy requires only a simple feature table which is likely to available in many languages since these are commonly used for phonetic and phonological studies. This system is very convenient where a speech recognition system has to be developed.

Since an extra tree clustering is introduced in this paper, phonetic questions can be generated faster and more efficient. This allows us to include gender information in our feature table and model gender-dependent acoustic model. This gender-dependent model and our phonetic questions show better phone recognition accuracy.

Acknowledgements

This material is based upon works supported by the Science Foundation Ireland for the support under Grant No. 02/IN1/I100. The opinions, findings and conclusions or recommendations expressed in this material are those of the authors and do not necessarily reflect the views of Science Foundation Ireland.

We also would like to thank Dr. Lorraine McGinty for AI aspect discussion and Mr. Moritz Neugebauer for reviewing our paper.

References

1. Odell, J.J.: The Use of Context in Large Vocabulary Speech Recognition. Ph.D. Thesis. Cambridge University, Cambridge (1995)
2. Beulen K., Ney H.: Automatic Question Generation for Decision Tree Based State Tying. in Proc. Int. Conf. Acoust., Speech, Signal Processing, Vol. 2 (1988) 805-809
3. Singh, R., Raj, B., Stern, R. M.: Automatic Clustering and Generation of Contextual Questions for Tied States in Hidden Markov Models. in Proc. Int. Conf. on Spoken Language Processing. Vol. 1 (1999) 117-120
4. Geumann, A.: Towards a New Level of Annotation Detail of Multilingual Speech Corpora. in Proc. Int. Conf. on Spoken Language Processing. (2004)
5. Luksaneeyanawin, S.: Speech Computing and Speech Technology in Thailand. in Proc. The Symposium on Natural Language Processing. (1993) 276-321
6. Kanokphara, S., Geumann, A.,Carson-Berndsen, J.: Accessing Language Specific Linguistic Information for Triphone Model Generation: Feature Tables in a Speech Recognition System. Submitted to 2nd Language & Technology Conference: Human Language Technologies as a Challenge for Computer Science and Linguistics. (2005).

Speeding Up Dynamic Search Methods in Speech Recognition

Gábor Gosztolya and András Kocsor

MTA-SZTE Research Group on Artificial Intelligence,
H-6720 Szeged, Aradi vértanúk tere 1., Hungary
{ggabor, kocsor}@inf.u-szeged.hu

Abstract. In speech recognition huge hypothesis spaces are generated. To overcome this problem dynamic programming can be used. In this paper we examine ways of speeding up this search process even more using heuristic search methods, multi-pass search and aggregation operators. The tests showed that these techniques can be applied together, and their combination could significantly speed up the recognition process. The run-times we obtained were 22 times faster than the basic dynamic search method, and 8 times faster than the multi-stack decoding method.

In speech recognition enormous hypothesis spaces arise. To handle them we can use dynamic programming, where we can avoid calculating the same values several times, which leads to a dramatic speed-up of a speech recognizer system. But this is not enough for real-world applications, hence we have to look for other ways of making improvements while preserving the recognition accuracy. Here we carry out experiments using search heuristics, aggregation operators and multi-pass search, and apply ideas for speeding up the heuristic search.

1 The Speech Recognition Problem

We have a speech signal given by a series of observations $A = a_1 \dots a_t$, and a set of phoneme sequences W. We look for the word $\hat{w} \in W = arg \max P(w|A)$ which, via Bayes' theorem, is equivalent to $\hat{w} = arg \max(P(A|w) \cdot P(w))/P(A)$. $P(A)$ is the same for all w, so $\hat{w} = arg \max P(A|w)P(w)$. Let w be $o_1 o_2 \dots o_n$, as o_j is the jth phoneme of w. Let $A_1, \dots, A_n$ be non-overlapping segments of A. We assume that the phonemes are independent, i.e. $P(A|w)$ can be obtained from $P(A_1|o_1), \dots, P(A_n|o_n)$. To calculate $P(A|w)$, we can use aggregation operators at two levels: g_1 supplies the $P(A_j|o_j)$ values as $g_1(P(a_{t_{j-1}}|o_j), \dots, P(a_{t_j}|o_j))$, while g_2 is used to construct $P(A|w)$ as $g_2(P(A_1|o_1), \dots, P(A_n|o_n))$.

Instead of a probability p we will use a cost $c = -ln\ p$. g_1 will be the addition operator. A *hypothesis* is a pair of phoneme series and segment series. The dynamic programming method uses a table with the a_i speech frames indexing the columns and the phoneme-sequences indexing the rows. A cell holds the lowest cost of the hypotheses having its phoneme-sequence and ending at its frame. To compute the value of a cell we take the value of an earlier frame and its

M. Ali and F. Esposito (Eds.): IEA/AIE 2005, LNAI 3533, pp. 98–100, 2005.

phoneme-sequence without its last phoneme, and add up the cost of this last phoneme on the interleaving frames. The result is the minimum of these sums.

2 Speeding Up the Recognition Process

The dynamic programming search technique, despite its effectiveness, tends to be quite slow. In this section we discuss some methods that speed it up while keeping the recognition accuracy at an acceptable rate.

Heuristic Search Methods. These techniques fill only a part of the table. So the result will not always be optimal, but we can get a notable speed-up with little or no loss in accuracy. The multi-stack decoding algorithm fills a fixed number (*stack size*) of cells (the ones with the lowest costs) for a row. The Viterbi beam search fills the cell with the best value, and the cells close to it defined by a *beam width* parameter. Here we used the multi-stack approach.

Speed-Up Improvements. In earlier works [1] we presented some speed-up ideas for the multi-stack decoding algorithm, which we also want to use here.

i) One possibility is to combine multi-stack decoding with a Viterbi beam search. At each column, belonging to one time instance, we fill only a fixed number of cells, and also discard those which are far from the best-scoring value.

ii) Another approach is based on the fact that the later the time instance, the fewer hypotheses (and filled cells) are need. Thus we filled $s \cdot m^i$ cells belonging to the a_i frame, where $0 < m < 1$ and s is the original *stack size* parameter.

iii) Actually, we need to fill more cells at those speech frames close to pronounced phoneme bounds. We trained an ANN to estimate whether a given time instance was a phoneme bound or not. Then we constructed a function that approximates the stack size based on the output of this ANN.

Multi-pass Search. Multi-pass methods work in several steps: in the first pass the worse hypotheses are discarded because of some condition requiring low computational time. We reduced the number of phoneme groups for this reason. In later passes only the remaining hypotheses are examined, but with a more detailed phoneme grouping. The last pass ($\mathcal{P}_0$) uses the original phoneme set. To create the phoneme-sets first a distance function of the original $ph_1, \ldots, ph_m$ phonemes is defined: $d(ph_i, ph_j)$ is based on the ratio of ph_i-s classified as ph_j and vice versa. We can use the higher value (d^1) or the average (d^2) as the metric. The distance between phoneme-groups can be the minimum distance between their phones ($\mathcal{D}_{min}$), or the maximum ($\mathcal{D}_{max}$) [2]. The recognition steps using the resulting phoneme-sets were $\mathcal{P}_1$ and $\mathcal{P}_2$.

3 Tests and Results

The train database consisted of 500 speakers, each uttering 10 sentences via telephone. In the test database the 431 speakers uttered the name of a town.

Table 1. Recognition results. The basic dynamic search method resulted in 431,607.07 phoneme-identifications, while the Viterbi beam search produced 131,791.63

Phoneme group		$\mathcal{P}_0$	$\mathcal{P}_1$	$\mathcal{P}_2$	–	i	iii	ii
standard		•	○	○	169,330.43	72,199.19	58,735.97	55,702.61
d^1	$\mathcal{D}_{min}$	•	•	○	110,300.97	32,382.85	30,727.94	30,103.32
		•	○	•	–	–	–	–
		•	•	•	–	–	–	–
	$\mathcal{D}_{max}$	•	•	○	111,047.41	26,591.38	20,769.16	**19,306.91**
		•	○	•	135,975.42	62,053.11	53,021.70	51,019.48
		•	•	•	170,505.40	70,249.03	61,114.36	59,737.51
d^2	$\mathcal{D}_{min}$	•	•	○	111,042.23	26,920.40	20,857.46	19,327.69
		•	○	•	–	–	–	–
		•	•	•	–	–	–	–
	$\mathcal{D}_{max}$	•	•	○	91,889.07	47,328.51	38,515.23	36,914.01
		•	○	•	217,525.55	98,423.11	78,825.82	76,961.10
		•	•	•	216,652.05	107,467.50	88,106.10	87,416.17

(Column groups: Passes = $\mathcal{P}_0$, $\mathcal{P}_1$, $\mathcal{P}_2$; Used Improvements = –, i, iii, ii.)

The *HTK* system [3] yielded 92.11% here. We first improved the recognition rate with aggregation operators [1], then the multi-stack decoding algorithm was used with the lowest stack size that kept the optimal accuracy. Next, multi-pass tests were applied. After we used the speed-ups in the sequence described in [1]. The speed of a configuration was the lowest one with accuracy above 92%, and was measured in average phoneme-identifications normalized to the last pass. We see that only those multi-pass configurations including $\mathcal{P}_2$ were unsuccessful. Using both the multi-stack decoding algorithm and the Viterbi beam search (improvement i) resulted in a 48-76% reduction in running times. Improvement iii reduced running times by 20%, and improvement ii also produced a slight speed-up.

4 Conclusion

In this paper we examined a dynamic search method, and some ways of speeding up this search process. We employed several tools like heuristic search, aggregation operators, multi-pass search and other ideas, which resulted in a dramatic speed-up with the same level of accuracy. In the end our method proved to be 22 times faster than the dynamic search algorithm, 6 times than the Viterbi beam search, and 8 times faster than the multi-stack decoding method.

References

1. G. Gosztolya, A. Kocsor, *Aggregation Operators and Hypothesis Space Reductions in Speech Recognition,* Proc. of TSD, LNAI 3206, pp. 315-322, Springer, 2004.
2. G. Gosztolya, A. Kocsor, *A Hierarchical Evaluation Methodology in Speech Recognition,* Submitted to Acta Cybernetica, 2004.
3. S. Young et al., *The HMM Toolkit (HTK) (software and manual),* http://htk.eng.cam.ac.uk/

Conscious Robot That Distinguishes Between Self and Others and Implements Imitation Behavior

Tohru Suzuki, Keita Inaba, and Junichi Takeno

Department of Computer Science , Meiji University,
1-1-1 Higashimita , Tama-ku , Kawasaki-shi , Kanagawa , Japan
{t_suzuki, keita2, takeno}@cs.meiji.ac.jp

Abstract. This paper presents a clear-cut definition of consciousness of humans, consciousness of self in particular. The definition "Consistency of cognition and behavior generates consciousness" explains almost all conscious behaviors of humans. A "consciousness system" was conceived based on this definition and actually constructed with recurrent neural networks. We succeeded in implementing imitation behavior, which we believe is closely related to consciousness, by applying the consciousness system to a robot.

1 Introduction

Consciousness is currently studied in many areas of neuroscience, psychology, philosophy, etc. In the robot area, in particular, where these studies are integrated, a revolution is imminent in the research of consciousness.

J. Tani and his colleagues at RIKEN, who are engaged in the study of self and consciousness of self, contrived a system for understanding and forecasting the environment[1]. Y. Nakamura and his team at the University of Tokyo implement imitation behavior using a humanoid robot of the Hidden Markov Model[2].

The humanoid robot DB of M. Kawato and his colleagues at ATR acquires specific behaviors through learning by imitation[3]. And also, A.Billard conducted an experiment about imitative robot by DRAMA system. But he did not explain the relation between imitation behavior and consciousness[4].

Consciousness and imitation are actively studied in robotics but no paper has ever presented a good model explaining human consciousness. This paper presents a new definition of consciousness and shows the validity of our theory. We devised a consciousness-generating model based on the new definition and conducted experiments in which the robots implement imitation behavior using the model.

The next chapter introduces the consciousness system and explains why it is necessary for the consciousness model to implement imitation behavior.

2 General Description of the Consciousness System

2.1 Definition of Consciousness and the System

Consciousness is basically a state in which the behavior of self and others is understood. The behavior resultant from cognition is a part of consciousness.

M. Ali and F. Esposito (Eds.): IEA/AIE 2005, LNAI 3533, pp. 101 – 110, 2005.

We therefore define consciousness as being generated by consistency of cognition and behavior. Consciousness system is defined as the system for generating consciousness. Figure 1 shows a model diagram of the consciousness system that we propose. This chapter describes the structure of the consciousness system, compares it with conventional cognition and behavior systems and demonstrates the validity of the definition.

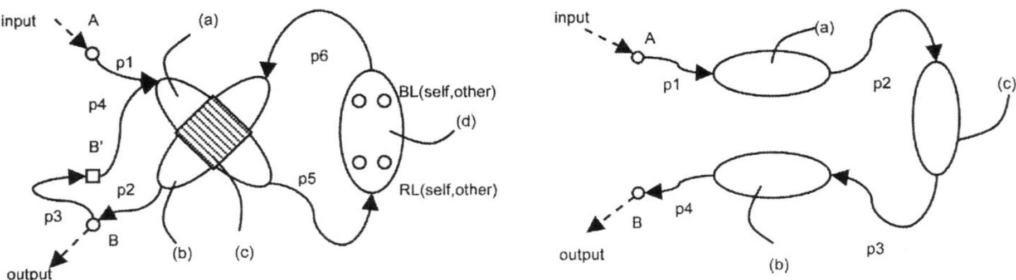

Fig. 1. Model of Consciousness System

Fig. 2. Mechatronics Model

2.2 Structure of the Consciousness System

In Fig. 1, the consciousness system comprises (a) cognition system, (b) behavior system, (c) primary representation, a common area for the cognition and behavior system, and (d) symbolic representation, (A) input and (B) output.

Cognition. External information enters the consciousness system at Input (A), passes p1 and reaches the Cognition System (a). This information, together with the information from BL of Symbolic Representation (internal information) derived from p6, is used for neural computation. The derived information is transmitted to RL of symbolic representation via p5. When BL and RL are in agreement, we define the system as being cognizant of the condition existent on the symbolic representation.

RL is a language label for cognized information. BL is dependent on RL and internal energy (internal information such as Kansei). BL is a language label for the next-expected behavior. The language labels of symbolic representation have different areas for understanding the condition of self and others. Accordingly, this consciousness system will distinguish between self and others.

Self and others are given externally to the consciousness system by supervised learning to facilitate understanding of the experiments. These functions may be generated internally by self-organization in the future.

Behavior. The behavior information from BL passes to the Behavior System (b) via p6. This information is added to input information and somatosensory information from p1 and p4 by neural computation. The resultant information is transmitted to Output (B) via p2 to implement a behavior.

Common. The primary representation, the common area for the cognition and behavior system, is the most important feature of the information flow in our consciousness system. The presence of the primary representation allows behavior learning during cognition and, conversely, cognition learning during behavior. The primary representation contains information on both cognition and behavior and each piece of information is correctly related to language labels of symbolic representation. Accordingly, the consciousness system brings a process of artificial thoughts as the process of information circulation through p5 and p6. That is, even in the absence of an input, the language labels can be triggered through the circulation route of p5 and p6. The circulation further allows the consciousness system to have expectations. For example, when information arrives from a language label of symbolic representation to primary representation via p6, information on cognition and behavior relevant to the language label is obtained. This information is considered an expectation because it refers to cognition and behavior of the next-arriving time.

Lastly, Output B is copied to B' via p3. Output B' enters the cognition system via p4, then the somatic sensation of self is used for cognition.

Example. The above information flow is explained below using the human language function as an example. Assume a conversation between self and other. The input hears the speech of both self and the other, cognizing that self and the other are talking. The symbolic language label behaves as such. Somatic sensation that self is talking (known from the motion of the lips, etc.) is fed back as input. This helps in the cognition that self is talking. Behavior of a new language label triggered by the p4-p5 circulation route gives rise to conversation through thinking and expectations. It may even be possible to offer new topics for conversation.

2.3 Comparison with Mechatronics Model

Conventional artificial intelligence and robots capable of cognition and behavior are mostly mechatronics models, such as that shown in Fig. 2. A mechatronics model comprises cognition system (a), behavior system (b), decision system (c), input (A) and output (B). Information from the input runs through p1, (a), p2, (c), p3, (b) and p4, eventually reaching the output. This means that cognition and behavior are implemented serially; there is no area similar to primary representation (d) of the consciousness system that we propose. Consistency of cognition and behavior is totally missing. The critical default of these behaviorist models is the complete inability to explain human consciousness. Imitation is impossible due to the lack of a common area for cognition and behavior. Absence of circulation routes makes it impossible for the robot to think and expect.

Our consciousness system provides for feedback of somatic sensation, and is better than mechatronics models just considering the cognition aspect alone.

2.4 Related Cases About Imitation

The consciousness system that we propose is superior to conventional mechatronics models in various aspects with regard to human consciousness as described above. We define consciousness as being born from consistency of cognition and behavior. Man has developed, evolved and generated consciousness through imitation behaviors as attested to by the various events introduced below.

2.4.1 Mirror Neuron

Mirror neurons are a special type of neuron discovered by Prof. G. Rizzolatti at the University of Parma, Italy, in the brain of monkeys[5]. The neuron fires when implementing a certain behavior by itself. It also fires upon observing others with the same behavior. This unique function is not limited to monkeys but exists in the human brain as well. This discovery led us to generating the new paradigm of "Consistency of Cognition and Behavior".

The primary representation in our consciousness system is the common area for cognition and behavior, which is equivalent to the mirror neuron. It is possible in our consciousness system to cognize the behavior of others and to learn it as our own behavior, or to imitate, because of the presence of this primary representation.

2.4.2 Mimesis Theory

From the mimesis theory, our ancestors must have existed without communication through language[6]. It is generally accepted that imitation was used as a means of communication. We call this mimesis communication, which is an information processing function to arbitrarily generate and cognize signals. To serve the purpose, people used their own and other people's bodies and the brain, as well as models of the external world to circulate information interactively.

In our consciousness system, imitation occurs while information circulates through primary and symbolic representation. The primary representation includes information derived from the cognition system and behavior system. This means that external information is integrated in the primary representation. The symbolic representation turns the external information into language labels. As previously stated, circulation of information through external models and one's own brain is necessary in mimesis communication. Circulation of information in primary and symbolic representation in our consciousness system is equivalent to this circulation of information in mimesis communication. Validity of our consciousness system can thus be shown by this mimesis theory.

2.5 Conclusion on Definition of Consciousness

The above discussion leads to the fact that imitation is an act of consistent cognition and behavior. It is also necessary that self and others be distinguished. Imitation means cognizing a behavior of others and instantly transferring it to self. Imitation is a function for understanding the conditions of self and others and cleverly integrating them. This is the source of consciousness. We therefore define that consciousness is born from consistency of cognition and behavior.

It is important, as the first stage of the study of consciousness, to distinguish between self and others and implement imitation behavior in the consciousness system. We believe that artificial consciousness shall be generated in a robot by further developing the consciousness system.

The following chapters describe learning in an actually constructed consciousness system and the experiments on imitation by robots using the consciousness system.

3 Learning in the Consciousness System

3.1 Purpose

In the experiment on imitation behavior, two robots learn imitation behavior through simulation on a PC using the consciousness system that we propose. The consciousness system is prepared in C language. It is a kind of recurrent neural network (Fig. 3). This chapter provides a detailed description of NN, a brief description of the flow of learning and the results of learning.

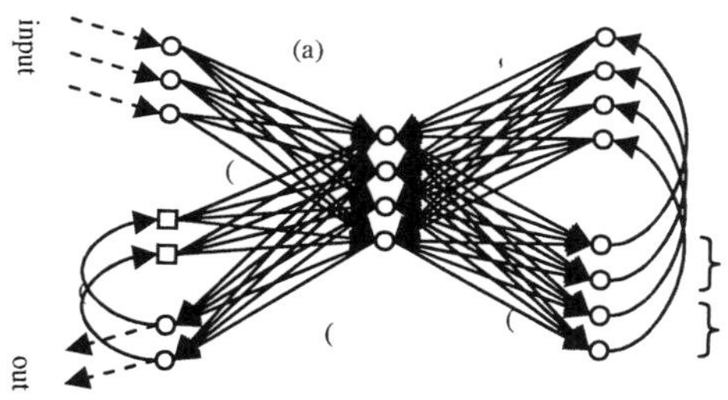

Fig. 3. NN of Consciousness System

3.2 Features of NN in the Consciousness System

NN has two structural features to implement consistency of cognition and behavior. One is recursiveness in which output M is copied to M' and returns to the circuit. Somatic sensation of behavior of self is fed back to enhance learning efficiency. The other feature is the presence of a common area (H) for cognition and behavior and data circulation through the circuit of H, (e), R, (f), B, (g) and H. This allows imitation learning and cognition of behavior of self and others at R.

3.3 Structure of NN in the Consciousness System

Sensor (S) is the input. There are five input patterns. Bit strings corresponding to patterns are written in S. The five patterns are:

(1) One of the two robots advances and approaches the other (001),
(2) Both advance (000),
(3) Both stop (010),
(4) One of the two robots backs up and moves away from the other (100), and
(5) Both back up and move away(111).

These five patterns were selected because the differential value of the quantity of reflected light on the IR sensor of the robot differs in these cases. Bit strings corresponding to the level of differential value measured by the IR sensor are input to NN.

The output is M (motor). The bit strings that correspond to advance(00), stop(01) and back up(11) are written. The value of output M is instantly copied to M'.

R receives the bit strings that correspond to the behavior of self and others(advance (00), stop(01) and back up(11)) that are neural-computed by S, M' and B. R has 4 bits. Two bits at r1 indicate behavior of self. The other two at r2 indicate behavior of others (Fig. 3). The B-value dictates the command for the next behavior from other superior consciousness system in the other cases. Naturally, S, M, R and B can be as interface channels of to the other consciousness systems for the purpose of making more complicated conscious system. It determines the next behavior to happen. To implement imitation behavior in this case, the R-value is copied to B. H is an intermediate layer for data circulation and is responsible for consistency of cognition and behavior.

3.4 Flow of Information in the Consciousness System

The flow of data in NN of the consciousness system is described below.

Bit strings of S, M' and B run the route of (a), (d) and (g), respectively, and the value of H is calculated. H follows the route of (b) and (e) and the values of M and R are calculated, respectively. Imitation behavior M is determined and implemented based on sensor value S (differentiated value), M' (condition of behavior of self) and B (condition of self and others cognized the previous time). This is equal to cognition of condition R of self and others at the present time. Lastly, the value M is copied to M' via (c) and R is copied to B via (f). Repeating this data flow, the consciousness system implements imitation behavior.

3.5 Learning Method of NN

Options for imitation learning by robots in the simulation were limited to three kinds of behavior: advance, stop and back up. This limitation was necessary because the small robot Khepera II report, to be actually used in the post-simulation experiment, has limited performance. The measuring range of the IR sensor built into Khepera II is approximately 5 cm; complex motion is difficult for detection. Imitation behaviors of advance, stop and back up, which are considered relatively simple, were selected for simulation.

The back up propagation (BP) method of supervised learning was used for NN learning through simulation. The weight of each arc was corrected by repeated learning until the error value was less than 0.01.

3.6 Result of Learning and Observations

Learning was actually conducted. Error convergence is shown in Fig. 4.

Both error_M (errors of M) and error_R (errors of R) converge when the order (number of learning) reached approximately 400. This convergence with a relatively small order attests to the good NN learning efficiency of the consciousness system, assisted by a small number of patterns in learning and a low error threshold value (0.01 or less).

Errors converged after approximately 40,000 times in a simulation with an increased threshold value of 0.0001. For the experiment, we selected the data that was learned with a 0.01 threshold value to save time in learning on the Khepera II.

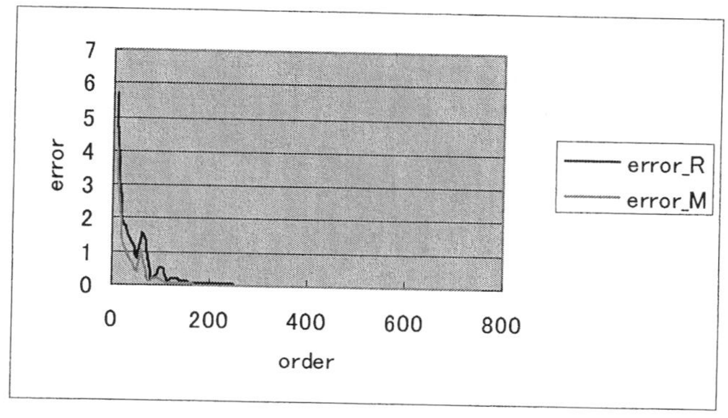

Fig. 4. Results of Imitation Learning

The above simulation showed that learning of imitation behavior would converge in the consciousness system with self and others distinguished. We were therefore confident that imitation behavior would be implemented if we conducted robot experiments using the learning method described in this chapter.

4 Robot Experiments

4.1 Purpose

Imitation behavior was experimented using two robots. The purpose of the experiment was to confirm that the robots installed with the consciousness system would implement imitation behavior correctly. The other purpose was to determine whether the corresponding R-values were correct, or whether the robots cognized the condition of self and others correctly at different times.

4.2 Description of Robots

Khepera II robots of 6 cm in diameter, as shown in Fig. 5, were used in the experiment. The robot is provided with four LED lamps on the IOturret to display four bits of R. The condition that Khepera cognizes, or the language label, is visible at a glance.

Fig. 5. Khepera II

4.3 Procedure of Experiment

One robot (A) imitates the behavior of the other (B). The robot (B) repeats forward and backward motions automatically in the order of advance, stop and back up. Each motion lasts 0.5s. Robot (A) is expected to imitate the forward and backward motion of robot (B). In concrete terms, NN of the consciousness system learns in the same way as in the computer simulation on Khepera II. According to the built-in program, a quantity of reflected light of the IR sensor enters NN; the R-value is used to light the LED to display the information cognized; and the NN output value is transmitted to the motor.

4.4 Results of Experiments and Observation

Experiments were conducted using the above-mentioned program. Figure 6 shows the change in bit strings for R (condition of self and others).

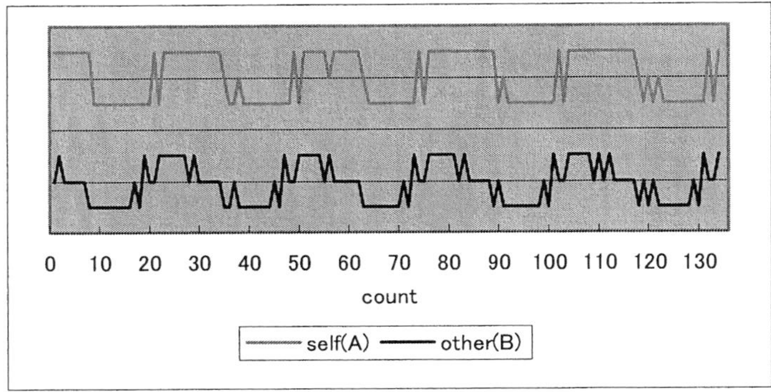

Fig. 6. Change of Bit Strings at R

In the graphs for self and others, the lowest represents 'advance,' the middle 'stop' and the highest 'back up.' COUNT shows the number of executions. Robot A cognizes forward and backward motion of Robot B and imitates its motion. Sometimes, the graph is instable and the smooth flow of cognition is disturbed. This is due to disturbance from the IR sensor; it is not a problem of the consciousness system. The graph further shows that behavior of self is slightly delayed compared to that of other. This time lag is because Robot A starts imitation after cognizing the behavior of Robot B.

This experiment showed that the consciousness system is able to distinguish between self and others and implement imitation behavior. We experimented only the advance, stop and back up imitation behavior using the Khepera II. We believe that our consciousness system is able to implement more complex imitation behavior in experiments conducted with a higher-level robot of the sensor system.

5 Conclusion

Believing that consciousness is born from consistency of cognition and behavior, we define the consciousness system as being a system to generate consciousness. The structure of the consciousness system was described to show that it is superior to mechatronics models of conventional cognition and behavior systems.

Mirror neurons and mimesis theory were discussed to prove the assertion that imitation behavior is closely related to the development of human consciousness. We also showed the validity of the definition that "consistency of cognition and behavior" generates consciousness and the consciousness system. Implementation of imitation behavior is important as the first stage of study of consciousness.

For simulation, Learning of imitation behavior converged on NN of the consciousness system after successfully distinguishing between self and others. Robot experiments were conducted using NN of the learned consciousness system. Distinction between self and others and imitation behavior were actually implemented in the experiment. Due to the restricted specifications of Khepera II, the robots imitated only the advance, stop and back up motions in the experiment. We believe that the consciousness system is capable of implementing all kinds of imitation behaviors.

References

1. Tani, J.: On the dynamics of robot exploration learning. Cognitive Systems Research (2002) 459-470
2. Nakamura, Y.: .An Integrated Model of Imitation Learning and Symbol Emergence basedon Mimesis Theory. The Robotics Society of Japan,vol22,No.2 (2004) 256-263
3. Kawato, M.: Using humanoid robots to study human behavior. IEEE Intelligent Systems: Special Issue on Humanoid Robotics,vol15 (2000) 46-56
4. Billard, A.and Hayes, G.: Learning to communicate through imitation in Autonomous robots. In proccedings of ICANN97, Seventh International Conference on Artificial Neural Networks (1997) 793-768
5. Gallese,V.,Fadiga,L.,Rizzolati,G.: Action recognition in the premotor cortex, Brain 119 (1996) 593-600
6. Donald, M.: [Origin of the Modern Mind] Harvard University Press, Cambridge, (1991).

7. Inaba, K., Takeno, J.: Consistency between recognition and behavior creates consciousness, proceedings of SCI'03 (The best paper of Systemics) (2003) 341-346
8. Takeno, J., Inaba, K., Suzuki, T.: Research related to imitation behavior using a consciousness machine, proceedings of CCCT'04 (2004) 268-273

Distance-Based Dynamic Interaction of Humanoid Robot with Multiple People*

Tsuyoshi Tasaki, Shohei Matsumoto, Hayato Ohba, Mitsuhiko Toda,
Kazuhiro Komatani, Tetsuya Ogata, and Hiroshi G. Okuno

Graduate School of Informatics, Kyoto University, Kyoto 606-8501, Japan
{tasaki, shohei_m, hayato, mtoda, komatani, ogata, okuno}
@kuis.kyoto-u.ac.jp
http://winnie.kuis.kyoto-u.ac.jp

Abstract. Research on human-robot interaction is getting an increasing amount of attention. Because almost all the research has dealt with communication between one robot and one person, quite little is known about communication between a robot and multiple people. We developed a method that enables robots to communicate with multiple people by selecting an interactive partner using criteria based on the concept of proxemics. In this method, a robot changes active sensory-motor modalities based on the *interaction distance* between itself and a person. Our method was implemented in a humanoid robot, *SIG2*, using a subsumption architecture. *SIG2* has various sensory-motor modalities to interact with humans. A demonstration of *SIG2* showed that the proposed method works well during interaction with multiple people.

1 Introduction

Studies of human-robot interaction with the robots *Robita* [1], *Robisuke* [2], *SIG* [3], *ASIMO* [4], *AIBO* [5], *Robovie* [6], and *Kismet* [7] have gotten much attention. Because almost all of them have dealt with only one-on-one communication between a robot and a person, quite little is known about the methodology for communications between a robot and multiple people. Robots must be able to interact effectively with multiple people at the same time if a human support robot is going to be developed. We present a design method for such human-robot communication.

The distance between a robot and each person is one of the most important issues in interaction with multiple people. If people are far away from the robot, their sound level is low. Since the robot usually hears a mixture of sounds, separating speech from the mixture and recognizing the separated sound is difficult. If the robot speaks to distant people, they will mistakenly think that the robot can hear them. Therefore, it should not speak but use gestures. On the other hand, if people are very close to the robot, it should speak. In addition, tactile sensors, such as skin sensors, may be used. Appropriate behaviors and sensory devices should be selected based on the interaction distance. We call this modality *sensory-motor modality* human-robot interaction.

* This research was partially supported by the Ministry of Education, Culture, Sports, Science and Technology, Grant-in-Aid for Scientific Research No.15200015 and No.1601625, and COE Program of Informatics Research Center for Development of Knowledge Society Infrastructure.

M. Ali and F. Esposito (Eds.): IEA/AIE 2005, LNAI 3533, pp. 111–120, 2005.

Robita is a conversation robot that can participate in group discussion [1]. Two people sitting on a chair interact with each other and Robita. *Robita* obtains auditory inputs through a headset microphone worn by each participant. Therefore, its interaction model does not depend on the interaction distance and uses the fixed sensory-motor modality. *SIG* tracks multiple people who are either talking or not talking by integrating visual and auditory localization [3]. It can performe various kinds of visual and auditory scene analyses including face localization and recognition, sound source localization and separation, and automatic speech recognition. Although it has various sensory-motor modalities, its behaviors are only passive; it can track and turn toward a speaker.

Basically, robots cannot communicate with multiple people at the same time except when the people can be regarded as one unit, such as an audience at a lecture. People select an interactive partner dynamically, based on various criteria such as "intimacy". People also change their interaction strategy of sensing and their behavior according to the situation. For example, if the distance between two people is small, they can identify the other individual easily, and speech recognition and facial expressions are effective for communication. If the distance between them is great, they would use gestures, etc. Thus, people's personal space, or interaction distance, is an important criterion for selecting appropriate sensory-motor modalities.

We design a method of human-robot dynamic communication in which the robot selects an interactive partner from multiple people by assigning priority based on the interaction distance. In this method, the robot refines its recognition and behavior by selecting appropriate sensory-motor modalities based on the interaction distance. The rest of the paper is orgranized as follows: In Section 2, we introduce proxemics, a social psychology theory, as the basic concept of our method and describe the details of our method. In Section 3, we explain the humanoid robot used in this study, and in Section 4, we present the implementation of the subsumption architecture used. In Section 5, we give some examples of the robot's behavior when communicating with multiple people. Section 6 concludes this paper.

2 Communication Based on Interaction Distance

We adopted proxemics [8] to design a methodology for a robot to interact appropriately with each person in a group of people based on the distance between the robot and each person. Proxemics is a social psychology theory which posits that two humans interact at an appropriate physical distance from one another based on their relationship. In this theory, an interaction distances are roughly classified into four groups, as follows:

- *Intimate distance* (approx. 50 cm): people can communicate via physical interaction and express strong emotions.
- *Personal distance* (approx. 50–120 cm): people can talk intimately.
- *Social distance* (approx. 120–360 cm): people maintain this distance when they are talking but do not know each other well.
- *Public distance* (approx. 360 cm or more): people who have no personal relationship with each other can comfortably coexist.

Table 1. Relationship between distance and function

Modalities	Intimate distance 50 cm or less	Personal distance 50 cm–1.2 m	Social distance 1.2 m–3.6 m	Public distance 3.6 m or more
Input	tactile sensor			
devices	face detection	face detection		
or	speech recognition	speech recognition		
sensors	face localization	face localization	face localization	face localization
	sound localization	sound localization	sound localization	sound localization
Output	normal speaker	normal speaker	normal speaker	normal speaker
devices			sound spotlight	sound spotlight
	tracking	tracking	tracking	tracking
	gesture	gesture	gesture	gesture
	hug			
			approach	approach

The distance values shown in parentheses are just typical examples. They depend on a person's personality and cultural background.

2.1 Categorization of Robot Functions Based on Proxemics

We divided the various functions of the humanoid robot into four groups based on the distances listed in Table 1. For input sensors, tactile sensors can be used within the reach of people. If a target person is standing far from the robot, the robot cannot use either speech recognition or face recognition because these functions require highly reliable sensory information. For output devices, normal loud speakers are not appropriate at long distances, because they deliver sounds to all the people around the robot. A sound spotlight based on a parametric loud speaker is used to deliver sounds to the people in a particular direction. The detailed sensory-motor modalities are explained later by giving concrete examples.

2.2 Robot Intimacy Based on Proxemics

Another factor in determining behaviors is *intimacy*. Proxemics suggests that the more intimate the communication, the nearer the target person stands. The parameter of intimacy is introduced to reflect the relationship between a robot and humans. The robot uses this parameter to determine communication priority among multiple in a situation, and then behaves according to its relationship with each person.

The parameter of intimacy, I, ranges from 0 to 1. It represents the intimacy of the relationship between a robot and a human. Since I changes dynamically during the communication, its level changes according to the following equations:

$$I(0) = P, \tag{1}$$

$$\frac{dI}{dt} = \left(\frac{I + P}{2}\right) \cdot D - I \cdot \left(\frac{P \cdot I + 1}{2}\right) + S_k. \tag{2}$$

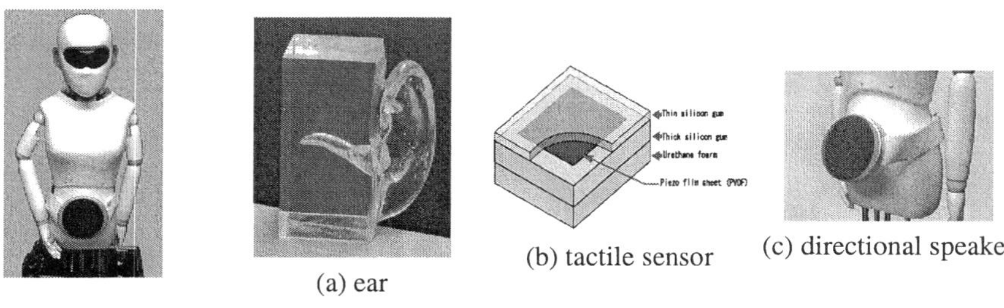

(a) ear (b) tactile sensor (c) directional speaker

Fig. 1. *SIG2* and its parts; (a) ear, (b) piezo tactile sensor, and (c) directional loud speaker

The term P is a constant parameter defined a priori as the robot personality. The first term or the right-hand side of Equation (2) shows the influence of the distance. The parameter of the distance, D, is defined as 0.04 and 0.02 for intimate and personal distances, respectively. For the other distances, D is defined as 0.0.

The term I is defined as the summation of the friendliness of the robot and intimacy of its relationship with a given person. If the robot recognizes the person as someone it is intimate with, I increases, and if the robot recognizes the person as someone it is not intimate with, I decreases. The second term of Equation (2) is a damping factor. If the robot has no communication with the person for a while, I converges to 0. The term S_k is a parameter of the influence of stimuli. It changes I based on the human's behavior.

3 Humanoid *SIG2* and Its Capabilities

We used the humanoid robot, *SIG2*, shown in Figure 1. *SIG2* has one microphone on each side of its head. Each microphone is embedded in the eardrum of a model of a human outer ear made of silicon (Figure 1-a). Its head and upper body are covered with soft skin-like material containing 19 patches of tactile sensors (Figure 1-b). A directional parametric speaker is located at its waist (Figure 1-c).

3.1 Tactile Sensors and Face Localization and Recognition

Each tactile sensor, which consists of piezo elements covered by silicon, can detect the pressure velocity of its patch. It can recognize three kinds of contact: *touch*, *rub*, and *hit*. Its velocity versus time for a hit and a rub are shown in Figure 2.

SIG2 can measure the distance to its partner using stereovision, which uses two cameras in its head. Since its visual processing detects multiple faces, then extracts, identifies, and tracks each face simultaneously, the size, direction, and brightness of each face changes frequently. We use MPIsearch [10] to attain robust face detection, as shown in Figure 3.

After an extracted face is identified, it is projected into the discrimination space, and its distance, d, from each registered face is calculated [3]. Since this distance depends on the degree (L, the number of registered faces) of the discrimination space, it is converted to a parameter-independent probability, P_v:

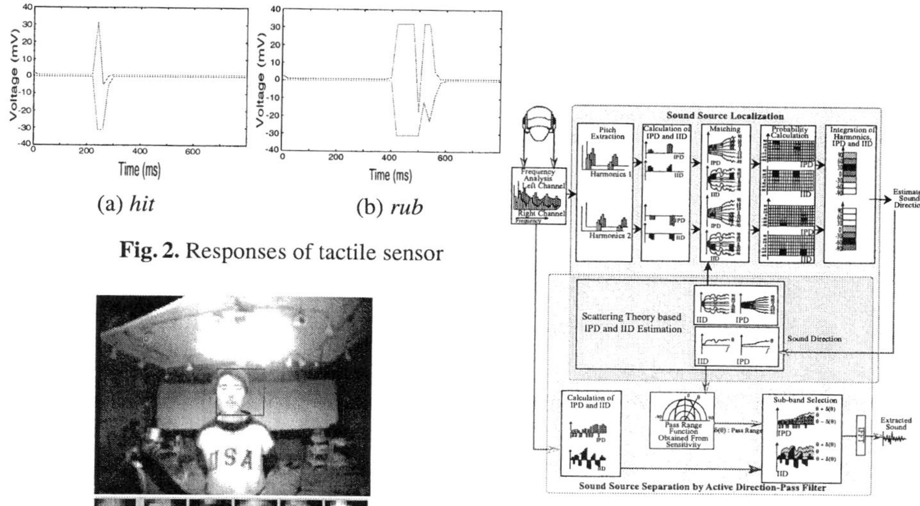

(a) *hit* (b) *rub*

Fig. 2. Responses of tactile sensor

Fig. 3. Face localization and recognition

Fig. 4. Sound source localization and separation system

$$P_v = \int_{\frac{d^2}{2}}^{\infty} e^{-t}\, t^{\frac{L}{2}-1} dt. \tag{3}$$

A discrimination matrix is created in advance or on demand from a set of variations of the face with an ID (name) using online linear discriminant analysis.

3.2 Sound Source Localization and Separation

Sound source localization is performed analogously to human perception; *SIG2* uses two microphones embedded in its head (Fig 1-a). To localize sound sources with the two microphones, first, a set of peaks are extracted for the left and right channels. Then, identical or similar peaks of the left and right channels are identified as pairs and each pair is used to calculate interaural phase difference (IPD) and interaural intensity difference (IID).

Because auditory and visual tracking involves motor movements, which cause motor and mechanical noises, audition should suppress or at least reduce such noises. In human-robot interaction, when a robot is talking, it should suppress its own speech. Nakadai and Okuno presented the *active audition* for humanoids to improve sound source tracking by integrating audition, vision, and motor controls [3]. They used their heuristics to reduce internal burst noises caused by motor movements.

Epipolar geometry with scattering theory is used to calculate the direction of a sound source from its IPD and IID [12]. The key ideas of Nakadai and Okuno's real-time active audition system are twofold; one is to exploit the property of the harmonic structure (fundamental frequency, $F0$, and its overtones) to find a more accurate pair of peaks in the left and right channels. The other is to search for the direction of the sound source by combining the belief factors of IPD and IID using the Dempster-Shafer theory.

3.3 Sound Source Separation Using ADPF

SIG2's sound source separation system uses an active direction-pass filter (ADPF), which separates out sound originating from a specified direction [11]. The architecture of the ADPF is shown in the lower dark area in Figure 4. The ADPF separates sound sources using a spectrum of input sound, the IPD and IID of the input sound, and the direction of the sound source. The details of the ADPF algorithm are as follows:

1. The pass range, $\delta(\theta_s)$, of the ADPF is specified by the pass range function, δ. Its minimum value is straight in front of *SIG2*, because the ADPF has its maximum sensitivity there. The function δ has a larger value at the periphery because of its lower sensitivity.
2. From a sound's direction, the IPD, $\Delta\varphi_E(\theta)$, and IID, $\Delta\rho_E(\theta)$, are estimated for each sub-band (i.e., FFT point) using auditory epipolar geometry.
3. The sub-bands are collected if the IPD and IID satisfy the pass-range conditions.
4. A wave consisting of collected sub-bands is constructed.

3.4 Speech Recognition for Separated Sound

We used automatic speech recognition (ASR) with multiple acoustic models to recognize sounds separated by the ADPF. In other words, the ADPF was used as front-end processing for ASR. Because making speech recognition robust against noises is one of the hottest topics in the speech community, approaches have been developed, such as multi-condition training and missing data [14, 15], that are, to some extent, efficient at recognizing speech with noise. However, these methods are of less use when the signal to noise ratio is as low as 0 dB, as occurs with a mixture of speech from different voices.

The Japanese automatic speech recognition software "Julian" was used for ASR. For acoustic models, words played by B&W Nautilus 805 loud speakers were recorded by *SIG2*'s pair of microphones. The speakers were installed in a 4 m × 6 m room, and the distance between *SIG2* and each speaker was 1 m. The training datasets were created based on the data separated from mixtures of two or three simultaneous speeches, using the ADPF. One loud speakers placed at 0° and one or two at every 10°, from -90° to 90°, were used to play two or three simultaneous utterances. Because there are 17 directions from -90° to 90° and we used three speakers, 51 training datasets were obtained.

In speech recognition, 51 ASRs with one of the resulting 51 acoustic models are processed against an input in parallel. Then the system integrated all the results of ASRs and output the most reliable result among them [11].

4 Design of Interaction-Distance Based Interaction

Our method dynamically determines the priority of various modalities of the sensory and motor systems, based on the interaction distance (Table 1).

- Public and social distances — *SIG2* can locate humans using skin color information from the vision system and can locate sound sources.
- Personal distance — Besides the functions mentioned above, *SIG2* separates sound sources and recognizes speech and faces.
- Intimate distance — Besides the functions mentioned for personal distance, *SIG2* recognizes three kinds of contact: *touch*, *rub*, and *hit*.

SIG2 has four degree-of-freedom in movement. Its movement functions include nod, incline, rotation of its neck, rotation of its body, movement using its cart, and utterance enabled by the two kind of speakers (directional and omnidirectional). Based on the distance to a person, *SIG2* selects movement functions:

- Intimate distance — *SIG2* uses the omni-directional (normal) loud speaker for utterances.
- Personal distance — Besides using the omni-directional loud speaker for utterances, speakers are tracked and gestures are facilitated by four motors.
- Social distance — Besides the functions used in personal distance, the directional loud speaker is used to talk to a person standing far away from *SIG2*.
- Public distance — Besides the functions used in social distance, *SIG2* can use the cart to get close to the target person or people.

4.1 Implementation Using Subsumption Architecture

A subsumption Architecture (SA) [9] is used to implement our method using the hierarchal structure in Table 1. This enables *SIG2* to process sensor information efficiently. All sensor information is sent to all action modules. Each action module processes input information in parallel to output results. The output of upper modules suppresses or inhibits that of lower modules to subsume the output of action modules. The top module, which inhibits the outputs of lower modules based on the interaction distance, is implemented to achieve dynamic modality-selection (see Figure 5).

5 Two Experiments to Check Effectiveness

5.1 Scenario 1: Selecting Sensory Modalities Based on Distance

In this experiment, *SIG2* interacted with two people who spoke from different distances, far and near, by changing input modalities. *SIG2* urged the farthest person from itself to approach. The structure of the SA used in this section is shown in Figure 6.

Step 1 Person A said "Hello, SIG2," at a social distance.
After localizing the sound, *SIG2* turned to Person A (turnFaceToSound), and after localizing the face, it continued looking at him (lookAtFace). It detected that he was positioned at a social distance by using the stereovision. Consequently, calling Person A's name (greetWithName) and replying with a greeting (replyGreet) were inhibited.

Step 2 Person B approached with in an intimate distance and said "Hello, SIG2."
After localizing the sound and face, *SIG2* turned to Person B and continued looking at him. Because Person B was positioned at an intimate distance, *SIG2* bowed slightly (item salute), called Person B's name, and greeted Person B.

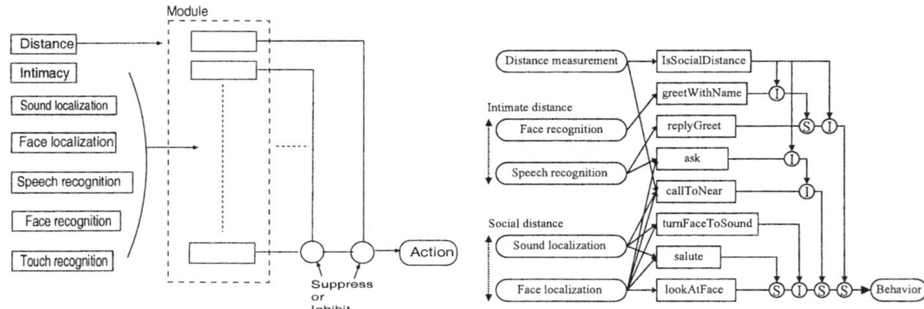

Fig. 5. System Overview

Fig. 6. Implemented Modules for Scenario 1

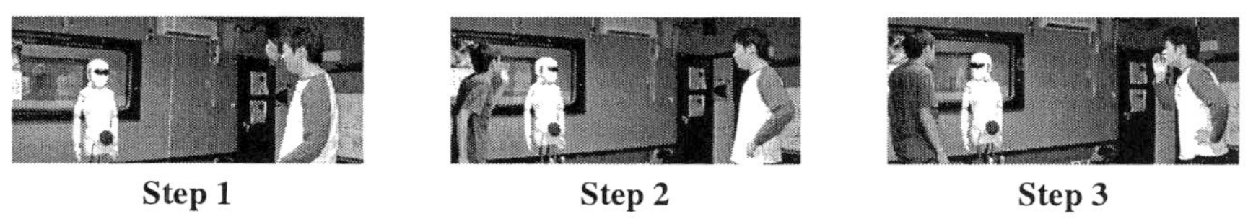

Fig. 7. Shapshots of Scenario 1

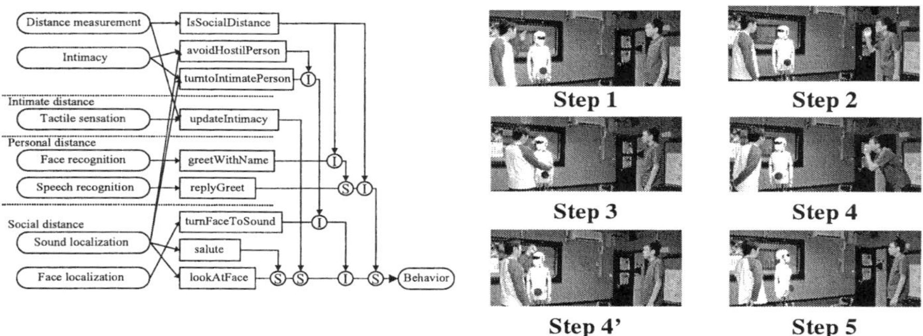

Fig. 8. Modules implemented for Scenario 2

Fig. 9. Snapshots of Scenario 2

Step 3 Person A called to *SIG2*.
After localizing the sound and face, *SIG2* turned to Person A and continueed looking at him. Greeting Person A was inhibited by the history of Person A's behavior. *SIG2* requested that Person A approach (callToNear). Asking about Person A's business (ask) became active, but was inhibited because of the social distance.

Step 4 Person A followed the instructions and approached *SIG2*.
After localizing the face, *SIG2* continued looking at Person A. *SIG2* detected that Person A was positioned at an intimate distance. Then it asked Person A's business. Requesting that Person A approach was inhibited.

5.2 Scenario 2: Changing Behavior Based on Intimacy

In this experiment, *SIG2*, between two people, changed its conversation partner based on intimacy. The SA used in this section is shown in Figure 8.

Step 1 Person A greeted *SIG2* from an intimate distance.
After localizing the sound and face. *SIG2* turned to Person A and continued looking at him. *SIG2* bowed slightly, called Person A's name, and replied to Person A because of their intimate distance. Its intimacy with Person A increased.

Step 2 Person B greeted *SIG2* from a social distance.
After localizaing the sound and face, *SIG2* turned to Person B and continued looking at him. Calling his name and offering a greeting was inhibited because of the social distance. *SIG2* compared the intimacy it experienced with Persons A and B, and then returned to Person A, with whom it had higher intimacy (turnToIntimatePerson).

Step 3 Person A rubbed *SIG2*.
The intimacy with Person A increased (updateIntimacy).

Step 4 Person B called to *SIG2* from a social distance.
After localizing the sound, *SIG2* turned to Person B with increasing frequency. However, *SIG2* continued looking at Person A because the intimacy with Person A was over the threshold value (turnToIntimatePerson). *SIG2* did not reply to Person B.

Step 5 Person A hit *SIG2*.
The intimacy with Person A decreased, and *SIG2* began avoiding him (avoidHostilePerson).

5.3 Discussion

The effects and observations of our method are summarized below:

(1) **Efficiency of design and operation** By selecting sensory modalities using distance information, we designed robot behaviors without considering all combinations of all modalities. Our method is also very efficient at computing costs compared to the method of selecting behavior in consideration of all possible modalities.

(2) **Efficiency of communication** We made a robot that avoids incorrect recognition by selecting sensors and behavior using distance information; therefore, it communicated exact information. This reduced the number of interactions and enabled efficient communication.

(3) **Priority based on interaction distance** The experiments with the humanoid robot showed that our method enables the robot to select an appropriate target person in communication using intimacy that dynamically changes. Demonstrations described in this paper would be natural styles for communication of a human support robot in the future.

6 Conclusion and Further Work

We presented a model of robot intimacy that interaction distance to determine the communication priority of multiple people. This method was implemented in a humanoid robot called *SIG2* using an SA. The demonstrations of *SIG2* showed the effectiveness of basing the design on proxemics.

Future work shoud focus on three main areas. First, the *reliability of sensory information* should be considered. Because the robot simply selects a sensor modality using our method, the unselected sensors are not used at all. The heterogeneous sensors should be integrated according to how reliable they generate appropriate robot behavior. Second, the definition of *intimacy* should be refined. The intimacy measure in our method completely depends on interaction distance. However, intimacy should be influenced by variations in communication. Last but not least, a *methodology of evaluation* for this kind of human-robot communication should be established. Most conventional studies of robot communication with a person have used subjective impressions derived from questionnaires as evaluation criteria. However, dealing with such subjective impressions of multiple people in a complete evaluation is quite difficult. We should consider methods of analysing of the dynamic transition of communication between a robot and multiple people.

Acknowledgements. The original *SIG2* was developed by the JST Kitano Symbiotic Systems Project. The authors thank Dr. Kazuhiro Nakadai of HRI-Japan and Dr. Hiroaki Kitano of the JST Kitano Project for their collaborations.

References

1. Matsusaka, Y.,Tojo, T., Kuota, S., Furukawa, K., Tamiya, D., Hayata, K., Nakano, Y., and Kobayashi, T.: Multi-person Conversation via Multi-modal Interface — A Robot who Communicates with Multi-user, *Proc. of EUROSPEECH-99*, 1723–1726, 1999.
2. Fujie, S. Ejiri, Y., Nakajima, K., Matsusakai, Y., and Kuota, S.: A Conversation Robot Using Head Gesture Recognition as Para-Linguistic Information, *Proc. of Ro-Man 2004*, 159–164.
3. Okuno, H.G., Nakadai, Lourens, T., and Kitano, H.: Sound and Visual Tracking for Humanoid Robot, *Applied Intelligence*, Vol.20, No.3 (May/June 2004) 253-266, Kluwer.
4. Sakagami, Y.,Watanabe, R., Aoyama, C., Matsunaga, S., Higaki, N., Fujimura, K.: The Intelligent ASIMO: System overview and integration, *Proc. of IROS-2002*, 2478–2483.
5. Kaplan, F., and Hafner, V.V.: The Challenge of Joint Attention, *Proc. of EpiRobo-2004*, 67–74, Lund Unviersity Cognitive Studies, 117, 2004.
6. Ishiguro, H., Miyashita, T., Kanda, T., Ono, T., and Imai, M.: Robovie: An interactive humanoid robot, *Video Proc. of IEEE ICRA-2002*, 2002.
7. Breazeal. C.L.: *Designing Sociable Robots, A Bradford Book*, 2001, ISBN 0262025108.
8. Hall, E.T.: *Hidden Dimension, Doubleday Publishing*, 1966.
9. Brooks, R.A.: A Robust Layered Control System For A Mobile Robot, *IEEE Journal of Robotics and Automation*, Vol.2, No.1 (1986) 14-23.
10. Fasel, I. and Movellan, J.R.: Comparison of neurally inspired face detection algorithms, UAM, 2002. *Proc. of ICANN 2002*, 1395–1401. 2002.
11. Nakadai, K., Hidai, K., Okuno, H.G., and Kitano, H.: Real-time speaker localization and speech separation by audio-visual integration, *Proc. of IEEE ICRA-2002*, 1043–1049. 2002.
12. Nakadai, K., Matsuura, D., Okuno, H.G, and Tsujino, H.: Improvement of Recognition of Simultaneous Speech Signals Using AV Integration and Scattering Theory for Humanoid Robots, *Speech Communication, in print*, Elsevier, Oct. 2004.
13. Dempster, A.: Upper and lower probabilities induced by a multivalued mapping. *Annals of Mathematical Statistics*, 38:325–339, 1967.
14. Barker, J., Cooke, M., and Green, P.: Robust asr based on clean speech models: *Proc. Of EUROSPEECH-2001*, 213–216. 2001.
15. Renevey, P., Vetter, R., and Kraus, J.: Robust speech recognition using missing feature theory and vector quantization. *Proc. of EUROSPEECH-2001*, 1107–1110. 2001.

Movement Prediction from Real-World Images Using a Liquid State Machine*

Harald Burgsteiner[1], Mark Kröll[2], Alexander Leopold[2], and Gerald Steinbauer[3]

[1] InfoMed/Health Care Engineering, Graz University of Applied Sciences, Eggenberger Allee 9-11, A-8020 Graz, Austria
[2] Institute for Theoretical Computer Science, Graz University of Technology, Inffeldgasse 16b/I, A-8010 Graz, Austria
[3] Institute for Software Technology, Graz University of Technology, Inffeldgasse 16b/II, A-8010 Graz, Austria

Abstract. Prediction is an important task in robot motor control where it is used to gain feedback for a controller. With such a self-generated feedback, which is available before sensor readings from an environment can be processed, a controller can be stabilized and thus the performance of a moving robot in a real-world environment is improved. So far, only experiments with artificially generated data have shown good results. In a sequence of experiments we evaluate whether a liquid state machine in combination with a supervised learning algorithm can be used to predict ball trajectories with input data coming from a video camera mounted on a robot participating in the RoboCup. This pre-processed video data is fed into a recurrent spiking neural network. Connections to some output neurons are trained by linear regression to predict the position of a ball in various time steps ahead. Our results support the idea that learning with a liquid state machine can be applied not only to designed data but also to real, noisy data.

1 Introduction

The prediction of time series is an important issue in many different domains, such as finance, economy, object tracking, state estimation and robotics. The aim of such predictions could be to estimate the stock exchange price for the next day or the position of an object in the next camera frame based on current and past observations. In the domain of robot control such predictions are used to stabilize a robot controller. See [1] for a survey of different approaches in motor control where prediction enhances the stability of a controller. A popular approach is to learn the prediction from previously collected data. The advantages are that knowledge of the internal structure is not necessarily needed, arbitrary non-linear prediction could be learned and additionally some past observations could be integrated in the prediction.

* Authors are listed in alphabetical order.

M. Ali and F. Esposito (Eds.): IEA/AIE 2005, LNAI 3533, pp. 121–130, 2005.

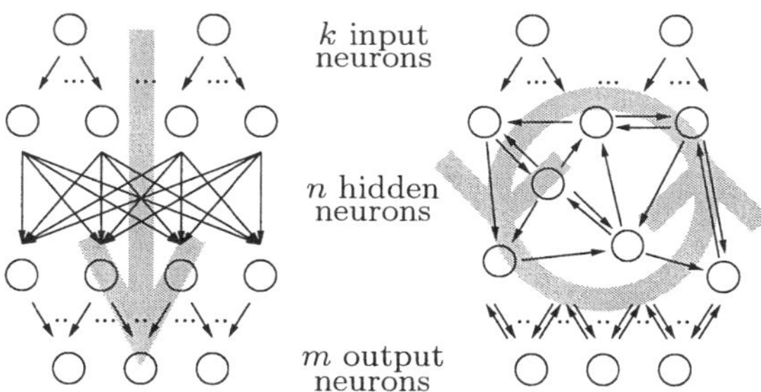

Fig. 1. Comparison of the architecture of a feed-forward (left hand side) with a recurrent neural network (right hand side); the grey arrows sketch the direction of computation

Artificial Neural Networks (ANN) are a common method used for this computation. *Feed-forward networks* only have connections starting from external input nodes, possibly via one or more intermediate hidden node processing layers, to output nodes. *Recurrent networks* may have connections feeding back to earlier layers or may have lateral connections (i.e. to neighboring neurons on the same layer). See Figure 1 for a comparison of the direction of computation between a feed-forward and a recurrent neural network. With this recurrency, activity can be retained by the network over time. This provides a sort of memory within the network, enabling it to compute functions that are more complex than just simple reactive input-output mappings. This is a very important feature for networks that will be used for computation of time series, because a current output is not solely a function of the current sensory input, but a function of the current and previous sensory inputs and also of the current and previous internal network states. This allows a system to incorporate a much richer range of dynamic behaviors. Many approaches have been elaborated on recurrent ANNs. Some of them are: dynamic recurrent neural networks, radial basis function networks, Elman networks, self-organizing maps, Hopfield nets and the "echo state" approach from [2].

Recently, networks with models of biologically more realistic neurons, e.g., spiking neurons, in combination with simple learning algorithms have been proposed as general powerful tools for the computation on time series [3]. In Maass et. al. [4] this new computation paradigm, a so called *Liquid State Machine* (LSM), was used to predict the motion of objects in visual inputs. The visual input was presented to a 8x8 sensor array and the prediction of the activation of these sensors representing the position of objects for succeeding time steps was learned. This approach appears promising, as the computation of such prediction tasks is assumed to be similar in the human brain [5]. The weakness of the experiments in [4] is that they were only conducted on artificially generated data. The question is how the approach performs with real-world data. Real data, e.g. the detected motion of an object in a video stream from a camera mounted on a moving robot, are noisy and afflicted with outliers.

In this paper we present how this approach can be extended to a real world task. We applied the proposed approach to the RoboCup robotic-soccer domain. The task was movement prediction for a ball in the video stream of the robot's camera. Such a prediction is important for reliable tracking of the ball and for decision making during a game. The remainder of this paper is organized as follows. The next section provides an overview of the LSM. Section 3 describes the prediction approach for real data. Experimental results will be reported in Section 4. Finally, in Section 5 we draw some conclusions.

2 The Liquid State Machine

2.1 The Framework of a Liquid State Machine

The "liquid state machine" (LSM) from [3] is a new framework for computations in neural microcircuits. The term "liquid state" refers to the idea to view the result of a computation of a neural microcircuit not as a stable state like an attractor that is reached. Instead, a neural microcircuit is used as an *online computation tool* that receives a continuous input that drives the state of the neural microcircuit. The result of a computation is again a continuous output generated by readout neurons given the current state of the neural microcircuit.

Recurrent neural networks with spiking neurons represent a non-linear dynamical system with a high-dimensional internal state, which is driven by the input. The internal state vector $x(t)$ is given as the contributions of all neurons within the LSM to the membrane potential of a readout neuron at the time t. The complete internal state is determined by the current input and all past inputs that the network has seen so far. Hence, a history of (recent) inputs is preserved in such a network and can be used for computation of the current output. The basic idea behind solving tasks with a LSM is that one does *not* try to set the weights of the connections within the pool of neurons but instead reduces learning to setting the weights of the readout neurons. This reduces learning dramatically and much simpler supervised learning algorithms which e.g. only have to minimize the mean square error in relation to a desired output can be applied.

The LSM has several interesting features in comparison to other approaches with recurrent circuits of spiking neural networks:

1. The liquid state machine provides "any-time" computing, i.e. one does not have to wait for a computation to finish before the result is available. Results start emitting from the readout neurons as soon as input is fed into the liquid. Furthermore, different computations can overlap in time. That is, new input can be fed into the liquid and perturb it while the readout still gives answers to past input streams.
2. A single neural microcircuit can not only be used to compute a special output function via the readout neurons. Because the LSM only serves as a pool for dynamic recurrent computation, one can use many different readout neurons to extract information for several tasks in parallel. So a sort of "multi-tasking" can be incorporated.

3. In most cases simple learning algorithms can be used to set the weights of the readout neurons. The idea is similar to support vector machines, where one uses a kernel to project input data into a high-dimensional space. In this very high-dimensional space simpler classifiers can be used to separate the data than in the original input data space. The LSM has a similar effect as a kernel: due to the recurrency the input data is also projected to a high-dimensional space. Hence, in almost any case experienced so far simple learning rules like e.g. linear regression suffice.
4. Last but not least it is not only a computational powerful model, but it is also one of the biological most plausible so far. Thus, it provides a hypothesis for computation in biological neural systems.

The model of a neural microcircuit as it is used in the LSM is based on evidence found in [6] and [7]. Still, it gives only a rough approximation to a real neural microcircuit since many parameters are still unknown. The neural microcircuit is the biggest computational element within the LSM, although multiple neural microcircuits could be placed within a single virtual model. In a model of a neural microcircuit $N = n_x \cdot n_y \cdot n_z$ neurons are placed on a regular grid in 3D space. The number of neurons along the x, y and z axis, n_x, n_y and n_z respectively, can be chosen freely. One also specifies a factor to determine how many of the N neurons should be inhibitory. Another important parameter in the definition of a neural microcircuit is the parameter λ. Number and range of the connections between the N neurons within the LSM are determined by this parameter λ. The probability of a connection between two neurons i and j is given by $p_{(i,j)} = C \cdot exp^{-\frac{D_{(i,j)}}{\lambda^2}}$ where $D_{(i,j)}$ is the Euclidean distance between those two neurons and C is a parameter depending on the type (excitatory or inhibitory) of each of the two connecting neurons. There exist 4 possible values for C for each connection within a neural microcircuit: C_{EE}, C_{EI},C_{IE} and C_{II} may be used depending on whether the neurons i and j are excitatory (E) or inhibitory (I). In our experiments we used spiking neurons according to the standard leaky-integrate-and-fire (LIF) neuron model that are connected via dynamic synapses. The time course for a postsynaptic current is approximated by the equation $v(t) = w \cdot e^{-\frac{t}{\tau_{syn}}}$ where w is a synaptic weight and τ_{syn} is the synaptic time constant. In case of dynamic synapses the "weight" w depends on the history of the spikes it has seen so far according to the model from [8]. For synapses transmitting analog values (such as the output neurons in our experimental setup) synapses are simply modeled as static synapses with a strength defined by a constant weight w. Additionally, synapses for analog values can have delay lines, modeling the time a potential would need to propagate along an axon.

3 Experimental Setup

In this section we introduce the general setup that was used during our experiments to solve prediction tasks with real-world data from a robot. As depicted in figure 2, such a network consists of three different neuron pools: (a) an input layer that is used to feed sensor data from the robot into the network, (b) a pool of neurons forming the LSM according to section 2 and (c) the output layer consisting of readout neurons which perform a linear combination of the membrane potentials obtained from the liquid neurons.

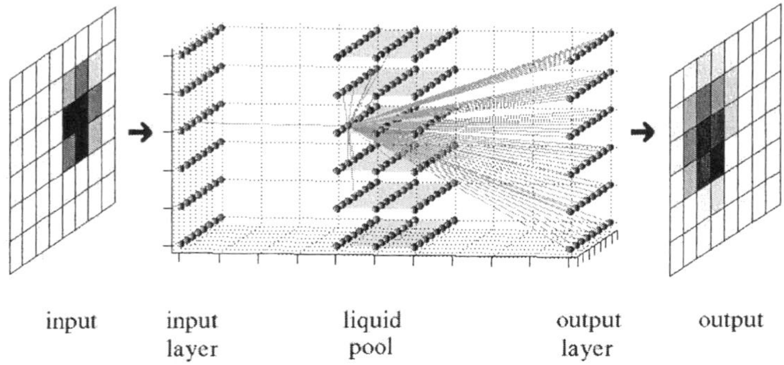

Fig. 2. Architecture of our experimental setup depicting the three different pools of neurons and a sample input pattern with the data path overview. Example connections of a single liquid neuron are shown: input is received from the input sensor field on the left hand side and some random connection within the liquid. The output of every liquid neuron is projected onto every output neuron (located on the most right hand side). The 8x6x3 neurons in the middle form the "liquid"

For simulation within the training and evaluation the neural circuit simulator *CSim*[1] was used. Parameterization of the LSM is described below. Names for neuron and synapse types all originate from terms used in the *CSim* environment. Letters I and E denote values for inhibitory and excitatory neurons respectively.

To feed activation sequences into the liquid pool, we use *External Input Neurons* that conduct an injection current I_{inject} via *Static Analog Synapses* (I_{noise} = 0nA, $w_{mean} = 3 * 10^{-8}$ (EE) or $6 * 10^{-8}$ (EI), $delay_{mean}$ = 1.5ms (EE) or 0.8ms (EI) with CV =0.1) into the first layer of the liquid pool. EE, EI, IE and II denote connections between the two types of neurons. Inspired from information processing in living organisms, we set up a cognitive mapping from input layer to liquid pool. The value of I_{inject} depends on the value of the input data, in this case the activation of each single visual sensor.

The liquid consists of *Leaky Integrate And Fire Neurons* (C_m = 30nF, R_m = $1M\Omega$, V_{thresh} = 15mV, $V_{resting}$ = 0mV, V_{reset} uniform distributed in the interval [13.8mV 14.5mV], V_{init} uniform distributed in the interval [13.5mV 14.9mV], $T_{refract}$ = 3ms (E) or 2ms (I), I_{noise} = 0nA, I_{inject} uniform distributed in the

[1] The software simulator *CSim* and the appropriate documentation for the liquid state machine can be found on the web page `http://www.lsm.tugraz.at/`

interval [13.5nA 14.5nA]), grouped in an $8 \cdot 6 \cdot 3$ cuboid, that are randomly connected via *Dynamic Spiking Synapses* ($U_{mean} = 0.5, 0.05, 0.25, 0.32$, $D_{mean} = 1.1, 0.125, 0.7, 0.144$; $F_{mean} = 0.05\text{s}, 1.2\text{s}, 0.02\text{s}, 0.06\text{s}$; $delay_{mean} = 1.5\text{ms}, 0.8\text{ms}, 0.8\text{ms}, 0.8\text{ms}$ with $CV = 0.1$; $\tau_{syn} = 3\text{ms}, 3\text{ms}, 6\text{ms}, 6\text{ms}$; for EE, IE, EI, II), as described above. The probability of a connection between every two neurons is modeled by the probability distribution depending on a parameter λ described in the previous section. Various combinations of λ (connection probability) and mean connection weights Ω (connection strength) were used for simulation. 20% of the liquid neurons were randomly chosen to produce inhibitory potentials. C was chosen to be 0.3 (EE), 0.4 (EI), 0.2 (IE) and 0.1 (II). Figure 2 shows an example for connection within the LSM.

The information provided by the spiking neurons in the liquid pool is processed (read out) by *External Output Neurons* (V_{init}, $V_{resting}$, I_{noise} are the same as for the liquid neurons), each of them connected to all neurons in the liquid pool via *Static Spiking Synapses* (τ_{syn} = 3ms (EE) or 6ms (EI), $w = -6.73 * 10^{-5}$ (e.g., set after training), $delay_{mean}$ = 1.5ms (EE) or 0.8ms (EI) with $CV = 0.1$). The output neurons perform a simple linear combination of inputs that are provided by the liquid pool.

We evaluate the prediction approach by carrying out several experiments with real-world data in the RoboCup Middle-Size robotic soccer scenario. The experiments were conducted using a robot of the "Mostly Harmless" RoboCup Middle-Size team [9]. The task within the experiments is to predict the movement of the ball in the field of view a few frames into the future. The experimental setup can be described as follows: The robot is located on the field and points its camera across the field. The camera is a color camera with a resolution of 320 times 240 pixel. The ball is detected within an image by simple color-blob-detection leading to a binary image of the ball. We can use this simple image preprocessing since all objects on the RoboCup-field are color-coded and the ball is the only red one. The segmented image is presented to the 8 times 6 sensor field of the LSM. The activation of each sensor is equivalent to the percentage of how much of the sensory area is covered by the ball.

We collect a large set of 674 video sequences of the ball rolling with different velocities and directions across the field. The video sequences have different lengths and contain images in 50ms time steps. These video sequences are transfered into the equivalent sequences of activation patterns of the input sensors. Figure 3 shows such a sequence. The activation sequences are randomly divided into a training set (85%) and a validation set (15%) used to train and evaluate the prediction. Training and evaluation is conducted for the prediction of 2 timesteps (100ms), 4 timesteps (200ms) and 6 timesteps (300ms) ahead. The corresponding target activation sequences are simply obtained by shifting the input activation sequences 2, 4 or 6 steps forward in time.

Simulation for the training set is carried out sequence-by-sequence: for each collected activation sequence, the neural circuit is reset, input data are assigned to the input layer, recorders are set up to record the liquid's activity, simulation is started, and the corresponding recorded liquid activity is stored for the

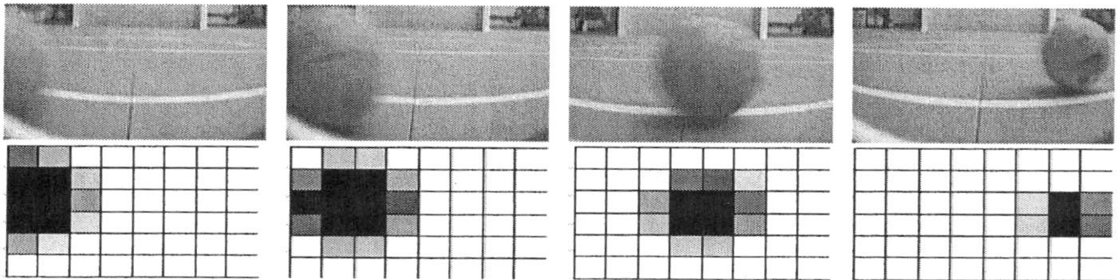

Fig. 3. Upper Row: Ball movement recorded by the camera. Lower Row: Activation of the sensor field

training part. The training is performed by calculating the weights[2] of all static synapses connecting each liquid neuron with all output layer neurons using linear regression.

Analogous to the simulation with the training set, simulation is then carried out on the validation set of activation sequences. The resulting output neuron activation sequences (*output sequences*) are stored for evaluating the network's performance.

4 Results

We introduce the mean absolute error and the correlation coefficient to evaluate the performance of the network. The mean absolute error is the positive difference between the activation values of target and output sequences of the validation set divided by the number of neurons in the input/output layer and the length of the sequence. This average error per output neuron and per image yields a reasonable measure for the performance on validation sets with different length. Figure 4 shows an example for a prediction and its error.

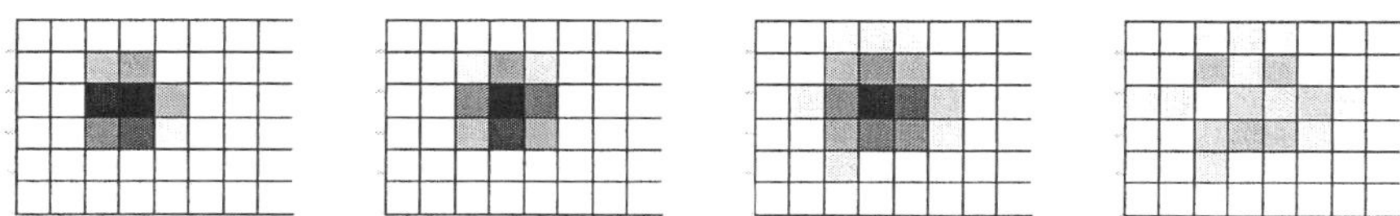

Fig. 4. Sensor activation for a prediction one timestep ahead. Input activation, target activation, predicted activation and error (left to right)

A problem which arises if only the mean absolute error is used for evaluation is that also networks with nearly no output activation produce a low mean

[2] In fact also the injection currents I_{inject} for each output layer neuron is calculated. For simplification this bias is treated as the 0th weight

absolute error - because most of the neurons in the target activation pattern are not covered by the ball and therefore they are not activated leading to a low average error per image. The correlation coefficient measures the *linear* dependency of two variables. If the value is zero two variables are not correlated. The correlation coefficient is calculated in similar way as the mean absolute error. Therefore the higher the coefficient the higher the probability of getting a correlation as large as the observed value without coincidence involved. In our case a relation between mean absolute error and correlation coefficient exists. A high correlation coefficient indicates a low mean absolute error.

In Figure 5 the mean absolute errors averaged over all single images in the movies in the validation set and the correlation coefficients for the prediction one timestep (50ms) ahead are shown for various parameter combinations. The parameter values range for both landscapes from 0.1 to 5.7 for Ω and from 0.5 to 5.7 for λ. If both Ω and λ are high, there is too much activation in the liquid. Remember, λ controls the probability of a connection and Ω controls the strength of a connection. We assume that this high activity hampers the network making a difference between the input and the noise. Both values indicate a good area if at least one of the parameters is low. Best results are achieved if both parameters are low (e.g. Ω=0.5, λ=1.0). The figure clearly shows the close relation between the mean absolute error and the correlation coefficient. Furthermore, it shows the very good results for the prediction as the correlation coefficient is close to 1.0 for good parameter combinations.

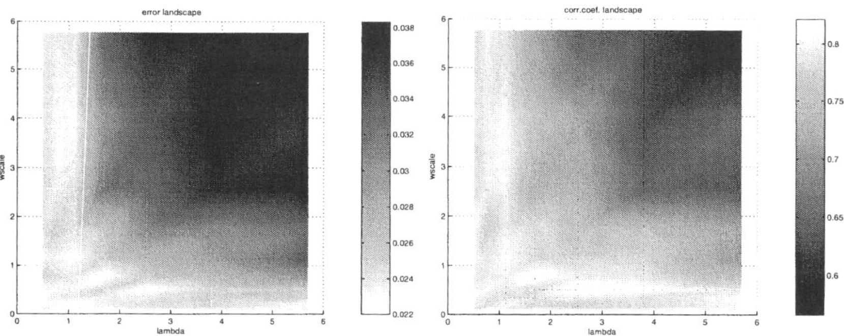

Fig. 5. Mean absolute error landscape on the left and correlation coefficient on the right for a prediction one time step ahead. Ω(*wscale*) [0.1,5.7], λ [0.5,5.7]

We also compare the results achieved with two (100ms) and four (200ms) time steps predicted. In order to compare the results of both predictions for different parameter combinations, we use again a landscape plot of the correlation coefficients. Figure 6 shows the correlation coefficient for parameter values range from 0.1 to 5.7 for Ω and from 0.5 to 5.7 for λ. The regions of good results remain the same as in the one timestep prediction. If at least one parameter - Ω

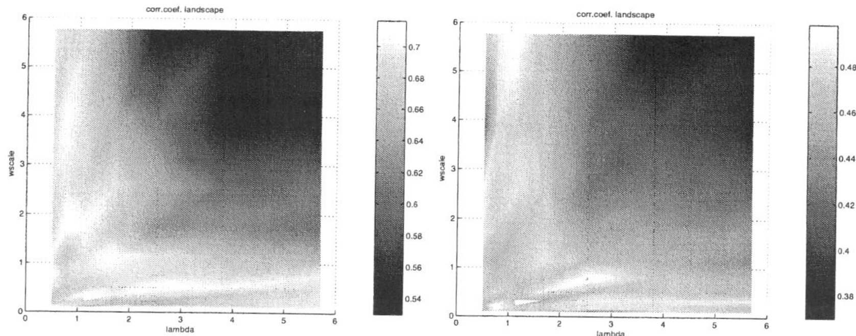

Fig. 6. Correlation coefficient landscape for two timesteps (100ms) on the left hand side and four timesteps (200ms) on the right hand side

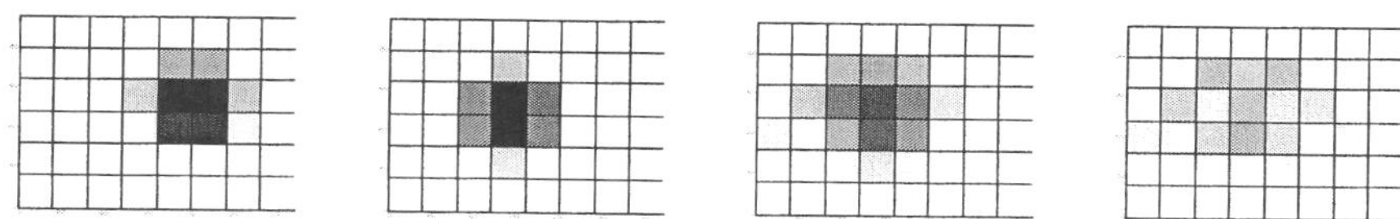

Fig. 7. Sensor activation for a prediction two timesteps ahead. Input activation, target activation, predicted activation and error (left to right). Parameter: Ω=1.0, λ=2.0

or λ - is low the correlation coefficient reaches its maximum (about 0.7 at two timesteps and about 0.5 at four timesteps). With increasing Ω and λ, the correlation coefficients decrease again. We believe that the too high activation is again the reason for this fact. Not surprisingly the maximum correlation compared to the one step prediction is lower because prediction gets harder if the prediction time increases. Nevertheless, the results are good enough for reasonable predictions.

Figure 7 shows an example for the activations and the error for the prediction of two timesteps ahead. It clearly shows that the center of the output activation is in the region of high activation in the input and the prediction is reasonable good. The comparison to Figure 4 also shows that the activation is more and more blurred around its center if the prediction time increases.

Furthermore we confronted the liquid with the task to predict 300ms (6 timesteps) without getting a proper result. We were not able to visually identify the ball position anymore. We guess this is mainly caused by the blur of the activation.

5 Conclusion and Future Work

In this work we propose a biologically more realistic approach for the computation of time series of real world images. The *Liquid State Machine (LSM)*, a new biologically inspired computation paradigm, is used to learn ball prediction within the RoboCup robotic soccer domain. The advantages of the LSM are that it projects the input data in a high-dimensional space and therefore simple learning methods, e.g. linear regression, can be used to train the readout. Furthermore, the *liquid*, a pool of inter-connected neurons, serves as a memory which holds the current and some past inputs up to a certain point in time (fading memory). Finally, this kind of computation is also biologically more plausible than other approaches like Artificial Neural Networks or Kalman Filters. Preliminary experiments within the RoboCup domain show that the LSM approach is able to reliably predict ball movement up to 200ms ahead. But there are still open questions. One question is how the computation is influenced by the size and topology of the LSM. Moreover, deeper investigation should be done for more complex non-linear movements, like balls bouncing back from an obstacle. Furthermore, it might be interesting to directly control actuators with the output of the LSM. We currently work on a goalkeeper, which intercepts the ball, controlled directly by the LSM approach.

References

1. M.I. Jordan and D.M. Wolpert. Computational motor control. In M. Gazzaniga, editor, *The Cognitive Neurosciences*. MIT Press, Cambridge, MA, 1999.
2. H. Jaeger. The echo state approach to analysing and training recurrent neural networks. Technical Report 148, GMD, 2001.
3. W. Maass, T. Natschlaeger, and T. Markram. Real-time computing without stable states: A new framework for neural computation based on perturbations. *Neural Computation*, 14(11):2531–2560, 2002.
4. W. Maass, R. A. Legenstein, and H. Markram. A new approach towards vision suggested by biologically realistic neural microcircuit models. In H. H. Buelthoff, S. W. Lee, T. A. Poggio, and C. Wallraven, editors, *Biologically Motivated Computer Vision. Proc. of the Second International Workshop, BMCV 2002*, volume 2525 of *Lecture Notes in Computer Science*, pages 282–293. Springer (Berlin), 2002.
5. M. F. Bear. *Neuroscience: Exploring the brain.* Williams and Wilkins, Baltimore, MA, 2000.
6. A. Gupta, Y. Wang, and H. Markram. Organizing principles for a diversity of gabaergic interneurons and synapses in the neocortex. *Science*, 287:273–278, 2000.
7. A.M. Thomson, D.C. West, Y. Wang, and A.P. Bannister. Synaptic connections and small circuits involving excitatory and inhibitory neurons in layers 2-5 of adult rat and cat neocortex: Triple intracellular recordings and biocytin labelling in vitro. *Cerebral Cortex*, 12(9):936–953, 2002.
8. H. Markram, Y. Wang, and M. Tsodyks. Differential signaling via the same axon of neocortical pyramidal neurons. *PNAS*, 95(9):5323–5328, 1998.
9. G. Fraser, G. Steinbauer, and F. Wotawa. A modular architecture for a multi-purpose mobile robot. In *Innovations in Applied Artificial Intelligence, IEA/AIE*, volume 3029 of *Lecture Notes in Artificial Intelligence*, Canada, 2004. Springer.

Robot Competition Using Gesture Based Interface

Hye Sun Park[1], Eun Yi Kim[2], and Hang Joon Kim[1]

[1] Department of Computer Engineering, Kyungpook National Univ., Korea
{hspark, hjkim}@ailab.knu.ac.kr
[2] Dept. of Internet and Multimedia Eng., NITRI (Next-Generation Innovative Technology Research Institute), Konkuk Univ., Korea
eykim@konkuk.ac.kr

Abstract. This paper developed a robot competition system using a gesture based interface. The used interface recognizes a gesture as meaningful movements from a fixed camera and controls a robot by transforming gesture commands. In the experiment, the used robot is *RCB-1* robot and the experimental results verify the feasibility and validity of the proposed system.

1 Introduction

Recently, there are significant amount of research on gesture recognition and its application to the robot control. Common robot control systems are controlled using additionally input devices like a joystick, remote control or sensor glove. However, theses methods are not only indirect and unnatural between a human and a robot, but also expensive and uncomfortable. Hence it is desirable to develop more intuitive and effective interface between the human and robot, without the additional tools [1-2].

For this, we developed a robot competition system using a gesture based interface. To assess the validity of the proposed system, we applied a real mobile robot, *KHR*-1. The results show that the proposed system can provide a convenient and intuitive interface and it has a potential to apply for the robot control.

2 Robot Competition System

Fig. 1 shows the proposed robot competition system in which the users control their robot using gestures. In our system, each camera, which is fixed on the desk, is connected to each robot, then the robot is controlled by processing the user's gestures obtained from the camera. In Fig.1, 'A'-user controls 'A'-robot through 'A'-interface using captured images from 'A'-camera. 'B'-user is also same as a case of 'A'-user.

The system controls mobile robots via the following 13 gestures: STAND UP, HOOK, TURN LEFT, TURN RIGHT, WALK FORWARD, BACK PEDAL, SIDE ATTACK, MOVE TO LEFT, MOVE TO RIGHT, BACK UP, BOTH PUNCH, LEFT PUNCH, RIGHT PUNCH. These gesture commands are basic commands for moving a robot.

M. Ali and F. Esposito (Eds.): IEA/AIE 2005, LNAI 3533, pp. 131 – 133, 2005.

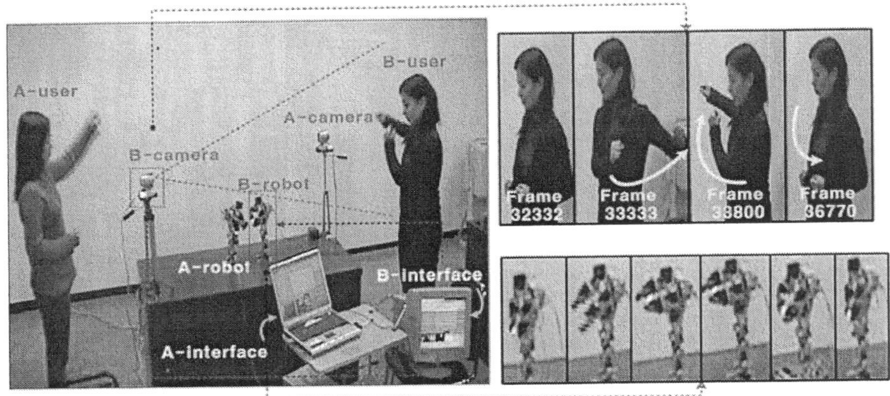

Fig. 1. The proposed robot competition system

3 Gesture Based Interface

The proposed system controls a robot using gesture-based interface. Fig.2 shows the outline of the gesture-based interface in our system.

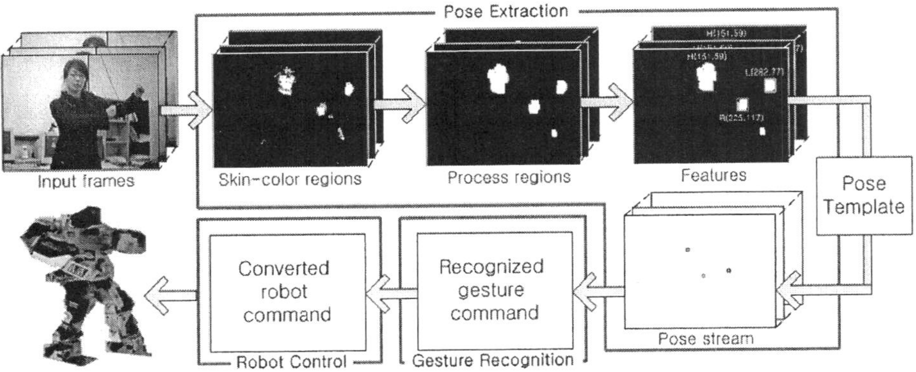

Fig. 2. The outline of the gesture based interface in the proposed system

A certain gesture in our system is represented by a pose symbol streaming, where a pose indicates the position of these body parts at a specific time. A pose symbol is represented as a vector $P = (F_x, F_y, L_x, L_y, R_x, R_y)$, where each element represents x-coordinate and y-coordinate of face, and left and right hands, respectively. Therefore, such poses are firstly extracted from input frames. The pose extraction step is performed by four steps: (1) we extracted skin-color regions using skin-color model that represented by 2-D Gaussian model, (2) the results are filtered using connected-component labeling, (3) positions of face, left hand, and right hand are obtained from

1st momentum of the respective components, (4) the extracted position vector is classified into a pose symbol by a template matching. After pose extraction step, the pose symbol streaming are recognized as gestures by the HMM which developed in [3]. The HMM processes a continuous stream as the input then segments and recognizes simultaneously. Thereafter, the recognized gestures are translated into commands to control a robot.

4 Experimental Results

The proposed system is implemented on Pentium IV using visual C++ language. The test images are captured at a frame rate of 10 (Hz) and the size of each color image was a 320 × 240.

For the experiments, each gesture was performed 100 times by 10 different individuals. The results show reliability of about 98.95% with false recognition of 1.05%. It is more interesting and friendly to control robot using a user movements than using additional input devices like a joystick or keyboard.

Consequently, the proposed system has a great potential to a variety of multimedia application as well as robot control.

5 Conclusions

In this paper, a robot competition system with a gesture-based interface has been successfully implemented on the mobile robot, *KHR*-1. The used gesture-based interface provides a more convenient and intuitive to control a mobile robot. Thus the user can form an intimacy with robot also feel more interests in controlling robot, by using the user gestures.

Acknowledgement

This research was supported by the MIC (Ministry of Information and Communication), Korea, under the ITRC (Information Technology Research Center) support program supervised by the IITA (Institute of Information Technology Assessment).

References

1. Chao Hu, Max Qinghu Meng, Peter Xiaoping Liu and Xiang Wang: Visual Gesture Recognition for Human-Machine Interface of Robot Teleoperation, IEEE/RSJ, (2003) 1560~1565.
2. Benoit, E., Allevard, T., Ukegawa, T. and Sawada, H.: Fuzzy sensor for gesture recognition based on motion and shape recognition of hand, VECIMS, (2003) 63-67.
3. H.S.Park, E.Y.Kim and H.J.Kim: A Hidden Markov Model for Gesture Recognition, Pattern Recognition, in review.

Agent Support for a Grid-Based High Energy Physics Application*

Aman Sahani, Ian Mathieson, and Lin Padgham

Intelligent Software Agents,
School of Computer Science and Information Technology,
RMIT University,
GPO Box 2476V, Melbourne, VIC 3001
{asahani, idm, linpa}@cs.rmit.edu.au

Abstract. This paper presents an agent system ASGARD-0, that provides monitoring for the success or failure of Grid jobs in a High Energy Physics application. This application area is one where use of the Grid is extremely well motivated as processes are both data and computationally intensive. Currently however there is no mechanism for automated monitoring of jobs and physicists must manually check to see whether the job has completed and whether it has done so in a successful manner. ASGARD-0 provides some initial services in this area and is also a proof of concept for a much more ambitious agent support system.

Keywords: Intelligent Agents, Intelligent Interfaces, Grid Support Services, Systems for Real Life Applications.

1 Introduction

This paper describes work done by the RMIT Intelligent Agents group in collaboration with the High Energy Physics (HEP) group at The University of Melbourne. The HEP group is keen to exploit the advantages offered by grid computing, but has been limited by the uninformative, immature nature of the underlying grid implementation: the current grid middleware provides no scheduling system or even an effective tool to split jobs across multiple machines. Compounding the problem is the lack of job progress monitoring provided.

This paper and the project in general looks at ways in which agents can assist with these problems, as well as assisting in other areas such as data discovery. Ultimately we aim to provide a fully-fledged system to allow an opaque interface to the grid that will allow physicists to perform experiments across various grid nodes. We refer to this future system as ASGARD (Agent Support for Grid Application Research and Development).

---

* Supported by VPAC Expertise grant EPPNRM121.2004, ARC Linkage grant LP0347025 in collaboration with the Australian Bureau of Meteorology and Agent Oriented Software P/L, ARC Discovery grant DP0346691 in collaboration with the RMIT Spatial Information Architecture Laboratory, and assisted by Tom Gamble.

M. Ali and F. Esposito (Eds.): IEA/AIE 2005, LNAI 3533, pp. 134–144, 2005.

The initial implementation, ASGARD-0, focuses upon providing the HEP community with feedback regarding the status of a job that has been or is currently running on a grid node, as currently they have no way of knowing whether their job has been successfully run or has failed.

2 The Application

One of the main challenges for High Energy Physics is to answer longstanding questions about fundamental particles and the forces acting between them. In particular the goal is to explain why some particles are much heavier than others, and why particles have mass at all.

The answer could reside in an all-pervading presence called the Higgs field, but at the moment there is no evidence of its existence. The University of Melbourne HEP group is participating in the BELLE experiment at the Japanese KEK-B asymmetric electron-positron collider, which generates huge amounts of B-meson decay data in search of evidence for the Higgs field. It is a highly collaborative project where multiple, geographically dispersed groups are using parts, or skims, of this dataset simultaneously.

There are two types of experiments conducted by the HEP group: simulations and analysis. A *simulation*, or Monte Carlo simulation, is essentially a data generation step. It is used to test and calibrate analysis code before running it on the actual BELLE data. An *analysis* is an experiment in which physicists look for particles of interest in a simulated or real dataset. Usually they are interested in a particular decay chain or particle and will perform data cuts or queries on the data to select the events of interest. The subsets of the full data set, containing only events exhibiting the decay chain being studied, are called *skims*.

Through the construction of increasingly sensitive and precise detectors, physicists have overcome to a large extent, the problem of generating useful data. Unfortunately this has led to an unresolved issue of how to extract meaningful information out of the resulting petabyte data collections. Filtering and querying of enormous magnitude is performed upon these massive datasets, leading to a bottleneck in terms of computational time and space.

Compounding the issue is that of the highly dispersed nature of the dataset. There are many organisations around the world involved in this project, each generating their own simulation data and skims from events collected by the BELLE detector. It is essential that the various organisations are able to share this data effectively.

The conventional single processor computational paradigm has proved inadequate in terms of both computational power and resource management/storage. Cluster-based computing, where a number of computers are devoted to the analysis takes advantage of the fact that it is possible to split these files into smaller sub files and perform independent analyses in parallel.

However, the data intensive nature of the HEP experiments, combined with the widely distributed scientific community, make availability of a grid resource highly desirable.

2.1 Problems

Grids clearly offer massive benefits to large projects such as the BELLE experiment. They allow data and resource sharing on an unprecedented level, leading to important collaborative work. However grids are also characterised by a number of problems:

- *Heterogeneity:* The programs and environment at each of the grid nodes are likely to be different.
- *Network Unreliability:* The network connection(s) between a local node and a remote host may go down during the execution of a job.
- *Network Cost:* It is costly to transmit large amounts of data.
- *Security:* Extra security and authentication procedures are required in order to guarantee computational integrity and authorise resource access.
- *Dispersed administration:* While having no central administration and monitoring facility is essential in some regards, it leads to the nodes on the grid being unreliable. Users submitting jobs to grid nodes may not know if that node is functioning correctly or at all.

All these can lead to a high failure rate of jobs that have been submitted to a grid. Our challenge is to reduce this failure rate by introducing an agent system capable of pre-empting failure through intelligent scheduling and submission, and intelligent recovery and resubmission following the failure of a node to successfully complete the job. Our initial implementation demonstrates an agent tool capable of detecting failure and reporting this in a meaningful way to the user.

2.2 Globus

The interest and need in grid computing has led to attempts to develop middleware capable of supporting grid applications. Globus [4] has become the most accepted (and indeed the default) standard for providing these services, although there are others (such as Legion [6]). The European Data Grid (EDG) has been developed as an extension of Globus, and is itself being extended to the "Large Hadron Collider" Grid (LCG) for a new set of experiments, known as ATLAS. The HEP group at the University of Melbourne has a test grid using the Globus Toolkit.

Globus defines an open source toolkit of low-level services for security, communication, resource location and allocation, process management and data access.

There are two major issues or problems that grid middleware, including Globus, have yet to address:

- *Lack of monitoring:* Globus allows an end user to check the status of a submitted job. Unfortunately this capability proved relatively primitive. There is no differentiation between failed and successfully completed jobs.

- *Lack of scheduling:* When a job is submitted to a Globus grid, the machine name of the remote host must be specified. An explicit mechanism for submitting to hosts is far from the goal of a system that has abstracted the underlying grid from the user.

These two problems do not mean that the Globus Toolkit is not useful, but emphasise the fact that the Toolkit is only a building block upon which developers can construct useful applications.

ASGARD has been built to use the Globus toolkit, but it should be readily adaptable to EDG and LCG, when physicists inevitably migrate, due to their similarities.

3 Agents for the Grid

Agents have been increasingly used in complex and dynamic applications [5]. Their proactive autonomous nature, combined with the ability to react to changing situations, makes them very suitable for grid environments , which are likely to be highly dynamic.

BDI (Belief Desire Intention) agent systems [1, 9] are particularly suitable due to their fault tolerant behaviour, and their commitment to continue to pursue a goal. These systems typically provide a number of plans with which an agent can attempt to achieve a given goal. This enables the agent to choose dynamically the most suitable plan for the given situation. If the plan unexpectedly fails, an alternative plan can be chosen in an attempt to achieve the goal. They can also monitor the environment and adapt the choice of plans accordingly. To encode this behaviour in a traditional system would be difficult at best, and probably result in a complex, brittle application, whereas it is innate in BDI style agent systems.

We have chosen to use JACK Intelligent Agents™ [2] as our BDI platform, as it is a well developed and robust system which is easily integrated into larger applications and provides extensive functionality.

A number of research groups are also working on agent support for the Grid. ARMS is a scheduling system for grid computing that uses the A4 design methodology and the PACE toolkit for internal resource scheduling. The A4 methodology describes each agent as a representative of a local grid resource.

AgentScape [7] provides middleware support (AOS) for developing agent applications via a virtual machine distributed across a WAN with heterogeneous hosts.

Both AgentScape and ARMS rely on the Grid having these systems installed on all Grid nodes. Our approach on the other hand does not rely on installing our agent system on all nodes. Rather the agent system operates at a local node, while communicating with the Grid infrastructure. This can be seen as a disadvantage and also an advantage. On the one hand a system such as AgentScape, with an AOS at every node has the potential to provide a great deal of information about the state of the grid, the network, and all the nodes in the grid.

However installing virtual machines across every node in the Grid is unlikely to be achievable in the near future as nodes are generally under varied institutional control. In this immature grid environment we believe our ASGARD architecture is more practical.

4 Overview of ASGARD Architecture and Design

ASGARD-0 has been designed using the Prometheus agent system design methodology [8] and the Prometheus Design Tool (PDT), then implemented using the JACK Development Environment (JDE) for JACK Intelligent Agents^{TM} [2] a multi-agent development environment based on the BDI model.

ASGARD devlivers intelligent support from *outside* the Grid. Thus it will eventually be able to monitor the commandline and act on the user's behalf.

Normally, after submitting a job to the BelleTestBed, the user would receive a *jobID* and manually check the BelleTestBed until the job appears `DONE`, then use the *jobID* to obtain the outputs from the experiment and visually inspect for signs of failure. Given that jobs can take hours or days to complete, this is an onerous task and is not efficient. ASGARD-0 abstracts this task of failure detection and diagnosis away from the user and returns the status of the job, along with the location of the data (if any).

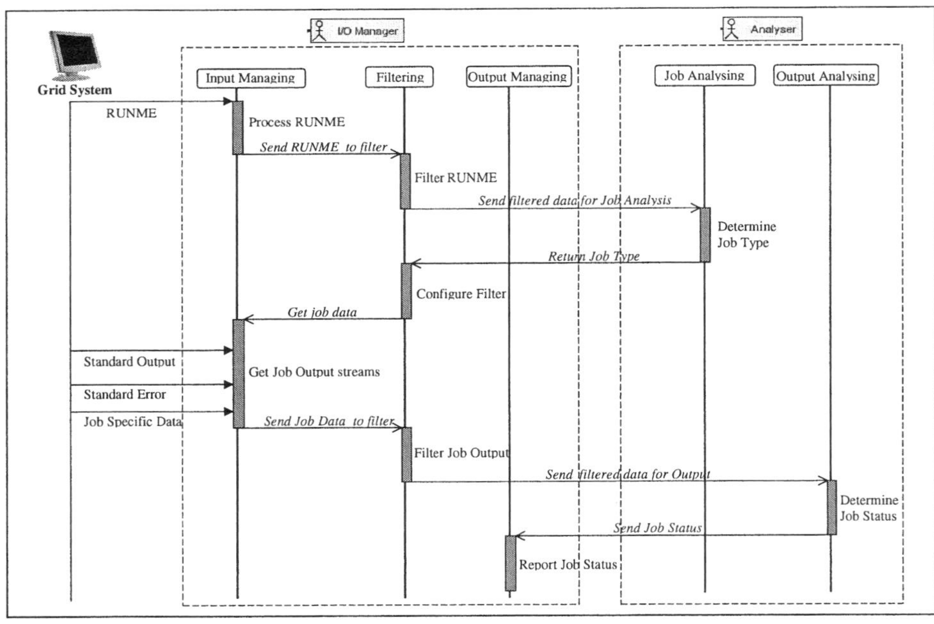

Fig. 1. Message flow within and between the ASGARD-0 agents and their capabilities

In our early experiments, we have concentrated on reasoning about specific problems which arise when using the BelleTestBed, rather than more general problems when connecting via Globus. Initial development was done using sample result files from previous executions on the BelleTestBed.

The system comprises two BDI agents. The *I/O Manager* agent is responsible for facilitating input and output exchanges with the environment and for filtering the data sent to the *Analyser*, which is responsible for reasoning about the job: before, during and after its execution (see Figure 1).

The *I/O Manager agent* acts to decouple the Analyser from the outside world, by controlling the manner in which inputs are obtained and forwarding only relevant material, as well as delivering any responses to the user. The filtering can be actively configured by the Analyser in response to the job description as well as during execution. The output can be reported in various forms including console messages, text reports, XML reports etc.

The *I/O Analyser agent* is responsible for determining the job type as well as reasoning about the job in order to determine the job status. The two distinct analysis phases, or aspects of the agent, are split into separate capabilities: Job Analysing and Output Analysing, also illustrated in Figure 1.

The *Job Analysing* capability receives the filtered job description data which helps the agent reason and determine the job type. Once the job type is determined a message is sent to the I/O manager agent in order to configure the filter.

The *Output Analysing* capability is the most important module of the system as its task is to determining the job status. It is discussed in more detail in the next section.

5 Output Analysis

This capability is the heart of the system, and requires the collection of input data, detection of potential errors and reporting of the job status upon successful termination of input. These tasks are delegated to the following sub-capabilities: Input Scanning, Error Handling, and Termination Handling, as shown in Figure 2.

The *Input Scanning* capability receives as input filtered job data from the standard output, standard input and other job specific files (if any) and stores this information about what it has seen as a set of beliefs, implemented as the JACK *beliefset* `JobOutputData` shown in Specific messages received may generate diagnosis goals which require further evaluation.

If potential error messages are encountered then a diagnosis goal causes plans to be chosen to try and ascertain the cause of the error These plans are part of the *Error Handling* capability to reason about the error and generate appropriate status messages. Similarly, if job termination messages are encountered then a goal is generated to determine whether or not the job has terminated successfully. The relevant plans then reason about the successful/unsuccessful termination of the job and report the status back to the I/O Manager agent. These plans are part of the *Termination Handling* capability.

The purpose of the *Error Handling* capability is to identify and analyse errors as and when they are encountered and to report the reasons responsible for them being generated. The goal which triggers this capability is *AnalyseError* (see Figure 2). Depending on the content of the message associated with a particular instance of this goal, different plans are chosen to reason about possible causes, or to monitor for future messages which may provide information about the cause.

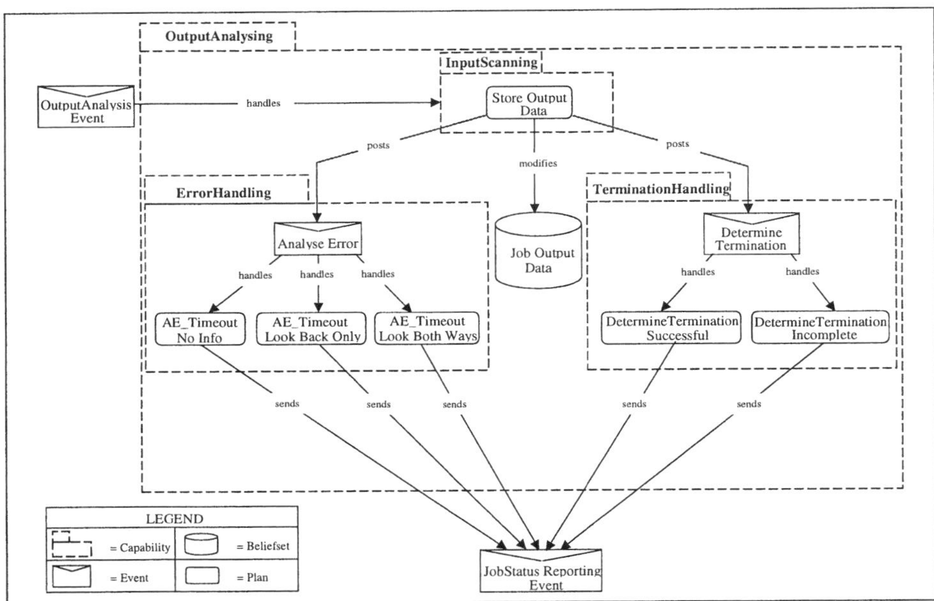

Fig. 2. Analyser capabilities, beliefsets and plans. Note that all plans have *read* access (not shown) to the beliefset, but only the StoreOutputData plan *modifies* the beliefset (as shown)

An example of a particular error is the "Timeout" error. In this case, the content of the message associated with the *AnalyseError* goal starts with the string `"FPDAGRID: ERROR - Timeout"`. There are three plans which attempt to find a cause for this error:

- AE_TimeoutLookBothWays (AE stands for Analyse Error),
- AE_TimeoutLookBackOnly, and
- AE_TimeoutNoInfo

These plans are all applicable for the situation where the error encountered is a timeout error. They are tried in the order shown above, where the

AE_TimeoutNoInfo plan is simply a default plan which provides (to the I/O Manager) the information that a timeout error has occured but the cause has not been determined while each of the first two plans look for certain messages in the beliefset that could have led to the timeout error being generated.

The first plan, AE_TimeoutLookBothWays, handles the most common situation. It does the following steps:

- wait until "event_server" error message is encountered.
- Access belief set data to look for additional information on reasons for the error.
- Report Error with details.

Once the "event_server" error message has been encountered, the plan can be certain that a "Timeout" error has occurred and can then, based on the information obtained, look in its beliefset for further information as to the cause. Items such as file availability messages and any corresponding errors that may be generated , provide further information about the sequence of events that have contributed to the "Timeout" error being generated.

TIMEOUT error messages are generated by low level library routines at the grid level and they indicate the possibility of an error. The "event_server" messages are generated from an application interfacing with the grid and they provide details about the error. However there is a possibility that an "event_server" error message may not be received, even though a TIMEOUT error has occurred. In this case, if EOF is encountered (in any of the input sources) prior to an "event_server" message being received, the first plan fails, and the agent will try the AE_TimeoutLookBackOnly plan in order to achieve the goal of analysing the "Timeout" error. This plan tries to look through the beliefset to find any evidence confirming the generation of a "Timeout" error, and associated information regarding causes. This is quite similar to the first plan but initially lacks conclusive evidence to help guide the further search for reasons. Once the evidence is gathered this plan then also tries to find further details of the error.

This plan tries to look for items such as server error responses in the beliefset. If such a message has occurred more than once then the plan succeeds at confirming the timeout error. The error detail (erroneous filename) is retrieved by looking up the Grid URL message and is reported back to the user.

In the unlikely event of the AE_TimeoutLookBackOnly plan failing as well as the AE_TimeoutLookBothWays plan, the AE_TimeoutNoInfo plan is executed. It simply reports that a "Timeout" error was observed but that no further information has been obtained. It reports only the detection of the error rather than diagnosing and specifying the details about it.

As new ideas on what to look for to try and diagnose each kind of error message are provided, these can readily be mapped to self contained plans which capture the analysis process.

Job Termination is handled by the *Termination Handling* capability. The goal is to determine the successful completion of the job upon job termination. This goal is represented by the *DetermineTermination* event (see Figure 2).

This capability has two alternative plans to achieve this goal. DetermineTermination_Successful and DetermineTermination_Incomplete in order of priority. These plans are considered if the following context conditions are *both* true:

- The agent has seen an EOF message from stdout (Job Status Message = EOF and Message Source = stdout).
- The agent has seen an EOF message from stderr (Job Status Message = EOF and Message Source = stderr).

If in addition the agent has seen the job status messages `"FPDAGRID: User Cleanup"` and `"Processing End....... Removing IPC.......... done"` then the DetermineTermination_Successful plan is chosen as appropriate and a successful execution message is reported back to the user via the I/O Manager agent.

If the job status messages `"FPDAGRID: User Cleanup"` and `"Processing End....... Removing IPC.......... done"` have not been seen by the agent (i.e. it is not the case that the beliefset contains these messages), then the DetermineTermination_Incomplete plan is appropriate and it simply reports an abnormal termination and execution incomplete status.

6 Conclusions and Future Work

ASGARD-0 is an initial but useful first step in providing intelligent agent assistance for grid computing, in the context of the HEP application. Being able to detect failures and reason about them (if not handle them) is useful, but our longer term aims are to provide more comprehensive support. Importantly we have demonstrated that it is possible to provide useful agent support services for the grid, without having the agents embedded tightly into the internal infrastructure of every grid node. In future work we hope to align with and make use of both our own and others' work within the world wide web research community.

The semantic grid is an extension of the semantic web, where the grid (or web) is defined as a service-oriented architecture in which services are provided to and from entities using an advertised contract system. These services are "advertised" through the use of standard Service Description Languages (SDLs). The Open grid Service Infrastructure (OGSI [10]) defines these WSDL specifications for use consistent with grid-based architectures. The ability to recognise and provide information about computation services on the grid is one aspect of the future development of ASGARD.

HEP analyses are typically very long processes, dealing with massive amounts of data. It is however possible that someone has already performed the analysis or simulation. If matching data exists somewhere on the grid, then it may make sense to locate and use this data, rather than reproduce it. An ASGARD agent could locate this data, by viewing the existing data as a service offered by grid nodes and avoid duplication.

If the analysis itself is viewed as a service, then it may be possible to further augment the BELLE process using ASGARD through semantic optimisation.

According to the physicists, "80% of computation is duplicated" with the early stages of many experiments being identical. However there is no way of getting access to other people's intermediate data. The cost of storage is the primary reason for this – it is completely infeasible to store even the output of a large number of experiments, much less the intermediate data. ASGARD could potentially recognise that two (or more) analyses were aligned in at least part of their process (more likely the earlier parts of the analysis) and run them as one single analysis, diverging them at the appropriate point. In the discourse of service composition: computation could be seen as the service, something supported by OGSI. Having each particular experiment advertise the type of analysis currently being undertaken, it may be possible to merge scheduled experiments.

The method we have used for providing intelligent agent services to grid applications indicates that this is an effective and relatively straightforward approach, as there is no necessity to obtain agreement from all nodes before the approach can be trialled. Even if it is desired at a later stage to integrate the services more fully within the grid infrastructure, the approach of having loosely attached agents in order to trial and refine such services is very promising.

References

1. Bratman, M. E.: *Intentions, Plans, and Practical Reason*, Harvard University Press, Cambridge MA, USA.
2. Busetta, P., Rönnquist, R., Hodgson, A., Lucas, A.: *Jack Intelligent Agents - Components for Intelligent Agents in Java*, Technical Report 1, Agent Oriented Software Pty. Ltd, Melbourne, Australia. See web site at `http://www.agent-software.com`.
3. Cao, J., Jarvis, S. A., Saini, S., Kerbyson, D. J., Nudd, G. R.: 'ARMS: An agent-based resource management system for grid computing' *Scientific Programming* **10**. (2002) 135–148 (Special Issue on Grid Computing)
4. Foster, I., Kesselman, C.: The Globus Project: A Status Report *in* 'Proceedings of the Seventh Heterogeneous Computing Workshop' IEEE Computer Society. (1998) 4–19 See web site at: `http://www.globus.org/`.
5. Jennings, N., Wooldridge, M.: Applications of Intelligent Agents *in* Jennings and Wooldridge 'Agent Technology: Foundations, Applications, and Markets', Springer. (1998) 3–28
6. Natrajan, A., Humphrey, M., Grimshaw, A. S.: Capacity and Capability Computing in Legion *in* 'Proceedings of International Conference on Computational Science (ICCS)', Lecture Notes in Computer Science **2073**, Springer Verlag. (2001) 273
7. Overeinder, B. J., Posthumus, E., Brazier, F. M. T.: Integrating Peer-to-Peer Networking and Computing in the AgentScape Framework *in* 'Proceedings of the 2nd IEEE International Conference on Peer-to-Peer Computing', IEEE Computer Society. (2002) 96–103 See web site at `http://www.iids.org/research/aos/`.
8. Padgham, L., Winikoff, M.: *Developing Intelligent Agent Systems: a practical guide*, John Wiley ands Sons, England. (2004)

9. Rao, A. S., Georgeff, M. P.: An Abstract Architecture for Rational Agents *in* C. Rich, W. Swartout, and B. Nebel, eds, 'Proceedings of the Third International Conference on Principles of Knowledge Representation and Reasoning', Morgan Kaufmann. (1992) 439–449
10. Tuecke, S., Foster I., Frey J., Graham S., Kesselman C., Maquire T., Sandholm T., Snelling D., Vanderbilt P.: *Open Grid Services Infrastructure (OGSI)*, Version 1.0, Global Grid Forum. See web site at `http://www.ggf.org/`.

Feasibility of Multi-agent Simulation for the Trust and Tracing Game

Sebastiaan Meijer and Tim Verwaart

Wageningen University and Research Centre, Burg. Patijnlaan 19, Den Haag, Netherlands
{sebastiaan.meijer, tim.verwaart}@wur.nl

Abstract. Trust is an important issue in trade. For instance in food trade, market actors have to rely on their trade partner's quality statements. The roles of trust and deception in supply networks in various cultural and organisational settings are subject of research in the social sciences. The Trust And Tracing game is an instrument for that type of study. It is a game for human players. Conducting experiments is time-consuming and expensive. Furthermore, it is hard to formulate hypotheses and to test effects of parameter changes, as this requires many participants. For these reasons the project reported in this paper investigated the feasibility of multi-agent simulation of the game and delivered a prototype. This paper briefly describes the game and introduces the process composition of the agents. The prototype uses simple, but effective models. The paper concludes with directions for refinement of models for agent behaviour.

1 Introduction

The Trust and Tracing game is a research tool designed to study human behaviour in commodity supply chains and networks. The issue of trust is highly relevant to the field of supply chain and network studies. In their paper founding the field, Diederen and Jonkers [3] list six core sources of value improvement for supply chains and networks. For four out of six sources trust is a major aspect in the way people deal with each other about these issues (transaction, property rights and value capture, social structure, and network externalities). For each of these four sources case studies have been done describing the importance of human relationships ([1], [13]).

Meijer [11] describes the appropriateness of using simulation games to facilitate the six sources of value improvement. The Trust and Tracing game is an example of such a game. This tool places the choice between relying on trust versus relying on complete information in trade environments at the core of a social simulation game. In research conducted, the game has been used both as a data gathering tool about the role of reputation and trust in various types of business networks, and as tool to make participants feed back on their own daily experiences in their respective jobs.

There are several disadvantages to playing games with human players for research purposes. Firstly it is impossible to control all parameters, as any person has social relationships and cultural bias [2]. Furthermore it is expensive and time-consuming to acquire enough participants [4], so the number of games that can be played in varying configurations is limited. A simulation model could prove useful for:

M. Ali and F. Esposito (Eds.): IEA/AIE 2005, LNAI 3533, pp. 145 – 154, 2005.

1. Validation of models of behaviour induced from game observations
2. Testing of hypotheses about system dynamics of aggregated results in relation to parameter changes in individual behaviour
3. Selection of useful configurations for games with humans (test design)

A multi-agent approach of the simulation is obvious because the weak notion of agency as formulated by Jennings and Wooldridge [8] applies to the players. The players pursue individual goals and take decisions individually (autonomy), they can react on offers of others (responsiveness), they plan their actions according to their private needs and preferences (pro-activeness), and they are aware of the identity of other players, negotiate with them, and maintain beliefs about them (social ability).

A brief description of the Trust And Tracing game will be given here. An extensive description is available in [10]. The focus of study is on trust in stated quality of commodities. The game needs a group of 12 up to 25 persons that play roles of producers, middlemen, retailers, or consumers (Fig. 1). The goal of producers and traders is to maximise profit. The consumers' goal is to maximise satisfaction.

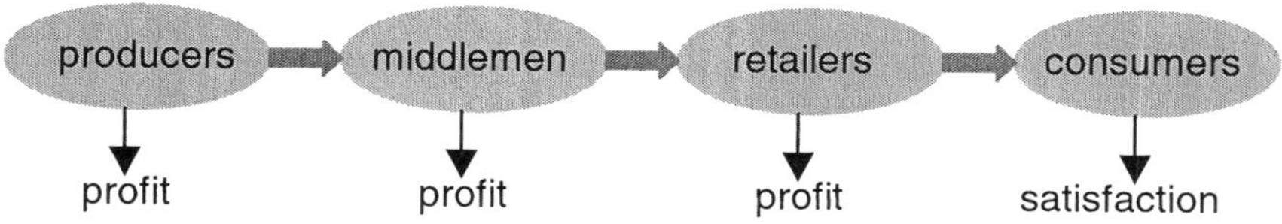

Fig. 1. Commodity flow and player's goals

Each player receives (artificial) money. Producers receive envelopes representing lots of commodities. Each lot is of a certain type of product and of either low or high quality. High quality products give more satisfaction points than low quality products. A ticket covered in the envelope (so it is not visible) represents quality. The producers know the quality. Other players have to trust the quality statement of their suppliers, or request a product trace at the cost of some money and some damage to the relations with their suppliers. The game leader acts as a tracing agency and can on request determine product quality. In case of deception the game leader will trace transactions and punish deceivers with a fine and public disgrace.

This paper describes the design of a prototype for the multi-agent simulation. Section 2 describes the design of the agents and their process composition and information exchange. Section 3 describes the simple models of behaviour implemented in this prototype and an example of simulation results. Section 4 discusses the feasibility of multi-agent simulation and directions for refinements of the behavioural models.

2 Agent Design

This section first introduces the agents and the information flow between agents. After the introduction it focuses on the internal structure (process composition and information flow) of the trading agents.

The types of agents acting in the game are the trading agents (producers, middlemen, retailers and consumers) and the tracing agency. Fig. 2. depicts the information exchange between the agents.

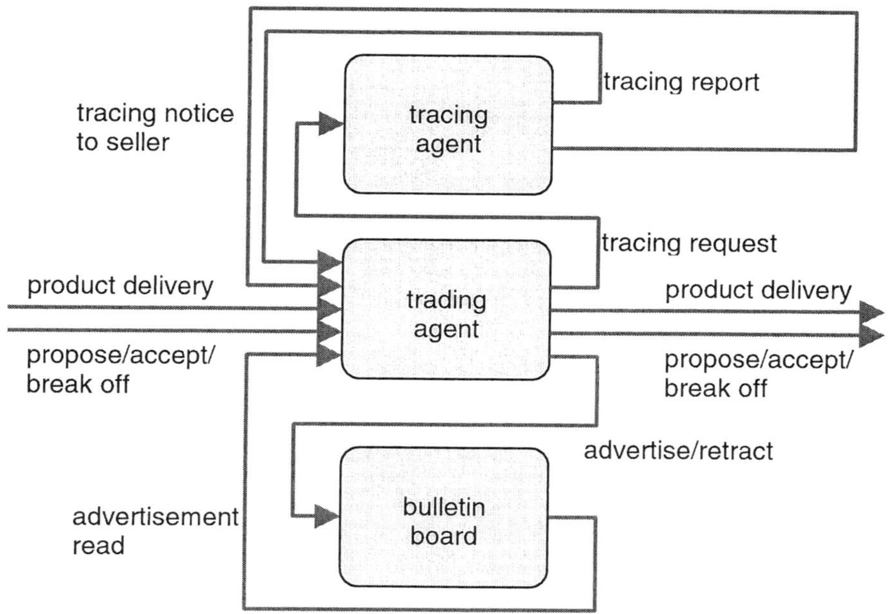

Fig. 2. Information exchange between agents

We choose to use a simple model for partner selection for the prototype. Trading agents may offer their products by advertising on a bulletin board. The agent offering may retract its advertisements. All agents can read all advertisements. An agent interested in buying a product proposes negotiations by sending a proposal to the offering agent. Agents negotiate by exchanging proposals until one of them accepts the last offer made or breaks the negotiation cycle. After a successful negotiation the product can be delivered. Together with the product the history of the lot arrives. The history contains the real quality and quality as stated by previous sellers as hidden attributes, which can be revealed by the tracing agent solely. A buying agent may request a trace. The tracing agent reveals hidden information for the requestor and informs the seller that a trace has been requested. In case of deception the tracing agent punishes all deceivers with a fine. Table 1 shows the attributes of the information exchanged.

The remaining part of this section is devoted to the trading agents. Producers, middlemen, retailers, and consumers have different roles in the market. However, they may be thought of as having similar process composition. Fig. 3 presents a model for process composition and internal information links in trade agents. The processes will be briefly described.

Table 1. Attributes of information exchanged between agents

Message	Attributes
Advertise	reference to offering agent; product quality; asking price
Retract	reference to offering agent; product quality; asking price
advertismt. read	reference to offering agent; product quality; asking price
Propose	ref. to proposing agent; product quality; proposed price
Accept	ref. to accepting agent; product quality; accepted price
break off	reference to agent breaking off negotiations
product delivery	ref. to selling agent; stated product quality*; real quality (hidden)*; list of [reference to selling agent; *stated quality (hidden)*] containing data about previous deliveries *(hidden attributes to be revealed only by tracing agent)*
tracing request	ref. to requesting agent; reference to product delivery
tracing report	reference to product delivery; real quality
tracing notice	reference to requesting agent; *if applicable*: fine

The central process is *need determination*. It sets the priorities for buying or selling products. It uses information about the current levels of stock and financial resources. It sends orders to the processes *supplier search* and *customer search* to initiate buying or selling of products.

The *customer search* process advertises products, using market price beliefs to make product offers. It advertises and stops search or advertising if no response occurs within a reasonable time, or if a proposal has been received through the *negotiation* process. It will report expiration of advertisements to the *seller's beliefs maintenance* process.

The *supplier search* process reads advertisements and uses asking prices and partner belief information from the *buyer's beliefs maintenance* process to select the most promising candidate for negotiations. If it succeeds in selecting a potential supplier it forwards the advertisement to the *negotiation* process to make a proposal. If not, the failure is reported to *buyer's belief maintenance.*

The *negotiation* process exchanges proposals with negotiation partners. It informs the *customer* search process as soon as it has received a reply on an advertisement. It uses beliefs about market price from a buyer's point of view or seller's point of view, depending on its role. It has limited patience and will break off negotiations if no agreement has been reached in a preset time. The outcomes of negotiations will be sent to *buyer's beliefs maintenance* or *seller's beliefs maintenance*.

The *buyer' beliefs maintenance* process maintains beliefs about the market (maximal prices from a buyer's point of view), each of the trade partners (ease of bargaining, reliability with respect to quality statements), and the agent itself (patience, confidence, and risk-attitude). Based on experience from *supplier search*, *negotiation*, and tracing reports the beliefs may be updated, e.g. negotiation outcomes lead to updates of patience or price beliefs and tracing reports lead to updates of trust in the supplier. In response to product delivery, the buyer's trust in the supplier is used in the *trust or trace decision*. In case of a negative tracing report stock update messages will be sent to the *stock and cash beliefs maintenance* process to adjust the beliefs about the products in stock.

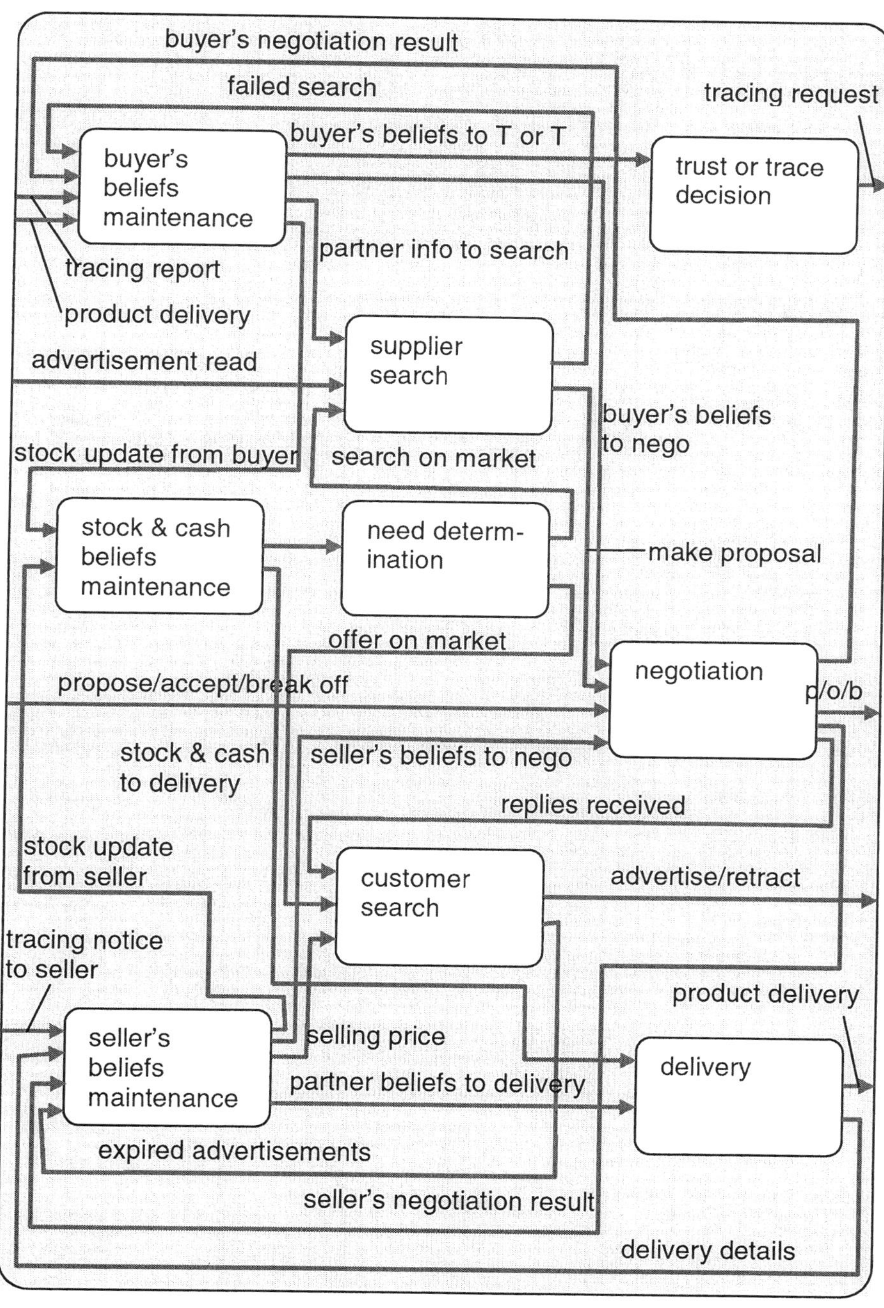

Fig. 3. Process composition and information links in trade agents

The *trust or trace decision* process evaluates the pros and cons of tracing. There is a tracing fee and tracing does damage to the interpersonal relation with the supplier if he is not deceiving. On the other hand the seller should not get the idea that the buyer is an easy prey. Also the seller might be deceived and deliver bad products in good faith. The decision depends mainly on the subjective estimate of seller's reliability and the buyer's confidence and reserve with respect to showing suspicion and buyer's willingness to take risk.

The *seller's beliefs maintenance* process maintains beliefs about the market (minimal prices from a sellers point of view), each of the trade partners (ease of bargaining, tracing frequency), and the agent itself (patience, honesty, and risk-attitude). Based on experience from *customer search*, *negotiation*, and tracing reports the beliefs may be updated, e.g. honesty may decay over time and be increased in response to a punishment; failing negotiations may lead to updates of patience or price beliefs. The *seller's beliefs maintenance* process forwards successful negotiation results to the *delivery* process, along with information about the relation with the buyer and honesty parameters.

The decision to deceive or to be truthful will be taken in the *delivery* process which sends product delivery information to the buyer. It can use the information provided by the *seller's beliefs maintenance* process to determine the intention to deceive, and information about stock and cash position to determine the opportunity to deceive.

The *stock and cash beliefs maintenance process* accumulates changes in cash and stock positions reported by the *buyer's* and *seller's beliefs maintenance* processes. The beliefs about quality of products in stock may be incorrect.

The next section presents a prototype that partially implements these processes, along with an example of simulation results.

Table 2. Traits and beliefs of TradeAgent in the prototype

Trait/Belief	Type	Range	Comments
patience	Integer	[1,∞)	Maximum number of time cycles an agent will take to achieve a result
m	Double	[0,1]	Lower bound for honesty (1: completely honest; 0: liar)
honesty	Double	[m,1]	Actual honesty, with experience based update
target	Integer	[0,∞)	Target number of products to get in stock, set for both product qualities
stock	Integer	[0,∞)	Target number of products to get in stock, maintained for both product qualities
cash	Integer	(-∞,∞)	Amount of money in cash
minSel	Integer	(0, ∞)	Belief about the minimal price for selling, maintained for both product qualities
maxBuy	Integer	(0, ∞)	Belief about the minimal price for selling, maintained for both product qualities
trust	Integer	[0,100]	Maintained for every other agent individually; < 50: unreliable, >50: reliable, 50: don't know

3 Prototype Implementation and Results

In this project we tested the feasibility of multi-agent simulation models for study of social aspects of supply chains and networks. We developed a prototype using the Swarm simulation environment [15]. The prototype partially implements the processes described earlier. This section presents the implementation and simple models for agent behaviour. The section concludes with an example of simulation results.

The agents are implemented as Java objects. The class TradeAgent has subclasses Producer, Middleman, Retailer, and Consumer, which differ in the type of partners they select for trading. Table 2 presents traits and beliefs of TradeAgents.

Swarm is a simulation environment based on time-cycles. In each time-cycle all agents are activated once by sending them the "step" message. Agents must implement a step-method that directs their activities. The prototype is based on three cycles, depicted in Fig. 4. Depending on the state of the agent the step-method executes one of the cycles, until it gets in a wait-state for next time-step.

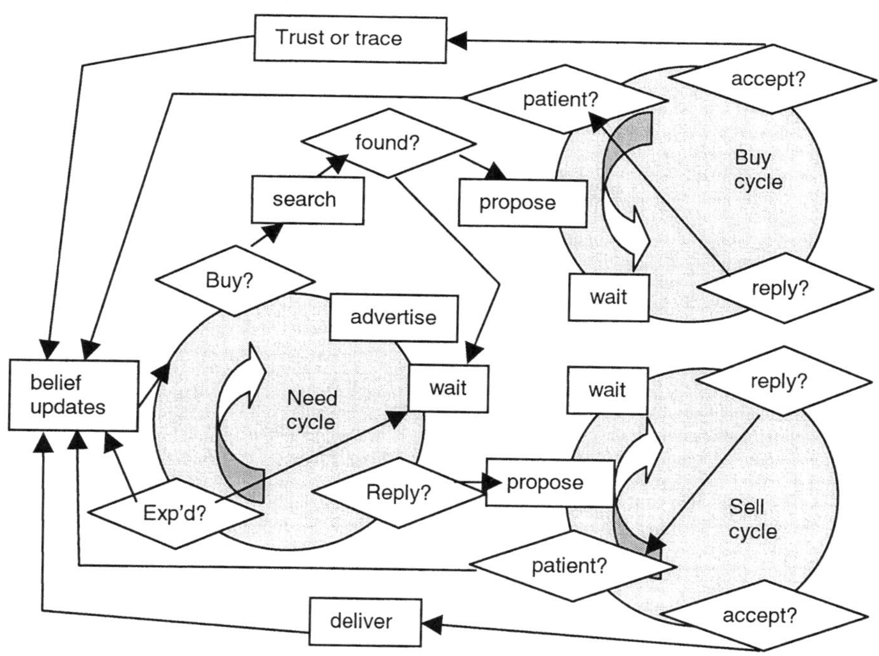

Fig. 4. TradeAgent: need-cycle, buy-cycle, and sell-cycle

In the need-cycle the agent checks for a reply to a current advertisement. If so, it will enter the sell-cycle. If an advertisement has been open for more cycles than the agent's patience, it will retract the advertisement and update beliefs (decrease minimum selling price and increase patience). If there is no advertisement, the agent has to decide to buy or sell. Only if stock is at target level for all qualities, an agent advertises a product of randomly selected quality (price=1.5*minSel) and waits for reply. Otherwise the agent will try to buy.

After the decision to buy, the agent searches a partner with best reliability advertising the desired quality. In case of success he makes a proposal (price=maxBuy/1.5). In the buy- and sell-cycles agents use a simple price negotiation model. If an agent runs out of patience he will break off and update price belief and patience. If an agreement is made in a number of time-steps half or less of patience, price belief and patience is updated in the opposite direction.

After an agreement has been reached, the selling agent has to deliver. If agreed product quality is high, and trust in partner < 55, and a random number in [0, 1] exceeds the current honesty, and it has cash to pay for the fine, it will cheat. The buying agent has to trust or trace. It will trace if product quality is high, and trust in partner < 55, and it has cash for the tracing fee. Table 3 summarises updates of honesty and trust that result from the decisions taken.

Table 3. Honesty and trust updates (trust limited in [0, 100]; honesty limited in [0, 1])

Event	Seller's trust	Seller's honesty	Buyer's trust
Successful negotiation	+1	0	+1
No trace requested	0	-0.02	0
Trace: truthful	-1	0	+3
Trace: deception	-5	+0.1	-5

The effect of reliable delivery on product flow is demonstrated in two simulations depicted in Fig. 5.

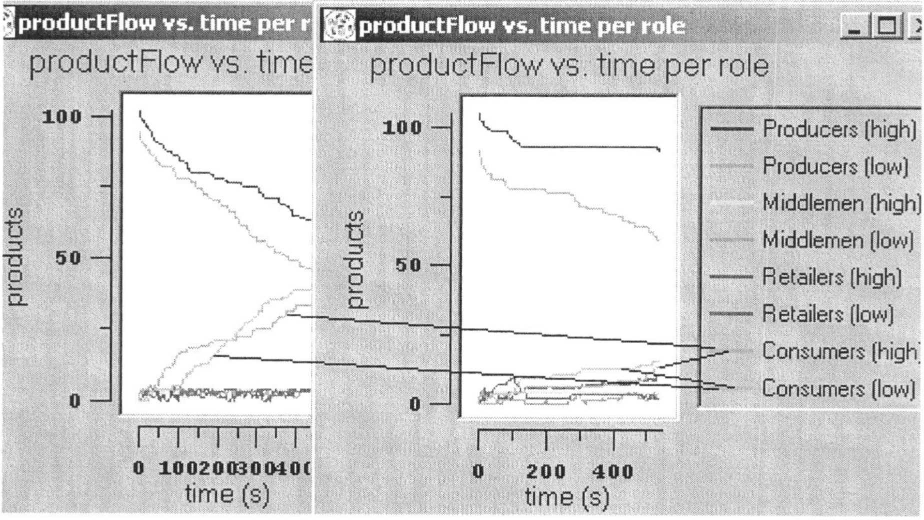

Fig. 5. Effect of honesty in the supply network. In the left hand run the honesty is set to 0.9 for all agents. Commodities flow rapidly from producers to consumers. In the right hand run honesty is set to 0.1. Hardly any products get to the consumers

4 Conclusion and Directions for Future Development

This research delivered a design and a working prototype based on simple models of agent behaviour in a Trust and Tracing game environment. The prototype captures the most characterising aspects of the human game [10], with bargaining, cheating, and deciding whether to trust or not. 'Trust' has been modelled as an opinion of the buyer about the chance a supplier will cheat. Multi-agent simulations of supply chains usually focus on techno-economic cooperation between agents. This prototype adds opinions about other agents to the economic reasoning implemented in other models (for instance [5], [6], [12]).

Initial experiments show that manipulation of the basic configuration parameters leads to attenuations in agent behaviour. The example given in this paper shows a faster trade when agents are honest. This is similar to observations in the real game and in real world business cases. We tested several other manipulations like increase of cheating behaviour, increase of supply and increase of honesty and found the simulation to react in a direction we expected from real game experiences.

Because of the limited detail in the models this prototype does not allow valid conclusions for the research purpose as the magnitude of changes has not been tested, nor modelled realistically. However, the prototype demonstrates the feasibility of multi-agent simulation for the Trust and Tracing game. The prototype proved sensitivity to manipulation of the major variables and showed similar changes in behaviour as observed in the human game.

The three contributions a multi agent simulation can make presented in the introduction (validation of models, testing of hypotheses and selection of useful game configurations) are yet unfulfilled. Future research should focus on more sophisticated models of behaviour in the game. The dimension of trust deserves special attention, as the human notion of trust and the agent definition will differ. The agent is not a social being, living in a complex society and culture. Furthermore, the current prototype implements a simple price negotiation model. Multi-attribute negotiation models like the one proposed by Jonker and Treur [9] support negotiation about price, quality, guarantee conditions, etc. simultaneously. Utility functions should involve risk assessment and trust. The cheating and trust or trace decisions should involve transaction cost economics [14]. For realistic modelling of beliefs maintenance Hofstede's synthetic cultures [7] can be used.

In a more sophisticated model of the Trust and Tracing game, the validation phase will require special attention. The complexity of human relationships cannot be caught fully in the simulation. Therefore the model should focus on theoretically correct outcomes. The validation phase will show where real humans differ from the theoretically correct agents.

The contribution of this research in the field of supply chain and networks research is a better insight in the working of trust on economic performance of chains and networks. Camps *et al* [1] show that long-term human relationships are of major importance in successful chains and networks. An empirically tested model of trust in long-term chain relationships will help understanding what happens in real world chains and networks and will facilitate design of the economic institutions.

Acknowledgement

The authors express their respect and gratitude to Martijn Haarman, Hans Klaverwijden, and Danny Kortekaas for their enthusiasm and for the great efforts they made to implement the prototype.

References

1. T. Camps, P. Diederen, G.J. Hofstede and B. Vos (ed), 2004, The emerging world of Chains and Networks, Reed Business Information.
2. D. Crookall, 1997, A guide to the literature on simulation / gaming, In: D. Crookall and K Arai, Simulation and gaming across disciplines and cultures, ISAGA
3. P.J.M. Diederen and H.L.Jonkers, 2001, Chain and Network Studies, KLICT paper 2415, 's Hertogenbosch, The Netherlands.
4. R.D. Duke and J.L. Geurts, 2004, Policy games for strategic management, pathways into the unknown, Dutch University Press, Amsterdam.
5. T. Eymann, 2001, Markets without Makers - A Framework for Decentralized Economic Coordination in Multiagent Systems. In: L. Fiege, G. Mühl, U. Wilhelm (Eds.), Electronic Commerce. Proc. of the Second Int. Workshop WELCOM 2001, LNCS 2232, Springer, 2001.
6. Y. Fu, R.Piplani, R.de Souza, J.Wu. Multi-agent Enabled Modeling and Simulation towards Collaborative Inventory Management in Supply Chains. In: J.A.Joines, R.R.Barton, K.Kang, P.A.Fishwick (Eds.): Proc. of the 2000 Winter Simulation Conference, ISBN:1-23456-789-0
7. G.J. Hofstede, P.B. Pedersen, G. Hofstede, 2002, Exploring cultures: Exercises, stories and synthetic cultures, Intercultural Press.
8. N.R. Jennings and M. Wooldridge, 1998, Applications of intelligent agents. In: N.R. Jennings and M. Wooldridge, Agent technology: Foundations, Applications, and Markets. 1998, Springer.
9. C.M. Jonker, J. Treur, 2001, An agent architecture for multi-attribute negotiation. In: B. Nebel (ed.), Proc. Of the 17th International Joint Conference on AI, IJCAI '01, 2001, pp 1195 – 1201.
10. S. Meijer, 2004, The usefulness of Chain Games, In: Proc. 8th Int. workshop on experimental learning, IFIP WG 5.7 SIG Conference, May 2004, Wageningen, The Netherlands.
11. S. Meijer and G.J. Hofstede, The Trust and Tracing game. In: Proc. 7th Int. workshop on experiential learning. IFIP WG 5.7 SIG conference, May 2003, Aalborg, Denmark.
12. T. Moyaux, B. Chaib-Dra, S. D'Amours, Multi-agent Simulation of Collaborative Strategies in a Supply Chain. In: Poc. Of AAMAS 2004, New-York, USA, 19-23 July 2004.
13. D. Pimentel Claro, 2004, Managing business networks and buyer-supplier relationships, Ph.D. thesis Wageningen University, 2004.
14. O.E. Williamson, 1998, Transaction Cost Economics: how it works, where it is headed. The Economist 146, No. 1. pp 23 – 58.
15. http://wiki.swarm.org/wiki/Main_Page

Multi-agent Support for Distributed Engineering Design

Camelia Chira, Ovidiu Chira, and Thomas Roche

Galway-Mayo Institute of Technology, Dublin Road, Galway, Ireland
camelia.chira@nuigalway.ie, ovichira@yahoo.com,
tom.roche@gmit.ie

Abstract. Characterised by geographical, temporal, functional and/or semantic distribution, today's enterprise models engage multiple design teams with heterogeneous skills cooperating together in order to achieve global optima in design. The success of this distributed design organization depends on critical factors such as the efficient management of the design related information circulated in the distributed environment and the support for the necessary cooperation process among participants dispersed across the enterprise. This paper proposes a multi-agent design information management system to support the synthesis and presentation of information to distributed teams for the purposes of enhancing design, learning, creativity, communication and productivity. Autonomous software agents and information ontologies enable the proposed system facilitating interoperation among distributed resources as well as knowledge sharing, reuse and integration.

1 Introduction

Emerging as a response to market demands and competitive pressures, distributed engineering design involves multidisciplinary teams of engineers dispersed over the computer network and requiring concurrent access to multiple system resources [1, 2]. These engineers have to collaborate in a distributed design environment in order to achieve the 'optimal' solution to the current design problem. Key aspects of this organization of engineering design that need to be addressed include the support of the cooperation process among participants dispersed across the enterprise and the efficient management of the design related information structures circulated within the distributed design environment.

This paper proposes a multi-agent architectural framework called IDIMS (Intelligent Multi-Agent Design Information Management System) to support the distributed engineering design organization by facilitating interoperation among distributed resources and knowledge sharing, reuse and integration. It is proposed to engage multi-agent systems, an important and fast growing area of Artificial Intelligence [3, 4], to cope with the inherent distribution of data, information, knowledge and expertise in the enterprise model of engineering design. In order to efficiently manage not only design data and information but also knowledge and make it readily available across the enterprise, ontologies have been employed to support the IDIMS architecture.

M. Ali and F. Esposito (Eds.): IEA/AIE 2005, LNAI 3533, pp. 155 – 164, 2005.

2 Distributed Engineering Design

Distributed engineering design brings together participants with heterogeneous skills [5], who, on sharing their skills, expertise and insight, create what is known as distributed cognition [1]. Enabled by distributed cognition, collaborative designs generally result in work products which are enriched by the multiple personalities of the designers engaged in the design task. Moreover, distributed engineering design aims to achieve benefits such as savings in project life-cycle and costs, added value to team efforts, access to a comprehensive knowledge-based system, reliable communication among design teams and members, flexible access and retrieval of information and timely connectivity with global experts [6, 7].

2.1 Distributed Engineering Design Characteristics

The main characteristics of distributed engineering design can be summarised as follows:

- The human and physical resources involved in the design process can be geographically, temporally, functionally and semantically distributed over the enterprise [2, 8, 9].
- The (teams of) human designers are highly heterogeneous (they may have different intent, background knowledge, area of expertise and responsibility) [5].
- Teamwork is playing a significant role in design projects becoming increasingly large, complex and long in duration [6, 7].
- The cooperation process among distributed teams of people is crucial for the successful location of the 'optimal' design solution [7, 10].
- The role of the computer for distributed design is that of a medium facilitating cooperation among distributed designers and also supporting the design process through various applications [11].

Characterised by distribution, cooperation, teamwork and being computer supported, distributed engineering design is an information intensive activity depending on the cooperation process of dispersed and multidisciplinary design teams with the aim of achieving a global 'optimal' design solution.

2.2 Problematic Aspects of Distributed Engineering Design

The potential benefits of distributed engineering design are often marginalized by the problems inherent in the process [12]. The big volume and dispersion of design data, information and knowledge [13] makes the design management process more difficult and impacts on the relevance of the information required for different design tasks [14]. Furthermore, the cooperation process in a distributed design environment is burdened by the inherent distribution and multidisciplinarity of the design teams involved in a project and by the heterogeneity of the resources supporting the decision making process [7, 15]. Another problematic aspect of distributed engineering design refers to the limited awareness and understanding of other designers and their work within the same project [16, 17]. Also, information and knowledge sharing among dispersed participants to the design process is difficult in a heterogeneous environment [11, 17]. Finally, current supporting software infrastructure of distributed design adds another dimension to the complexity of the problematic aspects of collaborative design due to their high heterogeneity and low integration [7, 18, 19].

It should be noticed that these problems are highly interconnected by the distributed design data, information and knowledge that needs to be managed, shared and understood by humans and machines within a collaborative environment. Computational design support is needed for communications and accessibility to design knowledge, past records and histories.

3 The Intelligent Multi-agent Design Information Management System (IDIMS) Architecture

Intended to address the main problems designers have when collectively working in a distributed environment in order to achieve global 'optima', the proposed IDIMS system aims to support the optimisation of the solution space of the collective dispersed design team. The requirements of the IDIMS system can be summarised as follows:

- The system should efficiently manage the design information circulated in a distributed environment by providing content related support in order to aid the designer in finding, accessing and retrieving required information.
- The system should aid distributed and multidisciplinary design teams to establish and maintain cooperation through an effective use of communication, co-location, coordination and collaboration processes.
- The system should address the integration of heterogeneous software tools used by designers by enabling the flow of information in the distributed environment.

In order to address these requirements, the design of the IDIMS architecture is supported by emerging technologies particularly those advanced in the Distributed Artificial Intelligence field. Traditional approaches such as the development of integrated sets of tools and the establishment of data standards cannot address the multifaceted problematic aspects of distributed engineering design [19]. Emphasizing the need for intelligent forms of technological support for distributed design, many of the relevant research studies [7, 15, 18] indicate that the complex activity of distributed engineering design may be effectively supported by the provision of a collection of interacting autonomous software components incorporating Artificial Intelligence specific problem-solving mechanisms. Moreover, software agents and multi-agent systems represent an effective method for providing support for the various tasks of distributed design [10, 19-21]. Considering knowledge sharing and reuse, ontologies [22-24] have been identified as the other supporting technological element of the proposed IDIMS system. These two emerging technologies are envisioned to form the next distributed computational environment, capable of managing inherent complex and inherent distributed systems.

3.1 Software Agents and Multi-agent Systems

Considered an important new direction in software engineering [4, 25], agents and multi-agent systems represent techniques to manage the complexity inherent in software systems and appropriate to domains in which data, control, expertise and/or resources are inherently distributed [4, 26, 27]. Although there is no universally accepted agent definition [3, 4, 25-28], most researchers agree that a software agent is a computer system situated in an environment (and able to perceive that environment) that autonomously acts on behalf of its user, has a set of objectives and takes actions in order to accomplish these objectives [3, 4, 25]. Autonomy is the most important property of an agent without which the notion of agency would not exist. Autonomous agents can take decisions without the intervention of humans or other systems based on the individual state and goals of the agent. Furthermore, many researchers consider that an agent should also be characterised by reactivity, pro-activeness, cooperation, learning, mobility and/or temporal continuity [3, 25-28]. The agents within a multi-agent system must coordinate their activities (to determine the organisational structure in a group of agents and to allocate tasks and resources), negotiate if a conflict occurs and be able to communicate with other agents [4]. Ideal for solving complex problems with multiple solving methods, perspectives and/or problem solving entities, multi-agent systems present many potential advantages including robustness, efficiency, flexibility, adaptivity, scalability, inter-operation of multiple existing legacy systems, enhanced speed, reliability and extensibility [4, 25, 27].

3.2 Ontologies

Ontologies specify content specific agreements to facilitate knowledge sharing and reuse among systems that submit to the same ontology/ontologies by the means of ontological commitments [22-24]. They describe concepts and relations assumed to be always true independent from a particular domain by a community of humans and/or agents that commit to that view of the world [22]. A merge of Gruber [24] and Borst et al [29] definitions is generally accepted by researchers, as follows: "Ontologies are explicit formal specification of a shared conceptualization" [23], where *explicit* means that "the type of concepts used, and the constraints on their use are explicitly defined", *formal* means that "the ontology should be machine readable, which excludes natural language", *shared* "reflects the notion that an ontology captures consensual knowledge, that is, it is not private to some individual, but accepted by a group" and *conceptualization* emphasizes the "abstract model of some phenomenon in the world by having identified the relevant concepts of that phenomenon" [23].

3.3 The IDIMS Architecture

From a high-level view, the proposed IDIMS architecture consists of two planes, i.e. the Ontological Plane and the Multi-Agent Plane (see Fig. 1). The Ontological Plane specifies the hierarchy of ontologies (i.e. Ontology Library) defining the concepts, relations and inference rules that compose the machine-enabled framework in which the system's information resources are circulated and stored. It also includes engineering knowledge instantiated according to the rules specified by the Ontology Library. The Multi-Agent Plane specifies the types and behaviours of the software agents required to enable the IDIMS functionality. It facilitates the access, retrieval, exchange and presentation of design information to distributed teams through agent systems such as the Object Interface Agents, the Instance Interface Agents and the Information Management Centre.

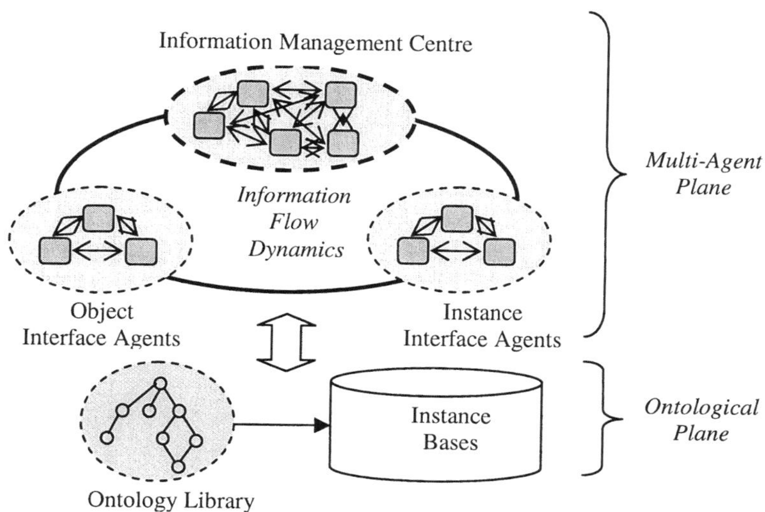

Fig. 1. A bi-plane view of the IDIMS architecture

A detailed view of the Multi-Agent Plane of the IDIMS architecture (see Fig. 2) shows exactly how multi-agent systems support distributed users within the collaborative environment during the design process.

The *Information Management Centre (IMC)* stays at the core of the IDIMS architecture coordinating all the other agent systems by handling requests generated by the Object Interface Agents and generating requests for the Instance Interface Agents. It consists of a set of mobile agents, supervised by one or more coordinator agents, that manage the request-response process.

The *Object Interface Agents* integrate the engineering design components to the IDIMS system. The Application Interface System Agent (AISA) is a set of autonomous agents that capture application specific information (e.g. part name, assembly name, material, dimensions regarding a product model managed with a CAD tool) and then appends it with the help of IMC and MA in a format that is consistent with the specific model ontology from the IDIMS Ontology Library. The User Interface System Agent (UISA) deals with any user specific aspect within a distributed design environment e.g. collaboration with other designers by providing an interface to the Collaborative Virtual Environment (CVE), captures of/requests for design knowledge. They are tailored and should be able to model themselves through learning according to specific user needs and preferences.

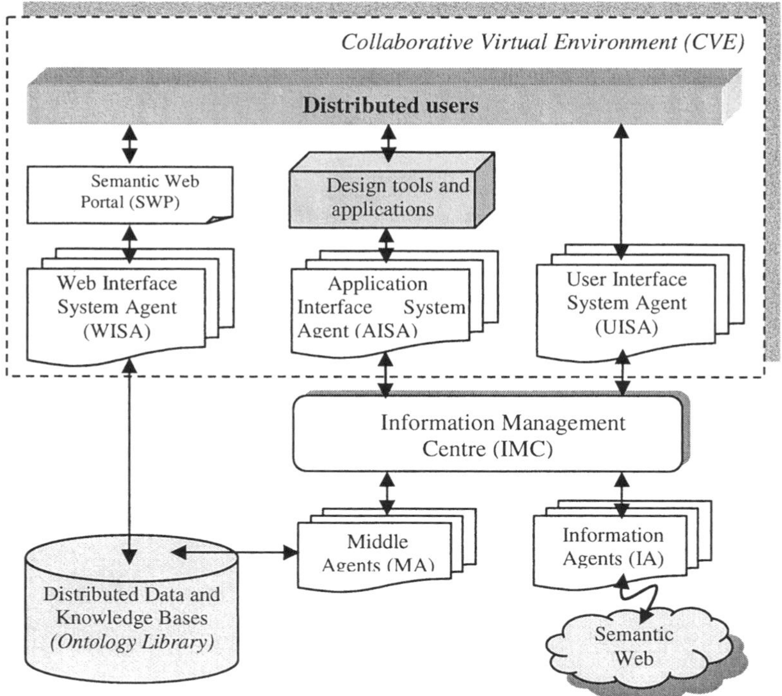

Fig. 2. Multi-agent Plane View of the IDIMS architecture

The *Instance Interface Agents* control the ontology-compliant data, information and knowledge instances managed within the IDIMS system. The Middle Agents (MA) manage the distributed data/information/knowledge hierarchy e.g. storing, structuring (according to the Ontology Library), correcting, updating, maintaining, retrieving and consistency checking of data, information and/or knowledge. This management activity is a bi-directional one, i.e. MA can extend the knowledge base from input data or information and can also identify and extract appropriate data and information from knowledge. The Information Agents (IA) exploit the vast amount of information available in wide area networks and retrieve specific required information. These agents will reach their true potential when the web will be semantically[1] enabled.

Adding further support to the distributed designer, the *Semantic Web Portal (SWP)* provides secured web access to the comprehensive IDIMS knowledge base and supports collaboration within the CVE through services such as instant messaging, audio/video conference, document repository and whiteboard. The *Web Interface System Agent (WISA)* serves the web portal by managing all user requests through a direct semantic link to the IDIMS Ontology Library.

---

[1] Semantic Web is envisioned to form the next generation of web wide computational environment where information will be defined and linked in such a way that it can be used by people and processed by machines (http://www.semanticweb.org).

4 The IDIMS Prototype

The IDIMS architectural description informs the implementation of the IDIMS prototype presented in this section. The Ontology Library is stored and managed using the RDF/RDFS[2] model through the Protégé 2000[3] editor tool. Fig. 3 exemplifies the ontological plane of the IDIMS prototype with the product model ontology.

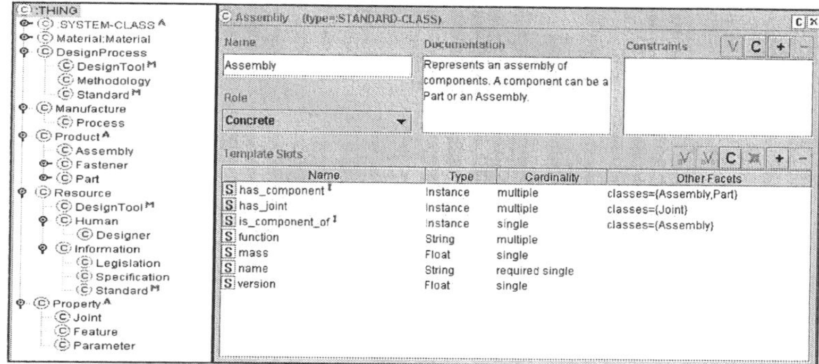

Fig. 3. Protégé ontology interface displaying class tree structure (*Assembly* class)

The Multi-Agent Plane implementation is supported by the Java programming language and the Java Agent DEvelopment Framework (JADE)[4]. All agents within the IDIMS multi-agent system submit to the Ontology Library facilitating knowledge sharing and reuse. The AISA system captures CAD model information (currently from the ProEngineer application). The UISA system assists the distributed design process by supplying services (e.g. search a specific instance base, browse the structure of product, initiate a chat session) for its clients or users. Upon activation, each UISA agent (identified with *username:AgentName*) sends a request message to IMC. Based on the received username, IMC retrieves the available services for this particular agent and sends them back to the UISA agent. In accordance with the returned messages, the UISA agent activates its GUI and waits for the user to request services. Fig. 4 presents an example of an UISA agent.

When the user requests one of the advertised services, the UISA agent finds through IMC an agent system that provides the requested service and sends out a REQUEST message. For example, if the user wishes to browse the Material ontological instances, IMC (supported by MA) will serve the REQUEST message sent by the UISA agent by creating a mobile agent that activates its GUI containing the requested information on the client machine (see Fig. 4 right).

---

[2] Resource Description Framework Schema (http://www.w3.org/rdf)

[3] http://protégé.stanford.edu

[4] Compliant with the FIPA (Foundation for Intelligent Physical Agents) specifications, JADE is a software framework fully implemented in Java that facilitates the development of multi-agent systems (http://jade.cselt.it).

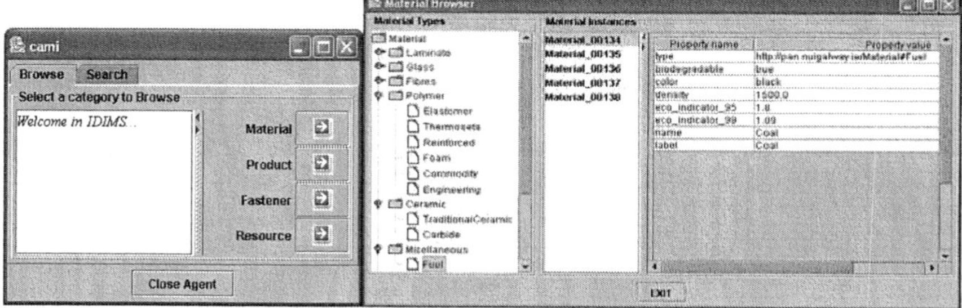

Fig. 4. The GUI of the UISA agent cami:MyAgent (for username cami). This agent provides the services of browsing and searching through materials, products, fasteners and resources (left). The Material Browser GUI presented to the requester (right)

Supported by Java Servlets technology (i.e. Apache Tomcat), the implementation of the WISA system offers dynamic creation of web pages into the Semantic Web Portal containing up-to-date information when requested by the designer. An example is presented in Fig. 5.

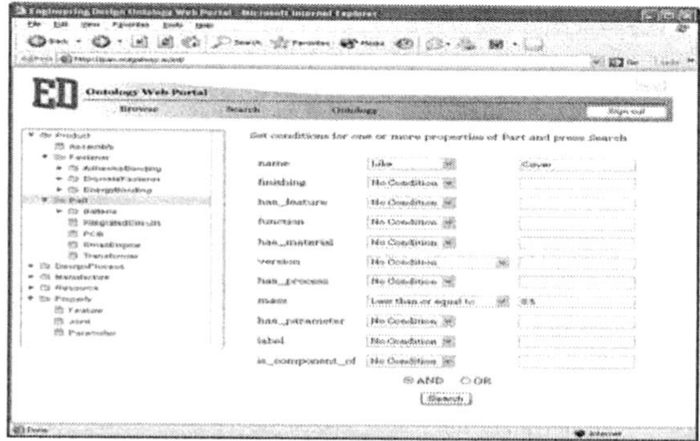

Fig. 5. Searching for specific parts with the Semantic Web Portal

Hidden to the user, the MA and IMC agent systems support and control the well functioning of the other agent systems within IDIMS through autonomous, proactive, cooperative and, where necessary, mobile software agents.

5 Conclusions and Future Work

Specified based on a careful analysis of distributed engineering design, the IDIMS ontological and multi-agent based system is intended to facilitate the management of the data-information-knowledge value chain efficiently in order to optimise engineering design operation and management. Providing robustness and efficiency, multi-agent systems coupled with ontologies are a potential solution for distributed design issues such as integration of heterogeneous software tools, interdisciplinary cooperation among distributed designers and exchange of design data, information and knowledge.

Current and future work focuses on completing the development of the ontology library and the implementation of the multi-agent system within the proposed architecture. The testing and validation of the implemented system is considered a crucial phase and links are currently formed with industrial companies to support this evaluation process.

References

1. Arias, E., Eden, H., Fischer, G., Gorman, A., Scharff, E.: Transcending the Individual Human Mind - Creating Shared Understanding through Collaborative Design. ACM transactions on Computer-Human Interaction, Vol. 7, No. 1 (2000) 84 - 113
2. Cross, N., Design as a Discipline. In Doctoral Education in Design: Foundations for the Future, D. Durling and K. Friedman (Eds). Staffordshire University Press Stoke-on-Trent. (2000)
3. Nwana, H.S.: Software Agents: An Overview. Knowledge Engineering Review, 11 (1996) 1-40
4. Jennings, N.R.: On agent-based software engineering. Artificial Intelligence, (2000)
5. Edmonds, E.A., Candy, L., Jones, R., Soufi, B.: Support for Collaborative Design : Agents and Emergence. Communications of the ACM, 37 (1994)
6. Iheagwara, C.,Blyth, A.: Evaluation of the performance of ID systems in a switched and distributed environment the RealSecure case study. Computer Networks, (2002)
7. Pena-Mora, F., Hussein, K., Vadhavkar, S., Benjamin, K.: CAIRO: a Concurrent Engineering Meeting Environment for Virtual Design Teams. Artificial Intelligence in Engineering, 14 (2000) 202-219
8. Weiss, G.: Multi-Agent Systems: A Modern Approach to Distributed Artificial Intelligence. London MIT Press (1999)
9. Bertola, P.,Teixeira, J.C.: Design as a knowledge agent. Design Studies, 24 (2003) 181-194
10. Liu, H., Tang, M., Frazer, J.H.: Supporting evolution in a multi-agent cooperative design environment. Advances in Engineering Software, 33 (2002) 319-328
11. MacGregor, S.P.: New Perspectives for Distributed Design Support. The Journal of Design Research, 2 (2002)
12. Huang, J.: Knowledge sharing and innovation in distributed design: implications of internet-based media on design collaboration. International Journal of Design Computing: Special Issue on Design Computing on the Net (DCNet'99), (1999)
13. Fischer, G.: Knowledge Management : Problems, Promises, Realities and Challenges. IEEE Intelligent Systems, (2002)
14. Viano, G. Adaptive User Interface for Process Control based on Multi-Agent approach. AVI 2000, Palermo, Italy (2000)
15. Cutkosky, M.R., Englemore, R.S., Fikes, R.E., Genesereth, M.R., Gruber, T.R., Mark, W.S., Tenenbaum, J.M., Weber, J.C., PACT: An Experiment in Integrating Concurrent Engineering Systems. In Readings in Agents, M.N. Huhns and M.P. Singh (Eds). Morgan Kaufmann San Francisco, CA, USA. (1997)

16. Nakakoji, K., Yamamoto, Y., Suzuki, T., Takada, S., Gross, M.: From Critiquing to Representational Talkback: Computer Support for Revealing Features in Design. Knowledge-Based Systems Journal, 11 (1998) 457-468
17. Thoben, K.-D., Weber, F., Wunram, M.: Barriers in Knowledge Management and Pragmatic Approaches. Studies in Informatics and Control, 11 (2002)
18. Anumba, C.J., Ren, Z., A.Thorpe, Ugwu, O.O., L.Newnham: Negotiation within a multi-agent system for the collaborative design of light industrial buildings. Advances in Engineering Software, 34 (2003) 389-401
19. Wang, L., Shen, W., Xie, H., Neelamkavil, J., Pardasani, A.: Collaborative conceptual design - state of the art and future trends. Computer Aided Design, 34 (2002) 981-996
20. Zhao, G., Deng, J., Shen, W.: CLOVER: an agent-based approach to systems interoperability in cooperative design systems. Computers in Industry, 45 (2001) 261-276
21. Chao, K.-M., Norman, P., Anane, R., James, A.: An agent-based approach to engineering design. Computers in Industry, 48 (2002) 17-27
22. Guarino, N. Formal Ontology and Information Systems. Formal Ontology in Information Systems. FOIS'98, 6-8 June 1998., Trento IOS Press, (1998)
23. Studer, R., Benjamins, V.R., Fensel, D.: Knowledge Engineering: Principles and Methods. Data and Knowledge Engineering, 25 (1998) 161-197
24. Gruber, T.R.: A Translation Approach to Portable Ontology Specification. Knowledge Aquisition, 5 (1993) 199-220
25. Wooldridge, M.,Ciancarini, P., Agent-Oriented Software Engineering: The State of the Art. In Agent-Oriented Software Engineering, P. Ciancarini and M. Wooldridge (Eds). Springer-Verlag (2001)
26. Oliveira, E., Fischer, K., Stepankova, O.: Multi-agent systems: which research for which applications. Robotics and Autonomous Systems, 27 (1999) 91-106
27. Bradshow, J.M., An Introduction to Software Agents. In Software Agents, J.M. Bradshow (Ed) MIT Press Cambridge. (1997)
28. Franklin, S.,Graesser, A. Is it an Agent, or just a Program?: A Taxonomy for Autonomous Agents. Proceedings of the Third International Workshop on Agent Theories, Architectures, and Languages, Springer-Verlag, 1996, Berlin, Germany (1996)
29. Borst, P., Akkermans, H., Top, J.: Engineering Ontologies. International Journal of Human-Computer Studies, 46 (1997) 365-406

Reliable Multi-agent Systems with Persistent Publish/Subscribe Messaging

Milovan Tosic and Arkady Zaslavsky

School of Computer Science and Software Engineering,
Monash University,
900 Dandenong Road,
Caulfield East, Victoria 3145,
Australia
{Milovan.Tosic, Arkady.Zaslavsky}@csse.monash.edu.au

Abstract. A persistent publish/subscribe messaging model allows the creation of an application-independent fault-tolerant layer for multi-agent systems. We propose a layer which is capable of supporting heterogenous agent platforms from different vendors. This layer is a three-tier application, which is accessible from multi-agent systems via web-services or a persistent publish/subscribe messaging system. We describe the design of the fault-tolerant layer, its messaging system, as well as the algorithm of fault-recovery procedure in the case of agent and/or host death. We also present performance analysis of the proposed solution, to justify its use in systems which demand different levels of reliability.

Keywords: autonomous agents, distributed problem solving, multi-agent osystems, reliability, fault-tolerance.

1 Introduction

Agents, as autonomous software entities which perform activities in a dynamic environment, can effectively be used in certain applications. They are able to sense their environment and conduct a set of activities to achieve the goals for which they were developed. Their social and coordination skills can help them solve problems which are too complex to be solved by a single agent. Mobility is a feature that allows agents to move between hosts and perform their activities locally, at a data source. Hosts provide agents with execution contexts, services and resources needed for task accomplishment.

Even though agents can be simple, their cooperation in multi-agent systems can form complex relationships. Multi-agent systems have proven their effectiveness in the areas of e-commerce, pervasive computing, artificial intelligence, telecommunications etc. However, they are also prone to weaknesses of their most unreliable components. We have to achieve a satisfactory level of multi-agent system reliability in order to be able to justify their application. A reliable system is able to perform its tasks under conditions which exist in its environment, even if those conditions cause software or hardware faults.

M. Ali and F. Esposito (Eds.): IEA/AIE 2005, LNAI 3533, pp. 165 – 174, 2005.

The main contribution of this paper, the proposed External Fault-Tolerant Layer (EFTL), is able to improve the reliability of supported multi-agent systems. It is an application and domain independent solution supporting heterogenous multi-agent systems based on agent platforms from different vendors. It is capable of supporting multiple agent systems simultaneously. Its support is negotiable, and the acceptance of its support depends on the estimated support costs. The EFTL fault-recovery procedures produce minimal overheads due to the use of context-aware messaging components, which conform to the persistent publish/subscribe Java Message Service (JMS) standard. EFTL is capable of solving the problems caused by agent and host death, agent unresponsiveness, agent migration faults, certain communication problems and faults caused by resource unavailability.

This paper is organized as follows: firstly, we present related work from the area of multi-agent system reliability. Then, we describe the architecture of EFTL. The fourth section focuses on the EFTL messaging system design, while the fifth section describes a recovery procedure used in the case of agent and/or host death. The last sections of this paper will present a performance analysis of EFTL, the conclusions and motivations for future work.

2 Related Work

We identify relevant groups of approaches which handle the sources of system failures. The biggest group is the one that handles the reliability of an agent as an individual entity. Some authors proposed checkpointing as a procedure which saves agent states to a persistent storage medium at certain time intervals. Later, if an agent fails, its state can be reconstructed from the latest checkpoint [2]. This approach depends on the reliability of hosts because we have the so-called blocking problem when the host fails. The agents which have been saved at a particular host can be recovered only after the recovery of that host [9]. The second approach that tries to ensure an agent's reliability is replication. In this approach, there are groups of agents which exist as replicas of one agent, and can be chosen to act as the main agent in case of its failure. In order to preserve the same view to the environment from all the members of the replica group, the concept of a group proxy has been proposed in [4]. A group proxy is the agent that acts as a proxy through which all the interactions between the group, and the environment, have to pass. When the proxy agent approach is broadened with the primary agent concept, as in [12, 13], then the primary agent is the only one which does all the computations until its failure. After the failure, all the slaves vote in another primary agent from their group.

In order to watch the execution of an agent from an external entity, some authors proposed the use of supervisor and executor agents [3, 8, 11]. The supervisor agents watch the execution of the problem-solving agents and detect all the conditions which can lead to, or are, the failures, and react upon detected conditions. Hosts can also be used as the components of fault-tolerant systems, as in [1]. Basic services which are provided by hosts can be extended by some services which help the agents achieve a desirable level of reliability. Depending on the implementation of the fault-tolerant system, it cannot cope with all kinds of failures. In order to determine the feasibility of the recovery, Grantner *et al.* proposed the use of fuzzy logic [5].

An approach that is also a type of execution monitoring is presented in [6]. Kaminka and Tambe focused on the monitoring of multiple agents using a centralised approach, with a single monitor agent, or a distributed approach, where problem-solving agents monitor each other. These authors introduced Socially Attentive Monitoring, where they detected irregularities in agent relationships, not in the fulfilment of their goals.

The benefits of the publish/subscribe messaging model in mobile computing have been presented in [10]. Their approach specifically concentrates on context-aware messaging, where an agent can subscribe to receive only the messages which satisfy its subscription filter. This solution leads us to a highly effective notification mechanism for the mobile agents.

Klein and Dellarocas introduced a fault-tolerant application-independent solution in [7]. They made a clear distinction between the problem-solving and the exception-handling agents. Their solution can be applied to any application domain with only small changes in the problem-solving agents, and is based on exception-handling services. These agents have to implement a set of interfaces in order to cooperate with the exception-handling agents. They also have to register their normal behavioural patterns with the fault-tolerant layer. Then the fault-tolerant layer is able to locate these behavioural patterns in its exception knowledge database.

3 EFTL Design

3.1 The EFTL Conceptual Architecture

EFTL's main design goal is to improve the reliability of multi-agent systems. Its messaging system is supposed to effectively reduce the messaging overheads. EFTL is capable of providing its services to more than one system at the same time. In its current state of development, EFTL improves reliability of systems implemented in the JADE[1] and Grasshopper[2] agent platforms.

Since every fault-tolerant solution is also prone to faults, we designed EFTL to work in an environment in which it would be able to inherit scalability and robustness of underlying J2EE application, HTTP web and messaging servers. In this paper, the term J2EE application server is used for a server program which hosts Enterprise Java Beans (EJBs) and provides a range of services to client applications. In order to provide the system with reliable communications and not to restrict agent autonomy, EFTL uses our altered persistent publish/subscribe messaging model which guarantees the exactly-once consumption of messages. In addition, EFTL's support to multi-agent systems is negotiable. An application can decide if the EFTL support costs are acceptable and can sign a support contract with EFTL. All the negotiations are performed via the EFTL web-services interface. The following sections of the paper describe some of the EFTL components, while the overall diagram of the system is presented in Fig. 1.

---

[1] http://jade.cselt.it
[2] http://www.grasshopper.de

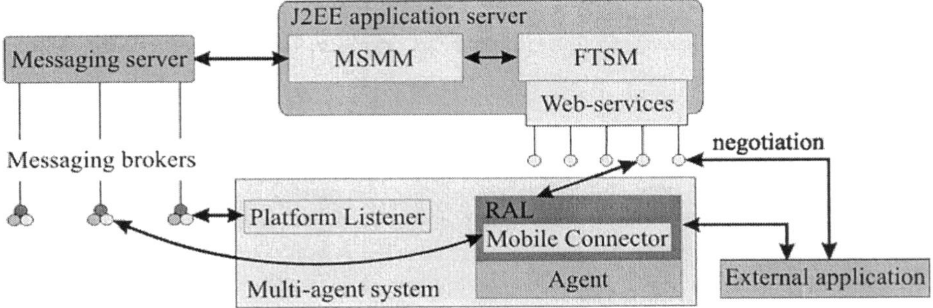

Fig. 1. Architecture of EFTL

3.2 The EFTL Components

The Fault-Tolerant System Manager (FTSM) is a component identified as the central functioning unit of EFTL. We developed it as a group of EJBs which are deployed in a J2EE application server. FTSM regularly checks whether certain conditions are being met in supported multi-agent systems, and reacts upon the discovery of any events which may be important for system reliability. It issues commands which must be performed by agents in order to improve the reliability of the system to which they belong. FTSM is a statefull component which saves all the data that describes multi-agent systems to the EFTL database.

The Reliable Agent Layer (RAL) is a platform-dependent component and a mandatory layer of each agent that is supported by EFTL. We have developed RAL for the JADE and Grasshopper agent platforms. This layer depends upon the properties which describe the data needed for this layer to cooperate with the rest of EFTL. Since one instance of FTSM is able to control more than one agent platform, both from the same and from different vendors, RAL provides FTSM with the data used to differentiate between those platforms. RAL performs activities at agent level, and they are initiated in order to improve the reliability of a particular agent or other agents in the system.

Our Messaging System Management Module (MSMM) is another component which is deployed in a J2EE application server. It is used to connect directly to a messaging server and to perform the creation or removal of messaging system users. When a new user is created, its credentials are forwarded to an agent's RAL. Then, the agent can make a durable subscription to the messaging topic of interest, and communicate with FTSM.

The Platform Listener's purpose is to detect the system-wide events which are important from a reliability viewpoint. These events can be the changes in an agent's life cycle: start-up, transfer, suspension, blocking, death etc. Following the detection of these events, the Platform Listener notifies FTSM about them. FTSM can then decide if any of the events are faults or can lead to faults, and can react by ordering agents to perform certain recovery activities.

4 The EFTL Messaging System Design

The publish/subscribe messaging model is common for performing asynchronous communication between publishers and subscribers, in a distributed system. A publisher sends its message to a specific JMS topic, at a message broker which in turn forwards the message to all the topic subscribers.

The persistent publish/subscribe messaging model guarantees the delivery of messages to mobile agents, since all the messages are saved to a persistent storage medium before they are being forwarded to subscribers. This model employs a retry scheme for the undelivered messages. In the case of a mobile agent, all the messages sent to it during its travel between hosts, would be forwarded to it as soon as the agent arrives at a new destination and reconnects to a message broker.

In EFTL, a lightweight messaging component that performs all the connecting and disconnecting agent activities to and from message brokers, in coordination with agent life-cycle changes, is called a Mobile Connector. Since agent platforms usually provide application level detection of life-cycle changes, it is not hard to disconnect an agent from a message broker before the next migration step, and to reconnect it after arrival at a new destination.

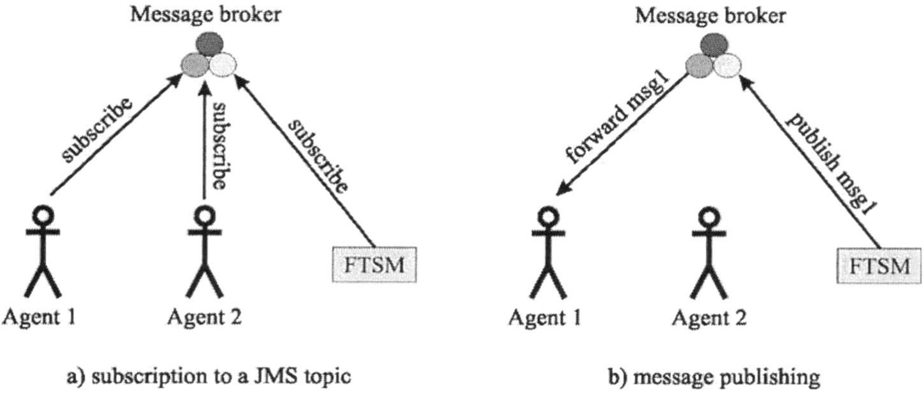

Fig. 2. Publish/subscribe messaging system

Any reliable agent, as well as the components of FTSM which are implemented as EJBs, can subscribe to a JMS topic, as in Fig. 2a. A subscription message, or a message selector, describes the rules which all the messages, which are forwarded to a subscriber, have to obey. In EFTL, every message, sent from FTSM, has a header with embedded information about the message recipient(s).

A message selector is a string which has a structure similar to the SQL-92 standard's '*where*' statement. If a messaging system provides clients with the possibility of message selection at its broker, as in the case of EFTL, then the clients can be context-aware. In that case, not all the messages published to a specific JMS topic would be sent to all subscribers, but only to those whose message selectors are satisfied, as is the case with Agent 1 in Fig. 2b. This functionality is very important for EFTL because it decreases the messaging overheads of the proposed fault-tolerant solution.

A JMS-compliant persistent publish/subscribe messaging system guarantees delivery of messages, but not within the exactly-once property. For example, a message receipt acknowledgement from an agent might not arrive at a message broker, due to a link failure. Then, the message broker will attempt to re-send the message to the agent. To prevent the multiple consumption of the same message, EFTL issues each message with a unique number. Agents keep track of the consumed message numbers and can simply discard the messages which are delivered to them more than once.

5 Recovery Procedure in the Case of Agent and/or Host Death

As an example of cooperation between agents and EFTL during fault-recovery, we present the procedure used in the case of agent and/or host death. Agent and/or host death is a common type of fault in multi-agent systems. An agent and/or a host can die due to a software or hardware fault. Other agents may not notice the disappearance of the failed agent and will be able to continue with the execution of their tasks. However, this type of fault can sometimes greatly affect the functioning of the whole system. The failed agent might have had to undertake an important task whose effects would be reflected in the overall system goal. Moreover, other agents might not be able to perform their activities without cooperation with the failed agent.

RAL periodically, before each migration, and after a resource update, saves local checkpoints of its agent. If a host does not support checkpointing, which can be a common case with handheld devices, RAL can send a compressed checkpoint, via the EFTL messaging system, to FTSM which saves it to the EFTL database. New checkpoints of a particular agent, at a host, overwrite its earlier checkpoints if they exist at that host. If the Platform Listener detects agent or host death, it informs FTSM about it. When a host dies, it causes the death of all the agents that resided in it. The failed agents cannot be recovered from the persistent storage medium of the failed host until that host is recovered. The problem of blocking is present when we have to wait for the recovery of a host, before we are able to recover agents. EFTL uses the algorithm described by the following pseudo-code to address this problem:

```
if(agent1 died at host1)
begin
   destination_host = host1;
   if(host1 is dead)
   begin
      list1 = hosts with resources most similar to
              host1;
      list2 = alive and reachable hosts from list1;
      if(list2 is not empty)
      begin
         list3 = sort list2 by the utilisation, in
                 descending   order;
         destination_host = the first host from list3;
```

```
        enod-if
        else
        begin
           destination_host = location of agent1's
           latest available checkpoint;
        end-else;
     end-if;
     agent2 = the closest agent to the location of
                agent1's latest available checkpoint;
     FTSM sends command to agent2 to recover agent1 from
            the checkpoint;
     FTSM orders agent1 to move to destination_host;
     FTSM resends all the messages sent to agent1 from
            the moment of its latest available checkpoint
            to the moment of its recovery;
end-if;
```

6 Performance Analysis

The reliability of multi-agent systems has to be measured differently from the reliability of other types of distributed systems. Multi-agent systems can be described with characteristics such as component autonomy, mobility and asynchronous execution. Therefore, system availability, as the measure of reliability, cannot be applied to them. We have to use another reliability model that can describe the events which can cause multi-agent system failures and allow us to evaluate our research proposals. As described in [8], reliability in multi-agent systems can be evaluated by measuring the reliability of each individual agent. An agent can either successfully complete its tasks or fail to do so. Therefore, the reliability of the whole system depends on the percentage of agents managing to achieve their goals. Lyu and Wong proposed that the agent tasks should be defined as scheduled round-trips in a network of agent hosts. Only the mobile agent which managed to visit all the functioning hosts in the network, and to arrive at the final host, can be considered a successful finisher. Consequently, the reliability can be calculated using the following expression:

$$R = \frac{F}{M} \cdot 100 \ [\%] \tag{1}$$

R – reliability
F – No. of successful finisher agents
M – No. of all mobile agents.

In the first group of experiments, which were conducted in JADE, the number of mobile agents and the number of JADE containers (hosts) were variable (10-100 agents, 5-20 containers). The mobile agents were created by a stationary agent that was not prone to failure. At the time of instantiation, the mobile agents queried the Agent Management System for the locations of all the containers registered within a platform. The containers were distributed to three different servers, connected to a local area network. We used AMD Athlon 1.67 GHz machines, each with 256 MB of RAM. The agents attempted to visit every JADE container present in their itineraries. They had to stay idle for five seconds in each of the visited containers. Their death rates were changed during the course of the experiment, but the times of failure occurrences were random. The agents were not prone to failures while they were in the initial and final hosts. In this experiment, the containers were not prone to failures, as we assumed that the probability of container death is much lower than the probability of agent death.

The average results of these experiments are presented in Fig. 3. The area filled with a line pattern represents the reliability of a system which is not supported by EFTL. On the other hand, the solid grey area in Fig. 3 represents reliability improvement of the same system when it is supported by EFTL. We can conclude that EFTL considerably improves the reliability of multi-agent systems. The trend of reliability improvement shows, approximately, uniform development. It does not depend on numbers of agents and hosts, and application domain. Levels of reliability achieve their maximum values in conditions where frequency and extent of faults is not high. Reliability slightly decreases when unfavourable events occur more often.

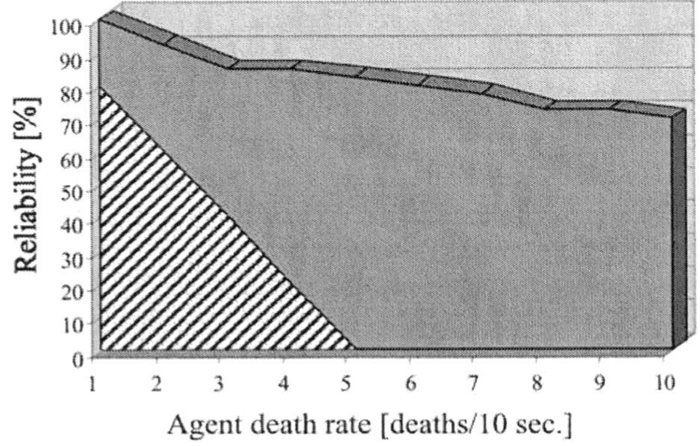

Fig. 3. Reliability improvement

The EFTL system entities are distributed across networks, and because of their communication, the evaluation of the costs, with which reliability improvement comes, has to include messaging overheads. To calculate messaging overheads, we conducted the experiments in the same environmental conditions as when we evaluated reliability improvement, except that the numbers of agents and JADE containers were constant (50 agents, 12 containers). These conditions allowed us to see if there was any relationship between messaging overheads and frequency of faults. We measured the overall size of messages exchanged via the publish/subscribe messaging system, because it is the only messaging infrastructure that EFTL uses. However, there was no dependence between messaging overheads and fault frequency. This is due to small EFTL message size and the low number of commands issued by FTSM in the case of agent and/or host death.

Another set of experiments included a variable number of mobile agents present in the system, and a constant agent death rate of one death per 10 seconds. Fig. 4 shows that the messaging overhead per agent declines as the number of agents in a system increases. FTSM disperses its commands to the agents which are most suitable to perform them. As the number of agents in a system becomes higher, the set of agents, which can execute EFTL commands, also becomes larger. Consequently, FTSM can choose to which agents it is going to send its commands. In that case, many of the agents never receive any sort of command or notification from FTSM, and the messaging overhead per agent drops.

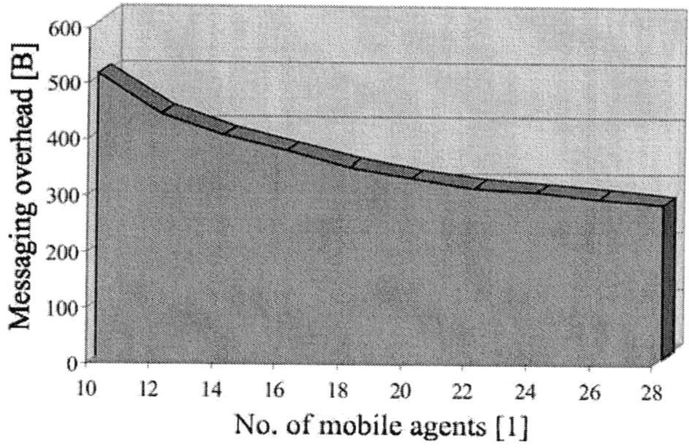

Fig. 4. Messaging overhead per agent

7 Conclusion and Future Work

The proposed system, called EFTL, allows negotiable fault-tolerant support, based on its costs. This solution significantly improves the reliability of supported systems. The implemented persistent publish/subscribe messaging model guarantees the exactly-once consumption of messages. The EFTL messaging system performs message filtering, based on agent subscriptions, at message brokers. Therefore, it reduces messaging overheads by introducing context-aware messaging in fault-tolerant multi-agent systems. Our future work will focus on the performance improvement of EFTL. A goal of supporting as many popular agent platforms as possible will determine our efforts to create a recognisable fault-tolerant system which improves the reliability of multi-agent systems.

References

1. Dake, W.; Leguizamo, C.P.; Mori, K., Mobile agent fault tolerance in autonomous decentralized database systems, Autonomous Decentralized System, The 2nd International Workshop on (2002) 192 – 199
2. Dalmeijer, M.; Rietjens, E.; Hammer, D.; Aerts, A.; Soede, M., A reliable mobile agents architecture, Object-Oriented Real-Time Distributed Computing, ISORC 98 Proceedings. First International Symposium on (1998) 64 – 72
3. Eustace, D.; Aylett, R.S.; Gray, J.O., Combining predictive and reactive control strategies in multi-agent systems, Control, Control '94., Volume 2., International Conference on (1994) 989 – 994

4. Fedoruk, A.; Deters, R., Improving fault-tolerance by replicating agents, Proceedings of the first international joint conference on Autonomous agents and multiagent systems: part 2, ACM Press New York, NY, USA, ISBN:1-58113-480-0 (2002) 737 – 744
5. Grantner, J.L.; Fodor, G.; Driankov, D., Using fuzzy logic for bounded recovery of autonomous agents, Fuzzy Information Processing Society, NAFIPS '97., Annual Meeting of the North American (September 1997) 317 – 322
6. Kaminka, G.; Tambe, M., I'm OK, you're OK, we're OK: Experiments in distributed and centralized socially attentive monitoring, Proceedings of the third annual conference on Autonomous Agents (April 1999) 213 – 220
7. Klein, M.; Rodriguez-Aguilar, J. A.; Dellarocas, C., Using domain-independent exception handling services to enable robust open multi-agent systems: The case of agent death, Proceedings of the seventh annual conference on Autonomous Agents, Kluwer Academic Publishers, Netherlands (2003) 179 – 189
8. Lyu, R. M.; Wong, Y. T., A progressive fault tolerant mechanism in mobile agent systems [online], Available: http://www.cse.cuhk.edu.hk/~lyu/paper_pdf/ SCI2003.pdf , [Accessed 25 April 2004]
9. Mohindra, A.; Purakayastha, A.; Thati, P., Exploiting non-determinism for reliability of mobile agent systems, Dependable Systems and Networks, DSN 2000. Proceedings International Conference on (June 2000) 144 – 153
10. Padovitz, A.; Zaslavsky, A.; Loke, S. W., Awareness and Agility for Autonomic Distributed Systems: Platform-Independent Publish-Subscribe Event-Based Communication for Mobile Agents, the 1st International Workshop on Autonomic Computing Systems, DEXA 2003, Prague, Czech Republic (September 2003)
11. Patel, R. B.; Garg, K., Fault-tolerant mobile agents computing on open networks [online], Available: http://www.caip.rutgers.edu/~parashar/AAW-HiPC2003/patel-aaw-hipc-03.pdf, [Accessed 18 April 2004]
12. Taesoon, P.; Ilsoo, B.; Hyunjoo, K.; Yeom, H.Y., The performance of checkpointing and replication schemes for fault tolerant mobile agent systems, Reliable Distributed Systems, 2002. Proceedings. 21st IEEE Symposium on (October 2002) 256 – 261
13. Zhigang, W.; Binxing, F., Research on extensibility and reliability of agents in Web-based Computing Resource Publishing, High Performance Computing in the Asia-Pacific Region, 2000. Proceedings. The Fourth International Conference/Exhibition on , Volume: 1 (May 2000) 432 – 435

A Strategy-Proof Mechanism Based on Multiple Auction Support Agents

Takayuki Ito, Tokuro Matsuo, Tadachika Ozono, and Toramatsu Shintani

Graduate School of Engineering, Nagoya Institute of Technology,
Gokiso, Showa-ku, Nagoya, 466-8555, Japan
{itota, tmatsuo, ozono, tora}@ics.nitech.ac.jp
http://www-toralab.ics.nitech.ac.jp/~itota/

Abstract. Agent-mediated electronic commerce has recently commanded much attention. Bidding support agents have been studied very extensively. We envision a future in which many people can trade their goods by using a bidding support agent on Internet auctions. In this paper, we formalize a situation in which people are trading their goods on Internet auctions and employing bidding support agents. Then, we prove that people who use a bidding support agent can successively win trades. Also, we prove that the situation in which every people use a bidding support agent can satisfied strategy proofness and Pareto optimality. Further, we present in the situation, unsupported bidders do not make a positive benefit.

1 Introduction

Agent-mediated electronic commerce has recently commanded much attention[7]. Software agents can act autonomously and cooperatively in a network environment on behalf of their users. There have been several agents that can support users to attend, monitor, and make bids at multiple auctions simultaneously, e.g., *BiddingBot*[8][9], Anthony's agent[1], and Preist's agent[14].

We envision a future in which many people trade their goods by using a bidding support agent on Internet auctions. In this paper, we formalize a situation in which goods are traded via Internet auctions and each user uses a bidding support agent in order to make reasonable contracts.

The question(or problem) is "if there are a lot of such bidding support agents, can people make trades reasonably ?" We try to answer "yes" in this paper. To do so, we assume the following situation and prove that people can make reasonable trades if they use a bidding support agent under the situation. In the assumed situation, all people use a bidding support agent. In particular, we prove that this situation, as a whole, can be seen as an strategy-proof mechanism. In a strategy-proof mechanism, the best strategy for each agent is to submit a true bid, i.e, to tell a truth. This means that by employing bidding support agents, we can realize a strategy-proof mechanism.

M. Ali and F. Esposito (Eds.): IEA/AIE 2005, LNAI 3533, pp. 175–184, 2005.

Computational mechanism designs [3][10][11][12] have recently commanded much attention. One of the main issues in the computational mechanism design is to construct strategy-proof and efficient mechanism. The situation we present in this paper is naturally seen as a such strategy-proof and efficient mechanism. In general, mechanisms constructed in these fields are very complex. However, the situation we present in this paper is very simple. The only thing people do is to employ a bidding support agent.

An auction consists of an auctioneer and bidders. In an auction, the auctioneer wants to sell an item and get the highest possible payment for it, while each bidder wants to purchase the item at the lowest possible price. The certain value of the utility that a user receives from an item is called its value to him. The user's estimate of its value is called the user's valuation[15]. English auction has been adopted by many online auction sites. In the English auction, each bidder is free to revise her bid upwards. When no bidder wishes to revise her bid further, the highest bidder wins the item and pays the price that she had bid[15].

The Vickrey auction[17] is one of the important auction protocols. In the Vickrey auction, the winner is the bidder who submitted highest bid. The winner's price for the auctioned item is the second highest price among submitted bids. The protocol is very simple but there is a significant advantage. The Vickrey auction can be satisfy strategy-proofness and Pareto optimality. Thus, in the mechanism design field, the Vickrey auction has gathered much attention.

In this paper, we focus on bidding support agents that can support users to monitor, attend, and make bids in **multiple** auction sites. Some auction sites offer users a simple proxy bid program. This proxy bid program resides on the auction site, and bids on a user's behalf. Users enter the maximum price that they can pay into this program, and it automatically submits the lowest possible bid to the auction site. Such proxy bid programs cannot participate in multiple auction sites.

In the current real world, if all participants in a single English auction site (e.g. eBay.com) use proxy programs, the situation is equivalent to Vickrey auction. This situation is a simple case of our situation presented in this paper. When a participant uses a proxy program, he inputs his maximum price to pay into the program. Then, the proxy program automatically increase his bid. In this case, the price that the winner needs to pay is the second price $P_{second} + \alpha$. α is a minimum price to increase. If we ignore α, the price to pay is the second price. When we use the Vickrey auction, the winning price is the second price. This means that, if all participants employ proxy programs in an English auction, the result is almost same as the result in Vickrey auction. In this paper, we extended the above case to multiple auction sites and more sophisticated proxy programs (agents).

The aims of this paper is to present that bidding support agents can assist an user to successibly win a trade, and the situation in which every people use a bidding support agent satisfies Pareto optimality and incentive compatiblity.

The paper consists of five sections. In section 2, we define the basic terms used in this paper. Then, we formalize an electronic commerce model in which people trade their good via multiple auction sites by using bidding support agents. In Section 3 we present Pareto optimality and strategy-proofness in terms of the situation described, and robustness against unsupported bidders. In Section 4, we discuss the other characteristics of the situation. In Section 5, we show the difference between our work and related work. Finally, we make some concluding remarks.

2 An E-Commerce Model Based on Multiple Auctions

2.1 Preliminaries

Below, we define the basic terms used in this paper.

Private Value Auctions: In this paper, we concentrate on private value auctions [13]. In traditional definitions[13], in private value auctions, each agent knows its own evaluation values of a good, which are independent of the other agents' evaluation values. Agent i's utility u_i is defined as the difference between the true evaluation value b_i of the allocated good and the monetary transfer t_i for the allocated good ($-t_i$ can be called the payment). Namely, $u_i = b_i - t_i$. Such a utility is called a *quasi-linear* utility.

Pareto Optimality: We say an auction protocol is Pareto optimal when the sum of all participants' utilities (including that of the auctioneer), i.e., the social surplus, is maximized in a dominant strategy equilibrium. In a more general setting, Pareto efficiency does not necessarily mean maximizing the social surplus. In an auction setting, however, agents can transfer money among themselves, and the utility of each agent is quasi-linear; thus the sum of the utilities is always maximized in a *Pareto optimal* allocation. If the number of goods is one, in a Pareto efficient allocation, the good is awarded to a bidder having the highest evaluation value corresponding the quality of the good.

Dominant Strategy: The strategy s is a *dominant strategy* if it is a player's strictly best response to any strategies the other players might pick, in the sense that whatever strategies they pick, his payoff is highest with s. In addition, strategy s' is *weakly dominated* if there exists some other strategy s'' for player i which is possibly better and never worse, yielding a higher payoff in some strategy and never yielding a lower payoff[15].

Strategy-proof: In a definition [13], an auction protocol is a strategy-proof, if bidding the true private values of goods is the dominant strategy for each agent, i.e., the optimal strategy regardless of the actions of other agents. For example, in the Vickrey auction, for each bidder, truth telling is the dominant strategy. We can say the Vickrey auction is strategy proof.

Bidding Support Agents: Bidding support agents are intelligent softwares that can support an user to monitor, attend, and make bids on multiple auction sites. Several bidding support agents have been proposed and developed. BiddingBot [8][9] we developed is one of bidding support agents that can support a user in simultaneous multiple English auction sites. Figure 1 shows the concept of BiddingBot.

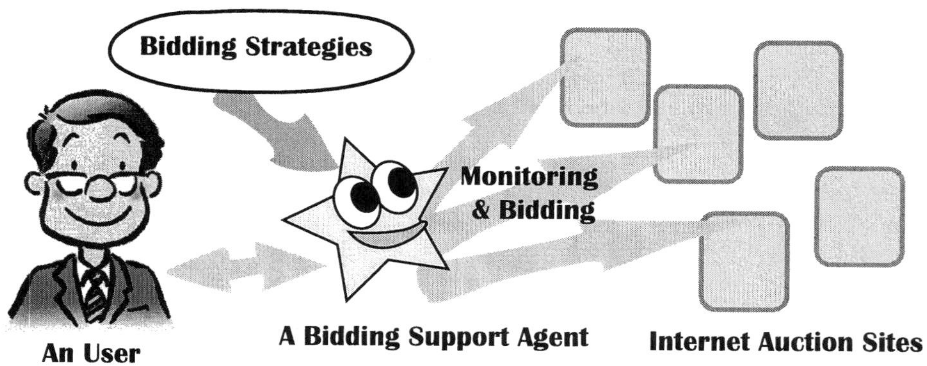

Fig. 1. The Concept of Bidding Support Agents

2.2 The Model

In this section, we define the model, several terms, and notations.

- A set of buyers is represented by $B = \{b_1, \ldots, b_n\}$.
- Buyer b_i's reservation price is represented by P_{b_i}.
- Each buyer has a bidding support agent a_{b_i}.
- A bidding support agent a_{b_i} exactly find the user's desired good and exactly submit a bid in the auction site that price is the lowest among multiple auction sites. Further, a bidding support agent a_{b_i} does not make a bid higher than the user's reservation price.
- A set of auction is represented by $S = \{s_1, \ldots, s_m\}$.
- Each auction site employs English auction.
- We assume the starting time of all auction sites is the same time.
- We assume the deadline time of all auction sites is the same time. This assumption is important for distinguishing the real situation with the ideal situation. If the deadlines are different, bidder support agents who have a good price prediction mechanism can tend to win auctions. In the ideal situation, we do not assume the price prediction mechanism.
- We assume the increasing price for each auction site is a small number α.
- We assume that $|B| - |S| \geq 1$. Namely, the number of bidders is larger than the number of auction. If $|B| - |S| \leq 1$, all buyers can succeed to win a good since supply is larger than demand.

3 The Characteristics of the Situation Where Multiple Bidding Support Agents Exist

3.1 Strategy Proofness and Pareto Optimality Under the Ideal Situation

In this section, we demonstrate that the ideal situation can satisfy strategy proofness and Pareto optimality.

Assumption 1. *In the ideal situation, all people employ a bidding support agent.*

Theorem 1. *Under the condition described in Section 2, the best strategy for each bidder is submitting a true value. Namely, participant's dominant strategy is telling a truth. Thus, we can say the situation based on the condition described in Section 2 is* **strategy proof**.

Proof. (Outline) As we can show in the example in Section 2, the awarding price is determined based on the price that is the highest among participants who failed to win a good. Concretely, in the Example in Section 2, the price for b_1 and b_2 is determined based on the b_3's price. b_3 failed to win a good. This is because all of auction sites employs the English auction protocol. Namely, since winners' prices do not depend on their bids, participant's dominant strategy is submitting a true value. The details are almost same as the proof for Vickrey auction protocol[15].

Theorem 2. *Under the condition described in Section 2, the situation satisfied Pareto optimality.*

Proof. Obviously, the goods are awarded to the bidders in order of the evaluation values submitted. Namely, the bidder who submitted higher value can be awarded.

Situation 1 to Situation 4 in Figure 2 show an example of multiple bidders in multiple auctions. Here, we assume three bidders, $B = \{b_1, b_2, b_3\}$, two auction sites, $S = \{s_1, s_2\}$, and $\alpha = 10$. Reservation prices are $P_{b_1} = 300$, $P_{b_2} = 200$, and $P_{b_3} = 100$. Situation 1 shows an initial state. "Current price" means the bidder's current price of the bid. "Current site" means the site in which the bidder has the highest bid. If a bidder does not have the highest bid in an auction site, "Current site" is "none". Situation 2 shows a situation in a certain time. Situation 3 also shows a situation where b_3 reached the reservation price. Situation 4 shows a final state. Here, b_3's bid was out-bided by b_1's bid that price is 110. The main point is that both of b_1's final price and b_2's final price is determined based on b_3's final price.

3.2 Robustness Against Unsupported Bidders

In this section, we relax the assumption in terms of the ideal situation. Here, we assume there exist bidders who do not employ bidding support agents. In

Bidder	b_1	b_2	b_3
Reservation price	300	200	100
Current price	0	0	0
Current item	-	-	-

Situation 1

Bidder	b_1	b_2	b_3
Reservation price	300	200	100
Current price	40	50	50
Current item	none	s_1	s_2

Situation 2

Bidder	b_1	b_2	b_3
Reservation price	300	200	100
Current price	90	110	100
Current item	none	s_1	s_2

Situation 3

Bidder	b_1	b_2	b_3
Reservation price	300	200	100
Current price	110	110	100
Current item	s_2	s_1	none

Situation 4

Fig. 2. An Example of Multiple Bidders in Multiple Auctions

this paper, while bidders who use bidding support agents are called "supported bidders" bidders who do not use bidding support agents are called "unsupported bidders".

Assumption 2. *In the semi-ideal situation, there are supported bidders and unsupported bidders. While supported bidders employ bidding support agents, unsupported bidders do not employ bidding support agents.*

The best strategy (dominant strategy) for unsupported bidders is to tell a true evaluation value since each auction is now same as Vickrey auction. We can prove that these unsupported bidders do not make a positive benefit in this situation.

Theorem 3. *If the unsupported bidder is rational, the unsupported bidder does not make a positive benefit in our situation.*

Proof (Outline). When the number of the selling item S is larger than the number of bidders B, i.e., $|S| \geq |B|$, then unsupported bidders play Vickrey auctions for each item while supported bidders can make bids to the items that can not be found by the unsupported bidders.

When the number of bidders B is larger than the number of the selling item S, i.e., $|B| > |S|$, then unsupported bidders pay the price that is higher than or same as that of the supported bidders. If there exist two or more unsupported bidders for a certain item, it is same as that they play a Vickrey auction. Thus, there is no benefit for them to tell false evaluation values. The price is the second price for their bids. This price can be higher than supported bidders. Even if there exist only one unsupported bidder for a certain item, he just participates in a Vickrey-like auction. Thus, even if he tell a false evaluation value, there is no benefit for him. The price can be same as the other supported bidders.

Figure 3 shows an example of the situation in which unsupported bidders exist. Here, we assume three bidders, $B = \{b_1, b_2, b_3', b_4'\}$, two auction sites,

Bidder	b_1	b_2	b'_3	b'_4
Reservation price	300	100	200	250
Current price	0	0	0	0
Current item	-	-	-	-

b_1&b_2 employ bidding support agents.
b'_3&b'_4 do not employ bidding support agents and, they only know item s_2.

Initial situation

Bidder	b_1	b_2	b'_3	b'_4
Reservation price	300	100	200	250
Current price	10	10	0	0
Current item	s_1	s_2	-	-

Situation 2

Bidder	b_1	b_2	b'_3	b'_4
Reservation price	300	100	200	250
Current price	10	10	10	0
Current item	s_1	s_3	s_2	-

Situation 3

Bidder	b_1	b_2	b'_3	b'_4
Reservation price	300	100	200	250
Current price	10	10	100	110
Current item	s_1	s_3	-	s_2

Situation 4

Bidder	b_1	b_2	b'_3	b'_4
Reservation price	300	100	200	250
Current price	10	10	200	210
Current item	s_1	s_3	-	s_2

Final situation

Fig. 3. An Example of the Situation in which Unsupported Bidders Exist

$S = \{s_1, s_2, s_3\}$, and $\alpha = 10$. Reservation prices are $P_{b_1} = 300$, $P_{b_2} = 100$, $P_{b_3} = 200$, and $P_{b_4} = 250$. Suppose there are 4 bidders, b_1, b_2, b'_3, and b'_4. Here b_1 and b_2 are supported bidders. b'_3 and b'_4 are unsupported bidders. b_1 and b_2 know items s_1, s_2, and s_3 that are being auctioned. On the other hand, b'_3 and b'_4 know only item s_3. For example, in Situation 2, b_1 and b_2 make bids, \$10, to s_1 and s_2, respectively. Then, in Situation 3, b'_3 makes a bid, \$10, to s_2. Here, b_2 know no one bid to s_3. Thus, b_2 change the item from s_2 to s_3, and make a bid, \$10, to s_3. Afterwards, in Situation 4, b_1 and b_2 do not need to make higher bids. On the other hand, since b'_3 and b'_4 know only s_2, they need to compete on s_2. Thus, in Situation 5, for example, b_1 and b_2 can win the items, s_1 and s_3, and b'_4 win the item s_2 at the price \$250.

4 Discussion

4.1 Different Deadlines

We assumed the deadlines are same so far. However, when we assume every people employ bidding support agents, and the bidding support agent do not predict prices, change the item, etc. after the deadline, then strategy-proofness and Pareto optimality can be satisfied. However, for bidding support agents, the prediction function on the deadline is actually very important, and there can be several strategies for prediction. Thus, the assumption that bidding support agents do not predict prices, change the item, etc. after the deadline is too strong to discuss the property of this situation.

4.2 Robustness Against Irrational Bidders

Irrational bidders do not select their dominant strategies. This means that irrational bidders do not make a true bid, i.e., tell a truth. In the situation we proposed here, even if there are irrational bidders, these irrational bidders do not make benefits. Further, even when all bidders are irrational, we can say they can not make a benefit by being irrational. Namely, while irrational players can make an negative utility, rational players do not make negative utility if they choose their dominant strategies, i.e., telling a truth. We clarify the above claim by presenting examples.

Figure 4 shows an example of all bidders are irrational. Resevation prices that are underlined are their true evaluation value. On the other hand, prices that are not underlined in reservation prices are their false bids. In this case, b_1 and b_3 can win the items. However, they can not get positive utilities.

Bidder	b_1	b_2	b_3
Reservation price	300 400	200 330	100 360
Current price	0	0	0
Current item	-	-	-

Initail situation

Bidder	b_1	b_2	b_3
Reservation price	300 400	200 330	100 360
Current price	340	330	340
Current item	s_1	none	s_2

Final situation

Fig. 4. An Example of All bidders are irrational

If b_1 makes a truthful bid, i.e., his dominant strategy, according to the theorem, he does not make any negative utility. Figure 5 shows an example of the situation in which only one bidder is rational. In this case, although b_1 does not win the item, the other bidders gets a negative utility by making false bids. On the other hand, b_1 does not suffer any loss.

5 Related Work

One of the most popular software agents is ShopBot[4]. ShopBot helps users to find desired shops or goods from the Internet. Jango[5] is an advanced ShopBot, and helps a user decide what and where to buy. The main function of ShopBot is to find a web site or a description of goods based on the user's preference. Greenwald[6] analyzed a future situation in which there are many ShopBots, and proposed PriceBot in order to enable sellers to price dynamically. However, ShopBot can not make a bid to multiple auctions. ShopBot mainly retrieve information from shop sites. Contrary, we focus on bidding support agents that can make bids to multiple auctions. Furthermore, while Greewald[6]'s analysis is based on a lot of information gathering agents, i.e., ShopBot, our analysis is based on a lot of bidding support agents.

The following related works handle multiple auction sites by using agent technology. In papers [1, 14], the authors discuss about the use of one single

Bidder	b_1	b_2	b_3
Reservation price	300 300	200 330	100 360
Current price	0	0	0
Current item	-	-	-

Initail situation

Bidder	b_1	b_2	b_3
Reservation price	300 300	200 330	100 360
Current price	300	310	310
Current item	none	s_1	s_2

Final situation

Fig. 5. Only one bidder is rational. The others are irrational

agent which monitors and submits bids in multiple auctions. The features of works [1, 14] are (a) the aim is to automate bidding: An agent is completely autonomous, (b) they assume one single agent, and (c) paper [1, 2] assumes a virtual auction world that consists of English auctions, Vickrey auctions, and Dutch auctions. Paper [14] assumes a virtual auction world that consists of modified English auctions. It is not known whether their methods can be used in real multiple Internet auctions. The above work does not have any insight on the situation we proposed in this paper.

6 Conclusions and Future Work

In this paper, we formalized a situation in which people are trading their goods on Internet auctions and employing bidding support agents. Then, we proved that in the above situation all participants need to submit true bids. This means that as a whole this situation can be seen as an strategy-proof and a Pareto optimal mechanism.

One of the main issues in the traditional mechanism design is to construct strategy-proof and efficient mechanism. The situation we present in this paper is naturally seen as a such strategy-proof and efficient mechanism. In general, mechanisms constructed in these fields are very complex. However, the situation we present in this paper is very simple. The only thing people do is to employ a bidding support agent.

As future work, we plan to relax the assumptions we described in Section 2. Namely, we assumed the starting time is same time, the increasing price is only α, and bidding support agents do not fail to win a good if he can win. In the real world, these bidding support agent may fail to make a bid due to something like noise or network jam. Thus, we plan to model such a situation and conduct some computer simulations.

References

1. Anthony, P., Hall, W., and Dang, V. D., "Autonomous agents for participating in multiple on-line auctions", In *Proc. of the IJCAI Workshop on E-Business and the Intelligent Web*, 54–64, 2001.
2. Anthony, P. and N. R. Jennings: 2002, 'Evolving Bidding Strategies for Multiple Auctions'. In: *Proc. of the 15th European Conference on Artificial Intelligence (ECAI2002)*.

3. R. K. Dash, N. R. Jennings, and D. C. Parks. Computational-mechanism design: A call to arms. *IEEE Intelligent Systems*, 18(6):40–47, 2003.
4. Doorenbos, R. B., Etzioni, O., and Weld, D. S., "A scalable comparison-shopping agent for the world-wide web", In *Proc. of Autonomous Agents 97*, 39–48, 1997.
5. Etzioni, O.: 1997, 'Moving Up the Information Food Chain: Deploying Softbots on the World Wide Web'. *AI magazine* **18**(2), 11–18.
6. Greenwald, R.R, and Kephart., J. O., "Shopbots and pricebots", In *Proceedings of the Sixteenth International Joint Conference on Artificial Intelligence (IJCAI-99)*, pp. 506–511, 1999.
7. Guttman, R. H., Moukas, A. G., and Maes, P. "Agent-mediated electronic commerce: A survey", *The Knowledge Engineering Review* 13(2):147–159, 1998.
8. Ito, T., Fukuta, N., Shintani, T., and Sycara, K., "*BiddingBot*: A multiagent support system for cooperative bidding in multiple auctions", In *Proc. of the 4th International Conference on Multi-Agent Systems (ICMAS-2000)*, pp. 399–400, 2000.
9. Ito, T., Hattori, H., and Shintani, T., "A Multiple Auctions Support System *BiddingBot* based on a Cooperative Bidding Mechanism among Agents", In journal of Japanese Society for Artificial Intelligence, Vol.17, No.3, 2002.
10. Ito, T., Yokoo, M., and Matsubara, S.: Designing an Auction Protocol under Asymmetric Information on Nature's Selection, in *Proc. of the 1st International Joint Conference on Autonomous Agents and Multi-Agent Systems (AAMAS02)*, pp. 61–68 (2002)
11. Ito, T., Yokoo, M., and Matsubara, S.: Towards a Combinatorial Auction Protocol among Experts and Amateurs: The Case of Single-Skilled Experts, in *Proc. of the 2nd International Joint Conference on Autonomous Agents and Multi-Agent Systems (AAMAS03)*, pp. 481–488 (2003)
12. Ito, T., Yokoo, M., and Matsubara, S.: A Combinatorial Auction among Versatile Experts and Amateurs, in *Proc. of the 3rd International Joint Conference on Autonomous Agents and Multi-Agent Systems (AAMAS04)*, pp. 378–385 (2004)
13. A. Mas-Colell, M. D. Whinston, and J. R. Green., *Microeconomic Theory.* Oxford University Press, 2nd edition, 1995.
14. Preist, C., Bartolini, C., and Phillips, I, "Algorithm design for agents which participate in multiple simultaneous auctions", In Dignum, F., and Cortes, U., eds., *Agent-mediated Electronic Commerce III*, LNAI 2003. Springer. pp. 139–154, 2001.
15. Rasmusen, E., "*Games and Information: An Introduction to Game Theory*", Blackwell Publishers, 2nd edition, 1989.
16. Varian, H.R., "Economic Mechanism Design for Computerized Agents", in *Proceedings of First Usenix Workshop on Electronic Commerce*, 1995.
17. Vickrey, W., "Counter Speculation, Auctions, and Competitive Sealed Tenders", Journal of Finance, Vol. 16, pp.8–37, 1961.

Automated Teleoperation of Web-Based Devices Using Semantic Web Services

Young-guk Ha[1], Jaehong Kim[1], Minsu Jang[1], Joo-chan Sohn[1], and Hyunsoo Yoon[2]

[1] Intelligent Robot Research Division, Electronics and Telecommunications Research Institute, 161 Gajeong-dong, Yuseong-gu, Daejeon, Korea
{ygha, jhkim504, minus, jcsohn}@etri.re.kr
http://www.etri.re.kr/e_etri/
[2] Computer Science Division, Korea Advanced Institute of Science and Technology, 373-1 Kusung-dong, Yuseong-gu, Daejeon, Korea
hyoon@camars.kaist.ac.kr

Abstract. In this paper, we present SWATS which supports task-oriented automated teleoperation of Web-based devices. The proposed system employs Semantic Web Services technology and AI planning technique to achieve operational automaticity.

1 Introduction

Internet-based teleoperation systems are mainly focused on remote control of networked devices, such as mobile robots or digital appliances through the Internet. In recent years, several attempts have been made to develop Internet-based teleoperation systems using the Web technology: i.e. USC's teleoperated excavation system Mercury and CMU's indoor mobile robot Xavier. In such systems, each control command generally provides a behavior-level control over the device with or without built-in autonomy. That is, to achieve a desired task, a human operator monitors remote devices through Web-cams or sensors, and manually sends a sequence of appropriate control commands and parameters with a Web browser as shown in Fig. 1-a.

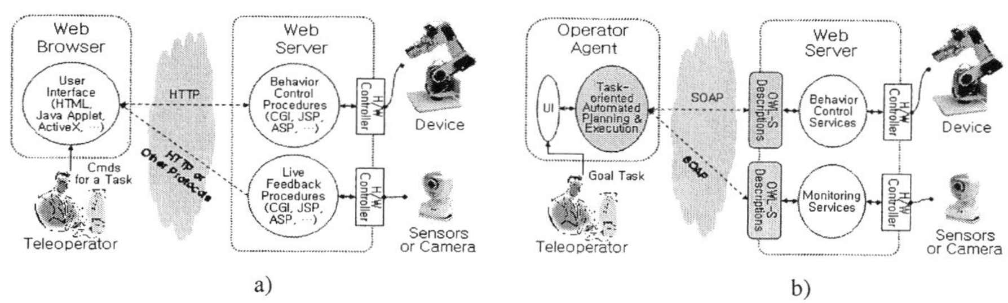

Fig. 1. Comparison of a) Traditional Web-based teleoperation and b) SWATS approach

In this paper, we propose SWATS (Semantic-Web-service-based Automated Teleoperation System) which supports task-oriented automated teleoperation of Web-

M. Ali and F. Esposito (Eds.): IEA/AIE 2005, LNAI 3533, pp. 185 – 188, 2005.

based devices. As shown in Fig. 1-b, SWATS employs Semantic Web Services technology [3] and automated planning to provide operational automaticity. That is, semantics of behaviors and interfaces for Web-based devices and sensors are encoded in OWL-S (Web Ontology Language for Services) [4] as Web services, so that operator agents can automatically plan operation processes for the requested tasks by reasoning about their semantics in OWL-S. And then the operator agents can achieve requested task goals by communicating with the devices and sensors through SOAP (Simple Object Access Protocol) messaging according to the operation processes.

2 Architecture of SWATS

Fig. 2 shows the architecture of SWATS. The OA, as an intelligent planning and service requester agent, plays the major role of automated teleoperation in SWATS architecture. A teleoperator inputs operation task as a goal to achieve and optionally initial operation contexts with the User Interface. Based on the input task and initial contexts, the Task Planning Module discovers required knowledge for planning through the Semantic Discovery Module and automatically generates a feasible task plan based on HTN (Hierarchical Task Network) planning [2]. To search the OKR for planning knowledge described in OWL-S, the Semantic Discovery Module generates appropriate semantic queries based on the input task description and sends them to the OKR. The Process Execution Module translates the task plan into the BPEL [1] process and executes the process through the Web services communication stack.

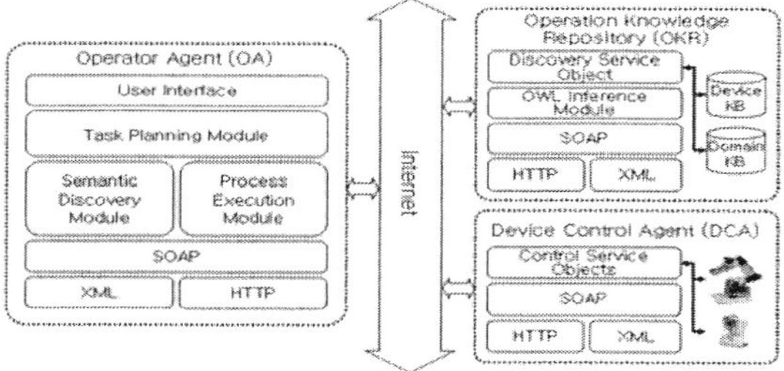

Fig. 2. The architecture of SWATS consists of three major components, which are Operator Agent (OA), Device Control Agent (DCA) and Operation Knowledge Repository (OKR)

The DCA is implementation of behavior control Web services for a device including monitoring services for sensor and camera devices. Each DCA can have Control Service Objects for one device or multiple devices which may work cooperatively, for instance an air-conditioning device and temperature sensors. And the DCA also has a Web services communication stack to communicate with an OA. The OKR contains KBs for task domain, device behaviors and interfaces which are used in automated task planning and process execution. The Domain KB stores OWL-S ontology of composite processes and internal data flows describing task domain knowledge. The Device KB stores OWL-S ontology of atomic processes and corresponding grounding descriptions as device service descriptions. The OKR includes the Discovery Service Object to handle knowledge discovery queries with semantic predicates. It uses the OWL Inference Module to reason about the semantic predicates. The OKR also includes a Web services communication stack because it works as a Web service itself. Fig. 3 shows automated teleoperation procedure of SWATS.

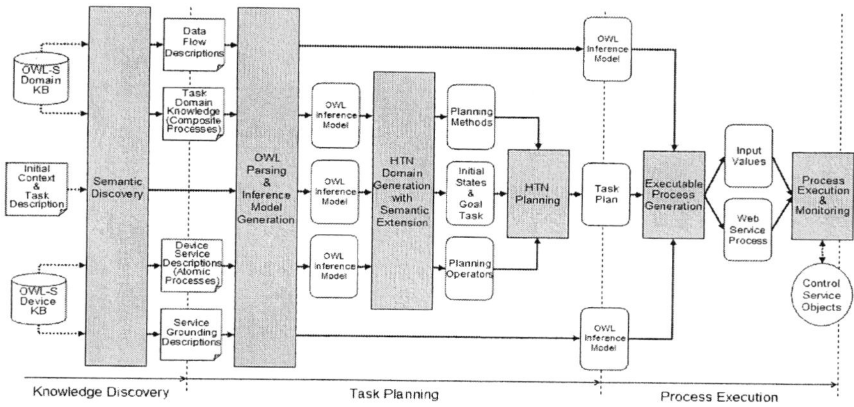

Fig. 3. Automated teleoperation procedure of SWATS consists of knowledge discovery, operational task planning and process execution phases

3 Implementation of SWATS

The prototype implementation of SWATS is shown in Fig. 4. The prototype DCA contains control service objects, i.e. MoveTo, GetImage, SendImage and etc, for the mobile robot. For an experiment, we generate OWL-S descriptions of the control services and task domain knowledge for home telesecurity services, i.e. ReportHomeStatus service which automatically operates a mobile robot to move to the specified place in the house, take a picture and send the picture to the outdoor user.

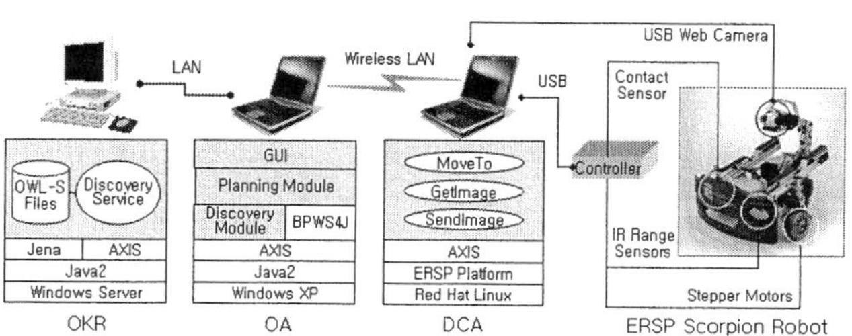

Fig. 4. The SWATS prototype implementation for automated home telesecurity services

References

1. Andrews, T., Curbera, F., Dholakia, H., Goland, Y., Klein, J., Leymann, F., et al.: BPEL for Web Services, http://www.ibm.com/developerworks/library/ws-bpel/ (2003)
2. Erol, K., Nau, D., Hendler, J.: UMCP: A Sound and Complete Planning Procedure for Hierarchical Task-Network Planning, AIPS-94, Chicago (1994)
3. McIlraith, S.A., Son, T.C., Zeng, H.: The Semantic Web Services, IEEE Intelligent Systems, Vol. 16, Issue 2, IEEE (2001) 46-53
4. The OWL Services Coalition: OWL-S 1.0 Release, http://www.daml.org/services/owl-s/1.0/ (2003)

Context Awarable Self-configuration System for Distributed Resource Management

Seunghwa Lee and Eunseok Lee

School of Information and Communication Engineering, Sungkyunkwan University
300 Chunchun jangahn Suwon, 440-746, Korea
{jbmania, eslee}@selab.skku.ac.kr

Abstract. Today's system administrator is forced to perform individual configuration and maintenance tasks (i.e. *installation, reconfiguration, update*) on numerous systems, in various formats. These tasks are time-consuming and labor intensive. Several research projects have attempted to resolve these issues with the development of an integrated, centralized management system. However, many tasks are still left to the system administrator for manual handling. A customized configuration system that reflects comprehensive context has not yet been fully realized. This paper proposes a context aware self-configuration system by employing multi-agents to collectively gather contextual information based on the system resources and user's system usage patterns. This proposed system, then analyzes the collected information and performs automatic configuration as and when required. This system will allow not only enable automation of the previously manual tasks, but also allow, in effect, a more customized configuration.

1 Introduction

While the performance capacity of computing devices is increasing with respect to the recent rapid development of IT technology, the price of these computing devices have been continuously declining. Coupled with the advent of *Ubiquitous Computing*, there has been an influx of more diverse computing devices in the market, hence an increase in the number of subjects to be managed as well as mounting complexity [1].

In these expanding computing environments, it is becoming increasingly challenging to handle and manage the expanding number of computing devices. Take for example a system managing and operating several hosts. In this case, each host requires installation of distinct software and also must bear the cost of time and the availability of human resources required to maintain these software application result in tremendous constraints. Novice end-users who are unfamiliar with their role often fail to conduct critical maintenance procedures such as OS patches or vaccine program updates, a negligence that often leads to system defects. In order to solve this resource management issue, technology to reduce the workload and automatic updates are being applied by various institutions. These technologies have arisen from studies regarding the centralized integration of management for distributed resources, and unattended installation [2][3]. However, these studies focus mainly on 'automation', which simply replaces the tasks currently processed manually. However, in this paper, we propose an adaptable self-management system that collects *system resources*, *user*

M. Ali and F. Esposito (Eds.): IEA/AIE 2005, LNAI 3533, pp. 189 – 191, 2005.

information, and *usage patterns* as contextual information and automates a large portion of the configuration tasks such as; *installation*, *reconfiguration*, and *update* the system, reducing the system maintenance burden on users. This paper is organized as follows. Section 2 describes the characteristics of the proposed system. Section 3 discloses the study's conclusion.

2 Proposed System

This paper defines configuration as the installation of necessary components that need to be managed, subsequently reconfiguring these components for specific tasks. The configuration process can be more specifically defined as follows:

- Installation: new installation of necessary components (OS, software, etc.)
- Reconfiguration: reconfiguration of installed components to fit unique situations
- Update: version management of applications or modification of components to correct defects. This also includes re-installation when parts of the configuration files have been corrupted due to virus attack or system error.

1) Installation
The proposed system will automatically write customized response files and specific preference values based on stored user data (user preferences gleaned from personal information, preference data of existing programs, and usage patterns).

For instance, when installing a new word processing program, the proposed system automatically sets default fonts as those, which are frequently selected by the user in similar applications. (The Ontology server stores the different expressions with identical meanings for each application and uses the data to identify preferences for other applications.) The system identifies automatic backup preferences from other applications to apply to the newly installed word processing application. User-specific preferences such as declining the creation of application icons on Windows and other GUI OS desktops are also reflected in the automated installation for newly installed applications. The proposed system identifies user preferences by analyzing preference values of similar applications and performing a customized installation process by directly writing and distributing an automated script or preference value, as described above. The system also observes user activity on a continual basis to see whether such settings are altered and if so, performs *Reinforcement learning* [5] by adjusting its policies following such negative feedback. It is also capable of generating a script to automatically select a minimal installation when sufficient space is not available, through gathered context data on system resources. The user is alerted and final decisions made, through which, the system learns and then reflects onto future tasks.

2) Reconfiguration
The proposed system gathers continually varying memory capacity as a contextual resource in order to adjust the application settings based on pre-defined rules, this continually refines service quality. This capability offers enhanced stability features for mobile devices and other devices in the domain of limited performance environments. The rules and information for adjusting the options for each application

is sent to the subject along with the application upon installation and is managed by the *Component Agent* that is embedded within the client device.

The Component Agent shuts down processes with high resource usage and restarts the process when sufficient resources become available. The processes are listed according to identified priority, based on application usage frequency and their correlation with other applications. These are updated on a regular basis to establish optimal rule sets through interaction with the Configuration System.

3) Update

The update priority is determined by monitoring the frequency of the components, through which the system facilitates the various tasks efficiently if the remaining storage or the time required for updating, is insufficient. Reflecting the *Astrolabe* [4] structure, each host organizes the components into zones, and these zones are organized hierarchically. A representative host of each zone collects a list of files on the individual hosts while a host requiring the file requests the location of a near host holding the file from the representative host. The host requiring the file receives it using peer-to-peer transmission. From this model, each host reduces the load of the centralized server, effectively increasing resistance to various difficulties, and quickly copies the required files. The update files copied within the zone are checked for consistency through comparing file sizes.

3 Conclusion

The proposed system provides a function of context adaptive self-configuration that collects system resources, user information, and usage patterns as contextual data. It has been applied to system *installation*, *reconfiguration*, and *update*. From the experiments, we can verify its effectiveness in terms of resource management by the ability to minimize human assistance, therefore decreasing workload. Peer-to-Peer communications is a solution to the inherent weaknesses of centralized distribution systems. This decreases central server load and simultaneously allows faster file distribution, resulting in more efficient updates. This system, along with the above described self-configuration features, offers a differentiated configuration process that employs both system and user contextual information. These features are expected to enhance usability and user satisfaction, relieving system administrators of the load they bear in this ubiquitous environment, offering enhanced computing convenience.

References

1. Paul Horn, "Autonomic Computing: IBM's Perspective on the State of Information Technology", IBM White paper, Oct.2001
2. http://www-306.ibm.com/software/tivoli
3. http://www.microsoft.com/technet/prodtechnol/winxppro/deploy/default.mspx
4. Robbert van Renesse, Kenneth Birman and Werner Vogels, "Astrolabe: A Robust and Scalable Technology for Distributed System Monitoring, Management, and Data Mining", ACM Transactions on CS., Vol.21, No.2, pp.164-206, May 2003
5. Richard S. Sutton, Andrew G. Barto, 'Reinforcement Learning: An Introduction (Adaptive Computation and Machine Learning)', The MIT Press, Mar.1998

A Decision Support System for Inventory Control Using Planning and Distributed Agents

Robert Signorile

Computer Science Department,
Boston College,
Chestnut Hill, MA,
USA 02467,
Phone: +1 617-552-3936
signoril@bc.edu

Abstract. Agent Technology has become very popular in the last few years as a new approach to developing software systems. Multi Agent Systems (MAS), a term used to describe the incorporation of multiple types of agents into various systems, is a way of designing and implementing a system with the advantages of agent entities. We chose to use agents as a decision support tool for use in a Retail Inventory Management System. Since the management of inventory is crucial to the success of most companies, and since we see a potential major role for agents in the business process management MAS seems a likely choice for a decision support platform. This work stems from our prior work in simulating a MAS inventory system, then implementing the system for production use.

Keywords: Decision Support Systems, Autonomous Agents, Multi-agent systems, Applications to Business.

1 Introduction

In this paper, we describe our approach in designing and implementing a Decision Support System for Inventory Management System with Agents. We discuss the advantages and disadvantages of incorporating Agents into such a system and whether it is beneficial or not. This work is an outgrowth of a system we developed to simulate multi agents in an inventory system.

Our production system can be used in two modes: completely autonomous mode (where agents perform all the inventory analysis, planning and ordering) or in human in the loop mode where the agents perform the pre-mentioned activities except ordering, which is the domain of the human manager or department head.

All agents will be given specific duties, which will be run at the local level. The agent itself will make all decision making for each agent's application. All agents are equal in their tasks.

The current scope of the inventory decision support system is the store itself, not the actual supply chain or any component of the supply chain. The current system uses agents to develop an optimal inventory plan (this would include lag time, warehousing and all aspects of the supply chain, which we make some simple assumptions about).

M. Ali and F. Esposito (Eds.): IEA/AIE 2005, LNAI 3533, pp. 192 – 196, 2005.

The architecture for this project is currently based on an agent hierarchy. There are the actual "physical agents" who represent real world objects or people and are static, and there are "logical agents" who are used to supply the "physical" agents with all information and materials they need to complete their tasks and are dynamic. This architecture seems to work very well, and keeps the decision-making local and allows the agents to keep their own individual tasks small.

2 Inventory Management

Inventory Management has three major parts [2]: Demand Forecasting, Inventory Control, and Replenishment; which we will discuss in detail in the next sub-sections. Our decision support system incorporates all three parts using agents.

2.1 Forecasting Inventory Demand

Forecasting calculates how much inventory is needed and when it will be needed. Its primary goal is to have the right products in the right positions at the right time. A forecasting system includes four elements: (1) an underlying model; (2) data, exploratory analysis, and calibration; (3) updates to the model; and (4) measurement of forecasting errors. [1]

2.2 Inventory Control

Inventory control does the basic record keeping that is the basis of which more complex decisions are made in the forecasting and replenishment modules. It involves the creation of inventory records, the practices dealing with the maintenance of these records, and the counting or auditing of inventory. It also deals with inventory administration, methods of valuating inventory, and evaluating inventory performance.

2.3 Replenishment of Inventory

The economic order quantity (EOQ) model is one technique used to determine the optimal quantity to order. The optimal ordering quantity, Q, can be found analytically. It occurs where the total annual holding cost equals the total annual ordering cost. [2]

3 Agents

Agents and multi-agent systems demonstrate a new way to analyze data and solve complex problems. With agent-based systems comes an entirely new vocabulary that describes how agents operate. The use of the word "agent" is so broad that some people argue that it can be made to mean almost anything. However, we focus on the unique characteristics that agents possess, and thus, we define agents based on these characteristics. We will see how agents work and what kinds of problems they are useful in solving.

4 How Agents Could Help Inventory Management Systems

"We see a potential major role for them (collaborative agents) in business process management." [6]

An Inventory Management System is extremely. Another issue is that the information the system manages needs to be accessed by many sources that could range from headquarters to the department level. An application needs to have two characteristics to be a suitable for a multi-agent system implementation: distribution and intelligence. [5] An inventory management system has both these characteristics. It needs to be distributed over the company's network where all managers, departments, etc. need access to it. And it also needs to be able to learn from past inventory histories, forecast histories, and replenishment histories. And it then applies what it learns by acting upon anything that it sees needs to be changed: such as changing the forecast technique and constants, changing the inventory control constants, changing the replenishment techniques and constants, and also to make sales on certain items when necessary. Since the system meets these two major requirements, it is a good candidate for a multi-agent system.

5 Our Decision Support System Using MAS

5.1 Specification

The decision support inventory management system using MAS is designed to manage the inventory of a retail store that sells only finished goods such as a chain of clothing stores. Effective inventory management includes forecasting, determining replenishment information, and controlling inventory levels. Agents will be used to carry out these functions are:

- Forecasting Agent: Forecasts demand using a simple moving average (MA) of the last n periods, depending on which n-month gives the least errors in the past.
- Inventory Control Agent: Record keeping agent that updates inventory when an item is sold or replenished.
- Replenishment Agent: determine the EOQ (Economic Order Quantity: how much to order and when) based on the demand forecast.
- Department Agent: there is one for each department and it controls the Forecast, Inventory Control, and the Replenishment agents.
- Manager Agent: One Manager Agent for each store to monitor the Department Agents.

6 Running the Inventory Management System

The overall system uses Java to construct the GUI, simulation and the report mechanism. As we mentioned, we constructed a simulation of this system [8], which modeled the actual system at the time. This motivated us to create the actual production system for the store. We implemented the system two modes. The first is an autonomous mode, which means the agents analyze the data database, inputs and generate the inventory plan. The second mode in the human in the loop mode, which means the agents create the inventory plan, but the management roles are humans and thus can override/modify any agent plan. In both modes, the system is capable of maintaining a database of inventory plans. We do this for future learning and analysis. This is most important for human in the loop mode, where the system can use the case in the future when a similar circumstance arises. We noticed increased efficiency in both inventory control (defined as minimizing the effect of too little or too much inventory) and perceived customer appreciation (defined as availability of goods due to size, color, style) when compared to traditional inventory control method. The reason for this is due to the gents learning ability and dynamic adjusting ability.

7 Conclusion

Agents can help design an Inventory Management System that is reliable, more accurate, intelligent, distributed, scalable, faster, and simpler in design. Such a system is very much needed in this time and in the future especially with the growing economy and the growth of the Internet. The future of such systems lies in creating a component that can negotiate online orders for restocking inventory with online suppliers. Our current decision support system is limited to the inventory system (excluding supply chain activities) for a medium sized department store in the United States. We plan to add to this system a simulation of the store's supply chain (or at least some part of it) to test how the inventory system will behave in a more dynamic scenario (i.e. testing various supply chain situations).

References

1. J.F. Robeson, W.C. Copacino and R.E. Howe, *The Logistics Handbook.* (NY: The Free Press, 1994).
2. E.A. Silver, D.F. Pyke, and R. Peterson, *Inventory Management and Production Planning and Scheduling*. (NY: John Wiley & Sons, 1998).
3. R.B. Chase, N.J. Aquilano, and F.R. Jacobs, *Production and Operations Management. Eighth Edition.* (Boston: Irwin McGraw-Hill, 1998).
4. N. R. Jennings and M. J. Wooldridge, *Agent Technology.* (Berlin: Springer, 1998).
5. R. Aylett, F. Brazier, N. Jennings, M. Luck, H. Nwana, and C. Priest, 1998. *"Agent Systems and Applications"*.
6. H. Nwana and D. Ndumu, 1996. *"An Introduction to Agent Technology"*.
7. Collis and J. Ndumu, *Zeus Agent Building Toolkit Manuals*, Intelligent Systems Research Group, BT Labs.
8. R. Signorile and M. Rawashdeh, ***"Inventory Management Simulation with Agents"***, Proceedings of HMS2000, Oct. 2000
9. R. Signorile and K. Lester, "Multi Agent Simualtion", Proceedings of SCI200
10. N. Jennings, K. Sycara, and M Wooldridge. A Roadmap of Agent Research and Development. Kluwer Academic Publishers, Boston, MA, 1998.
11. Signorile, R, and Segritch A., "Distributed Intelligent Agents for a Collaborative Web-based Simulation", In the *Proceedings of WEBSIM2000,* San Diego, CA, January, 2000

12. Signorile R. and McNulty, M., "Simulating the Use of Intelligent Agents in an Automated Distributed Multi-Constrained Scheduling System", In *Proceedings of the 11th European Simulation Symposium* (Germany), SCS
13. Signorile, R. "A Framework for Distributed Intelligent Agents in the Simulation of External Logistics of an Enterprise", In *the Proceedings of the HMS1999*, Genova, Italy, Oct. 1999.
14. Rosaria Conte, Jaime S. Sichman,G. Nigel Gilbert, Proceedings of the Multi-Agent Systems and Agent-Based Simulation : First International Workshop, Mabs '98, Paris, France, July 1998

Controlling Complex Physical Systems Through Planning and Scheduling Integration

Amedeo Cesta and Simone Fratini*

Institute for Cognitive Science and Technology,
Italian National Research Council,
Viale Marx 15, I-00137, Rome, Italy
name.surname@istc.cnr.it

Abstract. This paper presents a framework for planning and scheduling integration based on a uniform constraint-based representation. Such representation is inspired to time-line based planning but has the unique characteristic of conceiving both resource and causal constraints as abstract specifications that generate segments of temporal evolution to be scheduled on the time-line. This paper describes the general idea behind this type of problem solving, shows how it has been implemented in a software architecture called OMP, and presents an example of application for the generation of mission planning commands for automating the management of spacecraft operations.

1 Introduction

While planning and scheduling have been traditionally distinct research areas, both can be seen as an *abstraction* of well known real-world problems. Solving a planning problem means finding *how* to achieve a given goal, that is, computing a sequence of actions which achieve the goal. Relevance is given to the logical reasoning on "what is needed for" without giving emphasis to time and resource constraints. The generation of a sequence of moves in the Blocks World domain is a typical example of planning problem. Solving a scheduling problem means determining *when* to perform a set of actions consistently with time and resource constraints specified within the domain. In a satellite domain for example, this could be the problem of deploying over time a set of downlink data operations from on-board a satellite to the on-ground station fulfilling constraints on visibility windows, channel data rates and on-board memory capacity.

Several planning architectures produced over the past two decades (see for instance O-PLAN [7], IxTeT [13], HSTS [14], RAX-PS [11], or ASPEN [6]) have already successfully included capabilities from both Planning and Scheduling (P&S) among their features. In particular, all these architectures have emphasized the use of a rich representation language to capture complex characteristics of the domain including time and resource constraints.

The particular perspective we are following is based on the observation that a P&S architecture should allow to model domains from a double perspective: (a) *planning with scheduling features*: in some domains the key factor is the representation of a

* Ph.D. student in Computer Engineering at DIS, University of Rome "La Sapienza", Italy.

M. Ali and F. Esposito (Eds.): IEA/AIE 2005, LNAI 3533, pp. 197–207, 2005.

causal description typical on planning reasoning with some additional scheduling requirements (i.e., actions require to share several resources to be executed, or should satisfy complex temporal relations); (b) *scheduling with planning features*: within a typical scheduling problem it is necessary to synthesize new activities (e.g., when a resource serves a certain activity, a specific process for producing additional resource should be generated). We report here examples from a space system because of our direct experience. In particular we describe a generic scenario where a spacecraft have to achieve some goals with its payloads, like taking pictures with a camera or gathering some specific data with other instruments. From a planning point of view this could be a typical domain where the modeler first describes which actions can be performed, then specifies some goals (object that have to be captured) and finally looks for a plan (a sequence of actions) that, when performed, allows the physical system to achieve the goals. In the reality this domain contains several restrictive constraints not easy to model from a pure planning perspective: for instance the case of a finite capacity for on-board memory or the fact that several communication channels have a pre-specified transmission rate that are used to download data to Earth. These situations are easier to capture in a scheduling framework, where you can model memory and channels as *resources*, then a solving process looks for a temporal sequence of upload and download operations that assure resources are never over-used. From the scheduling perspective you cannot simply describe the domain like a set of resources and activities, because it is not possible to allocate these activities over resources without considering that each activity needs some not trivial action combination to be performed: for instance when you allocate a download activity over a communication channel you need to be sure that the spacecraft is pointing to Earth and maybe you need to force the satellite to slew toward Earth by planning some actions for this purpose. The same perspective can be applied in general in those cases where complex physical systems should be controlled so the approach described is quite general and can also be used outside the space domain.

In the rest of the paper we first describe the constraint reasoning perspective our view on P&S integration is based on, and second present a problem solving architecture called OMP that makes such ideas operational. The spacecraft domain will be used as a running example throughout the paper.

2 Scheduling with a Causal Domain Theory

Our approach is grounded on constraint reasoning so we recall here the basic definition of a Constraint Satisfaction Problem (CSP) [15]. A CSP consists in a set of variables $X = \{X_1, X_2, \ldots, X_n\}$ each associated with a domain D_i of values, and a set of constraints $C = \{C_1, C_2, \ldots, C_m\}$ which denote the legal combinations of values for the variables such that $C_i \subseteq D_1 \times D_2 \times \cdots \times D_n$. A solution consists in assigning to each variable one of its possible values so that all the constraints are satisfied. The resolution process can be seen as an iterative search procedure where the current (partial) solution is extended on each cycle by assigning a value to a new variable. As new decisions are made during this search, a set of *propagation rules* removes elements from the domains D_i which cannot be contained in any feasible extension of the current partial solution.

Several approaches to P&S integration pursue the idea of stretching the planning domain definition language, and hence the reasoning capability of planners, to include temporal and resource reasoning [9]. We follow a rather opposite direction: starting from our background in CSP-based scheduling (see for example [5]), we focus on *causal reasoning* as a distinguishing factor between planning and scheduling and try to understand how a form of causal reasoning can be integrated in a CSP-based scheduler. The pursued idea is to have planning and scheduling reasoning working together in a common constraint-based environment.

In a typical scheduling problem a plan is given in advance composed by a set of *activities* that require different amount of *resources*, each with its own capacity, in order to be executed. Additionally a set of temporal constraints is imposed between these activities – usually constraints are specified from duration to simple precedence, and minimal and maximal quantitative separation between pairs of activities. The problem is to find *when* to start each activity in order to ensure the temporal constraints are satisfied and resources are never over or under used. Such problem can be represented in a CSP framework choosing temporal events (e.g., start and end of activities) as variables with a finite temporal horizon as domain. This CSP can be implemented in a constraint data-base in which the temporal constraints are represented as a Simple Temporal Problem (STP [8]), while resource constraints are reasoned upon with specialized data-structures on top of the STP. In Fig. 1(a) there is a sketchy abstract representation of the process behind all this for the case of a scheduling problem with a single resource: the problem's activities can be seen as a central layer connected in a precedence graph (Activity Network in the figure); all the temporal constraints are represented in the Temporal Network that is the lower layer of representation; at a higher level there are specialized representations for resource consumption over time called Resource Profiles. A solver for this problem "reasons" on this data-base and takes decisions. For example in a *Precedence Constraints Posting* (PCP) approach [5] reasoning on *resource profiles* it is possible to deduce a set of additional *precedence constraints* between activities that, when posted, ensure resource constraints are never violated. The same abstract schema can be used for implementing the resource propagation rules proposed in [12]. In these approaches the STP is polynomially propagated after each decision step. The schema can be "easily" extended to multiple resources by considering on top of a unique STP network several resource profiles. This equates to reasoning upon multiple activity networks that evolve over time as *concurrent threads* (see the three rectangles in the middle layer of Fig. 1(b) as an example). It is worth noting that such threads are each other independent until a single activity does not require more than one resource to be executed.

As said in the introduction, our aim is to go a bit further with respect to a pure scheduling problem and to model problems that also specify, for example, that scheduled activities need, in some cases, to satisfy causal relationships and in so doing require a generative reasoning step to add new activities to the plan. To allow the specification of such "causal laws" we use a domain specification paradigm first proposed in HSTS [14] and studied also in subsequent works [4, 11, 10]. It considers the relevant components of a domain as continuously evolving temporal automata that specify which sequences of states are logically allowed for any of such components. These sub-parts are called *state variables* because they are entities that keep track of what is going on

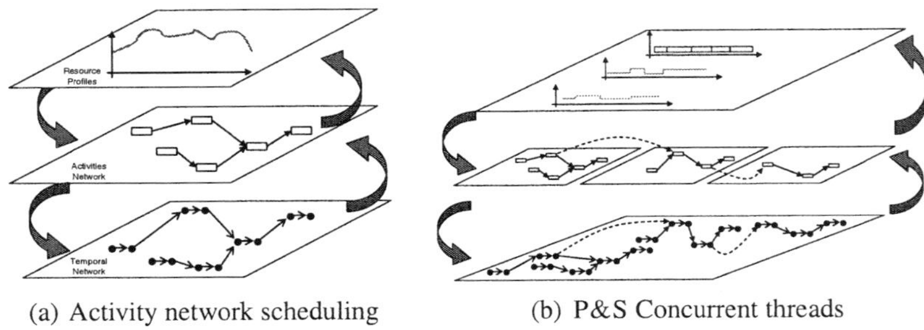

(a) Activity network scheduling (b) P&S Concurrent threads

Fig. 1. Extending a scheduler with causal reasoning

in the world by assuming sequences of values over a temporal interval as temporally ordered sequences of state transitions. Our current effort aims at reasoning upon such components, that we refer to as "causal components", similarly to the CSP resource reasoning sketched above. One main difference resides in the effects of activities: on resources effects are additive (a cumulative numeric consumption function is computed over time – see the two temporal profiles on to top layer of Fig. 1(b)) while on state variables decisions cause a state transition (so over time they assume sequences of states as temporal evolutions – see the last temporal function on the top layer of Fig. 1(b)).

We refer now to the basic example domain to clarify the idea of causal components and its associated temporal automata[1]. In the spacecraft domain if a certain activity consists of pointing a precise celestial body, the knowledge specification system may allow to specify such constraints to the problem solver. We formalize the different parts that compose the spacecraft physical system either as resources (same concept as in scheduling) or state variables (sub-parts whose temporal sequences are subject to transition laws formalized as "causal constraints"). For instance the on-board mass memory can be formalized as a multi-capacity resource, while a camera as a payload can be formalized, simplifying a similar example used in [14], as a causal component that may assume one of the states $\{Wait, WarmUp, Ready, TakePicture\}$. Similarly the spacecraft pointing-system may assume values in the set $\{Unlocked, Locked, Locking\}$. In order to perform experiments or to send data, the satellite have to be stably pointing toward a direction (state *Locked*), while to move from one stable target to another it assumes the state $Locking$. $Unlocked$ is an idle state. While for "resource components" we directly use the maximum and minimum capacity constraint specification, for causal components some additional formalism is needed to write down the legal transitions from state to state in order to obtain correct temporal evolutions. In our approach as a compact specification language for causal constraints we use temporal automata where labels are used to specify duration constraints for both states and transitions.

Why we choose to represent the domain causal laws as state transition systems instead of referring to $\langle precondition \rightarrow effect\rangle$ rules as in classical approaches to planning? Of course state variables can compactly represent the state of a domain, but this can be adopted also in classical planning representation as shown in [1]. We are interested in this approach based on components firstly because it allows to localize changes

[1] For an earlier treatment of this aspects the reader may refer to [3].

in domain definition and refinement and secondly because it permits an easy integration of P&S in a CSP approach. Let us consider again the isomorphism between causal and resource components shown in Fig. 1(b). The figure sketches what we describe in detail in the rest of this paper: resources and state-variables are different types of concurrent threads represented on-top of a unique STP temporal network. Each concurrent thread (middle layer in the figure) can be thought of as a set of partially ordered activities. The additional constraint for the state-variables is that in any feasible solution they may assume a linear sequence of values (i.e., any legal sequence of states recognized by their own temporal automata specification).

3 OMP: The Open Multi-CSP Planner

OMP is an integrated constraint-based software architecture for planning and scheduling that is fully based on the ideas sketched in the previous section. Our design and implementation efforts has focused on two main directions: (1) a domain definition language that allows the user to naturally define the resource and causal components and their connected constraints; (2) an open layered software architecture that runs a CSP solver over different constraint based sub-systems that have to work together to solve an integrated planning and scheduling problem.

This paper shows the expressiveness of OMP by modeling a realistic scenario taken from the MARS-EXPRESS mission, a program of the European Space Agency that is currently operational around Mars. Our group has conducted a study for MARS-EXPRESS to develop MEXAR [2] an automated solver for synthesizing the downlink operations that allow Earth-bound transmission of the on-board telemetry (data produced by payload activities and by different on-board devices which monitor the conditions of the spacecraft) during downlink connections. The example domain we use here is grounded on knowledge of the spacecraft elicited during that study. While MEXAR solves a specific scheduling problem we are considering the domain from a wider perspective. In particular, here we try to cope with the whole life-cycle of mission planning, from deciding to schedule a certain payload operation, to addressing the associated data return problem. In this scenario the goal is to allocate over time (to *plan*) a set of observations, taking care of the fact that data they produce could be safely downloaded later (an associated scheduling problem because data are first stored on the on-board memory then transmitted to Earth). Reasoning only on which observation have to be performed without contextually taking into consideration the data download can easily generate data loss, while afford only the download problem means to work with a fixed set of activity without any way to perform a global optimization on the whole "mission control → satellite → observation → store → download" problem cycle. It is worth noting that also the pure planning problem is not trivial here because to some extent it requires to model the physics of the spacecraft in order to produce meaningful operative procedures.

3.1 The OMP Knowledge Modeling Language

In OMP the domain theory is described using DDL.2 as domain description language. This language, fully described in [3], extends a previous proposal called DDL.1 [4] by inserting resources as first citizen components in a domain specification. In DDL.2 a domain theory is specified to the solver by identifying resource and causal components for the domain. Then the relevant constraints that circumscribe the temporal evolution of such components should be defined. The solver goal is to synthesize a temporal evolution for each of the components that meets all the constraints specified in the domain theory.

Before modeling the MARS-EXPRESS domain further details on the causal component constraint specification are needed. Such components, called *state variables*, should satisfy a set of constraints that, to facilitate compactness, are expressed by defining a timed automata for the component. This means that a set of possible states, called *state-var values*, the state variable may assume over time is given, and the possible transitions between pair of states are defined. Each state-var value is specified with a name and a list of static variable types. As a consequence, in DDL.2 the possible state-var values consist of a discrete list of predicate instances of type $\mathcal{P}(x_1, \ldots, x_m)$. For each state variable it is possible to specify: (1) a name that uniquely indicate this kind of component; (2) a domain of predicates $\mathcal{P}(x_1, \ldots, x_m)$ and (3) a domain for each static variable x_j in the predicate.

The MARS-EXPRESS life-cycle problem can be represented in our framework using two resources, *Memory* and *Channel*, a state variable *Satellite* representing the main pointing status as previously sketched, a set of state variables model on board instrument, $\{Inst\_1, \ldots, Inst\_n\}$, and some particular state variables that describe visibility windows to both Earth ground stations and Mars interesting targets. The variables $Inst\_i$ may assume values *Observe(Target,Data)* and *DownloadMemory(Data)*. The variables *VisibilityEarth*, *VisibilityMars* assume a specific role, because their behavior is entirely specified by the user like a set of goals. The variable *VisibilityEarth* assumes as values *NotVisible* and *Visible(GroundStation)* while the variable *VisibilityMars* assumes *NotVisible* and *Visible(Target)*. These components, also called *uncontrollable state variable*, are used to model aspects that are not under control of the problem solver. The time intervals in which an uncontrollable state variable assumes the value *Visible* depend on decision of flight dynamics team (e.g., the particular orbits decided for the spacecraft). They are additional input to initialize a domain model description.

```
SV Satellite (Unlocked(),Locked(Pos),Locking(Pos))
{
COMP
{
STATE Unlocked() [1, +INF] {  MEETS { Locking (x:Pos)}
                              MET-BY { Locked (y:Pos)} }
STATE Locked(x) [1, +INF] {   MEETS { Unlocked (x)}
                              MET-BY { Locking (x)} }
STATE Locking(x) [1, +INF] {  MEETS { Locked (x)}
                              MET-BY { Unlocked (x)} }
}}
```

(a) sequence constraints on a variable

```
COMP
{
STATE Observe (Target,Data) [time(Target) , time(Target)]
SYNC
{
DURING VisibilityMars Visible(Target) [0,+INF] [0,+INF];
DURING Satellite Locked(Target) [5,+INF] [5,+INF];
BEFORE Inst_1 DownloadMemory(Data) [time(Data),time(Data)];
USE Memory memoryOcc(Data) [0, 0] [0, 0] AFTERSTART;
USE Channel memoryOcc(Data) [0, 0] [0, 0] FROMSTARTTOEND;
} }
```

(b) a SYNC compatibility

Fig. 2. Example of DDL.2 specification

While defining constraint for the resources is quite straightforward (e.g., maximum capacity of the on-board *Memory*), some additional syntactic constructs are needed to specify constraints on state variables, among different state variables, and among state variables and resources. DDL.2 uses for such constraints an adaptation of the concept of *compatibility* first introduced in [14]. In general compatibilities codify the temporal automata that describes a single component, the synchronization constraints among different automata and special resource requirements for state variable values.

In Fig. 2(a) we show a possible DDL.2 model for the causal component *Satellite*, where the type Pos (short for $Position$) assumes as values $Earth$, $Mars$, etc. For each state we specify the legal following state and the legal preceding state, expressing which state transition rules are legal for that component. The value $Unlocked()$ for instance should hold for at least one second and there is not upper limit to its duration (the statement $[1, +INF]$ represents the duration constraints for the value to be assumed). It can be followed (statement MEETS) by a value $Locking(x)$ with parameter the object x. Similarly the MET-BY statement allows to specify which value the component can assume just before the $Unlocked()$ value. Such a specification models a causal component whose behavior is an alternation of sequences $\ldots Unlocked() \rightarrow Locking(Pos) \rightarrow Locked(Pos) \rightarrow Unlocked() \ldots$ and so on.

Fig. 2(b) shows a more complex example of causal relations specification in DDL.2. It is the case of a synchronization (SYNC) compatibility for a generic instrument *Inst_1*[2]. It requires that when the payload *Inst_1* assumes the value *Observe(Target,Data)* the following events should be synchronized: (1) target on Mars should be visible; (2) the spacecraft must be locked on the same target – hence a temporal synchronization is required with the value *Locked(Target)* of the state variable *Satellite*; (3) observed data have to be downloaded to the Earth (then it must exist a following state *DownloadMemory(Data)* in the same component behavior)[3]; (4) you must have enough free memory and enough channel rate to perform your operation, then activities over the resources *Memory* and *Channel* must be allocated (construct USE in the figure). The amount of resource required from the activities depends on how much data the instrument produces or is able to transmit in a time unit.

After defined a domain theory, it is possible to formulate a problem to be solved according to that theory. This is done by specifying, as goals, tasks to be performed by instruments components[4], e.g., specifying some *Observe* states to be allocated over the causal components. It is possible to specify a desired time interval for the observation or to leave the solver free to allocate it on the state variable when constraints allows it. Compatibility constraints ensure that generated plans are feasible from both planning

---

[2] For the sake of space we do not include MEET and MET-BY statement. *time* and *memoryOcc* are two integer function to compute the duration of an observation and the amount of data it produces.

[3] It is worth observing that further complex constraints could be also specified using language features: for example, data downloadable not before a certain slack of time (in order to perform some elaboration on them) and not after another slack of time (in order to avoid information starving).

[4] In the current architecture that supports DDL.2 OMP provides a PDL (Problem Definition Language) designed to accommodate specific state-var values on causal components to hold during desired time intervals (goals over state variables) and a set of pre-defined activity that have to be allocated over resources in any feasible solution (goals over resources).

point of view (meaning that download follow observation and every operation is performed when the satellite is oriented in the right way) and the scheduling point of view (memory and channel are not overused).

3.2 The Software Architecture

OMP is an integrated constraint-based software architecture for planning and scheduling built around the ideas presented above. Starting from a domain theory expressed in DDL.2 OMP builds activity networks over a shared temporal network, and schedule them according to the current problem specification to determine temporal evolution of the resource and causal components that is compatible with all the domain constraints.

The OMP software architecture essentially implements, from an abstract point of view, the typical CSP solving loop, alternating decision and propagation steps, starting from a CSP specification of the problem. This architecture is composed by a *decision making* module that guides the search by incrementally posting constraints on a *constraints database* that maintains information about the current partial solution and propagates decision effects pruning the search space (see Fig.3). A set of database queries helps the decision module to reason on the current solution. The temporal problem is managed and solved only via constraint propagation using an All Pair Shortest Path algorithm on the STP. Resource and state variable management need both a constraint propagation and a search decision phase.

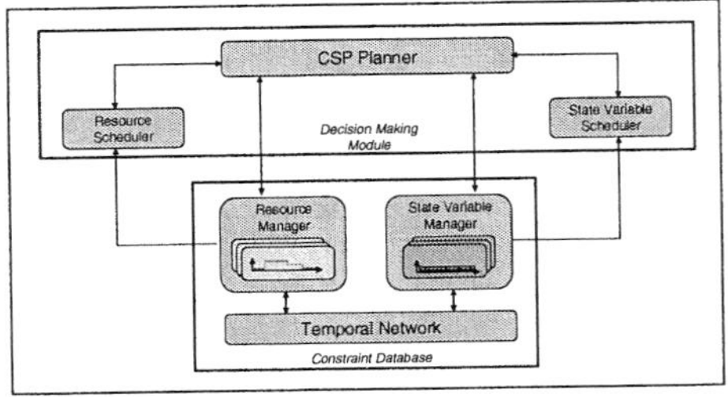

Fig. 3. OMP software architecture

Current search strategy in OMP follows a precedence constraint posting approach. An algorithm incrementally computes conflicts in the activity networks that represent the concurrent threads in the domain model, choose a critical conflict and try to solve it by adding additional precedence constraints between pairs of activities. The process is iterated according to a complete backtracking algorithm. The decision process is interleaved with a propagation step that make explicit some implicit or "forced" ordering between activities. For instance in the case of the two activities showed in the top part of fig 4(a), let us suppose they require, between their start and end points, two contradictory states of a causal component. The underlying temporal network shows that the first one can hold somewhere between the lower bound of its start time and the upper bound of its end time, while the second one can hold within an analogous bounded interval. We know that (1) they cannot overlap because a state variable must have at least one value in any final solution; (2) there is no way for the second activity to hold before the first one with respect to the temporal position of involved start and end points. The propagated temporal network gives us a *necessary* ordering constraints between them. As a consequence we force the second to hold strictly after the first one. The result is showed in the bottom part of the same figure.

In general there are cases in which a search step is necessary. For instance, the left side of fig. 4(b) shows situation with two activities that have to be scheduled again on a single state variable. But this time even analyzing the underlying temporal problem we are not able to compute any necessary precedence constraint between these two activities: *both* ordering are temporally feasible. Thus a search decision step must be made, basically between the two feasible ordering showed in the right side of the same figure. Of course constraints posted during the propagation step are necessary, so they cut only not feasible solutions, meaning that *any* feasible solution *must* contain these constraints. On the other hand scheduling precedence constraints are *search* decision, then they *could* cut some feasible solutions, opening the need for backtracking.

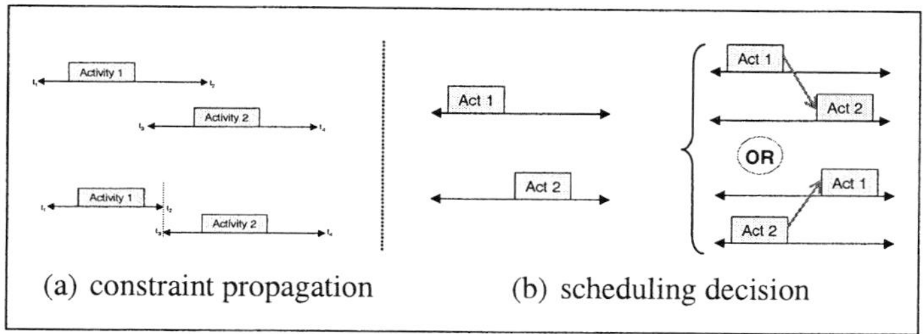

Fig. 4. Basic steps in the solving loop

To propagate and schedule resource and state variable activities there are in OMP two modules, the *resource manager* and the *state variable manager*, that manage networks performing specific constraints propagation. Strictly connected with these two *scheduling modules* are able to analyze resource and state variable constraints database and build the planner search space, where at each node the planner can choose among different activity orderings. Resource propagation algorithms from [12] are implemented in the resource manager, and specialized algorithms has been developed for the state variable manager. The *CSP planner* is the decision making module core: starting from some goals (actually activities that must appear in the final solution) it dynamically unfold the domain theory putting more resource and causal activities into the respective networks. Every time that a new activity is added we deduce, via propagation rules, new precedence constraints that affect the whole networks situation, due to the shared temporal model. Moreover the planner must make also chooses about which order to force among activities when propagations are not able to cut all not feasible orders (this set is computed by the scheduler modules). As a matter of fact we integrate planning and scheduling by interleaving scheduling and unfolding steps.

4 Conclusions

This paper describes our approach to planning and scheduling integration. It has been discussed how *Causal Knowledge* is the main distinguishing factor between planning and scheduling, thus building an architecture where both time/resource reasoning about activity scheduling and causal reasoning about planned actions can be modeled and managed. The proposed architecture shows a way to bridge the gap between these two AI research lines, extending from one hand pure planning schemes with quantitative time and resource reasoning and from the other hand extending pure scheduling schema with a domain theory.

Using this approach we built an operational prototype able to produce control sequences for MARS-EXPRESS, demonstrating how an integrated P&S framework allows to manage a wider problem with respect to a pure scheduling problem. We are still working on this environment, extending the model toward more complex specifications in order to further match real world features.

Acknowledgments. Authors would like to thank Angelo Oddi for common work on this topic and the other members of Planning and Scheduling Team [PST] at ISTC-CNR for creating the stimulating environment in which this research is developed.

References

1. C. Bäckström. *Computational Complexity of Reasoning About Plans*. PhD thesis, Linköping University, 1992.
2. A. Cesta, G. Cortellessa, A. Oddi, and N. Policella. A CSP-Based Interactive Decision Aid for Space Mission Planning. In *Lecture Notes in Artificial Intelligence, N.2829*. Springer, 2003.
3. A. Cesta, S. Fratini, and A. Oddi. Planning with Concurrency, Time and Resources: A CSPBased Approach. In I. Vlahavas and D. Vrakas, editors, *Intelligent Techniques for Planning*. Idea Group Publishing, 2004.
4. A. Cesta and A. Oddi. DDL.1: A Formal Description of a Constraint Representation Language for Physical Domains. In M. M.Ghallab and A. Milani, editors, *New Directions in AI Planning*. IOS Press, 1996.
5. A. Cesta, A. Oddi, and S. F. Smith. A Constraint-based method for Project Scheduling with Time Windows. *Journal of Heuristics*, 8(1):109–136, January 2002.
6. S. Chien, G. Rabideau, R. Knight, R. Sherwood, B. Engelhardt, D. Mutz, T. Estlin, B. Smith, F. Fisher, T. Barrett, G. Stebbins, and D. Tran. ASPEN - Automating Space Mission Operations using Automated Planning and Scheduling. In *Proceedings of SpaceOps 2000*, 2000.
7. K.W. Currie and A. Tate. O-Plan: Control in the Open Planning Architecture. *Artificial Intelligence*, 51:49–86, 1991.
8. R. Dechter, I. Meiri, and J. Pearl. Temporal Constraint Networks. *Artificial Intelligence*, 49:61–95, 1991.
9. M. Fox and D. Long. PDDL 2.1: An extension to PDDL for expressing temporal planning domains. *Journal of Artificial Intelligence Research*, 20:61–124, 2003.
10. J. Frank and A. Jonsson. Constraint based attribute and interval planning. *Journal of Constraints*, 8(4):339–364, 2003.
11. A.K. Jonsson, P.H. Morris, N. Muscettola, K. Rajan, and B. Smith. Planning in Interplanetary Space: Theory and Practice. In *Proceedings of the Fifth Int. Conf. on Artificial Intelligence Planning and Scheduling (AIPS-00)*, 2000.
12. P. Laborie. Algorithms for Propagating Resource Constraints in AI Planning and Scheduling: Existing Approaches and new Results. *Artificial Intelligence*, 143:151–188, 2003.

13. P. Laborie and M. Ghallab. Planning with Sharable Resource Constraints. In *Proceedings of the International Joint Conference on Artificial Intelligence (IJCAI-95)*, 1995.
14. N. Muscettola, S.F. Smith, A. Cesta, and D. D'Aloisi. Coordinating Space Telescope Operations in an Integrated Planning and Scheduling Architecture. *IEEE Control Systems*, 12(1):28–37, 1992.
15. E.P.K. Tsang. *Foundation of Constraint Satisfaction*. Academic Press, London and San Diego, CA, 1993.

Plan Execution in Dynamic Environments

Gordon Fraser, Gerald Steinbauer, and Franz Wotawa*

Technische Universität Graz, Institute for Software Technology,
Inffeldgasse 16b/II, A-8010 Graz, Austria
{fraser, steinbauer, wotawa}@ist.tugraz.at

Abstract. This paper deals with plan execution on agents/robots in highly dynamic environments. Besides a formal semantics of plan execution and a representation of plans as programs, we introduce the concept of plan invariants. Plan invariants are similar to loop invariants in imperative programs in that they have to be true during the whole plan execution cycle. Once a plan invariant fails the plan execution is stopped and other plans that are more appropriate in the current context are considered for execution instead. The use of plan invariants allows for an early detection of problems. Plan assumptions that are required for a plan to succeed are explicitly represented by plan invariants.

1 Introduction

For decades, autonomous agents and robots acting in dynamic environments have been subject of research in AI. The existence of exogenous events makes dynamic environments unpredictable. Several such domains are used as common test-beds for the application of AI techniques to robots acting in dynamic environments, e.g. robotic soccer, tour guide robots or service and delivery robots. These domains come close to the real world where the gathered data are error prone, agents are truly autonomous, action execution regularly fails, and exogenous events are ubiquitous.

Agents deployed in such domains have to interact with their environment. An agent has a belief about its environment and goals it has to achieve. Such beliefs are derived from domain knowledge and environment observations. While pursuing its goal by executing actions that influence the environment, the agent assumes these actions cause exactly the desired changes and that its belief reflects the true state of the environment. However, due to ambiguous or noisy observations and occlusions the belief of the agent and the state of the environment are not necessarily consistent. Furthermore, other agents or exogenous events may also affect the environment in an unpredictable way. Finally, actions might fail to achieve their desired effect. In this paper we present a solution to enable an agent to quickly react to such influences in order to be able to successfully achieve a given goal.

To investigate the advantages of the proposed solution, experiments were conducted using a robot architecture that can be outlined as follows: On the software side a three-layered architecture is used that separates hardware interfaces, numerical and symbolic

* Authors are listed in alphabetical order.

M. Ali and F. Esposito (Eds.): IEA/AIE 2005, LNAI 3533, pp. 208–217, 2005.

data processing. The symbolic layer hosts an abstract knowledge-base (belief), a planning system which is based on classical AI planning theories, and a plan executor. The representation language used is based on the well known STRIPS [1] representation language and incorporates numerous extensions thereof that have been presented in recent years, allowing the usage of first-order logic with only minor restrictions.

The execution of a plan's actions is twofold. For one, on an abstract layer execution is supervised in a purely symbolic manner by monitoring conditions. On a numerical layer, where none of the abstract layer's symbols are known, a set of elementary behaviors corresponding to the abstract action are executed. This behavioral approach for low-level action execution ensures that reactivity is achieved where needed, and incorporates tasks such as path planning or obstacle avoidance that are not of concern to the symbolic representation.

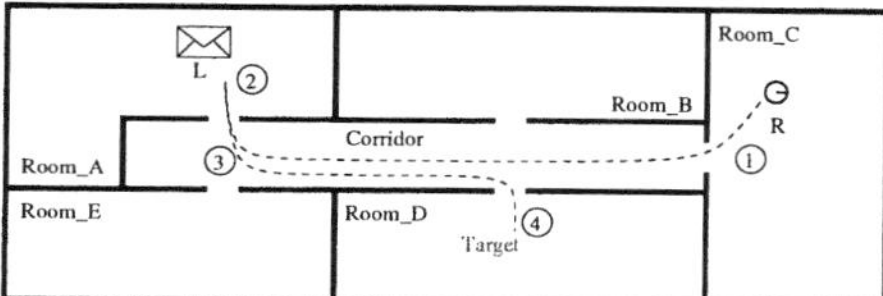

(a) Successful execution of the plan: (1) move to *Room_A*, (2) pick up letter, (3) move to *Room_D* and (4) release letter.

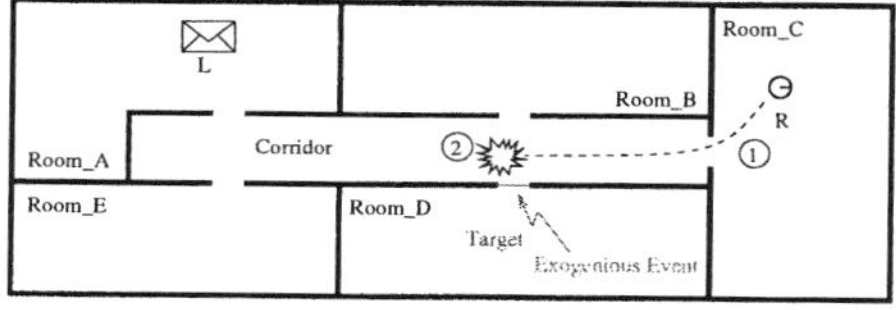

(b) During execution of action (1) the exogenous event, close door to $Room_D$, invalidates the plan (as the target is not reachable anymore). In (2) the robot detects the closed door and the violation of the plan invariant ($accessible(Room\_D)$). Due to the application of plan invariants the infeasibility of the plan is early detected.

Fig. 1. Plan execution using plan invariants for the delivery robot example

In this paper, we present the idea of plan invariants as a means to supervise plan execution. Plan invariants are conditions that have to hold during the whole plan execution. Consider a delivery robot, based on the above architecture. Its task is to transport a letter from room A to room D. This task is depicted in Figure 1. The robot believes that it is located in room C, the letter is in room A and all doors are open. Its goal is that the letter is in room D. The robot might come up with the following plan fulfilling the goal: (1) move to *Room_A*, (2) pick up letter, (3) move to *Room_D* and (4) release letter. In situation (a) no exogenous events occur, the belief of the agent is always consistent with the environment. Therefore, the robot is able to execute the plan and achieves the desired goal. In situation (b) the robot starts to execute the plan with action (1). Unfortunately, somebody closes the door to room D (2). As the robot is not able to open doors, its plan will fail. Without plan invariants the robot will continue to execute the plan until it tries to execute action (3) and detects the infeasible plan. If we use a plan invariant, e.g., room D has to be accessible, the robot detects the violation as it passes the closed door. Therefore, the robot is able to early detect invalid plans and to quickly react to exogenous events.

In the next section we discuss the advantages of plan invariants in more detail. In Section 3 we formally define the planning problem and plan execution. In Section 4 we formally introduce plan invariants. Finally, we discuss related research and conclude the paper.

2 Plan Invariants

Invariants are facts that hold in the initial and all subsequent states. Their truth value is not changed by executing actions.

There is a clear distinction between these plan invariants to action preconditions, plan preconditions and invariants applied to the plan creation process. Action preconditions have to be true in order to start execution of an action. They are only checked once at the beginning of an action. Similarly, plan preconditions (i.e., initial state) are only checked at the beginning of plan execution. Thus, preconditions reflect conditions for points in time whereas invariants monitor time periods. In the past, invariants have been used to increase the speed of planning algorithms by reducing the number of reachable states. (e.g. [2]). An invariant as previously described characterizes the set of reachable states of the planning problem. A state that violates the invariant cannot possibly be reached from the initial state. For example, this has been efficiently applied to Graphplan [3] as described in [4, 5]. Such invariants can be automatically synthesized as has been shown in [6, 7]. However, plan invariants are not only useful at plan creation time but also especially at plan execution time. To our best knowledge plan invariants have never been used to control plan execution.

There is a clear need for monitoring plan execution, because execution can fail for several reasons. Plan invariants can aid in early detection of in-executable actions, unreachable goals or infeasible actions.

3 Basic Definitions

Throughout this paper we use the following definitions which mainly originate from STRIPS planning [1]. A planning problem is a triple (I, G, A), where I is the initial state, G is the goal state, and A is a set of actions. A state itself is a set of ground literals, i.e., a variable-free predicate or its negation. Each action $a \in A$ has an associated pre-

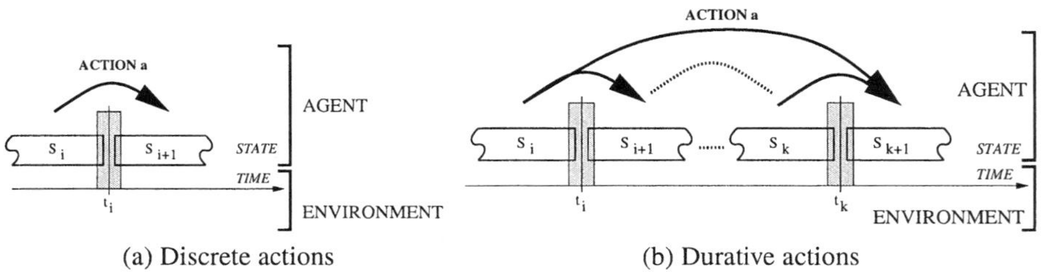

(a) Discrete actions (b) Durative actions

Fig. 2. Action execution with respect to time

condition $pre(a)$ and effect $eff(a)$ and is able to change a state via its execution. The pre-conditions and effects are assumed to be sets of ground literals. Execution of an action a is started if its pre-conditions are fulfilled in the current state S. After the execution all literals of the action's effect are elements of the next state S' together with the elements of S that are not influenced by action a. A plan p is a sequence of actions $< a_1, \ldots, a_n >$, that when executed starting with the initial state I results in goal state G.

For the delivery example the planning problem is defined as follows. The set of actions is A=$< move, pickup, release >$ with:

move(origin, dest):
pre: accessible(dest) $\wedge$ isat(R,origin) $\wedge \neg$ isat(R,dest)
eff: $\neg$ isat(R,origin) $\wedge$ isat(R,dest)
pickup(item):
pre: isat(R,item) $\wedge \neg$ hold(item)
eff: hold(item)
release(item):
pre: hold(item)
eff: $\neg$ hold(item)

The initial state is I:= isat(letter, Room_A) $\wedge$ isat(R,Room_C) and the goal is defined as G:= isat(letter, Room_D). As the names of constants and predicate are chosen quite intuitively, definitions are omitted due to space limitations.

A plan can be automatically derived from a planning problem and there are various algorithms available for this purpose. Refer to [8] for an overview. For the delivery example a planner might come up with the plan p=<move(Room_C, Room_A), pickup(letter), move(Room_A, Room_D), release(letter)>. The planning problem makes some implicit assumptions for plan computation. First, it is assumed that all actions are atomic and cannot be interrupted. Second, the effect of an action is guaranteed to be established after its execution. Third, there are no external events that can change a state. Only actions performed by the agent alter states. Finally, it is assumed that the time granularity is discrete. Hence, time advances only at some points in time but not continuously.

In the most simple way plan execution is done by executing each action of the plan step by step without considering problems that may arise, e.g., a failing action or external events that cause changes to the environment. Formally, this simple plan execution semantics is given as follows (where $[\![\ ]\!]$ denotes the interpretation function):

$$[\![< a_1, \ldots, a_n >]\!]\ S = [\![< a_2, \ldots, a_n >]\!]\ ([\![a_1]\!]\ S)$$
$$[\![a]\!]\ S = \begin{cases} eff(a) \cup \{x | x \in S \wedge \neg x \notin eff(a)\} \text{ if } pre(a) \subseteq S \\ \textbf{fail} \text{ if } pre(a) \not\subseteq S \end{cases}$$
$$[\![a]\!]\ \textbf{fail} = \textbf{fail}$$

Given the semantics definition of plan execution we can now state what a feasible plan is.

Definition 1. *A plan* $p =< a_1, \ldots, a_n > | a_i \in A$ *is a feasible plan for a planning problem* (I, G, A) *iff* $[\![p]\!]\ I \neq$ **fail** *and* $[\![p]\!]\ I \supseteq G$.

Planning algorithms always return feasible plans. However, feasibility is only a necessary condition for a plan to be successfully executed in a real environment. Reasons for a plan to fail are:

1. An action cannot be executed.
   (a) An external event changes the state so that the pre-condition cannot be ensured.
   (b) The action itself fails because of an internal event, e.g., a broken part.
2. An external event changes the state of the world in a way so that the original goal cannot be reached anymore.
3. The action fails to establish the effect.

In order to formalize a plan execution in the real world, we assume the following situation. A plan is executed by an agent/robot which has its view of the world. The agent can modify the state of the world via actions and perceives the state of the surrounding environment via sensors. The agent assumes that the sensor input is reliable, i.e., the perceived information reflects the real state of the world. Hence, during plan execution the effects of the executed actions can be checked via the sensor inputs. For this purpose we assume a global function **obs(t)** which maps a point in time t to the observed state. Note that we use the closed world assumption. Any predicate remains false until it is observed as true.

In order to define the execution of an action in the real world two cases need to be distinguished. Actions can last a fixed, known time. In this case, execution is considered done after that time has elapsed. On the other hand, actions can continue indefinitely, e.g., a move action in a dynamic environment can take unexpectedly long if changes in the dynamic environment require detours. Execution of such an action is considered to be finished as soon as its effect is fulfilled. Following the nomenclature previously used in [9], actions with fixed duration are called *discrete*, and indefinitely continued actions are called *durative*.

Figure 2 depicts the action execution with respect to time. A discrete action a is executable if its precondition $pre(a)$ is satisfied in state S_i, where a state $S_i = S_{i-1} \oplus obs(t_{i-1})$.

The function $S \oplus obs(t) = obs(t) \cup \{l | l \in S \wedge \neg l \notin obs(t)\}$ defines an update function for the agent's belief. The function returns all information about the current state that is available, i.e., the observations together with derived conditions during plan execution which are not contradicting the given observations.

An action lasts for a given time and tries to establish its effect $\mathit{eff}(a)$ in the succeeding state S_{i+1}. A durative action a is also executable if its precondition $pre(a)$ is satisfied in state S_i. In contrast to discrete actions a durative action a is executed until its effect $\mathit{eff}(a)$ is established in some following state S_{k+1}. At each time step t_j, $i \leq j \leq k+1$ a new observation is available, a new state S_j is derived $S_j = S_{j-1} \oplus obs(t_{j-1})$. For each state S_j the condition $\mathit{eff}(a) \subseteq S_j$ is evaluated. A durative action can possibly last forever if it is impossible to establish the effect $\mathit{eff}(a)$.

$$\text{if } \mathbf{discrete}(\text{a}) \text{ then } [\![a]\!]\,(S) =$$

$$= \begin{cases} S \oplus obs(t) \text{ if } \mathit{eff}(a) \subseteq (S \oplus obs(t)) \\ [\![\mathbf{exec}]\!](a, S \oplus obs(t)) \text{ if } pre(a) \subseteq (S \oplus obs(t)) \wedge \mathit{eff}(a) \not\subseteq (S \oplus obs(t)) \\ \mathbf{fail} \text{ otherwise} \end{cases} \tag{1}$$

In the above definition of the plan execution semantics for single actions we can distinguish three cases. The first line of the definition handles the case where the effect is fulfilled without the requirement of executing the action a. In the second line, the action a is executed which is represented by the $\mathbf{exec}(a, S)$ function.

$$[\![\mathbf{exec}]\!]\ (a, S) = \begin{cases} \mathit{eff}(a) \cup \left\{ x \,\middle|\, \begin{matrix} x \in (S \oplus obs(t) \wedge \\ \neg x \notin \mathit{eff}(a) \end{matrix} \right\} & \text{if action } a \text{ is executed} \\ & \textbf{fail} \text{ otherwise} \end{cases} \tag{2}$$

$\mathbf{exec}(a, S)$ returns **fail** if the action a was not executable by the agent/robot in state S. If action a is executed **exec** returns the effect of the action $\mathit{eff}(a)$ unified with all literals of state S not negated by $\mathit{eff}(a)$. t is the time after executing the action.

The last line of the execution semantics states that it returns **fail** if the precondition of the action is not fulfilled. The action **release** is an example for a discrete action. Once the action is triggered it either takes a certain amount of time to complete or it fails.

For durative actions, execution semantics can be written as follows:

$$\text{if } \mathbf{durative}(\text{a}) \text{ then } [\![a]\!]\ (S) = \begin{cases} S \oplus obs(t) \text{ if } \mathit{eff}(a) \subseteq (S \oplus obs(t)) \\ [\![a]\!]'\ (S \oplus obs(t)) \text{ if } pre(a) \subseteq (S \oplus obs(t)) \wedge \\ \qquad \mathit{eff}(a) \not\subseteq (S \oplus obs(t)) \\ \textbf{fail} \text{ otherwise} \end{cases} \tag{3}$$

with

$$[\![a]\!]'\ (S) = \begin{cases} S \oplus obs(t) \text{ if } \mathit{eff}(a) \subseteq (S \oplus obs(t)) \\ [\![a]\!]'\ (S \oplus obs(t))\ otherwise \end{cases} \tag{4}$$

The precondition of a durative action is checked only at the beginning of the action. We assume that one recursion of an durative action (equation 4) lasts for a time span greater than zero. The action **move** is an example for a durative action, as it executed until the robot reaches its destination. This may take different amounts of time or possibly may never occur.

Given a plan and a real-world environment we can now define what it means to be able to reach a goal after executing a plan.

Definition 2. *A plan* $p = < a_1, \ldots, a_n >$ *for a given planning problem* (I, G, A) *is successfully executed in a given environment if* $[\![< a_1, \ldots, a_n >]\!](I) \supseteq G$.

4 Extended Planning Problem

As outlined in Section 2, plan invariants are a useful extension to the planning problem. The addition of an invariant to a planning problem results in the following definition:

Definition 3. *An extended planning problem is a tuple* (I, G, A, inv) *where* inv *is a logical sentence which states the plan invariant.*

A plan p for an extended planning problem is created using any common planning algorithm. We call the tuple (p, inv) extended plan.

The plan invariant has to be fulfilled until the execution of the plan is finished (either by returning the goal state or **fail**). A plan invariant is a more general condition for feasible plans. It allows for considering exogenous events and problems that may occur during execution, e.g., failed actions. Automatic generation of such invariants is questionable. Invariants represent knowledge that is not implicitly contained in the planning problem, and thus cannot be automatically extracted from preconditions and effect descriptions. An open question is how more knowledge about the environment (e.g., modeling physical laws or the behavior of other agents) and an improved knowledge representation would enable automatic generation of plan invariants.

The execution semantics of such an extended plan can be stated using $||$ to denote parallel execution:

$$[\![(p, inv)]\!]\ (S) = [\![p]\!]\ (S) || [\![inv]\!]\ (S) \tag{5}$$

Communication between statements executed in parallel is performed through obs, S and the state of plan execution.

The semantics of checking the invariant over time is defined as follows:

$$[\![inv]\!](S) = \begin{cases} [\![inv]\!](S) \text{ if } inv \cup (S \oplus obs(t)) \not\models \bot \\ \textbf{fail} \qquad otherwise \end{cases} \tag{6}$$

where S is the current belief state of the agent and $obs(t)$ results in a set of observations at a specific point in time t. Hence, the invariant is always checked unless it contradicts the state of the world obs or the agent's belief S. For the delivery example inv = accessible(Room_D) $\wedge$ (accessible(Room_A) $\vee$ hold(letter)) would be a feasible invariant. The invariant states that as long as the robot does not hold the letter Room_A has to be accessible. Room_D has to be accessible during the whole plan execution.

Definition 4. *An extended plan* $p = (< a_1, \ldots, a_n >, inv)$ *is a feasible extended plan for a planning problem* (I, G, A) *iff* $[\![p]\!]\ I \neq$ **fail** *and* $[\![p]\!]\ I \supseteq G$*, and all states that are passed by the plan the invariant must hold, i.e.,* $\forall_{i=0}^{n}([\![a_1, \ldots, a_i]\!](I) \cup inv) \not\models \bot$.

Feasibility is again a necessary condition for extended plans to be executable. Hence, it must be guaranteed that the invariant does not contradict any state that is reached during plan execution. We now can easily extend Definition 2 for extended plans.

Definition 5. *An extended plan* $p = (< a_1, \ldots, a_n >, inv)$ *for a given planning problem* (I, G, A) *is successfully executed in a given environment if* $[\![(< a_1, \ldots, a_n >, inv)]\!](I) \supseteq G$.

Theorem 1. *An extended plan* $p = (< a_1, \ldots, a_n >, inv)$ *for a planning problem* (I, G, A) *is successfully executed in a given environment with observations obs if (1) the plan is feasible , (2)* $\forall_{i=0}^{n}([\![a_1, \ldots, a_i]\!](I) \cup inv) \not\models \bot$. *and (3) the set of believed facts resulting from execution of plan p with simple plan execution semantics is a subset of the set of believed facts resulting from execution in a real-world environment.*

Regarding Theorem 1 (3), in real-world environments, observations lead to believed facts that are not predictable from the plan execution, hence $[\![a]\!](S)$ differs.

Corollary 1. *Every feasible extended plan for a planning problem* (I, G, A) *is a feasible plan for the same planning problem.*

Concluding the execution of a plan does not relieve an agent of its duties. If the plan execution succeeds, a new objective can be considered. If plan execution fails, alternative designations need to be aimed at. Not all possible goals might be desirable, we therefore need a condition that decides about execution. This condition needs to be valid from the beginning of plan creation to the initiation of plan execution, hence the initial state I needs to fulfill this condition, the *plan problem precondition*. An agent is given a set of alternative planning problems $P_1, \ldots, P_n$ and nondeterministically picks one out of these that has a satisfied precondition C_i thus deriving an extended planning problem (I, G_i, A, inv).

$$\Pi = \left\{ \begin{array}{l} C_1 \rightarrow (I, G_1, A, inv) \\ \ldots \\ C_n \rightarrow (I, G_n, A, inv) \end{array} \right\}. \tag{7}$$

The knowledge base of an agent Π comprises of all desired reactions of the agent to a given situation. The preconditions trigger sets of objectives the agent may pursue in the given situation.

The execution semantics of this set of planning problems can be stated as follows:

$[\![\Pi]\!]\ (I) =$
do for ever
  select (I, G_i, A, inv) **when** $S \models C_i$
  $p_i =$ **generate_plan**(I, G_i, A, inv)
  $[\![(p_i, inv_i)]\!]\ (S)$
end do;

The function **generate_plan** generates a feasible plan. The plan could be generated by using any planning algorithm. The use of pre-coded plans is also conceivable. The function **select** nondeterministically selects one planning problem of the set of planning problems whose precondition is fulfilled. A heuristic implementation of the function is conceivable, if some measure of the performance/quality of the different planning problems is available.

5 Related Research

Invariants for planning problems have previously been investigated within the context of planning domain analysis. Planning domain descriptions implicitly contain structural features that can be used by planners while not being stated explicitly by the domain designer. These features can be used to speed up planning. For example, Kautz and Selman [10] used hand-coded invariants provided as part of the domain description used by Black-box, as did McCluskey and Porteous [11]. The use of such constraints has been demonstrated to have a significant impact on planning efficiency[12]. Such invariants can be automatically synthesized as has been shown in [6, 7, 4]. Even temporal features of a planning domain can be extracted by combining domain analysis techniques and model checking in order to improve planning performance [13]. Also noteworthy is Discoplan [14], a system that uses domain description in PDDL [15] or UCPOP [16] syntax to extract various kinds of state constraints that can then be used to speed up planning. Any forward- or backward-chaining planning algorithm can be enhanced by applying such constraints, e.g. Graphplan [3], as described in [5]. However, in [17] Baioletti, Marcugini and Milani suggest that such a constrained planning problem can be transformed to a non-constrained planning problem, which allows the application of any common planning algorithm. In [18] Dijkstra introduced the concept of guarded commands by using invariants for statements in program languages. This concept is similar to our proposed method except that we use it for plan execution.

6 Conclusion

In this article we have presented a framework for executing plans in a dynamic environment. We have implemented the framework in our autonomous robotic platform [19]. The framework is a three-tier architecture whose top layer comprises of the planner and the plan executor. We use the implementation on our robots in the RoboCup robotic soccer domain which led to promising results. We have further discussed the operational semantics of the framework and have shown under which circumstances the framework represents a language for representing the knowledge of an agent/robot that interacts with a dynamic environment but follows given goals. A major objective of the article is the introduction of plan invariants which allow for representing knowledge that can hardly be formalized in the original STRIPS framework. Summarizing, the main advantages gained by the use of plan invariants are:

Early recognition of plan failure - the success of an agent in an environment is crucially influenced by its ability to quickly react to changes that influence its plans.

Long-term goals - plan invariants can be used to verify a plan when pursuing long term goals, as the plan's suitability is permanently monitored.

Conditions not influenced by the agent - plan invariants can be used to monitor conditions that are independent of the agent. Such conditions are not appropriate within action preconditions.

Exogenous events - it is usually not feasible to model all exogenous actions that could occur, but plan invariants can be used to monitor significant changes that have an impact on the agent's plan.

Intuitive way to represent and code knowledge - as the agent's knowledge commonly has to be defined manually it is helpful to think of plan preconditions (the situation that triggers the plan execution) and plan invariants (the condition that has to stay true at all times of plan execution) as two distinct matters.

Durative actions - plan invariants can be used to detect invalid or unsuitable plans during execution of durative actions. Durative actions, as opposed to discrete actions, can continue indefinitely. Again, plan invariants offer a convenient solution.

References

1. Richard E. Fikes and Nils J. Nilsson. STRIPS: A New Approach to the Application of Theorem Proving to Problem Solving. *Artificial Intelligence*, 2:189–208, 1971.
2. Jussi Rintanen and Jörg Hoffmann. An overview of recent algorithms for AI planning. *KI*, 15(2):5–11, 2001.
3. Avrim Blum and Merrick Furst. Fast planning through planning graph analysis. In *Proceedings of the 14th International Joint Conference on Artificial Intelligence (IJCAI 95)*, pages 1636–1642, 1995.
4. M. Fox and D. Long. The automatic inference of state invariants in tim. *Journal of Articial Intelligence Research*, 9:367–421, 1998.
5. Maria Fox and Derek Long. Utilizing automatically inferred invariants in graph construction and search. In *Artificial Intelligence Planning Systems*, pages 102–111, 2000.
6. Jussi Rintanen. An iterative algorithm for synthesizing invariants. In *AAAI/IAAI*, pages 806–811, 2000.
7. G. Kelleher and A. G. Cohn. Automatically synthesising domain constraints from operator descriptions. In Bernd Neumann, editor, *Proceedings of the 10th European Conference on Artificial Intelligence*, pages 653–655, Vienna, August 1992. John Wiley and Sons.
8. Daniel S. Weld. Recent advances in ai planning. *AI Magazine*, 20(2):93–123, 1999.
9. Nils J. Nilsson. Teleo-reactive programs for agent control. *Journal of Artificial Intelligence Research*, 1:139–158, 1994.
10. Henry A. Kautz and Bart Selman. The role of domain-specific knowledge in the planning as satisfiability framework. In *Artificial Intelligence Planning Systems*, pages 181–189, 1998.
11. T. L. McCluskey and J. M. Porteous. Engineering and compiling planning domain models to promote validity and efficiency. *Artificial Intelligence*, 95(1):1–65, 1997.
12. Alfonso Gerevini and Lenhart K. Schubert. Inferring state constraints for domain-independent planning. In *AAAI/IAAI*, pages 905–912, 1998.
13. Maria Fox, Derek Long, Steven Bradley, and James McKinna. Using model checking for pre-planning analysis. In *AAAI Spring Symposium Model-Based Validation of Intelligence*, pages 23–31. AAAI Press, 2001.
14. Alfonso Gerevini and Lenhart K. Schubert. Discovering state constraints in DISCOPLAN: Some new results. In *AAAI/IAAI*, pages 761–767, 2000.
15. Maria Fox and Derek Long. *PDDL2.1: An Extension to PDDL for Expressing Temporal Planning Domains*. University of Durham, UK, 2003.
16. J. Scott Penberthy and Daniel S. Weld. UCPOP: A sound, complete, partial order planner for ADL. In Bernhard Nebel, Charles Rich, and William Swartout, editors, *KR'92. Principles of Knowledge Representation and Reasoning: Proceedings of the Third International Conference*, pages 103–114. Morgan Kaufmann, San Mateo, California, 1992.
17. M. Baioletti, S. Marcugini, and A. Milani. Encoding planning constraints into partial order planning domains. In Anthony G. Cohn, Lenhart Schubert, and Stuart C. Shapiro, editors, *KR'98: Principles of Knowledge Representation and Reasoning*, pages 608–616. Morgan Kaufmann, San Francisco, California, 1998.
18. Edsger W. Dijkstra. *A Discipline of Programming*. Series in Automatic Computation. Prentice-Hall, 1976.
19. Gordon Fraser, Gerald Steinbauer, and Franz Wotawa. A modular architecture for a multi-purpose mobile robot. In *Innovations in Applied Artificial Intelligence, 17th Conference on Industrial and Engineering Applications of Artificial Intelligence and Expert Systems, IEA/AIE*, volume 3029 of *Lecture Notes in Artificial Intelligence*, Ottawa, 2004. Springer.

Structural Advantages for Ant Colony Optimisation Inherent in Permutation Scheduling Problems

James Montgomery[1,*], Marcus Randall[1], and Tim Hendtlass[2]

[1] Faculty of Information Technology, Bond University, QLD 4229, Australia
{jmontgom, mrandall}@bond.edu.au
[2] School of Information Technology, Swinburne University, VIC 3122, Australia
thendtlass@swin.edu.au

Abstract. When using a constructive search algorithm, solutions to scheduling problems such as the job shop and open shop scheduling problems are typically represented as permutations of the operations to be scheduled. The combination of this representation and the use of a constructive algorithm introduces a bias typically favouring good solutions. When ant colony optimisation is applied to these problems, a number of alternative *pheromone representations* are available, each of which interacts with this underlying bias in different ways. This paper explores both the structural aspects of the problem that introduce this underlying bias and the ways two pheromone representations may either lead towards poorer or better solutions over time. Thus it is a synthesis of a number of recent studies in this area that deal with each of these aspects independently.

Keywords: heuristic search, planning and scheduling.

1 Introduction

Ant Colony Optimisation (ACO) is a constructive metaheuristic that uses an analogue of ant trail pheromones to learn about good features of solutions. ACO belongs to the class of model-based search (MBS) algorithms [1]. In an MBS algorithm, new solutions are generated using a parameterised probabilistic model, the parameters of which are updated using previously generated solutions so as to direct the search towards promising areas of the solution space. The model used in ACO is known as *pheromone*, an artificial analogue of the chemical used by real ants to mark trails from the nest to food sources. While pheromone used by real ants is deposited on the ground they traverse, artificial pheromone can often be associated with a variety of features that characterise and distinguish solutions. Choosing which features to associate pheromone with is an important

* Corresponding author.

M. Ali and F. Esposito (Eds.): IEA/AIE 2005, LNAI 3533, pp. 218–228, 2005.

design decision when adapting ACO to suit a particular problem. Indeed, recent work by Blum and Sampels [2] and Blum and Dorigo [3] has revealed that the choice of pheromone representation can introduce a distinct and potentially unhelpful bias to an ACO search.

This paper considers how the structure of a number of scheduling problems can actually assist the performance of ACO, especially if a particular pheromone representation is used. Previous work by Montgomery, Randall and Hendtlass [4] examines the structure of the space in which ants build solutions. In contrast, Blum and Sampels [2] and Blum and Dorigo [3] study the frequency with which individual pheromone values are updated given different pheromone representations. This paper is a synthesis of both approaches to understanding bias in ACO. The well-known job-shop and open-shop scheduling problems (JSP and OSP respectively) are used both to illustrate these biases and to highlight the interesting structure these problems exhibit when solved by ACO.[1] Understanding the mechanisms of these biases establishes that they are enduring features of these kinds of scheduling problems, which allows for the consistent and effective application of optimisation techniques such as ACO.

Section 2 describes the JSP and OSP and the way in which solutions to these problems are produced by ACO and other constructive algorithms. Section 3 describes the structural aspects of these problems that favour good solutions, while Section 4 considers the way different pheromone representations react to this structure and lead to the reinforcement of either poorer or better solutions. Section 5 summarises the findings.

2 ACO Applied to Shop Scheduling Problems

The JSP and OSP are well-known scheduling problems with applications in manufacturing [6]. An instance of either problem consists of a set of *operations* $\mathcal{O} = \{o_1, o_2, \ldots, o_{|\mathcal{O}|}\}$ partitioned into the *jobs* to which they belong $\mathcal{J} = \{J_1, J_2, \ldots, J_{|\mathcal{J}|}\}$ and the *machines* $\mathcal{M} = \{M_1, M_2, \ldots, M_{|\mathcal{M}|}\}$ on which they must be processed. In both problems, only one operation from a job may be processed at any given time, only one operation may use a machine at any given time and operations may not be pre-empted. In the JSP, precedence constraints impose a total ordering on the operations within each job (i.e., there is a fixed sequence in which operations must be processed), while operations may be processed in any order in the OSP. Each operation o_i has a non-negative processing time $p(o_i)$, and the aim of both problems is to minimise the total amount of time to complete all jobs, called the *makespan*. The makespan of a solution s is denoted by $C(s)$. Blum and Sampels [2] describe a generalisation of these problems where operations within each job are also partitioned into *groups*, with precedence constraints applying within groups. This generalisation is called the

[1] The JSP and OSP are also the subject of the work by Blum and Sampels [5] and Blum and Dorigo [3], which allows for concurrent validation of results presented in this paper.

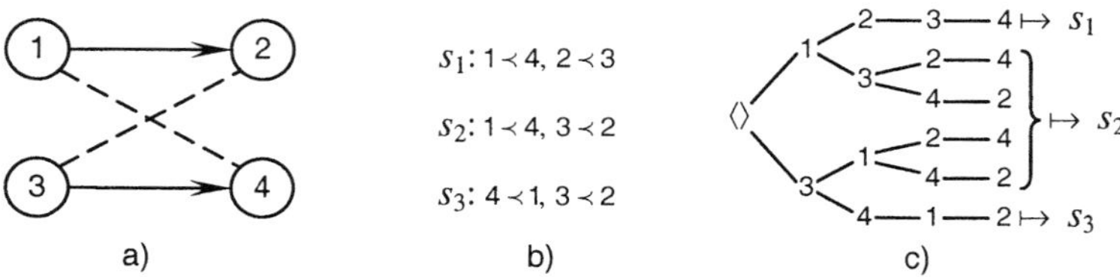

Fig. 1. A JSP instance described by Blum and Sampels [2]. a) A small JSP instance with $\mathcal{O} = \{1,2,3,4\}$, $\mathcal{J} = \{J_1 = \{1,2\}, J_2 = \{3,4\}\}$, $1 \prec 2$, $3 \prec 4$, $\mathcal{M} = \{M_1 = \{1,4\}, M_2 = \{2,3\}\}$, $p(1) = p(4) = 10$, $p(2) = p(3) = 20$. $i \prec j$ indicates i must be processed before j. b) The three solutions to this problem described in terms of the relative order of operations that require the same machine. $C(s_1) = C(s_3) = 60$, $C(s_2) = 40$. c) The construction tree for this problem showing the six sequences that may be produced and the solutions to which they correspond

group shop scheduling problem (GSP). In the JSP, each operation is assigned its own group (i.e., precedence constraints apply between operations), while in the OSP all operations within a job belong to a single group (i.e., there are no existing precedence constraints between operations). Given an existing JSP or OSP instance and adjusting the number, and hence size, of groups, a range of problem instances may be constructed with characteristics intermediate between the JSP and OSP.

It is common to represent instances of these problems as disjunctive graphs, where directed arcs indicate existing precedence constraints (as exist in the JSP for instance) and undirected arcs exist between operations that either require the same machine or are part of the same job but have no pre-existing precedence constraints between them. Operations connected by undirected arcs can be referred to as being *related* [5]. Fig. 1 shows the disjunctive graph representation of a small JSP instance consisting of two jobs, both of two operations each. A schedule for such problems may be created by assigning directions to undirected arcs in the disjunctive graph to create a directed acyclic graph. Each operation is then scheduled as early as possible given the precedence constraints imposed by this directed graph. The *list scheduler algorithm* is a constructive algorithm for these problems that ensures that cycles cannot be created in the disjunctive graph. The algorithm creates a permutation of the operations to be scheduled by successively choosing from those operations whose required predecessors have already been placed in the permutation. The relative order of related operations is determined by their relative positions in the permutation.

In ACO, solutions are built as sequences of *solution components*, which corresponds quite naturally with the list scheduler algorithm, provided that operations are used as solution components. In this paper a sequence of solution components is denoted by $\mathfrak{s}$, while the solution represented by the sequence is denoted by $X(\mathfrak{s})$ or s. The set of sequences that represent a solution s is denoted by $\mathfrak{S}(s)$.

3 Bias Inherent in Constructive Algorithms

At each step of a constructive algorithm a decision is made concerning which solution component to add to the sequence of solution components already built. The set of available solution components is determined by problem constraints and typically excludes those components already included in the partial sequence. Thus constructive algorithms implicitly explore a tree of constructive decisions, or construction tree, where the root corresponds to the empty sequence $\langle\rangle$ and leaves correspond to complete sequences and hence, to solutions. We denote a construction tree by $\mathcal{T}$.

The topology of the construction tree is defined by the nature of the problem being solved and the solution components used. The constructive algorithm also defines the mapping from sequences to solutions. When applying ACO to the GSP, the mapping from sequences to solutions is typically not uniform. Consider the JSP depicted in Fig. 1. There are three distinct solutions, yet six feasible sequences representing those solutions. Of these, four correspond to solution s_2, thereby introducing a *representation bias* [4] in favour of solution s_2.

Definition 1. *A constructive algorithm applied to a combinatorial optimisation problem is said to have a* representation bias *if there exist two solutions s_1 and s_2 such that $|\mathfrak{S}(s_1)| \neq |\mathfrak{S}(s_2)|$.*

The remainder of this section considers the use of a list scheduler algorithm which selects each solution component probabilistically using a uniform random distribution over the available components at each step. This algorithm is hereafter referred to as $\text{ACO}_{\text{undir}}$ (i.e., undirected ACO). Using such an algorithm, the probability of choosing a particular component at a given node in a construction tree is inversely proportional to the number of alternative components at that node. Consequently, sequences found on paths with fewer alternatives at each node are more likely to be discovered than those on paths with more alternatives at each node. In the example JSP, the probability of each of the sequences corresponding to solutions s_1 and s_3 is twice that for any of the four sequences corresponding to solution s_2, so that overall $P(s_1) = P(s_3) = 0.25$ while $P(s_2) = 0.5$. This constitutes a *construction bias* [4].

Definition 2. *A construction tree $\mathcal{T}$ has a* construction bias *if there exist two nodes in T such that their heights are equal yet their degrees are not equal.*

In problems where every sequence of solution components represents a feasible solution, the degree of nodes in the construction tree is uniform within each level. Such problems consequently do not have a construction bias. GSP instances with at least two groups for one of the jobs all have a construction bias, while the OSP (i.e., a GSP instance with one group per job) does not, as all permutations of operations are permissible.

Construction trees for the GSP have an interesting structure which places these two biases against each other, each in favour of one of two different kinds of solution.

In an investigation of the poor performance of ACO applied to the GSP when using certain pheromone representations, Blum and Sampels [2] found that sequences corresponding to poor solutions tend to have runs of operations from the same job. They measure this characteristic of sequences by introducing a *line scheduling factor*,[2] given by $f_{ls}(\mathfrak{s}) = \left(\sum_{i=1}^{|\mathcal{O}|-1} \delta(\mathfrak{s}, i)\right) / (|\mathcal{O}| - |\mathcal{J}|)$ where $\mathfrak{s}[i]$ is the operation in the ith position of $\mathfrak{s}$, and $\delta(\mathfrak{s}, i) = 1$ if $\mathfrak{s}[i]$ belongs to the same job as $\mathfrak{s}[i+1]$, 0 otherwise. Hence, the value of f_{ls} is in $[0, 1]$, where 1 indicates that all operations for each job are contiguous, while 0 indicates that no pairs of operations from the same job are adjacent in the sequence.

Sequences with a high line scheduling factor generally correspond to poor solutions to these problems. Intuitively this is to be expected as good schedules allow operations from different jobs to run in parallel. A sequence in which all operations from one job appear in a contiguous group can produce a schedule which contains lengthy delays for other jobs' operations, which must wait for operations from the first job to finish. This intuitive claim is born out by empirical results. The top row of Fig. 2 plots the mean f_{ls} value of sequences for each solution against the cost of the solution represented for a nine operation, three job, three machine JSP and OSP (both with a similar structure to the JSP depicted in Fig. 1).

In GSP instances that are not OSP instances, a construction bias always exists in favour of solutions with a high line scheduling factor. This is most evident in the JSP. In a JSP with n jobs, n operations are available to be added to the sequence at each step (i.e., one from each job) until all the operations from one of the jobs have been added to the sequence, after which $n - 1$ operations are available. As each job's set of unscheduled operations becomes empty, the number of available operations becomes smaller. Thus, selecting an operation from the same job as that last added to the sequence decreases the number of steps until that job's set of unscheduled operations becomes empty, and consequently makes it more likely that the same will have to be done with operations from other jobs later in solution construction. Consider a JSP with n jobs of m operations each. A sequence with $f_{ls} = 1$ can be produced on a path with m steps of n options, followed by m steps of $n-1$ options, m steps of $n-2$ options and so on, finishing with m steps of 1 option only. Denote this sequence by $\mathfrak{s}^{f_{ls}=1}$. Consider an alternative sequence constructed by selecting an operation from each job in a round-robin fashion, which accordingly has $f_{ls} = 0$. The path for such a sequence will have $(m - 1) \cdot n + 1$ steps at which every job has at least one remaining operation to be scheduled, followed by $n - 1$ steps with decreasing numbers of options, $n-1, n-2, \ldots, 1$, as each job's set of unscheduled operations becomes empty. Denote this sequence by $\mathfrak{s}^{f_{ls}=0}$.

The probability of a sequence being produced by $\text{ACO}_{\text{undir}}$ is the inverse of the product of the number of options at each step. Accordingly, $P(\mathfrak{s}^{f_{ls}=1}) = \left(\prod_{i=0}^{n-1} (n-i)^m\right)^{-1}$, while $P(\mathfrak{s}^{f_{ls}=0}) = \left(n^{(m-1)\cdot n+1} \cdot (n-1)!\right)^{-1}$. In general, $P(\mathfrak{s}^{f_{ls}=1}) > P(\mathfrak{s}^{f_{ls}=0}) \quad \forall\, m, n > 1$.

[2] Blum [7] also refers to this measure simply as a *sequencing* factor, denoted by f_{seq}.

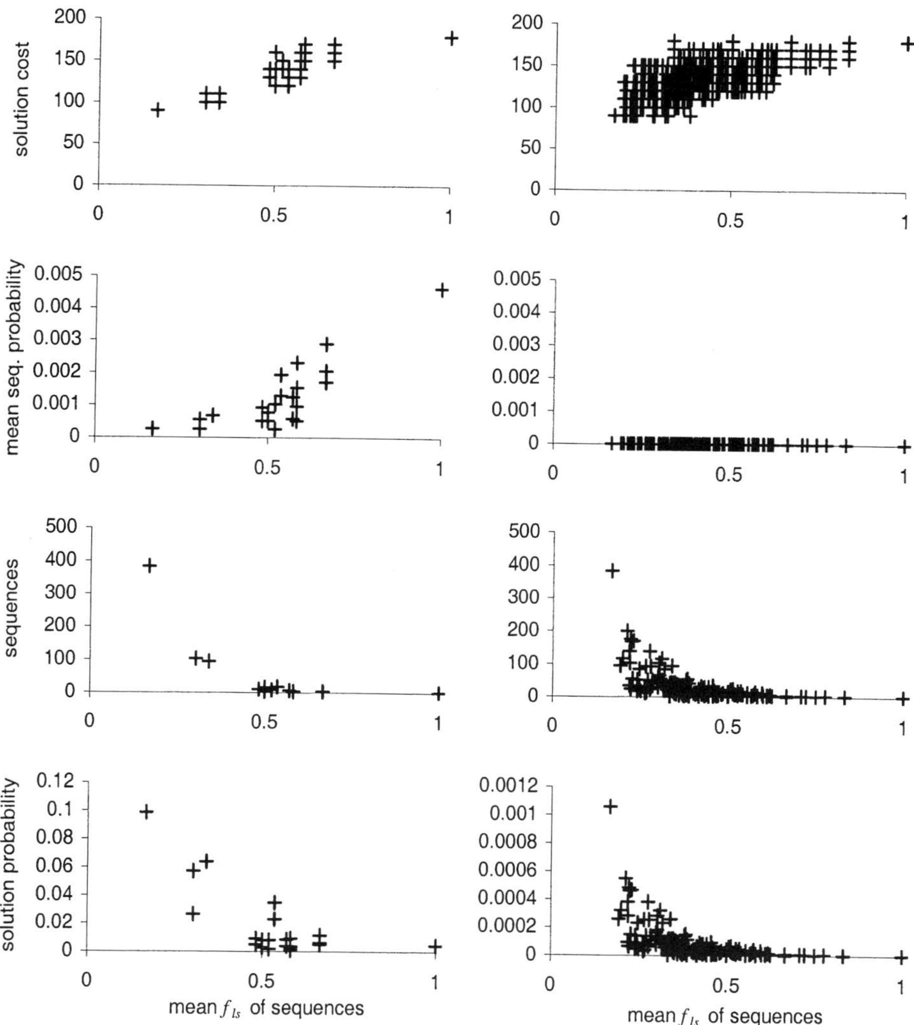

Fig. 2. Mean f_{ls} values of solutions' sequences against: solution cost (top row); mean probability of solutions' sequences (second row); number of sequences per solution (third row); and solution probability (bottom row) for a nine operation, three job, three machine JSP (left) and OSP (right)

The disparity in probability between sequences with $f_{ls} = 1$ and those with $f_{ls} = 0$ is greatest on the JSP, and diminishes as operation precedence constraints are eased (i.e., in GSP instances with groups containing increasing numbers of operations), becoming zero in OSP instances. Thus sequences corresponding to poor solutions, which typically have a high line scheduling factor, are likely to have a relatively high probability of being found in the construction trees for JSP and GSP instances (excluding OSP instances). This is illustrated in the second row of Fig. 2.

However, solutions represented by sequences with predominantly high line scheduling factors are generally represented by fewer sequences, across all GSP instances. The third row of Fig. 2 plots the mean line scheduling factor of solutions' sequences against the number of sequences representing that solution. Intuitively, sequences with a high f_{ls} value can tolerate only small perturbations before the solution represented changes. Certainly, in the JSP, a sequence with $f_{ls} = 1$ can only be altered slightly before the relative order of related operations is changed and the sequence represents a different solution. Accordingly, the lower the line scheduling factor, the easier it is to perturb the sequence without changing the relative order of related operations. This suggests that low cost solutions, which are generally represented by sequences with a low f_{ls} value, are overrepresented in the construction tree.

Indeed, the representation bias, which typically favours good solutions to these problems, can overwhelm the construction bias that typically favours poorer solutions. The fourth row of Fig. 2 plots the mean line scheduling factor of solutions' sequences against the overall probability of finding that solution using $\mathrm{ACO}_{\mathrm{undir}}$.

In moderate to large problem instances it becomes impossible to perform a complete exploration of the construction tree and hence to analyse the impact of construction and representation biases. While these biases must still be present, for the reasons given above, any search algorithm can at best produce a sample of the many feasible solutions to such instances. However, although the effects of these biases cannot be observed on larger instances, the mechanisms that drive them do have an impact on the different pheromone representations that an ACO algorithm may use.

4 Pheromone and Construction Biases

Constructive decisions in ACO are biased by pheromone information, which represents the learned utility of adding a particular solution component given the current state of the sequence and/or solution under construction.[3] A pheromone representation is a collection of pheromone values that individually correspond to some characteristic of either a sequence or the solution it represents. *Solution characteristics* may either correspond to the solution components used to build a solution or to some aggregate feature of a solution induced by a number of solution components [8]. Pheromone values for each solution characteristic are increased in proportion to the quality of the solutions with those characteristics

[3] Constructive decisions in ACO are also typically biased by a problem-specific heuristic measure of the utility of adding a component, but this is not considered here in order to simplify the analyses performed.

produced at each iteration of the algorithm. The relative value of pheromone associated with each solution characteristic influences the selection of solution components in later iterations.

Two pheromone representations for the GSP are considered in this paper. $\mathsf{PH}_{\mathsf{suc}}$, used in early ACO algorithms for these problems, associates a pheromone value with pairs of operations that may be placed in succession (including an artificial start node that is not part of the original problem description). Hence the solution characteristic (o_1, o_2) from $\mathsf{PH}_{\mathsf{suc}}$ relates to the learned utility of placing operation o_2 immediately after operation o_1 in a sequence. $\mathsf{PH}_{\mathsf{rel}}$, a recently developed pheromone representation introduced by Blum and Sampels [5], associates a pheromone value with pairs of *related* operations to learn which operation should precede the other. Hence the solution characteristic (o_1, o_2) from $\mathsf{PH}_{\mathsf{rel}}$ relates to the learned utility of scheduling o_1 before o_2, i.e., at any location in the sequence before o_2. When considering a candidate operation o_1, $\mathsf{PH}_{\mathsf{rel}}$ makes use of a number of pheromone values, as a candidate operation may be related to many as yet unscheduled operations. Blum and Sampels [5] take the minimum pheromone value associated with these characteristics.

In empirical work conducted by Blum and Sampels [2], and in the current investigation, $\mathsf{PH}_{\mathsf{suc}}$ was found to perform poorly on the GSP. Its performance is worst on the JSP, but improves as problem constraints are eased such that its performance is very good on the OSP. Blum and Sampels observed high f_{ls} values (up to 1) for sequences produced by $\mathsf{PH}_{\mathsf{suc}}$ applied to GSP instances other than the OSP. In contrast, f_{ls} values when using $\mathsf{PH}_{\mathsf{rel}}$ were consistently low (less than 0.1) across the JSP, GSP and OSP. This result has been found across a range of instances of varying size. As was found by Blum and Sampels, and illustrated in Section 3, sequences with a high f_{ls} value typically represent poor solutions to these problems, a result which holds regardless of problem size. Fig. 3 plots f_{ls} values against solution cost for sequences produced by ACO algorithms using $\mathsf{PH}_{\mathsf{suc}}$ and $\mathsf{PH}_{\mathsf{rel}}$ applied to the `la38` JSP instance.[4] Data were collected by sampling every 100th sequence produced by an ACO algorithm producing a total of 30,000 sequences.[5]

An insight into the strong bias $\mathsf{PH}_{\mathsf{suc}}$ exhibits towards solutions with a high f_{ls} value can be obtained in a number of ways. Blum [7] introduces the concept of a *competition balanced system*, which in terms of ACO is defined as a pheromone representation consisting of solution characteristics that appear in the same number of sequences produced by the algorithm. If a pheromone model applied to a particular problem instance is not a competition-balanced system, Blum states that bias may be observed. Certainly, when using $\mathsf{PH}_{\mathsf{suc}}$ with constrained GSP instances (such as the JSP), solution characteristics corresponding to placing two operations from the same job in succession appear in proportionally more sequences than those for which it is not the case. In contrast, solution

[4] This instance is part of a benchmark JSP set described by Lawrence [9].

[5] The actual algorithm used is a modification of Ant Colony System from which heuristic information and its greedy bias (q_0) have been removed.

characteristics from $\mathsf{PH}_{\mathsf{rel}}$ that are associated more strongly with sequences with a low f_{ls} value appear in a greater number of sequences than those characteristics that are not. Thus, in problems where a high f_{ls} value is strongly predictive of a high solution cost, use of $\mathsf{PH}_{\mathsf{suc}}$ will make good solutions increase the pheromone associated with poor solutions, whereas use of $\mathsf{PH}_{\mathsf{rel}}$ will result in even poor solutions increasing pheromone associated most strongly with good solutions.

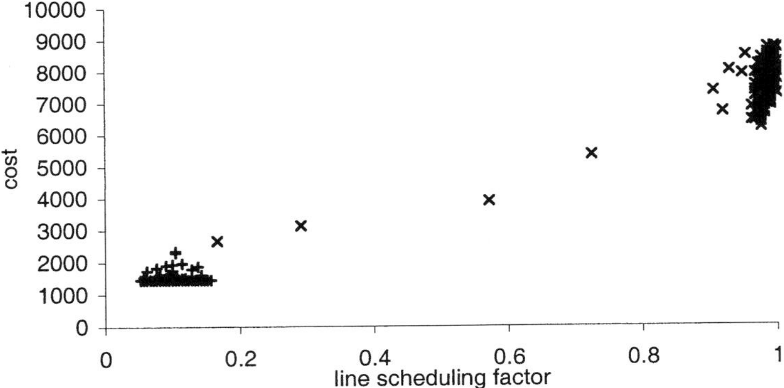

Fig. 3. f_{ls} values of samples of 300 sequences produced by ACO with $\mathsf{PH}_{\mathsf{suc}}$ (shown as $\times$) and $\mathsf{PH}_{\mathsf{rel}}$ (shown as $+$) against cost of solutions represented. All points for $\mathsf{PH}_{\mathsf{rel}}$ have $f_{ls} \in (0.05, 0.16)$

Consideration of the structure of these problems, described in Section 3, reveals why the solution characteristics from these two pheromones are so strongly biased towards different kinds of sequences and hence, solutions. Given that selecting an operation from the same job as that most recently selected decreases the likelihood that successive pairs of operations placed later will be selected from different jobs, those solution characteristics from $\mathsf{PH}_{\mathsf{suc}}$ that correspond to placing successive operations from different jobs are also less likely to appear in those sequences. In contrast, partially constructed sequences with a low f_{ls} value restrict the set of available operations less, and so still allow successive operations from the same job to be placed. Thus, the same mechanism that introduces a construction bias (which has little detectable effect on larger instances) does have an effect on the distribution of solution characteristics from $\mathsf{PH}_{\mathsf{suc}}$ in the construction tree. Conversely, many of the operation precedence relationships established by sequences with a high f_{ls} value are largely restricted to those sequences, and are not present in those sequences that may be perturbed while maintaining the solution represented. Sequences with a high f_{ls} value will still contain some of those operation precedence relationships that appear in better solutions, and so overall the number of sequences that these precedence relationships appear in is relatively high. The representation bias in these problems serves to accentuate the effect, as all sequences for a single solution exhibit the same solution characteristics in $\mathsf{PH}_{\mathsf{rel}}$.

5 Conclusions

The structure of the GSP, which includes the well-known JSP and OSP, serves to bias constructive searches towards good solutions. However, on medium to large instances the relative difference between competing solutions becomes negligible given the comparatively large number of solutions overall. Nevertheless, the presence of underlying biases in the construction trees for these problems produces a bias in the various pheromone representations that may be used by ACO. Associating pheromone with pairs of successive operations in a sequence ($\mathsf{PH}_{\mathsf{suc}}$) performs poorly because the construction path for those sequences that represent poor solutions necessarily restricts alternatives, thereby increasing the number of sequences in which solution characteristics of poor solutions appear. Conversely, learning the relative order of related operations ($\mathsf{PH}_{\mathsf{rel}}$) performs well because in that pheromone representation characteristics of poor solutions can only appear in a small number of sequences as small perturbations to those sequences change these characteristics. Understanding the mechanisms underlying these different behaviours of ACO applied to these problems establishes that they are enduring features, and so supports the effective application of ACO to these problems. The interesting and advantageous structure of these problems suggests the possible existence of other problems that have a structure that may be similarly exploited by the use of a carefully chosen pheromone representation to increase the probability of finding good solutions. It also suggests that there may be problems whose structure cannot be exploited and which require additional heuristic techniques to counter any inherent unfavourable biases.

References

1. Zlochin, M., Dorigo, M.: Model-based search for combinatorial optimization: A comparitive study. In: 7th International Conference on Parallel Problem Solving from Nature (PPSN 2002). (2002) 651–662
2. Blum, C., Sampels, M.: When model bias is stronger than selection pressure. In Guervós, J.M., et al., eds.: 7th International Conference on Parallel Problem Solving from Nature (PPSN2002). Volume 2439 of Lecture Notes in Computer Science., Springer-Verlag (2002) 893–902
3. Blum, C., Dorigo, M.: Deception in ant colony optimisation. In Dorigo, M., et al., eds.: 4th International Workshop on Ant Colony Optimization and Swarm Intelligence, ANTS 2004. Volume 3172 of Lecture Notes in Computer Science., Springer-Verlag (2004) 118–129
4. Montgomery, J., Randall, M., Hendtlass, T.: Search bias in constructive metaheuristics and implications for ant colony optimisation. In Dorigo, M., et al., eds.: 4th International Workshop on Ant Colony Optimization and Swarm Intelligence, ANTS 2004. Volume 3172 of Lecture Notes in Computer Science., Springer-Verlag (2004) 390–397
5. Blum, C., Sampels, M.: Ant colony optimization for FOP shop scheduling: A case study on different pheromone representations. In: 2002 Congress on Evolutionary Computation. (2002) 1558–1563

6. Blum, C., Sampels, M.: An ant colony optimization algorithm for shop scheduling problems. Journal of Mathematical Modelling and Algorithms **3** (2004) 285–308
7. Blum, C.: Theoretical and practical aspects of ant colony optimization. PhD thesis, Université Libre de Bruxelles, Belgium (2004)
8. Montgomery, J., Randall, M., Hendtlass, T.: Automated selection of appropriate pheromone representations in ant colony optimisation. Artificial Life (to appear)
9. Lawrence, S.: Resource constrained project scheduling: An experimental investigation of heuristic scheduling techniques (supplement). Technical Report, Graduate School of Industrial Administration, Carnegie Mellon University, Pittsburgh (1984)

Incrementally Scheduling with Qualitative Temporal Information

Florent Launay and Debasis Mitra

Florida Institute of Technology, USA
flaunay@fit.edu, dmitra@cs.fit.edu

Abstract. Scheduling is typically a quantitative engineering problem involving tasks and constraints. However, there are many real life situations where the input is qualitative in nature and any quantitative information is neither available nor cared for. We address here such a qualitative scheduling problem with disjunctive temporal constraints between the tasks. The problem we address is incremental in nature, where a new task is added to a committed schedule. We not only find a valid schedule when it exists, but also analyze the causes of inconsistency otherwise. This is new direction of research.

1 Introduction

There are various definitions of the scheduling problem depending on the nature of the tasks (temporal aspects, resource utilization aspects, etc.). We present here a type of scheduling of tasks on a time line when only qualitative and disjunctive temporal constraints are provided as input. In this work tasks are modeled as time intervals on a continuous time-line. The scheme we have presented here allows efficient Incremental Qualitative Scheduling (IQS), where new tasks are gradually added to the schedule sequentially. IQS problem is defined below: a set of intervals (or tasks) committed on a time line is provided as input: {*Old1, Old2, . . ., Old_n*}. It is a total order *T* of the boundary points of those intervals. An interval *I* is (*I*-, *I*+) on a time line. The input also provides qualitative temporal constraints between a *New* interval and some of the old intervals. The problem is to insert *New*- and *New*+ on the total order *T* following the constraints. Alternatively, the constraints may be inconsistent with respect to each other in which case the minimum number of constraints, which are responsible for inconsistency, is output as a set called *MinSet.*

The input temporal constraints are allowed to be disjunctive, i.e., for all the constraints R_i in (*New* R_i *Old_i*) $1 \le |R_i| \le 13$, e.g., (D {*overlaps* or *during* or *starts*} A) for intervals *D* and *A*, 13 being the total number of basic relations possible between a pair of intervals [Allen, 1983]. If $\forall$i, |Ri|=1, or one basic relation per constraint, then a simple topological sort would be able to find inconsistency (for a cycle) or be able to insert *New* in the total order *T*. If $\forall$i, |Ri|≈m, then m^n number of possibilities for *n* constraints may need to be checked before detecting any inconsistency.

2 Algorithms

The 13 basic relations that an interval can have with respect to another interval (X,Y) can be represented in a 2D space (Fig 1) [Ligozat 1996]. Their topological

M. Ali and F. Esposito (Eds.): IEA/AIE 2005, LNAI 3533, pp. 229 – 231, 2005.

relationships form a lattice (Fig 2). Any disjunctive relation, which can be represented as a range over this lattice, is called a *convex* relation, and if zero or more 1D relation (e.g., *f*) or the 0D relation (*eq*) is missing from an otherwise convex relation, then it is called a *preconvex* relation. A *Convex closure* of a preconvex relation *p* is when those missing relations (from otherwise the convex relation) are added back to *p*. While checking satisfiability of a set of constraints with arbitrary type of disjunctive relations is NP-hard, that with only preconvex relations is in P-class. Our following algorithms are for solving IQS problem with preconvex relations.

We first convert a given set of constraints into its *ORD-clause* form, which is a conjunctive normal form that uses only point relations {=, ≠, ≤} between the boundaries of the intervals. Next, we split the resulting point-constraints for the two boundaries *New+* and *New-*. Finally, we run point-insertion algorithm (*PoSeq*, developed before) for each of the two boundary points. In case of detecting inconsistency, the algorithm finds minimal set of constraints (for each boundary point) responsible for inconsistency and the corresponding union *MinSet* is reported to the user. We briefly describe the algorithms in this section.

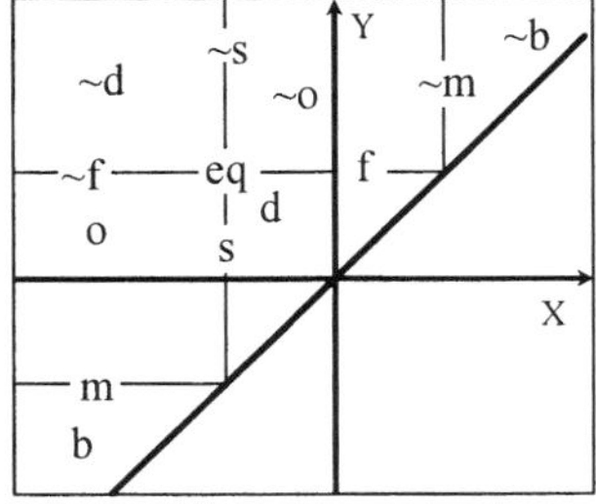

Fig. 1. Interval relations in 2D

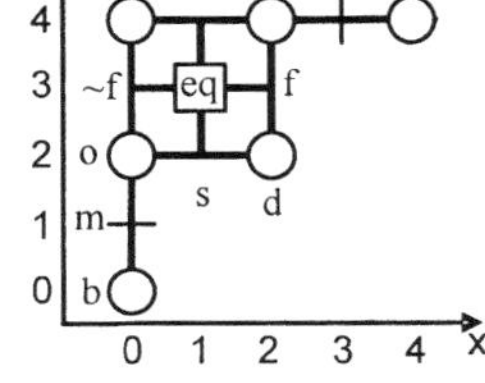

Fig. 2. Lattice of basic relations

The *normalization* algorithm converts each constraint into a clausal form. Then the convex closure for each constraint may be represented by a simple conjunction of two clauses on two axes (Fig 3), each being a range over the respective axis in Fig 2. The negations of the missing lower dimensional relations (Fig 4) are then added to the convex closure. For example, the preconvex constraint {*d, s, o, ~f, f*} has the convex closure {*d, s, o, ~f, f, eq*} (a range [*o, f*] over the lattice in Fig 2), where '*eq*' as the missing basic relation for {(New+ ≠ I+) ∨ (New- ≠ I-)}.

The following *sorter* algorithm primarily creates a conjunctive set by picking up the tightest constraint-literal from each clause. In the subsequent step we sort all the chosen literals from the previous steps into two groups: one set of point-relations involving the *New-* and another one involving *New+*.

Example: for the following committed set of intervals S = {A, B} where {A (before) B}, the sets of constraints: {New (*d, eq, o*) A} and {New (*m, o, d~, eq*) B} will produce the two sets L+ and L- as follows:

L- ={New- ≤ A+, A+ ≠ New-, New- ≤ B-, A- ≠ New-, B- ≠ New-} and
L+ = {New+ ≤ A+, A+ ≠ New+, A- ≤ New+, B- ≤ New+, B+ ≠ New+, B- ≠ New+}
and in addition, the total order *T* of relations between the committed intervals S:
{A- ≤ A+, A- ≠ A+, B- ≤ B+, B- ≠ B+, A+ ≤ B-, A+ ≠ B-, A- ≤ B+, A- ≠ B+}.

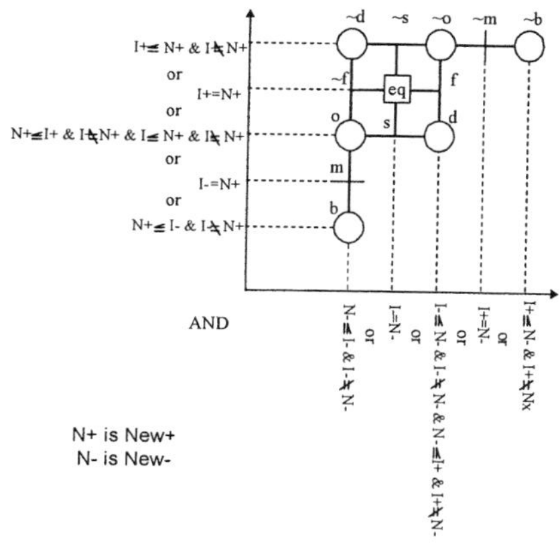

Fig. 3. Clausal representation of basic relations

!s	I+ $\leq$ New+ V I- $\neq$ New-
!~s	New+ $\leq$ I+ V I- $\neq$ New-
!f	New- $\leq$ I- V I+ $\neq$ New+
!~f	I- $\leq$ New- V I+ $\neq$ New+
!m	I- $\leq$ New- V I- $\neq$ New+
!~m	New+ $\leq$ I+ V I+ $\neq$ New-
!eq	I+ $\neq$ New+ V I- $\neq$ New-

Fig. 4. Conjugate of lower dimensional relations

Thus, our next task is to run the point sequencing algorithm *PoSeq* twice – (the *PoSeq* algorithm is described in [Mitra and Launay, 2004]), once over the point-constraint set for *New+* and then for the one for *New-*. The outputs are the valid regions for *New+* and *New-* over the total order *T*. If either (or both) of them produces inconsistency, then the minimal sets of constraints that cause the inconsistency are being returned. The union of these two sets (from the two runs of *PoSeq*) is *MinSet*.

Each of the algorithms described above, the *normalization,* the *sorter*, and the *PoSeq* algorithm are polynomial algorithms. However, in case of non-preconvex constraints, i.e., for the general unrestricted input, the *sorter* algorithm may have to backtrack when inconsistency is detected by the *PoSeq* algorithm.

Acknowledgement. A grant from the US NSF has initiated this work.

References

Allen, J. F., (1983). "Maintaining knowledge about temporal intervals". Communications of the ACM, v.26 n.11, p.832-843, Nov.

Ligozat, G., (1996). "A new proof of tractability for ORD-Horn relations". In Proceedings of the 13th National (US) Conference on Artificial Intelligence (AAAI-96). AAAI Press, Menlo Park, Calif., 395--401.

Mitra, D., Launay, F., (2004). "Problem of detecting the "culprit" conflicting constraints in temporal reasoning. " *Workshop on Spatial and Temporal Reasoning*, San Jose, California. AAAI.

New Upper Bounds for the Permutation Flowshop Scheduling Problem

Joanna Jędrzejowicz[1] and Piotr Jędrzejowicz[2]

[1] Institute of Mathematics, Gdańsk University, Wita Stwosza 57, 80-952 Gdańsk, Poland
jj@math.univ.gda.pl

[2] Department of Information Systems, Gdynia Maritime University, Morska 83, 81-225 Gdynia, Poland
pj@am.gdynia.pl

Abstract. The paper proposes an implementation of the population learning algorithm (PLA) for solving the permutation flowshop scheduling problem (PFSP). The PLA can be considered as a useful framework for constructing a hybrid approaches. In the proposed implementation the PLA scheme is used to integrate evolutionary, tabu search and simulated annealing algorithms. The approach has been evaluated experimentally. Experiment has produced 14 new upper bounds for the standard benchmark dataset containing 120 PFSP instances and has shown that the approach is competitive to other algorithms.

1 Introduction

In the permutation flowshop scheduling problem (PFSP) there is a set of n jobs. Each of n jobs has to be processed on m machines $1 \dots m$ in this order. The processing time of job i on machine j is p_{ij} where p_{ij} are fixed and nonnegative. At any time, each job can be processed on at most one machine, and each machine can process at most one job. The jobs are available at time 0 and the processing of a job may not be interrupted. In the PFSP the job order is the same on every machine. The objective is to find a job sequence minimizing schedule makespan (i.e., completion time of the last job).

In this paper a new implementation of the population learning algorithm designed to solving PFSP instances is proposed and evaluated experimentally.

2 Population Learning Algorithm and Its PFSP Implementation

Population learning algorithm introduced in [1] is a population-based technique with a decreasing population size and an increasing complexity of the learning procedures used at subsequent computation stages.

M. Ali and F. Esposito (Eds.): IEA/AIE 2005, LNAI 3533, pp. 232–235, 2005.

In the PLA an individual represents a coded solution of the considered problem. Initially, a number of individuals, known as the initial population, is generated. Once the initial population has been generated, individuals enter the first learning stage. The improved individuals are then evaluated and better ones pass to a subsequent stage. A strategy of selecting better or more promising individuals must be defined and applied. In the following stages the whole cycle is repeated. At a final stage the remaining individuals are reviewed and the best represents a solution to the problem at hand. The population learning algorithm applied to solving the PFSP instances makes use of genetic algorithm with cross-over and mutation, tabu search and simulated annealing.

3 Computational Experiment Results

The first part of the experiment was designed to compare the performance of the PLA with other state-of-the art techniques.

It has been decided to follow the experiment plan of [3] to assure comparability. Two PFSP implementations of the population algorithm denoted PLA1 and PLA2 have been considered. PLA1 is the version proposed in [2] and PLA2 is the new implementation described in Section 2. In both cases the algorithm iterated for the prescribed time, each iteration consisting of the full population learning algorithm cycle, starting with a reasonably small initial population. The final result represents the best solution found during all iterations. In both cases the initial population size has been set to 10 and the selection procedure discarded all individuals with fitness function valued below current average at each stage. The experiment involving both PLAs has been carried on a PC computer with the 2.4 GHz Pentium 4 processor and 512 MB RAM. The results obtained by applying the PLA1 and PLA2 are compared with the following [3]: NEHT - the NEH heuristic with the enhancements, GA - the genetic algorithm, HGA - the

Table 1. The average percentage increase over the currently known upper bound

instance	NEHT	GA	HGA	SAOP	SPIRIT	GAR	GAMIT	PLA1	PLA2
20×5	3.35	0.29	0.20	1.47	5.22	0.71	3.28	0.14	0.03
20×10	5.02	0.95	0.55	2.57	5.86	1.97	5.53	0.46	0.58
20×20	3.73	0.56	0.39	2.22	4.58	1.48	4.33	0.53	0.42
50×5	0.84	0.07	0.06	0.52	2.03	0.23	1.96	0.12	0.07
50×10	5.12	1.91	1.72	3.65	5.88	2.47	6.25	0.65	0.77
50×20	6.20	3.05	2.64	4.97	7.21	3.89	7.53	1.62	1.67
100×5	0.46	0.10	0.08	0.42	1.06	0.18	1.33	0.13	0.03
100×10	2.13	0.84	0.70	1.73	5.07	1.06	3.66	0.67	0.72
100×20	5.11	3.12	2.75	4.90	10.15	3.84	9.70	1.35	1.09
200×10	1.43	0.54	0.50	1.33	9.03	0.85	6.47	0.64	0.56
200×20	4.37	2.88	2.59	4.40	16.17	3.47	14.56	1.07	1.05
500×20	2.24	1.65	1.56	3.48	13.57	1.98	12.47	1.93	1.13
average	3.33	1.33	1.15	2.64	7.15	1.84	6.42	0.77	0.68

Table 2. Mean, max and min relative errors for the second part of the experiment

instance	MRE	max RE	min RE
20 × 5	-0.0081%	0.0000%	-0.0809%
20 × 10	-0.0073%	0.0000%	-0.0726%
20 × 20	0.0279%	0.0000%	-0.0476%
50 × 5	0.0000%	0.0000%	0.0000%
50 × 10	-0.0135%	0.0000%	-0.0349%
50 × 20	0.3059%	0.5382%	0.0269%
100 × 5	-0.0458%	0.0000%	-0.2350%
100 × 10	0.0724%	0.3475%	0.0000%
100 × 20	0.2357%	0.7425%	-0.1103%
200 × 10	0.0580%	0.1864%	0.0000%
200 × 20	0.1412%	0.5376%	-0.5779%
500 × 20	0.3384%	0.5333%	0.0941%
average	0.0921%	-	-

Table 3. New upper bounds found by the PLA2

Instance size	Instance number	Old upper bound	New upper bound	% improvement
20 × 5	5	1236	1235	0.0809%
20 × 10	4	1378	1377	0.0726%
20 × 20	2	2100	2099	0.0476%
50 × 10	2	2892	2891	0.0346%
50 × 10	3	2864	2863	0.0349%
50 × 10	4	3064	3063	0.0326%
50 × 10	8	3039	3038	0.0329%
100 × 5	8	5106	5094	0.2350%
100 × 5	9	5454	5448	0.1100%
100 × 5	10	5328	5322	0.1126%
100 × 20	7	6346	6339	0.1103%
100 × 20	9	6358	6354	0.0629%
200 × 20	2	11420	11354	0.5779%
200 × 20	3	11446	11424	0.1922%

hybrid genetic algorithm, SAOP - the simulated annealing algorithm, SPIRIT - the tabu search, GAR - another genetic algorithm and GAMIT - the hybrid genetic algorithm. The first part of the experiment was designed to compare the performance of the PLA with other state-of-the art techniques. For evaluating the different algorithms the average percentage increase over the currently known upper bound is used. Every algorithm has been run to solve all 120 benchmark instances and the data from a total of 5 independent runs have been finally averaged. As a termination criteria all algorithms have been allocated 30 seconds for instances with 500 jobs, 12 seconds for instances with 200 jobs, 6 seconds for instances with 100 jobs, 3 seconds for instances with 50 jobs and 1.2 seconds for instances with 20 jobs. The results obtained for all 120 instances from the OR-LIBRARY benchmark sets averaged over 5 runs are shown in Table 1.

It can be observed that the proposed population learning algorithm (PLA2) outperforms all other tested algorithms by a significant margin. Also PLA1 proposed in [2] performs better then the rest of algorithms even if it is inferior to PLA2 under the criterion used. The second part of the experiment has been designed with a view of using the PLA2 to obtain best possible results. Computation times varied from a few seconds for instances with 20 tasks up to more than 6 hours for instances with 500 tasks and 20 machines. These, however, have not been the focus of the experiment. Mean, max and min relative errors, as compared with the currently known upper bounds averaged for each of the 12 subsets of instances are shown in Table 2.

The experiment has also succeeded in finding new better upper bounds for 14 instances out of 120 instances in the benchmark dataset from the OR-LIBRARY. The newly found upper bounds are shown in Table 3.

The respective solutions (that is permutations of task numbers) representing new upper bounds are available at http://manta.univ.gda.pl/~jj/pla.txt.

4 Conclusions

Considering the results of the experiment in which the population learning algorithm has been used to solve all 120 PFSP instances from the standard benchmark dataset, the following conclusions can be drawn:

- Population learning algorithm provides a useful framework for constructing hybrid approaches to solving successfully difficult computational problems.
- A cocktail of proven metaheuristics can produce synergic effects leading to better solutions than produced by any homogenous approach.
- Population learning algorithm uses a scheme that produces a competitive performance with respect to two criteria - a good performance in a reasonable time and the best overall performance.

References

1. Jędrzejowicz P.: Social Learning Algorithm as a Tool for Solving Some Difficult Scheduling Problems, Foundation of Computing and Decision Sciences, **24** (1999) 51–66
2. Jedrzejowicz, J., Jedrzejowicz, P.: PLA-Based Permutation Scheduling, Foundations of Computing and Decision Sciences **28(3)** (2003) 159–177
3. Ruiz, R., Maroto, C., Alcaraz, J.: New Genetic Algorithms for the Permutation Flowshop Scheduling Problems, Proc. The Fifth Metaheuristic International Conference, Kyoto, 2003, 63-1–63-8

R-Tree Representations of Disaster Areas Based on Probabilistic Estimation

Hiroyuki Mikuri, Naoto Mukai, and Toyohide Watanabe

Department of Systems and Social Informatics,
Graduate School of Information Science, Nagoya University,
Furo-cho, Chikusa-ku, Nagoya, 464-8603, Japan
{hiro, naoto, watanabe}@watanabe.ss.is.nagoya-u.ac.jp

Abstract. In order to realize a navigation system for refugees in disaster areas, we must reduce computation costs required in setting escape routes. Thus, in this paper, we propose a method for reducing the costs by grasping whole danger regions in a disaster area from a global perspective. At first, we estimate future changes of dangerous regions by a simple way and link all regions with Danger Levels. Then, we index estimated dangerous regions by extended R-tree. In this step, we link the Danger Levels with depths of the extended R-tree and each Danger Level is managed at each depth of the extended R-tree. Finally, we show how our approach effects in setting escape routes.

1 Introduction

Recently, information technologies have been utilized in counter plans against natural disasters [1, 2], and a lot of systems for the plans have been proposed. Among the proposed systems, we pick up a navigation system for refugees in the area where an earthquake occurred. In the area, there are a lot of dangerous regions which refugees cannot go through safely and the regions change their forms and sizes as time advances. Therefore, the navigation system needs to set escape routes which avoid all dangerous regions and notify refugees of the routes. In this case, considering the number of refugees who need to escape, needs for prompt responses to escape route information requests from refugees, and limit of available computational capacity, the escape routes need to be set at low computational cost.

In this paper, we propose a method for reducing the costs by grasping whole dangerous regions in a disaster area from a global perspective. At first, we estimate future expansions of dangerous regions by a simple way. In this step, we approximate all dangerous regions and estimated dangerous regions by rectangles and link all regions in the area with Danger Levels. Then, we index estimated dangerous regions by extended R-tree. In the extended R-tree, each Danger Level is linked with each depth and regions which have higher Danger Level are basically managed in deeper depth. This structure enables the navigation systems to grasp whole dangerous regions in the area from a global perspective and to cut off searching escape routes in unpromising areas.

M. Ali and F. Esposito (Eds.): IEA/AIE 2005, LNAI 3533, pp. 236–238, 2005.

2 Approach

2.1 Estimating Future Changes of Dangerous Regions

In order to handle changes of dangerous regions and set escape routes which avoid dangerous regions, we estimate future changes of dangerous regions by a simple way. In this paper, we only deal with an example of estimated results.

In estimating, we approximate all dangerous regions by rectangles and use two assumptions as follows. One is that regions which once turned into dangerous regions remain to be dangerous regions for quite a while. The other is that no dangerous region emerges abruptly. Of course, these assumptions are not always true in actual environment. We simplify and approximate changes of all dangerous regions by them.

If we estimate the change of a known dangerous region using the theorems and classify regions around the known dangerous region by Danger Levels, we can get Fig. 1(a). In Fig. 1(a), Danger Level 1 corresponds to the known dangerous region. Danger Level 2 located around Danger Level 1 corresponds to the regions where are likely to be dangerous region in the future. Danger Level 3, 4, and 5 is expressed in a similar fashion. We express probabilistic spreads of the known dangerous region by the structure like Fig. 1(a).

2.2 Extended R-Tree

Outline of the extended R-tree. In order to manage probabilistic spreads of dangerous regions, we extend the R-tree [3]. Briefly speaking, estimated results like Fig. 1(a) become leaf node of the extended R-tree and each Danger Level is linked with each depth of the tree. In addition, regions which have higher Danger Level are basically managed in deeper depth in the tree. Therefore, in making an minimum bounding rectangle (MBR), we consider the Danger Level managed at the depth and make MBR of the Danger Level's rectangles.

Structure of the extended R-tree is expressed as Fig. 1(b). In Fig. 1(b), all nodes have Danger Levels which are managed at the node's depth. At each intermediate node, the density of the node is calculated. Here, the density means

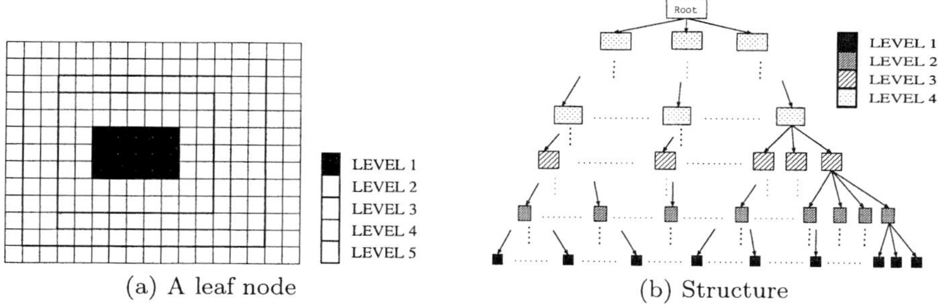

(a) A leaf node (b) Structure

Fig. 1. Extended R-tree

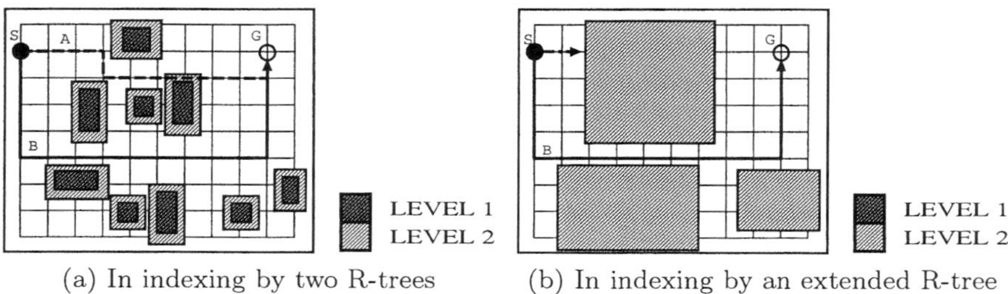

(a) In indexing by two R-trees (b) In indexing by an extended R-tree

Fig. 2. Simplified disaster area

how much the node is taken up by its child node. Then, whole area of the intermediate node is considered to be dangerous if the density of the node is high.

Escape Route Setting. We show how to set a escape route using the extended R-tree and how the extended R-tree effects in cutting off computational costs. We express a simplified disaster area by Fig. 2. In Fig. 2, there is a grid of streets. On the streets, start point of escape is expressed as `S` and goal point is expressed as `G`. We consider setting a escape route from `S` to `G`.

If we index Danger Level 1's regions and Danger Level 2's regions by two R-trees, this situation corresponds to Fig. 2(a). At first, an escape route which avoids Danger Level 2's regions is searched. In Fig. 2(a), route `B` is to be found. If there is no route which avoid all Danger Level 2's regions, an escape route which avoids Danger Level 1's regions is searched and route `A` is to be found. We can get one of the safest route by following these two steps. However, we have to search many points which are not used in the escape routes.

If we index Danger Level 1's regions and Danger Level 2's regions by an extended R-tree, the situation is grasped as Fig. 2(b) at the second deepest depth. We assume three Danger Level 2's rectangle's density are high enough. In this case, when we search an escape route which avoids Danger Level 2's regions, we can also get route `B`. The route we can get is same as the previous case but the number of searched points which are not used is not same. By grasping the situation as Fig. 2(b), we can cut off searching unpromising areas where have many dangerous regions and reduce computational costs for setting the escape route.

References

1. Kitano, H., Tadokoro, S., Noda, I., Matsubara, H., Takahashi, T., Shinjou, A., Shimada, S.: Robocup-rescue : Search and rescue in large-scale disasters as a domain for automous agents research. In: Proceedings of IEEE, IEEE Press (1999)
2. Ishida, T.: Digital city kyoto : Social information infrastructure for everyday life. Communications of the ACM(CACM) **45** (2002)
3. Guttman, A.: R-trees : A dynamic index structure for spatial searching. In: Proceedings of ACM SIGMOD'84, ACM (1984) 47–57

AI/NLP Technologies Applied to Spacecraft Mission Design

Maria Teresa Pazienza[1], Marco Pennacchiotti[1],
Michele Vindigni[1], and Fabio Massimo Zanzotto[2]

[1] Artificial Intelligence Research Group,
University of Roma Tor Vergata, Italy
{pazienza, pennacchiotti@info.uniroma2.it}
[2] University of Milano Bicocca, Italy
zanzotto@disco.unimib.it

Abstract. In this paper we propose the model of a prototypical NLP architecture of an information access system to support a team of experts in a scientific design task, in a shared and heterogeneous framework. Specifically, we believe AI/NLP can be helpful in several tasks, such as the extraction of implicit information needs enclosed in meeting minutes or other documents, analysis of explicit information needs expressed through Natural Language, processing and indexing of document collections, extraction of required information from documents, modeling of a common knowledge base, and, finally, identification of important concepts through the automatic extraction of terms. In particular, we envisioned this architecture in the specific and practical scenario of the Concurrent Design Facility (CDF) of the European Space Agency (ESA), in the framework of the SHUMI project (Support To HUman Machine Interaction) developed in collaboration with the ESA/ESTEC - ACT (Advanced Concept Team).

1 Introduction

An interesting field of application of information access technologies relates to scenarios in which several users work jointly to a common *project*, sharing their possibly different and specific knowledge, and providing their essential personal contribution to a common goal. Imagine, for instance, a *design process* in which a team of experts coming from different scientific disciplines, cooperates in a common task of designing and engineering a particular device, that requires their different competencies to be jointly used and intertwined. Moreover, they should be possibly supported during the process by a large repository of domain knowledge from which to extract information that can help in the design [1].

For instance, in designing a space missions (as it is the case of the SHUMI project [13]), the goal of the process is both to produce a spacecraft able to accomplish an envisioned mission and to plan the mission itself. The expert team, composed by engineers, physicians and other scientists, jointly works in the CDF. The planning

[1] This context is what specifically analyzed into SHUMI-ESA ESTEC funded study N.18149/04/NL/MV.

M. Ali and F. Esposito (Eds.): IEA/AIE 2005, LNAI 3533, pp. 239 – 248, 2005.

activity needs a fast and effective interaction of involved disciplines and requires the access to several kinds of documentations, among which scientific papers, studies, internal reports, etc., produced by experts of related disciplines all over the World (*pre-existing knowledge*). Thus, during a design process a large quantity of knowledge is usually accessed in order to satisfy the team information need. Moreover, the design process produces itself a large amount of information, such as meeting minutes and deliverables (*on-going knowledge*). Tools for retrieving and coherently organizing documents are then necessary as complementary resources for a design environment (such as the ESA - CDF). We propose a model of an architecture whose aim is to provide the team of experts with such tools, in order to speed-up the design process and to improve the quality of the resulting project. The proposed system can be intended as a *virtual assistant* helping the team to use the *pre-existing* and *on-going knowledge* repositories.

In order to help the experts during the design process, the system should thus be able to interpret the information need of the team expressed implicitly in the on-going knowledge repositories or explicitly through direct queries by the experts. It should be then able to satisfy these needs extracting the required information from the pre-existing knowledge repositories. IR and NLP (such as syntactic parsing and information extraction) are the most promising technologies to carry out these activities. Moreover, the system could provide a way to model and express in a *design process ontology* the overall relevant knowledge shared by the experts . Such a formal ontological *conceptualization* has two main goals: to represent how the project contributed to the systematic representation of the knowledge about the specific domain of interest, and to support a useful indexing of the documentation produced and gathered during the design process. Finally, as an additional feature, the system could offer the possibility of understanding the common "jargon" and terminology used in the design process, fixing it in the *design process ontology*. Indeed, it is plausible that some new concepts arise during the design process and assume a status of shared concepts, expressed through their linguistic expressions, that is *terms*.

The technological scenario for the information access framework is a *virtual assistant* as depicted in Fig.1. In the overall architecture it is envisioned a *proactive* system, that "listens" at the dialogues going on among the project participants (through the minutes of the meetings, for example) and extracts information needs, later on used to query information access systems able to retrieve documents where they can be satisfied. Once selected as relevant by users, retrieved documents contribute to the definition of the *design process ontology,* that embodies the knowledge relevant for the design project.

The overall system could result in facilitating: the access to the project related documentation and external information, the definition of terminology and knowledge involved in the process (through the ontology of the mission), the creation of a central view of the knowledge stored in the project related documentation using the proposed terminology. Such a system could be realized with technologies ranging from Information Retrieval engines, to knowledge based systems using complex natural language models. Either generic linguistic (such as WordNet [10]) or specific domain semantic knowledge can be used to empower document clustering and to interpret ambiguous and unknown terms. In the framework of the SHUMI project, a modular architecture able to satisfy all users needs has been defined, while allowing to reach final results at different levels of automation. It is possible to set up several different architectures where more functionalities can be added, starting from a "core" system, composed by an Information Retrieval engine plus the Document Clusterer.

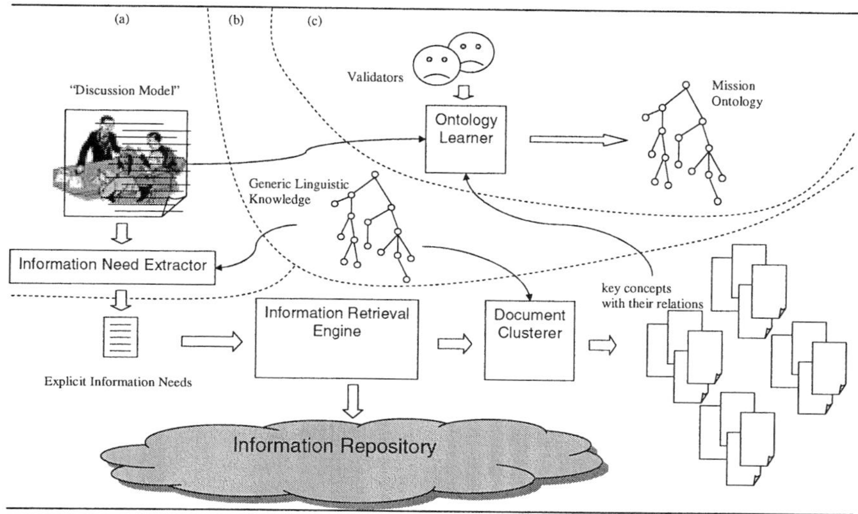

Fig. 1. A complete solution for an Automatic Assistant

Additional capabilities define more complex systems *((a),(b),(c))*:

- the system *(a)* behaves as an "active" information access system, "following" the conversation among experts and extracting *implicit* information needs (Sec. 2.2);
- the system *(b)* becomes more robust for lexical variations by using generic linguistic knowledge bases such as WordNet [10] (Sec. 2.3);
- the system *(c)* could acquire an explicit model of the knowledge embodied in processed documents as well as produced by the process. This explicit knowledge model is what has been called the design process ontology. It represents the memory the system has about the structure of the mission (Sec. 2.4).

All the linguistic processes carried out to implement the system are supported by an underlying modular syntactic parser (*Chaos*, [2]).

2 Architecture Components

In the following sections we describe existing technologies that could be integrated to implement the different proposed architectures.

2.1 Information Retrieval and Clustering (IR&C)

The "core" of the proposed architecture, as described in the previous section, is based on both an IR engine and an automatic cluster components (IR&C).

Clustering results of a given query is often seen as a way to better publish documents retrieved by an information retrieval engine, driving users to the relevant documents by using indexing techniques.

Clustering algorithms as well as information retrieval methods are generally based on a vector space model, where documents are represented in the bag-of-word fashion. Nothing prohibits to use more relevant, i.e. more readable, features, such as the one we propose in [11], where features like terms and simple relations (verb-object and verb-subject pairs) are used to represent document content. Due to modular approach in architectural design, our technology for IR&C may be substitute by other tools accessible on the market (commercial information retrieval engine with clustering capabilities as Vivisimo ©, RealTerm and e-Knowledge Portal™). As it is a very active area in information retrieval research [17], several products have been produced as a follow-up.

2.2 "Active" Information Access System

Aim of the "active" system is to follow the conversation in a project session (through the use of a Speech Recognizer module) and to "extract" an *implicit information need*, that will be in turn used to query and enhance the information retrieval core system.

As carrying out directly all these activities using NLP state of the art technologies still is a challenge to be faced, the basic idea is not to produce a complex information need extractor but a simple model taking advantages from stable technologies. Meanwhile, instead of a speech recognition module to produce minutes of the meeting, we can start from a manually provided version. The meeting minute is then used to feed an *Information Need Extractor* module able to extract the *implicit information needs*. A criterion to model how an implicit information need is expressed may be to investigate and give information on things and ideas where the communication fails, i.e. a concept that is not understood by two or more people in the same way. Repeated *terms* may suggest that a disagreement exists as the underlying concept is not shared. This may be an easy way to decide a sort of list of candidates to be searched. The Information Need Extractor can be thus intended as a simple module that, relying on a terminological repository is able to find the most frequent terms in the minutes and to query the IR&C system. Moreover, it should be able to enrich the repository with new terminological expressions contained in the minutes, using ad hoc methodologies, as described in Sec. 3.

As an example, imagine that during the meeting the experts are discussing about different option in building a lunch vehicle. From the automatic minute produced by the speech recognition module frequent terminological expressions could then emerge, such as "launch vehicle" and "mechanical parts". The Information Need Extractor should recognize these frequent terms and query the IR&C system using them as keywords. At the end of the process, the experts could thus be provided with relevant documents that could support their decisions, organized in topical clusters, such as "Test design" (containing documents on previous design of vehicles) and "Reusable Launch Vehicle" (documents on designing general purpose vehicles).

2.3 The Generic Linguistic Knowledge

Generic linguistic resources can be used to help the system in interpreting and disambiguating the content of both pre-existing and on-going knowledge repositories.

As natural language is rich of information and, as a consequence, very ambiguous, words may convey very different meaning while different words may be used to express the same concept. To tackle with this problem linguistic background knowledge resource such WordNet ([10]) can be used. These resources may be coupled with a graded activation of these relationships among words, that often take the form of probabilities [15], [6]. The use of the linguistic knowledge is particularly useful in the following phase of creating and enriching the domain ontology, as described in the next section.

2.4 The *Design Process* Ontology

As a further relevant step, the architecture can be enriched with a domain specific ontology, able to represent the knowledge emerging from the design process through pre-existing knowledge repositories and document retrieved by the IR module.

A few approaches have been proposed to learn automatically or semi-automatically a domain ontology from textual material (e.g. [1],[9]). Here, we propose a novel methodology, able to fix in a single structured and harmonized knowledge base different types of information: an upper-level ontology of domain concepts (*domain concept hierarchy, DCH*), an set of semantic relations among concepts (*relation type system, RTS*), aterminology extracted from the knowledge repositories (*terms*), a set of verbal relations among terms (*relational patterns*), and a generic linguistic knowledge (*linguistic knowledge base, LKB*).

The *DCH* formalizes the knowledge of the design process in a conceptual hierarchy (e.g. in SHUMI, concepts like *spacecraft* and *orbit* are here represented). The *RTS* hierarchy stores important *semantic relations* among concepts in the DCH (e.g. the event of a *spacecraft reaching an orbit*). *Terms* are defined as "surface linguistic forms of relevant domain concepts" ([12]): the terminology, automatically extracted from the knowledge repositories, thus represents a synthetic linguistic representation of domain concepts as embodied in documents. Terms are then linked to their corresponding concepts in the DCH (for example the term *Earth's_orbit* should be attached to the concept *orbit*). As terms are linguistic representation of concepts, in the same way *relational patterns* are (partially generalized) verbal relation prototypes that represent semantic relations in the RTS. For example the patterns *spacecraft gets close to Lunar orbit* (that can be a generalization of text fragments like *Shuttle gets close to Lunar orbit* and *Endeavour gets close to Lunar orbit*) should be associated to the semantic relation *spacecraft reaching an orbit*. As semantic relations are usually linguistically expressed through fragments governed by verbs, in our model they are supposed to be instantiated in text only by verbal patterns. The WordNet LKB represents a hierarchical linguistic repository of generic lexical knowledge: a link can be thus established between concepts in the DCH and synset in the LKB. For example the concept *spacecraft* can be associated with the synset *{spacecraft, ballistic capsule, space vehicle}*.

What we propose is an acquisition method that, starting from a pre-existing DCH and LKB , is able to derive the *linguistic interface* of the ontology (composed by the LKB, the relational patterns and the terms) suggesting linguistic patterns for known concepts and relations as well as to propose new concepts and new semantic relation. Knowledge textual repositories are the starting point of our analysis and are assumed to drive the discovery of new domain knowledge.

The overall learning process is organized as follows. Firstly terms and relational patterns are extracted from the corpus. Then, an analysis devoted to determine a concept hierarchy is applied to the more relevant concepts patterns extracted, making use of the pre-existing DCH. This activity generalizes the available evidence across the LKB and is called *Semantic Dictionary Building*. Domain concepts are also mapped into the general lexical database (we propose an automatic method, described in [5]). The resulting *concept hierarchy* can be successively used in the analysis and interpretation of relational patterns in the domain texts. This generalization allows to conceptually cluster the surface forms observed throughout the corpus. The derived generalizations can undergo the statistical processing during the *Domain Oriented Clustering* phase. The resulting generalized patterns can be organized according to their domain relevance score. The manual *Relation Type Definition* phase identifies a system of important domain concept relationships, which are in turn used for the manual or semi-supervised *Relational Pattern Classification* phase. The previously clustered relational patterns are thus mapped into the appropriate semantic relations. The result of this last activity is the set of linguistic rules for the matching and prediction of relations in RTS (*Linguistic Relation Interfaces*).

The ontological repository can be then used to support the design process, providing a central view of the overall knowledge. As a simple application, suppose for example that the team of experts is interested in finding all the textual material gathered so far (minutes and external documents previously queried via the IR&C) related to the modality of launch of spacecrafts. They could simply access the ontology to easily find the semantic relation "launching of spacecraft" navigating the RTS hierarchy. They would then retrieve all the relational patterns and the terms linked to the semantic relation and finally obtain the documents in which the patterns and the terms have been found.

3 Extracting Terms and Relational Patterns

As stated above, one of the primary tasks in building the ontology is to extract terms and relational patterns. At the present we do the simplifying assumption that semantic relations are expressed in the text only through verbal fragments as it usually happens. *Terms*, defined as surface (linguistic) representations of domain key concepts, are automatically extracted from texts using NLP techniques supported by statistical measures. Many approaches to terminology extraction have been proposed in the literature, ranging from purely linguistic (e.g. [7]) to purely statistical (e.g. [16]). Usually, mixed approach are the most reliable and used (e.g. [8], [12]): *candidate terms* are extracted from text as noun phrases having particular syntactic structure (e.g. *adjective+noun*, *noun+noun*) and then ordered according to a specific statistical measure that is supposed to capture the notion of *termhood* (the degree of reliability with which a text fragment is supposed to be a term). In our architecture a mixed approach has been chosen, mixing linguistic filters with a measure (frequency) that seems to capture the notion of termhood, according to different studies (e.g.[8],[14]) where a comparative analysis over different measures have been done.

Relational patterns are generalized forms of lexical knowledge that represent a sort of normalization of one or more actual textual *sentences*. In particular they are verb phrases, i.e., semantically generalized lexical fragments of text governed by a verb, representing the syntactic expressions of relational concepts. As for terms, also relational pattern extraction is carried out using a mix of linguistic and statistical methods [3]. In order to feed the ontology, once automatically extracted from the corpus, terms and relational patterns have to be validate by human experts.

3.1 Terminology and Relational Patterns Extraction

The architecture of our *Term Extractor*, includes the modules hereafter described.

A **pre-processing module** takes as input the corpus documents in textual format, converting them into XML files readable by the syntactic parser, checking for possible corrections and adaptations. The **parsing module** invokes Chaos, a robust and modular parser architecture developed at the AI laboratory of Roma Tor Vergata University [2]. The **terminology extraction module** extracts *admissible surface forms* from the previously parsed text: specific syntactic rules are used to select candidates, identifying sequences of words with specific syntactic properties: for instance, syntactic sequences like *JJ NN* (an adjective followed by a singular common noun, as *"lunar mission"*) and *NN NNP* (singular common noun followed by a plural common noun, as *"spacecraft projects"*) are retained as possible surface forms. Finally, the **terminology sorting module** sorts by relevance the list of previously produced candidates. Relevance is evaluated as the frequency with which each form has been met in the corpus. In fact, while many statistical measures have been proposed in the literature to estimate term importance (Mutual Information, T-score, TfIdf, etc.), frequency has been demonstrated in several frameworks to be a good approximated measure to express term relevance, as underlined in [8] and [14]. The list of produced forms is the *candidate* terminology, as the set of candidate terms that still needs a manual validation by a human expert.

In our framework, each term can be a simple sequence of words (e.g. *"spacecraft_mission"*) or a semantically generalized form. In the latter case the candidate term is formed by words and *Named Entities* (NE) (semantic generalizations representing important entities of a specific domain, such as people or organizations). As an example the candidate term *"entity#ne#_mission"* indicates a mission of a generic *entity*, that is an organization, a person or a specific object (e.g. *"ESA mission"*).

Relational patterns are extracted from text using a strategy similar to the one adopted for terms. The *Relation Extraction* extracts surface forms by using as background knowledge the terms extracted by the Term Extractor, since relational patterns are intended as relations among terms. An architecture similar to the Terminology Extractor is needed: corpus syntactic analysis is carried out to extract forms of interest.

The **relational pattern extraction module** analyses the parsed text produced by the parsing modules and extracts all verb phrases (text fragments): a list of *sentences* is thus produced, each of which is represented by the governing verb and its arguments. For each argument its lexical form and its syntactic role is indicated (for example *approach((SUBJ, the spacecraft), (OBJ,the orbit),(IN,ten minutes))*). The **relational pattern sorting module**, taking as input the corpus sentences, by first generalizes them into relational patterns, then ranks the patterns. The strategy we adopted for the generalization step is fully described in [3]. Once surface forms are produced, they are ranked accordingly to their frequency (calculated as the sum of the frequency of appearance of its corresponding sentences in the corpus). Candidate relational patterns are then validated by a human expert. An example of relational pattern that generalizes the above sentence, could be *approach((SUBJ, spacecraft), (OBJ,orbit))*.

It must be noticed that, as in the case of terms, NE are used in the extraction of relational patterns, producing pattern like *approach((SUBJ, mission#ne#), (OBJ,orbit))*, where *mission#ne#* represents the entity class of spacecraft missions. The pattern thus generalizes all the sentences which have "approach" as verb, "orbit" as object and any spacecraft mission as subject (i.e. "Mariner", "Voyager" etc.).

3.2 SHUMI Case Study: Preliminary Results

In order to estimate the validity of our term and relational pattern extraction methods, in the framework of the SHUMI project, we tested our architecture over a corpus of spacecraft design documents specifically provided by ESA, consisting in a collection of 32 ESA reports, tutorials and glossaries, forming 4,2 MB of textual material (about 673.000 words), fairly in line with other experiments in term extraction, such as [8] (240.000 words) and [7] (1.200.000 words). Extracted terms and relational patterns have been manually validated by a pool of ESA experts.

58.267 candidate terms have been extracted from the ESA corpus, among which 7821 (14%) have been retained as useful by the experts. Out of the 58.267 candidates, 4820 appear inside the corpus more than five times, with an accuracy of 38% (1814 terms retained). As the accuracy rises from 14% to 38%, a frequency of five can be thus empirically considered as a good threshold to automatically separate interesting term from spurious ones.

As outlined in [8] the most interesting and frequent terms are those composed by two *main items* (i.e., counting only meaningful words, such as noun, adjectives and adverbs): indeed, in our experiment roughly 60% of retained terms are 2-words. A list of the 10 *most relevant* terms (that is with highest frequency and retained by the experts) and a list of the 10 2-words most relevant terms is reported in Fig.2 (where entity#ne# is a generic NE standing for persons, companies and organizations), together with the list of 2-words non generalized most relevant terms (without NE). Terms as *"solar wind"* and *"magnetic field"* represent important concepts for an envisioned ontology for spacecraft design: those terms are in fact a useful hint both to identify concepts to insert into the ontology and to model the ontology itself.

For what concerns relational patterns, the system extracted 110.688 forms, among which the 21% has been retained by the experts (a quite good accuracy considering that the procedure of patterns extraction is affected by the problem of *overgeneration*,

Requirement	entity#ne#_system	application_datum
System	application_datum	magnetic_field
spacecraft	entity#ne#_packet	solar_wind
datum	entity#ne#_requirement	technical_requirement
test	entity#ne#_engineering	test_level
time	entity#ne#_state	source_packets
orbit	magnetic_field	source_datum
process	entity#ne#_model	launch_vehicle
operation	solar_wind	mechanical_part
design	entity#ne#_spacecraft	mission_phase

Fig. 2. Ten most relevant terms (left), ten most relevant *2-words* terms (center) and most relevant not generalized *2-words* terms (right)

that is, each verb sentence met in the corpus creates several related surface forms, some of which can be sometimes too general to be considered interesting). Fig.3 shows the most relevant (i.e. frequent) patterns.

```
perform((SUBJ,test))
conform((TO,requirement))
meet((DIROBJ,requirement))
conform((SUBJ,null),(TO,requirement))
do((SUBJ,service))
conduct((SUBJ,test))
conform((DIROBJ,null),(TO,'space_organization#ne#'))
conform((TO,'space_organization#ne#'))
conform((DIROBJ,null),(DIROBJ2,null),(TO,'space_organization#ne#'))
perform((SUBJ,analysis))
```

Fig. 3. Ten most relevant relational patterns validated by the experts

As it can be inferred from previous table, most of the surface forms retained by the experts are governed by verbs whose driven semantic *meaning in phrases* usually directly refers to events regarding planning and design. That is, these verbs, used in specific context (i.e. spacecraft design) assume a particular meaning. For example, the verb "meet", that in general can assume many senses and semantic values (10 according to *The Concise Oxford Dictionary*), in the analyzed spacecraft design context assumes a specific semantic value. This "sense restriction" has two important implications in the overall automatic process. From one side it underlies the importance of surface forms in order to build a correct DCH (it emerges how verbs behave either semantically or syntactically in specific domains). Moreover, verb senses a sort of *verb sense disambiguation* is automatically carried out.

4 Further Improvements

At the moment we are focusing our major efforts in modeling and implementing the ontology building process. We are trying to develop a framework in which semi-automatic techniques cooperate in learning the domain ontology using linguistic and semantic approaches (see [5]). The relational pattern semantic clustering activity is also a challenging issue we are still exploring, using Machine Learning techniques based on linguistic and semantic features ([4]). Techniques to cut down the need for human support is also an important point: so far, domain experts are in fact requested to validated terms and relational patters and to help in building at least the top levels of the DCH and RTS hierarchies. While the latter task is an unavoidable and "one time" step, the former is highly time consuming, as it involves a vast amount of data. We are thus developing interactive tools able to support and speed up validation.

References

1. Agirre, E., Ansa, O., Hovy, E., and Martinez, D. Enriching very large ontologies using the WWW. In: Proceedings of the Workshop on Ontology Construction of ECAI-00 (2000)
2. Basili, R., Pazienza, M.T., Zanzotto, F.M.: Customizable modular lexicalized parsing. In: Proc. of the 6th International Workshop on Parsing Technology (2000)
3. Basili, R., Pazienza, M.T., Zanzotto, F.M.: Learning IE patterns: a terminology extraction perspective. In: Workshop of Event Modelling for Multilingual Document Linking at LREC 2002, Canary Islands, Spain (2002)
4. Basili, R., Pazienza, M.T., Zanzotto, F.M.: Exploiting the feature vector model for learning linguistic representations of relational concepts. In: Workshop on Adaptive Text Extraction and Mining (ATEM 2003). Cavtat, Croatia (2003)
5. Basili,R., Vindigni, M., Zanzotto, F.M.: Integrating ontological and linguistic knowledge for Conceptual Information Extraction Web Intelligence (WI 2003) Halifax, Canada (2003)
6. Basili, R., Cammisa, M., Zanzotto, F.M.: A semantic similarity measure for unsupervised semantic disambiguation. In: Proceedings of the Language, Resources and Evaluation LREC 2004 Conference, Lisbon, Portugal (2004)
7. Bourigault, D.: Surface grammatical analysis for the extraction of terminological noun phrases. In: Proceedings of the Fifteenth International Conference on Computational Linguistics (1992) 977-981
8. Daille, B. : Approach mixte pour l'extraction de termilogie: statistique lexicale et filters linguistiques. PhD Thesis, C2V, TALANA, Universitè Paris VII (1994)
9. Hahn, U., Schnattinger, K.: Towards text knowledge engineering. In Proceedings of AAAI '98 / IAAI '98, Madison, Wisco (1998)
10. 10.Miller, G.A.: WordNet: A lexical Database for English. In: Communication of the ACM, 38(11) (1995) 39-41
11. 11.Moschitti, A., Zanzotto, F.M.: A robust summarization system to explain document categorization. In: Proceedings of ROMAND2002, Frascati, Italy July (2002)
12. 12.Pazienza, M.T.: A domain specific terminology extraction system. In: International Journal of Terminology. Benjamin Ed., Vol.5.2 (1999) 183-201
13. 13.Pazienza, M.T., Pennacchiotti, M., Vindigni, M., Zanzotto, F.M.: Shumi, Support To Human Machine Interaction. Technical Report. ESA-ESTEC cont.18149/04/NL/MV (2004)
14. 14.Pazienza, M.T., Pennacchiotti, M., Zanzotto F.M.: Terminology extraction: an analysis of linguistic and statistical approaches. In Knowledge Mining, Springer Verlag, 2005
15. 15.Resnik, P.: Using Information Content to Evaluate Semantic Similarity in a Taxonomy. In: Proceedings of the 14th International Joint Conference on Artificial Intelligence (1995)
16. 16.Salton, G., Yang, C.S., Yu, C.T.: A Theory of term importance in automatic text analysis. In: Journal of the American Society for Information Science 26(1) (1972) 33-44
17. 17.Wu,W., Xiong, H., Shekhar, S.: Clustering and Information Retrieval. Kluwer Academic Publishers, Boston (2003)

Automatic Word Spacing in Korean for Small Memory Devices

Seong-Bae Park, Eun-Kyung Lee, and Yoon-Shik Tae

Department of Computer Engineering,
Kyungpook National University,
702-701 Daegu, Korea
{sbpark, eklee, ystae}@sejong.knu.ac.kr

Abstract. Automatic word spacing will be a very useful tool in a SMS (simple message service) , if it can be commercially served. However, the problems of implementing it in the devices such as mobile phones are small memory and low computing power of the devices. To tackle these problems, this paper proposes a combined model of rule-based learning and memory-based learning. According to the experimental results, the model shows higher accuracy than rule-based learning or memory-based learning alone. In addition, the generated rules are so small and simple that the proposed model is appropriate for small memory devices.

1 Introduction

Many languages have their own word spacing rules for better readability and comprehension of the texts written by the languages. As online texts are getting massive, it gets easier and easier to find the texts with broken word spaces. What is worse, the writers sometimes break the rules on purpose. Thus, many text-based computer applications such as word processors have not only a spell-correcting tool but also an automatic word spacing tool. These two tools have a common feature that they require a large scale dictionary in their working.

Most digital devices with large memory such as personal computers are of no problem with the idea using a large scale dictionary. However, the idea is a practical obstacle in implementing an automatic word spacing tool for small memory devices such as mobile phones. Even though the mobile phones have more and more memory nowadays, they usually do not have memory enough to load a dictionary.

Nevertheless, since the SMS (Short Message Service) gets more and more important in the mobile environments, the effectiveness and necessity of an automatic word spacing tool are being increased. Especially in Korean mobile phone environments, there are major reasons for needs of the tool. First, the message length is limited to 80 bytes due to the practical reasons. As most Korean words have 2 or 3 syllables on average, the space usually takes 20$\sim$27 syllables among 80 bytes. Thus, it could occupy about 30 percent of total messages. That is, we could send more messages up to 30 percent without spaces. The second reason

M. Ali and F. Esposito (Eds.): IEA/AIE 2005, LNAI 3533, pp. 249–258, 2005.

is the difficulty of inputting syllables. In order to send a Korean message with a current mobile phone, a special button for producing a space must be pressed at each end of words. This inconvenience can be avoided by ignoring spaces.

To recover a message without a space, a device has to have word spacing ability. That is, it must decompose a message into words without a large scale dictionary in the mobile environments. When a sentence consists of n syllables, there could be theoretically 2^{n-1} kinds of decompositions. The easiest way to decompose a message is to take the most plausible one among these 2^{n-1} decompositions.

For this purpose, this paper proposes a combined model of two machine learning methods: *rule-based learning* and *memory-based learning*. To reduce the size of learning memory, this model is basically based on the rule-based learning. However, the performance of the rule-based learning is relatively low compared with other supervised machine learning algorithms. In our previous work, it is shown that a combination of rules and memory-based learning achieves high accuracy [9]. Thus, the rules trained are reinforced by the memory-based learning in the proposed model.

The rest of this paper is organized as follows. Section 2 surveys the previous work on automatic word spacing. Section 3 describes the proposed the *CORAM algorithm*, the combined model of rule-based learning and memory-based learning, and Section 4 presents the experimental results. Finally, section 5 draws conclusions.

2 Previous Work

There are basically two kinds of approaches to automatic word spacing in Korean: *analytic approach* and *statistical approach* [6]. The analytic approach is based on the results of morphological analysis. Kim et al. distinguished each word by the morphemic information of postpositions and endings [7], while Kang used the fundamental morphological analysis techniques in word spacing [5]. The main drawbacks of analytic approach is that (i) the analytic step is very complex, (ii) it is expensive to construct and maintain the analytic knowledge, and (iii) in many cases it requires a morphological analyzer. When a morphological analyzer is used for automatic word spacing, the frequent backtracking and error propagation must be gotten rid of. In addition, the morphological analyzer has problems in handling the unknown words unregistered in the dictionary.

In the other hand, the statistical approach extracts from corpora the probability that a space is put between two syllables. Since this approach can obtain the necessary information automatically, it does require neither the linguistic knowledge on syllable composition nor costs for knowledge construction and maintenance. In addition, the fact that it does not use a morphological analyzer produces solid results even for unknown words. Many previous studies using corpora are based on *bigram* information. According to Kang [6], the number of syllables that are used often in modern Korean is about 10^4, which implies that the number of bigrams reaches 10^8 ($= 10^4 \times 10^4$). Assuming that the frequency of each bigram is represented by two bytes, it requires 200 MBytes. Thus, it it impractical to load this information into memory in a small memory device. If *trigrams* are adopted rather than bigrams for higher accuracy, the memory requirement gets intractable.

To tackle this limit, machine learning methods have been also used in previous studies. Lee et al. adopted a *hidden Markov model* [8] as they thought that the automatic word spacing is locally equivalent to a part-of-speech tagging. This method considers the sequence of syllables and their contexts. As a result, it gives the state-of-the-art performance in this task. However, since it has a great number of states and transitions, it is not a suitable model for small memory devices, either.

3 Combining of Rule-Based Learning and Memory-Based Learning

3.1 Combined Model

Assume that a sentence S composed of n syllables,

$$S = w_1, w_2, \ldots, w_n$$

is given. Then, the word spacing can be considered to be a binary classification task from a viewpoint of machine learning. If we have a classifier $f(\Theta)$ parameterized by Θ, then it is formulated as

$$s_i^* = \underset{s \in \{split, nonsplit\}}{\arg\max} \quad (s = f(w_i, h_i)), \tag{1}$$

where h_i is a context of a syllable w_i.

This paper proposes a combined model of rule-based learning and memory-based learning for $f(\Theta)$ (see Figure 1). This model is basically based on the rule base designed by a rule-learning algorithm, and its decision is verified by the memory-based classifier. If the performance of the rules is high enough to trust their decisions, it is of no problem to use the rules only. However, the main drawback of the current rule learning algorithms is their low performance [10]. In general, the rule-based learning algorithms focus on the comprehensibility, and they have tendency to give lower performance than other supervised learning algorithms. Memory-based learning is thus adopted to handle the errors of the rules. In the training phase, each sentence is analyzed by the rules trained by a rule learning algorithm and its classification results are compared with the true labels $s \in \{split, nonsplit\}$. *split* implies that a space must be put after w_i, and *nonsplit* that w_i has to be concatenated with w_{i-1}. In cases of misclassification, the error is stored in the *error case library* with its true label. Since this error case library accumulates only the exceptions of the rules, the number of instances stored is small if the rules are general and accurate enough to represent the instance space well.

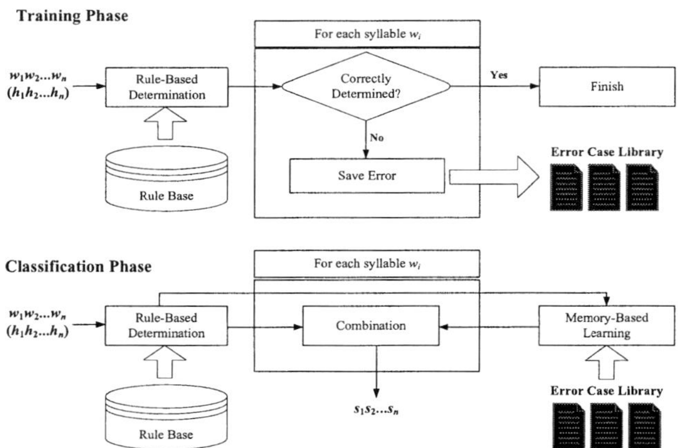

Fig. 1. The combined model of rule-based learning and memory-based learning

The classification phase determines the spacing s_i of each unknown syllable w_i given with its context h_i. First, it tries to determine s_i with the rules. Then, it is checked whether the current context h_i is an exception of the rules. This is because if h_i is an exception of the rules, the classification result of the rules is untrustworthy. If it is, the classification made by the rules is discarded and then is determined again by the memory-based classifier trained with the error case library. The reasons why memory-based classifier is used as an alternative classifier of the rules are that it has an ability to distinguish whether h_i is an exception of the rules and that its decisions are reliable even though it is trained with a small number of examples.

3.2 Training and Combining Algorithms

Figure 2 shows the training phase of the model. The first step is to train the rules with a training set `data`. For this purpose, the model uses `MODIFIED-IREP`, a modified version of the IREP [4]. The only difference between `MODIFIED-IREP` and the IREP is that `MODIFIED-IREP` does not have a rule pruning step. That is, in `MODIFIED-IREP`, the rules only grow and are never simplified. The role of the rule pruning is played by the memory-based classifier explained later. In the next step, the examples that are uncovered by `MODIFIED-IREP` are gathered into `ErrCaseLibrary`, and the memory-based learner is trained with them.

Since both rules and memory-based learning are used, it is important to determine when to apply rules and when to apply memory-based classifier. To make this decision, a threshold θ is used. The optimal value for θ is found by the following procedure. Assume that we have an independent held-out data set `HeldOutData`. Various value for θ is applied to the classification function described in Figure 3. The optimal value for θ is the one that outputs the best performance over `HeldOutData`.

```
function Support(RuleSet, data)
begin
   Err := φ
   for each (⟨w_i, h_i⟩, s_i) ∈ data do
      if RuleSet(⟨w_i, h_i⟩) ≠ s_i then
         Add (⟨w_i, h_i⟩, s_i) into ErrCaseLibrary.
      endif
   endfor
   MBL := Memory-Based-Learning(ErrCaseLibrary)
   return MBL
end

function Training-Phase(data)
begin
   RuleSet := MODIFIED-IREP(data)
   MBL := Support(RuleSet, data)
   θ := Get-Threshold-MBL(RuleSet, MBL, HeldOutData)
   return RuleSet + MBL + θ
end
```

Fig. 2. The training algorithm of the proposed combined model. s_i is the true label for $\langle w_i, h_i \rangle$

```
function Classify(x, θ, RuleSet, MBL)
begin
   s := RuleSet(x)
   y := the nearest instance of x in ErrCaseLibrary.
   if D(x, y) ≤ θ then
      s := MBL(x)
   endif
   return s
end
```

Fig. 3. The classification algorithm of the proposed combined model

Figure 3 depicts the classification phase of the proposed model. In `Classify`, $\mathbf{y}$ is the most similar to the given instance $\mathbf{x} = \langle x_1, \ldots, x_m \rangle$. To find $\mathbf{y}$, the similarity between $\mathbf{x}$ and all examples $\mathbf{y}_i$ in `ErrCaseLibrary` is computed using a *distance metric*, $D(\mathbf{x}, \mathbf{y}_i)$. That is, $\mathbf{y} = \underset{\mathbf{y}_i \in \texttt{ErrCaseLibrary}}{\arg\min} D(\mathbf{x}, \mathbf{y}_i)$. The distance from $\mathbf{x}$ and $\mathbf{y}_i$, $D(\mathbf{x}, \mathbf{y}_i)$ is defined to be

$$D(\mathbf{x}, \mathbf{y}_i) \equiv \sum_{j=1}^{m} \alpha_j \delta(x_j, y_{ij}), \tag{2}$$

where α_j is the weight of the j-th attribute and

$$\delta(x_j, y_j) = \begin{cases} 0 \text{ if } x_j = y_j, \\ 1 \text{ if } x_j \neq y_j. \end{cases}$$

When α_j is determined by *information gain*, the k-NN algorithm with this metric is called *IB1-IG* [3]. All the experiments performed by memory-based learning in this paper are done with IB1-IG.

If $\mathbf{x}$ and $\mathbf{y}$ are similar enough, $\mathbf{x}$ is considered to be an exception of the rules. Since all the instances in `ErrCaseLibrary` are the ones with which the rules

```
function IREP(data)
begin
  RuleSet := φ
  while ∃ positive examples ∈ data do
    Split data into grow and prune.
    rule := GrowRule(grow)
    rule := PruneRule(prune)
    Add rule to RuleSet.
    Remove examples covered by rule from data.
    if Accuracy(rule) ≤ P/(P+N) then
      return RuleSet
    endif
  endwhile
  return RuleSet
end
```

Fig. 4. The IREP algorithm. P is the number of positive examples in `data` and N is that of negative examples

make an error, small $D(\mathbf{x}, \mathbf{y})$ implies that $\mathbf{x}$ is highly possible to be an exception of the rules. Thus, if $D(\mathbf{x}, \mathbf{y})$ is smaller than the predefined threshold θ, the rules should not be applied. Since the memory-based learning (`MBL`) is trained with the instances in `ErrCaseLibrary`, it should be applied in this case instead of the rules.

As θ is a threshold value for $D(\mathbf{x}, \mathbf{y})$, $0 \leq \theta \leq \beta$ is always satisfied where $\beta \equiv \sum_{j=1}^{m} \alpha_j$. When $\theta = \beta$, the rules are always ignored. In this case, the generalization is done by only memory-based classifier trained with the errors of the rules. Thus, it will show low performance due to data sparseness. In contrast, only the rules are applied when $\theta = 0$. In this case, the performance of the proposed model is equivalent to that of the rules.

3.3 Rule-Based Learning

The performance of the proposed model depends basically on the rules. In order to construct high-quality rules, at least one human expert who have profound knowledge about the target task is needed. However, it is very expensive to work with such an expert. Thus, in machine learning community, a number of methods have been proposed that learn the rules from data. Clark and Niblett proposed CN2 program that uses the general-to-specific beam search [1], and Fürnkranz and Widmar proposed the IREP algorithm [4].

The rule-learning step of the proposed model is based on the IREP algorithm shown in Figure 4. This algorithm consists of two greedy functions: `GrowRule` and `PruneRule`. The first greedy function `GrowRule` constructs a rule at a time, and then removes from the training set all examples covered by the newly generated rule. The principle used in constructing a rule is that more positive examples and less negative examples should be covered by the rule. For this purpose, it partitions given a training set `data` into two subsets: `grow` and `prune`. In general, `grow` is two-thirds of `data`, and `prune` is one-third. `grow` is used to construct a rule in `GrowRule`, and `prune` is used to simplify it in `PruneRule`.

The function `GrowRule` generates a rule by repeatedly adding conditions to rule r_0 with an empty antecedent. In each i-th stage, a more specialized rule r_{i+1}

is made by adding single condition to r_i. The added condition in constructing r_{i+1} is the one with the largest information gain relative to r_i. The conditions are added until the information gain becomes 0.

In the second step PruneRule, the rule constructed by GrowRule is simplified again by dropping the conditions one by one. In PruneRule, the condition that maximizes the function $f(r_{i+1}) = \frac{T_{i+1}^{+} - T_{i+1}^{-}}{T_{i+1}^{+} + T_{i+1}^{-}}$ is removed. Here, T_i^+ and T_i^- are the number of positive and negative examples covered by r_i accordingly. After simplifying the rule, the pruned rule is added to RuleSet, and all examples covered by it are removed from data.

PruneRule plays a role of a validation step in IREP. That is, it avoids too specific rule being made. This role is not needed in the proposed model, since the errors made by too specific rules are accumulated in the error case library and then treated by the memory-based classifier separately. Thus, the function MODIFIED-IREP in Figure 2 is equivalent to IREP except that it does not have the PruneRule function.

4 Experiments

4.1 Data Set

There is no standard and publicly available dialogue corpus for Korean. Thus, in this paper, TV news scripts of three Korean broadcasting stations (KBS, MBC, and SBS) are used as a data set. This data set is a part of *Korean Information Base* distributed by KAIST KORTERM[1]. The reason why TV news scripts are chosen for experiments is that their style is far nearer to a colloquial style than that of newspaper articles which are widely available in Korea, even though they are not true dialogues.

Table 1. Statistics on a data set

	No. of Words	No. of Examples
Training (KBS + SBS)	56,200	234,004
Held-Out (KBS + SBS)	14,047	58,614
Test (MBC)	24,128	91,250

Table 1 summarizes the simple statistics on the data set. The news scripts of KBS and SBS are used to train the proposed model, while those of MBC are used as a *test set*. Since the proposed model needs a held-out set separated from the training set, 80% of the KBS and SBS news scripts are used as a *training set* and the remaining 20% are used as a *held-out set*. The number of words in the training set is 56,200, that of the held-out set is 14,047, and that of the test set is 24,128.

[1] http://www.korterm.org

Table 2. The comparison of the proposed model with various ML algorithms

Data Set	Accuracy
C4.5	92.2%
TiMBL	90.6%
RIPPER	85.3%
CORAM	**96.8%**

As a context information in determining the class of s_i of a syllable w_i in Equation (1), four left syllables and four right syllables are used. That is, $h_i = \{w_{i-4}, w_{i-3}, w_{i-2}, w_{i-1}, w_{i+1}, w_{i+2}, w_{i+3}, w_{i+4}\}$. Since a word are composed of several syllables in general, the number of examples used is far more than that of the words. The number of training examples is 234,004, while those of held-out and test examples are 58,614 and 91,250 respectively. And, the number of syllables used is just 1,284.

4.2 Experimental Results

In order to evaluate the performance of the proposed model, we compare it with RIPPER [2], C4.5 [11], and TiMBL [3]. RIPPER is a rule-based learning algorithm, C4.5 is a decision-tree learning algorithm, and TiMBL is a memory-based learning algorithm. Table 2 gives the experimental results. As stated above, the performance of rule-based learning algorithms is relatively low, while that of memory-based learning is relatively high. Therefore, RIPPER gives the lowest accuracy, and C4.5 and TiMBL have more than 90% of accuracy. However, the proposed model (**CORAM** in Table 2) shows 96.8% of accuracy. This is the best accuracy and is, on the average, higher than C4.5 by 4.6%, RIPPER by 11.5%, and TiMBL by 6.2%. Therefore, the proposed model shows higher performance than rule-based learning or memory-based learning alone.

How good is this accuracy? The number of *nonsplit* class in the test set is 67,122 among 91,250. Thus, the lower bound is 73.6% (= 67122/91250 · 100). As explained above, the proposed method consists of two learning algorithms. The accuracy of `MODIFIED-IREP` is 84.5%, and that of `MBL` is just 38.3%. However, the possibility that one of them predicts a correct class is 99.6%. That is, the upper bound is 99.6%. Therefore, $73.6 \leq Acc \leq 99.6$ should be met where Acc is the accuracy of the proposed model. As Acc is 96.8, it can be told that this is very close to the upper bound.

Why is the accuracy of `MBL` is so low although that of TiMBL is relatively high? The memory-based classifier, `MBL` in the proposed model is trained only with the error case library, `ErrCaseLibrary`. Since `MODIFIED-IREP` shows high accuracy, the number of errors made by it is just 36,270. These errors are the exceptions of the rules, and they do not cover all instance space. Thus, the hypothesis made by memory-based learning using these errors is not the general one, even though that made by TiMBL is very general.

Figure 5 shows some example rules learned by `MODIFIED-IREP`. Even though nine syllables (one for w_i and eight for h_i) are considered at each example,

```
IF w_{i-1} = "da" AND w_i = punctuation mark THEN class = split.
IF w_i = "ul" THEN class = split.
IF w_i = "nun" THEN class = split.
IF w_i = "yi" AND w_{i+1} = number THEN class = split.
IF w_i = "yi" AND w_{i-3} = "han" THEN class = split.
⋮
DEFAULT class = nonsplit.
```

Fig. 5. Some example rules that are learned by MODIFIED-IREP

Table 3. The comparison of information gain distributions

Feature	Training Set	Error Case Library
w_{i-4}	0.053	0.023
w_{i-3}	0.076	0.034
w_{i-2}	0.106	0.047
w_{i-1}	0.175	0.116
w_i	0.365	0.381
w_{i+1}	0.195	0.207
w_{i+2}	0.109	0.089
w_{i+3}	0.063	0.051
w_{i+4}	0.033	0.035

the generated rules have just one or two antecedents. In addition, the number of rules is only 179. In comparison with MODIFIED-IREP, C4.5 generates more than three million rules as it is trained with syllable features. In a word, the processing of the unlabeled instances by the rules can be fast since the rules are simple and the number of them is small. Thus, the proposed model is suitable for the devices with small memory and low computing power. Moreover, since they are reinforced by the memory-based classifier, the proposed model is very accurate.

As an additional information, Table 3 shows the information gain of nine syllables for the training set and the error case library. In accordance with the intuition, w_i is the most important syllable in determining s_i for both sets. The second most important syllable is w_{i+1}. And, the least important syllable is w_{i+4} for the training set and w_{i-4} for the error case library. In conclusion, the more distant from w_i the syllable gets, the less important in determining s_i it is.

5 Conclusions

In this paper we have proposed a combined model of rule-based learning and memory-based learning for automatic word spacing in small memory devices. It first learns the rules, and then memory-based learning is performed with the errors of the trained rules. In classification, it is basically based on the rules, and its estimates are verified by a memory-based classifier. Since the memory-based learning is an efficient method to handle exceptional cases of the rules, it supports the rules by making decisions only for the exceptions of the rules. That is, the memory-based learning enhances the trained rules by efficiently handling their exceptions.

We have applied the proposed model to Korean word spacing. The experimental results on TV news scripts showed that it improves the accuracy of RIPPER by 11.5%, C4.5 by 4.6%, and TiMBL by 6.2%, where RIPPER and C4.5 are rule-based learning algorithms and TiMBL is a memory-based learning algorithm. Therefore, the proposed model is more efficient than rule-based learning or memory-based learning alone. We also showed that the rules by the proposed model is small and simple. It implies that the proposed model is appropriate for the devices with small memory and low computing power such as mobile phones.

Acknowledgements

This research was supported by Korea Research Foundation Grant (KRF-2004-003-D00365).

References

1. P. Clark and T. Niblett, "The CN2 Induction Algorithm," *Machine Learning*, Vol. 3, No. 1, pp. 261–284, 1989.
2. W. Cohen, "Fast Effective Rule Induction," In *Proceedings of the 12th International Conference on Mahcine Learning*, pp. 115–123, 1995.
3. W. Daelemans, J. Zavrel, K. Sloot, and A. Bosch, *TiMBL: Tilburg Memory Based Learner, version 4.1, Reference Guide*, ILK 01-04, Tilburg University, 2001.
4. J. Fürnkfranz and G. Widmar, "Incremental Reduced Error Pruning," In *Proceedings of the 11th International Conference on Machine Learning*, pp. 70–77, 1994.
5. S.-S. Kang, "Eojeol-Block Bidirectional Algorithm for Automatic Word Spacing of Hangul Sentences," *Journal of KISS*, Vol. 27, No. 4, pp. 441–447, 2000. (*in Korean*)
6. S.-S. Kang, "Improvement of Automatic Word Segmentation of Korean by Simplifying Syllable Bigram," In *Proceedings of the 15th Conference on Korean Language and Information Processing*, pp. 227–231, 2004. (*in Korean*)
7. K.-S. Kim, H.-J. Lee, and S.-J. Lee, "Three-Stage Spacing System for Korean in Sentence with No Word Boundaries," *Journal of KISS*, Vol. 25, No. 12, pp. 1838–1844, 1998. (*in Korean*)
8. D.-G. Lee, S.-Z. Lee, H.-C. Rim, and H.-S. Lim, "Automatic Word Spacing Using Hidden Markov Model for Refining Korean Text Corpora," In *Proceedings of the 3rd Workshop on Asian Language Resources and International Standardization*, pp.51–57, 2002.
9. S.-B. Park and B.-T. Zhang, "Text Chunking by Combining Hand-Crafted Rules and Memory-Based Learning," In *Proceedings of the 41st Annual Meeting of the Association for Computational Linguistics*, pp. 497–504, 2003.
10. S.-B. Park, J.-H. Chang, and B.-T. Zhang, "Korean Compound Noun Decomposition Using Syllabic Information Only," In *Proceedings of the 5th Annual Conference on Intelligent Text Processing and Computational Linguistics*, pp. 146–157, 2004.
11. R. Quinlan, *C4.5: Programs for Machine Learning*, Morgan Kaufmann Publisher, 1993.

Generating Personalized Tourist Map Descriptions

B. De Carolis, G. Cozzolongo, and S. Pizzutilo

Dipartimento di Informatica -Università di Bari
http://www.di.uniba.it/intint

Abstract. When visiting cities as tourists, most users intend to explore the area looking for interesting things to see or for information about places, events, and so on. An adaptive information system, in order to help the user choice, should provide contextual information presentation, information clustering and comparison presentation of objects of potential interest in the area where the user is located. To this aim, we developed a system able to generate personalized presentation of objects of interest, starting from an annotated city-map.

1 Introduction

User-tailored information presentation has been one of the main goals of the research on adaptive systems: features such as the user interests, background knowledge and preferences were considered to settle, at the same time, the information to be included in the message and its 'surface' realisation [1,2,3]. With the evolution of devices (PDA, mobile phones, car-computers, etc.), network connections (GSM, GPRS, UMTS, WLAN, Bluetooth, ...) and localization technologies (GPS) for interacting with information services, users can access to these services potentially everywhere and anytime[4]. In this case, the main goal of an adaptive information system is deliver targeted information to the users *when* they need them, *where* they need them and in a form that is suited to their *situational interests* and to the technological context (*how* they need the information).

In general, achieving this objective requires the following system's capabilities:

- accessing the description of the domain data in order to select objects of interest and use their representation for generating related information presentation;
- accessing the description of the current context in order to understand the situation in which the user is (location, activity, device, etc.);
- modelling the situational interests of the user in order to use these data to personalize the selection and presentation of information [5];
- generating information presentation accordingly [6,7].

In this paper, we present a solution to the personalization of information presentation that combines the use of XML annotation for domain knowledge representation, ***Mobile User Profiles*** (MUP) for managing contextualized user preferences and interests, a media-independent content planner and a context-sensitive surface generator.

In order to show how the system works, we will use the tourist domain as an example. Indeed, as mobile phones and other portable devices are becoming more advanced, tourism is one obvious application area. Tourism has been a popular area for

M. Ali and F. Esposito (Eds.): IEA/AIE 2005, LNAI 3533, pp. 259–268, 2005.

mobile information systems. In particular, the Lancaster GUIDE system [8], and other systems based on mobile devices [9,10] are examples of application in this field.

When people visit cities as tourists most users intend to explore the area and find interesting things to see or information about places, objects, events, and so on. According to [11] most of the times they do not make very detailed and specific plans "so that they can take advantage of changing circumstances" and, moreover, when choosing where to go and what to see they tend to "pick up an area with more than one potential facility". According to these findings, it would be useful to support the user choice with contextual information presentation, information clustering and comparison presentation of object of potential interest in the same area.

The paper is structured as follows: after a brief illustration of the system architecture, we focus on the description of the process of generating personalized description of places of interest using an annotated town-map. In particular, we describe the structure of the map annotation scheme, the role of the MUP and the generation steps necessary to produce a personalized map description. Finally, conclusions and future work are discussed in the last session.

2 System Architecture

Let's consider the following situation: "a user is traveling for business purposes, she is in the center of a town and requires information about a place using a personal mobile device. She wants to know what is going on in that area."

In this case, the user is "immersed" in the environment and she is presumed to look for "context-sensitive" information. One of the most common ways for tourists for requesting information about places of interests in a particular town is to use a map. Then integrating information provision with a graphical map of the place is one of the most used metaphors supporting this type of interaction. However, if this map is only a graphical representation of the town, it cannot be "explained" to the user by an automatic system. In order to generate targeted information about places of interest, the map has to be annotated so as to define a correspondence between graphical objects and metadata understandable by the system that has to generate the presentation of information. With this aim, we developed a system that, starting from an XML representation of domain knowledge, decides which information to provide and how to present it either after an explicit user request or proactively in presence of interesting objects, events and so on.

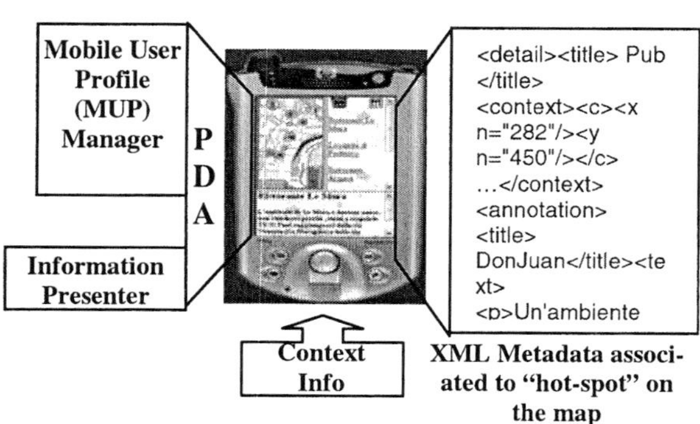

Fig. 1. Outline of the System

As outlined in Figure1, the system runs on a PDA and uses two other components: the Mobile User Profile (MUP) Manager and the Information Presenter. These components, given a metadata representation of a map, cooperates in establishing which information to present and the structure of the presentation according to the "user in context" features.

In this paper we will not discuss about information filtering, context detection and proactivity issues, but we will focus on the process of generating adaptive information presentation while interacting with the city-map. Let's see in more details which are the methods employed to implement the system.

2.1 Understanding the Map

Understanding a map means extracting and describing objects of particular interest with their descriptive features. Data annotation is a typical solution to achieve this objective. Since we do not use automatic image features extraction techniques, the description of the map components, their attributes and the relationships among them, is achieved using metadata.

In this case, the map image is annotated in a modality-independent way using a markup language and encapsulates tourist information in a XML structure. To build these metadata, we use a tool in Java (Inote [12]) that is available on line and provides a way of annotating images in a user-friendly way. Inote allows to attach textual annotations to a image and to store them in a XML file. Then, Inote's mark-up language is very general and may be applied to every kind of image. For instance, we have been using it for describing radiological images in another project [13].
With Inote it is possible to identify:

- a region of interest, a part of the image, called "<overlay>";
- each overlay may contain some objects of interest denoted as "<detail>" and
- each <detail> may have attributes;
- each attribute is denoted as "<annotation>", and may be given a name;
- a <text> may be associated with every annotation of every detail, in order to add the description of that attribute.

To tailor it to map description, we defined a parser able to interpret the tags according to the following ad hoc semantics (illustrated in Figure 2):

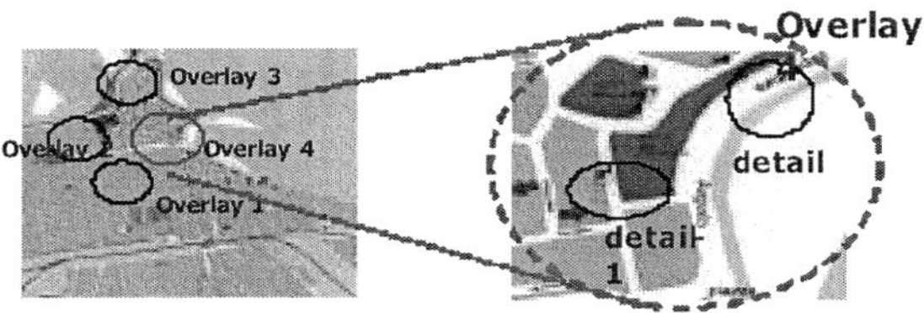

Fig. 2. Illustration of the Map Annotation Scheme

A map region has some "General Properties" that identify it: the name of the town, the described area, its coordinates, and so on. In this wide region it is possible to identify some areas of interest, these are denoted as overlays. The main information content of each overlay then consists in a list of details that correspond to the category of places of interest (eating places, art, nature, and so on); each place of interest is described by a set of attributes (type, position, etc.) denoted as "annotation" whose value is described by the "text" tag.

The following is an example of structure generated by Inote following this scheme:

```
<overlay><title>bari-zone1</title>
        <detail><title>eating<title>
                <annotation><title>type</title>
                <text>fast-food</text> </annotation>
                <annotation><title>name</title>
                <text>Bar Città Vecchia (da Cenzino)
                 </text> </annotation>
                <annotation><title>coordinates</title>
                <text>41°06'14.800"N 16°45'57.013"E </text>
                </annotation>
                <annotation><title>view</title> <text>historical center</text>
                </annotation>
                <annotation><title>wheelchair accessibility</title>
                <text>yes </text>
                </annotation>
   ...</detail></overlay>
```

2.2 Mobile User Profiles

The illustrated interaction scenario depicts a situation in which the user is interacting with the information system with a mobile device. Mobile personalization can be defined as the process of modeling contextual user-information which is then used to deliver appropriate content and services tailored to the user's needs. As far as user modelling is concerned, a mobile approach, in which the user "brings" always with her/himself the user model on an personal device, seems to be very promising in this interaction scenario [14]. It presents several advantages: the information about the user are always available, updated, and can be accessed in a wireless and quite transparent way, avoiding problems related to consistency of the model, since there is always one single profile per user.

Based on this idea, our user modeling component uses profiles that allows to:

- express context-dependent interests and preferences (i.e. "I like eating Chinese food when I'm abroad");
- allows to share its content with environments that can use it for personalization purposes following the semantic web vision [15].

Then, as far as **representation** is concerned, beside considering static long term user features (age, sex, job, general interests, and so on), it is necessary to handle information about more dynamic "user in context" features. Instead of defining a new a ontology and language for describing mobile user profiles, since this is not the main aim of our research, we decided to adopt UbisWorld [5] language as user model ontology of our user modeling component. In this way we have a unified language able to integrate user features and data with situational statements and privacy settings that better suited our need of supporting situated interaction. This language allows representing all concepts related to the user by mean of the UserOL ontology, to annotate these concepts with situational statements that may be transferred to an environment only if the owner user allows this according to privacy settings. An example of a situational statement is the following:

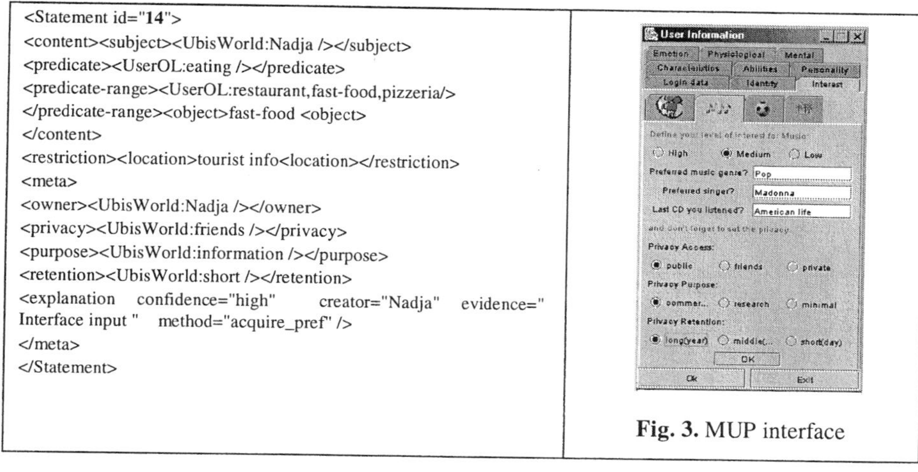

```
<Statement id="14">
<content><subject><UbisWorld:Nadja /></subject>
<predicate><UserOL:eating /></predicate>
<predicate-range><UserOL:restaurant,fast-food,pizzeria/>
</predicate-range><object>fast-food <object>
</content>
<restriction><location>tourist info<location></restriction>
<meta>
<owner><UbisWorld:Nadja /></owner>
<privacy><UbisWorld:friends /></privacy>
<purpose><UbisWorld:information /></purpose>
<retention><UbisWorld:short /></retention>
<explanation confidence="high" creator="Nadja" evidence="
Interface input " method="acquire_pref" />
</meta>
</Statement>
```


Fig. 3. MUP interface

User preferences, interests, etc. are collected in two ways:

- using a graphical interface (Figure 3) in which the user can explicitly insert her preferences and related privacy settings regarding particular domains,
- deriving other information (i.e. temporary interests) from user actions or from other knowledge bases (i.e. user schedules, agenda, etc. [16]).

User feedback and actions in the digital and real world may reproduce changes in the user model. The MUP manager observes the user actions: when new information about the user can be inferred, it updates or adds a new slot in the MUP and sets the "confidence" attribute of that slot with an appropriate value that is calculated by the weighted average of all the user actions having an impact on that slot. The confidence attribute may be set to low, medium and high.

2.3 Generating Context-Sensitive Information

The Architecture of the Information Presenter is based on the model of Natural Language Generation (NLG) systems [17]. Given a set of goals to be achieved in the selected domain (tourist information in this case), the Agent plans what to communicate to the user and decide how to render it according to the context. In this case, situational user preferences play an important role in order to adapt the description of object to the situation. As it has been already proven in previous research on language generation (e.g.,[7,18]), user-related information could be used to constrain generator's decisions and to improve the effectiveness and tailoring of the generated text. Such an information is useful at any stage of the generation process: i) for selecting relevant knowledge; ii) for organizing information presentation (the organisation strategies or plans can have preconditions dependent on user information); and iii) for the surface realisation (use of words which depends on the context).

3 Selecting Relevant Knowledge

Let's consider the following example: suppose the user is travelling for business reasons and, during lunch break, she is visiting the centre of the town. While she is there, information about places of interest close to where she is will be emphasized on the interactive map running on her personal device.

In this case, the Information Presenter will ask to MUP manager to select the situational statements regarding "time_of_day = lunch time" when "reason_of_travel=business purposes" and when the user "location=town-centre". In the set of selected statements, the one with the highest confidence value will be chosen.

Referring to the previously mentioned example, in the described context, the MUP Manager will infer that the user prefers to eat something fast but in a place with a nice view on the town center. Then, according to this preference, the Information Presenter will select, in the XML description of the map, all places (<details>) of category "eating" being "fast-foods" with coordinates that show that the place is relatively close to the user position (within 500 mt). Moreover, the system will check for other features matching the presumed user preferences (i.e. view="historical center"). Then a new xml structure containing the selected places will be generated to be used for the presentation. Selected items are then ordered on the bases of number of matched user features. As the user moves, the map is updated as well as the context information.

3.1 Organizing the Information Presentation

There are several computational approaches to planning "what to say" when presenting information. Important milestones in this research field were the introduction of *text schemata* [19] and *Rhetorical Structure Theory* (RST), as formulated by Mann and Thompson [20]. Meanwhile, RST has been operationalized by the application of a traditional top-down planner [21], and has been further refined by the introduction of intentional operators [22]. Planning, however, is an heavy computational task. Considering the need of dealing with real-time interaction on a *small* device, our approach is based on the idea of using a library of non-instantiated plan-recipes expressed in an XML-based markup language: DPML (Discourse Plan Markup Language [23]). DPML is a markup language for specifying the structure of a discourse plan based on RST: a discourse plan is identified by its name; its main components are the nodes, each identified by a name. Attributes of nodes describe the communicative goal and the rhetorical elements: role of the node in the RR associated with its father (nucleus or satellite) and RR name.

The XML-based annotation of the discourse plan is motivated by two reasons: i) in this way, a library of standard explanation plan may be built, that can be instantiated when needed and can be used by different applications, in several contexts; ii) XML can be easily transformed through XSLT in another language, for instance HTML, text or another scripting language driving for instance a TTS, favoring in this way the adaptation to different context and devices.

Once a communicative goal has been selected, explicitly as a consequence of a user request or implicitly triggered by the context, the Information Presenter selects the plan in this library that best suits the current situation. The generic plan is, then,instantiated by filling the slots of its leaves with data in the XML-domain-file that is associated with the map to describe. In this prototype we consider the following types of communicative goals:

- Describe(Ag, U, x) where x is a single object to be described;
- Describe(Ag, U, list_of(y_i)) where list_of(y_i) represent a set of objects of interest of the same type (i.e. restaurants) to be described;
- DescribeArea(Ag, U, list_of(z_i)) where list_of(z_i) represent a list of objects of interest belonging to different categories.

Considering the previous example, the Presentation Agent will select the plan correspondent to the Describe(Ag, U, list_of(y_i)) goal for listing the eating facilities matching the user preferences and then it will instantiate it with the selected data (fast foods close to where the user is, with a nice view and open at the current time). A small portion of the XML-Instantiated-Plan that was generated for describing some eating facilities in the area is shown in Figure 4.

```
<d-plan name="describe_set_of_objects">
<node name="n1" goal="Describe(where_to_eat, area1)" role="root" RR="Elab">
   <node name="n2" goal="Inform(existence(fast_foods))" role="nucleus" RR="null"/>
   <node name="n3" goal="Describe(fast_foods, area1)" role="sat" RR="ElabGenSpec">
         <node name="n4" goal="Inform(number(fast_foods, 3))" role="nucleus" RR="null"/>
         <node name="n5" goal="Describe(list(fast_foods))" role="sat" RR="OrdinalSequence">
         <node name="n5.1" goal=" Describe(fast_foods, "La Locanda di Federico")" role="nucleus"
         RR="ElabObjAttr">
               <node name="n5.1.1" goal="Inform(name, "fast_foods")" role="nucleus" RR="null"/>
         <node name="n5.1.2" goal="Describe(Specific Features, image)" role="nucleus"
         RR="OrdinalSequence">
               <node name="n5.1.2.1" goal="Inform(type, "osteria tipica barese")" role="nucleus"
         RR="null"/>
               <node name="n5.1.2.2" goal="Inform(rel_pos, "100 meter North")" role="nucleus"
         RR="null"/>
               <node name="n5.1.2.3" goal="Inform(timetable, "12.00-24.00")" role="nucleus" RR="null"/>
               <node name="n5.1.2.4" goal="Inform(telephone, "0805240202")" role="nucleus"
         RR="null"/>
               <node name="n5.1.2.5" goal="Inform(description, "a osteria where it is possible to eat
         good typical bari food....")" role="nucleus" RR="null"/>
         </node>
   </node>...
   </node>
...</node></d-plan>
```

Fig. 4. An example of XML-Instantiated-Plan

This plan first presents general information about the existences of open fast foods, then it lists them, describing in details their main features.

3.2 Rendering the Map Objects Description

Adaptation of layout (visible/audible) should support alternative forms of how to present the content, navigational links, or the presentation as a whole.

The appropriate transformation technology, especially when considering standard initiatives, is obviously XSL transformation (XSLT) in combination with DOM (Document Object Model) programming. XSLT is an effective way to produce output in form of HTML, or any other target language. Rule-based stylesheets form the essence of the XSLT language and build an optimal basis for the introduced adaptation mechanism.

The surface generation task of our system is then very simple: starting from the instantiated plan apply the appropriate template. This process is mainly driven by the type of the communicative goal and by the RRs between portions of the plan. The plan is explored in a depth-first way; for each node, a linguistic marker is placed between the text spans that derive from its children, according to the RR that links them.

For instance, the description: "There are 3 fast foods in this town area", in Figure 5, is obtained from a template for the Describe(Ag, U, list_of(yi)) where the Ordinal Sequence RR relates the description of the single objects in the list. We defined the templates' structure after an analysis of a corpus of town-map websites. At present, we generate the descriptions in HTML; however, our approach is general enough to produce descriptions in different formats and, therefore, for different interaction modalities [24].

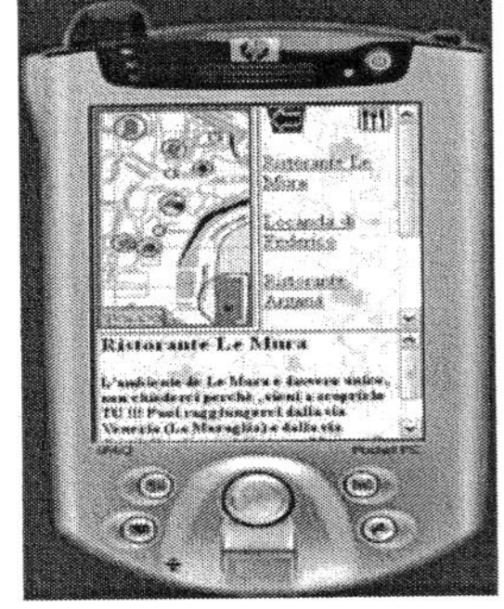

Fig. 5. List of eating places

In the example in Figure 5, the Information Presenter will display to the user a web page structured as follows: i) on the left side the portion of the map of the town area where the user is located and the graphical indications (icons denoting different categories of objects) about places of interests is displayed; ii)on the right side a description of those objects is provided; iii) on the bottom part, when the user selects one of the objects in the list, a detailed description of the selected object will be displayed. The user may access the same information directly clicking on the icons on the map.

Looking in more detail at the proposed information could be considered as a positive feedback in building the usage models. However, while this is important in the case of non-mobile information systems, when the user is moving in a real space, this is not enough. In this case, the digital action should be reinforced by the action in the real world: going to that place. We are still working on this issue since it is important to consider contextual events that may discourage the user to eat in that place (i.e. the restaurant is full). At the moment, for dealing with this kind of feedback, we ask directly to the user.

4 Conclusions and Future Work

In this paper, we described the prototype of a system able to generate context-sensitive description of objects of interest present in a map. Even if we selected the mobile tourism as a application domain to test our approach, the system architecture and employed methods are general enough to be applied to other domains. Moreover, the use of XML content modeling and domain-independent generation methods, allows the system to deal with the adaptation of the presentation modality. In this way, the provided information can be easily adapted to different devices and to the needs of user with disabilities. The system has been implemented in Java and XML related technologies. We tested on a iPAQ h5550 without GPS. We simulated the user location with an interface for managing context features.

In this phase of our work we are concerned more with the study of the feasibility of the proposed approach and employed methods than in evaluating the effectiveness of the generated description. At this stage we performed only an evaluation of the generated text against the descriptions present on Bari tourist guide and the results show a good level of similarity. However, this does not show any evidence that contextual information provision is more effective than non-contextual one. This will be the aim of our future user studies. After this study, in case there is an evidence that contextual information provision is effective, we will concentrate on the generation of comparative descriptions of places of interests in the same area.

Acknoledgements

Research described in this paper is an extension of the work we performed in the scope of the ARIANNA project. We wish to thank those who cooperated in implementing the prototype described in this paper: in particular, Gloria De Salve and Marco Vergara. In particular, we thanks Fiorella de Rosis for her useful comments on this work.

References

1. L. Ardissono, A. Goy, G. Petrone, M. Segnan and P. Torasso. Ubiquitous user assistance in a tourist information server. Lecture Notes in Computer Science n. 2347, 2nd Int. Conference on Adaptive Hypermedia and Adaptive Web Based Systems (AH2002), Malaga, pp. 14-23, Springer Verlag 2002.
2. Brusilovsky P.(1996).Methods and Techniques of Adaptive Hypermedia.UMUAI,6.87:129.
3. Wilkinson R., Lu S., Paradis F., Paris C., Wan S., and Wu M. Generating Personal Travel Guides from Discourse Plans. P. Brusilovsky, O. Stock, C. Strapparava (Eds.): Adaptive Hypermedia and Adaptive Web-Based Systems International Conference, AH 2000, Trento, Italy, August 2000. Proceedings LNCS 1892, p. 392 ff.
4. Weiser M. The Computer for the 21st Century. Scientific American, september 1991.
5. UbisWorld: http://www.u2m.org
6. De Carolis, B., de Rosis, F., Pizzutilo, S.: Generating User-Adapted Hypermedia from Discourse Plans. Fifth Congress of the Italian Association of Artificial Intelligence (AI*IA 97), Roma , (1997).
7. Paris, C. User modelling in Text Generation. Pinter Publishers, London and New York. 1993.
8. Cheverst K., Davies N., Mitchell K., Friday A. and Efstratiou, Developing Context-Aware Electronic Tourist Guide: Some Issues and Experiences, Proceedings of CHI'2000, Netherlands, (April 2000), pp. 17-24.
9. Gregory D. Abowd, Christopher G. Atkeson, Jason I. Hong, Sue Long, Rob Kooper, Mike Pinkerton: Cyberguide: A mobile context-aware tour guide. Wireless Networks 3(5): 421-433 (1997).
10. Pan, Bing and Daniel R. Fesenmaier (2000). "A Typology of Tourism Related Web Sites: Its Theoretical Background and Implications." In Fesenmaier, Daniel R., Stefan Klein and Dimitrios Buhalis (Eds.),Information and Communication Technologies in Tourism 2000 (pp. 381-396). Springer-Verlag.

11. B. Brown, M. Chalmers (2003) Tourism and mobile technology, In: Kari Kuutti, Eija Helena Karsten (eds.) Proeceedings of the Eighth European Conference on Computer Supported Cooperative Work, Helsinki, Finland, 14-18 September 2003., KluwerAcademic Press.
12. Inote: Image Annotation Tool. http://jefferson.village.edu/iath/inote.html.
13. De Salve, G., De Carolis, B. de Rosis, F. Andreoli, C., De Cicco, M.L. Image Descriptions from annotated knowledge sources. IMPACTS in NLG, Dagsthul, July 25-28, 2000.
14. Kobsa A., Generic User Modeling Systems. UMUAI vol. II nos.1-2 pp.49-63. Kluwer Academic Publisher. 2001.
15. A. Sinner, T. Kleemann, A. von Hessling: Semantic User Profiles and their Applications in a Mobile Environment. In Artificial Intelligence in Mobile Systems 2004.
16. Cavalluzzi A., De Carolis B., Pizzutilo S., Cozzolongo G.: Interacting with embodied agents in public environments. AVI 2004: 240-243.
17. Cozzolongo, G., De Carolis, B., Pizzutilo, S.. Supporting Personalized Interaction in Public Spaces. In Proceedings of the Artificial Intelligence in Mobile Systems 2004. Baus J., Kray, C., Porzel, R. (Eds.). Nottingham, UK, 2004.
18. Reiter E. and Dale R. Building Natural Language Generation Systems. Cambridge University Press. 2000.
19. McKeown, K. Text Generation: Using Discourse Strategies and Focus Constraints to Generate Natural Language Text. Cambridge University Press, Cambridge, England. 1985.
20. Mann W.C., Matthiessen C.M.I.M., Thompson S. (1989). Rhetorical Structure Theory and Text Analysis.ISI Research Report- 89- 242.
21. Hovy, E., (1988), Generating Natural Language under Pragmatic Constraints, Hillsdale, NJ: Lawrence Erlbaum Associates.
22. Moore J. and Paris C.. ``Planning Text for Advisory Dialogues: Capturing Intentional and Rhetorical Information." Computational Linguistics Vol 19, No 4, pp651-694, 1993.
23. De Carolis B., Pelachaud C., Poggi I. and Steedman M. APML, a Mark-up Language for Believable Behavior Generation. In H Prendinger and M Ishizuka (Eds): "Life-like Characters. Tools, Affective Functions and Applications". Springer, in press.
24. Palle Klante, Jens Krösche, Susanne Boll: AccesSights - A Multimodal Location-Aware Mobile Tourist Information System. ICCHP 2004: 287-294.

Haptic Fruition of 3D Virtual Scene by Blind People

Fabio De Felice, Floriana Renna, Giovanni Attolico, and Arcangelo Distante

Institute of Intelligent Systems for Automation – CNR
Via Amendola 122 D/O, 70126, Bari, Italy
{defelice, renna, attolico}@ba.issia.cnr.it

Abstract. Haptic interfaces may allow blind people to interact naturally and realistically with 3D virtual models of objects that are unsuitable for direct tactile exploration. The haptic interaction can be offered at different scales, by changing the relative size of probe and objects and by organizing different levels of details into the model. In addition, haptic interfaces can actively drive the user along the most effective exploration path around the scene. All these features can significantly help the synthesis and the understanding of the huge amount of tactile sensations (that blinds must collect serially) beyond the limits of the exploration in the real world. The paper describes an architecture (and its already realized modules for visualization, collision detection and force simulation) intended to generate a reliable simulation of the geometrical and physical interactions between the user's hand and a virtual 3D scene.

Keywords: Intelligent systems in education, systems for real life applications, Human-robot interaction.

1 Introduction

This paper describes the design and the on-going development of a system, based on a haptic device [1], that enables the exploration of 3D virtual models by visually impaired people. These models are intended to replace objects that for their location, dimension or sensitivity to damages cannot be offered to direct tactile exploration. Moreover, the enhanced interaction made possible by haptic tools is expected to improve the understanding of the collected sensorial data [2].

A haptic interface can offer a multi-resolution experience (a common property of vision) to blind people: the relative size of fingertips and objects can be dynamically changed and at higher level, the virtual model can be organized in different scales, each with a distinct amount and type of information and details [3].

Moreover, an efficient exploration path can significantly improve the understanding of the object. Haptic device can support the perception by applying suitable forces that suggest effective waypoints to the user.

An important application of the system is the fruition of cultural heritage (statues, architectural sites, ...). It is also intended to serve as a didactical support to access information (mathematical, biological, geographical, historical, artistic, ...) that currently need specifically prepared three-dimensional artifacts that can be touched by the blind but often prove to be not completely satisfactory.

M. Ali and F. Esposito (Eds.): IEA/AIE 2005, LNAI 3533, pp. 269 – 278, 2005.

The VRML language [4] has been chosen as the format for the input data. It represents the common representation used for three-dimensional information on the web and gives access to a large number of models in many different domains.

Next section presents the general architecture of the application. Then the principal characteristics of the modules already available (the visual rendering, the collision detection and the force simulator) and the problems that have been solved for their integration in an effective application are described. Finally some preliminary conclusions and current research required to complete the system and to reach the described goals are drawn.

2 General Architecture

To support a realistic tactile exploration of a 3D virtual model by blind people we have chosen the CyberForce system, manufactured by Immersion Corporation [5] and equipped with the CyberGrasp and CyberGlove devices.

The CyberForce is a desktop force-feedback system that conveys realistic grounded forces to the wrist of users by a 3 DOF armature. It can also provide complete position/attitude data about the users' wrist. The CyberGrasp by means of five actuators provides grasping force feedback roughly applied perpendicularly to each fingertip of the user's hand. The CyberGlove is a glove with flexion and abduction sensors transforming hand and fingers motions in digital data that allow the rendering of a graphical hand which mirrors the movements of the physical hand.

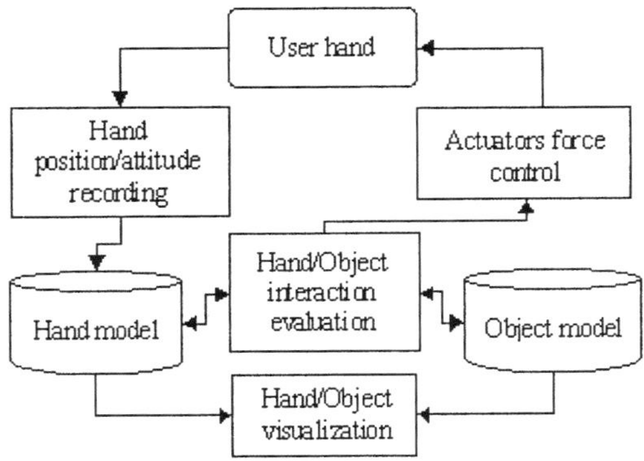

Fig. 1. The system architecture

The architecture of the system we are developing is reported in figure 1. The *Hand position/attitude recording* module continuously updates the hand model in the virtual scene on the basis of the data provided by the CyberGlove and by the CyberForce used as a 3D tracker [6]. The *Hand/object interaction evaluation* module analyses the relative geometry of the objects in the virtual scene and extracts the necessary information to simulate the physical forces generated in the virtual environment. The *Actuators force control* makes the necessary adaptation between these desired forces and the mechanical capability of the physical device to return a sufficient level of realism to the user.

To simplify and make the system more suited to the application, we have chosen to model the hand only in terms of its fingertips, each modelled by a sphere. In this first phase of the development only the CyberForce device, equipped with a stylus, has being used (Figure 2). In this way only the index distal phalanx is simulated.

Fig. 2. A picture of the system. The screen shows the virtual space in which the red dot at the center of the cross, an avatar representing the fingertip of the physical hand on the right, interacts with a sculpture. The system uses the haptic device held by the physical hand to return forces to the user whose sensations approximate the effect of exploring a real object having the same shape

A realistic perception depends on an effective interaction between the models of the hand and of the object which involves a controlled and homogeneous mapping between physical and virtual spaces. Previous activities [6] show that the accuracy and repeatability of the CyberForce as a 3D tracker are not homogeneous with respect to the distance from the base of the haptic device: nonetheless they can be used for the intended application in a significant region of the real space. The serial nature of the tactile exploration can be exploited to propose the part of interest of the model in the region of the physical space where the CyberForce provides better performance.

2.1 The Haptic Software Development Kit

The CyberForce system is equipped with the software development kit named Virtual Hand (VH) that handles the connection to the haptic hardware [7] and gives the basic tools to create a virtual environment and to organize its visual and haptic exploration [8]. VH provides a complete support for the visual rendering of the virtual hand but offers only simple geometrical primitives (such as cubes, spheres, ...) to describe the virtual environment. The collision detection is done by software packages that require the objects in the scene to be convex and composed by triangular faces.

Our project must consider scenes that can be quite complex and rich of non-convex components. Our application uses an essential model of the hand (only its fingertips) to be more effective. Moreover, a force model more reliable and realistic than the one offered by VH is needed for the interaction between the hand and the scene. All these requirements have suggested the customization of the environment and the integration and/or development of specific components to load complex VRML models, to enhance the flexibility and efficacy of collision detection and to return realistic forces to the user via the CyberForce device.

The VH remains the general framework of the application and is complemented by external packages to meet all our goals. The VH handles the entire system dynamics by a single class, the vhtEngine, intended as an easy to use framework for building user simulations. Primarily, the engine runs a vhtSimulation created by the user in its own execution thread. In addition to this, the engine maintains the link between the user simulation and the hand model.

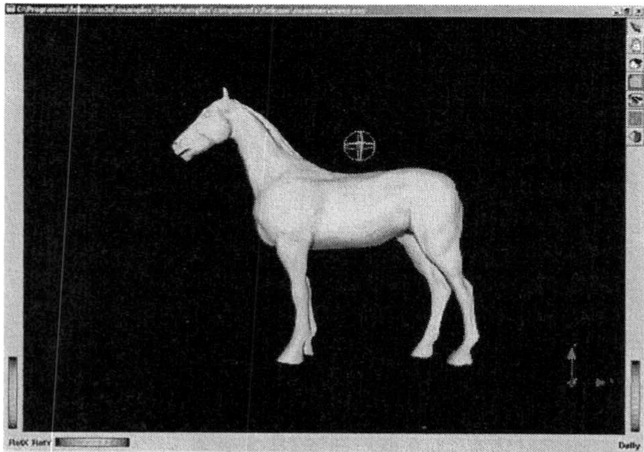

Fig. 3. Application GUI, with the 3D model of a horse and the red dot at the center of the cross representing the virtual counterpart of the physical fingertip. The user can flexibly control the rendering of the virtual scene: while useless for blind people the GUI is helpful for debugging the system and makes the system useful as an enhanced interface with virtual scene for normally seeing people

Another important component is the class vhtCollisionEngine designed to simplify and unify the collision detection tasks for a user specified scene graph. The collision engine builds and maintains all the data structures required for collision detection and manages all the calls to low level routines involved in this process. The user specifies the haptic scene graph (or sub-graph) that this engine must manage and calls collision check whenever it needs an updated list of collisions.

Following the guidelines suggested in [8], an entirely new parser has been written to fit the characteristics of Coin3D, the package used to load and visualize the VRML models. An efficient application GUI (Figure 3) offers visual tools (rotation and translation of the virtual camera or of the scene graph, ...) that help the debugging of the system and the visual understanding of the virtual scene. Furthermore, the modules required to catch the hand movements and to update accordingly in real time the visual scenario has been created.

In addition, specific methods to automatically extract from the nodes of the haptic scene graph the geometric data required by the collision detection package (Swift++) have been added to the classes of VH. Further features have been added to appropriately transform and exchange data between VH and Swift++ during the collision detection process, to manage the Decomposition pre-processing step required by Swift++ and to handle the data returned by each call to the Swift++ package. These features are thoroughly described in the following paragraphs.

2.2 The Visual Scene Graph Manager

The *Hand/object visualization* module may appear secondary in an application which addresses blind people. It has, instead, two important roles: it simplifies the debug, providing a visual perception of the geometries in the scene and allowing a check of the forces generated for each relative position of probe and object; it enables the same system to be used to provide an enhanced experience, as an integration of visual and tactile data, of virtual models to seeing people.

The functionalities required to the graphic library are fundamental: the creation of the scene graphs for the virtual scene and the hand, the fast and simple acquisition and modification of the scene graph data, the organization of multi-resolution descriptions and perceptions, the manipulation of models in real-time, the evaluation and rendering of the complete virtual environment (hand plus model). The Coin3D graphic library [9] has been chosen to handle the upload of the VRML models, their visual rendering and, in general, the entire graphic user interface. Coin3D is Open Source and is fully compatible with SGI Open Inventor 2.1 [10]. It includes the support for VRML1.0, VRML97, 3D sound and 3D textures, features not supported by the native Immersion graphic library.

A dynamical integration must be done to create a link between the visual scene graph, handled by Coin3d, and the haptic scene graph, handled by the VH environment, in order to enrich the virtual environment with the haptic counterpart. This link is realized by the so called Data Neutral Scene Graph (DNSG). It is composed by hybrid type nodes, called neutralNodes, whose structure maintains two pointers: one to a visual node and the other to the corresponding haptic node. The parser traverses the visual graph with a depth-first strategy, creates the related haptic nodes and links both of them to appropriate neutralNodes. This process continues until the entire visual tree has been processed and associated to a haptic tree [8] (Figure 4).

From a haptic point of view the only relevant information in the scene graph is geometrical: the coordinates of points composing the shape at hand, the way they are combined in triangular faces, the translation/rotation/scale of each component of the virtual environment. The information about the physical behavior of the object is not necessarily present in a VRML model and may requires specific data to be provided to the system. Therefore from a geometrical point of view the haptic counterpart of a given VRML model (coordinates, indexes and transformations) can be seen as a subset of the visual scene graph.

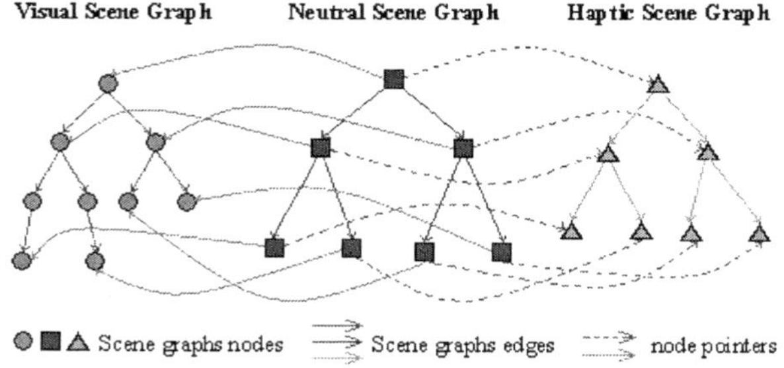

Fig. 4. Scene Graphs Mapping. The Neutral Scene Graph provides a link between the visual and the haptic Scene Graphs

To retrieve all this information, the parser must account for the differences in format between the VRML97 and the VRML 1.0, as well as the different configurations by which the scene features can be represented. Moreover several intermediate nodes providing data, primary oriented to visual goals, can occur. These nodes, that can make harder the search of transformation nodes, must be ignored by the parser because haptically redundant. The geometric data are generally contained in leaf nodes, and they simply need the appropriate discrimination between VRML 1.0 and VRML97 formats. The parser continues the analysis of the scene graph until all the data of interest, from all the models in the scene, have been collected. Currently the integration is able to handle a large number of different scene graph structures allowing new behaviors to be easily added when needed.

2.3 The Collision Detection Manager

The interactions among the objects moving in the virtual world are modeled by means of dynamic constraints and contact analysis that limit their movements. Users perceive the virtual objects as solid if no interpenetration between them is permitted. Therefore a realistic perception of the virtual world needs an accurate collision detection. For a depth collision detection investigation see [11] [12].

Collision detection must check all the potential collisions due to the user movements and may require a lot of time. A realistic interaction between the user and the system requires the algorithm to be fast enough to detect collisions at a high time rate.

To detect collisions in the virtual space we have chosen SWIFT++ (Speedy Walking via Improved Feature Testing for Non-Convex Objects) [13]. This library detects objects' intersections, performs tolerance verification, computes approximate and exact distances and determines the contacts between pairs of objects in the scene. Moreover, with respect to similar packages, SWIFT++ can flexibly import rigid polyhedral models, closed or with boundary and having any degree of non-convexity. It uses a preprocessing tool, the Decomposer, that translates a file describing the coordinates of the points and the indices of the triangular faces forming the shape of any complex model in a hierarchy of simpler convex bounding boxes that can be inserted in the virtual scene.

The collision detection architecture built-in the VH environment operates in two steps: the wide mode followed by the local mode. In the wide mode, the algorithm tries to cull as much as possible the set of potential collision pairs. In local mode, each pair of shapes is considered at the actual geometry level to determine detailed contact information (contacts normal, closest points and distance between them). This last phase can be customized to interface the VH environment with an external collision detection engine.

Therefore Swift++ implements the local phase giving the data on which the VH collision engine operates. The interface that enables this link includes two different mechanisms: one determines if two shape nodes in the haptic scene graph can collide and, if so, generates the corresponding collision pair structure; the second one analyzes the geometry of the shape and generates a geometry representation appropriate for the external collision detection package. A custom Swift++ interface has been developed which extends the VH geometry templates with methods for the creation, decomposition and insertion of shapes into a Swift++ scene.

The Swift++ geometry, for both the model and the probe, is built as follow: the geometric primitives, shape point coordinates and triangles indices from the related shape geometry are collected in a file. This file is preprocessed by the Decomposer program: this is a requirement of the Swift++ package in order to insert a simpler hierarchy of convex components in the Swift++ scene. This phase can be slow when the model is very complex (a large number of convex bounding boxes needs to be created): for this reason the results are saved in a hierarchical file that can be loaded again at any time without further processing. An extension of the basic local collision mechanism, called SwiftCollide, handles the collision loop and, for each collision, makes the query to Swift++ and returns the results to the corresponding collision pair structure that plays a fundamental role at runtime.

3 Runtime Main Loop

The main loop starts loading the chosen VRML model; during this first phase its scene graph is merged with the model of the probe. A new scene graph including these two components is created and loaded in the application. The models are loaded in a neutral initial position: their center of mass must coincide with the origin of the reference system of the scene. After this initialization, the visual and the haptic loops start as two separated threads and update the probe position by directly reading the position from the CyberForce used as a 3D tracker.

To visualize the probe on the screen following the hand movements in the real world, the event handling mechanism of Open Inventor has been used [14]: a software device needs to be set up to monitor the window messages for a given peripheral. This device generates an Open Inventor event for each event generated by the peripheral and dispatches it to the internal visual scene graph. Then the scene graph is traversed and the event is proposed to every node that, accordingly to its role, responds to or ignores it.

To this aim, our application creates a device to periodically read the finger position answering the WM_TIMER Windows message sent by a timer. As a new position is read, a corresponding SoMotion3Event [14] is created and sent to the visual scene graph. The manipulator node, acting as a transformation node for the probe, manages this event updating the probe position and attitude. On the other hand, the haptic loop reads the probe position directly from the CyberForce and the transformations of the haptic component representing the manipulator are updated accordingly.

The two scenes used for the visual rendering and for the haptic feedback have each its own reference frame. The center of the scene visualized on the screen coincides with the center of the probe/object in the virtual environment (local scene). The haptic scene follows the physical world the user moves into (global scene). This choice strongly simplify the visualization on the screen and the understanding of the scene by offering a close and well centered view of the observed objects.

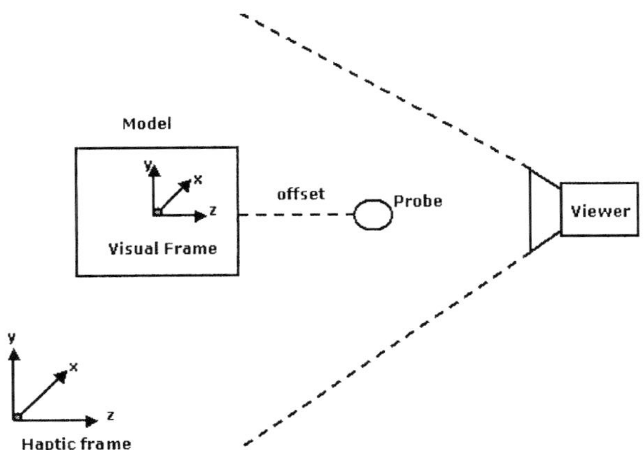

Fig. 5. Reference frames configuration. To separate the haptic and visual reference systems help in keeping for each of them the maximum flexibility: the user receives the better view of the virtual scene and the system exploits the most useful working region of the haptic device

The visual loop places the VRML model at the origin and the probe at an appropriate offset so that it starts near and in front of the object. The relative translations (differences between two successive finger positions) are applied to the transform node of the probe.

The haptic loop, on the other hand, places the probe at the physical position of the finger in the real world, as read by the CyberForce, and offsets the VRML model by a distance equal to the one set in the visual rendering loop. The resulting scene is given as the global transformation to the Swift++ scene. This configuration is illustrated in figure 4. At runtime there is no interaction between the two loops: the visual one is totally entrusted to the Coin/SoWin framework, while the haptic loop is managed by the VH/Swift++ framework.

The latter loop is composed by the user simulation that checks the valid collision pairs on which the SwiftCollide is activated for querying the Swift scene. For each colliding pair the query returns the coordinates of the nearest points, the normal directions at those points and their distance or –1 if the objects are interpenetrating. These collected data are sent to the relative collision pair and read by the user simulation to evaluate the collision response and the appropriate forces that need to be returned to the user.

The application must calculate and update the height interaction forces available in the system: five, one for each finger, plus three that are applied to the wrist, along the main axes. At the moment the single modeled fingertip is supposed to coincide with the wrist and only the last three forces are set. A first simple force feedback model has been applied starting from the well known spring law:

$$F = d * K \tag{1}$$

where d is the distance between the objects and K is the stiffness we want to reproduce for the object. The force feedback behaviour approximates a square wave step as much as possible: zero when probe and object are separated and K when they touch each other. To reduce the instability, that strongly reduces the realism of the simulation, an exponential law has been used to pilot the wave inclination.

This very simple force model has given good results for simply convex models as cubes and sphere, even if its performance decays for more complex geometries.

4 Conclusions

The paper presents a haptic system for the fruition of 3D virtual models by blind people. The exploration of virtual 3D models can be helpful when the direct tactile fruition is impossible: objects (artistic artworks, animals, plants, geographical or historical data, ...) that for dimension, location or sensitivity to damages cannot be touched, abstract representations of concepts (in biology, chemistry, mathematics, ...) that can be hardly translate in physical three-dimensional artefacts, ... Moreover, the flexibility of the haptic interaction can help to catch the meaning of tactile sensations which, in the physical world, are collected serially and at a single scale and require a huge effort for being synthesized and understood in the brain.

The architecture designed for the system and the complex integration of the visualization, collision detection and force feedback components have been explained. A simple force model used for starting the development of a realistic interaction between the user and the virtual scene has been introduced. To offer a realistic experience of VRML models with any degree of non convexity we have customized the environment. Suitable software for scene graph manipulation and for collision detection has been developed starting from available software packages: the native VH environment of the haptic device works only as a general manager inside the application. A specific module to load complex VRML models and an open framework for the investigation of force models in the virtual space have been realized. The current components allow a basic geometrical and physical interaction between the user (through the model of its hand) and the virtual scene. The future development will focus on the analysis of more realistic force models, on the virtual exploration through the complete hand (using an hand's model with realistic anatomical constraints and appropriate distribution of forces between the wrist and the five fingers), on the study of a multi-resolution interaction to support an exploration similar to the coarse to fine abilities of the human vision system.

Acknowledgements

This activity is supported by the Italian Ministry for University and Scientific Research (MIUR) under the grant "Cluster 22 Servizi al cittadino ed al territorio – Progetto N. 37 Un ponte tecnologico verso coloro che non vedono".

References

1. Salisbury, K., Conti, F., Barbagli, F.: Haptic Rendering: Introductory Concepts, Computer Graphics and Applications, IEEE, 24-32, (2004)
2. Magnusson, C., Rassmun-Grohm, K., Sjostrom, C., Danielsson H.: Haptic 3D object recognition – A study with blind users, Vision 2002, Goteborg, Sweden, (2002)
3. Magnusson, C., Rassmun-Grohm, K.: Non-visual zoom and scrolling operations in a virtual haptic environment, Proc. of the 3th International Conference Eurohaptics 2003, Dublin, Ireland, (2003)
4. http://www.web3d.org/x3d/specifications/vrml/
5. www.Immersion.com
6. Di Alessio, F.L., Nitti, M., Renna, F., Attolico, G., Distante, A.: Characterizing the 3D Tracking Performance of a Haptic Device, Proc. of the 4th International Conference EuroHaptics 2004, Germany, June 5-7, (2004), pp. 463-466
7. VHS Users Guide V2.7
8. VHS Programmers GuideV2.5
9. www.Coin3d.org
10. http://oss.sgi.com/projects/inventor/
11. Lin, M., Manocha, D.: Collision and Proximity Queries, Handbook of Discrete and Computational Geometry: Collision detection, (2003)
12. Greene, N.: Detecting intersection of a rectangular solid and a convex polyhedron, Graphics Gems IV. Academic Press, (1994)
13. http://www.cs.unc.edu/~geom/SWIFT++/
14. http://www-evasion.imag.fr/Membres/Francois.Faure/doc/inventorToolmaker/sgi_html/ndex.html
15. http://www-evasion.imag.fr/Membres/Francois.Faure/doc/inventorMentor/sgi_html

Ontology-Based Natural Language Parser for E-Marketplaces

S. Coppi[1], T. Di Noia[1], E. Di Sciascio[1], F.M. Donini[2], and A. Pinto[1]

[1] Politecnico di Bari, Via Re David, 200, I-70125, Bari, Italy
{s.coppi, t.dinoia, disciascio, agnese.pinto}@poliba.it
[2] Università della Tuscia, via San Carlo, 32, I-01100, Viterbo, Italy
donini@unitus.it

Abstract. We propose an approach to Natural Language Processing exploiting knowledge domain in an e-commerce scenario. Based on such modeling an NLP parser is presented, aimed at translating demand/supply advertisements into structured Description Logic expressions, automatically mapping sentences with concept expressions related to a reference ontology.

1 Introduction

We focus on an approach specifically aimed at translating demand / supply descriptions expressed in Natural Language (NL) into structured Description Logic (DL) expressions, mapping in an automated way NL sentences with concepts and roles of a DL-based ontology. Motivation for this work comes from the observation that one of the major obstacles to the full exploitation of semantic-based e-marketplaces, particularly B2C and P2P ones, lies in the difficulties average users have in translating their advertisements into cumbersome expressions or in filling several form-based web pages. Yet constraining a user to completely fill in forms is in sharp contrast with the inherent Open World Assumption typical of Knowledge Representation systems. We report here how we faced this issue in the framework of MAMAS demand/supply semantic-matchmaking service [11]. Distinguishing characteristics of our NL parser include the direct use of DLs to express the semantic meaning, without intermediate stages in First Order Logic Form or Lambda calculus. This has been possible because of the strong contextualization of the approach, oriented to e-commerce advertisements, which possess an ontological pattern that expresses their semantics and affects grammar creation. Such pattern is reflected both in the structure of the ontologies we built for e-commerce tasks and in the creation of the grammars. Two separate lexical category sets are taken into account; the first one for goods, the second one for their description. This choice allows to embed the problem domain into the parser grammar. Furthermore we designed the grammar in two separate levels. In this way we achieve more flexibility: the first level only depends on the ontology terminology, while the second one only on the particular DL used. Finally, our parser performs automatic disambiguation of the parsed sentences, interacting with the reasoner.

M. Ali and F. Esposito (Eds.): IEA/AIE 2005, LNAI 3533, pp. 279–289, 2005.

2 Description Logics and Natural Language Processing

To make the paper self-contained we begin by briefly revisiting fundamentals of DLs [3]. The basic syntax elements are *concept* names, such as, CPU, `device`; *role* names, such as `hasSoftware`, `hasDevice`; *individuals*, such as `HPworkstationXW`, `IBMThinkPad`. Concepts stand for sets of objects, and roles link objects in different concepts. Individuals are used for special named elements belonging to concepts. Formally, a semantic *interpretation* is a pair $\mathcal{I} = (\Delta, \cdot^{\mathcal{I}})$, which consists of the *domain* Δ and the *interpretation function* $\cdot^{\mathcal{I}}$, which maps every concept to a subset of Δ, every role to a subset of $\Delta \times \Delta$, and every individual to an element of Δ. The *Unique Name Assumption* (UNA) restriction is usually made, *i.e.*, different individuals are mapped to different elements of Δ, *i.e.*, $a^{\mathcal{I}} \neq b^{\mathcal{I}}$ for individuals $a \neq b$. Basic elements can be combined using *constructors* to form concept and role *expressions*, and each DL is identified by the operators set it is endowed with. Every DL allows one to form a *conjunction* of concepts, usually denoted as $\sqcap$; some DL include also disjunction $\sqcup$ and complement $\neg$ to close concept expressions under boolean operations. Expressive DLs [3] are built on the simple $\mathcal{AL}$ (Attributive Language) adding constructs in order to represent more expressive concepts. Allowed constructs in $\mathcal{AL}$ are: $\top$ *universal concept* (all the objects in the domain); $\bot$ *bottom concept* (the empty set); A *atomic concepts* (all the objects belonging to the set represented by A); $\neg A$ *atomic negation* (all the objects not belonging to the set represented by A); $C \sqcap D$ *intersection* (the objects belonging both to C and D); $\forall R.C$ *universal restriction* (all the objects participating to the R relation whose range are all the objects belonging to C); $\exists R$ *unqualified existential restriction* (there exists at least one object participating in the relation R). Expressions are given a semantics by defining the interpretation function over each construct. Concept conjunction is interpreted as set intersection: $(C \sqcap D)^{\mathcal{I}} = C^{\mathcal{I}} \cap D^{\mathcal{I}}$, and also the other boolean connectives $\sqcup$ and $\neg$, when present, are given the usual set-theoretic interpretation of union and complement. The interpretation of constructs involving quantification on roles needs to make domain elements explicit: for example, $(\forall R.C)^{\mathcal{I}} = \{d_1 \in \Delta \mid \forall d_2 \in \Delta : (d_1, d_2) \in R^{\mathcal{I}} \rightarrow d_2 \in C^{\mathcal{I}}\}$. Concept expressions can be used in *inclusion assertions*, and *definitions*, which impose restrictions on possible interpretations according to the knowledge elicited for a given domain. The semantics of inclusions and definitions is based on set containment: an interpretation $\mathcal{I}$ satisfies an inclusion $C \sqsubseteq D$ if $C^{\mathcal{I}} \subseteq D^{\mathcal{I}}$, and it satisfies a definition $C = D$ when $C^{\mathcal{I}} = D^{\mathcal{I}}$. A *model* of a TBox $\mathcal{T}$ is an interpretation satisfying all inclusions and definitions of $\mathcal{T}$. Adding new constructors to $\mathcal{AL}$ increases DL languages expressiveness, but may also make inference services intractable [5]. The allowed operators in a DL based an $\mathcal{AL}$ are indicated by a capital letter. For instance, $\mathcal{ALN}$ is a $\mathcal{AL}$ endowed with unqualified number restriction *i.e.*, $(\geq n\ R)$, $(\leq n\ R)$, $(= n\ R)$ (respectively the minimum, the maximum and the exact number of objects participating in the relation R); $\mathcal{ALC}$ allows full negation; in $\mathcal{ALE}$ there can be used the qualified existential restriction; in $\mathcal{ALEN}$ both existential and unqualified number restriction are defined and so on. Here we refer mainly to an $\mathcal{ALN}$ DL, which can be mapped in a subset of OWL-DL

[9]. Since the early days of terminological reasoners, DLs have been applied in semantic interpretation for natural language processing [12]. Semantic interpretation is the derivation process from the syntactic analysis of a sentence to its logical form – intended here as the representation of its context-dependent meaning. Typically, DLs have been used to encode in a knowledge base both syntactic and semantic elements needed to drive the semantic interpretation process. Several studies have been carried out aimed at building a good DL knowledge base for natural language processing [6, 7]. A linguistically well motivated ontology ought to be partitioned into a language-dependent part (the *upper model*) and a domain-dependent part (the *domain model*), but it is well known this result is theoretically very hard to achieve. Implemented systems rely on the so-called *multilevel semantics architecture* [1]. For a recent survey of NLP projects using DLs, see Chapter 15 in [3].

3 A Grammar for Parsing E-Commerce Advertisements

We started analyzing several advertisements related to different commerce domain *e.g.*, consumer electronics components, real estate services, job postings. As we expected, we noticed that advertisements present almost always, regardless of the domain, a characteristic structure and are strongly contextualized. Furthermore the lexicon often uses some jargon and is a finite and limited set of terms. With reference to the structure, there is always the good(s) to be bought/sold and related characteristics. Each good in the domain refers to a single *concept* in the knowledge domain but can be represented using different expressions, which are semantically equivalent. The same can be said for good characteristics. Hence, in each sentence there are at least two main lexical category: the good and its description. From a DL point of view, generic advertisement can be brought back to the following form:

$$C_1 \sqcap C_2 \sqcap ...C_n \sqcap \forall r_1.D_1 \sqcap \forall r_2.D_2 \sqcap ...\forall r_m.D_m$$

where C_i are the concepts related to the goods, and $\forall r_j.D_j$ to the goods description. This pattern can be also used as a guideline to model the task ontology for the specific marketplace. Atomic concepts representing a good are modeled as sub-concepts of a generic `Goods` concept. Notice that at least an $\mathcal{ALN}$ DL is needed to model a marketplace, in order to deal with concept taxonomy, disjoint groups, role restrictions ($\mathcal{AL}$), and particularly number restriction ($\mathcal{N}$) to represent quantity. The sentence structure led us to investigate techniques similar to *Semantic Grammars* [2] ones, where the lexical categories are based on the semantic meaning. We created two basic lexical category sets. One related to what we call Fundamental Nouns (FN), denoting nouns representing goods, the other one related to what we simply call Nouns (N), denoting nouns describing goods. The lexical categories built based on Ns can be identified because their names start with a capital D. For instance DP corrsponds to the *classical* NP but related to a noun phrase representing a good description. This distinction is useful during grammar rules composition (see 1) because it allows to determine if a sentence is acceptable or not in our scenario. It must contain at least a constituent of category FN, otherwise it means there are no goods to look for. Since the idea was to bind the grammar to the reference DL ontology, we enforced the relationship using features identifying the role of lexical categories within the ontology itself. In a way inspired by the use of a **TYPE** feature in a *Template Matching* [2] approach, we created three different features, respectively for concept names (`concept`), role names (`role`), operators (`op`), whose value is strictly related to the terminology used in the ontology. Using such features it is possible both to align the lexicon with the terms in the ontology and to obtain a limited number of rules associating a semantic meaning to the constituents.

3.1 Lexicon and Grammars

With the aim of building reusable elements to be easily adapted for different marketplaces and ontologies, we separated information related to the terminology, the lexical category of the terms, and the expressiveness of the DL used to model the ontology. The idea is to minimize changes and possibly to reuse both the lexical and the semantic information. In fact the parsing process is conceived in two stages, each one using a different (kind of) grammar. Using the first grammar, terms in the NL sentence are strictly related both to the terminology used in the ontology –atomic concept names and role names– and to the logical operators. With the Level 1 Grammar a parser is able to bind set of words to the correspondent element in the ontology. The Level 2 grammar uses the intermediate result produced during the Level 1 phase to build the logical form of the sentence with respect to a good/description model. In this parsing phase logical operators and quantifiers allowed by the DL used to built the ontology are used to link the basic elements. This subdivision allows more flexibility. Adapting the grammar to a new ontology (based on the same DL) requires major changes only in the Level 1 grammar, in which concept and role names appear, in order to remap the new Lexicon to the terminology used in the ontology. On the other hand if the adopted DL is changed, *e.g.*, from a $\mathcal{ALN}$ DL to a $\mathcal{ALEN}$ DL [3], major changes are requested only for Level 2 rules.
In the following we show how the logical form of the sentence is built with the aid of some examples, conceived with reference to the toy ontology in Fig. 1 [1].

Lexicon. First of all let us point out that, at the current stage of our work, we do not carry out any morphological analysis. In the lexicon, each term is endowed with the following features:

- `cat` represents the lexical category of the single word, *i.e.*, FN (noun indicating goods), N (noun describing goods), V (verb), ADJ (adjective), ADJN (numerical adjective), ADV (adverb), ART (article), CONJ (conjunction), PREP (preposition).

[1] In the ontology, for the sake of clarity, we do not model also `Processor`, `Monitor`, `Storage_Device` as subconcept of `Goods`. Even if in a real computer marketplace scenario these can be modeled as `Goods` to be sold/bought.

$\texttt{AMD\_Athlon\_XP} \sqsubseteq \texttt{Processor}$
$\texttt{Intel\_Pentium4} \sqsubseteq \texttt{Processor}$
$\texttt{Intel\_Celeron} \sqsubseteq \texttt{Processor}$
$\texttt{CD\_Reader} \sqsubseteq \texttt{Storage\_Device}$
$\texttt{CRT\_monitor} \sqsubseteq \texttt{Monitor}$
$\texttt{LCD\_monitor} \sqsubseteq \texttt{Monitor}$
$\texttt{CRT\_monitor} \sqsubseteq \neg\texttt{LCD\_monitor}$
$\texttt{Computer} \sqsubseteq \texttt{Goods}$
$\texttt{Desktop\_Computer} \sqsubseteq \texttt{Computer} \sqcap (= 1\ \texttt{hasCPU}) \sqcap \forall\texttt{hasCPU.Processor} \sqcap \exists\texttt{hasComponent} \sqcap \forall\texttt{hasComponent.Monitor} \sqcap \exists\texttt{RAM}$
$\texttt{Notebook} \sqsubseteq \texttt{Desktop\_Computer} \sqcap \forall\texttt{hasComponent.LCD\_monitor}$
$\texttt{Server} \sqsubseteq \texttt{Computer} \sqcap \forall\texttt{hasCPU.Processor} \sqcap (\geq\ 2\ \texttt{hasCPU}) \sqcap \forall\texttt{RAM.}(\geq\ 1\ 0)\texttt{00mb})$
$\texttt{Monitor} \sqsubseteq \neg\texttt{Processor}$
$\texttt{Monitor} \sqsubseteq \neg\texttt{Storage\_Device}$
$\texttt{Storage\_Device} \sqsubseteq \neg\texttt{Processor}$

Fig. 1. The toy ontology used for examples

- `concept`,`role` represent, respectively, the corresponding atomic concept, role in the ontology.
- `op` represents the corresponding logical operator in DL.
- `sw`, is set `true` if the term is a *stopword.*
- `aux` is an auxiliary field for a further customization of the grammars.

Level 1 Grammar. Actually, the mapping between the terms in the NL sentence and the ones in the ontology is not in a one to one relationship. There is the need to relate words set to the same concept or role within the ontology. In Fig. 2 a simple grammar is reported to deal with sentences related to our reference computer domain (see Fig. 1).

1) DPF[c,r,-] → N[c,r,-]
2) DP[-,r,x] → N[-,r,x]
3) DP[-,r,-] → N[-,r,-]
4) NP[c,-,-] → FN[c,-,-]
5) DP[-,r2,c1] → ADJN[c1,-,-] N[-,r2,-]
6) NP[concat(c1,c2),-,-] → N[c1=Desktop,-,-] FN[c2=Computer,-,-]
7) DP[-,hdd,-] → ADJ[-,r1=hard,-] N[-,r2=disk,-]
8) DPF[concat(c1,c2),r,-] → N[c1=LCD,r,-] N[c1=monitor,r,-]
9) DPF[concat(c1,c2),r,-] → V[-,r=hasStorageDevice,-] N[c1=CD,-,-] N[c1=Reader,-,-]

Fig. 2. Example Level 1 Grammar Rules

1) 2) 3) 4) map nouns N,FN to constituents NP,DP,DPF, which can contain more than one noun.

6) 7) 8) 9) deal with elements in the ontology represented by two or more words in the sentence. In particular, Rule 9) represents a role with its filler.

5) since number restriction are needed in e-commerce scenarios, as good descriptions, we allow to introduce them in this grammar. Role 5) creates a new DP constituent linking the role `mb` to its numerical restriction, *e.g.*, ($\geq$ 256 `mb`).

Level 2 Grammar. This grammar binds the sentence to the expressiveness of the DL chosen to model the ontology. The purpose of Level 2 rules is to put together single concepts and roles of the ontology, to form an expression in DL representing the logical model of the sentence, reflecting the structure of the good/description ontological pattern. With respect to the rules in Fig. 3 we obtain:

1) 2) 3) introduce the DL operators $\geq$ and $\forall$. Rule 1) states that if there is a constituent DPF, *e.g.*, with `role="hasComponent"` and `concept= "LCD_monitor"`, a new DPA (a descriptive constituent) is created with `concept` containing the DL expression: ∀`hasComponent.LCD_monitor`. The distinction, inspired by the *Semantic Grammars* approach, is useful to reduce ambiguity in the resulting logical form. In a similar way rule 2) introduces the operator ($\geq n\ R$) and the DPL category containing this operator. Rule 3) manages the case of an ($\geq n\ R$) nested in a $\forall R.C$ expression such as ∀`RAM.`($\geq$ 256 `mb`).

4) 6) are useful to compose contiguous constituents of the same type.

5) 7) state that a sentence is composed by a constituent NP representing the good of the advertisement, followed by descriptive constituents DPA or DPC.

1) DPA[(all r c)] → DPF[c,r]
2) DPL[(atLeast x r)] → DP[-,r,x]
3) DPA[(all r2 c1)] → DPL[c1,-] DP[-,r2]
4) DPC[c1 c2] → DPA[c1,-] DPL[c2,-]
5) S[(And c1 c2 c3)] → DPC[c1,-] NP[c2,-] DPA[c3,-]
6) DPA[c1 c2] → DPA[c1,-] DPA[c2,-]
7) S[(And c1 c2)] → NP[c1,-] DPA[c2,-]

Fig. 3. Example Level 2 Grammar Rules

3.2 Ambiguity Resolution Through Filtering

After the parsing process, more then one DL logical expression –corresponding to the NL sentence– can be produced. Interacting with the DL reasoner, the parser is able to reduce the number of expression to just one, thanks to the domain knowledge. This is performed through the application of a sequence of post-processing filters.

1. *Removing unsatisfiable descriptions.* Descriptions unsatisfiable with respect to the ontology are filtered out.
2. *Ontological pattern matching.* Checks whether the DL descriptions match a given ontological pattern. In the marketplace scenario it is verified if the

concept expressions keep the good/description structure via a subsumption check with a DL expression representing such structure.

3. *Subsumption relationship.* Given D_1, D_2 two different translations of the same advertisement, if $D_1 \sqsubseteq D_2$, the filter removes the more general description D_2, which is less specific than D_1.
4. After the application of the previous filters, there could yet be more than one DL expression $D_1, D_2, ..., D_n$ associated to the sentence. In order both to avoid the same sentence being described with logical formulas inconsistent with each other and to put together all the information extracted from the NL sentence, we model the final translation as the conjunction of all the translations remaining after previous stages. In this way, if two resulting descriptions, D_i,D_j model information incompatible with each other, *i.e.*, $D_i \sqcap D_j \equiv \bot$, then an error message is returned, stating that the parser is not able to find a unique semantic model of the sentence. Furthermore, in this way we are able to catch all available information, even if it is not present in every candidate expression associated to the sentence.

4 System and Results

The NL parser presented here was designed with the aim of making the system as flexible and modular as possible. It is implemented in Java and all configurations, including grammars, are provided as XML files; a snapshot of the Graphical interface is in Fig. 4. The parser is is part of the MAMAS[2] framework, a semantic-based matchmaking service, which uses a largely modified version of the NeoClassic reasoner to provide both standard inference services (*e.g.*, subsumption and satisfiability) and novel non-standard services, in an $\mathcal{ALN}$DL, especially tailored for e-marketplaces. Given a supply/demand advertisement *potential ranking* [11] retrieves a sorted list of *satisfiable* matching advertisements, ranked accordng to their mismatch semantic distance from the query; *partial ranking* [11] retrieves a sorted list of *unsatisfiable* matching advertisements, ranked according to their dissimilarity semantic distance from the query (basically useful when nothing better exists); *abduce* [10] provides descriptions of what is missing in a description to completely fulfill the query, *i.e.*, it extends subsumption providing an explanation. To provide a flavor of the system behavior, in the following we report matchmaking results with respect to the marketplace descriptions shown in Table 1. Notice that in the table *demand0* is not consistent with the knowledge modeled in the ontology because of processors number specification[3]. Hence, the ranked list below is related only to *demand1* versus *supply1*, *supply2*, *supply3*.

---

[2] Available at http://dee227.poliba.it:8080/MAMAS-devel/

[3] The ontology describes a desktop computer as a machine endowed with exactly 1 CPU (`Desktop_Computer` $\sqsubseteq$ ...(= 1 `hasCPU`) $\sqcap$ ...), then a notebook defined as a desktop computer (`Notebook` $\sqsubseteq$ `Desktop_Computer`...) cannot have two processors.

Table 1. Marketplace example

demands	**NL sentence/DL translation**
demand0	– *Looking for a Pentium4 biprocessor notebook with 256 mb RAM.* – `Request Incoherent w.r.t. the Ontology`
demand1	– *Desktop computer with 30 Gb hard disk, lcd monitor included.* – $\mathtt{Desktop\_Computer} \sqcap \forall \mathtt{hdd.}(\geq\ 30\ \mathtt{gb}) \sqcap \mathtt{hasComponentLCD\_monitor}$
supplies	**NL sentence/DL translation**
supply1	–*Offering Notebook with 40 Gb hard disk and 256 Mb ram.* – $\mathtt{Notebook} \sqcap \forall \mathtt{RAM.}(=\ 256\ \mathtt{mb}) \sqcap \forall \mathtt{hdd.}(=\ 40\ \mathtt{gb})$
supply2	– *Offering Desktop computer with 80 Gb hard disk and 512 mb ram equipped with cd reader.* – $\mathtt{Desktop\_Computer} \sqcap \forall \mathtt{RAM.}(=\ 512\ \mathtt{mb}) \sqcap \forall \mathtt{hdd.}(=\ 80\ \mathtt{gb})$ $\sqcap \forall \mathtt{hasStorageDevice.CD\_Reader}$
supply3	– *Offering Server with Pentium4 processors.* – $\mathtt{Server} \sqcap \forall \mathtt{hasCPU.Intel\_Pentium4}$

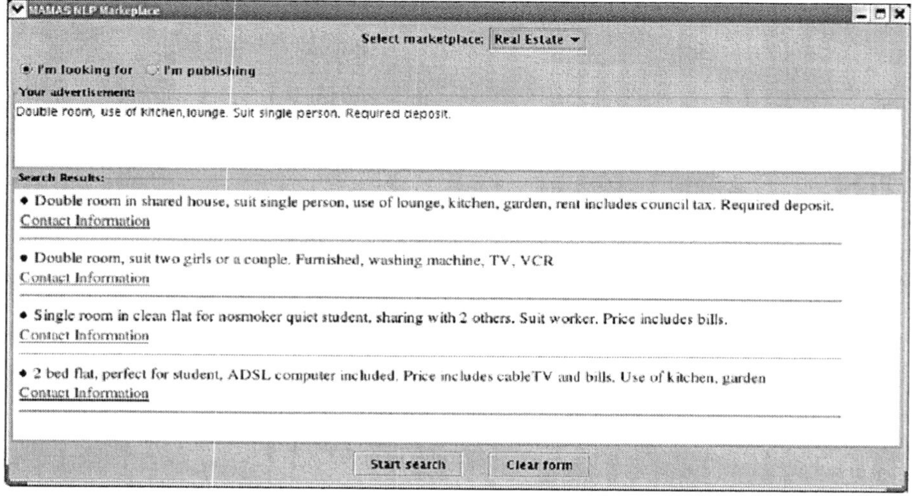

Fig. 4. Parser graphical user interface

Potential matches ranking list ([potential ranking] – [abduce] results):
supply1 vs. *demand1* [0] – [$\top$]
supply2 vs. *demand1* [1] – [$\forall \mathtt{hasComponent.LCD\_monitor}$]
Analyzing the above results, we see that *supply1* completely satisfies *demand1*, in fact the mismatch distance is 0, as there is a subsumption relation between *demand1* and *supply1*, as can be also argued by the $\top$ result for the related Concept Abduction Problem. With reference to *supply2*, in order to make it completely satisfy *demand1*, information on $\forall \mathtt{hasComponent.LCD\_monitor}$

Table 2. Test Results

Translated Advertisements	**89**
Completely translated	73
Incomplete translations	16
Wrong translation	**9**
Inconsistent translation w.r.t. the ontology	**2**

should be specified, then the distance computed w.r.t. the ontology is 1 (instead of 2, due to the axiom in the ontology stating that $\texttt{Desktop\_Computer} \sqsubseteq \ldots \sqcap \forall\texttt{hasComponent.Monitor}\ldots$).
Partial matches ranking list ([partial ranking] result): *supply3* vs. *demand1* [1]

To carry out a test of the parser performances, without any claim of completeness, we selected the domain of real estate advertisements. The domain knowledge was provided examining advertisements from several English newspapers and websites. The ontology built for this marketplace is composed by 146 concepts and 33 roles. The Lexicon is of 553 words, and Level 1 and Level 2 Grammars respectively have 79 and 58 rules. We randomly selected 100 advertisements (all different from those originally used during the domain definition) from various British websites and used them as test set. Results are summarized in Table 2.

5 Discussion and Conclusion

The Semantic Web intiative, which envisions ontology-based semantic markup both for interoperability between automated agents and to support human users in using semantic information, has provided a renovated interest towards NL based systems and approaches. Relevant recent works include *Aqualog* [8], which uses the GATE (http://gate.ac.uk) infrastructure and resources, extended by use of Jape grammars that add relations and question indicators to annotations returned by GATE. The input query in natural language is mapped to a triple-based data model, of the form ¡subject, predicate, object¿. These then are further processed by a dedicated module to produce ontology-compliant queries. If multiple relations are possible candidates for interpreting the query, they revert to string matching is used to determine the most likely candidate, using the relation name, eventual aliases, or synonyms provided by lexical resources such as WordNet. Swift et al. [13] proposed a semi-automatic method for corpus annotation using a broad-coverage deep parser to generate syntactic structure, semantic representation and discourse information for task-oriented dialogs. The parser, like the one we propose, is based on a bottom-up algorithm and an augmented context-free grammar with hierarchical features, but generates a semantic representation that is a flat unscoped logical form with events and labeled semantic arguments. This method builds linguistically annotated corpora semi-automatically by generating syntactic, semantic and discourse information with the parser, but the best parse has to be selected by hand from a set of alternatives. Our system, instead, uses a post-processing module that refers to an ontology and a reasoner to automatically select the final translated sentence. Semantic interpretation in our system is performed using a semantic grammar, which allows to produce constituents with both syntactic and semantic meanings; a similar approach is used by Bos et al. [4]; they apply *Combinatory Categorial Grammar* (CCG) to generate semantic representations starting from CCG parser. The tool they use to build semantic representations is based on the lambda calculus and constructs first-order representations from CCG derivations. In this work we exploited use of knowledge domain, to model task ontologies and grammars, making them both highly re-usable. We are currently working on the introduction of a morphological analysis in conjunction with WordNet for lexicon modeling, and on an extension of the approach to more expressive DLs.

Acknowledgments

The authors acknowledge partial support of projects PON CNOSSO, PITAGORA, and MS3DI.

References

1. A.Lavelli, B.Magnini, and C.Strapparava. An approach to multilevel semantics for applied systems. In *Proc. ANLP'92*, pages 17–24, 1992.
2. James Allen. *Natural Language Understanding (2nd ed.)*. The Benjamin Cummings Publishing Company Inc., 1999.
3. F. Baader, D. Calvanese, D. Mc Guinness, D. Nardi, and P. Patel-Schneider, editors. *The Description Logic Handbook*. Cambridge University Press, 2002.
4. J. Bos, S. Clark, and M. Steedman. Wide-coverage semantic representations from a ccg parser. In *Proc. COLING-04*, 2004.
5. R.J. Brachman and H.J. Levesque. The tractability of subsumption in frame-based description languages. In *Proc. AAAI-84*, pages 34–37, 1984.
6. J.A.Bateman. Upper modeling: Organizing knowledge for natural language processing. In *Proc. 5th Int. Workshop on Natural Language Generation*, pages 54–61, 1990.
7. K.Knight and S.Luk. Building a large knowledge base for machine translation. In *Proc. AAAI'94*, 1994.
8. V. Lopez and E.Motta. Ontology-driven question answering in aqualog. In *Proc. NLDB-04*, 2004.
9. T. Di Noia, E. Di Sciascio, and F.M. Donini. Extending Semantic-Based Matchmaking via Concept Abduction and Contraction. In *Proc. EKAW 2004*, pages 307–320. 2004.
10. T. Di Noia, E. Di Sciascio, F.M. Donini, and M. Mongiello. Abductive matchmaking using description logics. In *Proc. IJCAI-03*, pages 337–342, 2003.
11. T. Di Noia, E. Di Sciascio, F.M. Donini, and M. Mongiello. A system for principled Matchmaking in an electronic marketplace. *International Journal of Electronic Commerce*, 8(4):9–37, 2004.

12. R.Brachman, R.Bobrow, P.Cohen, J.Klovstad, B.Webber, and W.Woods. Research in natural language understanding, annual report. Technical Report 4274, Bolt Beranek and Newman, 1979.
13. M. D. Swift, M. O. Dzikovska, J. R. Tetreault, and J. F. Allen. Semi-automatic syntactic and semantic corpus annotation with a deep parser. In *Proc. LREC 04*, 2004.

Towards Effective Adaptive Information Filtering Using Natural Language Dialogs and Search-Driven Agents*

Anita Ferreira-Cabrera[1] and John A. Atkinson-Abutridy[2]

[1] Departamento de Español,
Universidad de Concepción, Concepción, Chile
aferreir@udec.cl
[2] Departamento de Ingeniería Informática,
Universidad de Concepción, Concepción, Chile
atkinson@inf.udec.cl

Abstract. In this paper, an adaptive natural language dialog model for Web-based cooperative interactions is proposed to improve the results in achieving a successful filtered search on the Web. The underlying principle, based on automatically generating language-driven interactions which take into account the context and the user's feedback is discussed. The preliminary working design and experiments, and the results of some real evaluations are also highlighted.

1 Introduction

The increasing use of Web resources in the last years has caused a need for more efficient and useful search methods. Unfortunately, the current mechanisms to assist the search process and retrieval are quite limited mainly due to the lack of access to the document's semantics and the underlying difficulties to provide more suitable search patterns.

Although keyword-based information retrieval systems can provide a fair first approach to the overall process so far, one of the next challenges will be to carry out these kind of tasks more precise and smarter in order to make good use of the user's knowledge (i.e., intentions, goals) so to improve the searching capabilities with a minimum of communicating exchanges. Our approach's main claims relies on the following working hypotheses:

- To decrease information overload in searching for information implies "filtering" that in an intelligent way in terms of the context and the user's feedback.

* This research is sponsored by the National Council for Scientific and Technological Research (FONDECYT, Chile) under grant number 1040500 "*Effective Corrective-Feedback Strategies in Second Language Teaching with Implications for Intelligent Tutorial Systems for Foreign Languages.*"

M. Ali and F. Esposito (Eds.): IEA/AIE 2005, LNAI 3533, pp. 290–299, 2005.

– To take into account the linguistic underlying knowledge as main working support can assist us to specify and to restrict the real user's requirements to capture the user knowledge.

The main working focus of this work is on improving the whole information searching paradigm with both a computational linguistics model and a more suitable search agent to filter and so to overcome the information overload issue. Our approach's backbone will be made of task-dependent discourse and dialog analysis capabilities as a major interactive searching system. While the original approach and implementation were carried out to deal with Spanish dialogs, we provide a model which can be easily adapted to other languages as long as the right grammar and pragmatic constraints are taken into account.

Our experiments, conducted in the context of a filtering system for Web documents, shows the promise of combine *Natural Language Processing* (NLP) techniques with simple inference methods to address an information searching problem. In what follows, we first motivate our work by discussing previous work. Next, the distinguishing features of our approach is described along with the analysis methods and used representation. Finally, details of some experiments and results are highlighted.

2 Information Filtering and Search

Several search engines use automated software which goes out onto the web and obtains the contents of each server it encounters, indexing documents as it finds them. This approach results in the kind of databases maintained and indexed by services such as *Alta Vista and Excite.* However, users may face problems when using such databases such as the relevance of the retrieved information, the information overload, etc.

Intelligent searching agents have been developed in order to provide a partial solution to these problems [7]. These agents can use apply spider technology used by traditional Web search engines, and employ this in new ways. Usually, these tools are "robots" which can be trained so to search the web for specific types of information resources. The agent can be personalized by its owner so that it can build up a picture of individual profiles or precise information needs.

These agents can learn from past experiences and will provide the users with the facility of reviewing search results and rejecting any information sources which are neither relevant nor useful. This information will be stored in a user profile which the agent uses when performing a search. For this, an agent can also learn from its initial forays into the web, and return with a more tightly defined searching agenda if requested. Some of the representative current tools using this technology include *FireFly*, *Webwatcher*, *Letizi*, etc. A common constraint of many search systems is the lack of a deeper linguistic analysis of the user's requirements and context to assist him/her in getting a more specific view about what he/she really wants.

Several approaches have been used to get into the document's "semantics", including *Foltz* which uses Latent Semantic Analysis to filter news articles, *IN-*

FOSCOPE which uses rule-based agents to watch the user's behavior and then to make suggestions, *MAXIMS* for collaborative electronic filtering, etc.

In this context, learning and adaptation capabilities become more important in a Information Filtering (IF) context rather than Information Retrieval (IR) because of the underlying environment's features: IF systems are used by huge groups of users who are generally not motivated information seekers, and so their interests are often weakly defined and understated.

On the language side, part of these problems could be overcame either by extracting deep knowledge from what the users are looking for or by interactively generating more explanatory requests to have users more focused in their interests. Although some research has been carried out using NLP technology to capture user's profiles, it has only been used in very restricted domains which use general-purpose linguistic resources [2].

Deeper approaches can be applied by making good use of NLP. In particular, *Natural Language Generation* (NLG) techniques can be used to allow the system to produce good and useful "dialogs" with the user. An important issue in this regard is on decreasing the number of generated conversation/interaction turns in order for the user to obtain the information (i.e., references to documents) he/she is looking for.

Over the last years, NLG research has strongly evolved due to the results obtained in the first investigations. Since then, the task of establishing and processing the discourse's content has been privileged [8]. A key issue issue here concerns the discourse planning in which, based on the speech acts theory [4], linguistic concepts are incorporated into the description of computer systems producing plans which contain sequences of speech acts [3]. In order to model NLG-based dialog interactions, some approaches have been identified including *Dialog Grammars*, *Dialog Plan based Theories*, *Dialogue as Cooperation*.

It is generally agreed that developing a successful computational model of interactive NL dialogue requires deep analysis of sample dialogues. Some of the types of dialogues include Human-Human dialogues in specific task domains, Human-Computer dialogues based on initial implementation of computational models, *Wizard of Oz (WOZ) dialogues* in which a human (the Wizard) simulates the role of the computer as a way of testing out an initial model [6].

While much knowledge can be gained from WOZ-based experimentation, this is not an adequate mean of studying all elements of human-computer NL dialogue. A simulation is plausible as long as humans can use their own problem-solving skills in carrying out the simulation. However, as the technique requires mimicking a proposed algorithm, this becomes impractical.

Despite of this potential drawback, this paper reports work that attempts to deal with WOZ techniques in a controlled experiment so as to conceive a task-specific dialog model.

3 Search-Driven Dialog Management

In coming up with suitable profiles or likes, current filtering systems allow the users to specify one or more sample documents as reflective of his/her interests [9] instead of requiring direct explicit definition of interest, whereas others attempt to learn those from the user's observed behavior. This kind of approach turns to be impractical as users are not focused in what they really want when they have not obtained documents matching their requirements.

Instead of providing samples or going through the Web looking for relevant information, we propose a new approach in which search requirements are focused by using a dialog-based discourse interaction system so to capture the user specific interests.

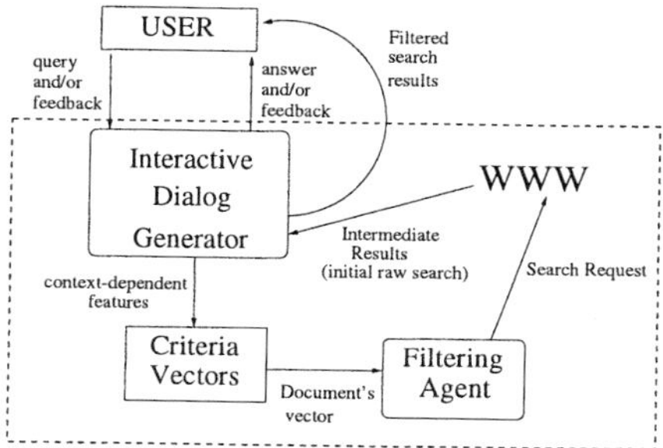

Fig. 1. The Overall Search-driven Dialog System

Our model for searching/filtering through discourse processing is shown in figure 1. The operation starts from Natural Language (NL) queries provided by the user (i.e., general queries, general responses, feedback, confirmation, etc) and then passed through the dialog manager so this generates the corresponding interaction exchanges ("turns") so to arrive into a more elaborated and specific search request. As the dialog goes on, the system generates a more refined query which finally is passed through a search agent. The results of the search are explicitly delivered to the user as soon as these have been appropriately filtered, which depends on previous interactions, the user's context and the features extracted from the queries.

3.1 Experiments with Web-Based Dialogs

A preliminary experimental stage consisted of recording, observing and establishing the dialogue structure produced by users in a communicating situation involving information searching on the Web. In order to classify explanatory and descriptive dialogs shown in a user-computer dialogue interaction, a set of experiments was carried to gather a corpora of dialogue discourses between user and computer. To this end, a series of activities were designed and then performed as case studies in a communicating situation involving natural language interaction.

As part of the methodology, dialog models can be built up from the data above using the WOZ technique. In our model, this method has been used to develop and to test the dialogue models. During each interaction, the human (*the Wizard*) simulates a system which interacts with the users who believe to be interacting with a system which (supposedly) handles natural language. Next, the dialogues are recorded, annotated and analyzed with the ultimate goal of improving the dialogue model and therefore, the interaction. In the actual experiments, WOZ has been used to gather dialogue corpus which allows us to analyze the transcriptions and to establish a dialogue structure based model that will support the planning and generation of interactive explanatory and descriptive discourse.

In the experimental sessions, a threshold of 20 minutes was considered to check for the user's communicating goal accomplishment with a total number of 20 non-expert subjects being involved. For this, the sample was divided into four groups, in which the first three ones were randomly selected whereas the fourth one was constituted by graduate students of linguistics. They were then required to perform the search and to provide explanations and descriptions from what they obtained from the search results.

3.2 Interactive Discourse Generator

The discourse generator relies on several stages which state the context, the participants' knowledge and the situation in which the dialogue discourse analyzed by the system is embedded. This also considers a set of modules in which input and output is delimited according to different stages of linguistic and non-linguistic information processing defined by the dialogue. This phase is strongly based on the linguistic proposal of a model to discourse processing and the discourse approach regarding the components of interaction and action.

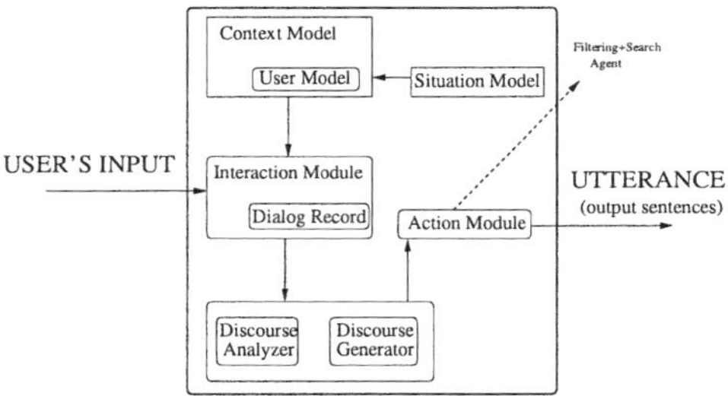

Fig. 2. The Interactive Dialog Processing Stage

In figure 2, the proposed model to generate discourse on bibliographic search on the Web is shown. This starts with the user's input (NL query) and produces either an output consisting on a NL conversation exchange to guide the dialog so to have the user more focused or a search request to be passed through the search agent.

In order to better understand the approach, the underlying working has been separated into different components as stated in figure 2:

- *The Context Model* deals with the information regarding the dialogue's participants. This is, the "user" who needs information from the Web and the "system" which performs the search. This model states the kind of social situation called "bibliographical queries on the Web" and the participants' goals: "find out information about some topic" and "assist the user on achieving her/his goal through collaborative dialog at searching the Web. Here, the *User Model* includes knowledge about the user (i.e., features) who the system will interact with.
- *The Interaction Module* is based on Grice's cooperative principle and collaborative maxims [5] and involves two-position exchange structures such as question/answer, greeting/greeting and so on. These exchange structures are subject to constraints on the system's conversation, regarding a two-way ability to transmit through the keyboard, suitable and understandable messages as confirmation acts.
- *The Discourse Analyzer* receives the user's query and analyzes the information contained in order to define the conditions which can address the system's response generation. This module's outcome is the query recognized and analyzed by the system.
- *The Discourse Generator* involves both the information from the search agent's *information recording module* and that coming from the *dialog recording module* to produce a coherent utterance on the current dialog state. As a first output, the module generates a question to the user about the information needed to produce the corresponding utterance to the dialog's conversational turn.

Dialog starts by generating the kind of utterance "query about information requested by the user". The system then considers two possible generations: an specific query for the communicating situation (`what topic do you want to search for?`) and a general one on the context of the different kinds of information available on the Web. Next, further user's requests can be divided into four general higher groups: request for information, positive/negative confirmation, specification of features, and specification of topic.

The discourse analyzer processes the user's input and gets the information needed to the search agent which performs the selected search itself. From the obtained information (i.e., references to documents) the NL generator addresses the dialog towards an explanatory generation into two kind of possible utterances: one aimed at having a more detailed specification of the user's query: *"Your query is too general, could you be more specific?"*, or one which requires the user to state some feature of the topic being consulted: *"I found too much information, in which one are you interested most?"*. The discourse analyzer again performs the analysis on the user's specific input in order for the agent to perform an suitable search.

The search actions are performed by an action generation module (figure 2) which receives the information analyzed from the discourse analyzer. At this point, the (discourse) analyzer processes the user's response in order for the generator to produce an output confirming or expressing the action done (i.e.,

"Did you find what you were looking for?"). Furthermore, the overall process starts by establishing a top goal to built down the full structure in the sentence level. Once the goal has been recognized, the corresponding speech acts are produced to guide the further NL generation.

3.3 Searching and Filtering Agent

Unlike traditional search engines or IR systems, we have designed a search agent which does not deliver all the information to the user in the very first interaction. The preliminary information is used to feed both the system's knowledge and the user's request and queries. As the dialog goes on, the agent refines the request and filters the initial information already obtained until a proper amount of information can be displayed at the page of the dialog.

This Filtering Agent (figure 1) is made of three components: the information searcher, the criteria analyzer which deals with the obtained information according to some parameters (criteria), and the information status recorder which keeps the information about the results of the analysis to be accessed by the discourse generator so to produce the output sentence. Both documents and user's queries are represented in a multidimensional space. Thus, when a query is processed this is then translated into a pattern representing a criteria vector.

Those criteria represent important context information related to obtained Web pages and so they can be useful in training the patterns and filtering the results. Initially, criterion X_0 will concern the subject or input's topic and the rest of the vector will remain empty (as the dialog proceeds and new search results are obtained, these slots are filled). In addition, each criterion has some "weight" which represents its contribution to a defined document or the importance of some features over others.

From these criteria, dialog samples and context information, it was possible to extract and synthesize the most frequent and useful search patterns. Some of them included the *URL Address of the Web page being selected, Documents' author, Language in which the document is written in, Document's source country, Type of document/page (commercial, education, etc), documents related to events, Technical documentation, Research groups, Products and Services*, and so on.

Decisions on specific actions to be taken given certain context knowledge (i.e., criteria) will depend on two kind of ground conditions: *information on the documents' slots/criteria (if any)*, and *simple inferences drawn when the previous information is not enough.* The later has to do with a rough statistical confidence of performing certain action given some criteria values (i.e., Bayesian inference). The result of this inference has two basic consequences: one affecting the information filtered and other assisting the sentence generation to look for criteria/features missed or incomplete.

In practice, the actions are translated into high level goals of pragmatic constraints which cause a particular kind of NL dialog to be generated (i.e., question, request, feedback,..).

4 Working Example and Results

The results of applying the model can be described in terms of two main issues regarding our initial goals and hypotheses. One hypothesis concerns the kind of utterance automatically generated by the system which suggests that the search-driven dialog generation can be plausible. A second issue concerns the benefits of using this kind of interaction to overcome the information overload so that the time spent by the user looking for information is decreased.

On the dialog processing side, a prototype was built in which the discourse generator was implemented and a restricted medium-size NL interface for user's input parsing was designed using the GILENA NL interfaces generator [1] which allowed us to tie the application with the Web resources.

In processing the rules implemented in the discourse generator, several discourse inputs were used. Thus, generating each rule involved producing the corresponding utterance. The analysis of results was based on the generation of 1000 dialog structure samples obtained from the discourse processing task carried out by the system. The discourse manager was able to generate dialog structures and to interact with the user starting from communicating goals as follows (**S** stands for the system's output, and **U** for the user's input, with the corresponding English translations):

ACTION: the system generates a kind of sentence/query on a topic requested by the user:

```
S: What are you interested in?
U: about linguistics
```

ACTION: "Specification of the results of the search topic" (the generation will involve a turn to request more specific information about the topic):

```
S: Your query is too broad, could you please be more specific? U:
bueno/Ok
```

ACTION: Search's results and dialog context dependent generation (the kind of utterance generated is fully adaptive so it varies from one interaction to other):

```
U: The information obtained is written in different languages,
 do you prefer it in Spanish? ..
U: There are twenty references about that topic, do you want
   to check all of them? ..
U: I found information about research groups, courses, etc,
    what are you interested in?
```

On the filtering side, the system performance was analyzed regarding the experiments evaluating the number of conversational turns in the dialog necessary to get a more accurate requirement and filtered information against the number of references/documents which matched these requirements. Initially, the set of possible candidate became more than 30000 document references but for the simplicity's sake the scope has been reduced to a maximum of 1000 references.

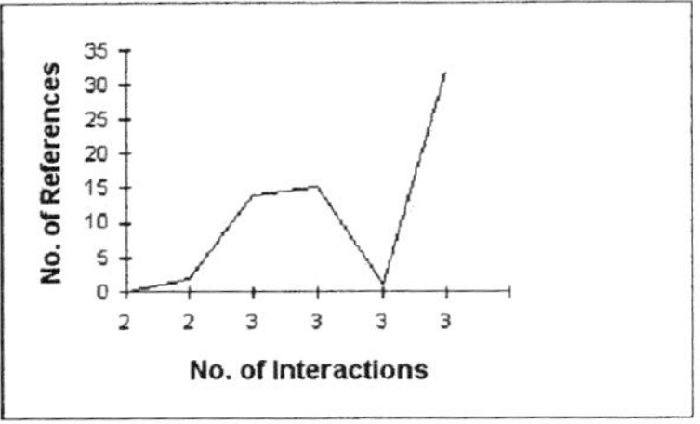

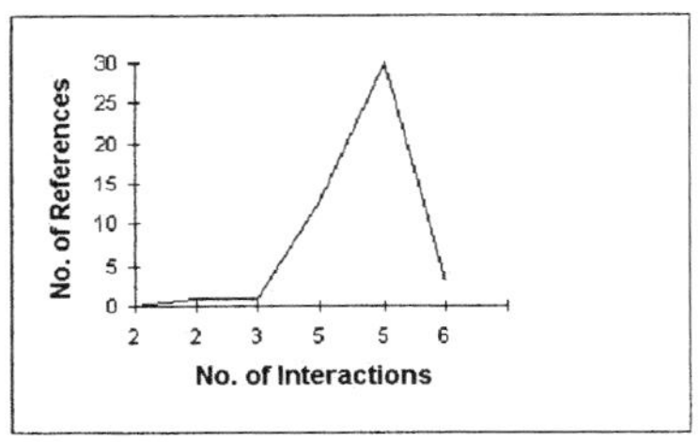

Fig. 3. Interactive Experiments: Number of Interactions vs Number of obtained References

Two experiments were carried out (figure 3). In a first one, one of the main topics of interest was around the focus `Object` (not the keyword), and the second, `Movies`. In order to better understand the analysis, each interaction is defined by one or more dialogs (exchanges) between user and system.

Interactions in experiment No. 1 showed an increase in the number of documents matched as more than three turns are exchanged. It does not come up by a chance: for the same number of interactions (i.e., five), different results are showed mainly due to the adaptive way the dialog continues. This is, the context and kind of the questions made by the agent are changing depending on the situation and the document's contents. Different results were obtained for the same number of interactions because the type of document searched for was changed as other features were restricted. A similar situation arises as the user states a constraint regarding the language, in which case, most of the references matched were not produced at all.

In the second experiment, something slightly similar happened. Even in dialogs with three exchanges, sudden increments were observed, going up from 1 to nearly 35 resulting references. One of the reasons for this growth is an inference drawn by the agent and a user's restriction related to the document's nature he/she is looking for (i.e., type of page, etc).

From both experiments, it can be seen that there is an important drop in the results obtained with a minimum of conversation turns due to constraints on the nature of the information finally delivered. Our prototype agent took into account the previous issues hence there are some classes of high level requests which are more likely to occur than others.

5 Conclusions

In this paper, we described a model for natural language based Web filtering and its cooperative strategies to deal with the problem of information overloading when interactions with the user are taken into account.

Initial hypotheses regarding user's feedback and the search agent's inference capabilities have been experimentally tested in medium-size situations. The analysis could have gone deeper, from an IR point of view, however our goal was to provide an integrated view in order to put together all the referred elements rather than concentrating on typical IR metrics as they mainly involves the surface side of the searching/filtering process (feedback loop is never considered).

From the underlying experiments, we hypothesize that a lot of time could be saved if we are were provided with weighted features usually presented on the information retrieved depending on its importance degree or usage. Whatever the situation, interactions (in form and content) will strongly rely on those factors, and this should not leave user's contributions apart from the decisions being made by the system. From a language-centered viewpoint, the current model based on dialog interactions suggest a promising work methodology to deal with more specific information searching requirements in which both designing and implementing a NLG system can easily be adapted to the current communicating situation. Even although there is a lot of NLG systems, as far as we know, this is the first attempt to integrate these technologies to address the problems of searching and filtering on the Web.

References

1. J. Atkinson and A. Ferreira. The design and implementation of the gilena natural language interface specification language. *ACM SIGPLAN*, 33(9):108–117, 1998.
2. E. Bloedorn and I. Mani. Using NLP for machine learning of user profiles. *Intelligent Data Analysis*, 1998.
3. J. Chu-Carroll. Mimic: an adaptive mixed initiative spoken dialogue system for informatio n queries. *Proceedings of the 6th Conference on Applied Natural Language Processin g, Seattle-USA*, 2000.
4. P. Cohen and H. Levesque. Performatives in a rationally based speech act theory. Technical Note 486, SRI International, 1990.
5. H. Grice. Logic and conversation. In *Syntax and Semantics*. Cole Morgan, 1975.
6. D. Jurafsky and J. Martin. *An Introduction to Natural Language Processing, Computational Linguistics, and Speech Recognition*. Prentice-Hall, 2000.
7. A. Levy and D. Weld. Intelligent internet systems. *Artificial Intelligence*, 11(8):1–14, 2000.
8. E. Reiter and R. Dale. *Building natural language generation systems*. Cambridge University Press, 2000.
9. L. Tong, T. Changjie, and Z. Jie. Web document filtering technique based on natural language understanding. *International Journal of Computer Processing of Oriental Languages*, 14(3):279–291, 2001.

Towards Minimization of Test Sets for Human-Computer Systems

Fevzi Belli and Christof J. Budnik

University of Paderborn,
Warburger Str. 100, 33098 Paderborn, Germany
{belli, budnik}@adt.upb.de

Abstract. A model-based approach for minimization of test sets for human-computer systems is introduced. Test cases are efficiently generated and selected to cover both the behavioral model and the complementary fault model of the system under test (SUT). Results known from state-based conformance testing and graph theory are used and extended to construct algorithms for minimizing the test sets.

1 Introduction

Testing is the traditional validation method in the software industry. This paper is a specification-oriented testing; i.e., the underlying model represents the system behavior interacting with the user's actions. The system's behavior and user's actions will be viewed here as *events,* more precisely, as *desirable events* if they are in accordance with the user expectations. Moreover, the approach includes modeling of the faults as *undesirable events* as, mathematically spoken, a complementary view of the behavioral model. Once the model is established, it "guides" the test process to generate and select test cases, which form *sets* of test cases (also called *test suites*). The selection is ruled by an *adequacy criterion,* which provides a measure of how effective a given set of test cases is in terms of its potential to reveal faults [10]. Most of the existing adequacy criteria are *coverage-oriented.* The ratio of the portion of the specification or code that is covered by the given test set in relation to the uncovered portion can then be used as a decisive factor in determining the point in time at which to stop testing (*test termination*). Another problem that arises is the determination of the test outcomes (*oracle problem*).

Based on [3], this paper introduces a novel graphical representation of both the behavioral model and the fault model of interactive systems. The number of the test cases primarily determines the test costs. Therefore sets of test cases (*test sets*) are constructed and minimized (*minimal spanning set for coverage testing*) by introduced algorithms. A *scalability* of the test process is given by the length of the test cases which are stepwise increased.

The next section summarizes the related work before Section 3 introduces the fault model and the test process. The minimization of the test suite is discussed in Section 4. Section 5 summarizes the results of different studies to validate the approach. Section 6 concludes the paper and sketches the research work planned.

M. Ali and F. Esposito (Eds.): IEA/AIE 2005, LNAI 3533, pp. 300 – 309, 2005.

2 Related Work

Methods based on finite-state automata (FSA) have been used for almost four decades for the specification and testing of system behavior [6], as well as for conformance and software testing [1, 15]. Also, the modeling and testing of interactive systems with a state-based model has a long tradition [16,17]. These approaches analyze the SUT and model the user requirements to achieve sequences of *user interaction* (*UI*), which then are deployed as test cases. A simplified state-based, graphical model to represent UIs is introduced to consider not only the desirable situations, but also the undesirable ones. This strategy is quite different from the combinatorial ones, e.g., *pairwise testing,* which requires that for each pair of input parameters of a system, every combination of these parameters' valid values must be covered by at least one test case. It is, in most practical cases, not feasible [18] to test UIs.

A similar fault model as in [3] is used in the mutation analysis and testing approach which systematically and stepwise modifies the SUT using *mutation operations* [8]. Although originally applied to implementation-oriented unit testing, mutation operations have also been extended to be deployed at more abstract, higher levels, e.g., integration testing, state-based testing, etc. [7]. Such operations have also been independently proposed by other authors, e.g., "state control faults" for fault modeling in [5], or for "transition-pair coverage criterion" and "complete sequence criterion" in [15]. However, the latter two notions have been precisely introduced in [3] and [21]. A different approach, especially for graphical UI (GUI) testing, has been introduced in [13]; it deploys methods of knowledge engineering to generate test cases, test oracles, etc., and to deal with the test termination problem. All of these approaches use some heuristic methods to cope with the state explosion problem.

This paper also presents a method for test case generation and selection. Moreover, it addresses test coverage aspects for test termination, based on [3], which introduced the notion of "minimal spanning set of complete test sequences", similar to "spanning set", that was also later discussed in [12]. The present paper considers existing approaches to optimize the round trips, i.e., the Chinese Postman Problem [1], and attempts to determine algorithms of less complexity for the spanning of walks, rather than tours, related to [20,14].

3 Fault Model and Test Process

This work uses *Event Sequence Graphs* (*ESGs*) for representing the system behavior and, moreover, the facilities from the user's point of view to interact with the system. Basically, an event is an externally observable phenomenon, such as an environmental or a user stimulus, or a system response, punctuating different stages of the system activity.

3.1 Preliminaries

Definition 1. An *Event Sequence Graph* $ESG=(V,E)$ is a directed graph with a finite set of *nodes* (*vertices*) $V \neq \varnothing$ and a finite set of *arcs* (*edges*) $E \subseteq V \times V$.

For representing user-system interactions, the nodes of the ESG are interpreted as events. The operations on identifiable components are controlled/perceived by input/output devices. Thus, an event can be a user input or a system response; both of them are elements of V and lead interactively to a succession of user inputs and system outputs.

Definition 2. Let V, E be defined as in Definition 1. Then any sequence of nodes $\langle v_0,\ldots,v_k\rangle$ is called an (*legal*) *event sequence* (*ES*) if $(v_i, v_{i+1}) \in E$, for $i=0,\ldots,k-1$.

Furthermore, α (*initial*) and ω (*end*) are functions to determine the initial node and end node of an ES, i.e., $\alpha(ES)=v_0$, $\omega(ES)=v_k$. Finally, the function l (*length*) of an ES determines the number of its nodes. In particular, if $l(ES)=1$ then $ES=\langle v_i\rangle$ is an ES of length 1. An $ES=\langle v_i, v_k\rangle$ of length 2 is called an *event pair* (*EP*). *Event triple* (*ET*), *event quadruple* (*EQ*), etc. are defined accordingly.

Example 1. For the ESG given in Fig. 1, *BCBC* is an ES of length 4 with the initial node *B* and end node *C*.

The assumption is made that there is at least one ES from a special, single node ε (*entry*) to all other nodes, and from all nodes there is at least an ES to another special, single node γ (*exit*) with (ε, $\gamma \notin$ V). Note that it can be $\varepsilon=\gamma$. The entry and exit, represented in this paper by '[' and ']', respectively, enable a simpler representation of the algorithms to construct minimal spanning test case sets (Section 4). Note that entry and exit are not considered while generating ESs.

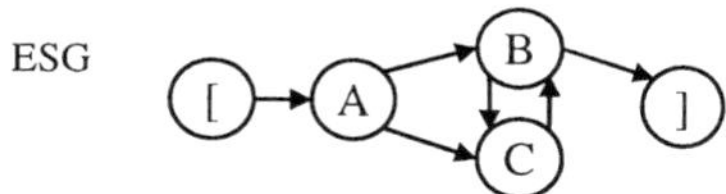

Fig. 1. An ESG with '[' as entry and ']' as exit

Example 2. For the ESG given in Fig. 1, *V* and *E* are: *V*={A,B,C}, *E*={(A,B), (A,C), (B,C), (C,B)}.

Definition 3. An ES is called a *complete* ES (*Complete Event Sequence*, *CES*), if $\alpha(ES)=\varepsilon$ is the entry and $\omega(ES)=\gamma$ is the exit.

Example 3. *ACB* is a CES of the ESG given in Fig. 1.

CESs represent *walks* from the entry '[' of the ESG to its exit ']'.

Definition 4. The node *w* is a *successor event* of *v* and the node *v* is a *predecessor event* of *w* if $(v,w) \in$ E .

Definition 5. Given an ESG, say $ESG_1 = (V_1, E_1)$, a *refinement* of ESG_1 through vertex $v \in V_1$ is an ESG, say $ESG_2 = (V_2, E_2)$. Let $N^+(v)$ be the *set of all successors* of *v*, and $N^-(v)$ be the *set of all predecessors* of *v*. Also let $N^-(ESG_2)$ be the *set of all EPs from start ('[') of* ESG_2, and $N^+(ESG_2)$ be the *set of all EPs from* ESG_2 *to exit (']') of* ESG_2. Then there should be given an *one-to-many mapping* from ESG_2 to ESG_1, $N^+(ESG_2) \rightarrow N^+(v)$ and $N^-(ESG_2) \rightarrow N^-(v)$.

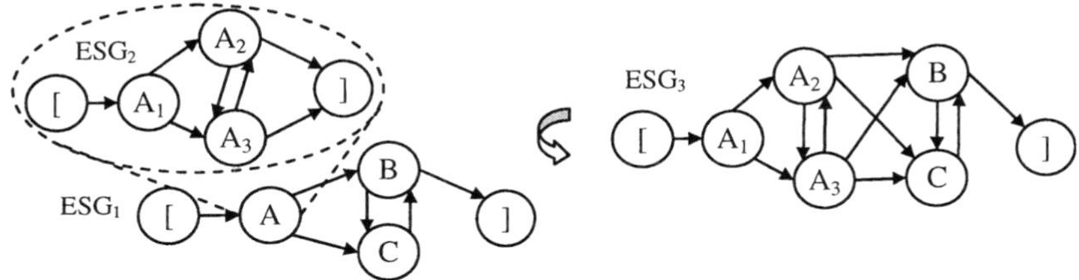

Fig. 2. A Refinement of the vertex *a* of the ESG given in Fig. 1

Fig. 2 shows a refinement of vertex *a* in ESG_1 given as ESG_2, and the resulting new ESG_3.

3.2 Fault Model and Test Terminology

Definition 6. For an ESG=(V, E), its *completion* is defined as $\widehat{ESG} = (V, \widehat{E})$ with $\widehat{E} = V \times V$.

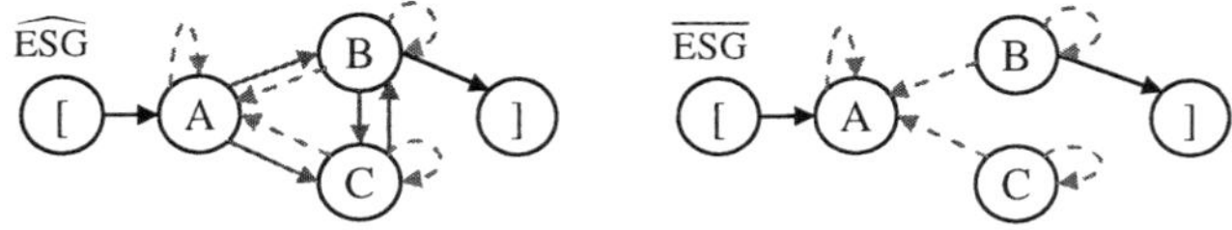

Fig. 3. The completion $\widehat{ESG}$ and inversion $\overline{ESG}$ of Fig. 1

Definition 7. The *inverse* (or *complementary*) ESG is then defined as $\overline{ESG} = (V, \overline{E})$ with $\overline{E} = \widehat{E} \setminus E$ (\: set difference operation).

Note that entry and exit are not considered while constructing the $\overline{ESG}$.

Definition 8. Any EP of the $\overline{\text{ESG}}$ is a faulty event pair (FEP) for ESG.

Example 4. *CA* of the given $\overline{ESG}$ in Fig. 3 is a FEP.

Definition 9. Let $ES=\langle v_0,\ldots,v_k\rangle$ be an event sequence of length $k+1$ of an ESG and $FEP=\langle v_k, v_m\rangle$ a faulty event pair of the according $\overline{ESG}$. The concatenation of the ES and FEP forms then a *faulty event sequence* $FES=\langle v_0,\ldots,v_k, v_m\rangle$.

Example 5. For the ESG given in Fig. 1, *ACBA* is an FES of length 4.

Definition 10. An FES will be called *complete* (*Faulty Complete Event Sequence, FCES*) if $\alpha(FES)=\varepsilon$ is the entry. The ES as part of a FCES is called a *starter*.

Example 6. For the ESG given in Fig. 1, the FE *CA* of Fig. 3 can be completed to the FCES *ACBCA* by using the ES *ACB* as a starter.

3.3 Test Process

Definition 11. A *test case* is an ordered pair of an input and expected output of the SUT. Any number of test cases can be compounded to a *test set* (or, a *test suite*).

The approach introduced in this paper uses event sequences, more precisely CES, and FCES, as test inputs. If the input is a CES, the SUT is supposed to successfully proceed it and thus, to *succeed* the test and to trigger a desirable event. Accordingly, if a FCES is used as a test input, a failure is expected to occur which is an undesirable event and thus, to *fail* the test. Algorithm 1 below sketches the test process.

Algorithm 1. Test Process

```
n:   number of the functional units (modules)
length:   length of the test sequences
FOR function 1 TO n DO
    Generate appropriate ESG and ESG-bar
    FOR k:=2 TO length DO                                    //see Section 4.2
        Cover all ESs of length k by means of CESs subject to
        minimizing the number and total length of the CESs   //see Section 4.1
    Cover all FEPs of by means of FCESs subject to
    minimizing the total length of the FCESs                 //see Section 4.3
Apply the test set to the SUT.
Observe the system output to determine whether the system response is in compli
ance with the expectation.
```

Note that the functional units *n* of a system in Algorithm 1 is given by the corresponding ESGs and their refinements (see Definition 5) that fulfill a well-defined task. To determine the point in time in which to stop testing, the approach converts this problem into the *coverage of the ES and FES of length k of the* $\widehat{ESG}$ whereby *k* is a decisive cost factor. Thus, depending on *k*, the test costs are to be scalable and stepwise increased by the tester in accordance with the quality goal and test budget.

4 Minimizing the Spanning Set

The union of the sets of CESs of minimal total length to cover the ESs of a required length is called *Minimal Spanning Set of Complete Event Sequences (MSCES).* If a CES contains all EPs at least once, it is called an *entire walk.* A legal entire walk is *minimal* if its length cannot be reduced. A minimal legal walk is *ideal* if it contains all EPs exactly once. Legal walks can easily be generated for a given ESG as CESs, respectively. It is not, however, always feasible to construct an entire walk or an ideal walk. Using some results of the graph theory [20], MSCESs can be constructed as the next section illustrates.

4.1 An Algorithm to Determine Minimal Spanning Set of Complete Event Sequences (MSCES)

The determination of MSCES represents a derivation of the *Directed Chinese Postman Problem (DCPP),* which has been studied thoroughly, e.g., in [1, 19]. The MSCES problem introduced here is expected to have a lower complexity grade, as the edges of the ESG are not weighted, i.e., the adjacent vertices are equidistant. In the following, some results are summarized that are relevant to calculate the test costs and enable scalability of the test process.

Fig. 4. Transferring walks into tours and balancing the nodes

For the determination of the set of minimal tours that covers the edges of a given graph, the algorithm described in [19] requires this graph be strongly connected. This can be reached for any ESG through an additional edge from the exit to the entry. The idea of transforming the ESG into a strongly connected graph is depicted in Fig. 4 as a dashed arc. The figures within the vertices indicate the balance of these vertices as the difference of the number of outgoing edges and the number of the incoming edges. These balance values determine the minimal number of additional edges from "+" to "-" that will be identified by searching the all-shortest-path and solving the optimization problem [2] by the Hungarian method [11]. The required additional edge for the ESG in Fig. 4 is represented as a dotted arc. The problem can then be transferred to the construction of the Euler tour for this graph [20]. Each occurrence of the ES=*][* in the Euler tour identifies another separate test case.

To sum up, the MSCES can be solved in $O(|V|^3)$ time. Example 8 lists a minimal set of the legal walks (i.e., CESs) for the ESG given in Fig. 4 to cover all event pairs.

Example 8. Euler tour=*[ABACBDCBC][* → MSCES=*ABACBDCBC.*

4.2 Generating ESs with Length >2

A phenomenon in testing interactive systems is that faults can often be detected and reproduced only in some context. This makes the consideration of test sequences of length>2 necessary since obviously only occurrences of some subsequences are expected to cause an error to occur and/or re-occur. For this purpose, the given ESG is "extended", leading to a graph the nodes of which can be used to generate test cases of length >2, in the same way that the nodes of the original ESG are used to generate event pairs and to determine its MSCES.

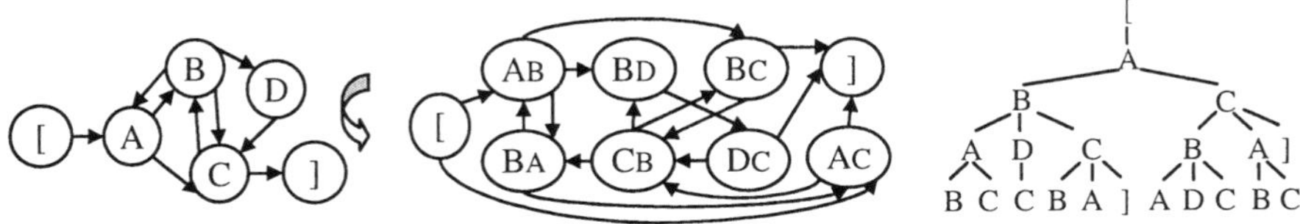

Fig. 5. Extending the ESG for covering ET and the reachability tree (not complete)

To solve this problem, the given ESG is transformed into a graph in which the nodes are used to generate test cases of length >2, in the same way that the nodes of the original ESG are used to generate EPs and to construct the appropriate MSCES. For this purpose, the reachability tree (Fig. 5) of the nodes is traversed to determine the sequences of adjacent nodes of length *n-1*, if any. The ESGs in Fig. 5 illustrates the generation of ESs of length=3, i.e., event triples (ETs). In this example adjacent nodes of the extended ESG are concatenated, e.g., *AB* is connected with *BD*, leading to *ABBD*. The shared event, i.e., *B*, occurs only once producing *ABD* as a ET. In case event quadruples (EQs) are to be generated, the extended graph must be extended another time using the same algorithm. This approach is given by Algorithm 2.

Algorithm 2. Generating ESs and FESs of length >2

```
Input:  ESG=(V, E); ε =[, γ=]; ESG'=(V', E') with V'=∅ , ε'=[, γ'=];
Output: ESG'=(V', E'), ε'=[, γ'=];

FOR all (i,j)∈E with i != ε AND j != γ DO
  add_node(ESG', (ES(ESG,i) ⊕ ω(ES(ESG,j))); // ⊕ : concatenation
  remove_arc(ESG, (i,j));
FOR all nodes i∈V' with i != ε' AND i != γ' DO
  FOR all nodes j∈V' with j != ε' AND j != γ' DO
    IF (ES(ESG',i) ⊕ ω(ES(ESG',j)) = α(ES(ESG',i)) ⊕ (ES(ESG',j)) THEN
        add_arc(ESG', (i,j))
  FOR all (k,l)∈E with k = ε DO
    IF (ES(ESG',i) = ES(ESG,l) ⊕ ω(ES(ESG',i)) THEN
        add_arc(ESG', (ε',i));
  FOR all (k,l)∈E with l = γ DO
     IF (ES(ESG',i) = α(ES(ESG',i))⊕ ES(ESG,k) THEN
        add_arc(ESG', (i,γ'));
RETURN ESG'
```

Therein the notation ES(ESG,i) represents the identifier of the node i of the ESG which can be concatenated with ("⊕"). Note that the identifier of the newly generated nodes to extend the ESG will be made up using the names of the existing nodes. The function `add_node()` inserts a new ES of length *k*. Following this step, a node *u* is connected with a node *v* if the last $n-1$ events that are used in the identifier of *u* are the same as the first $n-1$ events that are included in the name of *v*. The function `add_arc()` inserts an arc, connecting *u* with *v* in the ESG. The pseudo nodes '*[*', '*]*' are connected with all the extensions of the nodes they were connected with before the extension. In order to avoid traversing the entire matrix, arcs which are already considered are to be removed by the function `remove()`.

Apparently, the Algorithm 2 has a complexity of $O(|V|^2)$ because of the nested FOR-loops to determine the arcs in the ESG'. The algorithm to determine MSCES can be applied to the outcome of the Algorithm 2, i.e., to the extended ESG, to determine the MSCES for l(ES) >2.

4.3 Determination of Minimal Spanning Set for the Coverage of Faulty Complete Event Sequences (MSFCES)

The union of the sets of FCESs of the minimal total length to cover the FESs of a required length is called Minimal Spanning Set of Faulty Complete Event Sequences (MSFCES).

In comparison to the interpretation of the CESs as legal walks, illegal walks are realized by FCESs that never reach the exit. An illegal walk is minimal if its starter cannot be shortened. Assuming that an ESG has *n* nodes and *d* arcs as EPs to generate the CESs, then at most $u:=n^2-d$ FCESs of minimal length, i.e., of length 2, are available. Accordingly, the maximal length of an FCES can be n; those are subsequences of CESs without their last event that will be replaced by an FEP. Therefore, the number of FCESs is precisely determined by the number of FEPs. FEPs that represent FCES are of constant length 2; thus, they also cannot be shortened. It remains to be noticed that only the starters of the remaining FEPs can be minimized, e.g., using the algorithm given in [9].

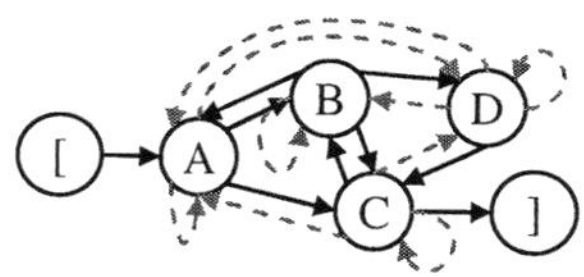

Fig. 6. Completion ESG of Fig. 4 to determine MSFCES

Example 9. The minimal set of the illegal walks (MSFCES) for the ESG in Fig. 6: *AA, AD, ABB, ACA, ACC, ACD, ABDB, ABDD, ABDA.*

A further algorithm to generate FESs of length >2 is not necessary because such faulty sequences are constructed through the concatenation of the appropriate starters with the FEPs.

5 Tool Support and Validation

The determination of the MSCESs/MSFCESs can be very time consuming when carried out manually. For that purpose the tool "GenPath" is developed to input and process the adjacency matrix of the ESG. The user can, however, input several ESGs which are refinements of the vertices of a large ESG to be tested.

For a comprehensive testing, several strategies have been developed with varying characteristics of the test inputs, i.e., stepwise and scalable increasing and/or changing the length and number of the test sequences, and the type of the test sequences, i.e., CES- and FCESs-based. Following could be observed: The test cases of the length 4 were more effective in revealing dynamic faults than the test cases of the lengths 2 and 3. Even though more expensive to be constructed and exercised, they are more efficient in terms of costs per detected fault. Further on the CES-based test cases as well as the FCES-based cases were effective in detecting faults.

The approach described here has been used in different environments [3]. A more detailed discussion about the benefits, e.g., concerning the number of detected errors in dependency of the length of the test cases, is given in [4]. Due to the lack of space, the experiences with the approach are very briefly summarized. Table 1 demonstrates that the algorithmic minimization (Section 4) could save in average about 65 % of the total test costs.

Table 1 . Reducing the number of test cases

Length	2	3	4	Average
Cost Reduction ES	58.5%	62.1%	74.7%	65.1 %

6 Conclusion and Future Work

This paper has introduced an integrated approach to coverage testing of human-computer systems, incorporating modeling of the system behavior with fault modeling and minimizing the test sets for the coverage of these models. The framework is based on the concept of "event sequence graphs (ESG)". Event sequences (ES) represent the human-computer interactions. An ES is complete (CES) if it produces desirable, well-defined and safe system functionality. An ESG is constructed to reflect the user expectations, the *user himself/herself* acted as an oracle of a high level of trustworthiness, de facto resolving the oracle problem.

The objective of testing is the construction of a set of CESs of minimal total length that covers all ESs of a required length. A similar optimization problem arises for the validation of the SUT under undesirable situations. To model the latter problem, faulty event sequences (FESs) are considered. These optimizing problems have been called determination of Minimal Spanning Sets of CESs and FCESs, respectively. The paper applied and modified some algorithms known from graph theory and conformance testing to the above mentioned problems. The research has shown that the complexity of algorithms that are necessary to solve them is expectedly less than the complexity of similar problems, e.g., Chinese Postman Problem, since the vertices of ESGs are equidistant and its edges have no attributes and weights.

The next step is to apply the approach to analyze and test *safety* features; in this case the risks originate from within the system due to potential failures and its spill-over effects causing potentially extensive damage to its environment. Another goal for future work is to design a defense action, which is an appropriately enforced sequence of events, to prevent faults that could potentially lead to such failures.

References

1. A. V. Aho, A. T. Dahbura, D. Lee, M. Ü. Uyar: An Optimization Technique for Protocol Conformance Test Generation Based on UIO Sequences and Rural Chinese Postman Tours. IEEE Trans. Commun. 39, (1991) 1604-1615
2. R. K. Ahuja, T. L. Magnanti, J. B. Orlin: Network Flows-Theory, Algorithms and Applications. Prentice Hall (1993)
3. F. Belli: Finite-State Testing and Analysis of Graphical User Interfaces. Proc. 12th ISSRE (2001) 34-43
4. F. Belli, N. Nissanke, Ch. J. Budnik: A Holistic, Event-Based Approach to Modeling, Analysis and Testing of System Vulnerabilities. Technical Report TR 2004/7, Univ. Paderborn (2004)
5. G. V. Bochmann, A. Petrenko: Protocol Testing: Review of Methods and Relevance for Software Testing. Softw. Eng. Notes, ACM SIGSOFT (1994) 109-124

6. Tsun S. Chow: Testing Software Designed Modeled by Finite-State Machines. IEEE Trans. Softw. Eng. 4 (1978) 178-187
7. M.E. Delamaro, J.C. Maldonado, A. Mathur: Interface Mutation: An Approach for Integration Testing. IEEE Trans. on Softw. Eng. 27/3 (2001) 228-247
8. R.A. DeMillo, R.J. Lipton, F.G. Sayward: Hints on Test Data Selection: Help for the Practicing Programmer. Computer 11/4 (1978) 34-41,
9. Edger. W. Dijkstra: A note on two problems in connexion with graphs. Journal of Numerische Mathematik, Vol. 1 (1959) 269-271
10. Hong Zhu, P.A.V. Hall, J.H.R. May: Software Unit Test Coverage and Adequacy. ACM Computing Surveys, 29/4 (1997)
11. D.E. Knuth: The Stanford GraphBase. Addison-Wesley (1993)
12. M. Marré, A. Bertolino: Using Spanning Sets for Coverage Testing. IEEE Trans. on Softw. Eng. 29/11 (2003) 974-984
13. A. M. Memon, M. E. Pollack and M. L. Soffa: Automated Test Oracles for GUIs, SIGSOFT 2000 (2000) 30-39
14. S. Naito, M. Tsunoyama: Fault Detection for Sequential Machines by Transition Tours, Proc. FTCS (1981) 238-243
15. J. Offutt, L. Shaoying, A. Abdurazik, and Paul Ammann: Generating Test Data From State-Based Specifications. The Journal of Software Testing, Verification and Reliability, 13(1), Medgeh (2003) 25-53
16. D.L. Parnas: On the Use of Transition Diagrams in the Design of User Interface for an Interactive Computer System. Proc. 24th ACM Nat'l. Conf. (1969) 379-385
17. R. K. Shehady and D. P. Siewiorek: A Method to Automate User Interface Testing Using Finite State Machines. in Proc. Int. Symp. Fault-Tolerant Comp. FTCS-27 (1997) 80-88
18. K. Tai, Y. Lei: A Test Generation Strategy for Pairwise Testing. IEEE Trans. On Softw. Eng. 28/1 (2002) 109-111
19. H. Thimbleby: The Directed Chinese Postman Problem. School of Computing Science, Middlesex University, London (2003)
20. D.B. West: Introduction to Graph Theory. Prentice Hall (1996)
21. L. White and H. Almezen: Generating Test Cases for GUI Responsibilities Using Complete Interaction Sequences. In Proc ISSRE, IEEE Comp. Press (2000) 110-119

Discovering Learning Paths on a Domain Ontology Using Natural Language Interaction

Roberto Pirrone[1,2], Massimo Cossentino[2], Giovanni Pilato[2], Riccardo Rizzo[2], and Giuseppe Russo[1]

[1] DINFO - University of Palermo Viale delle Scienze 90128 Palermo, Italy
[2] ICAR - Italian National Research Council Viale delle Scienze 90128 Palermo, Italy
pirrone@unipa.it
{cossentino, pilato, ricrizzo}@pa.icar.cnr.it

Abstract. The present work investigates the problem of determining a learning path inside a suitable domain ontology. The proposed approach enables the user of a web learning application to interact with the system using natural language in order to browse the ontology itself. The course related knowledge is arranged as a three level hierarchy: content level, symbolic level, and conceptual level bridging the previous ones. The implementation of the ontological, the interaction, and the presentation component inside the TutorJ system is explained, and the first results are presented.

1 Introduction

The present work regards the problem of managing the course knowledge for a web learning application aimed satisfy user's requests generating personalized learning paths. Such a systems has to rely on the definition of a domain ontology structuring the concepts related to the course domain. A learning path between the concepts is constrained by the relations holding among them. In particular, it is possible to devise two kinds of relations between concepts: structural, and navigation relations. Structural relations are the classical specialization and subsumption predicates plus some predicates that are specific for the particular domain. Navigation relations are related to the logical links between different pieces of knowledge: which argument is a prerequisite for another one, and so on. Moreover, given a concept, not all the other ones related to it concur in the same way to its explanation, so the links have to be tagged with respect to concepts relevance. A planning approach is needed to obtain an articulated learning path from such an ontology. Finally, such a system has to provide an intuitive interface, and to offer a strong interaction with the user. Previous considerations have been partially implemented in the TutorJ system[1], a tutoring tool for undergraduate students involved in a course about the Java language. The course related knowledge is arranged as a three level hierarchy. Multimedia information is managed at a content level as a set of HTML documents. The symbolic level corresponds to the ontology: a learning path is obtained browsing it. At the

M. Ali and F. Esposito (Eds.): IEA/AIE 2005, LNAI 3533, pp. 310–314, 2005.

intermediate level topics are represented by a concept map, implemented using a SOM network. The map is used to cluster the course materials, and to map them onto atomic concepts that can be instantiated at the ontological level.

2 The TutorJ System

The complete structure of the TutorJ system is detailed in figure 1. The internal Cyc inferential engine is used to generate learning paths. The architecture is

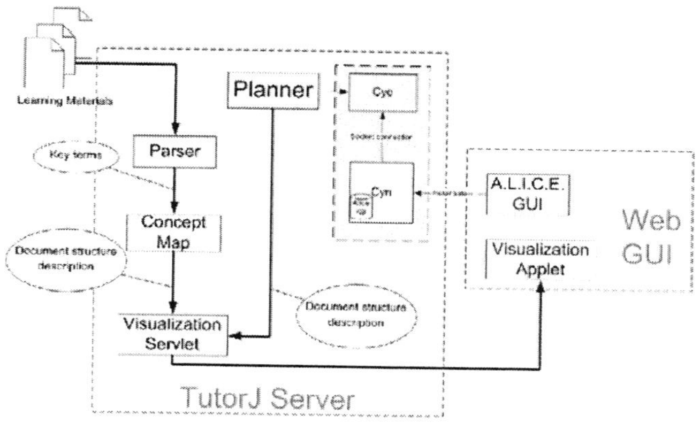

Fig. 1. The TutorJ architecture

based on the client-server paradigm, but the knowledge management block can run on a different host with respect to the rest of the server. Learning materials (lessons, documentation, source code for self-assessment tests) are processed by a *parser* that provides a representation of the key terms in a suitable vector space. Then a SOM is used to link the materials to the concepts developed: this map is what we called *concept map*. It must be noticed that, in TutorJ system, there are a lot of different learning materials that are not only tutorials and lessons , and as explained in [2], they can't be automatically clustered by the SOM algorithm. So the concept map is not simply a SOM network but a tool, based on the SOM, that can be updated by the teacher and it is capable to present the contained materials in a rich and flexible interface. Users issue their requests by means of the A.L.I.C.E. [1] chat-bot GUI whose dialog repository is enriched using the CyN version [3] of this tool to perform SubL queries containing the terms isolated from the dialog, that are passed to the knowledge base via direct connection to the TCP socket of the Cyc listener. The *visualization* system for the concept map is implemented as a couple servlet-applet.

[1] http://www.alicebot.org

3 Structure of the Ontology

We use OpenCyc to represent our word. OpenCyc represent the Knowledge Base at different levels of abstraction. OpenCyc makes easy to map a word to explain, or to investigate, using terms and concepts at a higher level of abstraction that are common to many fields. This gives us a shared vocabulary. All the information and the structure of the concepts in our Java Ontology, are organized and verified starting from the official Sun Microsystems document. The domain-specific theory in our representation has been partitioned essentially in two levels: the structure level and the navigation level. The first level realizes a structural definition of the ontology concepts, in terms of composition, definition of properties and all the other structural relation we need to represent our world. The navigation level gives the opportunity to tie down different concepts in a way to perform the operation of improving knowledge in our domain. In what follows the structural relations are reported.

- `(#$iscomposed #$Java #$Statement)`: a statement is a part of Java
- `(#$iscomposed #$Class #$ClassBody)`: the "class body" is a part of a class
- `(#$genls #$FloatingPoint #$Primitive)`: the Floating Point Type is an instance of Primitive Type
- `(#$isaMethodOf #$Equal #$String)`: equal is a method of the String Class
- `(#$isa #$Java #$ObjectOrientedProgrammingLanguage)`: Java is a OOP Language

The navigation relations are the following:

- `(#$isaPrerequisiteFor #$Class #$Object)`: the former concept (Class) is a prerequisite for the comprehension of the latter (Object)
- `(#$conceptuallyRelated #$String #$Length)`: the first concept is simply related (in some way) to the second

The predicate `isaPrerequisiteFor` has been implemented to obtain a backbone structure inside the ontology ensuring us the possibility of extracting meaningful learning paths on the basis of a sequence of precedence relations. The `conceptuallyRelated` enables a free exploration of the ontology using a less strong relation than `isaPrerequisiteFor`. To avoid a combinatorial explosion of search paths, we have introduced a tag system where every concept has an index representing his "importance" related to all the others. The tag system is related to the number of occurrences of a concept in the master document from which the ontology has been built. This "citation weight" can be used by the planner as a simple way to choose trajectories.

4 Learning Path Visualization

In TutorJ a large set of heterogeneous materials are used, so the interface should be capable to present not only different kinds of resources in correspondence of the same concept, but also complex information as the learning path. The

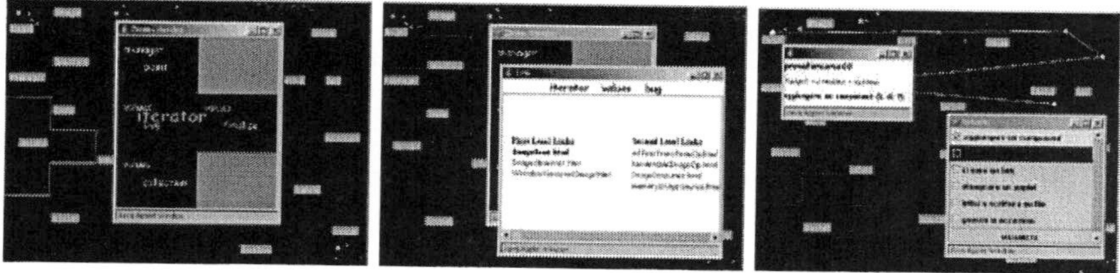

Fig. 2. From left to right: area, content, and learning path selection

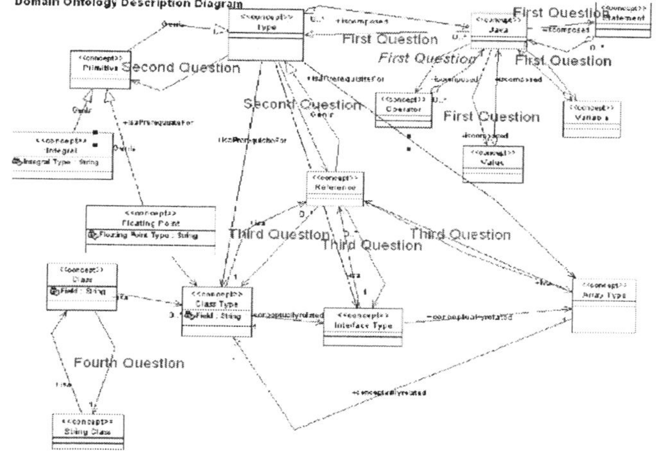

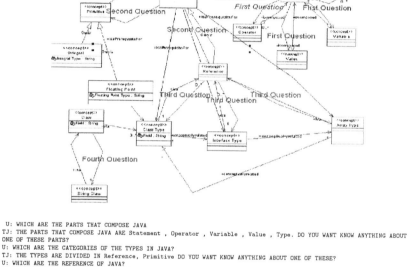

U: WHICH ARE THE PARTS THAT COMPOSE JAVA
TJ: THE PARTS THAT COMPOSE JAVA ARE Statement , Operator , Variable , Value , Type. DO YOU WANT KNOW ANYTHING ABOUT ONE OF THESE PARTS?
U: WHICH ARE THE CATEGORIES OF THE TYPES IN JAVA?
TJ: THE TYPES ARE DIVIDED IN Reference, Primitive DO YOU WANT KNOW ANYTHING ABOUT ONE OF THESE?
U: WHICH ARE THE REFERENCE OF JAVA?
TJ: THE REFERENCE OF JAVA ARE ClassType , InterfaceType , ArrayType. DO YOU WANT KNOW ANYTHING ABOUT ONE OF THESE ?
U: WHICH ARE THE CLASSTYPE OF JAVA?
TJ: THE CLASSTYPE OF JAVA ARE Class , Interface , Method. DO YOU WANT KNOW ANYTHING ABOUT ONE OF THESE ?
U: WHICH ARE THE CLASS OF JAVA?
TJ: THE CLASS OF JAVA ARE Object , StringClass , Byte , Short , Integer , Long , Character , Float , Double. DO YOU WANT KNOW ANYTHING ABOUT ONE OF THESE ?
U: WHAT ARE THE METHODS OF THE CLASS STRING?
TJ: THE METHODS OF THE CLASS STRING ARE Lenght , charAt , ToString , Equal , CountToken , NextToken , StringTokenizer , New

Fig. 3. Example of ontology browsing

map is inspired by the "StarryNight" interface[2]. On this interface we identify the different areas in the map, while the stars' density represents the number of documents in each area. Clicking on a specified area provides the visualization of its single cells, and the user can decide in which cell the desired documents or materials should be using the keywords that are associated to each cell. When a single cell is selected, its content is shown in another pop-up window. The content is organized in different sections that help to find the resource needed.

[2] http://rhizome.org/starrynight/

The learning paths can be visualized on the map as a set of links that connects related concepts.Figure 2 illustrates the GUI main functionalities.

5 Experimental Results

Two main approaches can be used to obtain information from TutorJ. The first one is a dialog aimed to to explore the CyC ontology. The used CyC predicates are: `isa`, `genls`, `isComposed`, `isMethodOf` (see figure 3). Besides the ontology exploration, the main goal of the chat-bot interface is to obtain the user profile in order to understand the concepts that the user desires to know. The predicates of the ontology for this task are `isaPrerequisiteFor` and `conceptuallyRelated`.

References

1. Pirrone, R., Cossentino, M., Pilato, G., Rizzo, R.: TutorJ: a web-learning system based on a hierarchical representation of information. In: II Workshop: Web Learning per la qualità del capitale umano, Ferrara, Italy (2004) 16–23
2. Brusilovsky, P., Rizzo, R.: Map-Based Horizontal Navigation in Educational Hypertext. Journal of Digital Information **3** (2002)
3. Coursey, K.: Living in CyN: Mating AIML and Cyc together with Program N (2004)

A Geometric Approach to Automatic Description of Iconic Scenes

Filippo Vella[1], Giovanni Pilato[2], Giorgio Vassallo[1], and Salvatore Gaglio[1,2]

[1] DINFO – Dipartimento di Ingegneria INFOrmatica
Università di Palermo
Viale delle Scienze - 90128 Palermo - Italy
vella@csai.unipa.it, {gvassallo, gaglio}@unipa.it
[2] ICAR - Istituto di CAlcolo e Reti ad alte prestazioni
Italian National Research Council
Viale delle Scienze - 90128 Palermo - Italy
pilato@pa.icar.cnr.it

Abstract. It is proposed a step towards the automatic description of scenes with a geometric approach. The scenes considered are composed by a set of elements that can be geometric forms or iconic representation of objects. Every icon is characterized by a set of attributes like shape, colour, position, orientation. Each scene is related to a set of sentences describing its content. The proposed approach builds a data driven vector semantic space where the scenes and the sentences are mapped. Sentences and scene with the same meaning are mapped in near vectors and distance criteria allow retrieving semantic relations.

1 Introduction

Many research attempts on scene description have been proposed to allow a verbal description of the objects present in the scene and relationship among them [4][5][6]. The reason can be found considering that spatial location is often expressed by closed-class forms and the concepts gained from this representation can act as fundamental structure in organizing conceptual material of different nature[6]. The LSA technique has been used in [3] for image annotation task. The procedure starts from representations with quantitative properties extracted from images and a set of associated labels attempting to catch the connection among these sub-image parameters and the labels.

The approach proposed in this paper is aimed to allow the detection of semantic relationship between scene and sentences based on a data driven semantic space where both of them are mapped. An LSA-like technique is applied where words have been replaced by sentences and documents by scenes. Experiments have been lead on a set of 150 scene and their related sentences and produced encouraging results in both image description and regularities retrieval.

M. Ali and F. Esposito (Eds.): IEA/AIE 2005, LNAI 3533, pp. 315 – 317, 2005.

2 The Proposed Approach

The proposed approach aims to represent heterogeneous entities like scene and sentences in the same vector space to let emerge the underlying connections among these entities. To extract these relationships, a matrix **W** is built considering a repository of images and a set of related sentences describing them. The *i*-th row of **W** is associated to the sentence referred with number *i* and the *j*-th column of **W** corresponds to the scene referred with number *j* in the repository. The element *(i,j)* of the matrix is 1 if the *i*-th sentence can be a predicate for the *j*-th scene.

To find the latent relationships among the set of scenes and the sentences a Latent Semantic Analysis (LSA)[1][2] like technique is applied to matrix **W**. While in traditional LSA the aim is to find relationships among singular words and topics of the documents, here the processing is applied to an heterogeneous space involving scenes and sentences. Accordingly to the LSA paradigm the matrix **W** is replaced with a low-rank (*R*-dimension) approximation generated by the truncated Singular Value Decomposition (TSVD) technique:

$$\mathbf{W} \approx \hat{\mathbf{W}} = \mathbf{U}\mathbf{S}\mathbf{V}^T \tag{1}$$

where **U** is the (*M*x*R*) left singular matrix, **S** is (*R*x*R*) diagonal matrix with decreasing values $s_1 \geq s_2 \geq \ldots \geq s_R > 0$ and **V** is the (*N*x*R*) right singular matrix. **U** and **V** are column-orthogonal and so they both identify a basis to span the automatically generated *R* dimensional space. Sentences describing the scenes (represented by $\mathbf{u}_i\mathbf{S}$) are projected on the basis formed by the column vectors of the right singular matrix **V.** The scenes (represented as $\mathbf{v}_i\mathbf{S}$) are projected on the basis formed by the column of the matrix **U** to create their representation in the *R*-dimensional space. The rows of **V** represent scenes and their components take into account their belonging to one of the clusters identified by the axes.

3 Experimental Results

The proposed approach allows to retrieve the latent connection among scene if some regularities are present. A set of 150 scenes has been created with rules for the colours of objects related to the presence or not of objects of the same type. For example, geometric shapes with corners (e.g. square, rhombus) were coloured cyan if they are in a scene with geometric shape of the same kind. They are coloured blue in the other cases. Evaluating the correlation between the vector representing the sentences dealing with the geometric shapes before and after the application of LSA, it can be seen that the presence of this rule brings the vector representation of the sentences in the Semantic Space nearer that in the original space. As an example the correlation between the sentence regarding the presence of a square and the sentence for the rhombus was -0.012 before the application of the proposed technique and became 0.854 when it was calculated between the corresponding vectors of the generated semantic space.

Experiments show that a trade-off must be found between the precision in retrieving correct sentences to scene. The precision increases when the dimension of the semantic space is also increased. On the contrary the power of regularities extraction is more evident when the value of R is decreased.

Table 1. Correctly associated sentences percentage

R	3	5	7	11
Correctly Retrieved Sentences	73%	81%	89%	96%
Regularities Derived Sentences	45%	36%	33%	21%

4 Conclusions and Future Works

An approach has been presented for the description of scene with natural language sentences. Experimental trials show that the proposed technique induces a data clustering based on semantic features and determines language referred groups.

Future works will include the test of the approach on extensive database of scenes coupled with sentences describing them and the mapping of new scenes in the semantic space with suitable metrics. This will allow the introduction of new images in the semantic space without recalculating the SVD for the new images set.

References

1. J. R. Bellegarda. Exploiting latent semantic information in statistical language modeling. *In Proceedings of the IEEE*, volume 88 No.8, pages 1279–1296, 2000.
2. S.T. Dumais T.K. Landauer. A solution to Plato's problem: the latent semantic analysis theory of acquisition, induction and representation of knowledge. *Psychological Review*, 1997.
3. F. Monay and D. Gatica-Perez. On image auto-annotation with latent space models. In *Proc. ACM Int. Conf. on Multimedia* (ACM MM), 2003.
4. T. Regier. *The human semantic potential*. MIT Press, 1996.
5. D. K. Roy. Grounded spoken language acquisition: Experiments in word learning. In *IEEE Transaction on Multimedia*, 2001.
6. L. Talmy. How language structures space. In Herbert Pick and Linda Acreolo, editors, In *Spatial Orientation: Theory, Research and Application*. Plenum Press, 1983.

Man-Machine Interface of a Support System for Analyzing Open-Ended Questionnaires

Ayako Hiramatsu[1], Hiroaki Oiso[2], Taiki Shojima[3], and Norihisa Komoda[3]

[1] Department of Information Systems Engineering, Osaka Sangyo University,
3-1-1 Nakagaito, Daito, Osaka, Japan
ayako@ise.osaka-sandai.ac.jp
[2] Codetoys K.K.
2-6-8 Nishitenma, Kita-ku, Osaka, Japan
oiso@codetoys.com
[3] Graduate School of Information Science and Technology, Osaka University,
2-1 Yamada-oka, Suita, Osaka, Japan
{shojima, komoda}@ist.osaka-u.ac.jp

1 Introduction

This paper proposes man-machine interface of support system for analyzing answers to open-ended questions supplied by customers of the mobile game content reply when they unsubscribe from the services. Since open-ended questions, however, place no restrictions on descriptions, the answers include an enormous amount of text data for the content provider. It is time-consuming to read all of the texts one by one. Since a large number of answers are identical to choices included in the multiple-choice questions or unnecessary opinions unconcerned with the game, there are few answers that should be read. Most opinions are needed to know only the number and the outline. However, the provider should not omit to read the unexpected opinion that is a minority. Additionally, since answers are input through cellular phones, they often include many symbols dependent on various kinds of terminals and grammatical mistakes, making them hard to understand. Our research, therefore, aims to create a system that supports the provider to analyze the answers of open-ended questions efficiently. The main function of the support system divides the answers into typical opinions and atypical opinions. Divided opinions are presented with different user interfaces, because the content providers can analyze the two type opinions with each way.

2 Support System for Analysis of Questionnaire Data

The answer of this open-ended question consists of two types: typical opinions and atypical opinions. Typical and atypical opinions are defined as follows. Typical opinions consist of 3 kinds: (a) Opinions having the same meaning as items of the multiple-choice questions. (e.g.: The packet charge is too expensive.) (b) Frequent opinions that the provider has already heard. (e.g.: My knowledge increased.) (c) Irrelevant opinions. (e.g.: I have a baby!) Atypical opinions are any opinions not typical. (e.g.: Quizzes for kids may be interest.)

The provider should fully read atypical opinions and manage typical opinions statistically. For analysis of open-ended questionnaire data, therefore, the provider

M. Ali and F. Esposito (Eds.): IEA/AIE 2005, LNAI 3533, pp. 318 – 320, 2005.

firstly judges if the opinion is typical or atypical. However, the borderline between the atypical and the typical is very ambiguous and also different by the provider's background knowledge. An atypical opinion might change to a typical opinion when the provider reads many opinions. Therefore, the support system should provide to be able to change the borderline flexibly by the provider.

Against atypical opinions, the provider reads text data and checks background data what kind of people wrote the opinions. If the provider reads just listed various atypical opinions, he/she just feels that there are something unique opinions. Therefore, if opinions do not have strong impacts, he/she maybe forget the opinions and will not reflect them to new strategies. To analyze atypical opinions, it is not only important to read raw opinions but also necessary to know what kind of opinions there are.

Typical opinions are not necessary to inspire new ideas properly. The provider need not read typical opinions carefully. The provider reads typical opinions quickly and feels the trend of the quantity of the same opinions. Therefore, the support system needs to classify typical opinions by meanings, and provides quantitative trend graphically to understand the change trend of customers' intention.

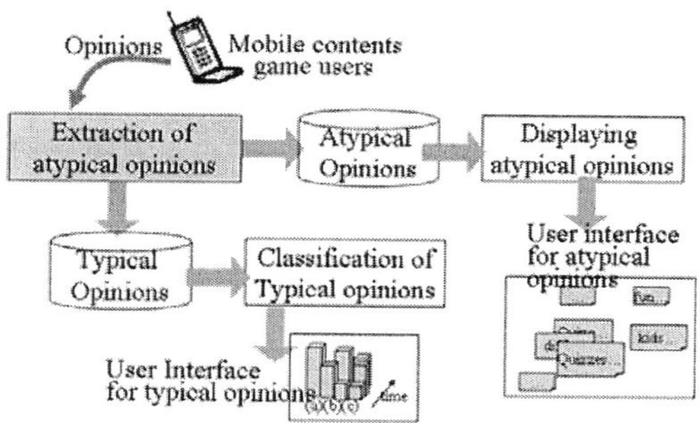

Fig. 1. Outline of the support system

The outline of the support system is shown in Fig. 1. The main purpose of this support system is that the provider easily takes a close-up of atypical opinions that are included only barely in huge number of opinions. The typical opinions need to be grouped to count the number of the same opinions. Therefore important functions of this support system are to extract atypical opinions from all opinions and to group typical opinions by contents. As the result of the extraction, opinions are divided into typical opinions and atypical opinions. Different user interfaces are necessary, because the direction for use differs in atypical opinions from typical opinions. Typical opinions are graphed to show time changes of the numbers of opinions that are grouped by the contents. A summary needs to be shown what kinds of content are included about atypical opinions. Thereupon, the result of the atypical opinion classified by representative keywords is placed as opinion cards on the screen. The novelty of opinions decides the coordinate. Based on decided coordinate, the opinion cards are displayed on the screen.

3 Interface of the Support System

The support system provides two types of user interfaces. The left in Fig.2 shows the user interface for analyzing typical opinions. There are three areas: Graph area, Category or month select area, and Text information area. These areas are linked each other. In the graph area, 3D graphs are shown. The 3 dimensions are number of opinions, months, and opinion groups. In the category or month select area, users can select categories and months for browsing graphs in the graph area. Users can change category and month by the tag that is in the upper part. By clicking the listed categories or months, users can select data for analysis. When users click a part of graph, raw text data is browsed in the text information area. If users click one raw text opinion, personal information of the opinion writer is shown in the right side windows. In the window of the lower right, to show the reason why the opinions are classified typical opinions and grouped certain category, keywords of the category are listed.

The right in Fig.2 shows the user interface for analyzing atypical opinions. There are three window areas: Classified result area, Opinion cards area, and Text information area. In the classified result area, categories of classified atypical opinion are listed. In the end of the category name, the number of opinions in the category is shown. When users select certain category by mouse operation, opinion cards are displayed by keyword novelty in the opinion cards area. In this area, only characteristic keywords are shown in the cards. When one card is clicked, raw text opinion and personal information of the opinion writer are shown in the text information area. To cope with vague changeable borderline between the typical and the atypical, users can add definition of typical opinions by dragging and dropping the card that users judge as the typical.

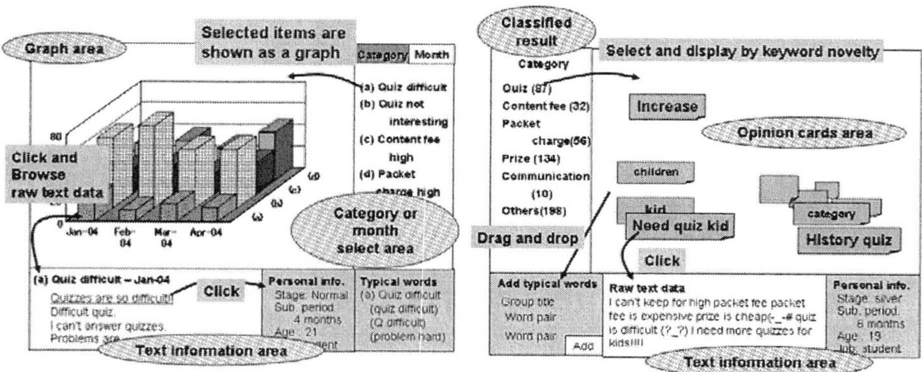

Fig. 2. User Interface of the support system

A Holistic Approach to Test-Driven Model Checking

Fevzi Belli and Baris Güldali

University of Paderborn,
Dept. of Computer Science, Electrical Engineering and Mathematics
belli@upb.de, baris@adt.upb.de

Abstract. Testing is the most common validation method in the software industry. It entails the execution of the software system in the real environment. Nevertheless, testing is a cost-intensive process. Because of its conceptual simplicity the combination of formal methods and test methods has been widely advocated. Model checking belongs to the promising candidates for this marriage. The present paper modifies and extends the existing approaches in that, after the test case generation, a model checking step supports the manual test process. Based on the *holistic* approach to specification-based construction of test suites, this paper proposes to generate test cases to cover both the specification model and its complement. This helps also to clearly differentiate the correct system outputs from the faulty ones as the test cases based on the specification are to succeed the test, and the ones based on the complement of the specification are to fail. Thus, the approach handles the *oracle problem* in an effective manner.

1 Introduction and Related Work

Testing is the traditional and still most common validation method in the software industry [3, 5]. It entails the execution of the software system in the real environment, under operational conditions; thus, testing is directly applied to software. Therefore, it is user-centric, because the user can observe the system in operation and justify to what extent his/her requirements have been met. Nevertheless, testing is a cost-intensive process because it is to a great extent manually carried out; the existing test tools are mostly used for test management and bookkeeping purposes, and not for test design and construction. Apart from being costly, testing is not comprehensive in terms of the validated properties of the system under test (SUT), as it is mainly based on the intuition and experience of the tester.

Testing will be carried out by *test cases*, i.e., ordered pairs of *test inputs* and expected *test outputs*. A *test* then represents the execution of the SUT using the previously constructed test cases. If the outcome of the execution complies with the expected output, the SUT *succeeds* the test, otherwise it *fails*. There is no justification, however, for any assessment on the correctness of the SUT based on the success (or failure) of a single test, because there can potentially be an infinite number of test cases, even for very simple programs.

The simplicity of this very briefly, but critically sketched test process is apparently the reason for its broad popularity. Motivated by this popularity during the last decades, the combination of formal methods and test methods has been widely advocated

M. Ali and F. Esposito (Eds.): IEA/AIE 2005, LNAI 3533, pp. 321 – 331, 2005.

[6]. Model checking belongs to the most promising candidates for this marriage because it exhaustively verifies the conformance of a specified system property (or a set of those properties) to the behavior of the SUT. Most of the existing approaches of combining testing and model checking propose to set up model checking to automatically generate test cases to be then exercised on the real, target system [1, 8, 11, 12].

Large software systems will, nowadays, be developed in several stages. The initial stage of the development is usually the requirements definition; its outcome is the specification of the system's behavior. It makes sense to construct the test cases and to define the test process (as a *test specification*) already in this early stage, long before the implementation begins, in compliance with the user's expectancy of how the system will behave. This test specification materializes "the rules of the game". Thus, tests can be run without any knowledge of the implementation (*specification-oriented testing*, or *black-box testing*). One can, of course, explore the knowledge of the implementation – if available – to construct test cases in compliance with the structure of the code, based on its data or control flow (*implementation-oriented,* or *white-box testing*).

Regardless of whether the testing is specification-oriented or implementation-oriented, if applied to large programs in the practice, both methods need an *adequacy criterion,* which provides a measure of how effective a given set of test cases is in terms of its potential to reveal faults. During the last decades, many adequacy criteria have been introduced. Most of them are *coverage-oriented*, i.e., they rate the portion of the system specification or implementation that is covered by the given test case set when it is applied to the SUT. The ratio of the portion of the specification or code that is covered by the given test set in relation to the uncovered portion can then be used as a decisive factor in determining the point in time at which to stop testing, i.e., to release SUT or to extend the test set and continue testing.

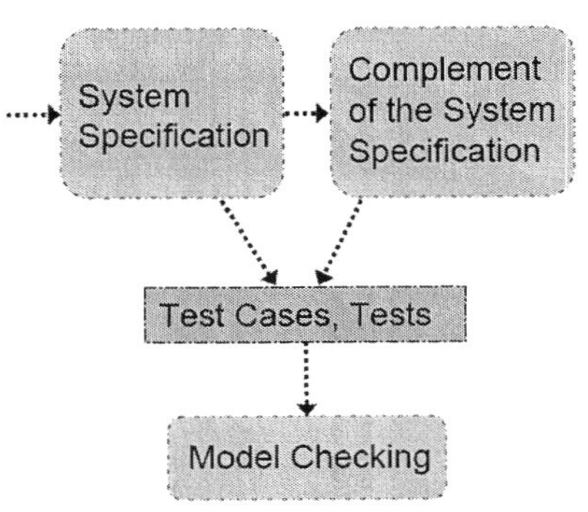

Fig. 1. Overall structure of the approach

In the *holistic* approach to specification-based construction of test case sets and tests, introduced in [4], one attempts to cover not only the model that is based on the specification, but also its complement. The aim is the coverage of all possible properties of the system, regardless of whether they are desirable or undesirable. The present paper modifies and extends this holistic approach in that, after the test case generation, a "model checking" step replaces the manual test process (Fig. 1). This has evident advantages: The manual exercising the vast amounts of test cases and observing and analyzing the test outcomes to decide when to stop testing, etc., is much more expensive than model checking that is to automatically run.

Model checking has been successfully applied for many years to a wide variety of practical problems, including hardware design, protocol analysis, operating systems, reactive system analysis, fault tolerance and security. This formal method uses graph theory and automata theory to automatically verify properties of the SUT, more precisely by means of its state-based model that specifies the system behavior. A *model checker* visits all reachable states of the model and verifies that the expected system properties, specified as temporal logic formulae, are satisfied over each possible path. If a property is not satisfied, the model checker attempts to generate a counterexample in the form of a trace as a sequence of states [2]. The following question arises when model checking is applied: Who, or what guarantees that all of the requirements have been verified? The approach introduced in this paper proposes to generate test cases to entirely cover the specification model and its complement. This helps also to clearly differentiate the correct system outputs from the faulty ones as the test cases based on the specification are to succeed the test, and the ones based on the complement of the specification are to fail. Thus, the approach elegantly handles a tough problem of testing (*oracle problem*). This is another advantage of the approach.

There are many approaches to generate test cases from finite-state machines [3, 5, 9]. The recent ones also attempt to extend and/or modify the underlying model, e.g., using mutation operations [1, 13, 15] but not the complement of the model. The mutation operations can bee seen as special cases of the complementing. Thus, the method presented in this paper is also different from the existing approaches in this aspect.

Section 2 summarizes the theoretical background we need to informally describe the approach, which then is explained in Section 3 along with a trivial, widely known example. To validate the approach and demonstrate the tool support, Section 4 introduces a non-trivial example, which is analyzed and automatically model-checked. Complexity of the approach is analyzed in section 5. Section 6 concludes the paper and gives insight into prospective future work.

2 Two Faces of Modeling

A model is always helpful when the complexity of the system under consideration exceeds a certain level. It is then appropriate to focus on the relevant features of the system, i.e., to abstract it from unnecessary detail. There are several kinds of models. During the development, a model prescribes the *desirable behavior* as it should be, i.e., the functionality of the system in compliance with the user requirements

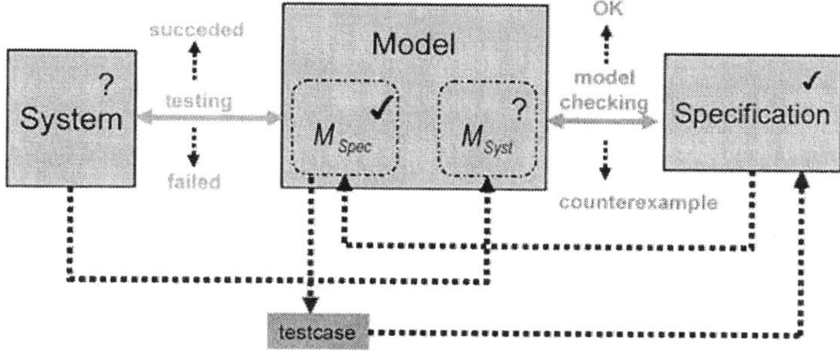

Fig. 2. Two faces of the modeling

(*specification model*). For validation purposes, one needs another model that describes the *observed behavior* of the system (*system model*).

Fig. 2 depicts different aspects and components of modeling. We assume that the specification is correct and has been correctly transferred to the specification model M_{Spec}. This will be symbolized by means of the symbol "✔." The implemented system, however, might not be in compliance with the M_{Spec}. Therefore, we put a question mark symbol "**?**" into the box that stands for the system; this means that the validity of the system must be checked.

The present approach suggests arranging testing, based on M_{Spec}, as a method for the system validation. Further, based on the system behavior observed by the user, a second model, M_{Syst}, is constructed. As no proof of the correctness of the system has been yet performed, the correctness of the M_{Syst} is, as a result, also questionable. Therefore, M_{Syst} is model checked, which is controlled by the generated test cases.

The testing approach in [4] proposes an additional, complementary view of the model M_{Spec}, which is used for generating additional test cases that are not based on the original specification. These new test cases represent the test inputs leading to situations that are undesirable, i.e., they transfer the system into a faulty state. This fact must also be taken into account by model checking.

M_{Spec} is represented in this paper by a finite state machine (FSM) as a quadruple $(S_{Spec}, R_{Spec}, s_{Spec0})$, where S_{Spec} is a (finite) set of states, $R_{Spec} \subseteq S_{Spec} \times S_{Spec}$ is a transition relation, and $s_{Spec0} \in S_{Spec}$ is an initial state.

Test cases will be generated from M_{Spec} and transferred to *the linear temporal logic (LTL) formulae* φ which is either of the following [10]:

- p, where p is an atomic proposition, or
- a composition $\neg\varphi$, $\varphi_1 \vee \varphi_2$, $\varphi_1 \wedge \varphi_2$, $\mathbf{X}\ \varphi_1$, $\mathbf{F}\ \varphi_1$, $\mathbf{G}\ \varphi_1$, $\varphi_1\ \mathbf{U}\ \varphi_2$, $\varphi_1\ \mathbf{R}\ \varphi_2$,

where the *temporal operators* used in this work have the following meaning over an infinite sequence of states, called a *path*:

- **X** (*neXt*) requires that a property hold in the *next* state of the path.
- **F** (*Future*) is used to assert that a property will hold at *some* state on the path.
- **G** (*Global*) specifies that a property hold at *every* state on the path.

M_{Syst} is presented in this paper as a Kripke structure that will be defined as follows [10]:

Let *AP* be a set of atomic propositions; a *Kripke structure M* over *AP* is a quadruple $(S_{Syst}, S_{Syst0}, R_{Syst}, L_{Syst})$ where S_{Syst} is a finite set of states, $S_{Syst0} \subseteq S_{Syst}$ is the set of initial states, $R_{Syst} \subseteq S_{Syst} \times S_{Syst}$ is a transition relation such that for every state $s \in S_{Syst}$ there is a state $s' \in S_{Syst}$ in that $R_{Syst}(s, s')$ and $L_{Syst}: S_{Syst} \rightarrow 2^{AP}$ is a function that labels each state with the set of atomic propositions that are true in that state.

3 Example

A simple example is used to illustrate the following approach. A traffic light system is informally specified by the sequence of the colors, red as the initial state:

$$\text{red} \rightarrow \text{red/yellow} \rightarrow \text{green} \rightarrow \text{yellow} \rightarrow \text{red} \rightarrow \ldots \qquad (1)$$

Fig. 3 transfers this specification to a model M_{Spec}.

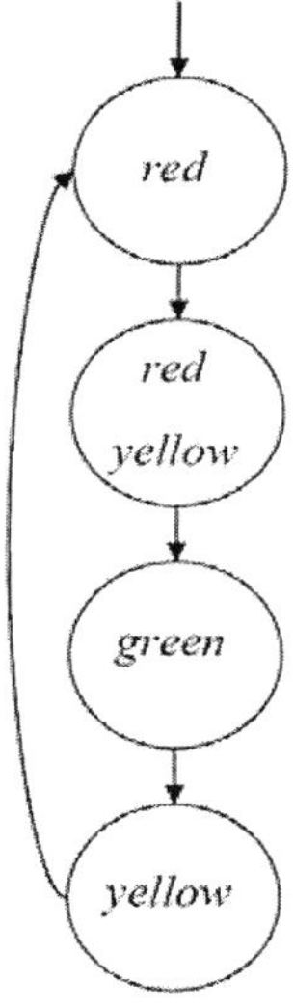

Fig. 3. Traffic light system as a FSM

In this graphic representation, the nodes of M_{Spec} can be interpreted as states or events. They can also be viewed as inputs that trigger events to occur or cause states to take place. Any transition and any transition sequence of this graph, e.g.,

$$(\text{red} \rightarrow \text{red/yellow}) \tag{2}$$

is valid (legal) in the sense of the specification M_{Spec}. As a test input, these sequences should cause the system to succeed the test. For the sake of simplicity, any single transitions will be considered as a test sequence that plays the role of a test input coupled with an unambiguous test output "succeeded". This is the way the approach handles the oracle problem.

The sequence in (2) can be transferred in an LTL formula:

$$\text{red}\rightarrow\text{red/yellow: } \varphi = \mathbf{G}(red \rightarrow \mathbf{X}(red \wedge yellow)) \tag{3}$$

This transformation has been intuitively carried out, with the following meaning: Globally, it must be satisfied that if in the present state the property "red" holds, in the next state the property "red and yellow" holds.

Adding the missing edges as dashed lines to the FSM of Fig. 3 makes the complementary view of the specification visible. In Fig. 4, the dashed lines are transitions that are not included in the M_{Spec} (Note that loops starting and ending at the same node are not considered to keep the example simple). Thus, these additional transitions are invalid (illegal). Invalid transitions can be included in sequences starting at a valid one, e.g.,

$$(\text{red} \rightarrow \text{red/yellow} \rightarrow \text{green} \rightarrow \textbf{red}) \tag{4}$$

The invalid transitions transfer the system into faulty states; thus, the test reveals a fault. Therefore, the expected test output is "failed". Accordingly, (5) represents the LTL format of the test case given in (4):

$$\text{green} \rightarrow \text{red: } \varphi = \mathbf{G}(green \rightarrow \mathbf{X}\neg red) \tag{5}$$

This formula has the following intuitive meaning: Globally, it must be satisfied that if in the present state the property "green" holds, in the next state it is not allowed that the property "red" holds.

We assume that the behavior-oriented model M_{Syst} of the system is given in Fig. 5. Please note the discrepancies to Fig. 3: We deliberately injected some faults we hoped that the model checking would reveal.

Fig. 6 transfers Fig. 5 into Kripke structure. The transition conserves the three states *red, green* and *yellow* of M_{Syst}, but renames them as s_1, s_2 and s_3. The atomic propositions *red, green,* and *yellow* are assigned to these states in combination of negated and not-negated form, expressing the color of the traffic light in each state of M_{Syst}.

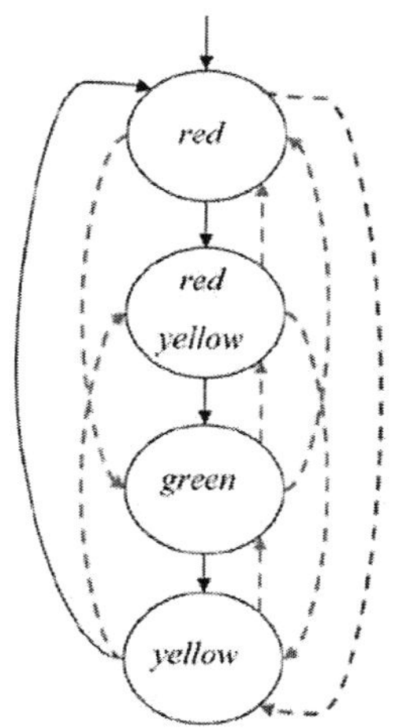

Fig. 4. Complementing (with dashed lines) of the FSM of Fig. 2

The manually model checking of the Kripke structure of Fig. 6 is sketched in Tab. 1. The results of the analysis of Table 1 can be summarized as follows:

- 1 of 4 legal tests led to inconsistencies in M_{Syst}.
- 1 of 8 illegal tests led to inconsistencies in M_{Syst}.

  We conclude that the model checking detected all of the injected faults.

- The system does not conduct something that is desirable (φ_1).
- The system
- conducts something that is undesirable (φ_6).

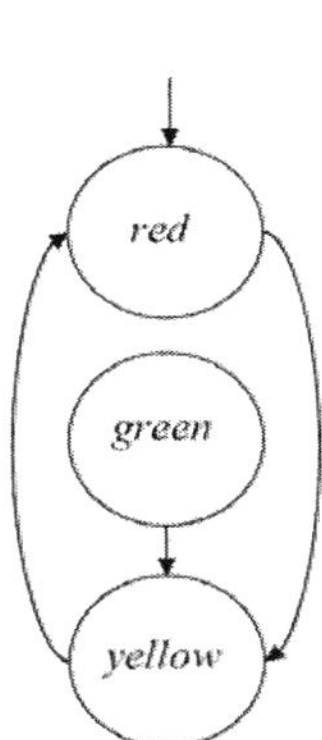

Fig. 5. Behavior-oriented system model M_{Syst}

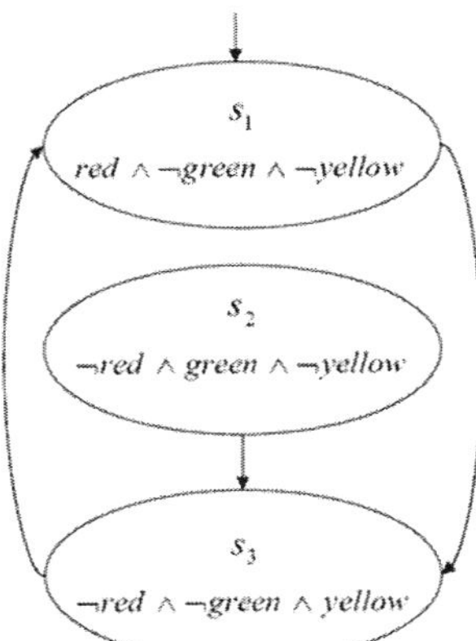

Fig. 6. Kripke structure for M_{Syst} of Fig. 4

Table 1. Manual model checking of the example

Valid Transitions		Invalid Transitions	
$\varphi_1 = G(red \rightarrow X(red \wedge yellow))$	-	$\varphi_5 = G(red \rightarrow X\neg green)$	+
$\varphi_2 = G((red \wedge yellow) \rightarrow Xgreen)$	+	$\varphi_6 = G(red \rightarrow X\neg yellow)$	-
$\varphi_3 = G(green \rightarrow Xyellow)$	+	$\varphi_7 = G((red \wedge yellow) \rightarrow X\neg red)$	+
$\varphi_4 = G(yellow \rightarrow Xred)$	+	$\varphi_8 = G((red \wedge yellow) \rightarrow X\neg yellow)$	+
Legend: -: the property is verified to be false +: the property is verified to be true		$\varphi_9 = G(green \rightarrow X\neg red)$	+
		$\varphi_{10} = G(green \rightarrow X\neg (red \wedge yellow))$	+
		$\varphi_{11} = G(yellow \rightarrow X\neg green)$	+
		$\varphi_{12} = G(yellow \rightarrow X\neg (red \wedge yellow))$	+

4 A Non-trivial Example and Tool Support

To validate the approach, the user interface of a commercial system is analyzed. Fig. 7 represents the utmost top menu as a graphical user interface (GUI) of the *RealJuke-*

box (*RJB*) of the RealNetworks. RJB has been introduced as a personal music management system. The user can build, manage, and play his or her individual digital music library on a personal computer. At the top level, the GUI has a pull-down menu that invokes other window components.

As the code of the RJB is not available, only black-box testing is applicable to RJB. The on-line user manual of the system delivers an informal specification that will be used here to produce the specification model M_{Spec}.

As an example, the M_{Spec} in Fig. 8 represents the top-level GUI to produce the desired interaction "Play and Record a CD or Track". The user can play/pause/ record/stop the track, fast forward (FF) and rewind. Fig. 8 illustrates all sequences of user-system interactions to realize the operations the user might launch when using the system. As the bold dashed line indicates, a transition from "Pause" to "Record" is not allowed. In the following, this property will be used as an example for model checking.

Fig. 7. Top Menu of the RealJukebox (RJB)

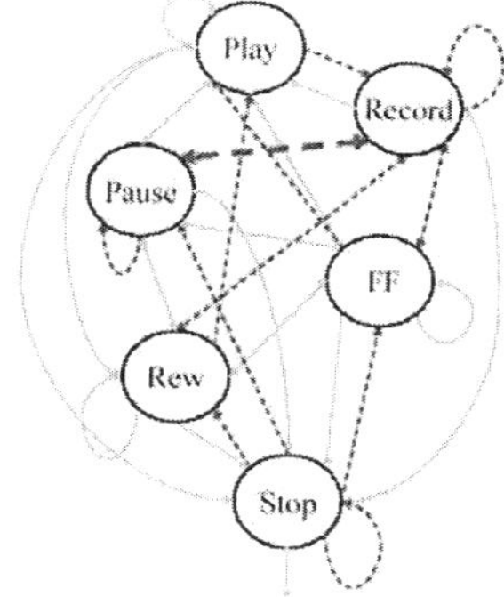

Fig. 8. M_{Spec} of the RJB

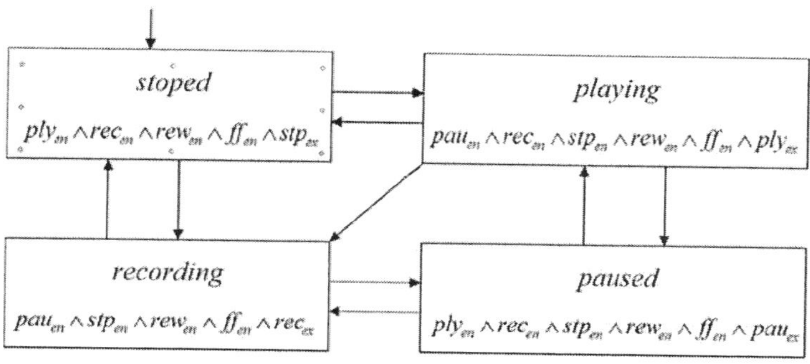

Fig. 9. M_{Syst} of the top GUI level of the RJB

As common in the practice, the user experiments with the system and finds out how it functions -- a process that leads to the production of the M_{Syst}. Fig. 9 depicts M_{Syst} as Kripke structure of the same abstraction level as Fig. 8.

The analysis process of the RJB delivers a variety of M_{Spec} *and* M_{Syst} of different abstraction levels that are handled by the approach as described in Section 3.

Because of the relatively large number of test cases and corresponding properties, an automated framework of tools is needed. This framework should explore the M_{Spec} and extract the legal and illegal test cases, convert them into properties, and model check these properties. For the latter step, SPIN [14] is deployed. The model checker SPIN is a generic verification system that supports the design and verification of asynchronous process systems. It accepts

- the system model described in PROMELA (a Process Meta Language) [14], and
- correctness claims specified in the syntax of standard LTL.

Fig. 10 contains screenshots of the user interface XSPIN of SPIN to demonstrate some steps of the tool deployment. Fig. 10a shows the PROMELA representation of the Kripke structure in Fig 9. A useful utility of XSPIN is the LTL property manager. It allows for the editing of LTL formula and the conversion of them automatically into a Büchi automata [7], which is then used to verify the defined property. Fig. 10b shows how LTL formula "$G(pau \rightarrow X \neg rec)$" is model-checked on M_{Syst} and verified as not being valid.

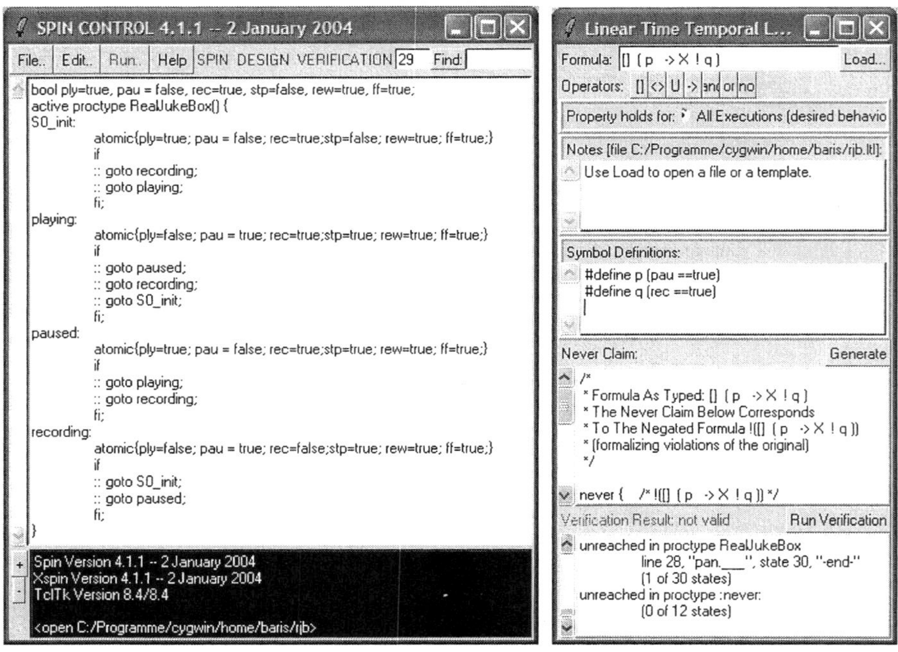

Fig. 10. XSPIN screenshots a) PROMELA definition of Kripke structure of Fig. 9b) LTL formula for $G(pau \rightarrow X \neg rec)$

Table 2. Detected faults and their interpretation corresponding to the system function "Play and Record a CD or Track"

No.	Fault Detected
1.	While recording, pushing the `forward` button or `rewind` button stops the recording process without a due warning.
2.	If a track is selected but the pointer refers to another track, pushing the `play` button invokes playing the selected track; the situation is ambiguous.
3.	During playing, pushing the `pause` button should exclude activation of `record` button. This is not ensured.
4.	`Track position` could not be set before starting the play of the file.

The command line Spin utilities can be used for a *batch processing* implemented by an additional script, where more than one LTL property are converted and verified. As an outcome, a protocol is desired including the verification result for each property. Tab. 2 excerpts the faults the approach detected.

5 Complexity Analysis of the Approach

[17] implies that the complexity of the automata-based LTL model checking algorithm increases exponentially in time with the *size of the formula* ($|\varphi|$), but linearly with the *size of the model* ($|S|+|R|$): $O(2^{|\varphi|}\times(|S|+|R|))$, where

- *size of the formula* ($|\varphi|$): the number of symbols (propositions, logical connectives and temporal operators) appearing in the representation of the formula,
- *size of the model* ($|S|+|R|$): the number of elements in the set of states S added with the number of elements in the set of transitions R.

Based on this result, the complexity of LTL model checking might be acceptable for short LTL formulas. Additionally the size of the model should be also controllable to avoid the state explosion problem.

For the present approach, LTL model checking is deployed for each formula φ generated from legal and illegal transitions of M_{Spec} for the verification of M_{Syst}. The number of all legal and illegal transitions is $|S_{Spec}|\times|S_{Spec}|=|S_{Spec}|^2$. The size of M_{Syst} is $|S_{Syst}|+|R_{Syst}|$. The complexity of the approach is $O(|S_{Spec}|^2) \times O(2^{|\varphi|}\times(|S_{Syst}|+|R_{Syst}|))$. As explained in section 3, the properties have always the same pattern: Globally, if some property p holds at some state, at the next state a property q should either hold in case of a legal transition ($\mathbf{G}(p \rightarrow \mathbf{X}q)$), or should not hold in case of an illegal transition ($\mathbf{G}(p \rightarrow \mathbf{X}\neg q)$). The size of the formulas ($|\varphi|$) is always constant. Because of this fact, we can ignore the exponential growth of the complexity of the approach, caused by the LTL property. The overall complexity of the approach is $O(|S_{Spec}|^2\times(|S_{Syst}|+|R_{Syst}|))$.

6 Conclusion and Future Work

An approach to combining specification-based testing with model checking has been introduced. Its novelty stems from (i) the holistic view that considers testing of not only the desirable system behavior, but also the undesirable one, and (ii) replacing the test process by model checking.

The approach has numerous advantages over traditional testing. First, model checking is automatically performed implying an enormous reduction of the costs and error-proneness that stemmed from manual work. Second, the test case and test generation are controlled by the coverage of the specification model and its complement. This enables an elegant handling of the test termination and oracle problems.

The complexity of the approach is exponential in the size of the specification model, but linear in the size of the system model, because of the constant size of the properties generated.

To keep the examples simple, test sequences of relatively short length have been chosen; checking with longer sequences would increase the likeliness of revealing more sophisticated faults.

There is much potential for a more efficient application of the approach in the practice: Automatically or semi-automatically transferring the test cases to LTL formulae. Also a report generator would enable the production of meaningful and compact test reports in accordance with the needs of the test engineer, e.g., on test coverage, time point of test termination, etc.

In this paper, an intuitive way of the construction of the system model has been considered. Proposals also exist, however, for formalization of the model construction, e.g., in [16], applying learning theory. Taking these proposals into account would further rationalize the approach.

Literature

1. P. Ammann, P. E. Black, W. Majurski, "Using Model Checking to Generate Tests from Specifications", ICFEM 1998, 46-54
2. P. Ammann, P. E. Black, and W. Ding, "Model Checkers in Software Testing", NIST-IR 6777, National Institute of Standards and Technology, 2002.
3. B. Beizer, "Software Testing Techniques", Van Nostrand Reinhold, 1990
4. F. Belli, "Finite-State Testing and Analysis of Graphical User Interfaces", Proc. 12th ISSRE, IEEE Computer Society Press, 2001, 34-43
5. R.V. Binder, "Testing Object-Oriented Systems", Addison-Wesley, 2000
6. J. P. Bowen, et al., "FORTEST: Formal Methods and Testing", Proc. COMPSAC 02, IEEE Computer Society Press, 2002, 91-101.
7. J. R. Büchi, "On a decision method in restricted second order arithmetic", Proc. Int. Cong. on Logic, Methodology, and Philosophy of Science, Stanford University Press, 1962 , 1-11
8. J. Callahan, F. Schneider, and S. Easterbrook, "Automated Software Testing Using Model-Checking", Proc. of the 1996 SPIN Workshop, Rutgers University, New Brunswick, NJ, 1996, 118–127.
9. T. S. Chow, "Testing Software Designed Modeled by Finite-State Machines", IEEE Trans. Softw. Eng., 1978, 178-187
10. E. M. Clarke, O. Grumberg, and D. Peled, "Model Checking", MIT Press, 2000
11. A. Engels, L.M.G. Feijs, S. Mauw, "Test Generation for Intelligent Networks Using Model Checking", Proc. TACAS, 1997, 384-398
12. A. Gargantini, C. Heitmeyer, "Using Model Checking to Generate Tests from Requirements Specification", Proc. ESEC/FSE '99, ACM SIGSOFT, 1999, 146-162

13. S. Ghosh, A.P. Mathur, „Interface Mutation", Softw. Testing, Verif.,and Reliability, 2001, 227-247
14. G. J. Holzmann, "The Model Checker SPIN", IEEE Trans. Software Eng., 1997, 279-295
15. J. Offutt, S. Liu, A. Abdurazik, P. Ammann, "Generating Test Data From State-Based Specifications", Softw. Testing, Verif.,and Reliability, 2003, 25-53
16. D. Peled, M. Y. Vardi, M. Yannakakis, "Black Box Checking", Journal of Automata, Languages and Combinatorics , 2002, 225-246
17. M.Y. Vardi, P. Wolper, "An automata-theoric approach to automatic program verification". In Proc. 1st IEEE Symp. Logic in Computer Science (LICS'86), IEEE Comp. Soc. Press, 1986, 332-244

Inferring Definite-Clause Grammars to Express Multivariate Time Series

Gabriela Guimarães and Luís Moniz Pereira

CENTRIA (Centre for Artificial Inteligence),
Universidade Nova de Lisboa, 2829-516 Caparica, Portugal
{gg, lmp}@di.fct.unl.pt
http://centria.di.fct.unl.pt/

Abstract. In application domains such as medicine, where a large amount of data is gathered, a medical diagnosis and a better understanding of the underlying generating process is an aim. Recordings of temporal data often afford an interpretation of the underlying pattens. This means that for diagnosis purposes a symbolic, i.e. understandable and interpretable representation of the results for physicians, is needed. This paper proposes the use of definitive-clause grammars for the induction of temporal expressions, thereby providing a more powerful framework than context-free grammars. An implementation in Prolog of these grammars is then straightforward. The main idea lies in introducing several abstraction levels, and in using unsupervised neural networks for the pattern discovery process. The results at each level are then used to induce temporal grammatical rules. The approach uses an adaptation of temporal ontological primitives often used in AI-systems.

1 Introduction

In several application domains, such as medicine, industrial processes, meteorology, often a large amount of data is recorded over time. The main aim lies in performing a diagnosis of the observed system. For example, consider an EEG recording to diagnose different sleep stages, or a chemical plant that goes through different process states, or the development of hail cells that possibly originate severe hailstorms, and so on. In all these cases, several types of processes are observed and problem specific diagnoses are searched for. Human beings, after a training phase, often develop the ability to recognise complex patterns in multivariate time series. The reason lies in their background knowledge, and in their experience to deal with standard and non-standard situations, thereby being able to make a diagnosis analysing the time series at different time scales.

The identification of complex temporal patterns is very hard to handle with technical systems. Classical approaches in the field of pattern recognition (PR) are very useful for feature extraction, where no temporal context has to be considered [5,21]. In order to interpret temporal patterns in time series, temporal dependencies between the primitive patterns (features) have to be taken into account. Syntactic PR views complex patterns as sentences of primitive patterns. Thus, techniques for syntactic PR strongly rely on the theory of formal languages [6]. New approaches in adaptive PR

M. Ali and F. Esposito (Eds.): IEA/AIE 2005, LNAI 3533, pp. 332–341, 2005.

and neurocomputing have recently been developed [3, 18], and enable a connection between the two approaches. In this paper we will show a way to extend adaptive PR-methods with Artificial Intelligence (AI) techniques.

Complex patterns in time series, as considered here, have to be seen in a temporal context. This requires context sensitive knowledge. And it means that context-free grammars are not powerful enough to parse context dependency in temporal series languages. Therefore, a powerful extension of context-free grammars, the so called definitive clause grammars (DCGs), is suitable. The advantage of DCGs, besides their context-dependency, lies in an easy implementation of their rules as logic statements [22]. Such an implementation enables an efficient parsing using a theorem prover like Prolog, or better still, XSB-Prolog, which can handle left recursion by means of tabling.

In section 2 related work is presented. Section 3 describes the main properties of DCGs and introduces the inference mechanism. An example in medicine to illustrate the extracted rules is given in section 4. Conclusions are presented in section 5.

2 Related Work

Approaches for the extraction of a rule-based description from time series in the form of grammars or automata usually employ a pre-classification of the signals, i.e. the time series are segmented and transformed into sequences of labeled intervals. The approaches differ in the way segmentation is performed or how rules are induced from the labeld time series.

Concerning the segmentation problem, approaches have been proposed where the main patterns in the time series are pre-defined, for instance already having a classification of P-waves or QRS-complexes of an ECG signal [14], or otherwise classified using simple algorithms, like the simple waveform detection operations of local minimum or negative slope [2], or of zero-crossings in the first derivatives, in order to segment the time series into increasing/decreasing and convex/concave parts [12], or of frequent episodes from a class of episodes [16]. Other approaches use more elaborate methods for segmentation, such as information-theoretic neural networks with changeable number of hidden layers, associated with different values of the corresponding input attribute applied to [15]. The connections represent associations rules between conjunctions of input attributes and the target attribute.

A strongly related approach that also uses SOMs in combination with recurrent neural networks for the generation of automata is presented in [7]. It was used to predict daily foreign exchange rates. One-dimensional SOMs are used to extract elementary patterns form the time series. This approach, however, is limited to univariate time series. SOMs are again used for knowledge discovery of time series satellite images [13]. The images are classified by a two-stage SOM and described in regard to season and relevant features, such as typhoons or high-pressure masses. Time-dependent association rules are then extracted using a method for finding frequently co-occurring term-pairs from text. The rules are stored in a database, which then allows for high-level queries.

3 Inferring Definitive Clause Grammars from Multivariate Time Series at Distinct Abstraction Levels

The induction of grammatical rules is an important issue in pattern recognition. It comprehends extraction, identification, classification, and description of patterns in data gathered from real and simulated environments. In pattern recognition this is handled at different levels, by handling primitive and complex patterns differently.

Primitive patterns are characterised and described by features. They are regarded as a whole and associated to a given class. Complex patterns always consist in a structural and/or hierarchical alignment of primitive patterns. In statistical pattern recognition, primitive patterns are identified using statistical methods [5, 21], and recently neural networks are also used [3,18]. No temporal constraints are considered here. This means pattern recognition is performed at a low-level, a data processing level.

Syntactical pattern recognition approaches, however, assume that primitive patterns have already been identified and thus are represented at a symbolic level. Primitive patterns are also building blocks of complex patterns. Here, the main goal lies in identifying and describing structural or hierarchical, and in our case temporal, relations among the primitive patterns. Methods from the theory of formal languages in computer science are suitable for this task, through regarding complex patterns as words and primitive patterns as characters of the language. The main aim is always to describe a large amount of complex patterns using a small number of primitive patterns and grammatical rules.

Definitive clause grammars (DCGs) are a powerful extension of context-free (cf-) grammars and therefore suitable for inducing temporal relations. Most applications of DCGs have been for many years in natural language parsing systems [4]. A good introduction to this formalism can be found in [20]. The use of DCGs for time series was for the first time proposed in [10].

Basically, DCGs are built up from cf-rules. In order to provide context-dependency, a DCG extends a cf-grammar by augmenting non-terminals with arguments. DCGs extend cf-grammars in three important ways [20]:

- DCGs provide *context-dependency* in a grammar, such that a word category in a text may depend on the context in which that word occurs in the text.
- DCGs allow arbitrary *tree structures* that are built up in the course of parsing, providing a representation of meaning of a text.
- DCGs allow extra conditions.

The advantage of DCGs in dealing with context-dependency lies in their efficient implementation of DCG-rules as logic statements by definitive clauses or *Horn clauses*. Now the problem of parsing a word of a language is reduced to a problem of proving a theorem in terms of a Prolog interpreter. In DCGs nonterminals are written as Prolog atoms and terminals as facts.

Inducing DCGs for multivariate time series not only affords a hierarchical and temporal decomposition of the patterns at different abstraction levels, but also an explicit temporal knowledge representation. At distinct levels, special unsupervised neural networks in an hierarchical alignment [9] allow for a successive and step-wise mining of the patterns, such that the obtained results can be converted into grammatical rules more easily. In this paper only a brief description of the abstraction levels is given. For a more detailed description of the method see [11].

The input to our system are multivariate time series sampled at equal time steps. As a result, we obtain the discovered temporal patterns as well as a linguistic description of the patterns (see Fig. 1), which can be transformed into a definite-clause grammar employed for parsing. Next, a description of the different abstraction levels is given.

Features. The feature extraction process exercises a pre-processing of all time series. Pre-processing can be applied to one (e.g. FFT) or more then one time series (e.g. cross correlation). A feature is then the value of a function applied to a selection of time series with a time lag.

Primitive patterns. Each primitive pattern (pp) is associated with a single point in time, forming an inseparable unit. pp´s are identified by clustering algorithms or unsupervised neural networks using features as input, and without taking time into consideration. A pp is then assigned to one of the clusters, i.e. a pp-class. Time points not associated with a pp-class are a kind of transition points or transition periods if they last long between succeeding pp´s of the same pp-class. A pp-channel is the allocation of the whole time lag with pp´s and transitions periods (i.e. a sequence of characters). We want to point out that it is possible and even desirable to perform several feature selections for the generation of several pp-channels. The selection depends highly on the application and reduces strongly the complexity, since not all time series are considered at the same time.

Successions. Temporally succeeding pp´s of the same pp-class are successions, each having a specific duration. The concept of duration and temporal relation is introduced here for the first time.

Events. Here the concept of approximate simultaneity, i.e. states ocurring more or less at the same time, is introduced. An event is identified by temporal overlapping sequences at distinct pp-channels. Recurring events then belong to the same event class. Regions not associated with an event-class are regarded as transitions periods. Since the duration of events belonging to the same class may differ, event classes have a minimal and a maximal duration in the context of a sequence.

Sequences. Recurrent sequences of events are the main structures in the time series, and describe a temporal order over the whole multivariate time series. Transition periods between sequences occur just as well, and also having a minimal and a maximal duration. Probabilistic automata can be used for the identification of sequences of events, where transition probabilities between events are identified and described.

Temporal patterns. Finallly, the concept of similarity results in the identification of temporal patterns. Similar sequences are sequences with a small variation of events in different sequences. This aggregation enables once again a simplification of the DCGs. String exchange algorithms are suitable for the identification of temporal patterns. Temporal patterns are the final result of the whole temporal mining process and describe the main temporal structures in the multivariate time series. Using the terminology of formal languages, primitive patterns can be regarded as characters used for forming words, or even complex words, in our case forming successions of characters or single ones, representing events. Sequences and temporal patterns are then composed by a sequence of events, like words form a sentence in a natural or a computer language.

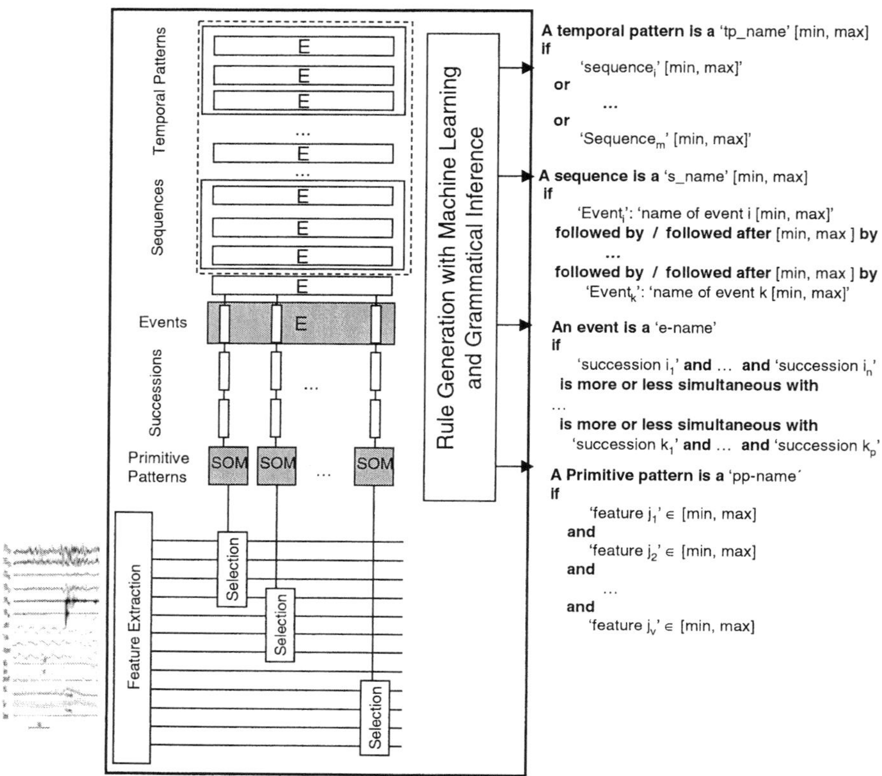

Fig. 1. A method with several abstraction levels for temporal pattern detection and for inferring Definite-Clause Grammars at distinct levels

As mentioned before, ML-algorithms are used to induce a rule-based and symbolic description of the pp´s. A parser for these rules can easily be implemented in Prolog [23]. A grammatical specification of events, sequences and temporal patterns presupposes that temporal dependences can be grammatically described, thus leading to the use of DCGs at higher abstraction levels. Before starting the induction process, however, an explicit temporal knowledge representation is needed. In AI a temporal reference is usually made up of a set of temporal elements, called ontological primitives (op). The main concepts for op´s are time points [17], time intervals [1], or a combination of both. For an overview to the main concepts on temporal reasoning, concerning logical formalisms in time in AI, ontological primitives, and concepts related with reasoning about action, see [24].

In this approach, a representation formalism related to Allen´s interval calculus is proposed. In the context of semi-automatic temporal pattern extraction Allen´s conception, with its 14 precedence relations, however, is far too complex and strict. For our purposes, a simpler forrmalism to describe an approximate simultaneity of events is needed, subsuming 10 of Allen´s precedence relation into a single one. Consequently, just a few op´s are needed to give a full description of the main concepts related to temporal patterns in multivariate time series. This leads to a simple and concise representation formalism built up by the following op´s:

- *and* for inclusion of features describing a primitive pattern
- *is more or less simultaneous with* describing an approximate simultaneity of successions
- *followed by* describing directly succeeding events
- *followed by ... after* describing succeeding events after a transition period
- *or* for alternative (temporal) sequences

4 An Example

This approach was applied to a sleep disorder with high prevalence, called sleep-related breathing disorders (SRBDs). For the diagnosis of SRBDs the temporal dynamics of physiological parameters such as sleep-related signals (EEG, EOG, EMG), concerning the respiration (airflow, ribcage and abdominal movements, oxygen saturation, snoring) and circulation related signals (ECG, blood pressure), are recorded and evaluated. Since the main aim is to identify different types of sleep related breathing disorders, mainly apnea and hypopnea, only the signals concerning the respiration have been considered [19]. Severity of the disorder is calculated by counting the number of apnea and hypopneas per hour of sleep, named respiratory disturbance index (RDI). If the RDI exceeds 40 events per hour of sleep, the patient has to be referred to therapy.

The different kinds of SRBDs are identified through the signals ´airflow´, ´ribcage movements´ and ´abdominal movements´, ´snoring´ and ´oxygen saturation´, as shown in Fig. 2, where a distinction between amplitude-related and phase-related disturbances is made. Concerning the amplitude-related disturbances, disturbances with 50%, as well as disturbances with 10-20%, of the baseline signal amplitude may occur. Phase-related disturbances are characterised by a lag between ´ribcage movements´ and ´abdominal movements´. An interruption of ´snoring´ is present at most SRBDs as well as a drop in ´oxygen saturation´.

For this experiment, 25 Hz sampled data have been used from three patients having the most frequent SRBDs. One patient even exhibited multiple sleep disorders.

In this paper we present an excerpt of the grammatical rules extracted from the results of the self-organizing neural networks at distinct abstraction levels, in order to demontrate how the algorithm for the generation of DCGs works. These rules can be transformed into Prolog rules and parsed at a symbolic level with a Prolog interpreter.

For the extraction of primitive pattern rules, the ML-algorithm sig* [23] was used, which generates rules for each class based on its most significant features. For instance,

```
a pp-class is a 'A4' if
        'strong airflow' ∈ [0.37, 1]
  and   'airflow' = 0
  and   'snoring intensity' ∈ [0.15, 1]
a pp-class is a 'B6' if
        'intense abdominal movements' ∈ [0.19, 1]
  and   'reduced ribcage movements' ∈ [0, 0.84]
  and   'intense ribcage movements' ∈ [0, 1]
```

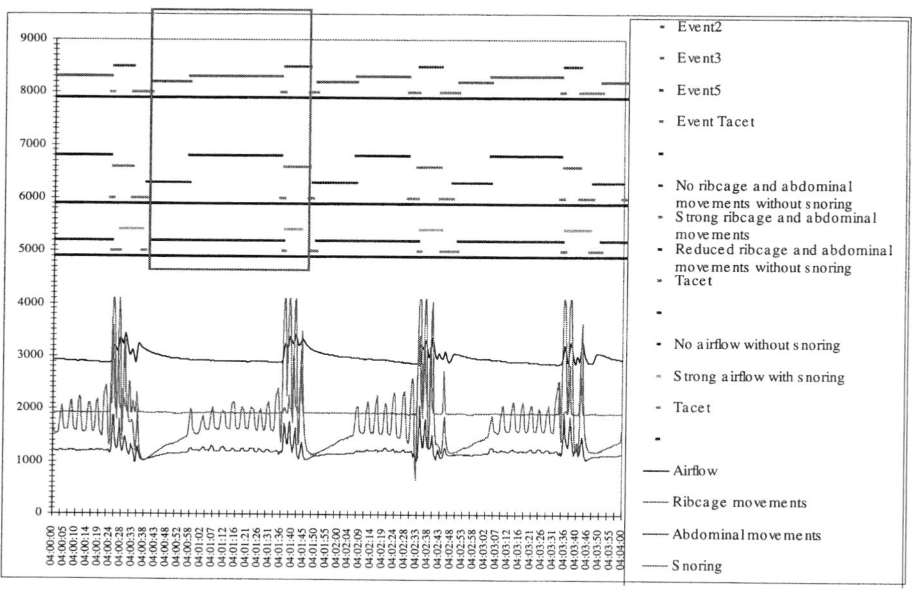

Fig. 2. Identified temporal pattern from a patient with SRBDs

These pp-classes were named A4: *strong airflow with snoring* and B6: *intense ribcage and abdominal movements*. For the other pp-classes rules were extracted as well, and meaningful names were given. These names can be used at the next level for the description of the event-classes. For instance,

```
an event-class is a 'Event5 'if
         ('strong airflow with snoring'
    or     'reduced airflow with snoring'
    or     'transition period')
  is more or less simultaneous with
        'intense ribcage and abdominal movements'
```

This event was named *strong breathing without snoring*. The names of the event-classes are then used at the next level for the descriptions of the sequences or temporal patterns.

```
a sequence is a 'Sequence1' [40 sec, 64 sec] if
       'Event2': 'no airflow with no chest and abdominal wall
        movements and without snoring' [13 sec, 18 sec]
  followed by
       'Event3': 'no airflow with reduced chest and no
       abdominal wall movements and without snoring' [20 sec,
       39 sec]
  followed after [0.5 sec, 5 sec] by
       'Event5':'strong breathing with snoring' [6 sec,
       12 sec]
```

The rules are simple and understandable for domain experts, since they provide a linguistic description of their domain. Experts can stay with their thought pattern. The domain expert can identify the above mentioned sequence as an *mixed apnoe* and

Event5 as an *hypopnoe*. Other temporal patterns were identified, namely *obstructive hypopnoe*, *mixed obstructive apnoe*, and *obstructive snoring*.

Next, a small excerpt of the DCG for the above mentioned temporal pattern is given.

```
Rules
  succession(S,D)  --> succ(S), op, duration(D), cp.
  ...
  transition(T,D)  --> trans(T), op, duration(D), cp.
  ...
  succes('E5',D1)  --> succession('A4',D) ; succession('A1',D) ;
                       transition(T,D).
  succes('E5',D2)  --> succession('B6',D).
  ...
  event('E5',D)  --> succes('E5',D1), simultaneity,
                     succes('E5',D2),range('E5',LR,UR),
                     {D is (D1+D2)/2, D<UR, D>LR}.
  ...
  sequence('S1',D)  --> event('S1',D1), followedby,
                  event('S1',D2),
                  followedafter, transition(T,D3),
                  event('S1',D4),{uplimit('S1',UD),
                  lowlimit('S1',LD), D is D1+D2+D3+D4, D<UD, D>LD}.
  ...
  duration(D)  --> [D],{number(D)}.
  range(D)  --> [D],{number(D)}.
  uplimit('S1',<value>).
  lowlimit('S1',<value>).
  ...
  Facts
  trans(T)  --> [transition,period].
  op --> ['['].
  cp --> [']',sec].
  and --> [and].
  or --> [or].
  followedafter --> [followed,after].
  followedby -->  [followed,by].
  simultaneity --> [is,more,or,less,simultaneous,with].
  succ('A4')  --> [strong,airflow,with,snoring].
  succ('A1')  --> [reduced,airflow,with,snoring].
  succ('B6')  --> [intense,ribcage,and,abdominal,movements].
```

A structured and complete evaluation of the discovered temporal knowledge at the different abstraction levels was made by questioning an expert. All events and temporal patterns presented to the physician described the main properties of SRBDs. All of the four discovered temporal patterns described very well the domain knowledge. For one of the patterns new knowledge was even found.

5 Conclusion

The recognition of temporal patterns in time series requires the integration of several methods, as statistical and signal processing pattern recognition, syntactic pattern recognition as well as new approaches like AI-methods and special neural networks. The main idea of this approach lies in introducing several abstraction levels, such that a step-wise discovery of temporal patterns becomes feasible. The results of the unsupervised neural networks are used to induce grammatical rules. Special grammars, named DCGs, have been used here, since they are a powerful extension of context-free grammars. The main advantage in using DCGs lies in augmenting non-terminals with arguments, such as temporal constraints, as required here.

If no temporal relations have to be considered, for instance for the generation of a rule-based description of the primitive patterns, then Machine Learning algorithms can be used straightforwardly. The main advantage of our approach lies in the generation of a description for multivariate time series at different levels. This permits a structured interpretation of the final results, where an expert can navigate between rules at the same level and, if needed, zoom in to a rule at a lower level or zoom out to a rule at a higher level. This procedure provides an understanding of the underlying process, first at a coarse and later on at more and more finer granulation.

Acknowledgment. We would like to thank Prof. Dr. J. H. Peter and Dr. T. Penzel, Medizinische Poliklinik, of the Philipps University of Marburg, for providing the data.

References

1. Allen, J.:Towards a General Theory of Action and Time. Artificial Intelligence 23 (1984) 123-154
2. Bezdek, J.C.: Hybrid modeling in pattern recognition and control. Knowledge-Based Systems 8, Nr 6 (1995) 359-371
3. Bishop, C.M.: Neural Networks for Pattern Recognition. Clarendow Press, Oxford (1995)
4. Bolc, L.: Natural Language Parsing Systems. Springer Verlag, New York (1987)
5. Duda, O., Hart, P.E.: Pattern Classification and Scene Analysis. John Wiley and Sons, Inc. New York (1973)
6. Fu, S.: Syntactic Pattern Recognition and Applications. Prentice-Hall, Englewood-Cliffs, N.J (1982)
7. Giles, C.L., Lawrence, S., Tsoi, A.C.: Rule Inference for Financial Prediction using Recurrent Neural Networks. In: Proceedings of IEE/IAFE Conf. on Computational Intelligence for Financial Engineering (CIFEr), IEEE, Piscataway, NJ (1997) 253-259
8. Gonzalez, R.C., Thomason, M.G.: Syntactic Pattern Recognition, Addison-Wesley (1978)
9. Guimarães, G.: Temporal knowledge discovery with self-organizing neural networks. In: Part I of the Special issue (Guest Editor: A. Engelbrecht): Knowledge Discovery from Structured and Unstructured Data, The International Journal of Computers, Systems and Signals (2000) 5-16
10. Guimarães, G.; Ultsch, A.: A Symbolic Representation for Patterns in Time Series using Definitive Clause Grammars. In: Klar,R., Opitz,R. (eds.): Classification and Knowledge Organization, 20th Annual Conf. of the Gesellschaft für Klassifikation (GFKl´96), March 6 - 8, Springer (1997) 105-111
11. Guimarães, G., Ultsch, A.: A Method for Temporal Knowledge Conversion. In: Hand, D.J., Kok, J.N., Berthold, M.R. (Eds.): Advances in Intelligent Data Analysis (IDA´99), The Third Symposium on Intelligent Data Analysis, August 9-11, Amsterdam, Netherlands, Lecture Notes in Computer Science 1642, Springer (1999) 369-380
12. Höppner, F.: Learning Dependencies in Multivariate Time Series. In: Proc. of the ECAI'02 Workshop on Knowledge Discovery in (Spatio-) Temporal Data, Lyon, France, (2002) 25-31
13. Honda, R., Takimoto, H., Konishi, O.: Semantic indexing and temporal rule discovery for time-series satellite images. In: Proceedings of the International Workshop on Multimedia Data Mining in conjunction with ACM-SIGKDD Conference, Boston, MA, 82-90, 2000

14. Koski, A., Juhola, M. Meriste, M.: Syntactic recognition of ECG signals by attributed finite automata. Pattern Recognition, The Journal of the Pattern Recognition Society 28, Issue 12, December (1995) 1927-1940
15. Last, M., Klein, Y., Kandel, A.: Knowlegde Discovery in time series databases. In: IEEE Transactions on Systems. Man and Cybernetics, Part B Cybernetics, Vol. 31, No. 1, (2001) 160-169
16. H. Mannila, H. Toivonen and I. Verkamo: Discovery of frequent episodes in event sequences. Data Mining and Knowledge Discovery 1, Nr. 3 (1997) 259-289
17. McDermott, D.: A Temporal Logic for Reasoning about Processes and Plans. Cognitive Science 6 (1982) 101-155
18. Pao, Y.-H.: Adaptive Pattern Recognition and Neural Networks. Addison-Wesley, New York (1994)
19. Penzel, T., Peter, J.H.: Design of an Ambulatory Sleep Apnea Recorder. In: H.T. Nagle, W.J. Tompkins (eds.): Case Studies in Medical Instrument Design, IEEE, New York (1992) 171-179
20. Pereira, F., Warren, D.: Definitive Clause Grammars for Language Analysis - A Survey of the Formalism and a Comparison with Augmented Transition Networks. Artificial Intelligence 13 (1980) 231-278
21. Tou, J.T., Gonzalez, R.C.: Pattern Recognition Principles, Addison-Wesley (1974)
22. Sterling, L., Shapiro, E.: The Art of Prolog. MIT Press (1986)
23. Ultsch, A.: Knowledge Extraction from Self-organizing Neural Networks. In: Opitz, O., Lausen, B., Klar, R. (eds.): Information and Classification, Berlin, Springer (1987) 301-306
24. Vila, L.: A Survey on Temporal Reasoning in Artificial Intelligence. Ai Communications 7, Nr 1 (1994) 4-28

Obtaining a Bayesian Map for Data Fusion and Failure Detection Under Uncertainty*

F. Aznar, M. Pujol, and R. Rizo

Department of Computer Science and Artificial Intelligence,
University of Alicante,
{fidel, mar, rizo}@dccia.ua.es

Abstract. This paper presents a generic Bayesian map and shows how it is used for the development of a task done by an agent arranged in an environment with uncertainty. This agent interacts with the world and is able to detect, using only readings from its sensors, any failure of its sensorial system. It can even continue to function properly while discarding readings obtained by the erroneous sensor/s. A formal model based on Bayesian Maps is proposed. The Bayesian Maps brings up a formalism where implicitly, using probabilities, we work with uncertainly. Some experimental data is provided to validate the correctness of this approach.

Keywords: Reasoning Under Uncertainty, Spatial Reasoning, Model-based Reasoning, Autonomous Agents.

1 Introduction

When an autonomous agent is launched into the real world there are several problems it has to face. The agent must have a model of the environment representing the real universe where it will interact. Nevertheless, it is necessary to bear in mind that any model of a real phenomenon will always be incomplete due to the permanent existence of unknown, hidden variables that will influence the phenomenon. The effect of these variables is malicious since they will cause the model and the phenomenon to have different behavioural patterns.

Reasoning with incomplete information continues to be a challenge for autonomous agents. Probabilistic inference and learning try to solve this problem using a formal base. A new formalism, the Bayesian programming (BP), [1],[2],[3] based on the principle of the Bayesian theory of probability, has been successfully used in autonomous robot programming. Bayesian programming is proposed as a solution when dealing with problems relating to uncertainty or incompleteness. A new probabilistic method that deals with the probabilistic modelling of an environment, based on BP, the Bayesian Maps (BM) [4],[5],[6] has been proposed recently as an incremental way to formalize the navigation of autonomous agents.

* This work has been financed by the Generalitat Valenciana project GV04B685.

M. Ali and F. Esposito (Eds.): IEA/AIE 2005, LNAI 3533, pp. 342–352, 2005.

Nowadays, the principal method used to model an environment is based on extracting a hierarchy of smaller models starting from a more complex and unmanageable model. In contrast, the BM uses simple models, which are combined to generate more complex models. Each BM sub model is built upon imbricate sensor motor relationships that provide behaviours. Obtaining such combinations of sensor motor models is also relevant to biologically inspired models, as it appears that no single metric model can account alone for large-scale navigation capacities of animals [5].

However, when the robot is performing within the environment another serious problem could occur, what would happen if one o more sensors provided erroneous readings? (We define an erroneous reading as a failure in the acquisition subsystem or in the data transmission from the sensor to the robot, not the reading variations produced by the physical properties of the environment). Erroneous readings make the robot's task more difficult, especially when working with autonomous agents in remote places (i.e. a lunar robot working to obtain information from the surface of Mars). In these circumstances it would be physically impossible to test if a sensor reading is correct or not. However, various readings, from one or more sensors, can be combined to obtain a better one. This process is called fusion. Data fusion provides more information than the individual sources and increases the integrity of the system.

In this paper an environment model for an autonomous agent based on the MB formalism is shown. The autonomous agent will develop a generic task working with uncertainly. Also, a method of obtaining sensor reliability in real time using an abstraction of various Bayesians maps will be defined. Next, the described models will be applied to a real robot. Finally, conclusions and future lines of investigation to be followed will be highlighted.

2 Adapting the Agent to the Uncertainty. From Bayesian Programming to Bayesian Maps

As commented above, using incomplete information for reasoning continues to be a challenge for artificial systems. Probabilistic inference and learning try to solve this problem using a formal base. Bayesian programming [1],[2],[3] has been used successfully in autonomous robot programming. Using this formalism we employ incompleteness explicitly in the model and then, the model's uncertainty chosen by the programmer, are defined explicitly too.

A Bayesian program is defined as a mean of specifying a family of probability distributions. There are two constituent components of a Bayesian program, presented in figure 1. The first is a declarative component where the user defines a description. The purpose of a description is to specify a method to compute a joint distribution. The second component is of procedural nature and consists of using a previously defined description with a question (normally computing a probability distribution of the form $P(Searched|\,Known)$). Answering this question consists in deciding a value for the variable *Searched* according to $P(Searched|\,Known)$ using the Bayesian inference rule:

$$\text{Program}\begin{cases}\text{Description}\begin{cases}\text{Spec}\,(\pi)\begin{cases}\text{Pertinent variables}\\ \text{Decomposition}\\ \text{Forms}\begin{cases}\text{Parametric}\\ \text{Programs}\end{cases}\end{cases}\\ \text{Identification based on Data}(\delta)\end{cases}\\ \text{Question}\end{cases}$$

Fig. 1. Structure of a Bayesian program

$$\begin{aligned} P\,(\text{Searched}|\,\text{Known}\otimes\delta\otimes\pi) = \\ \tfrac{1}{\Sigma}\times\sum_{\text{Unknown}} P\,(\text{Searched}\otimes\text{Unknown}\otimes\text{Known}|\,\delta\otimes\pi)\end{aligned} \tag{1}$$

Where $\frac{1}{\Sigma}$ is a normalization term (see [1] for details). It is well known that a general Bayesian inference is a very difficult problem, which may be practically intractable. However, for specific problems, it is assumed that the programmer would implement an inference engine in an efficient manner. More details about BP can be found in [1],[2].

2.1 Bayesian Maps

Bayesian Maps (BM) [4],[5],[6] are one of the models developed using the BP. A Bayesian map c is a description (see figure 2a) that includes four variables: a perception one (P), an action one (A), a location variable at time t (L_t) and a location variable at time t' where $t' > t$ ($L_{t'}$). The choice of decomposition is not constrained; any probabilistic dependency structure can therefore be chosen here. The definition of forms and the learning mechanism (if any) are not constrained, either.

For a Bayesian map to be interesting, it is necessary that it generates several behaviours. A series of questions is proposed to ensure that a given map will generate useful behaviours. These questions are: localization $P\,(L_t|\,P\otimes c)$, prediction $P\,(L_{t'}|\,A\otimes L_t\otimes c)$ and control $P\,(A|\,L_t\otimes L_{t'}\otimes c)$. A map is considered useful if these questions are answered in a relevant manner (their entropy is *far enough* of its maximum).

In [6] a method of constructing a Bayesian map using other maps (sub maps) is presented. The abstractor operator (see figure 2b) combines different maps c^i, which could cover different locations, in a new map c' (global map or abstract map) permitting the agent to develop long routes. In addition this operator allows us to create a hierarchy of maps from the simplest to the most complex. Moreover, since each map within the hierarchy is a full probabilistic model, this hierarchy is potentially rich.

As seen in [7], a Bayesian map is a general framework able to represent different models (for example Kalman filters and particle filters). Using a BM we can ask prediction questions $P\,(L_{t'}|\,A\otimes L_t\otimes c)$ which can form the basis of a

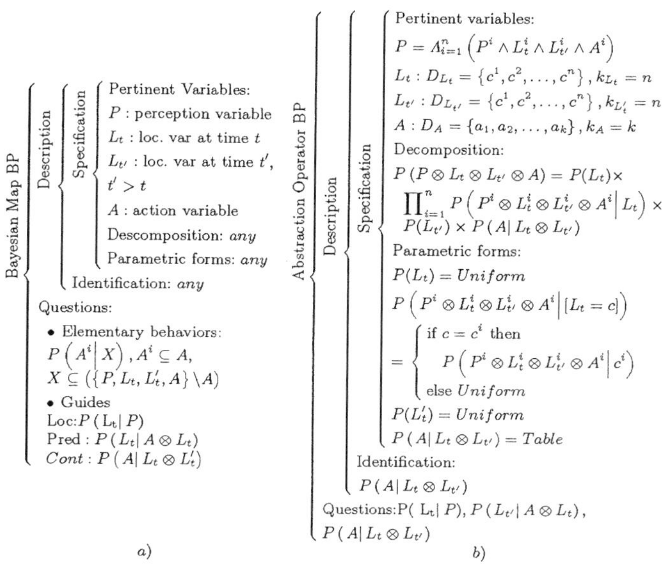

Fig. 2. a) Structure of a Bayesian Map. b) The Abstractor Operator. ($|c$ is omitted from the right hand of the formulation)

planning process. The resulting hierarchical models are built upon imbricate sensorimotor relationship that provide behaviours, thus departing from the classical *perceive, plan, act* control loop (see [4],[5],[6]).

3 Environment Model, Bayesian Map Proposed

In this part a generic Bayesian map is presented, this map will be used to represent the environment. Starting with a specific task, to be developed by our robot, will permit the deduction of the generic model.

The working environment of our robot is represented by this map (figure 3e). The robotic agent must serve as a connection between the rooms shown in the figure, gathering and providing material from one to others.

BM are a good approximation to solve this problem because uncertainty is directly specified in the model and they represent the knowledge in a hierarchical way. In order to formalize the task it was divided, and four subtasks defined:

- The robot is in a corridor (and has to advance along it)
- The robot recognizes a door on the right (and has to pass through it)
- The robot detects the end of the corridor (and has to turn 180 degrees)
- Finally the robot detects only a wall (and has to follow it)

3.1 Bayesian Maps

Once the task has been broken down the next step is to define a Bayesian map for each situation. In our case a Pioneer 1 robot with a seven sonar ring was used, defined by the perception variable $P = Px = \{P_1, P_2, ..., P_7\}$ and controlled by two action variables $A = \{Vrot, Vtrans\}$ representing the rotational and transactional velocity respectively.

The first proposed map c^{corr} describes the navigation along a corridor. For this map we define a localization variable L as $L = \{\theta, d\}$ where θ represents the angle between the robot and the corridor and d the distance to the nearest wall (see figure 3a). The angular distance is simplified in 5 regions from $\frac{\pi}{4}$ to $-\frac{\pi}{4}$ and the distance d represented as near, normal and far, $\lfloor\theta\rfloor = 5$, $\lfloor d\rfloor = 3$. This leads to a model that is compact yet sufficiently accurate to complete the proposed subtask.

In this way this joint distribution is defined with the following decomposition:

$$\begin{aligned}
&P(Px \otimes \theta \otimes d \otimes \theta' \otimes d' \otimes Vrot \otimes Vtrans|\, c^{corr}) = \\
&= P(Px|\, c^{corr}) \times P(\theta \otimes d|\, Px \otimes c^{corr}) \times P(\theta' \otimes d'|\, Px \otimes \theta \otimes d \otimes c^{corr}) \\
&\quad \times P(Vrot|\, Px \otimes \theta \otimes d \otimes \theta' \otimes d' \otimes c^{corr}) \\
&\quad \times P(Vtrans|\, Px \otimes \theta \otimes d \otimes \theta' \otimes d' \otimes Vrot \otimes c^{corr}) \\
&= P(Px|\, c^{corr}) \times P(\theta \otimes d|\, Px \otimes c^{corr}) \times P(\theta' \otimes d'|\, \theta \otimes d \otimes c^{corr}) \\
&\quad \times P(Vrot|\, \theta \otimes d \otimes \theta' \otimes d' \otimes c^{corr}) \times P(Vtrans|\, \theta \otimes d \otimes \theta' \otimes d' \otimes c^{corr})
\end{aligned} \tag{2}$$

Where the second equality is deduced from the conditional independence hypothesis. The next step is to identify the parametrical form of the previously defined joint distribution. $P(Px|\, c^{corr})$ and $P(\theta' \otimes d'|\, \theta \otimes d \otimes c^{corr})$ are uniform distributions (initially uniformity in readings and the environment are supposed). $P(\theta \otimes d|\, Px \otimes c^{corr})$ describes, using a reading, the angle and the distance that will determine the corridor. Despite being easier to work with the direct model $P(Px|\, \theta \otimes d \otimes c^{corr})$ than with the inverse one. This is because the distribution could be obtained directly using the robot (obtaining reading in the real environment). Even though, one distribution can be obtained from the other:

$$\begin{aligned}
P(Px|\, L \otimes c^{corr}) &= \tfrac{1}{\Sigma} \times \sum_{L'A} \begin{pmatrix} P(Px|\, c^{corr}) \times P(L|\, Px \otimes c^{corr}) \times P(L'|\, Px \otimes L \otimes c^{corr}) \\ \times P(A|\, Px \otimes L \otimes L' \otimes c^{corr}) \end{pmatrix} \\
&= \tfrac{1}{\Sigma} \times P(Px|\, c^{corr}) \times P(L|\, Px \otimes c^{corr}) \times \sum_{L'} P(L'|\, Px \otimes L \otimes c^{corr}) \times \\
&\qquad \times \sum_{A} P(A|\, Px \otimes L \otimes L' \otimes c^{corr}) \\
&= \tfrac{1}{\Sigma} \times P(Px|\, c^{corr}) \times P(L|\, Px \otimes c^{corr}) \\
&= \tfrac{1}{\Sigma'} \times P(L|\, Px \otimes c^{corr}), \text{where } L = \theta \otimes d
\end{aligned}$$

In this way the robot could be placed in different angles θ and at different distances d to obtain the Px values. Each sensor P_i will be represented by a Gaussian that shows the mean and the variation for each angle and distance.

$P(Vrot|\, \theta \otimes d \otimes \theta' \otimes d' \otimes c^{corr})$ and $P(Vtrans|\, \theta \otimes d \otimes \theta' \otimes d' \otimes c^{corr})$ shows the velocity (rotational or transactional) necessary to reach the required angle and distance at time t', when the initial angle and distance are given. These terms could be specified in an easy way using a table provided by the programmer.

This BM can be used by asking a question based on the joint distribution previously defined. For example it could be asked: $P(Vrot \otimes Vtrans | Px \otimes [\langle \theta, d \rangle = \langle 0, 1 \rangle])$. This question makes the robot follow the corridor between its walls obtaining the motor variables to perform this task. Using the same reasoning of this section the following Bayesian map is proposed (see figure 4).

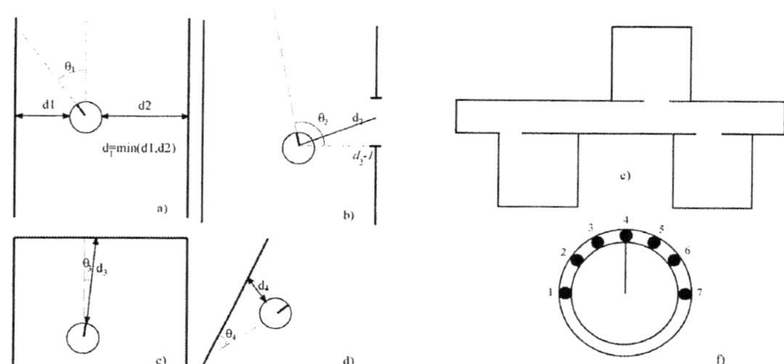

Fig. 3. a,b,c,d) Submap specification and variables for the submaps. e) Map where the robots moves. f) Sonar distribution in the Pionner 1 robot

Applying the decomposition proposed in this map, the next MB can be obtained taking into consideration that the localization variables are specific for each map (see figure 3).

4 Data Fusion and Incoherence Detection

Once the different parts of the environment where the Bayesian maps are going to work have been defined, they have to be combined. The combination or abstraction of maps is a method defined in [6] that is able to combine information (included in the sub map distributions we define) and generate a new map. This map is not only the combination of the individual sub maps but also provides a uniform model for the entire environment (even for places where the model is not specified).

Before applying the abstraction process, a method for combining the multiple sensor readings will be defined. We propose this sensor combination[1]:

$$P(Px | L) = \prod_i P(Px_i | L) \tag{3}$$

[1] In the next section we will omit $|c$ from the right hand side of the formulation.

We will assume independent sensorial elements (knowing the cause the consequences are independent). This is, indeed, a very strong hypothesis although it will be assumed because it provides a more robust system for malfunctions, improved signal quality and more efficient computation. Even so another question remains to be solved: How can the reliability distribution of one sensor be obtained? When the fusion process is defined as a product of a simpler terms related to each sensor we could obtain the sensor reliability in an easy way (for a given sub map):

$$P\left(Px_1^t \middle| Px_2^t \otimes Px_3^t \otimes ... \otimes Px_7^t \right) = 1 - \frac{1}{\Sigma} \sum_L \prod_i P\left(Px_i^t \middle| L \right) \tag{4}$$

It would be known if Px_1 is emitting incorrect readings if a reading in time t persists in being inconsistent with the readings of other sensors in a predetermined period. This inconsistency may be detected by a very low probability for Px_1^t.

BP Map Model
- Description
  - Specification
    - Pertienent Variables:
    - $P : Px = \langle P_1, ..., P_7 \rangle, L_t : \langle \theta_1, d_1 \rangle, L_{t'} : \langle \theta_1', d_1' \rangle$
    - $A : \langle Vrot, Vtrans \rangle$
    - Descomposition:
    - $P\left(Px \otimes \theta \otimes d \otimes \theta' \otimes d' \otimes Vrot \otimes Vtrans \middle| c \right) = P\left(Px \middle| c \right) \times$
    - $P\left(\theta \otimes d \middle| Px \otimes c \right) \times P\left(\theta' \otimes d' \middle| \theta \otimes d \otimes c \right) \times$
    - $P\left(Vrot \middle| \theta \otimes d \otimes \theta' \otimes d' \otimes c \right) \times P\left(Vtrans \middle| \theta \otimes d \otimes \theta' \otimes d' \otimes c \right)$
    - Parametric forms:
    - $P\left(Px \middle| c \right) \equiv$ Uniform; $P\left(\theta' \otimes d' \middle| \theta \otimes d \otimes c \right) \equiv$ Uniform
    - $P\left(\theta \otimes d \middle| Px \otimes c \right) \equiv G_{x,\theta,d}$, $P\left(Vrot \middle| \theta \otimes d \otimes \theta' \otimes d' \otimes c \right) \equiv$ Table;
    - $P\left(Vtrans \middle| \theta \otimes d \otimes \theta' \otimes d' \otimes c \right) \equiv$ Table
  - Identification:
  - $P\left(\theta \otimes d \middle| Px \otimes c \right) = \frac{1}{\Sigma} \underbrace{P\left(Px \middle| \theta \otimes d \otimes c \right)}_{\text{Learning}}$
- Questions:
- $P\left(L_t \middle| P \otimes c \right), P\left(L_t' \middle| A \otimes L_t \otimes c \right), P\left(A \middle| L_t \otimes L_t' \otimes c \right)$

Fig. 4. Generic Bayesian map proposed

As has been seen previously, combining maps using abstraction operators provides some advantages, one of them being an emergence of robustness (the abstract map is more robust than simply adding the individual robustness of the submaps). In this way a method to combine the sensorial reliability of the submaps is provided. In equation 4 we define how to calculate the reliability of a sensor in a Bayesian submap. This reliability only depends on the term $P\left(Px \middle| L \right)$. According to the definition of the abstract operator we can obtain this term for the abstraction of maps:

$$
\begin{aligned}
P(Px|\,L) &= \sum_{A\,L'} P(L)\prod_i P\left(P^i \otimes L^i \otimes L^{i'} \otimes A^i \middle| L\right) \times P(L') \times P(A|\,L \otimes L') = \\
&= P(L) \times \prod_i P\left(P^i \otimes L^i \otimes L^{i'} \otimes A^i \middle| L\right) \times \sum_{L'} P(L') \times \sum_{A} P(A|\,L \otimes L') = \\
&= \tfrac{1}{\Sigma}\prod_i P\left(P^i \otimes L^i \otimes L^{i'} \otimes A^i \middle| L\right)
\end{aligned}
$$

In the global map (the map obtained through the application of the abstraction operator) the localization depends not only on the submaps localization but also on the sensorial readings and the actions developed by the map. In this way the probability of sensor failure for the global map has been defined as:

$$
\begin{aligned}
PSF_1^t &= P(Px_1^t|\,Px_2^t \otimes Px_3^t \otimes \ldots \otimes Px_7^t \otimes c_{abstract}) = \\
1 - \tfrac{1}{\Sigma}\prod_n &\begin{pmatrix} P(P \otimes L \otimes L' \otimes A|\,[L = c_1]) \times \tfrac{1}{\Sigma'} \sum_{L_{c1}} \prod_i P(P_i|\,L) \times \\ \vdots \\ P(P \otimes L \otimes L' \otimes A|\,[L = c_n]) \times \tfrac{1}{\Sigma'} \sum_{L_{cn}} \prod_i P(P_i|\,L) \end{pmatrix}
\end{aligned} \tag{5}
$$

This computation can thus be interpreted as a Bayesian comparison of the relevance models with respect to the probability of the sensors failure.

Once the probability of sensor failure has been obtained it can be used to discard an erroneous sensor and then continue using the other ones. In order to discard a sensor a threshold has to be specified(any value over this threshold will be considered as a sensor failure). The failure of a sensor can be defined as:

$$
fail_{P_1} = \left(\frac{\sum_i P\left(P_i|\,S \otimes c^{abstract}\right)}{i} - PSF_1^t + \mu \right) < 0, \text{where } S \subseteq \left\{Px_i^t \backslash P_i\right\} \tag{6}
$$

To determine if a sensor is working correctly, a threshold is needed (provided by the programmer) and also a normalization term. This term is required in environments with high uncertainty (for example in environments where the agent is not prepared) because without this normalization the agent could think that all sensors are erroneous.

5 Experimental Validation

Using the provided maps and combining them with the abstract operator we have obtained the desired agent behaviour. In the next figure 5a, the path followed by the robot is shown for a complete route. As we see, the robot follows the corridor (landmark 1) until it finds the right door (landmark 3). Once the door is detected the robots passes through the door and turns 180 degrees so

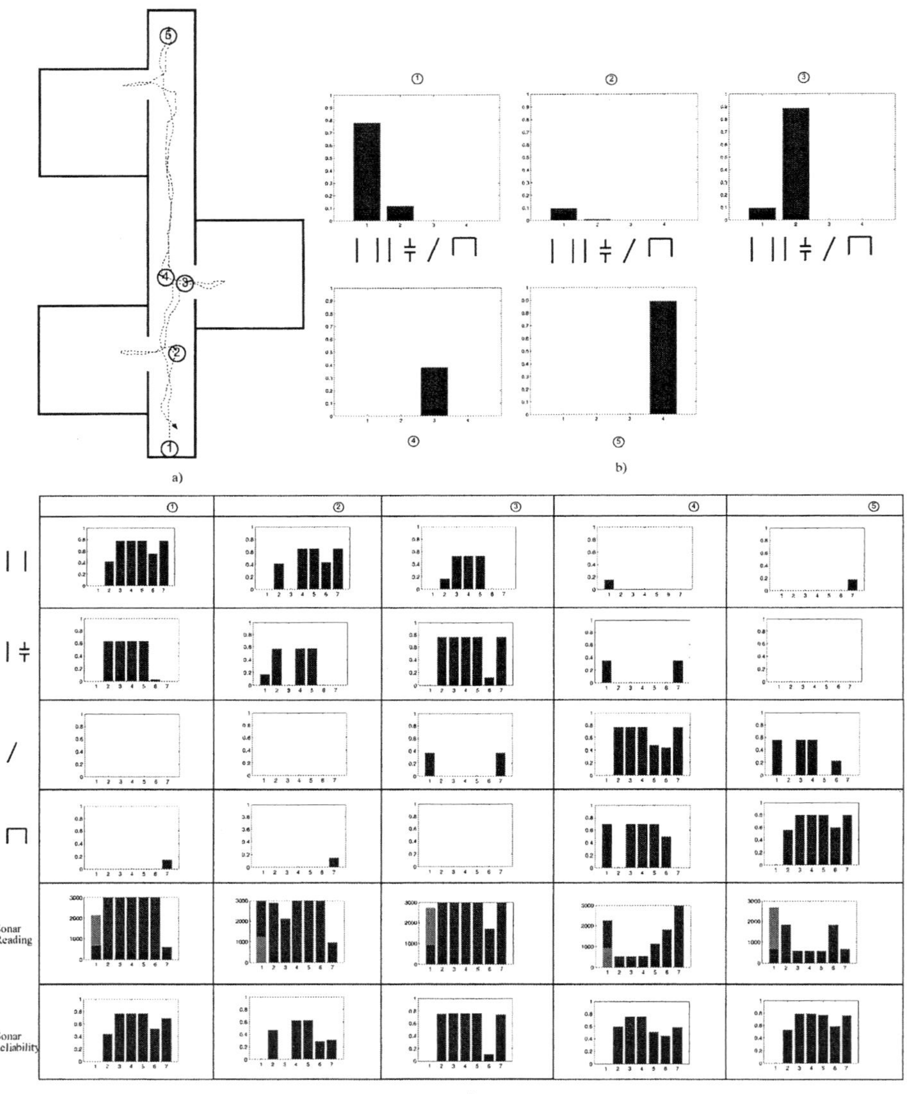

Fig. 5. a) Landmarks and route developed by the robot. The landmarks show the angle and the position where the tests are performed. b) $P(L|Px \otimes c_i)$ for each landmark and each map i (a map is represented by a symbol: corridor, door, wall and end of corridor). c) For each sonar (1...7) the reliability $P\left(Px_1^t \middle| Px_2^t \otimes Px_3^t \otimes ... \otimes Px_7^t\right)$ is obtained for each submap and each landmark. The global reliability in the final row is also shown. The tests are done contaminating the first sensor readings with impulsive noise. The red bar (the brightest) shows the noise value used, the blue bar is the real value detected by the sensor

that it sees a wall (landmark 4). The robot continues parallel to the wall and follows it until the corridor map reactives. Once it arrives to the end of the corridor (landmark 5) it turns 180 degrees to continue the route. The left door in landmark 2 complicates recognition (this situation not being pre prepared; the robot only learnt to recognise doors on the right) although the model works correctly (see figure 5b2).

Developing the same route, an impulsive noise is introduced in the furthermost left sensor (see sensor 1 in the figure 3c). A table summarizing the data collected by the experiment is provided where the following can be seen : the sensor readings, the value of $P(L|\, Px)$ for the global map and the sensor reliability for some selected landmarks. It is interesting to analyse the results represented in figure 5c. Firstly, it can be seen that the sensorial reliability for a landmark[2] varies with respect to the sub map used. This variation occurs because each map expects different readings according its internal model; therefore, the expected sensor reliability varies between models. Once sensor reliability for each sub map has been obtained applying (equation 5) they can be combined to obtain the common reliability for the landmark n. By observing the sixth row of the table (the global reliability) it can be seen how sensor 1 works incorrectly. The programmer is the person who must determine the threshold μ for discarding erroneous sensors.

6 Conclusions

In this paper a model has been presented based on Bayesian maps, in which a physical agent develops a generic task working under uncertainty. The possibility of detecting any failures in the sensorial system has been added to the model, thereby detecting if any sensor is returning erroneous readings.

Examples of both navigation and failure tolerance systems have been provided, which determine the correction of the models presented here.

In an uncertain world it is necessary to work taking this uncertainty into consideration. The models proposed here contain the uncertainty inside itself because they are rigorously based on the Bayes Theorem. Future studies will try to develop data fusion with different sensors sources using the same Bayesian paradigm.

References

1. Lebeltel, O., Bessière, P., Diard, J., Mazer, E.: Bayesian robots programming. Autonomous Robots **16** (2004) 49–79
2. Bessière, P., Group, I.R.: Survei:probabilistic methodology and tecniques for artefact conception and development. INRIA (2003)
3. Diard, J., Lebeltel, O.: Bayesian programming and hierarchical learning in robotics. SAB2000 Proceedings Supplement Book; Publication of the International Society for Adaptive Behavior, Honolulu (2000)

[2] In this example we see the reliability considering only the final 30 readings (taken at the same location) in order to make the data comparison easier.

4. Julien Diard, P.B., Mazer, E.: Hierarchies of probabilistic models of navigation: the bayesian map and the abstraction operator. Proceedings of the 2004 IEEE, Internationa Conference on Robotics & Automation. New Orleans, LA (April 2004)
5. J. Diard, P. Bessière, E.M.: Combining probabilistic models of space for mobile robots: the bayesian map and the superposition operator. Proc. of the Int. Advanced Robotics Programme. Int. Workshop on Service, Assistive and Personal Robots. Technical Challenges and Real World Application Perspectives p. 65-72, Madrid (ES) (October, 2003)
6. Julien Diard, P.B., Mazer, E.: A theorical comparison of probabilistic and biomimetic models of mobile robot navigation. Proceedings of the 2004 IEEE, Internationa Conference on Robotics & Automation. New Orleans, LA (April 2004)
7. Julien Diard, Pierre Bessière, E.M.: A survey of probabilistic models using the bayesian programming methodology as a unifying framework. In Proceedings International Conference on Computational Intelligence, Robotics and Autonomous Systems (IEEE-CIRAS), Singapore (2003)

Event Handling Mechanism for Retrieving Spatio-temporal Changes at Various Detailed Level

Masakazu Ikezaki, Naoto Mukai, and Toyohide Watanabe

Department of Systems and Social Informatics,
Graduate School of Information Science, Nagoya University,
Furo-cho, Chikusa-ku, Nagoya, 464-8603, Japan
{mikezaki, naoto, watanabe}@watanabe.ss.is.nagoya-u.ac.jp

Abstract. We propose an event handling mechanism for dealing with spatio-temporal changes. By using this mechanism, we can observe changes of features at diverse viewpoints. We formalize an event that changes a set of features. The relation between events has a hierarchical structure. This structure provides observations of spatial changes at various detailed level.

1 Introduction

Recently, a geographic information system (GIS) is used in various fields, and takes an important role as fundamental resources for our lives. However, in almost traditional researches on GIS, they focus on only local changing of geographic information. If GIS can treat global changes and dynamic aspects of geographic information, GIS may become a more useful tool in all fields in which GISs are used. There are some researches on dynamic aspects of geographic information ([1][2]). However, they have restriction in some degree. We propose an event handling mechanism. In our mechanism, the factor of changing features is defined as an event. We construct a hierarchical structure of events to observe changes of objects at diverse viewpoints.

2 Frame Work

2.1 Feature

We define a feature as an object that has shapes as spatial attributes and lifespan as temporal attributes. In Addition, generally any maps have specific scale corresponding to its detailed degree. Among maps with different scale, we can consider hierarchical structure. Additionally, we should consider themes of maps such as road, construct, intendancy, and so on. A Multi-Theme Multi-Scale map information model ([3]) had been proposed to maintain these hierarchical relations and themes without redundancy. Based on the M2 map information model,

M. Ali and F. Esposito (Eds.): IEA/AIE 2005, LNAI 3533, pp. 353–356, 2005.

each feature is assigned to appropriate level layer and appropriate theme. We denote the level of a layer and a theme to which feature o belongs by $Level_F(o)$ and $Theme(o)$.

2.2 Event Structure

Definition of Event. A feature changes as time passes. These changes often have a common factor. We call these common factors an event. There are two event types. One is primitive event (PE), and the other is composite event (CE). A primitive event $pe \in PE$ changes a set of features and a composite event $ce \in CE$ consists of an event set.

$$pe = (cf_1, cf_2, ;cf_n) \tag{1}$$

$$ce = \{ee_1, ee_2, ;ee_n | ee_i \in PE \vee ee_i \in CE\}. \tag{2}$$

In equation 1, cf_i represents a change of a feature such as "deletion of a building". In addition, a set of features affected by pe is denoted by $TargetOf(pe)$, and $Theme(pe)$ represents the set of themes to which each feature included in $TargetOf(pe)$. In equation 2, ee_i represents an element of a composite event. Additionally, a set of elements of ce and a set of features affected by ce are denoted as $Element(ce)$ and $TargetOf(ce)$, respectively. In addition, $Theme(ce)$ is represents the set of themes to which each element of ce belongs.

Relation Between Events. The relation between events has two types.

The relation between a composite event and its elements has hierarchical structure. Each event e in the event hierarchy assigned specified level, which is denoted as $Level_E(e)$. Formally levels of the event are calculated as follows.

$$Level_E(e) \geq Max(Level_F(f | f \subset TargetOf(e)) \tag{3}$$

The level of Event e must be higher than the level of the all features in $TargetOf(e)$. In addition, if $TargetOf(e_{i+1})$ is subset of $TargetOf(e_i)$, then event e_i is higher than e_{i+1}. We name the relation between e_i and e_{i+1} an Aggregate-Relation.

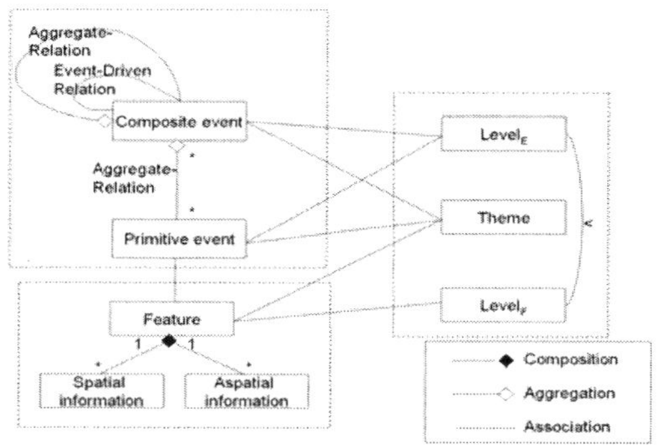

Fig. 1. Conceptual model of event structure in UML

In addition to Aggregate-Relation, we consider one more relation. In the world, most of events are driven by other events. For instance, an earthquake drives flood disasters. We name such a relation between events Event-Driven-Relation. The Event-Driven-Relation represents temporal relation, while Aggregate-Relation represents spatial relation. Fig.1 presents our framework in UML.

3 Multi-detailed Observation of Event

3.1 Retrieving Features with Common Factor

In the traditional models, even if each feature has same timestamp of changing, it is not clear that these changes are synchronized mutually. For instance, even if some building has lifespan from "1994-12-01" to "2004-11-14", it is not clear that these buildings are synchronized with each other when these buildings are deleted. In contrast, we can treat changes of features as synchronized changes in our model, features associated with the same event can be treated as a set one key feature or event.

3.2 Retrieving Feature with Interrelated Factor

In our model, the factors of changes of features have a hierarchical structure. Based on Aggregate-Relation, we can observe the changes at diverse viewpoints. If we trace to the upper event in event hierarchy, we can obtain the synchronized changes at upper layer. These changes are global changes. On the other hand, if we trace to the lower event in the hierarchical event structure, we can obtain the synchronized changes at lower layer. It pulls up a set of features that have strong tie each other. In addition, by using Event-Driven-Relation, it is possible to obtain the features with causal relation.

4 Conclusion

In this paper, we propose the event handling mechanism. The event has two types: one is a primitive event, and the other is composite event. The primitive event manages changes of features. The composite event consists of a set of events. The relation among events constitutes a hierarchical structure. Using this structure, we can observe changes of feature at diverse viewpoints. The upper event manages a set of global changes of features, while the lower event manages a set of local changes of features that has stronger tie each other.

References

1. Peuquet, D., Duan, N.: An event-based spatiotemporal data model (estdm) for temporal analysis of geographical data. International Journal of Geographical Information Systems **9** (1995) 7–24

2. JIANG, J., CHEN, J.: Event-based spatio-temporal database design. In: International Journal of Geographical Information Systems. Volume 32., Germany (1998) 105–109
3. Feng, J., Watanabe, T.: Effective representation of road network on concept of object orientation. Trans. IEE of Japan **122-C** (2002) 2100–2108

Fault Localization Based on Abstract Dependencies*

Franz Wotawa and Safeeullah Soomro**

Graz University of Technology, Institute for Software Technology,
8010 Graz, Inffeldgasse 16b/2, Austria
{wotawa, ssoomro}@ist.tugraz.at
http://www.ist.tugraz.at/wotawa/

1 Introduction

Debugging, i.e., removing faults from programs, comprises three parts. Fault detection is used to find a misbehavior. Within fault localization the root-cause for the detected misbehavior is searched for. And finally, during repair the responsible parts of the program are replaced by others in order to get rid of the detected misbehavior. In this paper we focus on fault localization which is based on abstract dependencies that are used by the Aspect system [1] for detecting faults. Abstract dependencies are relations between variables of a program. We say that a variable x depends on a variable y iff a new value for y may causes a new value for x. For example, the assignment statement `x = y + 1;` implies such a dependency relation. Every time we change the value of y the value of x is changed after executing the statement. Another example which leads to the same dependency is the following program fragment:

```
if ( y < 10) then x = 1; else x = 0;
```

In this fragment not all changes applied to y cause a change on the value of x, although x definitely depends on y. The Aspect system now takes a program, computes the dependencies and compares them with the specified dependencies. If there is a mismatch the system detects a bug and notifies the user. However, the Aspect systems does not pinpoint the root-cause of the detected misbehavior to the user.

We illustrate the basic ideas of fault localization using the faulty implementation of a multiplication operation `myMult` which has the following source code:

```
  int myMult (int x,y) {
    int result = 0;
    int i = 0;
    while ( i < x ) {
```

* The work described in this paper has been supported by the Austrian Science Fund (FWF) project P15265-INF and the Higher Education Commission(HEC), Pakistan.

** Authors are listed in reverse alphabetical order.

M. Ali and F. Esposito (Eds.): IEA/AIE 2005, LNAI 3533, pp. 357–359, 2005.

```
4.     result = result + x ; // Should be result = result + y
5.     i = i + 1; }
6.   return result;
  }
```

The bug lies in statement 4 where the variable x is used in the right hand side expression of the assignment instead of variable y. In order to detect the fault we first have to specify the abstract dependencies for the multiplication where the result should depend on both inputs. Hence, we specify that result depends on x and y which can be written as a rule: result $\leftarrow$ x, y or as binary relation $\{(\texttt{result}, \texttt{x}), (\texttt{result}, \texttt{y})\}$.

When approximating the dependencies from the source code of myMult using the Aspect system, we finally obtain a dependency relation $\{(\texttt{result}, \texttt{x})\}$ which fails to be equivalent to the specified dependency relation. The question now is how the root-cause of this misbehavior can be found. The idea behind our approach is the following. During the computation of abstract dependencies every statement has an impact to the overall dependency set. For example statement 4 says that result depends on result and x. When knowing the dependencies of result before statement 4, we can extend the relation. For myMult the variable result also depends on i (statement 3) and a constant 0 (statement 1). The variable i itself depends on i (statement 5), x (statement 3) and a constant 0 (statement 2). Hence, in this case all statements fail to deliver a relation $(\texttt{result}, \texttt{y})$ and are therefore candidates for a root-cause. Let us now extend our example by introducing an additional specified dependency i $\leftarrow$ i, x which is said to be valid for statements 3 to 6. In this case statements 2, 3, and 5 can no longer be candidates for the root-cause because they are necessary to compute dependencies for variable i which fulfill the specification. Hence, only 1 and 4 remain as potential root-causes.

All arguments for extracting root-causes have been done using only dependencies which are computed by analyzing statements. Hence, a adapted formalization of this process which allows for reasoning about statements and their influences on the computed abstract dependencies should lead to a system which extracts root-causes automatically from the source code of programs and the specified dependencies. During the rest of this paper we provide a framework for this purpose which is based on model-based diagnosis [2]. Model-based diagnosis provides the means for reasoning about statements and their influences which is necessary for our purpose.

2 Modeling

The model of the statements is based on abstract dependencies [1]. Similar to previous research in the domain of debugging using model-based diagnosis, e.g., [3], the model represents the abstract behavior of statements when they are assumed to be correct, i.e., bug free. In contrast the new model introduces an additional model for the case when we assume a statement to be faulty. The assumption that a statement s is faulty or not is represented by the predicate

$AB(S)$ and $\neg AB(S)$ respectively. This is the standard notation in model-based diagnosis [2] and is used by a diagnosis engine during the computation of fault locations. The second difference between previous research and ours is that we propagate dependencies that correspond to statements. A statement that is assumed to be correct contributes dependencies which are computed by using the work published by [1]. If a statement is incorrect the computed dependencies comprises only the pair (t, ξ) where ξ represents a model variable that represents different program variables.

For example, the model of an assignment statement $x = e$ is the following. For the correct behavior we introduce the rules $\neg AB(x = e) \rightarrow D(x = e) = \{(x, v) | v \in vars(e)\}$ and $\neg AB(x = e) \rightarrow M(x = e) = \{x\}$, where $vars(e)$ is a function returning all referenced program variables in expression e. For the faulty case, where we assume the statement $x = e$ to be incorrect, we obtain $AB(x = e) \rightarrow \{(x, \xi)\}$ and $AB(x = e) \rightarrow M(x) = \{x\}$ where ξ is a model variable that is unique for each statement. Consider the following short program fragement

```
1.  x = a;
2.  y = x + b;
```

and the specified dependencies after line 2 is given by: $\{(x, a), (y, a), (y, c)\}$. Assuming that line 1 is faulty and line 2 is not, we obtain the dependency set $\{(x, \xi), (y, b), (y, \xi)\}$. It is easy to see that there is no substitution for ξ which makes the given specification equivalent to the computed dependencies. Hence, the assumptions are not valid and line 1 is not faulty. If we assume line 1 to be correct and line 2 to be incorrect, we get a dependency set which is equivalent to the specification when substituting ξ with a and c. Hence, this assumption is consistent with the given specification and we obtain a diagnosis. This procedure can be automated using a model-based diagnosis engine like the one described in [2].

The described model for assignment statements can be easily extended to handle while-loops and conditionals. Moreover, as described in [1] models of pointers and arrays are also possible. They only need to be extended for the case where we assume a statement that comprises pointers or arrays to be incorrect. Beside the fault localization capabilities of our approach which only requires an abstract specification of the program in terms of specified dependencies the used model can be extracted directly from the source code. Hence, the whole diagnosis process can be fully automated.

References

1. Jackson, D.: Aspect: Detecting Bugs with Abstract Dependences. ACM Transactions on Software Engineering and Methodology **4** (1995) 109–145
2. Reiter, R.: A theory of diagnosis from first principles. Artificial Intelligence **32** (1987) 57–95
3. Friedrich, G., Stumptner, M., Wotawa, F.: Model-based diagnosis of hardware designs. Artificial Intelligence **111** (1999) 3–39

Freeway Traffic Qualitative Simulation[1]

Vicente R. Tomás and A. Luis Garcia

Applying Intelligent Agents Research Group
University Jaume I,
12071 Castellon, Spain
{vtomas, garcial}@icc.uji.es

Abstract. A new freeway traffic simulator based on a deep model behaviour is proposed. This simulator is defined and developed for helping human traffic operators in taking decisions about predictive control actions in situations prior to congestion. The simulator uses qualitative tags and cognitive events to represent the traffic status and evolution and the temporal knowledge base produced by its execution is very small and it has a high level of cognitive information.

1 Introduction

The main purpose of an Intelligent Traffic System (ITS) is to help human traffic operators to decide which measures and strategies should be activated anticipating traffic changes based on the current information available of the road network [1]. However, this purpose is very difficult to obtain because the intrinsic ill-defined nature of the road traffic behaviour. Moreover, in freeway traffic the domain is even more difficult: traffic information is distributed between several traffic management centres (TMC) and the management of incidents usually involves a coordination process between several administrations and TMCs. There are several quantitative proposed approaches to help human traffic operators for ITS [2][3], but the way and the results provided by these approaches are not easily understood by the human traffic operator. So, it is needed a new, more cognitive, approach for helping human traffic operators to easily interchange and understand traffic parameters and evolution.

2 The Deep Knowledge Freeway Traffic Simulator

Freeway traffic information is highly distributed, so it is needed to use a common ontology for traffic coordination measures definition and evaluation. The freeway traffic domain ontology is composed of three subdomains: 1) The road subdomain describes topological features of the roads. This subdomain is composed of the following objects: segments (a one way road sections with the same number of lanes) and links (points where adjacent segments are connected: origins, destinations, bifurcations, unions, weavings and merges); 2) The dynamic traffic information

[1] This research has been partly supported by the Spanish research projects CICYT DPI2002-04357-c03-02 and Fundacio Caixa- Castello P1 1B2003-36.

M. Ali and F. Esposito (Eds.): IEA/AIE 2005, LNAI 3533, pp. 360 – 362, 2005.

subdomain (basic traffic parameters, the relationships between them and the qualitative tags and quantitative intervals defined to deal with these traffic parameters); and 3) the sensor/actuator equipment subdomain (data capture stations, CCTV cameras, VMS and emergency phones).

The main parameter used to represent traffic status and evolution is dynamic traffic density and the qualitative tags defined for modelling traffic density are showed in figure 1b. The main idea behind the definition of the freeway traffic qualitative model is to model the spatio-temporal fluctuations in traffic levels by defining a discrete qualitative space. Every road point with the same density of vehicles defines a qualitative region. The spatio-temporal limit that divides two adjacent regions is represented by a straight line. The vertexes of each qualitative region are traffic cognitive events because they represent significant properties in the dynamics of the traffic. So, it is possible to achieve entities with cognitive meaning due to the selection of these events as primitive ones that represent the evolution of the system. Figure 1a shows an example of the application of this formalism to the freeway domain. The left image of figure 1a represents the quantitative traffic evolution of a union link. The right image of figure 1a represents the same traffic evolution by using constant traffic density qualitative values. It is showed that the increasing of traffic in the upper road branch (1) produces an increment of density around the union (2). In spite of the traffic flow in the down branch is constant, the overall increase of density affects the union and the new density zone grows up (3). This temporal qualitative evolution is the result (following the mass conservation principle) of the border speed interaction between every pair of qualitative regions.

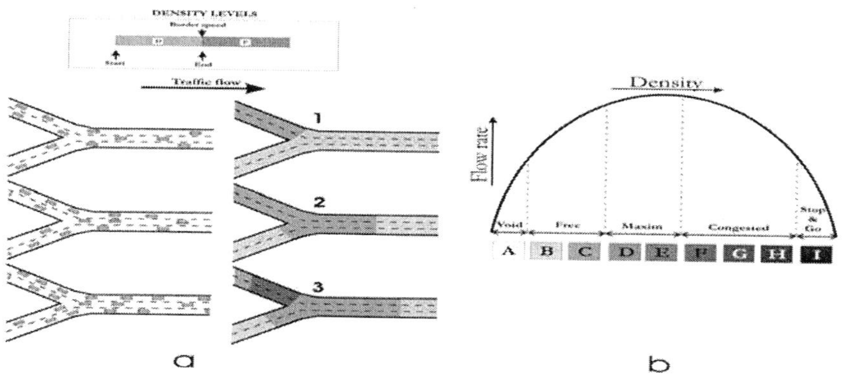

Fig. 1. (a) Quantitative and qualitative spatio-temporal representation of a traffic evolution on a union link. **(b).** Traffic density qualitative tags associated to traditional traffic levels of service

Let shows an example of how it is modelled the qualitative evolution on a bifurcation. A new qualitative region appears at the beginning of a bifurcation when a qualitative region arrives to the bifurcation. The initial value of the new qualitative region is function of the previous qualitative value at the bifurcation and the associated origin/destination matrix bifurcation.

The new inserted qualitative region must hold the traffic flow continuity principle or it will be sooner disappear. This principle restricts the range of possible qualitative values that can be assigned to adjacent regions. For example, if there is no traffic incidents it can not exists a qualitative region with a congestion value E followed by an adjacent qualitative region with a free value B. An additional set of heuristics is used to complete the bifurcation freeway traffic behaviour: 1) Traffic speed is always the fastest possible due to the behaviour of drivers; and 2) Qualitative value at the input segment of a bifurcation is usually bigger than the qualitative values of the possible output segments. This last fact is due to the traffic flow division between output segments.

The freeway traffic qualitative simulator works under the closed world assumption. It calculates, in an inductive way, when and which will be the next cognitive event to appear. Then, it is calculated the qualitative overall freeway traffic status associated to this cognitive event. The loop finishes when the time point of the next cognitive event to appear it is outside the temporal window of the simulator run.

3 Results, Conclusions and Future Work

A real freeway, that covers 30 Kms of the A-3 and A-31 Spanish freeways, has been modelled using the proposed qualitative simulator and the METANET[4] simulator. The accuracy of the freeway qualitative simulator results are as good as the results provided by METANET in this modelled network. Moreover, there are several good features to highligth of this simulator when compared with METANET: 1) the temporal knowledge base containing all the events produced by the simulator execution is very small and with a high level of cognitive information; 2) the defined qualitative tags and the way cognitive events are calculated are closer to the human traffic operator empirical knowledge, so they are suitable to be used as primitive traffic knowledge to be communicated between several TCM. However, the simulator does not deal with incidents traffic behaviour. The main purpose of the simulator is to be used for evaluating several alternative traffic routes in the absence of traffic incidents. We are now working on how several TMCs and administrations can begin to negociate the cooperative control actions to perform to deal with traffic incidents (e.g. meteorological incidents) with the use and the evaluation of the results provided by this qualitative simulator.

References

1. Transportation Research Board "Highway Capacity Manual", TRB 2000
2. Hoogendoorn et al. "Real-time traffic management scenario evaluation," Proc. of the 10th IFAC Symposium on Control in Transportation Systems (CTS 2003), Tokyo, Japan.
3. Smartest deliverable 3. "Simulation modeling applied to road transport European scheme tests. Review of micro-simulation models". Inst. of transport studies, Leeds University 1999.
4. Kotsialos, A. Papagoeorgiou et al. "Traffic flow modelling of large-scale motorway network using the macroscopic modelling tool Metanet". Proceedings of the TRAIl Expert Seminar on Recent Advances in traffic Flow Modelling and Control. Delft. The Netherlands. 1999

LEADSTO: A Language and Environment for Analysis of Dynamics by SimulaTiOn
(Extended Abstract)

Tibor Bosse[1], Catholijn M. Jonker[2], Lourens van der Meij[1], and Jan Treur[1]

[1] Vrije Universiteit Amsterdam, Department of Artificial Intelligence,
De Boelelaan 1081a, 1081 HV Amsterdam, The Netherlands
{tbosse, lourens, treur}@cs.vu.nl
http://www.cs.vu.nl/~{tbosse, lourens, treur}
[2] Nijmegen Institute for Cognition and Information, Division Cognitive Engineering,
Montessorilaan 3, 6525 HR Nijmegen, The Netherlands
C.Jonker@nici.ru.nl

Abstract. This paper presents the language and software environment LEADSTO that has been developed to model and simulate dynamic processes in terms of both qualitative and quantitative concepts. The LEADSTO language is a declarative order-sorted temporal language, extended with quantitative means. Dynamic processes can be modelled by specifying the direct temporal dependencies between state properties in successive states. Based on the LEADSTO language, a software environment was developed that performs simulations of LEADSTO specifications, generates simulation traces for further analysis, and constructs visual representations of traces. The approach proved its value in a number of research projects in different domains.

1 Introduction

In simulations various formats are used to specify basic mechanisms or causal relations within a process, see e.g., [1], [2], [3]. Depending on the domain of application such basic mechanisms need to be formulated quantitatively or qualitatively. Usually, within a given application explicit boundaries can be given in which the mechanisms take effect. For example, "from the time of planting an avocado pit, it takes 4 to 6 weeks for a shoot to appear".

In such examples, in order to simulate the process that takes place, it is important to model its *dynamics*. When considering current approaches to modelling dynamics, the following two classes can be identified: *logic-oriented* modelling approaches, and *mathematical* modelling approaches, usually based on difference or differential equations. Logic-oriented approaches are good for expressing qualitative relations, but less suitable for working with quantitative relationships. Mathematical modelling approaches (e.g., Dynamical Systems Theory [3]), are good for the quantitative relations, but expressing conceptual, qualitative relationships is very difficult. In this

M. Ali and F. Esposito (Eds.): IEA/AIE 2005, LNAI 3533, pp. 363 – 366, 2005.

article, the LEADSTO language (and software environment) is proposed as a language combining the specification of qualitative and quantitative relations.

2 Modelling Dynamics in LEADSTO

Dynamics is considered as evolution of states over time. The notion of state as used here is characterised on the basis of an ontology defining a set of properties that do or do not hold at a certain point in time. For a given (order-sorted predicate logic) ontology Ont, the propositional language signature consisting of all *state ground atoms* (or *atomic state properties*) based on Ont is denoted by APROP(Ont). The *state properties* based on a certain ontology Ont are formalised by the propositions that can be made (using conjunction, negation, disjunction, implication) from the ground atoms. A *state* S is an indication of which atomic state properties are true and which are false, i.e., a mapping S: APROP(Ont) → {true, false}.

To specify simulation models a temporal language has been developed. This language (the LEADSTO language) enables one to model direct temporal dependencies between two state properties in successive states, also called *dynamic properties.* A specification of dynamic properties in LEADSTO format has as advantages that it is executable and that it can often easily be depicted graphically. The format is defined as follows. Let α and β be state properties of the form 'conjunction of atoms or negations of atoms', and e, f, g, h non-negative real numbers. In the LEADSTO language the notation $\alpha \twoheadrightarrow_{e, f, g, h} \beta$, means:

If state property α holds for a certain time interval with duration g, then after some delay (between e and f) state property β will hold for a certain time interval of length h.

An example dynamic property that uses the LEADSTO format defined above is the following: "observes(agent_A, food_present) $\twoheadrightarrow_{2, 3, 1, 1.5}$ belief(agent_A, food_present)". Informally, this example expresses the fact that, if agent A observes that food is present during 1 time unit, then after a delay between 2 and 3 time units, agent A will believe that food is present during 1.5 time units. In addition, within the LEADSTO language it is possible to use sorts, variables over sorts, real numbers, and mathematical operations, such as in "has_value(x, v) $\twoheadrightarrow_{e, f, g, h}$ has_value(x, v*0.25)".

Next, a *trace* or *trajectory* γ over a state ontology Ont is a time-indexed sequence of states over Ont (where the time frame is formalised by the real numbers). A LEADSTO expression $\alpha \twoheadrightarrow_{e, f, g, h} \beta$, holds for a trace γ if:

$\forall$t1: [$\forall$t [t1−g ≤ t < t1 ⇒ α holds in γ at time t] ⇒ $\exists$d [e ≤ d ≤ f & $\forall$t' [t1+d ≤ t' < t1+d+h ⇒ β holds in γ at time t']

An important use of the LEADSTO language is as a specification language for simulation models. As indicated above, on the one hand LEADSTO expressions can be considered as logical expressions with a declarative, temporal semantics, showing what it means that they hold in a given trace. On the other hand they can be used to specify basic mechanisms of a process and to generate traces, similar to Executable Temporal Logic (cf. [1]).

The LEADSTO language has been used in a number of research projects in different domains. It has been used to analyse and simulate behavioural dynamics of agents in cognitive science, biology, social science, and artificial intelligence. For publications about these applications, the reader is referred to the authors' homepages.

3 Tools

The LEADSTO software environment consists of two programs: the *Property Editor* and the *Simulation Tool*. The Property Editor provides a user-friendly way of building and editing LEADSTO specifications. It was designed in particular for laymen and students. The tool has been used successfully by students with no computer science background and by users with little computer experience. By means of graphical manipulation and filling in of forms a LEADSTO specification may be constructed.

The Simulation Tool can perform the following activities:

- Loading LEADSTO specifications, performing a simulation and displaying the result.
- Loading and displaying existing traces (without performing simulation).

Apart from a number of technical details, the simulation algorithm is straightforward: at each time point, a bound part of the past of the trace (the maximum of all g values of all rules) determines the values of a bound range of the future trace (the maximum of f + h over all LEADSTO rules).

Figure 1 gives an example simulation trace within the domain of psychotherapy. It demonstrates the power of LEADSTO to combine quantitative concepts with qualitative concepts. The result is an easy to read (important for the communication with the domain expert), compact, and executable representation of an informal cognitive model.

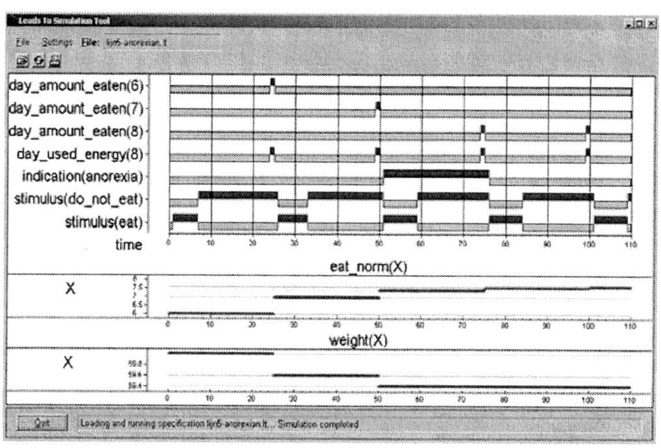

Fig. 1. Example simulation trace

4 Conclusion

This article presents the language and software environment LEADSTO that has been developed especially to model and simulate dynamic processes in terms of both qualitative and quantitative concepts. It is, for example, possible to model differential and difference equations, and to combine those with discrete qualitative modelling approaches. Existing languages are either not accompanied by a software environment that allows simulation of the model, or do not allow the combination of both qualitative and quantitative concepts.

Dynamics can be modelled in LEADSTO as evolution of states over time, i.e., by modelling the direct temporal dependencies between state properties in successive states. The use of durations in these temporal properties facilitates the modelling of such temporal dependencies. Main advantages of the language are that it is executable and allows for graphical representation.

The software environment LEADSTO proved its value for laymen, students and expert users in a number of research projects in different domains.

References

1. Barringer, H., M. Fisher, D. Gabbay, R. Owens, & M. Reynolds (1996). *The Imperative Future: Principles of Executable Temporal Logic*, Research Studies Press Ltd. and John Wiley & Sons.
2. Forbus, K.D. (1984). *Qualitative process theory*. Artificial Intelligence, volume 24, number 1-3, pp. 85-168.
3. Port, R.F., Gelder, T. van (eds.) (1995). *Mind as Motion: Explorations in the Dynamics of Cognition*. MIT Press, Cambridge, Mass.

Prediction-Based Diagnosis and Loss Prevention Using Model-Based Reasoning

Erzsébet Németh[1,2], Rozália Lakner[2], Katalin M. Hangos[1,2], and Ian T. Cameron[3]

[1] Systems and Control Laboratory,
Computer and Automation Research Institute, Budapest, Hungary
[2] Department of Computer Science,
University of Veszprém, Veszprém, Hungary
[3] School of Engineering, The University of Queensland, Brisbane, Australia

Abstract. A diagnostic expert system established on model-based reasoning for on-line diagnosis and loss prevention is described in the paper. Its diagnostic "cause-effect" rules and possible actions (suggestions) are extracted from the results of standard HAZOP analysis. Automatic focusing as well as "what-if" type reasoning for testing hypothetical actions have been also implemented. The diagnostic system is tested on a granulator drum of a fertilizer plant in a simulation test-bed.

1 Introduction

The importance of powerful and efficient fault detection and isolation methods and tools [1] for large-scale industrial plant cannot be overestimated. Prediction based diagnosis [7] is one of the most powerful approaches that utilizes a dynamic, quantitative and/or qualitative model of the plant.

Therefore, our aim has been to propose an expert system that is able to perform model-based on-line fault-detection, diagnosis and loss prevention [2] for large-scale process systems using a combination of model-based reasoning [6] and rule-base inference originating from a HAZOP (HAZard and OPerability) analysis, often available for large process plants.

2 The Knowledge Base and the Diagnostic Procedures

As dictated by the diversity of the knowledge sources, the methods and procedures used for diagnosis in our expert system are of two types. *Standard forward and backward reasoning on the rule-set derived from the HAZOP tables* is applied for cause-consequence analysis, and *model-based reasoning applied on dynamic engineering models* is used to predict the effect of faults and preventive actions.

Hierarchically Structured Dynamic Model. In fault detection and diagnosis, the prediction of a system's behaviour is used for deriving the consequences

M. Ali and F. Esposito (Eds.): IEA/AIE 2005, LNAI 3533, pp. 367–369, 2005.

of a state of the system in time and it is usually done in process engineering by dynamic simulation. In the case of *prediction-based diagnosis* [7], however, the faulty mode of the system can also be detected based on the comparison between the real plant data and the predicted values generated by a suitable dynamic model.

The best solution for addressing computational complexity of multiple fault diagnosis [4] is abstraction [2], where the approaches are usually hierarchical and the problem is presented at multiple levels. Faults are then isolated on one level with further focus at more finer levels as required. The *multi-scale modelling* [3] approach of describing dynamic process models, that are composite mathematical models describing phenomena at different characteristic time and/or length scales fits well to abstraction. This is because a multi-scale model is an ordered hierarchical collection of partial models.

HAZOP Table. The operational experience about the faulty behaviour of the system together with the reasons and the ways of correction of malfunctions are described in the proposed diagnostic system in the form of diagnostic and preventive action rules constructed from a HAZOP table [5] consisting of standard columns. The column *Guide word* identifies a measurable or observable variable, the deviation of which is associated to the hazard. The column *Deviation* describes the difference from the "normal behaviour" of the *Guide word* by using guide expressions. In the column *Possible causes* are the real primary causes of the deviation. In the column *Consequeces* the potentially harmful consequences are listed. The last column *Action required* gives actions that are recommended for eliminating or mitigating the hazard that can be regarded as preventive actions.

Symptoms. Symptoms are identified deviations from design or operational intention described in the form of inequalities, such as $level_{low} = (h < 2\ m)$ which is defined by using measurable level h. Symptoms can be derived from the columns *Guide word* and *Deviation* of the HAZOP table. Symptoms are time-varying quantities and they are naturally connected to the process model through their associated measurable variable. Thus the rule-base associated with symptoms is also naturally modularized and driven by the structure of the hierarchical process model.

Rule-Base. We have mapped the knowledge of human expertise and operation collected in the HAZOP table to "if – then" rules of two types. *Diagnostic rules* describe the possible "cause – consequence" type relationships between the root causes and symptoms. *Preventive action rules* are "(cause, consequences) – action" type relationships between the (symptoms, root causes) pairs and preventive actions.

The Integration of Fault Detection, Diagnosis and Loss Prevention Steps. In our diagnostic expert system the model-based fault detection, diagnosis and loss prevention steps are organized in a cyclic process consisting of the following main steps:

1. *Performing measurements and symptom detection:* Using the measured signals from the system and the relationships among them, the possible symptoms are determined with pattern matching.
2. *Focusing and primary fault detection:* Focusing is applied to find the proper hierarchy level and/or part of the model (the dynamic model augmented with structured rules) connected to the detected symptoms by using the model and rule hierarchy. Thereafter, the possible causes are derived by backward reasoning. Multiple symptoms connected to a common cause or multiple causes connected to common symptoms are also taken into account together with possible preventive actions for the possible causes.
3. *Fault isolation:* Comparing the measured data with the predicted values of the variables the spurious (cause, preventive action) pairs can be removed from the list of the possible (cause, preventive action) pairs.
4. *Loss prevention:* Multiple prediction (what-if type reasoning) is performed for each applicable (cause, preventive action) pair and a preventive action is suggested which drives the system back to its normal operation mode.

The Granulator Diagnosis Expert System. A diagnostic expert system based on the above principles is implemented in G2 that is tested on a granulator drum of a fertilizer plant in a simulation test-bed.

Acknowledgement. This research has been supported by the Hungarian Research Fund through grants T042710 and T047198, as well as the Australian Research Council International Linkage Award LX0348222 and Linkage Grant LP0214142.

References

1. Blanke, M., Kinnaert, M., Junze, J., Staroswiecki, M., Schroder, J., Lunze, J., Eds.: Diagnosis and Fault-Tolerant Control. Springer-Verlag. (2003)
2. Console, W. H. L., Hamscher, de Kleer, J. Eds.: Readings in Model-Based Diagnosis. Morgan Kaufmann, San Mateo, CA. (1992)
3. Ingram, G. D., Cameron, I. T., Hangos, K. M.: Classification and analysis of integrating frameworks in multiscale modelling. Chemical Engineering Science **59** (2004) 2171–2187
4. de Kleen, J., Williams, B. C.: Diagnosing multiple faults. Artificial Intelligence **32** (1987) 97–130.
5. Knowlton, R. E.: Hazard and operability studies : the guide word approach. Vancouver: Chematics International Company (1989)
6. Russell, S., Norvig, P.: Artificial intelligence, A modern approach. Prentice-Hall (1995)
7. Venkatasubramanian, V., Rengaswamy, R., Kavuri, S. N.: A review of process fault detection and diagnosis Part II: Qualitative models and search strategies. Computers and Chemical Engineering **27** (2003) 313–326

An Algorithm Based on Counterfactuals for Concept Learning in the Semantic Web

Luigi Iannone and Ignazio Palmisano

Dipartimento di Informatica,
Università degli Studi di Bari,
Via Orabona 4, 70125 Bari, Italy
{iannone, palmisano}@di.uniba.it

Abstract. Semantic Web, in order to be effective, needs automatic support for building ontologies, because human effort alone cannot cope with the huge quantity of knowledge today available on the web. We present an algorithm, based on a Machine Learning methodology, that can be used to help knowledge engineers in building up ontologies.

1 Introduction

Since Tim Berners-Lee coined the name Semantic Web (SW) for his personal vision of the brand new Web [1], a lot of effort from research community - especially Knowledge Representation & Reasoning (KRR) groups - has been spent in finding out the most promising formalism for representing knowledge in the SW. Semantic Web, in fact, stands as a stack of specifications for KR languages in order to make information (or, better, knowledge) directly processable by machines. This stack relies on very well known pre-existing Web technologies such as XML[1] or URI[2] and builds up on these standards a framework for representing metadata for enriching existing resources on the Web such as RDF[3]. In order to be interoperable, such metadata should come from shared *vocabularies* where they are defined with their properties and with the relationships with each other. The evolution of standard specification for expressing such *vocabularies* started form RDFSchema [2] and moved to OWL (Web Ontology Language) [3] making it clear that SW choice in representing metadata concepts and relationships was Description Logics [4]. The term *ontology* was borrowed from philosophy yet with a different meaning: that is "a specification of a conceptualization" [5].

This represents the consolidated evolution track of SW, that is that we currently have specifications for writing down portable documents (XML), to enrich them or other documents (e.g. HTML pages) with metadata (RDF), and to build metadata ontologies, that are collections of taxonomic and non taxonomic relationships among metadata classes. Since these ontologies are based

[1] eXstensible mark-up language http://www.w3.org/XML

[2] Uniform Resource Identifiers http://www.w3.org/Addressing/

[3] Resource Description Framework - http://www.w3.org/RDF

M. Ali and F. Esposito (Eds.): IEA/AIE 2005, LNAI 3533, pp. 370–379, 2005.

on Description Logics, they have formal semantics and, hence, they offer the possibility of implementing inferences on ontology based representations.

This being the settings, we will proceed now illustrating the rising issues in this big picture we want to tackle, motivating a machine learning approach to such problems (Section 2). Then we will illustrate our solution from a theoretical point of view (Section 3) and we will provide a practical example (Section 4). Finally (Section 5) some conclusions will be drawn and further enhancements to this work will be presented.

2 Motivation of Our Work

Semantic Web ensures semantic interoperability thanks to ontologies that specify the intended meaning of metadata in terms of their relationships with the entities compounding their domain. The problem is that, nowadays, Web has not yet been provided with a considerable number of ontologies. There are few of them available and on very few subjects. Moreover, building up an ontology from scratch can be a very burdensome and difficult task [6], and, very often, two domain experts would design different ontologies for the same domain. Though these differences could appear trivial, they can depend on various factors (level of granularity, different points of view), and cannot be easily harmonized by machines. Therefore, we need an approach for building ontologies that is:

- At least semi-automatic.
- Predictable and controllable, in the sense that, fixed some input parameters, does not produce different results at each run on the same domain.

We argue that a Machine Learning approach is very appropriate in this setting, providing both the necessary flexibility and the formal support for acquiring ontologies. In particular, we study the problem of building up a concept definition starting from positive and negative examples of the target concept itself. We will in the following (Section 5) see how this can later be applied to learn whole ontologies. However, a practical situation in which this algorithm can reveal itself useful is that in which one has an ontology that has to evolve and embed new definition. Knowledge engineers can follow two approaches:

- Writing the new concept intensional definition in the desired ontology language (e.g.: OWL).
- Use a supervised machine learning algorithm for inducing the new concept definition starting from positive and negative examples of the target concept.

Though the first solution could appear simpler, it may hide some undesirable drawbacks. For instance, none can guarantee that the new definition is consistent with the examples (instances/individuals) already present in the knowledge base. Moreover, in writing the definition engineers could miss some important features that could not be so evident without looking at the examples.

A practical case could be the extension of an interesting work by Astrova [7] in which the author proposes a methodology for building an ontology from a

Table 1. The constructors for $\mathcal{ALC}$ descriptions and their interpretation

NAME	SYNTAX	SEMANTICS
top concept	$\top$	$\Delta^{\mathcal{I}}$
bottom concept	$\bot$	$\emptyset$
concept negation	$\neg C$	$\Delta^{\mathcal{I}} \setminus C^{\mathcal{I}}$
concept conjunction	$C_1 \sqcap C_2$	$C_1^{\mathcal{I}} \cap C_2^{\mathcal{I}}$
concept disjunction	$C_1 \sqcup C_2$	$C_1^{\mathcal{I}} \cup C_2^{\mathcal{I}}$
existential restriction	$\exists R.C$	$\{x \in \Delta^{\mathcal{I}} \mid \exists y\ (x,y) \in R^{\mathcal{I}} \wedge y \in C^{\mathcal{I}}\}$
universal restriction	$\forall R.C$	$\{x \in \Delta^{\mathcal{I}} \mid \forall y\ (x,y) \in R^{\mathcal{I}} \rightarrow y \in C^{\mathcal{I}}\}$

relational database. Let us suppose that after the process one realizes that the resulting ontology lacks some classes (concepts) that can be built starting from the basic ontology formerly obtained. Instead of writing the missing definition from scratch, the knowledge engineer may properly select some positive and negative examples (that in this case are no more that tuples of some view in the database) and run the concept learning algorithm we propose.

3 Concept Learning Algorithm

In this section we illustrate our algorithm from a theoretical point of view, that is the learning of a definition in aforementioned family of KR formalisms called Description Logics (DL). In particular we show our results for a particular DL named $\mathcal{ALC}$. DLs differ from each other for the constructs they allow. In order to make this paper as much self contained as possible here we report syntax and semantics for $\mathcal{ALC}$; for a more thorough description please refer to [8].

In every DL, primitive *concepts* $N_C = \{C, D, \ldots\}$ are interpreted as subsets of a certain domain of objects (resources) and primitive *roles* $N_R = \{R, S, \ldots\}$ are interpreted as binary relations on such a domain (properties). More complex concept descriptions are built using atomic concepts and primitive roles by means of the constructors in Table 1.

Their meaning is defined by an *interpretation* $\mathcal{I} = (\Delta^{\mathcal{I}}, \cdot^{\mathcal{I}})$, where $\Delta^{\mathcal{I}}$ is the *domain* of the interpretation and the functor $\cdot^{\mathcal{I}}$ stands for the *interpretation function*, mapping the intension of concepts and roles to their extension.

A *knowledge base* $\mathcal{K} = \langle \mathcal{T}, \mathcal{A} \rangle$ contains two components: a T-box $\mathcal{T}$ and an A-box $\mathcal{A}$. $\mathcal{T}$ is a set of concept definitions $C \equiv D$, meaning $C^{\mathcal{I}} = D^{\mathcal{I}}$, where C is the concept name and D is a description given in terms of the language constructors. Actually, there exist general T-Boxes that allow also for axioms like $C \sqsubseteq D$ or $C \sqsupseteq D$ and for cycles in definition, but in this paper we restrict to what in literature are called *acyclic* T-Boxes in which there are only concept definitions. Such definitions are in the form $ConceptName \equiv D$ (one can easily show that they are equivalent to acyclic T-Boxes with complex concepts on the both sides of equivalence sign). $\mathcal{A}$ contains extensional assertions on concepts and roles, e.g. $C(a)$ and $R(a, b)$, meaning, respectively, that $a^{\mathcal{I}} \in C^{\mathcal{I}}$ and $(a^{\mathcal{I}}, b^{\mathcal{I}}) \in R^{\mathcal{I}}$.

The semantic notion of *subsumption* between concepts (or roles) can be given in terms of the interpretations:

Definition 3.1 (subsumption). *Given two concept descriptions* C *and* D *in* $\mathcal{T}$, C subsumes D, *denoted by* $C \sqsupseteq D$, *iff for every interpretation* $\mathcal{I}$ *of* $\mathcal{T}$ *it holds that* $C^{\mathcal{I}} \supseteq D^{\mathcal{I}}$. *Hence,* $C \equiv D$ *amounts to* $C \sqsupseteq D$ *and* $D \sqsupseteq C$.

Example 3.1. A possible concept definition in the proposed language is:
$Father \equiv Human \sqcap Male \sqcap \exists hasChild.Human$
which translates the sentence: *"a father is a male human that has some humans as his children"*.

A-box assertions look like:
$Father(Tom)$, $Father(Bill)$, $hasChild.Human(Bill, Joe)$ and so on.

Now, if we define two new concepts:
$FatherWithoutSons \equiv Human \sqcap Male \sqcap \exists hasChild.Human \sqcap \forall hasChild.(\neg Male)$
$Parent \equiv Human \sqcap (Male \sqcup Female) \sqcap \exists hasChild.Human$
then it is easy to see that $Father \sqsupseteq FatherWithoutSons$ and $Parent \sqsupseteq Father$, yet $Father \not\sqsupseteq Parent$ and $FatherWithoutSons \not\sqsupseteq Father$

Notice that subsumption imposes a partial order relationship on any set of DL concepts. In the following, in fact, we will consider a set of concepts definition ordered by subsumption as a search space $(\mathcal{S}, \succeq)$ in which the algorithm has to find out a consistent definition for the target concept. Our problem of induction in its simplest form can be now formally defined as a supervised learning task:

Definition 3.2 (learning problem). *In a search space* $(\mathcal{S}, \succeq)$
Given *a knowledge base* $\mathcal{K} = \langle \mathcal{T}, \mathcal{A} \rangle$ *and a set of positive and negative assertions* $\mathcal{A}_C = \mathcal{A}_C^+ \cup \mathcal{A}_C^-$ *regarding the membership (or non-membership) of some individuals to a concept* C *such that:* $\mathcal{A} \not\models_{\mathcal{T}} \mathcal{A}_C$
Find *a new T-box* $\mathcal{T}' = (\mathcal{T} \setminus \{C \equiv D\}) \cup \{C \equiv D'\}$ *such that:* $\mathcal{A} \models_{\mathcal{T}'} \mathcal{A}_C$

Thus, if a concept C is not defined in the terminology $\mathcal{T}$ we have a case of an *induction problem* requiring to find definitions $C \equiv D$ entailing the (new) assertions in $\mathcal{A}_C$. Conversely, when an existing definition in $\mathcal{T}$ proves to be incorrect i.e. it is not capable of entailing the positive assertions in $\mathcal{A}_C$ (*incomplete* definition) or it entails negative ones (*inconsistent* definition), this yields a *refinement problem* where a new correct definition $C \equiv D'$ is to be found on the ground of the previous one and the new examples.

Both problems can be cast as search problem on the space of all possible concept definitions in the give $\mathcal{ALC}$ DL. In order to traverse this space one needs operators that allow for moving across concepts in two directions (as we said that this kind of spaces are ordered by subsumption). In fact, given a concept definition in such a space one can:

- Obtain a more general one (upward refinement operator).
- Obtain a more specific one (downward refinement operator).

Depending on the target DL one can imagine many refinement operators. Typically they are operators that manipulate the syntactical structure of the concept that has been previously put in a particular *normal form*. This kind of syntactical way of re-writing concepts, usually, presents some nice features that result in simplified refinement operators and exists for any concept description in the target DL. Some examples of refinement operators can be found in [9] and in [10] for two different DLs.

From the theoretical point of view one can study some important properties of refinement operators that can guarantee that their implementation will be *effective* in traversing the search space. Such properties (in brief) are:

- Locally finiteness that means that the set of the possible concepts obtainable through refinement are finite in number.
- Properness that ensures that each refinement step would return a concept that is strictly more general (or specific depending whether we are considering upward or downward refinement) than the starting one.
- Completeness that guarantees that every concept subsumed (or subsumed by depending whether we are considering upward or downward refinement) the starting one is reachable through a refinement chain (i.e.: n refinement application proceeding from the starting concept through one of its refinement then recursively).
- Minimality that is each possible refinement from a concept cannot be reached through two different refinement chain (non redundancy of refinement).

An *ideal* refinement operator is the one that has the property of being locally finite, complete and proper. Yet for $\mathcal{ALC}$ none found out such an operator, neither a strategy of implementing a very redundant complete operator would make much sense in terms of efficiency. It would, in fact, result in a *generate and test* strategy that consists in generating all possible refinement of the input concept and testing which one is correct and consistent w.r.t. positive and negative examples in the learning problem.

This approach, beside being poor in performance, does not exploit the information available in the examples that can be used in building the concept refinement. In this paper we will illustrate, in particular, an example-based downward refinement operator, that is a way for specializing overly general definitions (definitions that include negative examples that should not be included instead), whereas generalization is intentionally left to the implementor as there are really efficient choices (especially in $\mathcal{ALC}$), as we will see in the remainder.

The idea that stands at the basis of the specialization is that, when examining an overly general definition, if, in order to refine it in a consistent way (w.r.t. negative examples it covers), one needs to *blame* the part of the concept definition that is responsible of the negative instances inclusion and eliminate it. An idea for *blame assignment* can consist in finding out the residual [11] among the wrong definition and the covered negative examples as explained later on. Then, once spotted, the responsible concept can be negated (since in $\mathcal{ALC}$ negation is allowed in front of complex concepts) and the intersection between the starting overly general concept and the negated residual can be computed. Obviously this is a downward refinement, since in set theory we have that if A, B are two sets then $A \cap B \subseteq A$ then take $A = C^I$ and $B = (\neg D)^I$, where C is the starting wrong concept and D the calculated residual then we have $C \sqsupseteq C \sqcup \neg D$. The negated residual is called *counterfactual* [12] and can be generalized in order to eliminate as much negative as possible from the inconsistent starting definition as specified in the following subsection.

3.1 The Algorithm

The learning process can start when there are examples and counterexamples in the A-box of a concept for which a new definition is required. Examples classification is assumed to be given by a trainer (the knowledge engineer). However, the methodology would apply also for a similar yet different setting, where there is a definition for the target concept in a given T-box, but it turned out to be incorrect (overly general) because it entails some (new) assertions that have been classified as being negative for the target concept. In order to carry out the latter task one can just call the second subroutine (counterfactuals) of the algorithm described in the following.

Each assertion is not processed as such: a representative at the concept language level (*single representation trick*) is preliminarily derived in the form of *most specific concept* (*msc*). The msc required by the algorithm is a maximally specific DL concept description that entails the given assertion. Since in some DLs it does not exist, we consider its approximations up to a certain depth [13]. Hence, in the algorithm the positive and negative examples will be very specific conjunctive descriptions.

The algorithm relies on two interleaving routines (see Figure 1) performing, respectively, generalization and counterfactuals, that call each other to converge to a correct concept definition.

The generalization algorithm is a greedy covering one: it tries to explain the positive examples by constructing a disjunctive definition. At each outer iteration, a very specialized definition (the msc of an example) is selected as a starting seed for a new partial generalization; then, iteratively, the hypothesis is generalized by means of the upward operator δ (here undefined but implementor should preferably choose one with a heuristic that privileges the refinements that cover the most of the positives) until all positive concept representatives are covered or some negative representatives are explained. In such a case, the current concept definition *ParGen* has to be specialized by some counterfactuals. The co-routine, which receives the covered examples as its input, finds a subdescription K that is capable of ruling out the negative examples previously covered.

In the routine for building counterfactuals, given a previously computed hypothesis *ParGen*, which is supposed to be complete (covering the positive assertions) yet inconsistent with respect to some negative assertions, the aim is finding those counterfactuals to be conjuncted to the initial hypothesis for restoring a correct definition, that can rule out the negative instances.

```
generalization(Positives, Negatives, Generalization)
input Positives, Negatives: positive and negative instances at concept level;
output Generalization: generalized concept definition
begin
ResPositives ← Positives
Generalization ← ⊥
while ResPositives ≠ ∅ do
        ParGen ← select_seed(ResPositives)
        CoveredPos ← {Pos ∈ ResPositives | ParGen ⊒ Pos}
        CoveredNeg ← {Neg ∈ Negatives | ParGen ⊒ Neg}
        while CoveredPos ≠ ResPositives and CoveredNeg = ∅ do
                ParGen ← select(δ(ParGen), ResPositives)
                CoveredPos ← {Pos ∈ ResPositives | ParGen ⊒ Pos}
                CoveredNeg ← {Neg ∈ Negatives | ParGen ⊒ Neg}
        if CoveredNeg ≠ ∅ then
                K ← counterfactuals(ParGen, CoveredPos, CoveredNeg)
                ParGen ← ParGen ⊓ ¬K
        Generalization ← Generalization ⊔ ParGen
        ResPositives ← ResPositives \ CoveredPos
return Generalization
end

counterfactuals(ParGen, CoveredPos, CoveredNeg, K)
input ParGen: inconsistent concept definition
      CoveredPos, CoveredNeg: covered positive and negative descriptions
output K: counterfactual
begin
NewPositives ← ∅
NewNegatives ← ∅
for each N_i ∈ CoveredNeg do
        NewP_i ← residual(N_i, ParGen)
        NewPositives ← NewPositives ∪ {NewP_i}
for each P_j ∈ CoveredPos do
        NewN_j ← residual(P_j, ParGen)
        NewNegatives ← NewNegatives ∪ {NewN_j}
K ← generalization(NewPositives, NewNegatives)
return K
end
```

Fig. 1. The co-routines used in the method

The algorithm is based on the construction of residual learning problems based on the sub-descriptions that caused the subsumption of the negative examples, represented by their msc's. In this case, for each model a residual is derived by considering that part of the incorrect definition *ParGen* that did not play a role in the subsumption. The residual will be successively employed as a positive instance of that part of description that should be ruled out of the definition (through negation). Analogously the msc's derived from positive assertions will play the opposite role of negative instances for the residual learning problem under construction.

Finally, this problem is solved by calling the co-routine which generalizes these example descriptions and then conjoining its negation of the returned result.

4 Running an Example

In this section we present a short example in order to illustrate the algorithm through its trace.

Example 4.1 (Supervised Learning). Suppose that the starting A-box is

$\mathcal{A} = \{M(d), r(d,l), r(j,s), \neg M(m), r(m,l), \neg M(a), w(a,j), r(a,s), F(d), F(j), \neg F(m) \neg F(a)\}$

(assuming $F \equiv$ Father, $M \equiv$ Man $r \equiv$ parentOf (role), $w \equiv$ wifeOf for this example, in order to give an understandable example)

F is the target concept, thus the examples and counterexamples are, respectively: *Positives* $= \{d, j\}$ and *Negatives* $= \{m, a\}$

The approximated msc's are:
$msc(j) = \exists r.\top$
$msc(d) = M \sqcap \exists r.\top$
$msc(m) = \neg M \sqcap \exists r.\top$
$msc(a) = \neg M \sqcap \exists r.\top \sqcap \exists w.\top$

The trace of the algorithm in this case follows:

generalize:
ResidualPositives $\leftarrow$ {msc(d), msc(j)}
Generalization $\leftarrow \bot$
/* Outer while loop */
ParGen $\leftarrow msc(d) = M \sqcap \exists r.\top$
CoveredPos $\leftarrow \{msc(d)\}$
CoveredNeg $\leftarrow \{\}$
ParGen $\leftarrow \exists r.\top$ /* M dropped in the inner loop */
CoveredPos $\leftarrow \{msc(d), msc(j)\}$
CoveredNeg $\leftarrow \{msc(m), msc(a)\}$
Call **counterfactuals**($\exists r.\top, \{msc(d), msc(j)\}, \{msc(m), msc(a)\}$)

counterfactuals:
$NewP_1 \leftarrow \neg M \sqcap \exists r.\top \sqcup \neg\exists r.\top = \neg M$
NewPositives $\leftarrow \{\neg M\}$
$NewP_2 \leftarrow \neg M \sqcap \exists r.\top \sqcap \exists w.\top \sqcup \neg(\exists r.\top) = \neg M \sqcap \exists w.\top$

NewPositives $\leftarrow \{\neg M, \neg M \sqcap \exists w.\top\}$
$NewN_1 \leftarrow M \sqcap \exists r.\top \sqcup \neg\exists r.\top = M$
NewNegatives $\leftarrow \{M\}$
$NewN_2 \leftarrow \top$
NewNegatives $\leftarrow \{M, \top\}$
Call **generalize**($\{\neg M, \neg M \sqcap \exists w.\top\}, \{M, \top\}$)
...

That results in $F = M \sqcap \exists r.\top$

5 Conclusion and Future Work

In this paper we have tackled the problem of constructing ontologies in a semi-automatic fashion. In particular we have presented an algorithm that is able to infer concept descriptions in the Description Logic ALC from concept instances available in an A-box.

The algorithm can represent the basis for a powerful tool for knowledge engineers. It has been implemented in a system called *YINYANG* (Yet another INduction Yelds to ANother Generalization), and, at the time of writing, it is being tested in order to extensively evaluate the applicability of this approach from an empirical point of view.

Moreover, in real problems it could be that case that A-boxes may turn out to be inconsistent, which would result in a failure of our method. Thus, another line for future research is the investigation on how to handle this problem.

Acknowledgments

This research was partially funded by National Ministry of Instruction University and Research Project COFIN 2003 "Tecniche di intelligenza artificiale per il reperimento di informazione di qualità sul Web".

References

[1] Berners-Lee, T., Hendler, J., Lassila, O.: The Semantic Web. Scientific American (2001)
[2] RDF-Schema: RDF Vocabulary Description Language 1.0: RDF Schema (2003) `http://www.w3c.org/TR/rdf-schema`.
[3] Horrocks, I., Patel-Schneider, P.F., van Harmelen, F.: From $\mathcal{SHIQ}$ and RDF to OWL: The making of a web ontology language. J. of Web Semantics **1** (2003) 7–26
[4] Baader, F., Calvanese, D., McGuinness, D., Nardi, D., Patel-Schneider, P., eds.: The Description Logic Handbook. Cambridge University Press (2003)
[5] Gruber, T.R.: A translation approach to portable ontology specifications (1993)
[6] Maedche, A., Staab, S.: Ontology learning for the semantic web. IEEE Intelligent Systems **16** (2001)

[7] Astrova, I.: Reverse engineering of relational databases to ontologies. In Bussler, C., Davies, J., Fensel, D., Studer, R., eds.: The Semantic Web: Research and Applications, First European Semantic Web Symposium, ESWS 2004, Heraklion, Crete, Greece, May 10-12, 2004, Proceedings. Volume 3053 of Lecture Notes in Computer Science., Springer (2004) 327–341

[8] Schmidt-Schauß, M., Smolka, G.: Attributive concept descriptions with complements. Artificial Intelligence **48** (1991) 1–26

[9] Badea, L., Nienhuys-Cheng, S.H.: A refinement operator for description logics. In Cussens, J., Frisch, A., eds.: Proceedings of the 10th International Conference on Inductive Logic Programming. Volume 1866 of LNAI., Springer (2000) 40–59

[10] Esposito, F., Fanizzi, N., Iannone, L., Palmisano, I., Semeraro, G.: Knowledge-intensive induction of terminologies from metadata. In McIlraith, S.A., Plexousakis, D., van Harmelen, F., eds.: The Semantic Web ISWC 2004: Third International Semantic Web Conference, Hiroshima, Japan, November 7-11, 2004. Proceedings. Volume 3298 of LNCS., Springer-Verlag Heidelberg (2004) 411–426

[11] Teege, G.: A subtraction operation for description logics. In Torasso, P., Doyle, J., Sandewall, E., eds.: Proceedings of the 4th International Conference on Principles of Knowledge Representation and Reasoning, Morgan Kaufmann (1994) 540–550

[12] Vere, S.: Multilevel counterfactuals for generalizations of relational concepts and productions. Artificial Intelligence **14** (1980) 139–164

[13] Brandt, S., Küsters, R., Turhan, A.Y.: Approximation and difference in description logics. In Fensel, D., Giunchiglia, F., McGuinness, D., Williams, M.A., eds.: Proceedings of the International Conference on Knowledge Representation, Morgan Kaufmann (2002) 203–214

Classification of Ophthalmologic Images Using an Ensemble of Classifiers*

Giampaolo L. Libralao, Osvaldo C.P. Almeida, and Andre C.P.L.F. Carvalho

Institute of Mathematic and Computer Science,
University of Sao Paulo - USP,
Av. Trabalhador Sao-carlense, 400 - CEP 13560-970, Sao Carlos, Sao Paulo, Brazil
{giam, pinheiro, andre}@icmc.usp.br

Abstract. The human eye may present refractive errors as myopia, hypermetropia and astigmatism. This article presents the development of an Ensemble of Classifiers as part of a Refractive Errors Measurement System. The system analyses Hartmann-Shack images from human eyes in order to identify refractive errors, wich are associated to myopia, hypermetropia and astigmatism. The ensemble is composed by three different Machine Learning techniques: Artificial Neural Networks, Support Vector Machines and C4.5 algorithm and has been shown to be able to improve the performance achieved). The most relevant data of these images are extracted using Gabor wavelets transform. Machine learning techniques are then employed to carry out the image analysis.

Keywords: Classifiers Combination, Ocular Refractive Errors, Machine Learning, Expert Systems, Hartmann-Shack Technique, Optometry.

1 Introduction

Frequently, an human eye presents refractive errors, like myopia, hypermetropia and astigmatism. Although there are several procedures able to diagnosis errors, previous studies have shown they are not efficient enough[17]. The available devices for refractive error detection require frequent calibrations. Besides, the maintenance of the current devices is usually expensive and may require technical support from experts[9].

In order to overcome the previous limitation, this paper presents an approach based on Machine Learning (ML). The authors believe that the approach developed is able to produce an efficient diagnosis solution. ML is concerned with the development and investigation of techniques able to extract concepts (knowledge) from samples[11]. In this work, ML techniques are applied for the classification of eye images.

The system developed employs images generated by the Hartmann-Shack (HS) technique. Before, their use by the ML techniques, the images are pre-

* The authors acknowledge the support received from FAPESP (State of Sao Paulo Research Funding Agency).

M. Ali and F. Esposito (Eds.): IEA/AIE 2005, LNAI 3533, pp. 380–389, 2005.

processed. The pre-processing is performed in order to eliminates image imperfections introduced during the acquisition process. Next, features are extracted from the image through the Gabor Wavelet Transform[6][3]. The use of Gabor transform reduces the number of input data (image pixels) to be employed by the ML algorithms, assuring that relevant information is not lost. Thus, a new data set is obtained where each sample is represented by a set of feature values. Experiments were also carried out with the PCA (Principal Component Analysis) technique[8], since the results obtained by the ensembles of classifiers were not as good as the Gabor results, only these are going to be presented in this article. Finally, ML algorithms are trained to diagnosis eyes images using this new data set.

In order to improve the performance achieved in the classification of eyes images, the authors combined different ML techniques in a committee. This article describes the ensemble proposed and a set of experiments performed to evaluate the performance gain due to the combination in the Refractive Errors Measurement System (REMS).

The article is organised as follows: Section 2 presents a brief review of Machine Learning (ML) techniques used in the classifiers ensemble; Section 2.4 discusses the main features of the ensemble investigated; Section 3 explains the proposed Refractive Errors Measurement System; Section 4 describes the tests performed and shows the experimental results obtained; finally, Section 5 presents the main conclusions.

2 Machine Learning Techniques

One of the main goals of ML is the development of computational methods able to extract concepts (knowledge) from samples[11]. In general, ML techniques are able to learn how to classify previously unseen data after undergoing a training process. The classification of samples that were not seen in the training phase is named generalization. ML algorithms are in general inspired on other research areas[15]: biological systems (as ANNs), cognitive processes (Case Based Reasoning), symbolic learning (Decision Trees), and statistical learning theory (Support Vector Machines).

2.1 Artificial Neural Networks

One of the ANNs used in this work is the MLP networks[14] which are one of the most popular ANN models. MLP networks present at least one hidden layer, one input layer and one output layer. The hidden layers work as feature extractors; their weights codify features from input patterns, creating a more complex representation of the training data set. There is no rule to specify the number of neurons in the hidden layers. MLP networks are usually trained by the Backpropagation learning algorithm[7].

The other ANN model investigated in this paper, RBF networks, were proposed by Broomhead and Lowe[2]. A typical RBF network has a single hidden layer whose neurons use radial base activation functions, which are in general

Gaussian functions. RBF networks are usually trained by hybrid methods, composed of an unsupervised and a supervised stage. The former determines the number of radial functions and their parameters. The later calculates the neuron weights. In general the K-Mean algorithm is used for the first stage. For the second stage, a linear algorithm is usually employed to calculate the values of the weights. RBF networks have been successfully employed for several pattern recognition problems[1].

2.2 Support Vector Machines

SVMs are learning algorithms based on the theory of statistical learning, through the principle of Structural Risk Minimization (SRM). They deal with pattern recognition problems in two different ways. In the first way, classification mistakes are not considered. Patterns that do not fit the typical values of their class will change the separation hyper-plane, in order to classify this pattern in the correct class. In the second, extra variables are established, so that patterns that do not fit the typical values of their group can be excluded, depending on the amount of extra variables considered, reducing, thus, the probability of classification errors. The high generalization capacity obtained by SVMs results from the use of the statistical learning theory, principle presented in the decade of 60 and 70 by Vapnik and Chernovenkis[18].

2.3 C4.5 Algorithm

The C4.5 algorithm is a symbolic learning algorithm that generates decision trees from a training data set. It is one of the successors of the ID3 algorithm[13]. The ID3 algorithm is a member of a more general group of techniques, known as Top-down Induction of Decision Trees (TDIDTs).

To build the decision tree, one of the attributes from the training set is selected. The training set patterns are then divided according to their value for this particular attribute. For each subset, another attribute is chosen to perform another division. This process goes on until each subset contains only samples from the same class, where one leaf node is created and receives the same name of the respective class.

2.4 Ensembles

Ensembles of classifiers aim to improve the overall performance obtained in a pattern recognition task by combining several classifiers individually trained[12]. Usually, such combination leads to more stable classifiers. However, it presents advantages and disadvantages as any other classification strategy.

The main disadvantage of ensembles is the increase of the problem complexity, which can be reduced by employing techniques to partition the problem among the classifiers. The choice of the number of classifiers to be combined depends on the main features of the problem investigated and the number of classes used.

The main emphasis of classifiers combination is the exploration of similarities and differences associated to each classifier. It is also very important to take into consideration the generalization capacity and the dependency among classifiers belonging to the combined set. Classifiers that produce similar errors are not recommended for a combination. Ensembles of classifiers can present lower classification error rates than those obtained by each classifier employed individually.

3 Refractive Errors Measurement System

This section presents the main features of the REMS (Refractive Errors Measurement System) proposed by Netto[9]. The REMS system has four modules:

1. *Image Acquisition Module.* The acquisition of the HS images was carried out by Prof. Dr. Larry Thibos from Optometry group of the Indiana University (USA), using an equipment built by his group, known as *aberrometer*;
2. *Image Pre-processing Module.* The ophthalmic images are generated in a format that does not allow their direct use by ML techniques. First the image data is normalized, then, the image is filtered by a pre-processing method to eliminate noise that may affect the feature extraction process;
3. *Feature Extraction Module.* This module aims the extraction of the main feature of an image in order to reduce the amount of input data for the analysis module. The extraction process uses a technique named Gabor Wavelet Transform;
4. *Analysis Module.* This module analyses patterns provided by the feature extraction module. The RBF and MLP networks, SVMs and the C4.5 algorithm were used to implement the analysis module. All these techniques are explained in Section 2. Classifiers combination developed is also part of this module.

This proposed computational system processes an image obtained by the HS technique and then analyses it extracting relevant information for an automatic diagnosis of the possible refractive errors that may exist in the eye using a ML technique. Once the images are obtained, these are filtered by a pre-processing method, which eliminates image imperfections introduced during the acquisition process. This method is based on histogram analysis and spacial-geometrical information of the application domain[16].

The eyes image dataset has 100 patients, six images for each patient, three images of the right eye and three of the left eye, which result in 600 images. Each image is associated to three measurements (spherical (S), cylindrical (C) and cylindrical axis (A)), which are used to determine refractive errors. The used data set possesses the following measurement spectrum: spherical, from -1.75D (Dioptres) to +0.25D; cylindrical, from 0.0D to 1.25D, and cylindrical axis, from $0°$ to $180°$. Negative values of spherical correspond to myopia, positive values of spherical indicate hypermetropia.

The resolution of a commercial auto-refractor is 0.25D for spherical (myopia and hypermetropia) and cylindrical (astigmatism), and $5°$ in cylindrical axis (astigmatism). The resolution adopted for the REMS is the same as commercial auto-refractors and the experimental data used in the experiments has also this resolution The aloud error for this kind of application is ±0.25D for S and C, and ±5° for A, the same resolution existent in commercial auto-refractors. The auto-refractor is fast and precise equipment in the analysis of refractive errors.

The measurements of original data set were divided into classes, according to a fix interval, based in a commercial auto-refractor's resolution. For spherical (S), 9 classes were created (the classes vary between -1.75D and +0.25D with interval of 0.25D), for cylindrical (C) were created 6 classes (the classes vary between 0.0D and +1.25D with interval of 0.25D), and for cylindrical axis (A), 25 classes were created (the classes vary between 0° and 180° with interval of 5°). Table 1 shows the distribution among classes for the C measurement, it is possible to note the adopted criterion do not aloud superposition between classes created, because it is based in a commercial auto-refractor's resolution.

Table 1. Quantity of exemplars for measurement C

C Measurement	Quantity of exemplars	Distribution among classes (%)
0.00	30	7.04%
0.25	229	53.76%
0.50	113	26.52%
0.75	31	7.28%
1.00	15	3.52%
1.25	8	1.88%

Before the image analysis, each image features are extracted using the *Gabor wavelet transform*[6], which allows an image to be represented by its most relevant features, storing the majority of the image information in a reduced data set. The use of Gabor has shown good results for the extraction of the most relevant features from images, as it is capable of minimize data noise in the space and frequency domains[5]. Then, the analysis module uses these extracted features as inputs for the proposed techniques, largely reducing the amount of information processed. Thus, input data to the classifiers combination modules developed are vectors created by Gabor transform, resulting in a final vector with 200 characteristics, this vector is first normalized before been presented to ML techniques analyzed. Details of the Gabor transform and the implemented algorithm can be found in Netto[9] and Daugman[5].

4 Tests and Results

The authors investigated random combinations of the ML techniques that presented the best individual performance. For the experiments, the Weka simulator[1], from University of Waikato, New Zealand, and the SVMTorch simulator[4],

[1] http://www.cs.waikato.ac.nz/ml/weka/index.html (accessed in January of 2004).

were used. It is important to highlight that three different sub-modules were developed foreach studied technique, in order to independently analyse each type of measurement (S, C and A). One set of experiments was devoted to interpret the data of S, another set of experiments for C and the last set for A.

The configurations of best arrangements of the ML techniques (MLPs, RBFs, SVMs and C4.5 algorithm) were combined into four different manners and their results presented to a final classifier, in order to obtain new final results better than those previously obtained by the system.

For training the random resampling method was applied. The data set (426 examples after leaving the patterns that presented measurement problems apart) was divided into 10 different random partitions. These 10 partitions were random generated, but keeping a uniform distribution for each measurement analyzed, S, C or A.

For the ANNs (MLPs and RBFs) and C4.5 algorithm, the partitions were subdivided into three subsets, one for training with 60% of the samples, another for validation, with 20% of the samples and the last for tests, with also 20% of the samples. For SVMs, the partitions were subdivided into two subsets, one for training and validation with 80% of the samples, and another for tests, with 20% of samples. The results obtained by the combined techniques were presented to a final classifier responsible to generate the final result of each module.

The four modules developed are composed by the following ML techniques:

- Module 1 combines two SVMs and one C4.5 classifier with C4.5 as final classifier;
- Module 2 has one SVM, one C4.5 classifier and one RBF with a SVM as final classifier;
- Module 3 has two C4.5 classifier and one SVM combined by a new SVM as final classifier;
- Module 4 has a MLP as final classifier of two SVMs and one C4.5 classifier.

The best results were obtained by the modules two and three, in which the final classifier was a SVM algorithm. These can be seen in tables 2 and 3. The C4.5 algorithm and the MLP networks did not achieve good performance as final classifiers and so these results will be omitted.

Table 2 shows the performance of SVM as a final classifier in data combination in the second module. It can be seen observed the efficiency of the SVM in the combination of the individual classifiers, better than any of the individual classifiers. Table 3 presents the results generated by module 3, which reinforces the results obtained in Table 2, since SVM again obtain high performance when acting as a final classifier. In both tables, the columm "Total of Exemplars" presents, for each class, the quantity of samples that exist in the test subset.

To determine the superiority of a particular technique, a statistical test was carried out[10]. The results obtained were used to decide which of the techniques presented better performance, with, for example, 95% of certainty. For such, the main task is to determine if the difference between the techniques As and Ap is relevant or not, assuming the normal distribution of error taxes[19]. For this, the

Table 2. Results for the second combination module (SVM)

Type of Measurement	Total of Exemplars	Tests	
		% Error	Standad Deviation
S	82	32.35%	±1.76%
C	83	19.20%	±1.43%
A	70	36.50%	±2.20%

Table 3. Results of third combination module (SVM)

Type of Measurement	Total of Exemplars	Tests	
		% Error	Standad Deviation
S	82	29.40%	±2.01%
C	83	19.40%	±1.70%
A	70	36.05%	±2.14%

average and the standard deviation of the error rates are calculated according to Equations 1 and 2, respectively. The absolute difference of standards deviations was obtained by Equation 3[11].

$$mean(As - Ap) = mean(As) - mean(Ap) \tag{1}$$

$$sd(As - Ap) = \sqrt{\frac{sd(As)^2 + sd(Ap)^2}{2}} \tag{2}$$

$$t_{calc} = ad(As - Ap) = \frac{mean(As - Ap)}{sd(As - Ap)} \tag{3}$$

Choosing the initial null hypothesis $H_\circ : As = Ap$ and the alternative hypothesis $H_1 : As \neq Ap$. If $ad(As - Ap)$ 0 then Ap is better than As; however, if $ad(As - Ap) \geq 2.00$ (boundary of acceptation region) then Ap is better than As with 95% of certainty. On the other hand, if $ad(As - Ap) \leq 0$ then As is better than Ap and if $ad(As - Ap) \leq -2.00$ then As is better than Ap with 95% of certainty. The boundary of acceptation region AR: (-2.00, 2.00) for these experiments are based in the distribution table *Student* t[10].

In order to compare efficiency of classifiers combination, two statistical tests were made comparing the performance of the modules 2 and 3, which presented better results, with the SVMs, which present best results in the experiments observed in Netto[9].

Table 4 presents the statistical tests comparing the second module of classifiers combination (Table 2) and the best results obtained by the SVM technique encountered in Netto[9]. This results show the SVM of the combination module achieved better results than any other SVM employed later, with more than 95% of certainty for the three measurements (S, C and A) analyzed.

Table 4. Results of the statistical comparison of SVM and the second module of combination

SVM (As) - Average error			**SVM (combination of classifiers) (Ap) - Average error**		
S	**C**	**A**	**S**	**C**	**A**
0.622 ±0.011	0.421 ±0.010	0.814 ±0.016	0.323 ±0.017	0.193 ±0.014	0.365 ±0.022

SVM and SVM from classifiers combination	$ad(As - Ap)$	**Certainty**	**Acceptation region**	**Hypothesis** H_1
S	20.88	95%	(-2.00, 2.00)	Accept
C	18.74	95%	(-2.00, 2.00)	Accept
A	23.34	95%	(-2.00, 2.00)	Accept

Table 5 presents the statistical tests comparing the third module of classifiers combination (Table 3) and the best results obtained by the SVM technique encountered in Netto[9]. This results show the SVM of the combination module achieve better results than any other SVM employed later, with more than 95% of certainty for the three measurements (S, C and A) analyzed.

Table 5. Results of the statistical comparison of SVM and the third module of combination

SVM (As) - Average error			**SVM (combination of classifiers) (Ap) - Average error**		
S	**C**	**A**	**S**	**C**	**A**
0.622 ±0.011	0.421 ±0.010	0.814 ±0.016	0.294 ±0.020	0.194 ±0.017	0.360 ±0.021

SVM and SVM from classifiers combination	$ad(As - Ap)$	**Certainty**	**Acceptation region**	**Hypothesis** H_1
S	20.32	95%	(-2.00, 2.00)	Accept
C	16.27	95%	(-2.00, 2.00)	Accept
A	24.31	95%	(-2.00, 2.00)	Accept

The results of the two applied statistical tests show that the modules of classifiers combination developed, based in SVM technique as a final classifier, improved the performance measured by REMS in the analysis of myopia, hypermetropia and astigmatism when compared to each classifier applied individually.

5 Conclusions

This article reports the application of classifiers combination to improve the performance of REMS described in Netto[9]. The classifiers combination uses ML techniques in order to carry out the analysis and improve the final performance achieved by the Analysis Module. The Analysis Module approach affects directly the system, so performance of this module is critical. Classifiers combination allowed this module and the hole system to become more refined.

The data set used for these experiments, HS images from the Optometry group of the Indiana University (USA), presents limitations, images has reduced measures spectra: for spherical (S), spectra varies between -1.75D and +0.25D and for cylindrical (C) between 0.0D and 1.25D (both with resolution 0.25D), with axis (A) varying between 5° and 180° (with resolution of 5°). In these spectra there are few exemplars of each class. Another important limitation of data set was that images of an eye from the same patient had differences in the measurements S, C and A. This is possibly caused by errors in the acquisition process.

The authors believe that a new data set without measurement errors and with a larger amount of representative exemplars uniformly distributed by the possible spectra of measurements (for example, S varying between -17.00D and 17.00D and C between 0.0D and 17.00D) would improve the performance obtained by the ML techniques individually and consequently the classifiers combination. Moreover, the set of images should have similar numbers of exemplars for each class.

The absence of preliminary studies in this kind of work does not alow the comparison between the REMS proposed in this article with those employed by similar systems. Nevertheless, these results show that the quality of the data set is crucial for the analysis performance.

In spite of the limitations of data set used, it is relevant to notice the classifiers combination achieved its objective, increasing the general performance of the system proposed. The results obtained were relevant and may encourage future researches investigating new approaches to improve even more the performance of the Analysis Module.

References

1. Bishop, C. M.. Neural Networks for Pattern Recognition, Oxford University Press.(1996).
2. Broomhead, D. S. and Lowe, D.. Multivariable functional interpolation and adaptative networks, Complex Systems. **2**(1988) 321-355.
3. Chang, T. and Kuo, C. J.. Texture Analysis and Classification with Tree-Structured - Wavelet Transform. IEEE Transaction on Image Processing. **2(4)** (1993) 429-441.
4. Collorbert, R. and Bengio, S.. SVMTorch: Support Vector Machines for Large Scale Regression Problems, Journal of Machine Learning Research, **1** (2001) 143-160. (http://www.idiap.ch/learning/SVMTorch.html).
5. Daugman, D.. Complete Discrete 2-D Gabor Transforms by Neural Networks for Image Analysis and Compression, IEEE Trans. on Acoustic, Speech, and Signal Processing, **36(7)** (1988) 1169-1179.
6. Gabor, D.. Theory of Communication. Journal of the Institute of Electrical Engineers. **93** (1946) 429-457.
7. Haykin, S.. Neural Networks - A Comprehensive Foundation, Prentice Hall, 2nd. edition.(1999).
8. Jolliffe, I. T.. Principal Component Analysis. New York: Spriger Verlag.(1986).

9. Libralao, G. L., Almeida, O. C. P., Valerio Netto, A., Delbem, A. C. B., and Carvalho, A. C. P. L. F.. Machine Learning Techniques for Ocular Errors Analysis. IEEE Machine Learning for Signal Processing Workshop 2004, Sao Luis, MA, September (2004). Proceedings in CD published by IEEE Computer Press.
10. Mason, R., Gunst, R., and Hess, J.. Statistical design and analysis of experiments, John Wiley and Sons. (1989) 330.
11. Mitchell, T.. Machine Learning, McGraw Hill. (1997).
12. Prampero, P. S. and Carvalho, A. C. P. L. F.. Recognition of Vehicles Using Combination of Classifiers. Proceedings of the IEEE World Congress on Computational Intelligence, WCCI'98. Anchorage, USA, May (1998).
13. Quinlan, J. R.. C4.5 Programs for Machine Learning. Morgan Kaufmann Publishers, CA. (1993).
14. Rumelhart, D. and Mcchelland, J. L.. Learning internal representations by error propagation. In: D.E. (1986).
15. Smola, A. J., Barlett, P., Scholkopf, B., and Schuurmans, D.. Introduction to Large Margin Classifiers, chapter 1, (1999) 1-28.
16. Sonka, M., Hlavac, V., and Boyle, R.. Image processing, analysis, and machine vision. 2nd. edition, PWS Publishing. (1999).
17. Thibos, L. N.. Principles of Hartmann-Shack aberrometry. Wavefront Sensing Congress, Santa Fe. (2000). (http://www.opt.indiana.edu/people/faculty/thibos/VSIA/VSIA-2000_SH_tutorial_v2/index.htm).
18. Vapnik, V. N. and Chervonenkis, A.. On the uniform convergence of relative frequencies of events to their probabilities. Theory of probability and applications, **16** (1968) 262-280.
19. Weiss, S. M. and Indurkhya, N.. Predictive Data Mining: A Practical Guide, Morgan Kaufmann Publishers, Inc., San Francisco, CA. (1998).

Comparison of Extreme Learning Machine with Support Vector Machine for Text Classification

Ying Liu[1], Han Tong Loh[1], and Shu Beng Tor[2]

[1] Singapore-MIT Alliance, National University of Singapore, Singapore 117576
{G0200921, mpelht}@nus.edu.sg
[2] Singapore-MIT Alliance, Nanyang Technological University, Singapore 639798
{msbtor}@ntu.edu.sg

Abstract. Extreme Learning Machine, ELM, is a recently available learning algorithm for single layer feedforward neural network. Compared with classical learning algorithms in neural network, e.g. Back Propagation, ELM can achieve better performance with much shorter learning time. In the existing literature, its better performance and comparison with Support Vector Machine, SVM, over regression and general classification problems catch the attention of many researchers. In this paper, the comparison between ELM and SVM over a particular area of classification, i.e. text classification, is conducted. The results of benchmarking experiments with SVM show that for many categories SVM still outperforms ELM. It also suggests that other than accuracy, the indicator combining precision and recall, i.e. F_1 value, is a better performance indicator.

1 Introduction

Automated text classification aims to classify text documents into a set of predefined categories without human intervention. It has generated interests among researchers in the last decade partly due to the dramatically increased availability of digital documents on the World Wide Web, digital libraries and documents warehouses [20].

Text classification (TC) is an area with roots in the disciplines of machine learning (ML) and information retrieval (IR) [1], [15]. Text mining has become a terminology very frequently used to describe tasks whose major concerns are to analyze high volumes of texts, detect interesting patterns and reveal useful information. TC has become one of the most important pillars of text mining.

In order to accomplish the TC tasks, one or more classifiers are needed. Most of current popular classifiers, i.e. support vector machine (SVM), neural network (NN), kNN, decision tree and decision rule, Naïve Bayes and so on, are built in an inductive learning way. Among them, SVM is acclaimed by many researchers for its leading performance [20]. Therefore, it has been widely used for TC purpose.

Most recently, a new learning algorithm, extreme learning machine (ELM), is available for the training of single layer feedforward neural network. The inventors of ELM have done a set of comprehensive experiments in regression and general classification to compare its performance with SVM [7]. The experimental results show that compared with classical learning algorithms in neural network, e.g. Back Propagation, ELM can achieve better performance with much shorter learning time [7].

M. Ali and F. Esposito (Eds.): IEA/AIE 2005, LNAI 3533, pp. 390 – 399, 2005.

Compared with SVM, ELM is sometimes better than SVM in terms of accuracy, though not always. But as the number of neurons available for each ELM machine is the only parameter to be determined, ELM is much simpler for parameter tuning compared with SVMs whose kernel functions are nonlinear, e.g. RBF functions, thus saving tremendous time in searching for optimal parameters. Currently, SVMs, even for those with linear kernel function only, have gained wide acceptance by researchers as the leading performer for TC tasks. Our interest in this research is to benchmark ELM and SVM with linear kernel function for TC tasks and see whether ELM can serve as an alternative to SVM in TC tasks.

Having described the motivation of comparison between ELM and SVM, the rest of this paper is organized as follows. Some previous work in TC field by using neural network and SVM is reviewed in section 2. A brief introduction to ELM is given in section 3. We explain the experiment details and discuss the results in section 4. Finally, conclusions are drawn in section 5.

2 Related Work

Since several years ago, Neural network (NN) has been applied to TC tasks as a classifier. A NN is composed of many computing units (neurons) interconnected with each other with different weights in a network. In TC domain, the inputs to NN are the weights of features, i.e. terms, in a text document. And the output is the desired category or categories of the text document [2], [20], [23], [24].

Perceptron, the simplest type of NN classifier, is a linear classifier and has been extensively researched. Combined with effective means of feature selection, perceptron has achieved a very good performance and remains as the most popular choice of NN [16]. A non-linear NN, on the other hand, is a network with one or more additional "layers" of neurons, which in TC usually represent higher-order interactions between terms that the network is able to learn [17], [18], [23], [24], [26]. The literature on comparative experiments relating non-linear NNs to their linear counterparts show that the former has yielded either no improvement or very small improvements [23]. With their flexible architectures, NNs are well suited for applications of hierarchy text classification also [24].

Compared with NN, support vector machine (SVM) is relatively new to researchers in the fields of machine learning and information retrieval. However, it has quickly become the most popular algorithm mainly due to its leading performance. It is invented by Vapnik [22] and first introduced into the TC area by Joachims [8], [9]. His SVM implementation, i.e. SVM Light, has become one of the most popular packages of SVM application and has been widely used for TC [5], [11], [20], [26]. According to Joachims [8], SVM is very suitable for TC purpose, because SVM is not very sensitive to the high dimensionality of the feature space and most of TC jobs can be linearly separated. Yang and Liu's experiments [26] over a benchmarking TC corpus show that compared with the assumption of non-linear separation, the linear separation case can lead to a slightly better performance and save much effort on parameter tuning.

Invented by Huang Guangbin, extreme learning machine (ELM) is a newly available learning algorithm for a single layer feedforward neural network [7]. ELM randomly chooses the input weights and analytically determines the output weights of the network. In theory, this algorithm tends to provide the good generalization performance at extremely fast learning speed. The regression and classification experiments conducted by the inventors have shown that compared with BP and SVM, ELM is easier to use, faster to learn and has the higher generalization performance [7].

3 Extreme Learning Machine

A standard single layer feedforward neural network with n hidden neurons and activation function $g(x)$ can be mathematically modeled as:

$$\sum_{i=1}^{n} \boldsymbol{\beta}_i g(\boldsymbol{w}_i \boldsymbol{x}_j + b_i) = d_j,\ j = 1,\ldots,N \tag{1}$$

where $\boldsymbol{w}_i$ is the weight vector connecting inputs and the ith hidden neurons, $\boldsymbol{\beta}_i$ is the weight vector connecting the ith hidden neurons and output neurons, d_j is the output from ELM for data point j.

With N data points in a pair as $(\boldsymbol{x}_j, \boldsymbol{t}_j)$, $\boldsymbol{x}_i \in R^n$ and $\boldsymbol{t}_i \in R^m$ where $\boldsymbol{t}_j$ is the corresponding output for data point $\boldsymbol{x}_j$, the ideal case is training with zero errors, which can be represented as:

$$\sum_{i=1}^{n} \boldsymbol{\beta}_i g(\boldsymbol{w}_i \boldsymbol{x}_j + b_i) = t_j,\ j = 1,\ldots,N \tag{2}$$

The above equations can be written compactly as:

$$\mathbf{H}\beta = \mathbf{T} \tag{3}$$

where

$$\mathbf{H} = \begin{bmatrix} g(\boldsymbol{w}_1 \boldsymbol{x}_1 + b_1) & \cdots & g(\boldsymbol{w}_n \boldsymbol{x}_1 + b_n) \\ \vdots & \cdots & \vdots \\ g(\boldsymbol{w}_1 \boldsymbol{x}_N + b_1) & \cdots & g(\boldsymbol{w}_n \boldsymbol{x}_N + b_n) \end{bmatrix}_{N \times n} \tag{4}$$

$$\beta = \begin{bmatrix} \beta_1^T \\ \vdots \\ \beta_n^T \end{bmatrix}_{n \times m} \text{ and } \mathbf{T} = \begin{bmatrix} t_1^T \\ \vdots \\ t_N^T \end{bmatrix}_{N \times m} \tag{5}$$

So the solution is:

$$\hat{\beta} = \mathbf{H}^{\dagger}\mathbf{T} \tag{6}$$

where $\mathbf{H}^{\dagger}$ is called Moore-Penrose generalized inverse [7].

The most important properties of this solution as claimed by the authors [7] are:

1. Minimum training error
2. Smallest norm of weights and best generalization performance
3. The minimum norm least-square solution of $\mathbf{H}\beta = \mathbf{T}$ is unique, which is $\hat{\beta} = \mathbf{H}^{\dagger}\mathbf{T}$.

So finally, the ELM algorithm is [7]:

Given a training set $\{(\boldsymbol{x}_i, \boldsymbol{t}_i) | \boldsymbol{x}_i \in R^n, \boldsymbol{t}_i \in R^m, i = 1,\ldots,N\}$, activation function $g(x)$, and N hidden neurons,

Step 1: Assign arbitrary input weights w_i and bias b_i, $i = 1,\ldots,n$.
Step 2: Calculate the hidden layer output matrix $\mathbf{H}$.
Step 3: Calculate the output weights β:

$$\beta = \mathbf{H}^{\dagger}\mathbf{T} \tag{7}$$

where $\mathbf{H}$, β and are as defined before.

4 Experiments

4.1 Data Set – MCV1

Manufacturing Corpus Version 1 (MCV1) is an archive of 1434 English language manufacturing related engineering papers. It combines all engineering technical

Table 1. The 18 major categories of MCV1

C01. Assembly & Joining	C07. Machining & Material Removal Processes	C13. Product Design Management
C02. Composites Manufacturing	C08. Manufacturing Engineering & Management	C14. Quality
C03. Electronics Manufacturing	C09. Manufacturing Systems, Automation & IT	C15. Rapid Prototyping
C04. Finishing & Coating	C10. Materials	C16. Research & Development / New Technologies
C05. Forming & Fabricating	C11. Measurement, Inspection & Testing	C17. Robotics & Machine Vision
C06. Lean Manufacturing & Supply Chain Management	C12. Plastics Molding & Manufacturing	C18. Welding

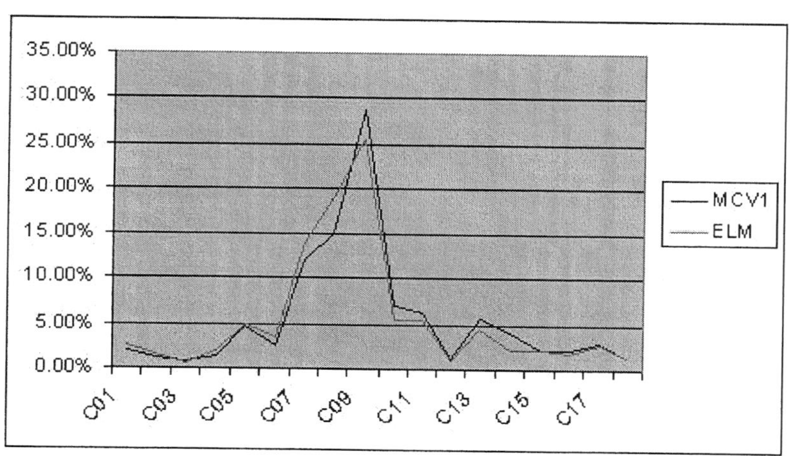

Fig. 1. Documents frequency distribution of MCV1 and ELM data set

papers from Society of Manufacturing Engineers (SME) from year 1998 to year 2000 [12]. There are 18 major categories of documents and two levels of subcategories below them. The 18 major categories are shown in Table 1:

Each document in MCV1 is labeled with one to nine category labels. For the purpose of this research, only one label is associated with each document. It is mainly because the current version of ELM only takes the highest value from output neurons as the prediction; it cannot handle the problem of multiclass classification using a single ELM machine.

Figure 1 shows that the documents frequency distribution in ELM data set matches very well with the original distribution in MCV1.

Table 2 shows the detailed distribution of 1434 documents from different categories.

Table 2. Percentage of documents of 18 categories in ELM data set

C01	**C02**	**C03**	**C04**	**C05**	**C06**
2.58%	1.47%	0.70%	1.81%	4.95%	3.63%
C07	**C08**	**C09**	**C10**	**C11**	**C12**
13.96%	19.12%	25.40%	5.51%	5.44%	1.05%
C13	**C14**	**C15**	**C16**	**C17**	**C18**
4.47%	2.30%	2.02%	1.74%	2.65%	1.19%

4.2 Experimental Setting

In the experiments, only the abstract of each paper is used. All standard text processing procedures are applied in the experiments, including stop words removal, stemming. By using the general *tfidf* weighting scheme, the documents are represented in vector format. Chi-square five fold cross validation is used to evaluate the features for ELM dataset.

In order to compare with SVM strictly, one ELM machine is built over each of 18 major categories. Document vectors sharing the same category label will be set as positive and all other vectors are set as negative. This way of building data set is generically the same as the one for SVM. In this paper, we call this "one-against-all". One-against-all is different from purely binary classification in the sense that the negative part is composed by many different categories, instead of from a single opposite category. Therefore, there are totally 18 datasets. For each of them, five fold cross validation is assessed. SVM Light is chosen as the SVM package with linear function as the kernel function. For ELM, all data points have been normalized to $(-1,1)$ and sigmoid has been chosen as the activation function. The way to search for the optimal size of neurons is suggested by the authors in [7]. With the starting size of 20, the number of neurons increases with a step of 20. Based on the output performance, the optimal size of neurons will be decided. Finally based on the optimal sizes of neurons, 50 more trials are performed in order to collect the best output.

4.3 Performance Indicator

Accuracy has been used as the performance indicator for classification comparison with SVM in [7]. However, if the datasets are formed as one-against-all, accuracy is not always a good indicator. A very obvious example for this argument is a dataset that might have some categories with very few documents. If the system predicts all data points as negative, it can still generate a very high accuracy value since the negative portion of this data set, which is composed by many different categories, occupies the large percentage of this data set. With the negative prediction for a document, it is still unclear which category it belongs to. The building of our dataset rightly fits into this case. In order to avoid this problem and show the real performance of both algorithms, the classic F_1 value which is defined as $F_1 = \frac{2pr}{p+r}$ is adopted, where p represents precision and r represents recall [1], [15], [20]. This performance indicator combines the effects of precision and recall, and it has been widely used in TC domain.

4.4 Results and Discussion

Figure 2 shows the relationship between the size of neurons and its performance for ELM machines built over major categories in MCV1. Obviously, with the increase of neurons, ELM machines achieve the best performance very quickly and remain stable

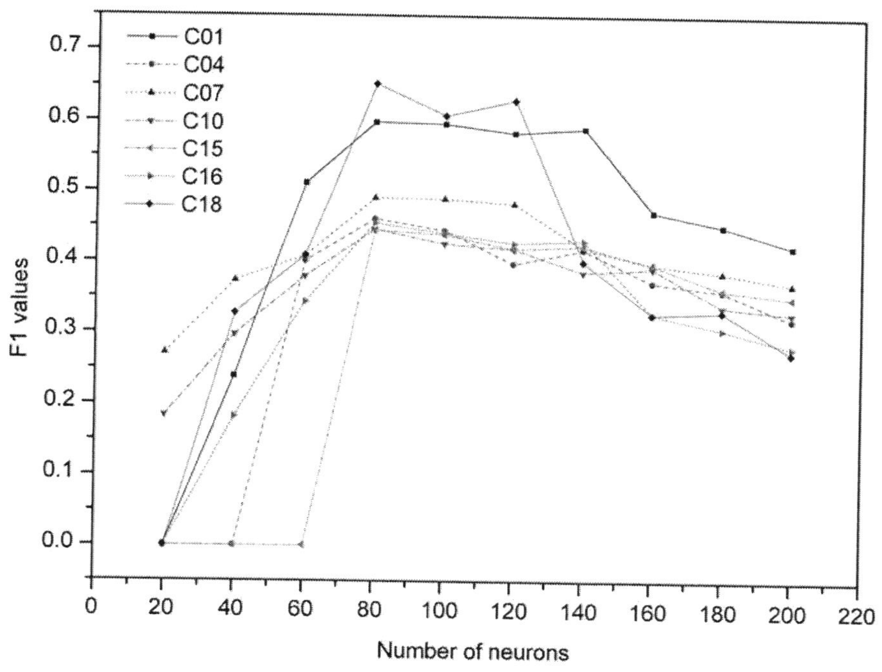

Fig. 2. Number of neurons vs. F_1 performance

for a wide range of neuron sizes. The broad spectrum of neuron size implies that ELM is robust to this critical parameter setting. It is also noted that for MCV1 dataset, 60-120 neurons can provide most categories with good performance in a few trials.

In the experiments, authors are curious whether feature selection still contributes towards the performance of ELM. Chi-Square five fold cross validation has been applied to select the salient features. With feature selection, the dimension has been dramatically reduced from over five thousand to less than one hundred. Table 3 shows the performance difference before and after feature selection. It is now clear that feature selection still has a critical role in ELM computation.

Table 3. Performance difference before and after feature selection

Category	No. of Documents	Percentage	F_1 ELM Before Feature Selection	F_1 ELM After Feature Selection
C01	37	2.58%	0.231	0.599
C02	21	1.47%	N/A	N/A
C03	10	0.70%	N/A	N/A
C04	26	1.81%	0.145	0.461
C05	71	4.95%	N/A	0.370
C06	52	3.63%	N/A	0.369
C07	200	13.96%	0.247	0.491
C08	274	19.12%	0.213	0.346
C09	364	25.40%	N/A	0.330
C10	79	5.51%	0.183	0.446
C11	78	5.44%	N/A	0.338
C12	15	1.05%	N/A	N/A
C13	64	4.47%	N/A	N/A
C14	33	2.30%	N/A	N/A
C15	29	2.02%	N/A	0.445
C16	25	1.74%	N/A	0.455
C17	38	2.65%	N/A	N/A
C18	17	1.19%	0.236	0.653

The most important results are F_1 values and accuracy values of SVM and ELM over 18 categories as shown in Table 4.

Note that SVM still outperforms ELM for the majority of categories. In some cases, the algorithms yield no results due to the lack of training samples or probably noise. In category C02, C03, and C14, when SVM does not work, ELM does not work as well. There are three categories, i.e. C12, C13, and C17, ELM does not work, while SVM still gives results. In two categories, i.e. C04 and C06, ELM slightly outperforms SVM and in two more categories, the performance from both are close to each other. It is also noted that the performance of both algorithms, evaluated by F_1

values, does not necessarily link to the values of accuracy. In many instances, even where the ELM has higher accuracy values, SVM still outperforms ELM in terms of F_1 values.

Table 4. F_1 values and accuracy values of SVM and ELM over 18 categories

Category	No. of Documents	Per	F_1 SVM	F_1 ELM	Accuracy SVM	Accuracy ELM	F_1 Difference (SVM-ELM)	Accuracy Difference (SVM-ELM)
C01	37	2.58%	0.699	0.599	0.980	0.984	0.099	-0.004
C02	21	1.47%	N/A	N/A	0.970	0.985	N/A	-0.014
C03	10	0.70%	N/A	N/A	0.986	0.994	N/A	-0.007
C04	26	1.81%	0.459	0.461	0.978	0.986	-0.002	-0.008
C05	71	4.95%	0.486	0.370	0.932	0.930	0.116	0.002
C06	52	3.63%	0.361	0.369	0.934	0.961	-0.007	-0.026
C07	200	13.96%	0.624	0.491	0.864	0.866	0.134	-0.003
C08	274	19.12%	0.548	0.346	0.684	0.800	0.202	-0.116
C09	364	25.40%	0.491	0.330	0.534	0.687	0.161	-0.153
C10	79	5.51%	0.485	0.446	0.927	0.944	0.039	-0.018
C11	78	5.44%	0.521	0.338	0.922	0.933	0.183	-0.011
C12	15	1.05%	0.511	N/A	0.977	0.988	>>	-0.011
C13	64	4.47%	0.225	N/A	0.884	0.953	>>	-0.069
C14	33	2.30%	N/A	N/A	0.959	0.976	N/A	-0.017
C15	29	2.02%	0.566	0.445	0.969	0.977	0.121	-0.008
C16	25	1.74%	0.558	0.455	0.987	0.986	0.104	0.001
C17	38	2.65%	0.267	N/A	0.953	0.970	>>	-0.018
C18	17	1.19%	0.709	0.653	0.988	0.990	0.056	-0.002

In our experiments, the CPU time spent by both ELM and SVM are trivial. As mentioned before in section 2, in TC tasks, many documents can be linearly classified in high dimensional space [8]. It is well known that with the sigmoid or RBFs as the kernel functions, SVM suffers from its tedious parameter tuning. So in TC tasks it is ideal for SVM to adopt a linear function as the kernel function to save much time on parameter tuning. By comparison, even with a single parameter to be tuned, the arbitrary assignment of initial weights requires ELM to search for the optimal size of neuron and run many times to get the average value [7]. In this case, ELM loses its edge over SVM.

5 Conclusion

In this paper, we have studied the performance of SVM and the newly available ELM algorithm for TC tasks. F_1 has been used to evaluate the performance because of its better suitability than accuracy as an indicator. While the ELM is easy to tune with a single parameter and is robust to the parameter settings, it is shown that SVM still outperforms ELM for the majority of categories in terms of F_1 values. Furthermore, accuracy does not have clear links with the performance evaluated by F_1. Compared to SVM with linear function as kernel function, the advantage of fast training of ELM is not significant in TC tasks.

References

1. Baeza-Yates, R. & Ribeiro-Neto, B.: Modern information retrieval. Addison-Wesley Longman Publishing Co., Inc. Boston, MA, USA, (1999)
2. Bishop, C. M.: Neural Networks for Pattern Recognition. Oxford University Press, (1996)
3. Burges, C. J. C.: A tutorial on support vector machines for pattern recognition. Data Mining and Knowledge Discovery, Vol. 2, (1998) 121-167
4. Cristianini, N. & Shawe-Taylor, J.: An introduction to Support Vector Machines: and other kernel-based learning methods. Cambridge University Press, (2000)
5. Dumais, S. & Chen, H.: Hierarchical classification of Web content. Proceedings of the 23rd annual international ACM SIGIR conference on Research and development in information retrieval (SIGIR2000), (2000)
6. Flach, P. A.: On the state of the art in machine learning: a personal review. Artificial Intelligence, Vol. 13, (2001) 199-222
7. Huang, G. B., Zhu, Q. Y. & Siew, C. K.: Extreme Learning Machine: A New Learning Scheme of Feedforward Neural Networks. International Joint Conference on Neural Networks (IJCNN'2004), (2004)
8. Joachims, T.: Text categorization with Support Vector Machines: Learning with many relevant features. Machine Learning: ECML-98, Tenth European Conference on Machine Learning, (1998)
9. Joachims, T.: Transductive Inference for Text Classification using Support Vector Machines. Proceedings of the 16th International Conference on Machine Learning (ICML), (1999)
10. Kasabov, N. Data mining and knowledge discovery using neural networks. 2002
11. Leopold, E. & Kindermann, J.: Text Categorization with Support Vector Machines - How to Represent Texts in Input Space. Machine Learning, Vol. 46, (2002) 423-444
12. Liu, Y., Loh, H. T. & Tor, S. B.: Building a Document Corpus for Manufacturing Knowledge Retrieval. Singapore MIT Alliance Symposium 2004, (2004)
13. Mangasarian, O. L.: Data Mining via Support Vector Machines. 20th International Federation for Information Processing (IFIP) TC7 Conference on System Modeling and Optimization, (2001)
14. Manning, C. D. & Schütze, H.: Foundations of Statistical Natural Language Processing. The MIT Press, (1999)
15. Mitchell, T. M.: Machine Learning. The McGraw-Hill Companies, Inc., (1997)
16. Ng, H. T., Goh, W. B. & Low, K. L.: Feature selection, perception learning, and a usability case study for text categorization. ACM SIGIR Forum , Proceedings of the 20th annual international ACM SIGIR conference on Research and development in information retrieval, (1997)
17. Ruiz, M. E. & Srinivasan, P.: Hierarchical Neural Networks for Text Categorization. Proceedings of the 22nd annual international ACM SIGIR conference on Research and development in information retrieval, (1999)

18. Ruiz, M. E. & Srinivasan, P.: Hierarchical Text Categorization Using Neural Networks. Information Retrieval, Vol. 5, (2002) 87-118
19. Schölkopf, B. & Smola, A. J.: Learning with Kernels: Support Vector Machines, Regularization, Optimization, and Beyond. 1st edn. MIT Press, (2001)
20. Sebastiani, F.: Machine Learning in Automated Text Categorization. ACM Computing Surveys (CSUR), Vol. 34, (2002) 1-47
21. Sun, A. & Lim, E.-P.: Hierarchical Text Classification and Evaluation. Proceedings of the 2001 IEEE International Conference on Data Mining (ICDM 2001), (2001)
22. Vapnik, V. N.: The Nature of Statistical Learning Theory. 2nd edn. Springer-Verlag, New York (1999)
23. Wiener, E. D., Pedersen, J. O. & Weigend, A. S.: A neural network approach to topic spotting. Proceedings of {SDAIR}-95, 4th Annual Symposium on Document Analysis and Information Retrieval, (1995)
24. Weigend, A. S., Wiener, E. D. & Pedersen, J. O.: Exploiting hierarchy in text categorization. Information Retrieval, Vol. 1, (1999) 193-216
25. Yang, Y.: An evaluation of statistical approaches to text categorization. Information Retrieval, Vol. 1, (1999) 69-90
26. Yang, Y. & Liu, X.: A re-examination of text categorization methods. Proceedings of the 22nd annual international ACM SIGIR conference on Research and development in information retrieval, (1999)

Endoscopy Images Classification with Kernel Based Learning Algorithms

Pawel Majewski and Wojciech Jedruch

Gdansk University of Technology,
Narutowicza 11/12, 80-952 Gdansk, Poland
{Pawel.Majewski, wjed}@eti.pg.gda.pl

Abstract. In this paper application of kernel based learning algorithms to endoscopy images classification problem is presented. This work is a part the attempts to extend the existing recommendation system (ERS) with image classification facility. The use of a computer-based system could support the doctor when making a diagnosis and help to avoid human subjectivity. We give a brief description of the SVM and LS-SVM algorithms. The algorithms are then used in the problem of recognition of malignant versus benign tumour in gullet. The classification was performed on features based on edge structure and colour. A detailed experimental comparison of classification performance for diferent kernel functions and different combinations of feature vectors was made. The algorithms performed very well in the experiments achieving high percentage of correct predictions.

1 Introduction

In recent years some research on processing and analysis of endoscopy information has been conducted at Gdansk University of Technology [5]. The research encompassed archivisation and recommendations based on the endoscopy data. Despite indeterminism in the data caused by several factors like: random position of the camera, many light reflexes and noise introduced by hue differences, air bubbles or slime the promising results were obtained. As an effect of the research efforts a dedicated application — Endoscopy Recommendation System (ERS) — was developed and deployed at Medical University of Gdansk. The system allowed to collect and process digital endoscopy data like movies, images and textual information. Additionally ERS has been equipped with a recommendation module to support the specialists when making a diagnosis of the gastrointestinal tract diseases. The recommendation system consisted of a set of associative rules using the standarized textual case description with help of the analysis of digital images.

This paper presents attempts to extend the existing recommendation system with image classification facility. The aim was to analyse kernel based learning algorithms in a classification problem of digital endoscopy images of benign and malignant tumour in gullet. The examined classification methods were applied to

M. Ali and F. Esposito (Eds.): IEA/AIE 2005, LNAI 3533, pp. 400–405, 2005.

the dataset of 90 endoscopy images. The algorithms exhibited highly satisfactory performance on the training set and showed its usefulness in real-life medical problems. The use of such a computer system could support the doctor when making a diagnosis and help to avoid human subjectivity.

2 Kernel Based Learning Algorithms

The kernel based learning algorithm [9] both in case of classification and function estimation, can be formulated as a problem of finding a function $f(x)$ that best "fits" given examples (x_i, y_i), $i = 1 \ldots N$. To measure the quality of fitting one can introduce a loss function $V(y, f(x))$. The loss function can be any function that expresses the difference between obtained and desired value. In practice convex loss functions are used. The problem of finding the appropriate function is then equivalent to minimizing the following functional:

$$I = \frac{1}{N} \sum_{i=1}^{N} V(y_i, f(x_i)) \tag{1}$$

and is usually reffered as *Empirical Risk Minimization* (ERM). In general ERM problem (1) is ill-posed, depending on the choice of the hypothesis space. Therefore instead of minimizing (1) one can minimize its regularized version. Many techniques developed for solving ill-posed problems are possible (Morozov [7], Ivanov [2], Pelckmans et al. [8]) but the classic approach involves Tikhonov [11] regularization. Following Tikhonov one obtains:

$$I_{reg} = \frac{1}{N} \sum_{i=1}^{N} V(y_i, f(x_i)) + \gamma \|f\|_k^2 \tag{2}$$

where γ is a positive real regularization parameter and $\|f\|_k^2$ is a norm in Reproducing Kernel Hilbert Space (RKHS) defined by the chosen kernel function k. The kernel function k can be any positive definite function that satisfies Mercer's conditions [6].

Regardless of the the loss function used, minimalization of (2) in case of two-class classification problem yields the solution of the form [9]:

$$f(\bullet) = sign\left(\sum_{i=1}^{N} \alpha_i k(x_i, \bullet)\right) \tag{3}$$

where α_i are coefficients found during learning process.

According to the choice of a particular loss function $V(y, f(x))$ one can obtain several learning algorithms. By applying Vapnik's ϵ-intensive loss function:

$$V_\epsilon(y, f(x)) = |y_i - f(x_i)|_\epsilon \tag{4}$$

the original SVMs [13] algorithm can be constructed. The learning problem becomes then equivalent to minimization of:

$$I_\epsilon = \frac{1}{N}\sum_{i=1}^{N} |y_i - f(x_i)|_\epsilon + \gamma \|f\|_k^2 \qquad (5)$$

and solution to (5) becomes a quadratic programming (QP) problem. Several efficient iterative algorithms have been developed to find solution to (5) even for large scale applications [3].

If the generic loss function $V(y, f(x))$ in (2) is substituted with a least squares function:

$$V_{LS}(y, f(x)) = (y_i - f(x_i))^2 \qquad (6)$$

another kernel algorithm, Least Squares Support Vector Machines (LS-SVM), can be constructed. LS-SVM were introduced by Poggio et al. [9] (named Regularization Networks) and later rediscovered by Suykens et al. [10]. With help of (6) learning problem can be formulated as a minimalization of following functional:

$$I_{LS} = \frac{1}{N}\sum_{i=1}^{N} (y_i - f(x_i))^2 + \gamma \|f\|_k^2 \qquad (7)$$

The resulting oprimization problem reduces to the solution of a set of linear equations instead of computationaly intensive QP in case of (5). One of the drawbacks of LS-SVMs, however, is lack of the sparseness of the solution. Efficient iterative methods for training LS-SVM are modifications of conjugate gradient (CG) methods [12].

3 Image Features Extraction

For the classification, a dataset of 90 digital endoscopy images was used. The images fell into one of two classes: MAL (malignant tumour in gullet) or BEL (benign tumourin in gullet). The MAL class consisted of 73 images and BEL was made of 17 images. Sample images from both classes are shown in Fig. 1.

Only fragments of the images contained relevant information for the classification purposes. To address this problem the interesting areas of the images were marked as the Region of Interest (ROI) [4]. ROIs were circles of adjustable diameters placed on the selected part of the image. There could be many ROIs on a single image but usually there was only one. Only pixels inside ROIs were considered for features extraction. The rest of the image was abandoned.

According to the knowledge aquired from professional medical staff the tumours could be distingushed by their edge and surface structure. BEL tumours are supposed to have smooth edges and soft surface while MEL tumours are usually irregular and slightly coarse. It should be noted, however, that sometimes it is not easy to distinguish the classes even for an experienced consultant. In our experiments algorithms based on edge structure and colour were employed.

The Water-Filling algorithm proposed by Zhou et al. [14] was used to extract information on the edge structure. It computes feature vector on edge map of the

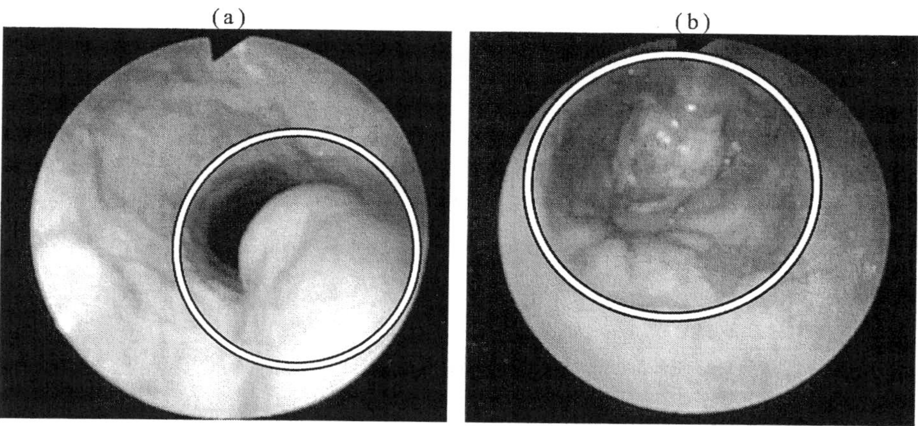

Fig. 1. Sample images from from training set with marked Regions of Interest (ROIs): (a) BEL (benign tumour) class sample; (b) MEL (malignant tumour) class sample

original image. The idea of this algorithm is to obtain measures of the edge length and complexity by graph traverse. The features generated by Water-Filling are more generally applicable than texture or shape features. The original version of Water-Filling works on grey-scale images only. Modification of the algorithm, Water-Filling Plus, incorporates some information on colour. Feature vectors produced by both versions of the algorithm contain some statistics on the edges and their structure in the image, namely edge length, number of forks, etc. The features are translation and rotation invariant and to some degree scaling invariant. Edge maps required by the Water-Filling algorithm were obtained with the Canny method [1].

The length of feature vectors secured with Water-Filling algorithm was 36. The Water-Filling Plus produced much longer vectors of 127 features. Additionally some simple features based on colour were extracted from the image. This includes mean values and standard deviations of the colour values derived from the RGB model. The values were computed on the pixels inside the ROIs only.

4 Experiments

In the experiments we compared the performance of classic SVM and LS-SVM. Four different feature vectors combined from the features described in the previous section were created and used for training. We experimented with polynomial and RBF kernels. The optimal model and kernel parameters (C and γ for models and σ, degree d and t for kernels) were found with the grid search. Before training all features were normalized to the range $[0, 1]$ to avoid domination of features with greater numeric ranges. To avoid overfitting a 5-fold cross-validation technique was used. As the image collection was really small and imbalanced all the

Table 1. Results of the experiments on the training set of 90 endoscopy images: 73 falling into MEL class and 17 into BEL class; degree of all polynomial kernels was set to 3 (optimal value found with cross-validation)

Features vector	Algorithm	Kernel function	Recall MEL	Recall BEL	Predictions rate MEL [%]	Predictions rate BEL [%]	Overal predictions rate [%]
Water-Filling	LS-SVM	Polynomial	57	8	78.08	47.06	72.22
	LS-SVM	RBF	73	9	100.00	52.94	91.11
	SVM	Polynomial	73	9	100.00	52.94	91.11
	SVM	RBF	73	7	100.00	41.18	88.89
Water-Filling Plus	LS-SVM	Polynomial	49	8	67.12	47.06	63.33
	LS-SVM	RBF	73	6	100.00	35.29	87.78
	SVM	Polynomial	73	9	100.00	52.94	91.11
	SVM	RBF	73	10	100.00	58.82	92.22
Water-Filling + Colour	LS-SVM	Polynomial	40	16	54.79	94.12	62.22
	LS-SVM	RBF	72	15	98.63	88.24	96.67
	SVM	Polynomial	72	16	98.63	94.12	97.78
	SVM	RBF	72	12	98.63	70.59	93.33
Water-Filling Plus + Colour	LS-SVM	Polynomial	47	13	64.38	76.47	66.67
	LS-SVM	RBF	73	6	100.00	35.29	87.78
	SVM	Polynomial	71	13	97.26	76.47	93.33
	SVM	RBF	73	11	100.00	64.71	93.33

images were used for training and testing. The results of the experiments can be found in table 1.

The best results for both SVM and LS-SVM algorithms were obtained with Water-Filling feature vectors extended with colour statistics. The rate of correct predictions reached over 97 per cent for SVM and over 96 per cent for LS-SVM. The Water-Filling Plus extended with colour features performed slightly weaker but at the higher computational cost due to almost four times longer input vectors. The experiments showed that classic SVM performed better with polynomial kernels while better results for LS-SVM were aquired when RBF kernels were used.

The computational cost of LS-SVM algorithm compared to SVM was significantly lower making the training less time-consuming. Faster training, however, did not influence the classification and generalization performance. Therefore it seems that LS-SVMs are more applicable to real-life applications then classic SVM. Especially, when the number of training set is relatively small and pruning techniques do not have to be used.

The experiments also showed the vulnerability to the correct placement of the ROIs. Classifications made on the whole images gave unsatisfactory results.

5 Conclusions

In this paper the results of experiments with kernel based algorithms on digital endoscopy images were presented. The classification methods were sketched as well as the feature extraction algorithms. Both applied algorithms demonstrated excellent performance on the used dataset reaching over 97 per cent of correct predictions. To support the claim the experiments should be repeated, as more examples are available.

Note that this is a preliminary approach to the problem and additional research should be done. The real accuracy of the presented method should also be assessed by professional medical staff in practice. Further work should go towards extension to multiclass classification.

References

1. Canny J.: A Computational Approach to Edge Detection, IEEE Transactions on Pattern Analysis and Machine Intelligence, **8**(6) (1986)
2. Ivanov, V., V.: The Theory of Approximate Methods and Their Application to the Numerical Solution of Singular Integral Equations, Nordhoff International (1976)
3. Keerthi, S., S., Shevade, S., K., Bhattacharyya, C., Murthy, K., R., K.: Improvements to Platt's SMO algorithm for SVM classifer design, Neural Computation, **13**(3) (2001) 637–649
4. Krawczyk, H., Knopa, R., Mazurkiewicz, A.: Parallel Procedures for ROI Identification in Endoscopic Images, IEEE CS, PARELEC, Warsaw (2002)
5. Krawczyk, H., Mazurkiewicz, A., Learning Strategies of Endoscopy Recommendation System, Journal of Medical Informatics & Technologies, **5** (2000) CS-3–CS-9
6. Mercer, J.: Functions of positive and negative type and their connection with theory of integral equations, Philos. Trans Roy. Soc, **209 A** (1909) 415–446
7. Morozov, V., A.: Methods for Solving Incorrectly Posed Problems, Springer-Verlag (1984)
8. Pelckmans K., Suykens J.,A.,K., De Moor, B.: Additive regularization : fusion of training and validation levels in Kernel Methods, Internal Report 03-184, ESAT-SISTA, K.U.Leuven (Leuven, Belgium) (2003)
9. Poggio, T., Smale, S.: The Mathematics of Learning: Dealing with Data, Noticies of AMS 50, **5** (2003) 537–544
10. Suykens, J., A., K., Van Gestel, T., De Brabanter, J.: Least Squares Support Vector Machines, World Scientific (2002)
11. Tikhonov, A., N., Arsenin, V., Y.: Solution of Ill-posed problems. W. H. Winston, Washington, DC (1977)
12. Van Gestel, T., Suykens, J., A., K., Baesens, B., Viaene, S., Vanthienen, J., Dedene, G., De Moor, B., Vandewalle, J.: Benchmarking least squares support vector machines classifiers, Machine Learning, **54**(1) (2004) 5–32
13. Vapnik, V., N.: Statistical Learning Theory, Wiley, New York (1998)
14. Zhou X. S., Rui Y., Huang T. S.: Water-Filling: A Novel Way for Image Structural Feature Extraction, IEEE International Conference on Image Processing, Kobe (1999)

Local Bagging of Decision Stumps

S.B. Kotsiantis[1], G.E. Tsekouras [2], and P.E. Pintelas[1]

[1] Educational Software Development Laboratory,
Department of Mathematics, University of Patras, Greece
{sotos, pintelas}@math.upatras.gr
[2] Department of Cultural Technology and Communication,
University of the Aegean, Mytilene, Greece
gtsek@ct.aegean.gr

Abstract. Local methods have significant advantages when the probability measure defined on the space of symbolic objects for each class is very complex, but can still be described by a collection of less complex local approximations. We propose a technique of local bagging of decision stumps. We performed a comparison with other well known combining methods using the same base learner, on standard benchmark datasets and the accuracy of the proposed technique was greater in most cases.

1 Introduction

When all training examples are considered when classifying a new test instance, the algorithm works as a global method, while when the nearest training examples are considered, the algorithm works as a local method, since only data local to the area around the testing case contribute to the classification [1]. Local learning [2] can be understood as a general principle that allows extending learning techniques designed for simple models, to the case of complex data for which the model's assumptions would not necessarily hold globally, but can be thought as valid locally. A simple example is the assumption of linear separability, which in general is not satisfied globally in classification problems with rich data. Yet any classification method able to find only a linear separation, can be used inside a local learning procedure, producing an algorithm able to model complex non-linear class boundaries.

When the size of the training set is small compared to the complexity of the classifier, the learning algorithm usually overfits the noise in the training data. Thus effective control of complexity of a classifier plays an important role in achieving good generalization. Some theoretical and experimental results [17] indicate that a local learning algorithm (that is learning algorithm trained on the training subset) provides a feasible solution to this problem. The authors of [7] proposed a theoretical model of a local learning algorithm and obtained bounds for the local risk minimization estimator for pattern recognition and regression problems using structural risk minimization principle. The authors of [9] extended the idea of constructing local simple base learners for different regions of input space, searching for ANNs architectures that should be locally used and for a criterion to select a proper unit for each region of input space.

M. Ali and F. Esposito (Eds.): IEA/AIE 2005, LNAI 3533, pp. 406–411, 2005.

In this paper, we propose a technique of local bagging of decision stumps. Usual bagging is not effective with simple learners with strong bias [5]. In the case of local bagging, this problem does not exist. We performed a comparison with other well known combining methods using the same base classifier, on standard benchmark datasets and the accuracy of the proposed technique was greater in most cases.

Current ensemble approaches and work are described in section 2. In Section 3 we describe the proposed method and investigate its advantages and limitations. In Section 4, we evaluate the proposed method on several UCI datasets by comparing it with standard bagging and boosting and other lazy methods. Finally, section 5 concludes the paper and suggests further directions in current research.

2 Ensembles of Classifiers

Empirical studies showed that classification problem ensembles are often much more accurate than the individual base learner that make them up [5], and recently different theoretical explanations have been proposed to justify the effectiveness of some commonly used ensemble methods [15]. In this work we propose a combining method that uses one learning algorithm for building an ensemble of classifiers. For this reason this section presents the most well-known methods that generate sets of base learners using one base learning algorithm.

Starting with bagging [8], we will say that this method samples the training set, generating random independent bootstrap replicates, constructs the classifier on each of these, and aggregates them by a simple majority vote in the final decision rule. Another method that uses different subset of training data with a single learning method is the boosting approach [12]. It assigns weights to the training instances, and these weight values are changed depending upon how well the associated training instance is learned by the classifier; the weights for misclassified instances are increased. After several cycles, the prediction is performed by taking a weighted vote of the predictions of each classifier, with the weights being proportional to each classifier's accuracy on its training set.

It was subsequently observed [13] that boosting is in effect approximating a stage-wise additive logistic regression model by optimising an exponential criterion. This leads to new variants of boosting that fit additive models directly. One such variant is Logitboost, which uses the Newton-like steps to optimise the loss criterion [13].

3 Proposed Algorithm

The proposed algorithm builds a model for each instance to be classified, taking into account only a subset of the training instances. This subset is chosen on the basis of the preferable distance metric between the testing instance and the training instances in the input space. For each testing instance, a bagging ensemble of decision stump classifier is thus learned using only the training points lying close to the current testing instance.

Decision stump (DS) are one level decision trees that classify instances by sorting them based on feature values [14]. Each node in a decision stump represents a feature in an instance to be classified, and each branch represents a value that the node can take. Instances are classified starting at the root node and sorting them based on their feature values. At worst a decision stump will reproduce the most common sense baseline, and may do better if the selected feature is particularly informative.

Generally, the proposed ensemble consists of the four steps (see Fig 1).

1) Determine a suitable distance metric.
2) Find the k nearest neighbors using the selected distance metric.
3) Apply bagging to the decision stump classifier using as training instances the k instances
4) The answer of the bagging ensemble is the prediction for the testing instance.

Fig. 1. Local Bagging of decision stumps

The proposed ensemble has some free parameters such as the distance metric. In our experiments, we used the most well known -Euclidean similarity function- as distance metric. We also used k=50 since about this size of instances is appropriate for a simple algorithm to built a precise model [11]. We used 10 iterations for the bagging process in order to reduce the time need for classification of a new instance.

Our method shares the properties of other instance based learning methods such as no need for training and more computational cost for classification. Besides, our method has some desirable properties, such as better accuracy and confidence interval.

4 Experiments Results

We experimented with 34 datasets from the UCI repository [4]. These datasets cover many different types of problems having discrete, continuous, and symbolic variables. We compared the proposed ensemble methodology with:

- K-nearest neighbors algorithm using k=50 because the proposed algorithm uses 50 neighbors.
- Kstar: another instance-based learner which uses entropy as distance measure [10].
- Local weighted DS using 50 local instances. This method differs from the proposed technique since it has no bagging process.
- Bagging DS, Boosting DS and Logitboost DS (using 25 sub-classifiers). All these methods work globally whereas the proposed method works locally.

In order to calculate the classifiers' accuracy, the whole training set was divided into ten mutually exclusive and equal-sized subsets and for each subset the classifier was trained on the union of all of the other subsets. Then, cross validation was run 10 times for each algorithm and the average value of the 10-cross validations was calculated. It must be mentioned that we used the free available source code for most of the algorithms by [19] for our experiments.

In Table 1, we represent as "v" that the specific algorithm performed statistically better than the proposed ensemble according to t-test with $p<0.05$. Throughout, we

Table 1. Comparing the algorithms

Dataset	Local Bagging DS	Local DS	50NN	Kstar	Bagging DS	Boosting DS	Logit-Boost DS
anneal	99,48	99,34	91,18 *	95,69 *	82,96 *	83,63 *	99,29
autos	76,37	74,82	48,18 *	72,01	44,95 *	44,9 *	81,47
badges	99,93	100	99,69	90,27 *	100	100	100
breast-c	73,66	72,68	70,75	73,73	73,38	71,55	68,62 *
breast-w	96,45	96,4	95,9	95,35	92,56 *	95,28	95,94
colic	81,77	80,87	84,04	75,71 *	81,52	82,72	82,15
credit-a	85,01	83,61	86,16	79,1 *	85,51	85,57	86,32
Credit-g	73,68	71,02 *	71,96	70,17 *	70 *	72,6	74,84
diabetes	74,54	73,2	74,68	70,19 *	72,45	75,37	75,09
Glass	70,96	70,58	56,16 *	75,31	45,08 *	44,89 *	72,52
haberman	71,18	69,81	72,91	70,27	73,07	74,06	72,73
heart-c	80,97	78,29	81,58	75,18 *	75,26	83,11	79,98
heart-h	79,69	79,17	83,98 v	77,83	81,41	82,42	80,72
heart-statlog	78,07	76,33	83,74 v	76,44	75,33	81,81	81,63
hepatitis	84,59	83,04	79,38 *	80,17	80,61	81,5	82,49
ionosphere	88,89	88,24	71,65 *	84,64 *	82,66 *	92,34 v	92,19
iris	93,87	94	90,53	94,67	68,87 *	95,07	93,53
kr-vs-kp	98,51	98,45	91,07 *	96,91 *	66,05 *	95,08 *	94,69 *
labor	87,57	85,3	64,67 *	92,03	81,97	90,57	91,37
lymphography	80,78	76,67	80,59	85,08	74,5	75,44	83,33
monk1	79,8	77,22	59,8 *	80,27	73,41 *	69,79 *	71,85 *
monk3	93,45	93,44	82,46 *	86,22 *	82,41 *	90,92	92,47
Nursery	97,75	97,52 *	96,05 *	96,88 *	66,25 *	66,25 *	91,6 *
primary-tumor	43,98	43,22	39,26	38,02 *	28,91 *	28,91 *	45,67
segment	96,97	96,68	90,43 *	97,09	56,54 *	28,52 *	97,16
sick	97,46	97,64	94,84 *	95,72 *	96,55 *	97,07	97,85
sonar	82,21	76,62 *	68,25 *	85,11	73,21 *	81,06	81,45
soybean	93,05	92,56	62,34 *	87,97 *	27,83 *	27,96 *	93,5
splice	91,65	89,6 *	88,89 *	78,84 *	62,38 *	86,24 *	95,81 v
titanci	78,99	79,05	77,56 *	77,56 *	77,6 *	77,83	77,83
vehicle	71,47	69,58	63,47 *	70,22	40,14 *	39,81 *	74,36
vote	95,72	95,4	90,41 *	93,22 *	95,63	96,41	96,39
wine	97,8	96,79	96,46	98,72	86,27 *	91,57 *	97,4
zoo	90,11	88,84	55,11 *	96,03 v	60,53 *	60,43 *	94,09
W/D/L		*0/30/4*	*2/13/19*	*1/16/17*	*0/13/21*	*1/20/13*	*1/29/4*

speak of two results for a dataset as being "significant different" if the difference is statistical significant at the 5% level according to the corrected resampled t-test [17], with each pair of data points consisting of the estimates obtained in one of the 100 folds for the two learning methods being compared. On the other hand, "*" indicates that proposed ensemble performed statistically better than the specific algorithm according to t-test with $p<0.05$. In all the other cases, there is no significant statistical difference between the results (Draws). In the last row of the table one can also see the aggregated results in the form (α/b/c). In this notation "α" means that the proposed ensemble is significantly less accurate than the compared algorithm in α out of 34 datasets, "c" means that the proposed algorithm is significantly more accurate than the compared algorithm in c out of 34 datasets, while in the remaining cases (b), there is no significant statistical difference.

In the last raw of the Table 1 one can see the aggregated results. The proposed ensemble is significantly more accurate than simple Bagging DS in 21 out of the 34 datasets, whilst it has significantly higher error rate in none dataset. In addition, the presented ensemble is significantly more accurate than single Local DS in 4 out of the 34 datasets, while it has significantly higher error rate in none dataset. What is more, the proposed ensemble is significantly more accurate than 50NN and Kstar in 19 and 17 out of the 34 datasets, respectively, whilst it has significantly higher error rate in 2 and 1 datasets. Furthermore, Adaboost DS and Logitboost DS have significantly lower error rates in 1 dataset than the proposed ensemble, whereas they are significantly less accurate in 13 and 4 datasets, respectively.

5 Conclusion

Local techniques are an old idea in time series prediction [3]. Local learning can reduce the complexity of component classifiers and improve the generalization performance although the global complexity of the system can not be guaranteed to be low. In this paper we proposed the local bagging of decision stumps and our experiment for some real datasets shows that the proposed combining method outperforms other well known combining methods that use the same base learner.

The benefit of allowing multiple local models is somewhat offset by the cost of storing and querying the training dataset for each test example that means that instance based learners do not scale well for the large amount of data. Local weighted learning algorithms must often decide what instances to store for use during generalization in order to avoid excessive storage and time complexity. By eliminating a set of examples from a database the response time for classification decisions will decrease, as fewer instances are examined when a query example is presented.

In a following work we will focus on the problem of reducing the size of the stored set of examples while trying to maintain or even improve generalization accuracy by avoiding noise and overfitting. In the articles [6] and [18] numerous instance selection methods can be found that can be combined with local boosting technique. It must be also mentioned that we will use local bagging with other weak base classifiers such as Naive Bayes.

References

1. Aha, D., Lazy Learning. Dordrecht: Kluwer Academic Publishers, (1997).
2. Atkeson, C. G., Moore, A. W. and Schaal, S., Locally weighted learning for control. Artificial Intelligence Review, 11 (1997) 75–113.
3. Atkeson, C. G., Moore, A. W. and Schaal, S., Locally weighted learning. Artificial Intelligence Review, 11 (1997) 11-73.
4. Blake, C. & Merz, C., UCI Repository of machine learning databases. Irvine, CA: University of California, Department of Information and Computer Science. [http://www.ics.uci.edu/~mlearn/MLRepository.html] (1998)
5. Bauer, E. and Kohavi, R., An empirical comparison of voting classification algorithms: Bagging, boosting and variants. Machine Learning, 36 (1999) 525–536.
6. Brighton, H., Mellish, C., Advances in Instance Selection for Instance-Based Learning Algorithms, Data Mining and Knowledge Discovery, 6 (2002) 153–172.
7. Bottou, L. and Vapnik, V., Local learning algorithm, Neural Computation, vol. 4, no. 6, (1992) 888-901.
8. Breiman, L., Bagging Predictors. Machine Learning, 24 (1996) 123-140.
9. Cohen S. and Intrator N., Automatic Model Selection in a Hybrid Perceptron/ Radial Network. In Multiple Classifier Systems. 2nd International Workshop, MCS 2001, pages 349–358.
10. John, C. and Trigg, L., K*: An Instance- based Learner Using an Entropic Distance Measure", Proc. of the 12th International Conference on ML, (1995) 108-114.
11. Frank, E., Hall, M., Pfahringer, B., Locally weighted naive Bayes. Proc. of the 19th Conference on Uncertainty in Artificial Intelligence. Acapulco, Mexico. Morgan Kaufmann, (2003).
12. Freund, Y. and Schapire, R., Experiments with a New Boosting Algorithm, Proc. ICML'96, (1996) 148-156.
13. Friedman, J. H., Hastie, T., Tibshirani. R., Additive logistic regression: A statistical view of boosting. The Annals of Statistics, 28 (2000) 337 – 374.
14. Iba, W. & Langley, P., Induction of one-level decision trees. Proc. of the Ninth International Machine Learning Conference (1992). Aberdeen, Scotland: Morgan Kaufmann.
15. Kleinberg, E.M., A Mathematically Rigorous Foundation for Supervised Learning. In J. Kittler and F. Roli, editors, Multiple Classifier Systems. First International Workshop, MCS 2000, Cagliari, Italy, volume 1857 of Lecture Notes in Computer Science, pages 67–76. Springer-Verlag, (2000).
16. Nadeau, C., Bengio, Y., Inference for the Generalization Error. Machine Learning, 52 (2003) 239-281.
17. Vapnik, V.N., Statistical Learning Theory, Wiley, New York, (1998).
18. Wilson, D., Martinez, T., Reduction Techniques for Instance-Based Learning Algorithms, Machine Learning, 38 (2000) 257–286.
19. Witten, I., Frank, E., Data Mining: Practical Machine Learning Tools and Techniques with Java Implementations. Morgan Kaufmann, San Mateo, CA, (2000.)

Methods for Classifying Spot Welding Processes: A Comparative Study of Performance

Eija Haapalainen, Perttu Laurinen, Heli Junno,
Lauri Tuovinen, and Juha Röning

Intelligent Systems Group, Department of Electrical and Information Engineering,
PO BOX 4500, FIN-90014 University of Oulu, Finland
{Eija.Haapalainen, Perttu.Laurinen, Heli.Junno,
Lauri.Tuovinen, Juha.Roning}@ee.oulu.fi

Abstract. Resistance spot welding is an important and widely used method for joining metal objects. In this paper, various classification methods for identifying welding processes are evaluated. Using process identification, a similar process for a new welding experiment can be found among the previously run processes, and the process parameters leading to high-quality welding joints can be applied. With this approach, good welding results can be obtained right from the beginning, and the time needed for the set-up of a new process can be substantially reduced. In addition, previous quality control methods can also be used for the new process. Different classifiers are tested with several data sets consisting of statistical and geometrical features extracted from current and voltage signals recorded during welding. The best feature set - classifier combination for the data used in this study is selected. Finally, it is concluded that welding processes can be identified almost perfectly by certain features.

1 Introduction

Resistance spot welding is one of the most important methods for joining metal objects. It is in widespread use in, for example, the automotive and electrical industries, where more than 100 million spot welding joints are produced daily in the European vehicle industry only [19].

Different combinations of welding machines used and materials welded constitute distinctive welding processes. In other words, welding processes could also be called production batches. In this study, various classification methods for identifying welding processes were examined for potential use in the quality control of spot welding.

The research done in the field until now has concentrated on quality estimation of individual welding spots, and typically, only one welding process at a time has been considered. The objective of our research, however, has been to utilise information collected from previously run processes to produce new welding spots of good quality. For this purpose, process classification is needed. In this paper, the aim is to search for viable features for classification and to

M. Ali and F. Esposito (Eds.): IEA/AIE 2005, LNAI 3533, pp. 412–421, 2005.

find the classifier that would give the best results in classifying welding processes. This study is a follow-up on a previous article by the authors, in which self-organising maps were used to identify welding processes [10]. The main advantage of self-organising maps was the graphical visualisation of the results they provided. However, as the number of processes used in the study increased, self-organising maps turned out inadequate as a classification method. Therefore, the benefit of easy visualisation was dropped, and the suitability of other classification methods was examined.

The aim of this study was to compare the characteristics of a sample from a new welding process to information collected from previously run processes to find a similar process. After that, the process parameters of the previous process already proven to lead to high-quality welding joints can also be applied to the new process. With this approach, good welding results can be achieved right from the beginning, and the time needed for the set-up of a new process can be significantly reduced. In addition, if a similar process is found, the quality control methods that proved viable for that process can also be used for the new process.

The research on computational quality assessment techniques in resistance spot welding has concentrated on quality estimation using neural networks and regression analysis. Artificial neural networks and regression models have been generated based on variation of resistance over time by, for example, [1] and [2]. In addition, studies using self-organising maps [9] and Bayesian networks [13] have been made. Self-organising maps have also been used for the detection and visualisation of process drifts by [20].

In this paper, the term 'process' is used differently from the previous studies discussing process control of spot welding. In our study, the properties of welding experiments that distinguish the different processes are the welding machine used, the materials welded and the thicknesses of the materials. However, changes in current, electrode force and electrode wear are thought to be internal changes of processes. In other studies, the term is used to refer precisely to the internal changes, including differences in electrode wear or shunting [15].

In addition, the term 'process identification' can be misunderstood. In our study, the term refers to the effort of finding similar processes stored in a database, whereas in some other application areas, such as the studies of [12] and [6], the term is used to refer to the development of mathematical models for processes.

In this paper, different classifiers are evaluated for their suitability to process identification. Welding samples are described using various geometrical and statistical features that are calculated from current and voltage signals recorded during welding. The features were chosen so as to represent the characteristics of the curves as precisely as possible.

2 The Data

The data used in this study were supplied by two welding equipment manufacturers. There are altogether 20 processes, of which 11 have been welded at

a)

b)

Fig. 1. a) Metal objects are joined using resistance spot welding. b) An example of a welded part

Harms+Wende GmbH & Co.KG [7] and 9 at Stanzbiegetechnik [18]. A total of 3879 welding experiments were covered. The experiments were done by welding two metal objects together using a resistance spot welding machine, (Fig. 1a)). An example of a welded part is shown in Fig. 1b). Each of the observations contains measurements of current and voltage signals recorded during the welding. The signals were measured at a sampling frequency of 25600 Hz.

The raw signal curves contained plenty of oscillatory motion and a pre-heating section, and they were therefore pre-processed before further processing. The pre-heating parts of the curves were cut off, so that all that remained was the signal curves recorded during the actual welding phase. In addition, the curves were smoothened using the Reinsch algorithm [16], [17]. An example of a signal curve before and after pre-processing is shown in Fig. 2.

a) b)

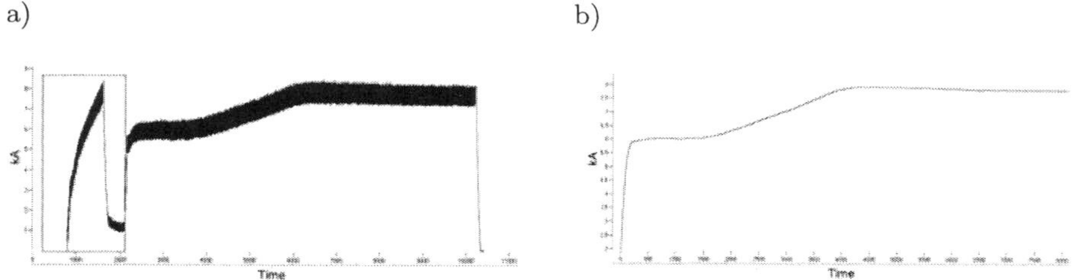

Fig. 2. a) A raw signal curve. The pre-processing section is outlined with a rectangle. b) The same curve after pre-processing

3 The Features

Since it was not feasible to use all the data points of the two signal curves relating to a single welding experiment in the classification, a more compact way to describe the characteristics of a curve had to be developed. This was resolved by extracting geometrical and statistical features of the curves. The geometrical features were chosen to locate the transition points of the curve as precisely as possible. The statistical features included the median of the signal, and the arithmetic means of the signal values calculated on four different intervals based on the transition points. In addition, the signal curve was divided into ten intervals of equal length, and the means of the signal values within these intervals were used as features. There were altogether 12 geometrical and 15 statistical features. The features extracted are demonstrated in Figs. 3 and 4.

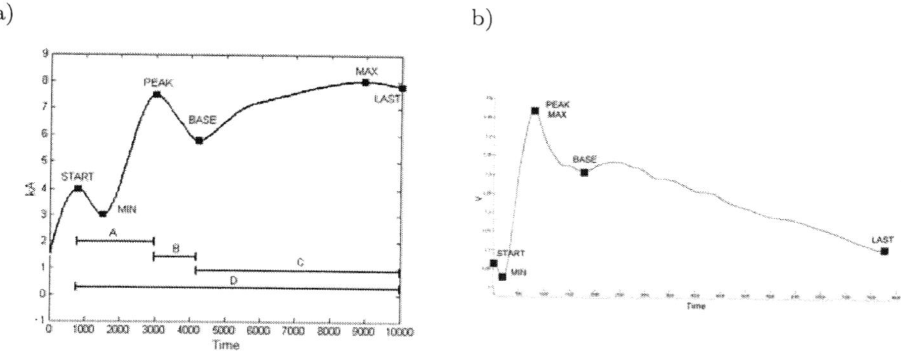

Fig. 3. a) The geometrical features on an artificial voltage curve. b) An example of how the geometrical features often partially overlap in practice. On this voltage curve, the features 'peak' and 'max' overlap

In practice, it often happens that some of the geometrical features overlap, and that the overlapping features vary from one curve to another. However, this can also be regarded as a characteristic of the curve. In Fig. 3a) all the geometrical features are demonstrated on an artificial curve simulating the real data. On this curve, the features do not overlap, but in other respects the curve is notably similar to genuine signal curves. Figure 3b) shows an example of the features calculated on a real signal curve. In Fig. 4, the calculation of the ten means is demonstrated.

Eight data sets were formed out of the feature data to be tested with the classifiers. The first set contained all of the features, while the second consisted of only the ten means. Since the number of features was rather high, and it was not known for sure that all of them contained information relevant to the classification, the feature data were compressed using principal component analysis (PCA). The aim was to pack most of the classification-related information into a relatively small number of features, to reduce the dimension of the feature space. This was done for both of these data sets, and two more sets were thereby obtained. Finally, the last four data sets were obtained by normalising each of the previous sets to have an average of zero and a standard deviation of one.

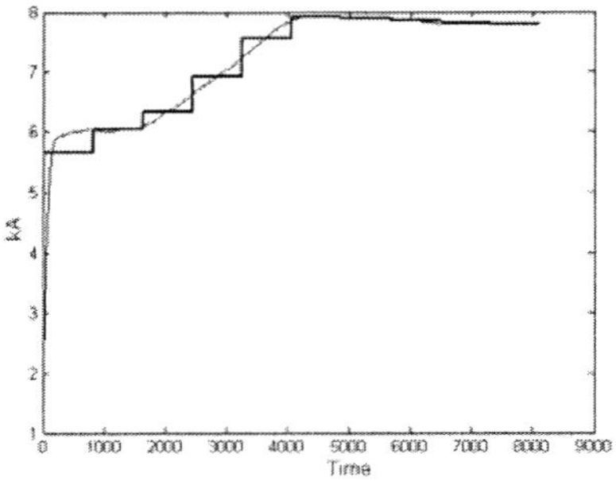

Fig. 4. Ten means of a current curve calculated on intervals of equal length

4 Classification Methods

Classification of the welding processes was carried out using five different classifiers. Since the distribution of the data was unknown, different types of classifiers were tested. The classifiers were chosen to represent both parametric and non-parametric methods. *Quadratic Discriminant Analysis* (QDA), *Linear Discriminant Analysis* (LDA) and *Mahalanobis Discrimination* (abbreviated as MD) are applications of the Bayes theorem. They model the class-conditional densities parametrically as multivariate normals.

QDA is based on the assumption that the samples originating from class j are normally distributed with mean vector μ_j and covariance matrix Σ_j. The classification rule is

$$g_{QDA}(x) = \underset{j=1,\dots,c}{\arg\max}\Big[-\frac{1}{2}\ln|\hat{\Sigma}_j| - \frac{1}{2}(x-\hat{\mu}_j)^T\hat{\Sigma}_j^{-1}(x-\hat{\mu}_j) + \ln\hat{P}_j\Big], \quad (1)$$

where the estimates $\hat{\mu}_j$ and $\hat{\Sigma}_j$ are the sample mean and the sample covariance of the vectors originating from class j, respectively. The a priori probabilities P_j are estimated by $\hat{P}_j = n_j/n$, where n_j denotes the number of class-j observations, and n is the total number of training samples.

In LDA, too, the different classes are assumed to be normally distributed with different mean vectors. However, covariances are now assumed to be equal, and the LDA rule is of the form

$$g_{LDA}(x) = \underset{j=1,\dots,c}{\arg\max}\Big[\hat{\mu}_j^T\hat{\Sigma}^{-1}(x - \frac{1}{2}\hat{\mu}_j) + \hat{P}_j\Big], \quad (2)$$

where $\hat{\Sigma} = \sum_{j=1}^{c}\hat{P}_j\hat{\Sigma}_j$. These classifiers are introduced in more detail in [4] and [8].

MD is similar to the previous methods, with the exception that the a priori probabilities are assumed to be identical, and the classification is performed merely based on squared Mahalanobis distances $(x-\hat{\mu}_j)^T\hat{\Sigma}_j^{-1}(x-\hat{\mu}_j)$.

The other two classification methods used in this study were the *k-nearest neighbour classifier* (kNN) [3] (with a small value of the parameter k) and *Learn-*

ing Vector Quantization (LVQ) [11]. These non-parametric methods are based on modelling of the classes using prototypes. In the case of LVQ the classification is performed according to the shortest distance to a prototype and in the case of kNN according to the shortest distances to k prototypes, respectively. The prototypes of kNN consist simply of the training vectors, whereas in LVQ the prototypes are composed of a more compact set of vectors formed from the training samples. There exist several variations of the LVQ algorithm that differ in the way the prototype vectors are updated.

In order to evaluate the classifiers, the data were divided into training and test data sets, which consisted of 2/3 and 1/3 of the data, respectively. The training data set was used to train each of the classifiers, and the test data set was used to evaluate their performance.

Before the actual classification, suitable initial parameter values for the kNN and LVQ classifiers had to be discovered. For the kNN classifier, the best value of the parameter k and the number of principal components used was sought out using tenfold cross-validation of the training data. In Fig. 5a), a surface plot of the results of the cross-validation is shown for one of the feature sets. It can be read from the plot that classification accuracy does not improve substantially after the inclusion of the five principal components. Likewise, it can be seen that the value 3 of the parameter k yields good results in the classification. The results for the other feature sets are similar.

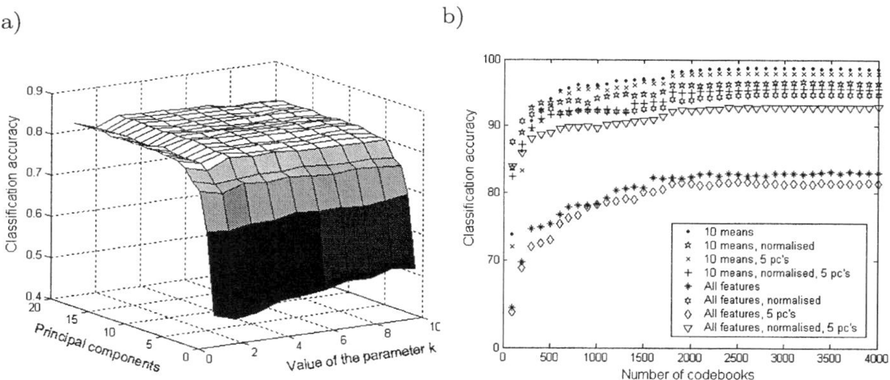

Fig. 5. a) A surface plot of the results of tenfold cross-validation of the parameter k and the number of principal components used. b) Results of tenfold cross-validation of the number of LVQ codebook vectors for the different feature sets

The number of LVQ prototype vectors, called codebooks, was also determined by tenfold cross-validation of the training data. The results are shown in Fig. 5b). It can be seen how an increase in the number of codebook vectors affects the accuracy of classification. The parameter value 2200 was selected because it seems to yield good classification results for all data sets.

5 Results

The classifiers were tested with the eight data sets, and the results for the test data are shown in Table 1. The percentages in the cells indicate the ratios of correctly classified processes; the cells left empty indicate invalid classifier - feature set combinations.

Classification accuracy appeared to be dependent on both the feature set and the classifier used. QDA seems to yield better classification results than LDA, and it can thus be concluded that the data support rather quadratic than linear decision boundaries. In addition, the MD method that classifies merely on the grounds of Mahalanobis distances performs approximately equally well as QDA. However, none of these classifiers compare with the two prototype classifiers, kNN and LVQ.

The kNN and LVQ classifiers gave the best classification results, and they performed approximately equally well. The performance of the three parametric methods was, generally speaking, inferior to that of the non-parametric ones. This can be explained by the diversity of the data. The non-parametric methods

Table 1. Comparison of classification accuracies for the 20 processes with different classifiers and feature sets. LDA = linear discriminant analysis, QDA = quadratic discriminant analysis, MD = Mahalanobis discrimination, kNN = k-nearest neighbours classifier and LVQ = learning vector quantization

	LDA	**QDA**	**MD**	**kNN, k = 3**	**LVQ,** 2200 **codebooks**
All features	92.96	-	-	84.13	84.52
All features, 5 pc's	62.46	75.23	72.37	83.20	82.51
All features, normalised	92.96	-	-	94.74	94.89
All features, normalised, 5 pc's	71.05	85.45	86.30	93.50	92.41
10 means	90.87	96.36	97.14	**98.53**	**98.07**
10 means, 5 pc's	82.12	94.27	94.35	97.76	97.06
10 means, normalised	90.87	96.36	97.14	95.43	96.13
10 means, normalised, 5 pc's	76.16	89.32	88.31	94.58	94.12

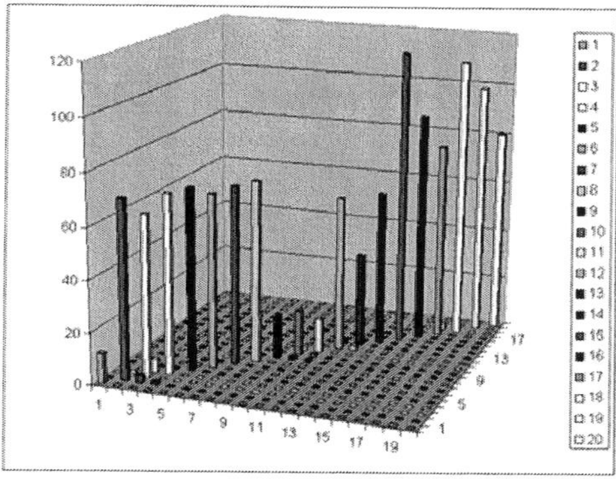

Fig. 6. A 3-D bar chart visualising the confusion matrix of the kNN ($k = 3$) classifier

performed better because they do not have any assumptions concerning the distribution of the data. These five classifiers tested yielded excellent process identification results, and there was hence no need to expand the study to other classifiers.

The kNN classifier turned out most suitable for this study due to its easy implementation in contrast to the LVQ classifier. The kNN classifier with 10 signal means as features was chosen as the best classifier - feature set combination with classification accuracy of over 98 %. Detailed results of the kNN (k=3) classifier for the 20 processes are shown in the 3-D bar chart of Fig. 6, which illustrates the confusion matrix of the test data.

6 Conclusions

Various classification methods were evaluated for the identification of resistance spot welding processes. Signal curves recorded during welding were preprocessed, and a number of statistical and geometrical features were extracted. The features were chosen to describe the characteristics of the curves as precisely as possible. Different combinations of the features were tested with all the classifiers. It was discovered that the kNN and LVQ classifiers yielded the best classification results with classification accuracy of over 98 %. After this, it was concluded that the kNN classifier was most suitable for this classification task. The best classification results were obtained using a data set consisting of means of the signal curves calculated on ten intervals of equal length. In the future, the work on process identification will be continued with classification of experiments that originate from processes not represented in the training data. In addition, the results of this study will be put to use on real spot welding production lines.

Acknowledgments

We would like to express our gratitude to our colleagues at Fachochschule Karlsruhe, Institut fr Innovation und Transfer, in Stanzbiegetechnik and in Harms + Wende GmbH & Co.KG for providing the data set and the expertise needed at the different steps of the research project and for numerous other things that made it possible to accomplish this work. Furthermore, this study has been carried out with financial support from the Commission of the European Communities, specific RTD programme "Competitive and Sustainable Growth", G1ST-CT-2002-50245, "SIOUX" (Intelligent System for Dynamic Online Quality Control of Spot Welding Processes for Cross(X)-Sectoral Applications). It does not necessarily reflect the views of the Commission and in no way anticipates the Commission's future policy in this area. Finally, we would like to thank Professor Lasse Holmström at the Department of Mathematical Sciences at the University of Oulu for the many words of advice and the ideas he has contributed to our study.

References

1. Aravinthan, A., Sivayoganathan, K., Al-Dabass, D., Balendran, V.: A Neural Network System for Spot Weld Strength Prediction. UKSIM2001, Conference Proceedings of the UK Simulation Society (2001) 156–160
2. Cho, Y., Rhee, S.: Primary Circuit Dynamic Resistance Monitoring and Its Application on Quality Estimation During Resistance Spot Welding. Welding Researcher (2002) 104-111
3. Devijver, P.A., Kittler, J.: Pattern Recognition - A Statistical approach. Prentice-Hall, London (1982)
4. Duda, R.O., Hart, P.E., Stork, D.G.: Pattern Classification. John Wiley & Sons, Inc., New York (2001)
5. Fachochschule Karlsruhe. <http://www.fh-karlsruhe.de/>, [Homepage of the University] (Referenced 3.11.2004)
6. Haesloop, D., Holt, B.R.: Neural Networks for Process Identification. IJCNN, International Joint Conference on Neural Networks **3** (1990) 429-434
7. Harms+Wende GmbH & Co.KG, <http://www.harms-wende.de>, 2004
8. Holmström, L., Koistinen, P., Laaksonen, J., Oja, E.,: Neural and Statistical Classifiers – Taxonomy and Two Case Studies. IEEE Transactions on Neural Networks **8**(1) (1997) 5–17
9. Junno, H., Laurinen, P., Tuovinen, L., Röning, J.: Studying the Quality of Resistance Spot Welding Joints Using Self-Organising Maps. Proceedings of the Fourth International ICSC Symposium on Engineering of Intelligent Systems (2004)
10. Junno, H., Laurinen, P., Haapalainen, E., Tuovinen, L., Röning, J., Zettel, D., Sampaio, D., Link, N., Peschl, M.: Resistance Spot Welding Process Identification and Initialization Based on Self-Organising Maps. Proceedings of the 1st International Conference on Informatics in Control, Automation and Robotics. **1** (2004) 296–299
11. Kohonen, T.,: Self-Organizing Maps. 2nd edition. Springer-Verlag, New York Berlin Heidelberg (1997)

12. Kulessky, R., Nudelman, G., Zimin, M.: Digital Electropneumatic Control System of Power Boiler Processes. Process Identification and Motion Optimization. Nineteenth Convention of Electrical and Electronics Engineers in Israel (1996) 507–510
13. Laurinen, P., Junno, H., Tuovinen, L., Röning, J.: Studying the Quality of Resistance Spot Welding Joints Using Bayesian Networks. Proceedings of Artificial Intelligence and Applications (2004) 705–711
14. McLachlan G.J.: Discriminant Analysis and Statistical Pattern Recognition. John Wiley & Sons, Inc., New York, (1992)
15. Mintz, D., Wen, J.T.: Process Monitoring and Control for Robotic Resistive Welding. Proceedings of the 4th IEEE Conference on Control Applications (28-29 Sept. 1995) 1126–1127
16. Reinsch C.H.: Smoothing by Spline Functions. Numerische Matematik **10** (1967) 177–183
17. Reinsch C.H.: Smoothing by Spline Functions, II. Numerische Matematik **16** (1971) 451–454
18. Stanzbiegetechnik, <http://www.stanzbiegetechnik.at>, [Web site of SBT] (Referenced 18.2.2004)
19. TWI World Centre for Materials Joining Technology: Resistance Spot Welding (Knowledge Summary), [www document], <http://www.twi.co.uk/j32k/protected/band_3/kssaw001.html> (Referenced 3.11.2004)
20. Zettel, D., Sampaio, D., Link, N., Braun, A., Peschl, M., Junno, H.: A Self Organising Map (SOM) Sensor for the Detection, Visualisation and Analysis of Process Drifts. Poster Proceedings of the 27th Annual German Conference on Artificial Intelligence (2004) 175–188

Minimum Spanning Trees in Hierarchical Multiclass Support Vector Machines Generation

Ana Carolina Lorena and André C.P.L.F. de Carvalho

Instituto de Ciências Matemáticas e de Computação (ICMC),
Universidade de São Paulo (USP),
Av. do Trabalhador São-Carlense, 400 - Centro - Cx. Postal 668,
São Carlos - São Paulo, Brazil
{aclorena, andre}@icmc.usp.br

Abstract. Support Vector Machines constitute a powerful Machine Learning technique originally designed for the solution of 2-class problems. In multiclass applications, many works divide the whole problem in multiple binary subtasks, whose results are then combined. This paper introduces a new framework for multiclass Support Vector Machines generation from binary predictors. Minimum Spanning Trees are used in the obtainment of a hierarchy of binary classifiers composing the multiclass solution. Different criteria were tested in the tree design and the results obtained evidence the efficiency of the proposed approach, which is able to produce good hierarchical multiclass solutions in polynomial time.

Keywords: Machine Learning, multiclass classification, Support Vector Machines.

1 Introduction

Multiclass classification using Machine Learning (ML) techniques consists of inducing a function $f(\mathbf{x})$ from a dataset composed of pairs $(\mathbf{x}_i, y_i)$ where $y_i \in \{1, \ldots, k\}$. Some learning methods are originally binary, being able to carry out classifications where $k = 2$. Among such methods, one can mention Support Vector Machines (SVMs) [5].

To generalize SVMs to multiclass problems, several strategies have been proposed [2, 4, 6, 8, 12, 15]. A standard method is the one-against-all (1AA) approach, in which k binary classifiers are built, each being responsible to separate a class i from the remaining classes [5]. Other common extension is known as all-against-all (AAA). In this case, given a problem with k classes, $k(k-1)/2$ classifiers are constructed, each one distinguishing a pair of classes i, j [8]. In another front, Dietterich and Bariki [6] suggested the use of error-correcting output codes (ECOC) to represent each class in the problem. Binary classifiers are then trained to learn these codes.

Several works also explored the combination of binary SVMs in a hierarchical structure. Among them, one can mention the DAGSVM approach [9], used

M. Ali and F. Esposito (Eds.): IEA/AIE 2005, LNAI 3533, pp. 422–431, 2005.

in the combination of pairwise classifiers, and the Divide-by-2 (DB2) method [15], which hierarchically divides the data into two subsets until all classes are associated to independent sets.

This work introduces the use of Minimum Spanning Trees (MST) in the generation of hierarchical multiclass SVM classifiers. Initially, information collected from data is used to build a weighted graph with k nodes, corresponding to the k classes in the problem. A MST algorithm is then applied to find a connected acyclic subgraph that spans all nodes with the smallest total cost of arcs [1]. The hierarchies of classes are found during the MST algorithm application, so that classes considered closest to each other are iteratively grouped.

This paper is structured as follows: Section 2 presents a brief description of the SVM technique. Section 3 describes some of the main developments in the multiclass SVM literature. Section 4 introduces the use of MSTs in multiclass SVM generation. Section 5 presents some experimental results, which are discussed on Section 6. Section 7 concludes this paper.

2 Support Vector Machines

Support Vector Machines (SVMs) represent a learning technique based on the Statistical Learning Theory [14]. Given a dataset with n samples $(\mathbf{x}_i, y_i)$, where each $\mathbf{x}_i \in \Re^m$ is a data sample and $y_i \in \{-1, +1\}$ corresponds to $\mathbf{x}_i$'s label, this technique looks for an hyperplane $(\mathbf{w} \cdot \mathbf{x} + b = 0)$ able of separating data from different classes with a maximal margin. In order to perform this task, it solves the following optimization problem:

$$\textbf{Minimize: } \|\mathbf{w}\|^2 + C \sum_{i=1}^{n} \xi_i$$

$$\textbf{Restricted to: } \begin{cases} \xi_i \geq 0 \\ y_i \left(\mathbf{w} \cdot \mathbf{x}_\mathrm{i} + b\right) \geq 1 - \xi_i \end{cases}$$

where C is a constant that imposes a tradeoff between training error and generalization and the ξ_i are slack variables. The former variables relax the restrictions imposed to the optimization problem, allowing some patterns to be within the margins and also some training errors.

The classifier obtained is given by Equation 1.

$$f\left(\mathbf{x}\right) = \mathrm{sign}\left(\sum_{\mathbf{x}_i \in \mathrm{SV}} y_i \alpha_i \mathbf{x}_i \cdot \mathbf{x} + b\right) \tag{1}$$

where the constants α_i are called Lagrange multipliers and are determined in the optimization process. SV corresponds to the set of support vectors, patterns for which the associated Lagrange multipliers are larger than zero. These samples are those closest to the optimal hyperplane. For all other patterns the associated Lagrange multiplier is null.

The classifier represented in Equation 1 is restricted by the fact that it performs a linear separation of data. In the case a non-linear separation of the dataset is needed, its data samples are mapped to a high-dimensional space. In this space, also named feature space, the dataset can be separated by a linear SVM with a low training error. This mapping process is performed with the use of Kernel functions, which compute dot products between any pair of patterns in the feature space in a simple way. Thus, the only modification necessary to deal with non-linearity with SVMs is to substitute any dot product among patterns by a Kernel function. A frequently used Kernel function is the Gaussian or RBF function, illustrated by Equation 2.

$$K(\mathbf{x}_i, \mathbf{x}_j) = \exp(-\sigma \|\mathbf{x}_i - \mathbf{x}_j\|^2) \tag{2}$$

3 Multiclass SVMs

As described in the previous section, SVMs were originally formulated for the solution of problems with two classes (+1 and -1, respectively). In order to extend them to multiclass problems, several strategies have been proposed.

The most straightforward of them is the one-against-all (1AA) decomposition. Given k classes, its principle lies in generating k binary predictors, each being responsible to distinguish a class i from the remaining classes. The final prediction is usually given by the classifier with the highest output value [14].

Another standard methodology, named all-against-all (AAA), consists of building $k(k-1)/2$ predictors, each differentiating a pair of classes i and j, with $i < j$. For combining these classifiers, a majority voting scheme can be applied [8]. Each AAA classifier gives one vote to its preferred class. The final result is then given by the class with most of the votes.

In an alternative strategy, Dietterich and Bariki [6] proposed the use of a distributed output code to represent the k classes associated with the problem. For each class, a codeword of length l is assigned. Frequently, the size of the codewords has more bits than needed in order to represent each class uniquely. The additional bits can be used to correct eventual classification errors. For this reason, this method is named error-correcting output coding (ECOC). A new pattern $\mathbf{x}$ can be classified by evaluating the predictions of the l classifiers, which generate a string s of length l. This string is then compared to the codeword associated to each class. The sample is assigned to the class whose codeword is closest according to a given distance measure. This process is also refered as decoding.

Several works also suggest the combination of binary SVMs in a hierarchical structure. Two examples of hierarchical classifiers for a problem with five classes are presented in Figure 1. In these predictors, each level distinguishes two subsets of classes. Based on the decision of previous levels new nodes are visited, until a leaf node is reached, where the final classification is given. In general, it can be stated that the hierarchical approaches have faster prediction times, since usually a lower number of classifiers need to be consulted for each prediction.

Figure 1a shows the representation of a Decision Directed Acyclic Graph SVM (DAGSVM) [9], used as an alternative combination of binary classifiers generated by AAA. Each node of the graph corresponds to one binary classifier for a pair of classes.

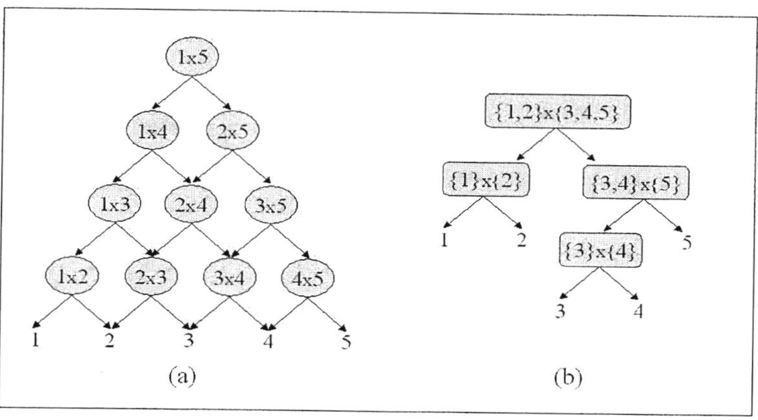

Fig. 1. Two examples of hierarchical classifiers for a problem with five classes

Figure 1b presents a binary tree hierarchical approach. Each node distinguishes two subsets of one or more classes. It should be noticed that a lower number of binary classifiers are induced in this case ($k-1$), so the time spent on the training of SVM classifiers is also reduced. This scheme is followed by the works of [12], [4] and [15]. They differenciate on the way the binary partitions of classes in each level of the tree are obtained.

In [12], the generation of the class hierarchies used the concept of confusion classes, which can be defined as subsets of classes whose patterns are similar. These classes were defined using the k-means algorithm.

In [4], a Kernel based SOM (KSOM) was used in the convertion of the multiclass problem into binary hierarchies. Two methods were then employed in the analysis of the results produced by the KSOM. In the first one, they were plotted on a 2-dimensional space and a human drawed lines separating the classes in two groups with minimum confusion. The second method made use of automatic grouping, maximizing a scattering measure calculated from the data. Overlaps between groups of classes were allowed, so the number of binary classifiers induced in this case can be higher than $k-1$.

In [15], the authors proposed a hierarchical technique named Divide-by-2 (DB2) and suggested three methods to divide the multiclass dataset hierarchically. The first one considers the application of the k-means algorithm. The second generates the hierarchies following a spherical shell approach. The third method considers the differences in the number of patterns between two subsets of classes, choosing partitions from the classes that minimize these differences. The authors pointed that the last method is useful either if the processing time has high importance or if the dataset has a skewed class distribution.

Using concepts from some of the previous works, this paper presents an alternative strategy for obtaining binary partitions of classes. The proposed strategy is described next.

4 Minimum Spanning Tress and Multiclass SVMs

Given an undirected graph $G = (V, E)$ with $|V|$ vertices, $|E|$ edges and a cost or weigth associated to each edge, a Minimum Spanning Tree (MST) T is a connected acyclic subgraph that spans all vertices of G with the smallest total cost of edges [1].

The MST problem can be used as a solution tool in several applications, such as cluster analysis, optimal message passing and data storage reduction [1].

In this work, the MST algorithm was employed as a tool for finding binary partitions of classes in a multiclass learning problem. For such, given a problem with k classes, information collected from the training dataset is used to obtain a weighted graph with k vertices and $k(k-1)/2$ edges connecting all pairs of vertices. Figure 2a illustrates an example of a graph for a problem with five classes, while Figure 2b shows the MST extracted from this graph.

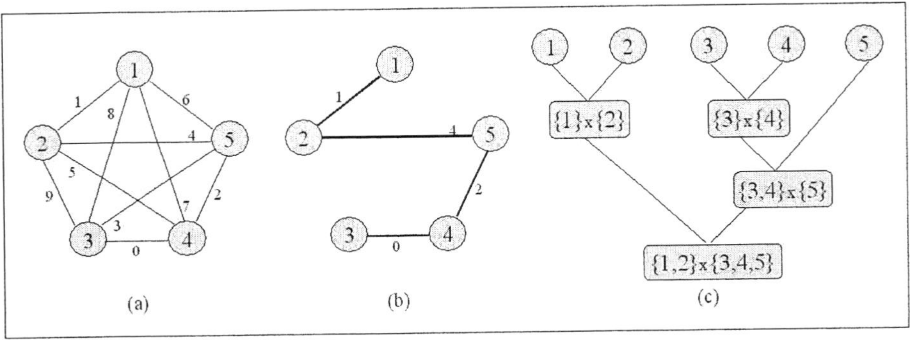

Fig. 2. (a) Graph for a problem with five classes; (b) Minimum Spanning Tree; (c) Multiclass hierarchical structure obtained

Various methods can be used to assign costs to the edges. In this work, the following approaches were investigated:

1. *Centroid distances*: each class is first represented by a centroid $\boldsymbol{\mu}_i$ determined by Equation 3, where $\mathbf{x}_k$ is a data sample and n_i is the number of samples from class i. The weight of an arc (i, j) is then given by the Euclidean distance between the centroids of classes i and j. Using this criterium, the MST will group in each level of the hierarchy subsets of one or more classes that are similar to each other according to their centroid.

$$\boldsymbol{\mu}_i = \frac{1}{n_i} \sum_{k:y_k \in \text{ class } i} \mathbf{x}_k \tag{3}$$

2. *Balanced subsets*: inspired by ideas presented in [15], this criterium acts by grouping classes that have similar data distribution. The weight of an arc (i, j) is then given by the difference among the number of patterns from classes i and j.

3. *Scatter Measure*: using concepts from [4], the weight of an arc (i, j) in this method is given by a scattering measure between classes i and j. This measure is calculated by Equation 4, where $\|\cdot\|^2$ represents the Euclidean norm, and $\mathbf{s}_i^2$ and $\mathbf{s}_j^2$ are the variances of data samples from classes i and j, respectively. The MST will then group classes considered less separated according to the scattering measure calculated.

$$s_m(i,j) = \frac{\left\|\boldsymbol{\mu}_i - \boldsymbol{\mu}_j\right\|^2}{\left\|\mathbf{s}_i^2\right\|^2 + \left\|\mathbf{s}_j^2\right\|^2} \tag{4}$$

Given the obtained weighted graph, an adapted version of the Kruskal algorithm [1] was applied in the multiclass tree determination. Next, a pseudocode of this algorithm is presented. The generation of the hierarchical structure operates in a bottom-up iterative way, as illustrated in Figure 2c for the graph of Figure 2a and MST of Figure 2b.

Multiclass Hierarchical classifier definition with Kruskal algorithm

```
{Given a graph G=(V,E) with |V| vertices and |E| edges};
  1. Sort edges in nondecreasing order
  2. Define sets Si = {Vi} for each vertice Vi
     Add these sets to the multiclass tree MT as leaves
  3. Define i=0 and j=0
  4. while i<|N|-1
     4.1 Take the jth edge acording to the weight ordering
     4.2 If the vertices of edge are in disjoint sets Sp and Sq
         4.2.1 Add a new node to the multiclass tree MT
               (define vertices in Sp as positive class
                and vertices in Sq as negative class)
               (the left branch of the new node must point to the
                tree node containing Sp and the right branch must
                point to tree node with Sq)
         4.2.2 Merge subsets Sp and Sq (Sp = Sp + Sq)
         4.2.3 Remove Sq
         4.2.4 Increment i
     4.3 End if
     4.4 Increment j
   5. end while
   6. return multiclass tree MT
```

The Kruskal algorithm has an $O(|E|+|V|log|V|)$ complexity plus the time for sorting [1]. Using Quick Sort, an average complexity of $O(|E|log|E|)$ is added. The merge of nodes in the multiclass tree can be implemented with $O(|V|log|V|)$. The weight assignment step can be performed in polynomial time. Thus, the proposed algorithm is efficient and allows a totally automatic determination of a multiclass hierarchical classifier structure from binary predictors.

5 Experiments

Three datasets were chosen to evaluate the effectiveness of the proposed multiclass technique. Table 1 describes them, showing for each dataset, the number of training and test samples (♯Train and ♯Test), the number of attributes (continuous and nominal), the number of classes, the average, minimum and maximum number of samples per class in the training set and the baseline error, which is the error rate for a classifier that always predicts the class with most samples.

The first two datasets from Table 1 were downloaded from the UCI benchmark repository. More details about them can be found in [13]. The last one is used for protein structural class prediction and was obtained from `http://www.nersc.gov/protein`. More information about its characteristics can also be found in [7]. All datasets attributes were normalized to null mean and unit variance.

The SVMs inductions were conducted with the LibSVM library [3]. A Gaussian Kernel was used. Different combinations of the C and std parameters were tested, being: $C = [2^{-1}, 2^0, 2^1, \ldots, 2^{12}]$ and $std = [2^{-10}, 2^{-9}, \ldots, 2^{-1}, 2^0]$. This gives a total of 154 combinations of parameters for each dataset. To perform this model selection process, the training datasets were divided with holdout (70% for training and 30% for validation). For each dataset, the hierarchical classifiers were then generated on the new training partition and tested on the validation set for all parameters combination. The (C, std) values were chosen as the ones that lead to maximum accuracy in the validation set. The multiclass hierarchical classifier was then generated using the whole training dataset with the parameters determined and tested on the independent test set. To speed up this model selection process, the same parameters were employed in all binary SVMs induced.

Table 2 shows the results obtained, presenting the best parameters (in parentheses, (C, std)) and also the accuracies of the multiclass classifiers. It also presents the results of 1AA, AAA with majority voting and ECOC decomposition strategies. The same model selection procedure previously described was also applied to these techniques.

The ECOC codes were generated by two criteria. For a number of classes $k \leq 7$, they were given by all $2^{k-1} - 1$ possible binary partitions of the classes. For $k > 7$, a method used in [2] was employed. It consists of examining 10000 random codes of size $\lceil 10\log_2(k) \rceil$ with elements from $\{-1, +1\}$ and choosing

Table 1. Datasets summary description

Dataset	♯Train	♯Test	♯Attributes (cont.,nom.)	♯Class	averag/min/max ♯samp. per class	Baseline Error
optical	3823	1797	64,0	10	382.3/376/389	0.11
satimage	4435	2000	36,0	6	739.2/415/1072	0.24
protein_struc	313	385	126,0	27	78.3/34/115	0.37

Table 2. Results (best rates bold-faced)

	Datasets		
Methods	optical	satimage	protein_struc
1	96.5 $(2^{12}, 2^{-7})$	90.9 $(2^{4}, 2^{-3})$	80.0 $(2^{2}, 2^{-9})$
2	96.9 $(2^{3}, 2^{-6})$	**91.9** $(2^{2}, 2^{-2})$	**83.1** $(2^{3}, 2^{-8})$
3	96.2 $(2^{4}, 2^{-6})$	91.8 $(2^{2}, 2^{-2})$	81.0 $(2^{3}, 2^{-10})$
1AA	**97.4** $(2^{2}, 2^{-6})$	91.4 $(2^{2}, 2^{-2})$	82.9 $(2^{1}, 2^{-8})$
AAA	96.9 $(2^{4}, 2^{-7})$	91.0 $(2^{4}, 2^{-3})$	81.0 $(2^{2}, 2^{-10})$
ECOC	97.3 $(2^{12}, 2^{-10})$	91.4 $(2^{2}, 2^{-2})$	81.0 $(2^{3}, 2^{-8})$

Table 3. Training and test time (train/test) of multiclass strategies (in seconds)

	MST methods			Decomposition Techniques		
Dataset	1	2	3	1AA	AAA	ECOC
optical	7.7/3.0	9.5/4.4	10.7/4.7	17.0/3.1	5.9/3.0	300.4/33.5
satimage	11.9/4.4	19.2/7.7	19.4/8.1	32.7/13.9	9.3/8.4	299.6/132.2
protein_struc	0.4/0.7	0.4/0.6	0.4/0.6	0.7/0.8	0.2/0.6	1.4/1.4

the one with the largest minimum Hamming distance between all pairs of rows and no identical columns. In decodifying the ECOC binary classifiers output, a distance measure proposed in [2] was used. It considers the margins of each SVM classifier in the prediction and was more accurate than Hamming distance in the experiments conducted.

The training and test times for each strategy (not considering the model selection time) were also calculated and are presented on Table 3. All experiments were carried out on a dual Pentium II processor with 330 MHz and 128 MB of RAM memory.

6 Discussion

The McNemar statistical test with Bonferroni adjustment [11] was employed to verify if the accuracy difference among all tested techniques in Table 2 was statistically significant. A significant difference at 95% of confidence level was found only in the optical dataset between strategies 1AA and hierarchical method 3. Thus, in general all approaches showed similar performance. Among the methods used in the graph generation process, Table 2 indicates that the balanced subsets criterium was the most effective in obtaining the hierarchical classifiers. It is also interesting to notice the good accuracy of the very simple 1AA technique, which is in accordance with the recent work of [10].

Although not shown in Table 2, the AAA technique can lead to unknown classifications, which occur when more than one class receives the same number of votes. The unknown rates verified were of 0.8, 0.4 and 1.3 for the optical, satimage and protein_struc datasets, respectively.

Concerning training time, the AAA technique was faster. Since only pairs of classes are involved in each binary classifier induction in this approach, a lower number of data is used in this process, speeding it up. Follows in sequence the hierarchical methods 1, 2 and 3. These techniques train $k-1$ SVMs, and in each level of the hierarchies the number of classes involved is reduced. The graph formation time was considered in computing these times. The 1AA strategy, with k SVM inductions using all data, showed higher training times than the previous approaches, followed by ECOC, that presented the highest times. Still according to Table 3, the hierarchical and AAA techniques were fast on test and the 1AA strategy was, in general, slower than these approaches. ECOC was the slowest in this phase.

One point that was not considered in this paper is that a graph may contain multiple MSTs if it has low cost edges with the same weights. Only one of such structures was investigated, but alternative trees could also be considered.

As a future interesting work, the parameters of each binary SVM composing the multiclass classifiers could be adjusted separately. As presented in [15], this approach can significantly improve the results of the multiclass predictors obtained. Leave-one-out error bounds for binary SVMs [5] could also be used in this model selection process.

The algorithm should also be evaluated for other datasets, especially with higher numbers of classes.

As another perspective, other types of similarity/dissimilarity measures between classes can be proposed and used in the graph phase formation. As an example based on the concept of confusion classes in [12], the results of a confusion matrix generated by other ML technique could be used in the weight assignment process, since these matrices offer an idea of which classes a classifier has more difficulty to distinguish.

A modification of the proposed algorithm is also under consideration. In this new proposal, each time two subsets of one or more classes are merged, the graph structure is modified accordinly. The vertices equivalent to these classes are grouped into one unique vertice, as well as the class information extracted from the data. Connections from other vertices are then adapted to the new node, with weights calculated based on the merged classes information.

7 Conclusion

This work presented an alternative technique for generating multiclass classifiers from binary predictors. It displaces predictors distinguishing two subsets of one or more classes in each node of a tree. This hierarchical structure has the atractives of fast training and test times. To obtain the hierarchies of binary subproblems in each level, an efficient Minimum Spanning Tree algorithm was employed. Different criteria were tested in the obtainment of the tree and others can also be adapted and used.

The proposed approach has also the attractive feature of being general. It can be employed to other machine learning techniques that generate binary classifiers.

Acknowledgements

The authors would like to thank the Brazilian research councils Fapesp and CNPq for their financial support.

References

1. Ahuja, R. K., Magnanti, T. L., Orlin, J. B.: Network Flows: Theory, Algorithms and Applications. Prentice Hall (1993)
2. Allwein, E. L., Shapire, R. E., Singer, Y.: Reducing Multiclass to Binary: a Unifying Approach for Margin Classifiers. In Proc of the 17th ICML (2000) 9–16
3. Chang, C.-C., Lin, C.-J.: LIBSVM : a library for support vector machines. http://www.csie.ntu.edu.tw/~cjlin/libsvm/
4. Cheong, S., Oh, S. H., Lee, S.-Y.: Support Vector Machines with Binary Tree Architecture for Multi-Class Classification. Neural Information Processing - Letters and Reviews, Vol. 2, N. 3 (2004) 47–50
5. Cristianini, N., Taylor, J. S.: An Introduction to Support Vector Machines. Cambridge University Press (2000)
6. Dietterich, T. G., Bariki, G.: Solving Multiclass Learning Problems via Error-Correcting Output Codes. JAIR, Vol. 2 (1995) 263–286
7. Ding, C. H. Q., Dubchak, I.: Multi-class Protein Fold Recognition using Support Vector Machines and Neural Networks. Bioinformatics, Vol. 4, N. 17 (2001) 349–358
8. Kreβel, U.: Pairwise Classification and Support Vector Machines. In B. Scholkopf, C. J. C. Burges and A. J. Smola (eds.), Advances in Kernel Methods - Support Vector Learning, MIT Press (1999) 185–208
9. Platt, J. C., Cristianini, N., Shawe-Taylor, J.: Large Margin DAGs for Multiclass Classification. In: Solla, S. A., Leen, T. K., Mller, K.-R. (eds.), Advances in Neural Information Processing Systems, Vol. 12. MIT Press (2000) 547–553
10. Rifkin, R., Klautau, A.: In Defense of One-Vs-All Classification. JMLR, Vol. 5 (2004) 1533–7928
11. Salzberg, S. L.: On Comparing Classifiers: Pitfalls to Avoid and a Recommended Approach. Data Mining and Knowledge Discovery, Vol. 1 (1997) 317–328
12. Schwenker, F.: Hierarchical Support Vector Machines for Multi-Class Pattern Recognition. In: Proc of the 4th Int Conf on Knowledge-based Intelligent Engineering Systems and Allied Technologies. IEEE Computer Society Press (2000) 561–565
13. University of California Irvine: UCI benchmark repository - a huge collection of artificial and real-world datasets. `http://www.ics.uci.edu/~ mlearn`
14. Vapnik, V. N.: Statistical Learning Theory. John Wiley and Sons, New York (1998)
15. Vural, V., Dy, J. G.: A Hierarchical Method for Multi-Class Support Vector Machines. In: Proc of the 21st ICML (2004)

One-Class Classifier for HFGWR Ship Detection Using Similarity-Dissimilarity Representation

Yajuan Tang and Zijie Yang

Radiowave Propagation Laboratory (RPL), School of Electronic Information,
Wuhan University, Wuhan 430079, Hubei, China
tangyj@vip.sina.com

Abstract. Ship detection in high frequency ground wave radar can be approached by one-class classifier where ship echoes are regarded as abnormal situations to typical ocean clutter. In this paper we consider the problems of feature extraction and representation problems. We first study characters of ocean clutter and ship echo, and find that initial frequency and chirp rate are two proper features to tell difference between ship echoes and ocean clutters. However to lower the probability of misjudging, we represent data examples in a combined similarity-dissimilarity space other than using these two features directly. A hypersphere with minimal volume is adopted to bound training examples, from which an efficient one-class classifier is established upon limited number of typical examples. The comparison result to a one-class classifier based on original feature representation is given.

1 Introduction

The high frequency ground wave radar (HFGWR) is a kind of remote sensor that transmits electromagnetic waves along the ocean surface [1]. Due to the low attenuation rates of HF electromagnetic waves when they are propagated over conductive ocean surface, HFGWR is capable of detecting surface ships beyond the horizon which is much farther than the detection range of microwave radar.

For HFGWR, target echo is emerged in ocean clutters. The primary disturbance to target detection is first-order ocean clutters called Bragg lines, which are produced by resonance between the decimetric ocean gravity waves and the incident HF wave [2]. To discriminate between ship echoes and ocean clutter, detection is performed in frequency domain based on their different Doppler shifts. However if the the Doppler shift of target is close to the Doppler shift of Bragg lines, target's echo is usually masked by Bragg lines as the energy of ocean clutter is so high that it often exceeds energy level of ships, resulting in a blind speed zone. To detecting target, most algorithms express radar returns as sinusoids by Fourier Transform and then detect moving target by comparing amplitude peaks in frequency domain with a threshold determined by constant false alarm rate (CFAR) technique [3, 4]. Sinusoid model implies that coherent integration time (CIT) should be short enough to guarantee an approximately

M. Ali and F. Esposito (Eds.): IEA/AIE 2005, LNAI 3533, pp. 432–441, 2005.

constant velocity of target during one CIT. However the length of CIT should also be long enough for spectrum estimation methods to obtain a high frequency resolution.

In this paper we provide a pattern classification based algorithm for ship detection in HFGWR. Our method replaces sinusoid by chirp and applies chirplet decomposition as an alternative of Fourier Transform to estimate parameters of chirp. As only information from one class, the ocean clutter class, are available in advance, this kind of problem is a typical one-class classification problems.

Our previous work is reported in [5], in which objects are represented by feature vectors composed of their chirplets parameters. Object representation is important in classification as it is the relationships between objects not the individual instance that are of interest. In this paper we provide a new representation method to describe data examples in a combined similarity-dissimilarity space. In this space, objects are expressed by their similarity as well as their dissimilarity to others that makes the difference between positive and negative examples more distinct. Therefore the probability rate of misjudging is reduced.

An experiment on radar returns measured by an HFGWR system OSMAR2000 [1] are used here to show that our feature extraction method based on chirplet decomposition and the combined similarity-dissimilarity representation result in a lower ocean clutter rejected rate, i.e. lower false alarm rate.

This paper is organized as follows. The background of HFGWR is introduced in section 2. Then in section 3 we provide our signal model and feature extraction method for constructing input vector of classifier. Section 4 discusses the similarity and dissimilarity representation, followed by our method of how to construct a similarity-dissimilarity space. Section 5 describes the experiment results. Finally a conclusion is made in section 6.

2 Background of HFGWR

HF radio waves are scattered from the ocean surface and Doppler shifted according to the phase speed of the ocean waves by an amount

$$f_d = \pm\sqrt{\frac{gf_c}{\pi c}} \tag{1}$$

where f_c is radar carrier frequency, g is gravity, c is velocity of light. As ocean waves travel either towards or away from radar station in the normal direction, positive and negative Doppler shifts both exist. The largest peak signals in the Doppler spectrum are associated with Bragg resonance from waves with half the radio wavelength. At this wavelength and higher multiples, the signals backscattered will be in phase with its neighbors, resulting in largest combined reflections. The Doppler spectrum of signals associated with this wavelength are named as first-order spectrum, and higher multiples are nth-order spectrum.

As illustrated in Figure 1, the Doppler spectrum of the backscattered signal contains two lines, which are first-order Bragg spectrum or Bragg lines. Known from Equation (1) the value of Bragg lines are fixed according to radar carrier. In general, due to an underlying surfacer current the two first-order peaks are away from the theoretical lines by a shift that is proportional to the radial surfacer current speed. In addition to Bragg lines, there is a much weaker but more complicated spectrum whose main parts are second-order spectrum.

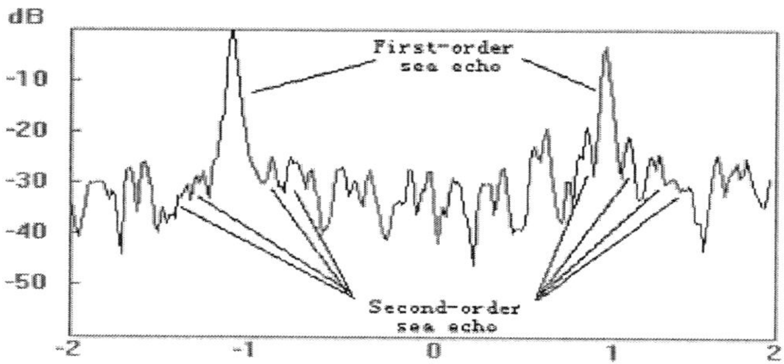

Fig. 1. Doppler Frequency

Ocean clutter has a great impact on low speed target detection. When spectrum of ship echo locates outside the first-order spectrum domain, the seconde-order ocean clutter becomes dominant noise background. However when the Doppler frequency of ship is close to the Doppler frequency of Bragg lines, it is often mistaken for Bragg lines as the energy of Bragg lines is generally as strong as or stronger than the energy of ship echoes [6]. To avoid high alarm rate, Bragg lines must be distinguished from targets. We can see from Equation (1) the frequencies of Bragg lines are fixed meanwhile targets move with unpredictable speeds, which motivates us to express the target detection problem as recognizing anomaly in Bragg lines and solve it by one class classifier.

3 Feature Extraction

3.1 Signal Model

A received signal s_{mn} from a target in the m'th radar range cell is expressed as [7]

$$s_{mn} = e^{j2\pi f_0 \frac{2v}{c} nT} \quad (2)$$

$$= e^{j2\pi f_0 \frac{2v}{c} t_n} \quad (3)$$

where f_0 is radar carrier, v is speed of target, c is velocity of light, t_n is within the coherent integration time (CIT) $[T, NT]$. Its FFT spectrum is

$$S_{mn}(f) = NT \frac{\sin\left[2\pi(f - \frac{2v}{c} f_0)NT/2\right]}{2\pi(f - \frac{2v}{c} f_0)NT/2} \quad (4)$$

If the target moves with a constant velocity in normal direction of radar station, S_{mn} is a Singer function with its highest peak locating at frequency $\frac{2v}{c}f_0$. This is the Doppler shift of a target with velocity v to radar carrier f_0. However, if the target's velocity varies with time which is possible during long CIT, the echoes of ship will smear in frequency domain and may be mistaken for second-order sea echoes or broadening part of the first-order Bragg peak.

To get local time-frequency structure of radar returns, it is proper to approximate them as multi-component chirp signals. Chirp signal is a general model that involves sinusoid as a special case whose chirp rate is zero. The velocity and acceleration of ship target can be obtained through its corresponding frequency and chirp rate respectively. Thus the radar returns can be expressed in a general manner as

$$s(t) = e^{j2\pi f_0 t + jmt^2} \tag{5}$$

3.2 Chirplet-Based Feature Extraction

Chirplets [8, 9] are chirp signals that have normalized Gaussian envelope

$$h_k(t) = \frac{1}{\sqrt{\sqrt{\pi}d_k}} \exp\{-\frac{1}{2}(\frac{t-t_k}{d_k})^2\} \exp\{(j2\pi f_k(t-t_k) + jm_k(t-t_k)^2)\} \tag{6}$$

where t_k, f_k, m_k and d_k represent the location in time, the location in frequency, the chirp rate and the duration, respectively. Chirplet decomposition represents a signal in terms of weighted chirplets as given below

$$s(t) = \sum_{k=1}^{\infty} c_k h_k(t) \tag{7}$$

The parameters of chirplet describe the information of target as well as Bragg lines in detail, thereby can be used to represent them through a vector $x(k) = [c_k, t_k, f_k, m_k, d_k]$. However not all of these five features are necessary to distinguish target echo and Bragg lines. First of all, the amplitude c_k explains nothing about them as the energy of target echo and Bragg lines are in a equal level. Secondly, when the signal appears and how long it lasts account little for differentiating between target echo and Bragg lines. It is highly possible that a ship exposes in the illuminating area during the whole CIT period as well as ocean. The really helpful features to discriminate them are initial frequencies f_0 and chirp rate m. As surface current always flows slowly, the chirplet corresponding to Bragg line has a known initial frequency and a very tiny chirp rate. On the contrary, ship travels with any possible velocity and acceleration, resulting in an unpredictable initial frequency and a chirp rate that can be any real number. Thus it is proper to use these two features to construct the input space of classifier as $x(k) = [f_k, m_k]$. Moreover, it is unfeasible for training set to model all possible information of target, resulting in a one-class classification problem.

4 Similarity and Dissimilarity Representation

Similarity or dissimilarity plays an important role in pattern classification problems because the basis assumption in classification is that an example of object belongs to one class if it is similar to examples of this class. The classification algorithm compares the degree of similarity of an example to a threshold and determines whether it is a class member or not.

Usually objects to be classified are represented by features and measured by dissimilarity based distance metrics [10, 11],such as Euclidean distance, squared Euclidean distance, Manhattan Distance, Chi-square Distance and so on, or similarity based metrics like inner product, Jaccard, simple matching and Chi-square similarity, etc. Suppose there are a number of training data $(x_1, y_1), (x_2, y_2), \ldots,$ $(x_m, y_m) \in \mathcal{X} \times \mathcal{Y}$. Here x_i is the feature observation, y_i is its corresponding label index where $y_i \in \{\pm 1\}$. In this paper we choose the most commonly used measurement for similarity and dissimilarity, that is the inner product $\langle x_i, x_j \rangle$ for measuring the degree of similarity and the Euclidean distance $\|x_i - x_j\|^2$ accounting for dissimilarity between two objects. In one-class classification problem, training set only consists of positive examples also known as target examples, the goal of training is to find a boundary that accepts target examples as much as possible, meanwhile minimizes chances of accepting negative ones, i.e. outliers.

Recently an alternative generalized kernel approach is proposed by Schölkopf [10] to represent similarity measurement. In most cases, we pay much attention to positive definite (pd) kernels. Due to the fact that a pd kernel can be considered as a inner product in feature space, i.e. $K(x, x') =<\rangle \phi(x), \phi(x') \langle$, it is natural to take it as (nonlinear) generalization of similarity measure. By means of kernel function, training example x_i is denoted by its similarity to the training set $R = \{x_1, x_2, \ldots, x_m\}$ as $S(x_i, R) = [S(x_i, x_1, S(x_i, x_2), \ldots, S(x_i, x_m)]^T$ which is equivalent to map input example $x_i \in \mathcal{X}$ into a similarity space $\mathcal{R}^m$. Schölkopf takes a further look at the squared distance in similarity space. The squared distance $d(\phi(x_i), \phi(x_j))$ between vectors $\phi(x_i)$ and $\phi(x_j)$ in similarity space are defined as

$$\begin{aligned} d(\phi(x_i), \phi(x_j)) &= \|\phi(x_i) - \phi(x_j)\|^2 \\ &= K(\phi(x_i), \phi(x_i)) + K(\phi(x_j), \phi(x_j)) - 2K(\phi(x_i), \phi(x_j)) \quad (8) \end{aligned}$$

This is the so-called kernel trick that expresses the distance in similarity space only by kernels without defining the mapping explicitly. Schölkopf claims that a larger class of kernels, the conditional positive definite (cpd) kernels can be used.

Pękalska [12] proposes another approach to represent objects based on dissimilarity values. A mapping $D(x, R)$ is applied to map input example $x \in \mathcal{X}$ into a dissimilarity space $\mathcal{R}^m$, in which x is represented in a dissimilarity manner as $D(x, R) = [D(x, x_1, D(x, x_2), \ldots, D(x, x_m)]^T$.

Either similarity or dissimilarity representation aims at measuring the degree of (dis)similarity between examples, on which a classification algorithm can depend to make a decision. Positive and negative examples locate far apart in this kind of feature space so that it is proper for one-class classifier to bound positive ones using a hypersphere with minimal volume [13,14,15] or separate them from the origin using a hyperplane as far as it can [16].

In order to get a better representation of positive and negative objects to exhibit difference between them entirely, we propose a method in this paper to denote data in a combined similarity-dissimilarity space $(S(x,R), D(x,R))$

$$SD(x,R) = [\sum_{i=1}^{m} S(x,x_i), \sum_{i=1}^{m} D(x,x_i)]^T \tag{9}$$

This representation expresses objects by their similarities and dissimilarities together to the whole training set. This representation can be interpreted as mapping data points in space $\mathcal{R}^n$ to a two dimensional space $\mathcal{R}^2$, in which two axes denote degree of similarity and dissimilarity respectively. Since our representation method gives attention to both similarity and dissimilarity, the difference between positive and negative classes are highlighted, which results in a lower misjudging rate.

If x is a negative example, its dissimilarity measure will be large to the representation set R, at the same time its similarity measure will be small. Then in this similarity-dissimilarity space, the mapped point of x, $SD(x,R)$, lies on the top left corner of the figure, as illustrated in Figure 2. Otherwise if x comes from the positive class, $SD(x,R)$ lies on the opposite direction of negative example because it is quite similar to most of the representation examples. We

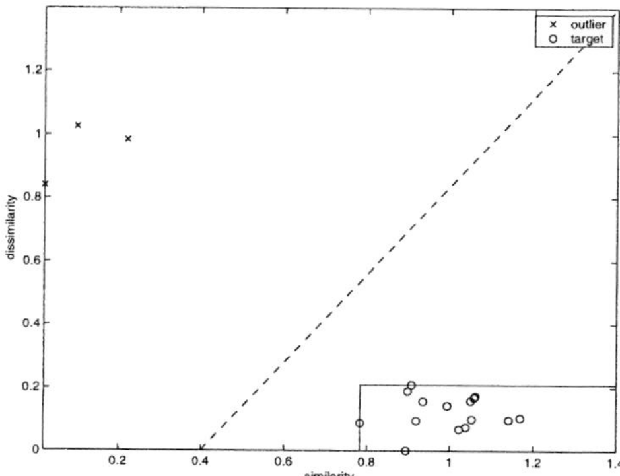

Fig. 2. data represented in similarity-dissimilarity space

can see from Figure 2 that positive examples are in an open rectangle with right side border unbounded. To describe the target class in this space, we should bound the points from both the left and top sides, which means we have two optimal problems to solve. This may be a complicated work. In practice as an object cannot be similar and dissimilar to one representation set R at the same time, mapped points just lie in a narrow line from top left corner to right down side. Therefore it's feasible to describe target class examples using just one hypersphere as usual.

Suppose the hypersphere has center a and radius R, it contains all the training objects inside and at the same time has the smallest volume. That is to solve the problem

$$\begin{aligned} \min \quad & R^2 + C\sum_i \xi_i \\ s.t. \quad & \|\phi(SD(x_i, R)) - a\|^2 \leq R^2 + \xi_i \\ & \xi_i \geq 0 \end{aligned} \tag{10}$$

Its dual problem is

$$\begin{aligned} \max \quad & \sum_i \alpha_i \phi(SD(x_i, R))\phi(SD(x_i, R)) - \sum_{i,j} \alpha_i \alpha_j \phi(SD(x_i, R))\phi(SD(x_j, R)) \\ s.t. \quad & 0 \leq \alpha_i \leq C \\ & \sum_i \alpha_i = 1 \\ & a = \sum_i \alpha_i x_i \end{aligned} \tag{11}$$

where α_i, $i = 1, \ldots, m$ are Lagrangian multipliers.

The distance from a test data z to the center is $\| z - a \|^2$, based on which a decision is made. If this distance is smaller than or equal to R^2, the test data is accepted as target class. Consequently the decision function is

$$\begin{aligned} f(z) = sgn(K(SD(z, R) \cdot SD(z, R)) - \sum_i \alpha_i K(SD(z, R), SD(x_i, R)) \\ + \sum_{i,j} \alpha_i \alpha_j K(SD(z, R), SD(x_i, R)) - R^2) \end{aligned} \tag{12}$$

5 Experiment

As the ocean wave spectrum nearly always contains ocean wavelengths of the order of the radar wavelength, the Bragg lines appear in every observation period of a given range cell. However, ship target travels in and out a range cell randomly with unpredicted velocity. Thereby radar returns are mainly consisted of ocean clutters, plus abnormal 'disturbance' of ship target echoes. The classifier must learn to distinguish them from positive examples. We extract information of signals through decomposing radar returns as combined chirplets and represent them by feature vectors composed of initial frequencies and chirp rates. Then we map the original representation to the similarity-dissimilarity space according to our new method described above. A hypersphere is used to bound the newly

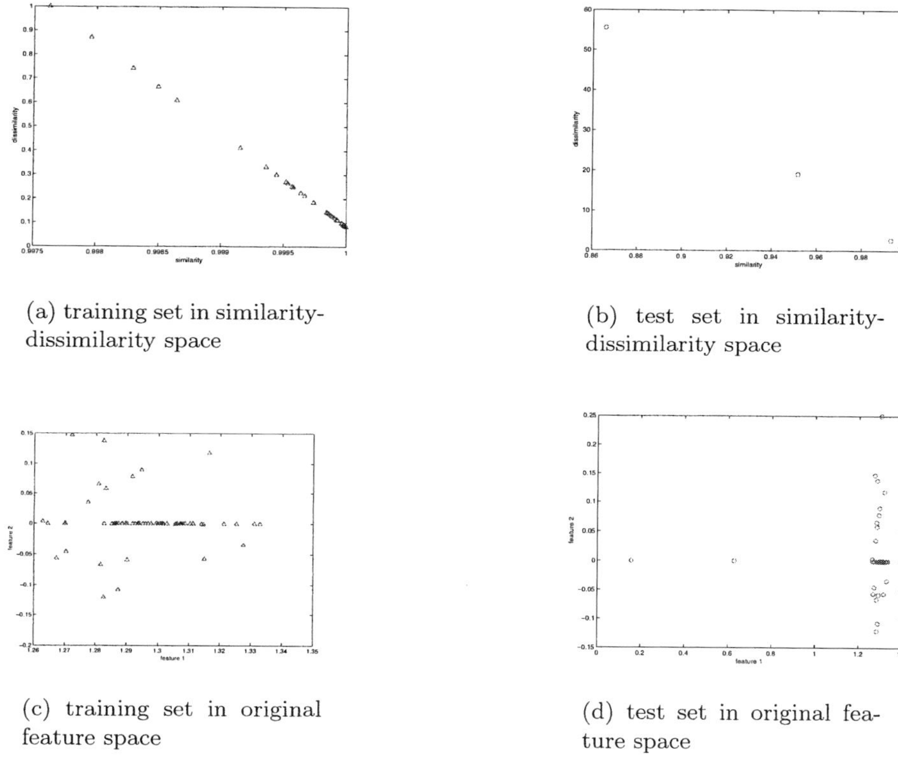

(a) training set in similarity-dissimilarity space

(b) test set in similarity-dissimilarity space

(c) training set in original feature space

(d) test set in original feature space

Fig. 3. Representation of training and test set

represented training objects to construct a one-class classifier. For a new data point, if it can not be accepted by this classifier, it is rejected as an instance of ship echo class. Otherwise it is accepted as belonging to ocean clutter class.

We test the new method with real measurement data collected by OSMAR2000 [17, 1]. OSMAR2000 is an HF radar illuminating the Chinese East Sea developed by Radiowave Propagation Laboratory (RPL), School of Electronic Information, Wuhan University.

The training data we use in this paper is taken on 24 December 2001, collected from 12:00 to 12:12, 90 to 100 kilometers away from radar station. We select data from ranges far away from radar station as training examples because the maximal detection range of clutter is larger than that of target [1]. As there are only ocean clutters in faraway ranges, it is proper to use them as training examples. Three simulated targets are added to the data from range cell that is 87.5 kilometers away from radar station to construct test data examples, in which one target travels almost the same as Bragg lines except for a little acceleration. According to the decomposing result, there are 70 and 13 examples in training and testing set, respectively. Since the values of frequencies are much larger than

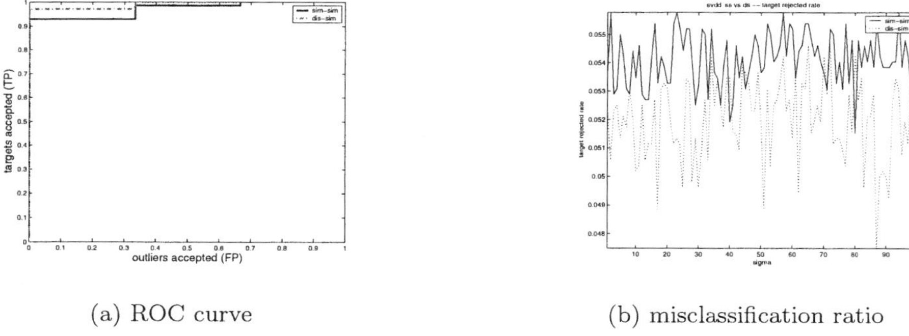

(a) ROC curve

(b) misclassification ratio

Fig. 4. Performance comparison

those of chirp rates, we normalize these two kinds of features to be in the range $[0, 1]$.

In Figure 3(a) and 3(b) the training set and testing set are represented in our similarity-dissimilarity space, where similarity is measured by RBF kernel, the dissimilarity is measured by Euclidean distance. As examples of training set are from the same class, their representations are highly concentrated in a small area with maximum value for dissimilarity is within 1, as illustrated in Figure 3(a). Figure 3(b) demonstrates representation of test examples. The three ship targets are obvious in this figure as their positions show remarkable difference to ocean clutter whose positions are so close to each other that they almost look like one point. Figure 3(c) and 3(d) represent the above two sets in original feature space. The pictures show that the difference between ship targets and ocean clutters is relatively not clear as in the similarity-dissimilarity space.

The ROC curve is used here to study the behavior of one class classifier. It is defined as a function of false positive versus the true positive ratio, i.e. outlier accepted vs target accepted. The threshold is determined by the training set and for all values of true positive ratio, the false positive ratio is measured [15]. We compare the performance of one-class classifier using our representation with that of using traditional RBF kernel based similarity representation. Results are illustrated in Figure 4. The dashed line in ROC curve of Figure 4(a) indicates a better performance than solid line. Figure 4(b) shows the ocean clutter rejected rate on the y-axis, versus Gaussian variance σ on the x-axis. In general, our method has a lower misclassification ratio than original feature vectors based method which means that less ocean clutter is rejected by the classifier, i.e. the false alarm rate is reduced effectively.

6 Conclusion

In this paper we have proposed a new algorithm that considers HFGWR ship target detection as pattern classification problems. The scattering signal of ship is modelled as chirp and decomposed into a linear combination of chirplets. The chirplet parameters are used to construct input vectors for classifier. Furthermore data examples are represented by their dissimilarity as well as similarity to the training set rather than original parameters. This representation can better express difference between ocean clutter and ship target, therefore lower the probability of misjudging ocean clutter as ship target. Experiments results show that its performance is well in practice.

References

1. Zijie, Y., Shicai, W., Jiechang, H., Biyang, W., Zhenhua, S.: Some problems in general scheme for hf ground wave radar engineering. Journal of Wuhan University (Natural-Science Edition) **47** (2001) 513–518
2. Barrick, D.E.: First-order theory and analysis of mf/hf/vhf scatter from the sea. IEEE. Trans. AP **20** (1972) 2–10
3. Turley, M.: Hybrid cfar techniques for hf radar. In: Radar 97. (1997) 36–40
4. Root, B.: Hf radar ship detection through clutter cancellation. In: Radar Conference. (1998)
5. Yajuan, T., Xiapu, L., Zijie, Y.: Ocean clutter suppression using one-class svm. In: 2004 IEEE Workshop on Machine Learning for Signal Processing, MLSP2004. (2004) Accepted.
6. Maresca, J.J., Barnum, J.: Theoretical limitation of the sea on the detection of low doppler targets by over-the-horizon radar. Antennas and Propagation, IEEE Transactions on [legacy, pre - 1988] **30** (1982) 837 – 845
7. Shicai, W., Zijie, Y., Biyang, W., etc: Waveform analysis for hf ground wave radar. Journal of Wuhan University (Natural Science Edition) **47** (2001) 528–531
8. Mann, S., Haykin, S.: Time-frequency perspectives: the 'chirplet' transform. In: IEEE International Conference on Acoustics, Speech, and Signal Processing. Volume 3. (1992) 417 – 420
9. Mann, S., Haykin, S.: The chirplet transform: physical considerations. IEEE Transactions on Signal Processing **43** (1995) 2745 – 2761
10. Schölkopf, B.: The kernel trick for distances. In: Neural Information Processing Systems. (2000) 301–307
11. Pekalska, E., Tax, D., Duin, R.: One-class lp classifier for dissimilarity representations. In: Neural Information Processing Systems. (2002)
12. Pękalska, E., Paclik, P., Duin, R.: A generalized kernel approach to dissimilarity-based classification. Journal of Machine Learning Research (2001) 175–211 Special Issue.
13. Tax, D., Duin, R.: Data domain description using support vectors. In: Proceedings of the European Symposium on Artificial Neural Networks. (1999) 251C256
14. Tax, D., Duin, R., Messer, K.: Image database retrieval with support vector data descriptions. In: the Fifth Annual Conference of the Advanced School for Computing and Imaging. (2000)
15. Tax, D.: One-class classification, Concept-learning in the absence of counter-examples. PhD thesis, Delft University of Technology (2001)
16. Schölkopf, B., Platt, J.C., Shawe-Taylor, J., Smola, A.J., Williamson, R.C.: Estimating the support of a high-dimensional distribution. Technical report, Max Planck Institute for Biological Cybernetics, Tübingen, Germany (1999)
17. Revell, J., Emery, D.: Hf surface wave radar simulation. In: Radar System Modelling, IEE Colloquium on. (1998)

Improving the Readability of Decision Trees Using Reduced Complexity Feature Extraction

Cesar Fernandez[1], Sampsa Laine[2], Oscar Reinoso[1], and M. Asuncion Vicente[1]

[1] Miguel Hernandez University, Av. Universidad s/n, 03202 Elche, Spain
c.fernandez@umh.es

[2] Helsinki University of Technology, P.O. Box 5400, FIN-02015 HUT, Finland
sampsa.laine@cis.hut.fi

Abstract. Understandability of decision trees depends on two key factors: the size of the trees and the complexity of their node functions. Most of the attempts to improve the behavior of decision trees have been focused only on reducing their sizes by building the trees on complex features. These features are usually linear or non-linear functions of all the original attributes. In this paper, reduced complexity features are proposed as a way to reduce the size of decision trees while keeping understandable functions at their nodes. The proposed approach is tested on a robot grasping application where the goal is to obtain a system able to classify grasps as valid or invalid and also on three datasets from the UCI repository.

1 Attribute Selection and Feature Extraction in Building Decision Trees

Performing an attribute selection step before building a decision tree helps discarding irrelevant or correlated attributes and, apparently, this step should improve both the readability and the classification accuracy of the resulting tree. However, experimental tests performed by previous researchers [1] show that while classification accuracy can be slightly improved, the number of tree nodes is usually increased, thus resulting is a loss of readability. On the other hand, performing a feature extraction step before building a decision tree is related to the generation of new attributes from the original attributes present in the dataset. The approach proposed in [2] obtains the new features as the hidden neurons of a MLP where a pruning algorithm is used to reduce them as much as possible: each new feature is a linear combination of some of the original attributes. The result is an increase in classification accuracy, but a decrease in tree readability (fewer but more complex nodes in the tree). A different approach is to perform the feature extraction process while building the tree, looking for the best features to perform the splits at each node. Previous studies following this methodology have used both linear [3][4] or non-linear functions [5] to obtain the new attributes. In all cases, the resulting trees are much smaller than those built on the original attributes, but no readable at all: each node of the

M. Ali and F. Esposito (Eds.): IEA/AIE 2005, LNAI 3533, pp. 442–444, 2005.

tree implements a complex function of all the original attributes. Considering all the possibilities, feature extraction before building the tree seems to be the best option. This is the methodology that will be further studied in the present paper, where a new approach based on non complex features is proposed. The goal is to build small trees with easily readable functions at their nodes.

2 Proposed Approach

In order to obtain non-complex functions at each node, the extracted features are restricted to combinations of just two attributes. In this way, the function at each node represents the relation between two variables, which is always an easily interpretable concept for the end user of the system. Besides, only four operators are considered: addition, subtraction, multiplication and division. Readability is, thus, assured. Under such restrictions, the class separation capability of the extracted features is clearly lower than that of features involving linear or non-linear combinations of all the attributes. In order to perform a fair comparison, the possible decision boundaries of the proposed approach are compared to those corresponding to linear combinations of two variables, which would represent a similar complexity at each node (slightly higher as a coefficient is also involved). Figure 1 shows the decision boundaries that can be obtained with a linear combination of two attributes ($y = k_1x_1 + k_2x_2$) and figure 2 shows the decision boundaries that can be obtained with the proposed approach. The result is a reduction in complexity at each node and a wider choice of decision boundaries.

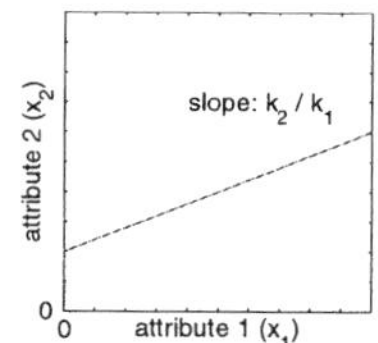

Fig. 1. Decision boundary for a linear feature of two attributes

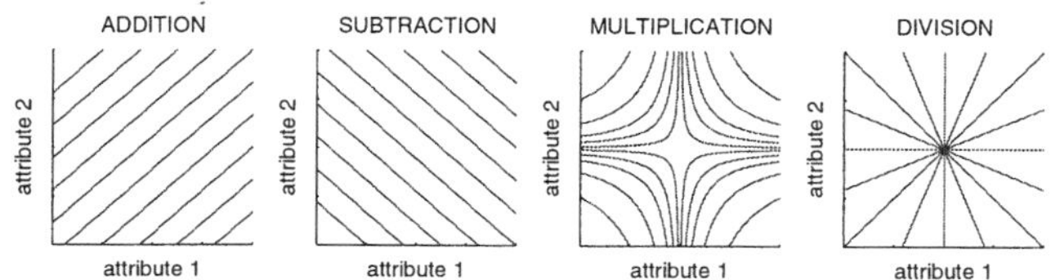

Fig. 2. Decision boundaries for the proposed features

3 Experimental Results

The proposed feature extraction system has been tested on three datasets from a robot grasping application where the goal is to obtain a system able to classify grasps as valid or invalid [6] and also on three other datasets from the UCI repository [7]. The C4.5 algorithm [8] was used for the tests: the classification accuracy and the tree complexity (total number of attributes in the tree) were measured at different values of the pruning confidence level, thus obtaining a relation between complexity and accuracy. The results obtained when the trees were built on the original attributes were compared to those obtained when the trees were built using both the original attributes and the extracted features. In most datasets, the complexity vs. accuracy ratio was improved; detailed results can be found in an internal report [9].

4 Conclusions

The main advantage of decision trees as classifiers is their readability, but sometimes trees generated from the original attributes became too large and complex, and thus are difficult to understand. A previous feature selection process reduces the number of features present in the tree, but not the tree size, which is usually increased. Feature extraction techniques reduce the tree size, but increase the complexity of each node. When the features extracted are (linear or non-linear) functions of multiple attributes, the resulting tree nodes are not understandable to the user. The proposed feature extraction method based on functions of only two attributes keeps node complexity reduced and usually produces small trees: the result is an improvement in tree readability.

References

1. Perner, P.: Improving the Accuracy of Decision Tree Induction by Feature Pre-Selection. Applied Artificial Intelligence, **15, 8** (2001) 747–760
2. Liu, H., Setiono, R.: Feature Transformation and Multivariate Decision Tree Induction. Proc. 1st Int. Conf. on Discovery Science (1998) 14–16
3. Murthy, S. K., Kasif, S., Salzberg, S.: A System for Induction of Oblique Decision Trees. Journal of Artificial Intelligence Research, **2** (1994) 1–32
4. Yildiz, O. T., Alpaydin, E.: Linear Discriminant Trees. Proc. of the 17th Int. Conf. on Machine Learning (2000) 1175–1182
5. Yildiz, O. T., Alpaydin E.: Omnivariate Decision Trees. IEEE Transactions on Neural Networks, **12, 6** (2001) 1539–1546
6. Fernandez, C., Vicente, M. A., Reinoso, O., Aracil, R.: A Decision Tree Based Approach to Grasp Synthesis. Proc. Int. Conf. on Intelligent Manipulation and Grasping (2004) 486–491
7. Blake, C. L., Merz, C. J.: UCI Repository of machine learning databases (http://www.ics.uci.edu/ mlearn/MLRepository.html) (1998)
8. Quinlan, J. R: C4.5: Programs for Machine Learning. M. Kaufmann Publ. Inc (1993)
9. Fernandez, C., Laine, S., Reinoso, O., Vicente, M. A.: Towards supervised and readable decision trees (http://lorca.umh.es/isa/es/personal/c.fernandez/dtrees) (2004)

Intelligent Bayesian Classifiers in Network Intrusion Detection

Andrea Bosin, Nicoletta Dessì, and Barbara Pes

Università degli Studi di Cagliari, Dipartimento di Matematica e Informatica,
Via Ospedale 72, 09124 Cagliari
andrea.bosin@dsf.unica.it
{dessi, pes}@unica.it

Abstract. The aim of this paper is to explore the effectiveness of Bayesian classifiers in intrusion detection (ID). Specifically, we provide an experimental study that focuses on comparing the accuracy of different classification models showing that the Bayesian classification approach is reasonably effective and efficient in predicting attacks and in exploiting the knowledge required by a computational intelligent ID process.

1 Introduction

An Intrusion Detection System (IDS) extracts relevant features from network audit data and applies some analysis techniques for detecting, as well as predicting, unauthorised activities. Traditionally, IDSs are being built on top of detection models, generally expressed in terms of a set of rules encoding the security knowledge of human experts. This approach leads to passive monitors that have proved to be insufficient [1, 2], as they limit the effectiveness and adaptability of the ID process in face of new attack methods or changed network configurations. In recent years, computational methods and data mining techniques [1, 2] have been proposed to extract relevant features from large amounts of audit data. This approach results in machine-learned detection models that are more "objective" and "generalizable" than the rules hand-picked by domain experts.

This paper presents an experimental study which compares the accuracy of different ID models derived from Bayesian networks. Two different Bayesian networks are evaluated: the first one, the Naive Bayes Network (NBN), assumes all features to be conditionally independent. The second one, the Adaptive Bayesian Network (ABN) [3], determines groups of attributes that are pair wise disjoint, i.e. the attributes belonging to the same group are correlated while attributes belonging to different groups are conditionally independent. Detection rules are automatically derived by the ABN to support a data analysis more knowledge based with respect to generic ID techniques that do not take into account the discovery of rules on attacks. The dataset we used originated from MIT's Lincoln Labs and was generated by DARPA [4]. It is considered a benchmark for off-line ID evaluations.

M. Ali and F. Esposito (Eds.): IEA/AIE 2005, LNAI 3533, pp. 445 – 447, 2005.

2 Experimental Study Cases

ID can be thought of as a classification problem: given a set of events belonging to different classes (normal activity, different types of attack), we look for a classifier that is capable of distinguishing among them as accurately as possible. Using both NBNs and ABNs, we are able to identify classifiers that may differ structurally and not necessarily imply the same set of independence relationships among attributes.

In our experiments we utilised ABN to determine groups of attributes (multi-dimensional features) that are conditionally independent and to assert the class label, i.e. the attack to be predicted. Interestingly, each multi-dimensional feature can be expressed in terms of a set of *if-then* rules enabling users to understand predictions.

Specifically, we developed the following models:

- the *multi-target model*, which was trained to identify single attacks and normal connections;
- the *five-target model*, which was trained to classify single connections according to the five categories they belong to (i.e. normal, dos, u2r, r2l, probing);
- the *binary-target model*, which was trained to separate normal and attack patterns.

Each model was built using both NBN and ABN. We trained and tested all models on the dataset originated from MIT's Lincoln Labs and developed by DARPA [4]. More precisely, we handled a *training dataset*, consisting of about 300000 records and containing both normal connections and attacks of 22 different types; a *test dataset*, consisting of about 150000 records and containing both normal connections and attacks of the 22 different types also present in the training dataset; an *unlabeled dataset*, consisting of about 300000 records and containing both normal connections and attacks of 39 different types.

We tested both NBN and ABN models against test and unlabeled datasets and we assumed the accuracy (i.e. the ratio between the number of correct predictions and the total number of predictions) as a measure of the model performance (Tables 1-2). The overall accuracy of the multi-target model on the test dataset is 99.0% for NBN and 98.8% for ABN. We observe that the five-target model performs best in predicting attack categories with a large number of training examples (dos, normal, probe). The accuracy is remarkably lower for attack categories (r2l and u2r) which are present in the training dataset with only a few instances, but this is not surprising.

Both NBN and ABN compare well with other "ad hoc" intrusion detection models proposed in the literature [1] and work well in detecting attacks they are trained for and poorly in detecting new types of attacks. We note that the difference in NBN and ABN accuracy tends to be very small and may not be statistically significant.

However, ABN outperforms NBN in building the five-target model because the NBN fails in classifying dos attacks, even with a sufficiently large number of training examples (Table 2). In our opinion, the key factor that affects this performance might be a strong conditional dependence among features of dos attacks. So, NBN performs poorly because it asserts, by assumption, the independence among features, while ABN performs best since it is capable of capturing these dependencies.

Table 1. Overall accuracy of five-target and binary-target models

Network	Five-target model		Binary-target model	
	Test dataset	**Unlabeled dataset**	**Test dataset**	**Unlabeled dataset**
NBN	94.5%	79.1%	98.6%	91.5%
ABN	98.9%	91.5%	99.3%	92.6%

Table 2. Performance of NBN and ABN five-target model on test dataset

Category	Number of records	NBN	ABN
dos	117632	93.9%	99.4%
normal	29132	96.7%	99.6%
probe	1215	96.5%	89.9%
r2l	336	94.0%	4.8%
u2r	21	52.4%	0%

Table 3. Some classification rules originated by the ABN multi-target model

IF (condition)	THEN (classification)
COUNT isIn (0 - 102.2) and SERVICE isIn (smtp) and PROTOCOL_TYPE isIn (tcp)	normal
COUNT isIn (408.8 - 511) and SERVICE isIn (ecr_i) and PROTOCOL_TYPE isIn (icmp)	smurf

While NBN models are faster both in learning and classification phases, ABN models are, on average, more accurate. Moreover, ABN has the advantage of providing a set of *if-then* rules (Table 3) which explain the inferred information in a human-readable form and allow easily extracting a more detailed knowledge on attack features. In our opinion, the integration between Bayesian inference and rule-based models could be very useful to improve the knowledge engineering approaches traditionally adopted in the domain of ID.

References

1. Lee W., Stolfo S. J., A Framework for Constructing Features and Models for Intrusion Detections Systems, ACM Transactions on Information and System Security, Vol. 3, No. 4, Nov. 2000, p. 227.
2. Lee, W.: Applying Data Mining to Intrusion Detection: the Quest for Automation, Efficiency, and Credibility, SIGMOD Explorations, 2002, Vol. 4, Issue 2.
3. Yarmus J.S., ABN: A Fast, Greedy Bayesian Network Classifier, 2003. http://otn.oracle.com/products/bi/pdf/adaptive_bayes_net.pdf.
4. UCI KDD Archive. http://kdd.ics.uci.edu/databases/kddcup99/kddcup99.html.

Analyzing Multi-level Spatial Association Rules Through a Graph-Based Visualization

Annalisa Appice and Paolo Buono

Dipartimento di Informatica,
Università degli Studi di Bari, Italy
{appice, buono}@di.uniba.it

Abstract. Association rules discovery is a fundamental task in spatial data mining where data are naturally described at multiple levels of granularity. ARES is a spatial data mining system that takes advantage from this taxonomic knowledge on spatial data to mine multi-level spatial association rules. A large amount of rules is typically discovered even from small set of spatial data. In this paper we present a graph-based visualization that supports data miners in the analysis of multi-level spatial association rules discovered by ARES and takes advantage from hierarchies describing the same spatial object at multiple levels of granularity. An application on real-world spatial data is reported. Results show that the use of the proposed visualization technique is beneficial.

1 Introduction

The rapidly expanding amount of spatial data gathered by collection tools, such as satellite systems or remote sensing systems has paved the way for advances in spatial databases. A spatial database contains (spatial) objects that are characterized by a geometrical representation (e.g. point, line, and region in a 2D context), a relative positioning with respect to some reference system as well as several non-spatial attributes. The widespread use of spatial databases in real-world applications, ranging from geo-marketing to environmental analysis or planning, is leading to an increasing interest in spatial data mining, i.e. extracting interesting and useful knowledge not explicitly stored in spatial databases.

Spatial association rules discovery is an important task of spatial data mining that aims at discovering interactions between reference objects (i.e. units of observation in the analysis) and one or more spatially referenced target-relevant objects or space dependent attributes, according to a particular spacing or set of arrangements. This task presents two main sources of complexity that is the implicit definition of spatial relations and the granularity of the spatial objects. The former is due to geometrical representation and relative positioning of spatial objects which implicitly define spatial relations of different nature, such as directional and topological. The second source of complexity refers to the possibility of describing the same spatial object at multiple levels of granularity. For instance, United Kingdom census data can be geo-referenced with respect to the hierarchy of areal objects ED $\rightarrow$ Ward $\rightarrow$ District $\rightarrow$ County, based on the internal relationship between locations. This suggests that taxonomic knowledge

M. Ali and F. Esposito (Eds.): IEA/AIE 2005, LNAI 3533, pp. 448–458, 2005.

on task-relevant objects may be taken into account to obtain multi-level spatial association rules (descriptions at different granularity levels).

A full-fledged system that copes with both these issues is ARES (Association Rules Extractor from Spatial data) [1] that integrates SPADA (Spatial Pattern Discovery Algorithm) [6] to extract multi-level spatial association rules by exploiting an Inductive Logic Programming (ILP) approach to (multi-) relational data mining [5]. ARES assists data miners in extracting the units of analysis (i.e. reference objects and task-relevant objects) from a spatial database by means of a complex data transformation process that makes spatial relations explicit, and generates high-level logic descriptions of spatial data by specifying the background knowledge on the application domain (e.g. hierarchies on target-relevant spatial objects or knowledge domain) and defining some form of search bias to filter only association rules that fulfill user expectations.

Nevertheless, ARES may produce thousands of multi-level spatial association rules that discourage data miners to manually inspect them and pick those rules that represent true nuggets of knowledge at different granularity levels. A solution can be found in the emerging field of visual data mining that combines achievement of data mining with visual representation techniques leading to discovery tools that enable effective data (pattern) navigation and interpretation, preserve user control, and provide the possibility to discover anything interesting or unusual without the need to know in advance what kind of phenomena should be observed [4].

While a lot of research has been conducted on designing association rules exploratory visualization [3], no work, in our knowledge, properly deal with multi-level spatial association rules. At this aim, we propose to extend the graph-based visualization presented in [2] in order to visualize, navigate and interpret multi-level spatial association rules by exploiting both the knowledge embedded on hierarchies describing the same spatial object at multiple levels of granularity and the number of refinement steps performed to generate each rule.

The paper is organized as follows. The problem of mining multi-level spatial association rules with ARES is discussed in Section 2, while the graph-based approach to visualize multi-level spatial association rules is presented in Section 3. An application to mine North West England 1998 census data is then discussed in Section 4. The goal is to investigate the mortality rate according to both socio-economic deprivation factors represented in census data and geographical factors represented in topographic maps. At this aim, multi-level spatial association rules discovery is combined with a graph-based visualization to pick those rules which may provide a guidance to recognize and balance the multiple factors affecting the mortality risk. Finally, conclusions are drawn.

2 Multi-level Spatial Association Rules Mined with ARES

The problem of mining multi-level spatial association rules can be formally defined as follows: *Given* a spatial database (SDB), a set S of reference objects, some sets R_k, $1 \leq k \leq m$, of task-relevant objects, a background knowledge BK including some spatial hierarchies H_k on objects in R_k, M granularity levels in the descriptions (1 is the highest while M is the lowest), a set of granularity assignments ψ_k which associate each object in H_k with a granularity level, a couple of thresholds minsup[l] and minconf[l] for each granularity level, a language bias LB that constrains the search space; *Find* strong multi-level spatial association rules, that is, association rules involving spatial objects at different granularity levels.

The reference objects are the main subject of the description, namely units of observation, while the task-relevant objects are spatial objects that are relevant for the task in hand and are spatially related to the former. Both the set of target object S and the sets of target relevant objects R_k typically correspond with layers of the spatial database, while hierarchies H_k define *is-a* (i.e., taxonomical) relations of spatial objects in the same layer (e.g. regional road is-a road, main trunk road is-a road, road is-a transport net). Objects of each hierarchy are mapped to one or more of the M user-defined description granularity levels in order to deal uniformly with several hierarchies at once. Both frequency of patterns and strength of rules depend on the granularity level l at which patterns/rules describe data. Therefore, a pattern P $(s\%)$ at level l is frequent if $s \geq minsup[l]$ and all ancestors of P with respect to H_k are frequent at their corresponding levels. The support s estimates the probability $p(P)$. An association rule $A \rightarrow C$ $(s\%, c\%)$ at level l is strong if the pattern $A \cup C$ $(s\%)$ is frequent and $c \geq minconf[l]$, where the confidence c, estimates the probability $p(C|A)$ and A (C) represents the antecedent (consequent) of the rule.

Since a spatial association rules is an association rule whose corresponding pattern is spatial (i.e. it captures a spatial relationship among a spatial reference object and one or more target-relevant spatial object or space dependent attributes), it can be expressed by means of predicate calculus. An example of spatial association rule is "*is_a(X, town), intersects(X, Y), is_a(Y, road)* $\rightarrow$ *intersects(X,Z), is_a(Z, road), Z*$\neq$*Y* (91%, 100%)" to be read as "if a town X intersects a road Y then X intersects a road Z distinct from Y with 91% support and 100% confidence", where X denotes a target object in town layer, while Y and Z some target-relevant object in road layer. By taking into account taxonomic knowledge on task-relevant objects in the road layer, it is possible to obtain descriptions at different granularity levels (multiple-level spatial association rules). For instance, a finer-grained association rules can be "*is_a(X, town), intersects(X, Y), is_a(Y, regional_road)* $\rightarrow$*intersects(X, Z), is_a(Z, main_trunk_road), Z*$\neq$ *Y* (65%,71%)", which states that "if a town X intersects a regional road Y then X intersects a main trunk road Z distinct from Y with 65% support and 71% confidence."

The problem above is solved by the algorithm SPADA that operates in three steps for each granularity level: i) pattern generation; ii) pattern evaluation; iii) rule generation and evaluation. SPADA takes advantage of statistics computed at granularity level l when computing the supports of patterns at granularity level $l + 1$.

In the system ARES[1], SPADA has been loosely coupled with a spatial database, since data stored in the SDB Oracle Spatial are pre-processed and then represented in a deductive database (DDB). Therefore, a middle layer is required to make possible a loose coupling between SPADA and the SDB by generating features of spatial objects. This middle layer includes both the module RUDE (Relative Unsupervised DiscrEtization) to discretize a numerical attribute of a relational database in the context defined by other attributes [7] and the module FEATEX (Feature Extractor) that is implemented as an Oracle package of procedures and functions, each of which computes a different feature. According to their nature, features extracted by FEATEX can be distinguished as geometrical (e.g. area and length), directional (e.g. direction) and topological features (e.g. crosses) [1]. Extracted features are then represented by extensional predicates. For instance, spatial intersection between two objects X and Y is expressed with *crosses(X,Y)*. In this way, the expressive power of first-order logic in databases is exploited to specify both the background knowledge BK, such as spatial hierarchies and domain specific knowledge, and the language bias LB. Spatial hierarchies allow to face with one of the main issues of spatial data mining, that is, the representation and management of spatial objects at different levels of granularity, while the domain specific knowledge stored as a set of rules in the intensional part of the DDB supports qualitative spatial reasoning. On the other hand, the LB is relevant to allow data miners to specify his/her bias for interesting solutions, and then to exploit this bias to improve both the efficiency of the mining process and the quality of the discovered rules. In SPADA, the language bias is expressed as a set of constraint specifications for either patterns or association rules. Pattern constraints allow to specify a literal or a set of literals that should occur one or more times in discovered patterns. During the rule generation phase, patterns that do not satisfy a pattern constraint are filtered out. Similarly, rule constraints are used to specify literals that should occur in the head or body of discovered rules.

In a more recent release of SPADA (3.1) new pattern (rule) constraints have been introduced in order to specify exactly both the minimum and maximum number of occurrences for a literal in a pattern (head or body of a rule). Moreover, an additional rule constraint has been introduced to eventually specify the maximum number of literals to be included in the head of a rule. In this way users may define the head structure of a rule requiring the presence of exactly a specific literal and nothing more. In this case, the multi-level spatial association rules discovered by ARES may be used for sub-group discovery tasks.

3 Multi-level Spatial Association Rules Graph-Based Visualization

A set R of multi-level spatial association rules can be naturally partitioned into $M \times N$ groups denoted by R_{ij}, where i $(1 \leq i \leq M)$ denotes the level of

[1] http://www.di.uniba.it/ malerba/software/ARES/index.htm

granularity in the spatial hierarchies H_k, while j ($2 \leq j \leq N$) the number of refinement steps performed to obtain the pattern (i.e. number of atoms in the pattern). Each set R_{ij} can be visualized in form of a graph by representing antecedent and consequent of rules as nodes and relationships among them as edges.

This graph-based visualization can be formally defined as follows: Given an association rules set R, a directed (not completely connected) graph $G = (N, E)$ can be built from R, such that:

- N is a set of couples (l, t), named *nodes*, where l denotes the conjunction of atoms representing the antecedent (A) or consequent (C) of a rule $A \rightarrow C \in R$, while t is a flag denoting the node role (i.e. antecedent, consequent or both of them).
- E is a set of 4-tuples (n_A, n_C, s, c), named edges, where n_A is a node with the role of antecedent; n_C is a node with the role of consequent, while s and c are the support and confidence of the rule $n_A.l \rightarrow n_C.l \in R$ respectively.

Each node of G can be visualized as a colored circle: a red circle represents a node n with the role of antecedent ($n.t = antecedent$) while a green circle represents a node n with the role of consequent ($n.t = consequent$). If the node has the role of antecedent for a rule and consequent for a different rule, it appears half red and half green. The label $n.l$ can be visualized in a rectangular frame close to the circle representing n. Conversely, each edge in G can be visualized by a straight segment connecting the node n_A with the node n_C. It corresponds with the rule $n_A.l \rightarrow n_C.l$ that exists in R. The confidence of this rule is coded by the length of the edge, the greater is the confidence, the longer is the edge. Conversely, the support is coded by color saturation of the edge: from light blue (low support) to black (high support). Support and/or confidence can be also visualized in a text label close to the edge (see Figure 1).

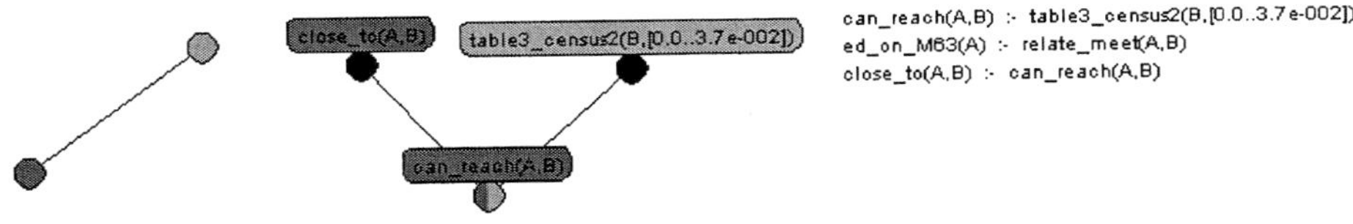

Fig. 1. Visualizing the graph of spatial association rules

As suggested by [2], this graph representation appears beneficial in exploring huge amount of association rules in order to pick interesting and useful patterns, since it takes advantages from human perceptual and cognitive capabilities to immediately highlight which association rules share the same antecedent or consequent with respect to the overall distribution of rules. Filtering mechanisms which permit to hide a sub-graph of G (i.e. subset of rules in R) according to either minimal values of support and confidence or the absence of one or more predicates in the rule provide a better interaction.

To explore multi-level spatial association rules discovered by ARES, this graph-based visualization should be further extended in order to enable data miners to navigate among several graphs G_{ij} according to either the levels of granularity i or the number of refinement steps j. In the former case, for each pair of granularity levels (i, h) with $1 \leq i < h \leq M$ $(1 \leq h < i \leq M)$ and number of refinement steps j $(2 \leq j \leq N)$, a specialization (generalization) operator $\rho_{i\downarrow h,j}$ $(\delta_{i\uparrow h,j})$ can be defined as follows:

$$\rho_{i\downarrow h,j} : R_{ij} \rightarrow \wp(R_{hj}) \ (\delta_{i\uparrow h,j} : R_{ij} \rightarrow \wp(R_{hj})),$$

where $\wp(R_{hj})$ denotes the power set of R_{hj}. For each spatial association rule $A \rightarrow C \in R_{ij}$, $\rho_{i\downarrow h,j}(A \rightarrow C) = \{A_1 \rightarrow C_1, \ldots, A_w \rightarrow C_w\}$, such that each $A_k \rightarrow C_k \in R_{hj}$ $(k = 1, \ldots, w)$ and $A_k \rightarrow C_k$ is a down-specialization (up-generalization) of $A \rightarrow C$.

To formally define the relation of down-specialization (up-generalization) between two spatial association rules, we represent each spatial rule $A \rightarrow C$ as $A_S, A_I \rightarrow C_S, C_I$, where A_S (C_S) includes all atoms in A (C) describing either a property (e.g. *area*$(X,$ [10..15]) or *cars*$(X,$ [150..1000])), a relationship (e.g. *intersect*(X, Y)) or an inequality (e.g. $X/=Y$). Conversely, A_I (C_I) includes all *is_a* atoms (e.g. $is\_a(X, road)$). Therefore, $A' \rightarrow C' \in R_{hj}$ is a down-specialization of $A \rightarrow C \in R_{ij}$ iff there exists a substitution θ (i.e. a function that associates a variable with a term) that renames variables in $A' \rightarrow C'$ such that $A_S = A'_S\theta$, $C_S = C'_S\theta$, and for each *is_a* atom of $A_I(C_I)$ in the form $is\_a(X, v_i)$, where X denotes a target relevant object in R_k and v_i is a node at level i of the spatial hierarchy H_k, there exists an atom $is\_a(X, v_h)$ in $A'_I\theta$ $(C'_I\theta)$ with v_h a node in the sub-hierarchy of H_k that is rooted in v_i. The up-generalization differs from down-specialization only in requiring that v_i is a node in the sub-hierarchy of H_k that is rooted in v_h and not vice-versa.

Example: Let us consider the spatial association rules:
$R1$: intersects($X1$, $Y1$), cars($X1$, [25, 120]),is_a($X1$, town), is_a($Y1$, road) $\rightarrow$ mortality($X1$, high).
$R2$: intersects($X2$, $Y2$), cars($X2$, [25, 120]), is_a($X2$, town), is_a($Y2$, main_trunk_road)$\rightarrow$ mortality($X2$, high).
where $R1.A_S$ is "intersects($X1$, $Y1$), cars($X1$, [25, 120])" and $R1.C_S$ is "mortality ($X1$, high)", while $R1.A_I$ is "is_a($X1$, town), is_a($Y1$, road)" and $R1.C_I$ is empty. Similarly $R2.A_S$ is "intersects($X2$, $Y2$), cars($X2$, [25, 120])" and $R2.C_S$ is "mortality ($X2$, high)", while $R2.A_I$ is "is_a($X2$, town), is_a($Y2$, main_trunk_ road)" and $R2.C_I$ is empty. R2 is a *down-specialization* of R1 since there exists the substitution $\theta = \{X2/X1, Y2/Y1\}$ such that $R1.A_S = R2.A_S\theta$, $R1.C_S = R2.C_S\theta$, and main_trunk_road is a specialization of road in the corresponding hierarchy. Conversely, R1 is an *up-generalization* of R2.

A different specialization (generalization) operator $\rho_{i,j\rightarrow h}$ $(\delta_{i,j\leftarrow h})$ can be further defined, for each granularity level i and pair of refinement step numbers (j, h) with $2 \leq j < h \leq N$ $(2 \leq h < j \leq N)$, such that:

$$\rho_{i,j\rightarrow h} : R_{ij} \rightarrow \wp(R_{ih}) \ (\delta_{i,j\leftarrow h} : R_{ij} \rightarrow \wp(R_{ih})),$$

In this case, for each spatial association rule $A \rightarrow C \in R_{ij}$, $\rho_{i,j\rightarrow h}(A \rightarrow C) = \{A_1 \rightarrow C_1, \ldots, A_w \rightarrow C_w\}$, where $A_k \rightarrow C_k \in R_{ih}$ $(k = 1, \ldots, w)$ and $A_k \rightarrow C_k$ is a right-specialization (left-generalization) of $A \rightarrow C$. More formally, a spatial association rule $A' \rightarrow C' \in R_{ih}$ is a right-specialization (left-generalization) of $A \rightarrow C \in R_{ij}$ iff there exists a substitution θ such that $A\theta \subset A'$ and $C\theta \subset C'$ $(A'\theta \subset A$ and $C'\theta \subset C)$.

Example: Let us consider the spatial association rules:
$R1$: is_a($X1$, town), intersects($X1$, $Y1$), is_a($Y1$, road) $\rightarrow$ mortality($X1$, high)
$R2$: is_a($X1$, town), intersects($X1$, $Y1$), is_a($Y1$, road), extension ($Y1$, [12..25]) $\rightarrow$ mortality($X1$, high).
R2 is a *right-specialization* of R1, since there exists the substitution $\theta = \{X1/X2, Y1/Y2\}$ such that $R1.A\theta \subset R2.A$ and $R1.C\theta \subset R2.C$. Conversely, R1 is a *left-generalization* of R2.

Consequently, by combining a multiple graph visualization with operators of both specialization and generalization defined above, data miners are able to navigate among the graphs G_{ij}. This means that it is possible to down(right)-specialize or up(left)-generalize the portion of the graph G_{ij} representing a specific rule $R \in R_{ij}$ and visualize the corresponding sub-graph of spatial association rules extracted at a different level of granularity or number of refinement steps.

This graph-based visualization has been implemented into a visualization tool, named ARVis (multi-level Association Rules Visualizer), which actively supports data miners in exploring and navigating among several graphs of multi-level association rules G_{ij} by highlighting the portion of graph that represents the down (right)-specialization or up(left)-generalization of a rule, zooming rules, dynamically filtering rules according to minimal values of support and/or confidence as well as presence or absence of some relevant predicate and visualizing details about a rule (e.g. support, confidence, patterns, rules).

4 An Application: Mining Geo-Referenced Data

In this section we present a real-world application concerning with both mining and exploring multi-level spatial association rules for geo-referenced census data interpretation. We consider census and digital map data stored into an Oracle Spatial 9*i* database provided in the context of the European project SPIN! (Spatial Mining for Data of Public Interest) [8]. This data concerns Greater Manchester, one of the five counties of North West England, which is divided into censual sections or wards, for a total of 214 wards. Spatial analysis is enabled by the availability of vectorized boundaries of the 1998 greater Manchester census wards as well as Ordnance Survey digital maps where several interesting layers are found (e.g. urban area or road net). Census data, geo-referenced at ward level, provide socio-economic statistics (e.g. mortality rate that is the percentage of deaths with respect to the number of inhabitants) as well as some measures describing the deprivation level (e.g. Townsend index, Carstairs index, Jarman index and DoE index). Both mortality rate and deprivation indices are

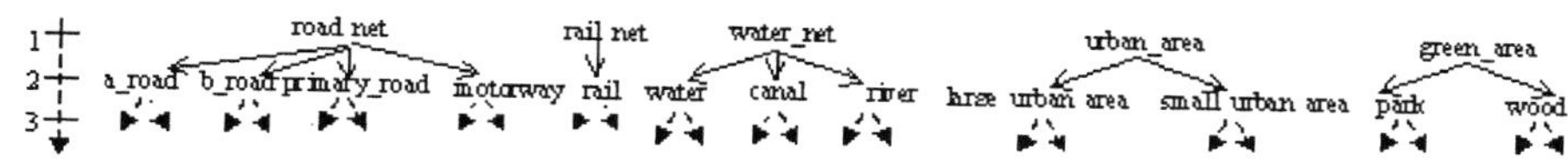

Fig. 2. Spatial hierarchies defined for five Greater Manchester layers: road net, rail net, water net, urban area and green area

all numeric. They can be automatically discretized with ARES. More precisely, Jarman index, Townsend index, DoE index and Mortality rate are automatically discretized in (low, high), while Carstairs index is discretized in (low, medium, high).

For this application, we decide to employ ARES in mining multi-level spatial association rules relating Greater Manchester wards, which play the role of reference object, with topological related roads, rails, waters, green areas and urban areas as task relevant objects. We extract 784,107 facts concerning topological relationships between each relevant object and task relevant object stored in the spatial database for Greater Manchester area. An example of fact extracted is *crosses(ward_135, urbareaL_151)*. However, to support a spatial qualitative reasoning, we also express a domain specific knowledge (BK) in form of a set of rules. Some of these rules are:

crossed_by_urbanarea(X, Y) : − crosses(X, Y), is_a(Y, urban_area).
crossed_by_urbanarea(X, Y) :- inside(X, Y), is_a(Y,urban_area).

Here the use of the predicate is_a hides the fact that a hierarchy has been defined for spatial objects which belong to the urban area layer. In detail, five different hierarchies are defined to describe the following layers: road net, rail net, water net, urban area and green area (see Figure 2). The hierarchies have depth three and are straightforwardly mapped into three granularity levels. They are also part of the BK. To complete the problem statement, we specify a language bias (LB) both to constrain the search space and to filter out uninteresting spatial association rules. We rule out all spatial relations (e.g. crosses, inside, and so on) directly extracted from spatial database and ask for rules containing topological predicates defined by means of BK. Moreover, by combining the rule filters *head_constraint([mortality_rate(_)],1,1)* and *rule_head_length(1,1)* we ask for rules containing only mortality rate in the head. In addition, we specify the maximum number of refinement steps as $J = 8$ and the minimal values of support and confidence for each granularity level as: *minsup[1]=0.1, minsup[2]=0.1, minsup[3]=0.05, minconf[1]=0.3, minconf [2]=0.2* and *minconf [3]=0.1*.

ARES generates 239 strong rules at first granularity level, 1140 at second granularity level and 15 at third granularity level. These rules are extracted from a set of 28496 frequent patterns describing the geographically distributed phenomenon of mortality in Greater Manchester at different granularity levels with respect to the spatial hierarchies we have defined on road, rail, water, urban area and green area layers. To explore this huge amount of multi-level spatial association rules and find which rules can be a valuable support to good public policy, we exploit the multiple graph-based visualization implemented in ARVis.

In this way, we are able to navigate among different graphs G_{ij} ($i = 1, \ldots, 3$ and $j = 2, \ldots, 8$) representing the group of rules R_{ij} discovered by ARES at i granularity level after j refinement steps. For instance, Figure 3 shows the graph of spatial association rules G_{15}. By graphically filtering rules in G_{15} according to confidence value, we identify the most confident rule $R1$ that is: *is_a(A, ward), crossed_by_urbanarea(A, B), is_a(B, urban_area), townsendidx_rate(A, high)* $\rightarrow$ *mortality_rate(A, high)* (c=39.71%, s=70.24%). This rule states that a high mortality rate is observed in a ward A that includes an urban area B and has a high value of Townsend index. The support (39.71%) and the high confidence (70.24%) confirm a meaningful association between a geographical factor such as living in deprived urban areas and a social factor such as the mortality rate. The same rule is highlighted in the graph G_{15} by filtering with respect

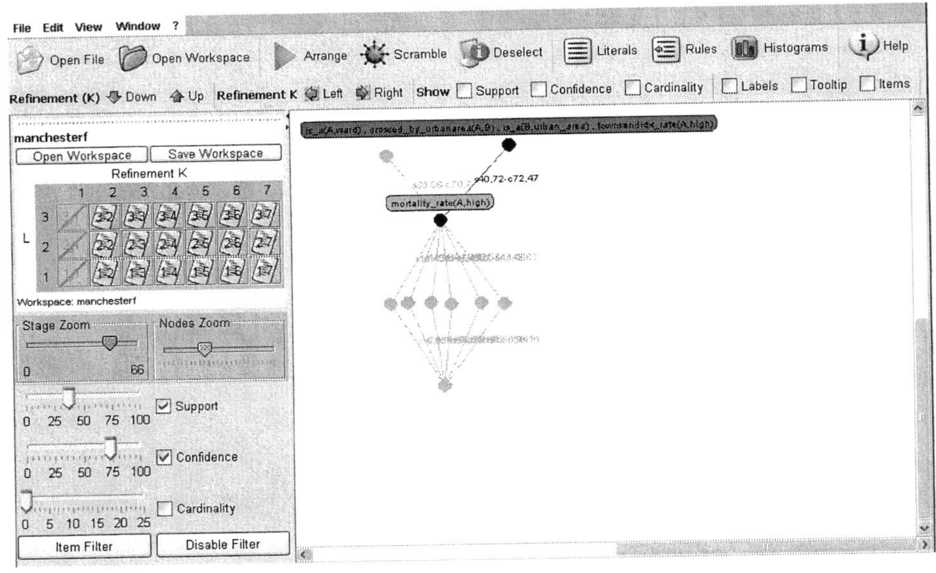

Fig. 3. Visualizing the graph of spatial association rules using ARVis

to increasing value of support. Moreover, by left-generalizing $R1$, we navigate from the graph G_{15} to a portion of the graph G_{14} and identify the rule $R2$ that is *is_a(A,ward), crossed_by_urbanarea(A,B), is_a(B, urban_area)* $\rightarrow$ *mortality_rate(A, high)* (54.67%, 60.3%). This rule has a greater support and a lower confidence. The same rule is highlighted in the entire graph G_{14} by graphically filtering with respect to increasing values of support and confidence. These two association rules show together an unexpected association between Townsend index and urban areas. Apparently, this means that this deprivation index is unsuitable for rural areas.

Conversely, we may decide to up-generalize $R1$ and move from the graph G_{15} to the portion of the graph G_{25} representing association rules which are up-generalization of $R2$ mined by ARES at second granularity level after four refinement steps. In this way, we discover that, at second granularity level, SPADA specializes the task relevant object B by generating the following rule which preserve both support and confidence: $R3$: *is_a(A, ward), crossed_by_urbanarea(A, B), is_a(B, urban_areaL), townsendidx_rate(A,high)* → *mortality_rate(A, high)* (39.71%, 70.24%). This rule clarifies that the urban area B is large. Similar considerations are suggested when we explore graphs of multi-level spatial association rules generated after more refinement steps.

We may explore spatial association rules characterizing low mortality wards. By visualizing G_{15} and moving the confidence filter slider, we discover that the highest confident rule with low mortality in the consequent is: *is_a(A, ward), crossed_by_urbanarea(A, B), is_a(B, urban_area), townsendidx_rate(A, low)* → *mortality_rate(A, low)* (19.15%, 56. 16%), stating that a low valued Townsend index ward A that (partly) includes an urban area B presents a low mortality.

5 Conclusions

In this paper we have presented a graph-based visualization specially designed to support data miners in exploring multi-level spatial association rules and finding true nuggets of knowledge. This new visualization extend traditional graph-based technique with operators of both generalization and specialization that allow data miners to navigate among different graphs of spatial association rules partitioned according with both the granularity level in spatial hierarchies and the number of refinement steps in generating the corresponding pattern. A real-world application shows that this visualization is beneficial for exploring multi-level spatial association rules discovered by ARES. Currently, usability testing are going on, and results will be provided in a future work.

References

1. A. Appice, M. Ceci, A. Lanza, F. A. Lisi, and D.Malerba. Discovery of spatial association rules in georeferenced census data: A relational mining approach, intelligent data analysis. *Intelligent Data Analysis*, 7(6):541–566, 2003.
2. D. Bruzzese and P. Buono. Combining visual techniques for association rules exploration. In M. F. Costabile, editor, *Proceedings of the Working Conference on Advanced Visual Interfaces AVI 2004*, pages 381–384. ACM Press, 2004.
3. D. Bruzzese and C. Davino. Visual post analysis of association rules. *Journal of Visual Languages and Computing*, 14(6):621–635, 2003.
4. M. F. Costabile and D. Malerba. Special issue on visual data mining, editor's foreword. *Journal of Visual Languages & Computing*, 14(6):499–501, 2003.
5. S. Džeroski and N. Lavrač, editors. *Relational Data Mining.* Springer, 2001.
6. F. Lisi and D. Malerba. Inducing multi-level association rules from multiple relations. *Machine Learning*, 55:175–210, 2004.

7. M. Ludl and G. Widmer. Relative unsupervised discretization for association rule mining. In D. Zighed, H. Komorowski, and J. Zytkow, editors, *Principles of Data Mining and Knowledge Discovery*, volume 1910 of *LNAI*, pages 148–158. Springer-Verlag, 2000.
8. M. May. Spatial knowledge discovery: The SPIN! system. In K. Fullerton, editor, *Proceedings of the EC-GIS Workshop*, 2000.

Data Mining for Decision Support: An Application in Public Health Care

Aleksander Pur[1], Marko Bohanec[2,5], Bojan Cestnik[6,2], Nada Lavrač[2,3], Marko Debeljak[2], and Tadeja Kopač[4]

[1] Ministry of the Interior, Štefanova 2, SI-1000 Ljubljana, Slovenia
aleksander.pur@policija.si
[2] Jožef Stefan Institute, Jamova 39, SI-1000 Ljubljana, Slovenia
{marko.bohanec, nada.lavrac, marko.debeljak}@ijs.si
[3] Nova Gorica Polytechnic, Nova Gorica, Slovenia
[4] Public Health Institute, Celje, Slovenia
[5] University of Ljubljana, Faculty of Administration, Ljubljana, Slovenia
[6] Temida, d.o.o. Ljubljana, Slovenia

Abstract. We propose a selection of knowledge technologies to support decisions of the management of public health care in Slovenia, and present a specific application in one region (Celje). First, we exploit data mining and statistical techniques to analyse databases that are regularly collected for the national Institute of Public Health. Next, we study organizational aspects of public health resources in the Celje region with the objective to identify the areas that are atypical in terms of availability and accessibility of the public health services for the population. The most important step is the detection of outliers and the analysis of the causes for availability and accessibility deviations. The results can be used for high-level health-care planning and decision-making.

Keywords: Data Mining, Decision Support, Knowledge Discovery, Knowledge Management, Applications to Health Care.

1 Introduction

Effective medical prevention and good access to health care resources are important factors that affect citizens' welfare and quality of life. As such, these are important factors in strategic planning at the national level, as well as in planning at the regional and local community level. Large quantities of data collected by medical institutions and governmental public health institutions can serve as a valuable source of evidence that should be taken into account when making decisions about priorities to be included in strategic plans.

The organization of public health care in Slovenia is hierarchical: the national Institute of Public Health (IPH) coordinates the activities of a network of regional Public Health Institutes (PHIs), whose functions are: monitoring public health, organizing the public health activities, and proposing and implementing actions for maintaining and improving public health. PHIs themselves coordinate a regional network of hospitals, clinics, individual health professionals and other health care resources. The

M. Ali and F. Esposito (Eds.): IEA/AIE 2005, LNAI 3533, pp. 459 – 469, 2005.

system of public health is thus organized at three levels: strategic (the Ministry of Health and the national IPH), managerial (regional PHIs) and operational (local hospitals, clinics, individual health professionals and other health care resources).

The network of regional PHIs, coordinated by the national IPH, collects large amounts of data, which require appropriate *knowledge management* [1]. Knowledge management is recognized as the main paradigm for successful management of networked organizations, aimed at supporting business intelligence [2] – a broad category of applications and technologies for gathering, storing, analysing, and providing access to data to help organizations make better decisions. In addition to the technological solutions, it needs to address organizational, economic, legislative, psychological and cultural issues [3].

Knowledge management can be supported by the use of knowledge technologies, in particular by *data mining* and *decision support* [4], which are in the focus of the work described in this paper. Data mining and decision support have a large potential for knowledge management in networked organizations, and have already proved to be successful in numerous applications. Data mining is typically applied to knowledge discovery in large and complex databases and has been extensively used in industrial and business problem solving, while its use in health care is still rare. In such a knowledge intensive domain, neither data gathering nor data analysis can be successful without using knowledge about both the problem domain and the data analysis process, which indicates the usefulness of integrating data mining with decision support techniques to promote the construction of effective decision criteria and decision models supporting decision making and planning in public health care.

This paper describes an application of data mining and decision support in public health care, which was carried out in Slovenia within a project called MediMap. Section 2 briefly overviews the two research areas, data mining and decision support, and proposes their integration to better solve data analysis and decision support problems. Section 3 presents the specific application of these techniques, which was developed for the Public Health Institute of the Celje region.

2 Data Mining and Decision Support in Knowledge Management

Data mining [5,4] is concerned with finding interesting patterns in data. Data mining includes predictive data mining algorithms, which result in models that can be used for prediction and classification, and descriptive data mining algorithms for finding interesting patterns in the data, like associations, clusters and subgroups.

Decision support [6,4] is concerned with helping decision makers solve problems and make decisions. Decision support provides a variety of data analysis, preference modelling, simulation, visualization and interactive techniques, and tools such as decision support systems, multiple-criteria modelling, group decision support and mediation systems, expert systems, databases and data warehouses. Decision support systems incorporate both data and models.

Data mining and decision support can be integrated to better solve data analysis and decision support problems. In *knowledge management* [1], such integration is interesting for several reasons. For example, in data mining it is often unclear which algorithm is best suited for the problem. Here we require some decision support for data mining. Another example is when there is a lack of data for the analysis. To ensure that appropriate data is recorded when the collection process begins it is useful to first build a decision model and use it as a basis for defining the attributes that will describe the data. These two examples show that data mining and decision support can complement each other, to achieve better results. Different aspects of data mining and decision support integration have been investigated in [4].

In MediMap, we mainly used descriptive data mining methods, and combined them with visualization and multiple-criteria techniques, as shown in the next section.

3 Data Mining and Decision Support: Health-Care Application

The main goal of the project MediMap was to establish a knowledge repository for supporting decisions in the field of planning the development of community health care centres (CHC) for a regional PHI Celje. We approached this goal in two phases: first, we analysed the available data with data mining techniques, and then, we used the acquired understanding of the data and the domain as leverage for a more elaborate study of the field with decision support techniques.

In the first phase, using data mining techniques, we focused on the problem of directing patients from the primary CHCs to the specialists. The main assumption was that similar CHCs should have comparable directing rates. For the similarity measure we took patients' age and social categories, as well as organization and employment structure of the CHCs. The results revealed that the deliberate aggregation of data, although justified for the primary purpose of data gathering, probably hid most of the interesting patterns that could be exposed in the data mining phase. Consequently, the need for additional data gathered from CHCs was forwarded to the national IPH. This data could be obtained at almost no additional costs, since it is already collected by CHCs, but aggregated too early in the data acquisition and reporting process. At the same time, we gained a substantial insight into the domain, which served as reinforcement for the further studies.

In the second phase we studied organizational aspects of public health resources in the Celje region. The goal was to identify the areas that are atypical in terms of availability and accessibility of the public health services for the population, which could provide valuable information to support decisions related to planning the future development of public health services. For the estimation of parameters from data, we used the same database as in the first phase. Additionally, we derived a model for estimating the availability and accessibility that incorporates several innovative criteria. Moreover, we gathered additional geographic information from several other data-sources, like statistical data for the population of a given area and distance measures between cities.

The most important step of the second phase was the detection of outliers and the analysis of the causes for different availability and accessibility figures. The result of the described process is summarized in Fig. 7, which can be used as a high-level information fusion tool for planning the requirements for the employees for health care services in the Celje region.

3.1 Analysis of Health Care Centres Data with Data Mining

First, we have tried to set up appropriate models and tools to support decisions concerning regional health care in the Celje region, which could later serve as a model for other regional PHIs. The requirements, formulated by the PHI Celje, fall into three problem areas: (1) health care organization (the PHI network, health care human resource distribution), (2) accessibility of health care services to the citizens, and (3) the network of health care providers. These requirements were made operational as five problem tasks:

- analysis of the public health providers network,
- analysis of public health human resources,
- analysis of public health providers workload,
- management and optimisation of the public health providers network, and
- simulation and prediction of the performance of the public health providers and human resource network.

The dataset for the analysis consisted of three databases: (1) the health care providers database, (2) the out-patient health care statistics database (patients' visits to general practitioners and specialists, diseases, human resources and availability), and (3) the medical status database.

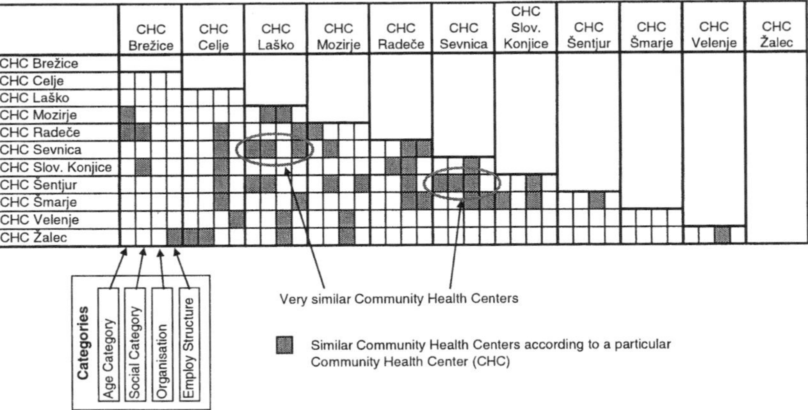

Fig. 1. The similarity matrix of community health centres (CHCs) in Celje

To model the processes of a particular CHC (the patient flow), data describing the directing of patients to other CHCs or specialists were used. Our intention was twofold: to detect the similarities between CHCs, and to detect the atypical CHCs. Similarities between CHCs were analysed according to four different categories: patient's age categories, patient's social categories, the organization of the community health centre, and employment structure of the community health centre. For each category, similarity groups were constructed using four different clustering methods: agglomerative classification [7], principal component analysis [7], the Kolmogorov-Smirnov test [8], as well as the quantile range test and polar ordination [9]. Averages over four clustering methods per category were used to detect the similarities between the CHCs of the Celje region (Fig. 1).

These results were evaluated by domain experts from PHI Celje. In several cases the results confirmed already known similarities, while the experts could not find any reasonable explanations for new knowledge described in the similarity matrix, as the data describing was too coarse (aggregated).

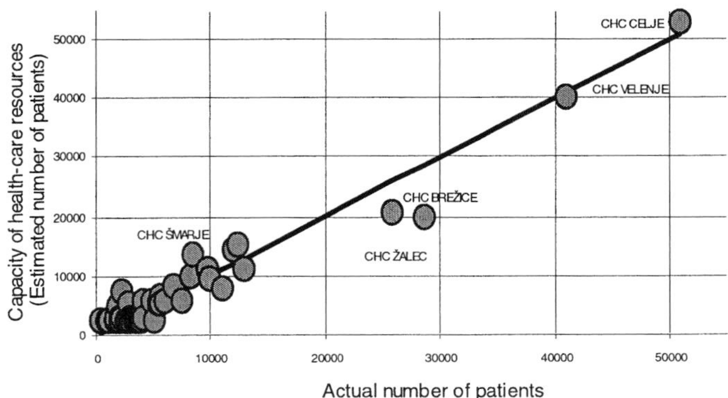

Fig. 2. Detecting atypical health care resources in Celje

The analysis of the typicality of CHCs was based on the comparison of the estimated number of patients that can be handled by a CHC (its capacity estimated by the number of employed staff), and the actual number of patients handled by the CHC. The outcome, which is shown in Fig. 2, was well appreciated by the experts. The figure presents some atypical CHCs, deviating from the diagonal line, such as CHC Brežice and Žalec, which have an insufficient number of staff compared to the number of actual patients.

3.2 Availability and Accessibility of Public Health Care Resources

The goal of this analysis was to detect the local communities that are underserved concerning general practice health services – this means that that the population in these areas have available less than a generally accepted level of services. We evaluated 34 local communities in the Celje region. The evaluation is based on the ratio of the capacity of health care services available to patients from the community and the demand for these services from the population of the same area. In our case, the *capacity* ability of health care services is defined as available time of health care services for patients in that community, and *demand* means the number of accesses to health care services from patient from the community. Therefore, our main criterion for the evaluation of health care system for patients in community c is actually the average time available in health services per access of a patient from this community. We call this criterion *AHSP* (Availability of Health Services for Patients):

$$AHSP = \frac{\sum t_i}{p_c} \tag{1}$$

Here, t_i denotes the total working time of health-care service i in community c, and p_c the number of accesses to health care services of patients from the community c.

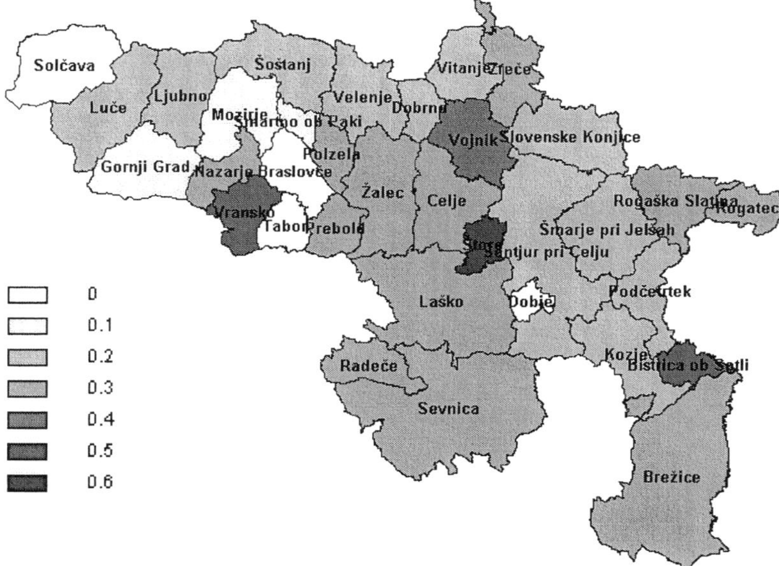

Fig. 3. Availability of health services (*AHSP*), measured in hours, in the Celje region in 2003

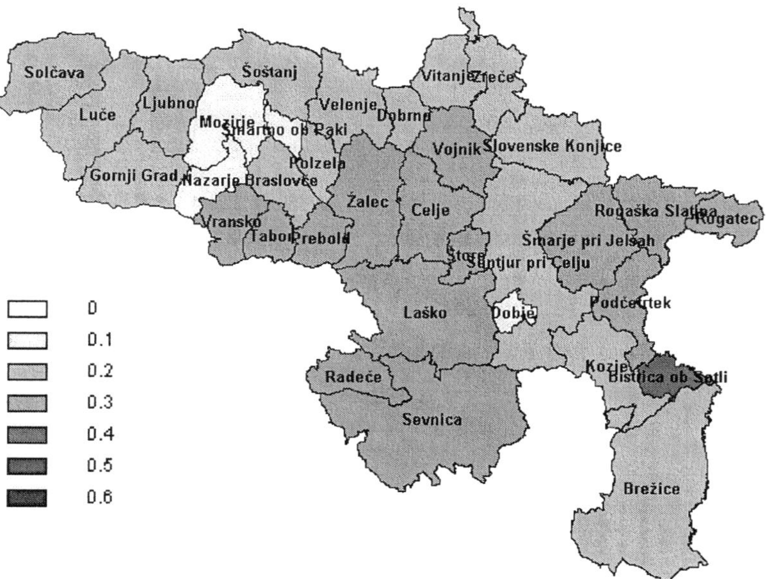

Fig. 4. Availability of health services in Celje in 2003, measured in hours, considering the migration of patients to neighbouring communities ($AHSP_m$)

AHSP does not take into account that many patients access health services in neighbouring communities. Moreover, some of communities do not have their own health care services at all. The migration of patients into neighbouring communities is considered in the criterion $AHSP_m$ as follows:

$$AHSP_m = \frac{1}{p_c} \sum_i a_i p_{ci} \qquad (2)$$

Here, a_i is the *available time* of health care service i per person, defined as the ratio of total working time of health-care services and total number of visits, p_c is the total number of accesses of patient from the community c, and p_{ci} is the number of accesses of patients from the community c to health service i.

The evaluation of some communities in the Celje region using the criteria *AHSP* and $AHSP_m$ is shown in Fig. 3 and Fig. 4, respectively. The colour of communities depends on the availability of health services for patients: the darker the colour, the higher the health care availability in the community (measured in hours). The main difference between the evaluations is noticeable in communities without their own health care services, like Braslovče, Tabor, Dobje and Solčava. If the migration of patients in neighbouring communities is not considered, then it looks like that the inhabitants of these communities are without health care (Fig. 3). Thus, $AHSP_m$ (Fig. 4) provides a more realistic evaluation criterion. Such a geographical representation of the results has been extremely well accepted by the health-care experts.

For even a clearer picture about the availability of health-care services and for the purpose of its visualization (Fig. 5), we introduce two additional criteria. The criterion *AHS* (Availability of Health Services) is defined as the availability of health care services for the population from community c. More precisely, *AHS* is defined as the available time of health care services per population g_c from the community c, considering the migration:

$$AHS = \frac{1}{g_c} \sum_i a_i p_{ci} \qquad (3)$$

The next criterion, *RAHS* (Rate of Accesses to Health Services), defines the rate of accesses to health care services for population g_c from the community c:

$$RAHS = \frac{p_c}{g_c} \qquad (4)$$

In this case, $AHSP_m$ is defined as the ratio between the availability of health services for population from community and the rate of visiting health service:

$$AHSP_m = \frac{AHS}{RAHS} \qquad (5)$$

All these criteria give us some very interesting indicators about health conditions and health care in communities. They can be conveniently presented as shown in Fig. 5. Four measurements are actually shown in the chart: *RAHS* along the horizontal axis, *AHS* along the vertical axis, $AHSP_m$ as dot colour, and the population size (g_c) as dot diameter. Communities with average values of *RAHS* and *AHS* appear in the middle of the chart. The outliers represent more or less unusual communities regarding health care. Communities on the left side of the chart have lower rate of access to health services and the ones on the right side have higher accessing rate. On the bottom are located the communities with lower values of *AHS* and on the top with higher. The dark-coloured communities have higher values of $AHSP_m$ than the light-coloured ones.

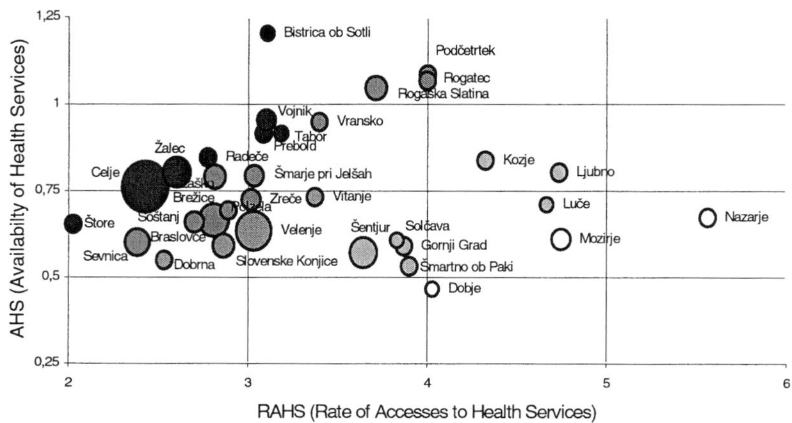

Fig. 5. Available time of health care services per population by community (2003)

Thus, Fig. 5 enables discovering implicit and interesting knowledge about health in communities. For example, the reason for high value of $AHSP_m$ in communities on the left side of the chart (e.g., Štore) could be the low rate of accesses to nearest health services, caused by inappropriate cure in these services. The reason for the low value of $AHSP_m$ in communities on the right side (Nazarje, Mozirje, Luče in Ljubno) is high rates of accesses to health services.

3.3 Decision Support for Planning Health Care Resources

Additional explanation of these rates can be provided by a chart as shown in Fig. 6. It shows the ratio of actual rate of accesses of health services and expected rate for age group of population in communities. This ratio is used in order to simplify detecting unusual rate of accesses to health services. The expected rate of accesses to health services is the average rate of population in age group. For example, the access to health services from population between 60 and 69 are almost five times as frequent as these between 20 and 29. The age group of population from communities is measured along the horizontal axis. Thus, the chart shows that the characteristic for these communities is unusual high rates of accesses to the health services of population under 20. Therefore we could presume that the main reason for the high value of $AHSP_m$ in these communities is the absence of paediatric services.

Further view on the disparity of health care in communities (Fig. 5) is provided in Fig. 7. There, the evaluation of health services is based on the ratio between the health-care capacity and demand. In our case the demand means the number of accesses to health services, and is measured along the horizontal axis. Capacity is proportional to the working time of health services, and is measured along vertical axis. Some of health services are denoted with identification number and community. Regression line in the chart represents the expected working time of health services, with respect to the number of accesses. The working time of the health services under the regression line, like Nazarje and Mozirje, is too short, and of these above the regression line is too long. Thus, this chart can serve for supporting decisions in planning the capacity and working time of health care services.

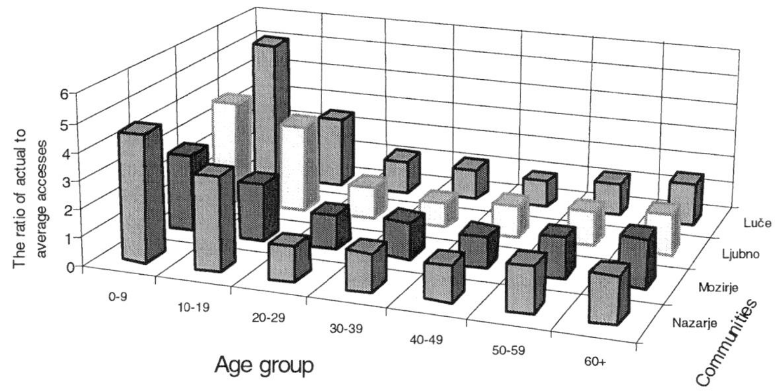

Fig. 6. The ratio between actual and average accesses (2003)

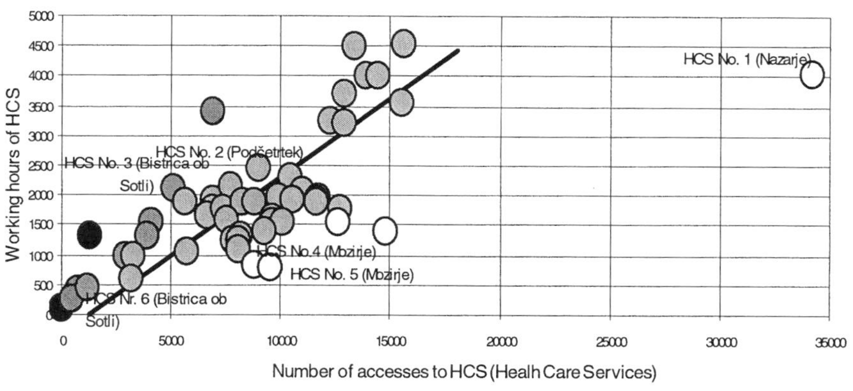

Fig. 7. The evaluation of health services: the ratio of health-care capacity and demand (2003)

4 Conclusion

Improved data mining and decision support methods lead to better performance in problem solving. More importantly, integrated data mining and decision support methods may further improve the performance of developed solutions and tackle new types of problems that have not been addressed before. A real-life application of this approach in public health care was shown in this paper.

In the MediMap project we have developed methods and tools that can help regional PHIs and national IPH to perform their tasks more effectively. Tools and methods were developed for the reference case of IPH Celje and tested on selected problems related to health care organization, accessibility of health care services to the citizens, and the health care providers work.

In the first part of the project, statistical and data mining methods were used in order to get acquainted with the problem domain and data sources. In the second part, we implemented decision support methods to the problem of planning the development of public health services. The main achievement was the creation of the model of availability and accessibility of the health services to the population of a given area. With the model it was possible to identify the regions that differ from average and to consequently explain the causes for such situations, providing many benefits for the health-care planning process.

In addition, the national IPH will use the results to identify missing data that should be included in the improved protocol of public health data gathering at the national level, as the study indicates that additional – more detailed, but relatively easy to obtain – data from the community health centres is needed. This finding is valuable for the IPH, which defines the national data model and prescribes data-gathering rules and procedures.

In further work, we will extend this analysis to other regions of Slovenia. We will focus on the development of decision support tools with the automatic modelling of health care providers using data mining. We wish to implement the developed methodology so that it can be regularly used for decision support in organisations reponsible for the health-care network: the Ministry of Health, the IPH, and PHIs.

Acknowledgements

We gratefully acknowledge the financial support of the Public Health Institute Celje, the Slovenian Ministry of Education, Science and Sport and the 6FP integrated project ECOLEAD (European Collaborative Networked Organizations Leadership Initiative). We also express our thanks to other members of the MediMap project team, in particular to Tanja Urbančič and Mitja Jermol, who have also contributed to the results described in this paper.

References

1. Smith RG, Farquhar A.: The Road Ahead for Knowledge Management: An AI Perspective. AI Magazine, Vol. 21, No. 4, 17–40 (2000)
2. Biere M.: Business Intelligence for the Enterprise. Prentice Hall PTR (2003)
3. McKenzie J, van Winkelen C.: Exploring E-collaboration Space. Henley Knowledge Management Forum (2001)
4. Mladenić D, Lavrač N, Bohanec M, Moyle S. (editors): Data Mining and Decision Support: Integration and Collaboration. Kluwer (2003)

5. Han J, Kamber M.: Data Mining: Concepts and Techniques. Morgan Kaufman (2001)
6. Mallach EG.: Decision Support and Data Warehouse Systems. McGraw-Hill (2000)
7. Legendre P, Legendre L.: Numerical Ecology. 317–341. Elsevier (1998)
8. Zar JH.: Bistatistical Analysis, 478-481. Prentice Hall (1999)
9. Ludwig JA, Reynolds JF.: Statistical ecology: A primer of methods and computing. Wiley Press, 337 (1988)

A Domain-Independent Approach to Discourse-Level Knowledge Discovery from Texts*

John A. Atkinson-Abutridy

Departamento de Ingeniería Informática,
Universidad de Concepción, Concepción, Chile
atkinson@inf.udec.cl

Abstract. This paper proposes a new approach for mining novel patterns from textual databases which considers both the mining process itself, the evaluation of this knowledge, and the human assessment. This is achieved by integrating Information Extraction technology and Genetic Algorithms to produce high-level explanatory novel hypotheses. Experimental results using the model are discussed and the assessment by human experts are highlighted.

1 Introduction

An important problem in processing real texts for text mining purposes is that this has been written for human readers and requires, when feasible, some natural language interpretation. Although full processing is still out of reach with current technology [6], there are tools using basic pattern recognition techniques and heuristics that are capable of extracting valuable information from free text based on the elements contained in it (e.g., keywords). This technology is usually referred to as **Text Mining**, and aims at discovering unseen and interesting patterns in textual databases [5]. Nevertheless, these discoveries are useless unless they contribute valuable knowledge for users who make strategic decisions. This leads then to a complicated activity referred to as *Knowledge Discovery from Texts* (KDT).

KDT can potentially benefit from successful techniques from Data Mining or KDD [4] which have been applied to relational databases. However, DM/KDD techniques cannot be immediately applied to text data for the purposes of TM as they assume a structure in the source data which is not present in free text. Hence new representations for text data have to be used. Also, while the assessment of discovered knowledge in the context of KDD is a key aspect for producing an

* This research is sponsored by the National Council for Scientific and Technological Research (FONDECYT, Chile) under grant number 1040469 "*Un Modelo Evolucionario de Descubrimiento de Conocimiento Explicativo desde Textos con Base Semántica con Implicaciones para el Análisis de Inteligencia.*"

M. Ali and F. Esposito (Eds.): IEA/AIE 2005, LNAI 3533, pp. 470–479, 2005.

effective outcome, the assessment of the patterns discovered from text has been a neglected topic in the majority of the KDT approaches. Consequently, it is not proved whether the discoveries are novel, interesting, and useful for decision makers.

The most sophisticated approaches to text mining or KDT are characterized by an intensive use of external electronic resources including ontologies, thesauri, etc., which highly restricts the application of the unseen patterns to be discovered, and their domain independence. In addition, the systems so produced have few metrics (or none at all) which allow them to establish whether the patterns are interesting and novel.

In terms of data mining techniques, Genetic Algorithms (GA) for Mining purposes has several promising advantages over the usual learning methods employed in KDT: the ability to perform global search, the exploration of solutions in parallel, the robustness to cope with noisy and missing data (something critical in dealing with text information as partial text analysis techniques may lead to imprecise outcome data), and the ability to assess the goodness of the solutions as they are produced.

In this paper, we propose a new model for KDT which brings together the benefits of shallow text processing and GAs to produce effective novel knowledge. In particular, the approach put together *Information Extraction* (IE) technology and multi-objective evolutionary computation techniques. It aims at extracting key underlying linguistic knowledge from text documents (i.e., rhetorical and semantic information) and then hypothesizing and assessing interesting and unseen explanatory knowledge. Unlike other approaches to KDT, we do not use additional electronic resources or domain knowledge beyond the text database.

2 Related Work

In the context of KDT systems, some current applications show a tendency to start using more structured or deeper representations than just keywords (or terms) to perform further analysis so to discover unseen patterns. Early research on this kind of approach is derived from seminal work by Swanson [8] on exploratory analysis from the titles of articles stored in the MEDLINE medical database. Swanson designed a system to infer key information by using simple patterns which recognize causal inferences such as `"X cause Y"` and more complex implications, which lead to the discovery of hidden and previously neglected connections between concepts. This work provided evidence that it is possible to derive new patterns from a combination of text fragments plus the explorer's medical expertise.

Further approaches have exploited these ideas by combining more elaborated IE patterns and general lexical resources (e.g., WordNet) [5] or specific concept resources (i.e., thesauri). They deal with automatic discovery of new lexicosemantic relations by searching for corresponding defined patterns in unrestricted text collections so as to extend the structure of the given ontology/thesaurus (i.e., new relations, new concepts).

A different view in which linguistic resources such as WordNet are used to assist the discovery and to evaluate the unseen patterns is followed by Mooney and colleagues [1] who propose a system to mine for simple rules from general documents by using IE extraction patterns. Furthermore, human subjects assess the real interestingness of the most relevant patterns mined by the system. The WordNet approach to evaluation has proved to be well correlated with human judgments. However, the dependence on a linguistic resource prevents the method from dealing with specific terminology leading to missing and/or misleading information.

3 Semantically-Guided Patterns Discovery from Texts

We developed a semantically-guided model for evolutionary Text Mining which is domain-independent but genre-based. Unlike previous approaches to KDT, our approach does not rely on external resources or descriptions hence its domain-independence. In addition, a number of strategies have been developed for automatically evaluating the quality of the hypotheses. This is an important contribution on a topic which has been neglected in most of KDT research over the last years.

Evolutionary computation techniques (i.e., GA) have been adopted in our model to KDT and others have been designed from scratch.

The proposed model has been divided into two phases. The first phase is the preprocessing step aimed to produce both training information for further evaluation and the initial population of the GA. The second phase constitutes the knowledge discovery itself, in particular this aims at producing and evaluating explanatory unseen hypotheses.

In order to generate an initial set of hypotheses, an initial population is created by building random hypotheses from the initial rules. The GA then runs for a number of generations until a fixed number of generations is achieved. At the end, a small set of the best hypotheses are obtained.

The description of the paper is organized as follows: section 3.1 presents the main features of the text preprocessing phase and how the representation for the hypotheses is generated. In addition, training tasks which generate the initial knowledge to feed the discovery are described. Section 3.2 highlights constrained genetic operations to enable the hypotheses discovery, and proposes different evaluation metrics to assess the plausibility of the discovered hypotheses.

3.1 Text Preprocessing and Training

An underlying principle in our approach is to be able to make good use of the structure of the documents for the discovery process. For this, we have restricted our scope somewhat to consider a scientific genre involving scientific/technical abstracts. These have a well-defined macro-structure (genre-dependent rhetorical structure) to "summarize" what the author states in the full document (i.e., background information, methods, conclusions, etc). From this kind of document's structure, important constituents can be identified such as *Rhetorical Roles*, *Predicate Relations*, and *Causal Relation(s)* [6].

In order to extract this initial key information from the texts, an IE module was built. Essentially, it takes a set of text documents, has them tagged through a previously trained Part-of-Speech (POS) tagger, and produces an intermediate representation for every document (i.e., template, in an IE sense) which is then converted into a general rule. A set of hand-crafted domain-independent extraction patterns were written and coded.

In addition, key training data are captured from the corpus of documents itself and from the semantic information contained in the rules. This can guide the discovery process in making further similarity judgments and assessing the plausibility of the produced hypotheses.

In order to obtain training information from the Corpus, we have designed a semi-structured Latent Semantic Analysis (LSA) representation [7, 3] for text data in which we represent predicate information (i.e., verbs) and arguments separately once they have been properly extracted in the IE phase. In addition, training information from the texts is not sufficient as it only conveys data at a word semantics level.

Accordingly, we perform two kinds of tasks: creating the initial population and computing training information from the rules. In computing training information, two kinds of key training data are obtained: correlations between rhetorical roles and predicate relations which establishes associations between rhetorical information and the predicate action performed (i.e., in certain domains, the *goal* of some hypothesis is likely to be associated with the *construction* of some component, etc) and the co-occurrences of rhetorical information, in which valid hypotheses are assessed in terms of their semantic coherence [7].

3.2 Mining and Evaluating Plausible Patterns

The approach to KDT is strongly guided by semantic and rhetorical information, and consequently there are some soft constraints to be met before producing the offspring so as to keep them coherent.

The GA will start from a initial population, which in this case, is a set of semi-random hypotheses built up from the preprocessing phase. Next, constrained GA operations are applied and the hypotheses are evaluated. In order for every individual to have a fitness assigned, we use a evolutionary multi-objective optimization strategy based on the SPEA algorithm [9] in a way which allows incremental construction of a Pareto-optimal set and uses a steady-state strategy for the population update.

Patterns Discovery. Using the semantic measure above and additional constraints discussed later on, we propose new operations to allow guided discovery such that unrelated new knowledge is avoided, as follows:

- *Selection:* selects a small number of the best parent hypotheses of every generation (*Generation Gap*) according to their Pareto-based fitness.

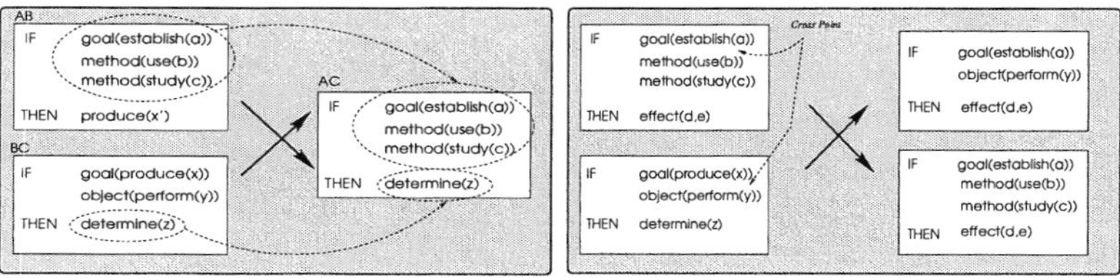

Fig. 1. (a) Semantically-guided Swanson Crossover. (b) Default Semantic Crossover

- *Crossover:* a simple recombination of both hypotheses' conditions and conclusions takes place, where two individuals swap their conditions to produce new offspring (the conclusions remain).
  Under normal circumstances, crossover works on random parents and positions where their parts should be exchanged. However, in our case this operation must be restricted to preserve semantic coherence. We use soft semantic constraints to define two kind of recombination:
  1. *Swanson's Crossover:* based on Swanson's hypothesis [8] we propose a recombination operation as follows:
     If there is a hypothesis (AB) such that "IF A THEN B" and another one (BC) such that "IF B' THEN C", (B' being something semantically similar to B) then a new interesting hypothesis "IF A THEN C" can be inferred, only if the conclusions of AB have high semantic similarity (i.e., via LSA) with the conditions of hypothesis BC.
     The principle above can be seen in Swanson's crossover between two learned hypotheses as shown in figure 1(a).
  2. *Default Semantic Crossover:* if the previous transitivity does not apply then the recombination is performed as long as both hypotheses as a whole have high semantic similarity which is defined in advance by providing minimum thresholds (figure 1(b)).
- *Mutation:* aims to make small random changes on hypotheses to explore new possibilities in the search space. As in recombination, we have dealt with this operation in a constrained way, so we propose three kinds of mutations to deal with the hypotheses' different objects: *Role Mutation*, *Predicate Mutation*, and *Argument Mutation:*.
- *Population Update:* we use a non-generational GA in which some individuals are replaced by the new offspring in order to preserve the hypotheses' good material from one generation to other, and so to encourage the improvement of the population's quality. We use a steady-state strategy in which each individual from a small number of the worst hypotheses is replaced by an individual from the offspring only if the latter are better than the former.

Assessment and Analysis. Since each hypothesis in our model has to be assessed by different criteria, usual methods for evaluating fitness are not appropriate. Hence *Evolutionary Multi-Objective Optimization* (EMOO) techniques which use the multiple criteria defined for the hypotheses are needed. Accordingly, we propose EMOO-based evaluation metrics to assess the hypotheses' fitness in a domain-independent way and, unlike other approaches, without using any external source of domain knowledge.

In order to establish evaluation criteria, we have taken into account different issues concerning plausibility, and quality itself. Accordingly, we have defined eight evaluation criteria to assess the hypotheses given by: **relevance, structure, cohesion, interestingness, coherence, coverage, simplicity, plausibility of origin**:

- **Relevance** (*How important is the hypothesis to the target question?*): measures the semantic closeness between the hypothesis' predicates and the target concepts. Relevance is then computed from compound vectors obtained in the LSA analysis which follows work by Kintsch on *Predication* [7]. We then propose an adaptation of the LSA-based closeness so to compute the overall relevance of the hypothesis in terms of the "strength" which determines how closely related two concepts are to both some predicate and its arguments.
- **Structure** (*How good is the structure of the rhetorical roles?*): measures how much of the rules' structure is exhibited in the current hypothesis. Since we have previous preprocessing information regarding bi-grams of roles, the structure is computed by following a Markov chain of the "bi-grams" of the rhetorical information of each hypothesis. From this model, it can be observed that some structures tags are more frequent than others.
- **Cohesion** (*How likely is a predicate action to be associated with some specific rhetorical role?*): measures the degree of "connection" between rhetorical information and predicate actions. The issue here is how likely some predicate relation P in the current hypothesis is to be associated with role r.
- **Interestingness** (*How interesting is the hypothesis in terms of its antecedent and consequent?*): Unlike other approaches to measure "interestingness" which use an external resource (e.g., WordNet) and rely on its organisation we propose a different view where the criterion can be evaluated from the semi-structured information provided by the LSA analysis. Accordingly, the measure for hypothesis H is defined as a degree of unexpectedness, that is, the semantic dissimilarity between the rule antecedent and consequent.
Here, the lower the similarity, the more interesting the hypothesis is likely to be. Otherwise, it means the hypothesis involves a correlation between its antecedent and consequent which may be commonsense knowledge.
- **Coherence:** This metrics addresses the question whether the elements of the current hypothesis relate to each other in a semantically coherent way, a property which has long been dealt with in the linguistic domain, in the context of *text coherence* [3].
As we have semantic information provided by the LSA analysis which is complemented with rhetorical and predicate-level knowledge, we developed a simple method to measure coherence, following work by [3] on measuring text coherence. Semantic coherence is calculated by considering the average semantic similarity between consecutive elements of the hypothesis.

- **Coverage:** The coverage metric tries to address the question of how much the hypothesis is supported by the model (i.e., rules representing documents and semantic information). For this, we say that a hypothesis covers an extracted rule only if the predicates of the hipothesis are roughly (or exactly, in the best case) contained in this rule. Once the set of rules covered is computed, the criterion can finally be computed as the proportion of rules covered by the hypothesis.
- **Simplicity** (*How simple is the hypothesis?*): shorter and/or easy-to-interpret hypotheses are preferred. Since the criterion has to be maximized, the evaluation will depend on the length (number of elements) of the hypothesis.
- **Plausibility of Origin** (*How plausible is the hypothesis produced by Swanson's evidence?*): If the current hypothesis was an offspring from parents which were recombined by a Swanson's transitivity-like operator, then the higher the semantic similarity between one parent's consequent and the other parent's antecedent, the more precise is the evidence, and consequently worth exploring as a novel hypothesis.

Note that since we are dealing with a multi-objective problem, there is no simple way to get independent fitness values as the fitness involves a set of objective functions to be assessed for every individual. Therefore the computation is performed by comparing objectives of one individual with others in terms of *Pareto dominance* [2] in which non-dominated solutions (Pareto individuals) are searched for in every generation.

Next, three important issues had to be faces in order to assess every hypothesis' fitness: Pareto dominance, fitness assignment and the diversity problem [2]. In particular, Zitzler [9] proposes an interesting method, *Strength Pareto Evolutionary Algorithm* (SPEA) which uses a mixture of established methods and new techniques in order to find multiple Pareto-optimal solutions in parallel, and at the same time to keep the population as diverse as possible. We have also adapted the original SPEA algorithm to allow for the incremental updating through a steady-state replacement method.

4 Analysis and Results

The quality (novelty, interestingness, etc) of the discovered knowledge by the model was assessed by building a Prolog-based KDT system. The IE task has been implemented as a set of modules whose main outcome is the set of rules extracted from the documents. In addition, an intermediate training module is responsible for generating information from the LSA analysis and from the rules just produced. The initial rules are represented by facts containing lists of relations both for antecedent and consequent.

For the purpose of the experiments, the corpus of documents has been obtained from the *AGRIS* database for agricultural and food science. We selected this kind of corpus as it has been properly cleaned-up, and builds upon a scientific area which we do not have any knowledge about so to avoid any possible bias and to make the results more realistic. A set of 1000 documents was extracted from which one third were used for setting parameters and making general adjustments, and the rest were used for the GA itself in the evaluation stage.

We then tried to provide answers a basic question concerning our original aims: How good are the hypotheses produced according to human experts in terms of text mining's ultimate goals: interestingness, novelty and usefulness, etc.

In order to address this issue, we used a methodology consisting of two phases: the system evaluation and the experts' assessment.

1. *System Evaluation:* this aims at investigating the behavior and setting the parameter values used by the evolutionary model for KDT.
   We set the GA by generating an initial population of 100 semi-random hypotheses. In addition, we defined the main global parameters such as *Mutation Probability* (0.2), *Cross-over Probability* (0.8), *Maximum Size of Pareto set* (5%), etc. We ran five versions of the GA with the same configuration of parameters but different pairs of terms to address the quest for explanatory novel hypotheses.
2. *Expert Assessment:* this aims at assessing the quality of the discovered knowledge on different criteria by human domain experts. For this, we designed an experiment in which 20 human experts were involved and each assessed 5 hypotheses selected from the Pareto set. We then asked the experts to assess the hypotheses from 1 (worst) to 5 (best) in terms of the following criteria: Interestingness (INT), Novelty (NOV), Usefulness (USE), Sensibleness (SEN), etc.

In order to select worthwhile terms for the experiment, we asked one domain expert to filter pairs of target terms previously related according to traditional clustering analysis. The pairs which finally deserved attention were used as input in the actual experiments (i.e., **glycocide and inhibitors**).

Once the system hypotheses were produced, the experts were asked to score them according to the five subjective criteria. Next, we calculated the scores for every criterion as seen in the overall results in table 1 (for length's sake, only some criterion are shown).

The assessment of individual criteria shows some hypotheses did well with scores above the average (50%) on a 1-5 scale. This is the case for hypotheses 11, 16 and 19 in terms of INT, hypotheses 14 and 19 in terms of SEN, hypotheses 1, 5, 11, 17 and 19 in terms of USE, and hypotheses 24 in terms of NOV, etc.

These results and the evaluation produced by the model were used to measure the correlation between the scores of the human subjects and the system's model evaluation. Since both the expert and the system's model evaluated the results considering several criteria, we first performed a normalization aimed at producing a single "quality" value for each hypothesis.

We then calculated the pair of values for every hypothesis and obtained a (Spearman) correlation $r = 0.43$ ($t - test = 23.75, df = 24, p < 0.001$). From this result, we see that the correlation shows a good level of prediction compared to humans. This indicates that for such a complex task, the model's behavior is not too different from the experts'.

In order to show what the final hypotheses look like and how the good characteristics and less desirable features as above are exhibited, we picked one of the best hypotheses as assessed by the experts (out of 25 best hypotheses) considering the average value of the 5 scores assigned by the user. For example, hypothesis 65 of run 4 looks like: **IF goal(perform(19311)) and goal(analyze(20811)) THEN establish(111)**

Table 1. Distribution of Experts' assessment of Hypothesis per Criteria

Criterion	No. of Hypotheses Negative $<$ Average	Positive $\geq$ Average
ADD	20/25 (80%)	5/25 (20 %)
INT	19/25 (76%)	6/25 (24 %)
NOV	21/25 (84%)	4/25 (16 %)
SEN	17/25 (68%)	8/25 (32 %)
USE	20/25 (80%)	5/25 (20 %)

Where the numerical values represent internal identifiers for the arguments and their semantic vectors, and its resulting criteria vector is $[0.92, 0.09, 0.5, 0.005, 0.7, 0, 0.3, 0.25]$ (the vector's elements represent the values for the criteria relevance, structure, coherence, cohesion, interestingness, plausibility, coverage, and simplicity) and obtained an average expert's assessment of 3.74. In natural-language text, this can roughly be interpreted as:

- The work **aims** at **performing** the genetic grouping of seed populations and investigating a tendency to the separation of northern populations into different classes.
- The **goal** is to **analyse** the vertical integration for producing and selling Pinus Timber in the Andes-Patagonia region.
- As a **consequence**, the best agricultural use for land lots of organic agriculture must be **established** to promote a conservationist culture in priority or critical agricultural areas.

The hypothesis appears to be more relevant and coherent than the others (relevance = 92%). However, this is not complete in terms of cause-effect. For instance, the methods are missing.

In addition, there is also qualitative evidence that there were other subjective factors which influenced some hypotheses' low scores, which was extracted from the experts' overall comments such as the origin and expertise of the experts, the hypotheses understanding, etc.

5 Conclusions

In this work we contribute a novel way of combining additional linguistic information and evolutionary learning techniques in order to produce novel hypotheses which involve explanatory and effective novel knowledge.

We also introduced a unique approach for evaluation which deals with semantic and Data Mining issues in a high-level way. In this context, the proposed representation for hypotheses suggests that performing shallow analysis of the documents and then capturing key rhetorical information may be a good level of processing which constitutes a trade off between completely deep and keyword-based analysis of text documents. In addition, the results suggest that the performance of the model in terms of the correlation with human judgments are slightly better than approaches using external resources. In particular criteria, the model shows a very good correlation between the system evaluation and the expert assessment of the hypotheses.

The model deals with the hypothesis production and evaluation in a very promising way which is shown in the overall results obtained from the experts evaluation and the individual scores for each hypothesis. However, it is important to note that unlike the experts who have a lot of experience, preconceived concept models and complex knowledge in their areas, the system has done relatively well only exploring the corpus of technical documents and the implicit connections contained in it.

References

1. S. Basu, R. Mooney, K. Pasupuleti, and J. Ghosh. Using Lexical Knowledge to Evaluate the Novelty of Rules Mined from Text. *Proceedings of NAACL 2001 Workshop on WordNet and Other Lexical Resources: Applications, Extensions and Customizations, Pittsburg*, June 2001.
2. Kalyanmoy Deb. *Multi-objective Optimization Using Evolutionary Algorithms*. Wiley, 2001.
3. P. Foltz, W. Kintsch, and T. Landauer. The Measurement of Textual Coherence with Latent Semantic Analysis. *Discourse processes*, 25(2):259–284, 1998.
4. J. Han and M. Kamber. *Data Mining: Concepts and Techniques*. Morgan-Kaufmann, 2001.
5. M. Hearst. Text Mining Tools: Instruments for Scientific Discovery. *IMA Text Mining Workshop, USA*, April 2000.
6. D. Jurafsky and J. Martin. *Speech and Language Processing: An Introduction to Natural Language Processing, Computational Linguistics and Speech Recognition*. Prentice Hall, 2000.
7. W. Kintsch. Predication. *Cognitive Science*, 25(2):173–202, 2001.
8. D. Swanson. On the Fragmentation of Knowledge, the Connection Explosion, and Assembling Other People's ideas. *Annual Meeting of the American Society for Information Science and Technology*, 27(3), February 2001.
9. E. Zitzler and L. Thiele. An Evolutionary Algorithm for Multiobjective Optimisation: The Strength Pareto Approach. Technical Report 43, Swiss Federal Institute of Technology (ETH), Switzerland, 1998.

An Efficient Subsequence Matching Method Based on Index Interpolation

Hyun-Gil Koh[1], Woong-Kee Loh[2], and Sang-Wook Kim[3]

[1] Department of Information and Communication Engineering,
Kangwon National University, Korea
gsp2@chollian.net

[2] Department of Computer Science,
Korea Advanced Institute of Science and Technology (KAIST), Korea
woong@mozart.kaist.ac.kr

[3] College of Information and Communications,
Hanyang University, Korea
wook@hanyang.ac.kr

Abstract. Subsequence matching is one of the most important issues in the field of data mining. The existing subsequence matching algorithms use windows of the fixed size to construct only one index. The algorithms have a problem that their performance gets worse as the difference between the query sequence length and the window size increases. In this paper, we propose a new subsequence matching method based on index interpolation, which is a technique that constructs the indexes for multiple window sizes and chooses an index most appropriate for a given query sequence for subsequence matching. We first examine the performance change due to the window size effect through preliminary experiments, and devise a cost function for subsequence matching that reflects the distribution of query sequence lengths in the view point of physical database design. Next, we propose a new subsequence matching method to improve search performance, and present an algorithm based on the cost function to construct the multiple indexes to maximize the performance. Finally, we verify the superiority of the proposed method through a series of experiments using the real and the synthetic data sequences.

Keywords: subsequence matching, index interpolation, window size effect, time-series database.

1 Introduction

Time-series data are the sequences of real values sampled at a fixed time interval, and the database storing time-series data is called a time-series database [1]. The typical examples of time-series data are stock prices, money exchange rates, temperatures, product sales amounts, and medical measurements [2, 4]. The similar sequence matching is to find the data sequences or subsequences

M. Ali and F. Esposito (Eds.): IEA/AIE 2005, LNAI 3533, pp. 480–489, 2005.

similar to a given query sequence from a time-series database, and is one of the most important issues in the field of data mining [1, 2, 4, 6].

Similar sequence matching is categorized into the whole matching and the subsequence matching [4]. The whole matching algorithm returns data sequences that are similar to a given query sequence Q from a time-series database, where the sequences in the database and the query sequence Q are of all the same lengths. The subsequence matching algorithm returns data sequences S that contain the subsequences X that are similar to a given query sequence Q from a time-series database, where the data sequences S and query sequence Q are of any arbitrary lengths. Since the subsequence matching can be used in wider applications than the whole matching, we focus on the subsequence matching in this paper.

The existing subsequence matching algorithms were proposed in [4, 6], which we call as *FRM* and *Dual-Match* in this paper, respectively. The algorithms extract *windows* of the fixed size from data sequences and query sequences of arbitrary lengths. The algorithms construct an index using the windows extracted from data sequences and perform subsequence matching by searching the index using the windows extracted from the given query sequences. FRM and Dual-Match are explained in more detail in Section 2. The size of window is one of the major factors that affect the performance of the subsequence matching. As the difference between the query sequence length and the window size increases, the performance tends to degrade. This phenomenon is called *window size effect* [6], and is explained through preliminary experiments in Section 3.

In this paper, we propose a new subsequence matching method based on index interpolation [5] to overcome the performance degradation due to the window size effect. Index interpolation is a technique that constructs multiple indexes and performs subsequence matching by choosing one index most appropriate for a given query sequence. Even though a subsequence matching method is based on index interpolation, its specific algorithms such as constructing multiple indexes, choosing an index, and searching similar subsequences using the chosen index can differ according to applications. The method proposed in this paper extends the existing FRM and Dual-Match algorithms, and dramatically enhances their performances.

The major contributions of this paper are summarized as follows: (1) Through preliminary experiments, we show the performance change according to the difference between the query sequence length and the window size in the existing subsequence matching algorithms. (See Section 3) (2) We propose a new subsequence matching method based on index interpolation to solve the problem of performance degradation due to the window size effect. (See Section 4.1) (3) We present a cost function for subsequence matching that reflects the distribution of query sequence lengths in the view point of physical database design. Based on the cost function, we present an algorithm to construct multiple indexes to maximize the performance of the proposed method given the number of indexes. (See Section 4.2) (4) We verify the superiority of the proposed method through a series of experiments using the real and the synthetic data sequences. (See Section 5)

2 Related Work

2.1 FRM

FRM [4] is an extension of the whole matching algorithm proposed in [1], and introduced the notion of a window of the fixed size. Figure 1 shows the sliding and disjoint windows extracted from a sequence S.

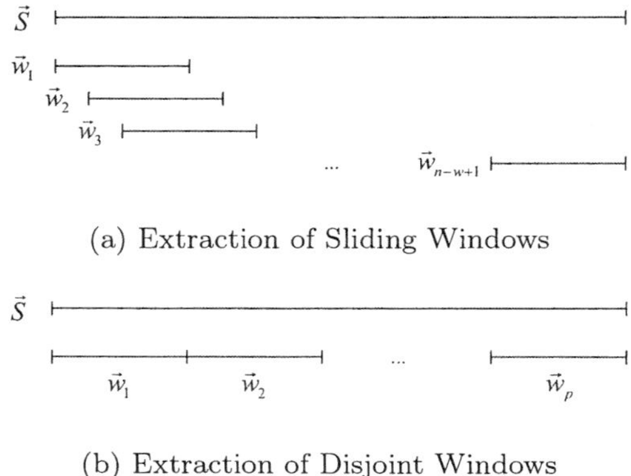

(a) Extraction of Sliding Windows
(b) Extraction of Disjoint Windows

Fig. 1. Extraction of Sliding and Disjoint Windows

In the indexing stage, FRM extracts sliding windows of size w from all the data sequences S in a database, which are called data windows. For efficient subsequence matching, the multi-dimensional index is used for indexing those data windows. The subsequence matching stage of FRM consists of the index search (IS) and the post-processing (PP) phases. In the IS phase, FRM divides a given query sequence Q into disjoint windows of size w, which are called query windows. For each query window, FRM searches for all the data windows that are close to the query window using the index constructed in the indexing stage. The candidate set is constructed with all the subsequences containing the data windows obtained in the IS phase. The candidate set contains false alarms, i.e., the subsequences that are *not* to be returned as the final query result. The PP phase is for removing such false alarms. FRM sets the window size w to be the minimum length $\min(Len(Q))$ of the query sequences Q in a specific application. It is proved in [4] that FRM does not cause false dismissal, i.e., the algorithm does not miss any subsequence that should be returned as the final query result.

FRM forms minimum bounding rectangles (MBRs) containing multiple data windows as shown in Figure 2, and stores the MBRs in the index. By storing the MBRs in the index instead of each data window individually, while it can reduce the necessary storage space, it can also dramatically increase the number of false alarms [6]. In Figure 2, q_i $(1 \leq i \leq p)$ is a query window and ϵ' is the search range from q_i. As shown in the figure, even though the data windows

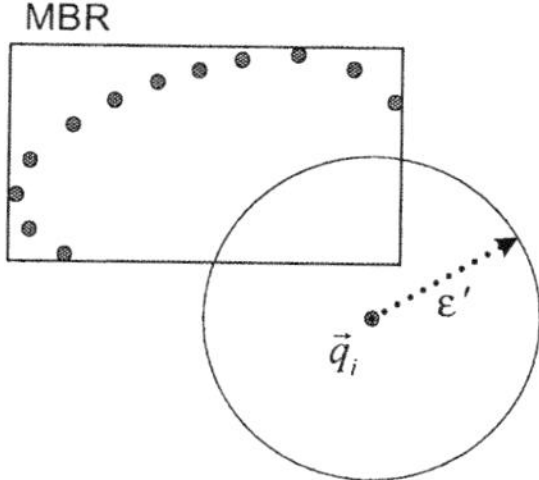

Fig. 2. MBR and Search Range in FRM

in the MBR are not actually within the search range centered with q_i, since the MBR overlaps the search range, the subsequences corresponding to the data windows are contained in the candidate set. Those windows increase the size of a candidate set and cause severe performance degradation.

2.2 Dual-Match

Dual-Match was proposed in [6] to overcome the weakness of FRM addressed above. Dual-Match extracts windows in the way opposite to FRM: It extracts disjoint windows from data sequences and sliding windows from a query sequence. In Dual-Match, instead of storing the MBRs containing multiple data windows as in FRM, each data window is individually stored in the index. By this way of constructing the index, Dual-Match can dramatically reduce the number of false alarms, and can obtain search performance much better than FRM. Usually, Dual-Match sets the window size w to be $\lfloor(\min(Len(Q)) + 1)/2\rfloor$. It is proved in [6] that Dual-Match does not cause false dismissal when using the window size.

3 Preliminary Experiments

3.1 Experiment Environments

We used 620 Korean stock price data sequences of length 1024 in the preliminary experiments. To generate query sequences, we randomly extracted and perturbed subsequences from the data sequences. We used the total execution time for subsequence matching for all the query sequences as the performance factor.

We performed two preliminary experiments. The first experiment used only one index of the fixed window size $w = 64$ and observed the tendency of subsequence matching performance while changing the query sequence length to $Len(Q) = 64$, 128, 256, 512, and 1024. The second experiment used the query sequences of the fixed length $Len(Q) = 1024$ and observed the tendency of subsequence matching performance while changing the window size to $w = 64$, 128, 256, 512, and 1024.

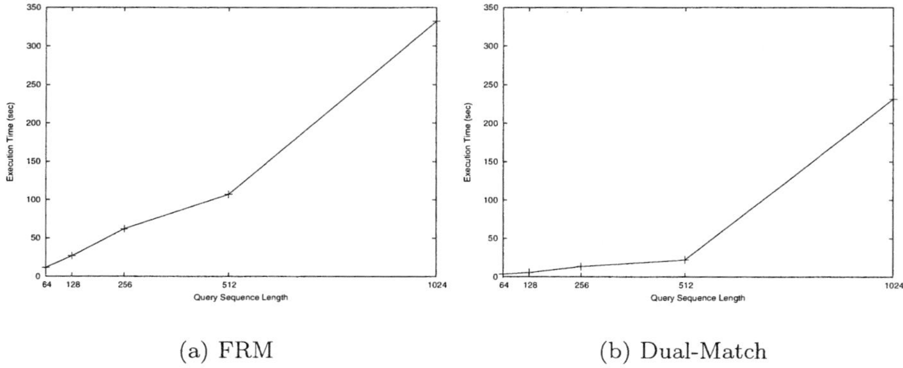

(a) FRM (b) Dual-Match

Fig. 3. Variation of Total Execution Time According to Query Sequence Lengths

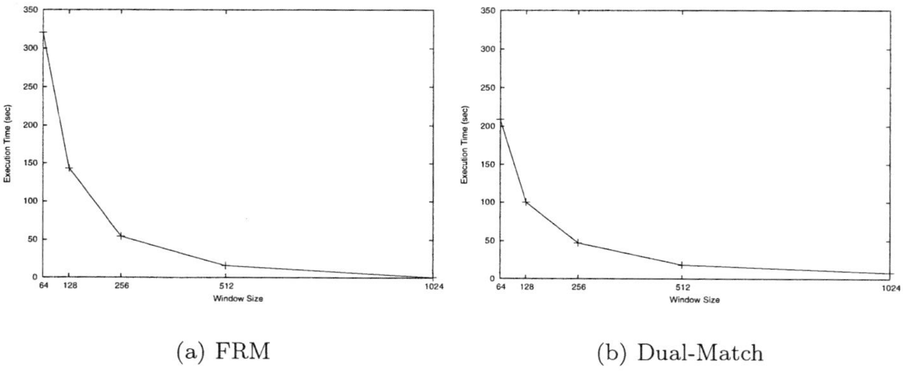

(a) FRM (b) Dual-Match

Fig. 4. Variation of Total Execution Time According to Window Sizes

3.2 Experiment Results and Analysis

Figures 3(a) and 3(b) show the results of the first preliminary experiment for FRM and Dual-Match, respectively. In the figures, the horizontal axes represent the query sequence length, and the vertical axes the total execution time expressed in the unit of seconds. Figures 4(a) and 4(b) show the results of the second preliminary experiment for FRM and Dual-Match, respectively. In the figures, the horizontal axes represent the window size.

According to the results of two preliminary experiments, the subsequence matching performance was found to be roughly proportional to the query sequence length and to be inversely proportional to the window size. By the shape of graphs in Figures 3 and 4, the execution time or cost T of subsequence matching can be expressed as the following Eq. (1):

$$T = c \cdot \frac{Len(Q)}{w} \; (c > 0) \; . \tag{1}$$

4 The Proposed Method

4.1 Basic Idea

Both FRM and Dual-Match use only one index constructed using the windows of a fixed size [4, 6]. Such an approach may result in a very poor search performance in the applications where query sequences are of various lengths. To obtain the satisfiable search performance, the subsequence matching method proposed in this paper constructs multiple indexes for windows of various sizes.

The index used in the proposed method is called the w-index [5]. Given a query sequence, subsequence matching is performed using one of the w-indexes chosen by the following Eq. (2):

$$w_{\max} = \begin{cases} \max\{w_i | w_i \le Len(Q)\ (1 \le i \le k)\} & \text{for FRM,} \\ \max\{w_i | w_i \le \lfloor (Len(Q)+1)/2 \rfloor\ (1 \le i \le k)\} & \text{for Dual-Match ,} \end{cases} \quad (2)$$

where k is the number of w-indexes, and w_i $(1 \le i \le k)$ are the window sizes for which w-indexes are constructed. Once $w_{\max}$ is chosen using Eq. (2), subsequence matching is performed using the w-index constructed using the windows of size $w_{\max}$.

The following Lemma 1 shows the robustness of the proposed method.

Lemma 1. The subsequence matching using the w-index chosen by Eq. (2) does not cause false dismissal.

Proof: We omit the proof due to the page limitation. □

```
Procedure GetWindowSizes
    Compute w_max(Q_1);
    for i = 2 .. k do
        for each possible w (≤ M) other than w_max(Q_j) (1 ≤ j < i) do
            Compute T;                    // using Eq. (3)
            if T is minimum then
                w_max(Q_i) = w;
            endif
        end for
    end for
end.
```

Fig. 5. Window Sizes Determination Algorithm

Even though it is possible to use the w-index for window size w' other than $w_{\max}$ chosen by Eq. (2), it provides the better search performance to use the w-index chosen by Eq. (2) than that for w'. If w' is smaller than $w_{\max}$, it holds that $w' < w_{\max} \le Len(Q)$ (for FRM) or $w' < w_{\max} \le \lfloor (Len(Q)+1)/2 \rfloor$ (for Dual-Match). Due to the window size effect, the search performance using the w-index for window size w' is worse than that for window size $w_{\max}$.

If w' is larger than $w_{\max}$, there must exist a query sequence Q whose length satisfies that $w' > Len(Q)$ (for FRM) or $w' > \lfloor (Len(Q)+1)/2 \rfloor$ (for Dual-Match). Since neither FRM nor Dual-Match can process the query sequence Q using the w-index for window size w', they should perform subsequence matching by the sequential scan. The search performance by the sequential scan is much worse than that using the w-indexes.

4.2 Construction of Multiple w-Indexes

In this paper, we discuss the index construction method using the physical database design approach. We assume that the query tendency in the future should be similar to that in the past in most applications. Given the distribution of the query sequence lengths in the past and the number k of w-indexes to be constructed, the proposed method determines the window sizes w_1, w_2, ..., w_k to construct the maximal w-indexes.

We first formulate the cost equation for subsequence matching for all the query sequences in an application. To compute the cost function, we partition all the query sequences into groups Q_1, Q_2, ..., Q_g by their lengths ($Len(Q_1) < Len(Q_2) < \ldots < Len(Q_g)$), where g is the number of the groups, i.e., the number of distinct lengths. We let the window sizes chosen by Eq. (2) for each group be $w_{\max}(Q_1), w_{\max}(Q_2), \ldots, w_{\max}(Q_g)$ ($w_{\max}(Q_1) \leq w_{\max}(Q_2) \leq \ldots \leq w_{\max}(Q_g)$). Here, we assume that the number of w-indexes k is less than or equal to the number of query sequence groups g.[1]

Under these configurations, we can compute the total cost T of subsequence matching based on index interpolation by extending Eq. (1) in Section 3 as the following Eq. (3):

$$T = \sum_{1 \leq i \leq g} \left(\frac{Len(Q_i)}{w_{\max}(Q_i)} \right) \cdot F_i \ , \tag{3}$$

where F_i ($1 \leq i \leq g$) is the frequency of each query sequence group Q_i, which can be computed by dividing the number of query sequences in a group Q_i by the number of all the query sequences.[2]

We next present an algorithm to determine the window sizes. If we consider all the combinations of window sizes, the time complexity should become $O(M^k)$, where M is the maximum query sequence length. The heuristic algorithm shown in Figure 5 is given the distribution of query sequence lengths and the number of w-indexes k, and returns the window sizes $w_{\max}(Q_i)$ ($1 \leq i \leq k$) that minimizes the total search cost T in Eq. (3). Since the algorithm has only two nested for-loops in the figure, the time complexity is $O(M \cdot k)$.

[1] If k is greater than g, there must exist at least $(k-g)$ w-indexes that are never used. So, we can discard such w-indexes and downsize the problem so that k is less than or equal to g.

[2] Unlike Eq. (1), Eq. (3) does not contain the positive constant c because the cost values computed by Eq. (3) are only relatively compared with one another in the algorithm in Figure 5.

5 Performance Evaluation

5.1 Experiment Environment

We used the real and the synthetic data sequences for performance evaluation in the experiments. The real data sequences, which were also used in Section 3, are 620 Korean stock price sequences of length 1024, and the synthetic data sequences are 5000 random walk sequences of length 1024.

The query sequences have lengths that are multiples of 32 in the range [64, 1024], and those with the same length belong to a group (31 groups in total). We unevenly distributed the query sequences over the groups, and Table 1 shows the distribution of query sequence lengths. We used the sum of execution times for the whole 216 query sequences as the performance factor, and adjusted the tolerance ϵ for each query sequence so that 20 subsequences should be returned as the final result.

We compared the performances of three methods in the experiments: (A) FRM and Dual-Match algorithms using only one index (the same as the original algorithms), (B) FRM and Dual-Match algorithms extended to use the w-indexes with the fixed interval, and (C) FRM and Dual-Match algorithms extended to use the w-indexes constructed by the proposed algorithm. Each of them is briefly called as method (A), (B), and (C) in this paper.

5.2 Experiment Results

We performed two experiments in this paper. First, we compared the performances of methods (A), (B), and (C) using the real data sequences changing the number of w-indexes. Second, we compared the performances using the synthetic data sequences changing the number of data sequences.

We performed the first experiment for FRM and Dual-Match independently. For FRM, we used only one index for $w = 64$ for method (A), five w-indexes for $w = 64, 304, 544, 784, 1024$ for method (B), and five w-indexes for $w = 64, 224, 384, 768, 896$ for method (C). For Dual-Match, we used only one index for $w = 32$ for method (A), five w-indexes for $w = 32, 152, 272, 392, 512$ for method (B), and five w-indexes for $w = 32, 112, 192, 384, 448$ for method (C). Figure 6 shows the result of the first experiment. In the figures, the horizontal

Table 1. Number of Query Sequences in Each Group

Number of query sequence groups	Number of query sequences in each group	Sub-total number of query sequences
4	30	120
5	10	50
6	5	30
16	1	16
Total: 31		216

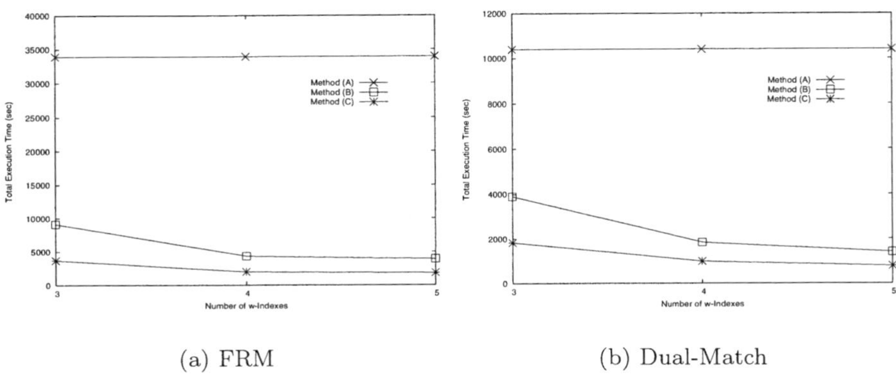

(a) FRM (b) Dual-Match

Fig. 6. Comparisons of Performances Changing the Number of w-Indexes

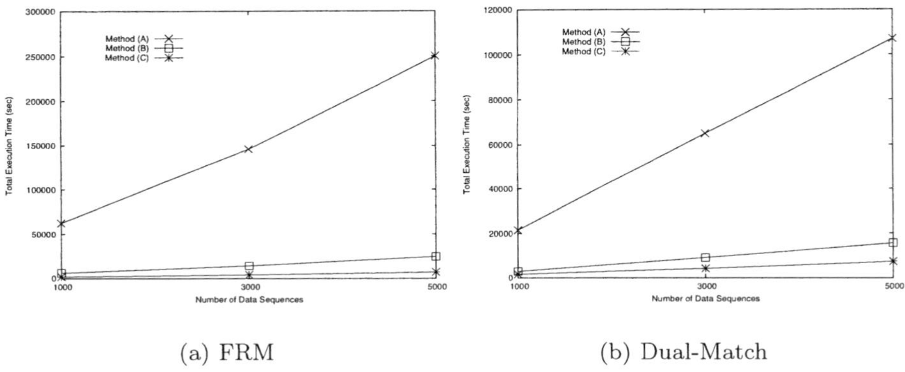

(a) FRM (b) Dual-Match

Fig. 7. Comparisons of Performances Changing the Number of Data Sequences

axes represent the number of w-indexes, and the vertical axes represent the total execution time in seconds. In Figure 6(a), when using five w-indexes, method (C) outperformed up to 18.4 times than method (A) and up to 2.1 times than method (B). In Figure 6(b), method (C) outperformed up to 13.3 times than method (A) and up to 1.8 times than method (B).

We performed the second experiment to observe the performances changing the number of synthetic data sequences to 1000, 3000, and 5000. For both FRM and Dual-Match, we used five w-indexes for methods (B) and (C) for the same window sizes w as in the first experiment. Figure 7 shows the result of the second experiment. In the figures, the horizontal axes represent the number of data sequences. In Figure 7(a), when using 5000 data sequences, method (C) outperformed up to 35.5 times than method (A) and up to 3.5 times than method (B). In Figure 7(b), method (C) outperformed up to 14.5 times than method (A) and up to 2.1 times than method (B).

6 Conclusions

In this paper, we proposed a new subsequence matching method based on index interpolation [5] to overcome the search performance degradation of the existing algorithms due to the window size effect. We formulated a cost function in the view point of physical database design, and presented a heuristic algorithm based on the cost function to construct multiple w-indexes that maximize the search performance of the proposed method. We showed the superiority of the proposed method upon the existing algorithms by a series of experiments.

Acknowledgment

This work has been supported by Korea Research Foundation under Grant (KRF-2003-041-D00486) and by the IT Research Center via Kangwon National University.

References

1. R. Agrawal et al., "Efficient Similarity Search in Sequence DataBases," In *Proc. Int'l Conf. on Foundations of Data Organization and Algorithms (FODO)*, pp. 69-84, Chicago, Illinois, Oct. 1993.
2. R. Agrawal et al., "Fast Similarity Search in the Presence of Noise, Scaling, and Translation in Time-Series Database," In *Proc. Int'l Conf. on Very Large Data Bases (VLDB)*, pp. 490-501, Zurich, Switzerland, Sept. 1995.
3. K. P. Chan and A. W. C. Fu, "Efficient Time Series Matching by Wavelets," In *Proc. Int'l Conf. on Data Engineering (ICDE)*, IEEE, pp. 126-133, Sydney, Australia, Mar. 1999.
4. C. Faloutsos et al., "Fast Subsequence Matching in Time-series Databases," In *Proc. Int'l Conf. on Management of Data*, ACM SIGMOD, pp. 419-429, Minneapolis, Minnesota, May 1994.
5. W. K. Loh et al., "A Subsequence Matching Algorithm that Supports Normalization Transform in Time-Series Databases," *Data Mining and Knowledge Discovery*, Vol. 9, No. 1, pp. 5-28, July 2004.
6. Y. S. Moon et al., "Duality-Based Subsequence Matching in Time-Series Databases," In *Proc. Int'l Conf. on Data Engineering (ICDE)*, IEEE, pp. 263-272, Heidelberg, Germany, Apr. 2001.

A Meteorological Conceptual Modeling Approach Based on Spatial Data Mining and Knowledge Discovery

Yubin Yang[1,2], Hui Lin[2], Zhongyang Guo[2], and Jixi Jiang[3]

[1] State Key Laboratory for Novel Software Technology, Nanjing University, Nanjing 210093, P. R. China
yangyubin@cuhk.edu.hk

[2] Joint Laboratory for Geoinformation Science, The Chinese University of Hong Kong, Shatin, N.T., Hong Kong

[3] National Satellite Meteorological Center, China Meteorological Administration, Beijing 100081, P. R. China

Abstract. Conceptual models play an important part in a variety of domains, especially in meteorological applications. This paper proposes a novel conceptual modeling approach based on a two-phase spatial data mining and knowledge discovery method, aiming to model the concepts of the evolvement trends of Mesoscale Convective Clouds (MCCs) over the Tibetan Plateau with derivation rules and environmental physical models. Experimental results show that the proposed conceptual model to much extent simplifies and improves the weather forecasting techniques on heavy rainfalls and floods in South China.

1 Introduction

Conceptual modeling is concerned with identifying, analyzing and describing the essential concepts and constraints of a domain with the help of modeling tools which are based on a small set of basic meta-concepts and derivation rules [1]. Conceptual models play an important part in a variety of areas. Especially as we are moving into the information age in which a vast amount of image data such as satellite images, medical images, and digital photographs are generated every day, concept extraction and modeling in those data-rich multimedia environment becomes much more important than before [2]. Therefore, how to extend the conceptual modeling techniques to those new emerged applications is an important research issue.

It is, however, well known that not all conceptualizations of a domain are equally suitable. Hence, the extraction of concept information requires a process of specifying data models or derivation rules that define the mapping from the actual data to the concepts that the domain users are interested. This process usually requires in-depth domain knowledge of relevant technologies.

In this paper, to address the conceptual modeling problem related to a real meteorological application, we propose a novel conceptual modeling approach based on a two-phase spatial data mining and knowledge discovery method, which aims at modeling concepts of the evolvement trends of Mesoscale Convective Clouds (MCCs) over the Tibetan Plateau by using their spatial environmental physical attributes and the meteorological satellite spatio-temporal imagery. The concept model consists of two

M. Ali and F. Esposito (Eds.): IEA/AIE 2005, LNAI 3533, pp. 490 – 499, 2005.

parts: derivation rules and environmental physical models, which correspond to the two data mining phases respectively. The proposed conceptual model is proved to simplify and improve the weather forecasting techniques on heavy rainfalls and floods in South China to much extent.

The rest of this paper is organized as follows. Firstly, the research background including some related work is shortly described in Section 2. Next, Section 3 proposes the architecture of our conceptual model describing the evolvement trends of MCCs. The two-phase spatial data mining and knowledge discovery process is then presented in Section 4 and experimental results are illustrated in Section 5. Finally, conclusion remarks with several future work issues are provided in Section 6.

2 Background and Motivation

2.1. Meteorological Background

The study of the life cycles, movement trajectories and evolvements of MCCs is always an important and challenging issue in the meteorological field. Especially in China, MCCs over the Tibetan Plateau were recently revealed to be the major factor resulting in the heavy rainfalls in Yangtze River Basin, which directly causes severe floods in South China [3]. Consequently, it is in high demand to make an appropriate conceptualization of the evolvement trends of MCCs over the Tibetan Plateau from the satellite data and image collections, in order to predict and evaluate the potential occurrences of strong precipitations effectively and efficiently.

Nowadays, meteorology community has already established some numerical weather forecasting systems based on different kinds of satellite imagery by using empirical numerical models. Examples are as follows. Souto et al. proposed a cloud analysis method aiming at rainfall forecasting in Spain by using a high-resolution non-hydrostatic numerical model applied to the satellite observations [4]. Arnaud et al. presented an automatic cloud tracking method based on area-overlapping analysis [5]. However, there are still many research issues, such as trajectory prediction and causation analysis, cannot be solved by numerical means. For this purpose, domain-specific concept models should be constructed with the goal of generalizing the properties and discovering the hidden associations from the data collections, by which the meteorological and geographical data can be transformed into information, inference, and even decision making.

2.2 Data Sources

Satellites with high spatial and temporal resolutions always provide a huge amount of meaningful data for meteorological research. The collection with large amount of data, as the foundation for spatial data mining and knowledge discovery, is indispensable for conceptual modeling of MCCs. For this purpose, satellite imagery, together with the brightness temperature (TBB) data taken by Geostationally Meteorological Satellite (GMS) 5, and High resolution Limited area Analysis and Forecasting System (HLAFS) data, which provides nine different kinds of environmental physical attributes including geopotential height (H), temperature (T), relative humidity (RH), vorticity (VOR), wind divergence (DIV), vertical wind speed (W), water vapor flux divergence (IFVQ), pseudo-equivalent potential temperature (θSE), K index (K), are used in the research of this paper as the target datasets. The data are from June 1998 to August 1998, a representative period when South China suffered from severe floods resulting from intensive heavy rainfalls, provided by China National Satellite Meteorological Center. The satellite imagery and TBB data are used for identifying and tracking MCCs, while the HLAFS data are actually employed to model the relationships between the evolvement trends of MCCs and their environmental physical models. Fig. 1 illustrates a snapshot of GMS-5 satellite cloud imagery. Since only the MCCs over the Tibetan Plateau are of our research interest, the actual spatial coverage of the data is from latitude 27°N to 40°N and longitude 80°E to 105°E.

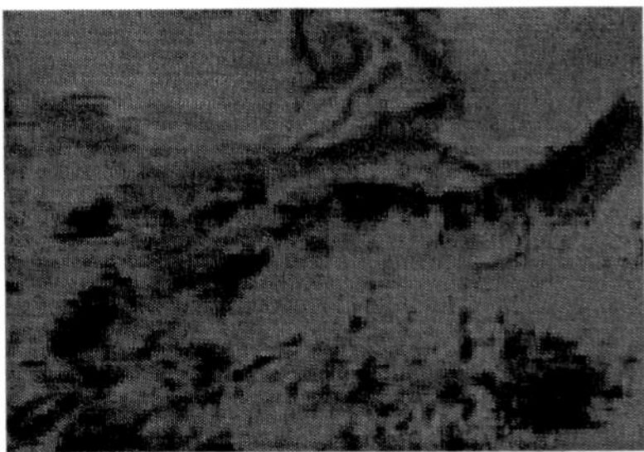

Fig. 1. GMS-5 Satellite Cloud Image

2.3 Cloud Tracking and Characterization

The MCC is the most essential and natural concept in the conceptual model targeting to explore the evolvement trends of MCCs over the Tibetan Plateau. Since the satellite imagery and data are spatio-temporal, we should firstly identify and track each MCC from the whole image sequences correctly and efficiently, then make necessary characterization by extracting their attributes from the corresponding data collections.

To address the above problems, we propose a fast tracking and characterization method of multiple moving clouds from meteorological satellite imagery based on feature correspondences [5,6]. The method is based on the fact that in a relative small time-span, the deformation of a MCC is progressive and detectable, which means that at two consecutive satellite images the same MCC will keep a relatively similar moving speed, shape, area and texture. Using the 8-connectivity chain code representation [7], each MCC is firstly segmented out from each satellite image, then the following features are computed: area, intensity, and protraction ratio. We also compute two kinds of morphological features, i.e. roundness and scattering degree based on Fourier Transformation [6]. In addition, spatial self-correlation function is also calculated for each cloud as its texture features. Then, we can make use of feature correspondences to identify and track the original MCCs in the time-varying satellite image sequences.

The first kind of feature correspondence is to compute the overlapping area ratio of two MCCs detected in two consecutive image windows of a pre-defined size. Those two MCCs are identified as the same original MCC if their overlapping area ratio is greater than the threshold value. The other feature correspondence is applied on morphological features and texture features, which are combined into a feature vector. We choose normalized Euclidean distance measurement to calculate their similarities, in terms of which two MCCs are identified whether they belong to the same original MCC.

Subsequently, in the characterization stage, the qualified MCCs are categorized into four types according to their evolvement trends on the satellite imagery, that is, MCCs moving out of the Tibetan Plateau in East (E), MCCs moving out of the Tibetan Plateau in Northeast (NE), MCCs moving out of the Tibetan Plateau in Southeast (SE) and MCCs staying in the Tibetan Plateau (STAY-IN).

3 Architecture of Conceptual Model

Conceptual model has reached a high maturity due to the availability of a sound and complete theory. However, we are entering an age where information content becomes a key concern. Therefore, data mining and knowledge discovery, i.e. the integration of data, information and knowledge, will be one of the very important future research directions of conceptual modeling [2]. By identifying valid, novel, interesting, useful, and understandable patterns in data, it allows to decrease complexity of processed data noticeably, and to focus on key factors of a conceptual model being created.

The conceptualization of the evolvement trends of MCCs over the Tibetan Plateau is a typical case facing one of the above challenges. From the satellite imagery and data, we should firstly infer the presence of objects, i.e., MCC structures, and the existence of a state of affairs, such as splitting, merging, vanishing and new-emergence of MCCs. Then, appropriate attributes of each object, including TBB value, HLAFS attributes and MCC's feature values, should be singled out to model the target concepts.

In this paper, we propose a data model called the Mesoscale Convective Cloud Conceptual Model (MC^3M), to map the satellite data into human perceived concepts related to the evolvement trends of MCCs. The objective of MC^3M is to enable the meteorologists to understand the data models easily and use them to perform forecasting tasks without worrying too much about technical details. The architecture of MC^3M conceptual model is shown in Fig. 2.

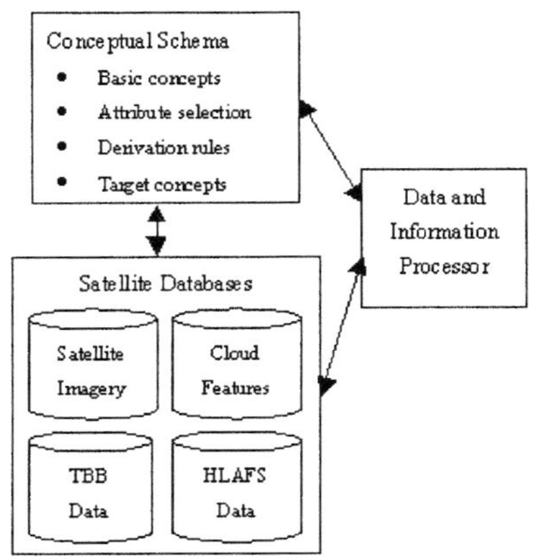

Fig. 2. Architecture of MC^3M Conceptual Model

The MC^3M conceptual model is specially designed to comprise the following three main components: (1) a multi-tier conceptual schema, (2) satellite databases, and (3) a data and information processor, which includes a two-phase spatial data mining and knowledge discovery process.

The satellite databases consist of all the attribute data related to the MCCs in the satellite imagery. The conceptual schema describes the concept hierarchy used to predict the evolvement trends of MCCs, composed of the following four parts: basic concepts, attribute selection, derivation rules and target concepts. Naturally, the tracked MCCs in the satellite imagery are represented as the basic concepts. On the other hand, from meteorologist's perspective, the evolvement trends of MCCs, especially the directions when they are moving out of the Tibetan Plateau, can be referenced as the firsthand proof for their weather analysis and forecasting decisions.

So the four categories of the qualified MCCs, i.e., E, NE, SE and STAY-IN, serve as the target concepts.

Furthermore, in MC^3M model, to implement the inference from the basic concepts to the target concepts, the conceptual schema should determine which kinds of attributes will be included in the construction of environmental physical models, and which ones will be ruled out. Moreover, a set of derivation rules should also be set up for this purpose. Those issues play a key role to make our conceptual modeling approach sound and practical. Therefore, data and information processor, the third component of MC^3M model, is thus introduced to address the above two issues effectively. The data and information processor implements a two-phase spatial data mining and knowledge discovery method, which is detailed in the next section.

4 Spatial Data Mining and Knowledge Discovery

One of the purposes of data mining and knowledge discovery technology is to aid in constructing valid conceptual model from the large data repositories. There are already researchers carried out their conceptual modeling process combining with data mining and knowledge discovery methodologies. For example, Goan proposed a method tightly coupling the knowledge discovery process with an explicit conceptual model to address the user interaction and collaboration problem [8]. With this method, the user can then use the explicit conceptual model to access different kinds of information.

In this paper, as stated above, spatial data mining and knowledge discovery technologies are employed to deal with two important issues to the conceptual model of MCCs, that is, environmental physical model construction and derivation rules generation. The meteorologists have revealed that the evolvement trends of MCCs have strong connections with some factors in the corresponding TBB data, HLAFS attributes and their representative features such as area, shape, etc. However, how to exactly find out what factors indeed contribute to the evolvement patterns of MCCs is really a problem. Moreover, to reveal how the selected attributes finally affect the evolvement trends of MCCs, that is, to establish the environmental physical models of MCCs is another tough work. So, aiming at solving these problems automatically, a two-phase spatial data mining and knowledge discovery method, which is naturally a data-driven approach with large-scale scientific databases, is proposed and implemented to relieve the meteorologists of the heavy burden of manual work. Supposing that all the data in satellite databases are defined as a set Ω, the attributes relevant to predicting the evolvement trends of MCCs are defined as a set Ψ, where Ψ is a subset of Ω, and the target concepts, i.e., the evolvement trends of MCCs, are defined as a set £, then the two-phase spatial data mining and knowledge discovery method we proposed can be represented as the following two mapping functions: f_{p1}: $\Omega \rightarrow \Psi$, and f_{p2}: $\Psi \rightarrow$ £.

The former function f_{p1} generates derivation rules using C4.5 decision tree algorithm [9,10], by which the evolvement trend of each MCC can be inferred provided that their TBB data and HLAFS attributes are extracted. The latter function f_{p2} then determine which HLAFS attributes are crucial to influence the evolvement trends of MCCs that will possibly cause heavy rainfalls in Yangtze River Basin, and plot the corresponding environmental physical model graphs based on those selected "relevant" HLAFS attributes.

4.1 Data Preprocessing from Spatial Perspective

Before spatial data mining and knowledge discovery steps are taken, the satellite data should be preprocessed according to certain domain-related prior knowledge. In order to analyze and discover the relationship and causality between MCCs and their attributes in terms of the knowledge from meteorologists, we should not only consider the geographical center point of a MCC, but also take into account, from a kind of spatial perspective, its adjacent geographical neighborhoods. This spatial perspective is illustrated in Fig. 3.

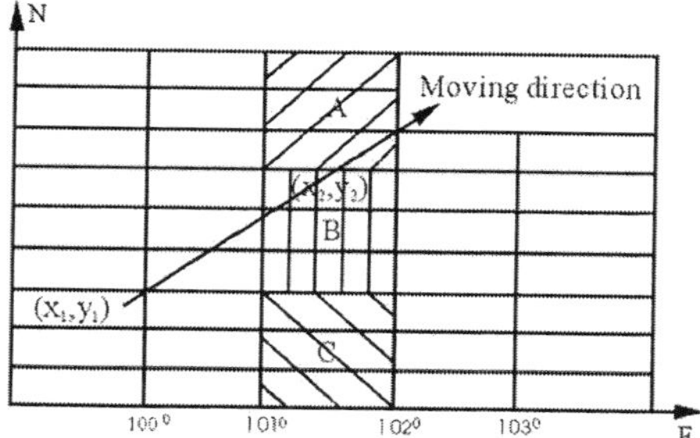

Fig. 3. Spatial Perspective in Data Mining

As we can see from Fig. 3, the geographical neighborhood regions of our interests are labeled as A, B and C, respectively, where the center of MCC is located in the central cell of region B. Each of the neighborhood region is in a size of 1°(longitude)×3°(latitude). For each MCC located in region B, the average values of HLAFS attributes for geographical region A, B and C are all computed. Next, we then calculate the difference value of each corresponding HLAFS attribute values in region B and A, which are denoted as a feature vector $D_{b\text{-}a}$, and those of region C and B, which are denoted as another feature vector $D_{c\text{-}b}$. Afterwards, a new feature vector consisting of the following attributes is generated for each MCC:

1) All the elements of feature vector $D_{b\text{-}a}$, which are related to HLAFS attributes including $H_{b\text{-}a}$, $T_{b\text{-}a}$, $RH_{b\text{-}a}$, $VOR_{b\text{-}a}$, $DIV_{b\text{-}a}$, $W_{b\text{-}a}$, $IFVQ_{b\text{-}a}$, $\theta SE_{b\text{-}a}$, and $K_{b\text{-}a}$;
2) All the elements of feature vector $D_{c\text{-}b}$, which are related to HLAFS attributes including $H_{c\text{-}b}$, $T_{c\text{-}b}$, $RH_{c\text{-}b}$, $VOR_{c\text{-}b}$, $DIV_{c\text{-}b}$, $W_{c\text{-}b}$, $IFVQ_{c\text{-}b}$, $\theta SE_{c\text{-}b}$, and $K_{c\text{-}b}$;
3) Area of each MCC;
4) Shape of each MCC, which is categorized into *Ellipse*, *Circle* or *other shapes* according to its morphological features;
5) Geographical position of each MCC represented as latitude and longitude values;
6) The lowest average TBB value of each MCC.

4.2 Phase I: Mining for Derivation Rules

The target concepts of our model can be defined to be a set of independently identified constructs composed of knowledge primitives and environmental physical models. The objective of data mining phase I is to conclude and abstract a set of independently identified knowledge primitives, which are used to predict the evolvement trends of MCCs based on their environmental physical field attributes, i.e., HLAFS attributes, and other extracted spatial features such as latitude, longitude and area, shape etc. Each of knowledge primitive is represented as a derivation rule explaining the relationship between those attributes of MCC and its evolvement trend. In Phase I, we make use of C4.5 decision tree algorithm to generate the derivation rules. The resulting rules define the patterns by which a concept, that is, the evolvement trends of MCCs, can be deduced.

The resulting rules is in the form as '$P_1\Lambda\ldots\Lambda P_m \rightarrow Q$', where $P_1,\ldots,P_m$ are different attribute data, and Q is one of the characterization categories of MCCs, i.e. "E", "NE", "SE" or "STAY-IN". The rule is interpreted as: "When the precondition '$P_1\Lambda\ldots\ \Lambda P_m$' comes into existence, then the pattern 'Q' is to be determined on the evolvement trends of the MCC with a certain probability".

One of the advantages of this method is that useful information and knowledge can be efficiently mined from large-scale databases, with high accuracy and relatively low computation burden. For each MCC, we can infer its evolvement trend using the knowledge represented as decision rules. Moreover, it can handle categorical and continuous attributes both employed in our data mining process, and the rules generated by C4.5 decision tree algorithm are quite easy to understand as well.

4.3 Phase II: Mining for Environmental Physical Models

The resulting derivation rules define the patterns by which the evolvement of MCCs can be deduced. However, that is not enough for predicting the possible heavy rainfall occurrences. Meteorologists always achieve their heavy rainfall prediction by eliciting and plotting the environmental physical model influencing the evolvement trends of MCCs that will possibly raise heavy rainfalls. Using environmental physical models, the influence of each relevant attribute on the evolvement trends of MCCs can be evaluated and then used to predict the real evolvement of new MCC.

Nevertheless, not all the attributes appearing as the precondition of the resulting derivation rules are relevant factors. We take advantage of the resulting C4.5 decision tree generated in Phase I to identify the relevant attributes, for it can clearly show which attributes are more important than others. We firstly make a simple statistic of all the preconditions of those result C4.5 rules, then select the HLAFS attributes that appear simultaneously at least in two rules as the variables used for constructing environmental physical models, which is also crucial to our conceptual modeling. Finally, all the values of each relevant HLAFS attribute corresponding to the identified MCCs are spatially averaged, which are then used to plot the corresponding environmental physical models for the heavy rainfall forecasting purpose.

It should be noted that the derivation rule part of the target concepts are based on each MCC. For each newly identified MCC, we can deduce their evolvement trend from the knowledge represented as decision rules. While for the environmental physical model, it targets on each individual attribute, where the attribute values of the same kind of MCCs are spatially averaged to provide a geographical relevance analysis of their evolvement trends. Both two parts are integrated and complementary components for modeling the concepts of the evolvement trends of MCCs.

5 Experimental Results

We concentrate on conceptual modeling issues under the "learning-from-data" paradigm. This paradigm requires large number of training and testing samples to derive meaningful results from data. We therefore carried on experiments of our meteorological concept modeling approach on a large-scale database, as mentioned in Section 2.2. The large size of those data provides the consistent and comprehensive archive of satellite data information, from which there are totally 320 qualified MCCs tracked and characterized for conceptual modeling purpose, among which 50 MCCs moved out of the Tibetan Plateau (105^0E): 37 MCCs for "E", 9 MCCs for "NE" and 4 MCCs for "SE". 70% of all the identified MCCs, that is, totally 224 MCCs, are used as training samples and the remaining 30% part are kept for testing. The attributes used in the data mining process are listed as follows: the nine different kinds of HLAFS attributes, area of MCC (km^2), the average lowest TBB value of MCC (°C), shape of MCC (*Ellipse*, *Circle*, *Others*) and geographical position of MCC (longitude and latitude coordinate values).

Table 1 lists the resulting decision rules of C4.5 algorithm, which have already been pruned, for classifying the evolvement trends of MCCs moving out of the Tibetan Plateau (at 500hPa level). After tree pruning process, the number of misclassification on test cases is 5 MCCs out of 96 MCCs, and the error rate is 5.2%.

Table 1. The Resulting Decision Rules for MCCs

Rule No.	Decision Rule
1	$101.5℃ < Longitude \leq 104℃ \wedge Area \leq 233750 \wedge IFVQ_{c\text{-}b} \leq -74 \rightarrow$ **NE(2/1)**
2	$101.5℃ < Longitude \leq 104℃ \wedge Area \leq 233750 \wedge H_{b\text{-}a} \leq 17 \wedge K_{b\text{-}a} \leq 12 \wedge T_{b\text{-}a} > 9 \wedge IFVQ_{c\text{-}b} > -74 \wedge DIV_{c\text{-}b} \leq 6 \rightarrow$ **E(10)**
3	$101.5℃ < Longitude \leq 104℃ \wedge Area \leq 233750 \wedge H_{b\text{-}a} > 17 \wedge K_{b\text{-}a} \leq 12 \wedge T_{b\text{-}a} > 9 \wedge IFVQ_{c\text{-}b} > -74 \wedge IFVQ_{b\text{-}a} > 2 \wedge DIV_{c\text{-}b} \leq 6 \rightarrow$ **E(3)**
4	$Longitude \leq 104℃ \wedge Area > 233750 \wedge K_{c\text{-}b} \leq 0 \rightarrow$ **NE(3/1)**
5	$Longitude \leq 104℃ \wedge Area > 233750 \wedge H_{b\text{-}a} \leq 9 \wedge \theta SE_{c\text{-}b} \leq 0 \rightarrow$ **SE(2/1)**
6	$Longitude \leq 104℃ \wedge Area > 233750 \wedge W_{b\text{-}a} \leq 138 \wedge H_{b\text{-}a} > 9 \wedge K_{c\text{-}b} > 0 \wedge \theta SE_{c\text{-}b} \leq 0 \rightarrow$ **E(8)**
7	$Longitude \leq 104℃ \wedge Area > 233750 \wedge W_{b\text{-}a} > 138 \wedge H_{b\text{-}a} > 9 \wedge K_{c\text{-}b} > 0 \wedge \theta SE_{c\text{-}b} \leq 0 \rightarrow$ **SE(3/1)**
8	$Longitude \leq 104℃ \wedge Area > 521250 \wedge \theta SE_{c\text{-}b} > 0 \wedge DIV_{b\text{-}a} > -10 \rightarrow$ **E(2)**
9	$104℃ < Longitude < 105℃ \wedge Area > 26250 \rightarrow$ **E(14)**
10	$104℃ < Longitude < 105℃ \wedge Latitude > 30.5 \wedge Area \leq 26250 \rightarrow$ **E(2)**

Therefore, from the above results shown in Table 1, the conclusions related to target concept modeling of MCCs, i.e. generating derivation rules and establishing environment physical models (at 500hPa air pressure level) can be summarized as follows:

(1) Attributes such as vorticity(VOR), relative humidity(RH), temperature(T) and MCC shape are less important for the evolvement trends of MCCs.
(2) If longitude of the centroid of a cloud is less than 104°E, then the evolvement trend of that MCC is mainly determined by attributes such as MCC area, K index(K) and water vapor flux divergence(IFVQ).
(3) If longitude of the centroid of a MCC is located between 104°E and 105°E, and the MCC area is greater than 26250 km^2, then that MCC will be much probable to move out of the Tibetan Plateau.

The results in Table 1 also illuminate that K, H, DIV and IFVQ are important and relevant HLAFS attributes influencing the evolvement trends of MCCs. The environmental physical models constructed using those HLAFS attributes, together with the C4.5 decision rules, constitute our concept model depicting the evolvement trends of MCCs. Fig. 4 gives an instance of the environmental physical model involved in IFVQ attribute, in which the black trail indicates the averaged evolvement trend of an identified class of MCCs.

The experimental results indicate that it is feasible to model and predict the evolvement trends of MCCs on the Tibetan Plateau based on their attribute values from the satellite databases. Moreover, it is also proved that our concept modeling approach provides an automatic and robust means for meteorologist to observe and analyze MCCs more effectively and efficiently, which is very important to reveal their unknown connections with intensive precipitations in the South China.

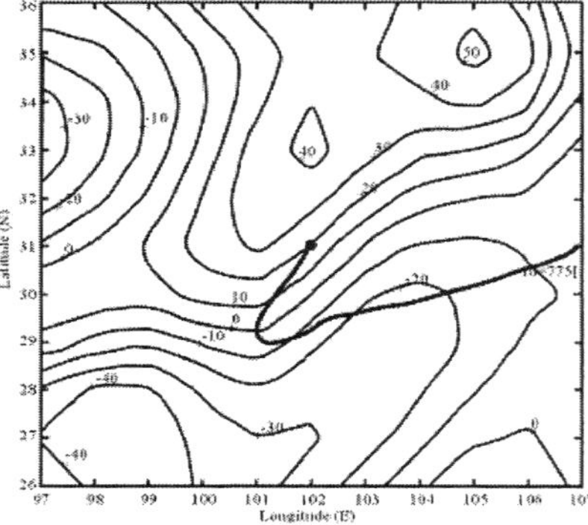

Fig. 4. The Environmental Physical Model

6 Conclusions

In this paper, to address the conceptual modeling problem related to a real meteorological application, we propose a novel conceptual modeling approach based on a two-phase spatial data mining and knowledge discovery method, which aims at modeling the concepts of the evolvement trends of MCCs over the Tibetan Plateau by using their spatial environmental physical attributes and the meteorological satellite spatio-temporal imagery. The concept model consists of two parts: derivation rules and environmental physical models, which correspond to the two data mining phases respectively. The proposed conceptual model is proved to simplify and improve the heavy rainfall forecasting process in South China to much extent.

However, it can also be clearly learned that there still has potential to further improve our research. Currently, the target concepts are categorized into only four types, that is, E, NE, SE and STAY-IN. In the future, this categorization will be refined with finer granuity to model the target concepts more accurately. Moreover, how to apply conceptual modeling approach to reveal the unknown patterns of intensive precipitations is still another important issue worth of more considerations.

Acknowledgements

This research has been funded in part by the National Natural Science Foundation of P. R. China under grant No. 40371080 and the RGC grant from Hong Kong Research Grant Council under grant No. CUHK4132/99H. We also thank the collaborators in

Hong Kong Observatory for their suggestive discussions on the domain-specific knowledge and provision of many useful data sources.

References

1. Giancarlo, G., Heinrich, H., Gerd, W.: On the General Ontological Foundations of Conceptual Modeling. In: Spaccapietra, S., March, S.T., Kambayashi, Y. (eds.): Proceedings of ER 2002, Lecture Notes in Computer Science, Vol. 2503. Springer-Verlag, Berlin Heidelberg New York (2002) 65-78
2. Chen, P., Thalheim B., Wong L. Y.: Future Directions of Conceptual Modeling. In: Chen, P., Akoka, J., Kangassalo, H., Thalheim, B. (eds.): Conceptual Modeling: Current Issues and Future Directions, Lecture Notes in Computer Science, Vol. 1565. Springer-Verlag, Berlin Heidelberg New York (1999) 287-301
3. Jiang, J., Fan, M.: Convective Clouds and Mesoscale Convective Systems over the Tibetan Plateau in Summer. Atmosphere Science, (1) 2002 262-269 (in Chinese)
4. Souto, M.J., Balseiro C.F., Pérez-Muñuzuri V., Xue M., Brewster K.: Impact of Cloud Analysis on Numerical Weather Prediction in the Galician Region of Spain. Journal of Applied Meteorology, (42) 2003 129-140
5. Arnaud, Y., Desbios, M., Maizi, J.: Automatic Tacking and Characterization of African Convective Systems on Meteosat Pictures. Journal of Applied Meteorology. (5) 1992 443-453
6. Yang, Y.B.: Automatic Tracking and Characterization of Multiple Moving Clouds in Satellite Images. In: Thissen, W., Wieringa, P., Pantic, M., Ludema, M. (eds.): Proceedings of IEEE Conference on System, Man and Cybernetics, IEEE Press (2004) 3088-3093
7. Freeman, H.: Computer Processing of Line-drawing Image. Computing Surveys 6 (1) (1974) 57-97
8. Goan, T.: Supporting the User: Conceptual Modeling & Knowledge Discovery. In: Chen, P., Akoka, J., Kangassalo, H., Thalheim, B. (eds.): Conceptual Modeling: Current Issues and Future Directions, Lecture Notes in Computer Science, Vol. 1565. Springer-Verlag, Berlin Heidelberg New York (1999) 100-104
9. Quinlan, J.: C4.5: Programs for machine learning, Morgan Kaufman, San Francisco (1993)
10. Salvatore, R.: Efficient C4.5. IEEE Transactions on Knowledge and Data Engineering, (2) 2002 438-444

Mining Generalized Association Rules on Biomedical Literature

Margherita Berardi[1], Michele Lapi[1], Pietro Leo[2], and Corrado Loglisci[1]

[1] Dipartimento di Informatica – Università degli Studi di Bari
via Orabona 4 - 70126 Bari
[2] Java Technology Center - IBM SEMEA Sud
Via Tridente, 42/14 - 70125 Bari
{berardi, lapi, loglisci}@di.uniba.it
{pietro_leo}@it.ibm.com

Abstract. The discovery of new and potentially meaningful relationships between concepts in the biomedical literature has attracted the attention of a lot of researchers in text mining. The main motivation is found in the increasing availability of the biomedical literature which makes it difficult for researchers in biomedicine to keep up with research progresses without the help of automatic knowledge discovery techniques. More than 14 million abstracts of this literature are contained in the Medline collection and are available online. In this paper we present the application of an association rule mining method to Medline abstracts in order to detect associations between concepts as indication of the existence of a biomedical relation among them. The discovery process fully exploits the MeSH (Medical Subject Headings) taxonomy, that is, a set of hierarchically related biomedical terms which permits to express associations at different levels of abstraction (generalized association rules). We report experimental results on a collection of abstracts obtained by querying Medline on a specific disease and we show the effectiveness of some filtering and browsing techniques designed to manage the huge amount of generalized associations that may be generated on real data.

1 Introduction

In biomedicine, the decoding of the human genome has increased the number of online publications leading to information overload. Every 11 years, the number of researchers doubles [10] and Medline, the main resource of research literature, has been growing with more than 10,000 abstracts per week since 2002[1]. Therefore, it becomes more and more difficult for researchers in biomedicine to keep up with research progresses. Moreover, the data to be examined (i.e. textual data) are generally unstructured as in the case of Medline abstracts and the available resources (e.g. PubMed, the search engine interfacing Medline) do not still provide adequate mechanisms for retrieving the required information. The need to analyze this volume

[1] http://www.nlm.nih.gov/pubs/factsheets/medline.html

M. Ali and F. Esposito (Eds.): IEA/AIE 2005, LNAI 3533, pp. 500–509, 2005.

of unstructured data and to provide knowledge to improve retrieval effectiveness makes biomedical text mining a central bioinformatic problem and a great challenge for data mining researchers.

In this paper we present the application of association rule mining to Medline abstracts in order to detect associations between concepts as indication of the existence of a biomedical relation but without trying to find out the kind of relation. The discovery process fully exploits the MeSH (Medical Subject Headings) taxonomy, that is, a set of hierarchically related biomedical terms which permits to mine multi-level association rules (*generalized association rules*). Considering the hierarchical relations reported in the MeSH taxonomy allows the discovery algorithm to find associations at multiple levels of abstraction from one side, but generally leads to a huge amount of generalized associations from the other side. The two-fold aim of the paper is to investigate how taxonomic information can be profitably used in the task of concept relationship discovery and to evaluate the effectiveness of some filtering and browsing techniques designed to manage the huge amount of discovered associations.

The paper is organized as follows. Section 2 illustrates the background on our work and some related works on biomedical text mining. Section 3 presents the problem of mining generalized association rules and some filtering methods. In Section 4, some experimental results on a collection of abstracts obtained by querying Medline on a specific disease are reported. Finally, some conclusions are drawn and some possible directions of future work are also presented.

2 Background and Related Works

In our previous work [3], we presented a data mining engine, namely MeSH Terms Associator (MTA), that was employed in a distributed architecture to refine a generic PubMed query. The idea is to support users by offering them the possibility of iteratively expanding their query on the basis of discovered correlations between their topic of interest and other terms in the MeSH taxonomy. A natural extension of this initial work is to enable an association discovery process that takes advantage of the MeSH taxonomy defined on biomedical terms. Kahng et al. [6] have already investigated an efficient algorithm for generalized association rule mining using the MeSH taxonomy. In this seminal work, no processing on Medline abstracts is performed but a MeSH-indexed representation (in Medline, to every record a set of relevant MeSH terms is manually associated as representation of the content of the document the record is about) is adopted. Moreover, the evaluation of the interestingness of mined associations with respect to the task of improving PubMed retrieval capabilities is not an issue considered by the authors. A different perspective is taken by Srinivasan [13] and Aronson et al. [2], who state the importance of query expansion to improve retrieval effectiveness of the PubMed engine. In particular, for the indexing process they both use a MeSH-indexed representation, while for the query expansion process, Srinivasan exploits a statistical thesaurus containing correlations between MeSH terms (MeSHs) and text, and Aronson et al. use the MetaMap system to associate UMLS (Unified Medical

Language System, that is, a semantic classification of the MeSH dictionary) Metathesaurus concepts to the original query.

For what concerns the application of association rule mining to the biomedical literature, an interesting work has been carried out by Hristovski et al. and implemented in the BITOLA system [5]. They tailor their work for the discovery of new relations involving a concept of interest, where the novelty of the relation is evaluated by matching transitive associations. Indeed, they first find all the concepts Y related to the concept of interest X, then all the concepts Z related to Y and finally, they check if X and Z appear together in the biomedical literature. If they do not appear together, the system has discovered a potentially new relation that will be evaluated by the user. The search of associations is constrained to associations involving only two terms (i.e. the concept of interest and a new related concept) and can be limited by the semantic type to which terms belong with respect to the UMLS dictionary. In particular, they exploit an association rule base gathered by the UMLS vocabulary on which the discovery of new associations will be performed. As document representation, a MeSH-indexed representation is used and no knowledge about the MeSH taxonomy is exploited.

The idea of applying the transitivity property on correlations in order to discover relations between concepts has been widely investigated also from a different perspective. Indeed, in [14] transitive knowledge is exploited not only for the discovery of new relations with an input topic but also for the discovery of connections between two given topics of interest that are bibliographically disjointed (e.g. two topics that have been studied independently and may belong to two different sub-areas of research). In both cases, the intermediate level of correlations is used as a transitivity level between topics in order to both discover "hidden" connections and provide the set of correlating concepts. In this work, correlations are extracted on the basis of co-occurrences computed in profiles of topics, where a profile is built in form of a vector of MeSH term vectors, that is, a vector that for each UMLS semantic type reports MeSHs weights (a measure of the conditional importance of each MeSH term). Srinivasan approach is inspired by the pioneer work of Swanson [15], who first explored potential linkages via intermediate concepts starting from two given topics. Many other works inspired to Swanson's approach mainly differs for the document processing phase. While Swanson restricted the analysis only to titles of Medline records, others consider the MeSH-indexed representation of abstracts or the whole abstracts as free-text. In this case, n-grams may be extracted and evaluated by means of different weighting schemes (e.g. TFIDF) as indexing method [9] or a UMLS-indexed representation may be obtained by applying the natural language processing capabilities of the MetaMap system [17, 11].

All these works aim at capturing connections between distinct sub-areas of biomedical literature in order to gain new knowledge on a single topic of interest or on the relation between two topics of interest. This leads to restricting the discovery to only two-term associations as in [5], which means extraction of knowledge only about co-occurrences, or to restricting the discovery to three-term associations as in the case of Swanson and works inspired by him, which means extraction of knowledge not only about co-occurrences but also about correlating terms. Moreover, in discovered associations, the topic (topics) of interest has (have) to be directly involved in the associations. On the contrary, we are interested in mining associations involving an unknown number of terms, which should be quite certain with respect to the distribution of associations and which may directly involve the topic of interest or not. Besides, we are not interested in discovering literature connections on an unknown segment of Medline but we intend to use the topic of interest directly as a query to retrieve from Medline the segment of related abstracts and then perform an "unbiased" mining on MeSHs contained in this set of abstracts, aiming at capturing the knowledge they share.

3 The Approach

In this section we present the general problem of mining association rules and the extension to the use of taxonomic knowledge on data. Moreover, some filtering techniques are discussed.

3.1 Mining Association Rules

Association rules are a class of regularities introduced by [1] that can be expressed by an implication:

$$X \rightarrow Y$$

where X and Y are sets of items, such that $X \cap Y = \emptyset$. The meaning of such rules is quite intuitive: Given a database D of transactions, where each transaction $T \in D$ is a set of items, $X \rightarrow Y$ expresses that whenever a transaction T contains X than T probably contains Y also. The conjunction $X \wedge Y$ is called pattern.

Two parameters are usually reported for association rules, namely the support, which estimates the probability $p(X \subseteq T \wedge Y \subseteq T)$, and the confidence, which estimates the probability $p(Y \subseteq T \mid X \subseteq T)$. The goal of association rule mining is to find all the rules with support and confidence exceeding user specified thresholds, henceforth called *minsup* and *minconf* respectively. A pattern $X \wedge Y$ is large (or *frequent*) if its support is greater than or equal to *minsup*. An association rule $X \rightarrow Y$ is *strong* if it has a large support (i.e. $X \wedge Y$ is frequent) and high confidence.

Srikant and Agrawal [12] have extended this basic mechanism in order to mine associations at the right level of a taxonomic knowledge defined on items. For this purpose, they have defined generalized association rules as association rules $X \rightarrow Y$ where no item in Y is an ancestor of any item in X in the taxonomy. The basic algorithm to mine generalized association rules extends each transaction of the database to include each ancestor of the items contained in the transaction.

3.2 Filtering Association Rules

Although discovered association rules are evaluated in terms of support and confidence measures, which ensure that discovered rules have enough statistical evidence, the number of discovered association rules is usually high and even considering only those rules with high confidence and support it is not true that all of them are interesting. It may happen that some of them correspond to prior knowledge, refer to uninteresting items or are redundant. On the other hand, the presentation of thousands of rules can discourage users from interpreting them in order to find nuggets of knowledge. Furthermore, it is very difficult to evaluate which rules might be interesting for end users by means of some simple statistics, such as support and confidence. Therefore, an additional processing step is necessary in order to clean, order or filter interesting patterns/rules, especially when the mining is performed at different level of abstraction on items because it intrinsically introduces a degree of complexity in the amount of discovered patterns/rules.

Two different approaches can be applied to structure the set of discovered rules and filter out interesting ones, automatic and semiautomatic methods. The former allows to filter rules without using user knowledge, while the latter allows to strongly guide the exploration of the set of discovered rules on the basis of user domain knowledge. An automatic method which aims at removing redundancy in rules has been already investigated in our previous work, namely association rule covers proposed by [16]. Carrying on the work on the automatic approach, we have then investigated the effectiveness of some measures proposed by [8], which aim at evaluating the interestingness of rules from a statistical point of view different from classical support and confidence measures. In this work, the definition of interestingness of a rule is based on the following statement:

Let Π be a statistical property of a set of association rules, $M\Pi$ its mean value, $\sigma\Pi$ its standard deviation and p a coefficient[2], two different behaviours for a rule can be defined: rules behaving in a *standard* way in relation to the property Π, that is rules whose value of Π is less than or equal to $M\Pi + (p*\sigma\Pi)$ and rules behaving in a *rare* way in relation to Π, that is rules whose value of Π is greater than $M\Pi + (p*\sigma\Pi)$.

In order to use this definition of interestingness of a rule, two statistical properties of rules have been considered. In particular, the three formulations of the dependency property and the statistical surprise as defined in [8] are used.

In order to augment automatic methods with user knowledge, some semiautomatic approaches have also been investigated. Indeed, in our previous work user-defined templates proposed by [7] are illustrated. An example of the template mechanism according to which the user can select and filter all the rules that satisfy a criterion specified in form of a template is reported. Considering the *inclusive* template *"Analytical Diagnostics and Therapeutic Techniques and Equipment"* → *Mental Disorders*, some rules satisfying it are the following:

"Analytical Diagnostics and Therapeutic Techniques and Equipment" → *Mental Disorders*
"Analytical Diagnostics and Therapeutic Techniques and Equipment" → *Dementia*
Therapeutics → *Mental Disorders*
Therapeutics → *Dementia*
Therapeutics → *Alzheimer Disease.*

Nevertheless, templates seem to be a quite dispersive method because it is useful to select all the rules satisfying a certain criterion but in this way, a large number of rules in any case could be proposed to the user. For this reason, we have also provided to the user a browsing functionality which allows to look at the set of

[2] Its value is often assumed to be equal to the maximum value of the statistical surprise property.

discovered rules as a set of subspaces of rules, where for each subspace a representative rule is identifiable.

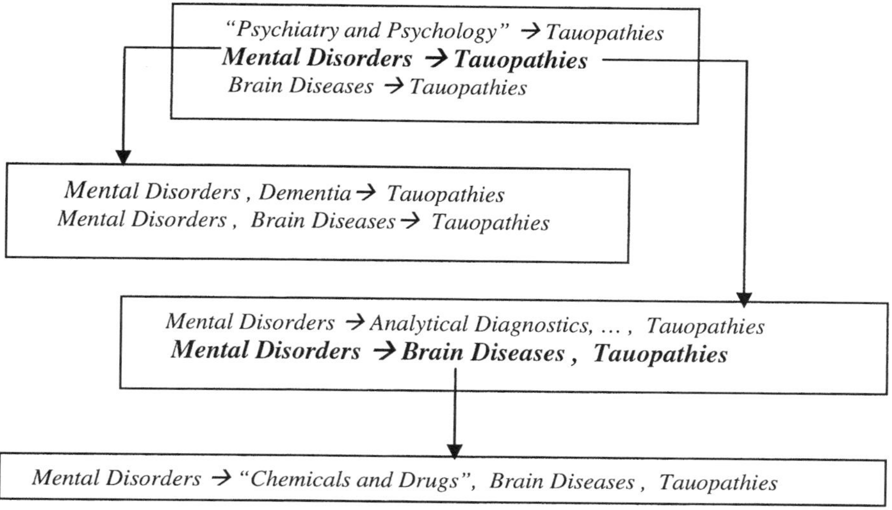

Fig. 1. Exploration of a set of rules by means of subspaces of rules. Rules that are representative of each subspace are reported in boldface. The exploration is based on the enhancement of one of the side of the representative rule

Then, the user can visit the rule space following his/her interest and moving towards more and more specific subspaces. An example of the exploration of a rule set by means of subspaces is shown in Fig. 1. In particular, on the basis of the users' interest (e.g. the set of rules involving the *Tauopathies* MeSH term), he/she can explore subspaces of rules at different level of specialization by selecting which side of the rule should be enhanced.

4 Experimental Results

In this section, we intend to compare results on *generalized* and *flat* association rule discovery on datasets generated by means of PubMed queries formulated by experts in the biomedical sector. An example of PubMed query formulated by biomedical researchers may ask for discovering the factors related to the reactions to Diabetes treatments (i.e. "Diabetes Drugs Response").

Submitting the query to PubMed, a set of retrieved abstracts is found out and initially annotated by the BioTeKS Text Analysis Engine (TAE) provided within the IBM UIM Architecture [4], by using a local MeSH terms dictionary. For each query, a single table of a relational database is created and fed with MeSHs occurring in the corresponding set of retrieved abstracts. In particular, each transaction of a single table is associated to an individual abstract and is described in terms of items that correspond to MeSHs. The simplest representation, namely the boolean representation, is adopted in order to represent the occurrence of a MeSH term in an abstract. More precisely, we consider only the most frequent MeSHs (about 50) with respect to the set of retrieved abstracts and we use the "canonical" form of each MeSH term, which is available in the MeSH dictionary. This allows to introduce a light control on redundancy in the data, since many MeSHs may occur referring to the same canonical term. The MeSH taxonomy is organized in 15 distinct hierarchies structured in a tree form that is about 11 levels deep.

In this study, two segments of Medline have been considered, that is the sets of abstracts related to two queries, namely *"Hypertension Adverse Reaction Drugs"* and *"Alzheimer Drug Treatment Response"*. We have retrieved 130 abstracts by running the first query while 653 abstracts by running the second query. For each set of abstracts, the contingency table has been created. Depending on the set of MeSHs occurring in a set of abstracts, a different part of the MeSH taxonomy should be considered. Indeed, for the *"Hypertension Adverse Reaction Drugs"* query five hierarchies (*Diseases, Biological Science, "Chemicals and Drugs", "Psychiatry and Psychology", "Analytical Diagnostics and Therapeutic Techniques and Equipment"*) have been used; while for the *"Alzheimer Drug Treatment Response"* query six hierarchies (*Diseases, Biological Science, "Chemicals and Drugs", "Psychiatry and Psychology", "Analytical Diagnostics and Therapeutic Techniques and Equipment", Anatomy*) have been used.

In Fig. 2, the number of discovered associations is drawn by varying both *minsup* and *minconf* values. The great difference in the number of generalized association rules compared with the number of flat association rules is a quite obvious observation considering that flat association rule discovery corresponds with generalized association rule discovery restricted to leaves of the taxonomy.

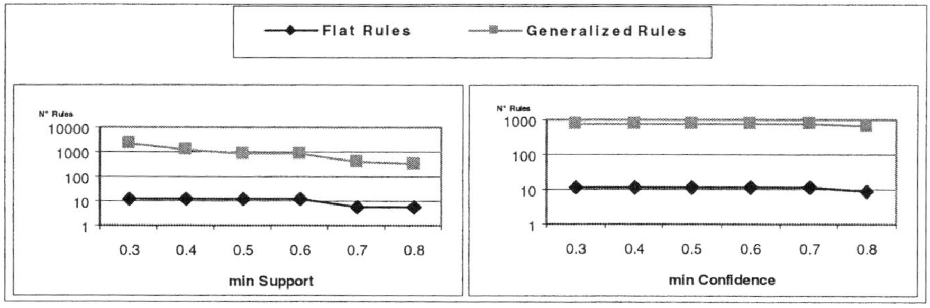

Fig. 2. Number of discovered rules varying *minsup* and *minconf*

Generally, association rules with low support express only a casual information since it is knowledge not statistically justified. Indeed, flat rules generated with low *minsup* often express this kind of knowledge. In contrast, generalized association rules generated with low *minsup* may represent knowledge with a probabilistic evidence as well. An example comes from considering the following two rules that have been both discovered with low (0.4) as well as with high (0.8) value of *minsup* by means of generalized association rule mining.

Tauopathies → *Alzheimer Disease, Delirium, Dementia, Amnesic Cognitive Disorders*
0.807 support, 1 confidence
Neurodegenerative Diseases → *Mental Disorders, Brain Diseases*
0.807 support, 1 confidence

Moreover, by means of generalized association rule discovery it is possible to check whether a rule is a specific case of a more general one. Thus, though a certain rule has been discovered with low *minsup* value, in any case it is statistically justified, because its related generalized rule is statistically justified too. For instance, if we consider the flat rule

Therapeutics → *Alzheimer Disease* 0.621 support, 0.813 confidence

and the corresponding one discovered by generalized association discovery

Therapeutics → *Alzheimer Disease* 0.621 support, 0.813 confidence

we can explore the following ancestor rules and verify that the most general one has in any way enough probabilistic evidence.

Therapeutics → *Dementia* 0.663 support, 0.868 confidence
Therapeutics → *Mental Disorders* 0.669 support, 0.876 confidence
"Analytical Diagnostics and Therapeutic Techniques and Equipment" →
Mental Disorders 0.717 support, 0.925 confidence

Moreover, we discover association rules from datasets which contain only the 50 most frequent MeSHs. Therefore, it is possible that an association rule that has low support in these datasets may correspond with a pattern that is strongly supported in the datasets containing all the MeSHs.

When we compare results on flat association rules and generalized rules on the same dataset, an interesting observation can be made about some rules that are generally considered as "trivial" rules except if the knowledge about ancestor rules is provided. Indeed, the MeSH taxonomy sometimes presents nodes that are duplicate in different part of the hierarchies. It aims to represent a different perspective of the same term. For instance, it may happen that discovered rules capture associations like X → X, where X is a MeSH that belongs to two different hierarchies in the MeSH structure. In the case of flat rules they should be discarded, while in the case of generalized rules, by exploring their ancestor rules the user may justify this kind of rules.

5 Conclusion and Future Work

In this paper the application of generalized association rule mining to biomedical literature has been presented. Given a biomedical topic of interest as input query to PubMed, the set of related abstracts in Medline is retrieved and a MeSH-based representation of them is produced by exploiting the annotation capabilities of

BioTeKS TAE. Associations are generated on a single set of abstracts with the aim of discovering potentially meaningful knowledge in form of relations among MeSHs. We assume that discovered associations play the role of relevant knowledge shared by the set of abstracts under study and that can be profitably used to expand the query on the topic of interest. Some browsing and filtering techniques have also been used to support the user in the complex task of evaluating the huge amount of discovered associations. Nevertheless, a number of improvements on this work are worth to be explored. In particular, further work on the document processing phase is necessary to evaluate how the document representation model affects the quality of discovered rules. Currently, we are working on the elimination of the threshold on the number of MeSHs to consider in the contingency table and on the application of feature selection methods in order to improve the MeSH-based representation. For instance, instead of representing the simple boolean occurrence of a MeSH, the occurrence frequency is employed and a TFIDF selection of MeSHs is performed. An interesting extension can be the exploitation of some form of "context" in which a term occurs. A solution is to use n-grams rather than single terms, in combination with a weighting schema that allows to evaluate the relevance of the n-grams for the set of abstracts. Another solution is to investigate the use of natural language processing techniques in order to extract information from sentences where terms occur. By using these techniques, we can also aspire to gain information about the kind of relation among co-occurrent MeSHs and to explore the application of multi-relational approaches to association rule mining. From the other hand, further work on the evaluation of the quality of the rules is in progress. In fact, we are working on a visualization technique based on the computation of similarity measures between rules which can help biomedical experts in the interpretation of rules.

Acknowledgments

This work has been funded by the IBM Faculty Award 2004 recently received from IBM Corporation to promote innovative, collaborative research in disciplines of mutual interest.

References

1. Agrawal, R., Srikant, R.: Fast Algorithms for Mining Association Rules. Proceedings of the Twentieth International Conference on Very Large Databases, Santiago, Cile (1994).
2. Aronson, A. R., Rindflesch, T. C.: Query expansion using the UMLS Metathesaurus. Proceedings of AMIA, Annual American Medical Informatics Association Conference, Nashville, TN (1997) 485-489.
3. Berardi, M., Lapi, M., Leo, P., Malerba, D., Marinelli, C., Scioscia, G.: A data mining approach to PubMed query refinement. 2nd International Workshop on Biological Data Management in conjunction with DEXA 2004, Zaragoza, Spain (2004).
4. Ferrucci, D., Lally, A.: UIMA: An Architectural Approach to Unstructured Information Processing in the Corporate Research Environment. Natural Language Engineering, 10(3-4), (2004) 327-348.

5. Hristovski, D., Stare, J., Peterlin, B., Dzeroski, S.: Supporting discovery in medicine by association rule mining in Medline and UMLS. Proceedings of MedInfo Conference, London, England, 10(2), (2001) 1344-1348.
6. Kahng, J., Liao, W.-H. K., McLeod, D.: Mining Generalized Term Associations: Count Propagation Algorithm. KDD, (1997) 203-206.
7. Klemettinen, M., Mannila, H., Ronkainen, P., Toivonen, H., Verkamo, A. I.: Finding Interesting Rules from Large Sets of Discovered Association Rules. Proceedings of the 3rd International Conference on Information and Knowledge Management, Gaithersburg, Maryland, (1994) 401-407.
8. Kodratoff, Y., Azé, J.: Rating the Interest of Rules Induced from Data within Texts. Proceedings of Twelfth International Conference On Database and Expert Systems Application, Munich, Germany (2001).
9. Lindsay, R. K, Gordon, M.D.: Literature-based discovery by lexical statistics. Journal of the American Society for Information Science, 50(7), (1999) 574-587.
10. Perutz, M. F.: Will biomedicine outgrow support? Nature 399, (1999) 299-301.
11. Pratt, W., Yetisgen-Yildiz, M.: LitLinker: Capturing Connections across the Biomedical Literature. Proceedings of the International Conference on Knowledge Capture (K-Cap'03), Florida, (2003).
12. Srikant, R., Agrawal, R.: Mining Generalized Association Rules. Proceedings of the 21st International Conference on Very Large Databases, Zurich, Switzerland, (1995).
13. Srinivasan, P.: Query expansion and MEDLINE. Information Processing and Management, 32(4), (1996) 431-443.
14. Srinivasan, P.: Text Mining: Generating Hypotheses from Medline. Journal of the American Society for Information Science, 55 (4), (2004) 396-413.
15. Swanson, D.R.: Fish oil, Raynaud's syndrome, and undiscovered public knowledge. Perspectives in Biology and Medicine, 30, (1986) 7-18.
16. Toivonen, H., Klemetinen, M., Ronkainen, P., Hatonen, K., Mannila, H.: Pruning and grouping discovered association rules. MLnet Workshop on Statistics, Machine Learning, and Discovery in Databases, (1995) 47-52.
17. Weeber, M., Klein, H., Berg, L., Vos, R.: Using concepts in literature-based discovery: simulating Swanson's Raynaud-Fish Oil and Migraine-Magnesium discoveries. Journal of the American Society for Information Science, 52(7), (2001) 548-557.

Mining Information Extraction Rules from Datasheets Without Linguistic Parsing*

Rakesh Agrawal[1], Howard Ho[1], François Jacquenet[2], and Marielle Jacquenet[2]

[1] IBM Almaden Research Center,
650 Harry Road,
San Jose CA 95120 - USA
{ragrawal, ho}@almaden.ibm.com
[2] Université de Saint-Etienne,
23 rue du docteur Paul Michelon,
42023 Saint-Etienne Cedex 2 - France
{Francois. Jacquenet, Marielle. Jacquenet}@univ-st-etienne.fr

Abstract. In the context of the Pangea project at IBM, we needed to design an information extraction module in order to extract some information from datasheets. Contrary to several information extraction systems based on some machine learning techniques that need some linguistic parsing of the documents, we propose an hybrid approach based on association rules mining and decision tree learning that does not require any linguistic processing. The system may be parameterized in various ways that influence the efficiency of the information extraction rules we discovered. The experiments show the system does not need a large training set to perform well.

Keywords: Text Mining, Information Extraction.

1 Introduction

Information extraction is subject to many efforts for some years [3]. The availability of a large amount of digital documents leads to the need to automatically extract information available in these one. The MUC conference series[1] contributed to the design of many successful theories and systems applied in various kinds of applications. Information extraction has been defined by Grishman in [18] as the identification of instances of a particular class of events or relationships in a natural language text, and the extraction of the relevant arguments of the event or relationship. The core of information extraction systems is a set of extraction rules that identify, in each text, the information to be extracted. This information may then be used to instantiate some slots of a template.

Let us consider an information extraction task which aims at extracting information from classifieds such as the address, the category, the rental and

* This work was supported in part by the PASCAL Network of Excellence, IST-2002-506778. This publication only reflects the authors' views.

[1] http://www.itl.nist.gov/iaui/894.02/related_projects/muc/

M. Ali and F. Esposito (Eds.): IEA/AIE 2005, LNAI 3533, pp. 510–520, 2005.

some extra features. Given the following ad: *"BLOSSOM HL 1bd & 2bd,Remod! Bonus, pool, covpkg. 1221 Blossom Hill$995-$1200 408 978-9618"*, an efficient information extraction tool is able to extract the address (1221 Blossom Hill), the category (1bd & 2bd), the rent ($995-$1200) and the extra features (pool, covpkg). Such information may then be stored in a database and used for other specific tasks such as SQL queries, data mining, etc.

Information extraction systems may be classified in several ways depending on their ability to process free, semi-structured or structured texts. Structured documents have a defined format and various information may be easily discovered because the system know where to find them. Semi-structured documents, such as HTML documents, do not have such rigid format as structured documents but they have a sufficiently regular structure to allow the system to find information in some particular areas of the document. Finally, free texts do not rely on any rule concerning their structure or content, which make them difficult to process.

From the mid-1990s, some researches began to focus on the problem of automatically learning information extraction rules using some machine learning techniques. The early years of machine learning for information extraction have seen the design of several systems such as AutoSlog [26], CRYSTAL [29] or LIEP [19]. These systems performed quite well but were based on a pre-processing step that involved sophisticated linguistic processes. In 1997 Kushmerick introduced the term *Wrapper induction* in [23] for the first time and opened an important field of researches. Several systems tried to use some first order logic features and proposed some frameworks based on inductive logic programming [25]. RAPIER [5], designed by Califf and Mooney was able to process structured and semi-structured texts. The extraction patterns learned by RAPIER were based on delimiters and content description and were expressed in the form of rules that exploit the syntactic and semantic information. RAPIER needed a part-of-speech tagger and a lexicon in order to provide such information. Designed by Freitag, SRV [16] also dealt with structured and semi-structured texts. In [30], Soderland presented the WHISK system which was the first system able to deal with structured, semi-structured and free texts. Nevertheless, in order to process free texts the system used some syntactic and semantic information. Moreover, even with such information, WHISK performed badly on free texts. Sasaki also proposed to apply some ILP techniques in order to generate information extraction rules [27] but his system also requires some linguistic processing of the texts. From the beginning of this decade, the number of researches that aim at discovering rules for information extraction has increased. Several works have been based on grammatical inference techniques such as [17] or [8, 7] but they only dealt with structured or semi-structured documents. Based on various other frameworks but also only dealing with structured or semi-structured texts, we can cite Pinocchio or (LP)2 by Ciravegna [10–12], the WhizBang site wrapper from Cohen [13], the Wrapper Induction systems of Kushmerick [21, 22], Bouckaert's system based on Baeysian networks [4], Yang's system [32] or Lin's work [24] to design wrappers induced from Web pages. Some recent systems can deal with free texts such as ALLiS from Déjean [14] at Xerox or Chieu's system [9] but they need some linguistic pre-processing steps in order to be efficient.

In fact, what can be noticed from the study of all these systems is that either they deal with free texts and they need some syntactic and/or semantic pre-processing, or they do not need any linguistic process but then they only deal with structured or semi-structured documents. The assessment is that no existing system can efficiently deal with free texts without integrating a linguistic process.

As we will see in the next section, our data consist in ASCII files containing many unknown words and they rely on no linguistic structure so none of the approaches previously listed may be used in our context. Thus we choose to design a system that is able to deal with free texts but without any linguistic parsing. In the remaining of the paper, we show the way we combine frequent pattern mining and decision tree learning in order to mine technical documents to discover information extraction rules for a specific task. In the next section we describe the context of this research, that is the Pangea project at IBM. Then, in section 3 we present the architecture of the system we designed and the main algorithm we implemented. In section 4, some experiments show the efficiency of our system in term of precision and recall. Finally we conclude and give some future directions for this work.

2 Context of the Project

That work was part of the Pangea project which aimed at designing an experimental B2B e-marketplace in the domain of electronic components and is quite similar to [6].

2.1 Global Architecture of the Pangea System

Figure 1 gives a simplified architecture of the system. It is based on a sophisticated interface to a database of electronic components [28] and at the first use of the system, only information from the database is available. Nevertheless, a Web crawler was designed in order to continuously discover, from the Web, new information about electronic components in the form of pdf files. A classifier was incorporated, based on the Athena tool designed at IBM [1], in order to classify the datasheets about electronic components based on their functionality (resis-

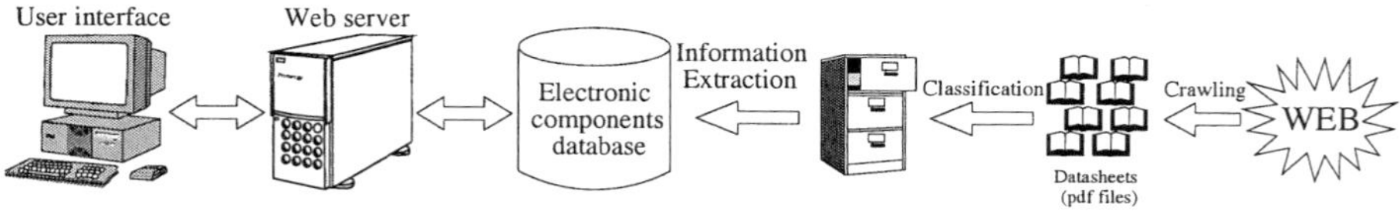

Fig. 1. Simplified architecture of the pangea system

tor, ...). The ultimate goal is to use the information contained in the datasheets crawled from the Web in order to enrich the evolving database. With such a system, the users are always sure to find an up-to-date information about electronic components. If we want the system to be as much automatic as possible, we have to automatically extract the useful information from the new datasheets crawled from the Web. That leads us to design an information extraction module.

2.2 Information Extraction in Pangea

The main task for incorporating the datasheets in the database is to be able to index them using the names of the components they describe. Such names are called part-numbers in the remaining of the paper. Thus automatically extracting, from datasheets, the part-number of an electronic component described in these datasheets was the task we had to solve. Datasheets that are crawled from the Web are mainly in pdf format. Because pdf files are often encrypted and pdf specifications are more than 1100 pages, it was chosen to convert pdf files into ASCII files and to design an information extraction tool that processed these ASCII files. Nevertheless, this process leads to an important loss of information and these files do no more rely on any syntactic and semantic structure. On pdf files, it would be possible to use some of the systems that were cited in the previous section in order to extract rules from structured documents. On ASCII files, as no more structure remains, no efficient linguistic processing can be performed. Thus we had to look at thousands of datasheets trying to manually (visually) discover some underlying rules for each kind of datasheets. Obviously this task quickly appeared to be tedious, boring and time consuming. Thus we decided to experiment some text mining techniques in order to automatically build the information extraction rules without the help of linguistic processing.

3 Mining Information Extraction Rules

Following Feldman [15], we can see a part of the Pangea project as a Knowledge Discovery from Textual databases (KDT) process.

3.1 Knowledge Discovery from Texts

The first step of this KDT process is a *selection* step that aims at selecting pdf files about electronic components from the huge amount of pdf files available from the Web. The second one is a *cleaning* step that aims at deleting redundant files, files that are corrupted, etc. The third one is a *transformation* step that converts the resulting files into ASCII files. Then for each file we do a labelling step, manually assigning the part-number of the electronic component described in this file. This task is quite easy to do as we have the associated pdf files that are very explicit about the part-number and as we see later, our process doesn't require a large amount of labelling. From this set of pairs of ASCII files and part-numbers, we use some text mining techniques – described in the next section – in order to discover information extraction rules. Then, given a new pdf file, we only need to convert it into the ASCII format and run the rules on it. Then, the result of this inference step is the part-number of the electronic component described in this new datasheet.

3.2 Basic Principle of the System

We now focus on the module of Pangea designed for discovering information extraction rules and Figure 2 shows the various steps of the process.

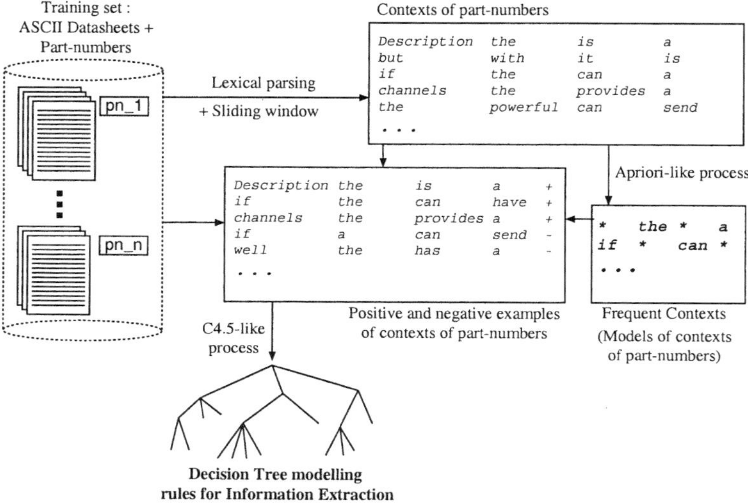

Fig. 2. Flow of data in our IE rule mining system

A very basic lexical parser traverses each ASCII file and returns a flow of tokens. Then, for each part-number that appears in the file, the system extracts the n words before and n words after the part-number, n beeing defined by the user. For a given part-number, we call these $2n$ words its context (of size n). Then, using an apriori-like algorithm [2], we mine the frequent contexts, that is, contexts that occur more than a threshold (called support) fixed by the user. At the end of this process we get a set of models of contexts. Of course, such patterns may also be models of contexts of tokens that are not part-numbers. So we scan the ASCII files using our models of contexts in order to find the context of part-numbers and the context of non part-numbers matching them. Hence, we get some positive and negative examples of contexts of part-numbers. We can then build a decision tree using a classical C4.5-based algorithm. Finally, given this decision tree, we can use it in order to extract the part-number of a new ASCII datasheet. From this datasheet we just have to collect all the contexts of all the tokens and for each one we use the decision tree in order to decide either the token is the part-number of the electronic component described in that datasheet or not.

3.3 Algorithm for Discovering Information Extraction Rules

We now present the core algorithm integrated in the system in order to implement the architecture of Figure 2. It is parameterized by several constants: the number of pages processed per datasheet, the size of the context of a token and the support threshold for the apriori algorithm. It takes as input a set

Input: *np*, the number of pages scanned per datasheet
sc, the size of the contexts of the part-numbers
minsup, the support threshold for the apriori algorithm
D, the set of pairs (d, pn) where *d* is a datasheet
and *pn* is the part-number of the component it describes

Output: *Tree*, a decision tree for Information Extraction.

```
begin
    Contexts ← EXTRACT_CONTEXTS(D,np,sc)
    Models_of_contexts ← apriori(Contexts,minsup)
    Positives ← GENERATE_POSITIVE(Model_of_contexts)
    Negatives ← GENERATE_NEGATIVE(D,Model_of_contexts,np,sc)
    Tree ← C4.5(Positives,Negatives)
end
```

Algorithm 1. Mining Information Extraction Rules

D of pairs of datasheets and their corresponding part-numbers. It extracts all the contexts of part-numbers from *D* and then call an apriori-like algorithm to mine some patterns from them, producing the models of contexts. These models are then used to generate the positive and the negative examples of contexts of part-numbers. Finally a C4.5-like algorithm (from the Weka library[2]) is called to build a decision tree from positive and negative examples of contexts.

Extracting the contexts of part-numbers (function EXTRACT_CONTEXTS) from each datasheet is simply done using a sliding window technique. For each datasheet, each time the system finds a part number at the middle of the window of words, it stores the words before and after the part-number as a context of this one.

In fact, these contexts may be real contexts of part-numbers but also context of tokens that are not part-numbers. For example, if we get [The,large,is,a] as a context for the part-number *TA87G48*, this one can also be a context for the token *chip* which is not a part-number. In order to discover the contexts of tokens that are not part-numbers (that we call negative examples) we have to scan the ASCII datasheets once again. Here again we use a sliding window technique and each time a context of a token that is not a part-number matches a model of context, we label this context as a negative example (function GENERATE_NEGATIVE).

---

[2] http://www.cs.waikato.ac.nz/~ml/

Concerning the positive examples (function GENERATE_POSITIVE), that is the contexts of part-numbers, we do not need to process the database once again because we already stored the contexts in the set *Contexts*. Nevertheless, some contexts of part-numbers may not be an instance of any model of contexts because, having a too small support, they did not succeed in generating a frequent set, and thus a model of context, during the use of the apriori algorithm. From that fact, we need to traverse the set of contexts of part-numbers in order to label as positive examples only the contexts which are an instance of a model of contexts.

3.4 Extracting a Part-Number Using the Decision Tree

Hence we built the decision tree that models a set of information extraction rules, we can use it in order to extract a part-number from a new datasheet. Once again we use a sliding window and process every contexts of the new datasheet with the decision tree. For each context, the tree will state if it is a context of part-number or not. In the first case, we store the part-number that has been discovered. At the end of the process, we get a set of candidate part-numbers associated with the datasheet. A simple heuristic is then used in order to choose the true part-number from that set: we choose the part-number that appears the most frequently in the set of candidates. We can note that, even if the system shows some good performances – as shown in the next section – a better strategy could be implemented here in order to increase even more the efficiency of the system.

4 Experiments

We evaluate the efficiency of our system using the usual values named *recall* and *precision* [31]. The first one is the percentage of useful information correctly extracted by the system and the second one is the percentage of information extracted by the system which is correct. The higher those values are, the better the system is. In fact, in the previous section we have seen that our system is parameterized by various constants. Thus it is interesting to observe its behavior as we tune these constants.

4.1 Impact of the Support Threshold

In this experiment we extracted the contexts of part-numbers scanning the three first pages of each datasheet and fixed the size of the contexts to three words. The training set contains 120 datasheets (with their corresponding part-number) and the test set approximately 100 datasheets. We run the system and observe the values of recall and precision of the system as we change the support threshold value in the apriori algorithm while extracting models of contexts. The support threshold has obviously some effects on the number of models of contexts generated by the apriori algorithm. From that fact, the value of support has also some effects on the number of positive and negative examples the system generates as shown on figure 3(a). Figure 3(b) shows the changes of recall and precision according to the support threshold for the apriori algorithm.

We may observe that recall and precision change according to the inverse changes of the ratio $card(E^-)/card(E^+)$, where E^+ et E^- are respectively the set of positive and negative examples. We can explain this by the fact that the largest the set of negative examples is with respect to the set of positive

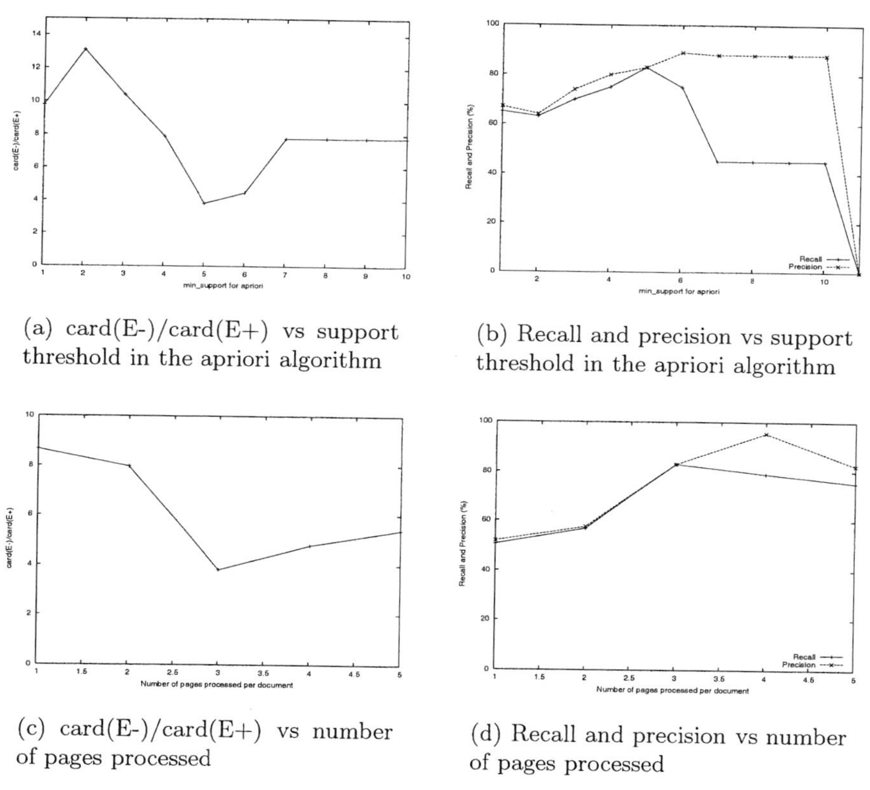

(a) card(E-)/card(E+) vs support threshold in the apriori algorithm

(b) Recall and precision vs support threshold in the apriori algorithm

(c) card(E-)/card(E+) vs number of pages processed

(d) Recall and precision vs number of pages processed

Fig. 3.

examples, the most it will have an harmful impact in the decision tree built by the system. Nevertheless, if the number of negative examples tends to be equal to the number of positive examples, the decision tree becomes more efficient and the performances of the system quite good. Such a phenomenon is not surprising and some researches have already been done in order to solve such a problem for example by Kubat, Holte and Matwin, in [20].

4.2 Impact of the Number of Pages Scanned per Datasheet

In this experiment we generated the models of contexts considering a support threshold equal to 5% for the apriori algorithm. The size of the contexts was equal to three words and the training set and test set had the same size as in the previous experiment.

We ran the system and observed the values of recall and precision as we changed the number of pages used for each datasheet by the system. Once again, we may observe on Figure 3(c) that the number of pages processed by the system has also an effect on the number of positive and negative examples the system generates. Figure 3(d) shows the changes of recall and precision according to the number of pages processed per datasheet. We observe again a variation in recall and precision according to the inverse changes of the value $card(E^-)/card(E^+)$.

5 Conclusion

In this paper we presented a system that is able to discover information extraction rules from technical datasheets of electronic components. Our system is based on a combination of frequent pattern mining and decision tree learning. The main advantage and originality of our approach is that it does not require any linguistic process to deal with free texts. The experiments show that our system performs quite well, in term of precision and recall, for extracting part-numbers from datasheets and it can efficiently replace a manually designed information extraction tool.

In the future we would like to discover information extraction rules that extract many other features from the datasheets. We also think our method may be applied to other domains such as bioinformatics where we could learn, for example, to extract gene names from texts.

References

1. R. Agrawal, R.J. Bayardo, and R. Srikant. Athena: Mining-based interactive management of text database. In *Proceedings of EDBT 2000*, LNCS 1777, pages 365–379, March 2000.
2. R. Agrawal and R. Srikant. Fast algorithms for mining association rules in large databases. In *Proceedings of VLDB'94*, pages 487–499, September 1994.
3. D.E. Appelt. Introduction to information extraction. *AI Communications*, 12(3):161–172, 1999.
4. R.R. Bouckaert. Low level information extraction, a bayesian network based approach. In *Proceedings of the Workshop on Text Learning*, Sydney, 2002.
5. M.E. Califf and R. Mooney. Relational learning of pattern-match rules for information extraction. In *Proceedings of AAAI'99*, pages 328–334, 1999.
6. M. Castellanos, Q. Chen, U. Dayal, M. Hsu, M. Lemon, P. Siegel, and J. Stinger. Component advisor: A tool for automatically extracting electronic component data from web datasheets. In *Workshop on Reuse of Web Information at WWW7*, 1998.
7. B. Chidlovskii. Wrapping web information providers by transducer induction. In *Proceedings of ECML'2001*, LNCS 2167, pages 61–72, September 2001.
8. B. Chidlovskii, J. Ragetli, and M. de Rijke. Wrapper generation via grammar induction. In *Proceedings of ECML 2000*, LNCS 1810, pages 96–108, June 2000.

9. H.L. Chieu, H.T. Ng, and Y.K. Lee. Closing the gap: Learning-based information extraction rivaling knowledge-engineering methods. In *Proceedings of the 41st Annual Meeting of the ACL*, pages 216–223, July 2003.
10. F. Ciravegna. Adaptive information extraction from text by rule induction and generalization. In *Proceedings of IJCAI 2001*, pages 1251–1256, Seattle, Washington, USA, August 2001. Morgan Kaufmann.
11. F. Ciravegna. (lp)2, an adaptive algorithm for information extraction from web-related texts. In *Proceedings of the IJCAI-2001 Workshop on Adaptive Text Extraction and Mining*, ,Seattle, August 2001.
12. F. Ciravegna and A. Lavelli. Learningpinocchio: Adaptive information extraction for real world applications. *Journal of Natural Language Engineering*, 10(2), 2004.
13. W. Cohen and L.S. Jensen. A structured wrapper induction system for extracting information from semi-structured documents. In *Proceedings of the IJCAI-2001 Workshop on Adaptive Text Extraction and Mining*, Seattle, August 2001.
14. H. Déjean. Learning rules and their exceptions. *Journal of Machine Learning Research*, 2:669–693, march 2002.
15. R. Feldman and I. Dagan. Knowledge discovery in textual databases (KDT). In *Proceedings of KDD'95*, pages 112–117. AAAI Press, August 1995.
16. D. Freitag. Multistrategy learning for information extraction. In *Proceedings of ICML'98*, pages 161–169, 1998.
17. D. Freitag and A. McCallum. Information extraction with HMM structures learned by stochastic optimization. In *Proceedings of AAAI'2000 and IAAI'2000*, pages 584–589. AAAI Press, August 2000.
18. R. Grishman. Information extraction : Techniques and challenges. In *Information Extraction : A Multidisciplinary Approach to an Emerging Information Technology*, pages 10–27. Springer, 1997.
19. S. Huffman. Learning information extraction patterns from examples. In S. Wermter, E. Riloff, and G. Scheller, editors, *Connectionist, Statistical and Symbolic Approaches to Learning for Natural Language Processing.* Springer, 1996.
20. M. Kubat, R. Holte, and S. Matwin. Learning when negative examples abound. In *Proceedings of ECML'97*, LNCS 1224, pages 146–153, April 1997.
21. N. Kushmerick. Wraper induction: Efficiency and expressiveness. *Artificial Intelligence*, 118(1-2):15–68, 2000.
22. N. Kushmerick and B. Thomas. Adaptive information extraction: Core technologies for information agents. In *Intelligent Information Agents - The AgentLink Perspective*, LNCS 2586, pages 79–103, 2003.
23. N. Kushmerick, D.S. Weld, and R.B. Doorenbos. Wrapper induction for information extraction. In *Proceedings of IJCAI'97*, pages 729–737, 1997.
24. S.H. Lin and J.M. Ho. Discovering informative content blocks from web documents. In *Proceedings of KDD 2002*, pages 588–593, July 2002.
25. S. Muggleton and L. De Raedt. Inductive Logic Programming : Theory and Methods. *Journal of Logic Programming*, 19-20:629–679, 1994.
26. E. Riloff. Automatically constructing a dictionnary for information extraction tasks. In *Proceedings of AAAI'93*, pages 811–816, 1993.
27. Y. Sasaki and Y. Matsuo. Learning semantic-level information extraction rules by type-oriented ILP. In *Proceedings of COLING 2000*, pages 698–704. Morgan Kaufmann, August 2000.
28. J.C. Shafer and R. Agrawal. Continuous querying in database-centric Web applications. In *Proceedings of the 9th International W3 Conference*, May 2000.
29. S. Soderland. *Learning Text Analysis Rules for Domain-Specific Natural Language Processing.* PhD thesis, University of Massachusetts, Amherst, 1997.

30. S. Soderland. Learning information extraction rules for semi-structured and free text. *Machine Learning*, 34(1-3):233–272, 1999.
31. J.A. Swets. Information retrieval systems. *Science*, 141:245–250, 1963.
32. J. Yang and J. Choi. Knowledge-based wrapper induction for intelligent web information extraction. In Y. Yao N. Zhong, J. Liu, editor, *Web Intelligence*, pages 153–172. Springer-Verlag, May 2003.

An Ontology-Supported Data Preprocessing Technique for Real-Life Databases

Bong-Horng Chu[1,3], In-Kai Liao[2], and Cheng-Seen Ho[2,4]

[1] Department of Electronic Engineering, National Taiwan University of Science and Technology, 43 Keelung Road Sec.4, Taipei 106, Taiwan
ben@ailab2.et.ntust.edu.tw

[2] Department of Computer Science and Information Engineering, National Taiwan University of Science and Technology, 43 Keelung Road Sec.4, Taipei 106, Taiwan
cheng-seen.ho@ieee.org

[3] Telecommunication Laboratories, Chunghwa Telecom Co., Ltd. 11 Lane 74 Hsin-Yi Road Sec.4, Taipei, 106, Taiwan
benjamin@cht.com.tw

[4] Information School, Chung Kuo Institute of Technology, 56 Hsing-Lung Road Sec.3, Taipei, 116, Taiwan
shawnho@mail.ckitc.edu.tw

Abstract. In this paper we propose an ontology-supported technique to preprocess the remark fields in real-life customer servicing databases in order to discover useful information to help re-categorize misclassified service records owing to human ignorance or bad design of problem categorization. This process restores the database into one with more meaningful data in each record, which facilitates subsequent data analysis. Our experience in applying the technique to a real-life database shows a substantial quality improvement can be obtained in mining association rules from the database.

1 Introduction

Customer servicing databases appear in all customer relationship management systems. They are usually designed to contain domain-specific categorizing fields, which take on proper values to reflect the physical semantics of a service record. But the predefined field values are hardly exhausted and therefore values like "others" have to be introduced. Categorizing fields containing scattered "others" values inevitably hamper subsequent analysis. Fortunately, the database usually also contains one or more remark fields to remember extra information about a service record. We humans thus can retrieve significant information embedded in those fields to help discover the real meaning behind the "others" values.

In this paper, we develop this process into a formal technique. Taking a troubleshooting database of a GSM system as an example, we first preprocess the database to discover significant values from the remark fields with ontology's support, and then revise the database by replacing the "others" values with these significant values. To prove the technique is viable, we finally conduct a mining process on the

M. Ali and F. Esposito (Eds.): IEA/AIE 2005, LNAI 3533, pp. 521 – 523, 2005.

revised database and make comparison on how the process helps discover better association rules.

2 Ontology-Supported Data Preprocessing

The trouble shooting database for a GSM system contains three categorizing fields, one *symptom* field to record customer's complaints, one *cause* field to put down the causes behind the symptoms, and one *process* field to describe the processes the representatives take to resolve the causes. There are two remark fields, one associated with the *symptom* field, and the other associated with both the *cause* and *process* fields. Before performing data preprocessing, we followed the guidance of the construction procedures proposed by Noy and McGuinness' work [1] to develop three ontologies related to *symptoms*, *causes*, and *processes*, namely *GSMSO* (*GSM-trouble Symptom Ontology*), *GSMCO* (*GSM-trouble Cause Ontology*) and *GSMPO* (*GSM-trouble Process Ontology*), respectively, to define the conceptual terminologies and concept hierarchies in the GSM trouble shooting domain. Our approach to data preprocessing includes three steps: Remarks Grouping, Keyword Extraction, and Terms Substitution. We will describe the steps using the refinement of *symptom* field as the example.

Remarks Grouping retrieves symptom remarks from the records that have value "others" in the *symptom* field, groups those remarks into different documents according to their *causes*, and tokenizes the texts in each document by MMSEG [2].

After tokenizing, we found many Chinese terms in the GSM trouble-shooting domain cannot be discriminated very well. Keyword Extraction is thus introduced to fix the problem. With the support of the *GSMSO* ontology, it first fixes the wrongly segmented tokens and then re-names them according to the symptom terms in the ontology. It finally eliminates the terms which cannot be found in the ontology. Only ontology terms or their synonyms can stay in the document after this step.

Terms Substitution starts by utilizing TFIDF [3] to calculate a weight for each term in the documents of symptom remarks, and then identifies most significant terms, which contains weights over a pre-defined threshold. With these significant terms, we can replace "others" with proper new terms in every record. Note the replacement is done in accord with what significant terms are contained in the *symptom remark* field of a record.

3 Empirical Evaluation

We apply the technique to revise a real-life GSM trouble shooting historical database, taken from one of the major telecommunication company in Taiwan. The revised database is then subjected to a data-mining module [4] for discovering implicit trouble-shooting rules. Two sets of rule are discovered, namely, rules in terms of *symptom→cause* and rules in terms of *cause→process*. Our experimental results show, the total accuracy rate of the *symptom→cause* rules has been improved from 38.2% (before data preprocessing) to 79.5% (after data preprocessing), and the total accuracy rate of the *cause→process* rules has been improved from 33.4% to 72.5% [5].

4 Conclusion

The proposed ontology-supported data preprocessing technique can revise a customer-servicing database so that further data analysis can obtain better results. The technique is ontology supported and hence can successfully identify significant terms from properly grouped remark fields, which are grouped together according to the semantics of related fields. The technique is text mining-based and hence can discover most significant terms from the grouped remark fields. The most significant terms then can be used to replace meaningless "others" values and make service records more meaningful. Our experience shows the technique can facilitate better association rules mining from a revised real-life trouble-shooting database.

References

1. Noy, N.F., McGuinness, D.L.: Ontology Development 101: A Guide to Creating Your First Ontology. Stanford Knowledge Systems Laboratory Technical Report KSL-01-05 and Stanford Medical Informatics Technical Report SMI-2001-0880, March (2001)
2. Tsai, C.H.: MMSEG: A Word Identification System for Mandarin Chinese Text Based on Two Variants of The Maximum Matching Alforithm. Availible at http://www.geocities.com/hao510/mmseg/ (1996)
3. Joachims, T.: A Probabilistic Analysis of the Rocchio Algrithm with TFIDF for Text Careagorization. Technical Report of CMU-CS-96-118, Department of Computer Science, Carnegie Mellon University, Pennsylvania, USA, March (1996)
4. Liao, B.C.: An Intelligent Proxy Agent for FAQ Service. Master Thesis, Department of Electronic Engineering, National Taiwan University of Science and Technology, Taipei, Taiwan, R.O.C. (2003)
5. Liao, I.K.: Ontology-Supported Data Preprocessing and Mining Techniques for Trouble Shooting of GSM Systems. Master Thesis, Department of Computer Science and Information Engineering, National Taiwan University of Science and Technology, Taipei, Taiwan, R.O.C. (2004)

A Fuzzy Genetic Algorithm for Real-World Job Shop Scheduling

Carole Fayad and Sanja Petrovic

School of Computer Science and Information Technology,
University of Nottingham, Jubilee Campus, Wollaton Road, Nottingham NG8 1BB UK
{cxf, sxp}@cs.nott.ac.uk
http://www.cs.nott.ac.uk/~cxf,~sxp

Abstract. In this paper, a multi-objective genetic algorithm is proposed to deal with a real-world fuzzy job shop scheduling problem. Fuzzy sets are used to model uncertain due dates and processing times of jobs. The objectives considered are average tardiness and the number of tardy jobs. Fuzzy sets are used to represent satisfaction grades for the objectives taking into consideration the preferences of the decision maker. A genetic algorithm is developed to search for the solution with maximum satisfaction grades for the objectives. The developed algorithm is tested on real-world data from a printing company. The experiments include different aggregation operators for combining the objectives.

Keywords: job shop scheduling, fuzzy logic and fuzzy sets, genetic algorithms.

1 Introduction

Scheduling is defined as the problem of allocation of machines over time to competing jobs [1]. The *m* x *n* job shop scheduling problem denotes a problem where a set of *n* jobs has to be processed on a set of *m* machines. Each job consists of a chain of operations, each of which requires a specified processing time on a specific machine.

Although production scheduling has attracted research interest of operational research and artificial intelligence community for decades, there still remains a gap between the academic research and real world problems. In the light of the drive to bridge this gap, we consider in this work a real-world application and focus on two aspects in particular, namely uncertainty inherent in scheduling and multi-objective scheduling.

Scheduling parameters are not always precise due to both human and machine resource factors [2]. As a result, classical approaches, within a deterministic scheduling theory, relying on precise data might not be suitable for representation of uncertain scenarios [3]. Consequently, the deterministic scheduling models and algorithms have been extended to the stochastic case, mainly to models that assume that processing times are random variables with specified probability distributions [1]. However, probabilistic characteristics of processing times and other scheduling parameters are often not available in manufacturing environments. That is the reason why standard stochastic methods based on probability are not appropriate to use. Fuzzy sets and

M. Ali and F. Esposito (Eds.): IEA/AIE 2005, LNAI 3533, pp. 524 – 533, 2005.

fuzzy logic have been increasingly used to capture and process imprecise and uncertain information [4,5]. For example, Chanas et al. consider minimization of maximum lateness of jobs in a single machine scheduling problem [6] and minimization of maximal expected value of the fuzzy tardiness and minimization of the expected value of maximal fuzzy tardiness in a two-single machine scheduling problem [7]. Itoh et al. [8] represent the execution times and due dates as fuzzy sets to minimize the number of tardy jobs.

Real-world problems require the decision maker to consider multiple objectives prior to arriving at a decision [9, 10]. Recent years have seen an increasing number of publications handling multi-objective job shop scheduling problems [11]. A survey on available multi-objective literature is given in [9] and a review on most recent evolutionary algorithms for solving multi-objective problems is given in [12].

This paper deals with a real-world job shop scheduling problem faced by Sherwood Press, a printing company based in Nottingham, UK. It is a due date driven client-oriented company. This is reflected in the objectives of minimizing average tardiness and number of tardy jobs. The durations of operations on the machines, especially the ones involving humans are not known precisely. Also, due dates are rigid and can be relaxed up to a certain extent. Fuzzy sets are used to model imprecise scheduling parameters and also to represent satisfaction grades of each objective. A number of genetic algorithms with different components are developed and tested on real-world data.

The paper is organized as follows. In Section 2, the fuzzy job shop problem is introduced together with the objectives and constraints; then, the real-world problem at Sherwood Press is described. The fuzzy genetic algorithm with the fitness function, which aggregates multiple objectives, is given in Section 3. Experimental results obtained on real-world data are discussed in Section 4 followed by conclusions in Section 5.

2 Problem Statement

In the job shop problem considered in this research, n jobs $J_1,...,J_n$ with given release dates $r_1,...,r_n$ and due dates $d_1,...,d_n$ have to be scheduled on a set of m machines $M_1,...,M_m$. Each job Jj j=1,…,n consists of a chain of operations determined by a process plan that specifies precedence constraints imposed on the operations. Each operation is represented as an ordered pair (i, j), i=1,..,m and its processing time is denoted by pij.

The task is to find a sequence of operations of n jobs on each of m machines with the following objectives:

(1) to minimize the average tardiness C_{AT}:

$$C_{AT} = \frac{1}{n}\sum_{j=1}^{n} Tj ; \quad Tj = \max\{0, Cj - dj\}; \quad j = 1,...,n \text{ and } Cj \text{ is the completion} \tag{1}$$

time of job J_j on the last machine on which it requires processing.

(2) to minimize the number of tardy jobs C_{NT}:

$$C_{NT} = \sum_{j=1}^{n} u_j \; ; u_j = 1 \text{ if } T_j > 0, \text{ otherwise } u_j = 0 \tag{2}$$

The resulting schedule is subject to the following constraints: (1) the precedence constraints which serve in ensuring that the processing sequence of operations of each job conforms to the predetermined order, (2) the capacity constraints which ensure that a machine processes only one job at a time and its processing cannot be interrupted.

Any solution satisfying all above listed constraints is called a feasible schedule.

2.1 A Real-World Job Shop Problem

In this section, a job shop problem faced by a printing company, Sherwood Press Ltd, is described. There exist 18 machines in the shopfloor, which are grouped within 7 work centers: Printing, Cutting, Folding, Card-inserting, Embossing and Debossing, Gathering, Stitching and Trimming and Packaging. Jobs are processed in the work centres, following a pre-determined order. A 'Job Bag' is assigned to each order to record the quantity in units to be produced and the 'Promised delivery date' of the order (referred to as due date).

Processing times of jobs are uncertain due to both machine and human factors. Consequently, the completion time of each job is uncertain. In addition, as it is not always possible to construct a schedule in which all jobs are completed before their due dates, some of the jobs may be tardy. The model should allow the decision maker to express his/her preference to the tardiness of each job. Fuzzy sets are used to model uncertain processing times of jobs and the decision maker's preference to the tardiness of each job.

Unlike a conventional crisp set, which enforces either membership or non-membership of an object in a set, a fuzzy set allows grades of membership in the set. A fuzzy set $\tilde{A}$ is defined by a membership function $\mu_{\tilde{A}}(x)$ which assigns to each object x in the universe of discourse X, a value representing its grade of membership in this fuzzy set [13]:

$$\mu_{\tilde{A}}(x) : X \rightarrow [0,1] \tag{3}$$

A variety of shapes can be used for memberships such as triangular, trapezoidal, bell curves and s-curves [13]. Conventionally, the choice of the shape is subjective and allows the decision maker to express his/her preferences.

The 'estimation' of processing time of each operation is obtained taking into consideration the nature of the machines in use. While some machines are automated and can be operated at different speeds, others are staff-operated and therefore the processing times are staff-dependent. Uncertain processing times $\tilde{p}_{ij}$ are modeled by triangular membership functions represented by a triplet (p_{ij}^1, p_{ij}^2, p_{ij}^3), where p_{ij}^1 and

p_{ij}^{3} are lower and upper bounds of the processing time while p_{ij}^{2} is so-called modal point [13]. An example of fuzzy processing time is shown in Fig.1. A trapezoidal fuzzy set (TrFS) is used to model the due date $\tilde{d}_j$ of each job, represented by a doublet (d_j^1, d_j^2), where d_j^1 is the crisp due date and the upper bound d_j^2 of the trapezoid exceeds d_j^1 by 10%, following the policy of the company. An example of a fuzzy due date is given in Fig.2.

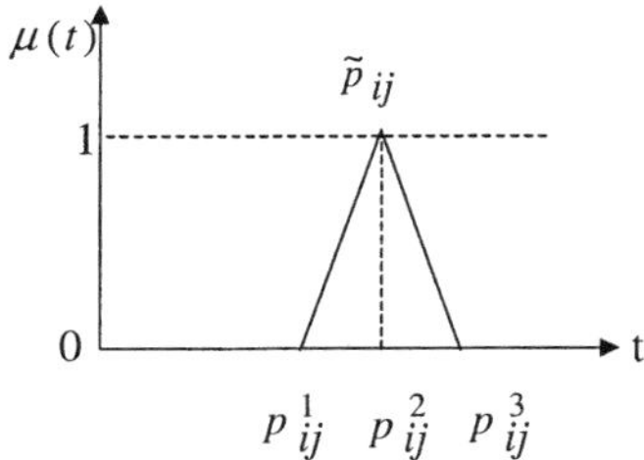

Fig. 1. Fuzzy processing time

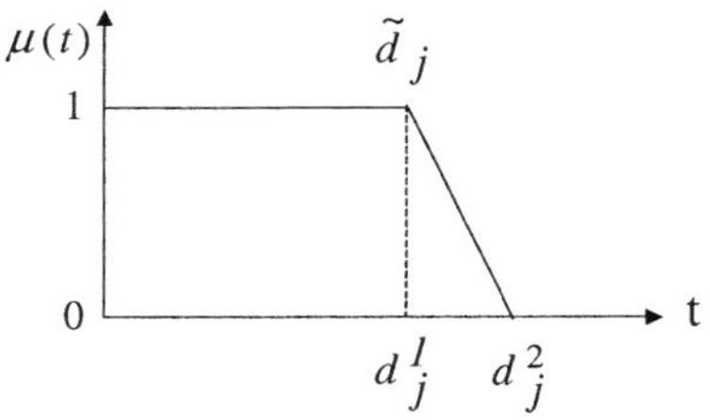

Fig. 2. Fuzzy due date

3 A Fuzzy Genetic Algorithm for the Job Shop Scheduling Problem

A genetic algorithm (GA) is an iterative search procedure widely used in solving optimization problems, motivated by biological models of evolution [14]. In each iteration, a population of candidate solutions is maintained. Genetic operators such as mutation and crossover are applied to evolve the solutions and to find the good solutions that have a high probability to survive for the next iteration.

The main characteristics of the fuzzy GA developed for job shop scheduling are described below:

- Chromosome: Each chromosome is made of two sub-chromosomes of length *m*, named machines sub-chromosome and dispatching rules sub-chromosome. The genes of the first sub-chromosome contain machines, while genes of the second sub-chromosome contain the dispatching rules to be used for sequencing operations on the corresponding machines.
- Initialization: The machine sub-chromosome is filled in by randomly choosing machines *i*, *i=1,..,m*. The initialization of the dispatching rules sub-chromosome is done by choosing randomly one among the following four rules: Early Due Date First, Shortest Processing Time First, Longest Processing Time First, Longest Remaining Processing Time First.
- Crossover operator: This operator is applied with a certain probability in order to combine genes from two parent sub-chromosomes and create new children sub-

chromosomes, taking care that machines are not duplicated in the machine sub-chromosome [11].

- Mutation operator: A randomly chosen pair of genes exchange their positions in a sub-chromosome. Mutation is applied independently in both sub-chromosomes.
- Selection: A roulette-wheel-selection technique is used for selection of chromosomes to survive to the next iteration. The probability of a survival of the chromosome is proportional to its fitness.
- Elitist strategy: In each generation, the best chromosome is automatically transferred to the next generation.
- Fitness function: The genetic algorithm searches for the schedule with highest fitness, where the fitness function is used to assess the quality of a given schedule within the population. The fitness function aggregates the Satisfaction Grade (SG) of two objectives. The satisfaction grades are calculated taking into consideration the completion times of the jobs. Fuzzy processing times of job operations imply fuzzy completion times of jobs. The question arises how to compare a fuzzy completion time of a job with its fuzzy due date, i.e. how to calculate the likelihood that a job is tardy. Two approaches are investigated: (1) based on the possibility measure introduced by Dubois et al [5] and also used by Itoh et al [8] to handle tardy jobs in a job shop problem, and (2) based on the area of intersection introduced by Sakawa in [2].

1. The possibility measure $\pi_{\tilde{C}_j}(\tilde{d}_j)$ evaluates the possibility of a fuzzy event, $\tilde{C}_j$, occurring within the fuzzy set $\tilde{d}_j$ [8]. It is used to measure the satisfaction grade of a fuzzy completion time $SG_T(\tilde{C}_j)$ of job J_j:

$$SG_T(\tilde{C}_j) = \pi_{\tilde{C}_j}(\tilde{d}_j) = \sup \min\{\mu_{\tilde{C}_j}(t), \mu_{\tilde{d}_j}(t)\} \qquad j=1,..,n \tag{4}$$

where $\mu_{\tilde{C}_j}(t)$ and $\mu_{\tilde{d}_j}(t)$ are the membership functions of fuzzy sets $\tilde{C}_j$ and $\tilde{d}_j$ respectively. An example of a possibility measure of fuzzy set $\tilde{C}_j$ with respect to fuzzy set $\tilde{d}_j$ is given in Fig.3.

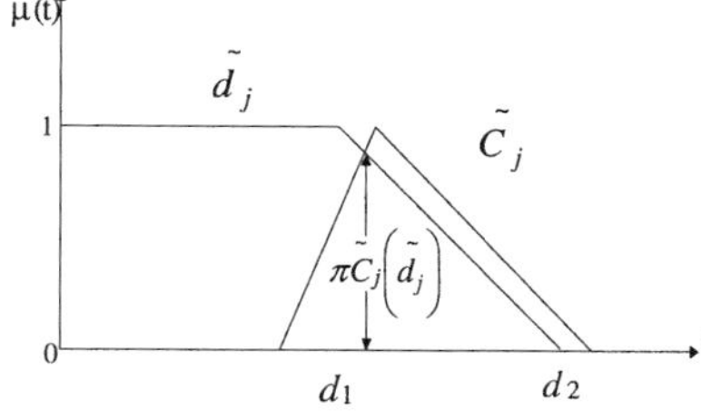

Fig. 3. Satisfaction Grade of completion time using possibility measure

2. Area of Intersection measures the portion of $\tilde{C}j$ that is completed by the due date $\tilde{d}_j$ (Fig. 4). The satisfaction grade of a fuzzy completion time of job J_j is defined:

$$SG_T(\tilde{C}_j) = (\text{area } \tilde{C}_j \cap \tilde{d}_j) / (\text{area } \tilde{C}_j) \quad (5)$$

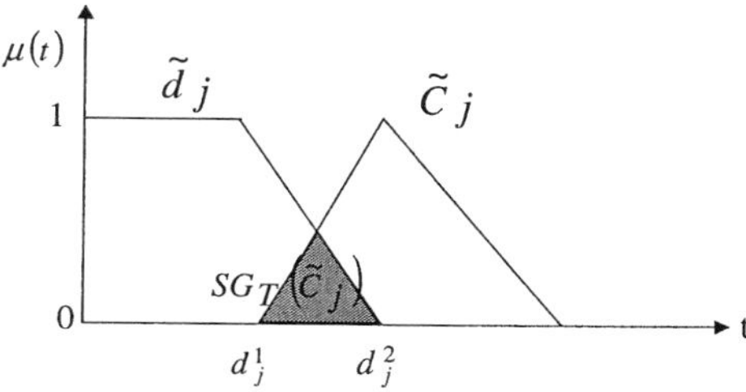

Fig. 4. Satisfaction Grade of completion time using area of intersection

The objectives given in (1) and (2) are transformed into the objectives to maximize their corresponding satisfaction grades:

(1) Satisfaction grade of Average Tardiness: $S_{AT} = \frac{1}{n} \sum_{j=1}^{n} SG_T(\tilde{C}_j)$ (6)

(2) Satisfaction grade of number of tardy jobs: A parameter λ is introduced such that a job J_j $j=1,\ldots,n$ is considered to be tardy if $SG_T(\tilde{C}_j) \leq \lambda$, $0 \leq \lambda \leq 1$. After calculating the number of tardy jobs *nTardy*, the satisfaction grade S_{NT} is evaluated as:

$$S_{NT} = \begin{cases} 1 & \text{if } nTardy = 0 \\ (n'' - nTardy)/n'' & \text{if } 0 < nTardy < n'' \\ 0 & \text{if } nTardy > n'' \end{cases} \quad (7)$$

n''= 15% of n, where n is the total number of jobs.

We investigate three different aggregation operators, which combine the satisfaction grades of the objectives:

1. Average of the satisfaction grades: $F_1 = 1/2\ (S_{AT} + S_{NT})$
2. Minimum of the satisfaction grades: $F_2 = \text{Min}\ (S_{AT}, S_{NT})$
3. Average Weighted Sum of the satisfaction grades: $F_3 = 1/2\ (w_1 S_{AT} + w_2 S_{NT})$, where $w_k \in [0,1]$, $k=1,2$, are normalized weights randomly chosen used in the GA and changed in every iteration in order to explore different areas of the search space [10].

Apart from handling imprecise and uncertain data, fuzzy sets and fuzzy logic enable multi-objective optimization in which multiple objectives that are non-commensurable are simultaneously taken into consideration. In this problem, objectives, the number of tardy jobs and the average tardiness of jobs are measured in different units but have to be used simultaneously to assess the quality of schedules.. Values of objectives are mapped into satisfaction grades, which take values from [0,1] interval and can be combined in an overall satisfaction grade.

4 Performance of the GA on Real-World Data

The developed GA algorithms were tested on real-world data collected at Sherwood Press over the period of three months denoted here by February, March and April. The load of each month is given in Table 1.

Table 1. Datasets

Month	Number of Jobs	Number of Operations
February	64	214
March	159	549
April	39	109

The experiments were run on a PC Pentium with 2 GHz and 512 MB of RAM, using Visual C++ .Net. The parameters used in the GAs are given in Table 2.

Table 2. Genetic algorithm parameters

Population size	50
Length of the chromosome	$2m$, where m = number of machines
Probability crossover	0.8
Mutation crossover	0.3
Termination condition	250 iterations

4.1 Experiments with Different Values of λ

The first sets of experiments are conducted with the aim of investigating what an effect changing the value λ has on the solution. A higher value of λ leads to higher number of tardy jobs. This is illustrated in Fig. 5, in which two values are used for λ: λ =0.3 and λ =0.7. Let J_j be a job with a fuzzy due date $\tilde{d}_j$ that could complete at

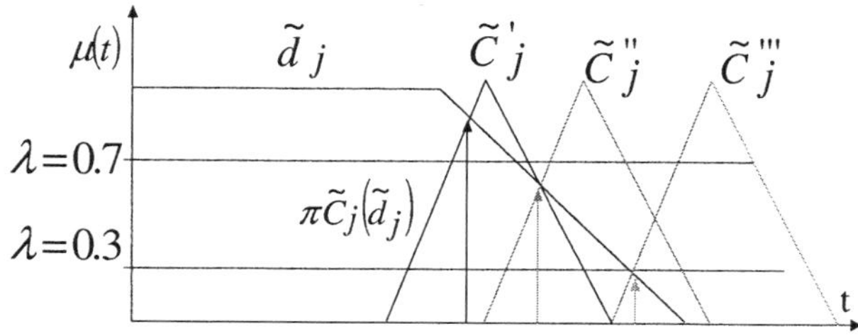

Fig. 5. Assessment of job tardiness with different completion times and values of λ

$\tilde{C}'_j$, $\tilde{C}''_j$ or $\tilde{C}'''_j$: If it completes at $\tilde{C}'_j$, then $\pi_{\tilde{C}_j}(\tilde{d}_j) \geq 0.7$; therefore, J_j is not tardy for both λ=0.3 & λ=0.7. If job J_j completes at $\tilde{C}''_j$, it is tardy if λ=0.7 and not tardy if λ=0.3. If it completes at $\tilde{C}'''_j$, J_j is tardy for both λ=0.3 & 0.7.

As an illustration, Fig. 6 shows the satisfaction grades of the objectives obtained on the March data, where the aggregation operator Average is used together with the possibility measure to determine tardy jobs. It can be seen that, S_{NT} converges to a higher value (S_{NT} =0.54) faster when λ=0.3 then when λ=0.7.

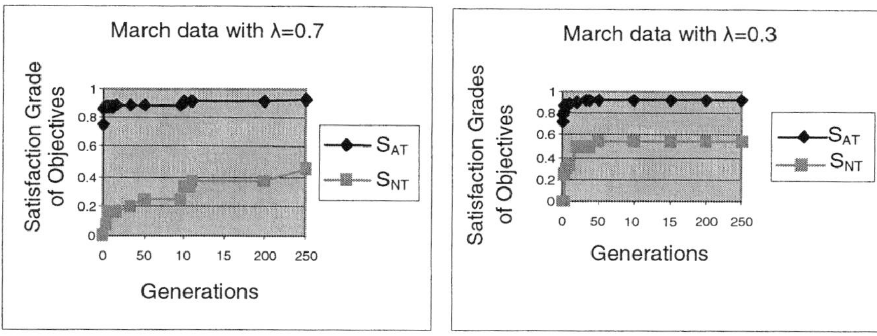

Fig. 6. The convergence of the values of objectives for different λ values

4.2 Experiments with Different Variations of the Genetic Algorithm

Six different variations of the genetic algorithm were developed at λ =0.7, with different approaches to determine tardy jobs, using possibility measure (Pos) and area of intersection (Area), and different aggregation operators, using Average, Min and WSum. For illustration purposes, results obtained on March data set running the different GA variations 20 times each are given in Table 3. The data in column FF shows the best/average value of the Fitness Function; of course, these values cannot be compared due to the difference in the nature of the aggregation operators. The columns S_{NT} and S_{AT} show the corresponding best/average values of satisfaction grades of the objective functions, while C_{NT} shows the corresponding values of the objective function of number of tardy jobs. However, three different aggregation operators enable the decision maker to express his/her preferences. Average aggregation operator allows compensation for a *bad* value of one objective, namely a higher satisfaction grade of one objective can compensate, to a certain extent, for a lower satisfaction grade of another objective. On the contrary, Minimum operator is non-compensatory, which means that the solution with a *bad* performance with respect to one objective will not be highly evaluated no matter how *good* is its performance with respect to another objective.

The possibility measure reflects more *optimistic* attitude to the jobs' tardiness than the area of intersection because the former measure considers the highest point of intersection of the two fuzzy sets regardless of their overall dimensions, while the area of intersection considers the proportion of the fuzzy completion time that falls within the fuzzy due date.

Table 3. Best and average values of satisfaction grades

Variations of GA	FF	S_{AT}	S_{NT}	C_{NT}
AverageArea	0.641/0.62	0.911/0.908	0.371/0.331	14/15
MinArea	0.371/0.264	0.904/0.893	0.371/0.264	14/17
WSumArea	0.43/0.415	0.907/0.893	0.371/0.26	14/17
AveragePos	0.69/0.66	0.923/0.913	0.455/0.41	12/13
MinPos	0.455/0.342	0.914/0.903	0.455/0.342	12/15
WSumPos	0.435/0.425	0.919/0.902	0.455/0.316	12/15

5 Conclusion

This paper deals with a multi-objective fuzzy job shop scheduling problem, where uncertain processing times and due dates are represented by fuzzy sets. The objectives considered are average tardiness and the number of tardy jobs. Six variations of the genetic algorithm are developed combining three aggregation operators for objectives and two different methods to determine tardiness of jobs. The results obtained highlight the differences of these aggregation operators in terms of compensation of objectives and the influence of the parameter λ in expressing an attitude toward the tardiness of jobs.

Our future research work will be focused on investigation of splitting jobs into lots and combining two or more jobs to be processed at the same time on the machine and processing different jobs of the same category, one after the other to reduce cost of set-up times.

Acknowledgments

The authors would like to thank the Engineering and Physics Science Research Council (EPSRC), UK, Grant No. GR/R95319/01 for supporting this research. We also acknowledge the support of the industrial collaborator Sherwood Press Ltd, Nottingham.

References

1. Pinedo, M., 'Scheduling Theory, Algorithms, and Systems,' Prentice Hall, Second Edition, (2002).
2. Sakawa, M. and Kubota, R., 'Fuzzy Programming for Multiobjective Job Shop Scheduling with Fuzzy Processing Time and Fuzzy Duedate through Genetic Algorithms', European Journal of Operational Research 120 2 (2000) 393-407.

3. Foretemps, P., 'Jobshop Scheduling with Imprecise Durations: A Fuzzy Approach', IEEE Transactions on Fuzzy Systems 5 4 (1997) 557-569.
4. Slowinski, R. and Hapke (Eds), M., Scheduling Under Fuzziness, Physica-Verlag, New York (2000).
5. Dubois, D. and Prade H., Possibility Theory: an Approach to Computerized Processing of Uncertainty, New York (1988).
6. Chanas, S. and Kasperski, A., 'Minimizing Maximum Lateness in a Single Machine Scheduling Problem with Fuzzy Processing times and Fuzzy Due Dates,' Engineering Applications of Artificial Intelligence 14 3 (2001) 377-386.
7. Chanas, S. and Kasperski, 'On Two Single Machine Scheduling Problems with Fuzzy Processing Times and Fuzzy Due Dates, European Journal of Operational Research, 147 2 (2003) 281-296.
8. Itoh, T. and Ishii, H., 'Fuzzy Due-date Scheduling Problem with Fuzzy Processing Time,' International Transactions in Operations Research 6 (1999) 639-647.
9. Nagar, A., Haddock, J. and Heragu, S., 'Multiple and Bi-criteria Scheduling: A Literature Survey', European Journal of Operational Research, 81 (1995) 88-104.
10. Murata, T., Ishibuchi, H. and Tanaka, H., 'Multi-Objective Genetic Algorithm and its Applications to Flowshop Scheduling,' Computers Industrial Engineering, 30 4 (1996) 957-968.
11. Bagchi, T., Multi-Objective Scheduling by Genetic Algorithms, Kluwer Academic Publish ers (1999).
12. Coelho, Carlos., Van Veldhuizen, D. and Lamont, G., Evolutionary Algorithms for Solving Multi-Objective Problems, Kluwer Acedmic Publishers (2002).
13. Klir, G. and Folger, T., Fuzzy Sets, Uncertainty and Information, Prentice Hall, New Jersey, (1988).
14. Reeves, C., Genetic Algorithms, in V.J. Rayward-Smith (Eds), Modern Heuristic Techniques for Combinatorial Problems, McGraw-Hill International, UK, ISBN 0-07-709239-2 (1995) 151-196.

Pareto-Optimal Hardware for Digital Circuits Using SPEA

Nadia Nedjah and Luiza de Macedo Mourelle

Department of Systems Engineering and Computation,
Faculty of Engineering, State University of Rio de Janeiro, Brazil
{nadia, ldmm}@eng.uerj.br

Abstract. In this paper, we focus on engineering $Pareto-optimal$ digital circuits given the expected input/output behaviour with a minimal design effort. The design objectives to be minimised are: hardware area, response time and power consumption. We do so using the Strength Pareto Evolutionary Algorithms. The performance and the quality of the circuit evolved for some benchmarks are presented then compared to those of single objective genetic algorithms as well as to the circuits obtained by human designers.

1 Introduction

Digital circuit design is a well-established area with a variety of on-the-shelf design methods and techniques. These tools, however, worry only about fulfilling the expected input/output behaviour of the circuit with the exception of some of them, which allow engineering circuits of relatively reduced size, i.e. the number of gate used. With the latter, the designer counterpart is a considerable designing effort.

The problem of interest consists of how can one design optimal circuits that implement a given input/output behaviour without much designing effort. The obtained circuits are expected to be minimal in terms of space, time and power requirements: The circuits must be *compact* i.e. uses a reduced number of gates, *efficient*, i.e. produces the output in a short time and *easy* or *not demanding*, i.e. consumes little power. The response time and power consumption of a circuit depends on the number and the complexity of the gates forming the longest path in it. The complexity of a gate depends solely on the number of its inputs. Furthermore, the design should take advantage of the all the kind of gates available on reconfigurable chip of field programmable gate array (FPGAs).

In this work, we design innovative and efficient evolutionary digital circuits. Circuit evaluation is based on their possible implementation using CMOS technology [2]. The produced circuits are balanced i.e., the trade-off between the required hardware area, the propagation time of the circuit output signals and the power consumption is the best. We do so using multi-objective evolutionary optimisation. We exploit the Strength Pareto Evolutionary Algorithm (SPEA) presented in [1]. SPEA is the most recent and efficient multi-objective evolutionary algorithm [5].

M. Ali and F. Esposito (Eds.): IEA/AIE 2005, LNAI 3533, pp. 534–543, 2005.

The rest of this paper is organised in five sections. First, in Section 2, we define multi-objective evolutionary hardware and introduce the characteristics of the basic components allowed. Subsequently, in Section 3, we present the multi-objective evolutionary algorithm used to perform the evolution i.e., the strength Pareto evolutionary algorithm [1]. Thereafter, in Section 4, we describe the circuit encoding and the genetic operator used followed with the definition and implementation of the circuit fitness evaluation with respect to all three considered objective. Then, in Section 5, we evaluate the performance of the evolutionary process and assess the quality of the evolved Pareto-optimal digital circuits. Also, we compare the area, time and power requirements to those of circuit designs engineered by human designers and single objective genetic algorithm. Last but not least, in Section 6, we summarise the content of the paper and draw some useful conclusions.

2 Principles of Multi-objective Evolutionary Hardware

Evolutionary hardware consists simply of hardware whose design was evolved using genetic algorithms, wherein individuals represent circuit designs. In general, evolutionary hardware designs offer a mechanism to get a computer to provide a design of circuit without being told exactly how to do it. In short, it allows one to automatically create circuits. It does so based on a high level statement of the constraints the yielded circuit must respect. The input/output behaviour of the expected circuit is generally considered as an omnipresent constraint. Furthermore, the generated circuit should have a minimal size, minimal response time or minimal power consumption. However, this is the case in single objective evolutionary computation. Throughout the paper, we assume that $\mathcal{C}_{\mathcal{B}}$ be the set of all possible circuits that implement a given input/output behaviour $\mathcal{C}_{\mathcal{B}}$.

Starting form random set of circuit designs, which is generally called *initial population*, evolutionary hardware design breeds a population of designs through a series of steps, called *generations*, using the Darwinian principle of natural selection. Circuits are selected based on how much they adhere to the specified constraints. *Fitter* individuals are selected, recombined to produce off-springs which in turn should suffer some mutations. Such off-springs are then used to populate of the next generation. This process is iterated until a circuit design that obeys to all prescribed constraints is encountered within the current population.

Each circuit within the population is assigned a value, generally called *fitness*. A circuit design is fit if and only if it satisfies the imposed input/output behaviour. In single objective optimisation, a circuit design is considered *fitter* than another if and only if it has a smaller size, shorter response or consumes less power, depending of the optimisation objective size, time or power consumption minimisation respectively. In multi-objective optimisation, however, the concept of fitness is not that obvious. It is extremely rare that a single design optimises all objectives simultaneously. Instead, there normally exist several designs that provide the same *balance*, *compromise* or *trade-off* with respect to the problem objectives.

Table 1. Node operators together with the corresponding size and delay

Name	Symbol	Gate	Delay	Name	Symbol	Gate	Delay
NOT	$\bar{\ }$	1	0.0625	NAND	$\odot$	1	0.1300
AND	$\cdot$	2	0.2090	NOR	$\mp$	1	0.1560
OR	$+$	2	0.2160	XNOR	$\ominus$	3	0.2110
XOR	$\oplus$	3	0.2120	MUX	[ ]	3	0.2120

A circuit $C_1 \in \mathcal{C}_\mathcal{B}$ *dominates* another circuit $C_2 \in \mathcal{C}_\mathcal{B}$, denoted by $C_1 \succ C_2$ (interchangeably C_2 *is dominated by* C_1) if and only if C_1 is no worse than C_2, i.e. $area(C_1) \leq area(C_2)$, $time(C_1) \leq time(C_2)$ and $power(C_1) \leq power(C_2)$, and C_1 is strictly better than C_2 in at least one objective, i.e. $area(C_1) < area(C_2)$, $time(C_1) < time(C_2)$ or $power(C_1) < power(C_2)$. Otherwise, C_1 does not dominate C_2 (interchangeably C_2 is not dominated by C_1).

The usual interpretation of the term optimum in multi-objective optimisation is the *Pareto* optimum that was first proposed by Francis Y. Edgeworth [6] and later generalised by Vilfredo Pareto [7]. A circuit $C \in \mathcal{C}_\mathcal{B}$ is *Pareto-optimal* if and only if there exists no other circuit $C' \in \mathcal{C}_\mathcal{B}$ such that C' dominates C.

Both in single and multi-objective optimisation, an important aspect of evolutionary hardware design is thus to provide a way to evaluate the adherence of evolved circuits to the imposed constraints as well as the corresponding quality. First of all, the evolved circuit design must fulfil the input/output behaviour, which is given in a tabular form of expected results given the inputs. This is the truth table of the expected circuit. Second, the circuit must Pareto-optimal. This constraint allows us to yield digital circuits with optimal trade-offs regarding area, time and power consumption.

We estimate the necessary area for a given circuit using the concept of *gate equivalent*. This is the basic unit of measure for digital circuit area complexity [2]. It is based upon the number of logic gates that should be interconnected to perform the same input/output behaviour. This measure is more accurate that the simple number of gates [2]. For response time estimation purposes, the circuit is viewed as a pipeline. Each stage in this pipeline includes a set of gates. We approximate the propagation delay of the output signals by the maximum delay imposed by the pipeline. The number of gate equivalent and output signal propagation delay for each kind of gate are given in Table 1. The data were taken form [2]. Note that only 2-input gates NOT, AND, OR, XOR, NAND, NOR, XNOR and 2:1-MUX are allowed. The power consumption of a circuit is computed using a rough estimation of the circuit switching activity [3, 4]. Details of how the multiple objectives of the optimisation are evaluated are given in Section 4.

3 SPEA: Strength Pareto Evolutionary Algorithms

In single-objective optimisation, the concept of optimality is clear. The optimal solution is the one that satisfies all the imposed constraints and optimise the unique objective. In multi-objective optimisation, however, that concept is not that obvious. In the section, we give the necessary definitions and the inherent terminology to formalise the concept of optimality within a multi-objective optimisation problem.

The *s*trength *P*areto *e*volutionary *a*lgorithm (SPEA) was proposed by Zitzler and Thiele [1]. It uses the Pareto dominance to preserve the population diversity. Besides the generational population, it maintains an external continuously updated population. This population is kept up-to-date with evolved solutions that are non-dominated within the generational population. When the number of non-dominated solutions, which are stored externally, exceeds a pre-specified size, a clustering is applied to prune the population. The fitness evaluation of individuals is done considering only the individuals of the the external population. The individuals selected to participate of the reproduction process are drawn from both the generational and external populations. SPEA applies a new sharing method to compute the fitness of individuals that appear in the same niche. The SPEA proceeds as described in Algorithms 1.

Algorithm 1. SPEA procedure
Input. Tournament size $Tsize$ and generation number $Gsize$
Output. Pareto set S

$Initialise(P)$; $generation := 1$; $S := \emptyset$;
do
  $S := \{C | \nexists D \in P,\ C \succ D\}$; $S := S \setminus \{C | \exists D \in S,\ D \succ C\}$;
  if $|S| < Tsize$ **then** $Prune(S)$;
  $Fitness(P, S)$; $generation := generation + 1$;
  $Mutation(Crossover(Select(P, S, Tsize)))$;
while $generation \neq Gsize$;
return S;
end.

In Algorithm 2, function $Initialise(P)$ allows the building of an initial population in P, function $Prune(S, Psize)$ prunes the Pareto set S reducing its size down to $Psize$. It does so using a clustering procedure, which is explained later in this section and function $Fitness(P, S)$ computes the fitness of the individuals in P and S. The tournament selection is used.

The clustering performed by SPEA uses cluster analysis [8]. This computation is described in Algorithm 2. In this algorithm, Δ_{l_1,l_2} represents the distance between clusters l_1 and l_2, which is computed as the average distance between all the possible pairs of individuals across the two clusters. The measure $\delta_{i,j}$ is the Euclidean distance between individuals i and j [9]. The computation in line 7 of the clustering algorithm allows the construction of the reduced Pareto set by selecting from each cluster a representative individual, i.e. that with minimal average distance to all other individuals within the cluster.

A central concept to the way SPEA evaluates individual fitness consists of the so-called individual *strength*. This is defined only for the individuals that are part of the Pareto set (external population). The *strength* of an Circuit C in the Pareto set P is the non-negative real number in [0,1), proportional to the number of individuals in P that are dominated by C. We denote circuit C's strength by θ_C [1].

Algorithm 2. SPEA clustering procedure - *Prune*
Input. Pareto set S, tagret size $Psize$
Output. Pruned Pareto set P

$L := \bigcup_{s \in S} \{\{s\}\}$; $P := \emptyset$;
while $|L| > Psize$ **do**
  for each pair of clusters $(l_1, l_2) \in L \times L$ **do**
    $\Delta_{l_1,l_2} := \frac{1}{|l_1| \times |l_2|} \times \sum_{(s_1,s_2) \in l_1 \times l_2} \delta_{s_1,s_2}$;
    $L = L \setminus \{l_1, l_2\} \cup \{l_1 \cup l_2\}$ where $\Delta_{l_1,l_2} = \min_{(x,y) \in L \times L} \Delta_{x,y}$;
  for each cluster $l \in L$ **do**
    $P := P \cup \{s\}$ where $\frac{\sum_{x \in l} \delta_{x,s}}{|l|} = \min_{y \in l} \left(\frac{\sum_{z \in l} \delta_{y,z}}{|l|} \right)$;
return P;
end.

The fitness evaluation in SPEA is computed for all the individuals including those in the generational and Pareto set. There is a difference, however. The individuals in the external population are ranked using the corresponding strength while those that belong to the generational population are given a specific fitness value instead. The fitness of an individual is obtained summing up the strengths of all the individuals in the Pareto set that dominates it and adding 1 so that solutions in the external population will always have a better fitness. This is because we assume a minimisation problem and so individuals with smaller fitness are better. The *fitness* function is described in Algorithm 3.

Algorithm 3. SPEA fitness evaluation procedure - *fitness*
Input. Population P, Pareto set S
Output. Fitness measure of individuals $Fitness$

for each individual $C \in S$ **do** $F[C] := \theta_C$;
for each individual $C \in P$ **do**
  $Fitness[C] := 1$;
  for each individual $D \in S | D \succ C$ **do** $Fitness[C] := Fitness[C] + \theta_D$;
  $Fitness[C] := Fitness[C] + 1$;
return F;
end.

4 Evolving Pareto-Optimal Digital Circuits

In general, two main important concepts are crucial to any evolutionary computation: individual encoding and fitness evaluation. In evolutionary multi-objective optimisation, individual fitness is understood as its dominance regarding the solutions of the pool. Considering Definition 1 and Definition 2, one needs to know how to appreciate the solutions with respect to each one of the multiple objectives. So In the section, we concentrate on these two aspects for evolving Pareto-optimal digital circuits.

4.1 Circuit Encoding and Genetic Operators

We encode circuit schematics using a matrix of cells that may be interconnected. A cell may or may not involved in the circuit schematics. A cell consists of two inputs or three in the case of a MUX, a logical gate and a single output. A cell may draw its input signals from the output signals of gates of previous rows. The gates includes in the first row draw their inputs from the circuit global input signal or their complements. The circuit global output signals are the output signals of the gates in the last raw of the matrix.

Crossover of circuit schematics, as for specification crossover, is implemented using a variable four-point crossover. The mutation operator can act on two different levels: gate mutation or route mutation. In the first case, a cell is randomised and the corresponding gate changed. When a 2-input gate is altered by another 2-input gate, the mutation is thus completed. However, when a 2-input gate is changed to a 3-input gate (i.e. to a MUX), the mutation operator randomise an additional signal among those allowed (i.e. all the input signals, their complements and all the output signals of the cells in the rows previous). Finally, when a MUX is mutated to a 2-input gate, the selection signal is simply eliminated. The second case, which consists of route mutation is quite simple. As before, a cell is randomised and one of its input signals is chosen randomly and mutated using another allowed signal. (For more details on the genetic operators used see [10].)

4.2 Circuit Evaluation

As introduced, we aim at evolving Pareto-optimal digital circuit regarding four objectives: soundness, hardware area, response time and power dissipation.

In order to appreciate the qualities of an evolved circuit with respect to the optimisation objectives, let C be a digital circuit that uses a subset (or the complete set) of the gates given in Table 1. Let $Gates(C)$ be a function that returns the set of all gates of C. On the other hand, let $Value(T)$ be the Boolean value that C propagates for the input Boolean vector T assuming that the size of T coincides with the number of input signal required for C.

The soundness of circuit C is evaluated as described in (1), wherein X represents the input values of the input signals while Y represents the expected output values of the output signals of C, n denotes the number of output signals that C has. Function *Soundness* allows us to determine how much an evolved circuit adheres to the prescribed input/output behaviour. For each difference between the evolved circuit output values and the expected output signals, penalty ξ is accumulated. Note that the smaller the returned value the sounder is the considered circuit. Thus, for sound circuits (i.e. those that implement the specified input/output behaviour), function *soundness* returns 0. Note that objective *soundness* is not negotiable, i.e. only sound individuals are considered as solutions.

$$Soudness(C) = \sum_{j=1}^{n} \left(\sum_{i|Value(X_i) \neq Y_{i,j}} \xi \right) \quad (1)$$

The hardware area required for the implementation of circuit C is evaluated as described in (2), wherein function $Gates(C)$ returns the set of all gates of circuit C while function $GateEquiv(g)$ provides the number of gate equivalent to implement gate g.

$$Area(C) = \sum_{g \in Gates(C)} GateEquiv(g) \quad (2)$$

The response time of circuit C is given in (3), wherein $Levels(C)$ be a function that returns the set of gates of C grouped by level. Levels are ordered. Notice that the number of levels of a circuit coincides with the cardinality of the list expected from function $Levels$. Function $Delay$ returns the propagation delay of a given gate as shown in Table 1.

$$Time(C) = \sum_{l \in Levels(C)} \max_{g \in l} Delay(g) \quad (3)$$

Unlike soundness, area and response time, the evaluation of the dissipated power by a given digital circuit is not simple as it depends on the values of the input signals. Several estimation model were elaborated [4]. The average power dissipation for a digital circuit C is given in (4), wherein V_{dd} is the supply voltage, T is the global clock period, $Transitions(g)$ represents the times the output of gate g switches from 0 to 1 and vice versa and $Capacitance(g)$ represents the output or load capacitance of gate g.

$$Power_{avg}(C) = \frac{V_{dd}^2}{2 \times T} \times \sum_{g \in Gates(C)} (|Transitions(g)| \times Capacitance(g)) \quad (4)$$

In the (4), the first term of the product is the same for all circuits so can be discarded. Thus the average power can be represented by the summation term. The Switching activity at gate g, which determines $Transition(g)$, depends on the input signal changes. To avoid this dependency, we enumerate all possible transition times for each gate. A gate output switches each time one of its input signals switch.

For a two-input gate g, if its input signals switch at times $\{t_1^1, t_1^2 \ldots, t_1^m\}$ and $\{t_2^1, t_2^2 \ldots, t_2^n\}$ respectively, then the output signal of gate g will switch at times $\{t_1^1 + Delay(g), \ldots, t_1^m + Delay(g)\} \cup \{t_2^1 + Delay(g), \ldots, t_2^n + Delay(g)\}$. Note that the primary inputs are supposed to switch only once during a given cycle period. So assuming that these input signals all switch at time 0, consequently gate g at the first level of the circuit will switch only once at time $Delay(g)$. For the sake of practicality and without loss of generality, we assume that the load capacitance of a gate by the corresponding number of fanouts. Also, we ignore the first factor in (4) as it is the same for all circuits.

5 Performance Results

In this section, we compare the Pareto-optimal evolutionary circuits yield by our multi-objective optimisation to those designed by a human as well as to those evolved by single objective genetic algorithms [11]. Here, we use four benchmarks and the symbol of Table 1.

Both the first and second benchmarks need a 4-bit input signal $X = \langle x_3 x_2 x_1 x_0 \rangle$ and yield a single-bit output signal Y. The third and fourth benchmarks also requires a 4-bit input signal X but the respective circuits propagate a 4-bit and 3-bit output signal respectively. The truth tables of the four benchmarks are summarised in Table 2 below. Note that the fourth benchmark is a simple 2-bit multiplier of $X = \langle x_3 x_2 \rangle$ times $Y = \langle x_1 x_0 \rangle$. (The notation of the input signals is purely for space sake!) For the first benchmark, we were able to evolve several

Table 2. Truth tables of the used benchmarks

Input				1nd	2rd	3th Benchmark				4th Benchmark		
x_3	x_2	x_1	x_0	$y^{(1)}$	$y^{(2)}$	$y_3^{(3)}$	$y_2^{(3)}$	$y_1^{(3)}$	$y_0^{(3)}$	$y_2^{(4)}$	$y_1^{(4)}$	$y_0^{(4)}$
0	0	0	0	1	1	0	0	0	0	1	0	0
0	0	0	1	1	0	0	0	0	0	0	1	0
0	0	1	0	0	1	0	0	0	0	0	1	0
0	0	1	1	1	0	0	0	0	0	0	1	0
0	1	0	0	0	1	0	0	0	0	0	0	1
0	1	0	1	0	0	0	0	0	1	1	0	0
0	1	1	0	1	1	0	0	1	0	0	1	0
0	1	1	1	1	1	0	0	1	1	0	1	0
1	0	0	0	1	1	0	0	0	0	0	0	1
1	0	0	1	0	1	0	1	0	0	0	0	1
1	1	1	0	1	1	0	1	1	0	1	0	0
1	0	1	1	0	0	0	1	1	0	0	1	0
1	0	0	0	0	0	0	0	0	0	0	0	1
1	1	0	1	1	1	0	0	1	1	0	0	1
1	1	1	0	0	1	0	1	1	0	0	0	1
1	1	1	1	0	1	1	0	0	1	1	0	0

Pareto-optimal digital circuits. The specifications of one of these circuits is given by the signal assignment of (5). The characteristics (i.e. area, time and power) of the circuit are (13, 0.783, 11).

$$y^{(1)} \Longleftarrow ((x_2 \cdot x_3) \cdot x_0) \ominus ((x_1 \ominus x_2) \mp (x_2 + x_3)) \tag{5}$$

For the second benchmark, as for the first one, we were able to evolve several Pareto-optimal digital circuits. The specifications of one of these circuits is given by the signal assignments of (6). The characteristics (i.e. area, time and power) of the circuit are (9, 0.639, 7).

$$y^{(2)} \Longleftarrow [x_0 \ominus x_3, x_1, x_2] + (x_1 \mp x_3) \tag{6}$$

For the third benchmark, we were also able to evolve several Pareto-optimal digital circuits. The specifications of one of these circuits is given by the signal assignments of (7). The characteristics (i.e. area, time and power) of the circuit are (16, 0.425, 13).

$$\begin{aligned} y_3^{(3)} &\Longleftarrow (x_2 \cdot x_0) \cdot (x_3 \cdot x_1) \\ y_2^{(3)} &\Longleftarrow (x_3 \cdot x_1) \cdot (x_0 \odot x_2) \\ y_1^{(3)} &\Longleftarrow (x_3 \odot x_0) \oplus (x_2 \odot x_1) \\ y_0^{(3)} &\Longleftarrow (x_2 \cdot x_0) + x_0 \end{aligned} \tag{7}$$

For the fourth benchmark, we evolved several Pareto-optimal digital circuits. The specifications of one of these circuits is given by the signal assignments of (8). The characteristics (i.e. area, time and power) of the circuit are (17, 0.685, 12).

$$\begin{aligned} y_2^{(4)} &\Longleftarrow (x_0 + \overline{x_2}) \cdot ((\overline{x_0} + x_2) \odot (x_1 \odot \overline{x_3})) \\ y_1^{(4)} &\Longleftarrow (\overline{x_0} + x_2) \cdot ((x_0 + \overline{x_2}) \odot (x_1 + \overline{x_3})) \\ y_0^{(4)} &\Longleftarrow ((\overline{x_0} + x_2) \odot (x_1 \odot \overline{x_3})) \mp ((x_0 + \overline{x_2}) \odot (x_1 + \overline{x_3})) \end{aligned} \tag{8}$$

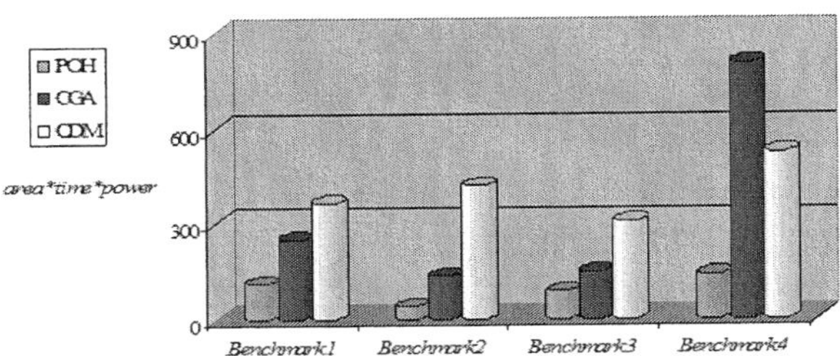

Fig. 1. Graphical comparison of the $area \times delay \times power$ factor for the three methods

Figure 1 shows a comparison between the fittest circuits engineered by a human designer, Coello's genetic algorithm and our genetic algorithm, which is based on genetic programming. In this figure, POH stands for *P*areto-*O*ptimal *H*ardware, CGA for *C*oello *G*enetic *A*lgorithm and CDM for *C*onventional *D*esign *M*ethods. We observed that big majority of the circuits we evolved dominate Coello's and the conventionally designed ones. Furthermore, the remaining circuits are not dominated neither by Coello's nor by the conventionally designed ones.

6 Conclusion

In this paper, we designed Pareto-optimal innovative evolutionary digital circuits. The produced circuits are balanced in the sense that they exhibit the best trade-off between the required hardware area, propagation time of output signals and power dissipation. We did so exploiting the strength Pareto evolutionary algorithm which is the most recent and efficient multi-objective evolutionary algorithm. The Pareto-optimal circuits obtained for a set of benchmarks present the best $area \times time \times power$ factor when compared to both circuits that were designed using conventional methods as well as to those genetically evolved by Coello's in [11]. The big majority of the circuits we evolved dominates the ones that were compared with and the rest is not dominated by neither of the circuits in comparison. A future work consists in performing a massive evolution for the used benchmarks which should yield all Pareto-optimal circuits for each benchmark. This would allow us to identify the Pareto fronts and its 3D representations.

References

1. Zitzler, E. and Thiele L., Multi0objective evolutionary algorithms: a comparative case study and the strength Pareto approach, IEEE Transactions on Evolutionary Computation, vol. 3, no. 4, pp. 257–271, 1999.
2. Ercegovac, M.D., Lang, T. and Moreno, J.H., Introduction to digital systems, John Wiley, 1999.
3. Hsiao, M.S., Peak power estimation using genetic spot optimization for large VLSI circuits, Proc. European Conference on Design, Automation and Test, pp. 175–179, March 1999.
4. Najm, F. N., A survey of power estimation techniques in VLSI circuits, IEEE Transactions on VLSI Systems, vol. 2, no. 4, pp. 446–455, December 1994.
5. Coello, C.A., A short tutorial on evolutionary multi-objective optimisation, Proc. First Conference on Evolutionary Multi-Criterion Optimisation, 2001.
6. Edgeworth, F. Y., Mathematical psychics: an essay on the application of mathematics to the moral sciences, Augustus M. Kelley, New York, 1967.
7. Pareto, V., Cours d'économie politique, volume I and II, F. Rouge, Lausanne, 1896.
8. Rosenman, M.A. and Gero, J.S., Reducing the Pareto set in multi-criterion optimisation, Engineering Optimisation, vol. 8, no. 3, pp. 189–206, 1985.
9. Horn, J., Nafpliotis, N. and Goldber, D., A niched Pareto genetic algorithm for multi-objective optimisation, Proc. IEEE Conference on Evolutionary Computation, IEEE World Congress on Computational Intelligence, Vol. 1, pp. 82–87, 1994.
10. Nedjah, N. and Mourelle, L.M., A Comparison of Two Circuit Representations for Evolutionary Digital Circuit Design, Lecture Notes in Computer Science, vol. 3029, pp. 351–360, 2004.
11. Coelho, A., Christiansen, A. and Aguirre, A., Towards automated evolutionary design of combinational circuits, Comput. Electr. Eng., vol. 27, pp. 1–28, 2001.

Application of a Genetic Algorithm to Nearest Neighbour Classification

Semen Simkin, Tim Verwaart, and Hans Vrolijk

Lei Wageningen UR, Burg. Patijnln. 19, den Haag, Netherlands
{semen.simkin, tim.verwaart, hans.vrolijk}@wur.nl

Abstract. This paper describes the application of a genetic algorithm to nearest-neighbour based imputation of sample data into a census data dataset. The genetic algorithm optimises the selection and weights of variables used for measuring distance. The results show that the measure of fit can be improved by selecting imputation variables using a genetic algorithm. The percentage of variance explained in the goal variables increases compared to a simple selection of imputation variables. This quantitative approach to the selection of imputation variables does not deny the importance of expertise. Human expertise is still essential in defining the optional set of imputation variables.

1 Introduction

All member states of the European Union run a Farm Accountancy Data Network (FADN). An FADN is a system for collecting data about financial position, financial results, technical structure, environmental data, labour, etcetera, on a sample of farms. The sample is drawn from an agriculture census containing data such as land use, livestock, and labour force. The sample is designed to minimise the standard error of some important variables on a national aggregation level. However, many research and policy questions apply to smaller regions or branches of agriculture.

Data fusion based on nearest neighbour approximation is a promising technique for small area estimation. The census gives data about land use, livestock, and labour force for each farm in the small area. The missing data about financial results, environmental data, etcetera, can be imputed from FADN sample farms selected from a larger area. The distance in terms of some variables known in both census and sample is the criterion for matching sample records to census farms. An example of this approach can be found in [1].

Determining optimal variables for distance measurement is a general problem in nearest neighbour classification. [2] introduces the application of genetic algorithms to select morphological features for the classification of images of granite rocks. The conclusion drawn there is that using only 3 out of 117 candidate features for distance measurement gives best recognition performance. This result confirms experience from application of agriculture data: adding more features to measure distance does not always improve the approximation. This paper reports the application of a genetic algorithm for optimisation of feature selection and feature weight for nearest neighbour selection to small area estimation in agricultural statistics.

M. Ali and F. Esposito (Eds.): IEA/AIE 2005, LNAI 3533, pp. 544 – 546, 2005.

2 Description of Datasets and Method

Datasets extracted from the Dutch agriculture census 1999 and the Dutch FADN sample 1999 were used for the experiments. The dataset selected from the census contains the variables listed below for N=26626 specialised dairy farms.

Total area (ha)	Farmer's age	Cows per ha	Ec size poultry	Nr of chicken
Farm type	Grassland area	Economic size	Nr of breedpigs	Nr of cattle
Region	Feed crops area	Ec size pigs	Nr of fatting pigs	Labour force(fte)
County	Nr of dairy cows	Ec size cows	Nr of peepers	

The sample dataset contains the variables listed above as well as the variables listed below for n=395 dairy farms.

N supply	N cattle	Cost fertilizer	Total cost	Entrepr. income
N manure	N products	Cost petrol	Net farm result	Family farm inc.
N fertilizer	N residue	Cost petroleum	Labour result	Total income
N concentrates	Cost pesticides	Cost diesel	Nr entrepren.s	Savings
N feed	Cost energy	Use diesel	Net result	Investments
N removal	Cost manure	Total revenue	Labour result f	

Into each record of the census, data were imputed from the sample record with minimal Euclidean distance d_E over a weighted selection of the census variables.

$$d_E = \sum_{i=1}^{j} w_i (x_i - y_i)^2 \qquad (1)$$

where w_i denotes the user-specified weight of the i-th out of j imputation variables and x_i and y_i denote standardised values of the i-th imputation variable in the census and the sample, respectively.

The quality of the approximation for some goal variable can be estimated by leave-one-out cross-validation [3]. For this purpose we impute into each sample record from the nearest different sample record and compute the coefficient of determination R^2.

$$R_g^2 = \frac{\sum_{i=1}^{n} \left(z_{gi} - \overline{z_g}\right)^2}{\sum_{i=1}^{n} \left(y_{gi} - z_{gi}\right)^2 + \sum_{i=1}^{n} \left(z_{gi} - \overline{z_g}\right)^2} \qquad (2)$$

where y_{gi} denotes the original value of the g-th goal variable of the i-th sample record and z_{gi} denotes its imputed value.

A genetic algorithm using leave-one-out-R^2 as a fitness function was applied to optimize the selection of distance variables and weight, configured as follows:

Initialisation	At random
Population size	10
Parent selection	Select two at random
Recombination mechanism	One-point crossover
Recombination probability	100%
Mutation mechanism	Randomly reinitialize with 10% probability
Mutation probability	100%
Number of offspring	10
Survivor selection	Best of merged population and offspring
Termination	After 100 generations

3 Experimental Results and Conclusion

Table 1 shows that there is no single optimal configuration for approximation of a set of variables. However, this type of table is very useful for a researcher selecting the imputation variables for a particular research project. The researcher can judge the importance of the goal variables for the project and can use his expert knowledge about relations between variables in order to select a good set of imputation variables.

The pattern of selected imputation variables differs across goal variables, although some imputation variables are selected more frequently than others. The last row of Table 1 gives the frequencies of selection in the optimisation. One might be tempted to use the frequencies for selection of imputation variables. However, tests show that combining most frequently selected variables decreases quality of approximation for individual goal variables, and does not necessarily result in a better estimate.

The results of the research reported in this paper show that the measure of fit can be improved by selecting variables with help of a genetic algorithm. The percentage of variance explained in the goal variables increases compared to intuitive selection of imputation variables. The example also illustrates that the optimal estimation of different goal variables requires the selection of different sets of imputation variables.

The quantitative approach to the selection of imputation variables does not deny the importance of expertise. Human expertise is still essential in defining the optional set of imputation variables. Furthermore the human expert should judge the face validity of the results in order to guarantee the acceptance of the outcomes.

Table 1. Optimal combination of imputation variables for distance measurement for some goal variables (Euclidean distance, all variables having equal weight)

Goal variable	R^2	Use census variable for distance (1) or not (0)
N supply	0.67	0 0 1 0 0 0 0 1 0 1 1 1 0 0 1 0 1 0 1
N manure	0.77	0 0 1 0 0 0 1 0 0 1 0 1 0 0 1 1 0 0 0
N fertilizer	0.75	0 1 0 0 1 0 0 0 0 1 0 0 1 0 0 0 1 0 0
N feed	0.46	1 0 1 0 1 0 0 1 0 1 0 1 0 1 0 0 0 0 1
N residue	0.72	0 0 1 0 1 0 1 0 0 1 0 1 0 0 0 0 0 0 0
Total cost	0.71	0 0 0 0 1 0 1 1 0 1 1 1 0 0 0 0 0 0 1
Net farm result	0.41	1 0 0 0 0 1 0 0 0 1 0 0 0 0 1 0 1 1 0
Family farm income	0.43	0 0 1 1 0 0 0 1 0 1 0 0 0 0 1 0 0 0 0
Savings	0.43	0 0 1 1 1 1 1 1 1 0 0 1 0 0 0 0 0 1 1
Investments	0.42	1 0 0 0 1 0 0 1 0 1 1 0 0 1 0 0 0 0 1
Frequency		3 1 6 2 6 2 4 6 1 9 3 6 1 2 4 1 3 2 5

References

1. H.C.J.Vrolijk, STARS: statistics for regional studies. In: K.J.Poppe (Ed.), Proc. of Pacioli 11 New roads for farm accounting and FADN, LEI, The Hague, 2004, ISBN 90-5242-878-6.
2. V.Ramos, F.Muge, Less is More: Genetic Optimisation of Nearest Neighbour Classifiers. In: F.Muge, C.Pinto, M.Piedade (ed), Proc. of RecPad'98 , Lisbon, 1998, ISBN 972-97711-0-3.
3. M.Stone, Cross-validatory choice and assessment of statistical predictions. Journal of the Royal Statistical Society, Vol.B, 36, pp.111-147, 1974.

Applying Genetic Algorithms for Production Scheduling and Resource Allocation. Special Case: A Small Size Manufacturing Company

A. Ricardo Contreras, C. Virginia Valero, and J.M. Angélica Pinninghoff

Informatics Engineering and Computer Science Department,
University of Concepción, Chile
rcontrer@udec.cl

Abstract. This paper describes a Genetic Algorithm approach to solve a task scheduling problem at a small size manufacturing company. The operational solution must fulfill two basic requirements: low cost and usability. The proposal was implemented and results obtained with the system lead to better results compared to previous and non-computerized solutions.

1 Introduction

Small companies are not generally able to invest in extensive computing resources and in these cases planning is typically a non-computerized activity. The core idea of this work is to model a low cost computer-aided solution keeping in mind the idea of portability. The hypothesis here is that it is possible to obtain good results for small productive companies and that the experience can be replicated by similar companies. In this work we are operating under the assumption that pure genetic algorithms can give rise to good solutions, and that those solutions could be improved later, and because of this we suggest direct constraint handling [2]. Once the genetic algorithm gives a feasible solution, the next step is to improve this solution by exploring a bounded space through tabu search. Tabu search is a meta-heuristic that guides a local heuristic search procedure to explore the solution space beyond local optimality [1]. The local procedure is a search that uses an operation called move to define the neighborhood of any given solution [3], [4].

2 The Problem

In this experiment we have chosen a small foundry. This company does not handle inventory systems and products are produced on demand for customers. The production line has six stages and there is an expert in charge of daily production planning. The expert is a production chief and decisions he makes are based only on his own experience. In figure 1 we show the production line.

M. Ali and F. Esposito (Eds.): IEA/AIE 2005, LNAI 3533, pp. 547–550, 2005.

A product remains at a given stage a variable time, depending on many factors (basically physical features), and operations that are to be accomplished at each stage depend on human and/or machine resources. The most crucial stage is Fusion, which encompasses Molding and Shoot Blasting. This stage is always done on site. For other stages it may be possible to outsource if an excessive workload occurs.

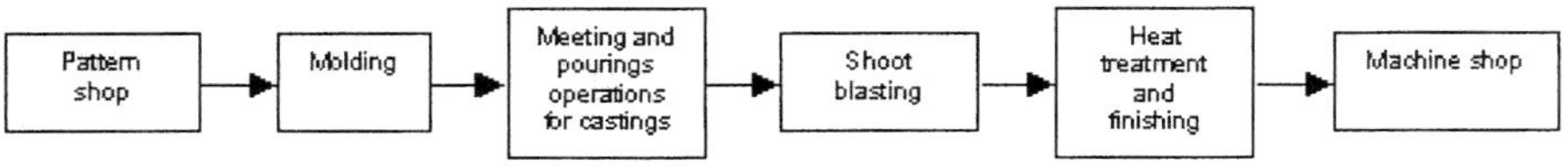

Fig. 1. Production line

Purchase orders (PO) are the core element of production planning. A purchase order contains a key, customer data, product data as well as specifying the necessary production processes, costs and delivery dates. Each order could contain from one to n products, each product having a variable quantity of component parts. Planning is focused on obtaining the optimal yield of the critical resource (alloy) as well as completing the PO in the shortest possible time.

3 The Proposal

The core idea is to generate an optimal production plan for m purchase orders, each one of them having from 1 to n products (with p parts) all of them having the same material (alloy). The purchase order specifies the different stages each product must go through and the estimated time to complete each stage. Solution is represented as a complete population in which manufacturing time is minimal. The population consists of a set of products and the associated resources for each production stage, having one product as a minimum. This product can be produced in one production stage (minimum), some of the stages or all of them.

The chromosome is defined as the minimal unit for considering all the products, always having the same size, as a means to facilitate crossover, containing k production stages; if a particular stage is not required for a specific product, the processing time for this stage is zero. Each production stage, is associated with a corresponding resource (i.e. for stage 1 only type 1 resources are considered).

The model was implemented considering the particular constraints the company imposes, trying to obtain a portable solution for applying to similar companies. In doing so, a special module was created to configure general parameters as resources, capabilities and so on. Once the genetic algorithm gives a feasible solution, the next step is try to improve this solution by exploring a bounded space through tabu search, in which case, only short term adaptive memory is used, because we are interested in the neighborhood related to the selected solution and not to explore new neighborhoods.

4 Solution Using Genetic Algorithms

By considering a pure genetic treatment, a simple crossover is accomplished based on resources. Mutation is not a valid alternative at this developmental stage, because a change in a chromosome should lead to a non valid plan.

Initial population generation is created in a deterministic fashion. The number of chromosomes is determined by the quantity of products to be manufactured, one chromosome per product.

In general, when working with genetic algorithms we have a population of individuals and the objective is to evaluate each one of these individuals to select the best of them. In our case, although individual evaluation is important, we need to evaluate the whole population because it represents company planning. In particular, we are interested in finding the optimal makespan which is defined as the time in which the last product finished its manufacturing process. So, fitness for the population is defined as follows:

$$Fitness(P(t)) = max\{t_f(X_{1n}^t), ...t_f(X_{kn}^t)\} - min\{t_i(X_{11}^t), ...t_i(X_{k1}^t)\}$$

Where $max\{t_f(X_{1n}^t), ..., t_f(X_{kn}^t)\}$ apply on the ending time for the last productive stage; $min\{t_i(X_{11}^t), ...t_i(X_{k1}^t)\}$, apply for the initial time of the first production stage. In this way we get an integer number representing time units (minutes) allowing us to compare two different populations.

The general parameters are *number of generations* 2500; *roulette wheel* is the selection technique, *crossover percentage* is 75, and *mutation* doesn't apply.

Once the genetic algorithm generates a feasible solution, a new heuristic is implemented to verify if it is possible to obtain an improved result. The selected heuristic is Tabu Search and the analyzed neighborhood for the solution considers the following parameters: *Move* is resource exchange; *Tabu list size* is 10; *number of neighbors generated* is 30% of total products; *general depth* is 50; *partial depth* is 50% of General depth; *stopping rule* is a solution better than the GA solution is found; and finally, *aspiration criteria* is: if neighbor fitness is better that actual best fitness, removes configuration from tabu list.

5 Tests and Results

To analyze the system performance a small family test consisting of 15 products was considered, with each product having a variable number of component parts (up to 200). The system was able to find, in 50% of considered situations, better results than obtained in an experts initial planning.

For different crossover percentages the best value is always reached, but the frequency of the best value appears to be variable.

By considering tabu search, given a pure genetic algorithm solution, and considering only the closer neighborhood, parameters are a general depth varying from 50 to 80 iterations. In general there is no change in results so the general depth is arbitrarily set to 50. For partial depth the test considered from 1/3 to 2/3 of general depth; as no changes were detected the final value is set to 50

In each search step, a number of neighbors equivalent to 30% of population are generated; although the test considered variations from 20% to 50% of population. A higher value for this parameter is not recommended because of memory considerations.

Performance of the system found improvements in 10% of considered cases. In testing, each parameter set was executed ten times and for each execution the best ten values (or the average) were considered, distributed in variable size sets depending on general depth, i.e., for a general depth of 50, the size for each set is 5, and analyzing the best value and the average of those 5 values.

6 Conclusions

Obtained results are satisfactory because planning obtained represents an improvement over non-computerized planning. In addition, there were no capital costs associated with new equipment as the computer was already in use for general management tasks. The use of tabu search improves only slightly the pure genetic algorithm solution. The crossover operator results in a large variability. Initial population is deterministically generated by trying to optimize resource assignment. Evaluation function (fitness) doesn't consider problem constraints once they are handled in a direct way. Classic selection strategy was modified to guarantee that each product is to be selected only once. The roulette wheel was chosen as an adequate mechanism to support the necessary variability.

Acknowledgement

This work has been partially supported by Project DIUC 203.093.008-1.0, University of Concepción, Chile.

References

1. A. Abraham, R. Buyya, and B. Nath. Nature's heuristics for scheduling jobs in computational grids. *Proceedings of the 8th IEEE International Conference on Advanced Computing and Communication*, pages 45–52, 2000.
2. A. Eiben. Evolutionary algorithms and constraint satisfaction: Definitions, survey, methodology and research directions. *Theoretical Aspects of Evolutionary Computation*, pages 13–58, 2001.
3. F. Glover and M. Laguna. *Tabu Search.* Kluwer Academic Publishers, USA, 1999.
4. P. Lorterapong and P. Rattanadamrongagsorn. Viewing construction scheduling as a constraint satisfaction problem. *Source Proceedings of the 6th International Conference on Application of Artificial Intelligence to Civil and Structural Engineering. Stirling, Scotland.*, pages 19–20, 2001.

An Efficient Genetic Algorithm for TSK-Type Neural Fuzzy Identifier Design

Cheng-Jian Lin[1,*], Yong-Ji Xu[1], and Chi-Yung Lee[2]

[1] Department of Computer Science and Information Engineering,
Chaoyang University of Technology,
No.168, Jifong E. Rd., Wufong Township,
Taichung County 41349, Taiwan
cjlin@mail.cyut.edu.tw

[2] Dept. of Computer Science and Information Engineering,
Nankai College,
Nantou County, 542 Taiwan, R. O. C.

Abstract. In this paper, an efficient genetic algorithm (EGA) for TSK-type neural fuzzy identifier (TNFI) is proposed for solving identification problem. For the proposed EGA method, the better chromosomes will be initially generated while the better mutation points will be determined for performing efficient mutation. The adjustable parameters of a TNFI model are coded as real number components and are searched by EGA method. The advantages of the proposed learning algorithm are that, first, it converges quickly and the obtained fuzzy rules are more precise. Secondly, the proposed EGA method only takes a few population sizes.

1 Introduction

Recently, GA appears to be better candidates for solving dynamic problem [1]-[4]. In this paper, we propose an efficient genetic algorithm (EGA) for TSK-type neural fuzzy identifier (TNFI) to solve the above problems. Compared with traditional genetic algorithm, the EGA uses the sequential-search based efficient generation (SSEG) method to generate an initial population and to decide the efficient mutation points. This paper is organized as follows. The proposed efficient genetic algorithm (EGA) is presented in Section II. In Section III, the proposed EGA method is evaluated using an example, and its performances are benchmarked against other structures. Finally, conclusions on the proposed model are summarized in the last section.

2 Efficient Genetic Algorithm

The proposed EGA consists of two major operators: initialization, mutation. Before the details of these three operators are explained, coding and crossover are discussed. The coding step is concerned with the membership functions and fuzzy rules of a

* Corresponding author.

M. Ali and F. Esposito (Eds.): IEA/AIE 2005, LNAI 3533, pp. 551 – 553, 2005.

TSK-type neural fuzzy system [1]. The crossover step is adopted two-point crossover in the proposed EGA. The whole learning process is described step by step below.

a. Initialization Step: The detailed steps of the initialization method are described as follows:

•**Step 0:** The first chromosome is generated randomly.
•**Step 1:** To generate the other chromosomes, we propose the SSEG method to generate the new chromosomes. In SSEG, every gene in the previous chromosomes is selected using a sequential search and the gene's value is updated to evaluate the performance based on the fitness value. The details of the SSEG method are as follows:
(a) Sequentially search for a gene in the previous chromosome.
(b) Update the chosen gene in (a) according to the following formula:

$$Chr_j[p]= \begin{cases} \mathrm{Chr_j}[p]+\Delta(\mathit{fitness\_value}, m_{\max}-\mathrm{Chr_j}[p]), \mathit{if}\,\alpha>0.5 \\ \mathrm{Chr_j}[p]-\Delta(\mathit{fitness\_value}, -\mathrm{Chr_j}[p]-m_{\min}), \mathit{if}\,\alpha<0.5 \end{cases}$$
$$\text{where } p=1, 3, 5, \ldots, 2*n-1 \tag{1}$$
$$Chr_j[p]= \begin{cases} \mathrm{Chr_j}[p]+\Delta(\mathit{fitness\_value}, \delta_{\max}-\mathrm{Chr_j}[p]), \mathit{if}\,\alpha>0.5 \\ \mathrm{Chr_j}[p]-\Delta(\mathit{fitness\_value}, -\mathrm{Chr_j}[p]-\delta_{\min}), \mathit{if}\,\alpha<0.5 \end{cases}$$
$$\text{where } p=2, 4, 6, \ldots, 2*n \tag{2}$$
$$Chr_j[p]= \begin{cases} \mathrm{Chr_j}[p]+\Delta(\mathit{fitness\_value}, w_{\max}-\mathrm{Chr_j}[p]), \mathit{if}\,\alpha>0.5 \\ \mathrm{Chr_j}[p]-\Delta(\mathit{fitness\_value}, -\mathrm{Chr_j}[p]-w_{\min}), \mathit{if}\,\alpha<0.5 \end{cases}$$
$$\text{where } p=2*n+1, \ldots, 2*n+(1+n) \tag{3}$$
$$\text{where } \Delta(\mathit{fitness\_value}, v)=v*\lambda*(1/\mathit{fitness\_value})^{\lambda} \tag{4}$$

where $\alpha, \lambda \in [0,1]$ are the random values; $\mathit{fitness\_value}$ is the fitness computed using Eq (5); $[\sigma_{\min}, \sigma_{\max}], [m_{\min}, m_{\max}]$ *and* $[w_{\min}, w_{\max}]$ represents the rang that we predefined to generate the chromosomes; *p* represents the *p*th gene in a chromosome; and *j* represents *j*th rule, respectively. If the new gene that is generated from (b) can improve the fitness value, then replace the old gene with the new gene in the chromosome. If not, recover the old gene in the chromosome. After this, go to (a) until every gene is selected.
•**Step 2:** If no genes are selected to improve the fitness value in step 1, than the new chromosome will be generated according to step 0. After the new chromosome is generated, the initialization method returns to step 1 until the total number of chromosomes is generated.

In this paper, the fitness value is designed according the follow formulation:

$$\text{Fitness}=1/(1+E(y,\bar{y})), \text{where } E(y,\bar{y})=(y_i-\bar{y}_i)^2$$
$$\text{for } i=1,2,\ldots.N \tag{5}$$

where y_i represents the true value of the *i*th output, $\bar{y}_i$ represents the predicted value, $E(y,\bar{y})$ is a error function and *N* represents a numbers of the training data of each generation.

b. Mutation Step: In EGA, we perform efficient mutation using the best fitness value chromosome of every generation. And we use SSEG to decide on the mutation points. When the mutation points are selected, we use Eqs. (1) to (4) to update the genes.

3 Illustrative Examples

To verify the performance of the proposed EGA method, we use the examples given by Narendra and Parthasarathy [2]. We shall compare the performance of the EGA method to that of other approaches based on this example. After 500 generations, the final RMS error of the output approximates 0.003. In this example, we compared the performance of the EGA with the traditional symbiotic evolution (TSE) [3] and the traditional genetic algorithm (TGA) [4]. Figures 1 (a) show the outputs of the EGA methods. Figure 1 (b) shows the learning curves of the three methods. In this figure, we find that the proposed EGA method converges quickly and obtains a lower rms error than others.

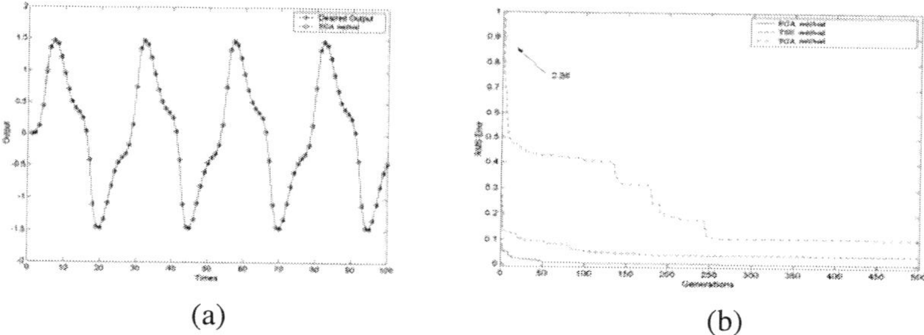

(a) (b)

Fig. 1. (a)Results of the desired output and the proposed EGA. (b) The learning curves of the proposed EGA method, the TSE [3] and the TGA [4]

4 Conclusion

In this paper, a novel genetic algorithm, called efficient genetic algorithm (EGA), was proposed to perform parameter learning. The EGA uses the sequential-search based efficient generation (SSEG) method to generate an initial population and to decide the efficient mutation points. Computer simulations have shown that the proposed EGA method obtained a better and quicker convergence than other method.

References

1. C. T. Lin and C. S. G. Lee: Neural Fuzzy Systems: A neural-fuzzy synergism to intelligent systems., Englewood Cliffs, NJ: Prentice-Hall, May 1996. (with disk).
2. C. F. Juang and C. T. Lin: An on-line self-constructing neural fuzzy inference network and its applications, IEEE Trans. Fuzzy Syst., vol. 6, no. 1, pp. 12-31, 1998.
3. C. F. Juang, J. Y. Lin and C. T. Lin: Genetic reinforcement learning through symbiotic evolution for fuzzy controller design, IEEE Trans. Syst., Man, Cybern., Part B, vol. 30, no. 2, pp. 290-302, Apr. 2000.
4. C. L. Karr: Design of an adaptive fuzzy logic controller using a genetic algorithm, in Proc. 4th Conf. Genetic Algorithms, pp. 450-457, 1991.

Hardware Architecture for Genetic Algorithms

Nadia Nedjah[1] and Luiza de Macedo Mourelle[2]

[1] Department of Electronics Engineering and Telecommunications,
Faculty of Engineering, State University of Rio de Janeiro, Brazil
nadia@eng.uerj.br

[2] Department of Systems Engineering and Computation,
Faculty of Engineering, State University of Rio de Janeiro, Brazil
ldmm@eng.uerj.br

Abstract. In this paper, we propose an overall architecture for hardware implementation of genetic algorithms. The proposed architecture is independent of such specifics. It implements the fitness computation using a neural networks.

1 Introduction

Generally speaking, a *genetic algorithm* is a process that evolves a set of *individuals*, also called *chromosomes*, which constitutes the *generational population*, producing a new population. The individuals represent a solution to the problem in consideration. The freshly produced population is yield using some genetic operators such as *selection*, *crossover* and *mutation* that attempt to simulate the natural breeding process in the hope of generating new solutions that are *fitter*, i.e. adhere more the problem constraints.

Previous work on hardware genetic algorithms can be found in [2, 4, 5]. Mainly, Earlier designs are hardware/software codesigns and they can be divided into three distinct categories: *(i)* those that implement the fitness computation in hardware and all the remaining steps including the genetic operators in software, claiming that the bulk computation within genetic evolution is the fitness computation. The hardware is problem-dependent; *(ii)* and those that implement the fitness computation in software and the rest in hardware, claiming that the ideal candidate are the genetic operators as these exhibit regularity and generality [1]. *(iii)* those that implement the whole genetic algorithm in hardware [4]. We believe that both approaches are worthwhile but a hardware-only implementation of both the fitness calculation and genetic operators is also valuable. Furthermore, a hardware implementation that is problem-independent is yet more useful.

2 Overall Architecture for the Hardware Genetic Algorithm

Clearly, for hardware genetic algorithms, individuals are always represented using their binary representation. Almost all aspects of genetic algorithms are very

M. Ali and F. Esposito (Eds.): IEA/AIE 2005, LNAI 3533, pp. 554–556, 2005.

attractive for hardware implementation. The selection, crossover and mutation processes are generic and so are problem-independent. The main issue in the hardware implementation of genetic algorithms is the computation of individual's fitness values. This computation depends on problem-specific knowledge. The novel contribution of the work consists of using neural network hardware to compute the fitness of individuals. The software version of the neural network is trained with a variety of individual examples. Using a hardware neural network to compute individual fitness yields a hardware genetic algorithm that is fully problem-independent. The overall architecture of the proposed hardware is given Fig. 1. It is massively parallel. The selection process is performed in one clock cycle while the crossover and mutation processes are completed within two clock cycles.

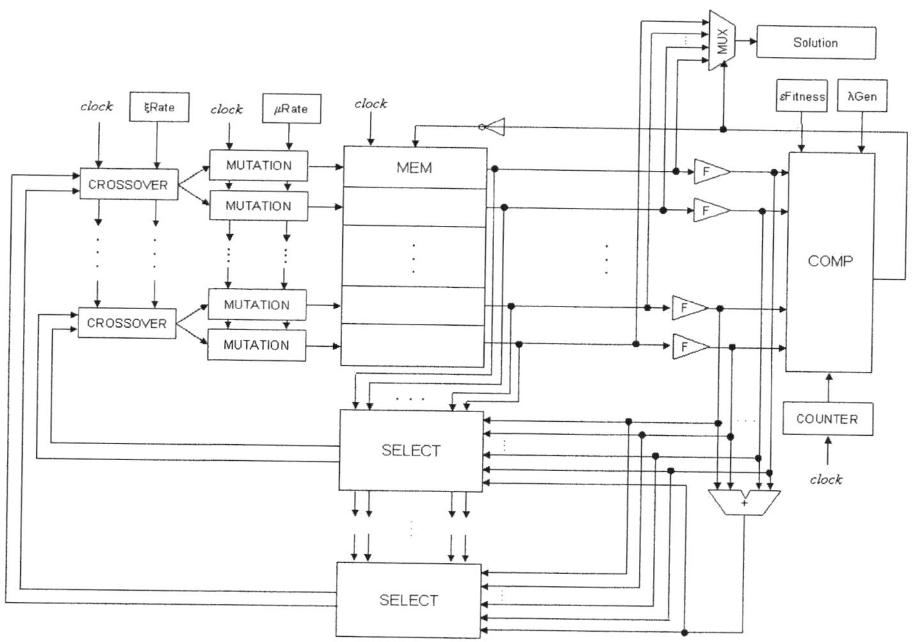

Fig. 1. Overall architecture of the hardware genetic algorithm proposed

3 Fitness Evaluation Component

The individual fitness measure is estimated using neural networks. In previous work, the authors proposed and implemented a hardware for neural networks [3]. The implementation uses stochastic signals and therefore reduces very significantly the hardware area required for the network. The network topology used is the fully-connected feed-forward. The neuron architecture is given in Fig. 2. (More details can be found in [3].) For the hardware genetic implementation, the number of input neurons is the same as the size of the individual. The output

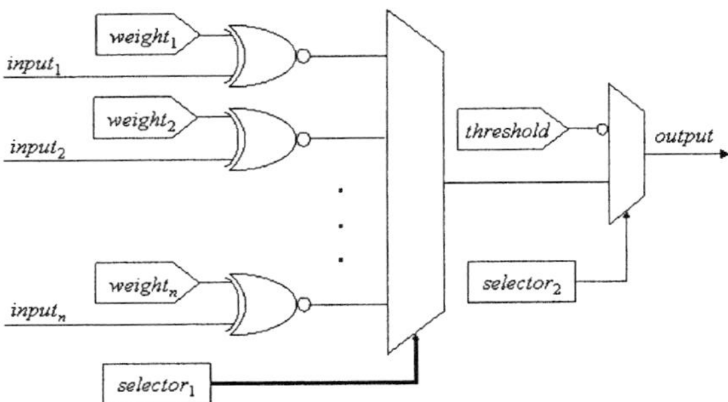

Fig. 2. Stochastic bipolar neuron architecture ([3])

neuron are augmented with a shift register to store the final result. The training phase is supposed to be performed before the first use within the hardware genetic algorithm.

4 Conclusion

In this paper, we proposed a novel hardware architecture for genetic algorithms. It is novel in the sense that is massively parallel and problem-independent. It uses neural networks to compute the fitness measure. Of course, for each type of problem, the neuron weights need to be updated with those obtained in the training phase.

References

1. Bland, I. M. and Megson, G. M., Implementing a generic systolic array for genetic algorithms. In Proc. 1st. On-Line Workshop on Soft Computing, pp 268–273, 1996.
2. Liu, J., A general purpose hardware implementation of genetic algorithms, MSc. Thesis, University of North Carolina, 1993.
3. Nedjah, N. and Mourelle, L.M., Reconfigurable Hardware Architecture for Compact and Efficient Stochastic Neuron, Artificial Neural Nets Problem Solving Methods, Lecture Notes in Computer Science, vol. 2687, pp. 17–24, 2003.
4. Scott, S.D., Samal, A. and Seth, S., HGA: a hardware-based genetic algorithm, In Proc. ACM/SIGDA 3rd. International Symposium in Field-Programmable Gate Array, pp. 53–59, 1995.
5. Turton, B.H. and Arslan, T., A parallel genetic VLSI architecture for combinatorial real-time applications – disc scheduling, In Proc. IEE/IEEE International Conference on genetic Algorithms in Engineering Systems, pp.88–93, 1994.

Node-Depth Encoding for Evolutionary Algorithms Applied to Multi-vehicle Routing Problem

Giampaolo L. Libralao, Fabio C. Pereira, Telma W. Lima, and Alexandre C.B. Delbem

Institute of Mathematical and Computer Science, University of Sao Paulo, USP
Trabalhador Sao Carlense, 400, 13560-970, Sao Carlos, SP, Brazil
{giam, telma, acbd}@icmc.usp.br
fly@grad.icmc.usp.br

1 Introduction

The Multi-Vehicle routing problem (MVRP) in real time is a graph modification problem. In order to solve this kind of problems, alternative approaches have been investigated. Evolutionary Algorithms (EAs) have presented relevant results. However, these methodologies require special encoding to achieve proper performance when large graphs are considered. We propose a representation based on NDE [Delbem et al., (2004a); Delbem et al., (2004b)] for directed graphs. An EA using the proposed encoding was developed and evaluated for the MVRP.

2 Node-Depth Encoding

This encoding is based on the concept of *node depth* in a graph tree and consists basically of a linear list containing the tree **nodes** and their **depths**, creating an array of pairs (n_x, d_x), where n_x is a node and d_x its depth.

Reproduction operators were developed in [Delbem et al., (2004a)] to produce new spanning forests from an undirected graph. This Section presents two operators (named operator 1 and operator 2) to generate new spanning forests using the NDE. Both operators generate a spanning forest F' of a directed graph G when they are applied to another spanning forest F of G.

The operator 1 requires two nodes previously determined: the prune node p, which indicates the root of the subtree to be transferred; and the adjacent node a, which is a node of a tree different from T_{from} and that is also adjacent to p in G. The operator 2 requires three nodes previously determined: the prune node p, the adjacent node a, and the new root node r of the subtree.

Next Section explains both operators considering that the required set of nodes were previously determined. Efficient procedures to find adequate nodes p, r, a are presented in [Delbem et al., (2004b)]. For directed graphs, the choice

M. Ali and F. Esposito (Eds.): IEA/AIE 2005, LNAI 3533, pp. 557–559, 2005.

of an adequate node r requires a procedure different from that presented in [Delbem et al., (2004b)]. First, pick up randomly a node from the pruned subtree (range (i_p+1)-i_l, see Section 2.1), and call it r. Then, verify if there is a path from r to p using an adjacent list with predecessors of each node. If there is no path, pich up randomly another r; otherwise, r is determined.

2.1 Operator 1

In the description of the operator 1, we consider that the NDE were implemented using arrays. Besides, we assume that p, its index i_p in the array T_{from}, a, and its index i_a in the array T_{to} are known.

The operator 1 can be described by the following steps:

1. Determine the range $(i_p$-$i_l)$ of indices in T_{from} corresponding to the subtree rooted at the node p. Since we know i_p, we only need to find i_l. The range $(i_p$-$i_l)$ corresponds to the node p at i_p and the consecutive nodes x in the array T_{from} such that $i_x > i_p$ and $d_x > d_p$, where d_x is the depth of the node x;
2. Copy the data in the range i_p-i_l from T_{from} into a temporary array T_{tmp} (containing the data of the subtree being transferred). The depth of each node x from the range i_p-i_l is updated as follows: $d_x = d_x - d_p + d_a + 1$;
3. Create an array T'_{to} containing the nodes of T_{to} and T_{tmp} (i.e., generate a new tree connecting the pruned subtree to T_{to});
4. Construct an array T'_{from} comprising the nodes of T_{from} without the nodes of T_{tmp};
5. Copy the forest data structure F to F' exchanging the pointers to the arrays T_{from} and T_{to} for pointers to the arrays T'_{from} and T'_{to}, respectively.

2.2 Operator 2

The operator 2 possesses the following arguments: nodes p, r, a, and the trees T_{from} and T_{to}. The nodes p, r are in the tree T_{from} and a is in T_{to}. The differences between operator 1 and operator 2 are in the steps 2 and 3 (see Section 2.1), i.e. only the formation of pruned subtrees and their storing in temporary arrays are different.

The procedure of copy of the pruned subtree for the operator 2 can be divided into two steps: The first step is similar to the step 2 for the operator 1 and differs from it in the exchanging of i_p by i_r. The array returned by this procedure is named T_{tmp1}.

The second step uses the path from r to p (see the introduction of Section ??). The nodes from this path, i.e. $r_0, r_1, r_2, \ldots, r_n$, where $r_0 = r$ and $r_n = p$, are considered as roots of subtrees. The subtree rooted at r_1 contains the subtree rooted at r_0 and so on. The algorithm for the second step should copy the subtrees rooted at r_i $(i = 1, \ldots, n)$ without the subtree rooted at r_{i-1} and store the resultant subtrees in a temporary array T_{tmp2}.

The step 3 of the operator 1 creates an array T'_{to} from T_{to} and T_{tmp}. On the other hand, the operator 2 uses the array $[T_{tmp1}\ T_{tmp2}]$ to construct T'_{to}.

3 Tests

Multi-Vehicle Routing [Brayasy, (2001); Liu et al., (1998)] in Real Time was used to evaluate the EA using the NDE for directed graphs. Several tests were performed using a large graph corresponding to the city of Sao Carlos, Brazil. This graph has about 4,700 nodes. For all the tests the EA performed 3,000 evaluations. The tests were carried out using a Dual Intel Xeon 2GHz with 4GRAM.

The first set of tests evaluated the capacity of the evolutionary approach of finding the best route for the one-vehicle routing problem. The obtained results show that the proposed approach can find optimal (obtained by Dijkstra) or near optimal routes. Table 1 shows the tests for three origins and two destinations, which shows the proposed approach can obtain proper solutions in relatively short running time.

Table 1. Results for different origins and destinations

Test	Origin	Destination	Cost 1	No. Nodes
15	2259	297	7456	84
16	2856	297	7827	89
17	2302	297	5719	60
18	2259	4051	2128	27
19	2856	4051	3265	40
20	2302	4051	4508	49

References

Brayasy, (2001). Brayasy, O., Genetic Algorithms for the Vehicle Routing Problem with Time Windows, Arpakannus 1/2001: Special issue on Bioinformatics and Genetic Algorithms, University of Vaasa, Finland, 2001

Delbem et al., (2004b). Delbem, A.C.B., Carvalho, A., Policastro C.A., Pinto, A.K.O., Honda, K. and Garcia, A.C., (2004). Node-depth Encoding Applied to the Network Design. Genetic Algorithm and Evolutionary Computation Conference - GECCO 2004, vol. 3102, pp. 678-687.

Delbem et al., (2004a). Delbem, A.C.B., Carvalho, A., Policastro C.A., Pinto, A.K.O., Honda, K. and Garcia, A.C., (2004). Node-depth Encoding Applied to the Degree-Constrained Minimum Spanning Tree. In Proceedings of 1st Brazilian Workshop on Evolutionary Computation, Maranhao, Brasil.

Liu et al., (1998). Liu, Q., H.C. Lau, D. Seah and S. Chong, An Efficient Near-Exact Algorithm for Large-Scale Vehicle Routing with Time Windows, In Proceedings of the 5th World Congress on ITS , Korea, 1998

Novel Approach to Optimize Quantitative Association Rules by Employing Multi-objective Genetic Algorithm

Mehmet Kaya and Reda Alhajj

Dept of CENG, Fırat University, Elazığ, Turkey
Dept of CS, University of Calgary, Calgary, AB, Canada
kaya@firat.edu.tr, alhajj@cpsc.ucalgary.ca

Abstract. This paper proposes two novel methods to optimize quantitative association rules. We utilize a multi-objective Genetic Algorithm (GA) in the process. One of the methods deals with partial optimal, and the other method investigates complete optimal. Experimental results on Letter Recognition Database from UCI Machine Learning Repository demonstrate the effectiveness and applicability of the proposed approaches.

1 Introduction

The optimized association rules problem was first introduced by Fukoda et al [3]. Recently, Rastogi and Shim [4] improved the optimized association rules problem in a way that allows association rules to contain a number of uninstantiated attributes. In this paper, we introduce two kinds of optimized rules. These are partial optimized rules and complete optimized rules. For this purpose, we used a multi-objective GA based method. In partial optimal, the number of intervals is given, and multi-objective GA based optimized rules are found by adjusting the boundary values for the given number of intervals. In complete optimal, the boundary values of the intervals along with their numbers are unknown. But, the sum of the amplitudes of the intervals gives all the domain of each relevant attribute regardless of the number of intervals. In other words, each value of an attribute certainly belongs to an interval. These intervals are adjusted so good that the most appropriate optimized rules are obtained. Experimental results conducted on the Letter Recognition Database from UCI Machine Learning Repository demonstrate that our methods give good results.

The rest of the paper is organized as follows. Sections 2 introduces our multi-objective optimization methods. Experimental results are reported in Section 3. Section 4 is the conclusions.

2 Partially and Completely Optimized Rules

As partially optimized rules are concerned, given the number of intervals for each attribute, optimized rules are found with respect to three important criteria. These are support that indicates the percentage of records present in the database and have positive participation for the attributes in the considered rule, confidence and amplitude, which is computed according to the average amplitude of the intervals belonging to the itemset. The latter parameter can be formalized as:

M. Ali and F. Esposito (Eds.): IEA/AIE 2005, LNAI 3533, pp. 560–562, 2005.

$$Amplitude = \frac{\text{Sum of Maximum Amplitudes} - \text{Average Amplitude}}{\text{Sum of Maximum Amplitudes}}$$

$$\text{Sum of Maximum Amplitudes} = \sum_{i=1}^{k} \max(D_i) - \min(D_i) \text{ and } \text{Average Amplitude} = \frac{\sum_{i=1}^{k} u_i - l_i}{k},$$

where k is the number of attributes in the itemsets and l_i and u_i are the limits of the intervals corresponding to attribute i. By this method, the rules with smaller amplitude of intervals are generated.

Complete optimization method handles all the intervals together in a way where no value of the attribute will stay out. In this case, some intervals generate stronger rules, and the others extract weaker rules. The objective measures of this method are support, confidence and interval, which can be defined as:

$$\text{Interval} = \frac{\text{Maximum Interval} - \text{Average Interval Number}}{\text{Maximum Interval}} \text{ and } \text{Average Interval Number} = \frac{\sum_{i=1}^{k} t_i}{k},$$

where t_i is the number of the interval for attribute i.

3 Experimental Results

All the experiments were conducted on a Celeron 2.0 GHz CPU with 512 MB of memory and running Windows XP. As experimental data, we used the Letter Recognition Database from UCI Machine Learning Repository. The database consists of 20K samples and 16 quantitative attributes. We concentrated our analysis on only 10 quantitative attributes. In all the experiments, the GA process started with a population of 60 for both partial and complete optimized rules. Also, crossover and mutation probabilities were chosen as 0.8 and 0.01, respectively; 5 point crossover operator has been used in the process.

Table 1. Number of rules generated vs. number of generations for 2 intervals (partial optimal)

Number of Generations	Number of Rules
250	83
500	99
750	111
1000	115
1250	118
1500	118

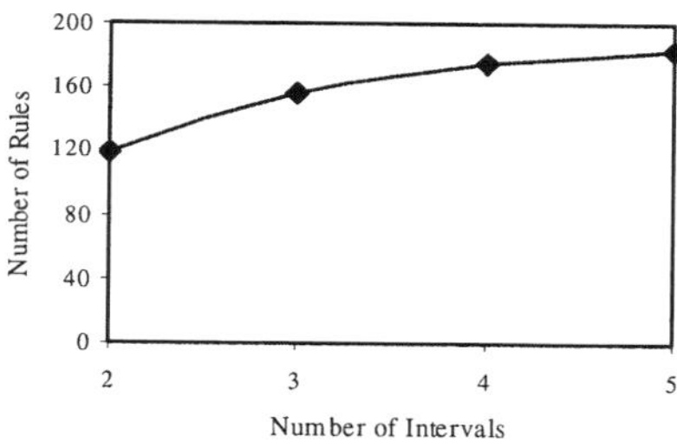

Fig. 1. Number of rules found for different number of intervals (partial optimal)

The first experiment finds the number of rules generated for different number of generations. The results are reported in Table 1. It can be easily seen from Table 1 that almost after 1250 generations, the GA does not produce more rules, i.e., it converges. In the second experiment, we obtained the number of rules for different number of intervals in the case of partial optimal. The results are reported in Figure 1. The curve is almost smooth after 4 intervals. This simply tells that no much gain will be achieved when the number of intervals increases beyond 4.

The second set of experiments handles complete optimized rules. The results of the conducted experiments are given in Table 2 and Figure 2. Table 2 shows that the GA process almost converges after 1200, or say 1500 generations. Figure 5 demonstrates that the run time increases almost linearly as the number of transactions increases. This somehow supports the scalability of the proposed approach.

Table 2. Number of rules generated vs. number of generations in the case of complete optimal

Number of Generations	Number of Rules
300	127
600	162
900	189
1200	201
1500	205
2000	207

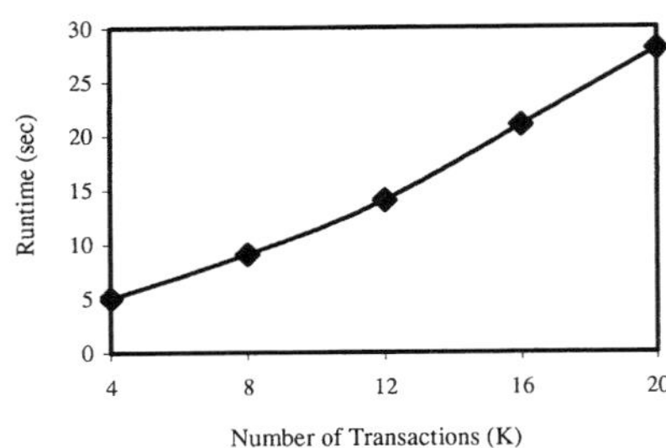

Fig. 2. Runtimes in different number of transactions (complete optimal)

4 Conclusions

In this paper, we contributed to the ongoing research by proposing two multi-objective GA based optimization methods. Each approach uses three measures as the objectives of the method: Support, Confidence and Amplitude or Interval. The results obtained from the conducted experiments demonstrate the effectiveness and applicability of the optimized rules. Currently, we are investigating the optimization of fuzzy association rules by applying these methods.

References

[1] M. Kaya, R. Alhajj, F. Polat and A. Arslan, "Efficient Automated Mining of Fuzzy Associ\ation Rules," *Proc. of the International Conference on Database and Expert Systems with Applications,* 2002.

[2] M. Kaya and R. Alhajj, "Facilitating Fuzzy Association Rules Mining by Using Multi-Objective Genetic Algorithms for Automated Clustering," *Proc. of IEEE ICDM*, Melbourne, FL, 2003.

[3] 9 T. Fukuda, Y. Morimoto, S. Morishita and T. Tokuyama, "Mining Optimized Association Rules for Numeric Attributes," *Proc. of ACM SIGACT-SIGMOD-SIGART PODS*, 1996.

[4] 12 R. Rastogi and K. Shim, "Mining Optimized Association Rules with Categorical and Numeric Attributes," *IEEE TKDE*, Vol.14, No.1, pp.29-50, 2002.

GMDH-Type Neural Network Modeling in Evolutionary Optimization

Dongwon Kim and Gwi-Tae Park*

Department of Electrical Engineering, Korea University, 1, 5-ka, Anam-dong, Seongbukku, Seoul 136-701, Korea
{upground, gtpark}@korea.ac.kr

Abstract. We discuss a new design of group method of data handling (GMDH)-type neural network using evolutionary algorithm. The performances of the GMDH-type network depend strongly on the number of input variables and order of the polynomials to each node. They must be fixed by designer in advance before the architecture is constructed. So the trial and error method must go with heavy computation burden and low efficiency. To alleviate these problems we employed evolutionary algorithms. The order of the polynomial, the number of input variables, and the optimum input variables are encoded as a chromosome and fitness of each chromosome is computed. The appropriate information of each node are evolved accordingly and tuned gradually throughout the GA iterations. By the simulation results, we can show that the proposed networks have good performance.

1 Introduction

System modeling and identification is important for system analysis, control, and automation as well as for scientific research. So a lot of attention has been directed to developing advanced techniques of system modeling. As one of modeling techniques, there is a GMDH-type algorithm. Group method of data handling (GMDH) was introduced by Ivakhnenko in the early 1970's [1-3], which has been extensively used for prediction and modeling complex nonlinear processes. The main characteristics of the GMDH are that it is a self-organizing and provides an automated selection of essential input variables without a prior information on a target system [4]. Self-organizing polynomial neural networks (SOPNN) [5] is a GMDH-type algorithm and one of useful approximator techniques, which has an architecture similar to feedforward neural networks whose neurons are replaced by polynomial nodes. The output of the each node in SOPNN structure is obtained using several types of high-order polynomial such as linear, quadratic, and modified quadratic of input variables. These polynomials are called as partial descriptions (PDs). The SOPNN shows a superb performance in comparison to the previous modeling methods. But it has some drawbacks to be solved. The performances of SOPNN depend strongly on the number of input variables to the model as well as polynomial types in each PD. They must be

* Corresponding author.

M. Ali and F. Esposito (Eds.): IEA/AIE 2005, LNAI 3533, pp. 563 – 570, 2005.

chosen in advance before the architecture of SOPNN is constructed. In most cases, they are determined by the trial and error method with a heavy computational burden and low efficiency. Moreover, the SOPNN algorithm is a heuristic method so it does not guarantee that the obtained SOPNN is the best one for nonlinear system modeling. Therefore, more attention must be paid to solve the above mentioned drawbacks.

In this paper we will present a new design methodology of SOPNN using evolutionary algorithm (EA) in order to alleviate the above mentioned drawbacks. We call this EA-based SOPNN. The EA is employed for determining optimal number of input variables to each node, optimal input variables among many inputs for each node, and an appropriate type of polynomial in each PD.

2 Design of EA-Based SOPNN

The SOPNN is based on the GMDH algorithm [1] and utilizes a class of polynomials. Depending on the polynomial order, three different polynomials were employed. The fundamentals of SOPNN have been explained in detail [5]. Instead of repeating them, they are briefly stated here. As stated earlier, the SOPNN employs a class of polynomials called the PDs. As an illustrative example, specific forms of a PD in the case of two inputs are given as

$$\begin{aligned} \text{Type 1} &= c_0 + c_1x_1 + c_2x_2 \\ \text{Type 2} &= c_0 + c_1x_1 + c_2x_2 + c_3x_1^2 + c_4x_2^2 + c_5x_1x_2 \\ \text{Type 3} &= c_0 + c_1x_1 + c_2x_2 + c_3x_1x_2 \end{aligned} \qquad (1)$$

where c_i is called regression coefficients.

PDs in the first layer are created by given input variables and the polynomial order. The coefficients of the PDs are determined by using the training data and typically by means of the least square method. The predictive ability of constructed PD is then tested with the test data. After constructing all PDs, several of them are selected in order of the predictive ability. This process is repeated for the subsequent layers. It should be noted that in this case the predicted outputs from the chosen PDs in the first layer are used as the new input variables to a PD in the second layer. When the stopping criterion is satisfied, only one node in the final layer characterized by the best performance is selected as the output node. The remaining nodes in that layer are discarded. Furthermore, all the nodes in the previous layers that do not have influence on the selected output node are also removed by tracing the data flow path on each layer.

When we design the SOPNN using EA, the most important consideration is the representation strategy, that is, how to encode the key factors of the SOPNN into the chromosome. We employ a binary coding for the available design specifications. We code the order and the inputs of each node in the SOPNN as a finite-length string. Our chromosomes are made of three sub-chromosomes. The first one is consisted of 2 bits for the order of polynomial (PD), which represents several types of order of PD. The relationship between bits in the 1st sub-chromosome and the order of PD is shown in

Table 1. Thus, each node can exploit a different order of the polynomial. The second one is consisted of 3 bits for the number of inputs of PD, and the last one is consisted of N bits which are equal to the number of entire input candidates in the current layer. These input candidates are the node outputs of the previous layer, which are concatenated a bit of 0's and 1's coding. The input candidate is represented by a 1 bit if it is chosen as input variable to the PD and by a 0 bit it is not chosen. But if many input candidates are chosen for model design, the modeling is computationally complex, and normally requires a lot of time to achieve good results. For the drawback, we introduce the 2nd sub-chromosome into the chromosome to represent the number of input variables to be selected. The number based on the 2nd sub-chromosome is shown in the Table 2.

Table 1. Relationship between bits in the 1st sub-chromosome and order of PD

Bits in the 1st sub-chromosome	Order of PD
00	Type 1
01 10	Type 2
11	Type 3

Table 2. Relationship between bits in the 2nd sub-chromosome and number of inputs to PD

Bits in the 2nd sub-chromosome	Number of inputs to a PD
000	1
001 010	2
011 100	3
101 110	4
111	5

The relationship between chromosome and information on PD is shown in Fig. 1. The PD corresponding to the chromosome in Fig. 1 is described briefly as Fig. 2. The node with PD corresponding to Fig. 1 is can be expressed as (2)

$$\hat{y} = f(x_1, x_6) = c_0 + c_1 x_1 + c_2 x_6 + c_3 x_1^2 + c_4 x_6^2 + c_5 x_1 x_6 \quad (2)$$

where coefficients c_0, c_1, …, c_5 are evaluated using the training data set by means of the LSM. Therefore, the polynomial function of PD is formed automatically according to the information of sub-chromosomes.

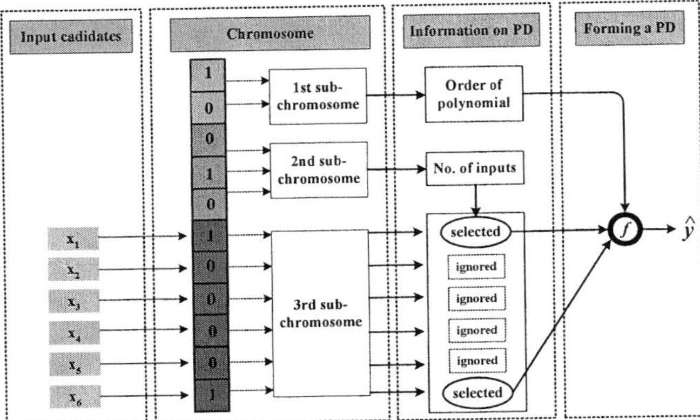

Fig. 1. Example of PD whose various pieces of required information are obtained from its chromosome

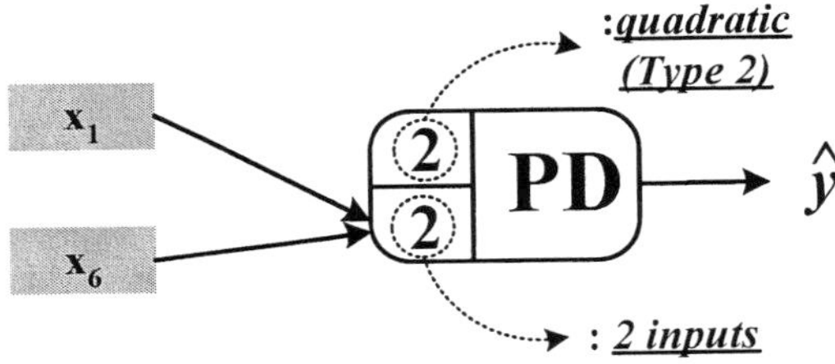

Fig. 2. Node with PD corresponding to chromosome in Fig. 1

The design procedure of EA-based SOPNN is shown in Fig. 3. At the beginning of the process, the initial populations comprise a set of chromosomes that are scattered all over the search space. The populations are all randomly initialized. Thus, the use of heuristic knowledge is minimized. The assignment of the fitness in EA serves as guidance to lead the search toward the optimal solution. After each of the chromosomes is evaluated and associated with a fitness, the current population undergoes the reproduction process to create the next generation of population. The roulette-wheel selection scheme is used to determine the members of the new generation of population. After the new group of population is built, the mating pool is formed and the crossover is carried out. We use one-point crossover operator with a crossover probability of P_c (0.85). This is then followed by the mutation operation. The mutation is the occasional alteration of a value at a particular bit position (we flip the states of a bit from 0 to 1 or vice versa). The mutation serves as an insurance policy which would recover the loss of a particular piece of information. The mutation rate used is fixed at 0.05 (P_m). After the evolution process, the final generation of population consists of highly fit bits that provide optimal solutions. After the termination condition is satisfied, one chromosome (PD) with the best performance in the final generation of population is selected as the output PD. All remaining other chromosomes are discarded and all the nodes that do not have influence on this output PD in the previous layers are also removed. By doing this, the EA-based SOPNN model is obtained.

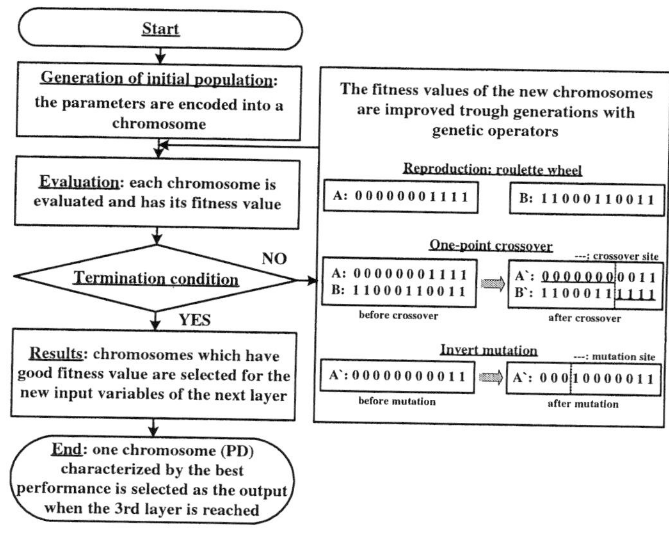

Fig. 3. Block diagram of the design procedure of EA-based SOPNN

The important thing to be considered for the EA is the determination of the fitness function. To construct models with significant approximation and generalization ability, we introduce the error function such as

$$E = \theta \times PI + (1-\theta) \times EPI \tag{3}$$

where $\theta \in [0,1]$ is a weighting factor for PI and EPI, which denote the values of the performance index for the training data and testing data, respectively. Then the fitness value [6] is determined as follows:

$$F = \frac{1}{1+E} \tag{4}$$

Maximizing F is identical to minimizing E. The choice of θ establishes a certain tradeoff between the approximation and generalization ability of the EA-based SOPNN.

3 Simulation Results

We show the performance of the EA-based SOPNN model for nonlinear time series modeling and prediction. The gas furnace process [7] has been intensively studied in the previous literature [8-11]. In this paper, we consider u(t-3), u(t-2), u(t-1), y(t-3), y(t-2), y(t-1) as input variables, and y(t) as the output variable. The total data set consisting of

296 input-output pairs is divided into two parts. The first 148 pairs are used for training purpose and the others serve for testing purpose. PI and EPI are calculated by

$$PI(EPI) = \frac{1}{148}\sum_{i=1}^{148}(y_i - \hat{y}_i)^2 \quad (5)$$

where y_i is the actual output, $\hat{y}_i$ is the output of the EA-based SOPNN.

The design parameters of EA-based SOPNN for modeling are shown in Table 3. In the 1st layer, 20 chromosomes are generated and evolved during 40 generations, where each chromosome in the population is defined as corresponding node. So 20 nodes are produced in the 1st layer based on the EA operators. All nodes are estimated and evaluated using the training and testing data sets, respectively. They are also evaluated by the fitness function of (4) and ranked according to their fitness value. We choose nodes as many as a predetermined number w from the highest ranking node, and use their outputs as new input variables to the nodes in the next layer. In other words, The chosen PDs (w nodes) must be preserved and the outputs of the preserved PDs serve as inputs to the next layer. The value of w is different from each layer, which is also shown in Table 3. This procedure is repeated for the 2nd layer and the 3rd layer.

Table 3. Design parameters of EA-based SOPNN for modeling

Parameters	1st layer	2nd layer	3rd layer
Maximum generations	40	60	80
Population size:(w)	20:(15)	60:(50)	80
String length	11	20	55
Crossover rate (P_c)		0.85	
Mutation rate (P_m)		0.05	
Weighting factor: θ		0.1~0.9	
Type (order)		1~3	

Table 4 summarizes the values of the performance index, PI and EPI, of the proposed EA-based SOPNN according to weighting factor. These values are the lowest value in each layer. The overall lowest value of the performance index is obtained at the third layer when the weighting factor is 0.5. When the weighting factor θ is 0.5, Fig. 4 depicts the trend of the performance index produced in successive generations of the EA.

Table 4. Values of performance index of the proposed EA-based SOPNN

Weighting factor (θ)	1st layer		2nd layer		3rd layer	
	PI	EPI	PI	EPI	PI	EPI
0.1	0.0214	0.1260	0.0200	0.1231	0.0199	0.1228
0.25	0.0214	0.1260	0.0149	0.1228	0.0145	0.1191
0.5	0.0214	0.1260	0.0139	0.1212	0.0129	0.1086
0.75	0.0214	0.1260	0.0139	0.1293	0.0138	0.1235
0.9	0.0173	0.1411	0.0137	0.1315	0.0129	0.1278

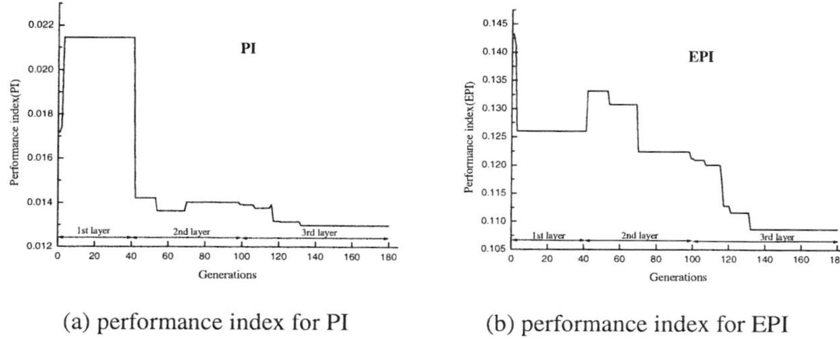

(a) performance index for PI (b) performance index for EPI

Fig. 4. Trend of performance index values with respect to generations through layers (θ=0.5)

Fig. 5 shows the actual output versus model output. The model output follows the actual output very well. Where the values of the performance index of the proposed method are equal to PI=0.012, EPI=0.108, respectively.

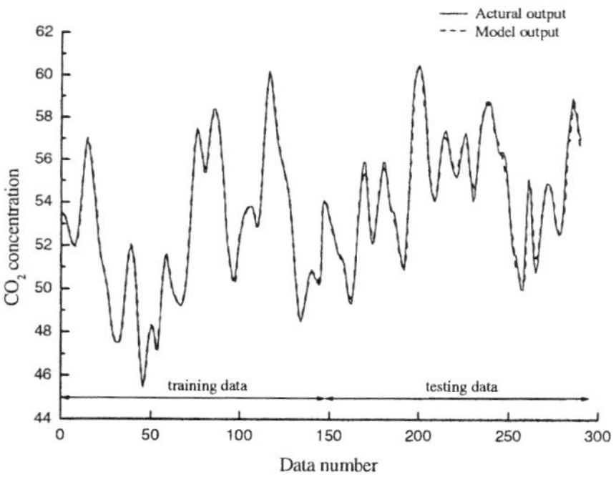

Fig. 5. Actual output versus model output

4 Conclusions

In this paper, we propose a new design methodology of SOPNN using evolutionary algorithm. We can see that the proposed model is a sophisticated and versatile architecture which can construct models for poorly defined complex problems. Moreover, the architecture of the model is not predetermined, but can be self-organized automatically during the design process. The conflict between overfitting and generalization can be avoided by using fitness function with weighting factor.

Acknowledgment. The authors thank the financial support of the Korea University. This research was supported by a Korea University Grant.

References

1. Ivakhnenko, A.G.: Polynomial theory of complex systems. IEEE Trans. Syst. Man Cybern. **1** (1971) 364-378
2. Ivakhnenko, A.G., Ivakhnenko, N.A.: Long-term prediction by GMDH algorithms using the unbiased criterion and the balance-of-variables criterion. Sov. Automat. Contr. **7** (1974) 40-45
3. Ivakhnenko, A.G., Ivakhnenko, N.A.: Long-term prediction by GMDH algorithms using the unbiased criterion and the balance-of-variables criterion, part 2. Sov. Automat. Contr. **8** (1975) 24-38
4. Farlow, S.J.: Self-Organizing Methods in Modeling, GMDH Type-Algorithms. New York, Marcel Dekker (1984)
5. Oh, S.K., Pedrycz, W.: The design of self-organizing Polynomial Neural Networks. Inf. Sci. **141** (2002) 237-258
6. Kim, D. W.: Evolutionary Design of Self-Organizing Polynomial Neural Networks. Master's thesis Dept. Control Instrum. Wonkwang Univ. (2002)
7. Box, G.E.P., Jenkins, F.M, and Reinsel, G.C.: Time Series Analysis: Forecasting and Control 3rd ed. Prentice-Hall (1994)
8. Leski, J., Czogala, E.: A new artificial neural networks based fuzzy inference system with moving consequents in if-then rules and selected applications. Fuzzy Sets Syst. **108** (1999) 289-297
9. Kang, S.J., Woo, C.H., Hwang, H.S., Woo, K.B.: Evolutionary Design of Fuzzy Rule Base for Nonlinear System Modeling and Control. IEEE Trans. Fuzzy Syst. **8** (2000)
10. Kim, E., Lee, H., Park, M., Park, M.: A simple identified Sugeno-type fuzzy model via double clustering. Inf. Sci. **110** (1998) 25-39
11. Lin, Y., Cunningham III, G.A.: A new approach to fuzzy-neural modeling. IEEE Trans. Fuzzy Syst. **3** (1995) 190-197

Predicting Construction Litigation Outcome Using Particle Swarm Optimization

Kwokwing Chau

Department of Civil and Structural Engineering, Hong Kong Polytechnic University, Hunghom, Kowloon, Hong Kong
cekwchau@polyu.edu.hk

Abstract. Construction claims are normally affected by a large number of complex and interrelated factors. It is highly desirable for the parties to a dispute to know with some certainty how the case would be resolved if it were taken to court. The use of artificial neural networks can be a cost-effective technique to help to predict the outcome of construction claims, on the basis of characteristics of cases and the corresponding past court decisions. In this paper, a particle swarm optimization model is adopted to train perceptrons. The approach is demonstrated to be feasible and effective by predicting the outcome of construction claims in Hong Kong in the last 10 years. The results show faster and more accurate results than its counterparts of a benching back-propagation neural network and that the PSO-based network are able to give a successful prediction rate of up to 80%. With this, the parties would be more prudent in pursuing litigation and hence the number of disputes could be reduced significantly.

1 Introduction

By its very nature, the construction industry is prone to litigation since claims are normally affected by a large number of complex and interrelated factors. The disagreement between the involving parties can arise from interpretation of the contract, unforeseen site conditions, variation orders by the client, acceleration and suspension of works, and so on. The main forums for the resolution of construction disputes are mediation, arbitration, and the courts. However, the consequence of any disagreements between the client and the contractor may be far reaching. It may lead to damage to the reputation of both sides, as well as inefficient use of resources and higher costs for both parties through settlement. The litigation process is usually very expensive since it involves specialized and complex issues. Thus, it is the interest of all the involving parties to minimize or even avoid the likelihood of litigation through conscientious management procedure and concerted effort.

It is highly desirable for the parties to a dispute to know with some certainty how the case would be resolved if it were taken to court. This would effectively help to significantly reduce the number of disputes that would need to be settled by the much more expensive litigation process. The use of artificial neural networks can be a cost-effective technique to help to predict the outcome of construction claims, on the basis

M. Ali and F. Esposito (Eds.): IEA/AIE 2005, LNAI 3533, pp. 571 – 578, 2005.

of characteristics of cases and the corresponding past court decisions. It can be used to identify the hidden relationships among various interrelated factors and to mimic decisions that were made by the court.

During the past decade, the artificial neural networks (ANN), and in particular, the feed forward backward propagation perceptrons, are widely applied in different fields [1-2]. It is claimed that the multi-layer perceptrons can be trained to approximate and accurately generalize virtually any smooth, measurable function whilst taking no prior assumptions concerning the data distribution. Characteristics, including built-in dynamism in forecasting, data-error tolerance, and lack of requirements of any exogenous input, render it attractive for use in various types of prediction. Although the back propagation (BP) algorithm is commonly used in recent years to perform the training task, some drawbacks are often encountered in the use of this gradient-based method. They include: the training convergence speed is very slow; it is easily to get stuck in a local minimum. Different algorithms have been proposed in order to resolve these drawbacks, yet the results are still not fully satisfactory [3-5].

Particle swarm optimization (PSO) is a method for optimizing hard numerical functions based on metaphor of human social interaction [6-7]. Although it is initially developed as a tool for modeling social behavior, the PSO algorithm has been recognized as a computational intelligence technique intimately related to evolutionary algorithms and applied in different areas [8-11].

In this paper, a PSO-based neural network approach for prediction of the outcome of construction litigation in Hong Kong is developed by adopting PSO to train multi-layer perceptrons, on the basis of characteristics of real cases and court decisions in the last 10 years.

2 Nature of Construction Disputes

The nature of construction activities is varying and dynamic, which can be evidenced by the fact that no two sites are exactly the same. Thus the preparation of the construction contract can be recognized as the formulation of risk allocation amongst the involving parties: the client, the contractor, and the engineer. The risks involved include the time of completion, the final cost, the quality of the works, inflation, inclement weather, shortage of materials, shortage of plants, labor problems, unforeseen ground conditions, site instructions, variation orders, client-initiated changes, engineer-initiated changes, errors and omissions in drawings, mistakes in specifications, defects in works, accidents, supplier delivery failure, delay of schedule by subcontractor, poor workmanship, delayed payment, changes in regulations, third-party interference, professional negligence, and so on.

Prior to the actual construction process, the involving parties will attempt to sort out the conditions for claims and disputes through the contract documents. However, since a project usually involves thousands of separate pieces of work items to be integrated together to constitute a complete functioning structure, the potential for honest misunderstanding is extremely high. The legislation now in force requires that any disputes incurred have to be resolve successively by mediation, arbitration, and the courts [12].

3 Multi-layer Feed-Forward Perceptron

A multi-layer feed-forward perceptron represents a nonlinear mapping between input vector and output vector through a system of simple interconnected neurons. It is fully connected to every node in the next and previous layer. The output of a neuron is scaled by the connecting weight and fed forward to become an input through a nonlinear activation function to the neurons in the next layer of network. In the course of training, the perceptron is repeatedly presented with the training data. The weights in the network are then adjusted until the errors between the target and the predicted outputs are small enough, or a pre-determined number of epochs is passed. The perceptron is then validated by presenting with an input vector not belonging to the training pairs. The training processes of ANN are usually complex and high dimensional problems. The commonly used gradient-based BP algorithm is a local search method, which easily falls into local optimum point during training.

4 Particle Swarm Optimization (PSO)

Particle swarm optimization (PSO) is an optimization paradigm that mimics the ability of human societies to process knowledge. It has roots in two main component methodologies: artificial life (such as bird flocking, fish schooling and swarming); and, evolutionary computation. The key concept of PSO is that potential solutions are flown through hyperspace and are accelerated towards better or more optimum solutions.

4.1 PSO Algorithm

PSO is a populated search method for optimization of continuous nonlinear functions resembling the movement of organisms in a bird flock or fish school. Its paradigm can be implemented in a few lines of computer code and is computationally inexpensive in terms of both memory requirements and speed. It lies somewhere between evolutionary programming and genetic algorithms. As in evolutionary computation paradigms, the concept of fitness is employed and candidate solutions to the problem are termed particles or sometimes individuals. A similarity between PSO and a genetic algorithm is the initialization of the system with a population of random solutions. Instead of employing genetic operators, the evolution of generations of a population of these individuals in such a system is by cooperation and competition among the individuals themselves. Moreover, a randomized velocity is assigned to each potential solution or particle so that it is flown through hyperspace. The adjustment by the particle swarm optimizer is ideally similar to the crossover operation in genetic algorithms whilst the stochastic processes are close to evolutionary programming. The stochastic factors allow thorough search of spaces between regions that are spotted to be relatively good whilst the momentum effect of modifications of the existing velocities leads to exploration of potential regions of the problem domain.

There are five basic principles of swarm intelligence: (1) proximity; (2) quality; (3) diverse response; (4) stability; and, (5) adaptability. The n-dimensional space calculations of the PSO concept are performed over a series of time steps. The population is responding to the quality factors of the previous best individual values and the previous best group values. The allocation of responses between the individual and group values ensures a diversity of response. The principle of stability is adhered to since the population changes its state if and only if the best group value changes. It is adaptive corresponding to the change of the best group value.

In essence, each particle adjusts its flying based on the flying experiences of both itself and its companions. It keeps track of its coordinates in hyperspace which are associated with its previous best fitness solution, and also of its counterpart corresponding to the overall best value acquired thus far by any other particle in the population. Vectors are taken as presentation of particles since most optimization problems are convenient for such variable presentations. The stochastic PSO algorithm has been found to be able to find the global optimum with a large probability and high convergence rate. Hence, it is adopted to train the multi-layer perceptrons, within which matrices learning problems are dealt with.

4.2 Adaptation to Network Training

A three-layered preceptron is chosen for this application case. Here, $W^{[1]}$ and $W^{[2]}$ represent the connection weight matrix between the input layer and the hidden layer, and that between the hidden layer and the output layer, respectively. When a PSO is employed to train the multi-layer preceptrons, the i-th particle is denoted by

$$W_i = \{W_i^{[1]}, W_i^{[2]}\} \tag{1}$$

The position representing the previous best fitness value of any particle is recorded and denoted by

$$P_i = \{P_i^{[1]}, P_i^{[2]}\} \tag{2}$$

If, among all the particles in the population, the index of the best particle is represented by the symbol b, then the best matrix is denoted by

$$P_b = \{P_b^{[1]}, P_b^{[2]}\} \tag{3}$$

The velocity of particle i is denoted by

$$V_i = \{V_i^{[1]}, V_i^{[2]}\} \tag{4}$$

If m and n represent the index of matrix row and column, respectively, the manipulation of the particles are as follows

$$V_i^{[j]}(m,n) = V_i^{[j]}(m,n) + r\alpha[P_i^{[j]}(m,n) - W_i^{[j]}(m,n)] + s\beta[P_b^{[j]}(m,n) - W_i^{[j]}(m,n)] \tag{5}$$

and

$$W_i^{[j]} = W_i^{[j]} + V_i^{[j]} \tag{6}$$

where j = 1, 2; m = 1, …, M_j; n= 1, …, N_j; M_j and N_j are the row and column sizes of the matrices W, P, and V; r and s are positive constants; α and β are random numbers in the range from 0 to 1. Equation (5) is employed to compute the new velocity of the particle based on its previous velocity and the distances of its current position from the best experiences both in its own and as a group. In the context of social behavior, the cognition part $r\alpha[P_i^{[j]}(m,n) - W_i^{[j]}(m,n)]$ represents the private thinking of the particle itself whilst the social part $s\beta[P_b^{[j]}(m,n) - W_i^{[j]}(m,n)]$ denotes the collaboration among the particles as a group. Equation (6) then determines the new position according to the new velocity [6-7].

The fitness of the i-th particle is expressed in term of an output mean squared error of the neural networks as follows

$$f(W_i) = \frac{1}{S}\sum_{k=1}^{S}\left[\sum_{l=1}^{O}\{t_{kl} - p_{kl}(W_i)\}^2\right] \tag{7}$$

where f is the fitness value, t_{kl} is the target output; p_{kl} is the predicted output based on W_i; S is the number of training set samples; and, O is the number of output neurons.

5 The Study

The system is applied to study and predict the outcome of construction claims in Hong Kong. The data from 1991 to 2000 are organized case by case and the dispute characteristics and court decisions are correlated. Through a sensitivity analysis, 13 case elements that seem relevant in courts' decisions are identified. They are, namely, type of contract, contract value, parties involved, type of plaintiff, type of defendant, resolution technique involved, legal interpretation of contract documents, misrepresentation of site, radical changes in scope, directed changes, constructive changes, liquidated damages involved, and late payment.

Some of the 13 case elements can be expressed in binary format; for example, the input element 'liquidated damages involved' receives a 1 if the claim involves liquidated damages or a 0 if it does not. However, some elements are defined by several alternatives; for example, 'type of contract' could be remeasurement contract, lump sum contract, or design and build contract. These elements with alternative answers are split into separate input elements, one for each alternative. Each alternative is represented in a binary format, such as 1 for remeasurement contract and 0 for the others if the type of contract is not remeasurement. In that case, only one of these input elements will have a 1 value and all the others will have a 0 value. In this way, the 13 elements are converted into an input layer of 30 neurons, all expressed in binary format. Table 1 shows examples of the input neurons for cases with different types of contract. The court decisions are also organized in an output layer of 6 neurons expressed in binary format corresponding to the 6 elements: client, contractor, engineer, sub-contractor, supplier, and other third parties.

In total, 1105 sets of construction-related cases were available, of which 550 from years 1991 to 1995 were used for training, 275 from years 1996 to 1997 were used for testing, and 280 from years 1998 to 2000 were used to validate the network results with the observations. It is ensured that the data series chosen for training and validation comprised balanced distribution of cases.

Table 1. Examples of the input neurons for cases with different types of contract

Input neuron	Cases		
	Remeasurement	Lump sum	Design and build
Type of contract - remeasurement	1	0	0
Type of contract - lump sum	0	1	0
Type of contract – design and build	0	0	1

Sensitivity analysis is performed to determine the best architecture, with variations in the number of hidden layers and number of hidden neurons. The final perceptron has an input layer with thirty neurons, a hidden layer with fifteen neurons, and output layer with six neurons. In the PSO-based perceptron, the number of population is set to be 40 whilst the maximum and minimum velocity values are 0.25 and -0.25 respectively.

6 Results and Discussions

The PSO-based multi-layer ANN is evaluated along with a commonly used standard BP-based network. In order to furnish a comparable initial state, the training process of the BP-based perceptron commences from the best initial population of the corresponding PSO-based perceptron. Figure 1 shows the relationships between the normalized mean square error and fitness evaluation time during training for PSO-based and BP-based perceptrons. Table 2 shows comparisons of the results of network for the two different perceptrons.

The fitness evaluation time here for the PSO-based perceptron is equal to the product of the population with the number of generations. It is noted that testing cases of the PSO-based network are able to give a successful prediction rate of up to 80%, which is much higher than by pure chance. Moreover, the PSO-based perceptron exhibits much better and faster convergence performance in the training process as well as better prediction ability in the validation process than those by the BP-based perceptron. It can be concluded that the PSO-based perceptron performs better than the BP-based perceptron. It is believed that, if the involving parties to a construction dispute become aware with some certainty how the case would be resolved if it were taken to court, the number of disputes could be reduced significantly.

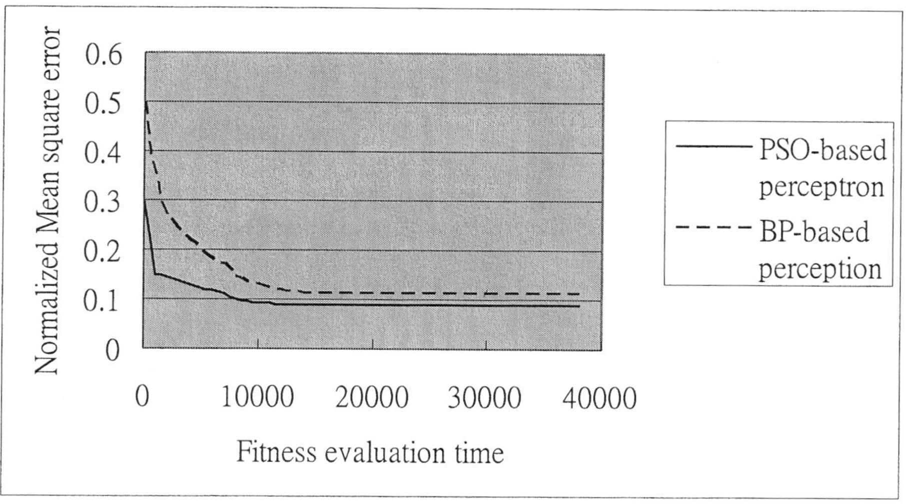

Fig. 1. Relationships between the normalized mean square error and fitness evaluation time during training for PSO-based and BP-based perceptrons

Table 2. Comparison of prediction results for outcome of construction litigation

Algorithm	Training		Validation	
	Coefficient of correlation	Prediction rate	Coefficient of correlation	Prediction rate
BP-based	0.956	0.69	0.953	0.67
PSO-based	0.987	0.81	0.984	0.80

7 Conclusions

This paper presents a PSO-based perceptron approach for prediction of outcomes of construction litigation on the basis of the characteristics of the individual dispute and the corresponding past court decisions. It is demonstrated that the novel optimization algorithm, which is able to provide model-free estimates in deducing the output from the input, is an appropriate prediction tool. The final network presented in this study is recommended as an approximate prediction tool for the parties in dispute, since the rate of prediction is up to 80%, which is much higher than chance. It is, of course, recognized that there are limitations in the assumptions used in this study. Other factors that may have certain bearing such as cultural, psychological, social, environmental, and political factors have not been considered here. Nevertheless, it is shown from the training and verification simulation that the prediction results of outcomes of construction litigation are more accurate and are obtained in relatively short computational time, when compared with the commonly used BP-based perceptron. Both the above two factors are important in construction management. It can be concluded that the PSO-based perceptron performs better than the BP-based perceptron.

Acknowledgement

This research was supported by the Central Research Grant of Hong Kong Polytechnic University (G-T592) and the Internal Competitive Research Grant of Hong Kong Polytechnic University (A-PE26).

References

1. Arditi, D., Oksay, F.E., Tokdemir, O.B.: Predicting the Outcome of Construction Litigation Using Neural Networks. Computer-Aided Civil and Infrastructure Engineering **13(2)** (1998) 75-81
2. Thirumalaiah, K., Deo, M.C.: River Stage Forecasting Using Artificial Neural Networks. Journal of Hydrologic Engineering, ASCE **3(1)** (1998) 26-32
3. Govindaraju, R., Rao, A. (Ed.): Artificial Neural Networks in Hydrology. Kluwer Academic Publishers, Dordrecht (2000)
4. Liong, S.Y., Lim, W.H., Paudyal, G.N.: River Stage Forecasting in Bangladesh: Neural Network Approach. Journal of Computing in Civil Engineering, ASCE **14(1)** (2000) 1-8
5. Chau, K.W., Cheng, C.T.: Real-time Prediction of Water Stage with Artificial Neural Network Approach. Lecture Notes in Artificial Intelligence, **2557** (2002) 715-715
6. Kennedy, J., Eberhart, R.: Particle Swarm Optimization. Proceedings of the 1995 IEEE International Conference on Neural Networks. Perth (1995) 1942-1948
7. Kennedy, J.: The Particle Swarm: Social Adaptation of Knowledge. Proceedings of the 1997 International Conference on Evolutionary Computation. Indianapolis (1997) 303-308
8. Clerc, M., Kennedy, J.: The Particle Swarm—Explosion, Stability, and Convergence in a Multidimensional Complex Space. IEEE Transactions on Evolutionary Computation **6(1)** (2002) 58-73
9. Kennedy, J., Eberhart, R., Shi, Y.: Swarm Intelligence. Morgan Kaufmann Publishers, San Francisco (2001)
10. Chau, K.W.: River Stage Forecasting with Particle Swarm Optimization. Lecture Notes in Computer Science **3029** (2004) 1166-1173
11. Chau, K.W.: Rainfall-Runoff Correlation with Particle Swarm Optimization Algorithm. Lecture Notes in Computer Science **3174** (2004) 970-975
12. Chau, K.W.: Resolving Construction Disputes by Mediation: Hong Kong Experience. Journal of Management in Engineering, ASCE **8(4)** (1992) 384-393

Self-organizing Radial Basis Function Network Modeling for Robot Manipulator

Dongwon Kim[1], Sung-Hoe Huh[1], Sam-Jun Seo[2], and Gwi-Tae Park[1,*]

[1] Department of Electrical Engineering, Korea University, 1, 5-Ka Anam-Dong, Seongbuk-Gu, Seoul 136-701, Korea
{upground,gtpark}@korea.ac.kr
[2] Department of Electrical & Electronic Engineering, Anyang University, 708-113, Anyang 5dong, Manan-gu, Anyang-shi, Kyunggi-do, 430-714, Korea

Abstract. Intelligent and adaptive approach to model two links manipulator system with self-organizing radial basis function (RBF) network is presented in this paper. The self-organizing algorithm that enables the RBF neural network to be structured automatically and on-line is developed, and with this proposed scheme, the centers and widths of RBF neural network as well as the weights are to be adaptively determined. Based on the fact that a 3-layered RBF neural network has the capability that represents the nonlinear input-output map of any nonlinear function to a desired accuracy, the input output mapping of the two link manipulator using the proposed RBF neural network is shown analytically through experimental results without knowing the information of the system in advance.

1 Introduction

As the developments of mechatronics and computer controlled systems, many kinds of manipulator systems are widely used in various application areas, and especially, the modeling and control of arm manipulators have attracted the attention of many researchers in the past few years[1-2]. To control an arm manipulator with a systematic approach, the mathematical model for the controlled system is necessary and to be derived by using the physical dynamic laws governing the motion characteristics [3]. However, this approach is much complex and sometimes infeasible. The main goal of the system modeling is to obtain a mathematical model whose output matches the output of a dynamic system for a given input. Because the solution to the exact matching problem is extremely difficult, in practical cases, the original problem is relaxed to developing the model whose output is to be as close as possible to the output of the real dynamic system. Recently, many kinds of schemes for the system modeling have been developed [4-5]. Owing to its modeling performance with simple structure, fast computation time and higher adaptive performance, radial basis function network (RBFN) is one of the most promising.

* Corresponding author.

M. Ali and F. Esposito (Eds.): IEA/AIE 2005, LNAI 3533, pp. 579 – 587, 2005.

The construction of RBFN involves three different layers: *Input layer* which consists of source nodes, *hidden layer* in which each neuron computes its output using a radial basis function (RBF) and *output layer* which builds a linear weighted sum of hidden layer outputs to supply the response of the network. The RBFN is basically trained by some learning strategies. The learning strategies in the literature used for the design of RBFN differ from each other mainly in the determination of centers of the RBF [6-8]. However, the general training methods share some fundamental drawbacks. One of them is that the general RBF neural network has no ability to get the proper structure. Moreover, most of the current research results on identification or control of uncertain nonlinear systems do not present an on-line structuring scheme. Generally, it is difficult to find a proper structure of RBFN in the case that identified systems are totally unknown. In that case, an on-line structuring algorithm is highly required in which a proper structure of the network is searched during a learning phase and it is the current issue which has been actively researched.

In this paper, we propose a self-organizing RBFN as an identifier of two-link robot manipulator system. The propose RBFN has no need of an initialization and has the ability to change its own structure during learning procedure. The proposed network initially has only one node in the hidden layer, but during the learning process, the network creates new nodes, and annexes similar nodes if they are needed. Identification results of the two-link robot manipulator will be showed to demonstrate the performance and efficiency of the scheme.

2 Self-organizing Radial Basis Function Network

RBFN is a three-layer neural networks structure. The structure of the RBFN is shown in Fig. 1. In RBFN, each hidden neuron computes the distance from its input to the neuron's central point, c, and applies the RBF to that distance, as shows in Eq (1)

$$h_i(x) = \phi(\|x - c_i\|^2 / r_i^2) \tag{1}$$

where $h_i(x)$ is the output yielded by hidden neuron number i when input x is applied; ϕ is the RBF, c_i is the center of the ith hidden neuron, and r_i is its radius.

The neurons of the output layer perform a weighted sum using the outputs of the hidden layer and the weights of the links that connect both output and hidden layer neurons

$$o_j(x) = \sum_{i=0}^{n-1} w_{ij} h_i(x) + w_{0j} \tag{2}$$

where $o_j(x)$ is the value yielded by output neuron number j when input x is applied: w_{ij} is the weight of the links that connects hidden neuron number i and output neuron number j, w_{0j} is a bias for the output neuron, and finally, n is the number of hidden neurons.

In the conventional design procedure, we have to set the initial structure before starting the learning of the network. In particular, it is hard to specify this initial structure in advance due to the uncertain distribution of on-line incoming data. We approach this problem using a self-organizing RBFN inspired by [10]. In what follows, $N(t)$ stands for the number of units at time t, and is zero initially.

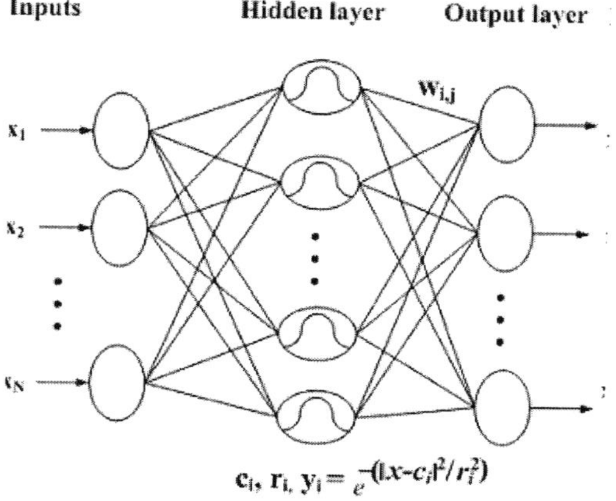

Fig. 1. Structure of the radial basis function network

2.1 Similarity Measure

Suppose the μ_A and μ_B as the activation functions of neurons A and B, respectively.

$$\begin{aligned} \mu_A(x) &= \exp\{-(x-m_1)^2 / \sigma_1^2\} \\ \mu_B(x) &= \exp\{-(x-m_2)^2 / \sigma_2^2\} \end{aligned} \tag{3}$$

And consider a criterion for the degree of similarity of two neurons, $S(\cdot,\cdot)$. Then, $S(\cdot,\cdot)$ takes the values in [0, 1], and the higher $S(A, B)$ is, the more similar A and B are. For self-organizing learning the similarity measure for bell-shaped membership functions is used as follows.

$$S(A, B) = \frac{|A \cap B|}{|A \cup B|} = \frac{|A \cap B|}{\sigma_1\sqrt{\pi} + \sigma_2\sqrt{\pi} - |A \cap B|} \tag{4}$$

$$|A| + |B| = |A \cap B| + |A \cup B|$$

where,

$$|A \cap B| = \frac{1}{2}\frac{h^2(m_2 - m_1 + \sqrt{\pi}(\sigma_1 + \sigma_2))}{\sqrt{\pi}(\sigma_1 + \sigma_2)} + \frac{1}{2}\frac{h^2(m_2 - m_1 + \sqrt{\pi}(\sigma_1 - \sigma_2))}{\sqrt{\pi}(\sigma_2 - \sigma_1)} + \frac{1}{2}\frac{h^2(m_2 - m_1 - \sqrt{\pi}(\sigma_1 - \sigma_2))}{\sqrt{\pi}(\sigma_1 - \sigma_2)} \tag{5}$$

$$h(x) = \max\{0, x\}$$

2.2 Creating a New Neuron

The procedure for creating new neuron is consists of several steps. The steps are as follows;

Step 1: Get the input $\mathbf{x}(t)$ and calculate the ϕ vector Shown in Fig. 2

$$\phi = \begin{bmatrix} \phi_1 & \phi_2 & \cdots & \phi_{N(t)} \end{bmatrix}^T \tag{6}$$

where ϕ_q, $q = 1, 2, \cdots, N(t)$ is the output value of each hidden neuron.

Step 2: Find the unit J having the maximum response value shown in Fig. 3

$$\phi_J = \max_{q=1,N(t)} \phi_q \tag{7}$$

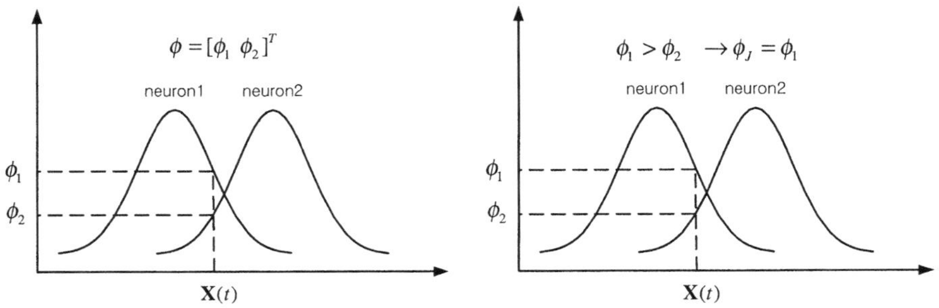

Fig. 2. Schematic representation of step 1 **Fig. 3.** Schematic representation of step 2

Step 3: Determine whether a new neuron is added or not according to the following criterion shown in Fig. 4

$$\begin{cases} if \ \phi_J \geq \bar{\phi} & \rightarrow \ J \text{ is winner (Do nothing).} \\ if \ \phi_J < \bar{\phi} & \rightarrow \ \text{Create a new unit.} \end{cases} \tag{8}$$

where $0 \leq \bar{\phi} < 1$ is a threshold value. We set this 0.750

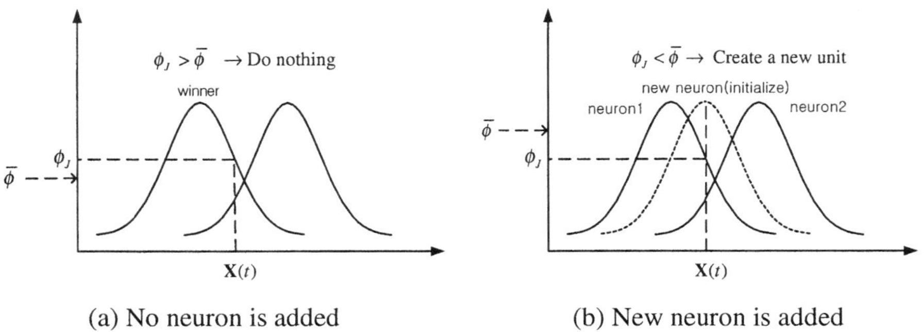

(a) No neuron is added (b) New neuron is added

Fig. 4. Schematic representation of step 3

Step 4: Modify or initialize parameters.

1) If J th neuron is the winner (Do nothing),

$$\begin{aligned} &n_J(t) = n_J(t-1) \\ &\alpha_J(t) = \frac{1}{n_J(t)} \\ &N(t) = N(t-1) \\ &\mathbf{m}_J(t) = \mathbf{m}_J(t-1) + \alpha_J(t)\left[u(t) - \mathbf{m}_J(t-1)\right] \end{aligned} \tag{9}$$

where α_J is the local gain

The local gain, α_J , governs the speed of the adaptive process for center, $\mathbf{m}_J$ and is inversely proportional to the active frequency, n_J , of the Jth unit up to the present time instant.

2) If a new neuron is created, we initialize parameters.

$$\begin{aligned} &N(t^+) = N(t) + 1 \\ &\mathbf{m}_{N(t^+)} = \mathrm{x}(t) \\ &\sigma_{N(t^+)} = \sigma_J \\ &\boldsymbol{\theta}_{N(t^+)i} = 0, \ i = 1, \ldots, n \end{aligned} \tag{10}$$

where t^+ indicates the time right after t.

2.3 Annexing Two Neurons

Step 5: Find the similarity set for annexation shown in Fig. 5. If we have *N(t)* neuron at time instance *t*, the similarity set is

$$S_{annexation} = \{S(1,2), S(1,3), \cdots S(N(t)-1, N(t))\} \tag{11}$$

where *S(i, j)* is the similarity between *i*th and *j*th neuron.

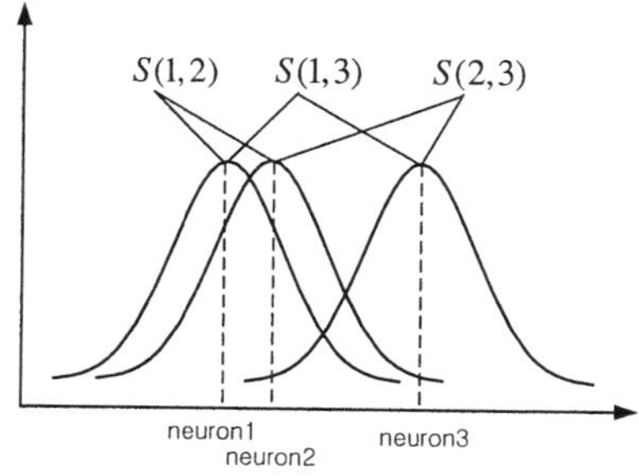

Fig. 5. Schematic representation of step 5

Step 6: In the similarity set, if there are elements which satisfy $S(i, j) > S_0$, ith and jth neuron are annexed. We set S_0 0.980. The annexed neuron has the center, slope and weight determined as

$$
\begin{aligned}
&N(t^+) = N(t) - 1 \\
&\mathbf{m}_{annex}(t^+) = \frac{\mathbf{m}_i(t) + \mathbf{m}_j(t)}{2} \\
&\sigma_{annex}(t^+) = \frac{\sigma_i(t) + \sigma_j(t)}{2} \\
&\boldsymbol{\theta}_{annex,k}(t^+) = \frac{\boldsymbol{\theta}_{ik}(t)\phi_i(t) + \boldsymbol{\theta}_{jk}(t)\phi_j(t)}{\phi_{newi}(t^+)}, \quad k = 1,\ldots,n
\end{aligned}
\tag{12}
$$

In step 4 and step 6, the new weight $\boldsymbol{\theta}_{N(t^+)k}$ and $\boldsymbol{\theta}_{annex,k}(t^+)$, $k = 1,\ldots,n$ are set to have no effect on the output of the RBF neural network by creation or annexation, that is $\hat{\mathbf{y}}(t) = \hat{\mathbf{y}}(t^+)$. The RBF neural network gets to find proper structure with above procedures step 1- step 6 going on.

3 Application to Robot Manipulators

Let us consider a two degree-of-freedom planar manipulator with revolute joints. Its figure and specification are shown in Fig. 6 and Table 1, respectively. For the identification of the two-link robot manipulator in this paper, the input vectors of the self-organizing RBFN consist of angle, angular velocity and torque input for each axis, and all of them are to be measured with experimental setup. The output vector is the estimated angle and angular velocity for each axis.

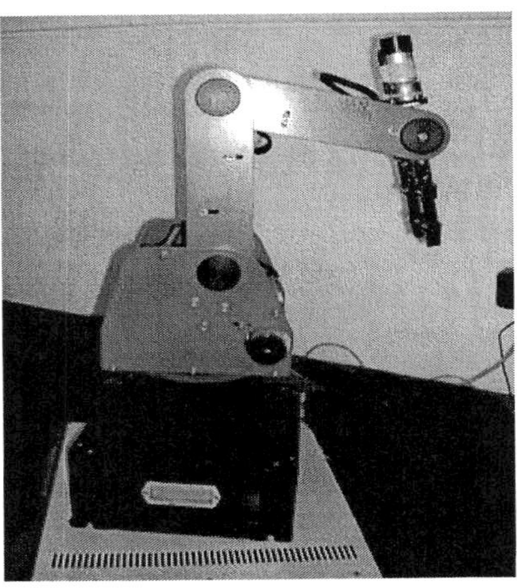

Fig. 6. Modeled two degree-of-freedom robot manipulator

Table 1. Specification of robot manipulators

	1-axis	2-axis
Motor	DC 24V/4.6W	DC 24V/4.6W
Encoder	200pulse / rev	200pulse/rev
Gear ratio	144:1	144:1
Operation range	± 65°	± 130°

Because the pre-information about the robot manipulators is unknown, measuring procedure for real input-output vector is necessary. For that purpose, a simple experimental environment connecting to the manipulator is set up. Its simple block diagram is shown in Fig. 7.

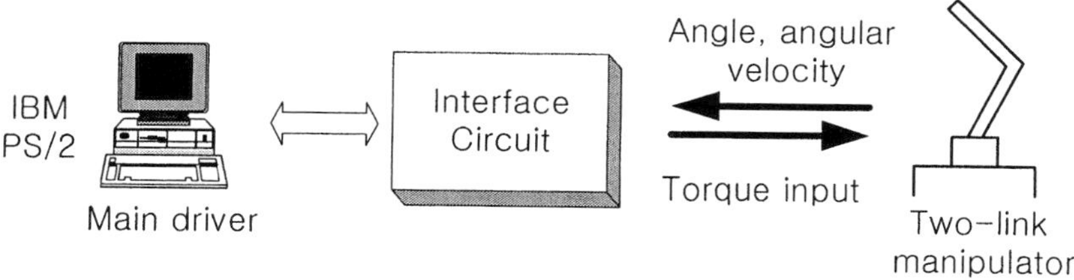

Fig. 7. Block diagram of the experimental environment

The experimental results are illustrated in Figs. 8-10. In the figures, the real (measured) and estimated values of angle and angular velocity of each axis, and their errors are presented. And the variation of the number of neurons in the hidden layer is also displayed. From the figures, we can see that the estimated values track well the original measured values. The RBFN has one neuron at the beginning, but the number of neurons increases gradually, and when the RBFN has enough neurons, the number of neurons is not increased any more.

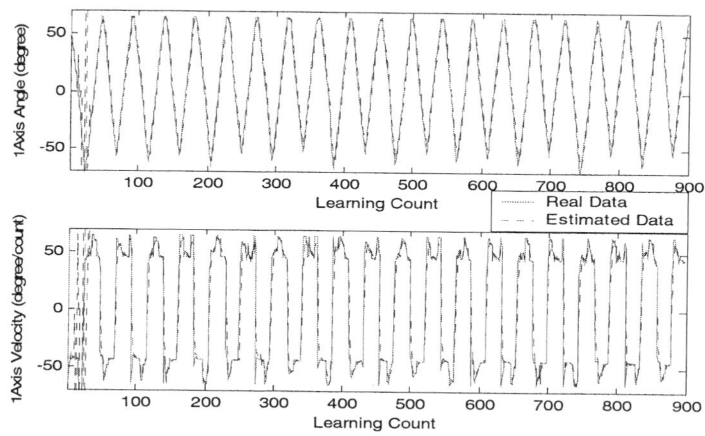

Fig. 8. Angle, angular velocity in 1-axis

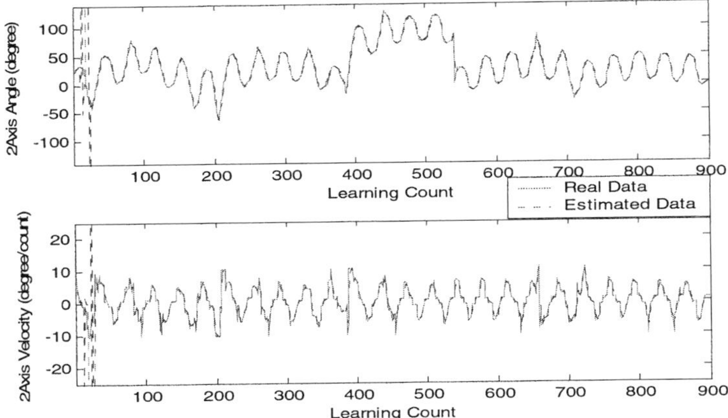

Fig. 9. Angle, angular velocity in 2-axis

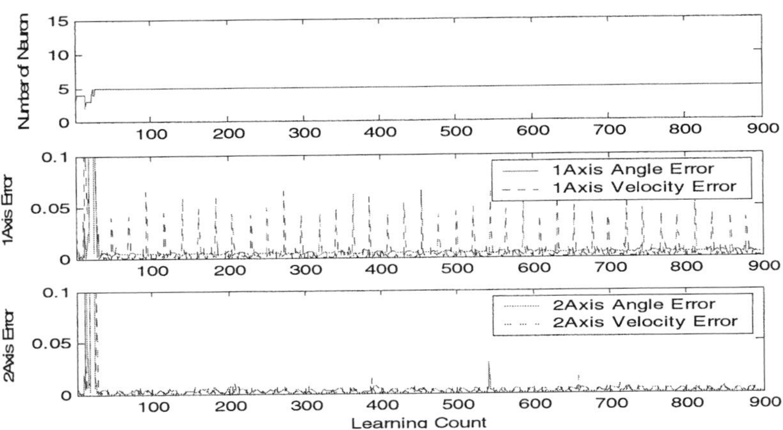

Fig. 10. No. of neurons and errors of angle and angular velocity of each axis

4 Conclusions

In this paper, an intelligent and adaptive approach to identify a two-degree-of-freedom robot manipulator system with self organizing radial basis function network is presented and experimentally verified. The RBFN creates and annexes neurons on-line and automatically during the identification procedure. And the centers and widths of RBFN as well as the weights are to be adaptively determined. If the input vector is too far away from the existent neurons, the new neuron will be created, and if the two neurons are too close each other, these neurons will be annexed.

Using this scheme, robot manipulators are modeled well and performance and efficiency are demonstrated.

Acknowledgment. He authors thank the financial support of the Korea University. This research was supported by a Korea University Grant.

References

[1] Gurkan, E., Erkmen, I., Erkmen, A.M.: Two-way fuzzy adaptive identification and control of a flexible-joint robot arm. Inf. Sci. 145(2003) 13-43

[2] Munasinghe, S.R., Nakanura, M., Goto, S., Kyura, N.: Optimum contouring of industrial robot arms under assigned velocity and torque constraints. IEEE Trans Syst., Man and Cybern. 31(2001) 159-167

[3] Craig, J.J.: ROBOTICS mechanics and control. 2nd edn Addison-Wesley, 1989.

[4] Grossberg, S.: On learning and energy-entropy dependency in recurrent and nonrecurrent signed networks. Journal of Stat Physics 1(1969) 319-350.

[5] Seshagiri,S., Khalil, H.K.: Output feedback control of nonlinear systems using rbf neural networks. IEEE Trans Neural Network 11(2000): 69-79.

[6] Chen, S., Cowan, C.F., and Grant, P.M.: Orthogonal least squares learning algorithms for radial basis function networks. IEEE Trans. Neural Networks 2(1991) 302-309

[7] Moody, J.E., and Darken, C.J.: Fast learning in networks of locally tuned processing unitsNeural Comput., 1(1989) 281-294

[8] Uykan, Z., Guzelis, C., Celebi, M. E., and Koivo, H.N.: Analysis of Input-Output Clustering for Determining Centers of RBFN. IEEE Trans, Neural Networks 11(2000) 851-858

[9] Slotine, J.E., Weiping, Li.: Applied nonlinear control. Prentice Hall (1991)

[10] Nie, J., Linkens, D. A.: Learning control using fuzzified self-organizing radial basis function network. IEEE Trans. Fuzzy Syst. 1(1993) 280-287

A SOM Based Approach for Visualization of GSM Network Performance Data

Pasi Lehtimäki and Kimmo Raivio

Helsinki University of Technology,
Laboratory of Computer and Information Science,
P.O. Box 5400, FIN-02015 HUT, Finland

Abstract. In this paper, a neural network based approach to visualize performance data of a GSM network is presented. The proposed approach consists of several steps. First, a suitable proportion of measurement data is selected. Then, the selected set of multi-dimensional data is projected into two-dimensional space for visualization purposes with a neural network algorithm called Self-Organizing Map (SOM). Then, the data is clustered and additional visualizations for each data cluster are provided in order to infer the presence of various failure types, their sources and times of occurrence. We apply the proposed approach in the analysis of degradations in signaling and traffic channel capacity of a GSM network.

Keywords: data mining, neural networks, visualization, self-organizing map, telecommunications.

1 Introduction

The radio resource management in current wireless communication networks concentrates on maximizing the number of users for which the quality of service (QoS) requirements are satisfied, while gaining the maximal profitability for the operator [12]. In practice, the goal is to obtain an efficient usage of the radio resources (i.e. maximal coverage and capacity with the given frequency spectrum) while keeping the infrastructure costs at the minimum. Currently, the variety of services is developing from voice-oriented services towards data-oriented services, causing new difficulties for the network resource management due to the increased diversity of QoS requirements.

The most severe performance degradations of wireless networks from the user point of view involve the reduced availability (blocking) of the services as well as the abnormal interruption of the already initiated services (dropping). In principle, such performance degradations may result from unpredictable hardware breakdowns or temporary changes in the operating environment (i.e in traffic flow), but on the other hand, they may originate from incorrect (or unsuitable) network configuration, causing bad performance more regularly.

The system knowledge required to optimize GSM system performance is very difficult to formalize as a mathematical model and therefore, automatic control

M. Ali and F. Esposito (Eds.): IEA/AIE 2005, LNAI 3533, pp. 588–598, 2005.

of many configuration parameters is unfeasible. Instead, the network optimization is carried out by application domain experts having a long experience in the problem field. In such a case, it is more efficient to exploit the existing expert knowledge and to try to represent the most informative portion of the measurement data in an efficient form in order to support performance optimization.

In this paper, an analysis process based on Self-Organizing Map (SOM) to visualize GSM network performance data is presented. The SOM has been applied in the analysis of 3G network performance, including advanced network monitoring and cell grouping [7, 6].

Next, the basic SOM algorithm is presented. Then, the overall SOM based analysis process for GSM performance data is outlined. Then, we demonstrate the use of the analysis process in two problem scenarios in which the capacity problems in the signaling and traffic channels are analyzed.

2 Methods

2.1 Self-organizing Map

One of the most widely used neural network algorithms is the Kohonen's Self-Organizing Map [5]. It consists of neurons or map units, each having a location in a continuous multi-dimensional measurement space as well as in a discrete two-dimensional output grid. During the so-called training phase, a multi-dimensional data collection is repeatedly presented to the SOM until a topology preserving mapping from the multi-dimensional measurement space into the two-dimensional output space is obtained. This dimensionality reduction property of the SOM makes it especially suitable for data visualization.

The training phase of SOM consist of two steps: the winner map unit search, followed by application of an update rule for the map unit locations in the measurement space. In winner search, an input sample $\mathbf{x}$ is picked up randomly from the measurement space and the map unit c closest to the input sample $\mathbf{x}$ is declared as the winner map unit or the best-matching map unit (BMU):

$$c = \arg\min_i ||\mathbf{x} - \mathbf{m}_i||, \tag{1}$$

in which $\mathbf{m}_i$ is the location of the ith map unit in the measurement space and c is the index of the winner map unit in the output grid of SOM.

After the winner search, the locations of the map units in the measurement space are updated according to the rule:

$$\mathbf{m}_i(t+1) = \mathbf{m}_i(t) + \alpha(t)h_{ci}(t)[\mathbf{x}(t) - \mathbf{m}_i(t)], \tag{2}$$

in which $0 < \alpha(t) < 1$ is a learning rate factor and $h_{ci}(t)$ is usually the Gaussian neighborhood function

$$h_{ci}(t) = \exp\left(-\frac{||\mathbf{r}_c - \mathbf{r}_i||}{2\sigma^2(t)}\right), \tag{3}$$

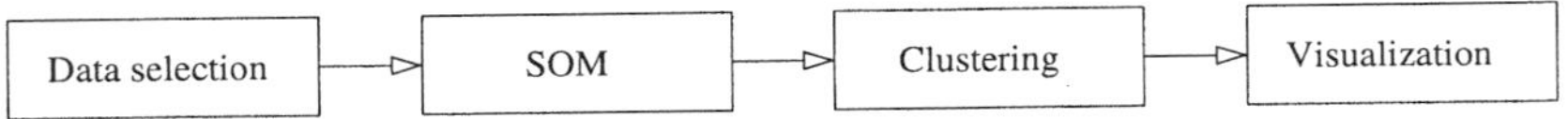

Fig. 1. A block diagram illustrating the phases of the proposed analysis process

where $\mathbf{r}_c$ is the location of the winner unit and $\mathbf{r}_i$ is the location of the ith map unit in the discrete output grid of SOM. The learning rate factor $\alpha(t)$ and the neighborhood radius $\sigma(t)$ are monotonically decreasing functions of time t.

2.2 The Overall Analysis Process

The proposed SOM based analysis process is illustrated in Figure 1. Next, the steps of the analysis process are discussed in detail.

Data Selection. The GSM system consists of large amount of base stations (BSs), each serving the users on distinct geographical areas (cells). The performance of the BSs is described by a large amount of variables called Key Performance Indicators (KPIs) with typical sampling frequency of one hour. For each KPI, an objective value can be defined by the network operator in order to define the acceptable performance of the network.

When projection methods such as the SOM are used in data visualization, all samples usually have equal priority when determining the projection (dimensionality reduction) function. In many trouble shooting tasks, however, more accurate visualizations of failures would be more appropriate at the expense of samples representing normal operation. When analyzing the performance degradations of a GSM network, the data subset to be used in projection function determination can be selected by choosing the KPIs of interest and removing the samples that represent normal operation (the objective values for the selected KPIs are met). For example, if an accurate visualization of traffic channel problems are desired, it would be justified to use only the samples in which traffic channel blocking or traffic channel drop rate exceed some pre-selected threshold.

SOM Training. After the subset of data of interest is selected, the data is normalized in order to make all variables equally important independently on the measurement unit. Then, the normalized data is used as the input data in the SOM training. The training procedure for the SOM was described in Section 2.1. The trained SOM is used to visualize the multi-dimensional input data using the component plane representation of SOM [10].

Clustering. The clustering of the data aims in partitioning the data into "natural" groups, each (hopefully) describing different types of failures present in the GSM network. Therefore, the clustering of the data allows the analysis process to be divided into subproblems in which different types of failures are analyzed separately. We have adopted a clustering approach in which the clustering process is carried out for the map units of SOM (in the measurement space) instead of the original data subset [11]. We have used the k-means clustering algorithm [2] for different values of k (the number of clusters in which the data is divided). The best clustering among different values of k is selected according to the Davies-Bouldin index [1].

Visualization. After the SOM training and clustering, a visualization of the selected multi-dimensional input data is obtained. This information helps the application domain expert to make inferences about the possible problem scenarios present in the data. The cluster analysis based on SOM component planes reveals the variety of failures faced by the network. It is relatively easy task for an expert to select the most important variables (KPIs) for each failure type. By analyzing the amount of samples in different fault clusters originating from each cell of the GSM network, the locations of the different failure types are efficiently obtained. Finally, the visualization of the times of occurrence of different fault types reveals additional temporal information about the faults. These three types of simple visualizations allows the selection of variables, cells and time periods that are taken into further analysis using conventional methods.

3 Experiments

3.1 Analysis of SDCCH Capacity Problems

In this section, we demonstrate the use of the presented analysis process by analyzing the capacity problems in the signaling channel. The available data set consists of several KPIs with sampling frequency of one hour. The measurements were made in 41 cells during 10-week time period, resulting in about 40 000 multi-dimensional data vectors. First, we selected a suitable data selection scheme in order to focus on the signaling channel capacity problems. The selected variable set consisted of SDCCH blocking and availability rates, uplink and downlink signal strengths and signal quality measurements, as well as the amount of circuit switched traffic in the cell.

We applied an inequality constraint with SDCCH Blocking > 0 % in order to filter the uninformative (normal operation) samples from the analysis. Then, we applied histogram equalization based normalization method for the selected data set in order to obtain invariance w.r.t the scales of the variables. Then, we trained a SOM in which the map units were organized in a 15×10 hexagonal grid by applying 500 epochs of batch training and 500 epochs of sequential training.

For comparison purposes, we used Principal Component Analysis (PCA) [3] and Independent Component Analysis (ICA) [4] methods to obtain alternative coordinate axes in the original data space along which the data samples were to be projected. We compared the quality of the projections using the measures of trustworthiness and preservation of neighborhoods [9]. We found out that the SOM and PCA based projections were equally good, outperforming the ICA based projection in both measures. We evaluated the same accuracy measures for the same data subset in cases where the data selection had no impact on actual projection function (i.e all the data was used in forming the projection). We found out, that the SOM and ICA based projections lost in representation

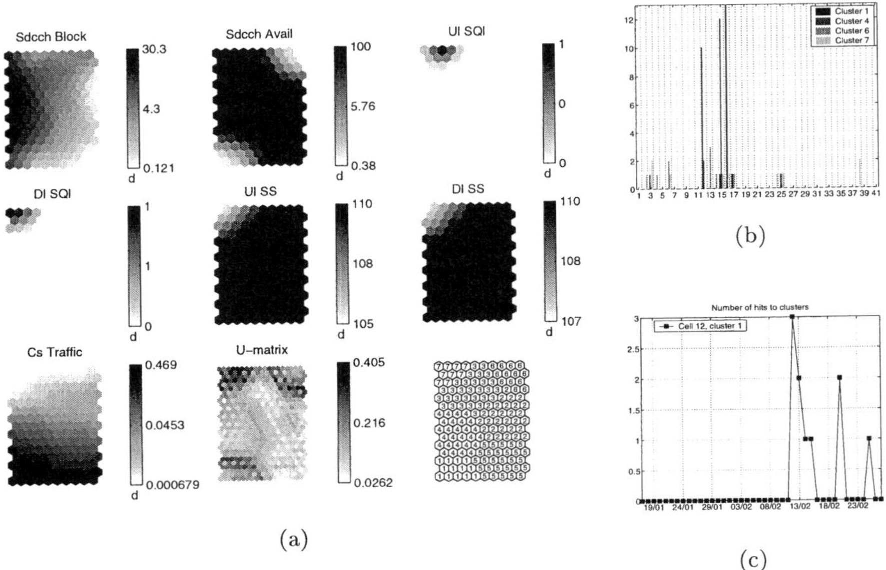

Fig. 2. (a) SOM of data samples representing possible signaling channel capacity problems. Clusters 1, 4, 6 and 7 represent possible signaling channel capacity problems. (b) Cells 12, 15 and 16 contribute the most to the fault clusters. (c) In cell 12, the failures appear mostly during a 4-day period

accuracy when data selection was not used. The PCA based projection performed equally well in both cases (with and without data selection).

In Figure 2(a), the so-called component planes of the SOM are shown. In order to visualize the cluster structure of the data, we clustered the map units of SOM using k-means clustering algorithm and plotted the resulted clustering with the U-matrix representation [8] of SOM. The numbers in the map units of SOM indicate the cluster memberships of the map units.

By analyzing the properties of each cluster using the component planes, four clusters that represent possible signaling channel capacity problems can be identified: cluster 4 contains high values for signaling channel blocking, with moderate amount of traffic. Clusters 1 and 6 represent behavior in which a drop in channel availability is likely to cause the high blocking values. Cluster 7 represents channel blockings that are likely to be a result of bad signal quality, i.e the connection is refused because the required channel quality could not be provided. The U-matrix reveals, that the clusters 1, 6 and 7 are located further apart from the other clusters.

By analyzing the number of hits into different fault clusters (see Figure 2(b)), it was evident that nearly all of the samples in the fault clusters were generated by only three cells of the network. Hits from other cells can be viewed instantaneous situations that do not give reasons to configuration adjustments and therefore can be ignored.

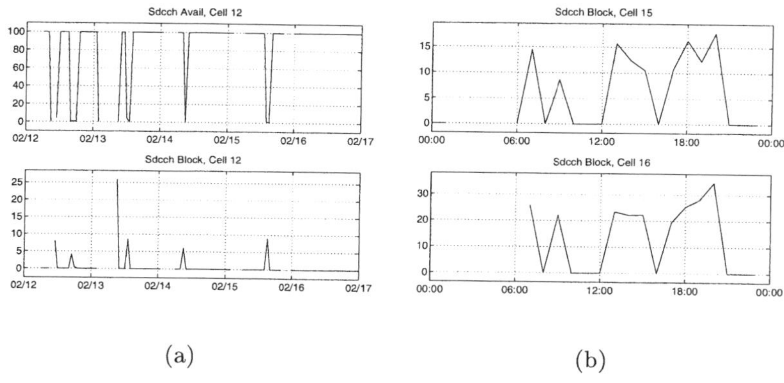

(a) (b)

Fig. 3. (a) In cell 12, peaks in signaling channel blocking appear during a drop in channel availability. (b) The blocking rates of the cells 15 and 16 are very correlating

When plotting the times of occurrences of the hits to the fault clusters from these three cells, it was found that the cell 12 had a 4-day period when most of the samples into fault cluster 1 were generated (see Figure 2(c)). This suggests that the signaling channel availability were temporarily reduced (i.e the amount of available channels dropped) and therefore, some of the channel requests were blocked. In order to verify this assumption, we plotted the signaling channel availability and blocking from that time period (see Figure 3(a)). According to this figure, it is even more clear that it is the drops in availability that causes the requests to be blocked.

Most of the samples of cluster 4 were generated by cells 15 and 16 (in the same site), suggesting that they suffer from signaling channel blocking at high amounts of users. In addition, these samples were generated mostly during one day. The signaling channel blockings of these cells from that day are shown in Figure 3(b). Clearly, the blocking rates of the two cells are strongly correlating. Such behavior can be due to a failure in a close-by cell, causing requests to originate from larger geographical area than normally. Therefore, the amount of channel requests is abnormally high. On the other hand, such increase in signaling channel traffic may also be caused by a configuration error leading to increased amount of location updates or paging traffic. It should be noted that the amounts of signaling traffic capacity problems in this network are relatively small (only less or equal to 10 hits per cell into any of the problem clusters).

3.2 Analysis of TCH Capacity Problems

In this experiment, we repeated the same analysis procedure for traffic channel data. The selected variables consisted of TCH blocking, dropping and availability rates, uplink and downling signal strengths as well as the amount of circuit switched data traffic. In addition, we applied the inequality constraint requiring that TCH Blocking > 0 % or TCH Drop Rate > 2 %.

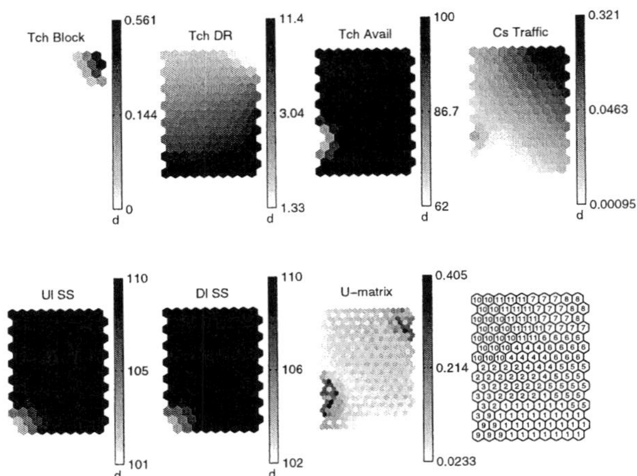

Fig. 4. The SOM of traffic channel capacity problems and the corresponding clusters on top of SOM

Then, a SOM was trained using the normalized data subset as the input data. The training procedure of SOM was similar to the one with the signaling channel data. Also, we trained SOMs with bigger map grids, but they did not provide any clear benefits over the map of size 15×10. When comparing the SOM based projection with the PCA and ICA projections, we found out that all the projections were equally good. The SOM based projection provided the worst values of trustworthiness measure with small neighborhoods, but the best values with large neighborhoods. Also, the ICA based projection gave worse values of preservation of neighborhoods as the size of the neighborhood increased. The importance of data selection in forming the projection function was not as clear as in the signaling channel capacity analysis. This is due to the fact that in the signaling channel capacity analysis, the data selection retained only 0.4 % of the samples, and in the traffic channel capacity analysis, the used data selection scheme retained up to 27 % of the samples.

In Figure 4, the SOM of the traffic channel capacity problems is shown with the corresponding clusters. From the figure, several fault clusters can be identified: cluster 1 represents samples with relatively high drop rate and low amount of traffic. Cluster 3 represents moderate amount of traffic channel drops and degraded traffic channel availability. In cluster 8, blocking appears with relatively high amount of traffic. Cluster 9 contains samples with high drop rate, low uplink and downlink signal strengths, and low amount of traffic.

Similarly to the signaling channel capacity analysis, the contributions of the cells into these clusters were analyzed. In the analysis, it was found that cells 39 and 9 generated many samples into cluster 3, stating that they suffer from call dropping due to low availability. By plotting the drop rate and channel availability as time series for both cells (not shown), it became clear that the drop rates in these cells were in the same level also when the availability was full.

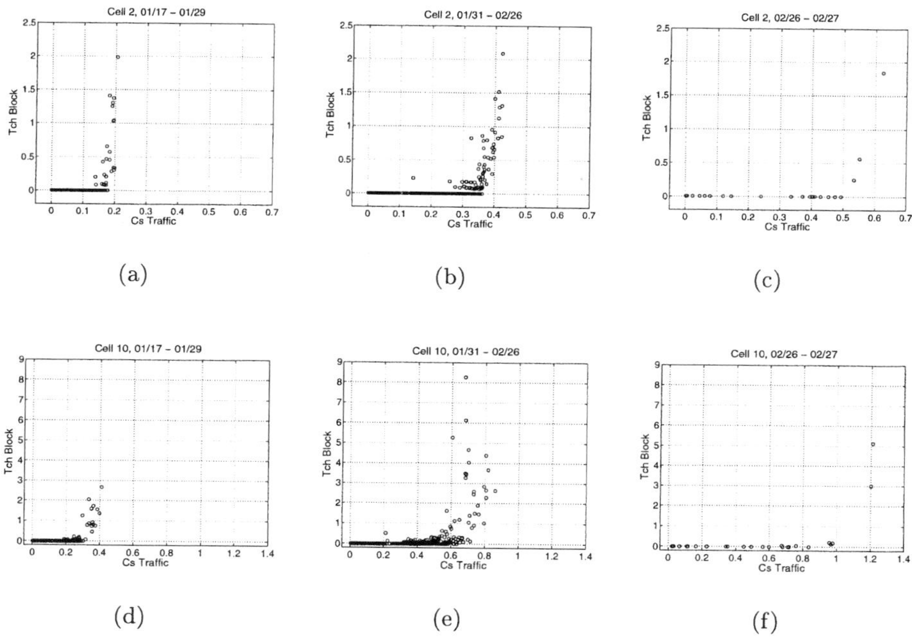

Fig. 5. The amount of traffic channel blocking at different amounts of traffic in cells 2 and 10. In these cells, the capacity is increased twice during the analyzed period

Therefore, the call dropping is not likely to be caused by the reduced channel availability. However, it is interesting that these problems appear simultaneously in these cells (see Figure 6(a)) and that they were located on nearly overlapping coverage areas.

Cells 2 and 10 generated most of the samples in cluster 8, i.e they seem to suffer from blocking at high amounts of traffic. The amount of resources (frequencies) may not be appropriate for these cells. They did not suffer from signal quality or channel availability problems, and therefore, the blockings are exclusively due to insufficient resources. Figure 5 shows the amount of blocking vs. the amount of traffic of these cells in three different time periods. In Figures 5(a) and (d), the first time period is shown. It is clear that the blockings start to increase when the amount of traffic in cell 2 is more than 0.15 Erlangs and in cell 10, more than 0.25 Erlangs. However, during the next time period shown in Figures 5(b) and (e), the blockings start to appear when the amount of traffic exceeds 0.3 Erlangs in cell 2 and 0.5 Erlangs in cell 10. It seems likely that the amounts of resources were increased between these two periods. However, blocking still appears. In Figures 5(c) and (f), the third time period is shown. This time period lasts only two days, but the same behavior seems to continue: blocking starts to appear when the amount of traffic exceeds 0.5 Erlangs in cell 2 and 1.0 Erlangs in cell 10.

Cells 6 and 26 generated most of the samples in cluster 9, indicating that they suffer from call dropping when the received signal strengths were low and the amount of traffic was low. Further analysis revealed that the low signal strengths did not explain the amount of dropping, since the variation in signal strengths did not cause variation in drop rates. Also, if low signal strength would have caused traffic channel dropping, power control should have increased the power levels in order to place it at appropriate level. Instead, these cells behave similarly to cells 4, 7, 12, 13, 18, 24, 26, 39, 40 and 41 that generated a lot of samples into cluster 1. Cluster 1 is essentially similar to the cluster 9, except the higher signal strength levels.

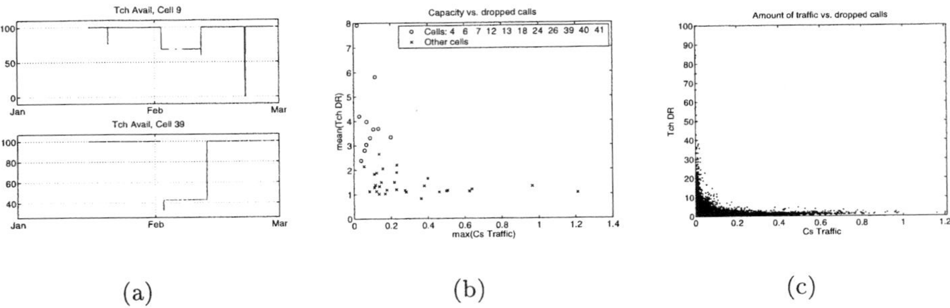

Fig. 6. (a) The drop in traffic channel availability in cells 9 and 39 was not explaining the inadequate drop rate values. Instead, the drop rate levels were high constantly. Interestingly, the channel availabilities dropped simultaneously in both cells. (b) The cells with lowest capacity tend to suffer from higher drop rates. (c) The highest drop rates occur at very low amount of traffic. This behavior is common to all cells

The key observation here is that all these cells suffer from high drop rates at low amount of traffic. There are at least two reasons that might explain this behavior. First, the so-called microcells characterized by low power levels, low capacity and small coverage areas are frequently positioned to cover the busiest locations such as city areas. Often, such areas also represent the most difficult propagation environments and the highest user mobility, causing serious variations in radio channel conditions. In Figure 6(b), the capacity of the cells (measured as maximum amount of traffic observed in the data) is plotted against the average drop rate. From the figure it is clear, that highest average drop rates are observed in the cells that also have the smallest capacity. As mentioned before, such small capacity cells are frequently used in hot-spot areas where user mobility is high and propagation conditions are difficult. Therefore, the call dropping in these cells are probably caused by physical constraints of the environment and it might be difficult to achieve better performance in such cells.

Secondly, it is evident that the highest drop rate values are observed when the amount of traffic is close to zero (see Figure 6(c)). When the amount of calls is very low, a drop of only a few connections may cause very high drop rates. This is due to the fact that the formula used to generate the traffic channel drop rate from several low-level counters exaggerates the seriousness of the fault at low number of calls during the measurement period. The inaccuracy of the traffic channel drop rate causes similar behavior in all cells, but is obviously more frequently present in the cells with higher drop rates at all amounts of traffic.

It can be concluded, that the traffic channel problems are much more regular than the signaling channel problems. The traffic channel problem clusters are hit about 50 - 500 times and the signaling channel problem clusters were hit at most 13 times. The most typical problem type was traffic channel dropping in low capacity cells.

4 Conclusion

In this paper, a SOM based approach to visualize GSM network performance data was presented. This visualization process allowed us to efficiently locate the problem cells and find the times of occurrences of problems, and to select the appropriate variables in order to continue the analysis by conventional analysis methods. By visualizing all the possible variable pairs over the whole time period from all the cells would have produced a very high number of graphs, making the manual analysis of such results unfeasible. Therefore, the use of the proposed analysis process helped to achieve a higher degree of efficiency in the analysis of multi-dimensional GSM network performance data.

References

1. D. L. Davies and D. W. Bouldin. A cluster separation measure. *IEEE Transactions on Pattern Analysis and Machine Intelligence*, 1(2):224–227, April 1979.
2. Brian Everitt. *Cluster Analysis.* Arnold, 1993.
3. Simon Haykin. *Neural Networks: a comprehensive foundation, 2nd edition.* Prentice-Hall, Inc., 1999.
4. A. Hyvärinen, J. Karhunen, and E. Oja. *Independent Component Analysis.* John Wiley and Sons., 2001.
5. Teuvo Kohonen. *Self-Organizing Maps, 3rd edition.* Springer, 2001.
6. Jaana Laiho, Kimmo Raivio, Pasi Lehtimäki, Kimmo Hätönen, and Olli Simula. Advanced analysis methods for 3G cellular networks. *IEEE Transactions on Wireless Communications (accepted)*, 2004.
7. Jaana Laiho, Achim Wacker, and Tomáš Novosad, editors. *Radio Network Planning and Optimisation for UMTS.* John Wiley & Sons, Ltd, 2002.
8. A. Ultsch and H. P. Siemon. Kohonen's self-organizing feature maps for exploratory data analysis. In *Proceedings of the International Neural Network Conference (INNC 90)*, 1990.
9. Jarkko Venna and Samuel Kaski. Neighborhood preservation in nonlinear projection methods: an experimental study. In *Proceedings of the International Conference on Artificial Neural Networks (ICANN)*, pages 485–491, 2001.

10. Juha Vesanto. Som-based data visualization methods. *Intelligent Data Analysis*, 3(2):111–126, 1999.
11. Juha Vesanto and Esa Alhoniemi. Clustering of the self-organizing map. *IEEE Transactions on Neural Networks*, 11(3):586–600, May 2000.
12. Jens Zander. *Radio Resource Management for Wireless Networks*. Artech House, Inc., 2001.

Using an Artificial Neural Network to Improve Predictions of Water Levels Where Tide Charts Fail

Carl Steidley, Alex Sadovski, Phillipe Tissot, Ray Bachnak, and Zack Bowles

Texas A&M University–Corpus Christi,
6300 Ocean Dr.
Corpus Christi, TX 78412
steidley@falcon.tamucc.edu

Abstract. Tide tables are the method of choice for water level predictions in most coastal regions. In the United States, the National Ocean Service (NOS) uses harmonic analysis and time series of previous water levels to compute tide tables. This method is adequate for most locations along the US coast. However, for many locations along the coast of the Gulf of Mexico, tide tables do not meet NOS criteria. Wind forcing has been recognized as the main variable not included in harmonic analysis. The performance of the tide charts is particularly poor in shallow embayments along the coast of Texas. Recent research at Texas A&M University-Corpus Christi has shown that Artificial Neural Network (ANN) models including input variables such as previous water levels, tidal forecasts, wind speed, wind direction, wind forecasts and barometric pressure can greatly improve water level predictions at several coastal locations including open coast and deep embayment stations. In this paper, the ANN modeling technique was applied for the first time to a shallow embayment, the station of Rockport located near Corpus Christi, Texas. The ANN performance was compared to the NOS tide charts and the persistence model for the years 1997 to 2001. This site was ideal because it is located in a shallow embayment along the Texas coast and there is an 11-year historical record of water levels and meteorological data in the Texas Coastal Ocean Observation Network (TCOON) database. The performance of the ANN model was measured using NOS criteria such as Central Frequency (CF), Maximum Duration of Positive Outliers (MDPO), and Maximum Duration of Negative Outliers (MDNO). The ANN model compared favorably to existing models using these criteria and is the best predictor of future water levels tested.

1 Introduction

In recent years the importance of marine activities has grown steadily. With the growth of the economy, the shipping industry has seen its activity increase leading to a push towards larger and deeper draft vessels. The operation of such vessels in ports where shallow water is a concern would greatly benefit from accurate advanced water level related information. Coastal communities would greatly benefit from such forecasts as well. A comparison of measured water levels with tidal forecasts is

M. Ali and F. Esposito (Eds.): IEA/AIE 2005, LNAI 3533, pp. 599 – 608, 2005.

presented in Fig. 1. The Division of Nearshore Research (DNR) at Texas A&M University–Corpus Christi has taken on two main tasks: the design of a model that will provide more accurate results than the currently relied upon tide charts, and to make the results from this model accessible to the marine community.

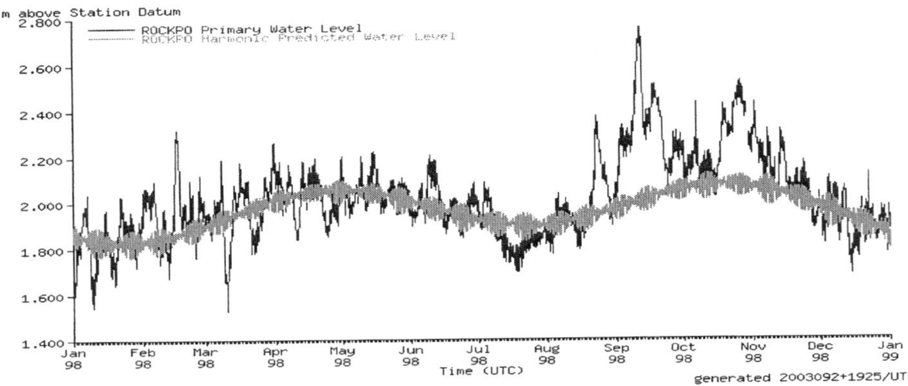

Fig. 1. Comparison of the Rockport Tide Chart predictions (gray) and the actual water level measurements (black) in 1998. (Notice the discrepancy between the predicted and actual values.)

The area of interest for this work is Rockport, TX., a coastal community of 7385 people, with a maximum elevation of only two meters. In general, all tourist activities, restaurants, and entertainment facilities are located near the water, no more than a few inches above the water level in Aransas Bay, a particularly shallow embayment (See Fig. 2).

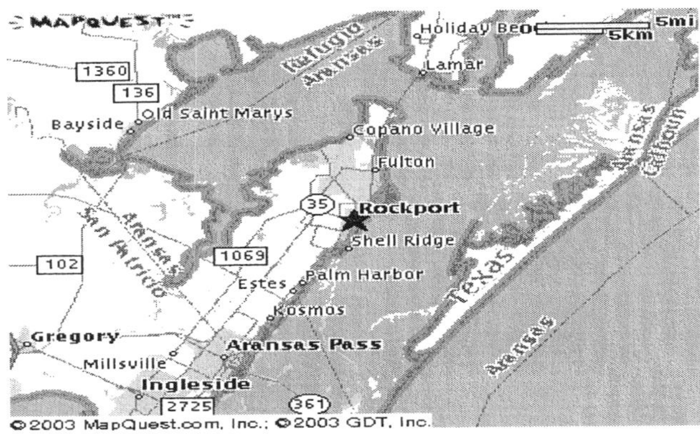

Fig. 2. Rockport, TX. The city is located 35 miles from Corpus Christi, one of the nations most active ports

Several approaches have been considered to solve the task of providing a more accurate model. This paper is focused on Artificial Neural Networks (ANN), which to date, have provided more accurate results for open coast and deeper embayments, but had not been tested for such shallow embayment. The ANN took into account the astronomical tide information in addition to time series of measured water levels, wind speeds and wind directions and barometric pressures.

The input data had been queried from data compiled for more than 10 years in the real-time database of the TCOON [2] (See Figs. 3,4). The models were trained over large data sets, and all the results were then compared using the National Ocean Service skill assessment statistics, with an emphasis on the Central Frequency. Central Frequency is the ratio of predictions that are within plus or minus X cm from the actual measurement. For NOS to consider a model operational, its Central Frequency of 15 cm must be equal or greater than 90%. The tide charts (the current method of water level predictions) for the entire coast of Texas did not pass the standard. The deficiency of the tide charts and the reason for the deficiency are known by the National Oceanic and Atmospheric Administration (NOAA). As the agency has stated, "...presently published predictions do not meet working standards" when assessing the performance of the tide charts for Aransas Pass, Texas [3].

The first test for a new model to be accepted is that it must improve upon the performance of a benchmark model called the persisted difference or "Persistence" model. The persistence model relies on the inference that a presently observed distance between the tide chart prediction and the actual water level will persist into the future. The Persistence model basically takes an offset and applies it to the tide charts for the prediction. It is simple and yet considerably more effective than the tide charts in predicting water levels along the Texas Gulf coast. Once this benchmark was incorporated, the objective shifted to the development and assessment of an ANN model applied to various locations along the Gulf Coast and within shallow estuaries and embayments.

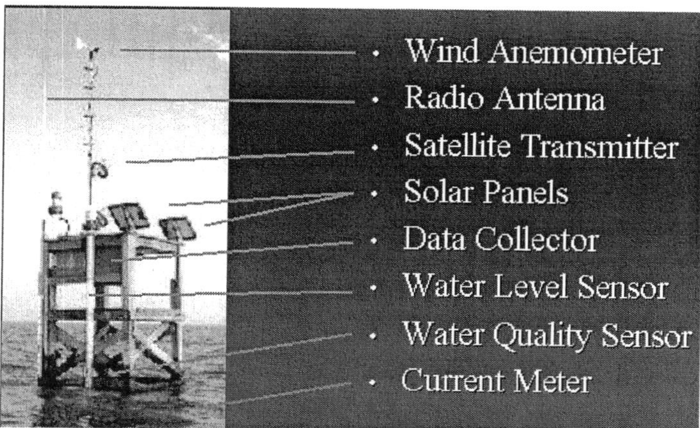

Fig. 3. A typical TCOON station. Each station records a variety of time series data then transmits the data to the TCOON database

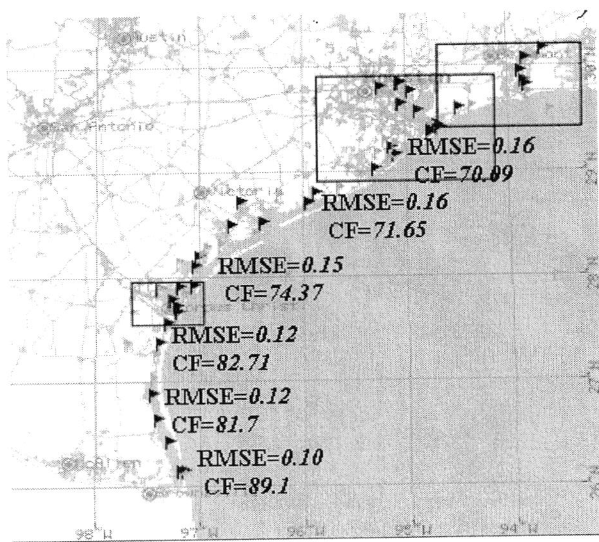

Fig. 4. Comparison of six coastal stations and their respective RMSE and Central Frequency for the tide charts. The NOS standard is 90%, and the best value is 89.1%

2 Site Description, Model Topology, and Training

Rockport, Texas, the central area of interest for this paper, is most directly affected by Aransas Bay, which is linked to the Gulf of Mexico through Aransas Pass (See Fig. 2). The barrier island protecting Rockport from the effects of the Gulf is called San Jose Island, which is also connected to Matagorda Island. The shallow waters between the barrier islands and the Rockport coastline lead to a delay between the observed water level trends in the Gulf and in Rockport. In general, what is observed in the Gulf takes a few hours to register in the affected bays. Most of the directly observed water level changes had been correlated with strong winds and frontal passages [3, 4]. This made it important to test the inclusion of winds as part of the input to the ANN model, but many other factors must also be considered. The presently used ANN model includes previous water levels measurements, tidal forecasts, previous wind speed and wind direction measurements, wind forecasts, and barometric pressure. A schematic of the model is presented in Fig. 5. Although a plethora of other time series data is available, it was shown by way of factor analysis that only a few components were actually necessary to model the water level changes [1]. Five years of hourly data between 1997 and 2001 were chosen to train and test the ANN model. Less than 2% of the data was missing for each of the data series (See Table 1) used in this work except for the Bob Hall Pier 1999 data set where 2.2% of the wind data was missing. The gaps were filled by linear interpolation within the

Table 1. Availability of data for the Rockport station from 1996-2001, and a summary of the missing data

Data Set Year	Data Set Span	Data Available	%pwl Missing	Max Dur Miss Data (pwl)
Rockport				
Data is hourly				
1996	1/1/96 - 12/31/96	pwl, wtp, harmwl, sig	**1.40%**	112 pts.
1997	1/1/97 – 12/31/97	pwl, wtp, harmwl, sig	**0.53%**	22 pts.
1998	1/1/98 – 12/31/98	pwl, wtp, harmwl, sig	**0.43%**	23 pts.
1999	1/1/99 – 12/31/99	pwl, wtp, harmwl, sig	**0.13%**	4 pts.
2000	1/1/00 – 12/31/00	pwl, wtp, harmwl, sig	**0.14%**	7 pts.
2001	1/1/01 – 12/31/01	pwl, wtp, harmwl, sig	**0.05%**	1 pt.

gaps for wind data and for water level gaps, the tidal component of the water level was first subtracted, then the gap was filled by interpolation, and finally the tidal component was added back in. All water level measurements were in reference to mean low water levels because the main audience for our predictions is ship captains, and many nautical charts use this as their reference point. The tidal forecasts, water levels, and all meteorological data were downloaded from the TCOON database. The tide forecasts were computed using a years worth of water level data and 26 harmonic constituents, using NOAA procedures. The information from the different inputs was scaled to a [-1.1, 1.1] range and inserted into the first or hidden layer of the ANN (See Fig. 5). A set of random numbers was picked to start the training process, then weights and biases were progressively optimized to adjust to the desired output or target. The number of layers could be varied with each case, but previous studies in Galveston Bay and Corpus Christi Bay showed that simple ANN using only one hidden and one output layer to be the most effective [5].

All ANN models had been developed, trained, tested, and assessed in a MatLab R13 environment and using the Neural Network Toolbox. The computers using MatLab ranged in processor speed from 450 MHz to 2.6 GHz. The Levenberg-Marquardt algorithm was used to train the model. The model was trained over one year of data, then applied to the other four years to create five training sets and twenty testing sets. The average performances were computed over the testing sets. The effectiveness of the models were determined using the National Ocean Service skill assessment statistics (See Table 2).

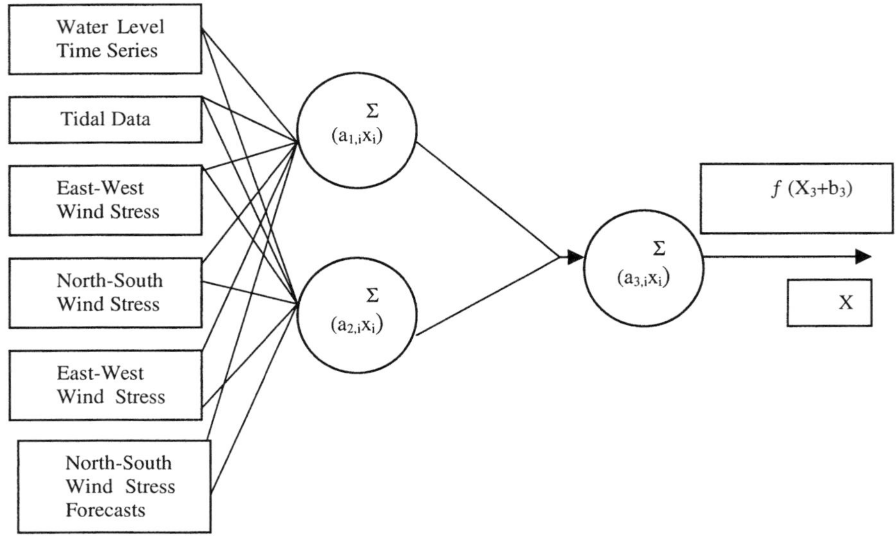

Fig. 5. Schematic of Artificial Neural Network Model

3 Optimization and Application

The first step in the optimization of the Artificial Neural Network was to find the number of previous water levels optimizing the accuracy of the water level forecasts. The average Central Frequency (CF) was used to evaluate the accuracy of the forecast. Previous water levels were added to the model in increments of three previous hours until the optimum CF was reached for that forecast, then the same process was repeated for increased forecasting times. Once the optimum number of previous water levels was found, the typical methodology would have been to include previous winds. However, since the database for the Rockport station did not have wind data for the period of this study this step was eliminated. The next step in the optimization was to find the best number of previous water levels for another nearby station. We decided to use the Bob Hall Pier, an open coast station. The same process was used for these previous water levels until the best combination of water levels from Bob Hall Pier and Rockport was found. Then, using the optimal water levels from Rockport, the third station, Port Aransas, was also evaluated. Once again, previous water levels were increased until the optimum number was found. Bob Hall Pier and Port Aransas have complete wind data, so once the optimal water levels were established, the winds for these stations could be incorporated into the model. Previous winds were added in the same fashion aswater levels: increasing the number of previous winds by three hours at a time until the optimum or 48 previous hours is reached. The final step in the optimization was incorporating the wind forecasts. In the operational models the wind forecasts will be provided by the National Center for Environmental Predictions (NCEP) Eta-12 of this study, wind forecasts were created

Table 2. NOS Skill assessment statistics. (The Central Frequency is the main performance assessment)

Error	The predicted value p minus the observed value r
SM	Series Mean; the mean value of a time series y
RMSE	Root Mean Square Error
SD	Standard Deviation
CF(X)	**Central Frequency; % of errors within the limits of -X and X**
POF(2X)	Positive Outlier Frequency; % of errors greater than X
NOF(2X)	Negative Outlier Frequency; % of errors less than –X
MDPO(2X)	Maximum Duration of Positive Outliers
MDNO(2X)	Maximum Duration of Negative Outliers

using the actual wind measurements. The performance of the ANN for the Rockport station was significantly improved when the wind forecasts from Bob Hall Pier were included, but not when including wind forecasts from the Port Aransas station. Changing the number of neurons was also a possibility in finding the optimized model, but previous studies showed no significant improvement in the results [6]. In general more accurate forecasts were observed when larger numbers of previous water levels were used. The optimal ANN model changes slightly for different forecast times, but in general, using 24 hours of previous water levels at Rockport, 24 hours of previous water levels at Bob Hall Pier, and 12 hours of previous wind speeds and wind directions at Bob Hall Pier lead to the most accurate water level forecasts without using wind forecasts. This model resulted in a CF(15 cm) of 99.59% for a 3-hour forecast, 99.20% for a 12-hour forecast, 97.85% for a 24-hour forecast, and 91.33% for a 48-hour forecast. Even for a two-day water level forecast, the model stays about 1.3% above the NOS criteria for a successful model or 90%. The tide charts, however had a CF(15 cm) of 85%, and the Persistence Model, 87.18% for 48-hour forecasts. Both of which were below the standard for a NOS acceptable model. Adding the Bob Hall Pier wind forecasts to the model increased the CF by 3.6%, which emphasized the importance of having wind forecasts available for the operational model.

4 Discussion

The performance of the ANN at the Rockport station showed significant improvement over all other discussed models. The 91.33% CF for 48-hour forecasts is a significant improvement over the other models considered (85% for the tide charts and 87%

forthe Persistence model). It was interesting to find that data from Bob Hall Pier was more helpful in improving forecasts than data at Port Aransas. Since geographically, Port Aransas is closer to Rockport and Port Aransas, like Rockport, is shielded from the Gulf of Mexico by the barrier islands.

The importance of winds can be observed in the increase in accuracy when this information is added to the model. A 0.4% increase in CF was observed when wind data was incorporated, and although this seems like a small difference, practically this represents an additional day and a half for which the predictions will be within the ± 15cm range. When wind forecasts were used there was a 3.6% increase in effectiveness, which corresponds to an additional 13 days of acceptable water level predictions. Archived wind forecasts were not available throughout this research, so the forecasts were obtained from actual measurements. The real-time model will utilize the Eta-12 wind forecast database, made available through a collaboration with the Corpus Christi Weather forecasting Office [7]. These forecasts have already been tested in a separate study of three local stations: Bob Hall Pier, Naval Air Station, and Port Aransas [8]. This study and a related study on Galveston Island showed that the difference between wind forecasts and wind measurements was not significant for the model, and that the water level predictions were not significantly affected by the likely differences between forecasts and measurements. Incorporating accurate wind forecasts will be particularly important when predicting water levels during frontal passages. The ANN has difficulty in catching very rapid changes in water levels without the association of wind forecasts during sudden changes in wind speeds and wind directions.

5 Conclusions

The Rockport station was the first of the TCOON shallow water stations upon which ANN models were tested. The results showed that the ANN outperforms all present models for the Rockport station [2]. The tide charts and the Persistence models do not meet the NOS criteria, while the Linear Regression model and the Neural Network Models (one with wind forecasts and one without) showed accuracy above the 90% CF criteria with the ANN model including wind forecasts having the best performance at 94.5%. The effectiveness of the model shows that a strong correlation can be established between water level forecasts and meteorological factors. The optimal model is a combination of the previous water levels at both Rockport and Bob Hall Pier, and previous wind information from the same coastal station. In this case, 24 hours of previous water levels at both Rockport and Bob Hall Pier, and 12 hours of previous winds at Bob Hall Pier. Wind forecasts significantly improve the water level forecasts and efforts are being made to incorporate Eta-12 wind information into the model. The simplicity and effectiveness of the tested Artificial Neural Network models has shown that this powerful and flexible modeling technique have benefited the marine community since the predictions of these models were made available on the World Wide Web in late Fall, 2003.

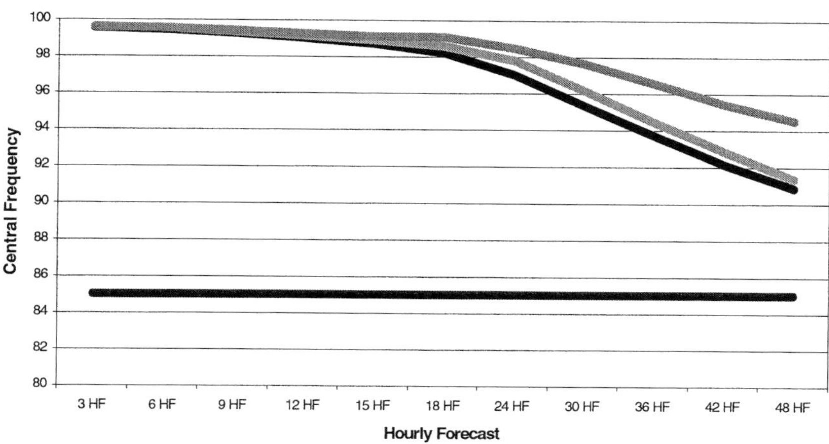

Fig. 6. The effects of the inclusion of wind forecasts. The top line is the ANN model using Rockport previous water levels, Bob Hall Pier previous water levels and wind measurements, and Bob Hall Pier wind forecasts, which led to an increase in CF(15cm) of 3.5%. The second line is using information from Port Aransas, and the third line is using information from Rockport only. The bottom line is the tide chart prediction

Acknowledgements

NASA Grant # NCC5-517

References

1. Sadovski, A. L., C. Steidley, A. Mostella, P.Tissot, "Statistical and Neural Network Modeling and Predictions of Tides in the Shallow Waters of the Gulf of Mexico," WSEAS Transactions on Systems, Issue 8, vol. 3, WSEAS Press, pp.2686-2694.
2. Michaud P. R., G. Jeffress, R. Dannelly, and C. Steidley, "Real-Time Data Collection and the Texas Coastal Ocean Observation Network," Proceedings of Intermac '01 Joint Technical Conference, Tokyo, Japan, 2001.
3. NOAA, 1991: NOAA Technical Memorandum NOS OMA 60. National Oceanic and Atmospheric Administration, Silver Spring, Maryland.
4. Garvine R., "A Simple Model of Estuarine Subtidal Fluctuations Forced by Local and Remote Wind Stress," Journal Geophysical Research, **90(C6)**, 11945-11948, 1985.
5. Tissot P.E., D.T. Cox, and P. Michaud, "Neural Network Forecasting of Storm Surges along the Gulf of Mexico," Proceedings of the Fourth International Symposium on Ocean Wave Measurement and Analysis (Waves '01), 1535-1544, 2002.
6. Tissot, P.E., P. R. Michaud, and D. T. Cox, "Optimization and Performance of a Neural Network Model Forecasting Water Levels for the Corpus Christi, Texas, Estuary," 3rd Conference on the Applications of Artificial Intelligence to Environmental Science, Long Beach, California, February 2003.

7. Patrick, A.R., Collins, W.G., Tissot, P.E., Drikitis, A., Stearns, J., Michaud, P.R., "Use of the NCEP MesoEta Data in a water Level Predicting Neural Network," Proceedings of the 19th AMS Conference on Weather Analysis and Forecasting/15th AMS Conference on Numerical Weather Prediction, 369-372, San Antonio, Texas, August 2002,.
8. Stearns, J., P. E. Tissot, P. R. Michaud, A. R. Patrick, and W. G. Collins, "Comparison of MesoEta Wind Forecasts with TCOON Measurements along the Coast of Texas," Proceedings of the 19th AMS Conference on Weather Analysis and Forecasting/15th AMS Conf. on Numerical Weather Prediction, J141-J144, August 2002, San Antonio, Texas.

Canonical Decision Model Construction by Extracting the Mapping Function from Trained Neural Networks[1]

Chien-Chang Hsu and Yun-Chen Lee

Department of Computer Science and Information Engineering,
Fu-Jen Catholic University,
510 Chung Cheng Rd., Hsinchuang, Taipei, Taiwan 242

Abstract. This work proposes a decision model construction process by extracting the mapping function from the trained neural model. The construction process contains three tasks, namely, data preprocessing, hyperplane extraction, and decision model translation. The data preprocessing uses the correlation coefficient and canonical analysis for projecting the input vector into the canonical feature space. The hyperplane extraction uses the canonical feature space to train the neural networks and extracts the hyperplanes from the trained neural model. The genetic algorithm is used to adjust the slop and reduce the number of hyperplanes. The decision model translation uses the elliptical canonical model to formulate the preliminary decision model. Finally, the genetic algorithm is used again to optimize the canonical decision model.

1 Introduction

Decision modeling is a key element in most decision support systems. It has been used to support the decision maker in selecting different alternative during decision activity. However, the decision model development is not a simple task. It must capture enough of the reality to make it useful for the decision makers. Many methods have been proposed for developing the decision model, such as, optimization, statistical estimation, decision tree, linear programming, decision theory, and simulation. However, the traditional methods contain the following shortcomings. First, the decision modeling can be cumbersome if there are many alternatives or goals need to choice. The large amount of data may cause the analysis task become intractable. Moreover, the generalization ability of the decision model is also another problem for solving unseen situations. Exceptions may cause the fragile decision model. Finally, an optimal solution may not guarantee to be generated through the modeling process.

Neural networks are endowed with the parallel-distributed capability that can be used to modeling the large amount of data and generating the optimal solutions for the decision makers. This work proposes a decision model construction process by extracting the mapping function from the trained neural networks. The construction

[1] This project is partly supported by National Science Council of ROC under grants NSC 93-2745-E-030-004-URD.

M. Ali and F. Esposito (Eds.): IEA/AIE 2005, LNAI 3533, pp. 609 – 612, 2005.

process contains three tasks, namely, data preprocessing, hyperplane extraction, and decision model translation. The data preprocessing uses the correlation coefficient and canonical analysis to project the input vector into the canonical feature space. The hyperplane extraction uses the canonical feature space to train the neural networks and extracts hyperplanes from the trained neural networks. The decision model translation uses the elliptical canonical model to build the preliminary decision model. Finally, the genetic algorithm is used to optimize the canonical decision model.

2 Decision Model Construction

The decision model construction contains three main tasks, namely, data preprocessing, hyperplane extraction, and decision model translation. The data preprocessing projects the input data into the canonical feature space. The data preprocessing uses the correlation coefficient analysis to find the variable with the maximum correlation coefficient as the decision attribute. The data preprocessing then uses the decision attribute to sort the data in ascending order. The sorting process generates a maximum distance between different set of data. Moreover, the data preprocessing uses the maximum summation of correlation coefficient between the classes to partition the variables into two clusters. The data preprocessing then unifies the variables in each cluster into a canonical attributes [1]. The hyperplane extraction then uses the reduced canonical data to train the neural networks. The hyperplane extraction extracts the hyperplanes from the trained neural networks. The hyperplane extraction uses the weights between the input and hidden layer of the feedforwad neural networks. Moreover, the hyperplane extraction uses the genetic algorithm to adjust the slop and reduce the number of hyperpalnes. The decision model translation constructs use the elliptical canonical model to construct the elliptical canonical model. The decision model translation uses the elliptical shapes to cover the canonical data in the hyperplanes decision regions. Finally, the decision model translation then uses the genetic algorithm to optimize the canonical decision model.

3 Data Preprocessing

The data preprocessing conducts two subtasks, namely, data classification and canonical analysis transformation. The data classification uses the correlation coefficient analysis to do the data sorting and data clustering. First, the data sorting computes the coefficient dependence between attributes to construct the correlation coefficient matrix. It selects the attribute with the maximum correlation coefficient as the decision attribute. It then uses the decision attribute to sort the data in ascending order. The sorting process generates a maximum distance between different set of data. Specifically, the data sorting computes the maximum correlation summation value of each attribute in the attribute correlation coefficient matrix [2]. Moreover, the data clustering uses the correlation coefficient analysis again to find the maximum distance between two classes that are far away [2]. Finally, the canonical analysis transformation unifies the attributes of each cluster into canonical attributes. The canonical formula, C_1 and C_2, transforms the variables in each cluster into the following formula.

$$C_1 = s_1u_1 + s_2u_2 + s_3u_3 + s_4u_4 \tag{1}$$

$$C_2 = t_1v_1 + t_2v_2 + t_3v_3 + t_4v_4 \tag{2}$$

where u_i and v_i are the ith variable in the cluster 1 and 2, s_i and t_i are the ith canonical coefficient of the canonical attribute 1 and 2.

4 Hyperplane Extraction

The hyperplane extraction is responsible to train the neural networks and extract the hyperplanes from the trained neural networks. The neural networks training uses the reduced canonical data to train the neural networks. The hyperplane extraction then uses the weights between the input and hidden layers of the trained feedforward neural networks to construct the hyperplanes. The hperplanes can be extracted from the hidden layer of the feedforward neural networks directly. It partitions the input space into many decision regions. The genetic algorithm is used to refine these hyperplanes. It adjusts the slope or reduces the number of the hyperplanes to achieve better classification. Fist, it simplifies the variables in the hyperplane formula into two for reducing the number of chromosome by Eq. 3.

$$x_1 + s_j x_2 - t_j = 0 \tag{3}$$

where s_j and t_j are the normalized coefficients. The chromosome then uses binary value to represent the hyperplane variables. Ultimately, the genetic algorithm uses the crossover and mutation operators to optimize the slope of the hyperplanes [2].

5 Decision Model Transformation

The decision model construction conducts two subtasks, namely, canonical model transformation and canonical decision model optimization. The canonical model transformation is responsible for transforming the decision regions from the trained neural model into the elliptical canonical model. The shape of the decision region is a polygon divided by the hyperplanes. The elliptical canonical model transformation then uses the coordination of each vertex for transforming the polygon into a elliptical canonical model. The ellipse model can represent the data distribution in the decision regions using the following equation.

$$\left(\frac{(x-h)\cos\theta-(y-k)\sin\theta}{a}\right)^2+\left(\frac{(x-h)\sin\theta+(y-k)\cos\theta}{b}\right)^2-1=0 \tag{4}$$

where h and k are the center of the ellipse, a, b, and θ are the length of the semi-major ellipse axis, the length of semi-minor ellipse axis, and the ellipse angle rotated clockwise [2]. The angle degree of the ellipse ranges between of $-\pi/2$ and $\pi/2$. The canonical neural model then uses the elliptical pattern to cover the data in each decision boundary. A polygon is transformed into an ellipse. The center of the ellipse is the center of the polygon. Eq. 5, 6, 7, and 8 represent the transformation of above, where a and b are the length of semi-major axis and the length of semi-minor axis of ellipse [2]. Finally, the genetic algorithm is used to refine the accuracy of the canonical neural model.

$$(h,k)=\left(\frac{\sum_{i}^{m}x_i}{m},\frac{\sum_{i}^{m}y_i}{m}\right) \tag{5}$$

$$a=\frac{\max(x_i)-\min(x_i)}{2} \tag{6}$$

$$b=\frac{\max(y_i)-\min(y_i)}{2} \tag{7}$$

$$\theta=\cos^{-1}\frac{T}{(S^2+T^2)^{1/2}} \tag{8}$$

6 Conclusions

This work proposes a decision model construction process by extracting the mapping function from the trained neural model. The construction process contains three tasks, namely, data preprocessing, hyperplane extraction, and decision model translation. The proposed canonical decision model construction system exhibits the following interesting features. First, the system projects the training data into the canonical feature space for reducing the dimension complexity. The decision model can be interpreted by human directly in the feature space. This method is much the same as the kernel function used in the support vector machine. Moreover, the system unlocks the mapping function black box in the neural networks. The system uses the canonical model to represent the mapping function of the neural networks. The canonical decision model uses elliptical shapes to cover the problem decision regions. The modeling is performed according to the construction process of canonical decision model. Finally, the proposed system uses the genetic algorithm to adjust the slope of the hyperplanes and elliptical shapes in the decision region, regarded as changing the synaptic weights in a neural model. The optimization process enhances the accuracy and generalization ability of the decision model.

References

1. Kuss, M., Graepel, T.,: The Geometry of Kernel Canonical Correlation Analysis. Max Planck Institute for Biological Cybernetics Technical Report, 108 (2003) Available at http://www.kyb.tuebingen.mpg.de/techreports.html
2. Lee, Y. C.,: The Design and Implementation of Transplant Neural Networks Modeling. Master Thesis, Fu-Jen Catholic University Taiwan (2004)

Detecting Fraud in Mobile Telephony Using Neural Networks

H. Grosser, P. Britos, and R. García-Martínez

Intelligent Systems Laboratory. School of Engineering, University of Buenos Aires,
Software & Knowledge Engineering Center (CAPIS) Graduate School, ITBA,
Computer Science PhD Program, Computer Science School, University of La Plata
rgm@itba.edu.ar

Abstract. Our work focuses on: the problem of detecting unusual changes of consumption in mobile phone users, the corresponding building of data structures which represent the recent and historic users' behaviour bearing in mind the information included in a call, and the complexity of the construction of a function with so many variables where the parameterization is not always known.

1 Description of the Problem

The existing systems of fraud detection try to consult sequences of CDR's (Call Detail Records) by comparing any field function with fixed criteria known as Triggers. A trigger, when activated, sends an alarm which leads to fraud analysts' investigation. These systems make what are known as a CDR's absolute analysis and they are used to detect the extremes of fraudulent activity. To make a differential analysis, patterns of behavior of the mobile phone are monitored by comparing the most recent activities to the historic use of the phone; a change in the pattern of behavior is a suspicious characteristic of a fraudulent act. In order to build a system of fraud detection based on a differential analysis it is necessary to bear in mind different problems: (a) the problem of building and maintaining "users' profiles" and (b) the problem of detecting changes in behavior. Pointing the first problem, in a system of differential fraud detection, information about the history together with samples of the most recent activities is necessary. An initial attempt to solve the problem could be to extract and encode Call Detail Records (CDR) information and store it in a given format of record. To do this, two types of records are needed; one, which we shall call CUP (Current User Profile) to store the most recent information, and another, to be called UPH (User Profile History) with the historic information [1, 2]. When a new CDR of a certain user arrives in order to be processed, the oldest arrival of the UPH record should be discarded and the oldest arrival of the CUP should enter the UPH. Therefore, this new, encoded record should enter CUP. It is necessary to find a way to "classify" these calls into groups or prototypes where each call must belong to a unique group. For the second problem, once the encoded image of the recent and historic consumption of each user is built, it is necessary to find the way to analyze this information so that it detects any anomaly in the consumption and so triggers the corresponding alarm.

M. Ali and F. Esposito (Eds.): IEA/AIE 2005, LNAI 3533, pp. 613 – 615, 2005.

2 Description of the Suggested Solution

In order to process the CDR's, a new format of record must be created containing the following information: IMSI (International Mobile Subscriber Identity), date, time, duration and type of call (LOC: local call, NAT: national call, INT: international call). For constructing and maintaining the "user's profiles", we have to fix the patterns that will make up each of the profiles. The patterns must have information about the user's consumption. We propose the use of SOM (Self Organizing Map) networks to generate patterns (creating resemblance groups) to represent LOC, NAT, and INT calls respectively [3]. The user's profile is built using the patterns generated by the three networks. The data used to represent a pattern are the time of the call and its duration. The procedure to fill the patterns consists of taking the call to be analyzed, encoding it and letting the neural network decide which pattern it resembles. After getting this information, the CUP user profile must be adapted in such a way that the distribution of frequency shows that the user now has a higher chance of making this type of calls. Knowing that a user's profile has K patterns that are made up of L patterns LOC, N patterns NAT and I patterns INT, we can build a profile that is representative of the processed call and then adapt the CUP profile to that call. If the call is LOC, the N patterns NAT and the I patterns INT will have a distribution of frequency equal to 0, and the K patterns LOC will have a distribution of frequency given by the equation $v_i = e^{-\|X-Q_j\|} / \left(\sum_{j=1}^{L} e^{-\|X-Q_j\|} \right)$ [2] where X is the encoded call to be processed; v is the probability that X call could be i pattern and Qi is the pattern i generated by the neural LOC network. If the call were NAT, then L must be replaced by N and the distribution of LOC and INT frequencies will be 0; if the call were INT, then L must be replaced by I and the distribution of LOC and NAT frequencied will be 0. The CUP and UPH profiles are compared using the Hellinger distance [3] in order to settle whether there have been changes in the pattern of behavior or not. The value of distance will establish how different must CUP and UPH be, in order to set an alarm going. By changing this value, there will be more or fewer alarms set off.

3 Results

The generated patterns after the training of the neural networks (LOC, NAC, INT) are shown as follows: Fig.1 shows 144 patterns corresponding to local calls, Fig.2 shows 64 patterns corresponding to national calls and Fig. 3 shows the 36 patterns corresponding to international calls. The construction of profiles and detection of changes in behavior are shown as follows: Fig. 4 shows a user's CUP at the moment an alarm was set off. It can be observed that the distribution of frequencies indicates a tendency to make local calls (patterns 1 to 144) and International calls (patterns 209 to 244), Fig. 5 shows the same user's UPH at the moment the alarm was set off. It can also be observed that the distribution of frequencies indicates a major tendency to make INT calls only (patterns 209 to 244).

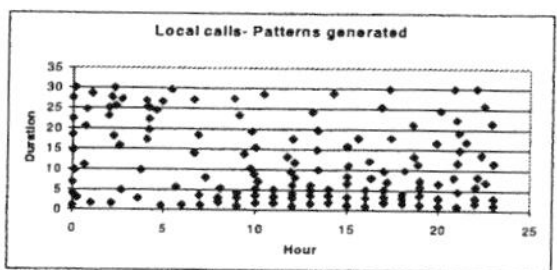

Fig. 1. LOC Patterns

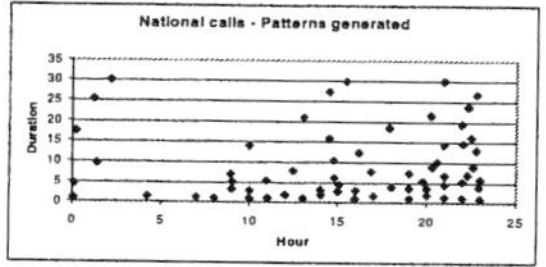

Fig. 2. NAC Patterns

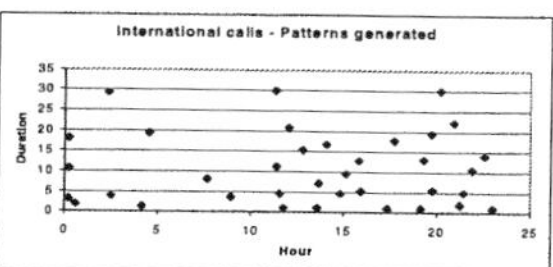

Fig. 3. INT Patterns

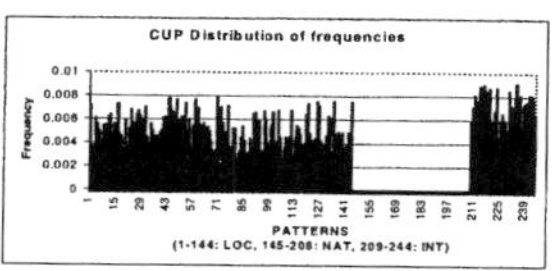

Fig. 4. User's CUP when an alarm was set off

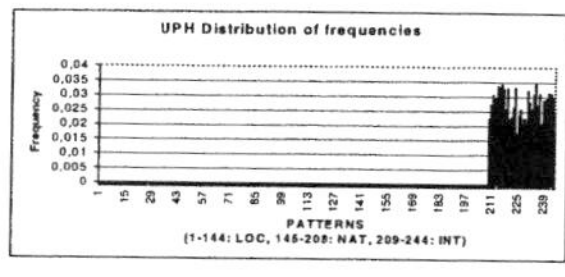

Fig. 5. User's UPH when an alarm was set off

By analyzing the detail of this user's calls from dates previous to the triggering of the alarm to the day it was set off, there is evidence that the alarm responded to the user's making only international calls till the moment that he started making local calls. When the number of local calls modified the CUP in the way illustrated by the graph, the alarm was triggered. If the user pays his invoice for international calls, this alarm is not an indicator of fraud, but it is an indicator of a sensitive change of behaviour in the pattern of user's consumption, and that is exactly what this system searches.

4 Conclusions

Though the change in behaviour does not necessarily imply fraudulent activity, it manages to restrict fraud analysts' investigation to this users' group. Applying to this group other types of techniques [1], it is possible to obtain, with a high degree of certainty, a list of users who are using their mobile phone in a " not loyal" way. It is also proven, with the experiences carried out, that the differential analysis provides with much more information than the absolute analysis, which can only detect peaks of consumption and cannot describe the user behavior in question.

References

1. ASPeCT. 1996. Advanced Security For Personal Communications Technologies. http://www.esat.kuleuven.ac.be/cosic/aspect/
2. Burge, P. and Shawe-Taylor, J. 2001. An Unsupervised Neural Network Approach to Profiling the Behaviour of Mobile Phone Users for Use in Fraud Detection. Journal of Parallel and Distributed Computing 61(7):pp. 915-925.
3. Hollmen J. 1996. Process Modeling using the Self-Organizing Map, Master's Thesis, Helsinki University of Technology, 1996.

An Intelligent Medical Image Understanding Method Using Two-Tier Neural Network Ensembles*

Yubin Yang[1,2], Shifu Chen[1], Zhihua Zhou[1], Hui Lin[2], and Yukun Ye[3]

[1] State Key Laboratory for Novel Software Technology, Nanjing University, Nanjing 210093, P. R. China
yangyubin@cuhk.edu.hk
[2] Joint Laboratory for Geoinformation Science, The Chinese University of Hong Kong, Shatin, N.T., Hong Kong
[3] Nanjing Bayi Hospital, Nanjing 210002, P. R. China

Abstract. This paper proposes an intelligent medical image understanding method using a novel two-tier artificial neural network ensembles framework to identify lung cancer cells and discriminate among different lung cancer types by analyzing the chromatic images acquired from the microscope slices of needle biopsy specimens. In this way, each neural network takes the shape and color features extracting from lung cancer cell images as the inputs and all the five possible identification results as its output.

1 Introduction

Lung cancer is one of the most common and deadly diseases in the world. Therefore, lung cancer diagnosis in early stage is crucial for its cure [1]. In this paper, a novel medical image understanding method is proposed to identify lung cancer cells and discriminate among different lung cancer types, by constructing a two-tier artificial neural network ensembles framework input by low-level image features. The method has already successfully implemented and applied to a Lung Cancer Cell Image Analysis System (LC^{2}IAS) developed for early stage lung cancer diagnosis.

2 System Architecture

The hardware configuration mainly includes a medical electron microscope, a digital video camera, an image capturer, and the output devices including a printer and a video display. The video frames are captured and saved as 24 bit RGB color images, on the basis of which the image understanding software identifies and discriminates among different lung cancer cells automatically according to the diagnosing flow as follows.

* This research has been funded in part by the National Natural Science Foundation of P. R. China under grant No.39670714 and grant No.60273033.

M. Ali and F. Esposito (Eds.): IEA/AIE 2005, LNAI 3533, pp. 616–618, 2005.

Firstly, the RGB image is projected into a one-dimensional gray level space in 256-scale using an algorithm customized for lung cancer cell images [2]. Then, image processing techniques including smoothing, contrast enhancement, mathematic morphological operations and color enhancement are utilized to improve image quality. After that, the image is thresholded and an 8-connectivity chain code representation [3] is used to mark all the possible cells in it. At the same time, color information of all the possible cells and the whole image is simultaneously kept for later use. Finally, the shape and color features of all the possible cells are extracted to feed in a trained two-tier neural network ensembles framework, in order to identify whether lung cancer cells exist in the specimen or not. If there exist lung cancer cells, a further diagnosis will be made to indicate which type of lung caner the specimen case may have.

The extracted shape features include perimeter, size, major axis length, minor axis length, aspect ratio, roundness degree, protraction degree and the variance of all the pixel values of a cell, which can be easily computed based on 8-connectivity chain code representation [4]. The extracted color features include the means and variances of red, green and blue components of RGB color space, and hue, illumination and saturation components of HIS color space [4], both of each individual cell and of the whole slice image. Moreover, a self-defined C_{ratio} component, which represents the ratio of blue component in a cell, is also derived from the medical fact.

3 Two-Tier Neural Network Ensembles

The proposed neural network ensembles framework comprises two independent neural network ensembles at two different tiers, which is illustrated in Fig. 1. The first tier takes the extracted shape features as its input, and the second tier takes the color features as its input. This kind of ensemble simulates the professional diagnosis experiences so well that the accuracy and performance can both be improved.

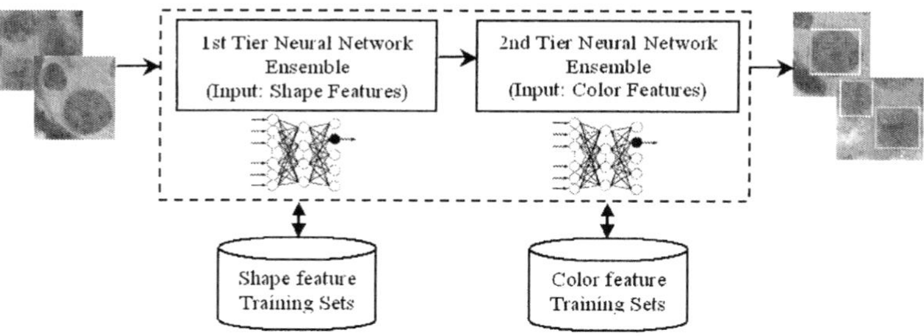

Fig. 1. The Neural Network Ensemble Framework

We choose error Back-Propagation (BP) learning algorithm for each individual neural network at each tier. Each BP neural network has three layers, taking normalized image feature vectors, shape or color, as its input units, and having five output units representing all the possible diagnosis results: *adenocarcinoma*, *squamous cell carcinoma*, *small cell carcinoma*, *abnormal cell*, and *normal cell*, each associated with a computed output value. The hidden units are configured by experience, where the first tier has seven and the second tier has ten.

4 Experimental Results

We have used 676 cells from 312 stained slice images collected from Department of Pathology, Nanjing Bayi Hospital as the experimental data set. All the samples are well-archived real cases ever diagnosed by medical experts. The data set is divided into two sets: a training set containing 550 cells (among which 321 are for the first ensemble tier while the remainder (229) are for the second ensemble tier), and a test set (126 cells). The experimental results are listed in Table 1.

Table 1. Experimental results of individual neural network ensemble and the two-tier method

Ensemble Type	General-error	False Negative	False Positive	Cross-error
1st tier	15.9%	7.9%	4.8%	3.2%
2nd tier	24.6%	13.5%	4.0%	7.1%
Two-tier method	8.7%	3.2%	4.0%	1.6%

In Table 1, there are totally four error measures. *General-error* measures the rate of overall false identifications, consisting of *False Negative*, *False Positive*, and *Cross-error*. *False Negative* measures the rate of false negative identifications that are cancer cells but erroneously identified as normal cells or abnormal cells. *False Positive* measures the rate of false positive identifications that are not cancer cells but erroneously identified as cancer cells. *Cross-error* is defined to measure the rate of false discriminations among different cancer types.

We can learn from Table 1 clearly that the two-tier method outperforms both individual ensembles by obtaining more satisfied values in all of the four measures. Moreover, the most noticeable and crucial improvement is that *False Negative* and *Cross-error* are both well controlled. It can be seen from Table 1 that *False Negative* is decreased to 3.2% and *Cross-error* is decreased to 1.6%, making the two-tier method more reliable in routine diagnosis. This is because the two-tier framework is able to combine the two ensembles to make use of the relative strengths of each and achieve the optimization of errors.

References

1. Ye Y.K., Shao C., Ge X.Z. et al.: Design and Clinical research of a Novel Instrument for Lung Cancer Early-stage Diagnosis. Chinese Journal of Surgery, 30 (5) (1992) 303-305
2. Yang Y.B., Li N., Chen S.F., Chen Z.Q.: Lung Cancer Identification Based on Image Content. In: 6th International Conference for Young Computer Scientists. (2001) 237-240
3. Freeman H.: Computer Processing of Line-drawing Image. Computing Surveys 6 (1) (1974) 57-97
4. Yang Y.B., Chen S.F., Lin Hui, Ye Y.K.: A Chromatic Image Understanding System for Lung Cancer Cell Identification Based on Fuzzy Knowledge. In: IEA/AIE'04, Lecture Notes in Computer Science, Springer-Verlag, 3029 (2003) 392-401

The Coordination of Parallel Search with Common Components

Stephen Chen[1] and Gregory Pitt[2]

[1] School of Analytical Studies and Information Technology, York University
4700 Keele Street, Toronto, Ontario M3J 1P3
sychen@yorku.ca
http://www.atkinson.yorku.ca/~sychen
[2] Department of Mathematics, York University
4700 Keele Street, Toronto, Ontario M3J 1P3
greg@pittresearch.com

Abstract. The preservation of common components has been recently isolated as a beneficial feature of genetic algorithms. One interpretation of this benefit is that the preservation of common components can direct the search process to focus on the most promising parts of the search space. If this advantage can be transferred from genetic algorithms, it may be possible to improve the overall effectiveness of other heuristic search techniques. To identify common components, multiple solutions are required – like those available from a set of parallel searches. Results with simulated annealing and the Traveling Salesman Problem show that the sharing of common components can be an effective method to coordinate parallel search.

Keywords: Parallel Algorithms, Heuristic Search, Simulated Annealing, Genetic Algorithms, Combinatorial Optimization, and Traveling Salesman Problem.

1 Introduction

Genetic algorithms are a heuristic search procedure modelled after Darwinian evolution and sexual reproduction. To implement this model, a genetic algorithm (GA) uses a population of solutions, fitness-based selection, and crossover [7][9]. Fitness-based selection over a population of solutions imitates the process of "survival of the fittest", and crossover simulates sexual reproduction to create new offspring solutions. Compared to other evolutionary computation techniques (e.g. [6][18]), the distinguishing feature of a genetic algorithm is the crossover operator.

It is generally believed by many GA researchers (e.g. [5][7][19]) that recombination is "the overt purpose of crossover" [19]. However, this emphasis helps overshadow the remaining mechanisms of a crossover operator: "respect" and "transmission" [14]. Specifically, in crossing two parents, the offspring should only be composed of components that come from the parents (transmission), and it should preserve all of the features that are common to the two parents (respect).

M. Ali and F. Esposito (Eds.): IEA/AIE 2005, LNAI 3533, pp. 619–627, 2005.

Respect, or the preservation of common components, has recently been isolated and demonstrated to be a beneficial feature of crossover operators [2]. Building on the commonality hypothesis which suggests that "schemata common to above-average solutions are above average", one interpretation of this benefit is that the preservation of common components will focus changes to the uncommon/below-average components of a solution [4]. This focus increases the probability that a given change will lead to an improvement in the overall solution (see figure 1). Subsequently, a search procedure which preserves common components should be more effective than one that does not.

Since multiple solutions are required to identify common components, a point-search technique like simulated annealing [11] is not normally capable of benefiting from respect. However, multiple solutions become available with parallel search. Therefore, the preservation of common components holds promise as a method to coordinate and improve the performance of parallel search techniques.

A parallel implementation of simulated annealing has been developed for the Traveling Salesman Problem (TSP). Experiments have been run in three modes: no coordination (i.e. run n trials and keep the best), coordination by transferring complete solution, and coordination by sharing common components. In these experiments, the best performance was achieved when the parallel search processes were coordinated by the sharing of common components.

2 Background

The benefit of crossover has traditionally been attributed to the mechanism of recombination [5][7][19]. If two parents each have a unique beneficial feature, then crossover can combine these two features into a "super offspring" that has both of these features. However, combinatorial optimization problems are not generally decomposable, so two good sub-solutions will not always recombine well.

```
Parent 1:     1 0 1 1 0 1 0 1 1 1
Parent 2:     1 1 0 1 0 1 1 1 0 1

Common:       1     1 0 1   1   1

Uncommon 1:     0 1         0   1
Uncommon 2:     1 0         1   0
```

Fig. 1. In the OneMax problem, the objective is to have all 1's. A solution is improved when a 0 is turned into a 1. In the above example, changing a component at random has only a 30% chance of improving a parent solution. When changes are restricted to uncommon components, the probability of an improvement increases to 50% [4]

A newly isolated benefit of crossover is the preservation of common components [2]. When common components are preserved, changes to the parent solutions are restricted to the uncommon components. Compared to unrestricted changes, these restricted changes are more likely to lead to improvements (see figure 1). This advantage of crossover should also apply to combinatorial optimization problems that have "big valley" fitness landscapes (e.g. the TSP).

In a big valley fitness landscape, random local optima are more similar than random solutions, the similarities among local optima increase with their quality, and the global optimum is in the "centre" of the cluster of local optima [1][12]. Starting from a local optimum, a search path that reduces solution similarities is likely to be heading away from the centre of this big valley. Conversely, a search operator that maintains solution similarities by preserving common components has a greater probability of directing the search process towards the better solutions found at the centre of the big valley.

3 Parallel Simulated Annealing

Simulated annealing [11] is an iterative improvement technique based on the physical process of metal annealing. Compared to hill climbing, simulated annealing is designed to allow probabilistic escapes from local optima. Assuming a minimization objective, the simulated annealing process can be visualized as a ball rolling downhill through a landscape of peaks and valleys. Depending on how much "energy" is in the ball, it has the ability to "bounce out" of local minima. When the temperature/energy approaches zero, the ball will come to rest in a final minimum – ideally the global minimum if the cooling schedule has been slow enough.

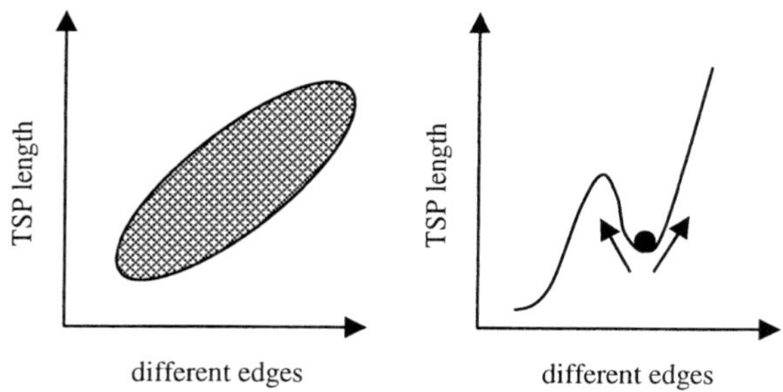

Fig. 2. In a typical distribution of local minima for the TSP (shown on the left), the best solutions have more common edges [1]. When escaping from a local minimum, simulated annealing will normally consider only the increase in the objective function. However, among moves that increase the objective function, the moves that create additional different edges are more likely to be leading the search process away from the centre of the big valley than the moves that preserve common components

Simulated annealing (SA) does not normally specify how the "ball" will escape from local minima – it can climb any valley wall with equal probability. This feature of SA is well-suited to problems with randomly distributed local minima. However, for problems that have big valley fitness landscapes, it may be beneficial to concentrate the search efforts of simulated annealing on the most promising part of the search space at the centre of the big valley. This focusing of the search effort can be achieved by using a search operator that preserves common components (see figure 2).

To identify/preserve common components, multiple solutions are required – like those available in a parallel implementation. In experiments using a fixed amount of computational effort, it has previously been shown that the preservation of common components can improve the performance of simulated annealing [2]. However, the efficacy of this form of communication as a means to coordinate parallel search procedures has not yet been fully analyzed.

4 The Traveling Salesman Problem

GA and SA researchers often use the Traveling Salesman Problem (TSP) as a standard combinatorial optimization problem. In addition to being well-defined (find the least-cost Hamiltonian cycle in a complete graph of N cities), many benchmark problems are readily available through TSPLIB [16]. The following experiments are conducted on 5 symmetric TSPLIB instances (i.e. pcb1173, pcb3038, fl1400, fl1577, and fl3795) that offer a good range of sizes. In general, instances below 1000 cities are no longer interesting [10], and instances above 4000 cities were too large for the current implementation[1].

5 The Experiments

The following experiments will compare three means of coordinating parallel search: no coordination, coordination by transferring complete solutions, and coordination by sharing common components. The base case of no coordination is equivalent to "run n trials and keep the best". Transferring complete solutions and sharing common components should allow both of these coordination methods to direct more search effort towards the most promising parts of the search space. However, sharing common components should maintain greater diversity and allow a "continuous" redirection of the search process towards the centre of the big valley.

5.1 Simulated Annealing for the TSP

The base SA application for the TSP (BaseSA) was developed with the following parameters. BaseSA starts from a random solution, uses a geometric cooling schedule (μ = 0.9) with 100 temperature cycles/annealing stages, applies two million two-opt swaps per stage[2], and returns to the best found solution at the end of each temperature cycle. Since a fixed number of annealing stages are used, the temperature is not decreased if the best solution does not improve during that annealing stage. To determine the initial temperature, a preliminary set of 50 two-opt swaps where only improving steps are accepted is used. At the end of this set, the initial temperature starts at the average length of the attempted backward steps / ln(0.5).

---

[1] Source available at http://www.atkinson.yorku.ca/~sychen/research/search.html

[2] In general, the number of two-opt swaps performed during each temperature cycle should increase with the problem size (e.g. [17]). However, the performance degradation caused by using a fixed number of two-opt swaps should help highlight any benefits (e.g. improved efficiency) of coordination

The above implementation of simulated annealing was run in sets of n = 1, 2, 4, and 8 independent parallel runs. After all individual runs in a set are complete, the best solution found by any of these runs is returned as the final solution. Thirty independent trials are run for each value of n, and the results are reported as percent distance above the known optimal solution. (See Table 1.)

Table 1. Average percentage above optimal for 30 independent trials of BaseSA with two hundred million total two-opt swaps performed per parallel run

Instance	n = 1		n = 2		n = 4		n = 8	
	avg	std dev	avg	std dev	avg	std dev	avg	std dev
pcb1173	8.55	1.03	8.07	0.72	8.05	0.53	7.49	0.59
fl1400	5.82	2.05	4.33	1.38	3.58	1.15	2.86	0.89
fl1577	10.97	3.11	9.09	2.84	7.69	1.94	6.91	1.55
pcb3038	15.34	1.64	15.13	1.08	14.59	0.81	13.66	0.50
fl3795	24.09	5.15	22.04	5.24	19.68	2.36	17.22	2.46

5.2 Coordination with Complete Solutions

Information among parallel searches can be shared by transferring complete solutions (e.g. [12][17]). In the following experiments, each process stores its best solution and queries a random parallel run for its best stored solution at the end of each temperature cycle. The better of these two solutions is used as the starting point for the next temperature cycle.

Coordination with complete solutions was tested with sets of n = 2, 4, and 8 parallel processes. Results are again reported as percent distance above the known optimal solution. (See Table 2.) The total number of two-opt swaps is held constant, but the communication overhead increases the actual runtimes (of each process) by about 2% compared to using no coordination.

Table 2. Average percentage above optimal for 30 trials of SA coordinated by transferring complete solutions with two hundred million total two-opt swaps performed per parallel run

Instance	n = 2		n = 4		n = 8	
	avg	std dev	avg	std dev	avg	std dev
pcb1173	8.28	0.65	7.85	0.67	7.29	0.63
fl1400	4.91	1.64	4.03	1.02	4.69	1.74
fl1577	9.40	2.77	8.83	2.30	7.76	2.82
pcb3038	14.65	0.97	13.83	1.12	13.15	0.77
fl3795	21.97	3.70	20.04	3.96	19.53	4.93

5.3 Coordination with Common Components

Transferring complete solutions can overly concentrate the search effort which may subsequently reduce the individual contributions of each parallel process. Conversely, sharing common components can help direct the search efforts of each SA implementation towards the centre of the big valley without sacrificing diversity. Specifically, a two-opt swap replaces two current edges with two new edges. To help preserve solution similarities and direct the search process towards the centre of the big valley, the replaced edges should be uncommon edges.

Similar to the experiments coordinated with complete solutions, each process stores and returns to its best solution at the end of each temperature cycle. The best stored solution of a random parallel process is examined, but each process continues with its own solution – only common edges are recorded from the shared solution. During the next temperature cycle, 90% of the two-opt swaps will ensure that one of the replaced edges is an uncommon edge [2].

Coordination with common components was tested with sets of n = 2, 4, and 8 parallel processes. Results are again reported as percent distance above the known optimal solution. (See Table 3.) Compared to using no coordination, the communication overhead and the cost of identifying and preserving common components have increased the actual runtimes of each parallel process by about 10%.

Table 3. Average percentage above optimal for 30 trials of SA being coordinated by sharing common components with two hundred million total two-opt swaps performed per parallel run

Instance	n = 2		n = 4		n = 8	
	avg	std dev	avg	std dev	avg	std dev
pcb1173	5.08	0.64	4.88	0.65	4.40	0.55
fl1400	3.15	1.33	2.45	0.90	1.94	0.47
fl1577	2.48	1.12	2.19	0.87	1.49	0.48
pcb3038	11.06	0.73	10.83	0.72	10.33	0.57
fl3795	11.27	2.17	10.10	1.89	8.86	1.44

6 Results

The basic test for a coordination method is to determine if it performs better than having no coordination at all. Surprisingly, coordination with complete solutions was often less effective than no coordination, and the occasional improvements were not highly significant (as determined by one-tailed t-tests). (See Table 4.) Conversely, the improvements observed when coordinating with common components are consistent and significant. This coordination strategy receives the benefits of both search diversification (n independent processes) and search concentration (each process uses the others to help direct it to the centre of the big valley). Overall, coordination with common components is clearly the most effective of the three coordination strategies.

The absolute performance of the above SA implementations is not particularly strong (e.g. [2][10][17]), and the difference with [2] is primarily attributed to starting from a random solution. Although additional tuning of BaseSA could be done, this is neither critical nor highly relevant to the purpose of the experiments. In particular, the diverse absolute results help highlight the consistent improvements in performance

Table 4. Results of one-tailed t-tests comparing methods of coordination. Values indicate percent probability that results achieved by the first coordination method are the same as those achieved by the second method (- indicates that the expected improvement was not observed)

Instance	n = 2		n = 4		n = 8	
	complete vs. none	common vs. none	complete vs. none	common vs. none	complete vs. none	common vs. none
pcb1173	-	0.00	13.57	0.00	9.92	0.00
fl1400	-	0.09	-	0.01	-	0.01
fl1577	-	0.00	-	0.00	-	0.00
pcb3038	5.76	0.00	0.27	0.00	0.52	0.00
fl3795	47.84	0.00	34.14	0.00	-	0.00

that are achieved by coordinating parallel runs through the sharing of common components. Specifically, the effectiveness of this coordination strategy is visible early (e.g. fl3795) and late (e.g. fl1577) in the search process.

7 Discussion

The benefit of parallel search is minimal if there is no coordination among the processes. Clearly, each process should have some information about the progress of other processes (e.g. a copy of their best solution). However, how this information is used can have a significant effect on the efficiency and/or effectiveness of the resulting parallel search strategy.

For example, parallel search processes could be coordinated by using recombination (e.g. [8][20]) which is more traditionally viewed as the primary advantage of crossover and genetic algorithms [5][7][19]. However, population search procedures lead to a fair amount of convergence (i.e. speciation) which is not necessarily a desirable feature for parallel search. When using recombination, the diversity among the parallel searches would have to be limited to avoid the situation where "crossover can be compared to the very unpromising effort to recombine animals of different species" [20]. Conversely, medical experiments for humans are often performed on a diverse set of animals that we would not likely receive any benefit if we were to recombine with them (e.g. rats, monkeys, etc). In a similar fashion, the coordination of parallel search with common components allows each process to share information on its key structures without sacrificing diversity.

Coordinating parallel search with complete solutions also sacrifices diversity. With respect to the goal of balancing exploration and exploitation in the search process, the copying of complete solutions eliminates one path in favour of another. Arguably, if that second search path has no chance of finding a better solution than the first path, then there is no point to expend any additional effort on exploring that path. When measuring the efficiency of parallel search for a given level of effectiveness (e.g. [17]), copying complete solutions may be a reasonable method of coordination. However, if the processing power is available, coordination with common components has been shown to be significantly more effective.

In many combinatorial optimization problems, the solution space resembles a big valley [1]. Specifically, there are many good solutions in the vicinity of other good solutions, and this is the premise behind search techniques like memetic algorithms [13][15]. However, memetic algorithms do not necessarily exploit the feature that defines the big valley – common components [3]. The coordination of parallel search processes with common components explicitly uses this feature in an attempt to direct each search process towards the centre of the big valley. For the TSP, the results indicate that this attempt has been quite successful.

8 Conclusions

There are two goals for any strategy to coordinate parallel search: greater efficiency and greater effectiveness. The experiments conducted with a simulated annealing implementation for the Traveling Salesman Problem demonstrate that sharing information on common components can be an effective way to coordinate parallel search. Compared to no coordination and coordination with complete solutions, coordination with common components has been significantly more effective.

Acknowledgements

The authors have received funding support from the Natural Sciences and Engineering Research Council of Canada and from the Atkinson Faculty of Liberal and Professional Studies, York University.

References

1. Boese, K.D.: Models for Iterative Global Optimization. Ph.D. diss., Computer Science Department, University of California at Los Angeles (1996)
2. Chen, S.: SAGA: Demonstrating the Benefits of Commonality-Based Crossover Operators in Simulated Annealing. Working paper. School of Analytical Studies and Information Technology, York University (2003)
3. Chen, S., Smith, S.F.: Putting the "Genetics" back into Genetic Algorithms (Reconsidering the Role of Crossover in Hybrid Operators). In: Banzhaf W., Reeves, C. (eds.): Foundations of Genetic Algorithms 5, Morgan Kaufmann (1999)
4. Chen, S., Smith, S.F.: Introducing a New Advantage of Crossover: Commonality-Based Selection. In GECCO-99: Proceedings of the Genetic and Evolutionary Computation Conference. Morgan Kaufmann (1999)
5. Davis, L.: Handbook of Genetic Algorithms. Van Nostrand Reinhold (1991)
6. Fogel, L.J., Owens, A.J., Walsh, M.J.: Artificial Intelligence through Simulated Evolution. Wiley (1966)
7. Goldberg, D.: Genetic Algorithms in Search, Optimization, and Machine Learning. Addison-Wesley (1989)
8. Hiroyasu, T., Miki, M., Ogura, M.: Parallel Simulated Annealing using Genetic Crossover. In Proceedings of the IASTED International Conference on Parallel and Distributed Computing and Systems. ACTA Press (2000)

9. Holland, J.: Adaptation in Natural and Artificial Systems. The University of Michigan Press (1975)
10. Johnson, D.S., McGeoch, L.A.: Experimental Analysis of Heuristics for the STSP. In: Gutin G., Punnen A.P. (eds.): The Traveling Salesman Problem and Its Variations. Kluwer Academic Publishers (2002)
11. Kirkpatrick, S., Gelatt Jr., C.D., Vecchi, M.P.: Optimization by Simulated Annealing. In Science, Vol. 220 (1983) 671-680
12. Mühlenbein, H.: Evolution in Time and Space--The Parallel Genetic Algorithm. In: Rawlins, G. (ed.): Foundations of Genetic Algorithms. Morgan Kaufmann (1991)
13. Norman, M.G., Moscato, P.: A Competitive and Cooperative Approach to Complex Combinatorial Search, Caltech Concurrent Computation Program, C3P Report 790 (1989)
14. Radcliffe, N.J.: Forma Analysis and Random Respectful Recombination. In Proceedings of the Fourth International Conference on Genetic Algorithms. Morgan Kaufmann (1991)
15. Radcliffe, N.J., Surry, P.D.: Formal memetic algorithms. In: Fogarty, T. (ed.): Evolutionary Computing: AISB Workshop. Springer-Verlag (1994)
16. Reinelt. G.: The Traveling Salesman: Computational Solutions for TSP Applications. Springer-Verlag (1994)
17. Sanvicente, H., Frausto-Solís, J.: MPSA: A Methodology to Parallel Simulated Annealing and its Application to the Traveling Salesman Problem. In Proceedings of the Second Mexican International Conference on Artificial Intelligence: Advances in Artificial Intelligence. Springer-Verlag (2002)
18. Schwefel, H.-P.: Numerical Optimization of Computer Models. Wiley (1981)
19. Syswerda, G: Uniform Crossover in Genetic Algorithms. In Proceedings of the Third International Conference on Genetic Algorithms. Morgan Kaufmann (1989)
20. Wendt, O., König, W.: Cooperative Simulated Annealing: How much cooperation is enough? Technical Report, No. 1997-3, School of Information Systems and Information Economics at Frankfurt University (1997)

A Decision Support Tool Coupling a Causal Model and a Multi-objective Genetic Algorithm

Ivan Blecic[1], Arnaldo Cecchini[1], and Giuseppe A. Trunfio[2]

[1] Department of Architecture and Planning, University of Sassari, Italy
{ivan, cecchini}@uniss.it
[2] Center of High-Performance Computing, University of Calabria, Rende (CS), Italy
trunfio@unical.it

Abstract. The knowledge-driven causal models, implementing some inferential techniques, can prove useful in the assessment of effects of actions in contexts with complex probabilistic chains. Such exploratory tools can thus help in "fore-visioning" of future scenarios, but frequently the inverse analysis is required, that is to say, given a desirable future scenario, to discover the "best" set of actions. This paper explores a case of such "future-retrovisioning", coupling a causal model with a multi-objective genetic algorithm. We show how a genetic algorithm is able to solve the strategy-selection problem, assisting the decision-maker in choosing an adequate strategy within the possibilities offered by the decision space. The paper outlines the general framework underlying an effective knowledge-based decision support system engineered as a software tool.

1 Introduction

When undertaking actions and strategies, a decision-maker normally has to cope with the complexity of the present and future context these strategies will fall in. For the purpose of our research, we can assume that "acting" is always explicitly or implicitly oriented with the intent to make a desirable future scenario more probable (and make the undesirable one less probable). However, the frequently complex interactions among possible social, natural or technological factors can make extremely difficult to take decisions, especially if there are strong constraints. This difficulty can be related to the fact the actors tend to consider only the first-order, or at most the second-order potential effects, being unable to cope intuitively with long cause-effect chains and influences, such that could sometimes bring about quite counter-intuitive and unexpected consequences. For the purpose of adequately taking into account and of coping reliably with the actual system's complexity, it might show useful to build a causal model and its related computational technique.

A widely used approximate technique is the so called Cross-Impact Analysis (CIA) [1], which provides estimated probabilities of future events as the result of the expected (i.e. estimated) interactions among them. Such approach was originally proposed by Helmer and Gordon in the 1966. Subsequently, Gordon and Hayward have developed a stochastic algorithmic procedure, capable of proving quantitative results [2]; the idea had number of variants and applications [3-6]. Such causal models and the related computational-inferential techniques made possible the simulation of

M. Ali and F. Esposito (Eds.): IEA/AIE 2005, LNAI 3533, pp. 628 – 637, 2005.

effects of subsets of implemented actions on the probability of the final scenarios. However, that brought about the issue of the inverse problem: given a desirable scenario, how to find the optimal set of actions in terms of effectiveness and efficiency, which could make the desirable scenario most probable?

In this paper we will propose and exploit a multi-objective genetic algorithm (MOGA) approach in the search for the best set of actions and the related budget allocation problem in the outlined probabilistic context. The computational framework described here, coupling the causal model and the MOGA, has been implemented is a software tool and is being used as an effective knowledge-based decision support system (DSS).

2 The Dynamics of a System of Events

Let us consider a time interval Δt and the set

$$\Sigma = \{e_1, \ldots, e_N\} \tag{1}$$

whose elements we will call *non recurrent events*, events which can occur at most once in the time interval $[\, t_0,\ t_0 + \Delta t\,]$. Furthermore assume that, during the given time interval, the occurrence of an event can modify the probability of other events (i.e. the set Σ represents a system). Noticeably, the interactions among events can be significantly complex, given the possibility of both feedbacks and memory-effect (i.e. the events' probability can depends on the *order* of occurrences of events).

We can define the *state* of Σ as an N-dimensional vector $\mathbf{s}=(s_1,\ldots,s_N)$, where $s_i=1$ if the i-th event has occurred, otherwise $s_i=0$ (i.e. every occurrence of an event triggers a state transition). Between the initial time t_0 and the final time $t_0 + \Delta t$, the system Σ performs, in general, a number of state transitions before reaching the final state.

Every non occurred event e_i in a state $\mathbf{s}_k$ has, with respect to the next state transition, a probability of occurrence p_i which can vary during the system's evolution.

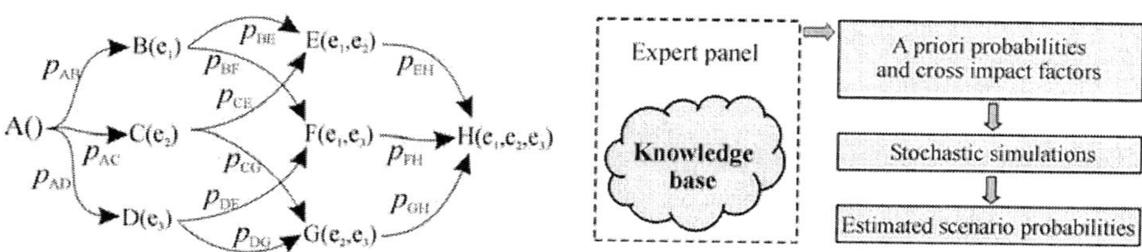

Fig. 1. The state-transition diagram for a three-event system without memory

Fig. 2. A scheme of the Cross Impact Analysis approach

As an example, let us consider the three-event no-memory system $\Sigma = \{e_1, e_2, e_3\}$. The state-transition diagram is represented in the Fig. 1, where all states are labelled using letters from A to H. When the system is in the state C, it has the transition probability p_{CE} (i.e. the current p_1) to switch to the state E.

Eventually, at the end the system reaches a state called *scenario* where, in general, we may observe that some events have occurred during the given time interval. In particular, observing the entire evolution of the system over time, we can define the probability of occurrence of the event e_i, which will be indicated as $P(e_i)$, or the probability of non-occurrence, indicated as $P(\neg e_i)$. Also, it is possible to determine the joint probabilities, such as $P(e_i \wedge \neg e_j \wedge \cdots \wedge e_k)$.

Clearly, only the knowledge of all transition probabilities allows us to determine such probabilities referred to the whole time interval. Unfortunately, given N events, the number of possible state transitions is $N2^{N-1}$ (e.g. 5.120 for 10 events) in a non memory-dependent system, and about $eN!$ (e.g. about 10 millions for 10 events) in a memory-dependent system [4]. As numbers grow, the problem becomes increasingly intractable. Nevertheless, as explained in detail further below, an alternative is given by applying Monte Carlo-like stochastic simulations on the cross-impact model [2].

2.1 An Approximate Solution: The Cross-Impact Analysis Approach

As widely known [7], a stochastic simulation procedure permits the estimation of probabilities from a random series of scenarios generated by a causal model. Hence, a possible approach to the former problem is to develop a causal model such as the CIA [1,2], which allows the execution of a stochastic inferential procedure (see Fig. 2). In the majority of cross-impact schemes [2,3,4], every event first gets attributed an initial probability and then it is assumed that, during the system's evolution along the time interval, an event occurrence can modify other events' probability. Thus, the model is specified with the assignment of N^2 probabilities:

- for each event e_k with k=1...N, an initial *a priori* probability $\hat{\Pi}(e_k)$ is assigned, estimated under the hypothesis of the non-occurrence of all the other events;
- for each ordered couple of events (e_i, e_j), with $i \neq j$, an *updated probability* $\Pi_j(e_i)$ is assigned, defining the causal influence of e_j over e_i, and representing the new probability of e_i under the assumption of the occurrence of e_j.

It is important to point out that the updated probabilities introduced above are not the conditional probabilities as defined in the formal probability theory. Instead, they should be intended as new *a priori* probabilities based upon a newly assumed knowledge on the state of the system [4]. Also, it is worth noting that there are formalised procedures allowing a panel of experts to produce knowledge-based estimates of the above probabilities (e.g. see [8]).

Frequently [2,4], the updated probabilities $\Pi_j(e_i)$ are not assigned explicitly, but using a relation $\Pi_j(e_i) = \phi(\Pi(e_i), f_{ij})$, where $\Pi(e_i)$ is the probability of e_i before the occurrence of e_j, while f_{ij} is an *impact factor* specifying the "intensity" of the effects of the e_j over the probability of occurrence of e_i.

As shown elsewhere [2], defining the elements of the model (i.e. the initial probabilities $\hat{\Pi}(e_k)$ and the probability updating relations) is the basis for executing M stochastic simulations of the system's evolution. The procedure is briefly illustrated in the Algorithm 1. In a Monte Carlo fashion, at the end of the execution procedure, the matrix $\boldsymbol{Q}$ contains M stochastically generated scenarios, making possible to estimate the probability of an arbitrary scenario as the frequency of occurrence.

1. A $N \times M$ integer matrix $\mathbf{Q}$ and the integer k are initialised by zeros;
2. **while** ($k<M$)
   2.1 all events are marked as non-tested;
   2.2 **while** (there exist non tested events)
      2.1.1 a non-tested event e_i, which has probability $\Pi(e_i)$, is randomly selected and is marked as tested;
      2.1.2 a random number $c \in [0,1]$ is generated;
      2.1.3 **if** ($c < \Pi(e_i)$) **then**
         - $\mathbf{Q}[i,k] \leftarrow \mathbf{Q}[i,k]+1$;
         - all probabilities are updated using the equation $\Pi_i(e_j) = \phi(\Pi(e_j), f_{ji})$;
      2.1.4 **endif**
   2.3 **end while**
   2.4 $k \leftarrow k+1$;
3. **end while**

Algorithm 1. The stochastic procedure for the scenario probabilities estimation

The cross-impact model employed by us presents some differences with respect to the classical formulations. In particular, for the purpose of a better representation of a decision-making context, we are assuming that the system's entities are differentiated and collected into three sets

$$\Sigma =< \mathbf{E}, \mathbf{U}, \mathbf{A} > \tag{2}$$

where **E** is a set of N_{E} events; **U** is a set of N_{U} *unforeseen events*, i.e. external events (exogenous to the simulated system) whose probability can not be influenced by the events in **E**; **A** is a set of N_{A} *actions*, which are events whose probabilities can be set to one or zero by the actor, and can thus be considered as actions at his/her disposal. We assume that the occurrence of events (normal and unforeseen) and actions can influence the probabilities of $e_i \in \mathbf{E}$. In particular the causal model is specified with:

- the N_{E} events $e_i \in \mathbf{E}$, each characterised by its initial probability $\hat{\Pi}(e_i)$, estimated assuming the single event as isolated;
- the N_{U} unforeseen events $u_i \in \mathbf{U}$, each defined by a constant probability $\hat{\Pi}(u_i)$;
- each action $a \in \mathbf{A}$ is defined as $a =< \mu, I_\mu >$, where $\mu \in I_\mu$ is an *effort* representing the "resources" invested in an action (e.g. money, time, energy, etc.).

The interactions among entities are defined by three impact factor groups and some interaction laws. In particular we have three matrices, $\mathbf{F}_{\mathrm{UE}}$, $\mathbf{F}_{\mathrm{EE}}$, and $\mathbf{F}_{\mathrm{AE}}$, whose generic element $f_{ij} \in [-f_{MAX}, f_{MAX}]$ determines, as explained below, a change of the probability of the event e_i, respectively caused by the occurrence of the unforeseen event u_j, by the occurrence of the event e_j and by the implementation of the action a_j.

The impact factors affect the change of the events' probabilities as follows:

$$\Pi_j(e_i) = \begin{cases} \Pi(e_i) + \dfrac{1-\Pi(e_i)}{f_{MAX}} \times f_{ij}, & f_{ij} \geq 0 \\ \Pi(e_i) \times \left(1 + \dfrac{f_{ij}}{f_{MAX}}\right), & f_{ij} < 0 \end{cases} \tag{3}$$

where $\Pi_j(e_i)$ is the *updated* probability (see Fig. 3-*a*). Note that the expression (3) works in a common-sense fashion: the resistance to change grows as the values gets closer to its limits.

In order to account for the different kinds of effort-impact responses, each action a_i is characterised by an *impact intensity* ψ_i expressed as a function of the action effort (see Fig. 3-*b*). The actual action's impact factors are obtained multiplying the maximum action impact factor in $\mathbf{F}_{AE}$ by ψ_i. The idea is that the more an actor "invests" in an action, the greater is the action's influence on the system. In particular, for each action, the *effective effort interval* is defined as $\Omega_i = [\alpha_i\overline{\mu}_i, \overline{\mu}_i]$, with $\alpha_i \in]0,1[$, where $\overline{\mu}_i$ and $\alpha_i\overline{\mu}_i$ are the efforts corresponding to respectively the 99% and the 1% of the maximum action's impact. Clearly, the α_i can be close to 1 in case of actions which are not reasonably scalable. Hence the impact intensity $\psi(\mu)$ is defined as:

$$\psi(\mu) = \frac{1}{1+e^{-a\mu-b}}, \text{ where } a = \frac{c_2 - c_1}{(\alpha-1)\overline{\mu}} \text{ and } b = \frac{c_1 - \alpha\, c_2}{\alpha - 1} \tag{4}$$

with $c_1 = \ln[(1-0.01)/0.01]$ and $c_2 = \ln[(1-0.99)/0.99]$.

As in the classical cross-impact models, defining all model's entities, parameters and equations, allows us to perform a series of *M* stochastic simulations using the procedure illustrated in the Algorithm 1. Subsequently, any scenario probability can be estimated as the frequency of occurrence.

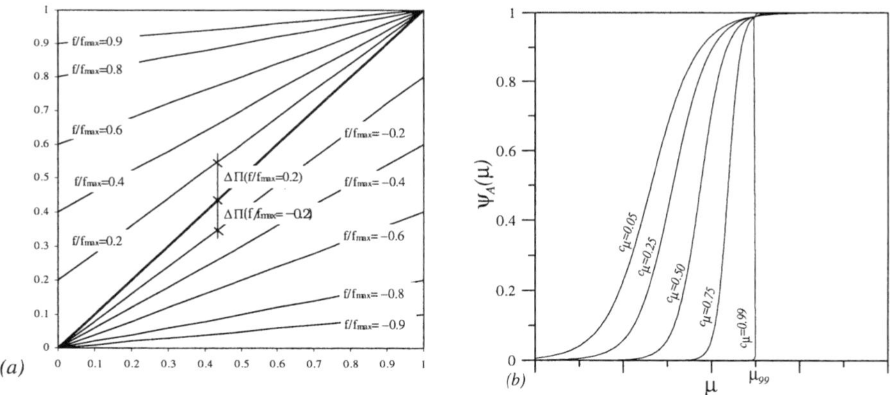

Fig. 3. (*a*) how the impact factor *f* affects probabilities of events; (*b*) how the action's effort μ affects the impact intensity of actions

3 Searching for the Best Strategies

When the system is highly complex, some aid for the automatic scenario analysis is required. In particular, the most frequent need is the determination of a strategy (i.e.

efforts to allocate on every potential action) which is optimal with respect to some objective functions. The problem can be stated as follows.

First we can assume that a joint probability P (i.e. the probability of a scenario) is expressed as a probabilistic function of the *effort vector* $\mathbf{m} = (\mu_1, \mu_2, \ldots, \mu_{N_A})$ representing a *strategy*, being μ_i the effort "invested" in a_i. Then, let us consider a partition of the set **E** in three subsets: **G**, the set of the positive events; **B**, the set of the negative events; **I** = **E** \ **G** U **B**, the set of neutral events.

Assuming that events belonging to the same subset are equally important, we want to find the strategy **m** able to simultaneously maximise the joint probability of events belonging to **G** and minimise the joint probability of events belonging to **B**. The search may include the strategy effort minimisation, and some effort constraints. Hence:

$$\begin{cases} \max\limits_{\mathbf{m}\in\Omega} \delta_{\mathbf{G}}(\mathbf{m}), & \delta_{\mathbf{G}}(\mathbf{m}) = P(e \quad \forall e \in \mathbf{G}) \\ \max\limits_{\mathbf{m}\in\Omega} \delta_{\mathbf{B}}(\mathbf{m}), & \delta_{\mathbf{B}}(\mathbf{m}) = P(\neg e \quad \forall e \in \mathbf{B}) \\ \min\limits_{\mathbf{m}\in\Omega} \delta_{\mu}(\mathbf{m}), & \delta_{\mu}(\mathbf{m}) = \sum\limits_{1}^{N_A} m_i \end{cases} \tag{5}$$

with the constraint $\delta_\mu(\mathbf{m}) \leq \mu_{\max}$, where Ω is the parameter space and $\mu_{\max}$ is the maximum allowed effort.

The objective functions in (5) are not available in explicit form, and their values can be computed only executing a complete simulation, as illustrated under 2.1. That makes the use of a classic optimisation methods, such as those gradient-based, rather difficult. All that suggests the employment of a technique based on the local function knowledge such as Genetic Algorithms (GAs). In our case, a GA is used to evolve a randomly initialised population, whose generic element is a chromosome representing the N_A-dimensional vector **m**. The *i*-th gene of the chromosome is obtained as the binary encoding of μ_i, using a suitable bit numbers and its interval of definition I_i. Each chromosome can be decoded in a strategy **m** and, performing the stochastic simulation, the objective functions in (5) can be computed.

In general, the constrained optimisation problem of q scalar functions $\phi_i(\mathbf{x})$, where $\mathbf{x} \in \Omega$, being Ω the decision space, can be stated as:

$$\max_{\mathbf{x}\in\Lambda} \phi_i(\mathbf{x}) \quad \text{with} \quad i = 1 \ldots q, \qquad \text{where: } \Lambda = \{a \in \Omega: \ g_i(a) \leq 0, \ i = 1 \ldots m\} \tag{6}$$

Often, the conflicts among criteria make difficult to find a single optimum solution. Methods for reducing the problem (6) to a single criteria exist, but they are too subjectively based on some arbitrary assumption [9].

In a different and a more suitable approach, the comparison of two solutions with respect to several objectives may be achieved through the introduction of the concepts of Pareto optimality and dominance [9-13]. This avoids any *a priori* assumption about the relative importance of individual objectives, both in the form of subjective weights or as arbitrary constraints. In particular, considering the optimisation problem (6), we say that a solution **x** *dominates* the solution **y** if:

$$\forall i \in \{1,\ldots,m\},\ \ \phi_i(\mathbf{x}) \geq \phi_i(\mathbf{y}) \ \ \wedge \ \ \exists\, k \in \{1,\ldots,m\} : \phi_k(\mathbf{x}) > \phi_k(\mathbf{y}) \tag{7}$$

In other words, if **x** is better or equivalent to **y** with respect to all objectives and better in at least one objective [10,11]. A non-dominated solution is optimal in the Pareto sense (i.e. no criterion can be improved without worsening at least one other criterion). On the other hand, a search based on such a definition of optimum almost always produces not a single solution, but a set of non-dominated solutions, from which the decision-maker will select one.

In the present work, the employed approach for the individual classification is the widely used Goldberg's 'non-dominated sorting' [10]. Briefly, the procedure proceeds as follows: *(i)* all non-dominated individuals in the current population are assigned to the highest possible rank; *(ii)* these individuals are virtually removed from the population and the next set on non-dominated individuals are assigned to the next highest rank. The process is reiterated until the entire population is ranked.

The MOGA (see Algorithm 2) proceeds on the basis of such ranking: every individual belonging to the same rank class has the same probability to be selected as a parent. The employed GA makes use of elitism as suggested by the recent research in the field [13], which means that from one generation to another, the non-dominated individuals are preserved. This allows us to extract the Pareto-set from the last population. In order to maximise the knowledge of the search space, the Pareto-optimal solutions have to be uniformly distributed along the Pareto front, so the GA includes a diversity preservation method (i.e. the procedure *Filter* in Algorithm 2). Just as in single-objective GAs, the constraints are handled by testing the fulfilment of the criteria by candidate solutions during the population creation and replacement procedures.

1. Initialise randomly the population P of size N_P accounting for the constraints
2. $k \leftarrow 0$
3. **while** ($k < K$)
   - 3.1 Evaluate the objective functions for each individual in P
   - 3.2 Execute the non-dominated sorting and rank the population P
   - 3.3 Copy in the set C all elements $x \in P$ which have the highest rank
   - 3.4 $C \leftarrow$ *Filter*(C)
   - 3.5 **while** ($\#C < N_P$)
     - 3.5.1 Select randomly from P, on the basis of their rank and without replacement, the two parents $x_0, y_0 \in P$;
     - 3.5.2 Perform the uniform crossover producing two children x_1, y_1 ;
     - 3.5.3 Perform the children mutation with probability p_m producing $\overline{x}_1, \overline{y}_1$;
     - 3.5.4 **if** (the constraints are fulfilled) **then** $C \leftarrow C \cup \{\overline{x}_1, \overline{y}_1\}$;
     - 3.5.5 **else** $C \leftarrow C \cup \{x_0, y_0\}$;
   - 3.6 **end while**
   - 3.7 $P \leftarrow C$;
   - 3.8 $k \leftarrow k+1$;
4. **end while**
5. $C \leftarrow$ Non-dominated elements of P

Algorithm 2. The used elitist multi-objective GA. The *Filter* procedure eliminates the elements which are closer than an assigned radius, using the Euclidean distance in the decision space. At the end of the procedure, the set C contains the Pareto-optimal solutions

4 An Example Application

The coupled CIA-GA presented here has been adopted in a DSS, developed in C++. The software can visualise the definition of the model as a directed graph (see Fig. 4.), and its main outcome is the best-strategy set, computed on the basis of the user's classification of events.

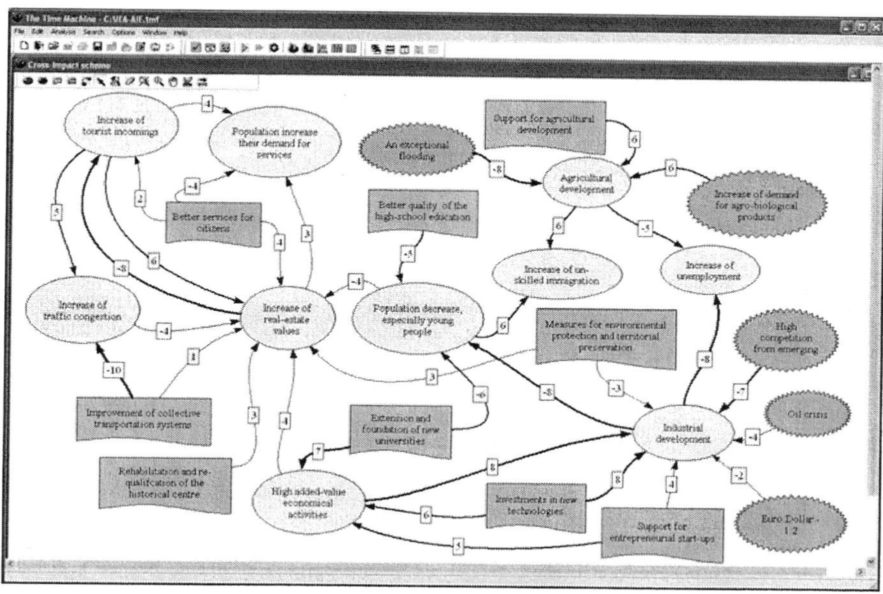

Fig. 4. The presented example graph and impact factors in the DSS software

Table 1. The entity characteristics in the presented example

	Id	*Set*	*Description*	Π
Events	e_1	G	Increase of tourist incomings	0.26
	e_2	B	Population decrease, especially young people	0.35
	e_3	I	Increase of un-skilled immigration	0.12
	e_4	G	High added-value economical activities	0.08
	e_5	B	Increase of traffic congestion	0.42
	e_6	G	Industrial development	0.41
	e_7	G	Increase of real-estate values	0.40
	e_8	I	Population increase their demand for services	0.20
	e_9	G	Agricultural development	0.50
	e_{10}	B	Increase of unemployment	0.25

	Id	*Description*	Π
Unforeseen events	u_1	An exceptional flooding	0.06
	u_2	Increase of demand for agro-biological products	0.64
	u_3	High competition from emerging countries	0.39
	u_4	Euro:Dollar - 1:2	0.02
	u_5	Oil crisis	0.21

	Id	*Description*	λ	α_{max}
Actions	a_1	Better quality of the high-school education	0.30	50
	a_2	Support for entrepreneurial start-ups	0.10	80
	a_3	Better services for citizens	0.30	50
	a_4	Investments in new technologies	0.60	40
	a_5	Rehabilitation and re-qualification of the historical centre	0.75	50
	a_6	Measures for environmental protection and territorial preservation	0.50	20
	a_7	Extension and foundation of new universities	0.80	40
	a_8	Improvement of collective transportation systems	0.80	30
	a_9	Support for agricultural development	0.20	20

The example application discussed here is related to a policy-making case-study. The Table 1 reports all entities included in the model and their estimated characteristics, as well as the events' rating (i.e. positive, negative and neutral sets). The cross-impact factors are shown in the Fig. 4.

The randomly initialised GA population was composed of 200 chromosomes, each coding a strategy (i.e. the 9 effort values relative to the available actions). For each effort value a 12-bit string was employed.

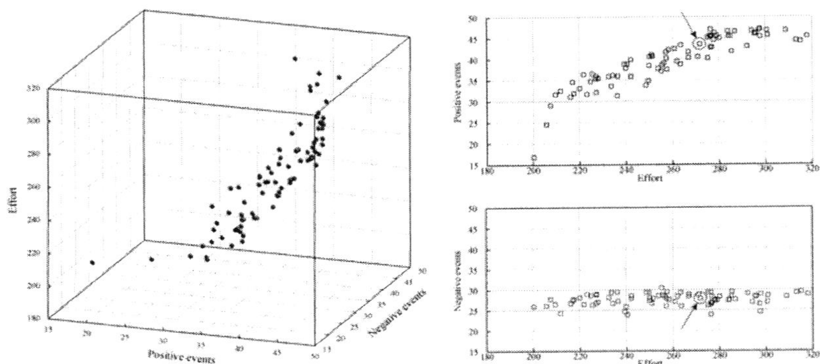

Fig. 5. The set of computed non-dominated solutions in the space of the objective functions defined in Eq. 5. The selected solution is indicated by the two arrows

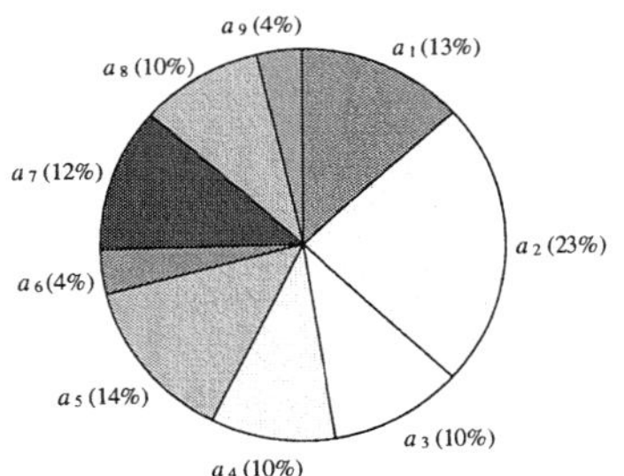

Fig. 6. Effort allocation in the selected solution (the total effort is 272)

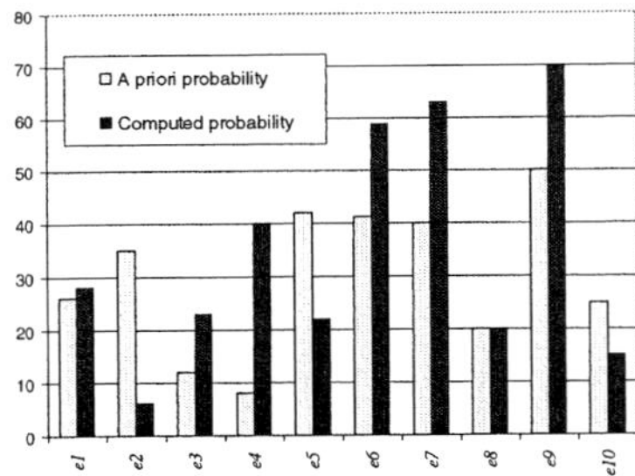

Fig. 7. How the event probabilities change in case of the selected solution

The objective function was evaluated performing a 200-iteration Monte Carlo simulation for each individual in the population. Given that the adopted GA was of elitist kind, the values of the objective function relative to the current Pareto set are conveniently stored from one generation into its successors (i.e. the simulations are not re-performed). In every generation, after the ranking, for each selected couple a one-site cross-over and subsequently a children mutation with probability p_m=0.003 were applied. In this example, in order to explore the whole decision space, the effort constraints were not considered. The computation was simply terminated after 20 generations (the software allows a real-time monitoring of the Pareto-set evolution). Using a standard PC, less than ten minutes were required for the total computation.

The Fig. 5, representing the final non-dominated set, shows how the proposed multi-objective approach allows the user to select a solution from a variety of possibilities. Clearly the final selection must be performed on the basis of some additional subjective decision. The selected strategy in our case, corresponding to 272 effort units, is highlighted in Fig. 5. In particular, the Fig. 6 reports the suggested effort allocation and the Fig. 7 reports the variation of the estimated probabilities corresponding to the solution.

5 Conclusions

We have presented a decision support tool coupling a classical causal model and a multi-objective genetic algorithm. While coupling a causal model with a single-objective GA is not a novelty (e.g. see [14]), we have shown that the use of a MOGA approach offers the decision-maker the choice of an adequate strategy, extending the knowledge about the variety of possibilities offered by the decision space. In particular, our application shows that the proposed DSS can be particularly useful in assisting the decision-making processes related to the future probabilistic scenarios.

References

1. Stover, J., Gordon, T.J. Cross-impact analysis. *Handbook of Futures Research*, ed. J. Fowles. Greenwood Press, 1978
2. Gordon, T.J., Hayward, H. Initial experiments with the cross-impact method of forecasting. *Futures* 1(2), 1968, 100-116
3. Helmer, O. Cross-impact gaming. *Futures* 4, 1972, 149–167
4. Turoff, M. An alternative approach to cross-impact analysis. *Technological Forecasting and Social Change* 3(3), 1972, 309-339
5. Helmer, O. Problems in Future Research: Delphi and Causal Cross Impact Analysis. *Futures* 9, 1977, 17-31
6. Alarcòn, L.F., Ashley, D.B. Project management decision making using cross-impact analysis. *Int. Journal of Project Management* 16(3), 1998, 145-152
7. Pearl, J. Evidential Reasoning Using Stochastic Simulation of Causal Models. *Artificial Intelligence*, 32, 1987, 245-257
8. Linstone, H.A., Turoff, M. (editors). The Delphi Method: Techniques and Applications, 2002, *Available at: http://www.is.njit.edu/pubs/delphibook/index.html*
9. Fonseca, C.M., Fleming, P.J. An overview of evolutionary algorithms in multiobjective optimization. *Evolutionary Computation* 3 (1), 1995, 1–16
10. Goldberg, D. Genetic Algorithms and Evolution Strategy in Engineering and Computer Science: Recent Advances and Industrial Applications, 1998, Wiley & Sons
11. Sawaragi Y, Nakayama H, Tanino T. Theory of multiobjective optimization. 1985, Orlando, Florida: Academic Press.
12. Srinivas N, Deb K. Multiobjective function optimization using nondominated sorting genetic algorithms. *Evolutionary Computation* 2(3), 1995, 221-248.
13. C.A. Coello Coello, D.A. Van Veldhuizen, G.B. Lamont, Evolutionary Algorithms for Solving Multi-Objective Problems, Kluwer Academic Publishers, 2002
14. L. M. de Campos, J. A. Gàmez, and S. Moral. Partial abductive inference in bayesian belief networks using a genetic algorithm. *Pattern Recogn. Lett.*, 20(11-13):1211–1217, 1999.

Emergent Restructuring of Resources in Ant Colonies: A Swarm-Based Approach to Partitioning

Elise Langham

Biomedical Sciences, University of Leeds, UK
A.E.Langham@leeds.ac.uk

Abstract. In this article partitioning of finite element meshes is tackled using colonies of artificial ant–like agents. These agents must restructure the resources in their environment in a manner which corresponds to a good solution of the underlying problem. Standard approaches to these problems use recursive methods in which the final solution is dependent on solutions found at higher levels. For example partitioning into k sets is done using recursive bisection which can often provide a partition which is far from optimal [15]. The inherently parallel, distributed nature of the swarm-based paradigm allows us to simultaneously partition into k sets. Results show that this approach can be superior in quality when compared to standard methods. Whilst it is marginally slower, the reduced communication cost will greatly reduce the much longer simulation phase of the finite element method. Hence this will outweigh the initial cost of making the partition.

1 Introduction

The problems tackled in this paper arise in the application of the Finite Element Method (FEM) which is used in branches of engineering such as fluid dynamics. Numerical simulation using techniques such as the Finite Element Method discretises the domain into a mesh consisting of a set of geometrical elements. It then solves for quantities of interest at the element nodes. Due to the large computational expense of such simulations, parallel implementations may be required, with the discretised domain partitioned or divided among several processors, in a manner that attempts to balance the load and minimise the communication between processors. This arises because the solution for a given element requires information from neighbouring elements that share edges, or points. With only two processors the graph partitioning problem becomes a graph bisection problem, where given a graph $G = (V, E)$ with vertices V equivalent to nodes in the mesh and edges E equivalent to connected nodes in the mesh, a partition $V = V_1 \cup V_2$ must be found such that $V_1 \cup V_2 = 0$, $|V_1| \simeq |V_2|$ and the number of cut edges $|E_c|$ is minimised, where $E_c = \{(v_1\ v_2) \in E \mid v_1 \in V_1, v_2 \in V_2\}$.

The emergent organisation known as *stigmergy*, seen in insect colonies, was first observed by Grassé in 1959 [3], who postulated that only indirect commu-

M. Ali and F. Esposito (Eds.): IEA/AIE 2005, LNAI 3533, pp. 638–647, 2005.

nication is used between workers, through their environment. Partitioning problems have been tackled, using the brood sorting capabilities seen in colonies of *Leptothorax Unifasciatus.* Deneubourg et al. [1] produced such sorting behaviour in a colony of ant-like agents. Ants move on a 2–D grid and can pick-up and drop objects. The probability of picking up an object is proportional to the isolation of that object, whereas the probability of dropping an object is proportional to similarity of objects in the local environment. Kuntz and Snyers [12] extended this to clique partitioning by relating the similarity of nodes to connectivity in the graph. Here the larger number of shared nodes two vertices have the more similar they are. Another approach adopted by Kuntz and Snyers [13] uses the spatial colonisation of nodes in a graph by a number of competing colonies of animats. The vertices are mapped onto a grid and competing species attempt to colonise nodes by having the most animats present. The vertices colonised by each species corresponds to a set in the graph partitioning problem.

Most partitioning methods employ recursive bisection which can often provide a partition which is far from optimal [15]. What seems optimal at the top level of recursion may provide a poor partition at lower levels given the benefit of hindsight. Recently many methods have been generalised to partition into more than two sets at each stage of recursion [5], [7]. However, results have been relatively poor in comparison. The best partitioning algorithms generally employ a combination of global and local methods. Global methods [14] use the structure of the graph whilst local methods [9, 2] try to improve a partition by swapping nodes between sets. Furthermore, multilevel versions of these methods have been shown to outperform their single level counterparts [8], [6]. Here, the graph is first coarsened down to a small number of vertices, by grouping sets of nodes to form the vertices of the new graph. A partition of this smaller graph is computed and this partition is projected back towards the original graph by refining the partition at intermediate levels of coarseness.

2 Method

Our approach is based on competing Ant colonies which must restructure their environment in a manner reflecting a good solution of the underlying problem. Initially, two competing colonies of ants are considered. Each colony is centred around a fixed cell on a grid which represents the environment in which the ants can navigate. The ants must learn to forage for food, each piece of food on the grid represents a node in the mesh which is being partitioned. The ants must find all the food and place it in the appropriate nest such that the set of nodes represented by the food in $Nest_1$ forms a set V_1 and the set of nodes in $Nest_2$ forms a set V_2. The mesh partitioning problem is equivalent to a graph bisection problem, where given a graph $G = (V, E)$ with vertices V, equivalent to nodes in the mesh, and edges E equivalent to connected nodes in the mesh, a partition $V = V_1 \cup V_2$ must be found such that $V_1 \cap V_2 = \emptyset$, $|V_1| \approx |V_2|$ and the number of cut edges $|E_c|$ is minimised where $E_c = \{(v_1, v_2) \bigm| v_1 \in V_1, v_2 \in V_2\}$.

2.1 The Ant Foraging Strategy

The Program used to govern movement of the ants is derived by Genetic Programming [10, 11] and is known as the Ant Foraging Strategy (AFS). Initially, all ants are located in their respective nests. Each iteration involves one movement of each ant in each colony according to this Program. AFS allows the ants to collect food and place it around the appropriate nest so that it represents a good partition of the underlying mesh. Each iteration represents one action by each ant in each colony. The possible actions are described below. Each grid cell holds a variable amount of food but may contain any number of ants. Each colony must collect food and hence an emergent co-operation between ants in the same colony is needed which is provided by pheromone trails. Each trail has a decay rate and hence must be reinforced or will disappear and because food sources are relatively constant this rate is quite low.

Control Algorithm.

if(Carrying Food) **then**
  if (In Nest Locus) **then** (Drop Food)
  else (Move To Nest)
else
  if(Food Here) **then** (Pick Up Food)
  else
    if(Food Ahead) **then** (Move Forward)
    else
      if(In Nest Locus) **then** (Move To Away Pheromone)
      else
        if (Help Signal) **then** (Move To Help)
        else (Follow Strongest Forward Pheromone)

Movement and Pheromone Trails. All ants are placed on the grid cell representing the colony nest at time t=0. They are initialised to face in a random direction i.e. North, South, East or West. During each time step (iteration), an ant can move only to one of the four adjacent neighbouring grid squares. `move_forward` causes an ant to move one grid square in the direction it is facing. There are also directional actions, `turn_right` and `turn_left` which cause the ant to change the direction it is pointing by rotating clockwise or anticlockwise 90 degrees. `move_random` causes the ant to point in a random direction and move forward one grid square in that direction. When an ant tries to move off the grid, it is forced to turn left or right with equal probability. By preventing the ants from wrapping around to the other side of the grid, a colony will be less likely to collect food corresponding to a disconnected partition of the graph which is mapped structurally onto the grid.

To partition the graph, each colony must collect a set of food pieces so that the associated nodes assigned to each colony correspond to a good global partition of the graph. To do this, ants must forage for food and bring it back to the nest.

When food is picked up, it disappears off the map. It can only be dropped if the ant is near the nest. `in_nest_locus` is True if an ant is within a distance of 2 grid squares from the colony nest. `drop_food` causes the food to reappear on the map, it is placed around the nest cell using a clockwise search to find the first cell with enough space to hold the node corresponding to the food piece.

To co-ordinate the activity of each colony, pheromone trails are used. These act as implicit communication signals which can be detected only by ants from the same colony. Pheromone is dropped only when an ant is carrying food, hence other ants can follow trails to find regions of the grid containing a high density of food. The amount of pheromone deposited, (Pheromone Strength Ph) is 100.0 units and the Decay Rate Ph_{decay} is 5% each iteration. `move_to_strong_forward_pheromone` which causes the ant to move forward one square. The probability of movement in each direction is proportional to the amount of pheromone in each grid square associated with that direction. A cumulative probability distribution is used to decide which direction is chosen. For example, if the ratio of pheromone in the 3 grid squares is 1:1:2 representing the relative amounts of pheromone in left:right:forward grid squares, then, for a given random number r between 0 and 1, the direction chosen would be dependent on the distribution as follows:

$$\texttt{movement} = \begin{cases} \texttt{move left} & \text{if } 0 \leq r \leq 0.25 \\ \texttt{move right} & \text{if } 0.25 < r \leq 0.50 \\ \texttt{move forward} & \text{if } 0.5 < r \leq 1.00 \end{cases}$$

`move_to_away_pheromone` causes the ant to move away from the nest in one of two *away directions*. The horizontal away direction can be either East or West according to which direction would increase the horizontal distance between the ant and the nest. Similarly, the vertical away direction can be either North or South.The away direction is chosen probabilistically and is proportional to the amount of pheromone in the grid squares corresponding to each away direction. For each pheromone action a small positive value of 90.0 is used when the amount of pheromone in a square is 0.0. This allows a small amount of exploration for new food sources.

Picking Up and Dropping Food. An ant can pick up food if `food_here` is True. This occurs when there is food on the current grid square which has not already been collected and assigned to the ant's colony. This stops ants trying to pick up food already assigned to that colony. Ants can pick up both unassigned food which has not yet been picked up and assigned food which has been placed in another colony's nest. These two eventualities in `pick_up_food` are governed by different rules and are known as *foraging* and *raiding*.

As stated previously, unassigned food is given a weight which relates to the number of cuts which will be created if the selected node is assigned to the ant's colony. The total number of cuts depends upon which colonies the connected nodes in the graph have been assigned. If all connected nodes are unassigned there are no cuts created. The edge weights between nodes correspond to the number of cuts produced if each node is placed in a different set. The total number of cuts produced by assigning the node are calculated as a proportion of all possible cuts i.e., the total edge weight. If this proportion is greater than 0.5 the ant cannot pick up the food piece. Otherwise the food is assigned a weight corresponding to the proportion of cuts produced. This weight indicates how many ants are needed to pick up and carry the food. Hence, the less cuts the easier it is for the ants to collect a piece of food.

The proportion of cuts produced, p_c, determines the weight of the food. If a weight of greater than 1 is assigned to a piece of food, an ant must send out a help signal, which can be detected by other ants from the same colony. `if_help_signal` is True if there is a signal within a distance of H_l grid squares. The help signal is used to attract other ants as food can only be picked up if the appropriate number of ants are present to lift the weight.

$$Weight = \begin{cases} 1 \text{ if } p_c & = 0.2 \\ 2 \text{ if } p_c & = 0.35 \\ 3 \text{ if } p_c & = 0.5 \end{cases}$$

Assigned food is always given a weight of 1. The probability of pick-up is dependent on the change in the proportion of cuts produced when a piece of food is reassigned to another colony. As with the unassigned food, the cuts are calculated as a proportion of the total possible cuts and an ant can pick it up with a greater probability if the proportion of cuts decreases when food is reassigned. If the proportion of cuts increases it can be picked up with a much lower probability.

The reason for this, is to encourage a better partition by making it easier for ants to pick up food which decreases the proportion of cuts. However, if the ants can only reassign food which reduces the proportion of cuts, then the system could easily get stuck in local minima. So, moves which increase the proportion of cuts are allowed with a low probability to improve the search mechanism. Hence, the probability of picking up an assigned piece of food is related to δp_c, the change in the proportion of cuts which is produced by reassigning the food, (δp_c is equal to the current p_c minus the new p_c). The probability of picking up food which increases the proportion of cuts is related to the number of cuts produced by reassigning the node and the appropriate deterioration constant $C_1 = 1.0$ or $C_2 = 6.0$.

$$Prob = \begin{cases} 1.0 & \text{if } \delta p_c \geq 0.0 \\ 1.0/(C_1 * (p_c)^2) & \text{if } -0.166 < \delta p_c < 0.0 \\ 1.0/(C_2 * (p_c)^2) & \text{if } -0.5 < \delta p_c \leq -0.166 \\ 0.0 & \text{if } \delta p_c \leq -0.33 \end{cases}$$

Unsuccessful pick-up leads to a `move_random` action. Ants can sense food in the immediate and adjacent squares using the functions, `if_food_here`, and `if_food_ahead`. It is also assumed that they can remember the position of the colony nest. `move_to_nest` makes an ant move one step towards the nest whereas `move_to_help` which moves the ant one step towards the nearest help signal.

Preprocessing. In order to produce a good k-way partition we map the structure of the graph onto the grid environment (i.e connected nodes are placed next to each other to reflect the spatial layout of the underlying graph) and then place the colony nests in a position to take advantage of this structure. Hence important global information is embedded in the grid environment such that ants need only use information in their local environment to find a good initial partition. Hence our method utilises both global and local information. In order to take advantage of the structural information provided by the layout of food on the grid we attempt to place each nest at the centre of roughly the same amount of food. To do this we use a primitive recursive bisection technique. A multilevel approach is adopted in which an initial coarse-grained graph (each node corresponds to a cluster of nodes in the original graph) is partitioned and the resulting partition is projected back through less coarse-grained graphs until the original graph is reached.

Run Parameters. This method produces high quality results over a range of parameter values. However we have tried to reduce the time taken by tuning certain parameters as described below. To reduce the search we eliminate unwanted partitions such as unbalanced and disconnected sets which cause a high number of cuts. This is done by defining an upper bound on the number of nodes a colony can collect. Each colony can exceed the upper bound (relating to the number of nodes in a balanced partition) by one piece of food. We also define a lower bound (relating to 90% of a balanced partition) which must be present in a colony before an ant from another colony can raid the food. We adopt a multilevel approach to cut down the search space and intermittent greedy phases where ants can only pick up food if the resultant partition would be the same as, or better quality than, the existing partition. At each successive level of the algorithm the blocks of nodes are split in two, doubling the number of blocks on the grid. After producing the new set of blocks each successive level consists of a greedy phase followed by a non-greedy phase until the node level is reached.The convergence interval is 300 iterations at each level for both the greedy and non-greedy phases. If no improvement is seen the next phase or level is started. To further speed up the algorithm we reduce the grid from $20 * 20$ at the first level to $10 * 10$ for subsequent levels.

3 Results

We have compared the results of our k-way algorithm (ML-AFS) against both single level and multilevel partitioning methods involving both recursive bisection and k-way methods. In particular we compare our results with Recursive Spectral Bisection (RSB) [14] and Multilevel Kernighan Lin (ML-KL) [6], a multilevel version of RSB using the Kernighan Lin heuristic (KL) for local improvement of partitions at each successive level. K-way versions of these algorithms use higher eigenvectors to partition the graph into k parts and a k-way version of KL to swap nodes between sets. Table 1 compares our method against RSB

Table 1. Comparison of Results with Recursive Bisection Methods from Chaco - showing number of cuts created by 8 Sets partitions and percentage improvement in quality of ML-AFS over these methods

Test Case	RSB	ML-KL	ML-AFS	% Improvement of ML-AFS over (ML-KL)
Airfoil2067	388	355	310	12.7
Rectangle925	269	233	221	5.2
Circle3795	547	499	442	11.4
Cascade885	208	187	161	13.7
Saddle1169	263	247	230	6.8
Naca4000	522	489	443	9.4
Spiral4680	559	531	476	10.3
La3335	310	287	271	5.6
PsSquare2298	448	388	353	8.9
PsSquare635	150	153	129	15.5

Table 2. Comparison of Results with Main Methods from Chaco Package - showing number of cuts created by 8 sets partitions and time taken in brackets

Test Case	RSB	RSB+KL	ML-KL	RSB	RSB+KL	ML-KL	ML-AFS
Scheme	Rb	Rb	Rb	Kway	Kway	Kway	Kway
Airfoil2067	388	353	355	358	341	357	310
(time)	(2.45)	(2.54)	(0.83)	(2.5)	(2.5)	(1.28)	(5.02)
Rec925	269	225	233	270	258	256	221
(time)	(0.86)	(0.94)	(0.57)	(0.72)	(1.24)	(0.85)	(2.90)
Circle3795	547	517	499	550	516	509	442
(time)	(4.6)	(5.3)	(1.15)	(3.6)	(4.62)	(2.06)	(9.13)
Cascade885	208	194	187	262	210	209	161
(time)	(0.72)	(0.89)	(0.46)	(0.72)	(1.4)	(1.0)	(2.84)
Saddle1169	263	251	247	309	270	288	230
(time)	(1.1)	(1.16)	(0.7)	(0.91)	(1.65)	(1.24)	(6.99)
Naca4000	522	492	489	524	517	528	443
(time)	(6.24)	(6.34)	(1.19)	(3.78)	(4.74)	(1.41)	(9.04)
Spiral4680	559	534	531	592	563	570	476
(time)	(6.73)	(7.84)	(1.53)	(5.11)	(5.76)	(1.58)	(9.21)
La3335	310	287	287	331	310	386	271
(time)	(5.26)	(5.32)	(1.13)	(4.31)	(4.82)	(2.18)	(11.11)
PsSquare2298	448	401	388	455	424	418	353
(time)	(2.99)	(2.9)	(0.94)	(2.04)	(2.74)	(1.22)	(7.39)
PsSquare635	150	137	153	178	174	189	129
(time)	(0.48)	(0.55)	(0.41)	(0.51)	(0.65)	(0.47)	(2.82)

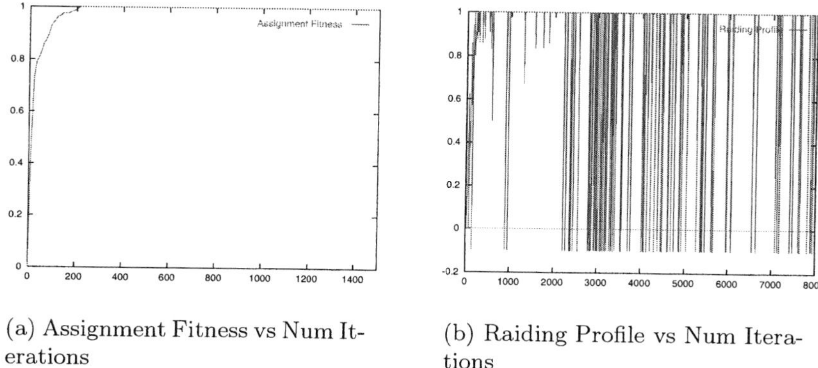

(a) Assignment Fitness vs Num Iterations

(b) Raiding Profile vs Num Iterations

Fig. 1. Assignment Fitness and Raiding Profile for an 8 Set partition of Film286 (-ve value means no food collected)

and ML-KL from the Chaco Package [4]. We show the percentage improvement of our method over Chaco's ML-KL as this gives the best results out of all methods in the Chaco Package. ML-KL is coarsened to 200 nodes as recommended by Hendrickson and Leyland. Table 2 shows a comparison with all the main methods

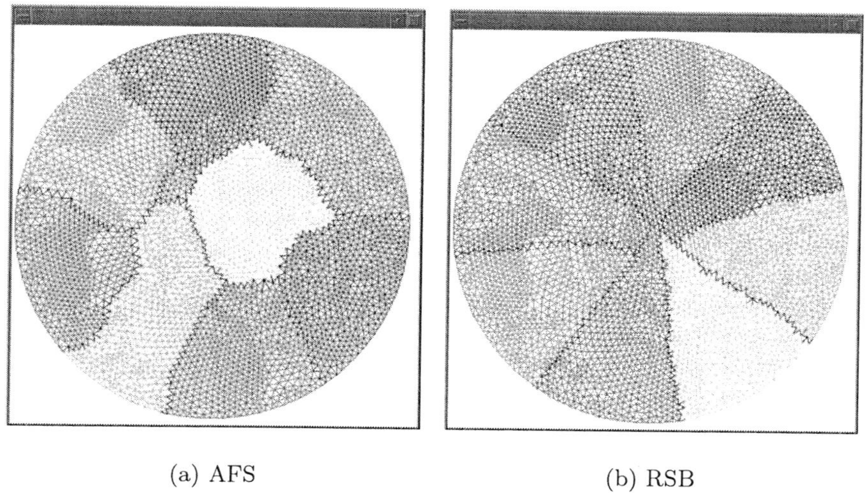

(a) AFS

(b) RSB

Fig. 2. 8 Sets Partitions for Circle3795

in the Chaco Package including RSB, RSB combined with KL (RSB+KL) and ML-KL. All results for our k-way algorithm (ML-AFS) are the best partition found during a run. Example partitions produced by ML-AFS are displayed alongside those produced by RSB in Figure 2.

4 Discussion

We have presented an algorithm which can take advantage of a rough initial partition and provide k-way search for a high quality initial partition which can be significantly better than recursive bisection approaches. It can be seen that ML-AFS is up to 15.5% better than those provided by ML-KL. This is because useful structural information is embedded into the environment so that each colony can find a good start point for the k-way partition with minimal search. However, analysis of the algorithm shows that a relatively high amount of raiding takes place whilst the initial partition is created. This is shown in Figure 1 which gives the Assignment Fitness (proportion of the total nodes assigned to a colony) and the Raiding Profile (proportion of nodes collected which are raided from another colony nest over intervals of 10 iterations) for a Finite Element mesh with 286 nodes. Hence, the crude recursive bisection scheme for nest placement does not determine the initial partition but merely gives a useful start point.

The upper and lower set bounds also help to reduce the search space by cutting out partitions with unbalanced sets. Furthermore, the combination of non-greedy and greedy local improvement allows the algorithm to successively refine this partition over various levels of granularity without the search getting stuck in local minima or lost in undesirable regions of the fitness landscape. Other swarm-based methods [12, 13] suffer from a lack of structural information and are hence relatively inefficient as they generally start from a random configuration. In our algorithm important structural information is embedded into the grid environment and a multilevel approach is used. This facilitates high quality partitions whilst greatly reducing the search space. Kuntz and Snyers use much larger grids and numbers of agents, making them unviable for partitioning graphs with over 500 nodes. They report run times of up to 15 minutes on graphs with known cluters of high connectivity and results are not compared with standard methods, hence direct comparison is difficult.

5 Conclusions

Our results show that the distributed swarm-based approach taken has provided much better quality results than standard methods which take a recursive approach such that the final solution is dependent on solutions found at higher levels of recursion.It is between approximately 6 and 10 times slower than standard ML methods. However the saving in communication cost over two consecutive recursive 8-way partitions would be approximately between 10 and 30 percent. As the simulation phase is generally very much longer than the partitioning phase this could lead to large overall savings in time as communication costs can drammatically slow down the solution process.

References

1. J.L. Deneubourg, S. Goss, N. Franks, A. Sendova-Franks, C. Detrain, and L. Chretien. The dynamics of collective sorting: Robot–like ants and ant–like robots. In J.A. Meyer and S.W. Wilson, editors, *Proceedings of the First International Conference on Simulation of Adaptive Behaviour: From Animals to Animats*, pages 356–363. MIT Press, 1990.
2. C.M. Fiduccia and R.M. Mattheyses. A linear time heuristic for improving network partitions. In *Proceedings of the 19th Design Automation Workshop*, page 175, July 1982.
3. P. Grassé. La réconstruction du nid et les coordinations interindividuelles; la théorie de la stigmergie. *IEEE Transactions on Evolutionary Computation*, 35:41–84, 1959.
4. B. Hendrickson and R. Leyland. The Chaco user's guide, version 2.0. Technical report, Sandia National Laboratories, 1993.
5. B. Hendrickson and R. Leyland. An improved spectral load balancing method. *Parallel Processing for Scientific Computing*, 1:953–961, 1993.
6. B. Hendrickson and R. Leyland. A multilevel algorithm for partitioning graphs. Technical report, Sandia National Laboratories, 1993.
7. B. Hendrickson and R. Leyland. An improved spectral graph partitioning algorithm for mapping parallel computations. *SIAM Journal of Scientific Computing*, 16, 1995.
8. G. Karypis and V. Kumar. A fast and high quality multilevel scheme for partitioning irregular graphs. Technical report, Dept. of Computer Science,University of Minnesota,Minneapolis,MN, 1995.
9. B.W. Kernighan and S. Lin. An efficient heuristic procedure for partitioning graphs. *Bell Systems Technical Journal*, 49(2):291–308, September 1970.
10. J.R Koza. *Genetic Programming: On the Programming of Computers by Natural Selection.* MIT Press, 1992.
11. J.R Koza. *Genetic Programming 2: Automatic Discovery of Reusable Programs.* MIT Press, 1994.
12. P. Kuntz, P. Layzell, and D. Snyers. A colony of ant–like agents for partitioning in VLSI technology. In P. Husbands and I. Harvey, editors, *Proceedings of the Fourth European Conference on Artificial Life*, pages 417–424. MIT Press, 1997.
13. P. Kuntz and D. Snyers. Emergent colonisation and graph partitioning. In D. Cliff, P. Husbands, J. Meyer, and S.W. Wilson, editors, *Proceedings of the Third International Conference on Simulation of adaptive behaviour: From Animals to Animats 3*, pages 494–500. MIT Press, 1994.
14. H.D. Simon. Partitioning of unstructured problems for parallel processing. *Computer Systems in Engineering*, 2:135–148, 1991.
15. H.D. Simon and S.H. Teng. How good is recursive bisection? Technical report, NAS Systems Division, NASA,CA, 1993.

The Probabilistic Heuristic In Local (PHIL) Search Meta-strategy

Marcus Randall

Faculty of Information Technology, Bond University,
QLD 4229, Australia

Abstract. Local search, in either best or first admissible form, generally suffers from poor solution qualities as search cannot be continued beyond locally optimal points. Even multiple start local search strategies can suffer this problem. Meta-heuristic search algorithms, such as simulated annealing and tabu search, implement often computationally expensive optimisation strategies in which local search becomes a subordinate heuristic. To overcome this, a new form of local search is proposed. The Probabilistic Heuristic In Local (PHIL) search meta-strategy uses a recursive branching mechanism in order to overcome local optima. This strategy imposes only a small computational load over and above classical local search. A comparison between PHIL search and ant colony system on benchmark travelling salesman problem instances suggests that the new meta-strategy provides competitive performance. Extensions and improvements to the paradigm are also given.

Keywords: heuristic search, combinatorial optimisation, meta-heuristic.

1 Introduction

Local search is a classical approach to solving combinatorial optimisation problems (COPs). There have been numerous instances of local search algorithms being used by themselves to solve COPs (e.g., [3, 5, 10, 12]) (usually as a means of implementing a control strategy); as the basis of meta-heuristic search strategies (e.g., simulated annealing (SA) [14] and tabu search (TS) [8]); or as an adjunct heuristic to other heuristics/meta-heuristics (e.g., ant colony optimisation (ACO) [4], greedy randomised adaptive search procedures (GRASPs) [6]). While the iterative meta-heuristic search strategies (such as SA and TS) are able to use local search to overcome local optima (usually at the expense of long runtimes), the settling in local minima or maxima for the classical approach is a limitation. However, the cost for using meta-heuristic strategies is that they can require significant amounts of computational runtime beyond that of the local search component. The Probabilistic Heuristic In Local (PHIL) search is designed to extend classical local search by augmenting it with a computationally inexpensive probabilistic branching strategy. This branching strategy is a recursive one that continues the search process from a point within the current search trajectory.

M. Ali and F. Esposito (Eds.): IEA/AIE 2005, LNAI 3533, pp. 648–656, 2005.

The remainder of the paper is organised as follows. Section 2 discusses other extensions to local search while Section 3 describes the extensions to the classic algorithm that constitute PHIL search. Section 4 presents the results of the computational experiments using benchmark travelling salesman problem (TSP) instances. Additionally, a comparison to an implementation of ant colony system (ACS) is provided. Finally Section 5 provides a discussion of some of the extensions and enhancements that are possible for the new search strategy.

2 Local Search

There have been a number of variations of local search that have been extended from the previously described classical forms. Some of the more notable approaches are described below.

Guided Local Search (GLS) [9, 15] is a nominal extension to classical local search that enables it to become a meta-strategy. Once local search becomes stuck in a local optimum, the meta-strategy component is activated. The weights/penalties in an augmented objective function are increased so as to guide the local search out of the particular local optimum. This is a form of search space transformation that has only been applied to a few combinatorial optimisation problems. An extended version of the algorithm in which tabu style aspiration criteria and random moves are added gives comparable performance on the quadratic assignment problem to standard TS approaches [9].

The Affine Shaker algorithm of Battiti and Techolli [1, 2] works by successively sampling sub-regions of search space. Each region is defined by a central starting point (i.e., the region surrounds this point equally). This region is then sampled to generate a new tentative point. Depending on whether this new point is of better or worse quality, the sampling area is expanded or compressed (respectively). If the sampling is able to produce a better solution, this becomes the new starting point, and the sub-region is relocated around this point. Thus the process can continue for a number of iterations. The affine shaker algorithm has been applied to problems within neural networking back propagation [2] and as part of continuous reactive tabu search solving benchmark functions [1].

Paquette and Stützle [10] present an enhancement of local search called Iterated Local Search (ILS) that optimises problems, such as the graph colouring problem, in which there are two optimisation criteria. In terms of this problem, ILS first attempts to find feasible colourings for successively smaller chromatic numbers. At each iteration of the algorithm, a complete local search based heuristic (such as classic hill climbing or tabu search) is executed. The procedure terminates once a legal colouring cannot be found and hence returns the chromatic number of the previous colouring. The authors reported receiving comparable results to state of the art heuristics and meta-heuristics on benchmark problems.

Yuret and de la Maza's [16] Dynamic Hill Climbing algorithm is a population based approach that uses genetic algorithm mechanisms of reproduction and selection in order to modify solutions. It also adds two elements to the search. These are: a) the dynamic alteration of the search space co-ordinate system and

b) the exploitation of local optimum. The first is necessary when the search encounters a local optima. It re-orients the search space co-ordinate system in order to compute an escape trajectory. In terms of the latter, the local optima found by the search process are recorded. If the population becomes stuck, a diversification measure is enacted. A new starting point point is generated by maximising the Hamming distance between the nearest recorded local optimum. At this stage, the search process is restarted and the list of local optima is reset. Dynamic hill climbing has been applied to De Jong's set of continuous test functions and has provided competitive performance [16].

Unlike the previously described local search methods, Complete Local Search [7] implements a local search having a memory component. The strategy keeps a finite list of previously visited solutions. This list is used to prohibit the search process from exploring the neighbourhoods of these solutions at a later stage. Experimental evaluation on the travelling salesman and subset sum problem instances [7] suggest that though its execution times are efficient, its overall performance is not yet comparable with standard heuristic and meta-heuristic implementations.

3 The PHIL Search Algorithm

PHIL search is an extension of classical local search. It resembles multistart local search as it performs multiple local searches. The key difference is that instead of starting at a random point in state space, PHIL search probabilistically chooses a point within the recently completed local search trajectory. The rationale for this is that the point will at least be better than the starting point and may lead to a superior end point. At this point, the new local search (referred to as a branch) chooses the next best transition operation[1] and proceeds until no more improvement is possible (i.e., the classic local search termination condition). Moreover, this is a recursive process as once a local search trajectory has been explored (in terms of the generation of probabilistic branch points), the strategy will return to the branch from which the current branch was initiated. This is consistent with depth first search behaviour.

Termination of the overall algorithm is either after a certain number of individual PHIL searches have been executed, or when a particular solution cost has been obtained. In terms of the former, an individual PHIL search is completed once the root branch (the original local search trajectory) has explored all its branch points. These may be referred to as search trees. The only parameter required by PHIL search (referred to as α) is the probability of branching at a point on the local search trajectory. A high probability will produce dense search trees, while the reverse is true for a low probability.

Algorithms 1-4 give the combined pseudocode description of PHIL search. The first presents the framework in which PHIL search is executed. The termination condition used here represents the number of search trees generated. The

[1] Any standard local search operator can be used within PHIL search.

Algorithm 1 The initialisation phase of PHIL search

```
Get user parameters(α, num_restarts)
for trial = 1 to num_restarts do
    x = Generate a random initial feasible solution
    cost = Find_cost(x)
    Initialise all of index array elements to 0
    cost = Perform_phil(x, α, cost, index, 1)
    if cost < best_cost then
        best_cost = cost
    end if
end for
Output best_cost
end
```

Algorithm 2 The PHIL search strategy

```
Perform_phil(x, α, cost, index, level)
x' = x
cost, trail_length = Perform_local_search(x', cost, tran_list1, tran_list2)
index[level] = Probabilistic_find_branch_point(x, α, tran_list1, tran_list2)
if index[level] ≠ dead_branch then
    index[level] = index[level] + 1
    level = level + 1
    Perform_phil(x, α, cost, index, level)
    level = level − 1
else
    return cost
end if
end Perform_phil
```

overall PHIL strategy is given in Algorithm 2 while Algorithm 3 corresponds to a standard local search procedure. The final part of PHIL search probabilistically chooses a branching point on the current local search trajectory. Fig. 1 provides an explanation of some of the terms used within the overall algorithm.

4 Computational Experience

The methodology and results of testing PHIL search are described herein. The target application for this initial study is the TSP. The local search operator is the inversion operator, as it has been shown to be effective by Randall and Abramson [12].

Initial experimentation with the α parameter suggests that appropriate values of it are a function of the size of the problem. In this case, the term "appropriate" refers to values that tend to produce good quality solutions. Using a linear regression model on a subset of the test problem instances revealed that $\alpha = -0.008n + 0.925$ (where n is the number of cities and the minimum bound of

Algorithm 3 The local search component of PHIL search

```
Perform_local_search(x, cost, tran_list_1, tran_list_2)
new_cost = cost
index = 1
while new_cost < cost do
    cost = new_cost
    neighbours = Evaluate_neighbours(x)
    tran_list_1[index] = neighbours[1]
    if there is a second best transition then
        tran_list_2[index] = neighbours[2]
    end if
    Apply_transition(x, tran_list_1[index])
    new_cost = Find_cost(x)
    index = index + 1
end while
return new_cost and index
end Perform_local_search
```

Algorithm 4 The probabilistic branching strategy within PHIL search

```
Probabilistic_find_branch_point(x, trail_length, α, tran_list_1, tran_list_2, index)
Perform all transitions up to and including the index^th
while found = false And index < trail_length do
    Apply_transition(x, tran_list_1[index])
    q = unif_rand()
    if q ≤ α And tran_list_2[index] is present then
        Apply_transition(x, tran_list_2[index])
        return index
    end if
    index = index + 1
end while
return dead_branch
end Probabilistic_find_branch_point
```

the equation is 0.005) is a good overall function for the TSP. The investigation of this parameter will receive further attention in future studies.

4.1 Methodology and Problem Instances

The computing platform used to perform the experiments is a 2.6GHz Red Hat Linux (Pentium 4) PC with 512MB of RAM.[2] Each problem instance is run across ten random seeds.

The experiments are used to compare the performance of PHIL search to a standard implementation of ACS (extended details of which can be found in Randall [11]). As the amount of computational time required for an ACS iteration is different to that of a PHIL search iteration, approximately the same

[2] The experimental programs are coded in the C language and compiled with gcc.

Fig. 1. Terms used within the PHIL search algorithm

x is the solution vector,
Find_cost evaluates the objective function,
dead_branch signifies a branch that has been explored,
Evaluate_neighbours evaluates all the neighbours of a solution using a defined local search operator,
neighbours is an ordered array of transition attributes of the neighbours,
$tran\_list_1$ refers to the list of best transitions at each stage of the local search while $tran\_list_2$ is the list of the second best,
Apply_transition() applies a transition to a solution using a set of transition attributes and
unif_rand() produces a uniform random number.

Table 1. Problem instances used in this study

Name	Size (cities)	Best-Known Cost
hk48	48	11461
eil51	51	426
st70	70	675
eil76	76	538
kroA100	100	21282
bier127	127	118282
d198	198	15780
ts225	225	126643
pr299	299	48919
lin318	318	42029

amount of computational time per run is given to both strategies. This is based on 3000 ACS iterations. It must be noted that the ACS solver applies a standard local search (using inversion as the operator) to each solution that is generated.

Ten TSP problem instances are used to test both the ACS strategy and PHIL search. These problems are from TSPLIB [13] and are given in Table 1.

4.2 Results and Comparison

The results for the ACS and PHIL search strategies (in terms of objective cost and the amount of computational time required to reach a run's best objective value) are given in Tables 2 and 3 respectively. In order to describe the range of costs gained by these experiments, the minimum (denoted "Min"), median (denoted "Med") and maximum (denoted "Max") are given. Non-parametric descriptive statistics are used as the data are highly non-normally distributed. Additionally, each cost result is given by a relative percentage difference (RPD) between the obtained cost and the best known solution. This is calculated as $\frac{E-F}{F} \times 100$ where E is the result cost and F is the best known cost.

Table 2. The results of the ACS strategy on the TSP instances. Note that Runtime is recorded in terms of CPU seconds

Problem	Cost (RPD)			Runtime		
	Min	Med	Max	Min	Med	Max
hk48	0	0.08	0.08	0.04	1.29	16.32
eil51	0.47	2	2.82	0.08	0.49	40.69
st70	0.15	1.33	2.07	36.39	43.48	87.56
eil76	0.19	1.3	2.42	0.08	70.23	114.73
kroA100	0	0	0.54	8.67	34.58	192.17
bier127	0.32	0.72	1.87	58.64	253.21	855.28
d198	0.16	0.33	0.6	154.53	1723.34	2422.52
ts225	0.63	1.15	1.93	513.65	3019.9	5484.59
pr299	0.42	0.92	2.68	10139.87	10794.69	13470.37
lin318	1.39	1.92	3	10388.72	14185.36	16090.43

Table 3. The results of the PHIL search strategy on the TSP instances

Problem	Cost (RPD)			Runtime		
	Min	Med	Max	Min	Med	Max
hk48	0	0.25	0.44	3.89	31.38	53.01
eil51	0	0.7	1.64	1.74	22.91	48.37
st70	0.15	0.3	0.74	19.73	127.04	264.78
eil76	1.12	2.42	3.35	56.7	138.69	309.24
kroA100	0.05	0.44	0.84	7.92	466.59	714.43
bier127	0.66	1.57	1.76	12.92	204.48	304.76
d198	1.12	1.66	1.86	17.26	1213.02	2172
ts225	0.34	0.61	0.93	173.25	2570.73	3602.72
pr299	2.13	2.64	3.7	455.17	6479.34	13885.99
lin318	2.96	3.86	4.51	5423.68	14961.38	19807.22

Given that PHIL search is a new technique, its overall performance is good in terms of solution quality and consistency. Both strategies can find solutions in all cases within a few percent of the best known costs. For the larger problems, PHIL search's performance is slightly behind that of ACS. However, it must be bourne in mind that this ACS (as is standard with ant colony techniques) also executes local searches for each solution that it constructs. It is suspected that a greater exploration of the mechanics and the parameters of the new technique will yield still better results. This is discussed in the next section.

5 Conclusions

A new meta-strategy search technique, based on local search, has been proposed in this paper. PHIL search uses a recursive branching strategy, based on previous points within a search trajectory, to generate new searches. The advantage to this technique is that the branching strategy is computationally light in comparison to the characteristic mechanics of other meta-heuristics, particularly TS and ACO. Additionally, it only requires one parameter. The performance of PHIL search on benchmark TSP instances is encouraging. It can achieve solution costs within a few percent of best known costs and it is comparable to an ACS implementation.

In principle, PHIL search can be applied to any combinatorial optimisation problem that has been solved by traditional techniques (such as SA, TS and ACO). The development of the procedure is still in the initial stages. Some of the larger issues include the mechanics of the branching strategy and PHIL search's performance on a wider range of COPs. The former will involve the investigation of alternative strategies such as those based on heuristic strategies rather than just probabilities. As for the latter, the performance of PHIL search needs to be benchmarked against other meta-heuristics, especially on larger and more difficult problems. Of interest will be the incorporation of constraint processing within the strategy. Additionally, it is also possible to replace the local search branches with either tabu searches or simulated annealing.

References

1. Battiti, R., Tecchiolli, G.: The continuous reactive tabu search: blending combinatorial optimization and stochastic search for global optimization. Technical Report UTM 432, Department of Mathematics, University of Trento (1994)
2. Battiti, R., Tecchiolli, G.: Learning with first, second and no dervatives: a case study in high energy physics. Neurocomputing **6** (1994) 181–206
3. Crauwels, H., Potts, C., van Wassenhove, L.: Local search heuristics for the single machine total weighted tardiness scheduling problem. INFORMS Journal on Computing **10** (1998) 341–350
4. Dorigo, M.: Optimization, Learning and Natural Algorithms. PhD. thesis, Politecnico di Milano (1992)
5. Ernst, A., Krishnamoorthy, M.: Solution algorithms for the capacitated single allocation hub location problem. Annals of Operations Research **86** (1999) 141–159
6. Feo, T., Resende, M.: Greedy randomised adaptive search procedures. Journal of Global Optimization **51** (1995) 109–133
7. Ghosh, D., Sierksma, G.: Complete local search with memory. Journal of Heuristics **8** (2002) 571–584
8. Glover, F., Laguna, M.: Tabu Search. Kluwer Academic Publishers, Boston, MA (1997)
9. Mills, P., Tsang, E., Ford, J.: Applying an extended guided local search to the quadratic assignment problem. Annals of Operations Research **118** (2003) 121–135
10. Paquete, L., Stützle, T.: An experimental investigation of iterated local search for colouring graphs. In Cagnoni, S., Gottlieb, J., Hart, E., Raidl, G., eds.: Proceedings of EvoWorkshops 2002. Volume 2279 of Lecture Notes in Computer Science., Springer Verlag (2002) 122–131

11. Randall, M.: A systematic strategy to incorporate intensification and diversification into ant colony optimisation. In: Proceedings of the Australian Conference on Artificial Life, Canberra, Australia (2003)
12. Randall, M., Abramson, D.: A general meta-heuristic solver for combinatorial optimisation problems. Journal of Computational Optimization and Applications **20** (2001) 185–210
13. Reinelt, G.: TSPLIB - A traveling salesman problem library. ORSA Journal on Computing **3** (1991) 376–384
14. van Laarhoven, P., Aarts, E.: Simulated Annealing: Theory and Applications. D. Reidel Publishing Company, Dordecht (1987)
15. Voudouris, C.: Guided Local Search for Combinatorial Optimisation Problems. PhD. thesis, Department of Computer Science, University of Essex (1997)
16. Yuret, D., de la Maza, M.: Dynamic hill climbing: Overcoming the limitations of optimization techniques. In: The 2nd Turkish Symposium on Artificial Intelligence and Neural Networks. (1993) 208–212

Search on Transportation Network for Location-Based Service

Jun Feng[1], Yuelong Zhu[1], Naoto Mukai[2], and Toyohide Watanabe[2]

[1] Hohai University, Nanjing, Jiangsu 210098 China
fengjun-cn@vip.sina.com
[2] Nagoya University, Nagoya, Aichi 464-8603 Japan

Abstract. The issue of how to provide location-based service (LBS) is attracted many researchers. In this paper, we focus on a typical situation of LBS which is to provide services for users in cars that move in a road network. To provide such kinds of services, an integrated method for representing transportation information in addition to road map is proposed. Based on the datasets generated by this method, queries in LBS applications can be responded efficiently.

1 Introduction

With the improvements of geographic positioning technology and the popularity of communication methods such as Internet and ad hoc network, new personal services are proposed and realized, many of which serve the user with desired functionality by considering the user's geo-location. This kind of service is also called as location-based service (LBS). A typical example is to provide services for users in cars that move in a road network. To provide such kinds of services, a variety of types of queries should be considered, such as range queries, nearest neighbor queries, path search query and so on. All these queries should be based on the transportation information on the road network, including transportation route and current travel cost (e.g., travel time) on the segments of road network. Therefore, how to represent the road network with transportation information and support efficient mobile services should be considered.

Transportation information is different from the information of road network. It is important to identify one-way roads with attributes of links, traffic constraints (e.g., no-left-turn and no-U-turn) information about turns between links, or access conditions from one link to another [1]. Moreover, for some important route planning problems, the turn costs are also taken into consideration [2], encountered when we make a turn on a cross-point. A typical method [3] represents the transportation network using a directed graph. In the graph, each edge depicts a one-way road and each node corresponds to a junction. Two-ways roads can be presented as a pair of edges: one in each direction. However, extra nodes should be added to the graph when there are any access limitations (constraints of specific traffic controls). In other words, one node on the road network may be represented with several vertices corresponding to the junctions, and they

M. Ali and F. Esposito (Eds.): IEA/AIE 2005, LNAI 3533, pp. 657–666, 2005.

are independent with each other. Since this representation method ignores the spatial attributes of map objects, only the routing queries are applicable well on this model.

An architecture was proposed in [4] for keeping traffic information on nodes of road network. However, the information of traffic constraints and turn costs on the nodes is omitted in their discussion. To represent the traffic cost and the turn cost, a method in [2] was proposed. The turn cost is represented by a pseudo-dual graph with additional nodes and links, which leads to the high cost of search algorithms (e.g., Dijkstra's algorithm [5]). Moreover, the pseudo-dual graph is insufficient (and needs the reference to the primary graph) for route drawing.

The fundamental objective in this paper is to propose an integrated representation method of transportation network to support mobile services that the user movement is restricted to the transportation network.

This paper is organized as follows. The representation method for integrated management of traffic conditions and spatial information about road network is proposed in Section 2. Section 3 describes the queries based on the previous representation method. Section 4 analyzes our method and Section 5 makes a conclusion on our work.

2 Modeling of Transportation Network

Not only the kinds of information but also the management method of transportation information affect the processing efficiency of queries in ITS applications. In this section, we propose a representation method for integrating traffic information and spatial information about road network by considering the followings terms:

1) The traffic conditions change continuously, and the snapshot of conditions is recorded as traffic information. In comparison with the traffic information, the map of road network is seldom updated, and can be regarded as static information. Therefore, if the static information is managed by an efficient structure, the changes of traffic information associated with the road map should not disturb the stability of the structure.
2) The integrated representation should not only support the spatial query on road network and the temporal query on traffic information, but also support the interaction between these two kinds of queries.

A road network with nodes and links representing respectively the crosses and road segments can be regarded as an un-directed graph G, $G = (V, L)$, where V is a set of vertices $\{ v_1, v_2, ...v_n\}$, and L is a collection of lines $\{ l_1, l_2, ...l_m\}$. Traffic information on the road network is regarded as a directed graph G', $G' = (V, A)$, where V is a set of vertices $\{ v_1, v_2, ...v_n\}$, and A is a collection of arcs $\{ a_1, a_2, ...a_p\}$.

Figure 1 depicts these two kinds of graphs. In the un-directed graph of Figure 1 (a) road segments are represented by lines, while in the directed graph of Figure

1 (b) junctions are represented by arcs. One line for road segment in Figure 1 (a) may be corresponded to two arcs in Figure 1 (b) with two-directions traffic information. In addition to the directions of traffic, there are usually traffic controls (constraints) on road network to constrain the action of traffic. An example of cross-node, v_k, with constraints of no left-turn and no U-turn is given in Figure 2. Road junctions are represented by using [3]'s model in Figure 2(1), where each edge depicts a one way road and each node corresponds to a junction. Extra nodes are added to the graph, here v_k is split into four nodes. Considering the shortcomings of this model, we propose *super-node* representation method for integrating junctions (including traffic cost and traffic constraints) and road network.

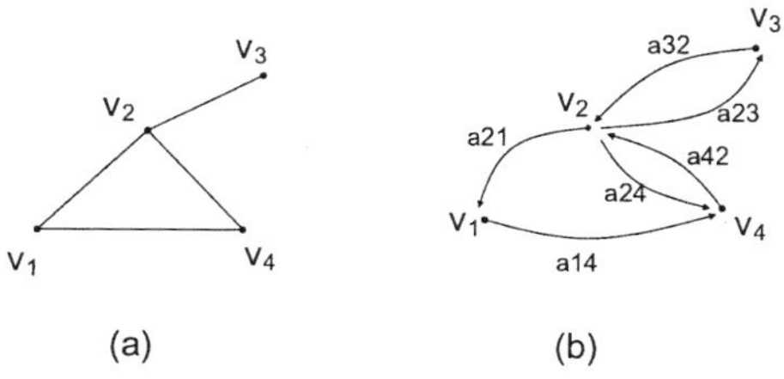

Fig. 1. Road segment and traffic arc

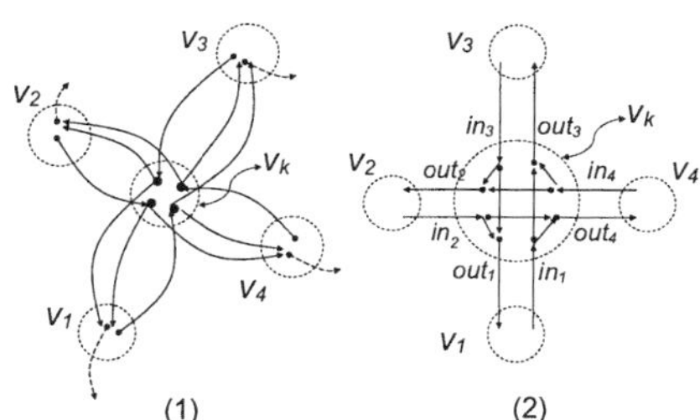

Fig. 2. Cross node with constraint

A *super-node* can be regarded as a node in road network with multiple corresponding junctions, for example, v_k in Figure 2 (2). We define a *super-node* v_k, or simply a *node*, as a triple (p, ca, cm). The first element p belongs to R^2 and is the position of v_k. Arcs connected to v_k are divided into two types. The arcs which have v_k as their final vertex are called *in-arcs* for v_k, denoted as in_i, and similarly the arcs which have v_k as their initial vertex are *out-arcs*, denoted as out_j. The number of those arcs are called as *in-degree* and *out-degree*, respectively. Every *out-arc* is defined as a *cost-arc*. The second element of v_k triple, ca, is the set of (*cost-arc*, v_i, *cost*) triples. Every *cost-arc* is a *out-arc* of v_k whose final vertex is v_i and traffic cost is *cost*. Consider the cross-node v_k in Figure 2(2), ca is a set like this: { (out_1, v_1 $cost_{k1}$), (out_2, v_2 $cost_{k2}$), (out_3, v_3 $cost_{k3}$),(out_4, v_4 $cost_{k4}$)}.

The third element of v_k, cm, is a *constraint-matrix*. For each pair of *in-arc* and *out-arc*, (in_i, out_j), of v_k, cm specifies whether it is allowed to move from in_i to out_j, i.e., cm: $ca^{in} \times ca^{out} -> \{0,1\}$, where 0 and 1 indicate that movement is prohibited and allowed, respectively. The matrix values reflect the specific traffic regulations that apply to the particular node. *constraint-matrix* for v_k in Figure 2 (2) is:

$$\begin{array}{c} \\ in_1 \\ in_2 \\ in_3 \\ in_4 \end{array} \begin{array}{c} \begin{array}{cccc} out_1 & out_2 & out_3 & out_4 \end{array} \\ \begin{pmatrix} 0 & 0 & 1 & 1 \\ 1 & 0 & 0 & 1 \\ 1 & 1 & 0 & 0 \\ 0 & 1 & 1 & 0 \end{pmatrix} \end{array}$$

which reflects that there is traffic constraints of no-left-turn and no-U-turn on v_k. Here, $cm(in_1, out_2) = 0$ indicates that it is not allowed to move from v_1 to v_2 via v_k, while $cm(in_1, out_3) = 1$ indicates that it is allowed to move from v_1 to v_3 via v_k.

Moreover, our method is able to process the turn cost by extending *constraint-matrix* to a *turn-cost/constraint-matrix*, t_cm, i.e., t_cm: $ca^{in} \times ca^{out} -> t\_cost$, $0 \leq t\_cost \leq MAX$. A value less than MAX specify the turn cost from in_i to out_j, and MAX specifies there is restriction from in_i to out_j.

For example, the *turn-cost/constraint-matrix* for v_k in Figure 2 (2) may be like this:

$$\begin{array}{c} \\ in_1 \\ in_2 \\ in_3 \\ in_4 \end{array} \begin{array}{c} \begin{array}{cccc} out_1 & out_2 & out_3 & out_4 \end{array} \\ \begin{pmatrix} MAX & MAX & 40 & 10 \\ 10 & MAX & MAX & 30 \\ 40 & 10 & MAX & MAX \\ MAX & 30 & 10 & MAX \end{pmatrix} \end{array}.$$

This method decreases the redundancies of nodes and traffic arcs in the database by adopting a complex node representation. For the basic road network, the additional information for traffic information is managed on every node. When the number of nodes and traffic arcs keep the same, the modification to any of the traffic information does not injure the stability of spatial index structure (i.e., R-tree [6]) for road network. Therefore, a kind of queries in ITS application, which refer to the spatial information, can be solved by taking advantages of the spatial index. Another kind of queries, which refer to traffic information, can also be solved effectively. In the next section, we center on solving the second kind of queries.

3 Queries on Transportation Network

Within computer science, past research has covered the efficient support for variety of types of queries, including different types of range queries, nearest neighbor queries and reverse nearest neighbor queries [7, 8, 9]. However, this line of research generally make simple assumptions about the problem setting – much work assumes that data and mobile objects are points embedded in, typically, two-dimensional Euclidean space. The result is inadequate for many LBSs, which is based on transportation network and at least the distance should computed based on the path length or cost. Though there was work based on road network [10, 4, 11], only the computation based on path length was talked about. In this section, we propose methods for searching on transportation network with the examples of region query, path search query and continuous nearest neighbor search query. All the queries are based on the path cost, in other word, traffic cost.

3.1 Path Search Regions on Road Network

The length of every road segment of a road network can be regarded as static value in a path search process. When the traffic cost on every road segment is approximated with a value in direct proportion with the length of segment, there are two propositions on the transportation network for nearest object search.

[Proposition 1] *For a source point S and a target object t, r is the path length from S to t, k is a parameter for computing traffic cost based on path length. When the path cost from S to t is $k \times r$, any target object which is with less cost from S than $k \times t$ can only be found inside a circle region, denoted as r-region, whose center is S and whose radius is r (Figure 3(a)).* □

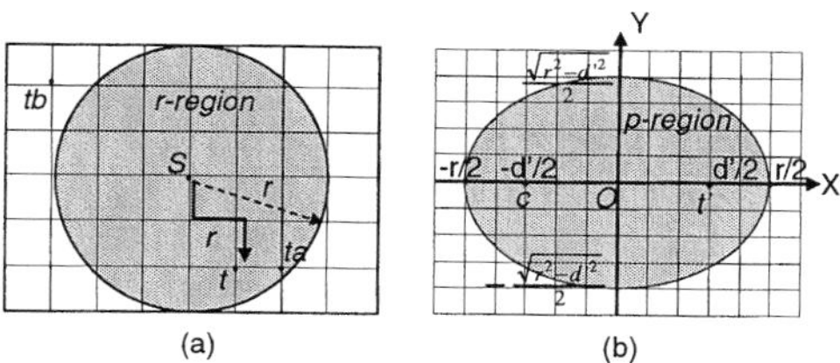

Fig. 3. (a) *r-region*; (b) *p-region*

We leave the proof out in this paper, as it can be convinced by the fact that any road segment outside *r-region* can only lead to a path longer than r from S and the traffic cost greater then $k \times r$.

[Proposition 2] *For two points S and t on the road network with straight-line distance d, the test of whether there is a path shorter than r from S to t can be based on a path search region, denoted as p-region, the sum of the straight-line distance between any nodes inside this region and S and that between this node and t is not longer than r.* □

For an easy description we define a coordinate for them in Figure 3(b), and there is:

$$p - region = \{(x, y) | \sqrt{(x + d/2)^2 + y^2} + \sqrt{(x - d/2)^2 + y^2} \leq r\}. \quad (1)$$

By taking using these two propositions, queries on transportation network can be transformed to the search on road network, which is based on the spatial information of road network. Queries based on spatial information can take advantage of the spatial structures (e.g., R-tree [6]) and achieve an efficient process. However, when there is no direct proportion between traffic cost and path length, An "ink-blot" search method is considered. The "ink-blot" search method solves a path search from v_i to v_t likes this: it begins from expanding v_i's connecting nodes in the sequence of the *cost* on the *cost-arc*; if the target node has not been expanded, the search goes on by expanding the nodes connected by those expanded nodes. By using this method, the region query and the nearest neighbor queries can be responded, efficiently.

3.2 Region and CNN Queries

Region query based on traffic cost is simplified as a tuple (q, c), q belongs to R^2, depicts a query point, the center of the query region. r is the *radius* (*costlimit*, in other word) of the query region. Basd on the transportation network, c can be specified as the travel cost from q.

The point of this kind of query is to decide the region or the shape of the region – because it is not a circle when the distribution of road segments and the cost on them are not uniform. Because all the connection and cost information are managed in nodes, delimit the "ink-blot" algorithm with c, the region can be decided quickly.

Continuous Nearest Neighbor search (CNN-search) along a predefined route is a typical query for LBS based on transportation network. The predefined route from a start point v_1 to an end point v_n is given by an array $Route(v_1, v_n) = (v_1, v_2, ..., v_{n-1}, v_n)$, and the target object set $\{t_a, t_b, ...\}$ is managed by a spatial index structure (e.g., R-tree). We center on the *super-node* representation method and its influence on CNN-search. The *super-node* dataset consists of information about road network and traffic cost on the network. To simplify the explanation, we first use an abstract *cost* on road network, and in the next section analyze the concrete examples of *cost*.

We make observations of the *super-node* dataset in CNN-search process:

1) Every vertex in the *super-node* dataset keeps the cost information of the possible out-arcs, so the cost of traveling from a vertex v_i on $Route(v_1, v_n)$ to the following vertex v_{i+1} is kept on vertex v_i and denoted as $v_i.cost_{i+1}$. If the nearest neighbor (NN) of v_{i+1} is known as t_{i+1} with $cost(v_{i+1}, t_{i+1})$, the cost of traveling from v_i to its NN t_i is not larger than a value *Cost-limit* (v_i), which is computed by: *Cost-limit* $(v_i) = v_i.cost_{i+1} + cost(v_{i+1}, t_{i+1})$. *Cost-limit* (v_i) is used to set a region for the NN-search of v_i (e.g., in Figure 4), NN of v_i can only be found inside the dotted circle region. The region is defined as a circle with radius of *Cost-limit* (v_i) and center of v_i.
2) The nearest target object t_{i+1} of v_{i+1} is also the nearest one on the possible paths from v_i via v_{i+1}. In other words, t_{i+1} is the nearest one found on a path from v_i via $v_i.out_{i+1}$. If there is any object being nearer to v_i than t_{i+1}, the shortest path from v_i to this object does not pass through v_{i+1}. Certainly, it is possible that there is a path from v_i to t_{i+1} via v_j $(j \neq i+1)$, which is shorter than *Cost-limit* (v_i). This situation is depicted in Figure 4,

where v_{i-1} and v_{i+1} share the same NN t_{i+1}, but there is no overlap between the two paths p_{i+1} and p_{i-1}.

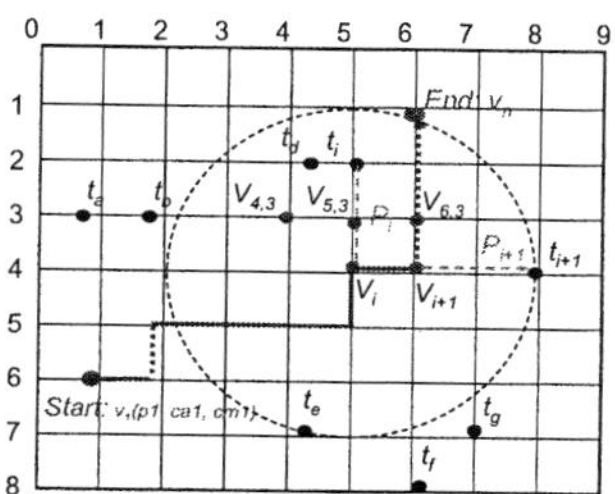

Fig. 4. NN-search for v_i with a limit

Based on the previous observations, it can be concluded that: 1) The path length from v_i to NN t_{i+1} of v_{i+1} can be set as a limit for NN-search of v_i. 2) NN-search of v_i can be executed along the out-arcs of v_i except for $v_i.out_{i+1}$.

Here, proof for these conclusions is omitted. We propose a method for CNN-search along $Route(v_1, v_n)$. Our method first searches t_n for the end vertex v_n; and then generates a search limit for the next computation vertex v_{n-1} based on the previous result, and checks whether there is an object nearer to v_{n-1} via the out-arcs of v_{n-1} except for $v_{n-1}.out_n$. These steps run in cycle until the computation vertex is v_1. NN-search for every vertex can be realized by adopting a priority queue to maintain the current frontier of the search. Any vertex with a higher cost from v_i than the limit value is not inserted into the queue. By expanding the vertex on the head of the queue, the algorithm ends when the head vertex connects to a target object.

4 Analysis

4.1 Characteristics of *Super-Node* Representation Method

In this subsection, we compare the features of traffic information represented by our method (denoted as *super-node* method) with those in the method used by [3, 2] (denoted as node-link method). These features lay the foundation for understanding the behaviors of these methods with respect to retrieval and storage.

For a n $(= m \times m)$ grid graph which represents a road network with m^2 nodes and $2m(m-1)$ links, Table 4.1 gives the number of objects (nodes, arcs and so on) managed in the datasets by using *super-node* method and *node-link* method in different conditions: 1) Without constraints: the transportation network is specified with travel cost and with/without turn costs; 2) With constraints: the transportation network is specified with travel cost, traffic constraints, and with/without turn costs. From this table, we can observe that on any conditions the number of arcs and nodes managed in the dataset keeps the same by using our

Table 1. Comparison of object numbers managed in different methods

		Without Constraints		With Constraints	
		Without turn costs	With turn costs	Without turn costs	With turn costs
Node-link method	nodes	m^2	$8\ m^2$ - $8\ m$	$4\ m^2 + 4$	$8\ m^2$ - $8\ m$
	arcs	$4\ m^2$ - $4\ m$	$40\ m^2$ $+\ 12\ m$ -4	$9\ m^2$ $+\ 8\ m$ - 5	$22\ m^2$ $+\ 4\ m$ - 2
Super-node method	Constraint-matrix	Null	Total elements in matrixes: $16\ m^2 + 36\ m$ - 20		
	nodes	m^2			
	arcs	$4\ m^2 + 4\ m$ - 3			

method. That is why our method supports the stability of the spatial index of the basic road networks. The stability of spatial index ensures that spatial searches can be realized efficiently and the searches on traffic information can also be performed with a steady cost. Contrary to this, in *node-link* method constraints or turn costs are represented with additional nodes and arcs. When there is no traffic constraint and turn cost on nodes, the traffic arcs can be represented only by the nodes on the road map; when there are traffic constraints, the number of nodes (arcs) is four times (duplicated); when there are turn costs, the number of them is even increased. With the increase, the search cost on traffic information is also increased.

4.2 Analysis of Traffic Cost

The abstract cost is used in the previous section. In this subsection, an analysis is given from a viewpoint of providing concrete examples of *cost*: when there is a uniform speed of traffic on the road network, *cost* can be the length of the road segment; otherwise, *cost* can be the travel time for every traffic arc on the road network. Certainly, there are other kinds of *cost*, for example, the toll of a path. Our method supports the search based on all these *cost* definitions.

The discussion and examples used in the previous sections can be regarded as the traffic arcs with the assumption that *cost* is equal to the length of the road segment, implicitly. If *cost* is the travel time on the traffic arc though the region may be not a circle on the road map, it is sure that a region can be generated with the same method and also NN-search for every vertex can be executed using the same program. This is because the region is actually realized by adopting the priority queue ordering on *cost*. The values of the turn cost can be used naturally in the process of search algorithm.

On the other hand, either kind of cost is adopted in the dataset, and the quantity of information on every vertex keeps the same. Therefore, when the road map is managed by some spatial index (e.g., R-tree), *cost-arc* and *constraint-matrix* associated to a vertex are stored into a fixed space of specific disk page. The update for traffic information does not injure the stability of the spatial index.

4.3 Prototype System

In this subsection, we compare our *super-node* representation method with the methods used by [2, 3]. The comparison is made on a part of our prototype system. The total number of nodes N_{num} is 42,062 and the number of links L_{num} is 60,349 in the basic road map.

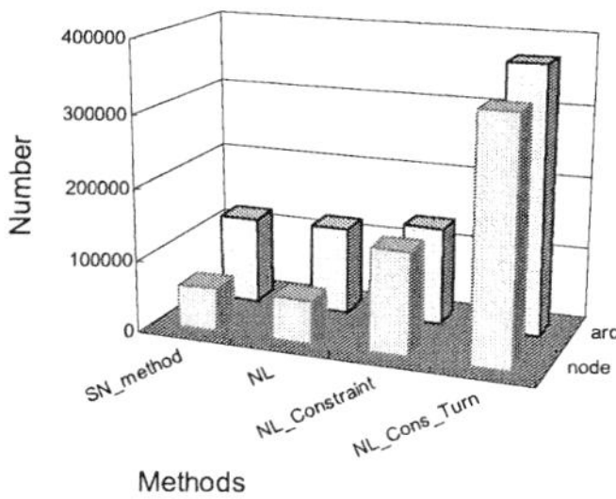

Fig. 5. Numbers of arcs and nodes managed by *super-node* and Node-link methods

The number of average traffic arcs connecting to a node is about 2.87 (=2 L_{num}/N_{num}). When there is no traffic constraint for the basic road map, in node-link method [3] there are 120,798 records (two times of link numbers in road maps). In our *super-node* method, the amount of information is related to the number of arcs in every node: here, the nodes with four, three, two and one out-arcs are about 24 : 51 : 13 : 12. The total arcs managed by SN method is 120,798. When there are traffic constraints, left-turn and U-turn are forbidden in about half of the cross and T-junction points. Then, in NL method there are about 142,423 nodes and 135,293 arcs; while in SN method the amount of information keeps the same on any situations. The number of arcs and nodes managed by *super-node* method (denoted as SN) and that by node-link method (denoted as NL) are given in Figure 5. In this figure, there are different values for different conditions of datasets in NL method. "Constraint" means there are traffic constraints and "Turn" means there are turn costs in the dataset. Because the number of nodes and arcs keep the same, the datasets generated by SN method shares the same value in this figure, which is denoted simply as SN_method. Just as the discussions in the previous subsection, the arc (node) number difference between SN_method and NL_Constraint comes from the traffic constraints on road network. Therefore, if there is no constraint on all road networks, the two methods would manage the same number of arcs (nodes). However, with the constraint increases, the differences between two methods increase, too. This is the situation in the real world: to ensure proper traffic fluency, more and more constraints on road network are set. Moreover, the cost of queries on transportation network (e.g., the cost of using Dijkstra's Algorithm for path search) is related to the number of road objects (nodes and arcs, here). The dataset created by NL method, which consists of more road objects than that in our method, leads to an inefficient query process.

5 Conclusion

In this paper, we proposed a representation method for transportation networks adaptable to location-based services. To attain efficient queries and stabile structure of managing the transportation information and spatial information of the road network, we proposed a *super – node* structure for representing the travel junctions (or traffic constraints), travel cost on road segments and turn corners. Based on the datasets generated by this method, queries in ITS applications can be responded efficiently. In our future work, the performance of the creation, modification and processing of the datasets created by our method will be evaluated, deeply.

References

1. M. F. Goodchild. Gis and transportation: Status and challenges. *GeoInformatica*, 4(2):127–139, 2000.
2. S. Winter. Modeling costs of turns in route planning. *GeoInformatica*, (4):345–361, 2002.
3. J. Fawcett and P. Robinson. Adaptive routing for road traffic. *IEEE Computer Graphics and Applications*, 20(3):46–53, 2000.
4. D. Papadias, J. Zhang, N. Mamoulis, and Y.F. Tao. Query processing in spatial network databases. *Proc. of VLDB 2003*, pages 802–813, 2003.
5. N. Christofides. *Graph Theory : An Algorithmic Approach.* Academic Press Inc.(London) Ltd., 1975.
6. A. Guttman. R-trees: A dynamic index structure for spatial searching. *Proc. of ACM SIGMOD'84*, pages 47–57, 1984.
7. V. Gaede and O. Gunther. Multidimensional access methods. *ACM Computing Surveys*, 30(2):170–231, 1998.
8. Z. X. Song and N. Roussopoulos. K-nearest neighbor search for moving query point. *Proc. of SSTD'01*, pages 79–96, 2001.
9. F. Korn and S. Muthukrishnan. Influence sets based on reverse nearest neighbor queries. *Proceedings of the 2000 ACM SIGMOD international conference on Management of data*, pages 201–212, 2000.
10. Y. F. Tao, D. Papadias, and Q. M. Shen. Continuous nearest neighbor search. *Proc. of VLDB'02*, pages 287–298, 2002.
11. J. Feng, N. Mukai, and T. Watanabe. Incremental maintenance of all-nearest neighbors based on road network. *Proc. of IEA/AIE 2004*, pages 164–169, 2004.

A Specification Language for Organisational Performance Indicators

Viara Popova and Jan Treur

Department of Artificial Intelligence, Vrije Universiteit Amsterdam,
De Boelelaan 1081a, 1081 HV Amsterdam, The Netherlands
{popova, treur}@few.vu.nl

Abstract. A specification language for performance indicators and their relations and requirements is presented and illustrated for a case study in logistics. The language can be used in different forms, varying from informal, semiformal, graphical to formal. A software environment has been developed that supports the specification process and can be used to automatically check whether performance indicators or relations between them or certain requirements over them are satisfied in a given organisational process.

1 Introduction

In organisational design, redesign or change processes, organisational performance indicators form a crucial source of information; cf. [6]. Within such processes an organisation is (re)designed to fulfill (better) the performance indicators that are considered important. In this manner within organisational (re)design processes performance indicators function as requirements for the organisational processes.

Within the domain of software engineering in a similar manner requirements play an important role. Software is (re)designed to fulfill the requirements that are imposed. The use of requirements within a software engineering process has been studied in more depth during the last decades; it has led to an area called requirements engineering; cf. [3][4][7]. Formal languages to express requirements have been developed, and automated tools have been developed to support the specification process (from informal to formal) and to verify or validate whether they are fulfilled by a designed software component.

In this paper it is investigated how some of the achievements in requirements engineering can be exploited in the field of organisational performance indicators. Inspired by requirement specification languages, a formal language to specify performance indicators and their relationships is proposed, and illustrated by various examples. It is shown how this language or subsets thereof can be used in informal, graphical or formal form. Performance indicators expressed in this language can be manipulated by a software environment to obtain specifications or to evaluate performance indicators against given traces of organisational processes.

The organization of the paper is as follows. First, in Section 2, the language is introduced. In Section 2 it is shown how the proposed language can be used to express indicators themselves, but also how they relate to each other and in what

M. Ali and F. Esposito (Eds.): IEA/AIE 2005, LNAI 3533, pp. 667 – 677, 2005.

sense they are desirable. Next, in Section 3, case studies of the use of the language for the logistics domain are presented. Section 4 is a discussion.

2 A Formal Specification Language for Performance Indicators

The starting point of this research is in the area of requirements engineering as applied within the process of design of software systems. The approach we adopt uses logic as a tool in the analysis (see for example [2][5][1]) and more specifically order-sorted predicate logic which employs sorts for naming sets of objects. Such an extension of first order logic by a sort hierarchy increases the clarity and intuitiveness in the description of the domain area.

In the following subsection we introduce the language by defining the sorts, predicates and functions included in it. We start with the simplest constructs on the level of the performance indicators and build on this basis to introduce constructs describing relationships between them and requirements imposed on the indicators.

2.1 Performance Indicators

First we consider single performance indicators and lists of indicators. The sorts that we define are given in Table 1.

Table 1. Sorts defined on indicators and lists of indicators

Sort name	Description
INDICATOR-NAME	The set of possible names of performance indicators
INDICATOR-LIST	The set of possible lists of performance indicators
INDICATOR-LIST-NAME	The set of possible names for lists of performance indicators

Based on these sorts we define a predicate that allows us to give names to lists of indicators for ease of reference:

IS-DEFINED-AS : INDICATOR-LIST-NAME × INDICATOR-LIST

In order to demonstrate the use of this and other predicates, we use a running example for the rest of this section. The domain area is logistics from the point of view of a logistics service provider. Table 2 gives the indicators included in the example.

Table 2. An example set of performance indicators

Indicator name	Indicator	Indicator name	Indicator
NC	Number of customers	ISC	Information system costs
NNC	Number of new customers	FO	% of failed orders
NO	Number of orders	SB	Salaries and benefits
ND	Number of deliveries	AP	Attrition of personnel
MP	Motivation of personnel		

The above defined predicate can be used as follows: IS-DEFINED-AS(COD, [NC, NO, ND]).

The definitions given in this subsection are fairly simple but they give us the basis for going one level higher and explore the possible relationships between indicators.

2.2 Relationships Between Performance Indicators

Performance indicators are not always independent. Often they are connected through complex relationships such as correlation (the indicators tend to change in a similar way) or causality (the change in one indicator causes the change in another). Often we would like to know whether these relationships are positive or negative, e.g. correlation can be positive (the indicators increase together) or negative (one increases and the other one decreases). Therefore we need a new sort given below.

Table 3. Additional sorts used in defining relationships between indicators

Sort name	Description
SIGN	The set {pos, neg} of possible signs that will be used in some relationship formulas

Now we are ready to define predicates for the relationships we would be interested in. First we define a predicate for correlation as follows:

CORRELATED : INDICATOR-NAME × INDICATOR-NAME × SIGN

Causality relation between two indicators is denoted with the following predicate:

IS-CAUSED-BY : INDICATOR-NAME × INDICATOR-NAME × SIGN

Examples: CORRELATED(NC, NO, pos), IS-CAUSED-BY(AP, MP, neg)

In a similar way we can define a predicate for cases where one indicator is included in another by definition, e.g. one indicator is the sum of a number of other indicators:

IS-INCLUDED-IN : INDICATOR-NAME × INDICATOR-NAME × SIGN

Example: IS-INCLUDED-IN (NNC, NC, pos)

Another predicate is used for indicating different aggregation levels of the same indicator, e.g. measured by day/month/year (temporal aggregation) or by employee/unit/company (organizational aggregation):

IS-AGGREGATION-OF : INDICATOR-NAME × INDICATOR-NAME

A set of indicators can be independent (no significant relationship plays a role) or conflicting (correlation, causality or inclusion in a negative way) denoted in the following way:

INDEPENDENT : INDICATOR-NAME × INDICATOR-NAME
CONFLICTING : INDICATOR-NAME × INDICATOR-NAME

Examples: INDEPENDENT (ISC, FO), ¬ CONFLICTING (NC, ISC)

It might also be the case that we can easily replace measuring one indicator with measuring another one if that is necessary – it is expressed as follows:

TRADE-OFF-SET : INDICATOR-NAME × INDICATOR-NAME

While the meaning of the indicators might be similar it might still be the case that measurement for one can be more expensive to obtain than for the other one. Such relationship is also important to consider when we choose which particular set of indicators to measure. It is denoted using the predicate:

IS-COSTLIER-THAN : INDICATOR-NAME × INDICATOR-NAME

The relationships discussed so far can be represented graphically using a conceptual graph (see [8][9]). Conceptual graphs have two types of nodes: concepts and relations. In our case the first type will represent the indicator names while the second type represents the relations between them. The nodes are connected by arrows in such a way that the resulting graph is bipartite – an arrow can only connect a concept to a relation or a relation to a concept. Some of the predicates that we defined have an additional attribute of sort SIGN. In order to keep the notation simple we do not represent it as a concept node but as an extra sign associated to the arc: '+' for positive relationships and '–' for negative ones. Figure 1 is a small example of how such a conceptual graph would look like. We use here the examples given to illustrate the predicates in this section and represent them in the graph.

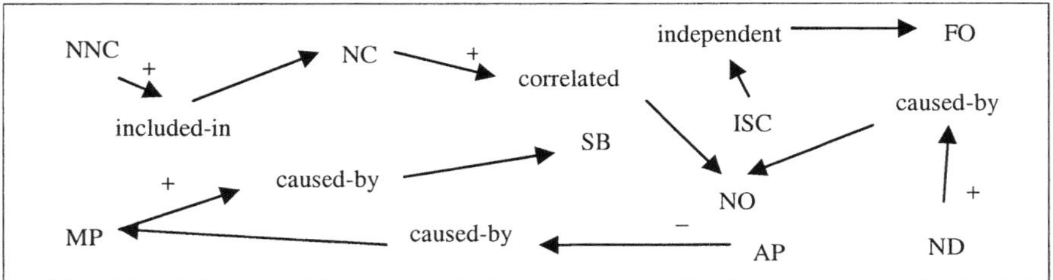

Fig. 1. The conceptual graph of relationships between the indicators

We now define one more predicate over a list of indicators. It will be used to indicate whether the set of indicators is minimal, where by minimal we imply that these three constraints are satisfied: no two indicators are replaceable, none is a different aggregation level of another and none is used in the definition of another:

MINIMAL : INDICATOR-LIST-NAME

Note that while such property of the indicator set is interesting to consider, it does not mean that we are only interested in minimal sets.

2.3 Requirements over Performance Indicators

The previous subsection concentrated on relationship between performance indicators. Going one more level higher we can define our own preferences over the set of indicators – what we prefer to measure and how we should evaluate the results. First we consider the second question by defining qualified expressions.

Qualified Expressions. Qualified expressions specify what we consider 'a success', i.e. when we consider one measurement of an indicator better than another one. Such specifications can be as simple as 'higher value is preferred over a lower one' or more complex such as 'the value should approximate a certain optimal value while never exceeding a predefined maximal value'.

The sorts that need to be added to our list are given in Table 4.

Table 4. The sorts concerning qualified expressions

Sort name	Description
VARIABLE	The set of possible variables over the values of indicators
INTEGER	The set of integers
INDICATOR-VARIABLE-EXPRESSION	The set of expressions over an indicator and its corresponding variable (see the definition below)
VARIABLE-EXPRESSION	The set of expressions over a variable (see examples below)
QUANTIFIER	The set of possible quantifiers (see the definitions below)
QUALIFIED-EXPRESSION	The set of possible qualified expressions (see below)
QUALIFIED-EXPRESSION-NAME	The set of possible names for qualified expressions
QUALIFIED-EXPRESSION-LIST	The set of possible lists of qualified expressions
QUALIFIED-EXPRESSION-LIST-NAME	The set of possible names for lists of qualified expressions

The sort VARIABLE-EXPRESSION contains expressions defining constraints over a variable as in the following examples:

v < maxKD (where v is a variable and maxKD is a constant),
v > minKD & v ≤ maxKD (where minKD is also a constant),
v ≤ minKD ∨ v > maxKD,
etc.

The sort INDICATOR-VARIABLE-EXPRESSION on the other hand contains expressions defining to which indicator the variable refers. Here we use the function:

has-value: INDICATOR × VARIABLE → INDICATOR-VARIABLE-EXPRESSION

For example the expression has-value(NNC, v) indicates that the variable v refers to the values of the indicator NNC. We now define the following functions that return objects of the type QUANTIFIER:

minimize, maximize: VARIABLE → QUANTIFIER
approximate: VARIABLE × CONSTANT → QUANTIFIER
satisfy: VARIABLE-EXPRESSION → QUANTIFIER

Examples: minimize(v), approximate(v, bestKD), satisfy(v < maxKD)

A qualified expression is identified by a quantifier and an indicator-variable expression. The following function given such a couple returns a qualified expression:

Qualified-expression: QUANTIFIER × INDICATOR-VARIABLE-EXPRESSION
→ QUALIFIED-EXPRESSION

As an example consider the expression Qualified-expression (min(v), has-value(ISC, v)), which should be read as: 'minimize the value v of the performance indicator ISC'. The following predicates can also be added to our set of predicates:

IS-DEFINED-AS : QUALIFIED-EXPRESSION-NAME × QUALIFIED-EXPRESSION
IS-DEFINED-AS : QUALIFIED-EXPRESSION-LIST-NAME × QUALIFIED-EXPRESSION-LIST

Example: IS-DEFINED-AS (q, Qualified-expression (max(v), has-value(NNC, v)))

Qualified Requirements. Building on the notion of qualified expressions, we can now define qualified requirements stating our preferences among the possible qualified expressions. We first introduce a number of new sorts:

Table 5. The sorts concerning qualified requirements

Sort name	Description
QUALIFICATION	The set of possible qualifications that can be used in a qualified requirement
QUALIFICATION-NAME	The set of possible names for qualifications
QUALIFIED-REQUIREMENT	The set of possible qualified requirements
QUALIFIED-REQUIREMENT-NAME	The set of possible names for qualified requirements
QUALIFIED-REQUIREMENT-LIST	The set of possible lists of qualified requirements
QUALIFIED-REQUIREMENT-LIST-NAME	The set of possible names for lists of qualified requirements

We can now define the following function which returns a qualified requirement:

Requirement: QUALIFICATION × QUALIFIED-EXPRESSION-LIST → QUALIFIED-REQUIREMENT

Example: Requirement(desired, Qualified-expression (max(v), has-value(NC, v)))

This can be read as: 'it is desired to maximize the value v of the performance indicator NC'. For simplicity, we abuse the notation by interchanging a qualified expression and a list of one qualified expression. Another example could look like:

Requirement(preferred-over, [Qualified-expression (max(v1), has-value(NC, v1)),
Qualified-expression (max(v2), has-value(NNC, v2))])

Here the list indicates that the first qualified expression (the head of the list) is preferred over the rest of the expressions (the tail of the list).

We define further a number of predicates:

IS-DEFINED-AS : QUALIFIED-REQUIREMENT-NAME × QUALIFIED-REQUIREMENT
IS-DEFINED-AS : QUALIFIED-REQUIREMENT-LIST-NAME × QUALIFIED-REQUIREMENT-LIST
CONFLICTING : QUALIFIED-REQUIREMENT-NAME × QUALIFIED-REQUIREMENT-NAME

Intuitively, CONFLICTING indicates that the two requirements cannot be satisfied together. More precisely that can happen when, due to correlation, causality or aggregation relationship, certain movement of one indicator is associated with certain movement of the other, however the corresponding requirements prescribe the opposite of this relation. An example would be two indicators that are positively correlated but the requirements specify one to be maximized and the other one to be minimized. Such relation over the set of requirement is important because often in practice conflicting needs arise and we must take special care in dealing with this.

A simple example can be given from the set of indicators listed in Table 2. The company management knows that the salaries and benefits contribute to the total costs and therefore reduce the profit. Thus the following requirement can be considered:

IS-DEFINED-AS (r1, Requirement(desired, Qualified-expression (min(v1), has-value(SB,v1))))

At the same time the management wants to minimize the attrition of employees as that increases the costs for teaching new employees and decreases the average productivity. Therefore another requirement can be considered:

IS-DEFINED-AS (r2, Requirement(desired, Qualified-expression (min(v1), has-value(AP,v1))))

But decreasing the salaries will lead to increase in the attrition of personnel, therefore the two requirements are conflicting: CONFLICTING (r1, r2).

We can now express rules such as this one – requirements over positively related indicators, where one is maximized and the other minimized, are conflicting:

∀ (i1, i2 : INDICATOR-NAME; L : INDICATOR-LIST-NAME; v1, v2 : INTEGER;
r1, r2 : QUALIFIED-REQUIREMENT-NAME)
(CORRELATED (i1, i2, pos) ∨ IS-INCLUDED-IN (i1, i2, pos) ∨
CAUSED-BY (i1, i2, pos) ∨ IS-AGGREGATION-OF (i1, i2)) &
IS-DEFINED-AS (r1, Requirement (desired, Qualified-expression (max(v1), has-value(i1,v1)))) &
IS-DEFINED-AS (r2, Requirement (desired, Qualified-expression (min(v2), has-value(i2,v2)))))
⇒ CONFLICTING (r1, r2)

3 A Case Study from the Area of Logistics

In this section we take a case study from the area of 3rd-party logistics (3PL) and apply the approach presented in the previous section. 3PL companies are specialized in providing logistics services to other companies. Important performance aspects typically include efficiency in transportation (e.g. reduction of transportation costs, improvement of route planning, equipment and labour utilization, etc.), customer satisfaction, employees satisfaction (in order to reduce the attrition of drivers), etc. Our case study includes performance indicators relevant for most of these aspects.

We first introduce the set of indicators and formulate how they are related to each other. Then we define the set of possible (meaningful) requirements over the list of indicators and analyze them concentrating on detecting conflicts.

3.1 Performance Indicators

The list of indicators is given in table 6. It is based on real-life indicator sets used in logistics and is augmented by several additional indicators used in 3rd-party logistics. Furthermore, we added a couple of indicators that usually remain implicit in real-life performance measurement and have to do with employees satisfaction and safety. Most of the indicators are typically numeric (costs, km, etc.), however, also non-numeric ones are included (employee motivation and safety). They can be modeled in different ways as long as the possible values are ordered in a consistent way.

Table 6. The list of performance indicators considered in the case study

Indicator name	Indicator	Indicator name	Indicator
TC	Total costs	TK	Total number of km
KD	Km/day	NT	Total number of trips
UV	Number of used vehicles	TO	Total number of orders
SO	% of served orders	R	Revenue
VO	% of violated orders	TP	Total profit TP = R - TC
TD	Trips per day	NA	Number of accidents
TT	Trips per truck	TS	Total amount for salaries
ST	Shops per truck	EM	Employee motivation (average)
NC	Number of clients	S	Safety
VP	% violations over the original plan	EP	Employee productivity (average)

3.2 Relationships

Looking closer at the indicators we see that many are not independent. The list below gives the most important relationships that we take into account.

RL1: IS-CAUSED-BY (TC, TK, pos)
RL2: IS-CAUSED-BY (TC, UV, pos)
RL3: CORRELATED (VO, SO, neg)
RL4: CORRELATED (TC, NT, pos)
RL5: CORRELATED (ST, TT, pos)
RL6: INDEPENDENT (SO, VP)
RL7: IS-CAUSED-BY (TC, VP, pos)
RL8: IS-INCLUDED-IN (R, TP, pos)
RL9: IS-INCLUDED-IN (TC, TP, neg)
RL10: IS-CAUSED-BY (R, TO, pos)
RL11: IS-CAUSED-BY (EP, EM, pos)
RL12: IS-CAUSED-BY (EM, KD, neg)
RL13: IS-INCLUDED-IN (TS, TC, pos)
RL14: IS-CAUSED-BY (EM, TS, pos)
RL15: CORRELATED (R, TK, pos)
RL16: IS-CAUSED-BY (TO, NC, pos)
RL17: IS-CAUSED-BY (R, NC, pos)
RL18: CORRELATED (NT, TO, pos)
RL19: IS-CAUSED-BY (EM, S, pos)
RL20: IS-CAUSED-BY (S, NA, neg)
RL21: IS-CAUSED-BY (TC, NA, pos)
RL22: IS-AGGREGATION-OF (TK, KD)
RL23: IS-AGGREGATION-OF (NT, TT)
RL24: IS-AGGREGATION-OF (NT, TD)

These relationships can be expressed graphically using conceptual graphs as discussed earlier. Fig. 2 gives the graph for our case study.

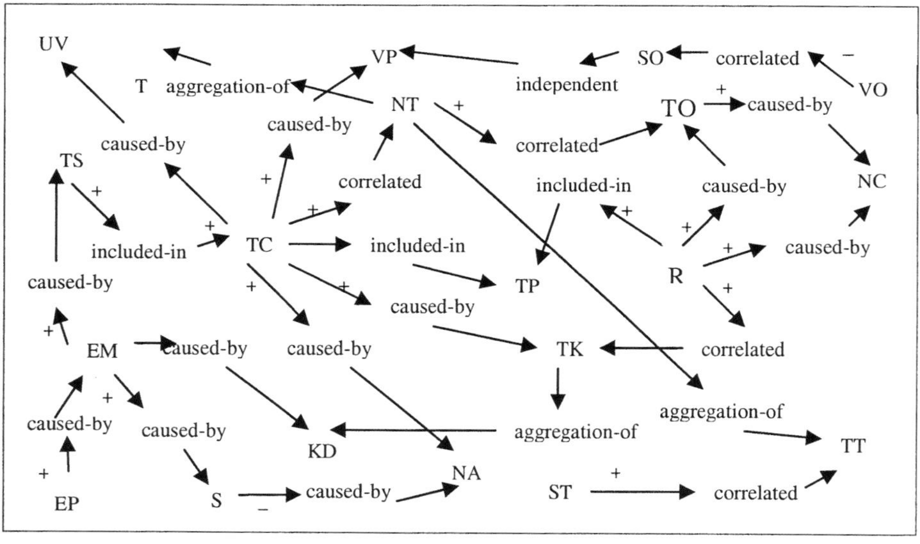

Fig. 2. The conceptual graph for the case study

3.3 Requirements

We can now formulate qualified requirements over the set of indicators. Most of the requirements are in a similar form as the ones given in the examples section 2.3. RQ12 and RQ13 however are a bit more complex. RQ12 states that the value of the indicator KD should approximate a given constant called bestKD. RQ13 on the other hand states that KD should not exceed another given constant maxKD. The intuition here is that the number of kilometers per day should approximate some pre-calculated optimal point but at the same time there exists a maximal value that does not allow the drivers to drive too much for health and safety reasons. Therefore the optimal point should be approximated in such a way that we do not exceed the maximal point.

RQ1: Requirement (desired, Qualified-expression (min(v), has-value(TC, v)))
RQ2: Requirement (desired, Qualified-expression (max(v), has-value(SO, v)))
RQ3: Requirement (desired, Qualified-expression (min(v), has-value(VO, v)))
RQ4: Requirement (desired, Qualified-expression (max(v), has-value(ST, v)))
RQ5: Requirement (desired, Qualified-expression (min(v), has-value(VP, v)))
RQ6: Requirement (desired, Qualified-expression (max(v), has-value(R, v)))
RQ7: Requirement (desired, Qualified-expression (max(v), has-value(TP, v)))
RQ8: Requirement (desired, Qualified-expression (max(v), has-value(EM, v)))
RQ9: Requirement (desired, Qualified-expression (max(v), has-value(EP, v)))
RQ10: Requirement (desired, Qualified-expression (min(v), has-value(TS, v)))
RQ11: Requirement (desired, Qualified-expression (max(v), has-value(TO, v)))
RQ12: Requirement (desired, Qualified-expression (approximate(v, bestKD), has-value(KD,v)))
RQ13: Requirement (desired, Qualified-expression (satisfy(v ≤ maxKD), has-value(KD,v)))
RQ14: Requirement (desired, Qualified-expression (max(v), has-value(NC, v)))
RQ15: Requirement (desired, Qualified-expression (max(v), has-value(S, v)))
RQ16: Requirement (desired, Qualified-expression (min(v), has-value(NA, v)))
RQ17: Requirement (preferred-over, Qualified-expression (min(v1), has-value(VO, v1)), Qualified-expression (max(v2), has-value(SO, v2)))
RQ18: Requirement (preferred-over, Qualified-expression (max(v1), has-value(NC, v1)), Qualified-expression (max(v2), has-value(TO, v2)))

3.4 Analysis of the Case Study

Looking at figure 2 and the list of formulated qualified requirements, we detect some inconsistencies. The indicator TC (total costs) is caused by TK (total number of km), which on the other hand is correlated with R (revenue). In our requirements we have indicated that TC should be minimized (RQ1). It is also indicated that R should be maximized (RQ6). Due to the correlation, maximizing R will lead to maximizing TK. Due to the causal relationship, maximizing TK leads to maximizing TC, which disagrees with RQ6. This can be expressed in the following way:

RL1 & RL15 ⇒ CONFLICTING (RQ1, RQ6)

In a similar way we consider ST (shops per truck), TT (trips per truck), NT (total number of trips) and TC (total costs). ST is positively correlated with TT while NT is aggregation of TT. Therefore maximizing ST (as in RQ4) will lead to maximizing TT which results in maximizing NT. However NT is positively correlated with TC and RQ1 requires TC to be minimized.

RL5 & RL23 & RL4 ⇒ CONFLICTING (RQ1, RQ4)

Another conflict involving TC can be detected in the path TC → NT → TO. TC is positively correlated with NT which is positively correlated with TO (total number of orders). Therefore there is a conflict between RQ1 and RQ11:

RL4 & RL18 ⇒ CONFLICTING (RQ1, RQ11)

The last conflict we detect arises from RQ8 and RQ10. RQ8 requires EM (employee motivation) to be maximized. EM is positively caused by TS, therefore changing TS will change EM in the same direction. RQ10 requires TS to be minimized which will lead to minimizing EM – conflict with RQ8.

RL14 ⇒ CONFLICTING (RQ8, RQ10)

4 Conclusions

Organisational performance indicators are crucial concepts in strategic management of an organisation, and in particular in the preparation of organisational change processes. They can occur in a variety of forms and complexity. In addition, often it is necessary to consider relations between performance indicators, and to express qualifications and requirements over them. Given these considerations, it is not trivial to express them in a uniform way in a well-defined specification language.

A similar situation is addressed in the area of requirements engineering which has developed as a substantial sub-area of software engineering. Also in the area of AI and design similar issues are addressed. Inspired by these areas, a specification language for performance indicators and their relations and requirements has been defined and presented in this paper. The language can be used in different forms, varying from informal, semiformal, graphical to formal. (The semantics of the language was left out from the scope of this paper and will be a subject of further research.) A software environment has been developed that supports the specification process and can be used to automatically check whether performance indicators or relations between them or certain requirements over them (those with quantifier satisfy) are satisfied in a given organisational process. The relevant complexity issues of the checking process are still a topic for future research.

For other types of requirements over performance indicators it may not be easy to automate the checking process. For example, that a certain performance indicator is minimal for a given organisational process requires comparison to alternative possible organisational processes. If a set of alternative processes is given, the software environment can handle the checking on minimality of one of these processes compared to the other ones. But in general such a set is hard to specify in an exhaustive manner. An alternative route is to make a mathematical analysis of this minimality criterion, and to formalize this analysis in the language so that it can be performed automatically. This is a subject for further research. Another direction for future investigation might be to provide assistance in the process of discovering missing or redundant requirements. The set of requirements is company-specific but it might be possible to provide some insight through scenario elicitation.

References

1. Bosse, T., Jonker, C.M., and Treur, J.: Analysis of Design Process Dynamics. In: Lopez de Mantaras, R., Saitta, L. (eds.): Proc. of the 16th European Conference on Artificial Intelligence, ECAI'04 (2004) 293—297
2. Brazier F.M.T., Langen P.H.G. van, Treur J.: A logical theory of design. In: Gero, J.S. (ed.): Advances in Formal Design Methods for CAD, Proc. of the Second International Workshop on Formal Methods in Design. Chapman & Hall, New York (1996) 243—266
3. Davis, A. M.: Software requirements: Objects, Functions, and States, Prentice Hall, New Jersey (1993)
4. Kontonya, G., and Sommerville, I.: Requirements Engineering: Processes and Techniques. John Wiley & Sons, New York (1998)
5. Langen, P.H.G. van: The anatomy of design: foundations, models and application. PhD thesis, Vrije Universiteit Amsterdam (2002)

6. Neely, A., Gregory, M., Platts, K.: Performance measurement system design: A literature review and research agenda. International Journal of Operations & Production Management, 15 (1995) 80—116
7. Sommerville, I., and Sawyer P.: Requirements Engineering: a good practice guide. John Wiley & Sons, Chicester, England (1997)
8. Sowa, J.F.: Conceptual Structures: Information Processing in Mind and Machine, Addison-Wesley, Reading, Mass. (1984)
9. Sowa, J.F., Dietz, D.: Knowledge Representation: Logical, Philosophical, and Computational Foundations, Brooks/Cole (1999)

A New Crowded Comparison Operator in Constrained Multiobjective Optimization for Capacitors Sizing and Siting in Electrical Distribution Systems

Salvatore Favuzza, Mariano Giuseppe Ippolito, and Eleonora Riva Sanseverino

Dipartimento di Ingegneria Elettrica Università di Palermo,
viale delle Scienze 90128 Palermo, Italia
{Favuzza, Ippolito, Eriva}@diepa.unipa.it

Abstract. This paper presents a new Crowded Comparison Operator for NSGA-II to solve the Multiobjective and constrained problem of optimal capacitors placement in distribution systems.

1 The Problem Formulation

For the multiobjective compensation system design, the objective functions economically express the following items: i) return on investment for the system compensation; ii) the voltage stability maximization. These can be translated into:

$$\max\{ROI\} = \max\left\{\frac{\mathrm{R}_{\Delta\mathrm{Et}} - C^{year}{}_{InstT}}{C_{instT}}\right\}. \tag{1}$$

$$\max\{fcar\} \tag{2}$$

Where ROI is the Return On Investment, $C^{year}{}_{InstT}$ is the investment cost per year and $R_{\Delta Et}$ is the economic benefit deriving from the reduced value of energy losses; whereas fcar is the loadability factor, whose maximization is related to the voltage stability maximization. The technical constraints include the limitation of the number of manoeuvres along the 24 hours of the capacitor banks and of the voltage drops. The relevant expressions are:

- *nman(**x**) <= max_man for each installation along the 24 hrs*
- $\Delta V(\mathbf{x}) > \Delta Vx$ *for each installation along 24 hrs*

2 The Algorithm NSGA-II and Constraints Handling

The constraint handling using NSGA-II [1], Non Dominated Sorting Genetic Algorithm-II, can be dealt with by considering them as further objectives, in terms of non dominance. Therefore the standard MO problem with inequality constraints:

Min $\{\mathbf{f_1(x)}, \mathbf{f_2(x)}, \ldots, \mathbf{f_m(x)}\}$; $\mathbf{x} \in \mathbf{X}$ Subject to: $\mathbf{g(x)} = \{ g_1(\mathbf{x}), \ldots g_s(\mathbf{x})\} \le 0$
turns into:
Min $\{f_1(\mathbf{x}), \ldots f_m(\mathbf{x}), \alpha_1(g_1(\mathbf{x})), \ldots, \alpha_s(g_s(\mathbf{x}))\}$ $\quad\quad \mathbf{x} \in \mathbf{X}$
where $\alpha_1(g_1(\mathbf{x})) = \{a+b*(max\_man-n_{man}(\mathbf{x}))\}$, $\alpha_2(g_2(\mathbf{x})) = \{a+d*(\Delta Vx-\Delta V(\mathbf{x}))\}$.

M. Ali and F. Esposito (Eds.): IEA/AIE 2005, LNAI 3533, pp. 678–680, 2005.

One of the most interesting operators in NSGA-II is the Crowded Comparison operator. It's definition allows the application of the Selection operator, which in this case is the Binary tournament Selection. Two different types of CCO are here proposed and compared. **The new CCO1,** ($\geq^*_n$): in this case, the constraints only take part in the ranking definition. **The CCO2,** ($\geq^{**}_n$), prizes in first place those solutions having lower constraints violation, then considering the rank order and finally the crowding factor. The measure for constraints violation has been considered to be the following:

$$\mathbf{CV = 0.5\,(\alpha_1(g_1(x)) + \alpha_2(g_2(x)))} \quad \textbf{if there is constraints violation}$$
$$\mathbf{CV = 0} \quad \textbf{if there is no constraints violation.}$$

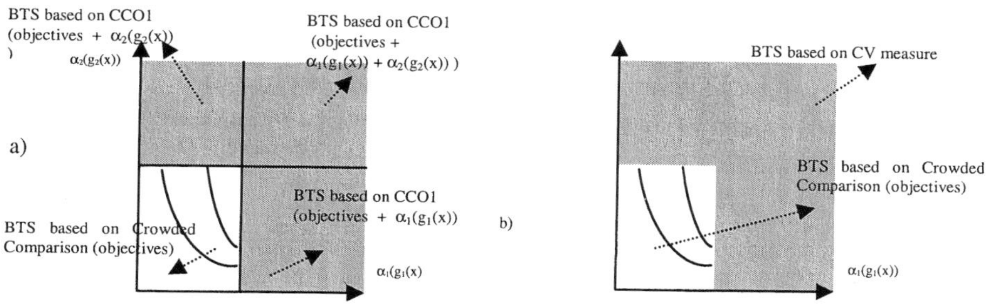

Fig. 1. The two Crowded Comparison operators. In a) the CCO1 operator, in b) the CCO2 operator are described

3 Applications

The tests concern the efficiency of the proposed CCO1 and CCO2 operators both on the problem of the design of the compensation system for an electrical MV network and on a difficult numerical test problem such as Tanaka. **Compensation system**

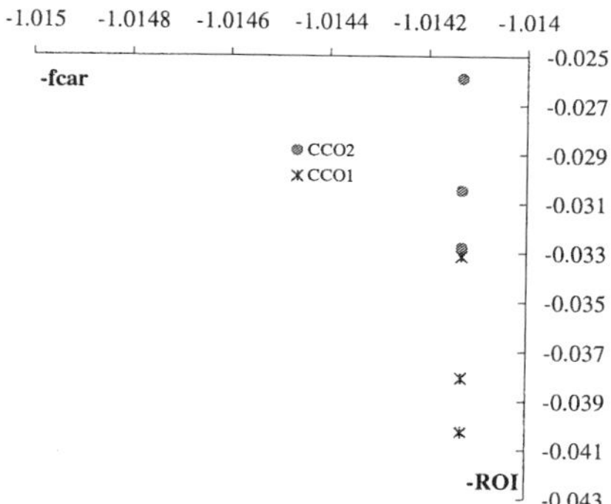

Fig. 2. A comparison of the two CCOs on the problem of optimal compensation for the considered test system

design for electrical distribution systems It is possible the installation of remotely controllable capacitor banks at MV load nodes, each step being 150 kVAR. The test systems has about 40 MV load nodes. The algorithm is always able to find feasible solutions. Ordering the solutions in the main objectives (ROI index and fcar index) non domination fronts, the feasible solutions can indeed be found in the lasts non domination fronts, since a reduction in the number of manoeuvres produces a large worsening in the optimization objectives, whereas the voltage drop decreases together with the main objectives.

Numerical test functions. The test problem introduced by Tanaka [2]. The results attained using the two CCOs are comparable.

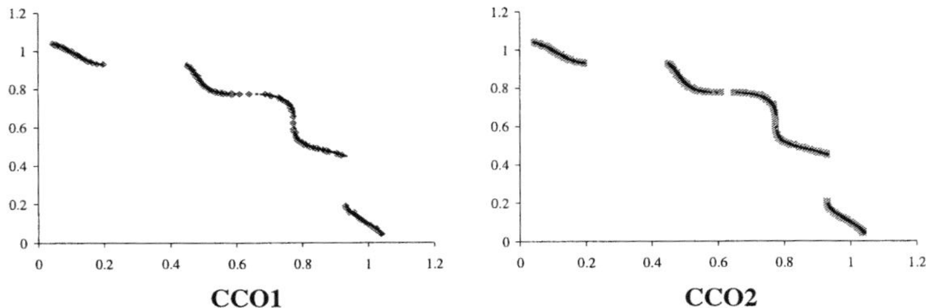

Fig. 3. Comparison of the two operators on TNK PF_{true}

	CCO_1	CCO_2
GD	0.000113	0.000128
HR	0.997123	0.99681

It can be observed that both indicators are worst in the case of CCO2.

References

1. Deb, K., Agrawal, S., Pratap, A., Meyarivan, T.: A Fast Elitist Non-Dominated Sorting Genetic Algorithm for Multi-Objective Optimization: NSGA-II, Proceedings of the Parallel Problem Solving from Nature VI Conference, 2000.
2. Deb, K.: Constrained test problems for Multi-objective Evolutionary Optimization. KanGAL Report 200005 Indian Institute of Technology, Kanpur, India.

A Two-Phase Backbone-Based Search Heuristic for Partial MAX-SAT – An Initial Investigation

Mohamed El Bachir Menaï

Artificial Intelligence Laboratory, University of Paris8,
2 rue de la liberté, 93526 Saint-Denis, France
menai@ai.univ-paris8.fr

Abstract. The Partial MAX-SAT Problem (PMSAT) is a variant of the MAX-SAT problem that consists of two CNF formulas defined over the same variable set. Its solution must satisfy all clauses of the first formula and as many clauses in the second formula as possible. This study is concerned with the PMSAT solution in setting a two-phase stochastic local search method that takes advantage of an estimated backbone variables of the problem. First experiments conducted on PMSAT instances derived from SAT instances indicate that this new method offers significant performance benefits over state-of-the-art PMSAT techniques.

1 Introduction and Background

Real-world problems in various applications such as scheduling [1] and pattern recognition [4], mostly contain hard and soft constraints. While hard constraints must be satisfied by any solution, soft constraints specify a function to be optimized. Cha *et al.* [2] introduced the Partial MAX-SAT (PMSAT) problem as a variant of MAX-SAT to formulate independently hard and soft constraints. It can be defined as follows. Let $X = \{x_1, x_2, \cdots, x_n\}$ be a set of n boolean variables. A clause c on X is a disjunction of literals. It is satisfied by an assignment $v \in \{0,1\}^n$ if at least one of its literals is satisfied by v, in such case the value of the clause equals 1, otherwise it is violated and its value equals 0. A formula f in conjunctive normal form (CNF) is a conjunction of m clauses. Given two CNF formulas f_A and f_B of m_A and m_B clauses, respectively over X. A PMSAT instance $P = f_A \wedge f_B$ asks to satisfy all the clauses of f_A and as many clauses in f_B as possible. P has a solution iff f_A is satisfiable.

Cha *et al.* [2] used a weighting-type local search algorithm to solve PMSAT by repeating n times each clause in f_A. In this way, the search always prefers a solution that satisfies all clauses of f_A regardless of the level of remaining clause violation. However, this can lead to an important increasing of total number of clauses when their number is initially large. Another approach for solving PMSAT described in [5], is based on recycling the model of f_A to satisfy the maximum number of clauses in f_B. The results reported indicate the overall superiority of this method w.r.t. a weighting-type local search algorithm.

An interesting property that influences the hardness of a satisfiability problem, is the *backbone variables* [6], a set of variables having fixed values in all

M. Ali and F. Esposito (Eds.): IEA/AIE 2005, LNAI 3533, pp. 681–684, 2005.

optimal solutions to the problem. Backbones are proven to be an important indicator of hardness in optimization and approximation [8], and subsequently heuristic search methods that identify backbone variables may reduce problem difficulty and improve performance [3, 9, 10]. The aim of this paper is to integrate a backbone guided moves to a local search algorithm for solving PMSAT. In a first time, both PMSAT formulas, $f_A \wedge f_B$, are solved together as a MAX-SAT instance using a backbone guided local search. In a second time, the best assignment found is recycled to the unsatisfied clauses in f_A to try to find a model using the backbone variables sampled in the previous phase. The effectiveness of this method is demonstrated empirically on some PMSAT instances created from SAT instances. In the next Section, we present the backbone-based local search method for PMSAT. The experimental results are presented in Section 3. We finally conclude and plan for future work in Section 4.

2 Backbone-Based Local Search Method

Let consider a PMSAT instance $P = f_A \wedge f_B$. The estimated backbone called *pseudo-backbone* [10] is performed using information extracted from local minima. Let Ω be a set of assignments on X, $S(x_i)$ the value of the variable x_i in the assignment S, and $C(S)$ the contribution of S defined as the total number of satisfied clauses in f_A and f_B: $C(S) = m_A \cdot Sat_A(S) + Sat_B(S)$, where $Sat_A(S)$ and $Sat_B(S)$ denote the number of satisfied clauses in f_A and f_B, respectively. A multiplier coefficient m_A is added to $C(S)$ to underline the priority of satisfying clauses of f_A. A variable frequency p_i of positive occurrences of x_i in all assignments of Ω is defined as $p_i = \left(\sum_{S \in \Omega} C(S) \cdot S(x_i)\right) / \sum_{S \in \Omega} C(S)$. We propose a two-phase algorithm for solving P called BB-PMSAT and summarized as follows. In the first phase, the algorithm begins by using a variant of the WalkSAT procedure [7] for MAX-SAT. It integrates a pseudo-backbone estimation using variable frequencies p_i to generate initial assignments as suggested in [9, 10]. The set of assignments Ω is updated at each time a new local minimum is reached. The second phase of the algorithm is performed if the best assignment found in the previous phase does not satisfy f_A. In such case, it is recycled to try to satisfy f_A using a variant of WalkSAT for SAT guided by the information in Ω.

3 Experimental Evaluation

PMSAT instances are generated using SAT instances from DIMACS[1] and SATLIB[2] archives since no PMSAT instances are publicly available. Four sets of randomly generated and structured SAT instances of n variables and m clauses are considered: uuf125-538* (100 'phase transition' hard 3-SAT instances of $n = 125, m = 538$), f* (3 large random 'phase transition' hard instances: f600

[1] http://dimacs.rutgers.edu/Challenges/

[2] http://www.informatik.tu-darmstadt.de/AI/SATLIB

($n = 600, m = 2550$), f1000 ($n = 1000, m = 4250$), f2000 ($n = 2000, m = 8500$)), par8-* (5 instances of SAT-encoded parity learning problem of $n = 350, 1149 < m < 1171$), and flat* (10 instances of SAT-encoded graph coloring problem of $n = 300, m = 1117$). PMSAT instances are generated using a partition of each SAT instance into two subsets f_A and f_B of $m_A = \lceil \alpha \cdot m \rceil + 1, 0 < \alpha < 1$, and $m_B = m - m_A$ clauses, respectively. Program code is written in C and run on a computer (Pentium IV 2.9 GHz with 1GBs of RAM running Linux). All of our results are averaged over 10 runs on each instance.

Table 1. Results of Algorithms BB-PMSAT ($\alpha = 0.3, r = 0.6, pb = 0.7n$) and WLS

Algorithm BB-PMSAT

Problem	#SAT	v(%)	CPU time		Flips	
			Mean	Std	Mean	Std
uuf*	10	0	0.411	0.053	4219.5	614.0
f600	9	0.0130	7.430	2.136	34474.6	5136.9
f1000	6	0.1129	20.856	3.505	86495.6	9435.9
f2000	7	0.1305	52.536	3.942	153601.1	11214.0
flat*	2.5	0.0982	3.419	0.210	28432.0	2162.2
par8-*	5.6	0.1348	6.517	1.021	45730.1	6879.3
Average	6.25	0.1029	11.723	1.495	53587.3	6295.9

Algorithm WLS

Problem	#SAT	v(%)	CPU time		Flips	
			Mean	Std	Mean	Std
uuf*	9.8	0.0123	0.845	0.205	8316.4	1485.0
f600	9	0.0130	10.620	2.010	47150.6	18420.0
f1000	6	0.1235	29.271	2.055	136171.0	19040.0
f2000	5	1.5764	60.028	5.601	265124.5	41190.0
flat*	2.1	0.2351	6.068	1.295	43166.3	9147.6
par8-*	3.2	0.4394	8.416	0.447	63290.7	3588.3
Average	4.79	0.4158	14.891	1.397	81638.2	10722.4

The total number of tries for each run of BB-PMSAT is shared between both phases. Let r be the first phase length ratio of the total run length, #SAT the average number of solutions to PMSAT instances over 10 runs, pb the ratio of pseudo-backbone size to n, and v the relative error of a solution S given by: $v(\%) = (1 - (Sat_B(S)/m_B)) \times 100$. BB-PMSAT is compared to a weighting-type local search algorithm for MAX-SAT, called WLS with RESET strategy [2]. WLS proceeds by adding weights to frequently violated clauses at local minima and resetting these weights when no improvement can be obtained. Computational results performed by BB-PMSAT and WLS are shown in Table 1. BB-PMSAT was tested using $\alpha = 0.3, r = 0.6$, and $pb = 0.7n$. The more significant gains in average number of solutions and total runtime are obtained on the problem par8-*. Indeed, the gain achieved by BB-PMSAT in average number of solutions on par8-* w.r.t. WLS is 75%. The fall in BB-PMSAT average total runtime cost for par8-* is 22.56% w.r.t. WLS. On all the problems, the average gain in BB-PMSAT number of solutions is 30.48% w.r.t. WLS, while the average fall in runtime cost is 21.27%. In summary, these first results show that BB-PMSAT can find high quality solutions, and performs faster than WLS on the considered set of instances.

4 Conclusion and Future Work

In this paper, we have described an incomplete local search method for solving the Partial MAX-SAT problem. In a first phase, the algorithm integrates a sampling of pseudo-backbone variables to the WalkSAT procedure to find good solution to a MAX-SAT instance. In a second phase, it tries to recycle the MAX-SAT solution to a PMSAT one using pseudo-backbone information. The performance of the algorithm is compared to a weighting-type local search algorithm (WLS) [2] proposed for solving PMSAT. The preliminary experimental results show that our algorithm can achieve significant gains both in average number of solutions and in total runtime cost. We are still working to solve larger SATLIB benchmark problems to further investigate the effectiveness of the algorithm. We plan to study the effect of varying the size of the peudo-backbone variables, and the ratio $m_A/(m_A + m_B)$ of the number of clauses in f_A to the total number of clauses, on the performance. Moreover, we intend to consider other local search heuristics within the same algorithmic framework.

References

1. Beck, J.C., Fox, M.S.: A genetic framework for constraint-directed search and scheduling. AI Magazine, 19(4), (1998) 101–130
2. Cha, B. Iwama, K., Kambayashi, Y., Miyasaki, S.: Local search for Partial MAX-SAT. In Proceedings of the 14th of AAAI-97, (1997) 263–265
3. Dubois, O., Dequen, G.: A backbone-search heuristic for efficient solving of hard 3-SAT formulae. In Proceedings of the 17th IJCAI, (2001) 248–253
4. Freuder, E., Wallace, R.: Partial constraint satisfaction. Artificial Intelligence, 58(1), (1992) 21–70
5. Menaï, M.B.: Solution reuse in Partial MAX-SAT Problem. In Proceedings of IEEE IRI-2004, (2004) 481–486
6. Monasson, R., Zecchina, R., Kirkpatrick, S., Selman, B., Troyansky, L.: Determining computational complexity from characteristic 'Phase Transition'. Nature, 400 (1999) 133–137
7. Selman, B., Kautz, H.A., Cohen, B.: Noise strategies for improving local search. In Proceedings of the 12th AAAI-94, (1994) 337–343
8. Slaney, J., Walsh, T.: Backbones in optimization and approximation. In Proceedings of the 17th IJCAI, (2001) 254–259
9. Telelis, O., Stamatopoulos, P.: Heuristic backbone sampling for maximum satisfiability. In Proceedings of the 2nd Hellenic Conference on AI, (2002) 129–139
10. Zhang, W., Rangan, A., Looks, M.: Backbone guided local search for maximum satisfiability. In Proceedings of the 18th IJCAI, (2003) 1179–1186

An Algorithm for Peer Review Matching Using Student Profiles Based on Fuzzy Classification and Genetic Algorithms

Raquel M. Crespo[1], Abelardo Pardo[1], Juan Pedro Somolinos Pérez[2], and Carlos Delgado Kloos[1]

[1] Departamento de Ingeniería Telemática, Universidad Carlos III de Madrid, Spain
{rcrespo, abel, cdk}@it.uc3m.es
www.it.uc3m.es

[2] Neoris, Madrid, Spain
juan.somolinos@neoris.com
www.neoris.com

Abstract. In the context of Intelligent Tutoring Systems, there is a potential for adapting either content or its sequence to student as to enhance the learning experience. Recent theories propose the use of team-working environments to improve even further this experience. In this paper an effective matching algorithm is presented in the context of peer reviewing applied to an educational setting. The problem is formulated as an optimization problem to search a solution that satisfies a set of given criteria modeled as "profiles". These profiles represent regions of the solution space to be either favored or avoided when searching for a solution. The proposed technique was deployed in a first semester computer engineering course and proved to be both effective and well received by the students.

1 Introduction

Intelligent Tutoring Systems [1] usually focus on adapting either content or the sequence in which it is presented according to what the user needs. Another typical approach focuses on providing automatic assessment and feedback to problems previously solved by the student.

However, the learning process is not limited to the simple exposition of contents to the student. Interaction with other actors involved in the process, both teachers and peer students, can be seen as a key factor. And so, as educational theories evolve, the learning process has moved from teacher to student centered, transforming the latter from a passive receptor into an active actor and main character of his/her own learning. Collaborative learning, with techniques such as team-working or peer learning, has risen with this evolution.

But before students can work together and benefit from the collaboration with their peers, group generation must be previously solved, and this phase is rarely paid the attention it deserves. Typical approaches use either random

M. Ali and F. Esposito (Eds.): IEA/AIE 2005, LNAI 3533, pp. 685–694, 2005.

matching or leave the students to create groups spontaneously. In reduced environments, teachers can guide this process and manually apply more complex criteria, matching students who probably will help more each other. But in situations such as courses with a large enrollment or in a distance learning environment, this manual approach soon becomes useless.

This document focuses on how to group students according to their profiles in a peer review context. More precisely, an algorithm for matching reviewers to authors depending on their characteristics in an educational peer review process, in order to generate the pairs according to a given pedagogical criterion is presented. The proposed model is generic enough to be applied in any other learning context requiring matching students together, such as team-working projects, or even outside the educational environment, in any scenario which involves grouping users.

2 Adaptive Peer Review

Peer Review consists of evaluating a colleague's work and providing feedback about it. It has been widely used in multiple contexts, ranging from childhood education to academic research. This paper focuses on peer review used in education, a field to which peer review has been typically applied, to virtually any level and subject. Supporting programs for peer review in educational environments are reported as early as 1995. More recent tools, like PG [2, 3], OASIS [4] or CPR [5], use the web to manage peer interaction.

Benefits as well as a detailed topology of peer review in education have been carefully studied (see [6] for an excellent survey). However, "how peer assessors and assessees should best be matched [...] is discussed surprisingly little in the literature", as noted in [6], cited again three years later in [7], and more recently in [8]. A taxonomy of matching procedures is described in [6], distinguishing between blind and non-blind and between electronic and non-electronic. A more detailed scheme of review-mapping strategies is sketched in [7] as well as the description of an algorithm for dynamically matching reviewers to authors, but it creates a match fitting a set of constraints. Dynamic matching is also used in [4] although no discussion is done, neither algorithms are provided, about which criteria is used or how to optimize the matching selection according to the user profiles and the process goals.

From our experience, it seems clear, though, that student characteristics have a deep influence in learning, both in how they learn themselves and from their peers. Student roles and adequateness have been frequently analyzed in collaborative work (see [9] for example). Influence of student preferences and learning styles in learning and team-working is reflected for example in [10]. In the context of peer review, diversification of peer-revision groups is reported in an experiment by [11]. Also, the influence of the quality of both works reviewed and received feedback in students learning is stated in [8].

As a consequence, it seems natural to adapt the peer review process to student needs and characteristics, and the matching process is the step where this adaptation can be done. In this paper, a generic algorithm for adapting the selection of reviewers is presented. The concrete criteria to apply depend on the context and goals pursued with the peer review process.

2.1 Extended Taxonomy of Mapping Criteria

Adaptive Peer Review leads to extend the taxonomy of mapping criteria. As it has been stated before, peer review systems care just about validity constraints assigned either statically or dynamically under request by the reviewers [12, 4]. The only requirement is that no violation of any restriction occurs. But aditional mapping criteria can be established beyond defining valid/non-valid maps, in order to be able to select between several valid maps which one is preferred for a given process.

A possible taxonomy for mapping criteria can be defined as follows:

- *Correctness*: constraints that must be satisfied by a map[1].
  - *Uniqueness*: Each submission must be assigned k_r *distinct* reviewers. In other words, a reviewer cannot be considered twice for the same submission.
  - *Equilibrium (load balancing)*: Only in certain circumstances it can be guaranteed that all reviewers are assigned exactly the same number of submissions, all potential reviewers should be assigned a similar number of submissions to evaluate. Formally, the difference between the maximum and the minimum number of submissions assigned to each reviewer must be less than or equal to 1.
  - *Self-exclusion*[2]: A submission cannot be reviewed by its author.
  - *Ad-hoc constraints*: Additional constraints specific to a given peer review process.
- *Optimization*: comparison criteria to evaluate mappings, allowing the process to be guided towards certain goals. In an educational environment these criteria can be further divided into:
  - Reliability: Promote the evolution towards accurate scores.
  - Pedagogical: Match students as to increase the understanding of the underlying concepts or the improvement of pursued skills (either social or subject-specific).

3 System Description

Mapping criteria can vary depending on the context. So, an important objective for a peer review system is to be easily configurable by the user. The definition of the mapping criteria should be as intuitive as possible for the teacher.

---

[1] These criteria correspond to a scenario in which each submission must be assigned a given number of reviewers, k_r. They can easily be adapted to the context where a fixed number of submissions is assigned to each reviewer.

[2] In certain cases, each submitted work must be reviewed by its author. In this situation, no algorithm is needed, therefore, it is considered as a special case.

The problem can be seen as an optimization problem. The objective is to find a mapping so that it is valid and maximizes the defined optimization criteria. Exhaustive search is discarded as the number of potential combinations explodes. An effective approach consists on using heuristics to directly build the solution (instead of searching the best combination among all possible ones). However, this approach has the drawback of not being easily configurable. Hard coded heuristics are difficult to adjust. Even if the user could change them by means of a set of rules, introducing all defining rules for the process could be very complex.

3.1 Mapping Criteria Implementation

An intuitive solution for the mapping problem consists on defining just the objectives, not the rules to reach them. That is, define a reduced set of author-reviewer pairs representing both desirable and undesirable assignments.

With this approach, the teacher simply introduces the profiles for a set of author-reviewers pairs (for example, four pairs), together with an interest measure for each of them. These pairs can be easily constructed cross-matching the typical students, representative of the different classes that can be distinguished.

Definition 1. *A prototype is defined as an individual that exhibits the essential features of a later type; a standard or typical example [13].*

Example 1. Match reviewers and authors with complementary profiles:
User model: student's proficiency score, normalized into [0..10] (see Figure 1).
User prototypes: 2 groups of students are defined: proficient and non-proficient. Representative profiles for each group are $\overrightarrow{ps} = (10)$ and $\overrightarrow{nps} = (0)$, respectively.
Author-reviewer prototypes: Cross-matching the student prototypes four typical pairings appear, as shown in Figure 1.

In order to implement the given mapping criterion (that is, matching authors to reviewers with complementary profiles), pairings similar to prototypes $\overrightarrow{B} = (\overrightarrow{nps}, \overrightarrow{ps})$ and $\overrightarrow{C} = (\overrightarrow{ps}, \overrightarrow{nps})$ must be promoted, whereas pairings similar to prototypes $\overrightarrow{A} = (\overrightarrow{nps}, \overrightarrow{nps})$ and $\overrightarrow{D} = (\overrightarrow{ps}, \overrightarrow{ps})$ must be discarded. So, prototypes $\overrightarrow{B}$ and $\overrightarrow{C}$ are assigned maximum positive interest (to attract pairings towards them) and prototypes $\overrightarrow{A}$ and $\overrightarrow{D}$ are assigned maximum negative interest (to steer assignments away from them).

Example 2. Match reviewers and authors with similar profiles:
User profile: learning style, normalized into $[-s..+s]$, where $-s$ means a global learning style and $+s$ a sequential learning style (see Figure 2).
User prototypes: Two learning styles are considered: sequential and global. Representative profiles for each group are $\overrightarrow{ss} = (+s)$ and $\overrightarrow{gs} = (-s)$, respectively.
Author-reviewer prototypes: Cross-matching the student prototypes four typical pairings appear, as shown in Figure 2.

In order to implement the given mapping criterion, pairings similar to prototypes $\overrightarrow{A} = (\overrightarrow{ss}, \overrightarrow{ss})$ and $\overrightarrow{D} = (\overrightarrow{gs}, \overrightarrow{gs})$ are promoted, whereas pairings similar to prototypes $\overrightarrow{B} = (\overrightarrow{ss}, \overrightarrow{gs})$ and $\overrightarrow{C} = (\overrightarrow{gs}, \overrightarrow{ss})$ are discarded. So, prototypes

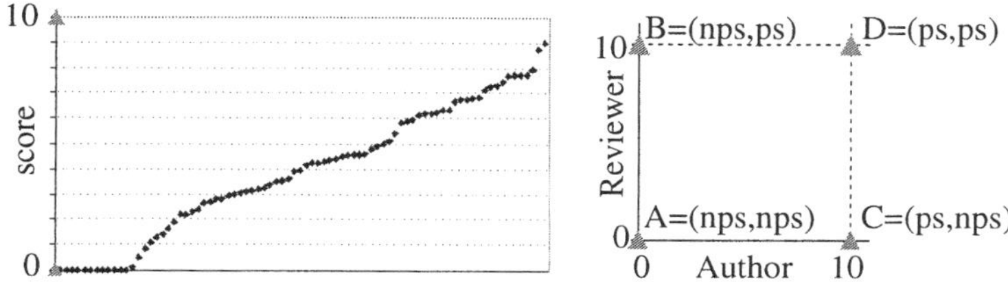

Fig. 1. (a) Students' scores (rhombus) and prototypes (triangles). (b) Prototypes of author-reviewer pairs

$\vec{A}$ and $\vec{D}$ are assigned maximum positive interest (to attract pairings towards them) and prototypes $\vec{B}$ and $\vec{C}$ are assigned maximum negative interest (to steer assignments away from them).

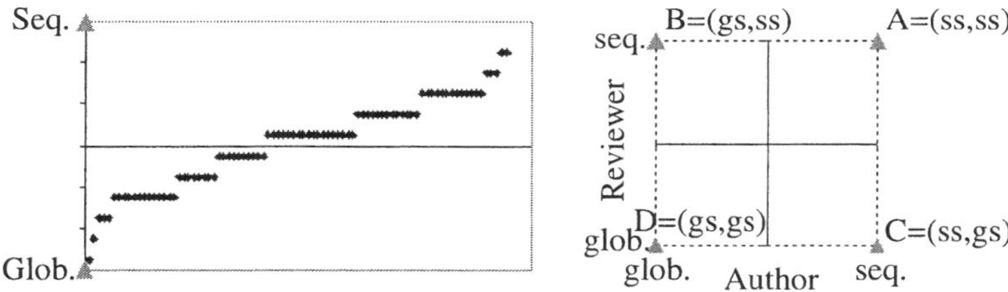

Fig. 2. (a) Students' learning styles (rhombus) and prototypes (triangles). (b) Prototypes of author-reviewer pairs

Prototypes define regions of interest (if positive interest) and regions to avoid (if negative interest) in the author-reviewer space. A given pair is selected or discarded depending on the region where it is located. Evaluation of an author-reviewer pair consists on classifying it with respect to the defined prototypes and assigning the corresponding interest.

A simple interest measure can be calculated for any author-reviewer pair, $\vec{X_i}=(\vec{au}, \vec{re})$, as the interest of the corresponding prototype:

$$interest_{CRISP}(\vec{X_i} = (\vec{au}, \vec{re})) = IP_i \tag{1}$$

being IP_i the interest assigned to prototype $\vec{P_i}$, representative of the class containing $\vec{X_i}$.

But in reality, student profiles rarely match exactly with ideal cases represented by the prototypes. Instead, student profiles are usually distributed through a wide range of values, without clear frontiers between classes, as it can be seen in Figures 1 and 2.

As a consequence, crisp classification is not an adequate approach, as it does not reflect the actual situation. The proposed system uses fuzzy regions, instead, which is more appropriate for the typical distributions found in a course.

The interest value of the matching point is then weighted with a measure of its similarity to the prototypes. Equation 1 is modified to consider fuzziness and multiple class membership in different degrees, as shown in Equation 2:

$$interest(\overrightarrow{X_i} = (\overrightarrow{au}, \overrightarrow{re})) = \sum_{i=0}^{N} m(\overrightarrow{X_i}, \overrightarrow{P_i}) \times IP_i \qquad (2)$$

being N the number of defined prototypes (classes), $\overrightarrow{P_i}$ the prototype representative of class i, IP_i the interest assigned to prototype $\overrightarrow{P_i}$ and $m(\overrightarrow{X_i}, \overrightarrow{P_i})$ a similarity measure between pairings $\overrightarrow{X_i}$ and $\overrightarrow{P_i}$: the membership degree of $\overrightarrow{X_i}$ to the class defined by prototype $\overrightarrow{P_i}$.

3.2 Searching Algorithm

Once the optimization criteria is implemented as an evaluation function which allows to compare mappings, an algorithm is needed to search the solution space for the optimal mapping. Exhaustive search is discarded due to the large solution space for the problem. Genetic algorithms proved to be effective to find a nearly-optimal solution at a reasonable cost in large solution spaces.

In order to map the proposed peer-matching algorithm to a genetic algorithm, some terms need to be defined.

Population: Evolution in genetic algorithms may work at different levels [14]: individual (try to build a single perfect specimen), population (try to create an entire population that maximizes global throughput when working in collaboration) or ecosystem ("co-evolve" several species that collaborate and compete with each other).

In the proposed system, each individual is a complete map (see Definition 2). So, evolution works at individual level, trying to build an optimal map for a given set of criteria.

Definition 2. *Given a set of submissions S, a set of reviewers R and the number of reviewers that must be assigned to each submission k_r, a map is defined as a function $\mathcal{M} : S \rightarrow R^{k_r}$, so that each submission $s_i \in S$ is assigned a set of k_r reviewers.*

Both sets S and R are represented in the system as arrays, so that each of their elements can be identified with the integer number representing its position.

A map $\mathcal{M}$ is represented in the system as a matrix of $|S| \times k_r$ dimensions, where each element $m[i]$ contains the k_r reviewers assigned to submission $s[i] \in S$; that is, each element $m[i][j]$ contains an integer $r_{ij} \in [0..|R|)$, representing the jth reviewer assigned to submission $s[i] \in S$, where $i \in [0..|S|)$ and $j \in [0..k_r)$.

As a first approach, each reviewer can be coded in the map matrix as its position in the reviewers array.

Example 3. Let us define:

$$A = R = \{u_0, u_1, u_2, u_3, u_4\} \; ; \qquad S = \{s_0, s_1, s_2, s_3, s_4\}$$

where A is the set of authors, R the set of reviewers, S the set of submissions and u_i is the author of s_i.

The matrix $\mathcal{M}_a = [3\,2\,1\,4\,0]$ represents the mapping where u_3 reviews s_0, u_2 reviews s_1, and so on.

Matrix $\mathcal{M}_b = [4\ 3\ 0\ 1\ 2]$ represents the mapping where u_4 reviews s_0, u_3 reviews s_1, and so on.

Fitness Function: The fitness function is derived from the interest function (see Equation 2). Given a map $\mathcal{M}$, it is calculated as the sum of the interest of each of the (author, reviewer) pairings contained in it:

$$fitness(\mathcal{M}) = \sum_{s_i \in S} \sum_{a_n \in A_i} \sum_{r_m \in R_i} interest(\overrightarrow{a_n}, \overrightarrow{r_m}) \tag{3}$$

being $A_i \subset A$ the set of authors of submission $s_i \in S$ and $R_i \subset R$ the set of reviewers assigned to s_i.

Genetic Operators: The crossover function consists on merging two maps to form a new generation. A breakpoint is randomly calculated and at that point each map is divided. The newly generated maps are the join of the beginning part of one map with the ending part of the other.

Example 4. Combining the two mappings defined in Example 3, the following maps are generated (supposing a breakpoint in position 3):

$$\begin{array}{l} \mathcal{M}_a = [3\,2\,1\ \|\ 4\,0] \searrow \mathcal{M}'_a = [3\,2\,1\ \|\ 1\,2] \\ \mathcal{M}_b = [4\,3\,0\ \|\ 1\,2] \nearrow \mathcal{M}'_b = [4\,3\,0\ \|\ 4\,0] \end{array}$$

It is really improbable that this approach reaches a valid solution. As illustrated in Example 4, load balancing is nearly impossible to maintain.

It is the same problem as the one found in [15] in genetic programming, mutations in the source code usually lead to individuals which do not compile. The subset of valid solutions is a too small subset of the search space.

Population Redefinition: Map coding is redefined to ensure load balancing and equiprobability between the reviewers. The absolute position of the reviewer in the reviewers array is no longer used. Instead, its position considering only *free* reviewers is used. Example 5 illustrates the mapping model implemented in the system.

The mutation operator is defined as randomly changing the value of one of the elements of the matrix, but always in the range of valid values for that position in the matrix.

Example 5. Using the relative model applied in the system, maps $\mathcal{M}_a$ and $\mathcal{M}_b$ defined in Example 3 are coded as follows:

$$\mathcal{M}_a = [3\,2\,1\,1\,0] \qquad \mathcal{M}_b = [4\,3\,0\,0\,0]$$

Reviewer of submission 3 in map $\mathcal{M}_a$ is coded now as 1 instead of 4, because at that point, only reviewers u_0 and u_4 are free. So, reviewer u_4 is in position 1 (starting from 0) in the array of *free* reviewers.

Applying the crossover operator, the following maps are generated:

$$\mathcal{M}'_a = [3\,2\,1 \parallel 0\,0] \qquad \mathcal{M}'_b = [4\,3\,0 \parallel 1\,0]$$

representing $[u_3\, u_2\, u_1\, u_0\, u_4]$ and $[u_4\, u_3\, u_0\, u_2\, u_1]$, respectively.

Non-valid mappings can still appear, as illustrated in $\mathcal{M}'_a$, in Example 5, where user u_4 reviews his/her own work. However, these non-valid individuals are not the majority of the search space, but a reduced subset. So, evolution discards naturally these mappings and tends towards valid solutions.

4 Experimental Results

The algorithm described has been implemented in a peer review matching system, which allows to define different mapping criteria to guide the author-reviewer matching process.

Figure 3 shows the resulting map obtained for the data of Example 1. Points are distributed near high-interest prototypes and completely avoid regions near negative-weighted prototypes. The described system has been deployed on a second semester computer engineering course. Three peer review cycles were executed. Assignments consisted on developing a complete software application. The coding phase was solved in teams, mostly in pairs, but reviews were assigned and done individually.

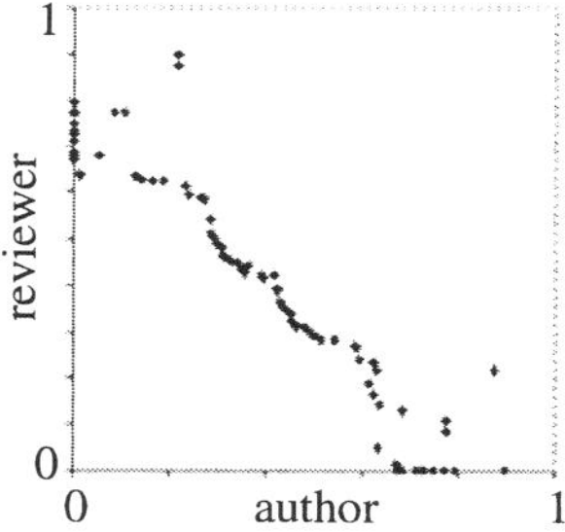

Fig. 3. Resulting map for Example 1

Using student scores as user profiles, each submission was assigned three reviewers, corresponding to three different criteria, as illustrated in Figure 4. The first reviewer was selected with a profile complementary to the author or, less probably, both proficient students. In the second, a reliable reviewer was preferred. The third reviewer was selected with similar profile to the author.

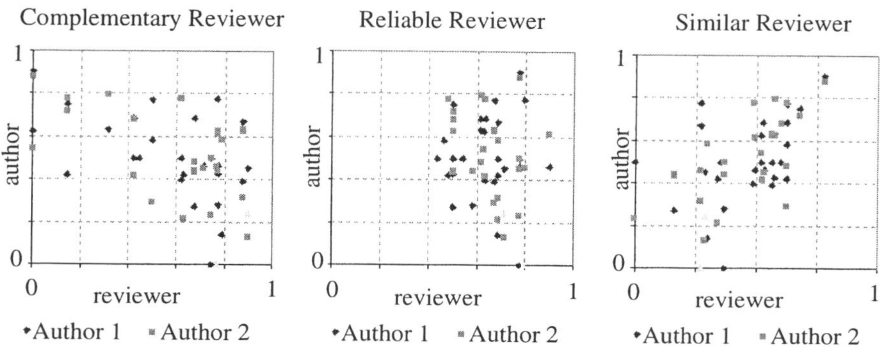

Fig. 4. Map applied in classroom experience

The three criteria were weighted, having the first one the highest priority and the third one the lowest.

Students opinions, requested both in surveys and informal talks, have been very positive. Moreover, experimental data confirm the expected correlation between learning and quality of work examined, both when reviewing applications ($\rho = 0.68$) and receiving feedback ($\rho = 0.58$).

5 Conclusions

In this paper, a novel algorithm is presented for matching authors and reviewers based on user profiles. Mapping criteria are easily configurable in the system, thanks to the intuitive approach based on student prototypes. Reviewers are selected based on their profiles, according to the previously defined mapping criteria.

Experimental application in the course has received a really positive reaction from the students. Results on student motivation and improvement are very promising.

As for future work, the range of courses where these techniques are applied is being widened. Alternative user models, as well as different criteria are being studied. More work is also needed on the analysis of the influence of student profiles in the process. Hopefully, the described system will make easier the analysis and comparison of different mapping criteria and their effects and influence in the peer review process.

Acknowledgment

Work partially funded by Programa Nacional de Tecnologías de la Información y de las Comunicaciones, project TIC2002-03635.

References

1. Lester, J.C., Vicari, R.M., Paraguaçu, F., eds.: Intelligent Tutoring Systems. 7th International Conf., ITS 2004 Proc. Volume 3220 of LNCS. Springer-Verlag (2004)
2. Gehringer, E.F.: Strategies and mechanisms for electronic peer review. In: Frontiers in Education Conference, ASEE/IEEE (2000)
3. Gehringer, E.F.: Electronic peer review and peer grading in computer-science courses. In: Proc. of the Technical Symposium on Computer Science Education, SIGCSE (2001) 139–143
4. Ward, A., Sitthiworachart, J., Joy, M.: Aspects of web-based peer assessment systems for teaching and learning computer programming. In: IASTED International Conference on Web-based Education. (2004) 292–297
5. : Calibrated peer review. cpr.molsci.ucla.edu (2004)
6. Topping, K.: Peer assessment between students in colleges and universities. Review of Educational Research **68** (1998) 249–276
7. Gehringer, E.F.: Assignment and quality control of peer reviewers. In: ASEE Annual Conference and Exposition. (2001)
8. Crespo, R.M., Pardo, A., Delgado Kloos, C.: An adaptive strategy for peer review. In: Frontiers in Education Conference, ASEE/IEEE (2004)
9. Inaba, A., Mizoguchi, R.: Learners' roles and predictable educational benefits in collaborative learning. an ontological approach to support design and analysis of cscl. In Lester, J.C., Vicari, R.M., Paraguaçu, F., eds.: Intelligent Tutoring Systems. 7th International Conference, ITS 2004 Proc. Volume 3220 of LNCS., Springer-Verlag (2004) 285–294
10. Feldgen, M., Clúa, O.: Games as a motivation for freshman students to learn programming. In: Frontiers in Education Conference, ASEE/IEEE (2004)
11. Nelson, S.: Teaching collaborative writing and peer review techniques to engineering and technology undergraduates. In: Frontiers in Education Conf. (2000)
12. Gehringer, E.F., Cui, Y.: An effective strategy for the dynamic mapping of peer reviewers. In: ASEE Annual Conference and Exposition. (2002)
13. : Merriam-webster online dictionary. www.m-w.com (2005)
14. Laramée, F.D.: Genetic Algorithms: Evolving the Perfect Troll. In: AI game programming wisdom. Charles River Media (2002) 629–639
15. Koza, J.: Genetic Programming-On the programming of the computers by means of natural selection. MIT Press (1992)

Pose-Invariant Face Detection Using Edge-Like Blob Map and Fuzzy Logic*

YoungOuk Kim[1,2], SungHo Jang[1], SangJin Kim[1], Chang-Woo Park[2], and Joonki Paik[1]

[1] Image Processing and Intelligent Systems Laboratory, Department of Image Engineering, Graduate School of Advanced Imaging Science, Multimedia, and Film, Chung-Ang University, 221 Huksuk-Dong, Tongjak-Ku, Seoul 156-756, Korea
`http://ipis.cau.ac.kr`

[2] Korea Electronics Technology Institute (KETI), 401-402 B/D 193. Yakdae-Dong, Wonmi-Gu, Puchon-Si, Kyunggi-Do, 420-140, Korea
`kimyo@keti.re.kr`
`http://www.keti.re.kr/~premech`

Abstract. We present an effective method of face and facial feature detection under pose variation in cluttered background. Our approach is flexible to both color and gray facial images and is also feasible for detecting facial features in quasi real-time. Based on the characteristics of neighborhood area of facial features, a new directional template for the facial feature is defined. By applying this template to the input facial image, novel edge-like blob map (EBM) with multiple strength intensity is constructed. And we propose an effective pose estimator using fuzzy logic and a simple PCA method. Combining these methods, robust face localization is achieved for face recognition in mobile robots. Experimental results using various color and gray images prove accuracy and usefulness of the proposed algorithm.

1 Introduction

This paper proposes face detection and facial features estimation methods that are suitable for mobile robot platform.

Previous face detection research [1, 2, 3, 4] mostly uses a fixed camera, where the face detection technology for "human robot interaction (HRI)" has unique properties in its embodiment. The face in the acquired image has significant pose variation due to the robot platform's mobility, located in cluttered background, and with significant amount of illumination changes.

For robust face detection we present a novel directional template for effective estimation of the locations of facial features; such as an eye pair and a mouth. This

* This research was supported by Korea Ministry of Science and Technology under the National Research Laboratory project, by Korea Ministry of Education under the BK21 project, and by Korean Ministry of Information and Communication under HNRC-ITRC program at Chung-Ang university supervised by IITA.

M. Ali and F. Esposito (Eds.): IEA/AIE 2005, LNAI 3533, pp. 695 – 704, 2005.

template will be applied to either still images or natural video to produce a new edge-like blob map(EBM) with multiple intensity strengths. The EBM will be shown to be robust in both pose variation and illumination change. And capable of estimating detailed locations of facial features without additional information.

Principle component analysis (PCA) [4] has been applied to face localization, coding and recognition but it is vulnerable to noise since the principle components maximize the variance of input data, resulting in undesired variations in pose, facial expression, and image orientation [5].

However, PCA can be made reliable if combined with fuzzy logic. This robust pose estimator can perform well up to 45 degree of face offset from the frontal viewpoint. In this paper we will show the appropriateness of the proposed method through experiments using the well-known gray-level database of facial images and various color images and natural scenes.

The main goal of face detection is locating position of face in an uncontrolled environment. Previous approaches [2, 3, 6] have limited their research goal to enhancing the detection performance as an individual process of face detection. On the other hand in the proposed approach, face detection process is taken as a prior step of face or expression recognition, considered from a viewpoint of the entire HRI process. In many research works related to detecting facial features, the use of facial color characteristics [8] is the most recent approach to pose-variant facial images. For the experiment of moderate or lower quality of color chrominance images, it is difficult to clearly distinguish facial features from each chromatic map of an eye or a mouth. Moreover, if a facial area or the eye and mouth features in face are very small, facial features can be concealed in facial color region and cannot be easily detected.

Many approaches use edge information for feature detection, and several related research works have been proposed recently, like the various type of 'edge map' images. For example, a method using edge orientation map (EOM) information can parameterize the local features in the facial area [8], and Line edge map (LEM) are defined and applied to recognize facial images [9]. However, these researches compose edge maps that are determined on the bases of frontal face edge figures and their similarity measures are computed from these frontal normal maps. Therefore, in the case of pose- variant or unknown-viewpoint facial images, correct detection rate is considerably decreased.

2 Scale and Pose-Invariant Face Detection

In this section, the proposed method for detecting face and its eye location is presented. The method can also be adapted for a gray image as well as color image inputs. According to the image type, additional step for preprocessing a facial image is included so that facial features can be detected more effectively. We also show robust pose-correction method, which is not a synthesizing technique but is an actual pose compensation method using fuzzy logic, simple PCA, and an active 3D camera system. Fig. 1 shows the overall process of the proposed algorithm.

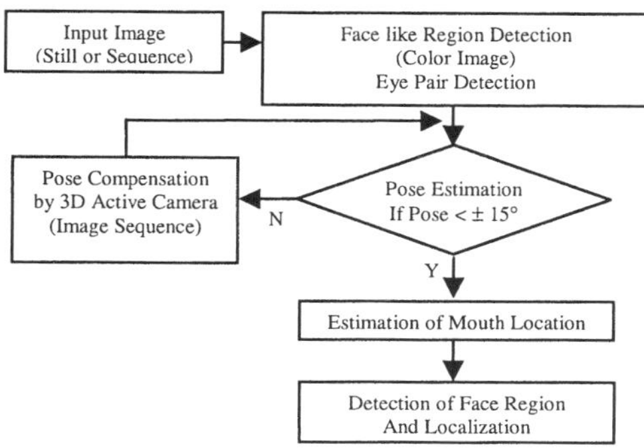

Fig. 1. The proposed pose invariant face detection algorithm

2.1 EBM for Eye Pair Detection

We present a novel approach that uses gray intensity of facial features, irrespective of their color characteristics. Two eyes have such an intensity property that the eye region is darker than neighboring facial regions. The ordinary near-eye region has distinctive shape of intensity. That is, the width of small darker intensity area of eye is longer than the height of the area; such shape is just similar to a horizontal 'blob' edge. We can estimate candidate location of features by using the new 'directional blob template'.

The template size is determined according to the size of the facial area, which is assumed as an appropriate area to be detected. Width of the template is usually larger than height as shown in Fig. 2. At the pixel, $P(x,y)$, in an intensity image of size $W \times H$, the center pixel, $P_{cent}(x_c, y_c)$, is defined as the one where the template is placed. From this center pixel, average intensity $\overline{I}_X$, given in (1) and (2), of eight-directions of feature template of size $h_{FF} \times w_{FF}$, is obtained, Finally intensity difference between $\overline{I}_X$ and I_{cent} (intensity value of P_{cent}) is also computed as (3). A directional template of facial features is shown in Fig. 2. The intensity value that has largest magnitude of intensity gradient is defined as the principal intensity $I_{\Pr}$ as (4).

$$\overline{I}_{Left} = \{\sum_{i=-w_{FF}/2+Xc}^{i=Xc} \sum_{j=Yc}^{j=Yc} P(x+i,y)/(w_{FF}/2)\} \quad \overline{I}_{Right} = \{\sum_{i=Xc}^{i=w_{FF}/2+Xc} \sum_{j=Yc}^{j=Yc} P(x+i,y)/(w_{FF}/2)\} \tag{1}$$

$$\overline{I}_{Top} = \{\sum_{i=Xc}^{i=Xc} \sum_{j=Yc}^{j=h_{FF}/2+Yc} P(x,y+j)/(h_{FF}/2)\} \quad \overline{I}_{Bottom} = \{\sum_{i=Xc}^{i=Xc} \sum_{j=-h_{FF}/2+Yc}^{j=Yc} P(x,y+j)/(h_{FF}/2)\}$$

$$\overline{I}_{NW} = \{\sum_{i=Xc-h_{FF}/2}^{i=Xc} \sum_{j=(-i)}^{j=(-i)} P(x+i,y+j)/(h_{FF}/2)\} \quad \overline{I}_{NE} = \{\sum_{i=Xc}^{i=Xc+h_{FF}/2} \sum_{j=(i)}^{j=(i)} P(x+i,y+j)/(h_{FF}/2)\} \tag{2}$$

$$\overline{I}_{SW} = \{\sum_{i=Xc-h_{FF}/2}^{i=Xc} \sum_{j=(i)}^{j=(i)} P(x+i,y+j)/(h_{FF}/2)\} \quad \overline{I}_{SE} = \{\sum_{i=Xc}^{i=Xc+h_{FF}/2} \sum_{j=(-i)}^{j=(-i)} P(x+i,y+j)/(h_{FF}/2)\}$$

$$\Delta I_{width} = (|I_{cent} - \overline{I}_{Left}| + |I_{cent} - \overline{I}_{Right}|)/2 \quad \Delta I_{height} = (|I_{cent} - \overline{I}_{Top}| + |I_{cent} - \overline{I}_{Bottom}|)/2 \tag{3}$$

$$\Delta I_{Diag1} = (|I_{cent} - \overline{I}_{NW}| + |I_{cent} - \overline{I}_{SE}|)/2 \quad \Delta I_{Diag2} = (|I_{cent} - \overline{I}_{NE}| + |I_{cent} - \overline{I}_{SW}|)/2$$

$$I_{\Pr} = \text{Max}\{\Delta I_{width}, \Delta I_{height}, \Delta I_{Diag1}, \Delta I_{Diag2}\} \tag{4}$$

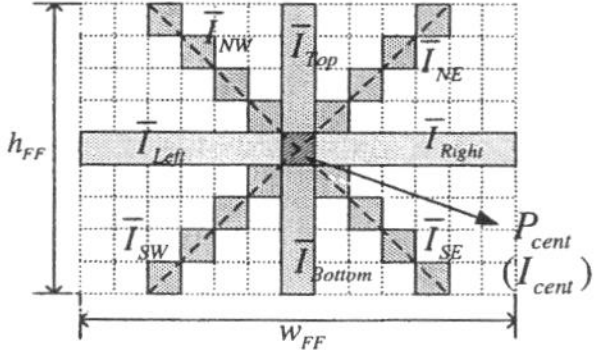

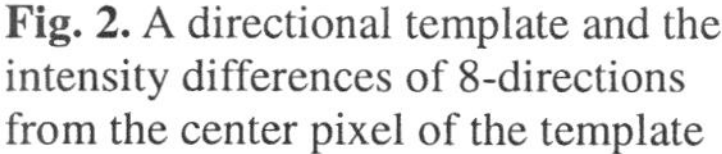

Fig. 2. A directional template and the intensity differences of 8-directions from the center pixel of the template

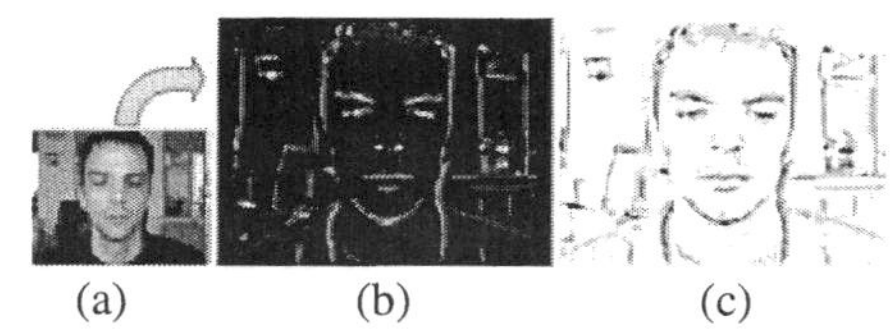

Fig. 3. An EBM from the original gray image and its negative image

Now, using principal intensity value I_{Pr}, EBM with multiple strength intensity is created as follows. For all locations of pixel, $P(x, y)$, in the entire intensity image, the masking operation with the directional template is applied to the intensity image. Using a threshold value that is weighted by the principal intensity I_{Pr}, multiple intensity strength of each pixel in the entire image is determined. For intensity difference, ΔI_{width}, of both sides of the horizontal direction at pixel $P(x, y)$; if a certain pixel intensity value is larger than α_{Pr}, weighted threshold given in (5), +1 level intensity strength is assigned. Next, for the vertical direction; if the pixel intensity value is larger than β_{Pr}, another weighted threshold in (5), then +1 level edge strength is also assigned. Similarly, for two diagonal directions at $P(x, y)$, as shown in Fig.3, if a pixel intensity value is larger than γ_{Pr}, weighted threshold, then +1 level edge strength is assigned in the same manner. From this process, the entire gray intensity image is converted into an EBM image that has different 4-level intensity strengths. Most bright edge-like blob pixels have its intensity level +4. Intensity value of each strength level has 40, 80, 120, and 200. Fig. 3(c) shown a negative EBM for highlighting the difference of the edge strengths rather than the original blob map image, as shown in Fig. 3(b).

$$
\begin{aligned}
&\text{For each pixel } p(x, y) \text{ in input image,} \\
&\textit{if } \Delta I_{width, P(x,y)} > \alpha_{\mathrm{Pr}} \mid I_{\mathrm{Pr}} \mid \text{ then add(+1) level strength intensity at } p(x, y) \\
&\textit{also if } \Delta I_{height, P(x,y)} > \beta_{\mathrm{Pr}} \mid I_{\mathrm{Pr}} \mid \text{ then add(+1) level strength intensity at } p(x, y) \\
&\textit{also if } \Delta I_{Diag1(2), P(x,y)} > \gamma_{\mathrm{Pr}} \mid I_{\mathrm{Pr}} \mid \text{ then add(+1) level strength intensity, each other} \\
&\qquad (\textit{where } \alpha_{pr} = 1.0, \beta_{\mathrm{Pr}} = 0.9,\ \gamma_{\mathrm{Pr}} = 0.8)
\end{aligned} \tag{5}
$$

From the edge-like blob map, eye analogue blob regions are marked and all probable eye-pair regions are selected. The eye-like region has more dark intensity property than other feature regions e.g., a mouth. So, we choose level 4 edge strength pixels only for candidate eye pixels. Above all, multiple intensity level blobs are divided into level 4 and level 1~3, and some properties of each small region, that is a blob, are acquired from the component labeling technique. Basic geometric conditions in (6) are applied to all candidate eye-blob regions, and only suitable eye blobs are marked. If the width and the height of the bounding rectangle of eye analogue blobs($width_{E.B.}$, $height_{E.B.}$)is smaller by 1.5 times either the width or the height of previous feature templates, except too noisy area ($area_{E.B}$ is below 6 pixels), these blobs are selected as candidate eyes.

$$\begin{aligned}&\text{Select certain blob as `candidate eye' blob (E.B.)}\\&\text{only if } \{width_{E.B} < c \cdot w_{ff}\} \cap \{height_{E.B} < c \cdot h_{ff}\} \cap \{area_{E.B} > \varepsilon\}\\&(where\ \ c = 1.5,\ \varepsilon = 6)\end{aligned} \tag{6}$$

All qualified eye-pairs are composed from above selected eye blobs, and only candidate eye pairs are selected according to whether facial geometric conditions is be satisfied. As shown in Fig. 4, the length of eye pair the distance, direction of eye-pair constructed vector, and the ratio of two eye regions are considered. Based on the area size of the detected face, suitable eye-pairs are chosen.

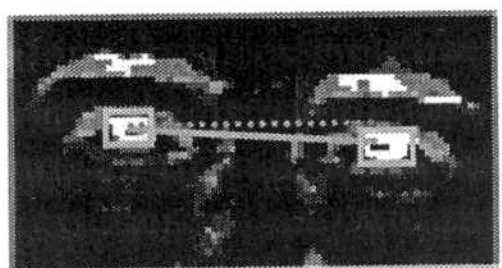

i) distance condition : $d_{Eye-pair}$ (green line)
ii) angular condition : $\angle \vec{d}_{Eye-pair}$ (green line vs. dot line)
iii) area ratio = $A_{LeftEye} / A_{RightEye}$ (two rectangular bounding box)

Fig. 4. Facial geometric conditions for eye-pair

Fig. 5. A result of eye-pair detection

Through both linear scaling of the eye patch region as shown in Fig.5 and histogram equalization, intensity properties of eye pairs can be robustly obtained. Fig. 5 shows an example of a candidate eye-pair patch region.

2.2 Pose Estimation using Fuzzy Logic and a 3D Active Camera

In this section we will present a pose compensation method using a 3D Active camera system. PCA and fuzzy logic have been applied to pose estimation. First, color segmentation in the HSV color space is performed to estimate face like regions. EBM is then applied to find the location of the eye pair. We can compose a face database with

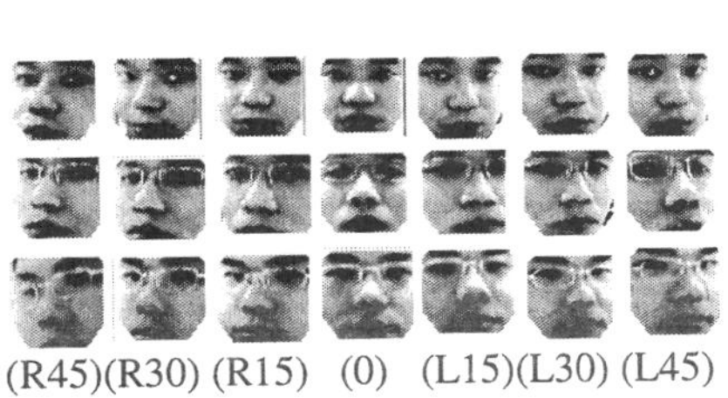

Fig. 6. A face database for pose estimation

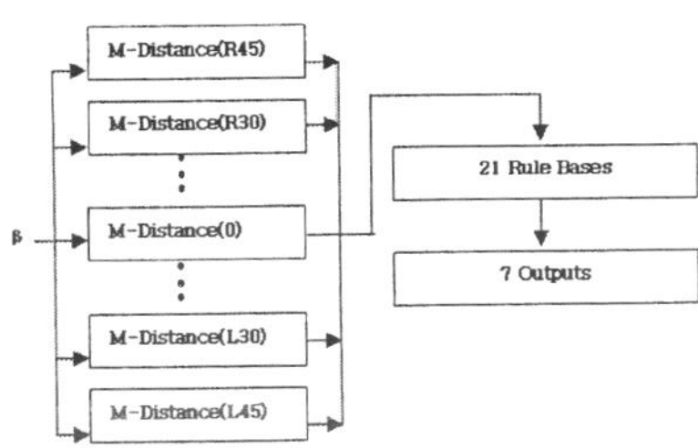

Fig. 7. Fuzzy inference engine

multiple viewing angles separated by 15 degree, such as -45°, -30°, -15°, 0°, 15°, 30°, and 45°, as shown in Fig. 6. The advantage of the proposed algorithm is that it uses only hardware compensation method, so it can minimize loss of facial information compared with the geometrical transform method.

The pose of rotated face can be estimated using PCA and the Mamdani's fuzzy inference [10]. In this case, we employed a seven inputs and seven outputs fuzzy inference engine. The input of the fuzzy engine is classified into 7 distances from PCA and the outputs are angle of rotated face as shown in Fig.7. In the figure β is a coefficient of the input vector that is inspected to eigenspace. The rule bases is given in (7).

$$\text{If } D(R_\theta) \text{ is } \begin{matrix}\text{ZERO}\\ \text{SMALL}\\ \text{LARGE}\end{matrix} \text{ Then } Output_\theta \text{ is } \begin{matrix}1.0\\ 0.5,\\ 0.0\end{matrix} \tag{7}$$

where, $R_\theta \in$ {-45°, -30°, -15°, 0°, 15°, 30°, and 45°}. The input membership function of the fuzzy inference engine is shown in Fig. 8.

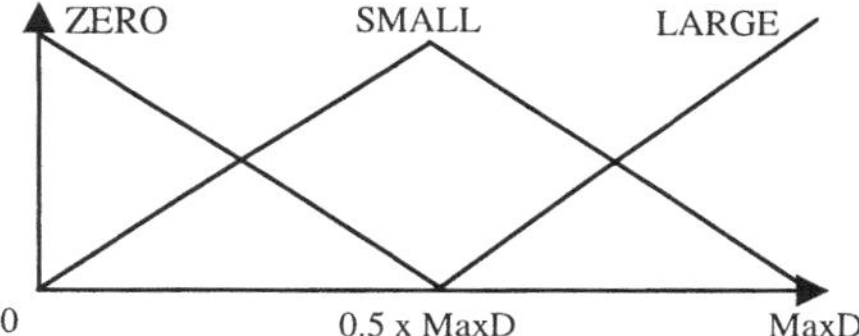

Fig. 8. Input membership function of the fuzzy engine

Finally, the estimated pose can be written using the singleton fuzzifier, the product inference engine, and the average defuzzifier.

$$\text{Pose} = -45°(1/\,Output_{-45°}) + -30°(1/\,Output_{-30°}) + \bullet\bullet\bullet + 30°(1/\,Output_{30°}) + 45°(1/\,Output_{45°}) \tag{8}$$

3 Face Localization for Recognition

For the case of a pose-varying face, we can compensate the pose for a nearby frontal view using a 3D active camera system. Since the input is still an image having differently rotated poses, this area shape is quite a variable form of a rectangular area. For this reason, estimating the location of a mouth as well as an eye-pair locations is also needed for detecting the precise facial region.

3.1 Estimation of Mouth Location

The edge-like blob for eye pair detection, presented in the previous section, is also effective in estimating the mouth location that is quite a variable shape of a facial feature. Similar to eye blobs the mouth area have also darker intensity compared with other facial regions. Owing to the various shape of a mouth's feature, edge strengths of the mouth in the EBM are not sufficiently prominent rather than those of eyes. Several candidate facial regions are decided by both pre-obtained eye pairs and the feasible locations of the mouth. Near these facial regions, the analysis of facial region similarity is performed in the next section.

The candidate locations of mouth are estimated as the positions where narrow and fairly strength edges exist in eye pair vector directions. Summary of estimation of probable locations of mouth is as follows.

(1) Determine normal vector to mouth locations on basis of eye pair vector,
(2) Form the area range of probable mouth locations (including from nose tip to jaw),
(3) Rotation of this area and normalization,
(4) Selecting probable locations at vertical direction if edge pixels that is above level 2 strength are larger than prescribed threshold at horizontal direction,
(5) Converting this area to vector image and component labeling for selected locations in 4),
(6) Determine candidate locations of mouth, if location blob thickness is below the prescribed threshold on basis of distance between eye pair,
(7) Choose up to three locations from the bottom

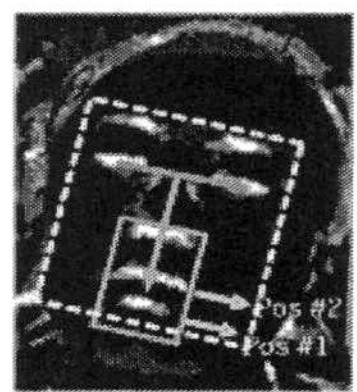

- Thick arrow – eye pair vector
- Thin arrow – its normal vector
- Dashed box
  – candidate area of face from eye and normal vector lengths
- Dotted box
  – boundary of possible locations of mouth
- position #1, position #2
  – candidate positions of mouth (from below)

Fig. 9. Various shapes of edge-like blob regions near the mouth area

3.2 Detection of Face Region and Localization of Facial Features

The similarity measure between candidate area and the predefined template of the standard face patch is calculated using the weighted correlation technique. At first, a normalized form of the candidate facial area must be prepared for measuring similarity with the predefined template. The preparation step is as follows: For the pre-obtained rectangular area that includes two eyes and a mouth, basic width is determined as shown in Fig.10. Basic height length is decided according to both eye-mouth distance and the basic width. This variable rectangle of obtained the facial area is 'two-stage' scaled to a fixed square patch of size 60×60 pixels. Although two-stage scale processes are performed, locations of two eyes and a mouth are always placed on a fixed position. For each eye-pair location, maximum three candidate facial areas are obtained according to multiple mouth locations, and their normalized square areas are compared to the standard face templates. Similarity measure between the area and templates is based on the basic form of correlation equations, given in (9). As shown in Fig.10(c), the weighted region of main facial features, that is circular region of dotted area, also defined. The modified correlations are computed with weighting values at the above region.

$$\rho_{I_{FD}}, I_{tmpl} = \frac{E[I_{FD} I_{tmpl}] - E[I_{FD}] \cdot E[I_{tmpl}]}{\sigma_{I_{FD}} \sigma_{I_{tmpl}}} \quad \textbf{(9)}$$

(where I_{FD} : obtained facial area, I_{tmpl} : face templates)

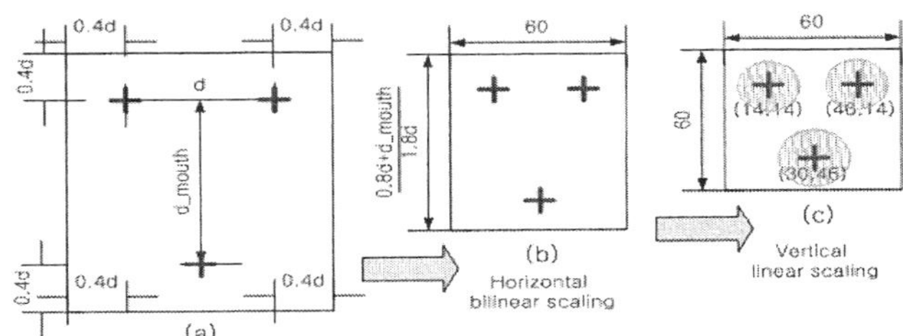

Fig. 10. Two-step scaling process of a rectangular facial region

We adopted 20 templates for improving accuracy of detection. Meanwhile, in the square regions in both candidate facial areas and standard templates, a non-facial part is often included, e.g., at the corner area of the patch. Using the fillet mask, some pixels of non-facial area in the normalized image patch is removed and histogram equalization is also performed on these patches. For these normalized face image patches, the region with the maximum average correlation in all standard facial templates represents the most likely face region, and is determined as the final face region. Three fixed positions in the face patch are also determined as the final facial feature's locations that correspond to pixel positions in the input image. These corresponding positions may construct a features' triangle of various configurations. The final facial features' triangle and the face region patch image are shown in Fig.11 and 12.

Fig. 11. Some face templates for modified correlation

Fig. 12. Detection result of a face area and the corresponding feature locations

4 Experimental Results

To present more practical results with various poses, BioID face database [11] is adopted. In the recent research of face detection, BioID face database has been advantageous for describing more realistic environments. These facial images contain quite a fairly degree of changes of face scales, pose variations, illuminations, and backgrounds. For a test set of BioID face database, entire facial image is converted to an EBM, and feasible locations of facial features are founded as shown in Fig.13. Some results of both successful and typical erroneous examples are also shown in Fig.14.

Natural scenes are also tested for pose compensation using the proposed system in Figs. 15 and 16.

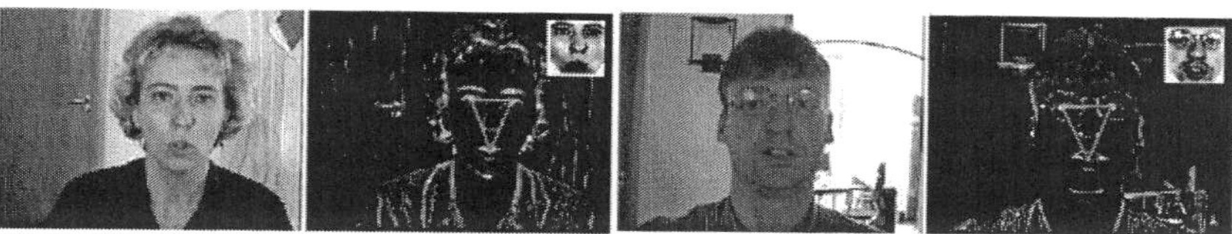

Fig. 13. Examples of detection results in 'Test set #2'-BioID face database

Fig. 14. Examples of correct and erroneous cases in Test set #2'-BioID

Fig. 15. The 3D Active camera system for pose compensation

Fig. 16. Process of pose compensation

5 Conclusion

We have presented pose-invariant face detection and the corresponding feature detection methods with robust pose estimation. Successful face detection can be achieved in complex background and additional estimation of facial feature locations is also possible, irrespective of a certain amount of pose variation. Especially, this method can be applied in gray images as well as color images. Thanks to this property of pliable type for input image, various input images can be used and also evaluated in widely used face databases.

References

1. C. Garcia and G. Tziritas, "Face Detection using Quantized Skin Color Regions Merging and Wavelet Packet Analysis," IEEE Trans. Multimedia, vol.1, no.3, pp.264-277, September 1999.

2. A. Nikolaidis and I. Pitas, "Facial Feature Extraction and Pose Determination," Pattern Recognition, vol. 33, pp. 1783~1791, 2000.
3. M. H. Yang, N. Ahuja, and D. Kriegman, "Mixtures of Linear Subspaces for Face Detection," Proc. Fourth Int. Conf. Automatic Face and Gesture Recognition, pp. 70-76, 2000.
4. B. Moghaddam and A. Pentlend, "Probabilistic Visual Learning for Object Recognition," IEEE Trans. Pattern Analysis, Machine Intelligence, vol. 19, no. 7 pp. 696-710, July 1997.
5. M. H. Yang, D. Kriegman, and N. Ahuja, "Detecting Face in Images: Survey," IEEE Trans. Pattern Analysis, Machine Intelligence. vol. 24, pp. 33-58, January 2002.
6. H . A. Rowley, S. Baluja, and T. Kanade, "Neural Network-based Face Detection," IEEE Trans. Pattern Analysis, Machine Intell., vol. 20, no. 1, pp. 23 ~38, January 1998.
7. R .L. Hsu, Mohamed Abdel-Mottaleb, and Anil K. Jain, "Face Detection in Color Images," IEEE Trans. Pattern Analysis, Machine Intell., vol. 24, pp. 696-706, may 2002.
8. B. Fr¨oba and C. K¨ublbeck, "Robust Face Detection at Video Frame Rate Based on Edge Orientation Features," Proc. 5th Int'l Conf. Automatic Face, Gesture Recognition, 2002.
9. Y. Gao and M. Leung, "Face Recognition Using Line Edge Map", IEEE Trans. Pattern Analysis, Machine Intell., vol. 24, no. 6, pp. 764-779, June 2002.
10. Y. Kim, C. Park, and Joonki Paik, "A New 3D Active Camera System for Robust Face Recognition by Correcting Pose Variation", Int. Conf. ICCAS pp. 1482-1487, August 2004.
11. The BioID face database; http://www.bioid.com/downloads/facedb/facedatabase.html

A Fuzzy Logic-Based Approach for Detecting Shifting Patterns in Cross-Cultural Data*

George E. Tsekouras[1], Dimitris Papageorgiou[1], Sotiris B. Kotsiantis[2], Christos Kalloniatis[1], and Panagiotis Pintelas[2]

[1] University of the Aegean, Department of Cultural Technology and Communication, Faonos and Harilaou Trikoupi Str., 81100, Mytilene, Lesvos, Greece, Tel: +301-2251-036631, Fax:+301-2251-0-36609, gtsek@ct.aegean.gr

[2] Efdlab, University of Patras, Department of Mathematics, Greece

Abstract. To assess the extent to which individuals adapt themeselfs in a strange cultural environement, the authors analyzed the adaptation process of a number of immigrants who live in Greece. Using categorical variables to represent certain cross-cultural adaptation indicators and employing fuzzy logic clustering, the authors detected and analyzed shifting patterns that are related to the cross-cultural adaptation of individuals.

1 Introduction

Cross-cultural movement has become a common place of our time. The pervasiveness of the movements of people across societies along with the technological changes, requires that we cope with numerous situations to which our previous experience simply does not apply. Because of its multiple facets and dimensions cross-cultural adaptation has been viewed from several conceptual angles and measured in various categories such as [1,2]: economic condition, perception, attitude, ethnocultural identity, social communication, and host communication competence.

In this paper we analyze cross-cultural data that are related to the last category: *the host communication competence*. The available data are categorical data and were generated by using a questionnaire over a number of immigrants who live in Greece. We elaborated these data using a fuzzy clustering algorithm to detect shifting patterns, which describe the adaptation process.

2 Host Communication Competence and Data Description

The concept of host communication competence can be examined by analyzing the following four key empirical indicators [1]: (1) Knowledge of the host communication

* This work was supported by the Greek Manpower Employment Organization, Department of Lesvos.

M. Ali and F. Esposito (Eds.): IEA/AIE 2005, LNAI 3533, pp. 705 – 708, 2005.

system, (2) Cognitive complexity in responding to the host environement, (3) Emotional and aesthetic co-orientation with the host culture, and (4) Behavioral capability to perform various interactions in the host environement.

We measured the above cross-cultural adaptation indicators using a questionnaire that consists of 8 questions (attributes). Each of the above attributes is assigned five possible answers (categories). The experiment took place between January 2001 and December 2002 in Lesvos, a famous Greek island, where 60 immigrants who live there provided answers to the questionnaire once per two months for 24 months. Thus, the total number of categorical data is equal to: n=720.

3 The Proposed Algorithm

Let $\boldsymbol{X}=\{\boldsymbol{x}_1,\boldsymbol{x}_2,...,\boldsymbol{x}_n\}$ be a set of categorical objects. The matching dissimilarity measure between two categorical objects $\boldsymbol{x}_k$ and $\boldsymbol{x}_l$ is defined as [3],

$$D(\boldsymbol{x}_k,\boldsymbol{x}_l)=\sum_{j=1}^{p}\delta(x_{kj},x_{lj})\quad(1\leq k\leq n,\ 1\leq l\leq n,\ \ k\neq l) \tag{1}$$

where p is the number of attributes assigned to each attribute, and $\delta(x,y)=0$ if x=y and $\delta(x,y)=1$ if $x\neq y$. The proposed algorithm uses an entropy-based clustering scheme, which provides initial conditions to the fuzzy c-modes, while after the implementation of the fuzzy c-modes applies a cluster merging process, which obtains the final number of clusters. A detailed analysis of the fuzzy c-modes can be found in [3].

3.1 Entropy-Based Categorical Data Clustering

The total entropy of an object $\boldsymbol{x}_k$ is given by the next equation [4],

$$\boldsymbol{H}_k=-\sum_{l=1}^{n}\left[E_{kl}\log_2(E_{kl})-(1-E_{kl})\log_2(1-E_{kl})\right]\qquad(l\neq k) \tag{2}$$

where,

$$E_{kl}=\exp\{-a\,D(\boldsymbol{x}_k,\boldsymbol{x}_l)\}\qquad k\neq l,\ \ a\in(0,1) \tag{3}$$

Based on (2) and (3), an object with small total entropy value is a good nominee to be a cluster center [4]. The entropy-based categorical data-clustering algorithm is:

Step 1) Using eq. (2) calculate the total entropies for all objects $\boldsymbol{x}_k$ $(1\leq k\leq n)$.

Step 2) Set c=c+1. Calculate the minimum entropy $\boldsymbol{H}_{\min}=\min_k\{\boldsymbol{H}_k\}$ and set the respective object $\boldsymbol{x}_{\min}$ as the center element of the c-th cluster: $\boldsymbol{v}_c=\boldsymbol{x}_{\min}$.

Step 4) Remove from $\boldsymbol{X}$ all the objects that are most similar to $\boldsymbol{x}_{\min}$ and assign them to the c-th cluster. If $\boldsymbol{X}$ is empty stop. Else turn the algorithm to step 2.

3.2 Cluster Merging Process

The weighted matching dissimilarity measure between pairs of clusters is [5],

$$D_w(v_i, v_j) = D(v_i, v_j)\sqrt{\sum_{k=1}^{n} u_{ik} \sum_{k=1}^{n} u_{jk} \Bigg/ \left(\sum_{k=1}^{n} u_{ik} + \sum_{k=1}^{n} u_{jk}\right)} \quad 1 \le i, j \le c \ (i \ne j) \quad (4)$$

Then, the similarity between two clusters is given as follows,

$$S_{ij} = \exp\{-\theta\, D_w(v_i, v_j)\} \quad (1 \le i, j \le c, \quad i \ne j) \qquad \text{with } \theta \in (0,1) \qquad (5)$$

4 Detecting and Analyzing Shifting Patterns

The implementation of the algorithm to the available data set gave c=5 clusters. Since each cluster (pattern) may share categorical objects with more than one sampling periods, it is assigned weight values, which are determined by the number of objects that belong both to the pattern and to each sampling period. Fig. 1 shows the resultant shifting patterns of the cross-cultural data as a function of time, where each of the labels corresponds to a specific cluster. Based on this figure we can see that as the time passes the individuals' adaptation becomes more and more efficient.

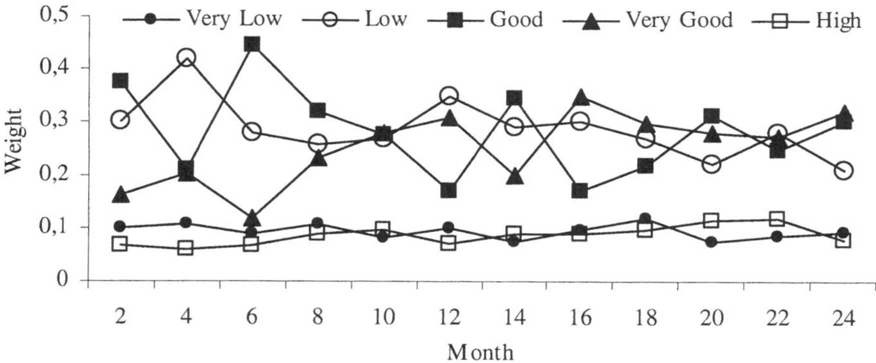

Fig. 1. Shifting patterns as a function of time

5 Conclusions

This paper presented a cross-cultural data analysis, where shifting patterns that correspond to certain levels of cross-cultural adaptation were detected and analyzed. The available data were categorical data, and were elaborated by a fuzzy clustering algorithm, which is able to automatically determine the final number of clusters.

References

1. Kim, Y. Y.: Communication and cross-cultural adaptation: and integrative theory, Multilingual Matters Ltd, England (1988)
2. Spicer, E. H.: Acculturation, In: D. L. Sills (Ed.): International Encyclopedia of Social Sciences, Macmillan, N. Y. (1968) 21-27
3. Huang, Z., Ng, M. K.: A fuzzy k-modes algorithm for clustering categorical data, IEEE Transactions on Fuzzy Systems 7 (4) (1999) 446-452
4. Yao, J., Dash, M., Tan, S.T., Liu, H., Entropy-based fuzzy clustering and fuzzy modeling, Fuzzy Sets and Systems 113 (2000) 381-388.
5. Mali, K., Mitra, S., Clustering of symbolic data and its validation, Lecture Notes in Artificial Intelligence 2275 (2002) 339-344.

Minimal Knowledge Anonymous User Profiling for Personalized Services

Alfredo Milani

Università di Perugia, Dipartimento di Matematica e Informatica,
Via Vanvitelli, 106100, Perugia, Italy
milani@unipg.it

Abstract. An algorithmic and formal method is presented for automatic profiling of anonymous internet users. User modelling represents a relevant problem in most internet successful user services, such as news sites or search engines, where only minimal knowledge about the user is given, i.e. information such as user session, user tracing and click-stream analysis is not available. On the other hand the ability of giving a personalised response, i.e. tailored on the user preferences and expectations, represents a key factor for successful online services. The proposed model uses the notion of fuzzy similarities in order to match the user observed knowledge with appropriate target profiles. We characterize fuzzy similarity in the theoretical framework of Lukasiewicz structures which guaranties the formal correctness of the approach. The presented model for user profiling with minimal knowledge has many applications, from generation of banners for online advertising to dynamical response pages for public services.

1 Introduction

The construction of user models is a basic activity in order to give personalized services based on user preferences and goals. A user model is relatively easy to build when the system as some mechanism (like login procedure) to identify users. Systems based on authorization have the opportunity to collect systematically information about users either by using questionnaires or by tracing his choices (like in click-stream analysis). Other methods, which relies upon user anonymity, are based on web server log file analysis [5] [3], collaborative filtering and multidimensional ranking [1]. Unfortunately there are many internet interactive services which don't offer the possibility of solid long term observation of users behaviour, while require an immediate user classification/personalised response.

1.1 User Profiling with Minimal Knowledge

In minimal knowledge hypothesis it is assumed to have only the data available from current HTTP request. From HTTP request it is possible a limited number of information which we assume are only the date/time of connection, one or more keywords in some language (directly issued by the user in a form or derived from the content tag of the current web-page), and location information derived from the IP number. Profile information are assumed to be expressed in a more flexible way, i.e. fuzzy constraints on time, keywords of interest, and personal social and economical parameters (i.e. religion, income, age etc.).

M. Ali and F. Esposito (Eds.): IEA/AIE 2005, LNAI 3533, pp. 709 – 711, 2005.

1.2 Fuzzy Similarity in Lukasiewicz Structure

Fuzzy similarity [6] can be used to evaluate and compare user profiles since it is a many-valued generalization of the classical notion of equivalence relation. Lukasiewicz structure [4] is the only multi-valued structure in which the mean of many fuzzy similarities is still a fuzzy similarity[2]. The various properties of user profiles to compare can be expressed through membership functions f_i valued between [0,1]. The idea is to define maximal fuzzy similarity by computing the membership functions $f_i(x_1)$, $f_i(x_2)$ for comparing the similarity of objects x_1 and x_2 on each property i and then combining the similarity values for all properties.

Definition. The *maximal fuzzy similarity* can be defined as

$$S < x_1, x_2 >= \frac{1}{n} \sum_{i=1}^{n} (f_i(x_1) \leftrightarrow f_i(x_2)).$$

where $x_1, x_2 \in X$, f_i are membership functions $i \in \{1,2,\ldots,n\}$ and $\leftrightarrow$ is the double residuum.

2 Algorithm for User Profile Matching

The goal of the algorithm is to determine the most appropriate profile for a given user. It is made by evaluating similarities between the observed data and a set of possible profiles. The data types which describe user profiles are the same data involved in the minimal knowledge hypothesis: keywords, connection date/time, IP/user location. The similarities values previously computed are finally composed to obtain the final result; [4]. The main elementary elements for profile comparison are:

- *user key-words similarity*: ontologies are used to classify and compare keywords according to their semantics. The similarity between two keyword k_1 and k_2 is based on the similarity of the corresponding classification paths v_1 and v_2 in the ontology tree, defined by

$$S_p(v_i, v_j) = \frac{1}{2L}(2L - d(v_i, v_j))$$

where L is the maximal depth of the ontology tree and $d(v_1, v_2)$ is a pseudo-metric which can be seen as a "dissimilarity" between v_1 and v_2.

- *evaluating connection time similarity*: a comparison is made between the crisp value of *observed* user date/time of connection (derived from HTTP request) and a fuzzy value taken from the profile, i.e. a set of trapezoidal time intervals; maximal fuzzy date/time similarity t_r is computed
- *evaluating user location/countries:* The information about country or user location is obtained from the IP address. The used technique, called amplification, consist in evaluating the similarity between two countries by comparing the additional information and properties (like annual income, population, religion etc.) which are associated to each country. Let ul_i ; the user location similarity degree for ùthe location/country for the profile *i*.

2.2 Combining Similarities

Once having n similarity values independently evaluated for different types of data finally it become possible to combine them in order to find the target profile which best matches the current user.

Let m_{ij} be the value of similarity for observed data and a profile *Pi*, and let w_{ij} are weights defined for every profile then a decision function can be defined:

$$up_i = \frac{1}{\sum_{j=1}^{n} w'_{ij}} (\sum_{j=1}^{n} w'_{ij} m_{ij})$$

Again w_{ij} are weights defined for every profile, they allow to express the relevance of the type of observed data for determining a certain profile. Finally, the profile most similar to the user observed data can be determined by considering maximum value (up) of upi. The profile such determined is then used to give a personalised response to the user issuing the request.

References

1. Burke, R.: Semantic ratings and heuristic similarity for collaborative filtering, AAAI Workshop on Knowledge-Based Electronic Markets, AAAI, (2000).
2. Luukka, P., Saastamoinen, K., Kononen, V., Turunen, E.: A classifier based on maximal fuzzy similarity in generalised Lukasiewicz structure,FUZZ-IEEE 2001, Melbourne, Australia (2001).
3. Martin-Bautista, M.J., Kraft, D.H., Vila, M.A., Chen, J., Cruz,, J. User profiles and fuzzy logic for web retrieval issues, Soft Computing, Vol. 6, No. 5, (2002).
4. Milani, A., Morici, C., Niewiadomski, R., Fuzzy Matching of User Profiles for a Banner Engine, Lecture Notes In Computer Science, LNCS 3045 (2004) 433-442
5. Spiliopoulou, M., Mobasher, B., Berent, B., Nakagawa, M.: A Framework for the Evaluation of Session Reconstruction Heuristics in Web Usage Analysis, INFORMS Journal on Computings 15 (2002).
6. Turunen, E.: Mathematics behind Fuzzy Logic, Advances in Soft Computing, Physica-Verlag, Heidelberg, (1999).

Formal Goal Generation for Intelligent Control Systems

Richard Dapoigny, Patrick Barlatier, Laurent Foulloy, and Eric Benoit

Université de Savoie, ESIA Laboratoire d'Informatique,
Sytèmes, Traitement de l'Information et de la Connaissance B.P. 806,
F-74016 ANNECY Cedex, France
Phone: +33 450 096529 Fax: +33 450 096559
listic@esia.univ-savoie.fr

Abstract. In the engineering context of control or measurement systems, there is a growing need to incorporate more and more intelligence towards sensing/actuating components. These components achieve some global service related with an intended goal through a set of elementary services intended to achieve atomic goals. There are many possible choices and non-trivial relations between services. As a consequence, both novices and specialists need assistance to prune the search space of possible services and their relations. To provide a sound knowledge representation for functional reasoning, we propose a method eliciting a goal hierarchy in Intelligent Control Systems. To refine the concept of goal with sub-concepts, we investigate a formalization which relies on a multilevel structure. The method is centered both on a mereological approach to express both physical environment and goal concepts, and on Formal Concept Analysis (FCA) to model concept aggregation/decomposition. The interplay between mereology and FCA is discussed.

1 Introduction

Goal elicitation is crucial in AI areas such as planning where planners are concerned with the problem of choosing a set of actions to achieve a given goal. Unfortunately, one of the problems faced in extending existing frameworks is the weak expressiveness of the representation of goals, actions and the external world. In this paper, the core objective is to propose a sound knowledge representation of goals with sufficient conceptual information in the context of engineering systems allowing for further reasoning. This knowledge representation is built with minimum interaction with the user. The foundations of the system modelling uses a structural and a functional representation and relies both on a mereo-topological formalism and on a set-based tool, i.e., Formal Concept Analysis (FCA) which is able to formalize the context. The mereological framework is crucial to clarify the users'intents about the potential inclusion of a given goal component in an inventory of the domain. The context of engineering system incorporates a network of Intelligent Control Systems (ICS) which are either sensing their physical environment or acting upon it and which

M. Ali and F. Esposito (Eds.): IEA/AIE 2005, LNAI 3533, pp. 712–721, 2005.

are able to exchange information with each other in order to achieve a global task. In each ICS several functioning *modes* (or micro-world) are designed, provided that at a given time, the ICS belongs to a single functioning *mode*. Each *mode* encapsulates a finite number of functionalities, known as *services*, that are teleologically related with the concepts of goal and action. In order to capture the various objectives that the engineering system should achieve, goals must represent different abstraction levels, and are formalized within a mereology.
In a second section, we discuss the selection of the relevant concepts involved in ICS and introduce the real-world application which will serve as a support for a clear understanding of the knowledge representation. The third section is dedicated to the goal representation where the concepts of universal and particular goals are detailed. The fourth section explains how the particular goals are extracted from the multi-context lattice while the fifth section describes the conceptual goal-subgoal hierarchy and the automaton which generates a sound goal mereology. Related work are discussed in the sixth section.

2 The Target Application

The real-world example concerns an open-channel hydraulic system which is controlled with (at least) two ICS as shown in figure 1. The control nodes are connected with a fieldbus (CAN network). Each active ICS referred as $\#n$, in the open-channel irrigation channel is located near a water gate and performs two pressure measurements from a Pitot tube (resp. in $SFArea_n$ and $DFArea_n$).

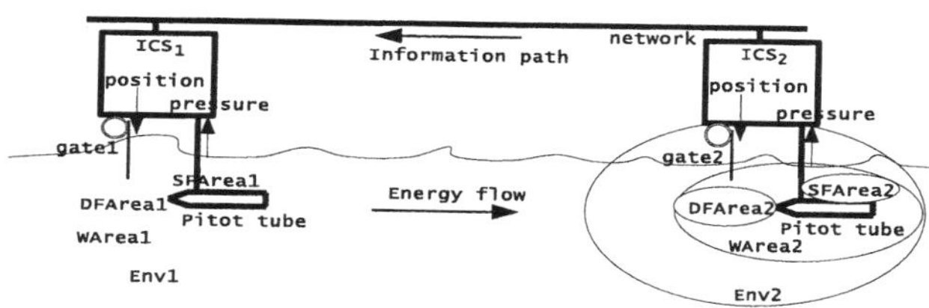

Fig. 1. The hydraulic control system with two Intelligent control nodes

In addition, it is able to react accordingly and to modify the gate position with the help of a brushless motor. Pairs of goal-program functions are the basic elements on which knowledge representation is built. While the basic functions are extracted from libraries, the goal/subgoal representation requires a particular attention. To each subgoal, one or several dedicated software functions can be either extracted from libraries or defined by the user. Goals and modes are user-defined. All functions handle variables whose semantic contents is extracted from the structural mereology (see). The selection process relates functions, while their goal/subgoal is semi-automatized, the user having the ability to force a given relation.

3 Theoretical Foundations

3.1 Mereology

As the goals appear to be parts of a composite structure, it is worth describing them by means of a part-whole theory (i.e., a mereology). A given concept is said to be a part of another iff all the atomic concepts of the first are also atomic concepts for the second. Therefore, the concept of goal seems to be a promising candidate to the design of a part-whole theory. Broadly speaking, the Ground Mereology (GM) supplies a binary predicate $P(Part - of)$ and corresponding partial order axioms, i.e., reflexivity, antisymmetry and transitivity to be regarded as the common basis for part-whole theories. The mereology of goals will only address the part-of primitive because identity of goals can occur if their associate structures have identical items. Some authors mention that multiple interpretations of the part-whole relation are possible and introduce different types of meronymic relations [7][6]. In the framework of ICS, a goal individual g is a teleological part of an individual G iff it is required to achieve the upper goal.

3.2 Formal Contexts and Formal Concepts

In FCA, each concept is expressed as a unit of thought comprising two parts, its extension and its intension [10]. The extension of a domain is composed by all objects to which the concept applies, whereas the intension denotes all properties (or attributes) defined for all those objects to which the concept applies. In other words, all objects in the extension share common properties which characterize that concept. FCA produces a conceptual hierarchy of the domain by exploring all possible formal concepts for which relationships between properties and objects hold. The resulting concept lattice, also known as Galois Lattice, can be considered as a semantic net providing both a conceptual hierarchy of objects and a representation of possible implications between properties.
A formal context C is described by the triple $C = (O, A, I)$, where O is a nonempty finite set of objects, A is a nonempty finite set of attributes and $I \subseteq O \times A$ is a binary relation which holds between objects and attributes. A formal concept (X, Y) is a pair which belongs to the formal context C if $X \subseteq O$, $Y \subseteq A$, $X = Y^I$ and $Y = X^I$. X and Y are respectively called the extent and the intent of the formal concept (X, Y). The ordered set $(\mathcal{B}(C), \leqslant)$ is a complete lattice [11] also called the concept (or Galois) lattice of the formal context (C).

Definition 1. *Given R, a nonempty set of physical roles, A, a nonempty set of potential actions verbs, and Φ, a nonempty set of mereological individuals, the physical entities,* [1] *we introduce two relations $I \subseteq \Phi \times R$ and $J \subseteq R \times A$ which are related with the respective contexts of semantic contents of ICS variables and universal goals.*

$$C_v = (\Phi, R, I), \quad C_g = (R, A, J) \tag{1}$$

[1] Which compose the energy stuff concerning the physical process.

Elementary goals can be joined to form more complex goals within conceptual hierarchies. For example, universal goal concepts can be described as follows:
$(\{pressure\}, \{to\_acquire\})$
$(\{level, speed\}, \{to\_compute, to\_compare, to\_send\})$

Definition 2. *Given two binary relations $I \subseteq \Phi \times R$ and $J \subseteq R \times A$, the compound relation $I \circ J \subseteq \Phi \times A$ is the binary relation such that for all $\varphi \in \Phi$ and for all $a \in A$, φ is related to a iff there is an element $r \in R$ such that $\varphi I r$ and $r J a$.*

Therefore, from the above definitions one can see that a binary relation exists between an action and a physical entity where the physical role is left implicit. The major benefit of that assertion holds in the fact that the formal context related to $I \circ J$ allows to extract formal concepts where we can easily derive the particular goals. Conceptually speaking, the particular goal extends the universal goal definition with an extensional part (i.e., the physical entity). These results suggest to generate particular goals from variable and universal goals contexts. In order to develop a goal formalization, a multi-context previously is introduced [12]. We focus on the concatenation of contexts C_v and C_g where the attribute set of C_v plays the role of the object set in C_g.

Definition 3. *Let a formal context $C_v = (\Phi, R, I)$ with $I \subseteq \Phi \times R$, and a second context $C_g = (R, A, J)$ with $J \subseteq R \times A$, the concatenation of contexts is defined as follows:*

$$C_v \odot C_g = (\Phi \dot{\cup} R, R \dot{\cup} A, I \cup J \cup (I \circ J) \cup (I * J)) \tag{2}$$

where $\dot{\cup}$ denotes the ordered union and $I * J = \bigcup_{r \in R} r^{JJ} \times r^{II}$.

	R	A
Φ	I	$I \circ J$
R	$I * J$	J

The concept lattice $\mathcal{B}(\Phi, A, I \circ J)$ related to the sub-context $(\Phi, A, I \odot J \cap \Phi \times A)$ is a complete lattice.

3.3 Knowledge Representation

To describe the physical behavior of physical entities, we must express the way these entities interact. The physical interactions are the result of energetic physical processes that occur in physical entities. Whatever two entities are able to exchange energy, they are said to be connected. Therefore, the mereology is extended with a topology where connections highlight the energy paths between physical entities. This approach extracts in a local database, energy paths stretching between computing nodes in the physical environment.

In ICS, the functional knowledge, through its teleological part, is represented by the concept of goal (goal), while the dynamic part is related to the concept of action [8]. We introduce the notion of universal goal relating an action verb and a physical role. By adding both a domain-dependent extensional item (i.e., the physical entity) to the universal goal and domain-based rules, we define the particular goals. In order to allow reuse and hierarchical conceptual clustering of goals, a goal mereology is derived. This mereology is elicited during a design step from the interaction with the user. For this purpose, an ICS conceptual database is built in two steps. First, a concept lattice is built with structural and functional information. A pruning algorithm using additional rules extracts atomic goal concepts from the lattice. Then these atomic goals are added with user-defined compound goals, and become intents of a second context where extents are composed of the variables semantic contents. The resulting lattice generates finally the functional mereology of the ICS.

4 The Goal Concept

4.1 Goal Representation

The goal modelling requires first to describe goal representation (i.e., data structures), and secondly to define how these concepts are related. In the context of engineering systems, any functional concept will be described by a (sub-)goal definition[2] which is related to the intensional aspect of function [1] and some possible actions (at least one) in order to fulfill the intended (sub-)goal [3][4]. The goal model defines the terms that correspond to actions expressing the intention (e.g., `to_generate`, `to_convert`, `to_open`, etc.) with the terms that are objects of the actions. Representation of intended goals as "*to do X*" has been used by several researchers such as [5] and we have extended that textual definition by relating actions and objects of these actions in a FCA framework. From the concept lattice $\mathcal{B}(\Phi, A, I \circ J)$ of the hydraulic control system, three concepts are highlighted each of them having an intent and an extent.

(1) **Intent** $\{Position, to\_move\}$
 Extent $\{Gate1, Position\}$
(2) **Intent** $\{Pressure, to\_acquire\}$
 Extent $\{Pressure, SFArea1, DFArea1\}$
(3) **Intent** $\{speed, level, to\_compare, to\_compute, to\_send\}$
 Extent $\{speed, level, WaterArea1, ExtEntity\}$

A particular goal is defined as follows:

Definition 4. *A particular goal concept g_i is a triple such as :*

$$g_i = (\{a_i\}, \{r_{ij}\}, \{\varphi_{ik}\}) \tag{3}$$

where $\{a_i\}$ is a singleton which denotes an elementary action, $\{r_{ij}\}$, a set of physical roles (at least one) and $\{\varphi_{ik}\}$, a set of physical entities (at least one) concerned by the action a_i.

[2] Assuming the teleological interpretation of functions.

In order to extract the basic goals by conceptual unfolding of concepts, some additional rules are required.

1. If the intent and the extent of the lattice concept share a common role, the role is added to the goal.
2. Each action of the intent is related to the role and distributed on each physical entity of the extent according to the universal goal arity (for instance, *to_compute*, *to_send*, *to_acquire* require one object while *to_compare* requires at least two objects).
3. For each action having a single physical entity, the presence of this entity is checked in the structural mereology. For all entities that are not present in the local mereology, the potential goal is removed. For actions working with several physical entities, all unknown entities generate a new goal $(\{to\_receive\}, \{role\}, \{ExtEntity\})$.

This last rule means that external data are required in order to complete the action at run-time and this, with a known conceptual content. Goals having identical actions and physical entity can merge their physical roles within a single compound goal. Applying these rules to the previous concepts leads to the following list of particular goals :

$g_1 = (\{to\_acquire\}, \{pressure\}, \{SFArea1\})$
$g_2 = (\{to\_acquire\}, \{pressure\}, \{DFArea1\})$
$g_3 = (\{to\_compute\}, \{speed, level\}, \{WaterArea1\})$
$g_4 = (\{to\_send\}, \{speed, level\}, \{WaterArea1\})$
$g_5 = (\{to\_compare\}, \{speed\}, \{WaterArea1, ExtEntity\})$
$g_6 = (\{to\_move\}, \{position\}, \{Gate1\})$
$g_7 = (\{to\_receive\}, \{speed\}, \{ExtEntity\})$

4.2 The Conceptual Goal Hierarchy

A close connection between FCA and mereology can be established by focusing on their basic topics, i.e., concept decomposition-aggregation and concept relationships. FCA helps to build ontologies as a learning technique [9] and we extend this work by specifying the ontology with mereology. The goal mereology is derived from the subsumption hierarchy of conceptual scales where the many-level architecture of conceptual scales [14] is extended taking into consideration the mereological nature of the extents. Higher level scales which relates scales on a higher level of abstraction provide information about hierarchy. Considering the particular atomic goals, the particular compound goals corresponding to the user intents, the ontological nature of the extents (i.e., the physical entities) and some basic assumptions, one can automatically produce the relevant instrument functional context. This context is required to produce the final concept lattice from which the functional mereology will be extracted.

As suggested in [14], the set of goals is extended with hierarchical conceptual scales such as the intent includes atomic and compound goals (i.e., services) and the ICS scale (highest level). Higher level scales define a partially ordered set. The formal context is filled in a two-stages process. In the first stage, we derive some rules from the structural mereology $\mathcal{S}$ which concerns the physical entities. To overcome difficulties about the conceptual equivalence between sets and mereological individuals, we make the assumption that a mereological structure can be reproduced within sets provided we exclude the empty set. Therefore, a set can be seen as an abstract individual which represents a class[3]. The part-of relation can be described as a conceptual scale which holds between the objects (i.e., extensions) related to the mereological individuals. Hierarchical conceptual scales are filled according to information input by the user concerning goals definitions (see table 1). Then the conceptual hierarchy highlights required inter-relations between concepts. For the hydraulic system, the user enters for example, the following goal specifications:

$G_1 = (\{to\_measure\}, \{speed, level\}, \{WaterArea1\})$
$G_2 = (\{to\_control\}, \{speed\}, \{WaterArea1\})$
$G_3 = (\{to\_manuallyMove\}, \{position\}, \{Gate1\})$
$extent(G_1) = \{g_1, g_2, g_3, g_4\}$
$extent(G_2) = \{g_1, g_2, g_3, g_5, g_6\}$
$extent(G_3) = \{g_6\}$

Finally, one can define a root (or ICS) level, which expresses the functional knowledge about the instruments'goals and goals that are achievable with the help of local variables. This level encapsulates all locally-achievable goals.
$ICS_1 = (\{to\_control\}, \{speed, level\}, \{Env1\})$
$extent(ICS_1) = \{all\ goals\ that\ deal\ with\ local\ variables\}$

Table 1. Instrument functional context for the open-channel irrigation canal

$\mathcal{F}$	g_1	g_2	g_3	g_4	g_5	g_6	g_7	G_1	G_2	G_3	ICS_1
(pressure, SFArea1)	x							x	x		x
(pressure, DFArea1)		x						x	x		x
(speed, WaterArea1)			x	x	x			x	x		x
(level, WaterArea1)			x	x				x	x		x
(position, Gate1)						x			x	x	x
(speed, ExtEntity)					x		x		x		

Finally, the concept lattice is transformed in a partial order with some elementary techniques:

step 1: to improve the readibility of the lattice, each object and each attribute are putting down only once at each node. The extent of a node can be found by following all line paths going downwards from the node [15]. in the lattice.
step 2: emphasize differences between wholes and parts through identical variables use i.e., $\{G_3, g_6\}$ will result in $P(g_6, G_3)$, where $P(x, y)$ denotes the Part-of relation.

[3] A class is simply one or more individuals.

step 3: extract common parts between set items, i.e., overlap relations.
step 4: create for each node a concept labelled with the intension of the lattice node [16]
step 5: remove the bottom element

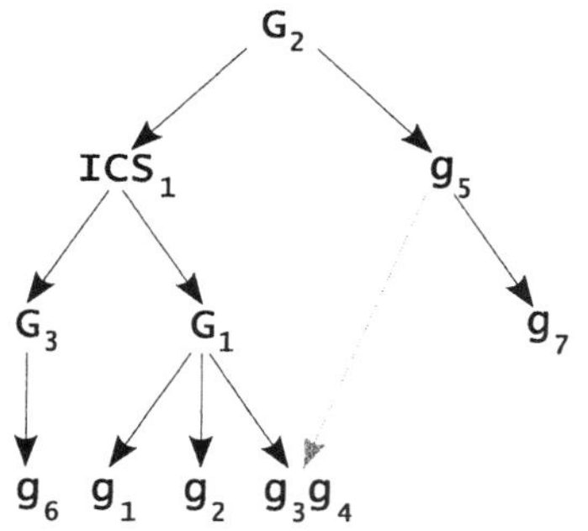

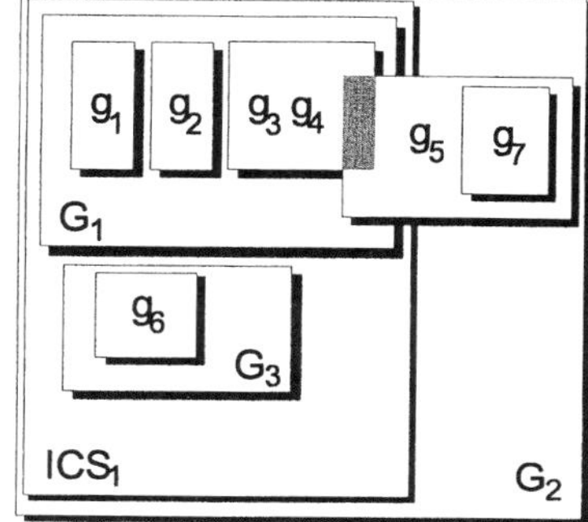

Step 1 : the pruned lattice   Step 2 : the goal mereology

Fig. 2. The goal mereology

In the reduced hierarchy, goals are mereologically ordered according to their physical variable extent[4] and generate the Var-mereology of the instrument. In this mereology, a first hierarchy of goals reflects the goals'use of variables until the node ICS. We notice that the goal G_2 subsumes the instrument node, which corresponds to the fact that G_2 requires external information whereas the instrument only deals with its local structural mereology. This entails that external information will be necessary at run-time. The common node g_3, g_4, g_5 points out that these goals share a common variable concept, i.e., $(\{speed\}, \{WaterArea1\})$. As a consequence, goals g_3, g_4, g_5 overlap according to the Var-mereology. The reduced lattice and the resulting mereology are sketched in figure 2 with overlap in green.

5 Related Work

Surprisingly, there is a lack of literature about goal modelling in software modelling and object-oriented analysis, excepted in requirements engineering. Modelling goals for engineering processes is a complex task. In [17] an acquisition assistant is proposed which operationalizes the goals with constraints. The structure of goals does not allow further reasoning and no automated support is provided. More recently, in [18] goals are represented by verbs with parameters,

[4] Other classifications are possible, using different object types.

each of them playing a special role such as target entities affected by the goal, resources needed for the goal achievement, ... Some tools are based on temporal logic and offer refinement techniques to link goals [19]. Based on the KAOS method, [20] used conditional assignments based on the application's variables in goal-oriented process control systems design with the B method. In this method no reasoning is performed at the system level due to the lack of semantic content for variables. For more general frameworks, [21] describes a logic of goals based on their relationship types, but goals are only represented with a label, and the reasoning is elicited from their relations only. In this article, we have emphasized the conceptual representation of goals which serves as a basis for further mereologic elaboration.

6 Conclusion

ICS are obviously intended for physicians or engineers. The use of simple techniques for eliciting knowledge from an expert tool without the mediation of knowledge or software engineers decreases drastically the cost and efficiency of such instruments. Alternatively, there is a growing need for a structured knowledge base to allow both reuse and distributed reasoning at run-time. The initial goal hierarchy supplied by the user provides through FCA, supplementary information about the data on a more general level. In particular, it allows to highlight global cross-scales relationships which are not easily recognized otherwise. Moreover, the bottom-up approach classifies concept-subconcept relations with conceptual scales and allows to obtain automatically the resulting mereology of goal-subgoals that holds for a given ICS. With this representation one may reason about goals at multiple levels of granularity, provided that the consistency between goal levels is achieved by mereological axioms. The major limitation holds in the restricted area of physical processes, however it seems possible to extend the physical role with any role and to replace the energy flow with an information flow. Future efforts include a formal modelling dedicated to run-time planning.

References

1. Lind M.: Modeling Goals and Functions of Complex Industrial Plant. Journal of Applied Artificial Intelligence **8** (1994) 259–283
2. Fikes R.: Ontologies: What are they, and where's the research?. Principles of Knowledge Representation and Reasoning. (1996) 652–654
3. Hertzberg J., Thiebaux S.: Turning an Action Formalism into a Planner: a case Study. Journal of Logic and Computation. **4** (1994) 617-654
4. Lifschitz V.: A Theory of Actions. Procs. of the 10th International Joint Conference on Artificial Intelligence (1993) 432-437
5. Umeda Y., et al.: Supporting conceptual design based on the function-behavior-state modeler. Artificial Intell. for Engineering Design, Analysis and Manufacturing. **10**(4) (1996) 275–288

6. Gerstl P., Pribbenow S.: A conceptual theory of part-whole relations and its applications. Data and Knowledge Engineering **20** (3) (1996) 305–322
7. Winston M.E., Chaffin R., Herrmann D.: A taxonomy of part-whole relations. Cognitive Science. **11** (1987) 417–444
8. Dapoigny R., Benoit E., Foulloy L.: Functional Ontology for Intelligent Instruments. Foundations of Intelligent Systems. LNAI 2871 (2003) 88–92
9. Cimiano P., Hotho A., Stumme G., Tane J.: Conceptual knowledge processing with formal concept analysis and ontologies. LNAI 2961. (2004) 189–207
10. Wille R.: Restructuring lattice theory: an approach based on hierarchies of concepts. Ordered sets. Reidel, Dordrecht-Boston. (1982) 445–470
11. Birkhoff G.: Lattice theory. (First edition) Amer. Math. Soc. Coll. Publ. 25. Providence. R.I. (1940)
12. Wille R.: Conceptual structures of multicontexts. Conceptual structures: knowledge representation as interlingua (Springer) LNAI 1115 (1996) 23–39
13. Ganter B., Wille R.: Applied lattice theory: formal concept analysis. Institut fr Algebra, TU Dresden, Germany. (1997)
14. Stumme G.: Hierarchies of conceptual scales. Procs. of the Work. on Knowledge Acquisition, Modeling and Managenent (KAW'99). **2** (1999) 78–95
15. Ganter B., Wille R.: Formal concept analysis - mathematical foundations (1999) Springer.
16. Cimiano P., Staab S., Tane J.: Deriving concept hierarchies from text by smooth formal concept analysis. Procs. of the GI Workshop LLWA (2003)
17. Dardenne A., van Lamsweerde A., Fickas S.: Goal-directed requirements acquisition. Science of computer programming. **20** (1993) 3–50
18. Rolland C., Souveyet C., Ben Achour C.: Guiding goal modelling using scenarios. IEEE Trans. on software eng. (1998) 1055–1071
19. Letier E.: Reasoning about agents in goal-oriented requirements engineering. Doct. dissertation. University of Louvain. (2001)
20. El-Maddah I., Maibaum T.: Goal-oriented requirements analysis for process control systems design. Procs. of MEMOCODE'03 (2003)
21. Giorgini P., Nicchiarelli E., Mylopoulos J., Sebastiani R.: Reasoning with goal models. Procs. of the int. conf. on conceptual modeling (2002)

MoA: OWL Ontology Merging and Alignment Tool for the Semantic Web

Jaehong Kim[1], Minsu Jang[1], Young-Guk Ha[1], Joo-Chan Sohn[1], and Sang Jo Lee[2]

[1] Intelligent Robot Research Division, Electronics and Telecommunications Research Institute, 161 Gajeong-dong, Yuseong-gu, Daejeon, 305-350, Korea
{jhkim504, minsu, ygha, jcsohn}@etri.re.kr
[2] Department of Computer Engineering, Kyungpook National University, 1370 Sankyuk-dong, Buk-gu, Daegu, 702-701, Korea
sjlee@knu.ac.kr

Abstract. Ontology merging and alignment is one of the effective methods for ontology sharing and reuse on the Semantic Web. A number of ontology merging and alignment tools have been developed, many of those tools depend mainly on concept (dis)similarity measure derived from linguistic cues. We present in this paper a linguistic information based approach to ontology merging and alignment. Our approach is based on two observations: majority of concept names used in ontology are composed of multiple-word combinations, and ontologies designed independently are, in most cases, organized in very different hierarchical structure even though they describe overlapping domains. These observations led us to a merging and alignment algorithm that utilizes both the local and global meaning of a concept. We devised our proposed algorithm in MoA, an OWL DL ontology merging and alignment tool. We tested MoA on 3 ontology pairs, and human experts followed 93% of the MoA's suggestions.

1 Introduction

The Web now penetrates most areas of our lives, and its success is based on its simplicity. Unfortunately, this simplicity could hamper further Web development. Computers are only used as devices that post and render information. So, the main burden not only of accessing and processing information but also of extracting and interpreting it is on the human user. Tim Berners-Lee first envisioned a Semantic Web that provides automated information access based on machine-processable semantics of data and heuristics that uses these metadata. The explicit representation of the semantics of data, accompanied with domain theories (that is, ontologies), will enable a Web that provides a qualitatively new level of services [1].

A key technology for the Semantic Web is ontologies, and these are widely used as a means for conceptually structuring domains of interest. With the growing usage of ontologies, the problem of overlapping knowledge in a common domain occurs more often and become critical. And also, even with an excellent environment, manually building ontologies is labor intensive and costly. Ontology merging and alignment

M. Ali and F. Esposito (Eds.): IEA/AIE 2005, LNAI 3533, pp. 722–731, 2005.

(*M&A*) can be the solution for these problems. Several ontology M&A systems & frameworks have been proposed, which we briefly review in section 2.

In this paper, we propose a novel syntactic and semantic matching algorithm. Our algorithm stems from the two general characteristics observed in most ontologies. First, concept names used in ontologies are mostly in multi-word formation: for example, CargoTruck, WhteWine, LegalDocument etc. Second, ontologies, even though they describe the same domain with a similar set of concepts, if different engineers design them, they possess different hierarchical structure.

The proposed algorithm is realized in MoA, an OWL DL ontology M&A tool for the Semantic Web. MoA consists of a library that provides APIs for accessing OWL ontology model, a shell for user interface and the proposed algorithm.

The remainder of the paper is organized as follows. In section 2, we briefly describe our basic approaches and the motivation for MoA. In section 3, we give an overall architecture of an ontology reuse framework as a showcase of MoA applications. Short descriptions on other tools that are employed in the framework are provided as well. The proposed core ontology M&A algorithm is described in detail in section 4. Section 5 provides the evaluation results of our algorithm. Section 6 summarizes the paper and concludes.

2 Basic Approaches and Motivations

This section provides the basic approaches and motivations of MoA. Basic approaches that MoA take are described by analyzing previous tools and are focused on the characteristics of tool itself. Motivations are mainly related to the algorithm that MoA uses to detect (dis)similarities between concepts.

2.1 Basic Approaches

The ontology M&A tools vary with respect to the task that they perform, the inputs on which they operate and the outputs that they produce.

First, the tasks for which M&A tools are designed differ greatly. For example, Chimaera [9] and PROMPT [6] allow users to merge two source ontologies into a new ontology that includes all the concepts from both sources. The output of ONION [10] is a set of articulation rules between two ontologies; these rules define what the (dis)similarities are [3]. The intermediate output of MoA is similar to the output of ONION, and the final output of MoA is a new merged ontology similar to that of Chimaera and PROMPT.

Second, different tools operate on different inputs. Some tools deal only with class hierarchies, while other tools refer not only to classes but also to slots and value restrictions [3]. MoA belongs to the latter category.

Third, since the tasks that the tools support differ greatly, the interaction between a user and a tool is very different from one tool to another. Some tools provide a graphical interface which allows users to compare the source ontologies visually, and accept or reject the results of the tool's analysis, the goal of other tools is to run the algorithms which find correlations between the source ontologies and output the results to the user in a text file or on the terminal, where the users must then use the results outside the tool itself [3]. In MoA, the correlations between the source ontologies are saved to a text file, and this can be viewed and edited in an editor. So, users can accept or reject the result by editing the file.

In brief, MoA takes hybrid approach of previous tools with respect to the tool itself. The detailed architecture of MoA is described in Section 3.

2.2 Motivations

In many ontology M&A tools and methods, linguistic information is usually used to detect (dis)similarities between concepts. Many of them are based on syntactic and semantic heuristics such as concept name matching (e.g., exact, prefix, suffix matching). This does work in most cases, but does not work well in more complex cases. We sorted out two major causes of the complex cases as follows, which are commonly observed in most ontologies.

First, multiple words are used to name a concept in lots of ontologies. Second, two ontologies designed by different engineers can have structural differences in their hierarchy even though they describe the same domain and contain similar concepts.

In the following figure, we can observe examples of multiple-word naming in class names: for example, ResearchAssistant, AdministrativeStaff and AssistantStaff. And we can see the same (or probably similar you may think) concepts are represented differently in their hierarchy (e.g., Administrative in O_1 and AdministrativeStaff in O_2).

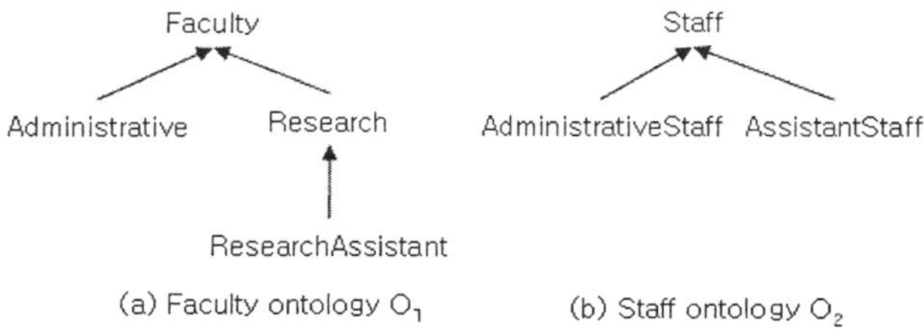

Fig. 1. Example ontologies

By addressing the two cases we just identified, we designed our MoA algorithm. Our algorithm is based on the concept of *local and global meaning*, which we describe in detail in Section 4.

3 Architecture

In this section, we present the architecture of our system. Fig. 2 shows the overall organization of our system. In our system, we assume that the source ontologies are in OWL DL.

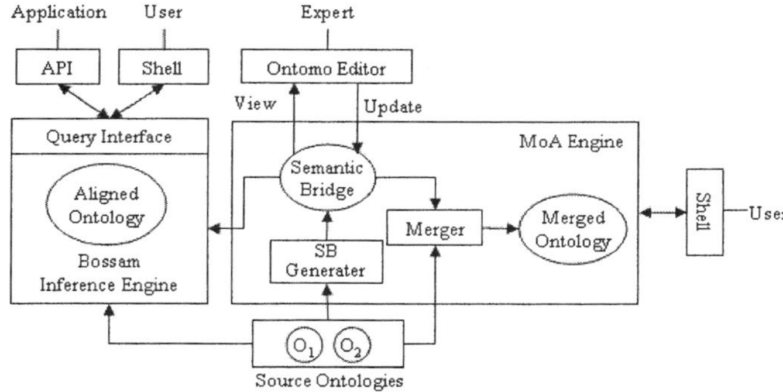

Fig. 2. Architecture of the MoA system. MoA engine, the core module of the architecture, is joined by *Bossam inference engine, Ontomo editor, and Shell.* They provide querying, editing, and user interfaces

Before we get into the details of the system architecture, some terms introduced in Fig. 2 need to be explained. *Source ontologies* are individual ontologies applied for merging or alignment. *Semantic bridge* is composed of the terms extracted from the source ontologies and the relationships between those terms. *Aligned ontology* is achieved by performing reasoning over the source ontologies and the semantic bridge. That is, it is the entailment produced from the semantic bridge and the source ontologies. *Merged ontology* is achieved by applying the actual physical merging process on the source ontologies with the semantic bridge as a hint. An aligned ontology exists as an in-memory data model, while a merged ontology is saved in a physical file. So, the aligned ontology is suitable for providing information retrieval facility on big related ontologies, while the merged ontology is suitable for developing new ontology by reusing existing ontologies.

3.1 MoA Engine

MoA engine is the primary focus of this paper. *SB generator* takes two source ontologies as input and generates a semantic bridge by taking terms from O_1 and maps each of them into a term of O_2 through a semantically meaningful relation. MoA uses two kinds of relations on the mapping: equivalency and subsumption. For labeling equivalency, OWL's equivalency axioms - "owl:equivalentClass", "owl:equivalentProperty" and "owl:sameAs" - are used. And for subsumption, "owl:subClassOf" and "owl:subPropertyOf" are used.

Every OWL equivalency or subsumption axiom appearing in the semantic bridge is interpreted as MoA's suggested equivalency or subsumption. The `SemanticBridge` algorithm presented in the Section 4 generates the *semantic bridge*. The *semantic bridge* is used by *Merger* to generate a *merged ontology.*

3.2 Bossam Inference Engine

Bossam [4] is a forward-chaining production rule engine with some extended knowledge representation elements which makes it easy to be utilized in the semantic web environment. Buchingae, a web-oriented rule language, is used to write rules - logic programs - for Bossam. You can write RDF queries or reasoning rules in Buchingae and run them with Bossam. Bossam provides a command-line user interfaces for users and querying API for applications.

3.3 Ontomo Editor

OntoMo (Ontology Modeler) is a visual ontology modeler that can handle OWL, DAML+OIL and RDFS documents. OntoMo provides graph-based visualization and editing environment, with which one can easily edit graph topology and graph node data. With OntoMo, users can load, edit and save ontology in above mentioned format, and visual editing of axioms and restrictions are possible. And, it has DB import and export functionality. The Semantic Bridge is also an OWL file, so it can be loaded, updated and saved in OntoMo editor. Domain experts use OntoMo to amend and correct problems found in the semantic bridge.

4 Ontology M&A Algorithm

We define basic terminologies, and describe the algorithm in detail and then show a running example of proposed algorithm.

4.1 Basic Definitions

We now define underlying terminologies for formal description of the core M&A algorithm. We begin by our own formal definition of ontology. As can be seen, our definition is not very different from others found in many semantic web literatures, but is presented here to put the cornerstone for the next definitions.

Definition 1. Ontology. An ontology is a 5-tuple $O:=(C,P,I,H^C,H^P)$ consisting of

- Three disjoint sets C, P and I whose elements are called classes, properties, and individuals, respectively.
- A class hierarchy $H^C \subseteq C x C$. $H^C(c_1,c_2)$ means that c_1 is a subclass of c_2.
- A property hierarchy $H^P \subseteq P x P$. $H^P(p_1,p_2)$ means that p_1 is a subproperty of p_2.

Definition 2. Lexicon. A lexicon for the ontology O is a 6-tuple $L:=(L^C,C^P,L^I,F,G,H)$ consisting of

- Three sets L^C, L^P and L^I whose elements are called ***lexical entries*** for classes, properties and individuals, respectively. For OWL ontology, a lexical entry corresponds to the ID of a class, a property or an individual. For example, L^C = {Staff, AdministrativeStaff, AssistantStaff} for the sample ontology O_2 of Section 2.2.

- Three relations $F \subseteq CxL^C$, $G \subseteq PxL^P$ and $H \subseteq IxL^I$ for classes, properties and individuals. Based on *F*, let for $c \in C$, $F(c)=\{l \in L^C | (c,l) \in F\}$. For class c_{Staff} in O_2, $F(c_{Staff})$ = {Staff}. *G* and *H* are defined analogously.

Definition 3. Naming functions. A naming function for an ontology *O* with lexicon *L* is a 5-tuple $N:=(W,T,LN,SI,GN)$ consisting of

- A set *W* whose elements are called ***tokens*** for lexicon. If a token is a registered keyword of *WordNet* [5], then it is called ***w-token***, otherwise ***nw-token***. A set *W* is the union of w-token set(W^W) and nw-token set(W^{NW}). W^W and W^{NW} are disjoint. For class $c_{AdministrativeStaff}$ in O_2, tokens are "Administrative" and "Staff".
- A set *T* whose elements are the set of tokens for lexical entry. A set {Administrative, Staff} is one of the elements of *T*.
- A set *LN* whose elements are function LN^C, LN^P and LN^I. Function LN^C:$C \rightarrow T$ called ***local names*** for class. For $c \in C$, $LN^C(c)=\{t \in T\}$. Function LN^C takes *c* as input and outputs the set of tokens constituting lexical entry $l(=F(c))$. For example, $LN^C(c_{AdministrativeStaff})$ = {Administrative, Staff}, $LN^C(c_{Administrative})$ = {Administrative}. NL^P and NL^I are defined analogously.
- Function $SI: W \rightarrow \{n | n \in N$, *N is a set of integers*$\}$ called ***semantic identifier*** for token. For $w \in W^W$, $SI(w)$ is the set of ***Synset offsets of WordNet*** for token *w*. For $w \in W^{NW}$, $SI(w)$ is the set of hash value for *w*. For example, $SI(Faculty)$={6859293, …}, $SI(Staff)$={…, 6859293, …}.
- A set *GN* whose elements are function GN^C, GN^P and GN^I. Function GN^C:$C \rightarrow T$ called ***global names*** for class. For $c \in C$, $GN^C(c)=\{t \in T\}$. Function GN^C takes $c \in C$ as input and outputs $\cup LN^C(c_i)$ where $\{c_i \in C | H^C(c,c_i) \vee (c_i=c)\}$. For example, $GN^C(c_{AdministrativeStaff})$={Administrative, Staff}, $GN^C(c_{Administrative})$={Administrative, Faculty}. GN^P is defined analogously. For individual, $GN^I(i \in I)=LN^I(i)$.

Definition 4. Meaning functions. A meaning function for an ontology *O* with lexicon *L* and naming function *N* is a 3-tuple $M:=(S,LM,GM)$ consisting of

- A set *S* whose elements are semantic identifier for tokens. A set {…, 6859293, …} is one of the elements of *S*.
- A set *LM* whose elements are function LM^C, LM^P and LM^I. Function LM^C:$C \rightarrow S$ called ***local meaning*** for class. For $c \in C$, $LM^C(c)=\{s \in S\}$. Function LM^C takes *c* as input and outputs the set of semantic identifier for each token of local names of *c*. $LM^C(c):=\{SI(w) | \forall w \in LN^C(c)\}$. For example, $LM^C(c_{Faculty})$ = {{6859293, …}}, $LM^C(c_{Staff})$ = {{…, 6859293, …}}. LM^P and LM^I are defined analogously.
- A set *GM* whose elements are function GM^C, GM^P and GM^I. Function GM^C:$C \rightarrow S$ called ***global meaning*** for class. For $c \in C$, $GM^C(c)=\{s \in S\}$. Function GM^C takes *c* as input and outputs the set of semantic identifier for each token of global names

of c. $GM^C(c):=\{SI(w) | \forall w \in GN^C(c)\}$. For example, $GM^C(c_{Administrative})$ = {{…}, {6859293, …}}, $GM^C(c_{AdministrativeStaff})$ = {{…}, {…, 6859293, …}}. GM^P is defined analogously. For individual, $GM^I(i \in I)=LM^I(i)$.

Definition 5. Semantic bridge. A semantic bridge for two ontologies $O_1:=(C_1,P_1,I_1,H^C{}_1,H^P{}_1)$ and $O_2:=(C_2,P_2,I_2H^C{}_2,H^P{}_2)$ with lexicon L, naming function N and meaning function M is a 5-tuple $B:=(SIE,ME,MS,EB,SB)$, consisting of

- Relation $SIE \subseteq SI \times SI$ for semantic identifier. $SIE(si_1, si_2)$ means that si_1 is semantically equivalent to si_2. $SIE(si_i, si_j)$ holds when $si_i \cap si_j \neq \{\}$. For example, $SIE(SI(Faculty),SI(Staff))$ holds.
- A set ME whose elements are relation LME and GME. Relation $LME \subseteq LM \times LM$ for local meaning. $LME(lm_1, lm_2)$ means that lm_1 is semantically equivalent to lm_2. $LME(lm_i,lm_j)$ holds when $|lm_i|=|lm_j|$ and for all si_i from lm_i, there exists exactly one si_j from lmj where meets $SIE(si_i,si_j)$. Relation $GME \subseteq GM \times GM$ for global meaning is defined analogously. For example, $LME(LM^C(c_{Faculty}),LM^C(c_{Staff}))$ and $GME(GM^C(c_{Administrative}),GM^C(c_{AdministrativeStaff}))$ holds.
- A set MS whose elements are relation LMS and GMS. Relation $LMS \subseteq LM \times LM$ for local meaning. $LMS(lm_1, lm_2)$ means that lm_1 is semantically subconcept of lm_2. $LMS(lm_i,lm_j)$ holds when $lm_i \supset lm_j$ after removing all si_i, si_j pairs that holds $SIE(si_i,si_j)$. Relation $GMS \subseteq GM \times GM$ for global meaning is defined analogously. For example, $GMS(GM^C(c_{RearchAssistant}),GM^C(c_{AssistantStaff}))$ holds.
- A set EB whose elements are relation EB^C, EB^P and EB^I. Relation $EB^C \subseteq C_1 \times C_2$ for classes. $EB^C(c_1,c_2)$ means that c_1 is equivalentClass of c_2. $EB^C(c_i,c_j)$ holds when $LME(LM^C(c_i),LM^C(c_j)) \vee GME(GM^C(c_i),GM^C(c_j))$. For example, $EB^C(c_{Faculty}, c_{Staff})$ and $EB^C(c_{Administrative}, c_{AdministrativeStaff})$ holds. $EB^P \subseteq P_1 \times P_2$ and $EB^I \subseteq I_1 \times I_2$ are defined analogously.
- A set SB whose elements are relation SB^C and SB^P. Relation $SB^C \subseteq C \times C(C_1 \times C_2$ or $C_2 \times C_1)$ for classes. $SB^C(c_1,c_2)$ means that c_1 is subClassOf c_2. $SB^C(c_i,c_j)$ holds when $LMS(LM^C(c_i),LM^C(c_j)) \vee GMS(GM^C(c_i),GM^C(c_j))$. For example, $SB^C(c_{ResearchAssistant}, c_{AssistantStaff})$ holds. $SB^P \subseteq P \times P$ for properties is defined analogously.

4.2 Algorithm

With definition 5, we can describe semantic bridge generation algorithm as follows.

Table 1. Semantic bridge generation algorithm and the semantic bridge for O_1 and O_2

<table>
<tr><td>Algorithm</td><td><pre>Ont SemanticBridge(Ont O1, Ont O2)
  Ont sb = new Ont(); // initialize semantic
bridge
  For all concept pairs from O1, O2
    if(EB^c(ci,cj) holds) then
      add owl:equivalentClass(ci,cj) to sb;
    if(EB^p(pi,pj) holds) then
      add owl:equivalentProperty(pi,pj) to
sb;
    if(EB^i(ii,ij) holds) then
      add owl:sameAs(ii,ij) to sb;
    if(SB^c(ci,cj) holds) then
      add owl:subClassOf(ci,cj) to sb;
    if(SB^p(pi,pj) holds) then
      add owl:subProperty(pi,pj) to sb;
  return sb;</pre></td></tr>
<tr><td>Semantic Bridge</td><td><pre>owl:equivalentClass(c_Faculty, c_Staff)
owl:equivalentClass(c_Administrative, c_AdministrativeStaff)
owl:subPropertyOf(c_ResearchAssistant, c_AssistantStaff)</pre></td></tr>
</table>

The following algorithm is a merging algorithm that is implemented in *Merger* to generate a *merged ontology*. The merging algorithm accepts three inputs: two source ontologies (O_1, O_2) and the *semantic bridge ontology* (sb).

Table 2. Ontology merge algorithm and the merged ontology for O_1 and O_2

<table>
<tr><td>Algorithm</td><td><pre>Ont Merge(Ont O1, Ont O2, Ont sb)
  Ont merged = new Ont(O1, O2);//initialize
merged ontology with all concepts from two
source ontologies
  For all semantic bridge instances from sb
   if(owl:equivalentClass(ci,cj)) then
merge(ci,cj);
   if(owl:equivalentProperty(pi,pj))
merge(pi,pj);
   if(owl:sameAs(ii,ij)) then merge(ii,ij);
   if(owl:subClassOf(ci,cj)) then
     add subClassOf(ci,cj) to merged;
   if(owl:subProperty(pi,pj)) then
     add subProperty(pi,pj) to merged;
 return merged;</pre></td></tr>
<tr><td>Merged ontology</td><td>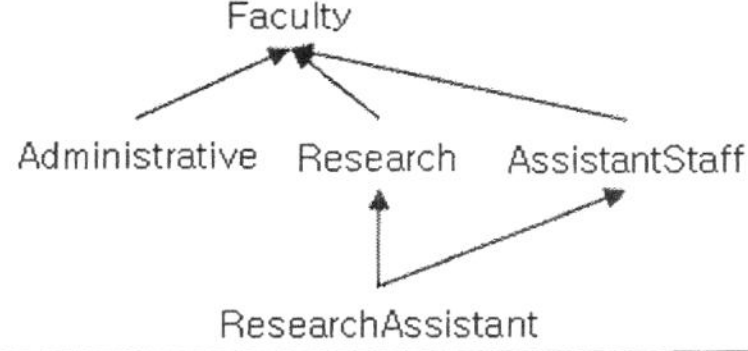
</td></tr>
</table>

5 Evaluation

We performed an experiment with three experts on three ontology pairs, and measured the quality of MoA's suggestions, which are used for semantic bridge generation. The three ontology pairs we applied for evaluation are as follows:

(A) two ontologies for simple air reservation and car rental [6]
(B) two organization structure ontologies [7] [8]
(C) two transportation ontologies, one of which is developed by Teknowledge Corporation and the other by CYC [8]

Domain experts were presented with the semantic bridge and were told to make a decision on the plausibility of each M&A suggestion. Some of the above ontologies are written in DAML, so, for the sake of experimentation, we converted them into OWL using a conversion utility, and then manually corrected some errors found in the converted result.

Table 3 shows some statistics of each ontology pair.

Table 3. Statistics on the ontologies used in the evaluation

	Pair A	Pair B	Pair C	Total
# of Classes	23	170	726	919
# of Properties	42	107	84	233
# of Individuals	0	12	40	52
Total	65	289	850	1204

Table 4 shows the final results of our experimentation. Precision is the ratio of the number of human experts' positive responses on MoA's suggestions to the total number of suggestions. As shown, human experts decided that 93% of MoA's suggestions are correct.

Table 4. Precision of the proposed algorithm

	Pair A	Pair B	Pair C	Average
Precision	93%	96.5%	90.5%	93.3%
Recall	58%	95%	87%[1]	80%

Through the experiment, we could conclude that MoA's M&A algorithm is highly effective in making ontology M&A decisions, though more exhaustive tests need to be done. Besides the correctness of the performance, MoA showed high execution efficiency with its *Merger* component executing most of the merging operations on its own.

[1] This includes only recall for equivalency relation, others(for A and B) include recall for both equivalence and subsumption relation.

6 Conclusion

We presented in this paper a linguistic-information based approach to ontology merging and alignment. Our approach is based on two observations and these observations led us to a merging and alignment algorithm that utilized both the local and global meaning of a concept. We devised our proposed algorithm in MoA, an OWL DL ontology merging and alignment tool. Our results show that MoA was very effective in providing suggestions: Human experts followed 93% of the MoA's suggestions. Even though its core algorithm was originally designed to cope with aforementioned specific cases, it performs well enough in general cases.

References

1. Fensel, D and Musen, M.A. The Semantic Web: A Brain for Humankind. *IEEE Intelligent Systems*, vol. 16, no. 2, pages 24-25, 2001.
2. G. Stumme and A. Mädche. FCA-Merge: Bottom-up merging of ontologies. In *17th International Joint Conference on Artificial Intelligence (IJCAI-2001)*, pages 225-230, Seattle, WA, 2001.
3. Noy, N.F and Musen, M.A. Evaluating Ontology-Mapping Tools: Requirements and Experience. http://www.smi.stanford.edu/pubs/SMI_Reports/SMI-2002-0936.pdf. 2002.
4. Minsu Jang and Joo-Chan Sohn. (2004). Bossam: An Extended Rule Engine for OWL Inferencing. In *Workshop on Rules and Rule Markup Languages for the Semantic Web at the 3rd International Semantic Web Conference (LNCS 3323)*, pages 128-138, Hiroshima, Japan, 2004.
5. Cognitive Science Laboratory at Princeton University. WordNet: a lexical database for the English Language. http://www.congsci.princeton.edu/~wn/.
6. Noy, N.F and Musen, M.A. PROMPT: Algorithm and Tool for Automated Ontology Merging and Alignment. In *17th National Conference on Artificial Intelligence (AAAI-2000)*, Austin, TX, 2000.
7. Noy, N.F and Musen, M.A. Anchor-PROMPT: Using non-local context for semantic matching. In *Workshop on Ontologies and Information Sharing at the 17th International Joint Conference on Artificial Intelligence (IJCAI-2001)*, Seattle, WA, 2001.
8. DAML. DAML ontology library. http://www.daml.org/ontologies/
9. D. L. McGuinness, R. Fikes, J. Rice, and S. Wilder. An environment for merging and testing large ontologies. In *Proceedings of the 7th International Conference on Principles of Knowledge Representation and Reasoning (KR2000)*, San Francisco, CA, 2000.
10. P. Mitra, G. Wiederhold, and M. Kersten. A graph-oriented model for articulation of ontology interdependencies. In *Proceedings Conference on Extending Database Technology 2000 (EDBT 2000)*, Konstanz, Germany, 2000.

Optimizing RDF Storage Removing Redundancies: An Algorithm

Luigi Iannone, Ignazio Palmisano, and Domenico Redavid

Dipartimento di Informatica, Università degli Studi di Bari,
Campus, Via Orabona 4, 70125 Bari, Italy
{iannone, palmisano, d.redavid}@di.uniba.it

Abstract. Semantic Web relies on Resource Description Framework (RDF). Because of the very simple RDF Model and Syntax, the managing of RDF-based knowledge bases requires to take into account both scalability and storage space consumption. In particular, blank nodes semantics came up recently with very interesting theoretical results that can lead to various techniques that optimize, among others, space requirements in storing RDF descriptions. We present a prototypical evolution of our system called RDFCore that exploits these theoretical results and reduces the storage space for RDF descriptions.

1 Motivation

One of the most important steps in the Semantic Web (SW) road map to reality is the creation and integration of ontologies, in order to share structural knowledge for generating or interpreting (semantic) metadata for resources. Ontologies and instances are to be expressed in RDF according to SW specifications. RDF relies on the least power principle; this imposes to have very simple structures as basic components. Indeed, it presents only URIs[1], blank nodes (i.e. nodes without a URI to identify them), literals (typed or not) and statements (often in this paper referred to as triples), thus leading to the obvious drawback that RDF descriptions tend to become very big as the complexity of the knowledge they represent increases. This can hamper the realization of scalable RDF-based knowledge bases; the existence of this issue encourages SW research to investigate toward the most effective solution to store RDF descriptions in order to minimize their size. Though this issue has been investigated somewhat in a thorough way, recently some theoretical results were issued both in [1] by W3C and in [2]. These results also apply to RDFS [2], but in this paper we will refer only to blank node semantics. In practice, these results offer the theoretical instruments to detect redundancies introduced by blank nodes presence within a RDF Description. Once detected, it can be shown that such redundancies can be eliminated by mapping blank nodes into concrete URIs or into different blank nodes,

[1] http://www.w3.org/Addressing/

[2] http://www.w3.org/TR/rdf-schema/

M. Ali and F. Esposito (Eds.): IEA/AIE 2005, LNAI 3533, pp. 732–742, 2005.

by preserving however the entire RDF graph (description) semantics. In other words, there are some cases in which a description meaning can be expressed with a smaller number of triples without losing anything in its formal semantics. Moreover, redundancy detection can be very useful in higher level tasks, such as the building of an ontology. For instance, let us suppose to have devised some classes (say in OWL) and, among them, a class that is a mere cardinality restriction. Let us suppose that somewhere in the ontology it has the name `ns:Test`, as depicted in Figure 1, and that somewhere else the same restriction is created without using a URI to identify it (which is a situation that could arise from the use of (semi-)automatic tools for ontology reconstruction from examples). In this case, we would have defined twice something unnecessarily, so intuitively we introduced redundancy. This kind of repetitions can be detected thanks to the blank node semantics and removed, thus improving readability of the ontology besides shortening its size.

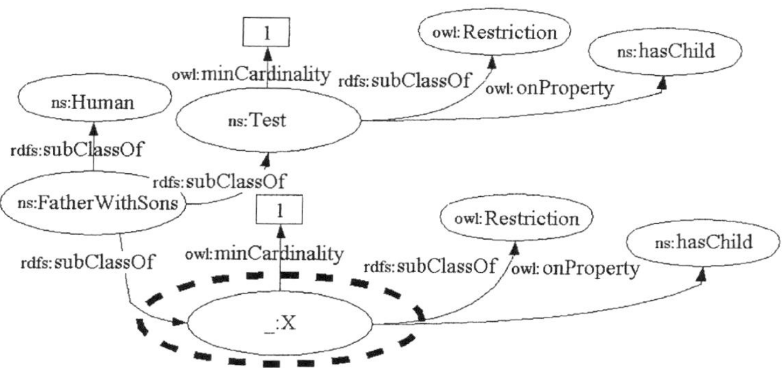

Fig. 1. Example of redundant Restrictions

In order to accomplish this, we will show a *correct* algorithm (in the sense that it produces descriptions equivalent to the starting ones) without claiming for its *completeness* (it will not be shown that it finds all possible equivalent descriptions) called REDD (REDundancy Detection). This algorithm has been integrated in our RDF management system: RDFCore [3] and implemented in the storage level to speed up the execution.

Effective storage of RDF has always been bound to another key issue: querying models. This was because no standard at the time of writing has been recommended by W3C for RDF description querying (see SPARQL [3]), and so different solutions were developed, each one with its own query language and related optimizations. Some components of RDF Data Access Group recently issued a report [4] in which six query engines were examined aiming to compare different

[3] `http://www.w3.org/2001/sw/DataAccess/rq23/`

[4] `http://www.aifb.uni-karlsruhe.de/WBS/pha/rdf-query/rdfquery.pdf`

expressive power of the underlying query languages. Regardless of the query language, it is obvious that querying a smaller model (often) can result in better performances than querying a bigger one; the work we present is therefore potentially useful in any system doing RDF storage. Actually, many different triple stores are available. Among them, we remark the toolkit from HP Semantic Web Lab, called Jena [4, 5]. At the time of writing, Jena supports RDQL as query language.

The remainder of this paper is organized as follows: Section 2 presents some necessary notions on RDF semantics, together with a brief survey on related work on RDF storage. In Section 3, the REDD algorithm is illustrated in detail; Section 4 describes RDFCore, the system in which we implemented the REDD algorithm, while some experimental results are illustrated in Section 5.

2 Basic Notions

We collect here some definitions and theorems; most of them have been taken from [1] and [2]. However, for the sake of brevity, we assume the reader familiar with RDF Concepts and Syntax[5]:

Definition 1 (RDF Graph). *A RDF Graph is a set of RDF statements. Its nodes are URIs or blank nodes representing subjects and objects of the statements. Its edges are labeled by URIs and represent the predicates of the triples. The edges are directed from subject to object, and there can be more than an edge from a subject to an object. Objects can also be literal values.*

Definition 2 (Mapping). *Let N be a set of URIs, blank node names and literals. A mapping is a function $\mu : N \rightarrow N$ that maps a node to another one.*

Notice that it is easier to think of *node-wise* mapping i.e.: mapping changing one node identifier (be it URI or blank node) at a time. Furthermore, when considering mappings useful for reducing graphs, the vocabulary of the URIs and blank nodes to use as candidate for the mapping is restricted to those already present in the original graph.

Definition 3 (Instance). *Let μ be a mapping from a set of blank nodes to some set of literals, blank nodes and URIs and G a graph, then any graph obtained from a graph G by replacing some or all of the blank nodes N in G by $\mu(N)$ is an instance of G.*

Definition 4 (Lean Graphs). *A RDF graph is lean if it has no instance which is a proper subgraph of the graph, i.e. a subset of the original statement set.*

The following results are proved in [1]:

Lemma 1 (Subgraph Lemma). *A graph entails all its subgraphs.*

[5] `http://www.w3.org/TR/rdf-concepts/`

Lemma 2 (Instance Lemma). *A graph is entailed by any of its instances.*

A small example illustrating the just presented lemmas:

```
  _:X    eg:aProp eg:a ENTAILS eg:aNode eg:aProp eg:a
eg:aNode eg:aProp eg:a
```

This means that every non-lean graph is equivalent to its *unique* [2] lean sub-graph. Relying on these notions we will present in Section 3 a correct algorithm that approximates lean sub-graphs.

3 Redundancy Detection

3.1 REDD Algorithm

Our redundancy detection algorithm is based on the notion of lean subgraph of a RDF graph. The lean subgraph is a subset of the RDF graph. It has the property of being the smallest subgraph that is *instance* of the original graph. It can be obtained from the original graph leaving untouched the ground part of the graph (i.e. every node that is not blank and any edge connecting non-blank nodes), and mapping from blank nodes to labels already existing in the graph or to different blank nodes.

Our approach consists of finding a mapping from the original blank nodes to labeled nodes or different blank nodes in the graph. As an example, let us consider a simple graph containing two statements, say:
`_:X ns:aGenericProperty ns:b`
`ns:a ns:aGenericProperty ns:b`
we can determine that the graph is not lean by considering the mapping
$\_ : X \rightarrow ns : a$
The result is a graph with a single statement
`ns:a ns:aGenericProperty ns:b`
which is lean by definition (being a graph with no blank nodes). More formally, called:

- *ORIGIN* the original graph
- *RESULT* the new graph we are going to build
- *X* the anonymous node we want to map

we define:

Definition 5 (SUBMODEL). *The graph extracted from* ORIGIN, *taking every statement in which* X *is the subject.*

Definition 6 (SUPERMODEL). *The set of statements that has* X *as object.*

```
FINDREDUNDANCIES(MODEL M)
 SET BLANKS, SUPERMODELS, SUBMODELS
FOR EACH SUBJECT S IN M BEGIN
 CREATESUPERMODEL(S,M)
 CREATESUBMODEL(S,M)
 IF S IS BLANK THEN ADD(BLANKS,S)
END
FOR EACH OBJECT O IN M BEGIN
 IF O IS RESOURCE THEN BEGIN
  CREATESUPERMODEL(O,M)
  CREATESUBMODEL(O,M)
  IF O IS BLANK THEN ADD(BLANKS,S)
 END
END
FOR EACH BLANK IN BLANKS BEGIN
 FINDCONTAININGSUPERMODELS(BLANK)
 IF BLANK HAS CONTAINING SUPERMODELS THEN
  BEGIN
  FINDCONTAININGSUBMODELS(BLANK)
  IF BLANK HAS CONTAINING SUBMODELS THEN
   REMOVETRIPLESCONTAINING(BLANK)
  END
 END
END


CONTAINSSUB(MODEL A, MODEL B)
FOR EACH S IN B BEGIN
 IF NOT EXISTS S IN A
   WITH S.PREDICATE AND S.OBJECT
    RETURN FALSE
END
RETURN TRUE
```

```
CREATESUBMODEL(SUBJECT S, MODEL M)
 IF SUBMODEL FOR S DOES NOT EXISTS THEN BEGIN
  FOR EACH STATEMENT IN M
   IF S IS SUBJECT OF STATEMENT THEN
    ADD(SUBMODEL, STATEMENT)
 END

CREATESUPERMODEL(OBJECT O, MODEL M)
 IF SUPERMODEL FOR O DOES NOT EXISTS THEN BEGIN
  FOR EACH STATEMENT IN M
   IF O IS OBJECT OF STATEMENT THEN
     ADD(SUPERMODEL, STATEMENT)
 END

FINDCONTAININGSUPERMODELS(NODE BLANK)
 FOR EACH SUPERMODEL IN SUPERMODELS BEGIN
  IF CONTAINSSUP(SUPERMODEL, SUPERMODEL(BLANK))
   THEN ADD(CONTAININGSUPERMODELS, SUPERMODEL)
 END

FINDCONTAININGSUBMODELS(NODE BLANK)
 FOR EACH SUBMODEL IN SUBMODELS BEGIN
  IF CONTAINSSUB(SUBMODEL, SUBMODEL(BLANK))
   THEN ADD(CONTAININGSUBMODELS, SUBMODEL)
END


CONTAINSSUP(MODEL A, MODEL B)
FOR EACH S IN B BEGIN
 IF NOT EXISTS S IN A
   WITH S.PREDICATE AND S.SUBJECT
    RETURN FALSE
END
RETURN TRUE
```

Fig. 2. Pseudo-code description of the REDD algorithm

Definition 7 (Containment). *A* SUBMODEL *(*SUPERMODEL*) A is contained in another* SUBMODEL *(*SUPERMODEL*) B iff for every statement in A there is a statement in B with the same predicate and object (predicate and subject).*

We then can check every possible mapping from X to a URI or to a blank node identifier already occurring in *ORIGIN* to obtain an instance of *ORIGIN* which is both an instance and a proper subgraph (an approximation of the lean subgraph) simply by checking that *SUBMODEL* of X is contained in *SUBMODEL* of the candidate node and *SUPERMODEL* of X is contained in *SUPERMODEL* of the candidate node (with the *Containment* relation we just defined). In fact, it can be easily proved that such a mapping does not produce any statement not contained in *ORIGIN*; *RESULT*, then, is a graph containing the same ground statements and a subset of the statements containing blank nodes. The missing statements are those containing the X node we just mapped. From the logical point of view, the information expressed by the graph is unchanged, since the mapping is equivalent to changing from: $\exists X.p(X,b)$ and $\exists a.p(a,b)$ to $\exists a.p(a,b)$ which are equivalent, not being stated that X is different from a. This mapping can be built for every redundant blank node in *ORIGIN*, but this does not include every redundant blank node in the graph. Indeed, as in Figure 3, it is

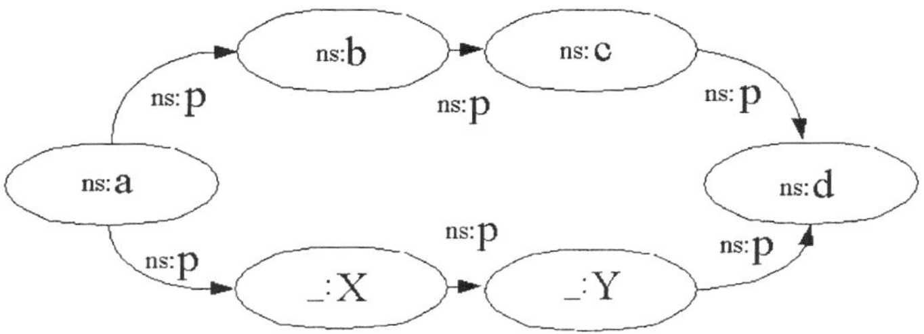

Fig. 3. Chained redundant blank nodes (not spottable with REDD)

possible to have a chain of redundant blank nodes which cannot be spotted with a one-level visit of the RDF graph as in REDD. In fact, in Figure 3, the two blank nodes represent the same structure as the two nodes labeled *b* and *c*, but it is not possible to use our algorithm to find this redundancy. The graph is not lean, but, in order to unravel its lean part (mapping, respectively X to a and Y to b), one should employ multi-level visits to blank nodes supergraphs and subgraphs. This problem can be cast as a search for unifying safe substitutions, thinking of blank nodes as variables and *URIs* as constants and predicates as first-order logic ones. The only constraint consists in imposing that those substitutions must not add triples not appearing in the starting graph. Though not formally evaluated, the complexity of the problem of matching multi-level graphs is intuitively bigger than that of our algorithm though it remains an interesting open issue for our future work.

3.2 REDD Computational Complexity

We will carry out an evaluation of the computational cost of REDD. We will keep as reference the pseudo code version of REDD in Figures 2. Obviously, the actual implementation, working natively on the storage layer (see Section 4), underwent some optimizations (not discussed here for the sake of brevity), hence calculations in this section represent an upper theoretical limit. In section 5, readers can find evaluations of REDD implementation performances.

In order to estimate computational cost we should start defining some metrics on RDF descriptions on which, as shown below, REDD complexity will depend.

Definition 8 (RDF Description metrics). *Be G a RDF description and n a generic node in G then*

- N_T^G *stands for the number of RDF triples within G*
- $\#_B^G$ *stands for the number of blank nodes within G*
- $outDeg(n)$ *stands for the number of outgoing edges from n (i.e. the number of triples in G of which node n is subject)*
- $inDeg(n)$ *stands for the number of ingoing edges into n (i.e. the number of triples in G of which node n is object).*

As shown in Figure 2 complexity of *FINDREDUNDANCIES* C_{FR} is:

$$C_{FR} = 2N_T^G(C_{SUP} + C_{SUB}) + \#_B^G(C_{FINDCSUP} + C_{FINDCSUB}) \qquad (1)$$

The following inequalities hold:

$$\begin{aligned} C_{SUP}, C_{SUB} &\leq N_T^G \\ C_{FINDCSUP} &\leq N_T^G outDeg(n) \\ C_{FINDCSUB} &\leq N_T^G inDeg(n) \end{aligned}$$

where C_{SUP} and C_{SUB} stand for complexity of *CREATESUPERMODEL* and *CREATESUBMODEL*; $C_{FINDCSUP}$ and $C_{FINDCSUB}$ stand for complexity of *FINDCONTAININGSUPERMODELS* and *FINDCONTAININGSUBMODELS*.

Furthermore, from graph theory we have $outDeg(n), inDeg(n) \leq N_T^G$ and $\#_B^G \leq 2N_T^G$, as graphs cannot have more nodes than two times their edges. Hence substituting in equation 1 we have the inequality

$$C_{FR} \leq 2N_T^G(N_T^G + N_T^G) + 2N_T^G((N_T^G)^2 + (N_T^G)^2) \qquad (2)$$

Therefore C_{FR} is polynomial in time and, more specifically $o((N_T^G)^3)$.

4 The RDFCore Component

The RDFCore component, presented in [3], is a component used for RDF descriptions storage and retrieval, including multiuser support and extensible support for query languages.

RDFCore has been adopted in the VIKEF Project as the basic component for RDF metadata storage in the VIKE (Virtual Information and Knowledge Environment) Framework, where its SOAP[6]-exposed services have been wrapped as a Web Service[7] for metadata storage, retrieval and querying.

RDFCore also has extensible support for different solutions for physical persistence. At the time of writing, there are four implementations of *RDFEngineInterface* (the basic interface to be implemented by plugins), two based on the already mentioned Jena Semantic Web Toolkit, one with MySQL RDBMS [8] as persistent storage, called *RDFEngineJENA*, and the other one using Microsoft SQL Server [9], using the resources by Erik Barke [10], called *RDFEngineMsSQL*. The third implementation is based on simple RDF/XML files, and is called *RDFEnginePlain*. The fourth implementation, called *RDFEngineREDD*, is the one in which we implemented the REDD algorithm natively in the storage level.

6 http://www.w3.org/2000/xp/Group/
7 http://www.w3.org/2002/ws/
8 http://dev.mysql.com/doc/mysql/en/index.html
9 www.microsoft.com/sql/
10 http://www.ur.se/jena/Jena2MsSql.zip

Fig. 4. Architecture of the RDFCore system

It uses Oracle[11] as RDBMS. In Figure 4 there is a small sketch of the system architecture.

5 Experimental Results

To evaluate the scalability of our implementation of the REDD algorithm in the *RDFEngineREDD* implementation of *RDFEngineInterface*, we built a set of Models to check some situations inspired by real models; the results of operations on these Models are in Table 5. The models come from different sources: the first two, *lean* and *nolean*, are from [1], where they are presented as basic examples of lean and non-lean graphs. *nolean2B* is a slight variation of *nolean*, with two redundant blank nodes. *cycleTest* is used to check the behavior of the algorithm when dealing with complex cyclic situations in graphs, while *blankChain* contains a chain of redundant blank nodes that cannot be spotted using our algorithm. *restriction* contains a redundant restriction class definition (as in Figure 1) together with a redundant union class definition (in OWL); the last Model, *daml*, contains a sketch of a DAML ontology, with some class definitions including both Restriction, Union and Intersection types.

For each model, we recorded the number of statements, the number of blank nodes present in the graph, the elapsed time to insert the models in our persistence, the elapsed time to execute REDD and the number of removable blanks in the graph. Since the size of these models is way too small to evaluate scalability on model size and complexity, we kept these test cases as correctness checks while developing the algorithm, and then created a parametric method to generate bigger models with known structure, in order to scale the size and complexity without having to check the correctness of the results (which can be a time consuming task for models with more than some tens of nodes). The parameters we used are: the number of blank nodes in a graph, the number of incoming/outgoing edges for each node, and the number of redundancies for each blank node (i.e. a blank node can be found redundant with one or more nodes in the graph). The test models were built scaling on the three parameters independently (showed in Tables 2, 3, 5), and in the last test case both the number of blank nodes and the number of redundancies per node is augmented. This is the case that produces the biggest models, as shown in Table 4.

[11] More specifically Oracle 9.2.0.1.0 also known as Oracle 9i Release 2 `http://otn.oracle.com/documentation/oracle9i.html`

Table 1. Fake models scaling on ingoing/ outgoing edges

Model id	Model size (# triples)	Blank node #	Blank node %	Storing time (ms)	REDD	Redundancies #	Removable blanks #	ingoing/ outgoing edges
0	120	1	0,83	1469	62	5	1	10
1	240	1	0,42	2469	94	5	1	20
2	360	1	0,28	3438	141	5	1	30
3	480	1	0,21	4515	188	5	1	40
4	600	1	0,17	5266	234	5	1	50
5	720	1	0,14	6328	297	5	1	60
6	840	1	0,12	7109	360	5	1	70
7	960	1	0,10	8172	437	5	1	80
8	1080	1	0,09	9203	594	5	1	90
9	1200	1	0,08	11016	625	5	1	100

Table 2. Fake models scaling on blank nodes number

Model id	Model size (# triples)	Blank node #	Blank node %	Storing time (ms)	REDD	Redundancies #	Removable blanks #	ingoing/ outgoing edges
10	200	5	2,50	1953	78	1	5	10
11	400	10	2,50	3766	125	1	10	10
12	600	15	2,50	5406	250	1	15	10
13	800	20	2,50	7203	219	1	20	10
14	1000	25	2,50	10000	281	1	25	10
15	1200	30	2,50	10860	375	1	30	10
16	1400	35	2,50	12828	407	1	35	10
17	1600	40	2,50	14844	469	1	40	10
18	1800	45	2,50	15969	563	1	45	10
19	2000	50	2,50	18047	750	1	50	10

Table 3. Fake models scaling on number of redundancies

Model id	Model size (# triples)	Blank node #	Blank node %	Storing time (ms)	REDD	Redundancies #	Removable blanks #	ingoing/ outgoing edges
20	120	1	0,83	2235	453	5	5	10
21	220	1	0,45	2235	93	10	10	10
22	320	1	0,31	3188	156	15	15	10
23	420	1	0,24	3828	188	20	20	10
24	520	1	0,19	4485	234	25	25	10
25	620	1	0,16	5047	266	30	30	10
26	720	1	0,14	5813	297	35	35	10
27	820	1	0,12	6907	546	40	40	10
28	920	1	0,11	7360	406	45	45	10
29	1020	1	0,10	8188	437	50	50	10

As can be seen, the insertion of new descriptions roughly scales linearly with the size of the descriptions. The performance overhead due to index updating, however, increases when the number of triples in a description increase, so the total complexity is more than linear. The heavy indexing, on the other side, enables us to obtain very good results when running the REDD algorithm on the data. About the real size reduction of the model after the removal of the blank nodes (which means the removal of every triple referring to these nodes),

Table 4. Fake models scaling on both blank nodes and redundancies number

Model id	Model size (# triples)	Blank node #	Blank node %	Storing time (ms)	REDD	Redundancies #	Removable blanks #	ingoing/ outgoing edges
30	600	5	0,83	4906	234	5	5	10
31	2200	10	0,45	18328	922	10	10	10
32	4800	15	0,31	39141	2187	15	15	10
33	8400	20	0,24	69578	4203	20	20	10
34	13000	25	0,19	118031	6078	25	25	10
35	18600	30	0,16	171563	10031	30	30	10

Table 5. Some real-world models tests

Model id	Model size (# triples)	Blank node #	Blank Node %	Storing time (ms)	REDD	Removable blanks #
lean	2	1	50,0%	140	32	0
nolean	2	1	50,0%	62	31	1
nolean2B	3	2	66,7%	46	47	2
blankChain	7	2	28,6%	94	31	0
cycleTest	15	2	13,3%	204	31	1
restriction	35	17	48,6%	500	93	7
daml	38	33	86,8%	718	282	16

it is not possible to draw general conclusions since the number of triples strongly depends on the graph; the only reasonable lower limit is two triples per blank node, since it is quite unusual to have a dangling blank node or a graph rooted in a blank node, and in these cases it is unlikely that the nodes are redundant (e.g. `ns:a ns:aProperty _:X` means that *ns:a* has a filler for the role *ns:aProperty*, but nothing else is known about this filler; adding another statement, `ns:a ns:aProperty _:Y`, would assert the same thing; unless stating that *_:X* is different from *_:Y*, REDD signals the nodes as redundant, and the same thing is likely to happen with a reasoner).

Acknowledgments

This research was partially funded by the European Commission under the 6th FP IST Integrated Project VIKEF (`http://www.vikef.net`) - Virtual Information and Knowledge Environment Framework (Contract no. 507173) Priority 2.3.1.7 Semantic-based Knowledge Systems.

References

1. Hayes, P.: RDF semantics (2004) W3C Recommendation 10 February 2004 `http://www.w3.org/TR/rdf-mt/`.
2. Gutierrez, C., Hurtado, C., Mendelzon, A.O.: Foundations of Semantic Web Databases. In: Proceedings of ACM Symposium on Principles of Database Systems (PODS) Paris, France, June 2004. (2004)

3. Esposito, F., Iannone, L., Palmisano, I., Semeraro, G.: RDF Core: a Component for Effective Management of RDF Models. In Cruz, I.F., Kashyap, V., Decker, S., Eckstein, R., eds.: Proceedings of SWDB'03, The first International Workshop on Semantic Web and Databases, Co-located with VLDB 2003, Humboldt-Universität, Berlin, Germany, September 7-8, 2003. (2003)
4. McBride, B.: JENA: A Semantic Web toolkit. IEEE Internet Computing **6** (2002) 55–59
5. Wilkinson, K., Sayers, C., Kuno, H.A., Reynolds, D.: Efficient RDF storage and retrieval in jena2. In Cruz, I.F., Kashyap, V., Decker, S., Eckstein, R., eds.: Proceedings of SWDB'03, The first International Workshop on Semantic Web and Databases, Co-located with VLDB 2003, Humboldt-Universität, Berlin, Germany, September 7-8, 2003. (2003) 131–150

Complementing Search Engines with Text Mining

Leszek Borzemski and Piotr Lopatka

Wroclaw University of Technology,
Wybrzeze Wyspianskiego 27,
50-370 Wroclaw, Poland
leszek.borzemski@pwr.wroc.pl

Abstract. A search engine called SearchService with text analysis functionality has been developed. It supports query sound and synonym expansion mechanisms. It also gives performance based result ranking.

We focus here on the application of text miming methods as they may support intelligent Web documents searching and help for user query processing. We also would like to introduce a new performance-based ranking for results lists which is built around the expected downloading time of targeted documents. Unlike other public search engines, our system called SearchService supports the means of query expansion mechanisms working on linguistic indexes, including sound and synonym expansions. It also gives performance data about searched pages, which can be used in result ranking. The system has been developed using the APIs for applications developers available in the IBM's Intelligent Miner for Text package [3].

Our search engine consists of: crawler, indexer, tool that serves user queries and a database, where all information is stored. The SearchService 'Query form' page is shown in Fig. 1. In the first row a query is entered. It may contain a group of words or phrase of interest. In the second row three selection lists are available. In the first one a number stands for the maximum replies to be returned. The second list specifies how to process the query. The following options are available: *Free Text* – relevance value is assigned to each document that contains at least one of non stop words in the query argument. Words in the argument, that occur close to each other form lexical affinities, which increase their relevance values. *Document* – this is a Boolean query in which all specified words need to occur in one document in order to return document. *Paragraph* – this is a Boolean query in which all specified words need to occur in one paragraph in order to return document. *Sentence* – this is a Boolean query in which all specified words need to occur in one sentence in order to return document.

The first option "Free Text" is the least restricted type of query and therefore usually returns far more replies, than others. In fact the options have been ordered from the least restricted to the most. The last option "Sentence" is the most demanding, because it requires having all non stop words in query term to appear in one sentence. The third selection list in the second row of a query form specifies additional linguistic processing applied. The following three options are available: *No expansion* – it includes only regular linguistic processing (stop words filtering, lemmatization etc.). *Synonym expansion* – additionally a request to search also for synonyms of the current

M. Ali and F. Esposito (Eds.): IEA/AIE 2005, LNAI 3533, pp. 743 – 745, 2005.

search term is made. Search engine uses synonyms defined in the language dictionary on the server workstation. *Sound expansion* – an option that requests to search additionally for terms that sound like the specified search term.

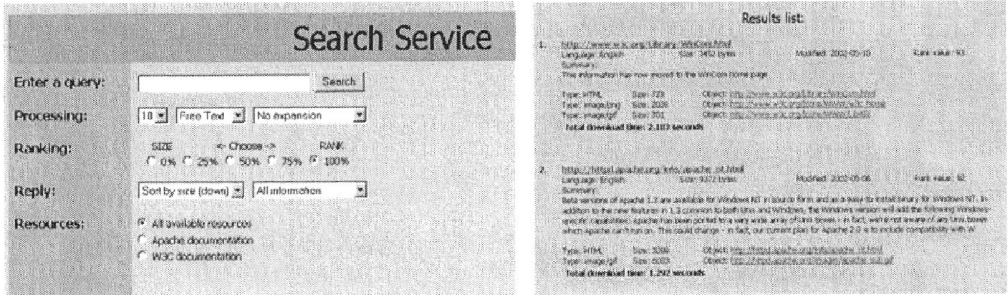

Fig. 1. 'Query form' page

Fig. 2. Results list

$$Ind(i) = \frac{size(i) - size\min}{size\max - size\min} * (100\% - weight) + \frac{rank(i) - rank\min}{rank\max - rank\min} * weight \quad (1)$$

$$Ind(i) = \frac{size(i) - size\min}{size\max - size\min} * (weight - 100\%) + \frac{rank(i) - rank\min}{rank\max - rank\min} * weight \quad (2)$$

We implemented indexes for two Web resources: Apache and W3C documentations. Using a radio button we can set what resources should be searched. Three options are available. First option joins these resources into one database. Second and third let the user select a single resource, specifically either Apache or W3C documentation resources. The next two options can be also set in a query form: (i) Ranking, and (ii) Reply. The ranking is a radio button option. Ranking sorts the results list. It lets specify whether the results ranking should be done according to 'rank value' returned with every document, or according to document's total size (with all embedded objects). If a user wants to sort a list of returned documents according to 'rank value' only, he or she should mark radio button at '100%'. On the contrary, if relevant documents are supposed to be sorted according to total size only, a user should mark radio button at '0%'. There is also a possibility to get an intermediate value and those two factors (*size* and *rank*) may have influence on the final document position with fixed contribution *weight*. The expressions (1) and (2) are used to calculate each documents indicator *Ind*. The higher indicator's value the higher document is put in the result list. When *weight* attribute is set on its one of bound values, only one factor (*size* or *rank*) contribute to final document positioning. In any other cases two factors contribute to final 'fixed' result. Expression (1) is used when 'sort by size (down)' option is chosen. Expression (2) is used when 'sort by size (up)' option is chosen. Additional option lets specify (in case documents are sorted by size), whether they should be placed in ascending or descending order. This can be done by choosing the option in the first drop down list in the 'Reply' section. 'Sort by size (down)' makes documents appear from the largest one to the smallest one. 'Sort by size (up)' works on contrary. The option Reply is also for selecting information provided with results list. The drop down list in 'Reply' section lets specify what kind of information about each document should be returned. The options are: - all information, - documents' details, - embedded objects, - download time (Fig. 2). When the second option 'documents' details' is chosen the following information is displayed about every document: - URL, - language, - size, - date of last modification, - rank value, - document summary. Document's size refers to the total document size including document itself and all embedded objects' together. The 'Embedded objects' option displays information only about embedded objects. For each document in the list the first line is always document's source file (bold line). The information given consists of the MIME type of the object, its size and URL. The 'All information' option joins two previously presented options. Information about language, summary, rank value and all embedded objects is presented. The last option "Download time" lets estimate time needed for Web page downloading. During displaying the search results an HTTP method 'GET' is called to every object. Time is stamped before sending the request and after the response is received. The difference is counted for each object and summed for a group of objects composing a Web page. In fact time provided with results list is burden with DNS lookup and cashing mechanisms. It is the time calculated for uploading the page by the server where the SearchService is running, not the client workstation. This should be remembered, when using this function. In the resulting page at the very beginning comes also a query specification. It contains a query that have been posted, processing conditions (type of query and possible expansions) and resource at which a query is aimed. Next a result list comes, which presents the most relevant documents that meet query criteria. In the first line a link to the document is placed. In the second line the document's attributes are presented: (i) document's language, (ii) document's size (in bytes), (iii) date of last modification (download date), (iv) rank value returned by the search engine. The last part of document's information is its summary. Summary can be produced only for English documents. If document is written in another language a note: "No summary available" is displayed.

Experienced user may take advantage of ranking based on document size to evaluate page downloading performance, enhancing features of such systems as Wing [2]. Using SearchService the user can decide what is more important at the moment, performance or information relevance (or both in some mixed sense) when accessing Web pages. The system may help users in finding yet relevant documents with superior expected downloading times. The automatic mechanism for getting documents which are expected to be downloaded fastest among documents in the results list with acceptable (same) relevance (rank) is now under development. It will employ our data mining approach for the prediction of Internet path performance [1].

References

1. Borzemski L.: Data Mining in Evaluation of Internet Path Performance. Proc. of IEA/AIE 2004. LNAI, Vol. 3029. Springer-Verlag, Berlin (2004) 643-652
2. Borzemski L., Nowak Z.: WING: A Web Probing, Visualization and Performance Analysis Service. Proc. of ICWE 2004. LNCS, Vol. 3140. Springer-Verlag, Berlin (2004) 601-602
3. Intelligent Miner for Text ver. 2.3. (1998)

A Decision Support Approach to Modeling Trust in Networked Organizations

Nada Lavrač[1,2], Peter Ljubič[1], Mitja Jermol[1], and Gregor Papa[1]

[1] Jožef Stefan Institute, Jamova 39, Ljubljana, Slovenia
[2] Nova Gorica Polytechnic, Nova Gorica, Slovenia

Abstract. The main motivation for organizations to e-collaborate is to enable knowledge sharing and learning in order to effectively address a new business opportunity by forming a Virtual Organization (VO) for solving the given task. One of the difficulties in VO creation is appropriate partner selection with mutual trust, as well as the support for the management of trust in a broader Virtual organization Breeding Environment (VBE) – a cluster of organizations willing to collaborate when a new business opportunity appears. This paper proposes an approach to modeling trust in a network of collaborating organizations, aimed at improved trust management in VBEs and improved decision support in the process of VO creation.

1 A Decision Support Approach to Trust Modeling

For trust modeling, the decision making problem of trust estimation can be decomposed into decision sub-problems. A mutual trust estimate can be performed by utility aggregation functions used in hierarchical multi-attribute decision support systems [1] in which values of top-level decision criteria are computed by aggregating values of decision criteria at lower levels of a hierarchical tree, which is used to decompose a decision making problem into sub-problems. Decision support system DEXi, used in our system for trust modeling, enables the development of qualitative hierarchical decision support models. DEXi is based on the DEX decision support system [1] which can be used to evaluate incompletely or inaccurately defined decision alternatives, by employing distributions of qualitative values, and evaluating them by methods based on probabilistic or fuzzy propagation of uncertainty.

Knowledge about mutual trust can be acquired through a simple questionnaire that a partner of a networked organization can fill-in to describe the competencies of its own organization and the collaborating partner's performance in previous joint collaborations (for organizations with which the partner has collaborated in past joint projects). For example, the relevant fields of a questionnaire could include:

- a list of partner's own competencies,
- a list of competencies of the collaborating partner, and
- collaborating partner's trust estimate based on (a) estimated collaborating partner's reputation (image, market share), (b) number of successful joint past collaborations, (c) estimate of the profit made in joint collaborations, (d) estimate of the partner's timeliness in performing assigned tasks, (e)

M. Ali and F. Esposito (Eds.): IEA/AIE 2005, LNAI 3533, pp. 746–748, 2005.

estimate of the partner's quality of performance and products, and (f) estimate of the partner's appropriateness of costs of performance and products.

2 Web-Based Trust Modeling: Estimating Research Reputation and Collaboration of Project Partners

A questionnaire-based approach is a preferred means for the estimation of trust between organizations that have known each other based on their experiences in past collaborations. An alternative approach to trust modeling is through the analysis of publicly available Web resources. A Web-based trust modeling approach, similar to the one proposed by [2], is more adequate for roughly estimating the reputation and joint collaborations of partners (individuals or organizations) when a consortium is build of numerous new partners whose past performance is not known. It is also an interesting approach to trust modeling in professional virtual communities and communities of practice.

This paper applies the proposed Web-based approach to modeling reputation and trust between partners of a large 6th FP integrated project ECOLEAD. The project has an ambitious goal of creating the foundations and mechanisms for establishing advanced collaborative and network-based industry society in Europe.

There are 102 registered individuals from 20 organizations participating in the ECOLEAD project. The left-hand side of Figure 1 shows the Web-based estimates of research reputation and joint collaborations of individuals of the ECOLEAD consortium. To model trust between project members, the following procedure was used:

1. Collect the information about partners' research *reputation*, based on the publications of each individual: WOS(Y) - the number of publications of author Y in journals with SCI or SSCI factor (obtained through the Web of Science system), and CITESEER(Y) - the number of citations of papers of author Y (obtained by the CiteSeer system).

2. Collect the information about past joint *collaborations* between each two individuals: CITESEER(X,Y) - the number of jointly written documents of authors X and Y (obtained by the CiteSeer system), and GOOGLE(X,Y) - the number of common appearances of individuals X and Y on the Web (obtained by Google search).

3. Finally, calculate *research trust,* estimated as weighted sum of reputation and joint collaborations estimates. The calculation of trust between two partners is performed using following function:

$$TRUST(X,Y) = w_p(w_{WOS}WOS(Y) + w_{CiteCit}CITESEER(Y)) + w_c(w_{CiteDoc}CITESEER(X,Y) + w_{Google}GOOGLE(X,Y))$$

where w_{WOS}, $w_{CiteCit}$, $w_{CiteDoc}$, w_{Google}, w_p, and w_c are weights of WOS publications, CiteSeer citations, joint publications in CiteSeer, and collaborations found by Google, respectively. In the model used in our experiment, all the weights were set to 0.5, while the numbers of publications, citations, joint publications and collaborations were normalized to values on the [0,1] interval. Note that the functions used for trust estimation are not commutative, so trust of X to Y and trust of Y to X must both be calculated. Having calculated the trust estimates, one is able to rank individual network partners according to their research reputation, joint collaborations and the overall trust estimate. The Web-based trust estimation model can be used also for other purposes: visualization of the entire trust network, as well as finding well-connected sub-graphs with high trust utility value, representing 'cliques' of partners with strong mutual trust.

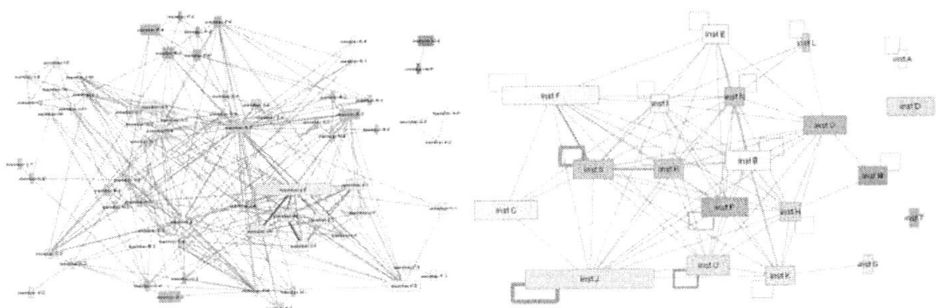

Fig. 1. Two graphs showing Web-based estimates of research reputation and joint collaborations of individual ECOLEAD researchers (left-hand side), and organizations constituting the ECOLEAD consortium (right-hand side). For anonymity, actual names of individuals and organizations have been replaced by neutral *member* and *institution* labels

In Figure 1, project and sub-project coordinators turn out to be in central positions according to collaborations. Some of the 102 individuals are not in the graph: those who have a few collaborations and/or low research reputation value. Some well collaborating individuals represent 'cliques' of individuals, e.g., researchers from the same organization (same color intensity of nodes) typically have more joint collaborations than researchers from different organizations. From the estimates of reputation and collaborations of individuals, research reputation and collaborations of organizations can be estimated.

Acknowledgements

This work was supported by the Slovenian Ministry of Higher Education, Science and Technology and the 6th FP integrated project ECOLEAD (European Collaborative Networked Organizations Leadership Initiative, 2004-2007).

References

1. Bohanec, M. and Rajkovič, V. DEX: An expert system shell for decision support, Sistemica 1(1): 145–157, 1990.
2. Matsuo, Y., Tomobe, H., Hasida, K. and Ishizuka, M. Finding social network for trust calculation. In *Proceeding of the 16th European Conference on Artificial Intelligence*, 510-514, IOS Press, 2004.

An Integrated Approach to Rating and Filtering Web Content

Elisa Bertino[1], Elena Ferrari[2], Andrea Perego[3], and Gian Piero Zarri[4]

[1] CERIAS, Purdue University, IN, USA
bertino@cerias.purdue.edu
[2] DSCPI, Università degli Studi dell'Insubria, Como, Italy
elena.ferrari@uninsubria.it
[3] DICo, Università degli Studi di Milano, Italy
perego@dico.unimi.it
[4] LaLICC, Université Paris IV/Sorbonne, France
gpzarri@paris4.sorbonne.fr

Abstract. In this poster, we will illustrate an integrated approach to Web filtering, whose main features are flexible filtering policies taking into account both users' characteristics and resource content, the specification of an ontology for the filtering domain, and the support for the main filtering strategies currently available. Our approach has been implemented in two prototypes, which address the needs of both home and institutional users, and which enforce filtering strategies more sophisticated and flexible than the ones currently available.

Web content filtering concerns the evalutation of Web resources in order to verify whether they satisfy given parameters. Although such definition is quite general, and it applies to diverse applications, Web filtering has been enforced so far mainly in order to protect users (e.g., minors) from possible 'harmful' content (e.g., pornography, violence, racism).

The filtering systems currently available can be grouped into two main classes. The former adopts a *list*-based approach, according to which Web sites are classified either as 'appropriate' (*white lists*) or 'inappropriate' (*black lists*). In the latter, Web resources are described by metadata associated with them, which are used for evaluating whether they can be accessed or not, depending on the preferences specified by the end user or a supervisor. Such approach is adopted mainly by the rating systems based on the PICS (Platform for Internet Content Selection) W3C standard [1], which defines a general format for *content labels* to be associated with Web sites.

Both such strategies have been criticized for enforcing a restrictive and rather ineffective filtering. In fact, their classification of Web resources is semantically poor, which does not allow to distinguish between categories concerning similar contents (e.g., pornography and gynecology). For the same reason, they often *under*- and/or *over*-block the access to the Web—i.e., respectively, they allow users to access inappropriate resources, or they prevent users from accessing appropriate resources. The metadata-based approach should overcome such drawbacks, since it would allow one to specify a precise and unambiguous description

M. Ali and F. Esposito (Eds.): IEA/AIE 2005, LNAI 3533, pp. 749–751, 2005.

of resources, but this is not true for the available metadata-based rating and filtering systems.

In order to address the issues of Web content rating and filtering, we developed an integrated approach which, besides supporting both the list- and metadata-based strategies, defines content labels providing an accurate description of Web resources and takes into account users' characteristics in order to enforce flexible filtering policies. The outcome of our work, formerly carried out in the framework of the EU project EUFORBIA[1], has been two prototypes, addressing the needs of institutional and home users, and an ontology (namely, the EUFORBIA ontology) for the specification of content labels.

The EUFORBIA ontology is an extension concerning the pornography, violence, and racism domains, of the general NKRL (Narrative Knowledge Representation Language) ontology [2]. NKRL is used to specify the EUFORBIA content labels, which consist of three sections: the first concerns the aims of the Web site, the second describes its relevant characteristics and content, whereas the third outlines the Web site's main sections. It is important to note that, differently from the currently available PICS-based content labels, a EUFORBIA label does not rate a Web site only with respect to the contents liable to be filtered, but, since the NKRL ontology is general purpose, it provides a precise and objective description of its content and characteristics. As a result, we can specify policies more sophisticated than, e.g., "user u cannot access pornographic Web sites", and it is possible to distinguish more precisely between, e.g., an actually pornographic Web site and a Web site addressing sexual topics and contents from a non-pornographic (e.g., medical) point of view.

The EUFORBIA ontology and the corresponding labels are used by two filtering prototypes which enforce complementary strategies for addressing end users' needs.

The former prototype, referred to as NKRL-EUFORBIA [3], allows end users to generate and associate EUFORBIA labels with Web resources, and to build a user profile by specifying NKRL-encoded filtering policies. NKRL-EUFORBIA can run either server- or client-side, and it consists of three main modules: the *Annotation Manager*, which allows the creation of well-formed NKRL 'conceptual annotations' to be used for encoding EUFORBIA labels, the *Web Browser*, which allows the definition of a user profile and a safe navigation over the Internet, and finally the *Web Filter*, which is used by the Web Browser module in order to determine whether the access to a requested resource must be granted or not.

The latter EUFORBIA prototype [3, 4], whose current version is referred to as MFilter [5], is a proxy filter specifically designed for institutional users, who must manage the access to Web content for a high number of heterogeneous users. MFilter implements a model according to which filtering policies can be specified on either users'/resource identity or characteristics. Users are characterized by associating with them *ratings*, organized into a hierarchy and denoted

---

[1] For detailed information concerning EUFORBIA, we refer the reader to the project Web site: `http://semioweb.msh-paris.fr/euforbia`

by a set, possibly empty, of attributes. An example of user rating system is depicted in Figure 1. Thus, differently from the available filtering systems, which make use of predefined and static profiles, MFILTER allows one to specify policies which take into account both user ratings and attribute values (e.g., "all the students whose age is less than 16").

Resources are rated according to the metadata-based strategy, with the difference that MFILTER makes use of multiple rating systems, for which a uniform hierarchical representation is adopted. Currently, MFILTER supports the EUFORBIA ontology and any PICS-based rating systems. Thanks to the hierarchical organization of both user and resource ratings, we can exploit a policy propagation principle according to which a policy concerning a given rating applies also to its children. As a result, we can dramatically reduce the number of policies that need to be specified. Moreover, MFILTER supports both positive and negative policies in order to allow for exceptions to the propagation principle mentioned above. Finally, since the decisions about what users can or cannot access may be shared among several persons (e.g., parents and teachers, in a school context), MFILTER enforces *supervised* filtering techniques, according to which the policies specified by the service administrator must be validated by *supervisors*.

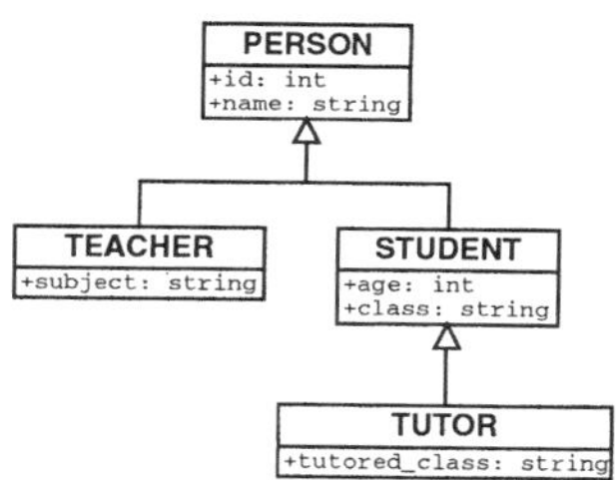

Fig. 1. A user rating system

The integrated approach we present in this poster is an attempt to enhance metadata-based rating and filtering in order to address the heterogeneous requirements of the Web users' community by supporting accurate content labels and flexible filtering policies. Moreover, our approach is fully compliant with the core Semantic Web technologies—namely, RDF and OWL—and it can be easily integrated into the W3C Web Service architecture, of which Web filtering is one of the main components.

References

1. Resnick, P., Miller, J.: PICS: Internet access controls without censorship. Communications of the ACM **39** (1996) 87–93
2. Zarri, G.P.: A conceptual model for representing narratives. In Jain, R., Abraham, A., Faucher, C., van der Zwaag, B., eds.: Innovations in Knowledge Engineering. Advanced Knowledge International, Adelaide (2003)
3. Zarri, G.P., Wu, P., Nallet, B., Pires, F., Abreu, P., Allen, D., Bertino, E., Ferrari, E., Perego, A., Mantegazza, D.: Report on the Final Enhancements to the EUFORBIA Demonstrator. EUFORBIA Deliverable D12, CNRS, Paris (2003) `http://semioweb.msh-paris.fr/euforbia/download/D12pdf.zip`.
4. Bertino, E., Ferrari, E., Perego, A.: Content-based filtering of Web documents: The Ma$\mathcal{X}$ system and the EUFORBIA project. International Journal of Information Security **2** (2003) 45–58
5. Bertino, E., Ferrari, E., Perego, A.: Web content filtering. In Ferrari, E., Thuraisingham, B., eds.: Web and Information Security. IDEA Group (2005) To appear.

Collaborative Case-Based Preference Elicitation

Paolo Avesani, Angelo Susi, and Daniele Zanoni

ITC-irst, Via Sommarive 18, I-38050, Povo, Trento, Italy
{avesani, susi, danzanoni}@itc.it

Abstract. Preference elicitation is a well known bottleneck that prevents the acquisition of the utility function and consequently the set up of effective decision-support systems. In this paper we present a new approach to preference elicitation based on pairwise comparison. The exploitation of learning techniques allows to overcome the usual restrictions that prevent to scale up. Furthermore, we show how our approach can easily support a distributed process of preference elicitation combining both autonomy and coordination among different stakeholders. We argue that a collaborative approach to preference elicitation can be effective in dealing with non homogeneous data representations.

The presentation of the model is followed by an empirical evaluation on a real world settings. We consider a case study on environmental risk assessment to test with real users the properties of our model.

Keywords: Decision Support, Machine Learning.

1 Introduction

Ranking a set of objects is an ubiquitous task that occurs in a variety of domains. Very often to define an order relation over a set of alternatives is a premise to enable a decision-making process.

Information filtering and recommendation systems are well known tasks where relevance assessment is achieved through a process of ranking a huge amount of alternatives. Nevertheless in such examples there is a bias in focusing the ranking process on the top of the list.

In other tasks, like risk assessment or requirement prioritization [9, 10], it is important to assess a total order that is homogeneously accurate over the whole set of alternatives.

The ranking process can be conceived as a task of preference elicitation. There are mainly two approaches to preference elicitation: ex-ante and ex-post. Ex-ante methods rely on the definition of an utility function that encodes a first-principle rational. Although such a kind of methods are quite effective, a strong restriction applies: the set of alternatives has to be homogeneously defined. Ex-post methods rely on case-based preference assessment. Users are involved in an interactive process to acquire their preferences on specific alternatives. Such approach, while overcomes the restriction above, doesn't scale up. The elicitation effort in charge of the users is quadratic with respect to the size of the set of alternatives. Both methods are not effective when the elicitation

M. Ali and F. Esposito (Eds.): IEA/AIE 2005, LNAI 3533, pp. 752–761, 2005.

process involves many stakeholders. Usually different stakeholders apply different criteria in ranking a set of alternatives. Two are the main current limitations: the former is concerned with the bias introduced by the engineer, the latter is the lack of coordination among the elicitation processes for different criteria.

In this paper we present a novel framework to enable a case-based preference elicitation process that interleaves human and machine efforts. The machine complements the partial acquisition of preferences from the users performing two tasks: first, scheduling the subset of alternatives that has to be analyzed by the users; second, completing the elicitation process over the remaining unspecified preferences.

The intuitive idea is to exploit machine learning techniques in the preference elicitation process. Case-based methods achieve a total rank over a set of alternatives by the elicitation of all the pairwise preference values, as in the Analytic Hierarchy Process (AHP) [11, 12] methodology. Part of these values can be acquired manually from the user, while the remaining part can be approximated through a learning step. An estimate of the unknown preference values is computed looking at known values, explicitly elicited by the user, and at other reference rankings.

Exploiting known rankings to approximate new target ranking is an intuition that has been already investigated, as in [7] where some techniques to support the preference elicitation by approximation are described; here the basic intuition relies on the paradigm of casebased reasoning [1] to retrieve a past similar order relation to generate an approximation for the current ranking problem. While this way of proceeding is quite appealing, nevertheless there are clear preconditions that most of the times it is difficult to satisfy. For example, let consider the scenario of risk assessment [4]. It is really difficult to refer to similar or past rankings for the same risk areas. More often the results for similar problem (e.g. environmental chemical emergencies) are available but for a different set of risky areas. Another kind of source for reference rankings can be the feature-based encoding of the alternatives. In this cases an order relation can be derived by ranking the set of alternatives with respect to the values of a given features. Of course two requirements are to be satisfied: the former is that does exist an order relation over the feature domain, the latter is that all the alternatives are homogeneously defined over the same set of features.

It is straightforward to notice that for real world problem it is really unusual to satisfy both these requirements. The consequence is that, although the learning approach to preference elicitation is appealing, case-based methods are not effective in practice.

In the following we define an architecture that supports a distributed process of preference elicitation. We show how this distributed architecture enables a collaborative approach to case-based ranking. We argue that a collaborative approach to preference elicitation allows to overcome the open issues mentioned above; open issues that up to now prevent a successful exploitation of learning techniques.

In our architecture many processes of preference elicitation are carried out in parallel to acquire many ranking criteria. Sharing of intermediate results enables a mutual benefit preserving the autonomy of preference elicitation. The single users can provide their preferences without any bias from other users' preferences. In the meanwhile an effective coordination occurs because the focus of elicitation is addressed towards relationships less evident.

In Section 2 we first give a formal definition of the problem and then we present the case-based ranking method. Section 3 show how collaborative case-based ranking can be enabled by a distributed preference elicitation architecture. Finally Section 4 and Section 5 show how the proposed architecture works in practice illustrating a case study performed on a real world settings.

2 Case-Based Ranking

We propose a framework that adopts pairwise prioritization technique and exploits machine learning techniques to produce ranking over the set of alternatives, using a binary rating. The machine learning techniques allow to approximate part of the pairwise preferences in order to reduce the elicitation effort for the user.

The framework, depicted in Figure 1, supports an iterative process for priority elicitation that can handle single and multiple evaluators and different criteria. In the following, we illustrate it considering the case of a set of users who collaborates to the prioritization of a set (of cardinality n) of instances, with respect to a common target rank criteria.

The types of data involved in the process are depicted as rectangles, namely: Data represents data in input to the process, that is the finite collection of instances that have to be ranked; Pair is a pair of candidate instances whose relative preference is to be specified; Preference is the order relation, elicited by the user, between two alternatives. The preference is formulated as a boolean choice on a pair of alternatives; Ranking criteria are a collection of order relations that represent rankings induced by other criteria defined over the set of alternatives; Final ranking represents the resulting preference structure over the set of instances. The final ranking, which results from the output of the process, represents an approximation of the target ranking. Notice that this ranking may become the input to a further iteration of the process.

The steps of the basic process iteration τ are depicted as ovals in Figure 1. In particular they are:

1. Pair sampling, an automated procedure selects from the repository a pair of alternatives and submits it to the user to acquire the relative priority. Notice that in this step, the selection of a pair takes into account information on the current available rankings (this information is stored in the data Preference, see the arrows between Preference and Pair sampling in Figure 1).
2. Preference elicitation, this step interleaves the involvement of the user in the loop: given a pair of alternatives the user chooses which one is to be preferred with respect to the target ranking criteria.
3. Ranking learning, given a partial elicitation of the user preferences, a learning algorithm produces an approximation of the unknown preferences and a ranking of the whole set of alternatives is derived.

If the result of the learning step is considered enough accurate or the manual elicitation effort is too demanding, the iteration halts and the latest approximated ranking is given as output; otherwise another cycle of the loop is carried on. The model is characterized by the fact that the preference elicitation is monotonic (i.e. the user does not see

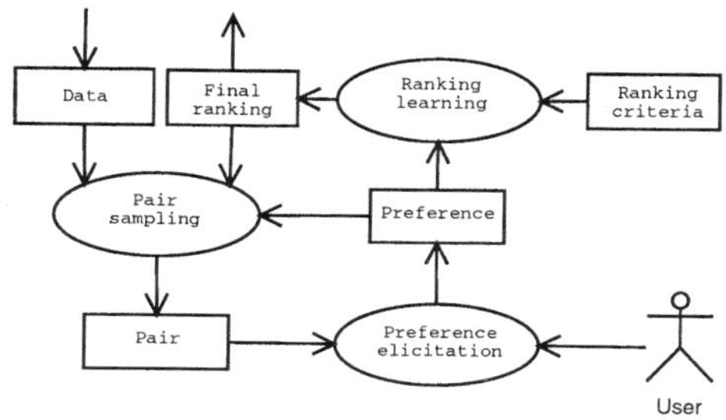

Fig. 1. The basic iteration of the requirements prioritization process

the same pair twice). Such a method aims at obtaining a lower human effort/elicitation, while increasing accuracy of the approximation.

The Ranking learning step produces an approximation of a preference structure, exploiting the boosting approach described in [5, 6]. In particular we have a finite set of alternatives $X = \{x_0, \ldots, x_n\}$, a finite set of m ranking criteria $F = (f_1, \ldots, f_m)$ describing the single alternative, inducing an ordering on the set X, where $f_j : X \to \overline{\mathbb{R}}$ ($\overline{\mathbb{R}} = \mathbb{R} \cup \{\perp\}$) and the interpretation of the inequality $f(x_0) > f(x_1)$ means that x_0 is ranked above x_1 by f_j and $f_j(x) = \perp$ if x is unranked by the functions in F. For example, if we consider the scenario of environmental risk assessment, a set of risk areas plays the role of the set of alternatives, while a ranking criterion could be represented by the order relation induced by the feature that describes the number of damaged people in a given area.

The target ranking represents the ideal risk areas ordering that we are interested in; it is defined as the function K where $K(x_0) > K(x_1)$ means that x_0 is ranked above x_1 by K. We define also the user feedback function, the sampling of the ranking target K at the iteration τ, $\Phi_\tau : X \times X \to \{-1, 0, 1\}$ where $\Phi_\tau(x_0, x_1) = 1$ means that x_1 be ranked above x_0, $\Phi_\tau(x_0, x_1) = -1$ means that x_0 be ranked above x_1, and $\Phi_\tau(x_0, x_1) = 0$ indicates that there is no preference between x_0 and x_1 (we assume $\Phi_\tau(x, x) = 0$ and $\Phi_\tau(x_0, x_1) = -\Phi_\tau(x_1, x_0)$ for all $x, x_0, x_1 \in X$). Related to the Φ we also define a density function $D : X \times X \to \mathbb{R}$ such that $D(x_0, x_1) = \gamma \cdot max(\{0, \Phi_\tau(x_0, x_1)\})$ setting to 0 all negative entries of Φ_τ; γ is a positive constant chosen such that D is a distribution, satisfying the normalization property[1] $\sum_{x_0, x_1} D(x_0, x_1) = 1$.

The goal of the learning step is to produce a ranking of all the alternatives in X. The ranking at the iteration τ is represented in the form of a function $H_\tau : X \to \mathbb{R}$ where x_1 is ranked higher than x_0 by H_τ if $H_\tau(x_1) > H_\tau(x_0)$. The function H_τ represents the approximate ordering of X induced by the feedback function Φ_τ using the information from the set of features F.

In our framework, the function H_τ is computed by a learning procedure based on boosting method that iteratively combines, via a linear combination, a set of partial

[1] Notice that $\Phi_\tau(x_0, x_1) = 0$ means that the pair hasn't been proposed to users, so this three valued functions allows to represent the boolean choice of the user.

Algorithm RankBoost
Input:
X: the set of requirements; F: the set of rankings support;
Φ_τ: the subest of known pairwise preferences at iteration τ;
D: the initial distribution over the pairwise alternatives
Output:
$H_\tau(x)$: the final Hypothesis

begin
$D_1 = D$;
For $t = 1, \ldots, T$:
Compute $h_t(X; F, \Phi_\tau, D_t)$;
Compute $D_{t+1}(X; D_t, h_t)$;
Compute $\alpha_t(X; D_t; h_t)$;
return $H_\tau(x) = \sum_{t=1}^{T} \alpha_t h_t(x)$;
end.

Fig. 2. A sketch of the RankBoost algorithm

order functions $h_t : X \rightarrow \mathbb{R}$, named weak rules, using a set of coefficients $\alpha = \{\alpha_1, \ldots, \alpha_t, \ldots\}$. The algorithm that computes H_τ, described in Figure 2, performs T iterations; it takes as input the initial distribution D and the set of functions F.

The basic iteration performs the three steps described below:

Step 1. Computation of a partial order h_t of the elements in X taking into account the user feedback function Φ_τ. The ranking hypothesis h_t is induced by the ranking criteria in F, that are used as possible models. The algorithm that computes h_t also uses the distribution D to emphasize sets of pairs that has to be ordered by h_t. To compute h_t we implemented the *WeakLearner* algorithm proposed in [5].

Step 2. Compute a new distribution D over the set of pairs already evaluated by the user, which is passed, on the next iteration, to the procedure that computes the partial order h; intuitively, distribution D represents the portion of relations where has been hardest to produce an accurate prediction till the present step, so it emphasize the relations that need to be ordered in the next steps. Moreover the information provided by the distribution D is given in input even to the pair sampling policy; in fact pairs whose priority relationship is supposed to be less accurate can be presented to the users for the next step of preference elicitation.

Step 3. Computation of a value for the parameter α_t, where $\alpha_t \in \mathbb{R}$. This value is a measure of the accuracy of the partial order h_t with respect to the final order H.

The number of iterations can be fixed a-priori or the algorithm stops when a stable ordering configuration has been found. More details on the algorithm in [2].

3 Collaborative Approach

In the architecture illustrated above, the key factor to get effective the learning step is the choice of the m ranking criteria, i.e. the set F. As discussed in [2] the number of ranking criteria is not crucial for enabling an accurate estimate of the target ranking. Therefore it is not important to scale up on the dimension of F; much more important is the relationships that hold between the target (and unknown) ranking and the single ranking criteria [3, 8].

The open issue is where these ranking criteria come from. In [2] the ranking criteria were derived looking at the feature based description of the alternatives. Given a set of alternatives and given a predefined feature, a ranking is obtained by the order relation induced by the feature values. Such a solution doesn't apply to symbolic features. However, the rankings derived from a feature-based description can be not related to the target ranking, providing a noisy support to the learning step. Last but not least this way of proceeding is not sustainable to manage a preference elicitation process over a set of alternatives not homogeneously described.

The basic idea of collaborative approach is to exploit at run time the intermediate ranking solutions generated by the preference elicitation process. First of all we can replicate such a process model many times, supporting a single user interaction. Therefore instead of collecting together preferences from three users to reduce the elicitation effort, we can setup a distributed process where each single user attends to her/his own process.

Each iteration of the cycle τ illustrated in Figure 1 produces a ranking hypothesis $H_\tau(x)$. If we replicate twice the model we will have at each iteration τ two ranking hypothesis $H^1_\tau(x)$ and $H^2_\tau(x)$. More in general we can have $H^u_\tau(x)$, with $u = 1, \ldots, U$. At a given step τ, the $U - 1$ ranking hypothesis $\{H^u_\tau(x)\}$, with $u = 2, \ldots, U$ can play the role of ranking criteria to support the learning step aimed to produce the ranking hypothesis $H^1_{\tau+1}(x)$. In a similar way all the ranking hypothesis for the $\tau + 1$ step for each user can be obtained looking at the intermediate hypothesis of other users.

After a bootstrap phase each user can accomplish the preference elicitation process taking advantage from other users effort. Therefore at run time a user can rely on a set of reference ranking defined over the same set X of alternatives. It is worthwhile to remark that each process work to build an accurate approximation of the target ranking for a given users. While the intermediate hypothesis $H^u_\tau(x)$ are shared among the different processes, each learning step aims to target only its own Φ^u_τ known preference set. Therefore each user doesn't have access to other users preferences, neither the learning step exploits a larger set of preferences merging different sources.

It is important to notice that such an architecture doesn't produce an unique ranking hypothesis and not necessarily the final hypothesis $H^j_\tau(x)$ will be the same as $H^i_\tau(x)$, where $j \neq i$. The ultimate goal is to produce an accurate ranking approximation tailored to a given user lowering the elicitation effort. The synthesis of a final ranking representative of all the users is not matter of this work.

4 A Case Study on Environmental Risk Assessment

The next step of our work has been the experimental evaluation on a real world problem. We have chosen the civil defense domain because both of the typical restrictions hold: first, it is usually difficult to have an homogeneous description of two different scenarios of risk, second, rankings over the same set of scenarios are not available.

The environmental systemic risk assessment is formulated as follows. There are a collection of risk areas. Each area represents a scenario of risk. Systemic risk refers to the capability of the social organization to react after an environmental emergency. The elapsed time of organizations reaction is a crucial point in the risk assessment. A quick answer can prevent that a moderate emergency will evolve in a high one. The systemic risk assessment is a really difficult task because the encoding of all the relevant factors is unsustainable. Much of this type of reasoning relies on background knowledge that very often is tacitly illustrated in a map. To perform a systemic risk assessment over a set of scenarios means to rank all these alternatives to support an intervention policy, for example scheduling high cost simulations.

We considered the systemic risk assessment on the Province of Vicenza, Italy. A preliminary recognition identified 40 scenarios of risk. Each risk scenario was defined by a feature-based description helpful to support non ambiguous reference. An annotated map provided a context sensitive characterization of the specific scenario.

We implemented a web-based interface to support a distributed access to a process model as depicted in Figure 1. We involved 4 experts, mainly geologists from a private company, that received the commitment to perform such a kind of assessment from the local government. We set up the system to support individual authenticated sessions for each expert. The typical session was organized as follows. An agenda of predefined paired scenarios was presented to the expert. After a pair selection, the expert was free to browse the map and to inquire the associated georeferenced database. Moreover they were free to annotate the map with a context sensitive information, useful to highlight the rational of risk assessment. The ultimate step was to resolve the relative risk value between the two alternative scenarios. They simply inputed a boolean value to elicit the pairwise preference.

The notion of target ranking was shared in advance by the different experts. The systemic risk has been established as a common criteria. Since this concept is not well defined, the single target rankings were not necessarily the same even though inspired by the same goal.

5 Empirical Evaluation

The evaluation of a preference elicitation process is a tricky step. It is important to remark that on-line evaluation strongly differs from off-line evaluation.

Off-line evaluation is based on simulation of the elicitation process. Therefore it is possible to assume that the target ranking is known in advance. Target ranking can be used as a correct model of the preference structure associated to a user. Such a model can be exploited to generate the preference values simulating the user behavior. At the end of the process the evaluation can be measured comparing the misalignment between the target ranking and the approximated ranking.

In on-line settings this way of proceeding is no more valid because there is no chance to know in advance the target ranking. For this reason we adopted an heuristic approach to evaluation assessment.

We proceeded as follows. We grouped the 4 experts into two teams. The first team, composed by three experts randomly selected, performed a collaborative preference

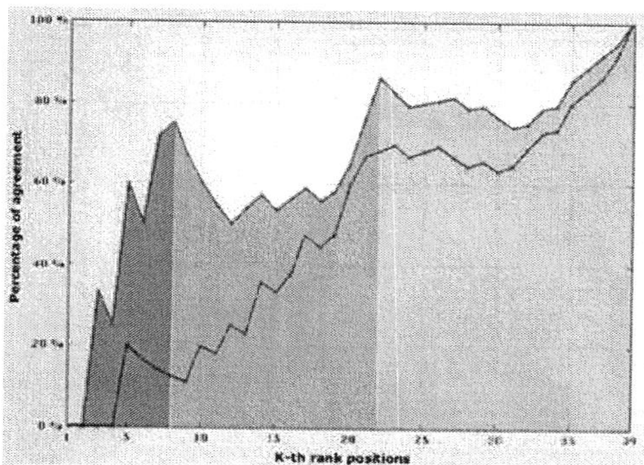

Fig. 3. The cumulative agreement on ranking hypothesis. The first curve represents the behavior of collaborative team while the second curve represents the behavior considering the solipsistic expert

elicitation process as described above. Each of them, autonomously attended the pairwise elicitation sessions without any contact with other experts of the team. Nevertheless, the learning step of their model has been set up to use the intermediate hypothesis of other two experts as ranking criteria. The process model of fourth expert has been set up differently. As ranking criteria were chosen few ranks derived from the feature-based description of the scenarios. At each cycle of the preference elicitation process, the learning step of the fourth expert takes in input the same ranking criteria.

All four experts performed a schedule of 6 sessions. In the first session they had an agenda of 20 pairs, then five more sessions with 8 pairs each. Experts independently and remotely accomplished their tasks with the only restriction of synchronization for the three of them. We have to remind that since the generation of new agenda of comparisons depends from the learning step, such a computation requires an intermediate alignment among the three different processes.

After the elicitation of 60 pairwise preferences for each expert, approximately the 8% of all the $|X|(|X|-1)/2$ possible pairs, we obtained four ranking hypothesis.

Starting from the four $H^i_\tau(x)$ ranking hypothesis we computed the curve of cumulative agreement of all the four experts and those of the team of three. Figure 3 show the behavior of such curves. On the x axis is plotted the $k-th$ rank position. On the y axis is plotted the percentage of agreement over the subset of scenario included between the first and the $k-th$ rank position. For example considering the first 8 positions the team achieved an agreement of 75%, that is all three of them placed the same 6 scenarios.

The first curve in Figure 3 shows the behavior of cumulative agreement for the collaborative team. All of them converge to a quite similar solution. The second curve shows the behavior considering all the four experts. It is quite evident that the fourth expert didn't converge to similar solution providing the same elicitation effort of other experts.

Of course we don't know whether the ranking hypothesis of the team are more closed to the target ranking than the fourth hypothesis. We are aware that the collaborative architecture tends to introduce a bias in the elicitation process. For these reasons we performed two additional test to assess whether the ranking hypothesis of the team are nearest to the target ranking.

The first test aimed at assessing whether there was a bias in the team formation. We considered for each user the first set of elicited preferences Φ_0^u, then we computed the first ranking hypothesis $H_0^u(x)$ free of every bias. Given the four ranking hypothesis we measured the correlation among all the possible subset of three experts. We detected that the four expert wasn't the outlier, on the contrary, the second expert belonging to the team was much less correlated to the others. Therefore we can argue that the divergence of the solipsistic expert isn't related to a significant variance on the notion of systemic risk.

The second test aimed to assess the agreement of the fourth expert on the results of the team. We invited the fourth expert to attend an additional session. We arranged an agenda of comparison as follows. We selected all the scenarios ranked by the team in the first 8 positions that the fourth expert ranked after the 8-th position. The fourth expert confirmed at least 75% of the ranking hypothesis of the team contradicting the response of his own ranking hypothesis. Therefore we can argue that, given the same amount of elicited preferences, a collaborative approach enables a much more effective approximation of the target ranking.

Off-line simulations allowed us to assess that this behavior is not related to the total amount of elicited preferences. To schedule a given amount of preferences acquisition among three experts or to assign the whole task to a single expert doesn't produce similar ranking hypothesis. There is trade off between the user effort and the accuracy of ranking hypothesis. When the size of alternatives increases the bootstrap of learning step increases too. Two are the strategies to have a quicker approximation of the target ranking: to provide much more elicited preference values or to provide much more accurate ranking criteria as support of the learning step. The second strategy results to be more effective in reducing the total elicitation effort while preserving an accurate approximated ranking.

The key factor of collaborative approach is twofold. The former is to provide to the learning step good reference rankings whose quality increases as the process proceeds. The latter is that the pair sampling policy address the acquisition of explicit preferences towards pairwise relationships that are more critical for the learner to approximate.

It is important to remark that we didn't make any restrictive assumption on the target ranking of different experts.

A useful by-product of the experimentation has been the detection of three main categories of risk. Looking at the curve of cumulative agreement, see Figure 3, it is possible to detect three main partitions where the agreement among the experts is locally maximum. This result seems to provide an evidence that the collaborative approach can be even much more performant if we adopt a rougher evaluation measure.

Finally it is worthwhile to remember that we didn't introduce any domain dependent assumption. The deployment of the collaborative architecture, the configuration of the elicitation process and the deployment of the application didn't require any additional effort related to the specific case study.

The merge of the three ranking hypothesis produced by the team of experts has been included in the environmental risk assessment report delivered to Province of Vicenza.

6 Conclusions

We have remarked how learning approach can be profitable to support large scale preference elicitation processes. Our contribution refers to a framework to support collaborative case-based preference elicitation. We argued how our proposal is effective in dealing with the scaling problem and the homogeneity restriction. Moreover we gave a solution to the lack of reference rankings, a premise to the exploitation of learning techniques. An experimental evaluation on a real world case study provided the empirical evidence of the performance of our method in practice.

Acknowledgments

We would like to thank the consultants of Risorse&Ambiente, M. Demozzi, F. Mutti, R. Bontempi and E. Crescini, that with their support made it possible the evaluation on a real environmental setting.

References

1. A. Aamodt and E. Plaza. Case-based reasoning: Foundational issues, methodological variations, and system approaches. *AI Communications*, 7(1):39–59, 1994.
2. Paolo Avesani, Sara Ferrari, and Angelo Susi. Case-Based Ranking for Decision Support Systems. In *Proceedings of ICCBR 2003*, number 2689 in LNAI, pages 35 – 49. Springer-Verlag, 2003.
3. G. Devetag and M. Warglien. Representing others' preferences in mixed motive games: Was schelling right? *Technical Report, Computable and Experimental Economics Lab, University of Trento*, 2002.
4. H. Kumamoto E. J. Henley. *Probabilistic Risk Assessment.* IEEE Press, New York, 1992.
5. Y. Freund, R. Iyer, R. Schapire, and Y. Singer. An Efficient Boosting Algorithm for Combining Preferences. In *Proceedings 15th International Conference on Machine Learning*, 1998.
6. Y. Freund and R. Schapire. A Short Introduction to Boosting, 1999.
7. Vu Ha and Peter Haddawy. Toward case-based preference elicitation: Similarity measures on preference structures. In Gregory F. Cooper and Serafín Moral, editors, *Proceedings of the 14th Conference on Uncertainty in Artificial Intelligence (UAI-98)*, pages 193–201, San Francisco, July 24–26 1998. Morgan Kaufmann.
8. S. Marcus. *Algebraic Linguistics: Analytical Models.* NY: Academic Press, 1967.
9. An Ngo-The and Günther Ruhe. Requirements Negotiation under Incompleteness and Uncertainty. In *Software Engineering Knowledge Engineering 2003 (SEKE 2003)*, San Francisco, CA, USA, July 2003.
10. G. Ruhe, A. Eberlein, and D. Pfahl. Quantitative winwin - a quantitative method for decisione support in requirements negotiation. In *Proceedings 14th International Conference on Software Engineering and Knowledge Engineering (SEKE'02)*, pages 159 – 166, Ischia, Italy, July 2002.
11. Thomas L. Saaty. Fundamentals of the analytic network process. In *Proceedings of International Symposium on Analytical Hierarchy Process*, 1999.
12. Thomas L. Saaty and Luis G. Vargas. *Decision Making in Economic, Political, Social and Technological Environments With the Analytic Hierarchy Process.* RWS Publications, 1994.

Complex Knowledge in the Environmental Domain: Building Intelligent Architectures for Water Management

Dino Borri, Domenico Camarda, and Laura Grassini

Dipartimento di Architettura e Urbanistica, Politecnico di Bari,
via Orabona 4, 70125 Bari, Italy
Tel. +39.080.5963347, Fax +39.080.5963348,
d.camarda@poliba.it

Abstract. The upcoming argumentative approach to environmental planning is increasingly spreading out, challenging the traditional strong and absolute rationality of planning. Aiming at structuring the complex issues of the environmental domain, rather than simplify problems, several agents need to interact, locate and share behaviours and knowledge, meanwhile learning from each others' attitudes and knowledge patterns. In this context, cybernetic rationality is being increasingly re-considered as a quite strong theoretical limitation to environmental planning, a background being founded on merely linear paths of elements and states which is hard to be removed. This rationality is indeed able to cope with deterministic processes, but unable to face the probabilistic and chaotic environmental phenomena, so making it extremely hard to point out elements, to schedule times, to respect consistencies. Given this starting conceptual condition, this paper discusses some theoretical and experimental issues for the development of cognitive architectures of intelligent agent communities in water resources management. This is done through the recognition of the common good nature of water resources, which in turn affects the features of social and individual cognitions involved, as well as the decisions processes. Throughout the paper, a special attention is paid to dilemmas of cognitive change and knowledge-in-actions development in multi-agent participatory environments, through references to both cognitive and organizational analysis.

1 Introduction[1]

Fundamental common goods – continental water, deserts, forests, oceans – are increasingly at risk in the planet Earth, as they are invested by populations and transformations exceeding their carrying capacities. As a consequence, scientific and political efforts to protect them are spreading. At the same time, public involvement

[1] The present study was carried out by the authors as a joint research work. Nonetheless, sections 2 and 5 were written by D.Borri, sections 3 and 4.2 by D.Camarda, sections 1 and 4.1 by L.Grassini.

M. Ali and F. Esposito (Eds.): IEA/AIE 2005, LNAI 3533, pp. 762 – 772, 2005.

in decision-making is increasingly seen as a cornerstone of democratic ideals and, besides, a necessary practical means of putting decisions into effect. In the water sector, in particular, both at the international and local levels, participatory arenas are increasingly being set up to build collaborative decisions and visions [10, 26]. However, traditional approaches to public involvement, which rely heavily on information campaigns, facilitated discussions, and public hearings for conveying information, frequently leave participants dissatisfied, so that new frameworks are needed to enable public participation into decision-making, especially if supported by ICT tools [22].

This paper discusses some theoretical and experimental issues for the development of cognitive architectures for water management. Special attention is paid to architectures and dilemmas of cognitions and actions implied by the participatory frames, that is by the situations in which power is shared among a number of agents.

In so doing, the present paper tries to explore the cognitive potentials of interaction, where cognition is considered an evolving frame on which interaction can play, perhaps, a major role in eliciting hidden relationships and attitudes. Which are the real potentials of multi-agent interactions in this respect? How far multi-agent interactions can really foster more in-depth explorations of any problematic situation and unravel aspects of individual and collective knowledge which remain hidden in the traditional mono-logic cognitive processes? These are the core questions that this paper tries to address, aiming at highlighting some promising research patterns by making reference either to theoretical debate and to empirical analysis.

The paper structure is made up as follows. After this introductory note, section 2 critically discusses the specific features of social and individual cognitions on common goods from the perspective of their interaction in participatory processes. This issue is further explored in section 3, where some issues for building effective cognitive architecture to support participatory decisions and knowledge-sharing for common goods are sketched out. In this section, some fundamental typologies of decisions in this field are discussed, making explicit references to decision processes and knowledge-in-action development. In the following section, cognitive change in participatory decision making for common goods are tackled, and mechanisms for change within organizations are discusses through references to research in both cognitive and organizational field. In section 5, some key aspects of the organization of forums are shown up, with a particular reference to cognitive exchanges involved. Finally, in section 6 some tools and cognitive architecture for Intelligent Agent Communities are discussed so leading to some concluding remarks in the last section.

2 Common Goods and Their Cognitions

From the point of view of multi-agent cognition and of communicative planning for use and protection of water resources, our interest goes to (i) exploring the ways in which a number of agents share basic cognitions about some fundamental common goods and (ii) starting from socially diffuse knowledge on common goods and from particular and/or contingent technical or political knowledge, developing – with the support of intelligent information technologies – integrated cognitive environments useful for local communities for sustainable resource management [1, 3, 4].

Social and individual cognitions about common goods – for aspects both fundamental and contingent – still lack of specific investigation, in particular from the point of view of the information technologies. Either belonging to a glacier or a river or a sea, water is well known in its essential sensorially – also emotionally – perceivable characteristics to the community living around and experiencing it. At the same time water reveales itself to scientific analysis through a set of characteristics – also not immediately perceivable – that are knowable through systematic reflection and experimentation[2]. The internal boundaries of this general – common and expert – knowledge are not easily definable, also because of the strong interrelation of the two components of the system.

What are the differences – if differences exist – in community cognitions relating to common goods or to particular goods? For the exploratory aims of this paper we assume that differences could only exist in the extent of the experience of these goods that is made by communities and individuals belonging to them (an extent, for example, which generates the monstruosities and fears often crowding wide waters or forests), which produces relevant basic cognitive frames, different from the modest ones often relating to particular goods or resources.

What are the peculiarities, on this terrain, of decisions and knowledges-in-action relating to common goods? This question does not have – as it is always for problems of cognition-in-action – absolute answers. One can observe, in the light of the above mentioned considerations, that – because of the fact that common goods perform roles of environmental dominants[3] – in this case decisions and knowledges-in-action are, on one side, captured within schemes and routines based on consolidated and traditional knowledges and experiences, accessible according to the models of libraries and related multi-objective and multifunction indexes. On the other side, they are driven towards innovative schemes and routines by concurrent strengths and by augmented probabilities of creative transformation of pieces of reality depending on the magnitude of the group of involved agents[4].

There is consequently a particular intense tension between tradition and innovation, between the conservative uses of schemes and routines – pieces of represented reality – stored in memories with basic features shared by cognitive-experiential multi-agents in the community and the transformative ones, whose variety increases with increasing numbers of involved agents.

In these processes, decisions and knowledges-in-action get basic co-ordination by some fundamentals of the common goods. They demand, however, further – more intentional and political – coordination. This is directed both to allow the development of autonomous initiatives of local agents on local phenomena of common goods not threatening global functional coherences of these common goods (that is, using an analogy, phenomena that are contained in the margins of resilience and adaptability of those common goods when we conceive them as systems) and to

---

[2] For the integration of experience and reflection, following Chomsky's suggestions, good references still come from the seminal works by Russell [18], Goodman [9], Quine [17].

[3] For the concept of environmental dominant see Maciocco [15, 16].

[4] For this quantitative-probabilistic view of creativity as transformation of reality starting from parts of it, and for the fundamental role played by memory in the transformation, see Borri, 2002.

find out wider functional or merely ideal field agreements[5] on those common goods in their wholes.

This is a co-ordination demanding the existence of dedicated agents when the elements that need to be co-ordinated exceed certain number, strength, and/or speed thresholds not definable in the abstract as they depend on the context of the communities and phenomena associated with the co-ordinations and their subjective and objective needs. Pre-existent or emerging constraints to decisions and knowledges-in-action, deriving from the control functions activated by the communities of agents and their institutions in order to preserve common goods, in complex ecological play of mutual equilibria [8], generally reduce the dimensions of problem spaces otherwise intractable.

3 The Organization of Forums

In setting up forum activities, agents are usually selected in order to respect a composition of stakeholders that is intended to be as broader as possible. From institutional to non-governmental, from working to non-working, from powerful to no-voice stakeholders are supposed to be invited to participate in forums, in order to coherently simulate the complexity of the domains involved in the decision-making process. Internet-based interactive platforms are also increasingly used, with the aim of involving as many agents as possible without pulling them away from their daily activity and, so having a larger process participation. The main aim is to build up distributed/shared interpretative platforms, where the interaction among stakeholders is long lasting, being possible to allow the collection and contextual comparison of the different forms of knowledge recognizable in different languages, representations and discourses [7, 12, 23].

Within the interaction process, the exclusion (or the over-inclusion) of stakeholders may imply an exclusion of several cognitive contributions from (or an over-inclusion in) the issues at hand, with possible related problems for democratic and effective decision-making. From the cognition standpoint, this means that the knowledge patrimony involved in multi-agent small-group interactions is strongly affected by a cognitive asymmetry toward some forms of knowledge, to the detriment of the others [19, 20]. In the environmental domain, intrinsically complex and characterized by a widely recognized presence of common, non-standardized, 'non-expert' forms of knowledge, an asymmetry to the advantage of 'expert' knowledge is able to affect the planning process making it ineffectual. In the domain of common goods, such as the water resource, where the need for grasping experiential, innate knowledge representations from communities is crucial to support decisions, the underestimation of non-standard cognitive contributions is even more dangerous, since it can induce false semantics, with the risk of allowing erroneous or unapt policy actions.

Notwithstanding such risks, in general, a character of casualness seems to inform the decision-making process, at least in its preliminary forum interaction stage. Stakeholders may join and leave the process with casual procedures and in casual

---

[5] For the concept of field agreement regarding the sharing of environmental values and intentions in human communities and their geographies, see Maciocco and Tagliagambe [14]; for the concept of operational agreement on partial truths in plans, see Borri [4].

times, but their contribution is always worthwhile and cannot be disregarded. This situation is able to challenge the intentionality that traditionally orients the setting up of planning processes, and poses questions about how to handle this apparent contradiction. This is not but a further aspect of the complexity of the environmental domain, that today's system architectures aimed at supporting decision-making need to address to achieve acceptable effectiveness.

4 Cognitive Architectures for Intelligent Agent Communities

4.1 Cognitive Mapping for Peripheral Reasoning

Cognitive maps are currently being used by our research group as an effective support for participatory cognitive interactions among multiple intelligent agents[6] [2, 5]. In particular, we have used cognitive maps as tools supporting participatory exercises within strategic process of environmental future scenario development at different levels. In general, we ask participant agents to draw themselves cognitive maps thanks to a user-friendly computer software[7] (Decision Explorer), so reducing the interference of the researcher and the ambiguities in interpreting the agents' comments. After drawing individual maps, each participant is then asked to read other

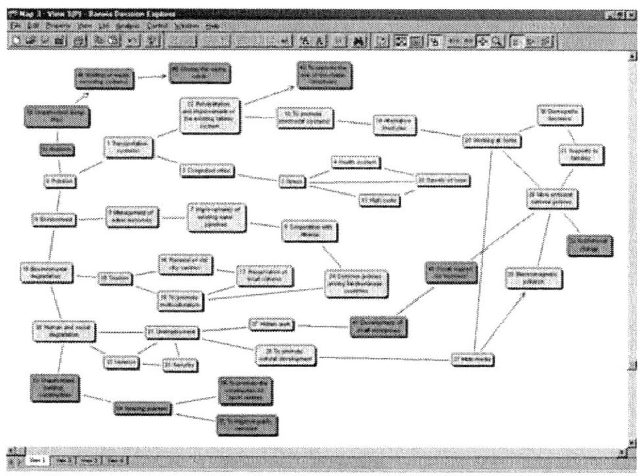

Fig. 1. Cognitive map before (light) and after (light & shaded) participants' interaction

[6] Today, cognitive maps are an important tool in the research field, and their use and applications have quite considerably changed during the last decades, particularly in cognitive-agents interactions [6, 24].

[7] The potential of cognitive mapping for architectures able to support effective participatory processes lies also in the increasing development of computer software able to manage them in a very easy and time-effective way. Decision Explorer© produces maps of concepts and relationships among them, so generating a visual representation of individual or group ideas.

agents' map and to make some changes in their own, if they liked. The results of our first experiments of this kind proved to be quite encouraging, with reference to the potential of cognitive maps to foster cognitive evolutions among participants. In fact, at the end of our experiments we usually found interesting hybridations happening on some benches of individual maps, especially on their peripheral areas. In fig. 1 there is an example of cognitive map drawn during a participatory process for the strategic development of some areas of the Apulia region; in that, shaded concepts are the ones added by participants after the interaction [5].

These first findings, together with the suggestions coming from previous discussions on cognitive reframing and conflict management, prompted us to take our experiments even further. In this light, while conflicts management issues were not specifically addressed in our first experiments, we have recently tried to explore potentials of cognitive maps as a means to foster institutional reframing for shared management of common goods in conflicting domains. In this perspective, we have tried to test if they could be a good support for the process of peripheral reasoning and cognitive change as a means to foster collaborative processes in conflicting communities.

This idea came from the analysis of the structure of cognitive maps, which is composed of nodes and links whose structure clearly shows a core part, storing fundamentals and strong ideas, and pieces of peripheral reasoning, which are linked to them in a tree-like structure. Our first aim was, thus, to organize a participatory experiment where to ask participant agents to draw their own map in order to use them not as holistic representations of agents' points of view but as a source of pieces of reasoning and cognitive branches to be shared among them without reference to the core ideas and values to which they were formally attacched. In this way, participants could get through other agents' cognitions without getting struck into conflicts on differences in core values and positions, while, at the same time, being allowed to attribute their own individual meanings to others' cognitive branches. In this way, we hoped, people could hybridize pieces of cognitions in an easier and less conflicting way.

Indeed, the case we choose, related to the already mentioned case of strategic planning for the Ofanto river basin, was not very successful since very few people got involved in the process, so our results are not robust enough to make general statements out of them. Nevertheless, first results encourages to make further attempt in the same direction and confirm the importance of cognitive maps as a precious tool for effective cognitive architectures for reframing within intelligent agent communities.

4.2 Working Agents in Operational DSS Architectures

Urged by the need of building up process architectures contextualized to different situations and spaces of decision, our research experiences witnessed a continuous modification of architectures themselves. In the general environmental domain, a possible structure should represent a hybrid combination of interoperable software tools and more traditional human-based steps, in the attempt of supporting the exchange of agents' cognitive contents and related frames (fig. 2).

The first step consists in the distribution of preliminary informational material about the subject. In fact, in standard multi-agent forum knowledge generation it is general rule to set up an explicit frame, variously wide and structured, usually exogenous, because of its preparation by the knowledge engineer who is responsible for the exercise and acts as 'intermediate agent' for knowledge facilitation, focusing, mediation [1, 5].

The second step aims at letting agents try to set up the problem space individually, as they perceive it, according to their own knowledge. Agents are stimulated to collect complex individual standpoints on the problem, structured as logical frames of nested concepts and ideas, that can be represented in a rich form [2].

In order to better clarify the concepts put down in the map, in step 3 agents are asked to explain individually the different typology of inferential rules among concepts (temporal, spatial, associative links, etc.). In doing so, they are forced to reflect on the relationships among concepts and, indirectly, to signify concepts themselves and make them more effective and manageable within the process [25]. With the same aim, agents are asked to further argue on one concept on which he/she is more emotionally involved, by using a software tool that manages idea generation, exchange and brainstorming [13].

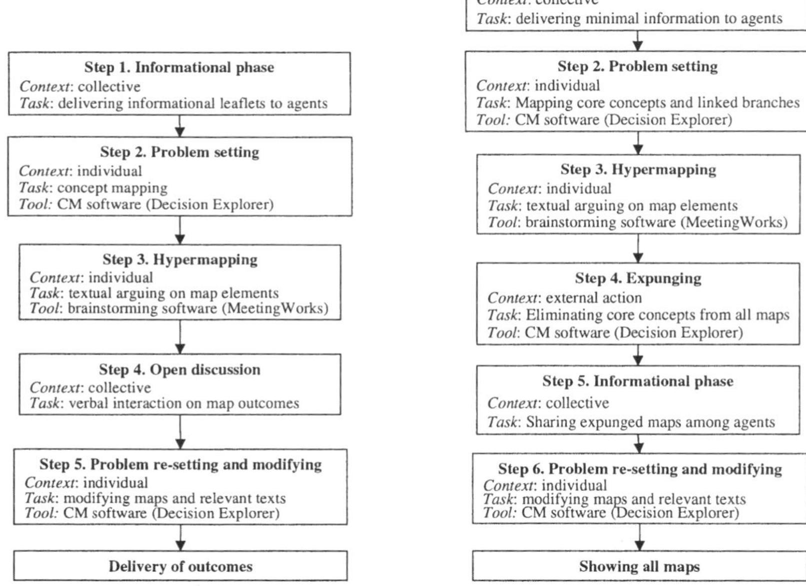

Fig. 2. Architecture for the environmental domain **Fig. 3.** Architecture for common goods management

Step 4 is a collective phase, in which agents are invited to discuss individual outcomes and compare different views, by looking at the collection of maps and textual statements. This step is similar to a sudden irruption of new information in the process, under the form of collective interaction, which lets each agent explore new elements and re-calibrate cognitive levels consequently. This irruption is supposed to modify contents, approaches, representations of the issues at hand: a 'card-shuffling' which should stimulates re-thinking in subsequent phases. This stage can be carried out by using the support of a software tool, as in the previous step: however, some experiences show that a verbal collective interaction is sometimes more able to exchange and clarify cognitive issues among agents, mainly because of emotional reasons [11].

The fifth step is intended to verify if substantial and/or cognitive changes have really occurred after the previous interaction. Agents are asked to modify maps in terms of either conceptual contents, or inferential rules, or value/fact categorization.

In the experimentation carried out in the case of the management of the Ofanto river basin, the space of decisions and of knowledge involved showed the typical characters of common goods. The process to support decision-making was therefore highly rooted on the experiential/innate dimension of knowledge, as said above. This means that the stages of the process should take into particular consideration the cognition frames of agents by, from the one side, enhancing their crucial contribution and, from the other side, preventing their ability to challenge creative modifications of frames themselves (fig. 3).

Also in this particular case, the first step represents the provision of an ex-ante informational picture set up to start the interaction process. However, this previous exogenous framing is not exempt from risks of frustrating the aspirations both to creativity and to democracy that inhere in cognitive exercises per se [21]. In dealing with the management of a river basin (a common good), this risk is to superimpose an exogenous representation of the context to individual cognitive frames, largely endogenous, so loosing the essential experiential/innate dimension of the cognition involved, that is so important in representing the complexity of the common good, as previously said. To minimize such risks, the first step may be only a phase of merely providing agents with the minimal information needed to express the problem space to be dealt with.

Steps 2 and 3 are aimed at the same purposes as in the general environmental case: therefore problem setting and 'hypermapping' are carried out with the same approach as in the general case.

Then, the subsequent stages of the process are channelled toward a really different path in the Ofanto river case study. Dealing with a common good, the handling of individual knowledge frames is important in many ways, as said before, so needing a particular approach to effectively process cognitive contents. With the aim of allowing the free development and restructuring of individual cognition contributions built up around core concepts, such core concepts are expunged from structured maps (step 4), leaving sub-concepts unlinked and available to all agents. Such libraries of free chains of (sub-)concepts are showed to agents as a new piece of information irrupting in the process to shock their frames (step 5), and represent cognitive cues usable to modify own original maps (step 6).

The rationale for this basic processual (and architectural) modification is connected to the fact that maps are the representation of strong individual cognitive frames on the river icon, and they can be overwhelmingly influential to structure developments. In this light, each frame is able to block the creative modifications of other individual frames: the expunging of core concepts from maps is aimed at letting agents exchange knowledge contributions, trying to limit that strong mutual influence. On the other side, each agent uses chains of concepts to enrich and develop own cognitive maps, so enhancing the complexity and de-prejudicialization of cognitive frames and, consequently, their crucial role in supporting decision-making.

Eventually, all modified maps are showed and made available as outputs in the process.

However, as mentioned before, casuality typically informs the real arenas of governance, and agents join and leave processes occasionally and unpredictably. DSS architectures, even hybrid and open, do reveal a certain degree of intrinsic rigidity at many levels, particularly unapt to handle those particularly complex kinds of casual events.

When a new agent joins an interaction session, s/he brings one or more cognitive frames along with her/him, stemming from either an exogenous/ autogenous sedimentation process, or a dynamical interaction with other agents, occurred in other sessions. Other agents in the 'room' are on an ongoing phase of looking for possible settings of a given problem, perhaps without finding coherent structures yet. The most probable contact may occur during this dynamic phase, and the new upcoming agent joins the process running into an existing cognition frame that is still fuzzy.

From this point on, a contact among different cognitive frames occurs. Unfortunately, the risk of a juxtaposition follows, rather than an integration, of frames is high, eventually resulting in a marginalization, or even a disregarding, of the new comer's contribution. In doing so, large part of the richness provided by the new comer can be lost, and the quest for grasping the complexity of problems fails. The reasons of a difficulty in managing the new comer's contribution are various, but often connected with the difficulty that existing agents show in catching the importance, the relevance of a new comer's contribution in real time. Often, the impossibility of understanding the 'quality' of the new cognition frame prevents the new comer from being considered as an 'equal among peers', which is a normal basic condition for a standard democratic forum to work.

In face-to-face forums, there are several informal, often unconscious mechanisms to filter and represent the backing knowledge, the previous experiential, social and cultural history (the cognitive frame) of the new comers. When dealing with on-line, even remote, computer-based forums, this mechanisms prove to be cryptic, and should be unveiled and made explicitly manageable within the process architecture -a hard multi-dimensional and multi-logic task, far from the working range of the toy-block world.

But even if the frames of the upcoming agent should be simplified and made manageable through ad-hoc architectures similar to what said before, the casuality of the joining event would prevent the singling out of definite points of the process in which the connection can be actually set up.

5 Conclusions

Decisions and cognitions-in-action relating to important environmental resources (common goods) provide relevant cues for the building of peculiar architectures of artificial cognitive agents. Questions of sharing and of integration of cognitions for action are confirmed by our initial experiments and insights. Such insights regard both the relevance of roles played by fundamental cognitions (experientially and innately derived) and the difficult tractability of integrative cognitions – as much essential as the fundamental ones – deriving from systematic reasoning and abstraction and logic categorisation abilities performed by integrated intelligent artificial agents.

The system architectures must allow complex co-ordinations of decisions and cognitions-in-action and also for this purpose they must be structured in various levels of abstraction more than concern. In those architectures the starting modules of the cognitive processing can be frames self-generated by the involved communities of agents.

A number of possible types of decisions and cognitions-in-action structure the architectures of multi-agent cognitive systems applied to important environmental resources. They are relevant both to the perceptions and mobilizations of needs and the related organisational chains affecting the communities of agents and the internal and/or external institutions which they refer to.

The systems which we are referring to are then connected in variously made networks and are highly influenced by casual phenomena.

The essential roles played by fundamentals and dominants pose problems of architectures of memories of the cognitions-in-action relating to the various agents involved and consequently of the capacities of transformation of elements of these memories. Interactions between socially shared and highly stable fundamentals – of innate type, lying at the core of the cognitive deposits – and integrative cognitions oriented to change located at the periphery of those deposits pose, in the end, further peculiar problems for the architecture of multi-agent cognitive systems engaged in decision and cognition-in-action tasks relating to common goods.

Also due to such major reasons, concrete examples of DSS architectures are still poorly available. Toward this operational aim further research effort is then needed, in order to attain more effective intelligent-agent-based decision support systems.

References

1. Barbanente, A., Monno, V.: Conoscenze Ambientali e Nuovi Scenari di Sviluppo per la Bassa Valle dell'Ofanto. Paper presented at the Conference "Acqua: Risorsa e Governo", Venice, April (2004).
2. Borri, A., Camarda, D., De Liddo, A.: Envisioning Environmental Futures: Multi-Agent Knowledge Generation, Frame Problem, Cognitive Mapping. In Luo Y. (ed.), Cooperative Design, Visualization and Engineering. Springer Verlag, Berlin (2004) 138-147.
3. Borri, D., Camarda, D.: Dealing with Multi-Agents in Environmental Planning: A Scenario-Building Approach. Studies in Regional and Urban Planning, forthcoming.
4. Borri, D.: Intelligent Learning Devices in Planning. Invited lecture at the Seminar on Computational Models in Design and Planning Support. Center for Advanced Spatial Analysis, University College London, London, September (2002).
5. Borri, D., Camarda, D., Grassini, L.: Distributed Knowledge in Environmental Planning: A Hybrid IT-based Approach to Building Future Scenarios. Paper presented at the 3rd Joint AESOP-ACSP Conference, Leuven, July (2003).
6. Eden, C., Ackermann, F.: Cognitive Mapping Expert Views for Policy Analysis in the Public Sector. European Journal of Operational Research, 152 (2004), 615-630.

7. Forester, J.: The Deliberative Practitioner. Encouraging Participatory Planning Processes. MIT Press, Cambridge (1999).
8. Friedmann, J.: Planning in the Public Domain. From Knowledge to Action. Princeton University Press, Princeton (1987).
9. Goodman, N.: Fact, Fiction and Forecast. Harvard University Press, Cambridge (1955).
10. GWP-TAC – Global Water Partnership/Technical Advisory Committee: Integrated Water Resources Management. TAC background papers, 4 (2000).
11. Khakee, A., Barbanente, A., Camarda, D., Puglisi, M.: With or Without? Comparative Study of Preparing Participatory Scenarios Using Computer-Aided and Traditional Brainstorming. Journal of Future Research, 6(4), (2002) 45-64
12. Laurini, R.: Information Systems for Urban Planning: A Hypermedia Co-operative Approach. Taylor & Francis, London (2001).
13. Lewis, F.L., Shakun, M.F.: Using a Group Support System to Implement Evolutionary System Design. Group Decision and Negotiation, 5 (1996) 319-337.
14. Maciocco, G., Tagliagambe, S.: La Città Possibile. Dedalo, Bari (1997).
15. Maciocco, G. (ed.): La Pianificazione Ambientale del Paesaggio. FrancoAngeli, Milano (1991).
16. Maciocco, G. (ed.): Le Dimensioni Ambientali della Pianificazione Urbana. FrancoAngeli, Milano (1991).
17. Quine, W.V.O.: Linguistics and Philosophy. In Hook S. (ed.), Language and Philosophy. New York University Press, New York (1969).
18. Russell, B.: Human Knowledge: Its Scope and Limits. Simon & Schuster, New York (1948)
19. Sardar, Z., Ravetz, J.R. (eds.): Cyberfutures: Culture and Politics on the Information Superhighway. New York University Press, New York (2001).
20. Shakun, M.: Consciousness, Spirituality and Decision/Negotiation in Purposeful Complex Adaptive Systems. Group Decision and Negotiation, 8 (1999) 1-15.
21. Shanahan, M.: Solving the Frame Problem. MIT Press, Cambridge (1997).
22. Stave, K.: Using System Dynamics to Improve Public Participation in Environmental Decisions. System Dynamics Review, 18 (2002) 139-167.
23. Talen, E.: Bottom-up GIS: A New Tool for Individual and Group Expression in Participatory Planning. Journal of the American Planning Association, 66 (2000) 279-294.
24. Tegarden, D.P., Sheetz, S.D.: Group Cognitive Mapping: A Methodology and System for Capturing and Evaluating Managerial and Organizational Cognition. Omega, 31 (2003) 113-125.
25. Warren, T., Gibson, E.: The Influence of Referential Processing on Sentence Complexity. Cognition, 85 (2002) 79-112
26. WSSCC – Water Supply and Sanitation Collaborative Council: Vision 21. A Shared Vision for Water Supply, Sanitation and Hygiene & a Framework for Future Action (1999).

An Expert System for the Oral Anticoagulation Treatment

Benedetta Barbieri[1], Giacomo Gamberoni[2], Evelina Lamma[2], Paola Mello[3], Piercamillo Pavesi[4], and Sergio Storari[2]

[1] Dianoema S.p.A., Via de' Carracci 93, 40100 Bologna, Italy
bbarbieri@ing.unife.it
[2] ENDIF, University of Ferrara, Via Saragat 1, 44100 Ferrara, Italy
{ggamberoni,elamma,sstorari}@ing.unife.it
[3] DEIS, University of Bologna, Viale Risorgimento 2, 40136 Bologna, Italy
pmello@deis.unibo.it
[4] Cardiologic Division, "Maggiore" Hospital, Largo Bartolo Nigrisoli 2, 40133 Bologna, Italy
piercamillo.pavesi@ausl.bologna.it

Abstract. Several attempts have been recently provided to define Oral Anticoagulant (OA) guidelines. These guidelines include indications for oral anticoagulation and suggested arrangements for the management of an oral anticoagulant service. They aim to take care of the current practical difficulties involved in the safe monitoring of the rapidly expanding numbers of patients on long-term anticoagulant therapy. Nowadays, a number of computer-based systems exist for supporting hematologists in the oral anticoagulation therapy. Nonetheless, computer-based support improves the quality of the Oral Anticoagulant Therapy (OAT) and also possibly reduces the number of scheduled laboratory controls. In this paper, we describe DNTAO-SE, a system which integrates both knowledge based and statistical techniques in order to support hematologists in the definition of OAT prescriptions to solve the limitations of the currently proposed OAT systems. The statistical method is used to learn both the optimal dose adjustment for OA and the time date required for the next laboratory control. In the paper, besides discussing the validity of these approaches, we also present experimental results obtained by running DNTAO-SE on a database containing more than 13000 OAT prescriptions. This paper is a better structured and complete version of a paper previously published in the "Intelligenza Artificiale" national italian journal edited by the AI*IA society [3].

1 Introduction

The Oral Anticoagulant Therapy (OAT) is an important treatment to prevent and treat thrombosis events, either venous or arterial. In the last few years these kinds of pathologies have been increased and, as a consequence, also the number of patients being treated with OA is growing. Several attempts have been provided recently to define guidelines for the correct management of Oral Anticoagulant Therapy (OAT). These guidelines include indications for oral anticoagulation and suggested

M. Ali and F. Esposito (Eds.): IEA/AIE 2005, LNAI 3533, pp. 773 – 782, 2005.

arrangements for the management of an oral anticoagulant service. They aim to take care of the current practical difficulties involved in the safe monitoring of the rapidly expanding numbers of patients on long-term oral anticoagulant therapy.

Nowadays, a number of computer-based systems exist (see [4,10,11] for instance) for supporting haematologists in OAT management. Nonetheless, computer-based support improves the OAT quality and also possibly reduces the number of scheduled laboratory controls. Most of these systems follow an algorithmic approach and do not allow as much flexibility as required by haematologists. On the other hand, they do not support haematologists in all the OAT therapy phases.

In this paper, we show how the integration of state-of-the-art artificial intelligence and statistical techniques can solve the limitation of such systems. Artificial intelligence techniques have been applied to the medical field since 1980, in order to develop intelligent knowledge based systems capable to support hospital personnel in many routine activities which require high quality levels and flexibility. Statistical techniques and, in particular, regression analysis have been used for 20 years to evaluate the relation between the prothrombin time against time following the loading dose of OA drug [10].

These techniques have been integrated and refined in a medical decision support system named DNTAO-SE which manages all the OAT therapy phases and helps haematologists in increasing the quality of their work. This quality improvement has been evaluated in a testing trial performed on 13000 OAT prescriptions performed by an hospital in Bologna (Italy) from January 2004 to December 2004.

The paper is organized as follows. In Section 2 we briefly introduce OAT and its phases. Section 3 describes DNTAO-SE objectives and architecture. Section 4 describes the experiments conducted for learning the regression model for automatic dose suggestion. Section 5 describes a test conducted in order to evaluate DNATO-SE suggestion reliability. Section 6 presents some related works. Finally Section 7 concludes and presents future works.

2 Oral Anticoagulant Therapy

The Oral Anticoagulant Therapy (OAT) is an important treatment to prevent and treat thrombotic events, either venous or arterial.

In the last few years these kinds of pathologies have been increased and, as a consequence, also the number of patients being treated with OA is growing: at this moment, patients being treated with OA in Italy are about 400000. In some clinical circumstances (stroke, atrial fibrillation, venous thrombosis etc.), the OA treatment has a determined period. In other pathologies, which are the greatest part of indications (mechanical prosthetic heart valve, recurrence of arterial thromboembolism, inherited thrombophilia), the treatments last the patient's entire life. In this case, treatment looks like a therapy for a chronic disease for patients of every age. It is necessary to keep the same decoagulation level of the blood to prevent occlusion, because in high-risk cases it can be fatal to the patient. This is the reason why patients under OAT are continuously under surveillance.

The International Normalized Ratio (INR) is the recommended method for reporting prothrombin time results for control of blood anticoagulation. A patient's

INR indicates to the doctor how to adjust the dose of Warfarin, or other oral vitamin K antagonist, trying to keep the INR near to the centre (target) of a fixed range of values, called therapeutic range. Therapeutic range is different from patient to patient, according to his cardiac disease, and is determined on the patient's therapeutic indication.

Therapy is based on three main phases: stabilization phase, maintenance phase, management of the INR excesses. The first objective of the therapy is to stabilize the patient's INR into the therapeutic range and then find the right dose of Warfarin needed on the second phase (maintenance phase) to keep INR in the range. The process of stabilization is very delicate and if it is badly managed, serious hemorrhagic events can occur. In this phase, the INR level must be checked daily and the next dose must be calibrated at every coagulation test, until the INR is stable. This objective is usually achieved within a week. Once stabilization is reached is necessary to find the maintenance dose: this dose is the one capable to keep the INR stable inside the range (when there are no other clinic complications that can modify the coagulation level). In this phase, control frequency can be reduced from daily to weekly and in some cases to monthly (if the patient shows a high grade of stability). If INR value gets off the therapeutic range more than the 25% of the range amplitude, specific dose adjustments are necessary.

The increasing number of OAT patients and the cutting of the INR evaluation points make necessary to improve the quality of the OAT prescriptions supporting the haematologists in the evaluation of each patient and in the adoption of international OAT guidelines. It also necessary to focus the haematologist and nurse's attention to the most critical cases which need a more detailed and accurate information collection. To reach these goals is becoming crucial the development of a software capable to provide a reliable OAT therapy support.

3 DNTAO-SE

DNTAO-SE, also described in details in [3], is a medical decision support system developed in order to improve DNTAO [5], an OAT data management system, by introducing as new functionality the automatic suggestion of the most suitable OAT prescription (dose and next control date).

The development of DNTAO-SE has been based on several considerations about the different steps followed by OA patients, nurses and haematologists for the execution of an OAT control. In the first step, a patient goes to the OAT control centre, where a nurse makes questions about the therapy status and other related events (Checklist) occurred after the last therapy prescription. In the second step, a blood sample is taken, and then is sent to a lab to be analyzed by an automatic device. The blood sample test is needed to measure the INR level. In the third step, a haematologist evaluates the checklist, the INR level, the patient clinical history (formerly INR levels and assigned doses in the previous prescriptions) and other relevant clinical information in order to define the next prescription.

DNTAO-SE supports the haematologist in the third step, automatically retrieving all the information previously described and applying a knowledge base and an

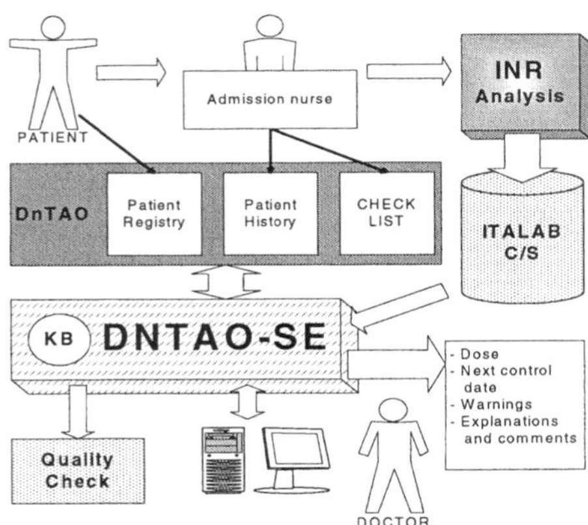

Fig. 1. Prototype architecture

inference engine to propose the most suitable next prescription. The proposed prescription is then manually revised by the haematologists in order to define the final one. The architecture of the DNTAO-SE prototype is shown in Fig. 1.

3.1 DNTAO-SE Knowledge Base

DNTAO-SE uses its knowledge base to subdivide patients in four categories: high risk patients; medium risk patients; low risk patients who need little therapy adjustment; low risk patients who do not need a therapy change.

DNTAO-SE defines a patient at high risk if almost one of these conditions is verified: he is starting the OAT therapy; he is restarting the therapy; he has delayed or anticipated the INR check; he has a very high or low INR level; he has an excessive INR change; he has the INR significantly out his therapeutic range. Each condition triggers a different therapy management.

The other patients may be at medium or low risk. A patient is at medium risk if almost one of these conditions is verified: he has alarms in his checklist; he had a high INR change; he is subjected to very low or very high drug doses; he was instable in almost one of the last three INR check; he has an INR out the therapeutic range. If none of these conditions are verified, the patient is defined at low risk.

For medium risk patient, DNTAO-SE automatically proposes a dose adjustment in order to reach the desired INR value. This dose adjustment is defined by using a regression model described in Section 4.

For low risk patient, DNTAO-SE confirms the drug dose assigned in the previous prescription and possibly proposes a temporary dose adjustment for the first two prescription days.

For what concerns the prescription length: for high risk patient, DNTAO-SE sets the next control date within a week; for medium and low risk patients, it computes the most frequent OAT prescription time length and sets the next control date within this time value (usually about two weeks for medium risk and four week for low risk).

3.2 Automatic Dose Adjustment for Medium Risk Patients

For medium risk patient DNTAO-SE automatically proposes a dose adjustment by using a regression model [2] that describes the behaviour of the INR with respect to some OAT variables. This model is learned from a database of OAT prescriptions. The development of this model is described in Section 4.

When DNTAO-SE have to propose a dose adjustment, it puts all the relevant information about the patient in the model, computes the difference between the measured INR and the target one and obtains from the model the dose change necessary to achieve the required INR change.

The models are periodically recomputed, in order to be improved by the new available information and to care of changes in the OAT biological process.

3.3 Prototype Implementation

The DNTAO-SE knowledge base and inference engine were developed by using Kappa-PC by Intellicorp [6]. All the conditions described in Section 3.1 were formalized in rules. An example of a DNTAO-SE rule is the following:

```
If      INR > EXTRangeUP          Or
        INR < EXTRangeDOWN
Then    INRoverextrarange = TRUE
```

This simple rule tests if the INR is significantly over the therapeutic range: it compares the INR value with the range border values *EXTRangeUP* e *EXTRangeDOWN* that usually are the ones of the therapeutic range augmented by 25%.

DNTAO-SE lets the haematologists tune the knowledge base, because it allows them to update for each rule, the structure and its parameters. The inference engine follows the forward chaining reasoning methodology.

During the prescription definition, the DNTAO-SE graphic user interface, shown in Fig. 2, presents to the haematologists the reasoning conclusions that can be accepted or discarded.

4 Models for Automatic Dose Prescription

As described in Section 3.2, one of the main objectives of DNTAO-SE is to efficiently manage medium risk patients. To reach this objective, we decided to use regression models [2] learned from dataset of OAT prescriptions.

In our experiments, the observations are composed by parameters which express the linkage between the prescribed anticoagulant dose and the induced INR. The initial available dataset was composed by more than 40000 OAT prescriptions (INR, OA drug dose and next control date) performed in four years at an italian hospital in Bologna on more than 1000 patients. Following the indications of some haematologists, we identified the target of the model (i.e. the parameter which has to be described) and the set of OAT parameters to be used as model variables.

The target is the dose variation percentage that represents the percentage of weekly dose variation between the new prescription and the previous one.

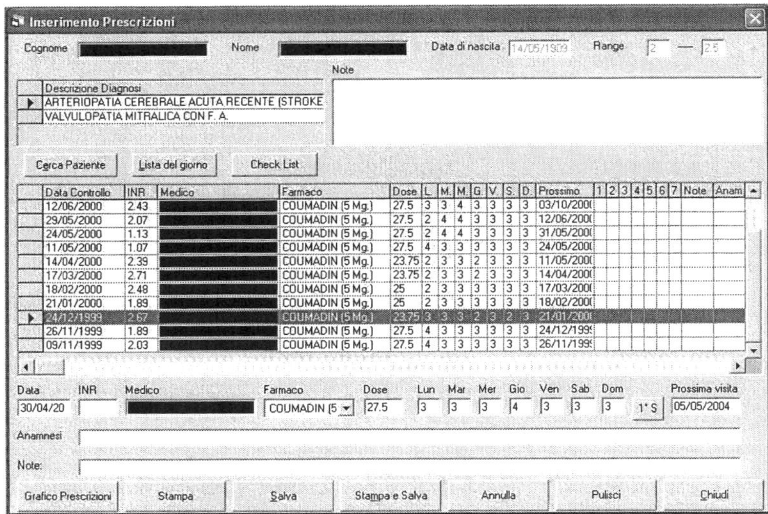

Fig. 2. DNTAO-SE graphic user interface

The most interesting OAT parameters to be considered are: the starting dose (the weekly anticoagulant dose (in mg) assumed since the previous OAT), referred as dose_start; the dose variation percentage (percentage of dose variation between the starting dose and the one assigned in the prescription), referred as delta_dose_perc; the INR variation percentage (percentage of INR variation induced by the dose variation), referred as delta_INR_perc; the therapeutic range assigned to the patient; the patient's age; the patient's sex; the main therapeutic indication (the diagnosis that has led the patient to start the OAT).

Given the OAT database, we grouped the ones associated to the same patient. Starting from this group of prescriptions, we decided to exclude some of them, considered unsuccessful. The exclusion criterion establishes that if the INR value found during the OAT control at time T, and induced by dose variation proposed during the OAT control at time T-1, is out of patient therapeutic range, then the prescription made by the haematologist at time T-1 is assumed to be unsuccessful and the relative prescription has not to be taken into account for regression model learning. We also consider only the prescription relative to the Warfarin drug because the DNATO-SE knowledge base contains only rules about its management. Applying these exclusion criteria, the number of prescriptions suitable for building a regression model was reduced to 23192: this set of prescriptions is referred in the paper as whole dataset (WD).

The starting point of our experiments was a simple regression model:

delta_dose_perc = f (dose_start * delta_INR_perc, delta_INR_perc)

Given this model (referred as general-DNTAO), we tried to develop a new model capable to achieve a significant improvement. The experiments, described in details in [7], was conducted in three steps: in the first, we modified the model function; in the second, we identified group of affine prescriptions, which requires a specific model; in the third, we combined the results achieved in the previous steps and built the final set of models used by DNTAO-SE.

Considering the results of the previous experiments, we decided to use in DNTAO-SE three models: one for starting dose less than 5 mg/week (referred as group1), one for starting dose greater than 50 mg/week (referred as group2) and one for the remaining prescriptions (named reduced dataset or RD).

For group1 and group2, the regression models use the same function as general-DNTAO but are obtained learning the model on the respective prescriptions.

About group3, performing further evaluations on this dataset, we observed that the relation between dose_start and the ratio of delta_dose_perc on delta_INR_perc is similar to a logarithmic function. For this reason we introduced a new model referred as ln-DNTAO:

$$\text{delta\_dose\_perc} = f\left(\frac{\text{delta\_INR\_perc}}{\ln(\text{dose\_iniz}/2)}, \text{delta\_INR\_perc}\right)$$

The ln-DNTAO performance on RD ($R^2 = 0.2667$)[1] improves the general-DNTAO one ($R^2 = 0.2386$) by 11.8% and involves the prescriptions in the reduced dataset (RD) that are the 96% of the ones in the whole dataset (WD).

5 DNTAO-SE Testing

In order to evaluate the performance of DNTAO-SE knowledge base and its regression model set (described in Section 4), we used a new dataset of approximately 13000 OAT prescriptions performed by an hospital in Bologna (Italy) from January 2004 to December 2004.

DNTAO-SE suggestions were compared with the haematologist's ones and the results are reported in Table 1. The central columns of this table report the average of days and doses difference (in percentage) among DNTAO-SE and haematologist suggestions. Analyzing these results, we observe that DNTAO-SE works very well on low (9.3% of the dataset prescriptions) and medium (69% of the dataset prescriptions) risk patients. The test provided many insights to haematologists too (we discovered some mistakes done by them).

Then we evaluated the DNTAO-SE ability to maintain the patient in medium or low risk. Table **2** shows that considering all the prescriptions made by haematologists, the patients stay in medium or low risk levels for 77.7% of the total therapy days. In the second row, you can see the statistics related to a prescription subset named concordant prescriptions (a prescription is concordant when the computer aided prescription is equal to the one prescribed by haematologists). DNTAO-SE maintains

---

1 In order to evaluate the performance of a regression model the literature introduces the linear determination coefficient R^2 [2], that gives the evaluation of the performance of a regression model:

- $R^2 = 1$, means that the regression model perfectly forecast the target variable;
- $R^2 = 0$, means that the regression model has a forecast accuracy level equal to that of the average of target variable.

the patient risk level medium or low in the 80.33% of their therapy time length. The third row shows the same statistics for discordant prescriptions. The concordant prescription performances are higher than the ones achieved by haematologists, when they disagree with the DNTAO-SE suggestion, and by the most representative OAT support systems in literature [10]. Staying for a long time in medium and low risk led to an improvement of the patient quality of life.

Table 1. Dosage and days difference between haematologist and DNTAO-SE prescriptions

Patient category	Number of prescriptions	Average date prescription difference (in days)	Average dose difference
Low risk	1297	3.48	6.97%
Medium risk	9550	5.04	3.99%
High risk	2993	8.88	27.78%

Table 2. Patient risk level induced by DNTAO-SE prescription suggestions

	Days	Days in medium-low risk level	Days in high risk level
Total prescriptions	228557	222904 (77.7%)	63653 (22.3%)
Concordant prescriptions	172958	138950 (80.33%)	34008 (17.67%)
Discordant prescriptions	113599	83954 (73.9%)	29645 (26.1%)

6 Related Work

Some computer systems are nowadays used for OAT management. Among the analyzed systems, we briefly describe PARMA [10]. PARMA (Program for Archive, Refertation and Monitoring of Anticoagulated patients) is a product of Instrumentation Laboratory [7] realized in collaboration with many hospitals in Parma (Italy). The basic characteristics of this system are: management of patient records, an algorithm for the automatic suggestion of OAT therapy; automated reporting; statistical analysis.

Comparing PARMA with DNTAO-SE, the most significant difference is in the adopted approach: the first uses a rigid algorithmic approach; the second uses a knowledge based approach that allow an high flexibility. DNTAO-SE allows haematologists to update its knowledge base by creating and modifying rule structures and parameters, increasing the system performances. DNTAO-SE also offers a more complete support for OAT patient and, in particular, high risk patients. The prescriptions proposed by DNTAO-SE for medium risk patient are reliable as they are defined by a refined and advanced regression model.

For a methodology comparison, in last years were developed several tools, in order to perform an intelligent management of medical guidelines. These approaches, e.g. ASGAARD [12], GLARE [13] and PROforma [6], give a graphic formalization tool by which the user can represent the different guidelines parts, and use this representation to assist the medical personnel in the evaluation of a clinic case.

DNTAO-SE, does not provide a graphical representation of the guideline, but formalizes this by mean of a rule set and an inference engine, giving decision support for therapy definition. Our approach is certainly more specific and less generalizable. This choice is due to our necessity of a fast implementation of a prototype, using a classical expert system development tool, for a trade off between readability and performance. Using one of these guideline formalization tools in this field can be very interesting in order to test their advantages, in particular the graphical management tool and the on-line valuation of consequence of the available actions.

Another approach in decision support system development is Case Based Reasoning [1]. A case based reasoner solves new problems by using or adapting solutions that were used to solve old problems. This approach is useful when there are no guidelines to follow. In our problem we literature proposes a lot of OAT guidelines that can be easily formalized in order to be used as rules of a knowledge base for a OAT decision support system. Nevertheless, our approach for managing medium risk patients is similar to the one used in CBR as we both use the old cases as knowledge for suggesting the best therapy for the new ones. We differ in the representation of this knowledge: CBR finds the old cases much closer to the new one and proposes a similar solution; DNTAOSE builds a regression model, based on past successful prescriptions, and uses this model to manage the new cases.

7 Conclusions and Future Work

In this paper we described a system for supporting haematologists in the definition of Oral Anticoagulant Therapy (OAT) prescriptions. DNTAO-SE automatically provides this support, retrieving all the information about the patient clinical history (formerly INR levels and drug doses in the previous prescriptions) and other relevant clinical information. Then it applies a knowledge base and an inference engine in order to propose the most suitable next therapy. During the reasoning, the patients are classified in three risk levels and for each level, a specific therapy definition method is used.

With respect to other OAT management systems (that usually can manage only therapy start and maintaining), DNTAO-SE offers a more complete support to haematologists, because it manages all the OAT phases included the return in the therapeutic range of patients with an INR level significantly out of it.

The suggestion of the most suitable therapy dose for medium risk patient is achieved by using a regression model learned on dataset of previous OAT prescriptions. Although this approach has been used also by other systems, the models used in DNTAO-SE are more sophisticated and can guarantee better performances. In the paper we described in details (see Section 4) every step of the development of these regression models.

The DNTAO-SE performance test, executed on a real dataset of prescriptions (see Section 5), has shown the reliability of its suggestions. This validation test also provided many insights to haematologists too (we discovered some of their mistakes).

In the future we plan to further improve the reliability of DNTAO-SE knowledge base and regression model, collecting more information about the patient anamnesis (structured checklist).

The approach described in this paper may be used in several domains in which guidelines are available. It allows a rapid prototyping: the guidelines can be quickly formalized in rules. These rules represent a knowledge base that aids the user managing a new case in a way compliant to the guideline. The paper also shows how regression may be used to represent and use knowledge about past cases, when a function model is needed, as in case of dosage adjustment.

Acknowledgements. This work has been partially supported by BMG Consulting S.r.l. under the regional project "Innovative actions in health care" Prot. AIA/PSE/03 n. 25281 19/8/03. The authors would like to thank Giuseppe Larosa for his help.

References

1. Aamodt, A., Plaza, E.: Case-based reasoning: Foundational issues, methodological variations and system approaches. AI Communications 7(1) (1994) 39–59
2. Anderson, D. R., Sweeney, D. J., Williams, T. A.: Introduction to Statistics concepts and applications, Third Edition, West Publishing Company (1994)
3. Barbieri, B., Gamberoni, G., Lamma, E., Mello, P., Pavesi, P., Storari, S.: Un sistema basato sulla conoscenza per la terapia anticoagulante orale. Intelligenza Artificiale 4, AIIA, (2004)
4. DAWN AC 6, see the web site: http://www.4s-dawn.com
5. Dianoema S.p.A., see the web site: http://www.dianoema.it
6. Fox, J., Johns, N., Rahmanzadeh, A., Thomson, R..: Disseminating medical knowledge: the PROforma approach. Artificial Intelligence in Medicine 14 (1998) 157-181
7. Gamberoni, G., Lamma, E., Mello, P., Pavesi, P., Storari, S.: Learning the Dose Adjustment for the Oral Anticoagulation Treatment. To be published in the proceedings of the 5th International Symposium on Biological and Medical Data Analysis (ISBMDA-2004), Springer LNCS 3337 (2004)
8. Instrumentation Laboratory, see the web site: http://www.il-italia.it/
9. Intellicorp Inc., see the web site: http://www.intellicorp.com
10. Mariani, G., Manotti, C., Dettori, A.G.: A computerized regulation of dosage in oral anticoagulant therapy. Ric Clin Lab 20 (1990) 119-25
11. Poller, L., Shiach, C.R., MacCallum, P.K.,. Johansen, A.M, Münster, A.M., Magalhães, A., Jespersen, J.: Multicentre randomised study of computerised anticoagulant dosage. The Lancet 352 (1998) 1505-1509
12. Shahar, Y., Mirksch, S., Johnson, P.: The Asgaard Project: a Task-Specific Framework for the Application and Critiquing of Time-Oriented Clinical Guidelines. Artificial Intelligence in Medicine 14 (1998) 29-51
13. Terenziani P., Molino, G., Torchio, M.: A Modular Approach for Representing and Executing Clinical Guidelines. Artificial Intelligence in Medicine 23 (2001) 249-276

Formal Verification of Control Software: A Case Study

Andreas Griesmayer[1], Roderick Bloem[1], Martin Hautzendorfer[2], and Franz Wotawa[1]

[1] Graz University of Technology, Austria
{agriesma, rbloem, fwotawa}@ist.tu-graz.ac.at
[2] Festo AG, Vienna, Austria
hautzendorfer@festo.at

Abstract. We present a case study of formal verification of control logic for a robotic handling system. We have implemented a system in which properties can be specified in the source code, which is then automatically converted to Java and checked using Java Path Finder. The model checker, working under the assumption of a nondeterministic environment, is able to efficiently verify critical properties of the design.

1 Introduction

Software errors can cause large amounts of damage, not only in safety-critical systems, but also in industrial applications. An error in the control program for a robot, for example, may cause damage to products and to the robot itself. In such areas as automotive engineering, both the robots and the products are very expensive. Moreover, the followup costs can be a multiple of the direct costs: the production line may have to be halted while a technician travels to the site to repair the problem.

The design of concurrent software is difficult. The environment strongly influences the order in which parts of the program are executed, which introduces a source of variation that makes testing difficult [LHS03].

To make sure that errors do not occur, formal techniques are required. Model checking [CGP99] in particular is a technique to prove adherence of a system to a given property, regardless of the behavior of the environment. Today, model checking is mainly employed in hardware [KG99], whereas research into model checking for software is still in its infancy [BR01, CDH+00, God97, VHB+03].

The benefits of model checking are

Full coverage. Unlike testing, model checking verifies all possible behavior.
Light-weight specification. Only properties of interest are stated and the specification need not be finished before the implementation is started.
Automatic proof. The user is not exposed to the mathematical details of the proof of correctness.
Reuse in testing. Properties written for formal verification and for testing can be shared.

In this paper, we present a case study of formal verification of control software for a robotic handling system. The software was built to show the capabilities of *DACS*, a

M. Ali and F. Esposito (Eds.): IEA/AIE 2005, LNAI 3533, pp. 783–788, 2005.

novel language for control software developed by Festo. Though small, it is a typical example of software written for an industrial handling system and can thus be used to check for the absence of typical errors.

We formulated safety properties (the robot arm does not move when blocked) as well as liveness properties (the robot does not get stuck in a given state). The model checker was able to prove absence of such bugs in the original system and to detect bugs in an altered system. In order to prove such properties for any environment behavior, we modeled a nondeterministic environment. Our system works by translating DACS code into JAVA, which is then fed to Java Path Finder [VHB+03]. Properties are specified directly in the DACS source code. We expect that the approach shown here is applicable to a large variety of control software.

Related research includes the work done by Bienmüller, Damm, and Wittke [BDW00], who verify automotive and aeronautic systems specified with state charts. State charts are a specification formalism, whereas our approach verifies the implementation directly. A specification is not always available, and verification on the implementation has the advantage that changes made to the implementation only are also verified. To our knowledge, direct verification of implementation code by translation to Java has not been attempted before.

In Section 2, we will describe the DACS language and the handling system. In Section 3, we discuss how correctness was verified, and we conclude with Section 4.

2 Handling System

The handling system is shown in Fig. 1. One robot arm takes products from the carrier and moves them to the conveyor belt and another one takes them back, forming a closed loop. The system consists of two belts and two robot arms with five actuators each to control the movements (raise and lower the arm, move the arm across, open and close the two grippers, and turn the grippers on the arm).

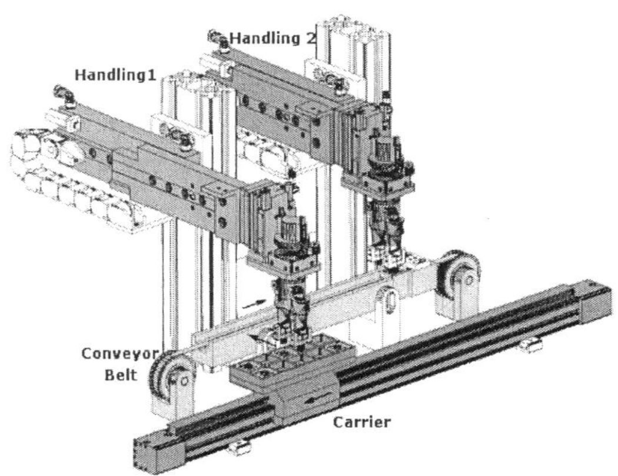

Fig. 1. the handling system

2.1 DACS

The control software has been implemented in DACS. The statements at hand are similar to familiar imperative languages like Java. Methods and variables regarding common objects are combined in classes. Each method is stored in its own file, and the static structure of the program is stored in a series of XML files containing the classes, their attributes and methods, and the instantiation of the objects. Each class is instantiated a finite, fixed number of times. Dynamic creation of objects and dynamic allocation of memory is not used because of time and memory constraints on an embedded system. This implies that the state space of the system is finite, which makes model checking easier.

A system consists of a hierarchical set of components, each described by a state machine. Each state machine executes one step (possibly staying in the same state) before passing control to its ancillary state machines, resulting in a program that can be run in one thread of control, but behaves like a set of parallel machines. A snipped of an state machine is given in Figure 2(a).

2.2 Properties

We checked two properties, each representative of a class.

safety. As an example for a safety-property we checked that the robot arms do not move horizontally while they are in their down position (because they might crash with a belt).

liveness. To provoke a liveness-failure, one of the conveyor-belts was "blocked" causing the system to wait infinitely to be allowed to proceed. This does not provoke a deadlock in the sense that no more events can be executed — the system loops through a couple of states — but it does not make a real progress either.

Fig. 2(a) shows the state machine controlling a single arm. *Vert* and *Hori* control the air-pressured cylinders that move the arm horizontally and vertically, respectively. When the robot arm is in its *Base* position, both are contracted, i.e., the arm is over the conveyor belt in the down position. The correct code first expands the *Vert* cylinder, moving the arm up and away from the belt, and then expands the *Hori* cylinder, moving the arm across, thus avoiding a crash with the carrier.

In the faulty version, shown in Fig. 2(b), we switched this order to provoke a crash. For the simulation of the liveness property we changed the implementation of the stepper motor of the carrier, which is part of the environment, to never report to reach its destination (not shown).

3 Verification

3.1 Translating the Handling System

For the case study, we developed a compiler which translates the DACS source code together with a set of properties to Java.

The Java Path Finder model checker (JPF) [VHB$^+$03] is based on a backtracking Java virtual machine. It searches the entire state space of the Java program, which in

```
SEQUENCE Handling
 STEP A.Base_0:
  Hold1.Base();
  Hold2.Base();
  NEXT_STEP;
 STEP A.Base_1:
  IF Hold1.InBase() AND
     Hold2.InBase() THEN
    Vert.Work();
    NEXT_STEP;
  END_IF;
 STEP Base_2:
  IF Vert.InWork() THEN
    Hori.Work();
    Turn.Work();
    NEXT_STEP;
  END_IF;
```

(a) original DACS code

```
SEQUENCE Handling
 STEP A.Base_0:
  Hold1.Base();
  Hold2.Base();
  NEXT_STEP;
 STEP A.Base_1:
  IF Hold1.InBase() AND
     Hold2.InBase() THEN
    Hori.Work(); // error
    NEXT_STEP;
  END_IF;
 STEP Base_2:
  IF Hori.InWork() THEN
    Vert.Work(); //error
    Turn.Work();
    NEXT_STEP;
  END_IF;
```

(b) safety fault introduced

```
switch(pos){
 case 1: //Base_0
  Hold1.Base();
  Hold2.Base();
  pos=pos+1;
 break;
 case 2: //Base_1
  if(Hold1.InBase()&&
     Hold2.InBase()){
    Vert.Work();
    pos=pos+1;
  }
 break;
 case 3://Base_2
  if(Vert.InWork()){
    Hori.Work();
    Turn.Work();
   pos=pos+1;
  }
 break;
}
```

(c) Java code

Fig. 2. In the correct code, STEP *A.Base_0* gives the command to open both grippers (*Hold*-cylinders). In *A.Base_1*, the vertical cylinder is moved to its top position when both Holds reached their base position. Finally, in *Base_2*, horizontal and turn cylinders are started. In the faulty version, we switched Vert and Hori to provoke a crash

our case is finite. JPF provides assertion methods, and properties can be included in the Java sources as calls to these methods.

Most statements, such as the `IF`-statement, function calls and assignments, are translated to Java in an obvious way — the corresponding Java statements provide the same functionality. State machines (`SEQUENCE`) are translated to a `switch-case`-statement and an extra member-variable keeping the current state. The structure of a DACS-program stored in its XML files is translated to a set of Java classes, one per DACS class. The instantiation of the objects is translated to a main() function and a set of default constructors, which instantiate the main class and the ancillary classes. The main() function also contains the code to drive the main state machine. Fig 2(c) gives the Java code corresponding to Fig. 2(a).

As JPF requires a closed system in order to do model checking, we implemented the environment directly in Java. The environment of the system was modeled using JPF's features for nondeterministic choice: hardware responds to a request in time that is finite but not predetermined.

Models for complex applications might exceed the size we can cope with. As the range of a variable has a strong impact on the size of the model, data abstraction techniques like those used in the Bandera framework [CDH$^+$00] replace it by a small number of tokens. If, for example, the rotation of the grippers is stored in degrees as integer, we could use *range abstraction* to replace all values smaller than zero and greater than

Table 1. results of model checking the control software

system	DFS				BFS			
	mem (MB)	time (s)	states	trace	mem (MB)	time (s)	states	trace
correct	72	18	161,023	N/A	85	1405	161,023	N/A
safety error	34	24	91,470	45,430	7.8	11	11,097	3,121
liveness error	13	4	4,257	4,256	37	4	74,790	3,992

359 by *invalid*, thus reducing the range to a fraction. Because we are only interested in two special positions, we may even increase the savings by *set abstraction*, which replaces the range by the tokens {*in_base, in_between, in_work, invalid*}. Further abstraction modes include *modulo-k abstraction*, which we can use to equate, for example, numbers that have the same remainder when divided by 360, and *point abstraction*, which drops all information by using a single token *unknown*.

3.2 Modeling Properties

JPF only offers checks for invariants. We translated liveness properties to invariants by the addition of a monitor which counts the time of no recognizable progress. Progress is perceived when the top-level state machine changes state. If the counter exceeds a fixed value, an assertion is violated and the error is reported. This value is easy to set: if the value is too small, a counterexample is shown in which progress still occurs, which is easily recognized by the designer. If the value is too large, a deadlock will still be caught, but the counterexample will be longer than strictly necessary.

We need to check the truth of an invariant between each two consecutive statements. To achieve this behavior, we exploit a characteristic of model checking concurrent threads: execution of events (statements) is interleaved nondeterministically. Hence, we perform the check of the safety-condition in a separate monitoring thread, which moves to an error state when the condition is violated. If a violation ever happens, there is a thread interleaving in which the monitoring thread moves to the error condition, and the model checker finds this interleaving.

Safety properties are specified by a new keyword, ASSERTGLOBAL, which takes a DACS-expression as argument. A second keyword, ASSERT, acts like the assert statement in the C language by ensuring that the given expression is satisfied at the respective position.

3.3 Case Study

The DACS sources of the control software consist of 1300 lines of code. Conversion to Java and implementation of the environment led to 12 Java classes with a total of 1340 lines.

Table 1 gives the results of our checks, for the three cases of the correct system, the system with the safety error, and the system with the liveness error. The memory (time) column gives the amount of memory (time) needed, the states column gives the number of states traversed, and the trace column give the length of the error trace, if applicable.

Experiments were performed on a Linux machine with a 2.8GHz Pentium IV and 2GB of RAM.

JPF uses Depth First Search (DFS) as its standard search order. The correct system had about 160,000 states and was checked in 18 seconds. DFS needs less memory and is far faster then Breadth First Search. The remaining test cases justify the use of BFS:

When an fault is found, JPF dumps an error trace consisting of executed statements and stops searching. BFS guarantees the shortest possible trace to an error by examining all states which are reachable in a given number of steps before increasing this number. This enhances the readability of the error trace and can significantly decrease the number of searched states, and thus amount of memory.

4 Conclusions

We have shown how control software for a robotic handling system can be verified automatically. Our example is typical of an industrial application. Though experiments with larger systems remain necessary, we have shown that translation to Java and verification by a general Java model checker leads to satisfactory results at a reasonable effort.

Robotic control software is hard to test off-site because of its concurrent behavior. Faults on-site, however, may be expensive. We believe that model checking can fill an important gap in securing the reliability of such systems.

References

[BDW00] T. Bienmüller, W. Damm, and H. Wittke. The Statemate verification environment, making it real. In E. A. Emmerson and A. P. Sistla, editors, *proceedings of the twelfth International Conference on Computer Aided Verification (CAV00)*, pages 561–567. Springer-Verlag, 2000. LNCS 1855.

[BR01] T. Ball and S. K. Rajamani. Automatically validating temporal safety properties of interfaces. In M.B. Dwyer, editor, *8th International SPIN Workshop*, pages 103–122, Toronto, May 2001. Springer-Verlag. LNCS 2057.

[CDH+00] J. C. Corbett, M. B. Dwyer, J. Hatcliff, S. Laubach, C. S. Pasareanu, Robby, and H. Zheng. Bandera: Extracting finite-state models from Java source code. In *22nd International Conference on Software Engineering (ICSE'00)*, pages 439–448, 2000.

[CGP99] E. M. Clarke, O. Grumberg, and D. A. Peled. *Model Checking*. MIT Press, Cambridge, MA, 1999.

[God97] P. Godefroid. Model checking for programming languages using verisoft. In *Symposium on Principles of Programming Languages*, pages 174–186, 1997.

[KG99] C. Kern and M. R. Greenstreet. Formal verification in hardware design: A survey. *ACM Transactions on Design Automation of Electronic Systems*, 4(2):123–193, April 1999.

[LHS03] B. Long, D. Hoffman, and P. Strooper. Tool support for testing concurrent java components. *IEEE Transactions on Software Engineering*, 29:555–566, 2003.

[VHB+03] W. Visser, K. Havelund, G. Brat, S. Park, and F. Lerda. Model checking programs. *Automated Software Engineering Journal*, 10:203–232, 2003.

GRAPE: An Expert Review Assignment Component for Scientific Conference Management Systems

Nicola Di Mauro, Teresa M.A. Basile, and Stefano Ferilli

Dipartimento di Informatica, University of Bari, Italy
{ndm, basile, ferilli}@di.uniba.it

Abstract. This paper describes GRAPE, an expert component for a scientific Conference Management System (CMS), to automatically assign reviewers to papers, one of the most difficult processes of conference management. In the current practice, this is typically done by a manual and time-consuming procedure, with a risk of bad quality results due to the many aspects and parameters to be taken into account, and on their interrelationships and (often contrasting) requirements. The proposed rule-based system was evaluated on real conference datasets obtaining good results when compared to the handmade ones, both in terms of quality of the assignments, and of reduction in execution time.

1 Introduction

The organization of scientific conferences often requires the use of a web-based management system (such as BYU [6], CyberChair [2], ConfMan [1], Microsoft CMT [3], and OpenConf [4])[1] to make some tasks a little easier to carry out, such as the job of reviewing papers. Some features typically provided by these packages are: submission of abstracts and papers by Authors; submission of reviews by the *Program Committee Members* (PCM); download of papers by *Program Committee* (PC); handling of reviewers preferences and bidding; web-based assignment of papers to PCMs for review; review progress tracking; web-based PC meeting; notification of acceptance/rejection; sending e-mails for notifications. When using these systems, the hardest and most time-consuming task is the process of assigning reviewers to submitted papers. Usually, this task is manually carried out by the *Program Committee Chair* (PCC) of the conference, that, generally, selects 3 or 4 reviewers *per* paper. Due to the many constraints to be fulfilled, such a manual task is very tedious and difficult, and sometimes does not result in the best solution. It can be the case of 300 submitted papers to be assigned to 30-40 reviewers, where some reviewers cannot revise specific papers because of conflict of interests, or should not revise papers about some conference topics due to their little expertise in that field; additionally, through the

[1] A list of other software, often developed *ad hoc* for specific events, can be found at `http://www.acm.org/sigs/sgb/summary.html`

M. Ali and F. Esposito (Eds.): IEA/AIE 2005, LNAI 3533, pp. 789–798, 2005.

bidding process reviewers generally express their preference in reviewing specific papers, and should be ensured some level of satisfaction in this respect. The more papers to be reviewed and constraints to be fulfilled, the more vain the hope to obtain a good solution is. Unfortunately, currently available software provides little support for automatic review assignment. Sometimes, they just support reviewers in selecting papers they wish to review, giving the PCC the possibility to use these preferences.

This paper describes GRAPE (Global Review Assignment Processing Engine), an expert component developed to be embedded in scientific Conference Management Systems (CMS). GRAPE, a successful real-life application, fully implemented and operational, performs a management activity by automatically assigning reviewers to papers submitted to a conference, additionally assessing the quality of the results of this activity in terms of profitability and efficiency. This system will become part of a web-based CMS, currently at prototype stage, whose main goal is to provide an easy-to-manage software package that features the traditional conference management functionality (e.g., paper submission, reviewer assignment, discussion on conflicting reviews, selection of papers, mailing to all actors, etc.) and addresses the weaknesses of other systems (such as automatic support for reviewers assignment, conference session management, etc.).

This paper is organized as follows. Section 2 introduces the main features of the CMS prototype in which GRAPE is embedded. In Section 3 the Reviewers Assignment Problem and its context are introduced, and some known systems that tackle it are presented. Section 4 describes GRAPE, whose experimental evaluation is discussed in Section 5. Finally, Section 6 will conclude the paper, with remarks and future work proposals.

2 The Conference Management System

Generally speaking, a CMS, among other basic services, can be seen as a system collecting documents (submitted) in electronic form, in PostScript (PS) or Portable Document Format (PDF), in a digital repository. The main characteristic of our CMS lies in its ability to understand the semantics of the document components and content. Intelligent techniques are exploited for the extraction of significant text, to be used for later categorization and information retrieval purposes. A preliminary Layout Analysis step identifies the blocks that make up a document and detects relations among them, resulting in the so-called layout structure. The next document processing step concerns the association of the proper logical role to each such component, resulting in so-called logical structure. This can enable a multiplicity of applications, including hierarchical browsing, structural hyperlinking, logical component-based retrieval and style translation. Our layout analysis process embedded in the CMS, sketched in Figure 1, takes as input a PDF/PS document and produces the initial document's XML basic representation, that describes it as a set of pages made up of basic blocks. Such a representation is then exploited by an algorithm, that collects

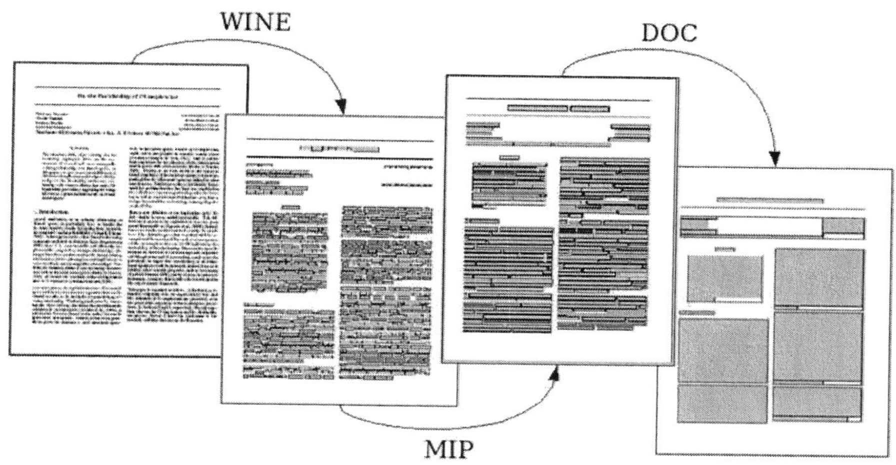

Fig. 1. Document Layout Analysis System

semantically related basic blocks into groups by identifying frames that surround them based on whitespace and background structure analysis.

When an Author connects to the Internet and opens the conference submission page, the received paper may undergo the following processing steps. The layout analysis algorithm may be applied, in order to single out its layout components, and then to classify it according to a description for the acceptable submission layout standards (e.g., full paper, poster, demo). A further step locates and labels the layout components of interest for that class (e.g., title, author, abstract and references in a full paper). The text that makes up each of such components may be read, stored and used to automatically file the submission record. The text contained in the title, abstract and bibliographic references, can be exploited to extract the paper topics, since we assume they concentrate the subject and research field the paper is concerned with.

3 The Conference Review Process

The review process on the contributions submitted by authors to a conference starts after the deadline for the paper submission phase. When the submission phase ends, suitable *PCM* are selected, which will act as *reviewers*, in order to evaluate the submitted papers. Hence, the PCC sends the collected submissions with review forms to individual reviewers. The review form consists of a set of questions to assess the quality of the paper, that the Reviewers must fill in and return it to the PCC. Each submission is typically examined and evaluated by 2 or 3 reviewers. Generally, the review process ends with the *Program Committee meeting*, where the papers are discussed on the basis of collected review forms, in order to their acceptance or rejection for presentation at the conference. After this meeting, anonymous extracts of the review forms (reviewer's comments) are typically sent back to all the authors, so that they can improve their paper, regardless of whether they were accepted or not. Finally, the authors of accepted papers may submit a new version of their paper, in the so-called *camera-ready* format, to the PCC, who will send them, together with the preface and the table of contents of the book, to the publisher in order to have the proceedings printed.

3.1 The Reviewers Selection

The process of identifying the right reviewers for each paper represents an hard task. In [7] O. Nierstrasz presented a small *pattern language*, that captures successful practice in several conference review processes. In this work we follow the patterns *ExpertsReviewPapers* and *ChampionsReviewPapers*, indicating that papers should be matched, and assigned for evaluation, to reviewers who are competent in the specific particular paper topics (*ExpertsReviewPapers*), and to reviewers who declared to be willing to review those papers in the bidding phase (*ChampionsReviewPapers*). As to the former pattern, the PCC can set up, before the submission phase of the conference starts, a list of research topics of interest for the conference. In order to get a match, generally, at first all reviewers are asked to specify which of the conference topics correspond to their main areas of expertise. Then, during the paper submission process, authors are asked to explicitly state which conference topics apply to their submissions. Such an information provides a first guideline for matching reviewers to papers. As to the latter pattern, as reported in [7], by distributing a list of titles, authors and abstracts to all reviewers, they may perform the so-called *bidding*, i.e. they may indicate which papers (i) they would like to review, (ii) they feel competent to review, and (iii) they do not want to review (either because they do not feel competent, or because they have a conflict of interest).

Finally, further information to match papers and Reviewers can be deduced from the papers. For example, related work by some reviewer explicitly mentioned in the paper may represent an indication of the appropriateness of that reviewer for that paper; conversely, if the reviewer is a co-author or a colleague of the paper authors, then a conflict of interest can be figured out.

Usually, the bidding preferences approach is preferred over the topics matching one. We give more value to the latter since the topics selected by a reviewer should refer to his background expertise, while specific preferences about papers could be due to matter of taste or some vague questions (e.g., the reviewer would like to revise a paper out of curiosity; the abstract that he has read is not very precise or misleading). We believe that if a paper preferred by a reviewer does not match his topics of expertise, this should be considered as an alarm bell.

3.2 Paper Distribution Systems

Most of the existent CMS, such as CMT [3] and CyberChair [2], provide tools for web-based paper submission and for review management. Both CMT and CyberChair have assignment functionalities. Specifically, CMT uses a greedy algorithm to assign a paper to the reviewers who gave the higher preference, but limiting the number of papers assigned to a reviewer by means of a threshold. When the system cannot find a reviewer for a paper, a matching of both the reviewers and paper topics is used. If this fails the result is unpredictable.

CyberChair [9], after the paper submission deadline, generates a paper distribution proposal for the PCC exploiting graph theory. This is done by combining the reviewer's expertise and willingness to review papers on certain topics with the preferences indicated by the reviewers when bidding for papers. The reviewer's expertise is obtained by asking the reviewers their expertise on the conference topics along with three levels: 1) expert on the topic, 2) not expert, but knowledgable in the subject area, 3) an informed outsider. CyberChair collects the bids, expertise levels and willingness to review papers on certain topics and the conflicts of interest of the reviewers, and it is tuned to assign as much as possible papers to reviewers based on their preferences. Each paper is assigned to the k reviewers with the least number of papers assigned so far, by using a list of the reviewers who indicated a *high* preference for the paper sorted according to the number of papers they have already been assigned so far. In case there are less than k reviewers, this process is repeated with the list of reviewers who indicated a *low* preference for the paper. In case there are not enough reviewers, the paper is assigned to the reviewers with the highest overall expertise.

An *ad-hoc* system is presented in [8], where the reviewers' assignment problem is compared to the more general problem of recommendation of items to users in web-based systems, and proposed a recommendation method based on collaborative filtering [8]. Such a method allows to compute a predicted rating for each pair (reviewer, paper), using a multi-step process which improves continuously the confidence level of ratings. In particular, each step consists of the following operations: (a) for each user, a sample of papers whose rating is expected to lead to the best confidence level improvement is selected, (b) each user is requested to rate the papers from its sample and (c) a collaborative filtering algorithm is performed to obtain a new set of predicted ratings based on the users ratings made so far. Step (c) results in a new level of confidence. The basic assumption is that each user provides a rating for each paper: Reviewers are required to rate the submitted papers based on title, abstract and authors information. These ratings are used by the algorithm to obtain the best possible assignment. This system relies on a variant of known techniques for optimal weighted matching in bipartite graphs [5], and delivers the best possible assignment. However, in practice, the number of papers is often large and it is difficult to ask for a comprehensive rating. Users rate only a small subset of the papers, and the rating table is sparse, with many unknown rating values. To overcome the problem in order to use the automatic assignment algorithm, they must then predict the missing rating values.

4 The GRAPE System

GRAPE (Global Review Assignment Processing Engine) is an expert system, written in CLIPS, for solving the reviewers assignment problem, that takes advantage from both the papers content (topics) and the reviewers preferences (biddings). It could be used exploiting the papers topics only, or both the paper topics and the reviewers' biddings. Its fundamental assumption is to prefer the topics matching approach over the reviewers' biddings one, based on the idea that they give assignments more reliability. Then, reviewers' preferences are used to tune paper assignments. Moreover, reviewers' preferences are useful because of the unpredictability of the distribution of reviewers and papers over the list of topics, which causes situations in which some papers have a lot of experts willing to review them, while some others simply do not have enough reviewers.

Let $P = \{p_1, \ldots, p_n\}$ denote the set of n papers submitted to the conference C, regarding t topics (*conference topics*, T_C), and $R = \{r_1, \ldots, r_m\}$ the set of m reviewers. The goal is to assign the papers to reviewers, such that the following *basic constraints* are fulfilled: 1) each paper is assigned to exactly k reviewers (usually, k is set to be equal to 3 or 4); 2) each reviewer should have roughly the same number of papers to review (the mean number of reviewers *per* reviewer is equal to nk/m); 3) papers should be reviewed by domain experts; and, 4) reviewers should revise articles based on their expertise and preferences. As regards constraint 2, GRAPE can take as input additional constraints MaxReviewsPerReviewer(r,h), indicating that the reviewer r can reviews at most h paper, that must be taken into account for calculating the mean number of reviews per reviewer.

We defined two measures to guide the system during the search of the best solutions: the *reviewer's gratification* and the *article's coverage*. The former represents the gratification degree g_{r_j} of a reviewer r_j calculated on his assigned papers. It is based on: a) the *confidence degree* between the reviewer r_j and the assigned articles: the confidence degree between a paper p_i, with topics T_{p_i} and the reviewer r_j, with expertise topics T_{r_j}, is equal to number of topics in common $T = T_{p_i} \cup T_{r_j}$; and, b) the number of assigned papers that the reviewer chose to revise (discussed in more details in Section 4.2). The article's coverage represents the coverage degree of an article after the assignments. It is based on: a) the *confidence degree* between the article and the assigned reviewers (the same as for Reviewer's gratification); and, b) the *expertise degree* of the assigned reviewers, represented by the number of topics. The expertise level of a reviewer r_j is equal to T_{r_j}/T_C. GRAPE tries to maximize both the reviewer gratification and the article coverage degree during the assignment process, in order to fulfill the third and fourth basic constraints. To reach this goal a fundamental prerequisite is that each reviewer must provide at least one topic of preference, otherwise the article coverage degree will be always null.

The two main inputs to the system are the set P of the submitted papers and the set R of the candidate reviewers. Each paper $p_i \in P$ is described by its title, author(s), affiliation(s) of the author(s) and topics T_{p_i}. On the other hand, each reviewer $r_j \in R$ is described by his name, affiliation and topics of interest T_{r_j}. Furthermore, the system can take as input a set of constraints CS indicating (i) the possibly specified maximum number of reviews *per* Reviewer (MaxReviewsPerReviewer(reviewer, h)), (ii) the papers that *must* be reviewed by a reviewer (MustReview(reviewer, paper)) indicated by the PCC. It can be also provided with a set of *conflicts CO* indicating which reviewers that cannot revise specific papers (CannotReview(reviewer, paper)) under suggestion of the PCC. Furthermore, the set of conflicts CO is enriched by GRAPE by deducting additional conflicts between papers and reviewers. Specifically, a conflict is assumed to exist between a paper p_i and a reviewer r_j if r_j is the (co-)author of p_i, or the affiliation of r_j is among the affiliation(s) reported in p_i.

Definition 1. *We say that* a reviewer r_j can revise a paper p_i with degree

$$\begin{cases} h \geq 1 & \textit{if the confidence degree between } r_j \textit{ and } p_i \textit{ is equal to } h \\ 0 \leq h < 1 & \textit{if the expertise degree of } r_j \textit{ is equal to } h \end{cases}$$

Definition 2. *Given a paper p_i, the number of* candidate reviewers *of p_i is the number of reviewers that can revise the paper with degree $k \geq 1$*

4.1 The Assignment Process

The assignment process is carried out into two phases. In the former, the system progressively assigns reviewers to papers with the lowest number of candidate reviewers (first those with only 1 candidate reviewer, then those with 2 candidate reviewers, and so on). This assures, for example, to assign a reviewer to papers with only one candidate reviewer. At the same time, the system *prefers* assigning papers to reviewers with few assignments. In this way, it avoids to have reviewers with zero or few assigned papers. Hence, this phase can be viewed as a search for reviews assignments by keeping low the average number of reviewers *per* reviewer and maximizing the coverage degree of the papers. In the latter phase, the remaining assignments are chosen by considering first the confidence levels and then the expertise level of the reviewers. In particular, given a paper p_i which has not been assigned k reviewers yet, GRAPE tries to assign it a reviewer r_j with a high confidence level between r_j and p_i. In case it is not possible, it assigns a reviewer with a high level of expertise.

4.2 The Bidding Process

The assignments resulting from the base process are presented to each reviewer, that receives the list A of the h assigned papers, followed by the list A' of the remaining ones (both, A and A' are sorted using the article's coverage degree). The papers are presented to the reviewer as virtually bid: the first $h/2$ papers of the list A are tagged *high*, and the following h papers are tagged *medium* (all the others are tagged *low*). Now, the reviewer can actually bid the papers by changing their tag: he can bid at most $h/2$ papers as *high* (*he would like to review*) and h as *medium* (*he feels competent to review*). Furthermore, he can bid $h/2$ papers as *no* (*he does not want to review*). All the others are assumed to be bid as *low* (*he does not feel competent*). Only papers actually bid by reviewers generate a preference constraint, of the form Bid(paper, level).

When all the reviewers have bid their papers, GRAPE searches for a new solution that takes into account these biddings. In particular, it tries to change previous assignments in order to maximize both article's coverage and reviewer's gratification. By taking the article's coverage high, GRAPE tries to assign the same number of papers bid with the same class to each reviewer. Then, the solution is presented to the reviewers as the final one.

It is important to say that, if the PCC does not like the solution, he can change some assignments to force the system to give another possible assignment configuration fulfilling these new preference constraints. In particular, he may: (i) assign a reviewer to a different paper; (ii) assign a paper to a different reviewer; (iii) remove a paper assignment; or, (iv) remove a reviewer assignment.

The main advantage of GRAPE relies in the fact that it is a rule-based system. Hence, it is very easy to add new rules in order to change/improve its behavior, and it is possible to describe background knowledge, such as further constraints or conflicts, in a natural way. For example, one can insert a rule that expresses the preference to assign a reviewer to the articles in which he is cited.

5 Evaluation

The system was evaluated on real-world datasets built by using data from a previous European conference and from this International conference. In order to have an insight on the quality of the results, in the following we present some interesting characteristics of the assignments suggested by GRAPE.

5.1 European Conference Experiment

This experiment consisted in a set of 383 papers to be distributed among 72 Reviewers, with $k = 3$ reviews *per* paper. The system was able to correctly assign 3 reviewers to each paper in 152 seconds. Obtaining a manual solution took about 10 hours of manual work from the 4 Program Chairs of that conference.

Each reviewer was assigned 14.93 papers on average (min 8, max 16) by topic (when there was confidence degree greater than 1 between the reviewer and the paper), and only 1.03 papers on average (min 0, max 8) by expertise degree (which is a very encouraging result). Table 1 reports the complete distribution of reviewers' assignments. The first row shows the number of assignments by type (Topics-Expertise). Noticeably, GRAPE made many good assignments: in particular, it assigned to 55 reviewers all 16 papers by topics (first row). The other rows refer to the topics of expertise of reviewers: the last two rows indicate that the system assigned an high number of papers by expertise to reviewers that had few topics.

The reviewers with highest gratification degree were r_{22}, r_{57}, and r_{20}. Indeed, they are the three reviewers that chose a lot of topics (r_{22} selected 11 topics, r_{57} selected 14, and r_{20} selected 17). On the other hand, the reviewers with the lowest gratification degree were r_{10} that selected few (and very rare among the papers) topics, and r_{56} that selected only two topics. As regards the papers, the best assigned papers with a high coverage degree were the p_{239} (concerning topics 1, 4, 15, 39 and 42), p_{231} (on topics 1, 2, 15, 30, 34 and 5), p_{303} (topics 1, 9, 11, 32 and 36), and p_{346} (topics 4, 15, 39 and 42). Table 2 reports the

Table 1. Reviewers' Assignments Distribution

Assignment	16-0	15-1	14-2	13-3	11-5	10- 5	8-8	8-6
#	55	3	2	3	3	1	4	1
Mean	5,73	2,67	2,5	2,67	1,67	1	1,5	1
Min	2	2	2	2	1	1	1	1
Max	18	3	3	4	2	1	2	1

Table 2. Reviewers per topic

Topic	1	2	4	9	11	15	30	32	34	36	39	42
Reviewers	17	14	10	5	5	12	11	5	3	7	20	17

Table 3. IEA/AIE 2005 Topics Distribution

ID	Topic	#r	#a	ID	Topic	#r	#a
1	Adaptive Control	3	11	18	Intelligent Interfaces	14	31
2	Applications to Design	3	19	19	Intelligent Systems in Educ.	11	12
3	Applications to Manufacturing	2	12	20	Internet Applications	12	24
4	Autonomous Agents	18	28	21	KBS Methodology	7	13
5	BioInformatics	9	8	22	Knowledge Management	16	30
6	Case-based Reasoning	9	4	23	Knowledge Processing	11	25
7	Computer Vision	3	20	24	Machine Learning	17	43
8	Constraint Satisfaction	6	9	25	Model-based Reasoning	6	11
9	Data Mining & Knowledge Disc.	24	44	26	Natural Language Process.	5	15
10	Decision Support	9	58	27	Neural Networks	11	29
11	Distributed Problem Solving	6	6	28	Planning and Scheduling	7	27
12	Expert Systems	15	28	29	Reasoning Under Uncertain.	4	20
13	Fuzzy Logic	4	13	30	Spatial Reasoning	7	9
14	Genetic Algorithms	5	29	31	Speech Recognition	2	8
15	Genetic Programming	2	6	32	System Integration	3	14
16	Heuristic Search	3	16	33	Systems for Real Life App.	10	41
17	Human-Robot Interaction	3	14	34	Temporal Reasoning	11	10

number of reviewers experienced in some topics of the conference. As one can see, there are lots of reviewers experienced with the topics appearing in papers with a high coverage degree. Papers with a low coverage degree were p_{15} (3 rare topics covered), p_{42} (2 rare topics) and p_{373} (0 topics).

5.2 IEA/AIE 2005 Experiment

In this experiment the dataset was built by using data from this conference[2], consisting of a set of 266 papers to be distributed among 60 Reviewers. The conference covered 34 topics as reported in Table 3, where #r represents the number

[2] IEA/AIE 2005 - The 18th International Conference on Industrial & Engineering Applications of Artificial Intelligence & Expert Systems

of reviewers experienced with the topic, and #a represents the papers regarding the topic. $k = 2$ reviews *per* paper were required. In solving the problem, the system was able to correctly assign 2 reviewers to each paper in 79.89 seconds.

GRAPE was able to assign papers to reviewers by considering the topics only (it never assigned a paper by expertise). In particular, it assigned 10 papers to 38 reviewers, 9 to 4 reviewers, 8 to 6 reviewers, 7 to 1 reviewer, 6 to 9 reviewers, 5 to 1 reviewer, and 2 to 1 reviewer, by considering some MaxReviewsPerReviewer constraints for some reviewers that explicitly requested ro revise few papers. The reviewers with the highest gratification degree, with 10 assigned papers, were r_{24} (that selected 7 topics), r_{32} (that selected 8 topics) and r_{41} (that selected 6 topics). As regards the papers, those assigned with highest coverage degree were p_{24}, p_{31}, p_{47}, p_{67}, p_{70}, p_{78}, p_{81}, p_{177}, p_{181}, p_{198}, p_{242} and p_{260}.

6 Conclusions

We presented the GRAPE expert system, specifically designed to solve the problem of reviewer assignments for scientific conference management. The proposed rule-based system was evaluated on real-world conference datasets obtaining good results when compared to the handmade ones, both in terms of quality and user-satisfaction of the assignments, and for reduction in execution time with respect to that taken by humans to perform the same process.

GRAPE is embedded in a web-based CMS in which we plan to insert some tools able to automatically extract the paper's topics from its title, abstract, and references, and the reviewer's topics by analyzing his previously written paper and web pages. Furthermore, we are planning to insert in our web-based CMS, a sessions manager system similar to GRAPE able to automatically propose sessions for the conference and the presentations for each session.

References

1. The confman software. `http://www.zakongroup.com/technology/openconf.shtml`.
2. The cyberchair software. `http://www.cyberchair.org`.
3. The microsoft conference management toolkit. `http://msrcmt.research.microsoft.com/cmt/`.
4. The openconf conference management system `http://www.zakongroup.com/technology/openconf.shtml`.
5. H.W. Kuhn. The hungarian method for the assignment problem. *Naval Research Logistic Quarterly*, 2:83–97, 1955.
6. Stephen W. Liddle. The byu paper review system. `http://blondie.cs.byu.edu/PaperReview/`.
7. O. Nierstrasz. Identify the champion. In N. Harrison, B. Foote, and H. Rohnert, editors, *Pattern Languages of Programm Design*, volume 4, pages 539–556. 2000.
8. Philippe Rigaux. An iterative rating method: Application to web-based conference management. In *ACM Intl. Conf. on Applied Computing (ACM-SAC'04)*, 2004.
9. Richard van de Stadt. Cyberchair: A web-based groupware application to facilitate the paper reviewing process. Available at www.cyberchair.org, 2001.

A Nurse Scheduling System Based on Dynamic Constraint Satisfaction Problem

Hiromitsu Hattori[1], Takayuki Ito[2], Tadachika Ozono[2], and Toramatsu Shintani[2]

[1] Dept. of Computer Science, University of Liverpool,
Peach Street, Liverpool, L69 7ZF United Kingdom
hatto@csc.liv.ac.uk

[2] Graduate School of Engineering, Nagoya Institute of Technology,
Gokiso-cho, Showa-ku, Nagoya, Aichi, 466-8555 Japan
{itota, ozono, tora}@ics.nitech.ac.jp

Abstract. In this paper, we describe a new nurse scheduling system based on the framework of Constraint Satisfaction Problem (CSP). In the system, we must deal with dynamic changes to scheduling problem and with constraints that have different levels of importance. We describe the dynamic scheduling problem as a Dynamic Weighted Maximal CSP (DW-MaxCSP) in which constraints can be changed dynamically. It is usually undesirable to drastically modify the previous schedule in the re-scheduling process. A new schedule should be as close to as possible to the previous one. To obtain stable solutions, we propose methodology for keeping similarity to the previous schedule by using provisional constraints that explicitly penalize changes from the previous schedule. We have confirmed the efficacy of our system experimentally.

1 Introduction

The nurse scheduling is a problem that is not easy to solve. In the nurse scheduling problem, various constraints, whose importance are different, must be taken into account (*e.g.*, legal regulations, organizational rules, nurses' requests). In this paper, we present a nurse scheduling system that helps hospital administrators to solve such complicated problems. There are several approaches to the nurse scheduling based on the framework of Constraint Satisfaction Problem (CSP) [1, 2]. For example, Abdennadher and Schenker express hard constraints and soft constraints by using a weight allocated to each constraint, and then using a search method that minimizes the number of unsatisfied soft constraints. They also constructed a practical scheduling system, called INTERDIP.

The nurse scheduling is achieved based on requests from all nurses. When nurses submit new requests, re-scheduling is required and the previous schedule could be drastically changed as a result of the re-scheduling. Therefore, we propose a scheduling method that can generate a stable schedule. In our method, we deal with changes to a problem by representing problems as a sequence of static CSPs based on Dynamic CSP [3, 4]. Because the nurse scheduling problems is often over-constrained, there would be no solutions that can satisfy all constraints. In this paper, we first represent

M. Ali and F. Esposito (Eds.): IEA/AIE 2005, LNAI 3533, pp. 799–808, 2005.

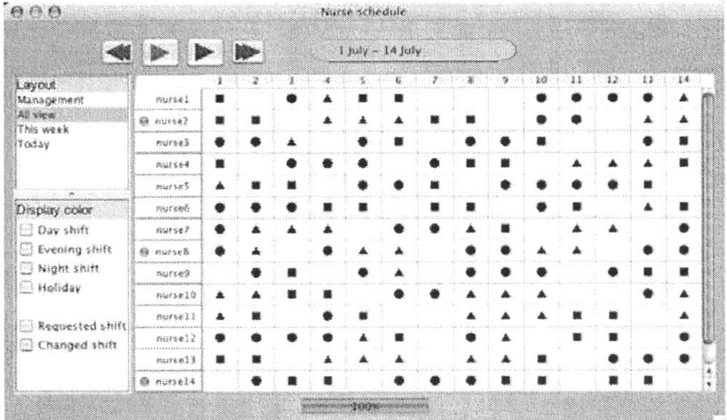

Fig. 1. An Example of a Roster

a problem at each time step as a Weighted Maximal CSP (W-MaxCSP), then represent a varying nurse scheduling problem as a Dynamic Weighted Maximal CSP (DW-MaxCSP). To obtain a stable schedule in our scheduling system, we introduce provisional constraints that explicitly penalizes changes from a previous schedule.

The structure of the rest of this paper is as follows. In the next section, we outline the nurse scheduling problem on which we focus in this paper, and in Section 3, we formalize this problem as a DW-MaxCSP. In Section 4, we shows the rescheduling process. In Section 5, we show the efficacy of our scheduling method and the system.

2 The Nurse Scheduling Problem

In a Japanese hospital, a new roster for each ward is usually generated monthly. There are two types of nurse rosters, a two-shift system and a three-shift system. In this paper, we focus on the 3-shift system. Each day consists of three units: a *day-shift*, an *evening-shift*, and a *night-shift*. Nurses have to be assigned to each shift or give holidays. The scheduling period is usually one month. An example of a roster generated by our nurse scheduling system is shown in Figure 1, where each row and column respectively express each nurse's schedule and working contents in each day. Circles, triangles, and squares respectively mean a day-shift, an evening-shift, and a night-shift. Blank cells means a holiday. Different constraints must be taken into account for generating a roster. We consider the following constraints:

- The number of nurses assigned to each working shift must be within the range of a certain maximum value and a certain minimum value (*e.g.*, at least four nurses must be working the evening-shift).
- The number of shifts assigned to each nurse must be within the limits of legal regulation (*e.g.*, the number of holidays which are assigned to each nurse should be about 2 days).

- Prohibited working patterns must be prevented. A "working pattern" is a sequence of working shifts over several days. An example of a prohibited working pattern is "the day-shift after the night-shift."
- Requests from nurses should be satisfied as much as possible. Specifically, both the required working shift and the nurses' requests for holidays should be considered.

As we mentioned above, the generation of a roster is based on a number of constraints. Therefore, even if a few schedules (*i.e.,* a value of one cell in a roster) are changed, many other schedules associated with these changed are affected.

3 Nurse Scheduling Based on Dynamic Weighted MaxCSP

3.1 Dynamic Weighted MaxCSP

When nurses submit new requests for their working shift, the scheduling problem is changed because constraints must be changed or added. We represent such dynamics by using the framework of Dynamic CSP [3, 4]. Because the real-life nurse scheduling problems are oftern over-constrained, we allocate a weight to each constraint and try to determine a schedule minimizing the total weight of unsatisfied constraints. That is, we formalize the problem , which is a sequence of over-constrained scheduling problems, as a DW-MaxCP. A DW-MaxCSP can be represented as a sequence of static W-MaxCSPs. When we let $\mathcal{WP}_i$ be a W-MaxCSP at time step i, we can represent the DW-MaxCSP as follows:

$$\mathcal{DP} = \{\mathcal{WP}_0, \mathcal{WP}_1, ..., \mathcal{WP}_i, ...\}$$

where $\mathcal{WP}_{i+1}$ is the problem generated from a previous problem $\mathcal{WP}_i$. Each W-MaxCSP is denoted as $\mathcal{WP}_i = (X_i, D_i, C_i, S, \varphi)$, where (X_i, D_i, C_i) is a classical CSP. The terms X_i, D_i, and C_i respectively represent a set of variables, a set of finite domains for the variables, and a set of constraints. $S = (E, \otimes, \succ)$ is a valuation structure, and $\varphi : C \to E$ is a valuation function that gives a valuation to each constraint. E is the set of possible valuations; $\succ$ is a total order on E; $\top \in E$ is the valuation corresponding to a maximal dissatisfaction, and $\perp \in E$ is the valuation corresponding to a maximal satisfaction; the aggregation operator $\otimes$ aggregates valuations. Let $\mathcal{A}$ be an assignment of values to all of the variables; that is a complete assignment. The valuation of $\mathcal{A}$ for the constraint c is defined as:

$$\varphi(\mathcal{A}, c) = \begin{cases} \perp & \text{if } c \text{ is satisfied by } \mathcal{A} \\ \varphi(c) & \text{otherwise} \end{cases}$$

and the overall valuation of $\mathcal{A}$ is given by

$$\varphi(\mathcal{A}) = \otimes_{c \in C} \varphi(\mathcal{A}, c).$$

The solution of W-MaxCSP is an allocation of values to all variables that can minimize the total weight of the unsatisfied constraints $\varphi(\mathcal{A})$.

In Dynamic CSPs, there is an important problem with solution stability. Solution stability is a property which makes new solutions close to the previous ones. According to Verfaillie and Shiex [5], a stable solution is one that keeps common allocations to previous solution as much as possible. Wallace and Freuder [6], on the other hand, say that a stable solution is one that is likely to remain valid after changes that temporarily alter the set of valid assignments, and they call the stability in [5] simply "similarity." Wallace and Freuder's concept of solution stability, however, includes that of Verfaillie and Shiex. Moreover, both concepts are elaborated to deal with the alteration of the problem even as the effectiveness of solution is kept. In this paper, we try to propose the method for re-scheduling considering "similarity".

3.2 Formalization Based on the DW-MaxCSP

The nurse scheduling problem with changes over time can be defined as a sequence of W-MaxCSPs each of which consists of some variables, the value of the variables and some constraints. Let $\mathcal{WP}_i = (X_i, D_i, C_i, S, \varphi)$ be a W-MaxCSP at time step i. Each element in a set of variables $X_i = \{x_{(1,1)}, x_{(1,2)}, ..., x_{(s,t)}\}$ represents a working shift of each nurse on each day. Each variable corresponds to a cell in a roster like taht in Figure 1, and $x_{(s,t)} \in X_i$ represents a shift of nurse s on date t. D_i represents a set of finite domains for the variables. In this paper, we suppose that the domains for all variables are common and that $d_{(s,t)} = \{0, 1, 2, 3\} \in D_i$, where the values 0, 1, 2, and 3 respectively correspond to "holiday," "day-shift," "evening-shift," and "night-shift". For a valuation structure $S = (E, \otimes, \succ)$, E is a set of integers, $\bot = 0$ and $\top = 9$. $\succ$ is a total order on E. Accordingly, when $\mathcal{A}$ is an assignment of values to all of the variables, $\varphi(\mathcal{A})$ represents the total weight of the unsatisfied constraints.

The form of a constraint included in a set of constraints C_i is defined as follows:

$$lim(min, max, List, w)$$

where min and max respectively represent the lower limits and the upper limits to the number of elements in an assignment $\mathcal{A}_i$ of values to all of the variables at time step i, which correspond to the elements in $List$. w represents the weight of the constraint and takes its value as an integer from 0 to 9. When the number n of elements in the same in $\mathcal{A}$ and $List$, and $min \leq n \leq max$, the constraint can be satisfied. For example, if a nurse s requires more than one and less than three holidays, such a condition is described by the following constraint:

$$lim(1, 3, \{x_{(s,1)} = 0, x_{(s,2)} = 0, ...\}, 5)$$

This constraint can be satisfied when more than one and less than three variables are allocated the value "0". If this constraint is not satisfied, a cost of 5 is added.

4 Re-scheduling Based on DW-MaxCSP

4.1 Solution Stability Based on the Provisional Constraint

Each $\mathcal{WP}_i$ can be solved in a manner which is similar to that used to solve an ordinary W-MaxCSP. Though each W-MaxCSP is solved while minimizing the total weight of unsatisfied constraints, there would be a few changes if some constraints assigned low weight were intentionally violated. Suppose, for example, there is a relatively weak constraint $lim(1, 1, \{x_{(s,t)} = 0\}, 1)$ for nurse s, who requires holiday on date t, and suppose there are many changes in the values of variables when this constraint is satisfied. If the number of changed variables is quite different depending on the satisfaction of constraint $lim(1, 1, \{x_{(s,t)} = 0\}, 1)$, it is appropriate, in light of the solution stability, to intentionally render this constraint unsatisfied and obtain a solution with a few changes. Moreover, if problems $\mathcal{WP}_{i-1}$ and $\mathcal{WP}_i$ are irrelevant in the calculation and do not affect each other, each of them is solved independently. The solution stability in DW-MaxCSP is obtained by inhibiting the change in the process of problem-solving for a sequence of W-MaxCSPs. Therefore, we need the method to render W-MaxCSPs dependent by using the previous solution for the solution stability.

We propose a method that introduces a provisional constraint. The provisional constraint can be used to keep values which are assigned in the last solution for all variables. Concretely, it is the weighted unary constraint in order to obtain the same value in the previous solution. For example, let $v_{(s,t)}$ be the value assigned to the variable $x_{(s,t)}$ in the last solution. Then the following provisional constraint is added:

$$lim(1, 1, \{x_{(s,t)} = v_{(s,t)}\}, w)$$

where w is a weight assigned to this provisional constraint. Since the provisional constraint can explicitly represent the penalty for changing a solution, it would be satisfied as a substitute for not satisfying the constraint that causes many changes of values. In that case, we can obtain a stable solution without many changes. Moreover, our method does not target only the last solution, but also all of previous solutions. Namely, some provisional constraints are added with respect to each rescheduling.

4.2 The Process of Re-scheduling

Suppose that problem $\mathcal{WP}_i$ changes to a new problem $\mathcal{WP}_{i+1}$ by addition of sets of constraints representing nurses' requirement C_{new} and C_{rev}. C_{new} is a set of constraints representing new requirements for the solution to $\mathcal{WP}_i$. C_{rev} is a set of constraints representing the adjustment for the shift in the solution to $\mathcal{WP}_i$. The process of rescheduling is as follows:

Step 1: The sets of new constraints C_{new} and C_{rev} are generated from nurses' requirements and are added to the current problem $\mathcal{WP}_i$. The problem then changes to $\mathcal{WP}_{i+1}$.

Step 2: For all variables, a set of the provisional constraints C^i_{prov} is generated and added to C_{prov}, which is generated in the previous scheduling process. That is,

$$C_{prov} = \bigcup_{j=0}^{i} C^j_{prov} \ (\forall j \ c \in C^j_{prov}, c \notin (C_{prov} \backslash C^j_{prov}))$$

Step 3: C_{prov} is added to $\mathcal{WP}_{i+1}$ and the temporary problem $\mathcal{WP}'_{i+1}$ is generated.

Step 4: For problem $\mathcal{WP}'_{i+1}$, a new schedule is determined according to a hill-climbing algorithm. Since the solution stability is already guaranteed by the addition of C_{prov}, the stable solution would be determined by simply solving $\mathcal{WP}'_{i+1}$.

$\mathcal{WP}_i = (X_i, D_i, C_i, S, \varphi)$: W-MaxCSP at time step i
$\mathcal{A}_i$: an assignment for $\mathcal{WP}_i$
C_{new}: a set of constraints which is added to $\mathcal{WP}_i$
C_{rev}: a set of revised constraints
C_{prov}: a set of provisional constraints
w: the weight of provisional constraint

1 **re_scheduling** $(\mathcal{WP}_i, \mathcal{A}_i, C_{new}, C_{rev}, C_{prov})$
2 $\quad ID_{new} \leftarrow$ ID of nurse associated with $c \in C_{new}$
3 $\quad DT_{new} \leftarrow$ date associated with $c \in C_{new}$
4 $\quad ID_{rev} \leftarrow$ ID of nurse associated with $c \in C_{rev}$
5 $\quad DT_{rev} \leftarrow$ date associated with $c \in C_{rev}$
6 $\quad C_i \leftarrow C_i - \{c\}$ (c is a constraint on the desire associated with $s \in ID_{rev}$)
7 $\quad C_{i+1} \leftarrow C_i \cup C_{new} \cup C_{rev}$
8 $\quad$ **for each** $x_j \in X_i$
9 $\quad\quad$ **if** $s \notin ID_{new} \vee t \notin DT_{new} \vee s \notin ID_{rev} \vee t \notin DT_{rev}$ **then**
10 $\quad\quad\quad C_{prov} \leftarrow C_{prov} \cup lim(1, 1, \{x_j = v_j\}, w)$
11 $\quad$ **end for**
12 $\quad C'_{i+1} \leftarrow C_{i+1} \cup C_{prov}$
13 $\quad \mathcal{A}_{i+1} \leftarrow$**hill_climbing**$(X_i, D_i, C'_{i+1}, S, \varphi)$
14 $\quad$ **for each** $c \in C_{prov}$
15 $\quad\quad$ **if** (c is not satisfied in $\mathcal{A}_{i+1}$) **then**
16 $\quad\quad\quad C_{prov} \leftarrow C_{prov} - \{c\}$
17 $\quad$ **end for**
18 $\quad \mathcal{WP}_{i+1} \leftarrow (X_i, D_i, C_{i+1}, S, \varphi)$
19 $\quad$ **return** $\mathcal{WP}_{i+1}$, $\mathcal{A}_{i+1}$ and C_{prov}

Fig. 2. An Algorithm for Re-scheduling

Step 5: After the problem is solved, C_{prov} is removed from $\mathcal{WP}'_{i+1}$ (the problem turns back to $\mathcal{WP}_{i+1}$) and all of satisfied provisional constraints are removed from C_{prov} in order to prevent overlapping of the provisional constraints in the later re-scheduling.

Figure 2 shows an algorithm for reshceduling. In line 1, there are five input data items: $\mathcal{WP}_i$, $\mathcal{A}_i$, C_{new}, C_{rev}, and C_{prov}. In line 6, some constraints representing requirements from nurses who require changes of their own shift. These are specified using the ID of each nurse, which is picked up in line 4. From line 8 to line 11, new provisional constraints, which are used to keep value $v_{(s,t)}$ in the schedule for $\mathcal{WP}_i$, are generated and added to C_{prov}. The provisional constraints for the target variables of C_{new} and C_{rev} are not generated. In the algorithm shown in Figure 2, although the weights to provisional constraints are identical and the value is predefined, it is possible to assign different weights to each constraint. In line 13, a schedule for $\mathcal{WP}_{i+1}$ is determined by the function **hill_climbing**. The argument of the function **hill_climbing**

$(X_i, D_i, C'_{i+1}, S, \varphi)$ expresses $\mathcal{WP}'_{i+1}$. C'_{i+1} is a union of C_{i+1} and C_{prov} which is generated in line 12. From line 14 to line 17, only satisfied constraints are removed from C_{prov}. Finally, in line 19, $\mathcal{WP}_{i+1}$, $\mathcal{A}_i$, and C_{prov} is outputted.

5 Evaluation

5.1 Experimental Results

We evaluated our method under the following conditions: a scheduling term was 2 weeks, and there are 15 nurses. Accordingly, the problem was to assign shifts (day/evening/night/holiday) to 210 variables. The constraints that have to be satisfied are the following:

(i) Essential constraints

- Constraints on the number of nurses for each working shift per day: For each shift, the number of nurses had to be within the range of maximum and minimum values (day: 4-6, evening: 3-5, night: 3-5).
- Constraints on prohibited working patterns– "day-shift after night-shift," "evening-shift after night-shift," "day-shift after evening-shift," and "3 consecutive night-shifts" – had to be avoided.

The constraints that had to be satisfied, if possible, are the following:

(ii) Desired constraints

- Numbers of working days and holidays (day-shift/evening-shift: over 2 days, night-shift: within 4 days, holiday: 3-5 days).
- Constraints on work patterns that were hopefully prohibited: "4 consecutive evening-shifts," "5 consecutive day-shifts," and "the holiday between some working shift"– should be avoided.

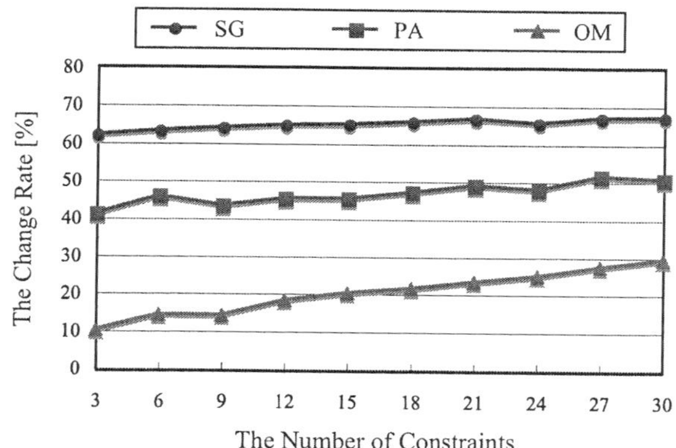

Fig. 3. Comparison on the Change Rate

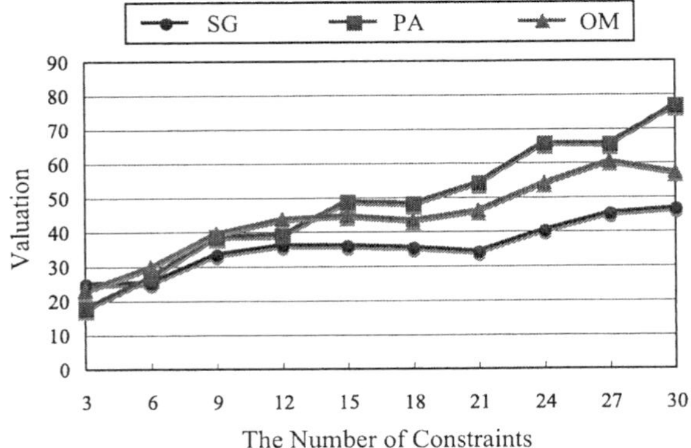

Fig. 4. Comparison on the Valuation

The weights of the essential constraints were set to 9 and those of the desired constraints were set to 4. For each nurse, the constraints, which represented each nurse's requests for two weeks, were generated. We assumed that the weights for these constraints were randomly distributed within the rage [1,9], then each constraints were randomly assigned any value within that range.

In the evaluation, we first generated an initial roster. Then some cells in a roster were randomly selected and constraints for the selected cells were generated. These constraints required the change of working shift and their weights were set to 9. Finally, rescheduling was achieved. In the process of re-scheduling, the weights of the provisional constraint were set to 2, and the upper limit of the search steps was set to 800. We compared our method (OM) to two other methods; one that simply generated a new schedule (SG), and another that used the previous assignment as an initial solution (PA). PA is described in [5, 7]

Figure 3 and Figure 4 respectively show the change rate and the valuation by varying the number of constraints, which requires changes, from 3 to 30. The change rate means the number of changed variables as a proportion of all other changed variables. These graphs show the averages for 30 different problems, each of which has the different number of constraints. In Figure 4, the valuation is calculated without including provisional constraints. As shown in Figure 3, in SG which did not absolutely consider the solution stability, over 60% of the remaining variables were changed. Although the change rate with PA was lower than that with SG, 50% of the remaining variables were changed. Accordingly, in these two methods, despite of the number of constraints requiring changes, many remaining variables were changed their value. In our method, on the other hand, the change rate increased as the number of constraints increased but was less than 10% in the easiest case and less than 30% in the most complicated case. Therefore, we can consider that our method can obtain stable solutions better than the other two methods can. As shown in Figure 4, the valuation of our method was better than that of PA. Although our method obtained worse valuation by comparison with SG, there was not much difference. Namely, our method can obtain stable and good-quality solutions. In this evaluation, the valuation obtained by PA was the worst, especially

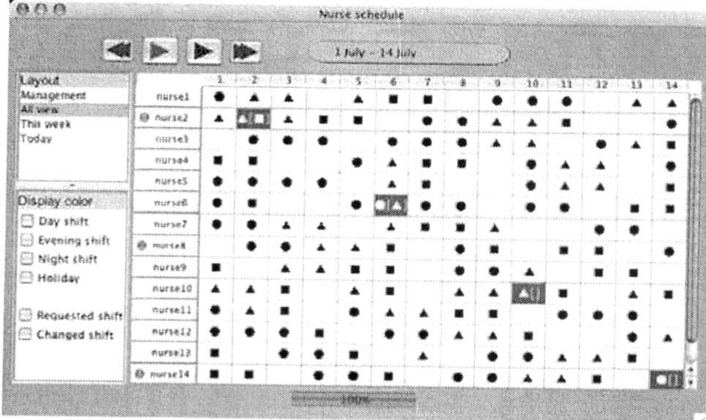

Fig. 5. A Roster before a Re-scheduling

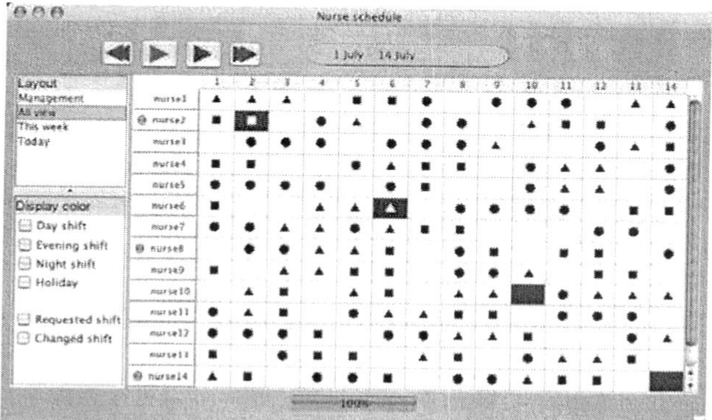

Fig. 6. A Roster after a Re-scheduling

when many changes were required (*i.e.,* a large number of constraints was considered) because the iterative improvement was no longer effective as a result of a large number of requirements for changes. Additionally, the valuation of our method was slightly worse than that of SG because in our method, even if there were better solutions, we could not obtain them because of the provisional constraint for solution stability.

We evaluated the computation time for the above three methods. We calculated the average time needed for 30 trials for problems in which there were 30 requests. In SG and PA, the computation time was not changed as the number of reschedulings increased. In our method, the larger the number of provisional constraints became, the more time-consuming the calculation of the new schedule got. Hence, we evaluated the computation time for the 10th rescheduling. We ran our experiments on a computer (PowerPC G5 1.6GHz) with a program written in Java. The computation time for OM was about 693 seconds and was about 487 seconds for the SG and PA. This difference was not large enough to prevent the practical use of our scheduling system. Moreover, the performance of our method with regard to solution stability can fully compensate this extra computation time.

5.2 System Examples

In this section, we show examples of schedules offered by our scheduling system. Figure 5 and Figure 6 respectively show rosters before and after re-scheduling. Each cell shows each nurse's working shift in the current schedule. Four colored cells are cells that need to have their value changed. The requirement is shown in the interior of "[ ]". For example, "nurse1" requires the working shift in his/her second cell to be changed from evening-shift to night-shift. In Figure 6, showing the result of a re-scheduling, cells in which values are changed in the re-scheduling are indicated by the circles. Additionally, the colored cells are ones in which the value was successfully changed by re-scheduling. As shown in this figure, the values of all required cells are changed appropriately.

6 Conclusion

In this paper, we presented a nurse scheduling system that can re-schedule effectively. To achieve solution stability in the re-scheduling process, we introduced provisional constraints. Provisional constraints can prevent drastic changes to schedules and are effective to keep values that are assigned in the previous solution for all variables. We experimentally confirmed the efficacy of our nurse scheduling system in practical use.

In this paper, we used the provisional constraints in a simple way. That is, we allocated the same weights to each of them. Thus, we are currently elaborating our method to determine and allocate appropriate weights to each provisional constraint.

References

1. Abdennadher, S., Schlenker, H.: Nurse scheduling using constraint logic programming. In: In Proc. of the 11th Annual Conference on Innovative Applications of Artificial Intelligence (IAAI-99). (1999) 838–843
2. Hofe, H.M.: Conplan/siedaplan: Personnel assignment as a problem of hierarchical constraint satisfaction. In: In Proc. of the 3rd International Conference on Practical Applications of Constraint Technologies (PACT-97. (1997) 257–272
3. Dechter, R., Dechter, A.: Belief maintenance in dynamic constraint networks. In: In Proc. of the 7th National Conference on Artificial Intelligence (AAAI-88). (1988) 37–42
4. Miguel, I., Shen, Q.: Hard, flexible and dynamic constraint satisfaction. Knowledge Engineering Review **14** (1999) 285–293
5. Verfaillie, G., Schiex, T.: Solution reuse in dynamic constraint satisfaction problems. In: In Proc. of the 12th National Conference on Artificial Intelligence(AAAI-94). (1994) 307–312
6. Wallace, R.J., Freuder, E.C.: Stable solutions for dynamic constraint satisfaction problems. In: In Proc. of the 4th International Conference on Principles and Practice of Constraint Programming. (1998) 447–461
7. Selman, B., Levesque, H., Mitchell, D.: A new method for solving hard satisfiability problems. In: In Proc. of the 10th National Conference on Artificial Intelligence (AAAI-92). (1992) 440–446

A Semi-autonomous Wheelchair with HelpStar

H. Uchiyama, L. Deligiannidis, W.D. Potter, B.J. Wimpey, D. Barnhard, R. Deng, and S. Radhakrishnan

Artificial Intelligence Center,
University of Georgia, Athens, Georgia, USA
{potter@uga.edu, ldeligia@cs.uga.edu}

Abstract. This paper describes a semi-autonomous wheelchair enabled with "HelpStar" that provides a user who is visually impaired with mobility independence. Our "HelpStar" enabled semi-autonomous wheelchair functions more like a personal assistant, allowing much greater user independence. When the user finds themself in an unforeseen circumstance, the "HelpStar" feature can be activated to allow a remote operator to use Virtual Reality technologies to provide helpful navigational instructions or to send commands directly to the wheelchair. This paper demonstrates the successful integration of assistive technologies that allow a person who is visually impaired and using a wheelchair to navigate through everyday environments.

Keywords: Systems for Real-Life Applications, Human-Robot Interaction, Robotics, Semi-autonomous Vehicles, Virtual Reality.

1 Introduction

A semi-autonomous (SA) wheelchair is an electric powered wheelchair that contains perceptual and navigational capabilities for assisting a person who is visually impaired and using a wheelchair. The goal of an SA wheelchair is to improve the independent mobility of individuals with multiple disabilities based upon integrated sensory information and human-machine interaction. In a nutshell, the SA wheelchair provides the user with enough information about the environment to allow the user to navigate effectively. This is similar to the assistance a sighted, human attendant might provide while assisting with moving the user from one location to another. The user actually controls the motions of the wheelchair but is directed by the attendant.

However, there are circumstances where the SA wheelchair user might need assistance with overcoming some unforeseen predicament. Usually, this requires the user to ask a passerby for assistance or to telephone a nearby friend to come help out. When owners of General Motors vehicles with the OnStar feature face some sort of difficulty while driving, they can request assistance from the OnStar service staff with the touch of a button. Likewise, stay-at-home customers of ADT's Companion Services contact the ADT 24-hour help staff by pressing the button on their personal alert device. Our virtual reality help system (called HelpStar) provides a similar feature but for a different type of user; the visually-impaired wheelchair user.

M. Ali and F. Esposito (Eds.): IEA/AIE 2005, LNAI 3533, pp. 809 – 818, 2005.

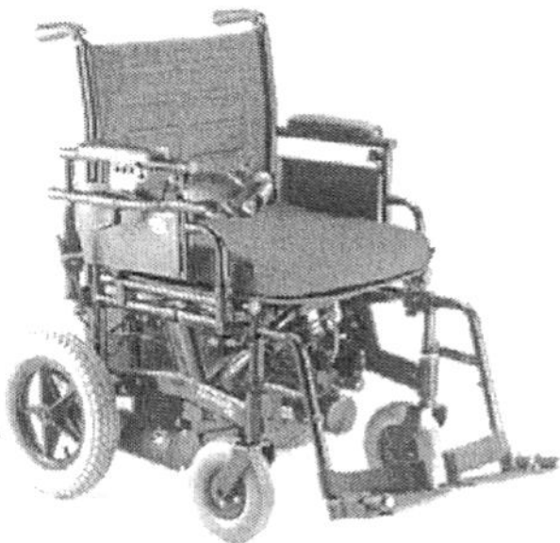

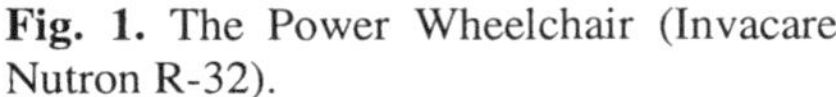

Fig. 1. The Power Wheelchair (Invacare Nutron R-32).

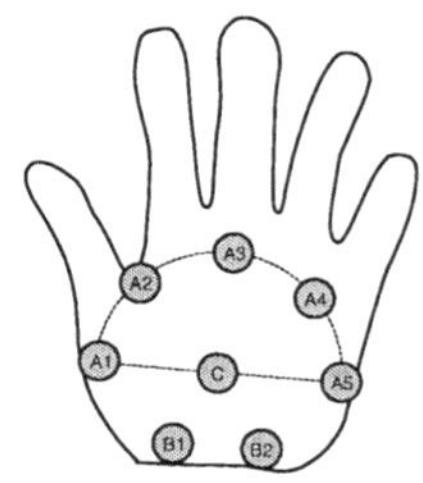

Fig. 2. The arrayed motors of the Vibrotactile Glove

With the touch of a button, a member of the HelpStar staff makes contact with the SA wheelchair user having difficulty. The sensory information routinely collected by the wheelchair is instantly forwarded to the HelpStar center. This information is used to establish a virtual environment in the HelpStar center that reflects the environment encountered by the wheelchair user. This allows the HelpStar staff to analyze, diagnose, and resolve the current problem faced by the user. Corrective feedback could either be in the form of commands to the user (similar to what a local human attendant might do), or commands directly to the SA wheelchair. In either case, the user's immediate problem is resolved with the minimum amount of local interference, and they are free to continue with their activity such as going to class.

The key concept behind the HelpStar project is independence. The SA wheelchair provides an enormous amount of mobility independence to the (essentially blind, using a wheelchair) user. HelpStar provides immediate assistance when the user encounters a problem. However, more importantly, HelpStar provides security and peace-of-mind to the user; if they need help, they know help is just a button push away. The remainder of this paper describes the approach we are taking to develop the HelpStar system. We discuss the major aspects of our semi-autonomous wheelchair, the sensory information acquisition systems, and the HelpStar virtual reality feature. We conclude the paper with a discussion of the current HelpStar prototype implementation.

2 Background

Most public institutions and facilities, such as universities, provide certain types of disability services. For example, the University of Georgia provides an on-campus curb-to-curb van transportation service to students with mobility, visual, and other health-related impairments. Students with disabilities need not worry with outdoor (building to building) transportation. However, no official attendant service is provided for navigating within a university building. This is typically the case on nearly all public university campuses. In addition, many universities have a rich heritage of historic building architecture. Unfortunately, many of these older buildings are not disability friendly. Even when situated in a disability friendly building, maneuvering to a particular destination is not an easy task without the aid of a sighted human attendant.

A number of studies have been conducted in the field of assistive technology which combine robotics and artificial intelligence to develop autonomous wheelchair control. Many of these autonomous wheelchairs are equipped with a computer and a set of sensors, such as cameras, infrared sensors, ultrasonic sensors, and laser rangers. This assortment of equipment is used to address a number of specific problems such as: obstacle avoidance, local environment mapping, and route navigation. With autonomous control, the system probes the environment, detects an obstacle, plans a navigation route, makes a decision, and actually controls the wheelchair. The user simply goes along for the ride. Consequently, the system is ultimately responsible for the results, which leaves the user totally dependent upon the equipment. Most of these autonomous wheelchairs have been employed for research purposes only. NavChair, developed at the University of Michigan [10], transports the user by autonomously selecting three different modes (tasks): obstacle avoidance, door passage, and wall following. The Tao series provided by Applied AI Systems Incorporated is mainly designed for indoor use and features escape from a crowd and landmark-based navigation behaviors in addition to the three common tasks accomplished by NavChair [6]. Tinman II [13] and Rolland [9] also provide similar functionalities. In each case, the user is not involved with the motion of the wheelchair but is a passenger.

3 The SA Wheelchair

Many users are very comfortable with the autonomous wheelchair transportation system. However, others want to be more involved with the process. They want to feel as if they are in control; to have some feeling of independence in both the decision making and the motion involved in their day to day transportation activities. A semi-autonomous wheelchair is more like a personal assistant; the user and the wheelchair cooperate in accomplishing a task. The degree of assistance can hopefully be determined by the user in a real time manner. Wheelesley, one of the early research efforts in this field [17], provided semi-autonomous control of an intelligent wheelchair with a graphical interface. This allows the sighted user to control the wheelchair by selecting from among several navigational tasks. Similarly SmartChair, designed at the University of Pennsylvania [15], consists of a vision-based human robot interface that allows computer-mediated motion control as well as total motion control by the user. Since the man-machine interaction of these intelligent wheelchairs relies on a graphical interface, it is inappropriate for our target audience: the visually impaired person using a wheelchair.

Our goal is to customize a standard wheelchair with enough information gathering capability to allow an unsighted user to effectively control it. Our base wheelchair is a standard power chair (Figure 1) that consists of two front pivot wheels, two rear motorized wheels, a battery pack, and a controller (joystick). The perceptual navigation system consists of a computer, a collection of sensors (e.g. ultrasonic, infrared, and CCD camera), and a man-machine interface.

An SA wheelchair automatically acquires sensory inputs from the environment, processes them, and provides navigational information transformed to fit the user's available sensory resources, such as audible or tactile perception. As a man-machine interface, we developed a tactile "display" designed for the back of the hand, which consists of an array of very small vibrating motors (Figure 2: the Vibrotactile Glove). The Vibrotactile Glove conveys relatively simple navigational and environmental information by activating one or more vibrating motors, which can be intuitively interpreted by the user. By wearing the Vibrotactile Glove connected to the SA wheelchair, the user is able to expand their limited sensory perception (i.e., combine their own sensory perceptions with those of the on-board sensors) for use with navigational decision making. In other words, the user has navigational control over the wheelchair, and uses available sensory information and system commands to pilot the wheelchair.

Our SA wheelchair is designed for users with multiple disabilities (mental disabilities are excluded), specifically users with a combination of physical and sensory disabilities. In the United States over two million individuals are bound to wheelchairs, 67% of which report suffering from two or more disabilities. Likewise 1.8 million people in the United States are counted as having impaired eye-sight including blindness, 63% of which have multiple disabilities (2000 US Census data). A growing number of elderly individuals in the United States and other countries are also potential users of the SA wheelchair.

The type of assistance required to operate a wheelchair varies according to the user's operating skill and physical condition, and an SA wheelchair must provide only as much assistance as the user really needs. We have targeted a typical SA wheelchair user with severe visual impairment or blindness but who is tactilely and audibly competent with fine motor control of the upper extremities. In fact, our research efforts have been influenced by a former student with exactly the disabilities we are targeting. The result of this collaborative effort enabled us to elucidate the specific and most important problems of interest:

Collision Avoidance (including movement in reverse)
Human Detection
Drop-Off Avoidance (e.g., stair steps or sidewalk curbs)
Portal Navigation (e.g., doorways and gates)
Directional-Information Acquisition (e.g., signs and room numbers)
Building Interior Navigation (e.g., inside navigation using map/landmark information)

The first three of those tasks (Collision Avoidance, Human Detection, and Drop-Off Avoidance) are safety oriented tasks and require real time responses, while the others (Portal Navigation, Directional-Information Acquisition, and Building Interior Navigation) are navigation oriented tasks and contain a large amount of cognitive, mapping, and planning processes.

The on-board system of our SA wheelchair attempts to accomplish two of these tasks (behaviors): Collision Avoidance and Portal Navigation, in cooperation with the user. On making decisions among the behaviors, a real-time response of the system is strongly required as well as a parallel processing capability. From an architectural point of view, modularity of the system, which enables us to easily add behaviors, is also an important factor. Based upon those demands, our control architecture for the on-board system [16] utilizes an extension of the Behavior-based control system, which is widely used in the robotics field [2, 3, 4; 11, 12].

Environmental information provided by our on-board system of sensors combined with decision making information is passed to the user in the form of navigational commands. The user receives these commands through the Vibrotactile Glove where different commands are presented as different vibration sequences via the small motors. However, there will surely be times when the user encounters a situation where they are in need of assistance. A human care attendant can assist with these sorts of emergencies, but having an attendant available all the time may not be possible and certainly does not improve independent mobility for the user. HelpStar is designed to provide the necessary assistance without the need for an attendant by utilizing virtual reality (VR) technology.

There are a number of studies that have been conducted, as well as some existing consumer applications, that employ the combination of VR with assistive technology. Most of these efforts focus upon training novice wheelchair users using a wheelchair simulator or virtual environment [1, 8]. Gundersen and his team [7] studied the use of virtual presence control on board a wheelchair at Utah State University. In their project, the on-board system was connected to the remote control booth via an RS-232 serial radio frequency (RF) link. Due to limitations with the RF band, the maximum range between the wheelchair and the remote center was approximately 1000 feet. The wheelchair was manipulated either by an attendant using the remote system or by the on-board (fully) autonomous control system. In either case, the user was not involved with control of the wheelchair.

Utilizing VR technology for remote attendance, we enrich our SA wheelchair control system by providing an "on-demand" care attendant to the SA wheelchair user. When the user hits the "HelpStar" button, the SA wheelchair control system connects to the remote attendant, the HelpStar staff member. The environmental information collected by the SA wheelchair's sensors, and the images acquired by the on-board camera(s) are transmitted to the HelpStar center via the Internet. The equipment available at the HelpStar center re-creates (in a virtual world) the situation encountered by the SA wheelchair user. Of course, the primary limitation is the necessary existence of a wireless cloud in the user's location. However, most college campuses (especially campus buildings and surrounding areas) are enclosed within a wireless cloud with direct access to the Internet.

The SA wheelchair user can select three modes of care attentiveness: observation mode, cooperation mode, and system override mode (Table 1). In observation mode, the HelpStar attendant takes on the passive role of an observer; providing no inputs to the SA wheelchair but simply observing what the wheelchair "senses" and the user's manipulations. The HelpStar attendant may provide some additional information or advice verbally through a headset to the user if they feel it is warranted. In cooperation mode, the HelpStar attendant actively controls the angles of the on-board cameras and ultrasonic sensors. Using the acquired information, the attendant may provide tactile or audible guidance to the SA wheelchair user. The user still manipulates the wheelchair movements. In the system override mode, in addition to controlling the on-board cameras and sensors, the HelpStar attendant can issue direct

Table 1. Attentiveness of the VR system

Mode	Sensor Control	Sensor Input	Vibrotactile Glove	Motion Control
Observation	SA wheelchair	SA wheelchair HelpStar attendant	On	User
Cooperation	HelpStar attendant	HelpStar attendant	On	User
System Override	HelpStar attendant	HelpStar attendant	Off	HelpStar attendant

wheelchair movement commands. This mode can be applied when the wheelchair user is unable to drive the wheelchair, or the user is required to do another task and wheelchair operation simultaneously.

4 Our Current Prototype

Our current prototype development efforts are divided into two directions: the SA wheelchair, and the HelpStar system. Our SA wheelchair is described in detail in [16]. This section discusses the HelpStar prototype; our proof of concept implementation. The hardware utilized for the current HelpStar platform is a commercially available robot kit called ER1, which is supplied by Evolution Robotics [5]. The robot kit includes control software, aluminum beams and connectors for constructing the chassis, two assembled nonholonomic scooter wheels powered by two stepper motors, one 360 degree rotating caster wheel, a power module, a 12V 5.4A battery, and a web-camera. A Dell Latitude C640 laptop computer (Intel Mobile Pentium 4 processor 2.0GHz with 512 MB RAM running Windows XP) is used as the controller device. Additional accessories were also used such as a one-dimension gripper arm, infrared sensors, and additional aluminum beams and connectors. The chassis is reconfigurable and this enables us to design a chassis that would meet our needs. The laptop is equipped with a PCMCIA card that provides four additional USB ports. The ports are utilized by the web-camera, the infrared sensors, the gripper, and the stepper motors.

The software that comes with the ER1 robot, which is called the "ER1 Robot Control Center", can be placed in three configurations.

1. Remotely control an ER1 using another instance of the Control Center on the remote machine.
2. Remotely control an ER1 using TCP/IP.
3. Control the ER1 by running behaviors.

The first configuration enables one to control the ER1 remotely from another computer using another instance of the Control Center on the remote computer. The second configuration enables one to open a TCP connection to a specified port on the Control Center and send ER1 commands to it such as move, open, close, etc. In the third configuration one can specify behaviors that the robot will execute such as find a specific object and then play a sound. More complex behaviors can be specified using

Evolution's toolkit called ERSP. With the behaviors, one can instruct the robot to find different objects or colors, and perform an action when certain conditions are met. The Control Center contains a module to recognize objects seen by the mounted web-camera. We instructed the Control Center to accept commands from a remote machine for its operations, configuration 2. We placed the camera a little bit behind the chassis in order for the gripper to be in the web-camera's field of view. We also placed the gripper as far as possible from the laptop to avoid dropping objects accidentally on top of the laptop.

5 Interacting with the Robot

We developed a new user interface based on Virtual Reality to remotely control multiple ER1 robots (the idea being that the HelpStar center might need to provide multiple concurrent assistance). The Virtual environment consists of three dimensional objects that each represents a robot (an SA wheelchair user). These 3D objects are referred to as TVs, (televisions). The position and orientation of these TVs in the Virtual Environment are unrelated to the physical position and orientation of the robots. The TVs could be any three-dimensional objects but we utilized simple cubes. The images from the robots' web-cameras are transmitted to the remote machine utilizing RTP (Real Time Protocol). These live feeds from the robots' web-cameras are converted into images that we texture map onto the TVs; we utilized Java's Media Framework (JMF) to implement this part of the application. This enables a fully immersed person (the HelpStar attendant) to walk around the TVs and see whatever the web-cameras of the robots see.

The live feeds from the robots' cameras are transmitted to the VR machine. The VR machine is attached to an electromagnetic tracking system, LIBERTY™ [14], which consists of a six-degree-of-freedom (6DOF) tracker with three sensors; LIBERTY™ supports up to eight sensors. One sensor is attached to the Head Mounted Display (HMD) and the other two sensors are attached to the attendant's left and right hands. We also utilize two Pinch Gloves™ provided by Fakespace Systems Incorporated to recognize gestures and send commands to the robots. We have a couple of HMDs where one of them has stereo capability. We also have three different PCs that are capable of driving the application, all of which are equipped with high end video cards. The VR machine is also attached to an eye-tracking machine. We currently use the eye-tracking machine to simply select a desired TV.

The fully immersed person (the HelpStar attendant) can pick up any of the TVs, move them, rotate them, and group them together to place related TVs together. The TVs have some decoration round them to easily distinguish the different TVs. The decoration could include some other objects around the TVs or the name of the user on top of the TVs. When the attendant's hand intersects with one of the TVs and the attendant performs the gesture shown in Figure 3, the selected TV follows the motion of the attendant's hand until they release the TV as shown in Figure 4. The attendant can utilize both of his/her hands to pick up two TVs, or simply pick up one TV with one hand and hand it over to the other hand; the application is aware of two hand interaction.

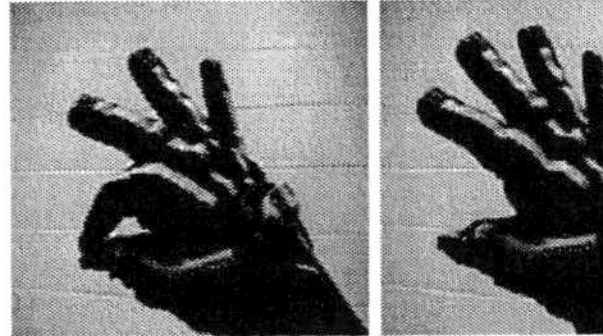

Fig. 3 & 4. Grasping and Releasing a TV

The HelpStar attendant using eye-tracking technology can select one of the three dimensional objects (TVs) that represents a robot. Since the attendant may simply look around and not want to select a particular TV, to select a TV they have to look at it and then perform another gesture to select the TV being looked at. When the TV is selected, the TV's position and orientation change dynamically so that it is always in front of the attendant, even if the attendant moves around. There could be only one TV selected. To deselect a TV the attendant performs the same gesture again.

The application has nine states and is aware of state transitions; actions may be performed on a state or at a state transition. The "Idle" state is a state that indicates no communication with the robots, besides that the application is receiving live feed from the robots' cameras, and no interaction between the attendant and the TVs. While in the "Idle" state, the attendant can pick up a TV with their left or right hand, or even both. The attendant needs to touch a TV and perform a gesture to attach the TV to their virtual hand; the gesture is: touch the thumb and the index finger. As soon as the attendant releases the touching fingers, the hand-TV relationship is terminated and the TV does not follow the attendant's hand anymore. The state machine reverts back to the "Idle" state. While in the "Idle" state, the attendant can also look at a TV and then touch and release the right thumb and middle fingers to select a TV. This transitions the state machine to the "Selected" state where the TV is locked in front of the attendant's field of view. As the attendant moves around, the TV appears in front and the attendant does not see the rest of the Virtual Environment that primarily consists of other TVs. This is the main state of the state machine where the attendant can either deselect the TV or send commands to the robot. To set the speed to slow or fast the attendant "pinches" the left thumb and index fingers and the left thumb and middle fingers respectively. The speed reflects the linear speed not the rotational/angular speed. Slow speed is the slowest the robot can move which is 5 cm/sec and the fast speed is the fastest the robot can move, which is 50 cm/sec. Note here that the speed is set at the transition from the "Speed_fast" or "Speed_slow" states to the "Selected" state. The gripper operates using the left thumb and the left pinky and ring fingers. As long as the state machine is in one of the "Gripper_open" or "Gripper_close" states, the gripper keeps opening or closing respectively. Upon releasing the fingers the state machine transitions to the "Selected" state at which point the "stop" command is transmitted. The stop command instructs the robot to cancel any operation that is being executed. This enables the attendant to partially open or close the gripper.

The other two states are used to maneuver, rotate left or right, and move forward or backwards, the robot. When the state machine transitions from either the "Move" or "Rotate" states to the "Selected" state the "stop" command is transmitted to stop the robot. We use two states, one for the rotation and one for the move because of the robot's limitations. An ER1 cannot move and at the same time rotate. So, either the attendant can instruct the robot to move straight (forward or backwards) or rotate (clockwise or counterclockwise). To instruct the robot to move forward, the attendant needs to simply lean forward and pinch the right thumb and pinky fingers. Similarly, to instruct the robot to move backwards the attendant simply needs to lean backwards and perform the same pinch. Since there is a Polhemus 3D sensor attached to the attendant's HMD to track their position and orientation in space, we define a plane in space that divides the space into two parts. We keep track of the attendant's position orientation continuously and upon the appropriate gesture we define the plane in space. The attendant can move between the divided space to instruct the robot to move forward or backwards.

To instruct the robot to rotate clockwise or counterclockwise, the attendant first needs to perform the right gesture for the state machine to transition to the "Rotate" state at which point the robot follows the rotation of the attendant's head. If the attendant rotates his/her head 20 degrees to the left, the robot also rotates 20 degrees to the left. Since the robot's motors are not as fast as the attendant's head rotation speed, the attendant should rotate slowly to give enough time to the robot to perform the rotation. The rotation angle we are tracking in real time is the rotation around the Y axis, which is pointing upwards.

The rotation or direction of the robot depends on local coordinates. That means that even if the attendant rotates his/her body 180 degrees, forward means forward to the robot and the attendant's left means left to the robot, something that is not true if one tries to maneuver the robot using a conventional mouse. Even if one uses the "Control Center" to remotely control the ER1, changing the speed of the robot would require multiple mouse clicks on different windows. However, utilizing a Virtual Reality interface makes operating an ER1 remotely seem more natural and the attendant can send more commands to the robot by simple gestures/postures.

6 Conclusions and Future Directions

HelpStar is our proposed system for remote assistance to a semi-autonomous wheelchair user using Virtual Reality as an invisible assistive service. The system is specifically designed for individuals who are visually-impaired, use a wheelchair, and want to be involved with their own mobility. A single HelpStar attendant can virtually see multiple users and provide immediate assistance to one or more of them. The SA wheelchair employed in the design allows the user to expand their limited sensory perception for use in navigational decision making. If the SA wheelchair user encounters an unusual situation, all they have to do is push a button to contact the HelpStar center. The key idea, the feature that makes this all worthwhile, is to provide mobility independence to the user.

To demonstrate the feasibility of this concept, the HelpStar prototype currently uses a commercially available robotics kit from Evolutionary Robotics called the ER1. The Virtual Reality environment enables a fully immersed person, the HelpStar attendant, to sense what the robots sense from a remote location. Upon selecting one robot using the PinchGloves, the attendant can control and move the ER1 using of any simple motion commands in a natural manner, perhaps to gain a better visual foothold situation. Once the SA wheelchairs are introduced into the equation, we will be able to begin actual field trials. We expect these to begin during the summer of 2005.

References

1. Adelola, I. A., Cox, S. L., and Rahman, A., (2002). Adaptive Virtual Interface for Powered Wheelchair Training for Disabled Children, In *Proc. of 4th Intl. Conference of Disability, Virtual Reality & Assoc. Technology*, Veszprém, Hungary, pp. 173-180.
2. Arkin, R. C., (1998). *Behavior-based robotics.* The MIT Press: Cambridge, Mass.
3. Brooks, R. A., (1991a). "How to Build Complete Creatures Rather than Isolated Cognitive Simulators." In K. VanLehn (ed.), *Architectures for Intelligence*, pp. 225-239, Lawrence Erlbaum Associates, Hillsdale, NJ.
4. Brooks, R. A., (1991b). "Integrated Systems Based on Behaviors." *SIGART Bulletin* 2, 2(4), pp. 46-50.
5. Evolution Robotics, (2004), Evolution Robotics ER1 Robot Kit, Retrieved October 12, 2004, from http://www.evolution.com/education/er1/
6. Gomi, T. and Griffith, A. (1998) Developing intelligent wheelchairs for the handicapped. In Mittal et al. eds., *Assistive technology and AI.* LNAI-1458, Berlin: Springer-Verlag, pp. 150-78.
7. Gundersen, R. T., Smith, S. J., and Abbott, B. A. (1996) Applications of Virtual Reality Technology to Wheelchair Remote Steering System, In *Proc. of 1st Euro Conf of Disability, Virtual Reality & Assoc. Technology*, Maidenhead, UK, pp. 47-56.
8. Inman, D. P., and Loge, K. (1995). Teaching Motorized Wheelchair Operation in Virtual Reality. In *Proceedings of the 1995 CSUN Virtual Reality Conference.* Northridge: California State University, Retrieved October 1, 2004 from http://www.csun.edu/cod/conf/1995/proceedings/1001.htm
9. Lankenau, A., Röfer, T. and Krieg-Bruckner, B. (2003) Self-localization in large-scale environments for the Bremen Autonomous Wheelchair. In Freksa and et al. eds., *Spatial Cognition III.* LNAI-2685. Berlin: Springer-Verlag, pp. 34-61.
10. Levine, S.P. and et al. (1999) The NavChair Assistive Wheelchair Navigation System. *IEEE Transactions on Rehabilitation Engineering* 7(4): pp. 443-51.
11. Matarić, M. J., (1991). "Behavioral Synergy without Explicit Integration." *SIGART Bulletin* 2, 2(4), pp. 130-133.
12. Matarić, M. J., (1992). "Behavior-Based Control: Main Properties and Implications." *Proc. of IEEE Int.l Conf. on Robotics and Automation, Workshop on Architectures for Intelligent Control Systems*, Nice, France, May, pp. 46-54.
13. Miller, D. (1998) Assistive robotics: an overview. In Mittal et al. eds., *Assistive technology and AI.* LNAI-1458. Berlin: Springer-Verlag, pp. 126-136.
14. Polhemus Inc., (2004), LIBERTY™ , Retrieved October 12, 2004, from http://www. polhemus.com/LIBERTY™ .htm
15. Rao, R. S. and et al. (2002) Human Robot Interaction: Application to Smart Wheelchairs. *Proc. of IEEE International Conference on Robotics & Automation*, Washington, DC, May 2002, pp. 3583-3588.
16. Uchiyama, H. (2003) Behavior-Based Perceptual Navigational Systems for Powered Wheelchair Operations, *Master Thesis Proposal at the University of Georgia*, Retrieved October 11, 2004, from http://www.cs.uga.edu/~potter/robotics/HajimeThesisProposal.pdf
17. Yanco, H. A. (1998) Integrating robotic research: a survey of robotic wheelchair development. *AAAI Spring Symposium on Integrating Robotic Research*, Stanford, California.

ST–Modal Logic to Correlate Traffic Alarms on Italian Highways: Project Overview and Example Installations

Stefania Bandini[1], Davide Bogni[2], Sara Manzoni[1], and Alessandro Mosca[1]

[1] Department of Computer Science, Systems and Communication, University of Milano Bicocca, Milano, Italy
[2] Project Automation S.p.A., Monza, Italy

Abstract. The paper describes and reports the results of a project that has involved Project Automation S.p.A. and the Italian highway company Società Autostrade S.p.A. The main aim of the project is to deliver a monitoring and control system to support traffic operators of Italian highways in their working activities. The main functionalities of the delivered system are: automatic detection of anomalous traffic patterns, alarm filtering according to peculiarities of the monitored highway section, atomic alarm correlation, and automatic control of traffic anomalies. In particular, the paper gives a general introduction to the System for Automatic MOnitoring of Traffic (SAMOT), its aims, design approach and general architecture. Moreover, more details will be given on the Alarm Correlation Module (MCA), a knowledge–based solution based on Modal Logic approach to the atomic alarm correlation and filtering. Finally, we will show three significant installations of the SAMOT system that are currently working to support traffic operators of some of the most important and traffic congested Italian highways.

1 Introduction

The paper describes and reports the results of a project that has involved Project Automation S.p.A. and the Italian highway company Società Autostrade S.p.A. The main aim of the project is to deliver a monitoring and control system to support traffic operators of Italian highways in their working activities. The main functionalities of the delivered System for Automatic MOnitoring of Traffic (SAMOT [1]) are: automatic detection of anomalous traffic patterns, alarm filtering according to peculiarities of the monitored highway section, atomic alarm correlation, automatic control of anomalies.

Traffic safety, congestion prevention and effective actions in case of emergencies can be supported today by the use of sophisticated technology that provides traffic monitoring and control. The aim of a traffic monitoring and control system is to detect traffic flow anomalies, to alert traffic operators and to support them in the management and control of emergencies [2, 3]. Different devices and technologies can be used for traffic anomaly detection (e.g. magnetic loop sensors, video–cameras, infrared, microwave radars, video image processors). In the last few years, the increase in demand for more diversified traffic information and more complex traffic control has lead to video–based detection systems and automatic incident detection systems. Image processing is a relatively new technology. It provides direct incident detection, automatic

M. Ali and F. Esposito (Eds.): IEA/AIE 2005, LNAI 3533, pp. 819–828, 2005.

storage of pre–incident images, as well as simultaneous monitoring of different lanes of traffic data [4]. The image processing technique is also characterized by flexibility to modifications and is suitable for different traffic monitoring applications. A lot of information can be derived from the analysis of traffic video images performed by Video Image Processors (VIP) [5].

When traffic flows are monitored automatically with video processing techniques, each peripheral VIP generates a set of data referring to its own point of observation. Each individual sensor records and transmits any monitored variation with respect to a set of sensitivity thresholds. VIP devices derive information about the traffic flow of the monitored lane (e.g. average speed, volume, occupancy, slowdowns, queues, wrong–way driving vehicles, stopped vehicles, vehicle gap and so on) according to algorithms for vehicle detection that, for instance, process differences of grey tone between background and car images. Artificial intelligence techniques like genetic algorithms and neural networks have often been employed to automatically derive from VIP elaborations atomic anomalous traffic conditions [6]. Traffic monitoring systems alert traffic operators every time an atomic anomaly is detected by VIPs, and automatically store several frames of the pre–anomaly images that can be extracted for analysis at a later stage. Different video detection algorithms have been proposed, and their comparison is usually based on Detection Rate (DR), False Alarm Rate (FAR) and Detection Time (DT). These evaluation parameters strongly influence one another: the shorter is the DT, the higher is the DR but, unfortunately, the higher is also the FAR [7].

One of the main problems in traffic anomaly detection is that generally only atomic anomalies are considered. According to a general framework for monitoring and control systems, correlation of heterogeneous data collected from the environment consists in merging and comparing true facts in different places at different time [8]. Correlation allows to exploit relations along space and time, inherent to the domain's structure, to draw more rich and informative inferences. In particular, alarm correlation is the integration of anomalous situations detected in the environment (i.e. the alarms detected by local agencies) along time. According to the above informal definition of correlation, a dedicated formal model has designed and applied within the SAMOT system in order to correlate atomic anomalous traffic patterns and to represent them as facts with respect to their relative space and time locations. The formal language based on Modal Logic in order to correlate those alarms has been described in [9, 8]. It allows the MCA module to reason on the adjacency relations among spatio–temporal locations of the single alarms and to interprete them as true facts with respect to specific space–time locations. The fundamental notion that the model introduces is that of spatio–temporal region (ST–region), on which propositions are evaluated. The Alarm Correlation Module (MCA) of SAMOT system bases its analysis, correlations and filtering of atomic traffic anomalies (detected by the VIP boards) according to the ST–region model. The main contribute of the MCA is *to logically deduce significant properties on spatio–temporal localized regions* and, thus, to improve traffic operators' awareness on the traffic dynamics. This improvement is mainly provided by the *filtering of non–significant alarms* that are not notified to SAMOT users that allows them to concentrate only on really dangerous situations. This advantage has been demonstrated by the system test during which it has been obtained both a reduction of the system FAR (False Alarm Rate) and an increase of its DR (Detection Rate) (without affecting the Detection Time).

After an overview of the System for Automatic MOnitoring of Traffic (SAMOT), the paper focuses on MCA module (giving an overview of its underlying model based on ST–modal logic) and on three significant instantiations of SAMOT that are currently working to support traffic operators of some of the most important and traffic congested Italian highways.

2 The SAMOT System

Traffic operators devoted to traffic monitoring and control of some of the more congested Italian highways are provided by the SAMOT system with a set of data about traffic situation of the monitored highway section and, when traffic anomalies are detected, they can undertake all the needed operations on SAMOT devices through the SAMOT user interface. For instance they can select, create and activate an adequate sequence of camera images to be shown on the Close–Circuit TV to verify the detected anomaly, or they can activate a message on Variable Message Panels (VMP) to inform motorists about traffic anomalies. The SAMOT system supports traffic operators in traffic control providing them with acoustic and visual warnings when anomalous traffic conditions are detected. Anomaly detection is performed by a set of Video Images Processing (VIP) boards that analyze images collected by video–cameras and identify according to vehicle velocity and road occupancy rate, anomalous traffic situations like *slow traffic*, *queue*, *stopped vehicle*, and *wrong–way driving vehicle*. Moreover, the system provides its users with some applications to configure, supervise and maintain the system. These applications allow to modify and verify the working status of system components and to modify system parameters. For instance, it is possible to modify the number of cameras and VIPs or the default video sequences that, when traffic anomalies are detected, are shown on operator CCTV in order to observe its dynamic. Finally, a dedicated knowledge–based module (Alarm Correlation Module - MCA) provides SAMOT users with an automatic alarm elaboration tool that correlates sequences of traffic situations, filters traffic anomalies and supports and provides traffic control.

2.1 SAMOT Overall Architecture

The two layers characterizing the architecture of the SAMOT system (*peripheral layer* and *central layer* in Figure 1) are connected by a Wide Area Network (WAN) and a Local Area Network (LAN). At the peripheral layer, close to the monitored road section, are located technological devices for image and traffic flow data acquisition (cameras and VIPs), video signal coding and transmission (codec MPEG-1 and multiplexers), and motorist information (Variable Message Panels - VMP). All the devices at the peripheral layer are linked to and managed by a set of Peripheral Processing Units (PPU) that are connected to the central layer through the WAN. At the central layer are located all the devices for video signal decoding into analogic format and for video display of images (decoder MPEG-1 and Front End), the Supervising Workstation and the Operator Workstations (Windows NT personal computer).

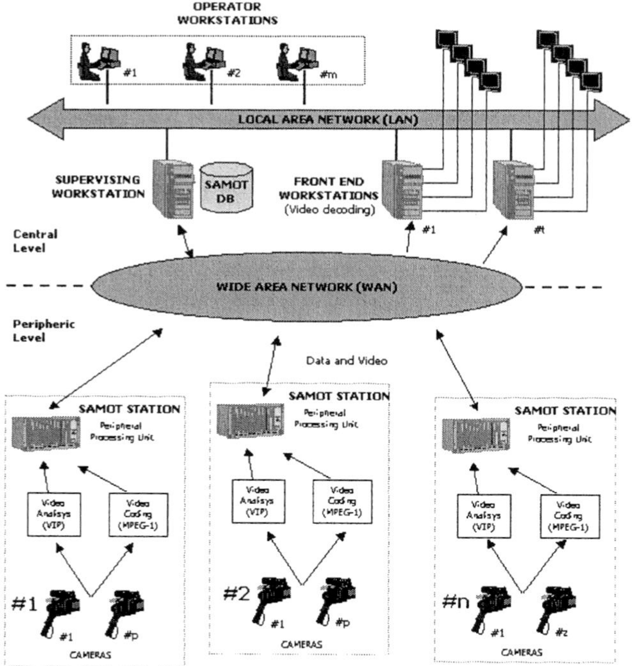

Fig. 1. SAMOT System Architecture

The quite modular, scalable and configurable SAMOT architecture provides device integration through the following modules:

SAMOT Remote: installed on Peripheral Processing Units, it provides an interface among peripheral devices for traffic image acquisition, coding and transmission, working status diagnosis and to execute action commands like messages on VMPs.

SAMOT FrontEnd: installed at the central layer on Front End Workstations, it decodes into the analogical format the MPEG–1 video flow received from the network in order to show it on operator Close–Circuit TVs.

SAMOT Supervisor: installed at the central layer on the Supervising Workstation, it manages the whole system by coordinating operator requests and their processing both at the peripheral layer (e.g. device configuration and messages on VMP) and at the central layer (e.g. video flow selection). Moreover, it manages and connects to other workstations SAMOT archive (SAMOT DB). SAMOT DB contains an image of the real system (e.g. number and type of PPUs, number and location of cameras, number of detecting devices) and it allows all SAMOT modules to be independent from development technologies.

SAMOT GUI: installed at central layer on each Operator Workstation, it provides the Graphical User Interface for data visualization, remote device control and diagnosis (e.g. cameras, multiplexers and VMPs), user profile management (security settings) and system configuration both from the physical viewpoint (e.g. type and number of devices) and the logical one (e.g. relation between alarms and adequate actions). In particular, it handles video flows adequately, organizing them according to automatically programmed scanning sequences. Many previously programmed sequences can be retrieved and directly updated through the SAMOT GUI.

SAMOT MCA: installed at central layer, it correlates atomic traffic situation, filters traffic anomalies taking into account their spatial and temporal location, and supports traffic operators in event–driven control actions.

2.2 The Correlation Module of SAMOT

Within SAMOT architecture, the role of video–cameras installed in the monitored field area is to capture images about their own portion of the monitored road. Images are on–line processed by VIPs that, according to techniques based on genetic algorithms' approach, identify several anomalous traffic situations that may occur on a highway section. Accordingly to VIP analysis, an alarm may be generated and notification (acoustic and/or visual) warning signals may be sent to traffic operators.

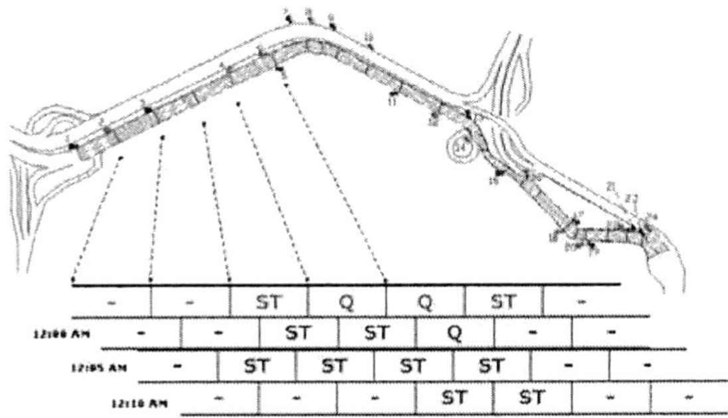

Fig. 2. Queue downflow: the transformation of a queue Q that characterizes two adjacent atomic ST–regions into a slow traffic situation (ST) and its following reduction

However, the correlation of atomic anomalous traffic conditions can give a wider perspective on what is happening on the highway and improve efficiency and effectiveness control actions' selection. MCA in particular supports traffic operators in their interpretation task on traffic situations, correlating atomic traffic anomalies and filtering them taking into account their spatial and temporal location. MCA manages acoustic and visual warnings and camera sequences on operators' videos and automatically displays adequate messages on VMP panels to inform motorists. Figure 2 shows a representation of a highway road section as a sequence of cameras that are installed along it and that monitor adjacent portions of the road (in particular, the representation in the figure refers to SAMOT installation on A10-A7 highway that will be described in Section 3). In this example, alarms generated by VIP boards are queue, slow traffic (other possible types of alarms are: stopped vehicle, wrong-way vehicle, camera failure).

Multiple atomic traffic anomalies that refer to adjacent video–cameras can sometimes be correlated and interpreted as Anomalous Traffic Patterns (ATP). An ATP represents a traffic anomaly referring to a sequence of atomic traffic situations detected by VIPs and referring to multiple cameras adjacently located. Each pair of rows represents the correlation of two traffic patterns that is, two sequences of atomic traffic anomalies, referring to consecutive time–stamps (i.e. T_0 and T_1). According to spatial and temporal relations among atomic traffic anomalies occurring on anomalous patterns, ATPs can be *created* (when two or more spatially adjacent road portions change their states from 'normal traffic' to 'anomalous traffic'), *deleted*, *extended* (when a portion of the road section adjacent to an already detected anomalous traffic pattern changes its state from 'normal' to 'anomalous' traffic), *reduced*, *shifted* (when an anomalous traffic pattern is reduced at an endpoint and extended at the other endpoint), *decomposed* into two patterns (when a portion of the road section within an anomalous traffic pattern, changes its state from 'anomalous' to 'normal' traffic) or *composed* by multiple patterns. The corresponding relations are fundamental to provide a qualitative comprehensive view over the current traffic situation according to its dynamic evolution; in this sense, the relevance of ATPs consists in the opportunity to be qualified by those relations.

Atomic space intervals, characterizing the space dimension in the semantics of ST–modal logic perfectly match with the succession of highway atomic sections monitored by a single camera in SAMOT. Each atomic section corresponds thus to a minimal space interval and the order of those sections in the highway is mapped into the space line that defines ST–regions. Since the monitored highway section is obviously finite, we can impose the space dimension to be a succession of elements as long as the number of VIPs on the highway. Time dimension in SAMOT is taken to be the time line determined by the system image acquisition rate. As it starts as the system is initialized, it can be assumed to be finite in the past, but not in the future. Thus, ST–regions correspond in SAMOT to the dynamic of the monitored section of the highway over time. Since atomic sections can be easily identified by a code, an example of an atomic ST–region is [(12.45:12.46),(T_{22}:T_{23})] (where the component (T_{22}:T_{23}) identifies the highway section that is monitored by a single VIP during the minute between 12.45 and 12.46) and [(12.45:12.46),(T_{22}:T_{26})] is an example of a non–atomic ST–region.

Fig. 3. A frame sequence taken by a single camera installed on the S. Donato Tunnel

The modal operators of the ST–modal logic allow referring to significant ST–regions in the SAMOT domain (see [8] for a definition of their meaning). An alarm, i.e. a traffic anomaly occurring over an atomic section at a specific time, is a true proposition in an atomic ST–region. According to the significant set of chosen alarms, a first set of primitive propositions consist of the following set: {*queue*, *slow_traffic*, *stopped_vehicle*, *ww_vehicle*, *f_camera*, *normal_t*}. The meaning of those propositions is almost intuitive. Less intuitive propositions are: *ww_vehicle*, that indicates the presence of a vehicle driving in the wrong–way direction; *f_camera*, that means that the camera is not properly working (all the VIP boards are equipped with an self–diagnosis component); and, *normal_t* indicating that no alarm has been generated. According to the set of the atomic propositions, we can then define a complex proposition ATS (Anomalous Traffic Situation), whose meaning is the following disjunction of alarms:

$$\mathtt{ATS} =_{\mathrm{def}} \mathit{queue} \vee \mathit{slow\_traffic} \vee \mathit{stopped\_vehicle} \vee \mathit{ww\_vehicle}$$

Note that the definition naturally implies a local closure of the domain relative to the set of possible traffic anomalies; furthermore, ATS and *normal_t* are mutually exclusive (i.e. $\mathit{normal\_t} \rightarrow \neg\, \mathtt{ATS}$). As an example, let us consider the following implications relative to the *creation* and *deletion* of anomalous traffic patterns, where the antecedents consist of particular configurations of atomic traffic anomalies along space and time dimensions:

$$\mathit{creation} \leftarrow \mathtt{ATS} \wedge \langle\overline{\mathbf{A^T}}\rangle \mathit{normal\_t}$$

$$\mathit{deletion} \leftarrow \mathit{normal\_t} \wedge \langle\overline{\mathbf{A^T}}\rangle \mathtt{ATS}$$

The true value of formulas about an atomic ST–regions is determined by the VIP signals: if an anomalous traffic condition is detected (an alarm is notified), the corresponding proposition is true, otherwise *normal_t* is true. Figure 3 represents a traffic situations flow detected by a single camera at adjacent time–stamps. The Alarm Correlation Module supports the deduction of dangerous ATP situations; for instance, in the above example the model axioms proof the *creation* at the fourth and ninth shots of the camera, where respectively a *slow_traffic* follows a *n_traffic* situation, and a *stopped_vehicle* follows a *slow_traffic* situation.

3 SAMOT Installations on Italian Highways

3.1 Installation at Connection of A10-A7 (Genova)

The first installation of the SAMOT system concerns the highway section between the Genova Aeroporto and Genova Ovest (East direction) at the conjunction of A10 and A7 Italian highways, managed by Autostrade per lItalia S.p.A. This highway section is really various and characterized by several critical sections: there are three tunnels of about one kilometer each, a bridge, some uphill sections where trucks usually keep slow speed and on the whole section (of about 2.8 km) there is no emergency lane. It is clear that any type of problems to any of the huge number of vehicles that everyday drive on this section and the slowness of vehicles can cause drastic traffic congestions.

This one has been the first installation of the SAMOT system, on which it has been performed the first field test that took 6 months [1]. The system for the whole period of its functioning has demonstrated its robustness in managing the huge amount of traffic anomalies detected each hour by VIPs (i.e. about one thousand per hour). Moreover, system users have evaluated as very useful and interesting the MCA alarm correlation and filtering functionality. The test results, for all the alarm types that the system was configured to detect, can be summed up as follows: Detection Rate (DR): $> 95\%$ and $> 99\%$ (in tunnels); False Alarm Rate (FAR) $< 2\%$; Detection Time (DT) $< 10sec$; Minimum extension of the monitored area: $\geq 400m$; System working time (scheduled system stop included) $> 99,5\%$

After the positive results of this test installation, the SAMOT system is now functioning on the same highway section and other installations have been performed by Project Automation S.p.A. (current system performances, in all the installations, are constant and do not significantly differ from the test results).

3.2 Installation on A1 Tunnel (S. Donato - MI)

This second installation of the SAMOT system is significative since it concerns a road section where two tunnels of the Italian A1 highway (at San Donato - Milano) are present. It concerns about 1 km and it has been classified as highly critical infrastructure from the traffic viewpoint, due to its structure and altitude that cause very different velocities of different types of vehicles and, thus, can cause slow traffic conditions and frequent incidents.

In this installation the peripheral unit is composed by two independent modules (one for each direction). Each module manages 8 video–cameras, 8 VIP boards, 1 board to record and control video sequences, 1 video matrix, 1 PC to control and compress videos in MPEG-1 format, 1 transmission interface to the network at 2 Mb/s. In this case video cameras able to ensure a high level resolution of videos also under the low light conditions of tunnels have been installed (an exwave sensor of 1//2"). The video signal is transferred on multimodal optic fiber in order to be processed by a Traficon VIP board that is configured in order to detect the following atomic anomalous traffic situations: stopped vehicle, slow traffic, wrong–way driving vehicle. The control board records digital videos related to anomalous traffic situations and concerning the period of 20 sec before the detected anomaly and of 20 sec after it. According to this analysis the system verifies the anomaly dynamics and defines possible actions to prevent the repetition of similar anomalies in the future. The video matrix either selects a video signal or manages a cycle of videos acquired by several cameras and send it to the control center. Thus the peripheral unit serves as signal collector, as sender to the central unit of alarms and video images, and as receiver and actuator of control actions.

The central unit is composed by four PCs, namely a director, a frontend and two client PCs. The director PC collects and stores into a relational database anomalous traffic situations, it analyzes them according to the MCA approach and manages outputs to operators and actuator devices. The frontend PC translates video signals into the PAL format in order to be visualized on monitor devices of 21". The client PCs, connected through a LAN to other system components, provides traffic operators with the user interface that has been specifically designed for this installation.

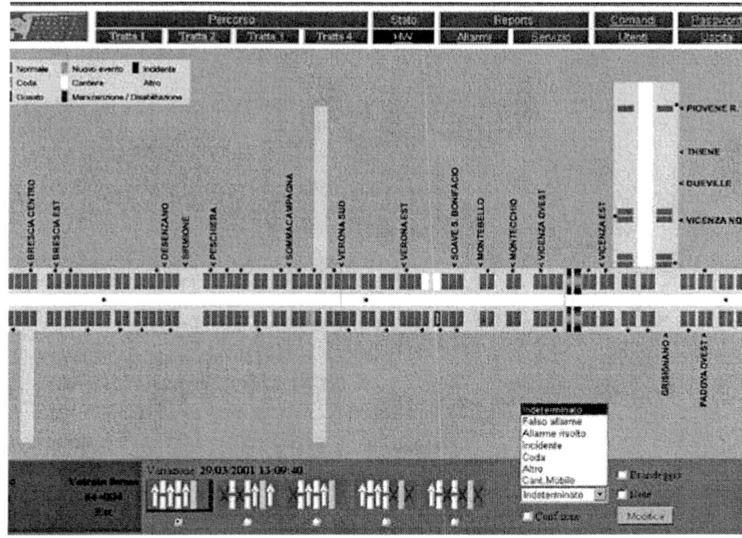

Fig. 4. SAMOT Web–based User Interface

3.3 Installation on A4 (Brescia - Padova)

The SAMOT installation that concerns A31 and A4 highways (section of about 182 kilometers between Brescia and Padova) is characterized by 89 standard cameras and 3 cameras that can remotely be managed by traffic operators. Each camera provides video images about both the highway directions (each one composed by three lanes and one emergency lane). VIP boards have been configured in order to detect anomalous situations together with the specific highway lane on which they occur. Moreover, the installed VIP boards allow their effective functioning on different weather conditions and daylights (during the night, vehicles are identified by their lights). Thus, this installation of the SAMOT system is quite particular from the hardware configuration viewpoint. Specific and innovative solutions have been provided also from the user interface and software viewpoints. The most significative software innovation refers to the presence of road sections characterized by different criticality levels. The specification of this feature for each road section can be conducted by traffic operators directly through SAMOT user interface and it allows MCA to behave according to this additional information and in a more effective way. The web–based user interface of the SAMOT system is shown in Figure 4. It allows traffic operators to monitor the highway sections, to be notified about anomalous situations and to classify them as either *critical* or *non–critical*. Moreover, alarm correlation about anomalous traffic conditions that refer to adjacent highway lanes is performed.

4 Concluding Remarks

SAMOT, System for Automatic MOnitoring of Traffic, has been presented. In particular, we have focused on its MCA (the SAMOT module that according to a Modal Logic model that correlates atomic traffic anomalies and filters them according to their spatial and temporal location) and on three installations of SAMOT on some of the most important Italian highways. Traffic control is achieved by the MCA that provides traffic operators with necessary information about the detected anomaly and directly shows adequate messages on variable message panels. For the MCA development a knowledge–based approach has been adopted. The knowledge acquisition campaign has been conducted on the team of traffic operators that are the current end–users of SAMOT. This knowledge has been acquired, formalized according to a Modal Logic approach and then, implemented into the MCA rule–based production system. The MCA has been integrated into the SAMOT general architecture and is now successfully installed and functioning on some of the main and traffic congested Italian highways. These installations have demonstrated the contribute of MCA to SAMOT according to all the parameters on which usually traffic monitoring and control are evaluated.

References

1. Bandini, S., Bogni, D., Manzoni, S.: Knowledge-based alarm correlation in traffic monitoring and control. In: Proceedings of the IEEE 5th International Conference on Intelligent Transportation Systems (ITSC02), September 3-6 2002, Singapore, IEEE Computer Society (2002)
2. Papageorgiou, M., Pouliezos, A., eds.: Transportation systems, Proceedings of the 8th IFAC/IFIP/IFORS symposium, Chania. Volume 1, 2, 3. (1997)
3. Ferrier, N., Rowe, S., Blake, A.: Real-time traffic monitoring. In: Proceedings of WACV94. (1994) 81–88
4. Ng, A., Ang, K., Chung, C., Gu, M., Ng, Y.: Change of image. Traffic Technology International (2002) 56–58
5. Egmont-Petersen, M., deRidder, D., Handels, H.: Image processing with neural networks a review. Pattern Recognition **35** (2002) 119–141
6. Bielli, M., Ambrosino, G., Boero, M., eds.: Artificial Intelligence Applications to Traffic Engineering, Utrecht, The Netherlands (1994)
7. Versavel, J.: Sparing lives, saving time. Traffic Technology International (2001) 189–194
8. Bandini, S., Mosca, A., Palmonari, M., Sartori, F.: A conceptual framework for monitoring and control system development. In: Ubiquitous Mobile Information and Collaboration Systems. Volume 3272 of Lecture Notes in Computer Science., Springer-Verlag (2004) 111–124
9. Bandini, S., Manzoni, S., Mosca, A., Sartori, F.: Intelligent alarm correlation. In: Proc. of System, Machine and Cybernetics, Special Session on Modelling and Control of Transportation and Traffic Systems, Washington. (2003) 3601–3606

Train Rescheduling Algorithm Which Minimizes Passengers' Dissatisfaction

Tomii Norio[1], Tashiro Yoshiaki[1], Tanabe Noriyuki[2], Hirai Chikara[1], and Muraki Kunimitsu[3]

[1] Railway Technical Research Institute,
2-8-38 Hikari-cho Kokubunji-shi Tokyo 185-8540 Japan
{tomii, ytashiro, hirai}@rtri.or.jp
[2] Hokkaido Railway Co., Ltd.,
1-1 Kita 11 Nishi 15 Chuo-ku Sapporo-shi Hokkaido Japan
[3] New Media Research Institute Co., Ltd.,
2-7-5 Yoyogi Shibuya-ku Tokyo Japan
muraki@nms-jg.co.jp

Abstract. Although computer systems which assist human experts in rescheduling disrupted train traffic is being practically used recently, they are not so helpful in decreasing the workload of human experts. This is because they are lacking in intelligence such as to automatically make rescheduling plans. In this paper, we propose an algorithm for automatic train rescheduling. Firstly, we propose to use passengers' dissatisfaction as a criterion of rescheduling plans and to regard the train rescheduling problem as a constraint optimization problem in which dissatisfaction of passengers should be minimized. Then we introduce an algorithm for train rescheduling designed as a combination of PERT and meta-heuristics. We also show some experimental results of the algorithm using actual train schedule data.

1 Introduction

In Japan, railways play the most significant role both in urban and intercity transportation. In fact, trains are operated every couple of minutes in many cities carrying a massive amount of commuters and even in Shinkansen high speed railway lines where trains run at the maximum speed of 300km/h, hundreds of trains a day are operated every three to four minutes [1]. Thus, it is strongly desired for railways to provide those people with a stable and reliable transportation.

Although Japanese railways are known to be the most punctual in the world, sometimes train traffic is disrupted when accidents, natural disasters, engine troubles happen. In order to restore the disrupted traffic, a series of modification of the current train schedule is done. This task is called "train rescheduling [2, 3]."

Recently, computer systems which help human experts in charge of train rescheduling (they are called train dispatchers) began to be put in a practical use. These systems, however, are lacking in a function to automatically make rescheduling plans.

Hence, train rescheduling is totally left to train dispatchers, and this is a heavy burden for them.

M. Ali and F. Esposito (Eds.): IEA/AIE 2005, LNAI 3533, pp. 829-838, 2005

In order to break through such a situation, it is required for train rescheduling systems to be equipped with an advanced function of automatic rescheduling.

To make train rescheduling plans, however, is an extremely difficult task [4]. Details will be described later in Chapter 2 but to name a few; objective criteria of rescheduling plans are diverse depending on the situations; it is a large size and complicated combinatorial problem in which hundreds or sometimes thousands of trains are involved; an urgent problem solving is required etc.

In this paper, we propose to treat the train rescheduling problem as a constraint optimization problem and introduce an algorithm which quickly produces a rescheduling plan. To this aim, we have to settle the following two issues.

1. To establish objective criteria of rescheduling plans.
2. To develop an algorithm which quickly produces a near optimal rescheduling plan.

To settle the first issue, we propose to use passengers' dissatisfaction as objective criteria of rescheduling plans. For the second issue, we introduce an algorithm combining PERT (Program Evaluation and Review Technique) and simulated annealing. This algorithm quickly produces a rescheduling plan in which passengers' dissatisfaction is minimized.

We analyze situations where passengers would complain and accumulate them in a file called a Claim File. Situations when passengers complain would be different depending on the characteristics of lines, times when accidents happened, severity of accidents etc. Thus, we prepare different Claim Files reflecting those characteristics and select an appropriate one before rescheduling plans are made. As mentioned earlier, criteria of rescheduling should be decided case-by-case basis, and we try to concur this problem by providing Claim Files appropriate for the situation.

This idea makes it possible to develop an intelligent algorithm which automatically produces a rescheduling plan, which was not realized in conventional works.

The overall structure of the algorithm is based on a combination of simulated annealing (SA) and PERT. One of the key idea of this algorithm is that SA does not explicitly deal with the departure/arrival times of trains and they only decide the outline of the schedule such as cancellation of trains, departing orders of trains etc., and the PERT technique calculates the arrival and departure times of trains so that there occur no conflict among them. This idea makes it possible to enormously reduce the search space of SA and get an algorithm which works quite fast.

In our algorithm, train schedules are expressed by Train Scheduling Networks, which is a kind of PERT networks. Then we propose an efficient rescheduling algorithm using a property that passengers' complaint relating with delays of trains could be eliminated by modification of the Train Scheduling Network focusing only on the critical paths in it.

We have implemented the algorithm on a PC and evaluated its effectiveness through several experiments using actual train schedule data. Then we have confirmed that our algorithm works good enough to produce rescheduling plans which are practically usable.

2 Train Rescheduling Systems: State of the Art

2.1 Why Train Rescheduling Is Difficult?

Methods of schedule modification employed in train rescheduling are shown in Table 1. We have to note that a combination of these methods are taken, not only one of them is used.

Train rescheduling is quite a difficult work. Major reasons of this are as follows:

(1) It is difficult to decide an objective criterion of rescheduling which is uniformly applicable. Criteria for rescheduling differ depending on various factors such as severity of accidents, time when the accident occurred, characteristics of the line such as whether it is a commuter line or an intercity railway line etc. To give an example, although delays of trains are usually considered to be undesirable, regaining the schedule is not so significant in railway lines where trains run with short intervals and it is considered to be more important to prevent the intervals from becoming too large. The criteria should be even different depending on the time accidents have happened. During the rush hours in the morning, to keep the constant intervals between trains is considered to be more important than to reduce delays, whereas in the afternoon, it is most important to regain the schedule before evening rush hours and sometimes a considerable number of trains are cancelled.

Table 1. Methods of rescheduling

Method	Contents of modification
Cancellation	To cancel operation of trains
Partly cancellation	To cancel a part of operating area of trains
Extra train	To operate an extra train which are not contained in the original schedule
Extension of train	To extend the operating section of a train
Change of train-set operation schedule	To change the operation schedule of a train-set
Change of track	To change the track of a train in a station
Change of departing order	To change the departing orders of trains (often, change the station where a rapid train passes a local train)
Change of meeting order	To change the meeting orders of trains (either in single track line or at a station where two lines come together)
Change of stop/pass	To make a train stop at a station which it was originally scheduled to pass
Change of train types	To change the type of a train (to change a rapid train to a local train, etc.)

(2) Train rescheduling is a large size combinatorial problem. In urban areas, the number of trains involved often reaches hundreds or even thousands. Moreover, in Japan, train schedules are prescribed by a unit of fifteen seconds (in urban lines, the time unit is five seconds). In making train rescheduling plans, we have to

determine departure/arrival times and tracks for each train, whether to cancel trains or not etc. This is quite a complicated and large size problem difficult to deal with. As a matter of fact, when trains are delayed about one hour, the number of required schedule modification sometimes reaches several hundreds.

(3) A high immediacy is required. Since train rescheduling plans are made in order to modify the schedule of trains which are running at that time, they have to be made quickly enough.

(4) All the necessary information cannot be always obtained. Some of the information necessary to make better rescheduling plans are; how crowded trains are/will be, how many passengers are/will be waiting for trains at stations, how many passengers will emerge at stations and so on. Under current technology, however, it is quite difficult or almost impossible to get or estimate such information.

To sum up, the train rescheduling problem is a so called ill-structured problem which is large size, complicated and whose criteria are full of ambiguity.

2.2 Problems of Current Train Rescheduling Systems

Since train rescheduling is such a difficult job, assistance by computer systems have been longed for, and nowadays train rescheduling systems are being practically used. Although they have a function to predict future train schedules, the problem is that they are very poor in automatic rescheduling. They only have a function to suggest changes of departing orders of trains and do not have a function to use other rescheduling methods of Table 1. So, to make rescheduling plans is totally left to train dispatchers.

The reason why current train rescheduling systems are lacking in intelligence is due to the reasons mentioned in 2.1. That is, objective criteria of train rescheduling are diverse and it is impossible to cope with it by a single criterion, thus a framework in which computers bear a routine work and human experts take charge of decision making is employed.

But train rescheduling systems developed under this framework is not useful to decrease the workload of dispatchers.

(1) It is often a time consuming work to input a large number of schedule modifications by hand. Sometimes, their inputs are too late to change the schedule.

(2) Current rescheduling systems adopt an algorithm to iterate a local change of schedules, hence they are lacking in a viewpoint to get a globally optimal solution.

3 Evaluation of Train Rescheduling by Passengers' Dissatisfaction

3.1 Previous Research on Evaluation of Train Rescheduling

In order to regard the train rescheduling problem as a combinatorial optimization problem, we first have to clarify objective criteria of the problem.

Until now, following ideas are proposed as the criteria [5-8].

(1) Delay time of trains should be minimized.

(2) Number of cancelled trains should be minimized.

(3) Time required until the train traffic is normalized should be minimized.
(4) Passengers' disutility should be minimized.
(5) Gaps of the service level between one which passengers expect and one passengers actually receive should be minimized.

None of these criteria, however, are satisfactory, because situations when train rescheduling is conducted are diverse. For example, an idea to use delay times of trains is not appropriate when a number of trains are cancelled. The more trains are cancelled, the less the delay would be, but passengers suffer from inconvenience, because trains are crowded and frequency of trains decreases. The idea to use the number of cancelled trains as a criterion has an opposite problem. Although it is true that cancellation of trains sometimes inconvenience passengers, this is the most effective method to restore disrupted schedule. Thus, it is often desirable to cancel appropriate number of trains and to normalize schedules especially when an accident happened before evening rush hours. Passengers' disutility and gaps of service level seem to be promising as the criteria from passengers' viewpoint but they are quite difficult to measure with existing technology.

3.2 Evaluation of Train Rescheduling Based on Passengers' Dissatisfaction

In this paper, we propose to use "passengers' dissatisfaction" as an objective criterion for train rescheduling. The background of this idea is as follows:

(1) Situations when train rescheduling is done are quite diverse and it is not a good idea to use a single criterion such as the total delays of trains, number of cancelled trains etc.
(2) Criteria for train rescheduling have to be set up from passengers' viewpoint, because in a situation where train schedules are disrupted, passengers' viewpoint is far more important than that of railway companies.
(3) At the present time, it is unrealistic to use the disutility of passengers because to estimate how much passengers will be inconvenienced is extremely difficult.

Table 2. Passengers' dissatisfaction

Dissatisfaction	Contents
Delay	A delay of an arrival of a train exceeds a certain threshold. A delay of a departure of a train exceeds a certain threshold.
Stoppage times	An increment of a stoppage time of a train exceeds a certain threshold.
Running times	An increment of a running time of a train exceeds a certain threshold (often occurs when a train is kept waiting before it arrives at a station because its scheduled track is occupied by some other train).
Frequency	An interval between trains exceeds a certain threshold.
Connection	Connection of trains usually kept is lost.

We first scrutinize in what cases passengers would complain considering conditions such as severity of accidents, characteristics of railway lines etc. Then these cases are accumulated in a file called the Claim File. Before our rescheduling algorithm starts, it chooses the most suitable Claim File.

Types of passengers' dissatisfaction we consider in this paper are shown in Table 2.

A weight is put to each dissatisfaction taking its content such as amount of delays etc. into account. We calculate an evaluation measure for a given rescheduling plan as a weighted sum of each dissatisfaction contained in the plan. We call this evaluation measure "dissatisfaction index."

From an alternative view, passengers' dissatisfactions defined above can be regarded as "constraints" to be satisfied. In this sense, we can say that we treat the train rescheduling problem as a sort of constraint optimization problem to find a schedule which observes the constraints defined in the Claim File as much as possible.

4 Train Rescheduling Algorithm Which Minimizes Passengers' Dissatisfaction

4.1 Overall Structure

Recently, for combinatorial optimization problems, a category of algorithms called meta-heuristics are attracting attention. There are many applications of meta-heuristics for scheduling problems which seem to have something common with the train rescheduling problems.

Table 3. Types of arcs in Train Scheduling Networks

Type	Meaning	Weight
Train	Operation of trains	Running time
Stoppage	Time necessary for passengers to get on and off at a station	Stoppage time
Train-set	Time needed to turn over	Turn over time
Track	Conflict of tracks	Minimum interval between trains
Departure	Departing orders of trains	Minimum interval between trains
Arrival	Arriving orders of trains	Minimum interval between trains
Number of trains	Maximum number of trains allowed to exist between stations	Minimum interval between trains
Crossover	Conflict of routes in a station	Minimum interval between trains
Schedule	Scheduled time of each train	Scheduled time

Table 4. Schedule modification methods reflecting arc types

Arc Type	Method of schedule modification
Departure	Exchange departing orders of trains which correspond to the both end nodes of the arc.
Arrival	Exchange arriving orders of trains which correspond to the both end nodes of the arc.
Track	Change a track of the train which corresponds to either end of the arc.
Train-set	Change the schedule of the train-set which corresponds to the arc.
	Cancel the train which corresponds to the arc.

Since a fast algorithm is required for the train rescheduling problems, we decided to apply the simulated annealing, which is one of the meta-heuristic algorithms.

The overall structure of the algorithm is shown in Fig. 1 and details will be introduced in the following sections.

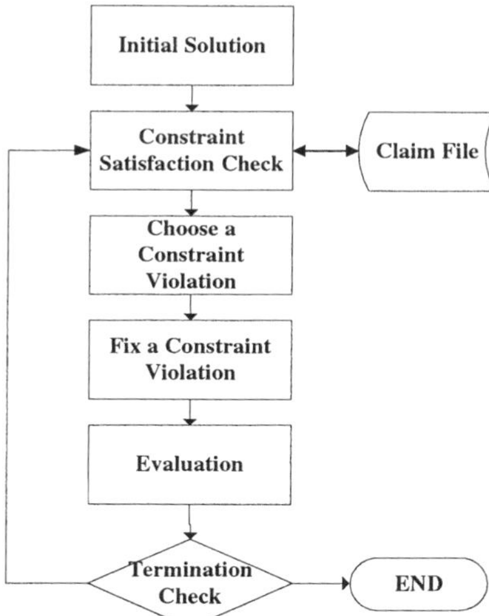

Fig. 1. Structure of Algorithm

4.2 Train Scheduling Network

We first introduce a network called a Train Scheduling Network (TSN) which is a kind of the PERT network. TSN is constructed as follows [9, 10]:

Node : a node is constructed corresponding either to an arrival of a train at a station or a departure of a train from a station. We also prepare a start node, which is used to express scheduled times of trains.

Arc : Chronological constraints between two nodes are expressed by an arc with a weight. The weight is the minimum time required for the two events of the both ends of the arc occur consecutively. Details are depicted in Table 3.

4.3 Details of the Algorithm

(1) Initial solution
The train schedule left as it is (namely, without giving any modification) is set as the initial solution. Let $S :=$ initial solution.

(2) Constraints satisfaction check
Check the schedule S whether the constraints defined in the Claim File are satisfied and if not, pick out all the portions in S which violate the constraints.

(3) Choose a constraint violation to be fixed.
Choose randomly a portion of S which violates a constraint.

(4) Try to fix a constraint violation and generate a new schedule.
   - Identify critical paths to the node which violates constraints in the Train Scheduling Network constructed from *S*.
   - Collect train-set, track, departure and arrival arcs in the critical paths.
   - Apply modification of the train schedule as described in Table 4.
   - Let *S'* := newly generated schedule.

(5) Evaluation of the newly generated schedule
   Calculate the dissatisfaction index of *S'* (we denote this | *S'* |) as $\sum w_i f(i)$, where *f* (*i*) is the number of violated constraint of type *i* and w_i is its weight.

(6) Decide whether to accept the newly generated schedule.
   If | *S'* | < | *S* | then let *S* := *S'*. Otherwise, let *S* := *S'* with a probability $exp(-\Delta/t)$, where Δ=| *S'* | - | *S* | and *t* is the *temperature* decided based on the idea of the simulated annealing [11].

(7) Termination
   If no improvement is observed during a prescribed iteration steps, the algorithm terminates and outputs the best schedule ever found. Otherwise, go to Step (2).

4.4 An Example of the Execution Process of the Algorithm

We show an example to show how the algorithm works using Fig. 2-5. Fig. 2 is a train schedule in which the departure of Train 3 from Station A is delayed (Train 3') for some reason and the departure of Train 1 from Station B is also delayed because it is scheduled to wait for Train 3 there. We set this schedule as the initial solution of our algorithm (Please note that Fig. 2, 4, 5 are drawn in the so called *train diagram* style, where the horizontal axis is the time axis and movements of trains between stations are depicted by diagonal lines).

Fig. 3 is the Train Scheduling Network created from the schedule of Fig. 2. The description inside each node means "Train-Station-departure/arrival." To avoid the figure becomes too complicated, weights of arcs are not shown.

Let us assume that the delay of the arrival of Train 1 at Station C is chosen as a constraint violation to be fixed. Critical paths from the node "Train1-StationC-arival" are looked for. In this case, the critical path is "1-C-*a* -> Track arc -> 4-C-d -> Train-set arc -> 3-C-*a* -> Train arc -> 3-B-*d* -> Stopage arc -> 3-B-*a* -> Train arc -> 3-A-*d*."

All the Track arcs and the Train-set arcs in the critical path are collected and one of them is chosen at random. Let us assume that the Track arc is chosen. Following the procedure in Table 4, either the track of Train 3-4 or that of Train 1-2 at Station C is to be changed. Let us assume that the track of Train 3-4 is changed to Track 2 (see Fig. 4). Iterating the similar process, the departing order of Trains 1 and 3 at Station B is changed and we get the schedule of Fig. 5.

5 Results of Experiments and Evaluation of the Algorithm

We have implemented our algorithm on a PC and evaluated its effectiveness.

(1) Data used in experiments

We selected a line in Tokyo urban area, which is about 40 km long and has 19 stations. We used a schedule of a whole day of this line which contains 564 trains. Time unit in making the timetable is fifteen seconds.

(2) Claim File

We created a Claim File considering delays at major stations, loss of connections, decrease of frequency of trains etc, which contains 265 records.

(3) Experiments

We have conducted experiments assuming two types of accidents: the first is a case in which a departure of one train is delayed due to an engine trouble and the second is a case in which a train is disturbed between stations due to an accident at a level crossing. We have conducted experiments ten times for each case.

(4) Results

We have confirmed that our algorithm produces a rescheduled plan which is practically usable in each trial. Since the space is limited, we only show the results of the first case. Fig. 6 is a schedule without rescheduling. Fig. 7 is an output of our algorithm (train schedules of two hours are shown). Observing Fig. 7, we can know that it was made by canceling an appropriate number of trains, changing tracks and departing orders of trains etc. The total number of modifications was thirty. Dissatisfaction index (DI) of the schedule in Fig. 6 is 942 and is reduced to 153 in Fig. 7.

Time needed for execution was approximately one minutes using a PC (Pentium 3.06 GB).

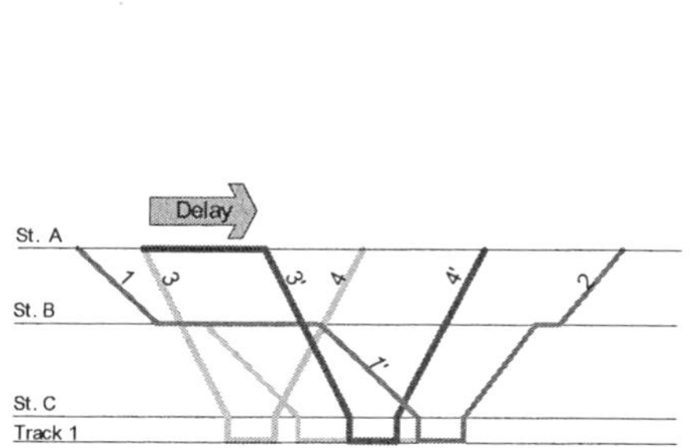

Fig. 2. Delayed schedule

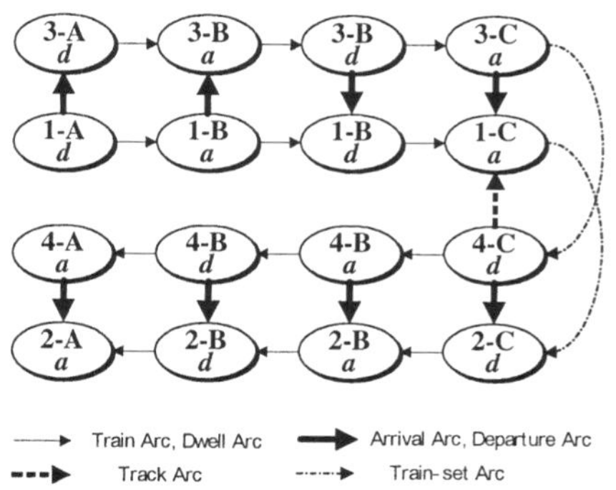

Fig. 3. Train Scheduling Network

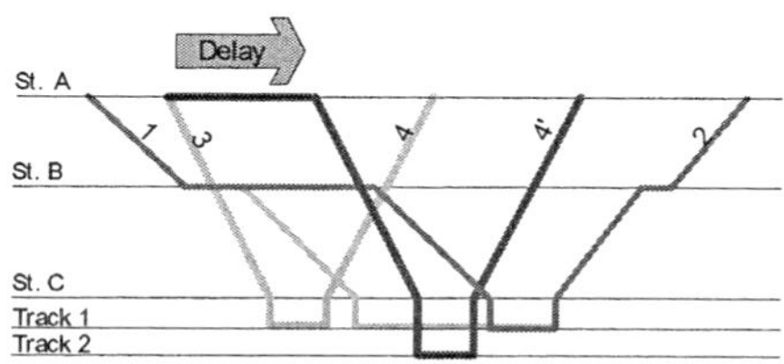

Fig. 4. Change of track

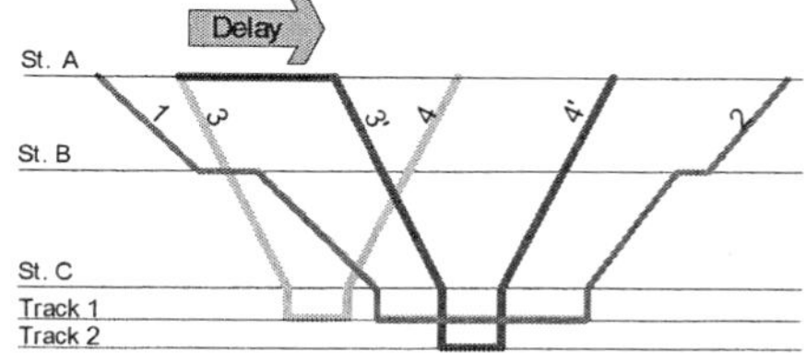

Fig. 5. Change of departing order

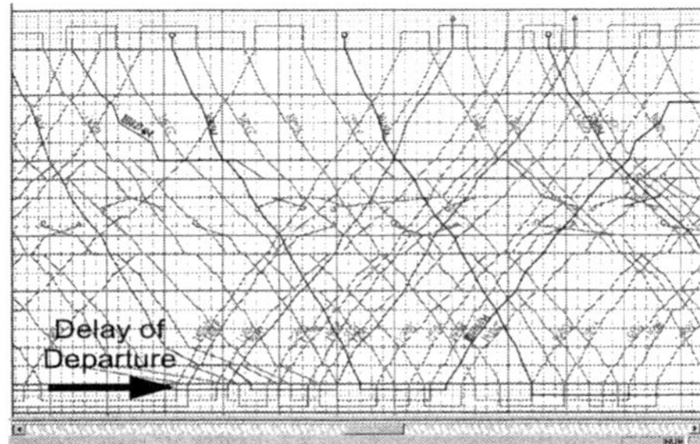

Fig. 6. Without rescheduling. DI=942

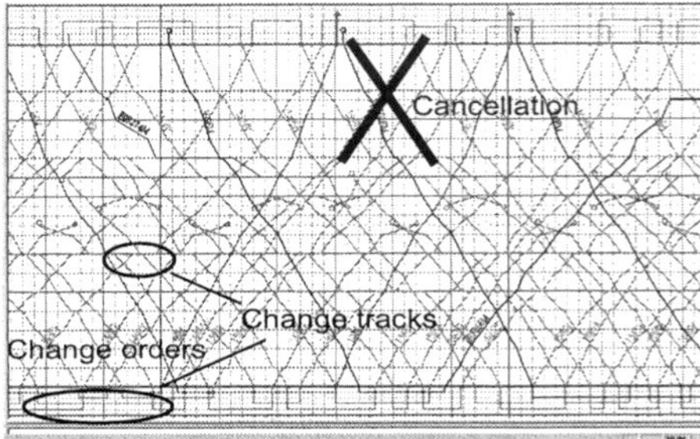

Fig. 7. Result of rescheduling. DI=153

6 Conclusions

We have proposed an idea to use passengers' dissatisfaction as the objective criteria of train rescheduling problems and introduced an efficient algorithm combining PERT and simulated annealing. This algorithm has a function to automatically make rescheduling plans for disrupted train traffic. Some of the characteristics of this algorithm are; it works quite fast and it supports versatile methods of rescheduling including cancellation, change of train-set operation schedule, change of tracks etc.

References

1. http://www.mlit.go.jp/english/white-paper/mlit03.html
2. TOMII, N.: *An Introduction to Railway Systems* (in Japanese), Kyoritsu Shuppan Co. (2001)
3. CORDEAU, J-F et al.: A Survey of Optimization Models for Train Routing and Scheduling *Transportation Science*, Vol.32, No.4 (1998)
4. Goodman, C. J. and Takagi, R.: Dynamic re-scheduling of trains after disruption, *Computers in Railways IX (COMPRAIL 2004)* (2004)
5. Hasegawa, Y. et al.: Experimental study on criteria of train rescheduling (in Japanese), *Proc. of 15th Symposium on Cybernetics in Railways* (1978)
6. Kobayashi R. et al.: Evaluation of train rescheduling from passengers' utility (in Japanese), *Proc. of J-Rail 2000* (2000)
7. Takano, M. et al.: Computer Assisting System to Propose and Evaluate Train-Rescheduling with a Function of Passenger-Path Allocation (in Japanese), *Proc. of J-Rail 2003* (2003).
8. Murata, S. and Goodman, C. J.: An optimal traffic regulation method for metro type railways based on passenger orientated traffic evaluation, *COMPRAIL 98* (1998)
9. Abe, K. and Araya, S.: Train Traffic Simulation Using the Longest Path Method (in Japanese), *Journal of IPSJ*, Vol. 27, No. 1 (1986)
10. TOMII, N. et al.: A Train Traffic Rescheduling Simulator Combining PERT and Knowledge-Based Approach," *European Simulation Symposium*, Elrangen (1995)
11. Aarts, E. and Korst J.: *Simulated Annealing and Boltzman Machines*, Wiley & Sons Inc. (1989)

Case-Based Reasoning for Financial Prediction

Dragan Simić[1], Zoran Budimac[2], Vladimir Kurbalija[2], and Mirjana Ivanović[2]

[1] Novi Sad Fair, Hajduk Veljkova 11, 21000 Novi Sad, Serbia and Montenegro
dsimic@nsfair.co.yu

[2] Department of Mathematics and Informatics, Faculty of Science, University of Novi Sad, Trg D. Obradovića 4, 21000 Novi Sad, Serbia and Montenegro
{zjb, kurba, mira}@im.ns.ac.yu

Abstract. A concept of financial prediction system is considered in this paper. By integrating multidimensional data technology (data warehouse, OLAP) and case-based reasoning, we are able to predict financial trends and provide enough data for business decision making. Methodology has been successfully used and tested in the management information system of "Novi Sad Fair".

1 Introduction

In order to help executives, managers, and analysts in an enterprise to focus on important data and to make better decisions, case-based reasoning (CBR - an artificial intelligence technique) is introduced for making predictions based on previous cases. CBR will automatically generate an answer to the problem using stored experience, thus freeing the human expert of obligations to analyze numerical or graphical data.

The use of CBR in predicting the rhythm of issuing invoices and receiving actual payments, based on the experience stored in the data warehouse is presented in this paper. Predictions obtained in this manner are important for future planning of a company such as the "Novi Sad Fair".

The combination of CBR and data warehousing, i.e. making an On-Line Analytical Processing (OLAP) intelligent by the use of CBR is a rarely used approach. The system also uses a novel CBR technique to compare graphical representation of data, which greatly simplifies the explanation of the prediction process to the end-user [1].

Performed simulations show that predictions made by CBR differ only for 8% in respect to what actually happened. With inclusion of more historical data in the warehouse, the system gets better in predictions.

In the following section we describe the illustrative problem that was used to demonstrate the advantages of our technique. The third section shortly describes our solution.

[1] 'Novi Sad Fair' has supported the first author. Other authors are partially supported by the Ministry of Science, Republic of Serbia, through a project 'Development of (intelligent) techniques based on software agents for application in information retrieval and workflow'.

M. Ali and F. Esposito (Eds.): IEA/AIE 2005, LNAI 3533, pp. 839–841, 2005.

2 The Problem

The data warehouse of "Novi Sad Fair" contains data about payment and invoicing processes in the past 4 years for every exhibition (25 to 30 exhibitions per year). The processes are presented as sets of points where every point is given with the time of the measuring (day from the beginning of the process) and the value of payment or invoicing on that day. These processes can be represented as curves.

The measurement of the payment and invoicing values was done every 4 days from the beginning of the invoice process in duration of 400 days - therefore every curve consists of approximately 100 points. By analyzing these curves one can notice that the process of invoicing usually starts several months before the exhibition and that the value of invoicing rapidly grows approximately to the time of the beginning of the exhibition. After that time the value of invoicing remains approximately the same till the end of the process. That moment, when the value of invoicing reaches some constant value and stays the same to the end, is called the *time of saturation for the invoicing process*, and the corresponding value – the *value of saturation*.

The process of payment starts several days after the corresponding process of invoicing (process of payment and invoicing for the same exhibition). After that the value of payment grows, but not so rapidly as the value of invoicing. At the moment of the exhibition the value of payment is between 30% and 50% of the value of invoicing. Then the value of payment continues to grow to some moment when it reaches a constant value and stays approximately constant till the end of the process. That moment is called the *time of saturation for the payment process*, and the corresponding value – the *value of saturation.*

The payment time of saturation is usually several months after the *invoice time of saturation*, and the *payment value of saturation* is always less than the *invoice value of saturation* or equal to it. The analysis shows that the payment value of saturation is between 80% and 100% of the invoice value of saturation. The maximum represents a total of services invoiced and that amount is to be paid. The same stands for the invoice curve where the maximum amount of payment represents the amount of payment by regular means. The rest will be paid later by the court order, other special business agreements or, perhaps, will not be paid at all (debtor bankruptcy).

The task was to predict the behavior of two curves for future exhibitions based on the data of the past exhibitions. This information was needed by financial managers of the Fair.

3 The Solution

The system first reads the input data from two data marts: one data mart contains the information about all invoice processes for every exhibition in the past 4 years, while the other data mart contains the information about the corresponding payment processes. After that, the system creates splines for every curve (invoice and payment) and internally stores the curves as the list of pairs containing the invoice curve and the corresponding payment curve.

In the same way the system reads the problem curves from the third data mart. The problem consists of the invoice and the corresponding payment curve at the moment of the exhibition. At that moment, the invoice curve usually reaches its saturation point, while the payment curve is still far away from its own saturation point. These curves are shown as the "Actual payment curve" and the "Actual invoice curve" (Fig. 1). Furthermore the CBR's prediction of payments saturation point is displayed as a big black dot in the picture. Detailed calculations are given in [2], [3].

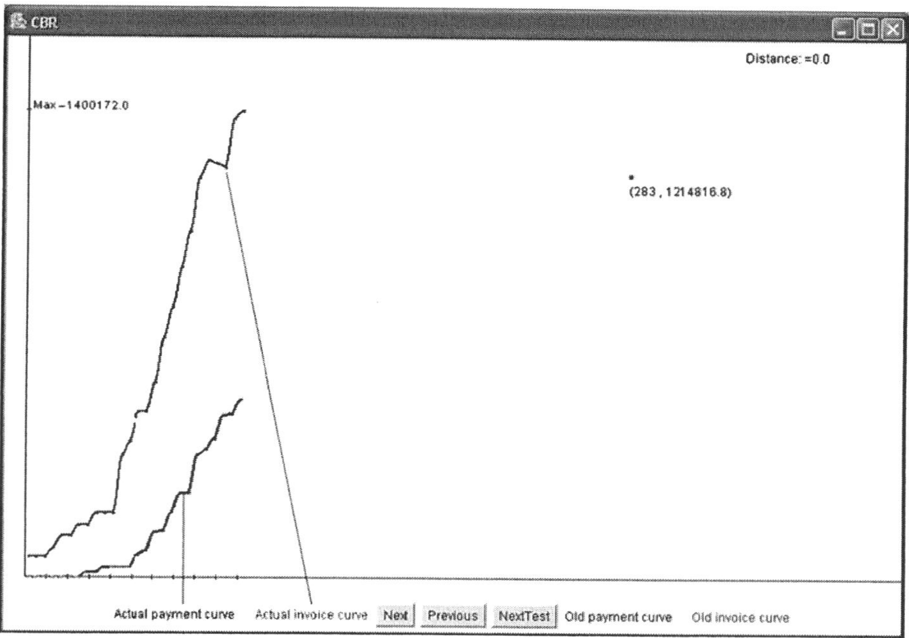

Fig. 1. Payment and invoice curves and the prediction for the payments saturation point

From the saturation point (given as the pair of the time and the payment value) the financial managers did get a prediction of: a) the time when the payment of a debt will be made, and b) the amount that will be paid regularly.

The error of our system is less than 8% with respect to what actually happens in practice, which is a result that financial managers find more than satisfactory.

References

1. Kurbalija, V.: On Similarity of Curves – Project Report, Humboldt University, AI Lab, Berlin (2003)
2. Simić, D.: Financial Prediction and Decision Support System Based on Artificial Intelligence Technology, Ph.D. thesis, Univ. of Novi Sad (2004)
3. Simić, D., Kurbalija, V., Budimac, Z.: An Application of Case-Based Reasoning in Multidimensional Database Architecture. In Proc. Of 5th International Conference on Data Warehousing and Knowledge Discovery (DaWaK), Lecture Notes in Computer Science, Vol. 2737. Springer-Verlag, Berlin Heidelberg New York (2003) 66 - 75.

The Generation of Automated Learner Feedback Based on Individual Proficiency Levels

Mariana Lilley, Trevor Barker, and Carol Britton

University of Hertfordshire, School of Computer Science,
College Lane, Hatfield, Hertfordshire AL10 9AB, United Kingdom
{M.Lilley, T.1.Barker, C.Britton}@herts.ac.uk

Abstract. Computer-adaptive tests (CATs) are software applications that adapt the level of difficulty of test questions to the learner's proficiency level. The CAT prototype introduced here includes a proficiency level estimation based on Item Response Theory and a questions' database. The questions in the database are classified according to topic area and difficulty level. The level of difficulty estimate comprises expert evaluation based upon Bloom's taxonomy and users' performance over time. The output from our CAT prototype is a continuously updated user model that estimates proficiency in each of the domain areas covered in the test. This user model was employed to provide automated feedback for learners in a summative assessment context. The evaluation of our feedback tool by a group of learners suggested that our approach was a valid one, capable of providing useful advice for individual development.

1 Introduction

The work reported in this paper follows from earlier research on the use of psychological student models in an intelligent tutoring system [3]. In this work, it was found that the approach was beneficial for learners and tutors, yet some global descriptors employed in the model had to be obtained co-operatively and thus inefficiently.

To overcome these efficiency issues, a statistical model was employed to dynamically estimate learners' proficiency levels. In the computer-adaptive test (CAT) introduced here, the level of difficulty of the questions was interactively modified to match the proficiency level of each individual learner. In previous work, we were able to show that the CAT approach was reliable and accurate [6] and that learners with different cognitive styles of learning were not disadvantaged by its use [2].

In spite of its benefits, expert evaluators indicated that the sole provision of a proficiency level index was unlikely to help learners detect their educational needs. Hence, the focus of this study was to investigate how the knowledge gained about learner performance in a CAT could be employed to provide individualised feedback on performance.

2 Prototype Overview

CATs are computer-assisted assessments that mimic aspects of an oral interview in which the tutor would adapt the interview by choosing questions appropriate to the

M. Ali and F. Esposito (Eds.): IEA/AIE 2005, LNAI 3533, pp. 842 – 844, 2005.

proficiency level of individual learners [9]. The CAT prototype described here comprised a graphical user interface, a question bank and an adaptive algorithm based on the Three-Parameter Logistic (3-PL) Model from Item Response Theory (IRT) [7, 9].

One of the central elements of the 3-PL Model is the level of difficulty of the question and/or task being performed by the user. All items in the question bank were classified according to topic and level of difficulty *b*. In this study, subject experts ranked the questions in order of difficulty, based upon their experience of the subject domain and Bloom's taxonomy of cognitive skills [4, 1]. Values for the difficulty *b* were refined over time, based on learners' performance. The cognitive skills covered by the question database were *knowledge* (difficulty *b* between -2 and -0.6), *comprehension* (difficulty *b* between -0.6 and 0.8) and *application* (difficulty *b* between 0.8 and 2).

3 The Study

A sample of 122 Computer Science undergraduate students participated in a summative assessment session using the CAT application. The assessment session took place in computer laboratories, under supervised conditions. Participants had 30 minutes to answer 20 questions organised into 6 topics within the Human-Computer Interaction subject domain. It was envisaged that all learners should receive feedback on: overall proficiency level, performance in each topic and recommended topics for revision.

The overall proficiency level section contained the proficiency level estimated for each individual learner, from -2 (lowest) to +2 (highest).

In addition to the overall performance proficiency level, the CAT application was used to estimate proficiency levels per topic. Sentences in this section of the feedback incorporated keywords from Bloom's taxonomy of cognitive skills [4, 1]. So, a proficiency level of 0.2 for one of the topics would be classified as *comprehension*. Keywords such as *classify* and *identify* would then be used to describe the estimated proficiency level. Keywords such as *apply* and *interpret* would, in turn, be used to provide a framework for future achievement.

The third section of the feedback document comprised a list of points for revision, based on the questions answered incorrectly by each learner. These statements comprised directive feedback and could optionally be supplemented by cues. Students were not provided with a copy of the questions answered incorrectly, as an underlying assumption was that this would not motivate learners to reflect on their mistakes and thus gain a deeper conceptual understanding of the subject domain.

Finally, the individual feedback analysis document was then sent to each learner by electronic mail.

4 Learner Attitude Towards the Feedback Format Used

A sample of 58 participants was asked to classify the feedback they received as "very useful", "useful" or "not useful". The results were split 50%/50% between "very useful" and "useful".

Participants were also asked to identify one benefit and one limitation of the approach. The most commonly identified benefits were provision of specific points for revision (64%) and feedback according to topic area (22%). The most commonly identified limitation was the absence of actual test questions (24%).

5 Summary

In this study we showed that a user model based on learners' proficiency levels was effective when applied to the generation of automated feedback. The importance of feedback as a tool to enhance learner's motivation and engagement is widely reported in the literature [5, 8]. In this paper, we have described an approach to the provision of automated feedback based on a user model developed using IRT [7, 9] and Bloom's model of learning [4, 1]. Our automated feedback prototype was evaluated positively by a group of learners. This supports the view that it successfully identified areas for improvement and provided useful advice for individual development.

References

1. Anderson, L.W. & Krathwohl, D.R. (Eds.) (2001). *A Taxonomy for Learning, Teaching, and Assessing: A Revision of Bloom's Taxonomy of Educational Objectives.* New York: Longman.
2. Barker, T. & Lilley, M. (2003). Are Individual Learners Disadvantaged by the Use of Computer-Adaptive Testing? In *Proceedings of the 8th Learning Styles Conference. University of Hull*, United Kingdom, European Learning Styles Information Network, pages 30-39.
3. Barker, T., Jones, S., Britton, C. & Messer, D. (2002). *The use of a co-operative student model of learner characteristics to configure a multimedia application.* User Modelling and User Adapted Interaction 12 (2/3), pages 207-241.
4. Bloom, B. S. (1956). *Taxonomy of educational objectives. Handbook 1, Cognitive domain: the classification of educational goals.* London: Longman.
5. Freeman, R. & Lewis, R. (1998). *Planning and implementing assessment.* London: Kogan Page.
6. Lilley, M., Barker, T. & Britton, C. (2004). The development and evaluation of a software prototype for computer adaptive testing. *Computers & Education Journal* **43**(1-2), pages 109-122.
7. Lord, F. M. (1980). *Applications of Item Response Theory to practical testing problems.* New Jersey: Lawrence Erlbaum Associates.
8. Mathan, S. A. & Koedinger, K. R. (2002). An empirical assessment of comprehension fostering features in an Intelligent Tutoring System. *LNCS* 2363, pages 330-343.
9. Wainer, H. (2000). *Computerized Adaptive Testing (A Primer).* 2nd Edition. New Jersey: Lawrence Erlbaum Associates.

A Geographical Virtual Laboratory for the Recomposition of Fragments

Nicola Mosca, Floriana Renna, Giovanna Carlomagno, Giovanni Attolico, and Arcangelo Distante

Institute of Intelligent Systems for Automation – C.N.R.
Via Amendola 122 D/O, Bari, Italy
{nmosca, renna, attolico}@ba.issia.cnr.it

Abstract. The paper describes a digital system for the virtual aided recomposition of fragmented frescos whose approach allows knowledge and experience of restorers to cooperate with computational power and flexibility of digital tools for image analysis and retrieval. The physical laboratory for the traditional recomposition is replaced by a geographically distributed client-server architecture implementing a virtual laboratory of fragments. Image processing and analysis techniques support the whole recomposition task. A properly designed engine for image indexing and retrieval enables the retrieval of fragments similar to suitably chosen sample images.

Keywords: Internet applications, Systems for real life applications.

1 Introduction

The proposed innovative approach to virtual aided recomposition of fragmented frescos is being developed and proved on the St. Matthew's fresco, painted by Cimabue, broken in more than 140.000 pieces during the earthquake in 1997.

The system, based on a client-server architecture, replaces the physical laboratory for traditional recomposition with a virtual laboratory spread over a geographical network, which transposes digitally most of the traditional manual recomposition process. With a short and easy training the knowledge and skills of operators can be fully exploited and integrated with the capabilities of the digital system. Image processing and analysis techniques support the restorers and a properly developed CBIR engine allows the efficient and effective management of the huge number of fragments. The tools can be applied also without a reference image so the system can be broadly used in all the fragments recomposition problems, regardless the pictorial documentation available about the painting before fragmentation.

2 The Virtual Laboratory

The client application runs on a Windows 2000 workstation equipped with three monitors and a special mouse with six degrees of freedom that allows to translate and rotate fragments simultaneously on the workspace: it includes the user interface and the local processing required by the recomposition. An OpenGL compatible graphics

M. Ali and F. Esposito (Eds.): IEA/AIE 2005, LNAI 3533, pp. 845 – 847, 2005.

card increases the performance of fragments manipulation in the workspace. The server application runs on a multi-processor Digital Alpha Unix system: it manages the database and the processing required to extract meta-data from the huge number of fragments and to execute the queries by examples of the users.

Fig. 1. The workstation for virtual aided recomposition. The left-side monitor represents the working area where fragments images are placed. On the other ones a scaled version of the whole fresco and a virtual container are shown

The user interface has been inspired by the elements in the physical laboratory [1]. Fragments, boxes used to organize fragments logically related to each other, tables covered by the image of the fresco at a real-scale size (if available) have their digital counterpart in the system. Fragments are represented by their two-dimensional picture [2]: the restorers cannot manipulate physical fragments to measure roughness, weight, characteristics of their back but any potential damage to the sensitive pictorial film is avoided. Fragments can be classified into virtual boxes and used by multiple restorers at the same time, increasing the efficiency of the work. Image processing techniques enhance visual characteristics (color, contrast, lightness, scale, ...) and the perception of details. Restorers can move fragments around to find their correct place in the workspace to which the image of the fresco, if available, can be superimposed to reproduce the condition of the physical laboratory. The system allows actions impossible in reality: visual properties of the reference image can be dynamically changed [3]; fragments can be shown in half-transparency for a better comparison with the background; already placed fragments can be hidden to improve the visual perception of the space; display scale can be decreased to evaluate larger parts of the fresco (up to the whole picture if needed) or increased to enhance visual details. A miniature image shows the whole fresco at low resolution to enable an easy navigation through the picture by naturally selecting the region of interest.

The tasks of the server are mainly related to evaluation of fragment similarity and management of central data (metadata describing the pictorial content of fragments; information shared between restorers such as common sets of fragments, placed fragments,...). The similarity evaluation is based on colour histograms, texture descriptions and fragment's dimension.

The system supports the retrieval of fragments using an incremental and iterative query-by-example modality: a set of images, fragments or details of the reference image, is used to index the database. The system returns the fragments most similar to the examples on the basis of the selected characteristics. The set can be changed and the process can be repeated until the operator's needs are fulfilled [4].

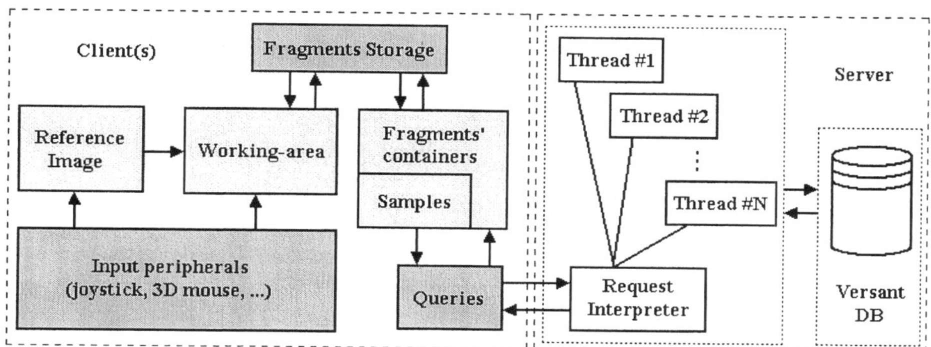

Fig. 2. Software modules of the developed system and their interactions. On the client some modules (yellow) handle the elements of user interface while others (green) grab user inputs and manage fragments and queries. On the server-side, the services manager accepts client requests and spans threads to accomplish them by accessing the database

Several restorers can work simultaneously on the same recomposition project from different places spread around the world. Clients and server communicate by TCP/IP and a custom protocol that minimizes the data exchanged over the network (the system runs also using 56k modems). Clients are unaware of methods used by the server to store and retrieve data associated with fragments and of the specific database.

Acknowledgement

The authors thank Marco Malavasi (Dip. Rapporti con le Regioni – CNR) for its important support; Giuseppe Basile, Lidia Rissotto, Angelo Rubino (ICR), Manuela Viscontini (Università della Tuscia) and Laura Cacchi for many valuable discussions.

References

1. Mosca, N., Attolico, G., Distante, A.: A digital system for aided virtual recomposition of fragmented frescos, http://www.icr.beniculturali.it/Strumenti/Documenti/Utopiareal3e.pdf
2. Renna, F., Carlomagno, G., Mosca, N., Attolico, G., Distante, A.: Virtual Recomposition of Frescos: Separating Fragments from the Background, IEEE ICPR2004, Cambridge, UK, 819-822, (2004)
3. Renna, F., Carlomagno, G., Mosca, N., Attolico, G., Distante, A.: Color Correction for the Virtual Recomposition of Fragmented Frescos, IEEE ICPR2004, Cambridge, UK, (2004)
4. Renna, F., Mosca, N., Carlomagno, G., Attolico, G., Distante, A.: A System for Aided Recomposition of Golden Images, Mirage 2005, INRIA Rocquencourt, France, (2005)
5. http://www.issia.cnr.it/htdocs%20nuovo/progetti/bari/restauro.html

A Meta-level Architecture for Strategic Reasoning in Naval Planning
(Extended Abstract)

Mark Hoogendoorn[1], Catholijn M. Jonker[2], Peter-Paul van Maanen[1,3], and Jan Treur[1]

[1] Department of Artificial Intelligence, Vrije Universiteit Amsterdam, De Boelelaan 1081a, 1081HV Amsterdam, The Netherlands
{mhoogen, pp, treur}@cs.vu.n
[2] NICI, Radboud University Nijmegen, Montessorilaan 3, 6525HR Nijmegen, The Netherlands
C.Jonker@nici.ru.nl
[3] Department of Information Processing, TNO Human Factors, P.O.Box 23, 3769ZG Soesterberg, The Netherlands

Abstract. The management of naval organizations aims at the maximization of mission success by means of monitoring, planning, and strategic reasoning. This paper presents a meta-level architecture for strategic reasoning in naval planning. The architecture is instantiated with decision knowledge acquired from naval domain experts, and is formed into an executable model which is used to perform a number of simulations. To evaluate the simulation results a number of relevant properties for the planning decision are identified and formalized. These properties are validated for the simulation traces.

1 Introduction

The management of naval organizations aims at the maximization of mission success by means of monitoring, planning, and strategic reasoning. In this domain, strategic reasoning more in particular helps in determining in resource-bounded situations if a go or no go should be given to, or to shift attention to, a certain evaluation of possible plans after an incident. An incident is an unexpected event, which results in an unmeant chain of events if left alone. Strategic reasoning in a planning context can occur both in *plan generation* strategies (cf. [4]) and *plan selection* strategies.
The above context gives rise to two important questions. Firstly, what possible plans are first to be considered? And secondly, what criteria are important for selecting a certain plan for execution? In resource-bounded situations first generated plans should have a high probability to result in a mission success, and the criteria to determine this should be as sound as possible.

In this paper a generic meta-level architecture (cf. [1, 2, 3]) is presented for planning, extended with a strategic reasoning level. Besides the introduction of a meta-level architecture, expert knowledge is used in this paper to formally specify executable properties for each of the components of the architecture. These properties are used for simulation and facilitate formal verification of the simulation results.

M. Ali and F. Esposito (Eds.): IEA/AIE 2005, LNAI 3533, pp. 848 – 850, 2005.

2 A Meta-level Architecture for Naval Planning

In Figure 1 the proposed generic architecture is shown for strategic planning applicable in naval planning organizations. The components denote processes, solid lines denote information, and the dotted lines denote a separation between meta-levels. In the middle part of the architecture, plans are executed in a deliberation cycle.. By comparing the perceived situation with the planned situation the Monitoring component generates evaluation information. In case the evaluation involves an

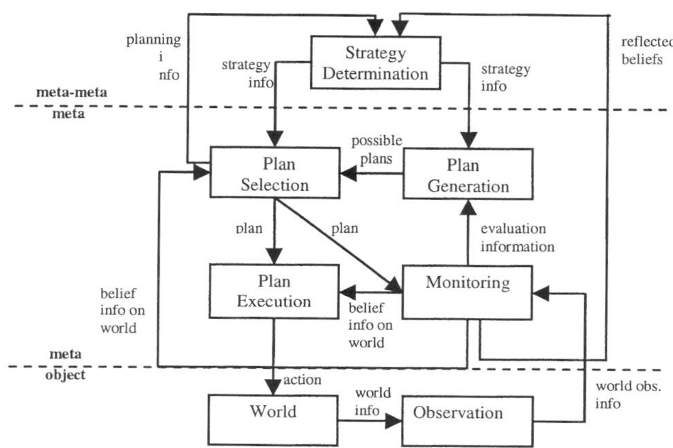

Fig. 1. Strategic planning processes applicable in naval organizations

exception PlanGeneration determines what the possible plans are, considering the situation. The conditional rules for the possible plans given a certain event are passed by the StrategyDetermination component. The possible plans are forwarded to the PlanSelection component which evaluates the plans taking the current beliefs on the world into consideration. In case an empty list of possible plans is received PlanSelection informs StrategyDetermination that no plan could be selected. The same is done when none of the plans passed the evaluation. The StrategyDetermination component can, in case of such a notification, provide PlanGeneration with additional conditional rules. It can also generate a new way to evaluate plans by means of different criteria rules. If a suitable plan has been found, it is passed to PlanExecution and becomes the current plan. The execution of the plan is done by means of the receipt of beliefs on the world and applying the plan to derive the next action. The actions that have been determined are passed to the World.

3 Case-Study in Naval Domain

The model presented in Section 2 has been applied in a case-study in the naval domain. Executable properties for each of the components have been specified for this particular domain and include PlanGeneration and PlanSelection strategies based on the candidate plans and criteria passed from StrategyDetermination. Selection criteria strategies incorporate mission success, safety and fleet moral, over which a weighed sum is calculated. Furthermore, candidate generation strategy determination is based on information from PlanSelection and PlanGeneration. Three different modes of operation are defined, which are *limited action demand*, *full preferred plan library*, and *exceptional action demand*. Finally, the StrategyDetermination component also includes executable properties that establish a change in the weights of the different selection criteria in case of failure to select an appropriate plan.

The above mentioned properties were used in a number of simulation runs. The results were formally verified by means the use of a developed software tool called *TTL checker*. These properties include upward and downward reflection (e.g., [3]), verifying whether no unnecessary extreme measures are taken, plans are not changed without a proper cause, and were all satisfied for the given trace.

4 Conclusion

This paper presents an architecture for strategic planning (cf. [4]) for naval domains. The architecture was designed as a meta-level architecture (cf. [1, 2, 3]) with three levels. The interaction between the levels is modeled by reflection principles (e.g., [2, 3]). The dynamics of the architecture is based on a multi-level trace approach as an extension to what is described in [2]. The architecture has been instantiated with expert naval domain decision knowledge. The resulting executable model has been used to perform a number of simulation runs. To evaluate the simulation results relevant properties for the planning decision process have been identified, formalized and validated. More simulation runs and the validation of properties for the simulation traces are expected to give more insight for future complex resource-bounded naval planning support systems.

Acknowledgements

CAMS-Force Vision funded this research and provided domain knowledge. The authors especially want to thank Jaap de Boer (CAMS-ForceVision) for his expert knowledge.

References

1. Davis, R., Metarules: reasoning about control, Artificial Intelligence 15 (1980), pp. 179-222.
2. Hoek, W. van der, Meyer, J.-J.Ch., and Treur, J., Formal Semantics of Meta-Level Architectures: Temporal Epistemic Reflection. *International Journal of Intelligent Systems*, vol. 18, 2003, pp. 1293-1318.
3. Weyhrauch, R.W., Prolegomena to a theory of mechanized formal reasoning, Artificial Intelligence 13 (1980), pp. 133-170.
4. Wilkins, D.E., Domain-independent planning Representation and plan generation. Artificial Intelligence 22 (1984), pp. 269-301.

A Support Method for Qualitative Simulation-Based Learning System

Tokuro Matsuo, Takayuki Ito, and Toramatsu Shintani

Department of Information Science and Engineering,
Nagoya Institute of Technology,
Gokiso-cho, Showa-ku, Nagoya, Aichi, 466–8555, Japan
{tmatsuo, itota, tora}@ics.nitech.ac.jp
http://www-toralab.ics.nitech.ac.jp/

Abstract. In this paper, we mainly present a support method of our proposed e-learning system. We employ qualitative simulations because this lets the learners understand the conceptual principles in economic dynamics. First, we define some qualitative values employed on simulation graph model that consists of nodes and arcs. Then, we show the support method using our learning system based on qualitative simulation.

1 Introduction

E-learning has been recognized as a promising field in which to apply artificial intelligence technologies[1][2]. Our paper describes how our system should support end-users learning in the economic education[3].

The advantages of qualitative reasoning in education are as follows. Student knowledge is formed and developed through learning conceptual foundations. If there are any mechanisms in the system, the user can understand these mechanisms using qualitative methods. Generally, students also understand dynamic systems through qualitative principles, rather than through mathematical formula. In our study, we developed our approach in least formula and took learning by non-specialist users into consideration.

The feature of our study is that users can learn without teacher. Our goal is developing a system in which users can understanding economic dynamics through their self-learning. We consider an approach and system in which non-specialist naive and novice users can use our system based on simple input. The contribution of our paper is the integration of theory and shows an approach to support method for qualitative simulation-based education system.

2 Qualitative Simulation Primer

The simulation primer uses a relation model between causes and effects expressed as a causal graph. Each node of the graph has a qualitative state value and each arc of the graph shows a trend in effects.

Qualitative States on Nodes: In economic qualitative simulations, it is difficult to decide landmark values because there aren't conceptions for landmark in conditions of

M. Ali and F. Esposito (Eds.): IEA/AIE 2005, LNAI 3533, pp. 851–854, 2005.

nodes. We provide three sorts of qualitative state values on nodes without fixed landmarks. In our system, the qualitative state $[x(t)]$ is defined as "High", "Middle" and "Low", that is the state values of nodes without landmarks. (node x at time t.)

State Trends Changing on Nodes: We define state trends changing on nodes that indicate the time differential. Three types of qualitative values are given. In our system, the qualitative changing state $[dx(t)]$ is defined as "Increase", "Stable", and "Decrease", that is the condition values of nodes. (node x at time t.)

Direction of Effects of Arcs: We show the direction of the effect nodes as influenced by the cause nodes. Two sorts of qualitative values are given. $D(x, y)$ is the direction of the effects from node x to node y. The directions are classified into two categories. $+$: When x's state value increases, y's state value also increases. / When x's state value decreases, y's state value also decrease. $-$: When x's state value decreases, y's state value increases. / When x's state value increases, y's state value decreases.

Transmission Speed of Effects on Arcs: We assume that transmission speed V_0 is used on the arc from node x to node y. When node x is influenced by other nodes and changes to a qualitative value, node y changes the value simultaneously. We assume that transmission speed V_1 is used on the arc from node x to node y. When node x is influenced by other nodes and changes to a qualitative value, node y changes the value with a one-step delay.

Integration of Multiple Effects on Nodes: The integration of multiple effects on nodes is defined as an addition of effects from multiple nodes. It is shown as adding among qualitative different values $[\delta X/\delta t]$ and $[\delta Y/\delta t]$. Namely, $Z = [\delta X/\delta t] + [\delta Y/\delta t]$.

For example, when $[\delta X/\delta t]$ is $+$ and $[\delta Y/\delta t]$ is $+$, the sum is $+$. On the other hand, when $[\delta X/\delta t]$ is $+$ and $[\delta Y/\delta t]$ is $-$, the qualitative sum value cannot be decided, namely its value is unknown. When there are multiple adjacent nodes connected to a node, the integration of multiple effects on nodes is defined as addition of changing state values among multiple nodes.

3 Supporting Procedure

Our system is intended for learners, such as elementary school students and junior high school students. Each student has each experience and knowledge concerned with economic activities. When such multiple users use our system, our system applies and decides how to support such users based on a process of users learning. When users construct a causal model, users behavior is difference based on each user's ability. If a user knows about some factors and its relationships partially, he/she tells finishing work and pushes the FINISH button (in our system) when he/she finishes making the causal graph. On the other hand, if a user doesn't know about some factors and its relationships, his/her work stops for minutes without his/her report. Thus, we decide conditions after making causal graph as follows. (a) After some operations, the operation stops for minutes, and (b) after some operations, the FINISH button is pushed.

When users don't operate in some minutes more than time in which a manager (teacher, mentor, ...) decides, our system judges (a). Our system asks whether the user's operation finished or not. If the user selects a button in which his/her work finished, our system asks the four questions as pop-up window, that is FINISH, HINT, GIVE UP and UNFINISH. When the user selects the UNFINISH button, the user continues making causal graph model. When the user selects the other buttons, our system check up a causal graph model constructed by the user and decides how to support the user's leaning. We classify the following sets based on the causal model. (1) The graph doesn't have both arcs and nodes, (2) the graph has less nodes, (3) the graph is constructed as a partial model, and (4) the graph has enough nodes and arcs.

Our system supports users based on a causal graph model constructed by the users. We define the following conditions based on a button pushed by the user. **F:** The user selects the FINISH button. **H:** The user selects the HINT button. **G:** The user selects the GIVE UP button.

We show the 9 sets of users situations in the users' graph making[1]. First, a user starts making causal graph. The graph construction window has a field of making causal graph, the UNFINISH button and the FINISH button. When the user finishes making simulation model, three buttons are provided, that is FINISH, HINT and GIVE UP. However, we don't provide the FINISH button at condition (1) to (3). The user can select HINT, GIVE UP and UNFINISH button at condition (1) to (3). Based on the option button selected by the user, our system supports user based on our support algorithm. After supporting at condition (1) to (3), the user retries making or completing causal graph model. In case of condition (4), our system checks the relationships between each node with arcs rule which are referred from database files. After the model is renewed, our system tries conducting simulation based on initial values input by the user.

Second, after the user remakes the causal graph model through our system's support, our system re-support the user based on the condition of model reconstructed by the user. We show an example of a process of completing causal graph model. The user starts making causal model and the user pushes the HINT button at condition (1). Our system shows some nodes, and the user selects the appropriate nodes from nodes shown by our system. Then, the user restarts making causal model and the user pushes the HINT button at condition (3). Our system drops hints as some relationship between nodes, the user uses appropriate arcs based on the hints. Finally, our system checks the causal model based on the rules concerned with the relationship between each node. The user try conducting an economic simulation based on the completed graph model.

4 Conclusion

In this paper, we proposed a support method of our e-learning support system based on qualitative simulation. When models and initial values are changed, users can know what influence its changing brings a result. Our system can be used without mentor, because users can input initial values easily in our system. Our system can be also a promising application as a self-learning system for a tele-education.

[1] http://www-toralab.ics.nitech.ac.jp/~ tmatsuo/research/model.jpg

References

1. Bredeweg, B., Forbus, K., "Qualitative Modeling in Education", AI magazine, Vol. 24, No. 4, pp.35-46, American Association for Artificial Intelligence, 2003.
2. Forbus, K. D., Carney, K., Harris, R. and Sherin, B. L., "A Qualitative Modeling Environment for Middle-School Students: A progress Report", in the proceedings of 11th International Workshop on Qualitative Reasoning, pp.17-19, 2001.
3. Matsuo, T., Ito, T., and Shintani, T.: A Qualitative/Quantitative Methods-Based e-Learning Support System in Economic Education, in the proceeding of the 19th National Conference on Artificial Intelligence (AAAI-2004) , pp.592-598, 2004.

Author Index